Social Psychology and Human Nature

SECOND EDITION

Social Psychology and Human Nature

Roy F. Baumeister

Florida State University

Brad J. Bushman

University of Michigan
VU University, Amsterdam, the Netherlands

WADSWORTH
CENGAGE Learning™

Australia • Brazil • Japan • Korea • Mexico • Singapore • Spain • United Kingdom • United States

Social Psychology and Human Nature, Second Edition

Roy F. Baumeister, Brad J. Bushman

Senior Publisher: Linda Schreiber

Executive Editor: Jon-David Hague

Senior Sponsoring Editor: Jane Potter

Managing Development Editor: Jeremy Judson

Assistant Editor: Trina Tom

Editorial Assistant: Alicia McLaughlin, Nic Albert

Media Editor: Lauren Keyes, Rachel Guzman

Executive Marketing Manager: Kim Russell

Marketing Manager: Liz Rhoden

Marketing Associate: Molly Felz

Executive Marketing Communications Manager: Talia Wise

Senior Content Production Manager: Pat Waldo

Creative Director: Rob Hugel

Senior Art Director: Vernon Boes

Print Buyer: Becky Cross

Text Permissions Editor: Mardell Glinski Schultz

Photo Permissions Editor: John Hill

Production Service: Lachina Publishing Services

Text Designer: Liz Harasymczuk

Photo Researcher: Roman Barnes

Cover Designer: Irene Morris

Cover Image: PhotoDisc

Compositor: Lachina Publishing Services

For product information and technology assistance, contact us at **Cengage Learning Academic Resource Center, 1-800-423-0563**

For permission to use material from this text or product, submit all requests online at **www.cengage.com/permissions** Further permissions questions can be e-mailed to **permissionrequest@cengage.com**

Library of Congress Control Number: 2009931070

Student Edition:
ISBN-13: 978-0-495-60133-3
ISBN-10: 0-495-60133-0

Brief Edition:
ISBN-13: 978-0-495-60265-1
ISBN-10: 0-495-60265-5

Advantage Edition:
ISBN-13: 978-0-495-90993-4
ISBN-10: 0-495-90993-9

Wadsworth
20 Davis Drive
Belmont, CA 94002-3098
USA

Cengage Learning is a leading provider of customized learning solutions with office locations around the globe, including Singapore, the United Kingdom, Australia, Mexico, Brazil, and Japan. Locate your local office at **www.cengage.com/global**

Cengage Learning products are represented in Canada by Nelson Education, Ltd.

To learn more about Wadsworth, visit **www.cengage.com/Wadsworth**

Purchase any of our products at your local college store or at our preferred online store **www.ichapters.com**

Printed in Canada
2 3 4 5 6 7 12 11 10

We dedicate this book to our mentors and to their mentors, in appreciation of the teaching of psychology through these relationships.

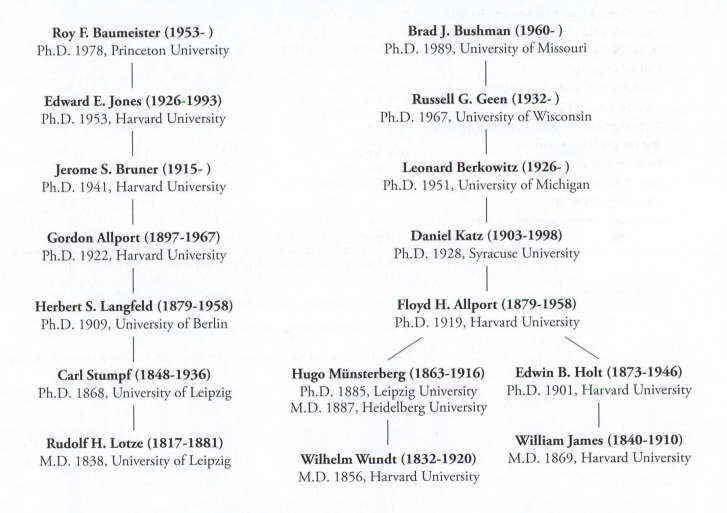

Roy F. Baumeister (1953-)
Ph.D. 1978, Princeton University

|

Edward E. Jones (1926-1993)
Ph.D. 1953, Harvard University

|

Jerome S. Bruner (1915-)
Ph.D. 1941, Harvard University

|

Gordon Allport (1897-1967)
Ph.D. 1922, Harvard University

|

Herbert S. Langfeld (1879-1958)
Ph.D. 1909, University of Berlin

|

Carl Stumpf (1848-1936)
Ph.D. 1868, University of Leipzig

|

Rudolf H. Lotze (1817-1881)
M.D. 1838, University of Leipzig

Brad J. Bushman (1960-)
Ph.D. 1989, University of Missouri

|

Russell G. Geen (1932-)
Ph.D. 1967, University of Wisconsin

|

Leonard Berkowitz (1926-)
Ph.D. 1951, University of Michigan

|

Daniel Katz (1903-1998)
Ph.D. 1928, Syracuse University

|

Floyd H. Allport (1879-1958)
Ph.D. 1919, Harvard University

Hugo Münsterberg (1863-1916)
Ph.D. 1885, Leipzig University
M.D. 1887, Heidelberg University

|

Wilhelm Wundt (1832-1920)
M.D. 1856, Harvard University

Edwin B. Holt (1873-1946)
Ph.D. 1901, Harvard University

|

William James (1840-1910)
M.D. 1869, Harvard University

about the authors

Roy F. Baumeister holds the Eppes Eminent Professorship in Psychology at Florida State University, where he is the head of the social psychology graduate program and teaches social psychology to students at all levels. He has taught introductory social psychology to thousands of undergraduate students. He received his Ph.D. from Princeton in 1978, and his teaching and research activities have included appointments at the University of California at Berkeley, Case Western Reserve University, the University of Texas at Austin, the University of Virginia, the Max Planck Institute in Munich (Germany), and the Center for Advanced Study in the Behavioral Sciences at Stanford. Baumeister is an active researcher whose work has been funded by the National Institutes of Health and by the Templeton Foundation. He has done research on the self (including self-esteem and self-control), the need to belong, sexuality, aggression, and how people find meaning in life. In 2005, the Institute for Scientific Information concluded from a survey of published bibliographies that he was among the most influential psychologists in the world. His publications have been cited over 5,000 times. The first edition of this textbook was his 300th publication, and he now has over 400. Baumeister lives with his wife and daughter by a small lake in Tallahassee, Florida. In his (very rare) spare time, he likes to play guitar and piano or go windsurfing.

Brad J. Bushman is Professor of Psychology and Communication Studies at the University of Michigan. He is also a professor at the VU University Amsterdam, the Netherlands, where he teaches and does research in the summer. He received his Ph.D. from the University of Missouri in 1989. He has taught introductory social psychology courses for about 20 years. Dubbed the "Myth Buster" by one colleague, Bushman's research has challenged several societal myths (e.g., violent media have a trivial effect on aggression, venting anger reduces aggression, violent people suffer from low self-esteem, violence and sex on TV sell products, warning labels repel consumers). His research has been published in the top scientific journals (e.g., *Science*, *Nature*) and has been featured on television (e.g., *ABC News 20/20*, Discovery Channel), on radio (e.g., NPR, BBC, CBC), in magazines (e.g., *Newsweek*, *Sports Illustrated*), and in newspapers (e.g., *New York Times*, *Wall Street Journal*). He lives in Ann Arbor, Michigan with his wife Tammy Stafford, and their three children Becca, Nathan, and Branden. In his spare time he likes to ride his bicycle (especially in Amsterdam), cross-country ski, and listen to jazz music (e.g., Miles Davis, John Coltrane, and the BBG Trio [Han Bennink, Michiel Borstlap, and Ernst Glerum]).

brief contents

Preface **xix**

CHAPTER 1 ▶ The Mission and the Method **1**

CHAPTER 2 ▶ Culture and Nature **25**

CHAPTER 3 ▶ The Self **57**

CHAPTER 4 ▶ Choices and Actions: The Self in Control **97**

CHAPTER 5 ▶ Social Cognition **125**

CHAPTER 6 ▶ Emotion and Affect **159**

CHAPTER 7 ▶ Attitudes, Beliefs, and Consistency **197**

CHAPTER 8 ▶ Social Influence and Persuasion **223**

CHAPTER 9 ▶ Prosocial Behavior: Doing What's Best for Others **255**

CHAPTER 10 ▶ Aggression and Antisocial Behavior **287**

CHAPTER 11 ▶ Attraction and Exclusion **323**

CHAPTER 12 ▶ Close Relationships: Passion, Intimacy, and Sexuality **351**

CHAPTER 13 ▶ Prejudice and Intergroup Relations **391**

CHAPTER 14 ▶ Groups **429**

Glossary **G1**

References **R1**

Name Index **N1**

Subject Index **S1**

contents

Preface **xix**

chapter 1   The Mission and the Method   1

A BRIEF HISTORY OF SOCIAL PSYCHOLOGY p. 3

WHAT DO SOCIAL PSYCHOLOGISTS DO? p. 6

SOCIAL PSYCHOLOGY'S PLACE IN THE WORLD p. 7

Social Psychology's Place in the Social Sciences p. 7
Social Psychology's Place Within Psychology p. 8

WHY PEOPLE STUDY SOCIAL PSYCHOLOGY p. 9
Curiosity About People p. 9
Experimental Philosophy p. 9
Making the World Better p. 10
Social Psychology Is Fun! p. 10

HOW DO SOCIAL PSYCHOLOGISTS ANSWER THEIR OWN QUESTIONS? p. 11
Accumulated Common Wisdom p. 11

Overview of the Scientific Method p. 11
Scientific Theories p. 12
Research Design p. 14

HOW MUCH OF SOCIAL PSYCHOLOGY IS TRUE? p. 20
Self-Correcting Nature of Science p. 20
Reliance on Student Samples p. 20
Cultural Relativity p. 21

CHAPTER SUMMARY p. 21

Food for Thought: Does Chicken Soup Reduce Cold Symptoms? **p. 12**

chapter 2   Culture and Nature   25

NATURE AND SOCIAL BEHAVIOR p. 27
Explaining the Psyche p. 27
Nature Defined p. 28
Evolution, and Doing What's Natural p. 28
Social Animals p. 30
The Social Brain p. 31

CULTURE AND HUMAN SOCIAL LIFE p. 32
Social Animal or Cultural Animal? p. 32
Culture Defined p. 33
Nature and Culture Interacting p. 35
What Makes Cultural Animals? p. 37
Are People the Same Everywhere? p. 39

IMPORTANT FEATURES OF HUMAN SOCIAL LIFE p. 41
The Duplex Mind p. 41
The Long Road to Social Acceptance p. 45

Built to Relate p. 45
Nature Says Go, Culture Says Stop p. 46
Selfish Impulse Versus Social Conscience p. 47
Tradeoffs: When You Can't Have It All p. 48
Putting People First p. 50

CHAPTER SUMMARY p. 53

Money Matters: Nature, Culture, and Money **p. 34**

Food for Thought: Virtuous Vegetarians **p. 35**

The Social Side of Sex: Sex and Culture **p. 36**

Tradeoffs: Political Tradeoffs **p. 50**

What Makes Us Human? Putting the Cultural Animal in Perspective **p. 53**

chapter 3   The Self 57

WHAT IS THE SELF? p. 59
The Self's Main Jobs p. 59
Who Makes the Self: The
    Individual or Society? p. 60
Self-Awareness p. 64

**WHERE SELF-KNOWLEDGE
    COMES FROM p. 67**
Looking Outside: The Looking-
    Glass Self p. 68
Looking Inside:
    Introspection p. 69

Looking at Others: Social
    Comparison p. 70
Self-Perception p. 71
The Fluctuating Image(s)
    of Self p. 71
Why People Seek
    Self-Knowledge p. 73

**SELF AND INFORMATION
    PROCESSING p. 77**
Anything That Touches
    the Self . . . p. 77
Can the Self-Concept
    Change? p. 78

**SELF-ESTEEM, SELF-
    DECEPTION,
    AND POSITIVE
    ILLUSIONS p. 81**
Self-Esteem p. 81
Reality and Illusion p. 82

How People Fool
    Themselves p. 83
Benefits of Self-Esteem p. 84
Why Do We Care? p. 85
Is High Self-Esteem Always
    Good? p. 87
Pursuing Self-Esteem p. 88

SELF-PRESENTATION p. 89
Who's Looking? p. 90
Making an Impression p. 91
Self-Presentation and Risky
    Behavior p. 93

    CHAPTER SUMMARY p. 94

Food for Thought: Eating
    Binges and Escaping the
    Self p. 66

Money Matters: Doing It for
    Money, Not Love p. 71

Tradeoffs: Self-
    Handicapping p. 75

The Social Side of Sex: Self-
    Esteem and Saying No to
    Sex p. 86

What Makes Us
    Human? Putting the
    Cultural Animal in
    Perspective p. 94

chapter 4   Choices and Actions: The Self in Control 97

**WHAT YOU DO, AND WHAT IT
    MEANS p. 99**
Making Choices p. 100
Why People Don't
    Choose p. 103
Choice and Change p. 104

**FREEDOM
    OF ACTION p. 106**
More or Less Free p. 106

Free Action Comes From
    Inside p. 106
Having an Out, Versus No Escape
    p. 107

**GOALS, PLANS,
    INTENTIONS p. 108**
Setting and Pursuing
    Goals p. 108
Hierarchy of Goals p. 109
Multiple Goals and Goal
    Shielding p. 110
Reaching Goals: What's
    the Plan? p. 111
Common Mistakes
    in Planning p. 112

SELF-REGULATION p. 113

**IRRATIONALITY AND SELF-
    DESTRUCTION p. 117**
Self-Defeating Acts: Being Your
    Own Worst Enemy p. 118
Suicide p. 119

    CHAPTER SUMMARY p. 122

Money Matters: How
    Money Can Trick You
    Into Making Bad
    Decisions p. 101

The Social Side of Sex:
    Gender, Sex, and
    Decisions p. 102

Food for Thought: Dieting
    as Self-Regulation p. 116

Tradeoffs: Now Versus
    Tomorrow: Delay of
    Gratification p. 120

What Makes Us
    Human? Putting the
    Cultural Animal in
    Perspective p. 122

chapter 5 Social Cognition 125

**WHAT IS SOCIAL
    COGNITION? p. 127**
Thinking About People: A Special
    Case? p. 127
Why People Think, and Why They
    Don't p. 128
Automatic and Controlled
    Thinking p. 129
Thought Suppression and Ironic
    Processes p. 134

**ATTRIBUTIONS: WHY DID
    THAT HAPPEN? p. 135**
It's Not My Fault: Explaining
    Success and Failure p. 136
You Looking at Me? The Actor/
    Observer Bias p. 137
The Attribution Cube and Making
    Excuses p. 139

**HEURISTICS: MENTAL
    SHORTCUTS p. 141**
Representativeness
    Heuristic p. 141
Availability Heuristic p. 142
Simulation Heuristic p. 143
Anchoring and Adjustment
    Heuristic p. 144

ERRORS AND BIASES p. 145
Confirmation Bias p. 147
Conjunction Fallacy p. 147

Illusory Correlation p. 148
Base Rate Fallacy p. 148
Gambler's Fallacy and the Hot
    Hand p. 149
False Consensus Effect p. 149
False Uniqueness Effect p. 150
Statistical Regression p. 150
Illusion of Control p. 151
Magical Thinking p. 151
Counterfactual Thinking p. 152

**ARE PEOPLE REALLY
    IDIOTS? p. 154**
How Serious Are
    the Errors? p. 154
Reducing Cognitive
    Errors p. 154

CHAPTER SUMMARY p. 156

Food for Thought: It's the
    Thought That Counts (or
    Doesn't Count!) the
    Calories p. 134

Money Matters: The
    Price of Being Mrs.
    Hisname p. 142

The Social Side
    of Sex: Counting Sex
    Partners p. 146

What Makes Us
    Human? Putting the
    Cultural Animal in
    Perspective p. 155

chapter 6 Emotion and Affect 159

WHAT IS EMOTION? p. 161
Conscious Emotion Versus
    Automatic Affect p. 162

**EMOTIONAL
    AROUSAL p. 162**
James–Lange Theory of
    Emotion p. 162
Cannon–Bard Theory of
    Emotion p. 163
Schachter–Singer Theory of
    Emotion p. 164
Misattribution
    of Arousal p. 164

**SOME IMPORTANT
    EMOTIONS p. 167**
Happiness p. 167
Anger p. 171
Guilt and Shame p. 174

**WHY DO WE HAVE
    EMOTIONS? p. 177**
Emotions Promote
    Belongingness p. 177
Emotions Cause Behavior—
    Sort Of p. 178
Emotions Guide Thinking and
    Learning p. 178
(Anticipated) Emotions Guide
    Decisions and Choices p. 180
Emotions Help and Hurt Decision
    Making p. 181
Positive Emotions Counteract
    Negative Emotions p. 181
Other Benefits of Positive
    Emotions p. 182

**GROUP DIFFERENCES IN
    EMOTION p. 183**
Are Emotions Different Across
    Cultures? p. 183
Are Women More Emotional Than
    Men? p. 185

**AROUSAL,
    ATTENTION, AND
    PERFORMANCE p. 186**

**EMOTIONAL INTELLIGENCE
    (EQ) p. 188**

**AFFECT
    REGULATION p. 189**
How to Cheer Up p. 189
Affect Regulation Goals p. 190
Gender Differences in Emotion
    Control Strategies p. 190
Is It Safe? p. 191

CHAPTER SUMMARY p. 193

The Social Side of Sex:
    Can People Be Wrong
    About Whether They Are
    Sexually Aroused? p. 165

Tradeoffs: Affect Intensity,
    or the Joys of Feeling
    Nothing p. 171

Food for Thought: Mood
    and Food p. 179

Money Matters: Emotions
    and Prices p. 182

What Makes Us
    Human? Putting the
    Cultural Animal in
    Perspective p. 192

chapter 7   Attitudes, Beliefs, and Consistency   197

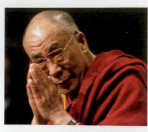

WHAT ARE ATTITUDES AND WHY DO PEOPLE HAVE THEM?   p. 200
Attitudes Versus Beliefs   p. 200
Dual Attitudes   p. 200
Why People Have Attitudes   p. 201

HOW ATTITUDES ARE FORMED   p. 202
Formation of Attitudes   p. 202
Polarization   p. 205

CONSISTENCY   p. 206
Heider's P-O-X Theory   p. 206
Cognitive Dissonance and Attitude Change   p. 206
Justifying Effort   p. 207
Justifying Choices   p. 208
Advances in Dissonance Theory   p. 210
Is the Drive for Consistency Rooted in Nature or Nurture?   p. 211

DO ATTITUDES REALLY PREDICT BEHAVIORS?   p. 211
Attacking Attitudes   p. 212
Defending Attitudes   p. 212
Conclusion: Attitudes in Action   p. 213

BELIEFS AND BELIEVING   p. 214
Believing Versus Doubting   p. 214
Belief Perseverance   p. 215
Belief and Coping   p. 215
Religious Belief   p. 217
Irrational Belief   p. 218

CHAPTER SUMMARY   p. 220

Money Matters: Would You Sell Your Soul for $1?   p. 208

Food for Thought: Would You Eat a Bug or a Worm?   p. 209

The Social Side of Sex: A–B Inconsistency and Erotic Plasticity   p. 213

What Makes Us Human? Putting the Cultural Animal in Perspective   p. 219

chapter 8   Social Influence and Persuasion   223

TWO TYPES OF SOCIAL INFLUENCE   p. 225
Being Liked: Normative Influence   p. 225
Being Correct: Informational Influence   p. 227

TECHNIQUES OF SOCIAL INFLUENCE   p. 228
Techniques Based on Commitment and Consistency   p. 228
Techniques Based on Reciprocation   p. 231
Techniques Based on Scarcity   p. 233
Techniques Based on Capturing and Disrupting Attention   p. 234

PERSUASION   p. 235
Who: The Source   p. 235
Says What: The Message   p. 237

To Whom: The Audience   p. 242
Two Routes to Persuasion   p. 244

RESISTING PERSUASION   p. 247
Attitude Inoculation   p. 248
Forewarned Is Forearmed   p. 249
Stockpile Resources   p. 249
Defenses Against Influence Techniques   p. 250

CHAPTER SUMMARY   p. 252

Money Matters: Even a Penny Will Help   p. 231

Food for Thought: Convert Communicators and Health Messages   p. 237

The Social Side of Sex: Scared Into Safe Sex?   p. 239

Tradeoffs: Should Speakers Talk Fast or Slow?   p. 247

What Makes Us Human? Putting the Cultural Animal in Perspective   p. 251

chapter 9   Prosocial Behavior: Doing What's Best for Others   255

WHAT IS PROSOCIAL BEHAVIOR?   p. 257
Born to Reciprocate   p. 259
Born to Be Fair   p. 259

COOPERATION, FORGIVENESS, OBEDIENCE, AND CONFORMITY   p. 261
Cooperation   p. 261
Forgiveness   p. 264

Obedience   p. 265
Conformity   p. 267

WHY DO PEOPLE HELP OTHERS?   p. 269
Evolutionary Benefits   p. 270
Two Motives for Helping: Altruism and Egoism   p. 271
Is Altruism Possible?   p. 273

WHO HELPS WHOM?   p. 274
Helpful Personality   p. 275
Similarity   p. 275
Gender   p. 275
Beautiful Victims   p. 275
Belief in a Just World   p. 276
Emotion and Mood   p. 277

BYSTANDER HELPING IN EMERGENCIES   p. 278
Five Steps to Helping   p. 278

Too Busy to Help?   p. 281

HOW CAN WE INCREASE HELPING?   p. 282
Getting Help in a Public Setting   p. 282
Educate Others   p. 282
Provide Helpful Models   p. 282
Teach Moral Inclusion   p. 283

CHAPTER SUMMARY   p. 285

Tradeoffs: The Prisoner's Dilemma   p. 262

Money Matters: Money, Prosocial Behavior, and Self-Sufficiency   p. 263

Food for Thought: Restaurants, Rules, and the Bad Taste of Nonconformity   p. 269

The Social Side of Sex: Helping, Sex, and Friends   p. 276

What Makes Us Human? Putting the Cultural Animal in Perspective   p. 284

chapter 10   Aggression and Antisocial Behavior   287

DEFINING AGGRESSION AND ANTISOCIAL BEHAVIOR   p. 289
Is the World More or Less Violent Now Than in the Past?   p. 292

IS AGGRESSION INNATE OR LEARNED?   p. 294
Instinct Theories   p. 294
Learning Theories   p. 295
Nature *and* Nurture   p. 296

INNER CAUSES OF AGGRESSION   p. 297
Frustration   p. 297
Being in a Bad Mood   p. 298
Hostile Cognitive Biases   p. 299
Age and Aggression   p. 299
Gender and Aggression   p. 300

INTERPERSONAL CAUSES OF AGGRESSION   p. 301
Selfishness and Influence   p. 301
Domestic and Relationship Violence: Hurting Those We Love   p. 301

EXTERNAL CAUSES OF AGGRESSION   p. 303
Weapons Effect   p. 303
Mass Media   p. 304

Unpleasant Environments   p. 306
Chemical Influences   p. 306

SELF AND CULTURE   p. 309
Norms and Values   p. 309
Self-Control   p. 310
Wounded Pride   p. 311
Culture of Honor   p. 312

OTHER ANTISOCIAL BEHAVIOR   p. 314
Lying   p. 314
Detecting Liars   p. 314
Cheating   p. 315
Stealing   p. 316
Littering   p. 317

CHAPTER SUMMARY   p. 319

Tradeoffs: Is Military Action an Effective Way to Fight Terrorism?   p. 292

The Social Side of Sex: Sexual Aggression   p. 302

Food for Thought: Is There a Link Between Diet and Violence?   p. 309

What Makes Us Human? Putting the Cultural Animal in Perspective   p. 319

chapter 11 Attraction and Exclusion 323

THE NEED TO BELONG p. 325
Belongingness as a Basic Need p. 325
Two Ingredients to Belongingness p. 328
Not Belonging Is Bad for You p. 329

Best Friends, Lovers, and . . . p. 329
ATTRACTION: WHO LIKES WHOM? p. 329
Similarity, Complementarity, Oppositeness p. 330
Social Rewards: You Make Me Feel Good p. 331
Tit for Tat: Reciprocity and Liking p. 332
You Again: Mere Exposure p. 333
Looking Good p. 335
REJECTION p. 338
Effects of Rejection: Inner Reactions p. 339

Behavioral Effects of Rejection p. 341
Loneliness p. 342
What Leads to Social Rejection? p. 343
Romantic Rejection and Unrequited Love p. 345
CHAPTER SUMMARY p. 348

Tradeoffs: Testosterone— A Blessing and a Curse p. 326
Money Matters: Is Manhood Measured in Dollars or Inches? p. 335
The Social Side of Sex: What Is Beauty? p. 337
Food for Thought: Social Rejection and the Jar of Cookies p. 340
What Makes Us Human? Putting the Cultural Animal in Perspective p. 347

chapter 12 Close Relationships: Passion, Intimacy, and Sexuality 351

WHAT IS LOVE? p. 354
Passionate and Companionate Love p. 354
Love and Culture p. 355
Love Across Time p. 356
Sternberg's Triangle p. 358

DIFFERENT TYPES OF RELATIONSHIPS p. 359
Exchange Versus Communal p. 359
Attachment p. 361
Loving People Who Love Themselves p. 364
MAINTAINING RELATIONSHIPS p. 365
I Love You More Each Day (?) p. 366
Investing in Relationships That Last p. 366
Thinking Styles of Couples p. 367

Being Yourself: Is Honesty the Best Policy? p. 369
SEXUALITY p. 372
Theories of Sexuality p. 372
Sex and Gender p. 374
Homosexuality p. 377
Extradyadic Sex p. 379
Jealousy and Possessiveness p. 381
Culture, Female Sexuality, and the Double Standard p. 386
CHAPTER SUMMARY p. 389

Tradeoffs: Sex In and Out of Marriage p. 357
Food for Thought: Eating in Front of a Cute Guy p. 378
Money Matters: Mating, Money, and Men p. 384
What Makes Us Human? Putting the Cultural Animal in Perspective p. 388

chapter 13 Prejudice and Intergroup Relations 391

ABCS OF INTERGROUP RELATIONSHIPS: PREJUDICE, DISCRIMINATION, AND STEREOTYPES p. 393
Common Prejudices and Targets **p. 396**

WHY PREJUDICE EXISTS p. 402
Us Versus Them: Groups in Competition **p. 403**

Ignorance? The Contact Hypothesis **p. 406**
Rationalizations for Oppression **p. 407**
Stereotypes as Heuristics **p. 407**
Prejudice and Self-Esteem **p. 408**

CONTENT OF PREJUDICE AND STEREOTYPES p. 409
Are Stereotypes Always Wrong, Mostly Wrong, or Mostly Right? **p. 409**
Are Stereotypes Always Negative? **p. 410**

INNER PROCESSES p. 411

OVERCOMING STEREOTYPES, REDUCING PREJUDICE p. 414
Conscious Override **p. 414**
Contact **p. 418**
Superordinate Goals **p. 418**

IMPACT OF PREJUDICE ON TARGETS p. 418
Self-Fulfilling and Self-Defeating Prophecies **p. 419**
Stigma and Self-Protection **p. 421**
Stereotype Threat **p. 422**

CHAPTER SUMMARY p. 425

Money Matters: Racial Discrimination in Sports—Paying More to Win **p. 394**

Food for Thought: Prejudice Against the Obese **p. 399**

The Social Side of Sex: Roots of Antigay Prejudice **p. 401**

Tradeoffs: Competition Versus Cooperation **p. 405**

What Makes Us Human? Putting the Cultural Animal in Perspective **p. 425**

chapter 14 Groups 429

WHAT GROUPS ARE AND DO p. 432

GROUPS, ROLES, AND SELVES p. 434

GROUP ACTION p. 436
Social Facilitation **p. 436**
Social Loafing **p. 439**
Punishing Cheaters and Free Riders **p. 441**

Deindividuation and Mob Violence **p. 441**
Shared Resources and the Commons Dilemma **p. 442**

HOW GROUPS THINK p. 443
Brainstorming, and the Wisdom of Groups **p. 443**
Why Do People Love Teams? **p. 445**
Transactive Memory: Here, You Remember This **p. 445**
Groupthink **p. 446**
Foolish Committees **p. 447**
Group Polarization and the "Risky Shift" **p. 447**

POWER AND LEADERSHIP p. 449
Leadership **p. 449**
Toxic Leaders **p. 450**
What Is Power? **p. 452**
Effects of Power on Leaders **p. 453**
Effects of Power on Followers **p. 456**
Legitimate Leadership **p. 456**

CHAPTER SUMMARY p. 457

Tradeoffs: Diversity in Groups **p. 432**

Food for Thought: Is Binge Eating Socially Contagious? **p. 439**

Money Matters: Money, Power, and Laughter **p. 454**

What Makes Us Human? Putting the Cultural Animal in Perspective **p. 457**

Glossary **G1**

References **R1**

Name Index **N1**

Subject Index **S1**

preface

This textbook is simultaneously an expression of love and rebellion. The love is our feeling toward our field. We followed different paths into social psychology, but over the years we have developed an affectionate appreciation for it. We agreed to write this textbook partly because we thought we could contribute to the field by covering what we love about it. The process of writing strengthened those positive feelings, by helping us see the remarkably diverse and creative work that our fellow psychologists have produced over the past several decades. We are also both very active social psychological researchers and teachers. We love doing social psychology research, and we love teaching students about the field of social psychology.

The rebellion part begins with the title. Maybe social psychology has sold itself short by clinging to the message "it's all about situations!" We think it's partly about situations, but to us social psychology is very much about people. We think students sign up for social psychology courses because they want to learn about people. And we think social psychologists actually have plenty to tell them about people. Hence the "human nature" part of our title.

In other words, we are rebelling against the old dogma that social psychology's truth requires treating people as blank slates who just respond to situations. Instead, we see people as highly complex, exquisitely designed, and variously inclined cultural animals who respond to situations. Our textbook will tell students plenty about the power of situations, but it also seeks to tell them about the people in those situations.

To us, the most exciting aspect of this project has been the attempt to "put the person back together," in the phrase that got us started on the book. We believe that social psychology can offer a remarkably new, coherent, and accurate vision of human nature.

In fact, this new vision of human nature was central to the story behind the book. Both of us had been approached many times by various publishers about possibly writing a social psychology textbook, and both of us had repeatedly brushed them off as quickly and thoroughly as possible. Back then we thought that writing a textbook sounded like a tedious, uncreative set of chores requiring reading and describing every part of the field, regardless of how interesting. Both of us loathe anything that is boring.

The turning point came when one of us spent a year at an interdisciplinary institute and embraced the task of trying to package what social psychology has learned that could be useful to other fields. Scholars in those fields mostly want to know about people and why they act as they do. The response to this took the form of a book for general audiences called *The Cultural Animal* (Baumeister, 2005), but the realization slowly dawned that this new, more integrated understanding of the human being might provide a powerful basis for a social psychology textbook.

We have used many different textbooks in our own social psychology courses. Many of them are quite good. One dissatisfaction with them, however, and indeed one that we have heard echoed by many other instructors and students, is that they end up being just narrative lists of findings grouped by topic, rather like a handbook or encyclopedia. We wanted more. We wanted an integrated, coherent vision. And now we had a basis in the form of a new understanding of human nature that put together the results of thousands of social psychology studies. So this time when publishers asked about writing a textbook, we thought it over. And then we decided to do it.

Some might think that explaining human nature isn't the job of social psychology and should be left to the personality psychologists. In our view, personality's claim to that question is not naturally any stronger than social psychology's. After all, personality psychologists mainly study differences between people, and so understanding the patterns common to all people isn't any more likely to arise from those data than from social psychology's data. Au contraire, learning about how people in general will respond to ordinary social dilemmas and events is at least as promising as studying individual differences in terms of being able to point toward general patterns of human nature.

Most general theories about human nature agonize over the competing explanations based on evolution and cultural influence. Our synthesis is based on the question "What sort of picture of the human being emerges from the results of thousands of social psychology experiments?" The answer is novel: Nature "made" human beings for culture. That is, we think human beings evolved specifically to belong to these complicated, information-using social systems that we call culture.

Our book has many themes that are mentioned occasionally in the various chapters to tie things together, and these are mostly derived from the theme of human beings as cultural animals. The theme of putting people first is a subtle way of conveying what is biologically unique about humans: whereas most animals get what they need from their physical environment, people get what they need from each other. This message was implicit even in the classic Asch conformity experiments, in which people would disregard the direct evidence of their physical senses in order to go along with what other people (even a collection of strangers!) were saying.

Another central theme is that inner processes serve interpersonal functions. The conventional wisdom in psychology, going back to its Freudian roots, has been more or less that what happens to people is a result of what's inside them. We think the research in social psychology points toward the need to turn that on its head. What is inside people is a result of what happens between them. Even in terms of what evolution has built into the human psyche, what is there inside the person is there to help people thrive in their social and cultural groups. People are built to relate to other people. Even the "self," much discussed and invoked throughout social psychology, is designed to cultivate social acceptance and other forms of success that are valued in human cultures.

This is not a book about evolution, nor is it a book about cultural differences. It is a book about people. Toward that end, we occasionally use insights that emerge from cultural and evolutionary studies. But those remain mostly on the sidelines. We differ from the evolutionists in that we focus more on how humans are different from other animals rather than how they are similar to other animals. We differ from the cultural psychologists in that we focus more on what cultures have in common than on how they differ. These are differences of emphasis, but they are fundamental and large ones.

The bottom line, for us, is a very positive view of human nature. Over the years, many of the major theories about people have emphasized the negative. They have depicted people as dominated by violent, destructive urges or by strivings for power, as souped-up rats in societal Skinner boxes, as spineless beings at the mercy of giant social forces or willy-nilly situational influences. We have been persuaded partly by the positive psychology movement that psychology loses much of its value when it focuses overly on the negative side. And, heck, we like people. So the integrated picture we offer is a generally positive one, though we give the dark side of human nature its due.

Hence one important feature of this book is that every chapter ends with a brief section entitled "What Makes Us Human? Putting the Cultural Animal in Perspective" that provides a quick review of what answers have emerged in that chapter. These were easy to write because we really do see that human social life is remarkably and importantly different from that of other animals. We do not shrink from discussing the flaws and biases in humanity, and we acknowledge humankind's vast capacity for petty malice and occasional capacity for great evil. But we think the final picture is mostly favorable. These end-of-chapter sections offer a brief reflection on what is special about human nature.

Concept Features

When we embarked on this book we listened long and hard to the complaints that fellow teachers of social psychology had regarding their textbooks and the way the field was taught. We also listened to the feedback from many students. Several features of our textbook are directly influenced by this feedback. We have sought to offer a new, positive alternative to existing textbooks.

The most common complaint, of course, was the lack of integration. Many instructors, and even those who liked their particular textbook, still felt that textbooks merely hopped from one finding and one phenomenon to another without any broad vision. Hence at the end of the term, as one colleague put it, the take-home message was "Social psychology is a large, interesting, and diverse field of study." Our overarching goal of putting the person back together was a direct response to this complaint and is, in our view, the defining feature of our book. The themes that run through the book help to flesh this out. These are developed in Chapter 2, "Culture and Nature," which we regard as the theoretical foundation of the book. We recommend that instructors assign this chapter early in the semester. That is why we put it early in our textbook. The subsequent chapters can be taught in almost any order. Thus, the book is not a linear sequence in which each chapter builds on the preceding one. We deliberately rejected that approach because we know many instructors like to adapt the sequence of topics to their own schedules, goals, and plans. Instead, the design of this book is like a wheel. Chapters 1 and 2 are the center, and all the other chapters are spokes.

Most chapters contain four box feature inserts. Although many textbooks have boxes, we are especially pleased with our set. In the first edition, they proved to be student favorites. We began with a fairly long list of possible boxes and gradually, based on input and feedback from students and instructors, trimmed these down to the list of four that run through the chapters. For the second edition, we kept three of the four boxes from the first edition. The fourth set, devoted to the broad theme that "bad is stronger than good," was also well received, but reluctantly we deleted that set to make room for an even more exciting set.

FOOD FOR THOUGHT

One box in every chapter has to do with eating. One of us recalls a conversation years ago with Peter Herman, who observed that "Eating is the perfect social psychology variable, because it is connected to almost every social variable or process you can think of!" As we researched the various chapters and thought about the findings, we came to see he was right, and so each chapter has a box that covers some findings showing how the chapter's topic influences or is influenced by eating. We thought this would be especially appealing to today's students, for whom college often presents a novel set of challenges and opportunities for eating, dieting, drinking, and related concerns. Eating is a microcosm of social processes. Following are the *Food For Thought* topics included in the book:

Does Chicken Soup Reduce Cold Symptoms?
(Chapter 1)
Virtuous Vegetarians (Chapter 2)
Eating Binges and Escaping the Self
(Chapter 3)
Dieting as Self-Regulation (Chapter 4)
It's the Thought That Counts (or Doesn't Count!) the Calories (Chapter 5)
Mood and Food (Chapter 6)
Would You Eat a Bug or a Worm? (Chapter 7)
Convert Communicators and Health Messages (Chapter 8)
Restaurants, Rules, and the Bad Taste of Nonconformity (Chapter 9)
Is There a Link Between Diet and Violence?
(Chapter 10)
Social Rejection and the Jar of Cookies
(Chapter 11)
Eating in Front of a Cute Guy (Chapter 12)
Prejudice Against the Obese (Chapter 13)
Is Binge Eating Socially Contagious?
(Chapter 14)
Fostering Healthy Eating (Module B)
Work Stress and Eating (Module C)

THE SOCIAL SIDE OF SEX

The same can be said for sex, and so each chapter has a box applying social psychology to sexuality. We suspect that few people leave college with their sexual selves unchanged since arrival, and so students' natural and personal interest in sexuality can be useful for illuminating many perspectives and patterns in social psychology. Our emphasis is, of course, not on the mechanics or techniques of sex but rather on the social context and influences, which the field of sexuality has often underappreciated. It is also helpful that human sexual behavior is a vivid, dramatic example of something that shows powerful influences of both nature and culture. Following are *The Social Side of Sex* topics included in the book:

Sex and Culture (Chapter 2)
Self-Esteem and Saying No to Sex (Chapter 3)
Gender, Sex, and Decisions (Chapter 4)
Counting Sex Partners (Chapter 5)
Can People Be Wrong About Whether They Are Sexually Aroused? (Chapter 6)
A–B Inconsistency and Erotic Plasticity
(Chapter 7)
Scared Into Safe Sex? (Chapter 8)
Helping, Sex, and Friends (Chapter 9)
Sexual Aggression (Chapter 10)
What Is Beauty? (Chapter 11)
Roots of Antigay Prejudice (Chapter 13)
Sex for Sale (Module A)
Increasing Condom Use and Safe Sex Practices (Module B)
Sexual Harassment (Module C)

TRADEOFFS

A third box presents tradeoffs. In this box we attempt to stimulate critical thinking. Many students come to social psychology wanting to find ways to change the world and solve its problems. We applaud that idealism, but we also think that many problems have their origin in the basic truth that solving one problem sometimes creates another. Many social psychology findings highlight tradeoffs in which each gain comes with a loss. Indeed, in other writings, we apply that principle to assorted issues, not least including gender differences: If men are better than women at something, they are probably worse at something else, and the two are interlinked. We hope that the students will come away from these boxes with a heightened integrative capacity to see both sides of many problems and behaviors. Following are the *Tradeoffs* topics included in the book:

Political Tradeoffs (Chapter 2)
Self-Handicapping (Chapter 3)
Now Versus Tomorrow: Delay of Gratification
(Chapter 4)
Affect Intensity, or the Joys of Feeling Nothing (Chapter 6)
Should Speakers Talk Fast or Slow? (Chapter 8)
The Prisoner's Dilemma (Chapter 9)
Is Military Action an Effective Way to Fight Terrorism? (Chapter 10)
Testosterone—A Blessing and a Curse
(Chapter 11)
Sex In and Out of Marriage (Chapter 12)
Competition Versus Cooperation (Chapter 13)
Diversity in Groups (Chapter 14)

Wrongful Convictions vs. Protecting Victims (Module D)

The Tragedy of the Commons (Module E)

MONEY MATTERS

New for the second edition is a series of boxes on money. This set was stimulated in part by listening to Paul Rozin, a thoughtful contrarian who has criticized psychology for being out of step with the interests of most people. He would hold up a copy of *USA Today*, "the nation's newspaper," and note that its four sections (politics/crime, money, sports, and life/style) are presumably what American citizens are most interested in reading—yet these topics are scarcely even mentioned in the indexes of most psychology textbooks.

Money is highly relevant to our theme of humans as cultural animals. Money is often spent on getting things that nature makes us want: food, shelter, warmth, comfort, and even health and sex. Social events, such as war, can greatly influence the value of money. Yet money is undeniably a cultural phenomenon. Thus, money shows how humankind has found cultural means of satisfying natural inclinations. Social psychologists (like intellectuals across the ages) have often been skeptical and critical of money, and especially of the desire for money. Yet money is a fact of life and an almost indispensable ingredient to the good life in modern society. We hope that this brand-new series of boxes will stimulate students to see money through the prism of social psychology's diverse interests. Following are the *Money Matters* topics included in the book:

Nature, Culture, and Money (Chapter 2)

Doing It for Money, Not Love (Chapter 3)

How Money Can Trick You Into Making Bad Decisions (Chapter 4)

The Price of Being Mrs. Hisname (Chapter 5)

Emotions and Prices (Chapter 6)

Would You Sell Your Soul for $1? (Chapter 7)

Even a Penny Will Help (Chapter 8)

Money, Prosocial Behavior, and Self-Sufficiency (Chapter 9)

Is Manhood Measured in Dollars or Inches? (Chapter 11)

Mating, Money, and Men (Chapter 12)

Racial Discrimination in Sports: Paying More to Win (Chapter 13)

Money, Power, and Laughter (Chapter 14)

The Costs and Benefits of Environmental Protection (Module E)

Other themes run through the book without being formally reflected in specific boxes. The "duplex mind," divided into the automatic/noncon-scious and the controlled/conscious sets of processes, has become a powerful theme in the field's thinking about a great many issues, and we want students to appreciate it. It is a profound insight into how the human mind is organized. "The long road to social acceptance" reflects how much work humans have to do to gain and keep their places in their social networks. "Nature says go, culture says stop" was not on our original list of themes but kept coming up as we wrote, and so we went back to revise our earlier chapters to recognize this one common way that nature and culture interact to shape human behavior.

Pedagogical Features

Our book has also benefited from input and suggestions for what can help students master the material. We have kept what has worked well in other textbooks, such as including glossaries, tables, and illustrations. In this edition we included more graphs from individual studies—roughly two graphs per chapter more than the first edition had. We created these graphs ourselves rather than having someone else do them for us. Several of the graphs are based on our own research. Each chapter also ends with a "Chapter Summary," where we present lists of bullet points summarizing key content in the chapter.

A more novel feature of our textbook is the inclusion of many self-quizzes. Each major header in each chapter ends with a series of multiple-choice questions. These were wildly popular with students in the first edition. We can understand why many books don't include them—they were an immense amount of work to prepare—but we think the effort was worth it. Every time students finish reading a section of a chapter, they can get a quick check on how well they understood it by answering those questions and verifying whether their answers are correct. For the second edition, we reworked all the quizzes and added more challenging questions.

Another exciting feature of this book is the set of application modules that can be assigned according to instructor preference. It is possible to get the book printed with or without these modules, or indeed with any combination of them. The five available with the first edition were: (Module A) Applying Social Psychology to Consumer Behavior, (Module B) Applying Social Psychology to Health, (Module C) Applying Social Psychology to the Workplace, (Module D) Applying Social Psychology to the Law, and (Module E) Applying Social Psychology to the Environment. We retained these same modules for the second edition. These modules enable an instructor to tailor a course that can encompass some of the most important applied fields of study that have had long, close relationships with social psychology.

More With Less

When we embarked on this textbook, we made "doing more with less" one of our guiding mottos. As we saw it, social psychology was approaching a turning point. The early textbooks often went into lively detail about many specific studies. That was possible because back then there wasn't a great deal of material to cover. Since then, the body of knowledge in the field has expanded year by year, with new findings being continuously documented in established journals along with new journals popping up all the time. It is no longer possible to cover all the influential studies in great detail.

Some textbooks have responded to information overload by packing more and more findings into the same amount of space. This plainly cannot go on forever. Either textbooks have to get longer and longer, or they have to become more and more selective. We chose the latter course. As things turned out, we were able to cover most of what has become standard in textbooks. But we do not claim or pretend to be exhaustive. Our model for this is introductory psychology. Once upon a time, perhaps, introductory textbooks could provide a comprehensive overview of psychology, but it has by now become standard practice for them merely to select a few topics for each chapter to illustrate rather than fully cover what that field has to offer. We think social psychology is reaching the same point and that the way forward is to accept the impossibility of covering it all.

To be sure, the review process did push us to be more thorough. One thing experts are very good at is saying, "Well, you could also cover X," and we heeded many such comments from our expert reviewers. But our goal all along has been to offer students an in-depth look at some information, with all its implications and connections highlighted, rather than to make sure to cite every relevant study. We hope instructors will add their personal favorites to the lectures, to augment what we have included. But to keep the book to a manageable length and still do justice to our goals, we had to leave out many important and worthy studies. Even some large topics ended up getting short shrift. Most notably, we devote fairly little space to the social neuroscience work that has become an important theme in the field. We don't dispute its importance. We simply think it is not what is best for introductory students.

Our recommendation is that universities offer a subsequent course that can focus on brain processes and their link to social behavior. For the first course, we think students would prefer to learn about the more familiar and more readily understood questions about how people think, feel, and act in recognizable social situations.

What's New in the Second Edition?

We were delighted with the positive reception of the first edition of our textbook, which sold nearly three times as many copies as the publisher's own official sales targets had hoped. We are full of gratitude toward all who have used the book. We heard from many instructors and students who made suggestions for material to cover, noticed typos or other things to fix, or simply wanted to express their liking for the book. Thanks to all.

In that happy spirit we set to work on the second edition. Our goals were to keep it current, to retain its core vision and best features, and to make substantial, targeted improvements in a few areas where we felt there were promising opportunities or recent developments in the field. Our treatment of the boxes (see earlier "Concept Features" section) exemplified this approach: We retained three of the four series, though we updated some individual boxes and replaced others. And we replaced one series of boxes ("Is Bad Stronger Than Good?") with an exciting new series ("Money Matters").

All chapters have come in for revision, especially updating their coverage with the addition of some recent research findings. Still, some chapters underwent more sweeping changes than others. Among these were Chapter 1, which includes a new section on graphs and how to interpret them (especially appropriate, given the addition of many more graphs than the first edition had). Chapter 2 also underwent extensive revision, which now sets out the book's core ideas and its grand context for understanding social behavior in a much more easily understandable and comprehensive manner. Chapter 4 has now a clearer focus on choice and decision making, along with other issues of control (e.g., self-regulation, reactance). The recent progress in research on emotion (Chapter 6) and power and leadership (Chapter 14) led to some of the more extensive revisions. The aggression chapter (Chapter 10) was also revised extensively, with a new opening vignette and current research on violent video game effects. We also added a section showing that although the world seems like a very violent place today (probably because the most violent stories are featured in the mass media), over time the world is actually becoming a more peaceful place. Chapter 10 also contains new material on lying due to the rising interest in lying in the popular media and culture (e.g., the new *Lie to Me* TV drama).

In a move to produce a more logical sequence and organization, we moved the chapter on social influence from its former place late in the book (Chapter 13) up to follow immediately after the Attitudes chapter (currently, Attitudes, Chapter 7, and Social Influence, Chapter 8).

We beefed up the very popular self-quiz feature by adding one relatively challenging item to each self-quiz, thereby providing a greater balance than the first edition so that students of all ability levels can find something useful and appropriate with which to check on their progress.

Some reviewers of the previous edition thought that including more graphs of research findings would improve the book. We agreed heartily with that suggestion and added a sizeable number of new graphs. Generally there are about two new such graphs per chapter.

We hope you will enjoy the second edition of our book. If you have suggestions for improvement or discover errors in the text, please let us know by dropping us an email (baumeister@psy.fsu.edu or bbushman@umich.edu). Again, we are deeply grateful for the opportunity to share our love of social psychology with students and teachers around the world.

Content Overview

CHAPTER 1: THE MISSION AND THE METHOD

The opening chapter explains what social psychologists do and why students may want to learn about it. It explains social psychology's place among the different fields that study human behavior. It offers a brief introduction to the methods social psychologists use to tell the difference between right and wrong theories.

CHAPTER 2: CULTURE AND NATURE

Chapter 2 sets up the big picture. How do we explain people? Departing from the old and tired battle of nature against nurture, this book follows a newly emerging understanding: nature and culture worked together, such that nature designed the human

being to be capable of culture. The stock notion of "the social animal" is shown to be correct but far too limited, whereas the "cultural animal" captures what is special about human beings.

This chapter then sets up many of the integrative themes that will run through the book to help make sense of the many facts and findings that will be covered.

CHAPTER 3: THE SELF

The human self is a complex and marvelous participant in the social world. This chapter provides a coherent understanding of the human self that is based on both classic and recent research in social psychology.

CHAPTER 4: CHOICES AND ACTIONS: THE SELF IN CONTROL

The self is not just an idea but also a doer. This chapter covers key social psychology topics of choice, decision making, self-regulation, and the psychology of action. The remarkable recent progress in this work lends extra excitement to this material.

CHAPTER 5: SOCIAL COGNITION

Social cognition revolutionized social psychology in the 1980s. Now it has settled into a core basis for understanding many spheres of social life. Cognition is vital to cultural animals, because cultures operate on the basis of information. This is a showcase for many of the great achievements of social psychology.

CHAPTER 6: EMOTION AND AFFECT

Studying emotion has proven much harder than studying cognition, and so Chapter 6 cannot compare with Chapter 5 in being able to point to a solid body of accepted knowledge. Despite that, much has been learned, and the "work in progress" flavor of the social psychology of emotion—combined with the natural human interest in emotion that students can readily share—should make this chapter an appealing read.

CHAPTER 7: ATTITUDES, BELIEFS, AND CONSISTENCY

The study of attitudes has a long and distinguished history in social psychology. This chapter brings together the influential early, classic studies with the latest advances.

CHAPTER 8: SOCIAL INFLUENCE AND PERSUASION

Social influence and attempted persuasion are deeply woven into the fabric of human social life, and indeed it is the rare social interaction that has absolutely none. As information-using cultural animals, humans often find themselves wanting to influence others or being the targets of influence. This chapter covers how people exert that influence, why they do—and how sometimes people manage to resist influence.

CHAPTER 9: PROSOCIAL BEHAVIOR: DOING WHAT'S BEST FOR OTHERS

In this chapter, we look at what people do in order to make possible the success of their cultural and social groups. Many textbooks have a chapter on helping. We cover helping in this chapter, but the broad focus is on all prosocial behavior. The integrative focus helps resolve some long-running debates, such as whether helping is genuinely altruistic and prosocial or merely egoistic and selfish. We also break with the Milgram tradition of depicting obedience and conformity as bad, because culture and thus human social life would collapse without them.

CHAPTER 10: AGGRESSION AND ANTISOCIAL BEHAVIOR

Just as Chapter 9 replaced the traditional, narrow focus on helping with a broader focus on prosocial behavior, this chapter replaces the traditional focus on aggression with a broader treatment of antisocial behavior. Aggression is treated here as a holdover from the social animal stage—which is why cultures mainly struggle to reduce and prevent aggression, favoring nonviolent means of resolving conflicts. Other antisocial behaviors covered include cheating, stealing, littering, and lying.

CHAPTER 11: ATTRACTION AND EXCLUSION

This chapter combines two very different but complementary sets of findings. The study of interpersonal attraction has a long history and, despite the occasional new finding, is a fairly well-established body of knowledge. The study of interpersonal rejection is far more recent but has become a thriving, fast-moving area. Together they constitute the two sides of the coin of people trying to connect with each other.

CHAPTER 12: CLOSE RELATIONSHIPS: PASSION, INTIMACY, AND SEXUALITY

In its first decades, social psychology mainly studied interactions among strangers—but most social life involves ongoing relationships. The study of close, intimate relationships blossomed in the 1980s from a small, underappreciated corner into a profound and exciting enterprise that changed the field. This chapter covers this work, much of it quite recent. It emphasizes romantic and sexual relationships, showcasing what social psychology has contributed to understanding of these grand, perennial human dramas. Human romance and sex are eternal problems that reveal our evolutionary background but also highlight the many striking ways in which humans are unique.

CHAPTER 13: PREJUDICE AND INTERGROUP RELATIONS

Prejudice occurs all over the world, often contributing to violence and oppression and other forms of misery. This chapter examines the many forms and faces of prejudice, ranging from the standard topics of racism and sexism to the less remarked prejudices against obese people, Arabs and Muslims, and homosexuals. Special emphasis is given to the emerging and uplifting work on how people overcome prejudice.

CHAPTER 14: GROUPS

All over the world, human beings live in small groups. This chapter takes a fresh and exciting look at the social psychology of groups. The first part addresses one often-overlooked but basic question, namely why are some groups more and others less than the sum of their parts? Classic material on group processes is mixed with new and exciting research.

Supplements

Annotated Instructor's Edition. Mary Johannesen-Schmidt, Oakton Community College. On nearly every page of this limited quantity instructor's edition, instructors will find annotations—25 to 30 annotations per chapter. Three kinds of tips appear: Teaching Tips, Discussion Tips, and Technology Tips. The technology tips direct instructors to specific websites. Exact URLs for the websites are available at the instructor's companion website.

Instructor's Resource Manual. Kelly Bouas Henry, Missouri Western State University. Each chapter of the manual includes the following elements:

- **Chapter outline.** Very detailed review of the chapter with key terms underlined and defined.
- **Lecture/discussion ideas.** Substantial prompts that provide helpful ways to address topics in the text, cover topics tangential to what is in the text, or provide alternative examples to what are presented in the text.
- **Class activity/demonstration ideas.** Substantial prompts for in-class activities.
- **Student projects/homework.** Short and longer term assignments. Substantial prompts for projects that students can do on their own as out-of-class assignments, or short-term projects.
- **Video clip suggestions.** Includes video clip suggestions from the *Social Psychology & Human Nature* DVD, the introduction to psychology ABC video collection, the Research in Action collection, and the Psychology in Film collection from Cengage Learning, as well as some YouTube video clip suggestions.
- **Video/DVD suggestions.** Includes helpful video resources available from third party sources for purchase or rental.
- **Handouts.** Each chapter includes helpful handouts that correlate with suggested activities and homework.

Test Bank. Kelly Bouas Henry, Missouri Western State University. For each chapter of the text, the print test bank includes the following features:

- Between 130 to 160 multiple-choice questions
- 15 true-false questions
- 15 completion questions
- 7 short essay questions
- Each question is coded with the following information: answer (ANS), difficulty level (DIF), question type (TYPE), main-text page reference (REF), and notation for questions on the website (WWW) and for questions new to the second edition (New).

ExamView. Computerized test-creation software on CD populated with all of the content from the Print Test Bank.

PowerLecture with JoinIn and ExamView.*
Fred W. Whitford, Montana State University. This

expansive DVD-ROM includes a wealth of intriguing social psychology videos. The Instructor DVD also includes PowerPoint lecture outlines and teaching tips embedded in "notes" and core text figures, photos, and extensive video clips. Exclusive "Author Lecture Launcher Videos" feature Baumeister and Bushman explaining key topics—"Why I Decided to Become a Social Psychologist," "Humans are Social and Cultural Animals," "What is Emotion?," "Effective Ways to Reduce Anger," "Public Self vs. Private Self," "Self-Esteem," and "Self-Control and Self-Regulation." Exclusive Wadsworth social psychology research videos introduce your students to a range of contemporary researchers such as Claude Steele, Vicki Helgeson, Roy Baumeister, Melanie Green, Greg Herek, Jeanne Tsai, Mahzarin Banaji, Rodolfo Mendoza-Denton, and Richard Moreland, among others. Instructors will find "ready-to-go" PowerPoint presentations with embedded graphics and videos, as well as separate asset files so that they can tailor their own lecture presentations. The DVD also includes electronic files for the print test bank and instructor's resource manual.

ABC Social Psychology Videos. High interest video clips from ABC covering various Social Psychology topics such as the Self-Esteem Movement, Venting Aggression, and more.

Classic and Contemporary Videos Student CD-ROM. High-interest video clips of classic and contemporary social psychology research.

Revealing Psychology. Real-world vignettes revealing human foibles and illustrating underlying psychological principles.

Social Psych in Film. Clips from the movies illustrating key ideas in social psychology

CengageNow for Baumeister and Bushman's *Social Psychology and Human Nature.* Multiple-choice pre- and post-tests that generate study plans for students. Student review of concepts is enhanced through interactive media modules.

Applying Social Psychology to Your Life: Personal Surveys. Includes instruments to gauge student attitudes for each chapter.

Study Guide. Fred W. Whitford, Montana State University. Each chapter of the study guide has five main parts: (a) Chapter Review, (b) Chapter Test, (c) Suggested Readings, (d) Key Terms, and (e) Answer Key. The Chapter Test covers all the major sections of the chapter. The Chapter Test includes the following elements: multiple-choice questions, true-

---

*The robust PowerLecture DVD-ROM is available to instructors upon adoption.

false questions, and short-essay questions. Suggested Readings include a list of additional resources that students can read for additional information.

Cultural Animal Reader. Joshua Feinberg, Saint Peter's College. Reader contains full text articles that relate to the overarching book themes with critical thinking questions for each chapter.

Webtutor Toolbox on WebCT and Blackboard. Online course management program.

Book Companion Website. Text-specific content for each chapter including glossary, flash cards, multiple-choice quizzing, weblinks, and more.

Acknowledgments

EDITORIAL BOARD

We are grateful to the members of the first edition editorial board for their guidance and suggestions.

Bruce Bartholow, University of Missouri
Jennifer Crocker, University of Michigan
Wendi Gardner, Northwestern University
Cheryl Kaiser, University of Washington
Marc Kiviniemi, University of Nebraska–Lincoln
Daniel Molden, Northwestern University
Richard Ryan, University of Rochester
Kennon M. Sheldon, University of Missouri
Jeff Sherman, University of California–Davis
Jean Twenge, San Diego State University
Kathleen Vohs, University of Minnesota

CONTENT AREA EXPERT REVIEWERS

We thank our colleagues for providing their expertise on specific chapters. Their comments sharpened and improved these chapters.

Craig A. Anderson, Iowa State University
James R. Averill, University of Massachusetts–Amherst
Donal E. Carlston, Carlston, Purdue University
Eddie M. Clark, St. Louis University
William D. Crano, Claremont Graduate University
Wind Goodfriend, Boise State University
Anne K. Gordon, Bowling Green State University
Michael Hogg, University of Queensland
Lee Jussim, Rutgers University
Marc Kiviniemi, University of Nebraska–Lincoln

Mark K. Leary, Duke University
George Levinger, University of Massachusetts–Amherst
Norman Miller, University of Southern California
Todd D. Nelson, California State University–Stanislaus
Laurie O'Brien, University of California–Santa Barbara
B. Keith Payne, University of North Carolina–Chapel Hill
Louis A. Penner, Wayne State University
Cynthia L. Pickett, University of California–Davis
Deborah Richardson, Augusta State University
Brandon J. Schmeichel, Texas A&M University
Peter B. Smith, University of Sussex
Jeff Stone, University of Arizona
Duane T. Wegener, Purdue University
Kipling D. Williams, Purdue University

MANUSCRIPT REVIEWERS

We thank our colleagues for their diligent and thoughtful readings of early drafts of the second edition chapters. Their suggestions pointed the way to make this a better book.

Gordon Bear, Ramapo College of New Jersey
Khanh Bui, Pepperdine University
Nilanjana Dasgupta, University of Massachusetts—Amherst
Kimberly Fairchild, Manhattan College
Jennifer Feenstra, Northwestern College
Joseph R. Ferrari, Vincent DePaul University
Kathleen McKinley, Cabrini College
Mark Muraven, University at Albany
Ernest Park, Cleveland State University
Ludmila Praslova, Vanguard University of Southern California
Christopher Robinson, University of Alabama, Birmingham
Heidi Wayment, Northern Arizona University

We thank our colleagues for their diligent and thoughtful readings of early drafts of the first edition chapters. Their suggestions pointed the way to make this a better book.

Nancy L. Ashton, The Richard Stockton College of New Jersey
Melissa Atkins, Marshall University
Kevin Bennett, Pennsylvania State University–Beaver
John Bickford, University of Massachusetts–Amherst
Kurt Boniecki, University of Central Arkansas
Thomas Britt, Clemson University

Jonathan Brown, University of Washington
Jeff Bryson, San Diego State University
Shawn Burn, California Polytechnic
 State University
Jennifer L. Butler, Wittenberg University
Keith Campbell, University of Georgia
Laurie Couch, Morehead State University
Traci Y. Craig, University of Idaho
Janet Crawford, Rutgers University
Layton Curl, Metropolitan State College of
 Denver
Deborah Davis, University of Nevada–Reno
John Davis, Texas State University–San Marcos
Dorothee Dietrich, Hamline University
Nancy Dye, Humboldt State University
Sarah Estow, Dartmouth College
Jennifer Feenstra, Northwestern College
Joe R. Ferrari, DePaul University
Lisa Finkelstein, Northern Illinois University
Phil Finney, Southeast Missouri State University
Wendi Gardner, Northwestern University
Bryan Gibson Central Michigan University
Tom Gilovich, Cornell University
Traci Giuliano, Southwestern University
Wind Goodfriend, Boise State University
Elizabeth Gray, Northpark University
Jeffrey D. Green, Soka University
Hillary Haley, Santa Monica College
Darlene Hannah, Wheaton College
Judith Harackiewicz, University of Wisconsin
Lora Harpster, Salt Lake City Community
 College
Helen C. Harton, University of Northern Iowa
Sandra Hoyt, Ohio University
Jon Iuzzini, University of Tennessee–Knoxville
Norine Jalbert, Western Connecticut State
 University
Robert Johnson, Arkansas State University
Deana Julka, University of Portland
Patrice Karn, University of Ottawa
Benjamin R. Karney, University of Florida
Timothy Ketelaar, New Mexico State University
Charles Kimble, University of Dayton
Linda Kline, California State University–Chico
Elisha Klirs, George Mason University
C. Raymond Knee, University of Houston
Susan Kraus, Fort Lewis College
Neil Kressel, William Patterson University
Joachim Kreuger, Brown University
Roger Kreuz, University of Memphis
Douglas Krull, Northern Kentucky University
Barry Kuhle, Dickinson College
Paul Kwon, Washington State University
Benjamin Le, Haverford College
Lisa Lockhart, University of the Incarnate Word
Britton Mace, Southern Utah University
Stephanie Madon, Iowa State University

Mark Muraven, State University of New York–
 Albany
Matt Newman, Bard College
Nelse Ostlund, University of Nevada–Las Vegas
Stephen Phillips, Broward Community College
Gregory Pool, St Mary's University
Jacqueline Pope-Tarrance, Western Kentucky
 University
Jack Powell, University of Hartford
Jim Previte, Victor Valley College
Mary Pritchard, Boise State University
Joan Rollins, Rhode Island College
Tonya Rondinone, St. Joseph College
Barry R. Schlenker, University of Florida
Brandon Schmeichel, Texas A&M University
Sherry Schnake, Saint Mary of the Woods
 College
Brian W. Schrader, Emporia State University
Gretchen Sechrist, State University of New
 York–Buffalo
Paul Silvia, University of North Carolina–
 Greensboro
Royce Singleton, Holy Cross University
Alexander Soldat, Idaho State University
Sam Sommers, Tufts University
Weylin Sternglanz, NOVA Southeastern
 University
Jeff Stone, University of Arizona
Rowena Tan, University of Northern Iowa
Stephanie Tobin, University of Houston
Tamara Towles-Schwen, Buffalo State College
David Trafimow, New Mexico State University
David Ward, Arkansas Tech University
Dolores Ward, Spring Hill College
Keith Williams, The Richard Stockton College
 of New Jersey
Kevin Woller, Rogers State University
Jennifer Yanowitz, University of Minnesota
Ann Zak, College of Saint Rose

CLASS TEST PARTICIPANTS

We express our gratitude to the instructors (and their students) who applied early drafts of the book to real-world classroom instruction, providing essential feedback to enhance the book's effectiveness for the best possible learning experience.

CONTRIBUTORS OF APPLYING SOCIAL PSYCHOLOGY MODULES

Special thanks go to our colleagues who wrote the application modules. These are specialized topics outside our own expertise, and we could not have done these ourselves even half as well. These modules add to the breadth and flexibility of what can be taught with this textbook.

Module A: Applying Social Psychology to Consumer Behavior. Traci Y. Craig, University of Idaho

Module B: Applying Social Psychology to Health. Regan A. R. Gurung, University of Wisconsin–Green Bay

Module C: Applying Social Psychology to the Workplace. Kathy Hanisch, Iowa State University

Module D: Applying Social Psychology to the Law. Margaret Bull Kovera, John Jay College of Criminal Justice, City University of New York

Module E: Applying Social Psychology to the Environment. Richard L. Miller, University of Nebraska at Kearney

AUTHORS OF THE SUPPLEMENTS

A textbook is far more than the book itself. We chose Wadsworth to publish our textbook in part because they showed imagination and commitment for getting a great total package to make the instructor's life easy and the student's experience fulfilling. We deeply appreciate the people who contributed these wonderful resources.

Annotated Instructor's Edition. Mary Johannesen-Schmidt, Oakton Community College

Instructor's Resource Manual. Kelly Henry, Missouri Western University

Test Bank. Kelly Henry, Missouri Western University

PowerLecture with JoinIn and Examview. Fred Whitford, Montana State University

Study Guide. Fred Whitford, Montana State University.

Cultural Animal Reader. Joshua Feinberg, Saint Peter's College

WADSWORTH TEAM

This book would not have been possible without the excellent in-house team at Wadsworth. Thanks to the following people for your belief in our vision for this book: Linda Schreiber, Senior Publisher; Jane Potter, Senior Sponsoring Editor; Jeremy Judson, Managing Development Editor; Trina Tom, Assistant Editor; Nic Albert, Editorial Assistant; Bessie Weiss, Managing Media Editor for Social Sciences; Lauren Keyes, Media Editor; Kimberly Russell, Executive Marketing Manager; Anna Andersen, Marketing Coordinator; Roman Barnes, Photo Researcher; Pat Waldo, Project Manager; Vernon Boes, Art Director; and Nicole Lee Petel of Lachina Publishing Services.

We acknowledge our appreciation and debt to this full team, but we must single out the two people who have had the most direct contact with us and who, at least from where we have sat for these several years, have made the most difference.

Jeremy Judson was a patient, thoughtful, intelligent, and diplomatic development editor who was remarkably effective at steering the manuscript through the nuts and bolts of the revision process. Often he would manage to sort through a dozen or more reviews, boiling the chaotic mass of suggestions down into the key targets for improvement and managing the process with reason and good humor. Jeremy stayed with us for the first and second edition of our book; we hope he will be around for the third edition too!

Last, and most of all, we thank Michele Sordi, our wonderful publisher who signed the book in the first place and oversaw the preservation and fulfillment of its original vision (no small feat!). We shall be ever grateful for her creativity, her energy, her resourcefulness, her intelligence, and her loyal support. We have also very much enjoyed working with our new editor, Jane Potter.

Social Psychology and Human Nature

chapter 1

The Mission and the Method

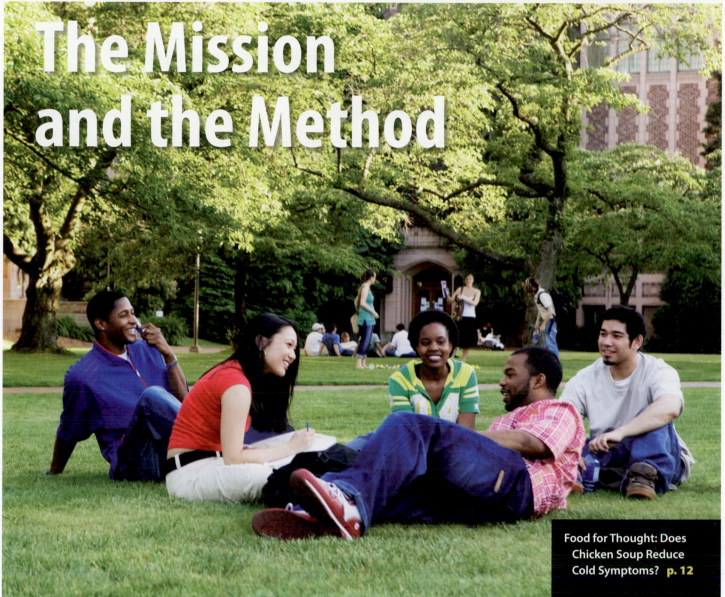

Food for Thought: Does Chicken Soup Reduce Cold Symptoms? **p. 12**

Andersen Ross/Getty Images

A BRIEF HISTORY OF SOCIAL PSYCHOLOGY p. 3

WHAT DO SOCIAL PSYCHOLOGISTS DO? p. 6

SOCIAL PSYCHOLOGY'S PLACE IN THE WORLD p. 7
Social Psychology's Place in the Social Sciences p. 7
Social Psychology's Place Within Psychology p. 8

WHY PEOPLE STUDY SOCIAL PSYCHOLOGY p. 9
Curiosity About People p. 9
Experimental Philosophy p. 9
Making the World Better p. 10
Social Psychology Is Fun! p. 10

HOW DO SOCIAL PSYCHOLOGISTS ANSWER THEIR OWN QUESTIONS? p. 11
Accumulated Common Wisdom p. 11

Overview of the Scientific Method p. 11
Scientific Theories p. 12
Research Design p. 14

HOW MUCH OF SOCIAL PSYCHOLOGY IS TRUE? p. 20
Self-Correcting Nature of Science p. 20
Reliance on Student Samples p. 20
Cultural Relativity p. 21

CHAPTER SUMMARY p. 21

Consider a few examples. In 2004, a rally for world peace was held in California. Sixteen thousand people came together from nine different countries to support the worthy cause of reducing violence and promoting harmony among all human beings. Many stayed up all night holding hands in a giant circle and praying for peace. Is it possible for human beings to live in peace? World War I was called "the war to end all wars," but after World War II that name went out of fashion. The colossal slaughter and destruction of World War II might have taught humanity some lessons about the importance of peace, yet wars continued; one expert calculated that during the 40 years after the end of World War II there were only 26 days of world peace, defined as the absence of international wars (Sluka, 1992). (Civil wars didn't count; if you count them, there were probably no days of peace at all.) World peace remains even today a hope of idealists, and we must be grateful for the efforts of campaigners such as those who rally for it. Yet it turns out that on the first day of the conference, several of the delegates got into an argument in the parking lot, and one beat another badly with a shovel. Why would people attending a rally for world peace start fighting each other?

Here are some stories from the news. A woman who was charged in the drunk-driving death of her son was sent to prison. The judge allowed her a leave for 24 hours to attend her son's funeral. Instead of attending the funeral, however, she went to a bar that was about a mile away from the church where the funeral was held. Another judge, in another country, removed a 9-year-old girl from her mother's home because he did not approve of the name the mother had given her child: "Talulah Does the Hula." He said such names humiliated children and should not be used. Other names were also rejected, such as Sex Fruit and, for twins, Fish and Chips. Still, not all weird names could be disallowed, and some children were named Number 16 Bus Shelter, Violence, and Midnight Chardonnay. In Santiago, Chile, a prostitute auctioned 27 hours of sex (she called it "love") and raised $4,000 for a charity event to help poor and disabled children.

Religion has been much in the news, but the coverage has been mixed. In Maryland, during the gasoline crisis of 2008, a community organizer held group meetings at gas stations, in which the group prayed for divine intervention to reduce fuel prices. Unfortunately, the prices remained high. (They did come down eventually.)

Another type of news story that created a minor furor in 2004 concerned the traffic signals in New York City. Many intersections had buttons for pedestrians to press in order to change the signals—to halt car traffic and activate the signal that it was safe to walk across the street. City officials admitted that many of these buttons were not even connected properly and did not work at all. Why did they have the buttons if they didn't work?

In Brussels, two Belgian beer fans (one a software designer, the other an electrical engineer) launched a video game called "Place to Pee." In one of the games,

This Chilean prostitute, Maria Carolina, auctioned 27 hours of sex to raise money for a disabled children's charity.

players can blow up aliens in outer space by aiming at sensors positioned on either side of the urinal. A specially designed paper cone allows women to play too!

Or consider the man who auctioned his "entire life" on eBay. He had recently divorced and wanted to make a new start. So he put up for bid his house in Australia and everything in it, his Mazda car, motorcycle, jet ski, parachuting gear, a trial run at his sales assistant job at a rug shop, and an introduction to his friends. The winning bid was 399,300 Australian dollars (about $389,000). He said, "I am relatively pleased but I thought it would go a bit higher, if I'm honest."

Or consider something much simpler, such as taking a coffee break. If your boss told you to make 10,000 decisions before you got your first cup of coffee, you'd probably think you had a mean boss! But the Starbucks chain of coffee shops has advertised that they offer 19,000 beverage options, if you count all the different coffees, teas, cold drinks, and all the things you could add to them. The recent addition of an "extra hot" option, in which the temperature of your chosen beverage is boosted by 30 degrees Fahrenheit, probably increases the number of choices to more than 25,000. In a sense, therefore, the customer who walks into a Starbucks shop for a morning drink is confronted with more than 25,000 decisions to make. Isn't that just a way to torture people? Why does Starbucks make money? Why don't their customers quit in protest? More to the point (at least for a social psychologist), how do people get by in a world that offers them thousands of options at every turn, even for the simplest decisions?

Social psychology is the scientific study of how people affect and are affected by others. Can social psychology help us make sense of the bizarre and baffling diversity of human behavior? The answer to this question is a resounding "Yes!" Whether you know it or not, social psychology can also help you make sense of your own social world. The material discussed in this book is intensely relevant to your life. For example, how many of

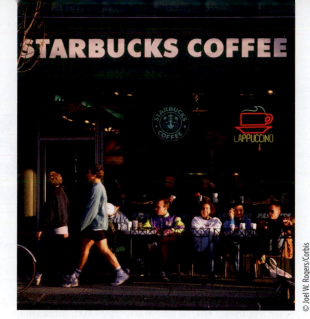

© Joel W. Rogers/Corbis

"Come on in and make a decision from 25,000 choices."

you have asked yourselves something along these lines: "How can I get him to go along with my plan?" "Should I ask her right up front to do this big favor, or is there a better way to get her to say yes?" "How can I bring them around to my way of thinking?" Chances are, something in this book will prove helpful to you in the future. This is not to say that social psychology is a cookbook for how to manipulate people. But social psychology can help you understand some basic principles of social influence, as well as many other principles of social behavior. And it is also just plain interesting to learn about how and why people act the way they do.

The point is that there are plenty of reasons why you ought to be interested in social psychology. As your reasons for learning about social psychology become deeper, your level of understanding will become deeper, and your enjoyment will become deeper. So let's plunge in by looking at a brief history of social psychology! ■

A Brief History of Social Psychology

It is hard to know what the first social psychology experiment was, but consider a few of the earliest ones we know about. One of the first social psychology experiments was conducted by Indiana University professor Norman Triplett (1897). While examining the cycling records for the 1897 season, he noticed that bicycle riders who competed against others performed better than those who competed against the clock. Triplett proposed that the presence of another rider releases the competitive instinct, which increases "nervous energy" and thereby enhances performance.

Triplett tested his hypothesis by building a "competition machine." He had 40 children wind up a fishing reel, alternating between working alone and working parallel to each other. The results showed that winding time was faster when children worked side by side than when they worked alone. Thus, the mere presence of another person enhanced performance on this simple task.

Another early social psychological experiment was conducted in the 1880s by a French professor of agricultural engineering named Max Ringelmann. He had men pull on a rope alone and as part of a group, and he

SOCIAL PSYCHOLOGY branch of psychology that seeks an understanding of how people affect and are affected by others

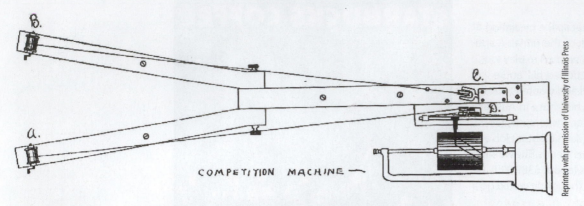

The competition machine Triplett created to test whether the presence of others affects individual performance.

measured the amount of effort exerted by each participant. He found that as group size increased, individual effort decreased. This study can explain why people tend to slack off when working on group projects.

These two seminal studies started a long chain of subsequent studies. Note, though, that the two studies pointed in opposite directions—one found that people worked harder in the presence of others, and the other found that people slacked off. Chapter 14 will try to resolve this seeming contradiction, but for now the point is to get used to the idea that social behavior is complicated.

The introduction of textbooks is an important milestone in the development of a field. In 1908, the first two books to bear the title *Social Psychology* were published, one by the sociologist Edward Ross and the other by the psychologist William McDougall. In 1924, Floyd Allport published another early social psychology book.

During the early part of the 20th century, many thinkers began to ponder where human society was going and why it had changed so much. The world wars, the rise of communism and fascism, the spread of automobiles, the rapid changes in romance and sexual behavior, the rise of advertising, popular fads, the population shift from farm to city life, and shocking economic events such as the Great Depression all challenged intellectuals to wonder what were the basic laws of how people relate to each other. They began to toss about various new and big ideas, including some that would shape the thinking of early social psychologists. One idea was that modern life makes people vulnerable to alienation and exploitation by giant social systems. Another idea was that we learn who we are from other people and our interactions with them. Still another idea was that modern humans act less on the basis of firm inner moral principles than on the basis of following the crowd.

Two ideas from this period stand out as having had a lasting influence on the direction social psychology took. One was Gordon Allport's observation that attitudes were the most useful and important concept in

social psychology. The study of attitudes dominated social psychology research for decades and is still centrally important today (see Chapter 7). (Allport also observed that the study of the self was going to be recognized as increasingly important in the coming years, and on that prediction he was also quite correct; see Chapter 3.)

The other key idea was Kurt Lewin's formula that behavior is a function of the person and the situation. Thus, if you want to predict whether Lenore will finish her school paper on time, you need two kinds of information. First, you must know something about Lenore: Is she lazy? Does she like her work? Is she smart enough to get the job done? Is she punctual? Second, you must know something about her situation: Is the task hard? Are other people bothering her? Is there a penalty for being late? Is her computer broken? Knowing only one kind of information without the other is an inadequate basis for predicting what will happen.

World War II stimulated a great deal of research in the social sciences, and in social psychology in particular. Several factors contributed to this rise in research. Some involved grand theoretical questions: Why did millions of citizens in a modern, civilized nation with a long tradition of religion, morality, and philosophy follow the cruel dictator Adolf Hitler in his policies that included systematic mass murder and violent invasion of neighboring countries? Other factors were more practical: Why did soldiers seem to have so many psychological problems with stress? What exactly motivates soldiers to continue doing their duty on modern battlefields where they could be killed at any moment? World War II also caused many researchers to leave Europe and migrate to the United States. The influx of influential thinkers (including Kurt Lewin, whom we already mentioned) supplemented American thinkers and helped make the United States a world leader in social psychology.

In fact, the terrible events during World War II in Nazi Germany were the impetus for the most famous social psychology study ever conducted. It was shortly after Adolf Eichmann (a high-ranking Nazi and SS officer) was captured, tried by an Israeli court, and hanged that Stanley Milgram conducted his study on obedience. During his trial, Eichmann did not dispute the facts of the Holocaust, but said he was only "following orders." He testified: "I never did anything, great or small, without obtaining in advance express instructions from Adolf Hitler or any of my superiors." Milgram (1974) asked: "Could it be that Eichmann and his million accomplices in the Holocaust were just following orders? Could we call them all accomplices?" In summarizing his findings, Milgram (1973) said: "I set up a simple experiment at Yale University to test how much pain an ordinary citizen would inflict on another person simply because he was ordered to by an experimental scientist. Stark authority was pitted against the subjects' strongest moral imperatives against hurting others, and, with the subjects' ears ringing with the screams of the victims, authority won more often than not." In Chapter 9 we describe Milgram's original study and subsequent studies in detail.

Social psychology began to come into its own as a field in the 1950s and 1960s. At the time, psychology was divided between two camps. One camp, known as **behaviorism**, sought to explain all of psychology in terms of learning principles such as reward and punishment. (Countless studies were conducted with white laboratory rats in order to establish these principles.) Behaviorists were opposed to talking about the mind, thoughts, emotions, or other inner processes, and they favored experiments and the scientific method. The other camp was **Freudian psychoanalysis**, which preferred elaborate interpretations of individual experiences (especially from clinical psychology) instead of systematic studies that counted behaviors. Social psychology was not really compatible with either camp. Social psychology was more congenial to the behaviorist camp in that it favored experiments and the scientific method, but it was sympathetic to the Freudian camp with its interest in inner states and processes. For a while it sought to steer a middle course. Eventually (by the 1970s and 1980s), social psychology found its own way, using scientific approaches to measure behavior but also trying to study thoughts, feelings, and other inner states scientifically.

What about the more recent past? Historians are generally uncomfortable writing about recent times, because main themes are easier to see from a distance than from up close. Still, we can make a few broad statements about the recent history of social psychology. The study of simple cognitive (mental) processes, such as attribution theory, evolved in the 1970s and 1980s into a large and sophisticated study of social cognition (how people think about people and the social world in general). This area of interest has continued up to the present.

Another huge development from the 1990s onward was a growing openness to biology. The influx of biology was boosted by evolutionary psychology, which sought to extend and apply the basic ideas of evolution to understanding human social behavior. It gained further momentum as some social psychologists began to study the brain in order to learn how its workings are related to social events.

The study of the self has been another central theme of social psychology since the 1970s. It is

Nick Koudis/Getty Images

In the 1960s people hardly ever used or cared about the term *self-esteem*.

hard to realize that in the 1960s people hardly ever used the term *self-esteem* or cared about it. In recent decades, social psychologists have explored many different aspects of the self—not only self-esteem but also self-regulation (also known as self-control), self-schemas, and self-presentation.

The field continues to change and evolve. In the 1980s, the conflict between the so-called free world and communist totalitarian systems was the dominant conflict in the world and the main focus of conflict studies. When the Soviet empire abruptly collapsed in 1989, the study of conflict between groups refocused on racial and ethnic conflict, which in the United States meant a sharp rise of interest in prejudice and stereotyping.

BEHAVIORISM theoretical approach that seeks to explain behavior in terms of learning principles, without reference to inner states, thoughts, or feelings

FREUDIAN PSYCHOANALYSIS theoretical approach that seeks to explain behavior by looking at the deep unconscious forces inside the person

2. Who published the first social psychology textbook?
   (a) Floyd Allport   (b) William McDougall
   (c) Edward Ross   (d) Both (b) and (c)

3. Who claimed that attitudes were the most important and useful concept in social psychology?
   (a) Gordon Allport   (b) Kurt Lewin
   (c) Edward Ross   (d) Norman Triplett

4. In the 1950s and 1960s, psychology was divided between what two camps?
   (a) Behaviorist and cognitive camps
   (b) Behaviorist and psychoanalytical camps
   (c) Cognitive and comparative camps
   (d) Comparative and psychoanalytical camps

What Do Social Psychologists Do?

You might think that social psychology focuses specifically on the study of groups or relationships. It does include those topics, but it studies much more. At present, social psychology aims for a broad understanding of the social factors that influence how human beings think, act, and feel. It focuses particularly on normal adult human beings, though some social psychologists do study children and people who suffer from mild mental illness (such as depression). Very little of what people do, other than those with severe mental illness, is off limits to social psychology.

Social psychology is concerned with the effect of other people (real or imagined) on our thoughts, feelings, and behaviors. These three dimensions or building blocks of social psychology are known as the **ABC triad** (see ▶ **FIGURE 1.1**). The **A** stands for Affect (pronounced 'af-ekt; note that this word is a noun, not a verb, which is pronounced ə-'fekt)—how people feel inside. Social psychologists are interested in how people feel about themselves (e.g., self-esteem), how they feel about others (e.g., prejudice), and how they feel about various issues (e.g., attitudes). The **B** stands for Behavior—what people do, their actions. Social psychologists are interested in all the various behaviors people engage in, such as joining groups, helping others, hurting others, working, playing, relaxing. The **C** stands for Cognition—what people think about. Social psychologists are interested in what people think about themselves (e.g., self-concept), what they think about others (e.g., forming impressions), and what they think about various problems and issues in the social world (e.g., protecting the environment).

And as Kurt Lewin suggested many years ago, social psychologists are concerned about the effects of personal and situational influences on these ABCs. Social psychology focuses especially on the power of situations. That is, when trying to explain some pattern of behavior, the first place social psychologists generally look is to the situation. In this focus, social psychology departed from two powerful traditions in psychology. Freudian psychoanalysis sought to explain behavior by looking at the deep unconscious forces inside the person, whereas behaviorist learning theory sought to explain behavior by looking at reinforcement histories (e.g., what behaviors were previously rewarded or punished). Social psychology emphasizes how people react to the world around them and how small changes in their immediate circumstances can produce substantial changes in behavior. Social psychologists study the influence of situational factors that people may not even be aware of. For example, participants in one study arranged scrambled words to form sentences (see Bargh, Chen, & Burrows, 1996). The study was said to be about how people use words in various, flexible ways. By the flip of a coin, participants received either words associated with the elderly (e.g., old, gray, wrinkled) or words not associated with the elderly (e.g., thirsty, clean, private). After participants completed the task, the researcher thanked them for participating and told them that the elevator was down the hall. Using a hidden stopwatch, the researchers timed how long it took participants to walk to the elevator. Participants who had unscrambled the elderly words took significantly longer to walk to the elevator than did participants who had unscrambled the neutral words. Somehow thinking about old people made them act like old people.

Another important feature of social psychology is that it embraces the scientific method. Most social psychologists conduct experiments, which are careful and systematic ways of testing theories. There are many ways to learn about people, such as reading a

▶ **FIGURE 1.1** Affect, Behavior, and Cognition are the ABCs of what social psychologists study.

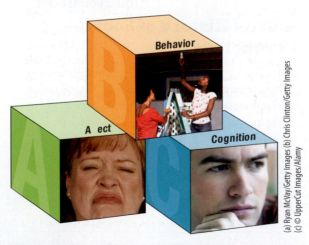

(a) Ryan McVay/Getty Images (b) Chris Clinton/Getty Images
(c) © UpperCut Images/Alamy

ABC TRIAD **A**ffect (how people feel inside), **B**ehavior (what people do), **C**ognition (what people think about)

novel, watching people at the airport, living in a foreign country, or talking with friends for hours at a time. All those approaches may yield valuable lessons, but the scientific method has important advantages over them. In particular, it is hard to know whether the insights gleaned from reading a novel or people-watching are correct. The scientific method is the most rigorous way of sorting out the valid lessons from the mistaken ones. We discuss the scientific method in detail in a later section.

[QUIZ YOURSELF]

What Do Social Psychologists Do?

1. Unconscious forces are to reinforcement histories as _____ is to _____.
   (a) affect; cognition
   (b) cognition; affect
   (c) behaviorism; psychoanalysis
   (d) psychoanalysis; behaviorism

2. What psychologist is primarily associated with psychoanalysis?
   (a) Floyd Allport   (b) Sigmund Freud
   (c) Kurt Lewin   (d) Norman Triplett

3. What are the components of the ABC triad?
   (a) Affect, behavior, cognition
   (b) Affect, beliefs, cognition
   (c) Attitudes, beliefs, compliance
   (d) Affect, behavior, conformity

4. What is the primary approach that social psychologists use to uncover the truth about human social behavior?
   (a) Reliance on authority figures
   (b) Introspection
   (c) Rationalism
   (d) Scientific method

Social Psychology's Place in the World

Social psychology is related to other social sciences and to other branches of psychology. It also differs from them in important ways.

SOCIAL PSYCHOLOGY'S PLACE IN THE SOCIAL SCIENCES

Social scientists study people and the societies in which people live. They are interested in how people relate to one another. The various social sciences focus on different aspects of social life.

Anthropology is the study of human culture. Human culture consists of the shared values, beliefs, and practices of a group of people. These values, beliefs, and practices are passed down from one generation to another. Not only are humans social animals, they are also cultural animals. This is one of the central themes of this book (see Chapter 2). Social psychologists cannot understand human behavior fully unless they understand the cultural context in which that behavior occurs.

Economics is the study of the production, distribution, and consumption of goods and services. Social psychologists are very interested in these topics. In fact, some social psychological theories are based on economic principles. For example, social exchange theory predicts commitment to relationships by considering factors such as the costs, rewards, investments, and the number of alternatives available. Economics also calls our attention to large social systems (such as the labor market or money system) and to how these systems shape behavior. Again, a full understanding of human behavior requires appreciating not just what goes on inside one person's head and what is happening in his or her immediate environment at the time, but also how the person's behavior fits into the larger social system.

History is the study of past events. For humans to progress, they should understand past events and learn from them. Society progresses when members can avoid repeating the same mistakes others have made. Social psychologists sometimes debate whether the behaviors they study have changed historically, but until recently there has been little interaction between social psychologists and historians.

Political science is the study of political organizations and institutions, especially governments. Social psychologists conduct research on political behavior. They study political issues such as voting, party identification, liberal versus conservative views, and political advertising. Political leaders can have a tremendous influence on the people they govern. Social psychologists are also interested in what makes some people better leaders than others (see Chapter 14).

Sociology is the study of human societies and the groups that form those societies. Although both sociologists and social psychologists are interested in how people behave in societies and groups, they differ in what they focus on. Psychologists tend to start from inside the individual and work outward, whereas sociologists start with large units such as countries,

---

ANTHROPOLOGY the study of human culture—the shared values, beliefs, and practices of a group of people

ECONOMICS the study of the production, distribution, and consumption of goods and services, and the study of money

HISTORY the study of past events

POLITICAL SCIENCE the study of political organizations and institutions, especially governments

SOCIOLOGY the study of human societies and the groups that form those societies

Psychology Subdiscipline	Description
Biological psychology	Biological psychologists focus on what happens in the brain, nervous system, and other aspects of the body.
Clinical psychology	Clinical psychologists focus on "abnormal" behavior.
Cognitive psychology	Cognitive psychologists focus on thought processes, such as how memory works and what people notice.
Developmental psychology	Developmental psychologists study how people change across their lives, from conception and birth to old age and death.
Personality psychology	Personality psychologists focus on important differences between individuals, as well as inner processes.
Social psychology	Social psychologists focus on how human beings think, act, and feel. Thoughts, actions, and feelings are a joint function of personal and situational influences.

*Data are from McGinnis and Foege; percentages are for all deaths. Source: Mokdad, Marks, Stroup, & Gerberding, 2004

religions, and organizations, and work from there. Some sociologists call themselves social psychologists, and the exchange of ideas and findings between the two fields has sometimes been quite fruitful because they bring different perspectives to the same problems.

SOCIAL PSYCHOLOGY'S PLACE WITHIN PSYCHOLOGY

Psychology is the study of human behavior. Psychology is like a big tree that contains many branches. Social psychology is just one of those branches, but it is intertwined with some of the other branches (see ▶ **TABLE 1.1**).

People are biological creatures, and everything that people think, do, or feel involves some bodily processes such as brain activity or hormones. **Biological** or **physiological psychology** and (more recently) **neuroscience** have focused on learning about what happens in the brain, nervous system, and other aspects of the body. Until recently, this

PSYCHOLOGY the study of human behavior

BIOLOGICAL PSYCHOLOGY (PHYSIOLOGICAL PSYCHOLOGY, NEUROSCIENCE) the study of what happens in the brain, nervous system, and other aspects of the body

CLINICAL PSYCHOLOGY branch of psychology that focuses on behavior disorders and other forms of mental illness, and how to treat them

COGNITIVE PSYCHOLOGY the study of thought processes, such as how memory works and what people notice

DEVELOPMENTAL PSYCHOLOGY the study of how people change across their lives, from conception and birth to old age and death

PERSONALITY PSYCHOLOGY the branch of psychology that focuses on important differences between individuals

work had little contact with social psychology, but during the 1990s (the "Decade of the Brain") many social psychologists began looking into the biological aspects of social behavior, and that interest has continued into the 21st century. Social neuroscience and social psychophysiology are now thriving fields.

Clinical psychology focuses on "abnormal" behavior, whereas social psychology focuses on "normal" behavior. Social psychological theory can shed a great deal of light on so-called normal behavior. Although abnormal and clinical cases may seem different, in fact social and clinical psychology have had a long tradition of exchanging ideas and stimulating insights into each other's fields.

Cognitive psychology is the basic study of thought processes, such as how memory works and what events people notice. In recent decades, social psychology has borrowed heavily from cognitive psychology, especially by using their methods for measuring cognitive processes. Under the rubric of "social cognition," social psychologists study how people think about their social lives, such as thinking about other people or solving problems in their world. Conversely, however, cognitive psychology has not borrowed much from social psychology.

Developmental psychology is the study of how people change across their lives, from conception and birth to old age and death. In practice, most developmental psychologists study children. Developmental psychology has borrowed much from social psychology and built on it, such as by studying at what age children begin to show various patterns of social behavior. Developmental psychology also has often borrowed social psychology theories. Until now, social psychology has not taken much from developmental psychology, though this may be changing. Social psychologists interested in self-regulation, emotion, gender differences, helping behavior, and antisocial behavior sometimes look to the research on child development to see how these patterns get started.

Personality psychology focuses on important differences between individuals, as well as inner processes. For example, some people are introverted and avoid social contact, whereas other people are extraverted and crave social contact. Social and personality psychology have had a long and close relationship (e.g., Funder, 2001), as reflected in the titles of three of the top scientific journals in the field: *Journal of Personality and Social Psychology*, *Personality and Social Psychology Bulletin*, and *Personality and Social Psychology Review*. The relationship between personality and social psychology has been sometimes complementary (personality psychologists looked inside the person, whereas social psychologists looked outside at the situation) and sometimes competitive (is it more important to understand the person or the situation?). In recent years, the line between these two fields has become blurred, as social psychologists have come to recognize the importance of inner processes and personality psychologists have come to recognize the importance of circumstances and situations.

There are many other branches of psychology (e.g., community psychology, educational psychology, forensic psychology). Our list is by no means exhaustive. But it should give you a feel for how social psychology differs from some other branches of psychology.

[QUIZ YOURSELF]

Social Psychology's Place in the World

1. A social psychologist is usually interested in studying the _____.
   (a) community   (b) group
   (c) individual   (d) institution

2. Social psychology has borrowed methodological tools most heavily from what other branch of psychology?
   (a) Cognitive   (b) Clinical
   (c) Counseling   (d) Developmental

3. A researcher is interested in studying how the annual divorce rate changes as a function of the unemployment rate. This researcher is probably a(n) _____.
   (a) anthropologist   (b) political scientist
   (c) psychologist   (d) sociologist

4. "Abnormal" behavior is to "normal" behavior as _____ psychology is to _____ psychology.
   (a) biological; cognitive   (b) clinical; cognitive
   (c) clinical; social   (d) personality; social

Why People Study Social Psychology

- -

CURIOSITY ABOUT PEOPLE

Some social events make you wonder. For example, why does the man usually pay for a date even when the woman earns as much as or more than he does? Why do so many people fail to vote in elections? Why are actors and celebrities so admired, when their success depends mainly on saying words that other people write for them and pretending to have emotions they do not really have? Why did the president of Kenya tell everyone in his country to abstain from sex for two years? (And do you think people obeyed him?) Why do the French live longer than people in just about any other country but also report much lower average happiness in life? Why do many people spend more than they earn?

One of the most highly respected and influential social psychologists, Edward E. Jones, was once asked how he could justify spending his entire life studying social psychology and interactions, even though his research did not translate directly into plans for how to cure suffering or make lots of money. He looked at his questioner with genuine puzzlement and explained that he, and presumably everyone else, had a "basic curiosity about people." For most people, this curiosity is merely a personal interest, but by becoming a social psychologist, Jones was able to make it his life's work. Jones thought that understanding people was an end in itself and did not need to be justified on other grounds (such as making money, though as a famous professor he earned a comfortable living). Only careful scientific research, like that practiced by social psychologists, can ultimately lead to a more reliable and valid understanding of people.

We think curiosity about people is still an excellent reason for studying social psychology. Social psychology can teach a great deal about how to understand people. If this book does not help you to understand people significantly better than before, then either you or we (or both) have failed. And if you do feel that this book and this course have improved your understanding of human nature, then that is worth quite a lot as an end in itself.

EXPERIMENTAL PHILOSOPHY

Philosophy (from the Greek *philo-sophia*) means "love of wisdom." Over the centuries philosophers have thought deeply about many of the most interesting and profound questions in the world. Most fields of study, including psychology, were originally part of philosophy. Psychology separated itself from philosophy around 1900, which in the context of Western civilization is pretty recent.

Psychology addresses many questions that pertain to the love of wisdom and that also interest philosophers: Why are human beings sometimes so cruel to each other? What is knowledge, and where does it come from? Is altruism (selflessly helping others) truly possible, or are helpers merely trying to feel better about themselves? What is virtue? Why do people so often give in to temptation? What is the nature of the self and identity?

What separates philosophy from psychology is psychology's heavy reliance on the scientific method. Philosophers deal with problems by thinking very carefully and systematically about them; psychologists address the same problems by systematically collecting data. Psychology, including social psychology, thus offers a marvelous opportunity to combine an interest in profound questions with the scientific method of seeking answers.

PHILOSOPHY "love of wisdom"; the pursuit of knowledge about fundamental matters such as life, death, meaning, reality, and truth

In the 2008 election, Republican presidential candidate John McCain and vice presidential candidate Sarah Palin emphasized drilling for oil as the immediate solution to the energy crisis, using the slogan "Drill, drill, drill." Drilling for oil can increase energy supplies and reduce energy costs, but it can also lead to environmental pollution and kill wildlife.

MAKING THE WORLD BETTER

Many social psychologists (and social scientists) are motivated by a wish to make the world a better place. They come to this field because they are troubled by injustice, violence, pollution, poverty, or the sufferings of some group. They want to understand the causes of these problems and perhaps begin to find ways of fixing them.

Hardly anyone thinks that our society is perfect. Changing it is often a tricky business, however, because many so-called remedies do not work, and sometimes the steps one takes to fix one problem end up creating a new or different problem. For example, drilling for oil can increase energy supplies and reduce energy costs, but it can also lead to environmental pollution.

Social scientists disagree among themselves as to the nature of many problems and the desired solutions, but most share a belief that better knowledge will in the long run enable society to deal with its problems more effectively. If a government passes new laws and makes new policies based on wrong information, those laws and policies are not likely to bring about the desired effects.

The desire to fix particular problems causes some social scientists to focus their study on a specific problem, such as the plight of welfare mothers, or why people don't wear seat belts, or how to get people to conserve electric power. These scholars are often called **applied researchers**, because their research is applied to a specific problem. Other scholars try to advance the cause of knowledge more generally, in the hope that creating a solid knowledge base will result in a better understanding of basic principles that can be applied to many different problems. When Kurt Lewin, one of the fathers of social psychology, was questioned as to whether his research had sufficient

practical value, he answered, "There is nothing as practical as a good theory" (Lewin, 1951, p. 169).

A passion to make the world a better place is a fine reason to study social psychology. Sometimes, however, researchers let their ideals or their political beliefs cloud their judgment, such as in how they interpret their research findings. Social psychology can only be a science if it puts the pursuit of truth above all other goals. When researchers focus on a topic that is politically charged, such as race relations or whether divorce is bad for children, it is important to be extra careful in making sure that all views (perhaps especially disagreeable ones, or ones that go against established prejudices) are considered and that the conclusions from research are truly warranted.

For example, Christina Hoff Sommers (1994) has written about pressures she faced regarding unpopular views. At the time, women's rights groups were campaigning for better treatment of adolescent girls, and they cited the high rate of girls' deaths from eating disorders as one sign of urgent need for intervention. Sommers discovered that there had been a huge error in reporting the frequency of these eating disorder deaths and that the real death toll was far less than reported. When she began to bring this up, Sommers said, many feminists told her that she should keep silent about it, because the reported numbers—even though wildly inaccurate—were helpful to their cause. Sommers was sympathetic to the desire to make life better for teenage girls, but she decided that spreading falsehoods was not a good means toward that end. Other researchers, however, were apparently quite willing to put their political ideals above the truth.

SOCIAL PSYCHOLOGY IS FUN!

Another reason to study social psychology is that it is fun. Not only do social psychologists get to spend their working lives dealing with many of the most

---

APPLIED RESEARCH research that focuses on solving particular practical problems

fascinating questions that occupy other people in their free time—but the process is also enjoyable.

To be good at social psychology, especially once you reach the stage of conducting research, it is helpful to be creative. The questions are exciting, but the challenge of testing them is often difficult. Social psychologists constantly try to come up with new and clever ways to test their ideas.

How Do Social Psychologists Answer Their Own Questions?

ACCUMULATED COMMON WISDOM

It turns out that world knowledge, or accumulated common wisdom, is loaded with social psychological "truths." Consider the adages your grandmother may have told you (Rogow, Carey, & Farrell, 1957):

-   "Idle hands are the devil's workshop."
-   "Absence makes the heart grow fonder."
-   "Birds of a feather flock together."
-   "Opposites attract."
-   "Out of sight, out of mind."

Note that some of these contradict each other! People were offering adages long before your grandma's

time. The problem with so-called common wisdom or common sense is that it allows us to happily and effortlessly judge adages as being true and, at the same time, judge their opposites as being true. For example, in one study, participants rated actual adages and their opposites (Teigen, 1986). The first version is authentic, whereas the second version is bogus. Yet both versions were rated as equally true.

-   "Fear is stronger than love."
-   "Love is stronger than fear."
-   "He that is fallen cannot help him who is down."
-   "He that is down cannot help him who is fallen."
-   "Wise men make proverbs and fools repeat them."
-   "Fools make proverbs and wise men repeat them."

Thus, human intuition is a poor method for discovering truth.

Common wisdom is probably right more often than it is wrong, but that is not good enough for science. In the long run, science can find the right answers to almost everything. (In the short run, scientists have to be content with slowly making progress toward the truth, such as replacing a partly right and partly wrong theory with another theory that is still partly wrong but a little more right.) Hence social psychologists do not rely too heavily on common sense or accumulated wisdom. If anything, they have often had to justify their scientific studies by finding patterns that go against common sense. Opposites do not attract. Instead, birds of a feather flock together (see Chapter 11). At most, common sense provides a good starting point for social psychologists to do their work. They can take ideas that everyone assumes to be true and find out which ones really are true, as opposed to which ones are always false. As for those that are sometimes true and sometimes false, social psychologists can study what factors determine when they are true and when they are false. For example, which absences do make the heart grow fonder, and which circumstances cause people to forget about their absent friends or lovers and refocus on the people around them?

OVERVIEW OF THE SCIENTIFIC METHOD

Most people think that science is chemistry or biology or physics. But science is a method for discovering truth, not a discipline. So what is the scientific method? What steps does it involve? The scientific method involves five basic steps.

1. The researcher states a problem for study.
2. The researcher formulates a testable hypothesis as a tentative solution to the problem. The Cambridge

Does Chicken Soup Reduce Cold Symptoms?

Dr. Stephen Rennard, a professor of medicine, and his colleagues applied the scientific method to the age-old observation that chicken soup makes people with colds feel better. Rennard wondered if something in chicken soup might reduce the upper respiratory inflammation that makes people with colds feel miserable. This was his hypothesis. Rennard designed a study to test the effect of chicken soup on white blood cells called neutrophils, the immune cells that cause congestion. He prepared a number of samples of chicken soup and fed them to participants.

Neutrophil counts were recorded before and after participants ate the soup. The dependent variable was neutrophil counts. The independent variable had two levels: before versus after eating chicken soup. Researchers call this a **within-subjects design** because each participant is exposed to all levels of the independent variable. In a **between-subjects design**, the research would have flipped a coin to determine who ate chicken soup and who did not. By carefully recording these observations, he collected data. As hypothesized, Rennard found that chicken soup reduced neutrophil counts. People were less congested after eating chicken soup than before.

Rennard wrote up exactly what he did and what he found in a formal manuscript (he even provided the recipe for the chicken soup) and submitted it to the editor of the scientific journal *Chest*. The editor sent the manuscript to other experts in the area for peer review. After reading the manuscript and the peer reviews, the editor decided that the study was good enough to be published. The article, titled "Chicken Soup Inhibits Neutrophil Chemotaxis *In Vitro*," is in the scientific journal *Chest*, Volume 118 (2000), pages 1150–1157. You (or anyone) can look it up. If you think the conclusion was mistaken, you are welcome to conduct a further experiment to show why. ●

Dictionary defines a **hypothesis** as "an idea or explanation for something that is based on known facts but has not yet been proved." Laypeople often define a hypothesis as an "educated guess." For example, one hypothesis is that homework improves grades.

3. The researcher designs a study to test the hypothesis and collects data. Anyone observing the data collection process should be able to replicate or repeat it.

4. A test is made of the hypothesis by confronting it with the data. Statistical methods are used to test whether the data are consistent or inconsistent with the hypothesis. No single study can prove anything beyond all doubt. There is always the possibility that the data turned out a certain way as a fluke, by random chance. Usually researchers test their hypotheses at the .05 (or 5%) significance level. If the test is significant at this level, it means that researchers are 95% confident that the results from their studies indicate a real difference and not just a random fluke. Thus, only 5% of research conclusions should be "flukes." Moreover, the pressures to replicate studies will sharply reduce the number and proportion of such false, invalid conclusions.

5. The researcher communicates the study results. The researcher submits a manuscript describing exactly what was done and what was found to the editor of a scientific journal. The editor then selects a few other experts in the area to review the manuscript. The editor reads the manuscript independently, reads the reviewers' comments, and then decides whether to accept the manuscript for publication. Only about 10–20% of manuscripts submitted to the best social psychology journals are accepted. These high standards help ensure that only the best research is published in social psychology journals. Once an article is published, it is in the public domain. If other social psychologists don't believe the results, they can replicate the study themselves to see if they obtain similar results. The *Food for Thought* box illustrates the various steps of the scientific method.

SCIENTIFIC THEORIES

Social psychologists are not content to know what people do; they also want to know *why* they do it. That is why psychologists derive their hypotheses from theories.

Theories are composed of constructs (abstract ideas or concepts) that are linked together in some logical way. Because constructs cannot be observed directly, the researcher connects them with concrete, observable variables using operational definitions. ▶ **FIGURE 1.2** illustrates the relationship between unobservable constructs (in dashed boxes) and

---

WITHIN-SUBJECTS DESIGN an experiment in which each participant is exposed to all levels of the independent variable

BETWEEN-SUBJECTS DESIGN an experiment in which each participant is exposed to only one level of the independent variable

HYPOTHESIS an idea about the possible nature of reality; a prediction tested in an experiment

THEORIES unobservable constructs that are linked together in some logical way

observable variables (in solid boxes). For example, one early theory proposed that frustration causes aggression (Dollard, Doob, Miller, Mowrer, & Sears, 1939). Frustration was defined as blocking someone from obtaining a goal. Aggression was defined as intentionally harming another person. In this theory, "frustration" is the theoretical stimulus, and "aggression" is the theoretical response.

The **independent variable** is any observable event that causes the person to do something. It is independent in the sense that its values are created by the researcher and are not affected by anything else that happens in the experiment. It is a variable because it has at least two levels, categories, types, or groups.

There is an important difference between manipulated independent variables and measured individual difference variables. Social psychologists have long recognized that behavior is a function of both situational and individual difference factors. Situational factors can be manipulated in experiments. Individual difference variables, such as gender, age, intelligence, ability, personality, and attitudes, can be measured but cannot be manipulated. For example, a researcher cannot manipulate whether participants will be male or female or whether they will be high or low in intelligence. Participants arrive for the experiment already possessing these attributes. A researcher can only draw cause–effect conclusions about the true independent variables that were manipulated in the experiment. This is important: We cannot ever really know that intelligence or gender *causes* a particular outcome, because only experimentation can establish causality, and those variables cannot be manipulated in an experiment. Still, we can learn a great deal about what typically correlates with gender or intelligence.

The **dependent variable** is any observable behavior produced by the person. It is "dependent" in the sense that its values are assumed to depend on the values of the independent variable. In a study of the effect of alcoholic and nonalcoholic beer on aggression, for example, aggression is the dependent variable. A researcher could use different measures of aggression (e.g., hostile verbal insults or physical acts such as hitting, kicking, or choking someone).

Researchers must at some point tie their unobservable constructs to concrete representations of those constructs. This is accomplished by using operational definitions. An **operational definition** classifies theoretical constructs in terms of observable operations, procedures, and measurements.

An example will help illustrate the abstract concepts described above. In one study that tested frustration–aggression theory, participants were waiting in long lines at various stores, banks, restaurants, ticket windows, and airport passenger check-in stands when a confederate crowded in front of them (Harris, 1974). (A **confederate** is somebody who is secretly

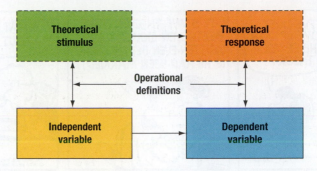

► FIGURE 1.2
Representation of a theoretical model. Unobservable constructs are represented as dashed boxes on the top level. Observable variables are in solid boxes on the bottom level.

working for the researcher.) By the flip of a coin, the confederate crowded in front of the 2nd person in line or in front of the 12th person in line. According to frustration–aggression theory, events are more frustrating if you are close to the goal (e.g., 2nd person in line) than if you are far from the goal (e.g., 12th person in line). It is especially frustrating if you can "almost taste it," but someone gets in your way. The confederate then recorded the participant's reaction. No response was coded 0; a somewhat aggressive response was coded 1 (e.g., participant tells confederate "Watch it!"); and a very aggressive response was coded 2 (e.g., participant pushes confederate). The results showed that participants who were 2nd in line responded more aggressively than did participants who were 12th in line, which is consistent with frustration–aggression theory. ► **FIGURE 1.3** shows the theoretical stimulus, theoretical response, independent variable, and dependent variable for this study.

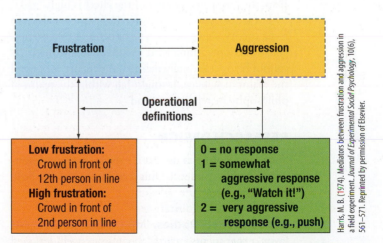

Harris, M. B. (1974). Mediators between frustration and aggression in a field experiment. *Journal of Experimental Social Psychology*, 10(6), 561–571. Reprinted by permission of Elsevier.

► FIGURE 1.3 Theoretical stimulus, theoretical response, independent variable, and dependent variable for the study on crowding in line that was used to test frustration–aggression theory (Harris, 1974).

INDEPENDENT VARIABLE the variable manipulated by the researcher that is assumed to lead to changes in the dependent variable

DEPENDENT VARIABLE the variable in a study that represents the result of the events and processes

OPERATIONAL DEFINITIONS observable operations, procedures, and measurements that are based on the independent and dependent variables

CONFEDERATE a research assistant pretending to be another participant in a study

Peanuts © United Feature Syndicate, Inc. Reprinted by permission.

Lucy's theory is not scientific because it cannot be tested.

Other factors can influence how aggressive people become when someone crowds in front of them in line. For example, participants in a similar study were more aggressive if the confederate who crowded in front of them wore a shirt that said "Drop Dead," and they were less aggressive if the confederate used a crutch or said "Please, I'm in a hurry" (Harris, 1976).

If the operational definitions of the constructs are valid, the study is said to have *construct validity* (Cook & Campbell, 1979). **Construct validity of the cause** means that the independent variable is a valid representation of the theoretical stimulus. **Construct validity of the effect** means that the dependent variable is a valid representation of the theoretical response. Consider our example in Figure 1.3. Is crowding in front of someone in line a valid way to define "frustration"? If so, the construct validity of the cause is high. Is pushing someone a valid way to define "aggression"? If so, the construct validity of the effect is high.

For a theory to be scientific, it must be testable. To test a theory, one must be able to define its theoretical constructs operationally. If the theoretical constructs cannot be operationally defined, the theory is beyond the realm of science. It might fall within the realm of philosophy or religion instead.

RESEARCH DESIGN

Social psychologists use both experimental and non-experimental studies. In this section we describe both types of studies.

Experimental Studies. Most social psychologists favor experiments, partly because a well-designed experiment can show causality. An **experiment** has two essential features. First, the researcher has control over the procedures. The researcher manipulates the independent variable and holds all other variables constant. All those who participate in an experiment are treated the same, except for the level of the independent variable they are exposed to. By exercising control, the researcher tries to make sure that any differences observed on the dependent variable were caused by the independent variable and not by other factors.

Second, participants are randomly assigned to the levels of the independent variable. A different group experiences each level of the independent variable. If the independent variable has two levels (e.g., experimental group versus control group), the researcher can flip a coin to assign participants to groups. If there are more than two groups, the researcher can draw a number from a hat or roll a die to assign participants to groups. **Random assignment** means that each participant has an equal chance of being in each group. By randomly assigning participants to groups, the researcher attempts to ensure that there are no initial differences between groups. Random assignment is the great equalizer, especially if there is a large number of participants in the study. Think about flipping a coin 20 times versus 200 times. Getting 20 heads in 20 flips is much more likely than getting 200 heads in 200 flips. If participants are randomly assigned to groups, the participants in one group should be no different—no smarter, no taller, no more liberal or conservative, no more mean-tempered, no more eager for love—than the participants in another group. If there are differences between groups of participants after the independent variable is manipulated, these differences should be due to the independent variable rather than to any initial, preexisting differences between participants.

If a researcher can manipulate an independent variable, but cannot use random assignment, the study is called a **quasi-experiment**. In a quasi-experiment, the researcher "takes people as they are." Researchers often use preexisting groups (e.g., classrooms, fraternity groups, athletic clubs) because random assignment is not possible. For example, if you wanted to learn about marriage, you would ideally like to assign

CONSTRUCT VALIDITY OF THE CAUSE the extent to which the independent variable is a valid representation of the theoretical stimulus

CONSTRUCT VALIDITY OF THE EFFECT the extent to which the dependent variable is a valid representation of the theoretical response

EXPERIMENT a study in which the researcher manipulates an independent variable and randomly assigns people to groups (levels of the independent variable)

RANDOM ASSIGNMENT procedure whereby each study participant has an equal chance of being in each treatment group

QUASI-EXPERIMENT a type of study in which the researcher can manipulate an independent variable but cannot use random assignment

people randomly to be married or single (and whom to marry), but this is clearly not feasible! So you rely on comparing people who are already married with those who happen to be single.

Suppose that a researcher is interested in determining whether a relationship exists between two variables, say X and Y. For example, a researcher might be interested in the relationship between exposure to violent video games (X) and aggression (Y). When two variables are related in a systematic manner, there are three possible explanations for the relationship: (a) X could cause Y; (b) Y could cause X; (c) some other variable (Z) could cause both X and Y.

The two essential features of an experiment (control and random assignment) allow the researcher to be fairly certain that the independent variable (X) caused differences in the dependent variable (Y). Note that one cannot conclude that Y caused X in an experiment. We know what caused X, and it wasn't Y. The experimenter caused X, because the experimenter manipulated X. Thus, we know that X preceded Y in time. In an experiment, it is also unlikely that some other variable (Z) caused both X and Y. The experimenter controlled many other variables by treating groups of participants identically. Random assignment is used to spread out the effect of other variables that cannot be controlled (e.g., the mood participants are in, their personalities).

A study is said to have **internal validity** if the researcher can be relatively confident that changes in the independent variable caused changes in the dependent variable (Cook & Campbell, 1979). Internal validity is usually very high in experimental studies.

Consider the violent video game example again. In a true experiment, the researcher doesn't ask participants if they would rather play a violent or a nonviolent video game. If the researcher let people choose what video game they wanted to play, people choosing the violent game might be very different from those choosing the nonviolent game. For example, people choosing the violent game might be more aggressive, less intelligent, or less socially skilled to begin with. That is why the researcher flips a coin to determine what video game people play. That way, the two groups should be the same before they play anything. If you flip a coin to determine what game people are assigned to play, it is very unlikely that all the aggressive people will end up playing the violent game, especially if there is a large number of people in the experiment. Suppose there are 200 participants in the experiment (100 in each group). There should be a 50–50 chance of an aggressive person playing a violent game. Think about flipping a fair coin 200 times. On average, you should get about 100 heads. It would be very unlikely to get 200 heads in a row, or even 150 heads out of 200 flips. Rare events are much less common when sample sizes are large. That is why

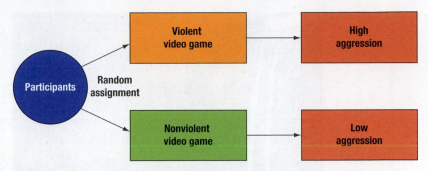

▶ **FIGURE 1.4** In an experimental study, participants are randomly assigned to groups, and then their responses are measured.

researchers try to test a large number of participants, rather than just a few.

Next, one group plays a violent game and the other group plays a nonviolent game. In all other respects, the researcher treats the two groups of participants identically. In a carefully conducted experiment, the violent and nonviolent video games would be matched on other dimensions that could increase aggression, such as how exciting they are. For example, if the violent video game is exciting, and the nonviolent video game is boring, any differences in subsequent aggressive behavior might be due to excitement, not to the violence. In other words, the effects of violence and excitement cannot be separated because the two variables are **confounded**. In addition, the researcher should use several different violent video games and several different nonviolent games. Otherwise, the comparison is between two particular video games (e.g., *Grand Theft Auto* versus *Sims*), not between violent and nonviolent video games in general.

Last, the researcher measures the aggressive behavior of both groups of participants. For example, participants are given an opportunity to hurt another person, such as by administering an electric shock. The "other person" is actually a confederate of the experimenter who is pretending to be another participant receiving the shock. If aggression levels are higher among those who play a violent game than among those who play a nonviolent game, what else could have caused the difference except what game they played? Random assignment ensures that the two groups were equally aggressive before they played anything. The researcher treats the two groups identically except for the type of game they played. In an experimental study, one can say that playing violent video games caused an increase in aggression. The only other possible explanation is a random fluke, but that should occur only 5% of the time. This process is depicted in ▶ **FIGURE 1.4**.

INTERNAL VALIDITY the extent to which changes in the independent variable caused changes in the dependent variable

CONFOUNDING occurs when the effects of two variables cannot be separated

Does frustration cause aggression?

Yellow Dog Productions/Getty Images

Factorial Designs. Human behavior is complex, and so are the causes of behavior. It is rarely the case that a single variable produces changes in behavior; generally, a number of variables act together to produce changes in behavior. Thus, researchers often must manipulate more than one independent variable in an experiment in order to produce changes in a dependent variable. If an experiment includes more than one independent variable or factor, it is called a **factorial design**. Analysis of the data from a factorial experiment allows researchers to examine two types of effects: main effects and interaction effects. A **main effect** is the effect of a single independent variable by itself, ignoring the effects of the other independent variables. An **interaction** refers to the joint effects of more than one independent variable. An interaction, as the term implies, means that the independent variables act together in a manner that differs

from that of either variable acting alone. Thus, an interaction occurs when the effect of one independent variable depends on the other independent variable.

As an example, consider another experiment that tested frustration–aggression theory (Fischer, Greitemeyer, & Frey, 2008, Study 3). The thought that one might not get a job after finishing college should be frustrating. Why waste four or five years attending college if there is little chance of employment afterwards? Participants in this study were German college students majoring in psychology. By the flip of a coin, participants read about a poll that found either high or low unemployment rates among college graduates with a degree in psychology. The other independent variable was self-awareness. Previous research has shown that self-awareness reduces aggression (e.g., Bailey, Leonard, Cranston, & Taylor, 1983). When people think about themselves, they become aware of their internal standards, such as being nice to others. The researchers manipulated self-awareness by having participants write a short essay about the positive and negative aspects of their personality. Participants in the high self-awareness conditions wrote the essay before aggression was measured, whereas participants in the low self-awareness conditions wrote the essay after aggression was measured. The measure of aggression was how long participants made a fellow student put their hand in ice-cold water. Participants were told that 15 seconds or longer could be "very painful." The researchers predicted a main effect for unemployment on aggression, with higher aggression levels for participants in the high unemployment group than for participants in the low unemployment group. The researchers also predicted an interaction between unemployment and self-awareness on aggression, with larger effects of unemployment on people low in self-awareness (who are not monitoring their aggression levels because they are not thinking about their internal standards) than on people high in self-awareness.

The average aggression levels for the four groups were: (1) 10.61 seconds for participants in the *low self-awareness/low unemployment* group; (2) 24.38 seconds for participants in the *low self-awareness/high unemployment* group; (3) 14.76 seconds for participants in the *high self-awareness/low unemployment* group; and (4) 18.89 seconds for participants in the *high self-awareness/high unemployment* group. These results are shown in ▶ **FIGURE 1.5**. In this study there was a *main effect* for unemployment: the average of the two red *high unemployment* bars [(24.38 + 18.89) / 2 = 21.64] is larger than the average of the two blue *low unemployment* bars [(10.61 + 14.76) / 2 = 12.69]. Note also that both of the red bars are higher than the pain level of 15 seconds. This main effect is consistent with frustration–aggression theory. Believing that one will be unemployed after earning a college degree in psychology is frustrating, and this frustration led to higher aggression against a fellow student.

▶ **FIGURE 1.5**
As can be seen in this figure, self-awareness reduces aggression in frustrated people who think they will be unemployed after finishing their college degree (Fischer et al., 2008).

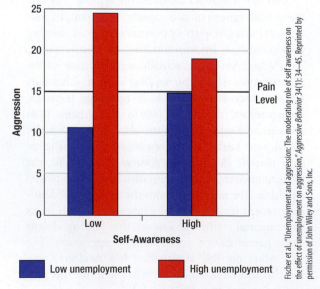

Fischer et al., "Unemployment and aggression: The moderating role of self awareness on the effect of unemployment on aggression," *Aggressive Behavior* 34(1): 34–45. Reprinted by permission of John Wiley and Sons, Inc.

FACTORIAL DESIGN an experiment that includes more than one independent variable or factor
MAIN EFFECT the effect of a single independent variable on the dependent variable, ignoring the effects of other independent variables
INTERACTION refers to the joint effects of more than one independent variable on the dependent variable

There is no main effect for self-awareness. The average of the two bars on the left side of Figure 1.5 for low self-awareness [(10.61 + 24.38) / 2 = 17.50] is not significantly different from the average of the two bars on the right side of Figure 1.5 for high self-awareness [(14.76 + 18.89) / 2 = 16.83]. However, there is an *interaction* between unemployment and self-awareness. As expected, the effects of unemployment on aggression were larger for people low in self-awareness than for people high in self-awareness. That is, the difference between high and low unemployment was greater in the low self-awareness conditions on the left side of Figure 1.5 (24.38 − 10.61 = 13.77) than in the high self-awareness conditions on the right side of Figure 1.5 (18.89 − 14.76 = 4.13).

Laboratory and Field Experiments. Have you ever had the experience of looking for a parking spot in a very crowded parking lot? There are no empty spots, but you see a shopper returning to her car and you decide to wait to get her spot when she leaves. Unfortunately, she takes a very long time to leave. She takes her time putting bags into her car. When she gets into the car, she puts on her seat belt, adjusts the mirror, arranges her hair, and so on. At long last, she starts the car. She lets it warm up awhile before pulling out. When she finally does pull out, it seems like a snail could do it faster. After she leaves, you zoom into the parking spot before somebody else grabs it.

Perhaps you have also had the converse experience. Your car is already parked in a lot, and some driver hovers over you waiting for you to leave. To teach the driver a lesson, you take your sweet time leaving. After all, it is your spot and you had it first.

These common experiences illustrate how territorial humans can be. People don't want others to encroach on their territory. An intruder creates a challenge to the occupant's control over the territory. According to psychological reactance theory (Brehm, 1966), people respond to such threats by experiencing an unpleasant emotional response called **reactance** that motivates them to defend their territory.

A field experiment was conducted to study territorial behavior in parking lots (Ruback & Juieng, 1997). Most experiments are conducted in laboratory settings, but some are conducted in real-world settings. An experiment conducted in a real-world setting is called a **field experiment**. In this field experiment, participants were drivers who were leaving their parking spaces at a mall. The researchers manipulated the level of intrusion. In the high intrusion condition, a confederate stopped four spaces from the departing driver's car, flashed his turn signal in the direction of the departing car, and honked his horn as soon as the departing driver sat behind the steering wheel. In the low intrusion condition, the confederate stopped four spaces from the departing car, but did not flash his turn signal or honk his horn. In the control condition,

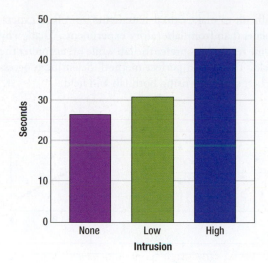

Drivers took their sweet time leaving a parking spot when an intruder was waiting to get it (Ruback & Juieng, 1997).

the researchers simply timed how long it took drivers to leave their parking space when there was no intruder present. The results showed that departing drivers took longer to leave when someone was waiting for their spot than when no one was waiting. In addition, drivers took longer to depart when the confederate flashed his turn signal and honked his horn than when he did not. These results are depicted in ▶ **FIGURE 1.6**.

The primary strength of a laboratory experiment is control over other variables that might influence the results; the primary weakness is that the setting is less realistic. Laboratory experiments do not have to be unrealistic, though. Actually, "realistic" can mean different things. The distinction between experimental realism and mundane realism is an important one (Aronson & Carlsmith, 1968). **Experimental realism** refers to whether participants get so caught up in the procedures that they forget they are in an experiment. **Mundane realism** refers to whether the setting physically resembles the real world. Laboratory experiments are generally low in mundane realism, but they can be high in experimental realism.

A study is said to have **external validity** if the findings are likely to generalize to other people and other settings (Cook & Campbell, 1979). Experimental realism is more important than mundane realism in determining whether the results of a study will generalize to the real world (Berkowitz & Donnerstein, 1982).

Field experiments are generally high in experimental and mundane realism, but they lack the tight control that laboratory experiments have. Thus, it is more

REACTANCE an unpleasant emotional response that people often experience when someone is trying to restrict their freedom

FIELD EXPERIMENT an experiment conducted in a real-world setting

EXPERIMENTAL REALISM the extent to which study participants get so caught up in the procedures that they forget they are in an experiment

MUNDANE REALISM the extent to which the setting of an experiment physically resembles the real world

EXTERNAL VALIDITY the extent to which the findings from a study can be generalized to other people, other settings, and other time periods

difficult to make causal statements from field experiments than from laboratory experiments. That's why some researchers prefer the lab while others prefer the field. There is no perfect method. Scientific progress is best served by using both lab and field.

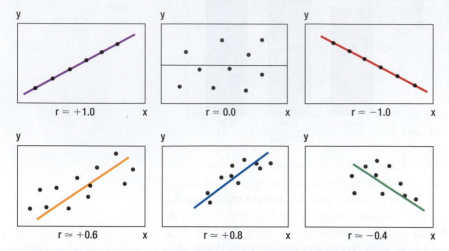

▶ **FIGURE 1.7** Visual depiction of values of correlation coefficients. One of the variables is plotted on the *x*-axis, and the other variable is plotted on the *y*-axis. The sign indicates the direction of the relation between the two variables (positive or negative). The value indicates how strongly the two variables are related—the stronger the relationship, the closer the points are to the line.

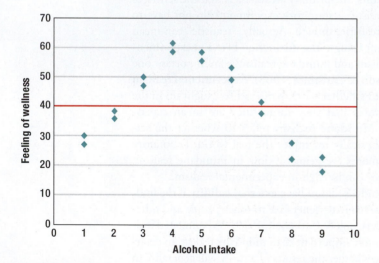

▶ **FIGURE 1.8** A situation in which a correlational approach is not appropriate. Correlation can only be applied when two variables are linearly related. In this graph, the relationship between alcohol intake and feeling well is not linear—it goes up, then down. Even though the correlation in this graph is 0 (denoted by the flat red line), there is a strong relationship between alcohol intake and feelings of wellness. As alcohol consumption increases to about 4 drinks, mood also increases. As the number of drinks increases beyond 4, mood decreases.

CORRELATIONAL APPROACH a nonexperimental method in which the researcher merely observes whether variables are associated or related

CORRELATION the relationship or association between two variables

CORRELATION COEFFICIENT (*r*) the statistical relationship or association between two variables

META-ANALYSIS a quantitative literature review that combines the statistical results (e.g., correlation coefficients) from all studies conducted on a topic

Nonexperimental Studies. Although social psychologists generally prefer experimental studies, sometimes they cannot be used. Recall that the two hallmarks of an experiment are control and random assignment. Some variables cannot be controlled for practical or ethical reasons, such as gender, race, ethnicity, marital status, and age. Sometimes random assignment cannot be used either. Suppose, for example, that a researcher is interested in the relationship between smoking cigarettes and lung cancer. It would be unethical to randomly assign participants to smoke or not smoke cigarettes.

Faced with such difficulties, social psychologists often adopt an alternative research technique known as the **correlational approach**. In this approach, the researcher does not try to control variables or randomly assign participants to groups. Instead, the researcher merely observes whether things normally go together. Such associations are called correlations. A **correlation** is a measure of the relationship or association between two variables. When a correlation is positive, as one variable goes up the other variable also goes up. For example, there is a positive correlation between smoking cigarettes and lung cancer: The more cigarettes people smoke, the more likely they are to get lung cancer (e.g., Wynder & Graham, 1950). When a correlation is negative, as one variable goes up the other variable goes down. For example, there is a negative correlation between time spent playing video games and grades in college: The more time college students spend playing video games, the lower their grade point average is (Anderson & Dill, 2000). When there is no correlation, the two variables are not related in a linear fashion. For example, there is no correlation between IQ scores and shoe size.

Mathematically, correlations are computed in terms of the **correlation coefficient**, denoted by *r*. A correlation coefficient can range from +1.0 (a perfect positive correlation) to −1.0 (a perfect negative correlation). A correlation coefficient of 0 indicates that the two variables are not linearly related. The closer a correlation is to +1 or −1, the stronger it is (see ▶ **FIGURE 1.7**).

A correlation of 0, however, does not mean that the two variables are unrelated. Consider the graph in ▶ **FIGURE 1.8**, showing the relationship between "Alcohol intake" (*x*-axis) and "Feeling of wellness" (*y*-axis). The correlation in this graph is 0 (i.e., the red line is flat), but there is a strong relationship between alcohol intake and feeling well. As alcohol consumption increases, feelings of wellness also increase (e.g., people become happier). After about 4 drinks, however, feelings of wellness decrease (e.g., people become sick or hung over).

A **meta-analysis** is a literature review that averages the statistical results (e.g., correlations) from different studies conducted on the same topic. It gives a "big picture" view of what all the studies show together.

GRAPHIC VIOLENCE IN THE MEDIA.

DOES IT GLAMORIZE VIOLENCE? SURE. DOES IT DESENSITIZE US TO VIOLENCE? OF COURSE. DOES IT HELP US TOLERATE VIOLENCE? YOU BET. DOES IT STUNT OUR EMPATHY FOR OUR FELLOW BEINGS? HECK YES.

DOES IT *CAUSE* VIOLENCE? ...WELL, THAT'S HARD TO PROVE.

THE TRICK IS TO ASK THE RIGHT QUESTION.

© 1995 Watterson/Dist. by Universal Press Syndicate

WATTERSON 2-15

Reprinted by permission of Universal Press Syndicate, Inc.

The main weakness of the correlational approach is that it does not allow the researcher to conclude that changes in one variable caused the changes in the other variable. Recall that when two variables (say X and Y) are correlated, any combination of three explanations is possible: (1) X could cause Y, (2) Y could cause X, or (3) some other variable (say Z) could cause both X and Y. For example, suppose a researcher finds a positive correlation between media violence (X) and violent crime (Y). At least three explanations are possible: (a) Media violence causes violent crime; (b) violent criminals like to consume violent media; and (c) some other variable (e.g., low intelligence, poverty, poor social skills) causes people to watch media violence and to commit violent crimes. The difficulty of drawing causal conclusions about media violence is reflected in the cartoon on this page. As this cartoon suggests, it is difficult to prove that media violence causes violent crime using the correlational approach. Of course, one cannot use the experimental approach either because it would not be ethical to give research participants guns or knives in the laboratory and watch to see if they commit violent crimes with the weapons! In Chapter 10 we will discuss in detail the effects of violent media on aggression and violence.

Consider another example. If you counted up the amount of ice cream eaten every day in Denmark and the number of people who drowned there each day, you might find a positive correlation—that is, there were more drownings on the days on which more ice cream was eaten. But you can't tell what causes what. It could be that eating more ice cream causes people to drown; perhaps people go swimming right after eating lots of ice cream, get cramps, and cannot swim back from deep water. Or it could be that drownings cause an increase in ice cream eating; maybe the friends of people who drown feel sad and try to console themselves by eating ice cream. (This seems doubtful on intuitive grounds, but without further information there is no way to be certain that it is wrong.) Or, most likely, changes in the weather might account for both ice cream eating and drownings. On hot days, more people swim and hence more people drown, and

hot days also promote ice cream eating. On snowy or rainy days, fewer people swim and fewer people eat ice cream. That's enough to produce a correlation.

[QUIZ YOURSELF]

How Do Social Psychologists Answer Their Own Questions?

1. A testable prediction about the conditions under which an event will occur is called a _____.
   (a) construct   (b) hypothesis
   (c) theory   (d) variable

2. Which of the following is an operational definition of racial prejudice?
   (a) A negative attitude toward individuals based on their membership in a particular race.
   (b) The number of negative traits the person selects from a list of traits when doing the list for his or her own race versus another race.
   (c) The tendency to believe that people of a particular race are less deserving than are people of another race.
   (d) All of the above could be operational definitions of prejudice.

3. With random assignment, each participant _____.
   (a) is exposed to all levels of the dependent variable
   (b) is exposed to all levels of the independent variable
   (c) has an equal chance of being exposed to each level of the dependent variable
   (d) has an equal chance of being exposed to each level of the independent variable

4. Which of the following correlations shows the strongest relationship between the variables?
   (a) The correlation between alcohol consumption and traffic deaths is $r = .36$.
   (b) The correlation between height and IQ is $r = 0$.
   (c) The correlation between time spent partying and grades among college students is $r = -.80$.
   (d) The correlation between watching media violence and aggression is $r = .20$.

How Much of Social Psychology Is True?

Many thousands of social psychology studies are done every year. On the one hand, this volume of activity gives the impression that a great deal is being learned and great progress is being made. On the other hand, the many arguments and controversies in the field create the impression that chaos and anarchy prevail and no progress is being made. Also, many people criticize social psychology experiments as not being good ways to learn about reality. The critics argue that social psychology laboratories are artificial settings, that social psychology measures are unrealistic, and that the participants tested (mainly college students) are not representative of real people. In other words, the critics claim that social psychology research lacks external validity. Accordingly, let us spend a little time reflecting on how much confidence we can have in what social psychologists learn—indeed, on how much one can believe what is presented in the rest of this book!

SELF-CORRECTING NATURE OF SCIENCE

As already mentioned, one source of concern about social psychology is that experts sometimes disagree. Sometimes both sides can point to experiments that seem to support their conflicting viewpoints. Moreover, some experiments can produce a wrong or misleading conclusion, possibly due to a hidden flaw in the experimental design. It is even possible that researchers occasionally fail to report their work correctly, and once in a great while it is found that researchers have lied about their work, perhaps to advance their careers by claiming to have produced some new discovery.

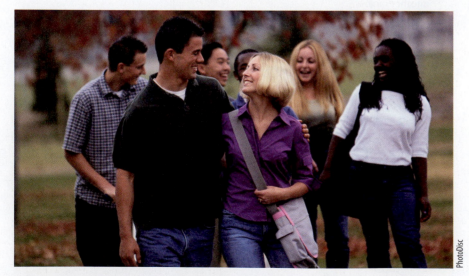

Studies show college students do not differ fundamentally from other people.

REPLICATION repeating a study to be sure similar results can be obtained

In the long run, these problems are corrected. Flawed experiments or misleading interpretations can arise, but in general new work builds on older work, and if there are mistakes in the older research, the newer research will find them and correct them. **Replication** means repeating an experiment, and many studies replicate earlier ones, so if the result of the earlier one was a fluke or a fraud, the replication will produce a different result, and gradually the correct answer will emerge from multiple studies. This is one of the great advantages of the sciences (including the social sciences) as opposed to the humanities (e.g., literary criticism): It is possible, eventually, to establish that some ideas or conclusions are wrong.

Hence some of the conclusions described in this book may turn out in the long run to be wrong or partly wrong. As each decade passes, the body of knowledge in the field becomes more complete and more correct. Social psychology, like almost all scientific fields, is a work in progress. But the progress is real.

RELIANCE ON STUDENT SAMPLES

Many people worry less about whether the findings of social psychology experiments are correct than about whether they are generalizable. These questions arise because most studies in social psychology are done with college students, who are easier to find for research (especially because most researchers are university professors). Some argue that students might not be typical of everyone else, so a social psychology based on college students might not generalize to other groups, such as the elderly, middle-aged corporate executives, or homeless people.

Periodically, social psychologists seek to replicate their studies using other groups. In general, the results are quite similar. College students do not differ fundamentally from other people in most respects. When they do differ, it is often more a matter of degree than of behaving according to different principles. A social psychology experiment typically seeks to establish whether or not some causal relationship exists (such as whether insults cause aggression). As it happens, college students do become more aggressive when insulted, but so do most other people. It might be that some groups will respond with more extreme aggression and others with less, but the general principle is the same: insults cause aggression.

Social psychology is also mainly interested in normal, typical people, as opposed to unusual groups that may have special characteristics (e.g., children or mentally ill persons). College students are drawn from a broad segment of normal people, so findings based on them typically can be generalized to other typical groups. But one should be careful generalizing from findings based on students (or on other normal groups) to very unusual groups.

When college students do differ from other people, these differences are probably limited to a few specific areas, and researchers interested in them should be cautious (Oakes, 1972; Sears, 1986). On average, college students may be more thoughtful than others, and more intelligent (because people of low intelligence are less likely to go to college). Their self-concepts may be less firmly established, because most students are still in the process of building their adult identities. They may have less experience with the burdens of responsibility than other adults who must cope with the demands of work and taking care of a family. They may come from slightly more affluent backgrounds and have somewhat smaller proportions of ethnic minorities than the population at large. None of these differences is likely to make students radically different from other people. Hence, social psychology's disproportionate reliance on studying college students does not represent a serious problem.

CULTURAL RELATIVITY

Most social psychology is done and published in the United States and a few other very similar Western countries (including Canada, the Netherlands, and Germany). Some people worry that findings based in these cultures would not apply to people who live in very different cultures, such as in sub-Saharan Africa, the Middle East, or central Asia.

We do not have enough evidence to know how serious this problem may be. Because Western countries dominate social psychology research (although much work is being conducted in Japan and elsewhere), we simply do not know how different people in other cultures may be. There is little evidence to suggest that people in other cultures fail to conform to certain basic patterns of social psychology—for example, that similarity promotes liking (see Chapter 11). But it is also true that no one has tested whether these same patterns can be found everywhere.

Although we are optimistic that much of what Western social psychologists find will prove to be true of people everywhere, we think it prudent to expect that some differences may exist. At present, it seems reasonably safe to generalize what social psychology knows to the vast majority of adult citizens in Western cultures, but to be cautious and hesitant about generalizing to people who live in very different cultures.

This book is based on the assumption that human nature has some basic, universal features. In other words, we do believe that some psychological facts and principles are true for people everywhere. But there are also cultural differences, and some of them are quite substantial and important. People may be born the same everywhere in many respects, but different cultures can build on these same basic traits in different ways and shape them according to different values. This theme is reflected in the next chapter, where we discuss humans as cultural animals.

[QUIZ YOURSELF]

How Much of Social Psychology Is True?

1. What concept allows science to be self-correcting over time?
   (a) Correlation (b) Generalizability
   (c) Random assignment (d) Replication

2. Most social psychological studies use participants from which continent?
   (a) Asia (b) Australia
   (c) North America (d) South America

3. What type of participants do most social psychologists use in their studies?
   (a) Children (b) College students
   (c) Senior citizens (d) White rats

4. Compared to the general population, college students _____.
   (a) are more extraverted
   (b) are more introverted
   (c) have less crystallized self-concepts
   (d) have more crystallized self-concepts

---

chapter summary

A BRIEF HISTORY OF SOCIAL PSYCHOLOGY

- Social psychology can help you make sense of your own social world.
- The mere presence of another person enhances performance on a simple task.

- Individual effort decreases as group size increases.
- Behaviorism seeks to explain all of psychology in terms of learning principles such as reward and punishment.

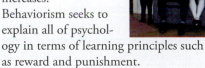

WHAT DO SOCIAL PSYCHOLOGISTS DO?

- Social psychology features experiments and the scientific method. It studies inner states and processes as well as behavior.
- Social psychology is concerned with the effect of other people on (mainly adult)

human beings' thoughts, feelings, and behaviors.

- The ABC triad in social psychology stands for
  - Affect, or how people feel inside (including emotion)
  - Behavior, or what people do, their actions
  - Cognition, or what people think about
- Social psychology focuses especially on the power of situations.

SOCIAL PSYCHOLOGY'S PLACE IN THE WORLD

- Social psychology is both similar to and different from other social sciences.
  - Anthropology is the study of human culture.
  - Economics is the study of the production, distribution, and consumption of goods and services.
  - History is the study of past events.
  - Political science is the study of political organizations and institutions, especially governments.
  - Sociology is the study of human societies and the groups that form those societies.
- Psychology is the study of human behavior. Several other areas of psychology are related to social psychology.
  - Biological psychology, physiological psychology, and neuroscience focus on the brain, nervous system, and other aspects of the body.
  - Clinical psychology focuses on abnormal behavior and disorders.
  - Cognitive psychology is the basic study of thought processes.
  - Developmental psychology focuses on how people change across their lives, from conception and birth to old age and death.
  - Personality psychology focuses on differences between individuals, as well as inner processes.
- What separates philosophy from psychology is psychology's heavy reliance on the scientific method.

WHY PEOPLE STUDY SOCIAL PSYCHOLOGY

- Social psychologists often find the topics they study to be intrinsically interesting.

- Applied researchers study a specific practical problem, usually outside the laboratory.

HOW DO SOCIAL PSYCHOLOGISTS ANSWER THEIR OWN QUESTIONS?

- To be a good social psychology researcher, it is helpful to be creative.
- Common sense can be mistaken.
- The scientific method involves five basic steps:

  - State a problem for study.
  - Formulate a testable hypothesis (educated guess) as a tentative solution to the problem.
  - Design a study to test the hypothesis and collect data.
  - Test the hypothesis by confronting it with the data.
  - Communicate the study's results.
- The independent variable is an observable event that causes a person in an experiment to do something. It has at least two levels, categories, types, or groups.
- In a between-subjects design, each participant is exposed to only one level of the independent variable; in a within-subjects design, each participant is exposed to all levels of the independent variable.
- A design that includes more than one independent variable or factor is called a factorial design.
- In a factorial design, a researcher can determine the effect of each individual independent variable on the dependent variable (called main effects) as well as the joint effects of more than one independent variable on the dependent variable (called interaction).
- The dependent variable is an observable behavior produced by a person in an experiment.
- An operational definition classifies theoretical variables in terms of observable operations, procedures, and measurements.
- For a theory to be scientific, it must be testable, so its theoretical constructs must be operationally defined.
- Two essential features of experiments are control and random assignment:
  - By exercising experimental control, the researcher tries to make sure that any differences observed on the dependent

variable were caused by the independent variable and not by other factors.
- Participants in an experiment must be randomly assigned to levels of the independent variable (assignment to groups is random if each participant has an equal chance of being in each group).
- A confederate is someone who helps the experimenter by pretending to be another participant.
- Experiments conducted in a real-world rather than a laboratory setting are called field experiments.
- Experimental realism refers to whether participants get so caught up in the procedures that they forget they are in an experiment (important for determining whether the results obtained in the experiment can be applied to the real world).
- Mundane realism refers to whether the setting and research procedures physically resemble the real world.
- In the correlational approach, the researcher does not try to control variables or randomly assign participants to groups, but merely observes whether things go together.
- A correlation is the relationship or association between two variables.
  - When a correlation is positive, as one variable goes up, the other variable also goes up.
  - When a correlation is negative, as one variable increases, the other variable decreases.
  - A correlation coefficient can range from +1.0 (a perfect positive correlation) to −1.0 (a perfect negative correlation).
- The main weakness of the correlational approach is it does not allow the researcher to conclude that changes in one variable caused the changes in the other variable.

HOW MUCH OF SOCIAL PSYCHOLOGY IS TRUE?

- Because research builds on older research, science is self-correcting.
- Some psychological facts and principles are true for people everywhere. But there are also cultural differences, and some of them are quite substantial and important.

Key Terms

ABC triad 6
Anthropology 7
Applied research 10
Behaviorism 5
Between-subjects design 12
Biological psychology 8
Clinical psychology 8
Cognitive psychology 8
Confederate 13
Confounding 15
Construct validity of the cause 14

Construct validity of the effect 14
Correlation 18
Correlation coefficient (*r*) 18
Correlational approach 18
Dependent variable 13
Developmental psychology 8
Economics 7
Experiment 14
Experimental realism 17
External validity 17
Factorial design 16

Field experiment 17
Freudian psychoanalysis 5
History 7
Hypothesis 12
Independent variable 13
Interaction 16
Internal validity 15
Main effect 16
Meta-analysis 18
Mundane realism 17
Neuroscience 8
Operational definitions 13
Personality psychology 8

Philosophy 9
Physiological psychology 8
Political science 7
Psychology 8
Quasi-experiment 14
Random assignment 14
Reactance 17
Replication 20
Social psychology 3
Sociology 7
Theories 12
Within-subjects design 12

[Quiz Yourself] Answers

1. A Brief History of Social Psychology
Answers: 1=c, 2=d, 3=a, 4=b

2. What Do Social Psychologists Do?
Answers: 1=d, 2=b, 3=a, 4=d

3. Social Psychology's Place in the World
Answers: 1=c, 2=a, 3=d, 4=c

4. Why People Study Social Psychology
Answers: 1=b, 2=b, 3=d, 4=c

5. How Do Social Psychologists Answer Their Own Questions?
Answers: 1=b, 2=b, 3=d, 4=c

6. How Much of Social Psychology Is True?
Answers: 1=d, 2=c, 3=b, 4=c

Media Learning Resources

Make sure you check out the complete set of learning resources and study tools below. If your instructor did not order these items with your new book, go to www.ichapters.com to purchase Cengage Learning print and digital products.

Social Psychology and Human Nature BOOK COMPANION WEBSITE

www.cengage.com/psychology/baumeister
Visit your book companion website, where you will find flash cards, practice quizzes, Internet links, and more to help you study.

CENGAGENOW™ JUST WHAT YOU NEED TO KNOW NOW!

Spend time on what you need to master rather than on information you have already learned. Take a pre-test for this chapter, and CengageNOW will generate a personalized study plan based on your results. The study plan will identify the topics you need to review and direct you to online resources to help you master those topics. You can then take a post-test to help you determine the concepts you have mastered and what you will still need to work on. Try it out! Go to www.cengage.com/login to sign in with an access code or to purchase access to this product.

CLASSIC AND CONTEMPORARY VIDEOS STUDENT CD-ROM

To see videos on the topics and experiments discussed in this chapter and to learn more about the research that social psychologists are doing today, go to the Student CD-ROM.

SOCIAL PSYCH LAB

These unique online labs give you the opportunity to become a participant in actual experiments, including re-creations of classic and contemporary research studies.

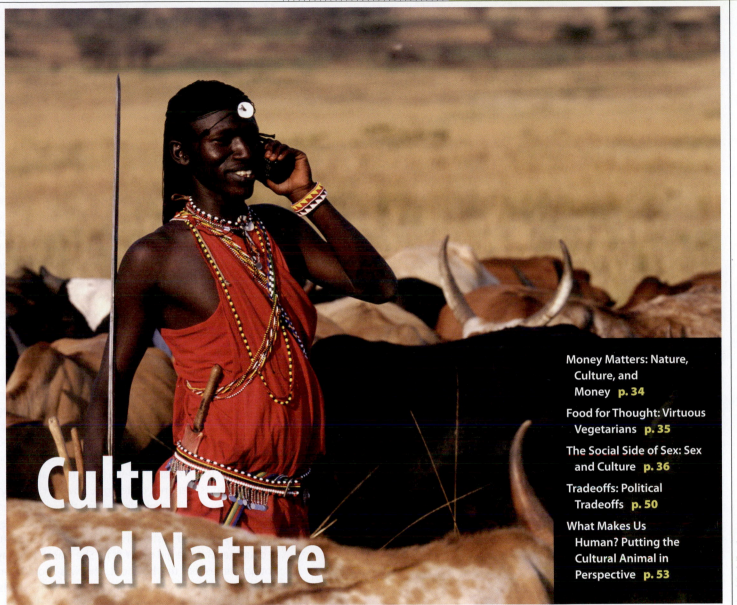

chapter 2

Culture and Nature

Money Matters: Nature, Culture, and Money **p. 34**

Food for Thought: Virtuous Vegetarians **p. 35**

The Social Side of Sex: Sex and Culture **p. 36**

Tradeoffs: Political Tradeoffs **p. 50**

What Makes Us Human? Putting the Cultural Animal in Perspective **p. 53**

Joseph Van Os/Getty Images

NATURE AND SOCIAL BEHAVIOR p. 27
Explaining the Psyche **p. 27**
Nature Defined **p. 28**
Evolution, and Doing What's Natural **p. 28**
Social Animals **p. 30**
The Social Brain **p. 31**

CULTURE AND HUMAN SOCIAL LIFE p. 32
Social Animal or Cultural Animal? **p. 32**
Culture Defined **p. 33**

Nature and Culture Interacting **p. 35**
What Makes Cultural Animals? **p. 37**
Are People the Same Everywhere? **p. 39**

IMPORTANT FEATURES OF HUMAN SOCIAL LIFE p. 41
The Duplex Mind **p. 41**
The Long Road to Social Acceptance **p. 45**
Built to Relate **p. 45**

Nature Says Go, Culture Says Stop **p. 46**
Selfish Impulse Versus Social Conscience **p. 47**
Tradeoffs: When You Can't Have It All **p. 48**
Putting People First **p. 50**

CHAPTER SUMMARY p. 53

A pair of healthy twin boys were born to a Canadian woman in 1965. When the boys were eight months old, they were taken to the hospital to be circumcised. Through a series of mishaps, one of the boys had his penis practically burned off by an electric cauterizing machine. ||||

Medical technology was not capable of repairing the damage. After some long and anxious conversations, the family and medical staff decided that the best thing to do was to remove the rest of the penis and raise the boy as a girl (Colapinto, 2000).

The decision was not taken lightly. The family consulted with leading experts on gender and sexuality. In the past, many psychologists and others had believed that men and women were innately different, but the feminist movement had challenged those beliefs as being mere rationalizations for oppressing women. Most expert opinion had come around to agree that boys and girls were not born different but were made different by how they were brought up. Many Canadian and American parents were themselves rethinking how to raise their children so as to undo the constraining stereotypes and perhaps produce more autonomous, stronger daughters and more sensitive, caring sons. If adult personality depended mainly on upbringing, then it should not matter much whether a child was born as a boy or a girl. It should therefore be possible to raise this baby boy as a girl with no untoward consequences. At most, the experts thought that the child would need some injections of female hormones around the time of puberty.

Little Brenda (as the child was named) was not told about the botched circumcision or the gender switch. She grew up wearing long hair and dresses, playing with other girls, and in other ways being introduced to the female sex role. The sex experts kept in touch and reported back to the scientific community that the experiment was working. Brenda was a normal girl.

The reports were not quite right, however. The parents were anxious to avoid displeasing the experts, and perhaps they also wanted to avoid admitting that they might have made a mistake in converting their son into a daughter. But the girl never fit in. She wanted to play rough games like the boys did. She was more interested in sports, race cars, and fighting toys than in dolls, makeup, or tea parties. Her dress was often dirty and disheveled, and her hair was tangled, unlike the other girls'. As the children approached puberty and began to play kissing games or to try dancing at parties, the tensions increased. Brenda did not know what was wrong, but she wanted no part of kissing boys or dancing with them. Her rebellious behavior increased.

Finally it came time for the hormone shots. By now Brenda was in regular therapy. She rebelled and absolutely refused to accept the injections. When her parents broke down and told her the full story of how she had been born as a boy, she finally felt as if she could understand herself. She immediately quit being a girl. She cut her hair, replaced her dresses with boys' clothes, and took a male name. He insisted on having lengthy, agonizing surgeries to remove his breasts and create a sort of penis from the muscles and skin of his legs. Although

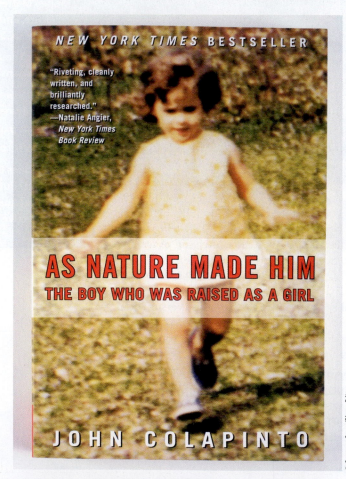

As Nature Made Him: The Boy Who Was Raised as a Girl, by John Colapinto.

his body could not biologically father a child, the former Brenda was even able to become a father by virtue of marrying a woman who already had children. But happiness proved elusive, and at age 38 he killed himself (Colapinto, 2000; also Joiner, 2005).

Later, investigative reporters uncovered other such cases. Each time, the person born as a boy and raised as a girl did not turn out to be a typical adult woman. One of them, for example, smoked cigars, refused to wear dresses and skirts, and worked as an auto mechanic. In a recent case, a 17-year-old named "Alex" from Australia, who was raised as a girl, was granted legal permission to have both breasts removed because Alex believes he is a boy ("Court grants," 2009).

These stories are important because they suggest limits to the power of socialization. In the 1970s and 1980s, most psychologists accepted the view that the differences between men and women were due to parental care and upbringing. Parents supposedly taught their sons to be aggressive while teaching their daughters to be passive and compliant. For a while, the early part of the "Brenda" story was reported in some textbooks as evidence that sex roles are entirely due to socialization, and Brenda was described as a normal and healthy girl. But the problems that emerged later suggested that the differences between male and female are partly innate. ("Innate" means something you are born with, as opposed to something you learned or acquired during your life. "Innate" is also understood to mean something that cannot be fully or easily changed.) There are limits to how much can be accomplished by teaching, upbringing, and other aspects of socialization.

None of this should be taken to mean that learning and culture are irrelevant. Boys and girls do learn from their culture how to act and how to understand themselves. But there are limits to the power of culture. Apparently people are predisposed to learn some things more easily than others. If gender identity were entirely a matter of learning, Brenda should have been a normal girl. Parents, teachers, psychologists, and others were all working together to raise her as a girl, and none of her peers or friends was told that she had once been a boy. At times she seemed to accept herself as a female and to act as girls were expected to act. However, the experiment failed. Apparently there are some parts of who you are that come from biology, regardless of what your parents and teachers tell you.

Social psychology is aimed at exploring how people think, feel, and act. The ultimate explanations for human behavior lie in nature and culture, and there have been many long, bitter debates over which of those is more important. The one clearly correct answer is that both are very important. In this chapter, we will consider the complementary influences of nature and culture. ■

Nature and Social Behavior

EXPLAINING THE PSYCHE

One approach to understanding how people think, feel, and act is to try to understand what the human psyche is designed for. (The **psyche** is a broader term for mind, encompassing emotions, desires, perceptions, and indeed all psychological processes.) To understand something, you have to know what it was designed to do.

Imagine someone who has grown up on a deserted island and has never met another human being or seen any man-made items. Then one day a box washes ashore containing an electric can opener. How would the person figure out what the can opener does? Having grown up on a deserted island, the person knows nothing about cans or electricity. This hypothetical person might take it apart, analyze it, observe its parts, and see what some of their properties are, but it would be almost impossible for this person to understand it properly.

Understanding the human psyche is somewhat like that. We want to understand and explain how it works. To do that, it is useful to know what the psyche/human mind is designed for. Hence we turn to nature and culture, because those are what made the psyche the way it is. If the psyche was designed for something in particular, then nature and culture designed it for that purpose. Accordingly, if we can learn what the purpose is, then we can understand people much better.

Why are people the way they are? Why is the human mind set up as it is? Why do people think, want, feel, and act in certain ways? Most of the explanations for human behavior ultimately lead back to two basic ways of answering these fundamental questions: nature and culture. The nature explanations say that people are born a certain way; their genes, hormones, brain structure, and other processes dictate how they will choose and act. In contrast, the culture explanations focus on what people learn from their parents, from society, and from their own experiences.

Such debates have raged over many other forms of social interaction and behavior. Are people born with a natural tendency to be aggressive, or is aggression something they pick up from watching violent films, playing with toy guns, and copying other people's actions? Are some people born to be homosexuals, or can people choose and change their sexual orientation? Is mental illness the result of how your parents treated you, or is it something in your genes?

PSYCHE a broader term for mind, encompassing emotions, desires, perceptions, and all other psychological processes

To understand how to work this device, you have to know what it is designed to do.

Thinkstock/Getty Images

What about whether someone likes to drink alcohol or gamble? What about heroism, especially when people risk their own lives to protect or save others? How many of the differences between men and women reflect their innate, genetic tendencies, and how many are the product of cultural stereotypes?

Many social scientists have grown tired of nature–nurture debates and wish to put an end to them, though others continue to pursue them vigorously. There has been an effort in recent years to say that both nature and culture have real influence. The most common resolution tends to favor nature as more important, however, because nature is indispensable. As Frans de Waal (2002) argued, nature versus culture isn't a fair fight, because without nature you have nothing. He proposed that the argument should be waged between whether a particular behavior is the direct result of nature or stems from a combination of nature and culture. Your body has to perceive what is happening, your brain has to understand events, and your body has to carry out your decisions (and brain and body are both created by nature). Put more simply, nature comes first, and culture builds on what nature has furnished. That is one view.

NATURE the physical world around us, including its laws and processes

THEORY OF EVOLUTION a theory proposed by Charles Darwin to explain how change occurs in nature

This book, however, favors the view that nature and culture have shaped each other. In particular, nature has prepared human beings specifically for culture. That is, the characteristics that set humans apart from other animals (including language, a flexible self that can hold multiple roles, and an advanced ability to understand each other's mental states) are mainly there to enable people to create and sustain culture. This interaction between nature and culture is the key to understanding how people think, act, and feel. But let's start by considering nature and culture separately.

NATURE DEFINED

Nature is the physical world around us, including its laws and processes. It includes the entire world that would be there even if no human beings existed. Nature includes trees and grass, bugs and elephants, gravity, the weather, hunger and thirst, birth and death, atoms and molecules, and all the laws of physics and chemistry. Nature made people too. (People who believe that the original humans were created by a divine power still recognize that the natural processes of reproduction and childbirth create today's people.)

Those who use nature to explain human behavior invoke the sorts of processes that natural sciences have shown. For example, neuroscientists look for explanations in terms of what happens inside the brain (chemical reactions, electrical activity). Behavior geneticists seek to understand behavior as the result of genes and show that people are born with tendencies to feel and act in certain ways. Above all, however, the advocates of nature in psychology turn to evolutionary theory to understand behavior patterns. The next section provides an introduction to this style of thinking.

EVOLUTION, AND DOING WHAT'S NATURAL

Over the past two decades, many social psychologists have begun looking to the theory of evolution to help explain social behavior. The **theory of evolution**, proposed by the British biologist Charles Darwin in the 1800s, focuses on how change occurs in nature. Over thousands of years, a type of plant or animal may evolve into a somewhat different kind of creature. Human beings and the great apes evolved from a common ancestor.

Human beings may be different from all other animals, but we are animals nonetheless. As such, we have many of the same wants, needs, and problems that most other animals have. We need food and water on a regular basis, preferably a couple of times every day. We need sleep. We need shelter and warmth. We need air. We suffer illnesses and injuries and must find ways to recover from them. Our interactions with others are sometimes characterized by sexual desire, competition, aggressive impulses, family ties, or friendly companionship. Sometimes we say that certain people are "acting like animals," but this is not surprising, because we are all animals. That phrase merely expresses the point that people can sometimes rise above their animal nature, but the animal parts are there inside all of us.

An important feature of most living things, including animals and hence humans, is the drive to prolong life. There are two ways to do this. Obviously, one way is to go on living. (Wouldn't you like to live forever? Death has always been a disturbing threat, and beliefs that death is not the end but merely a transition into a different kind of life, whether as a ghost, a spirit in heaven, or a reincarnated person, have been found all over the earth since prehistoric times.) The other is reproduction: Life makes new life. Indeed, you might say that nature was unable to create an immortal being and therefore settled on reproduction as the only viable strategy to enable any form of life to continue into the future.

Change is another common trait of living things. Each living thing changes as it grows older, but more important forms of change occur from one generation to the next: Children are different from their parents. Nature cannot plan ahead and design a certain kind of change. Instead, nature produces changes that are essentially random. That is, the complicated processes that mix the genes of two parents to produce a unique set of genes in the baby sometimes produce novel outcomes in the form of new traits. However, there are powerful forces that react to these random changes. As a result, some random changes will disappear, whereas others will endure. The process of **natural selection** decides which traits will disappear and which will continue.

For example, imagine that one baby was born with no ears, another with one leg longer than the other, and the third with eyes that could see farther than the average eye. Having no ears or having legs of unequal length would probably be disadvantages, and natural selection would not preserve these traits for future generations. (That's a polite way of saying that those babies would probably die before being able to pass on their genes by having offspring.) A significant improvement in vision might however be selected to remain, because the baby who grew up seeing better than other people would be able to find more food and spot danger from a safer distance. The genes for better vision would therefore remain in the gene pool (assuming that this baby would grow up and have babies), and so in future generations more and more people would enjoy this improvement.

Natural selection operates on the basis of two criteria: survival and reproduction. (Remember, these are the two ways of prolonging life.) A trait

off the mark.com   by Mark Parisi

DO THOSE SWEET SOUNDING BELLS SEEM TO BE GETTING CLOSER OR IS IT JUST ME?

NATURAL SELECTION AT WORK

that improves survival or reproduction will tend to endure for many generations and become more common. A trait that reduces one's chances for survival or reproduction will probably not become common. These are crucial themes, because the biological success of any trait is measured in those terms. A novel trait that makes someone happier, or gives the person higher self-esteem, or fosters a weird sense of humor, will not necessarily be passed on to future generations, unless those changes can translate into better survival or better reproduction.

Survival is not hard to understand. It means living longer. Darwin's contemporary Herbert Spencer coined the phrase "survival of the fittest" to describe natural selection. Animals compete against each other to survive, as in who can get the best food or who can best escape being eaten by larger animals. In a group of zebras, for example, the ones who run the slowest are most likely to be eaten by lions, so the ones born to be fast are more likely to live long enough to pass along their genes.

Survival depends in part on the circumstances in your environment. Consider the coloring of fish. Almost all fish have a relatively light colored belly and a relatively dark colored top or back. Why? That coloring is adapted for survival in the water. Most fish live until a bigger fish eats them, making the ability to hide from bigger fish an important trait for survival. Some big fish swim near the surface and

---

NATURAL SELECTION the process whereby those members of a species that survive and reproduce most effectively are the ones that pass along their genes to future generations
SURVIVAL living longer

off the mark.com   by Mark Parisi

I'M HAVING THE WORST LUCK...

SURVIVAL THROUGH EVOLUTION

Reprinted by permission of Atlantic Feature Syndicate/Mark Parisi.

look downward for food. The lower (deeper) you go in the water, the darker it gets. When a big fish looks downward, therefore, it can't see dark-colored fish very well, so fish who are dark on the top side are harder to see (and therefore safer). Meanwhile, some big fish lurk in the depths and look upward for their food. Looking upward is looking into the light, so the best way for a fish to blend in is to have a light coloring on its underside. Over millions of years, the fish who were dark on top and light on the bottom survived longest because they were the hardest for the bigger fish to see, so they were less likely to be eaten and, therefore, more likely to make more baby fish with the same coloring. As a result of this selection process, most fish have this coloring today.

Gradually, biologists have shifted their emphasis from survival to reproduction as the single most important factor in natural selection. Survival is important mainly as a means to achieve reproduction. **Reproduction** means producing babies—though the babies also have to survive long enough to reproduce. Reproductive success consists of creating many offspring who will in turn create many offspring. Put another way, nature judges you by how many grandchildren you produce.

For example, suppose there were a **mutation** (that is, a new gene or combination of genes) today that doubled the expected life span of a woman, from about 75 years to about 150. That is, one particular woman was born with the biological makeup to enable her to live 150 years. Would subsequent generations have more and more of this trait, and thus be more and more like this woman (and hence able to live longer?). Possibly not. If the woman was still done having babies around the age of 40, and if her longer life did not improve her quantity or quality of children and grandchildren, then her genetic traits would not spread. Now imagine another woman born with a mutation that doubled the number of children she produced, even though she would die at age 75 just like the others. Subsequent generations would contain more and more people like her.

Much of the recent work in evolutionary theory has focused on gender differences (Buss, 1994; Symons, 1979; Trivers, 1972). For example, evolution would likely select men to want more sex partners than women want. A woman can only have one baby a year no matter how many men she has sex with, but a man can father dozens of children each year if he has sex with many women. Moreover, a woman's children would be most likely to survive to adulthood if they were cared for by two parents rather than just their mother. Hence men today are probably descended from men who desired multiple partners, whereas today's women probably descended from female ancestors who preferred long-lasting monogamous relationships. Current research suggests that this pattern is found all over the world, in many different cultures: Men desire more sex partners than women (Schmitt, 2003).

How, exactly, does biological evolution produce changes? The causal processes depend entirely on random changes to physical entities, such as genes. The person (or other creature) is programmed to respond a certain way. Crucially, nothing has to be thought, understood, or spoken in order for these changes to occur. That is, meaning has nothing to do with it. Molecules, chemicals, electrical impulses in the body, and other physical mechanisms produce the results. Behavior changes because the physical makeup of the newborn individual is different. This is quite different from how culture works, as we shall see.

SOCIAL ANIMALS

Psychologists study people. Many psychologists have studied other animals, especially rats. But psychologists have never shown much interest in studying trees. Why not?

Trees, like people and all other living creatures, need to get certain things (e.g., water, nutrients) from the world around them. What is inside them is there to enable them to get what they need. The inside parts of trees enable them to draw water from the soil, chemicals from sunlight, and so forth. Trees, however, do not move around in search of food or

---

REPRODUCTION producing babies that survive long enough to also reproduce
MUTATION a new gene or combination of genes

to escape from predators. They take what comes to them where they are. Facing few decisions and being therefore essentially indifferent to other trees, they do not have much psychology. They don't have much in the way of thoughts, feelings, or behavior, because they don't need these things to survive and reproduce. (That's why psychologists don't find them interesting.)

Contrast this with animals who also live as loners. They have to find food, possibly kill it, and eat it. They need more food and produce more waste than trees do. They need to sleep and so must find safe places to do so. Reproduction is more complicated than it is for trees, so they may need to perform a particular set of behaviors in order to reproduce. Like trees, they need to interact with their world, but doing so is more complicated for animals, so what is inside them has to be up to the task. Psychologists start to get interested in these processes.

Many animals are not loners. They discovered, or perhaps nature discovered for them, that by living and working together, they could interact with the world more effectively. For example, if an animal hunts for food by itself, it can only catch, kill, and eat animals much smaller than itself—but if animals band together in a group, they can catch and kill animals bigger than they are. A pack of wolves can kill a horse, which can feed the group very well. Thus, there is more food available to the same animals in the same forest if they work together than if they work alone. There are other benefits of cooperation: They can alert each other to danger, can find more food (if they search separately and then follow the ones who succeed in finding food), and can even provide some care to those who are sick and injured. Mating and reproduction are also easier if the animals live in a group than if they live far apart.

In short, being social provides benefits. Being social is a strategy that enables some animals to survive and reproduce effectively. That is the biological starting point of social psychology: Being social improves survival and reproduction.

The downside of being social is that it is more difficult to achieve than solitary life. As with trees, what is inside social animals is there to enable them to get what they need from the environment. But to be social, one has to have quite a bit going on inside. (Hence psychologists can find much to study.) Social animals have to have something inside them that makes them recognize each other and want to be together. They must have something that prompts them to work together, such as automatic impulses to copy what the others are doing. (Hunting in groups doesn't happen by mere coincidence.) They must have ways to resolve the conflicts that inevitably arise in social life, as when two animals both want the same piece of food. They need something akin to

"So really, what are you like deep down inside?"

self-control to enable them to adjust to group life. In short, social animals need complex, powerful brains.

THE SOCIAL BRAIN

Trees don't need brains, and solitary creatures can get by with relatively simple ones. Social animals, however, require brains with additional, flexible capabilities.

The evolutionary anthropologist Robin Dunbar (1993, 1996) compared the brain sizes of many different species to see what behavioral differences went with bigger brains. (Brain size is always adjusted for body weight, because bigger animals generally have bigger brains. For example, human men have bigger brains than women, but that's mainly because men are bigger all over.) Did big-brained species eat better foods, or more complicated foods such as fruit (which ripens and turns rotten rapidly)? Did they roam over larger territories, so that they needed a bigger brain to maintain a more complex mental map? No. What Dunbar found was that bigger brains were mainly linked to having larger and more complex social groups. Small-brained animals tend to live alone or in small, simple groups, whereas bigger-brained, presumably smarter animals have more relationships with each other and more complicated groups (such as those with dominance hierarchies and competing allies).

This conclusion is highly important. The human brain did not evolve because it helped us outsmart lions and tigers and bears, or build better shelters, or invent calculus. It evolved mainly in order to enable human beings to have rich, complex social lives. The brain is not for understanding the physical world around us, so much as it is for understanding each other. It is not so much a calculating brain or a problem-solving brain as it is a social brain.

Again, what is inside is there to enable the creature to satisfy its needs and, ultimately, to survive and reproduce. Social animals (including humans) accomplish those things by means of social interaction. Much of what goes on inside the human mind is designed to help the person relate to others. Social psychologists spend much time studying people's inner processes, including their thoughts and feelings and, recently, how human brains work. They study those things because *inner processes serve interpersonal functions*. Remember that phrase; it will be one of the themes of this book, and it is a good basis for understanding social psychology.

off the mark.com   by Mark Parisi

WHEN I WAS A KID, WE DIDN'T HAVE BIG JUICY BRAINS TO PROBE ...NO... WE HAD TO GET BY ABDUCTING CAVE PEOPLE WITH PUNY BRAINS... ...AND HAIRY BODIES!

offthemark.com

Reprinted by permission of Atlantic Feature Syndicate/Mark Parisi.

[QUIZ YOURSELF]

Nature and Social Behavior

1. The finding that kids who watch violent TV programs become more aggressive as adults than do kids who watch nonviolent TV programs can best be explained in terms of _____ influences.
   (a) biological   (b) genetic
   (c) hormonal   (d) societal

2. Suppose that a new baby girl was born with no teeth. Unfortunately, because she had great difficulty eating, she died of starvation before she could have any children. Thus, the trait of having no teeth was not preserved for future generations. This process is called _____.
   (a) natural selection   (b) nurture
   (c) praxis   (d) None of the above

3. What term refers to a new gene or combination of genes?
   (a) Mutation   (b) Natural selection
   (c) Reproduction   (d) Survival

4. Some species have bigger brains (for their body weight) than other species. What do big-brained species primarily use their brains for?
   (a) Eating better foods
   (b) Roaming over larger territories
   (c) Have larger and more complex social structures
   (d) All of the above

Culture and Human Social Life

SOCIAL ANIMAL OR CULTURAL ANIMAL?

Social psychologists like to use the phrase "the social animal" to describe human nature. This phrase has been used by many influential thinkers, from the ancient Greek philosopher Aristotle right down to the modern social psychologist Elliot Aronson (2007). By calling people **social animals**, these thinkers are saying that people seek connections to others and prefer to live, work, and play together with other people.

People are indeed social animals, but using this label may miss the mark of what is special about human beings. Plenty of other animals are social, from ants to elephants (as Aronson and others acknowledge). Human beings are not the only and probably not even the most social animals.

Being social animals is not what is most special about human beings. What is special is being **cultural animals**. Some other animals have bits and scraps of culture, such as when a tribe of monkeys all use a certain group of stones to open nuts, or learn to rinse their potatoes in the stream to get the dirt off (de Waal, 2002), but none comes anywhere close to having the remarkably rich and powerful cultural systems that humans have. Moreover, human beings have culture everywhere; human life is almost impossible to imagine without it. Culture in animals is typically a bonus or a luxury, something they could live almost as well without. All humans use culture every day and depend on it for their survival.

Culture is thus the essence of what makes us human. Yes, we are social beings, but we have plenty of company in that respect. We are also deeply cultural beings, and in that respect we are unique. Let us therefore consider what culture is.

SOCIAL ANIMALS animals that seek connections to others and prefer to live, work, and play with other members of their species

CULTURAL ANIMAL the view that evolution shaped the human psyche so as to enable humans to create and take part in culture

CULTURE DEFINED

Culture is harder to define than nature. (In fact, Boyd and Richerson, 1985, listed 164 different definitions of culture that different thinkers have used!) The term originally referred to a system of farming (a usage one can still see in terms like *agriculture*). Then it came to refer to musical and artistic achievements, such as paintings and symphonies. Social scientists eventually began to use the term to refer to what a large group of people has in common. French culture, for example, refers to everything that French people share: language, values, food preferences, a style of government, a place (France), and a shared sense of connection to the artistic and historical achievements of other French people.

For present purposes, the important thing about culture is that it is a kind of social system. Just as a pack of wolves or a school of fish is a social system, so is France. But there are obvious differences. France is much more complex than a pack of wolves. It is rich in symbols, meanings, and information. There are more different kinds of relationships among the French people than among the wolves.

Culture is thus an advanced way of being social. If we think of evolution as proceeding from simple creatures such as plants, to solitary animals, to social animals, then cultural animals are a further step in that same direction.

Following are some important features of culture.

Shared Ideas. Culture is the world of shared ideas. Culture enables you to interact with people you have never met before; by virtue of belonging to the same culture, you have enough in common that you can do things together. If you travel to another city and meet new people, many interactions are possible because of culture: You might talk to them about sports or politics, or you might buy something from them in a store, or you might work together to sail a boat. To say that culture consists of "shared ideas" is to say that no single person has culture by himself or herself.

People may argue about many beliefs and practices, but the arguments occur on the basis of shared underlying beliefs. In the United States, for example, Democrats and Republicans argue about how best to run the country, but they share an underlying faith in certain ideas such as free elections, help for the sick and needy, a healthy economy, and good schools. They just disagree about how to provide these things and how to choose between two values when they conflict.

Culture as System. Culture exists as a network linking many different people. The idea of a network is useful because it captures the essential point that culture connects many people together and exists in what they share. The problem with the idea of a net-

French people share a sense of connection.

work is that it doesn't sufficiently capture the dynamic (changing) aspect of culture. Culture never sits still.

Instead of a network, therefore, it is useful to think of culture as a system consisting of many moving parts that work together. Think, for example, of how people get food nowadays: Farmers grow it, factories process it, truckers transport it, stores display it, people buy it and cook it. When a family sits down to dinner, it is likely that fifty or a hundred other people have directly helped get that food there (not to mention the thousands of others who were indirectly involved, including the management of the supermarket chain, the banks that financed the farms and the trucking company, the corporations that paid the mother and father the salaries they used

Not a good idea.

Nature, Culture, and Money

Money is such a familiar feature of human life that we take its existence and power for granted. All countries in the world today use money, so culturally it is nearly universal by now. Looked at from the perspective of nature, however, money is quite unusual. No species of plant or animal (other than humans) uses money. Money is thus a product of human culture, but it is estimated to be only about 3,000 years old (Davies, 2002), which means that early civilizations did not have it. It is much too recent to have shaped human nature biologically. There is no "money instinct."

Clearly people want money, and many people work long and hard to get it. Attempting to explain this in biological terms, Lea and Webley (2005) started with the analogy of a tool. Just as animals use tools to get what they want, people use money to get what they want. Biology has programmed humans (like other animals) to want things, so people also come to want money because it enables them to get these things. This part of the theory seems straightforward. Like any tool, money is desired not for itself but for what can be done with it.

But this analogy failed to explain the widespread human concern with money, as Lea and Webley soon recognized. For example, some people hoard money, obviously wanting to get it and keep it but not spend it. What good is a tool you never use?

So Lea and Webley produced a second analogy: Money is not just like a tool; it is also like a drug. People come to want it for its own sake, even though it does not confer any benefit that biology recognizes.

Drugs take advantage of the body's natural capacities for pleasure. People feel happy when they do something that will ultimately lead to survival or reproduction, such as when they have sex or fall in love or find something great to eat. Drugs in a sense trick the body, because when you take a drug, you might feel as good as if you had fallen in love, but whereas being in love might help you achieve survival and reproduction, being high on drugs will not normally accomplish either of these. In the same way, money comes to be desired for its own sake, rather than for the sake of the good things one gets for it. That's why people might hoard money, for example. It is as if they are addicted to money.

Although animals never develop money on their own, some of them seem capable of learning aspects of money, if humans teach them. Levitt and Dubner (2005) reported on studies done

PhotoDisc

by Keith Chen with monkeys. After several months of training, the monkeys learned to trade little coins for treats such as grapes. When the researchers changed the price, the monkeys adjusted their purchases accordingly. There wasn't much sign of monkeys' using money with each other, except for one enterprising male who managed to trade a coin for sex with a female (who then spent the coin on getting a grape, her favorite treat). Still, their grasp of money remained rudimentary, and the researchers reported that they sometimes tried to use cucumber slices as if they were coins, at least when trading with humans (who did not fall for the counterfeit). ■

to buy the food, the factories that built the refrigerator and stove, the suppliers of electricity, and so on).

The food system is an initial illustration of one theme of social psychology that we will call putting people first. (We will talk more about this later in the chapter, and throughout the book.) Most animals get their food directly from nature, at least after a brief period of infancy. In the modern world, most people get their food from other people. Human survival and success depend more on how we deal with each other than on how we deal with the natural world around us.

Culture as Praxis. Anthropologists now argue among themselves as to whether a culture should be understood more on the basis of shared beliefs and values or shared ways of doing things. (Many use the term **praxis** to refer to practical ways of doing things.) Almost certainly, the answer is both. The culture that people in Philadelphia share involves some shared values, such as the value of money, democracy, preferences for some kinds of food, aversion to crime, support for their local sports teams, and so forth. They also share ways of doing things: They drive on the same roads, use the same hospitals when they are sick, buy their food at local supermarkets, borrow money from the same banks, read the same newspapers, and so on. You will not live very well in Philadelphia if you refuse to shop at Philadelphia stores, or insist on driving your car on the left side of the road, or only go to a hospital to play billiards rather than to get treatment for illness.

Often the praxis depends on shared ideas. Money provides a good example: Certain round bits of metal and strips of colored paper are inherently worthless but, by virtue of shared ideas about them, acquire value and can be exchanged for all sorts of things. You can analyze the physics and chemistry of a dollar bill (e.g., its molecular structure) without gaining any clue to its value, because the value depends on shared social understandings. To learn more about the cultural significance of money, see the *Money Matters* box.

PRAXIS practical ways of doing things

Virtuous Vegetarians

Throughout this book, we will feature research relevant to eating. We have selected eating for this treatment because human eating is relevant to both nature and culture.

On the nature side, eating is natural; all animals eat. Eating is a vital means of getting what one needs for survival, which, as we saw, was a crucial goal of biological life. Social animals are social precisely because their social interactions help them get food and thereby to survive. Like other animals, humans feel bad when they do not have enough to eat, and these bad feelings motivate people to seek food. Also like other animals, humans quickly learn to dislike and avoid foods that make them sick.

Humans resemble other animals in their need to eat regularly. But eating has been transformed by culture. Unlike all other animals, humans go on diets, have elaborate systems of etiquette and table manners, cook their food, experiment endlessly with recipes, and sometimes serve meals to total strangers.

Another uniquely human trait is the tendency to reject certain categories of food based on ideas. Many religions, for example, prescribe or forbid particular foods, especially on certain days. Based on religious views, some people will eat beef but not pork, while others eat pork but not beef.

Vegetarianism is a revealing example. Some animals eat only plants, but that is the way nature made them. Humans are capable of eating meat and naturally do eat meat, yet cultural reasons convince many people to refuse to eat meat. For example, some people believe that it is morally proper to refuse to eat other animals (Blackwell & Hutchins, 1994; Frey, 1983; Ritson, 1802; Tansey & D'Silva, 1999; Walters & Portmess, 1999). That means that ideas convince them not to eat meat. These ideas include a belief that animals should have rights similar to humans, or a belief that it is better for the planet to have people eat only plant food (because land used for growing livestock is less productive than land used for growing plants).

Nothing like this has been seen in any other species. There is no evidence of any animal that naturally eats meat but sometimes decides, for moral or religious reasons, to eat only plant food.

RUBES®   By Leigh Rubin

www.creators.com
rubes2@earthlink.net   Creators Syndicate, Inc.
www.egreetings.com/rubes   © 1999 Leigh Rubin!   9-22

Early radicals of the Animal Rights Movement

Reprinted by permission of Creator's Syndicate, Inc.

Many human beings do precisely that, however. Such behavior is not found in nature but is well documented among human beings, and it reflects the power of meaning (ideas) to change and determine how people act. ●

Culture, Information, and Meaning. Another crucial aspect of culture is that it is based on meaningful information. All cultures use language to encode and share information. People act as they do because they process this information. People change their behavior based on information they get from the culture, such as laws and rules, religious teachings and moral principles, historical events, symbols, what they read in books or see on television, and what they learned in school. Nonhuman animals respond to very little information of those kinds.

Unlike squirrels, human beings can think about and plan for the future. If you dig up all a squirrel's nuts and cart them off, the squirrel just goes on burying more nuts at the same pace, not even trying to compensate for the loss. But if humans lose their stores—perhaps because of a power failure that causes all the food in the refrigerator to spoil—then people quickly compensate by replacing the lost supply.

Summary. What, then, is culture? The different components mentioned in this section can be summarized in this way: **Culture** is an information-based system, involving both shared understandings and praxis, that enables groups of people to live together in an organized fashion and to get what they need. Culture can have a significant influence even on basic human needs, such as food and sex. To learn more, read the *Food for Thought* and *The Social Side of Sex* boxes.

NATURE AND CULTURE INTERACTING

See what sort of explanation you can think of for this: Statisticians began noticing that a large number of professional hockey players in the National Hockey League had birthdays in January and February (Grondin, Deshaies, & Nault, 1984). Maybe being born in winter makes someone love winter sports more? Getting ice skates for your birthday? But November and December should also be good for that, and those months were marked by relatively few birthdays of NHL players. Also, the same pattern

---

CULTURE an information-based system that includes shared ideas and common ways of doing things

Sex and Culture

Like eating, sexual behavior will be featured through this book as an important category of behavior that is shaped by both nature and culture. Whereas food is needed for survival, sex is needed for reproduction.

Sex has been a bitter battleground between those who explain it on the basis of nature and evolution and those who emphasize cultural construction. Is sex a matter of genes and hormones causing people to feel desires the way nature has prescribed them? Or is culture the principal cause of who wants to do what to whom in bed?

Some features of sexuality are found everywhere and may well be rooted in nature. In all cultures, for example, men seem to desire a greater number of sexual partners than women (Pedersen, Miller, Putcha-Bhagavatula, & Yang, 2002). Sex is everywhere the main way (and usually the only way) to make babies. The same basic sex practices are known to most cultures. Sex historian Reay Tannahill (1980) observed that the sex manuals written thousands of years ago in ancient China covered almost all the same techniques one would find in a sex manual today, with only one exception (sadomasochism).

Some other universal aspects of sex reflect the influence of culture. All known cultures have rules about sex (Frayser, 1985). Cultures know that sex leads to making babies, and efforts to prevent pregnancy have been found all over the world, though the ancient means of preventing conception (except for abstaining from sex) are generally less effective than modern technologies such as the birth control pill and the IUD. Some form of prostitution, in which people pay money for sex, is found in most large cultures,

although many aspects of it (such as whether it is legally tolerated and what it costs) differ substantially.

Cultural differences in sex are also evident. In Guam, a law prohibits a woman from marrying while a virgin, so women who want to get married sometimes hire a man to deflower them. In Turkey, women are expected to be virgins until they marry, and until quite recently it was standard practice for many brides-to-be to have a medical examination to certify their virginity. Indonesian law prohibits masturbation and stipulates that anyone caught committing this "crime" should be beheaded. Lebanese men who have sex with male animals are likewise subject to the death penalty, but it is perfectly legal for them to have sex with female animals. In New Guinea, some tribes regard male–male sex as normal while people are growing up, and boys are expected to perform oral sex on young men as a way of acquiring fluids that produce masculine strength, but after marriage men are supposed to stop their homosexual activities and restrict themselves to their wives (Herdt, 1984). Liberty Corner, New Jersey, has a law prohibiting people from beeping the horn of a parked car during sexual intercourse; one can scarcely imagine what life must have been like in that town before that law restored peace and quiet. Another curious law comes from Liverpool, England: Topless salesgirls are forbidden to work in tropical fish stores, though not in other stores.

Last, there are plenty of differences within a culture too. In the United States today, there are people who reach their 30th birthday while still virgins, whereas others have had sex with more than a dozen people by the age of 15. Millions of people go through their entire lives having sex with only one person (their spouse) and only in the missionary position (man on top, woman on bottom), whereas some people have more than a thousand sex partners without ever using the missionary position. Genghis Kahn, perhaps the world's most successful lover, has more than 16 million direct male descendants alive today! Many people yearn for practices that others regard as dangerous perversions. Some people love to read about sex or watch films of people having sex, whereas others find those materials disgusting and want them to be outlawed.

Nature or culture? There is ample evidence of both in human sexuality. ■

© Shenval/Alamy

NO SEX

began to emerge in other sports as well, especially soccer, where the effect has been found all over the world (for review, see Musch & Grondin, 2001). It is statistically undeniable. What might cause it? Astrology? No.

The unequal birthday pattern emerges from a curious mix of nature and culture. In hockey, as in many sports, pro athletes generally got their start while they were children. Children's leagues are grouped by age, but rather than automatically moving from league to league on their birthday (which might disrupt teams), kids are grouped for each season based on a cutoff date—typically January 1st. Thus, when the season starts in November, if you're already 9 or will turn 9 by the end of December, you play with the 9-year-olds, but if your birthday isn't until after January 1st, you play with the 8-year-olds. Why does that matter? Nine-year-olds are usually bigger and stronger than 8-year-olds. Kids born late in the year grow up always being matched against others who are older, stronger, and faster, so they tend to drop out of the sport. Meanwhile, the lucky kids with birthdays in January will grow up always being among the oldest (and therefore biggest and strongest) children in their league, which puts them at a physical advantage. This advantage helps them be successful and makes the sport fun for them.

You might think the effect would wear off as children grow up. But many of the younger children have already dropped out. Moreover, coaching increases the problem. Coaches want to win, so they bestow their attention and more playing time on their best players—which often means their oldest (hence biggest, strongest, and most coordinated) ones. Children born after January 1st end up getting more training and more opportunities to compete, while those born late in the year spend more time on the bench.

The so-called relative age effect (Musch & Grondin, 2001) is not limited to sports. It has been shown in school performance also (Dickinson & Larsen, 1963; Hauck & Finch, 1993). Children who end up getting classified as gifted often benefited from starting school later than others, which made them older than their classmates (Maddux, Stacy, & Scott, 1981). Before you start planning to have your babies in January, however, note that school cutoff dates are different from sports ones. In many schools, it is the children born in the summer (just before school starts in September) who are destined to be always the youngest in their class and therefore suffer disadvantages in school (DeMeis & Stearns, 1992).

Sport in general is a combination of nature (innate physical abilities) and culture (practice, training, and arbitrary rules). Star pro athletes are thus neither made nor born: They need both the gifts of nature and the benefits of culture. And, it appears, the luck to be born on the right side of the cutoff date also helps!

This chapter began with the story of little Brenda. The failure to raise the boy as a girl suggests that being male has some elements of nature that are not easily overcome by culture. Yet manhood also has strong aspects of culture. Research on "precarious manhood" by Vandello, Bosson, Cohen, Burnaford, and Weaver (2008) showed some cultural differences in beliefs about being a man versus a woman. Many cultures require boys to prove themselves before they can claim to be men, whereas all girls grow up to be women. Even among modern American college students, manhood is regarded as more tentative and requiring of proof than womanhood. In one of their studies, students read about people who said they felt they were no longer a man, or no longer a woman. Loss of womanhood seemed difficult to fathom, and students thought it must mean that the woman had undergone a sex change operation. Loss of manhood was more readily seen as a result of social factors, such as not being able to provide for one's family.

Which child has the physical advantage over the others? The child whose birthday falls in January, according to relative age theory.

Thus, in a sense, society regards womanhood as a biological achievement, whereas manhood requires a cultural achievement. (Note that both are cultural opinions, however!) The need for men to prove themselves is relevant to many gender differences. In Vandello et al.'s studies, threats to a man's masculinity caused him to feel aggressive and anxious, whereas parallel threats to a woman's femininity produced no such response.

WHAT MAKES CULTURAL ANIMALS?

The human being is thus a product of both nature and culture. A traditional way of thinking has been that nature provides the foundation, and then culture builds on top of that. That style of thought puts nature first, culture second. However, recent theories have looked for ways to blend the two, such that nature and culture shape each other (e.g., Boyd & Richerson, 1985; Baumeister, 2005).

Many animals have a little bit of culture. Hence it is likely that culture existed on earth before humans evolved. If culture was already in the environment, then it could have guided natural selection to endow humans with traits that promoted culture.

Why is culture so rare or rudimentary in nonhuman animals? The answer lies almost certainly in the advanced psychological requirements for culture. We saw earlier that animals need more inner processes to be social than to be solitary. In the same way, they need more inner processes to be cultural than to be merely social. Most animals don't have enough brainpower to sustain culture.

What are some of the main differences between being social and being cultural (or, more precisely,

Studying for a college degree is a way of preserving knowledge.

between being merely social and being both social and cultural)? Social animals may act together, as when a swarm of bees or a pack of wolves or a herd of zebras all move together. This mass action is social because the animals know what the others are doing and coordinate their own behavior with it. In contrast, cultural animals often have elaborate division of labor, in which each individual performs a unique function. Compare the collective work of a corporation or a football team with that of a swarm of bees, for example. Although different bees might have different roles (e.g., the queen bee is the mother of all the bees in her hive, worker bees lack reproductive capacity but carry pollen back to the hive to feed the young), the roles are far simpler, less flexible, and fewer than roles in human society.

Alexander Graham Bell invented the telephone.

Social animals may figure out good ways of doing things and may possibly copy something they see another doing. Cultural animals (human beings) deliberately share their knowledge throughout the group, so that it can be preserved and passed on to the next generation. Humans are the only animals to have schools, universities, and libraries, for example. The preservation of knowledge allows for progress, too. One man (Alexander Graham Bell) invented the telephone, and even though he has been dead for decades, many people have and use telephones without having to invent them all over again. Among animals without culture, each problem has to be solved anew by each generation, and in some cases by each individual.

Social creatures can often communicate, such as with grunts and barks. Their communication refers mainly to events or entities that are present at that moment. Cultural animals use language, which enables them to communicate about many things that are far removed from the here and now. Human children often study history, for example, in which they learn about events that occurred centuries before they were born. Such communication is impossible for merely social animals.

Social animals may help each other, but in general helping is limited to relatives. It is quite rare for any nonhuman animal to make some sacrifice (such as willingly giving away food) in order to benefit another, even if the two animals are related (and especially if they aren't). In contrast, cultural animals have a broader sense of community and sometimes help total strangers. Some people donate large sums of money to alleviate hunger or sickness among people they have never met, who may be of a different race and may live on a faraway continent. Others help people even when it involves great danger to themselves.

When animals live and work together, some degree of conflict is probably inevitable. Social animals have few ways of resolving these disputes other than aggression. If two animals (not related to each other) want the same piece of food, the bigger and stronger one is likely to get it, by force if necessary. In contrast, culture offers many alternative means of resolving disputes. These include moral principles, compromise, and going before a judge in a court of law. Most social animals do not have that luxury. In fact, most cultures strongly discourage people from settling their disputes by resorting to violence.

Thus, the best approach to social psychology is to assume that people are products of both nature and culture. Nature has given humans certain traits and abilities, because over time those enabled some people to survive and reproduce better than others. And humans really do survive and reproduce by means of their culture. Hence we think that natural selection has shaped the human mind to "do" culture. In that sense, it is natural for humans to share information, seek to be together, form groups with multiple roles, communicate with each other about their inner thought processes, and more.

To review: Culture is a better way of being social. Being social, and thus being cultural, is a biological strategy. Biology measures success in terms of survival and reproduction. By those measures, human culture has been remarkably successful, even despite its problems such as war, pollution, social inequality, and oppression. Survival has improved remarkably. Indeed, by virtue of research (an important cultural activity), humans have nearly tripled their average life span—something no other species has been able to do. Meanwhile, the human population has risen from one woman about 200,000 years ago to about 7 billion people now. Our animal relatives such as the great apes all live near the equator, but humans have been able to live in mountains, forests, plains, in cold and snowy places, in deserts, in rain-soaked places, and others, thanks to cultural innovations such as clothing, heated homes, and cooked food.

Still no progress on cooked food, democracy, female liberation, social security, patent law, football, e-mail, or cosmetic surgery.

ARE PEOPLE THE SAME EVERYWHERE?

At first blush, people are very different. If you have ever visited a foreign country, especially one outside North America and Western Europe, you probably encountered striking differences. People speak different languages, read different books and magazines, and eat very different foods. These differences reflect the influence of culture.

What could be more natural than sleep? Yet there are important cultural differences in how people sleep. In the United States, most people sleep only at night and wake up with an alarm clock. Many consume coffee or some other substance containing a drug that wakes them up. In Mexico, it is customary for adults to take a nap (a siesta) in the middle of the day, and as a result they may not sleep as much at night. Some cultures and religions disapprove of consuming coffee and similar drugs, so people must wake up naturally.

Sleeping arrangements are also quite different, even though most people regard their own sleeping patterns as natural. For example, should small children sleep alone or with their parents? In the United States, the prevailing practice is to keep children out of their parents' bed and even in a separate bedroom. One study of white, middle-class, two-parent families in Cleveland, Ohio, found that only 3% of the babies slept in their parents' bedroom during their first year of life, and only 1% after that (Litt, 1981). In a more recent incident in the same city, a little girl mentioned to her friends in first grade that she slept with her father, and the friend told the teacher, who initiated a police investigation. Thus, having children sleep with parents is not only unusual, but some regard it as potentially a crime.

In other cultures, however, sleeping arrangements are quite different. In a survey of many different non-Western, nonindustrial societies, anthropologists found that the norm everywhere was for infants to sleep with their mothers (Barry & Paxson, 1971). Researchers in Japan confirmed that a typical Japanese person hardly ever sleeps alone at any point in life, nor does he or she want to. Roughly half of Japanese children ages 11 to 15 sleep in the same bed with their mother or father; others sleep with siblings. The only Japanese who normally sleep alone are unmarried young adults who are living away from home and old people whose spouse has died and whose children (and grandchildren) are living elsewhere.

People who are accustomed to the middle-class American system might regard it as dangerous, immoral, or even pathological (sick) to let children sleep with their parents. However, when Japanese or people from other cultures learn about the American practice, they have a similar reaction. They think that Americans must not love their children if they put them through the terrifying ordeal of making them sleep by themselves. Some point out that in the animal kingdom, too, babies want to be with their mothers, especially at night, and so it seems "natural" to them to do the same. The American practice thus seems dangerous, immoral, or wrong to them.

In these and countless other ways, people are different, both within and between cultures. Then again, in other respects people are much more similar. Nearly

In some cultures, babies rarely sleep alone.

© Digital Archive Japan/Alamy

everywhere, people love their children, try to get enough to eat, talk about the weather, wait their turn, make distinctions between right and wrong, compete for status, help each other (and help family and relatives more readily than strangers), worry about money, and drive their cars on the same side of the road. Usually they drive on the right, though in some countries (such as England and Australia) they drive on the left, but the important thing is that they share a rule that tells everyone to drive on the same side.

The question of whether people are the same everywhere, or differ in different cultures, is a vexing one for social psychology. By far the greatest amount of research is done in the United States, most of it at American universities with university students as participants. Some social psychologists despair that the cultural differences are so big that it is impossible to formulate any general conclusions, and some suggest that we should never generalize beyond American college students (or at least not without years of careful checking to verify what patterns are found everywhere).

Others are more optimistic. Although cultural differences are real and important, they are often merely matters of degree rather than opposites. For example, people respond more aggressively to insults and criticism than to praise, people are attracted to others similar to themselves more than to those who are different, and people get jealous when their romantic partners have sex with someone else. There are cultural differences in how these reactions are expressed and perhaps even in how strongly they are felt, but there is no known culture in which the opposite patterns (e.g., disliking similar others, or aggressing more in response to praise than insult) are found. Likewise, basic beliefs about people and the world have broadly similar consequences; for example, social cynicism (expecting that social life will often produce negative outcomes) goes with low conformity, low drive to achieve, and various negative attitudes toward leaders (Leung & Bond, 2004).

In this book, we will present some interesting findings of cultural differences. But our greater quest is for underlying similarities. For example, languages are very different from each other, but underneath they have great similarities, and all known human cultures have and use language. Hence we think the use of language is part of human nature. Moreover, evolution helped install the necessary equipment (vocal cords, ears that can tell thousands of words apart, and brains that can use grammar) for people to use language. Much of social psychology can be understood by assuming that the human psyche was designed by nature (via natural selection) for culture. This means that culture is in our genes, even though cultural differences may not be.

We started with the question of what the human psyche was designed for. Culture is a large, important part of the answer. That is, the human mind, including its emotions, was designed in part to enable it to take part in the advanced kinds of social life that humans have.

Important Features of Human Social Life

In this section, we will cover several features of human social life that set humans apart from other animals and that are crucial for understanding social interaction among humans. They reflect important ways that human life was shaped by nature to cope with human social life, including culture. These themes will come up repeatedly in the chapters that follow.

THE DUPLEX MIND

The human mind has two main systems. In a sense, this is what Freud said when he distinguished between the conscious ego and the unconscious. Most experts no longer accept Freud's account of how the mind is laid out, but there is a new and exciting version of the theory that the mind has two parts. We call this the **duplex mind**, as in a duplex house with two separate apartments.

Unfortunately, the experts don't agree about what to call these two systems or exactly what goes where. Here we will try to give you one summary version that combines many views, but you should be aware that many different variations exist and many details are disputed.

Two Systems. We can call the two systems the automatic and the conscious. The **automatic system** is outside of consciousness, though it is not a Freudian kind of unconscious full of repressed urges and thoughts you are afraid to think. Instead, it is like a team of little robots doing lots of simple jobs to make your life easier. You are not aware of the robots and the work they are doing. Whereas Freud thought that the unconscious often trips you up by making you say or do the wrong thing, the automatic system is usually very helpful. It handles the endless mundane tasks, such as interpreting, organizing, and categorizing all the information that comes in through your eyes and ears. For example, it might sort through the stream of babbling sounds that your ears hear in order to pick out the score of the game involving your favorite team, and it links that score

The automatic system even operates during sleep, which is why you can hear the alarm clock and wake up.

with relevant information in your memory, such as how your team is doing generally and whether today's outcome will help it qualify for the playoffs.

The **conscious system** is the other "half" of the duplex mind. (We put "half" in quotation marks because a precise comparison of sizes is not possible given the present state of knowledge. Most likely the automatic system is much bigger than the conscious system.) Though people sometimes think they are conscious of everything in their minds, in reality they are conscious of only one part—but that is a very important part.

The conscious system is what seems to turn on when you wake up and turn off when you go to sleep. The automatic system continues to operate during sleep, which is why you can hear the alarm clock and wake up. It also moves the body around in bed, as when you bump into your sleeping partner and roll away without waking up. It processes information, too: You will wake up to the sound of your own name spoken more softly than almost any other word, which means that your mind can tell the difference in the meanings of words even when asleep (Oswald, Taylor, & Treisman, 1960). Telling the difference is the job of the automatic system.

An influential article has called the two systems "impulsive" and "reflective," and these terms capture the gist of how they operate (Strack & Deutsch, 2004). The automatic system operates by impulse; you feel something and then do it, for example. The

---

DUPLEX MIND the idea that the mind has two different processing systems (conscious and automatic)

AUTOMATIC SYSTEM the part of the mind outside of consciousness that performs simple operations

CONSCIOUS SYSTEM the part of the mind that performs complex operations

Walking comes naturally for adults who can do it unconsciously. However, for children, learning how to walk takes a lot of conscious effort.

reflective system typically involves conscious deliberation about what would be the best thing to do.

What Is Consciousness For? Most people think their conscious minds are in charge of everything they do. They believe the conscious mind constantly directs their actions and their train of thought. These beliefs are false. The automatic system generally runs almost everything. Consider walking, for example, which is something that most people do over and over all day long. Do you consciously control the movements of your legs and feet? Does your conscious mind have to say, "Now pick up the left foot, swing it forward, hold it high enough so it doesn't bump the ground, set down the heel, roll forward, shift weight off the back foot," and so forth? Of course not. Some day watch a small child who is just learning to walk, and you may see what happens when the conscious mind tries to figure out how to make the legs walk. But after walking has been learned, the person almost never thinks about it again. Walking is done automatically.

Over the past couple of decades, there has been a huge shift in psychological theory about the role of consciousness. This change has been driven by the rise in research findings that show how much the automatic system does. Much of behavior is driven and directed by these automatic responses that occur outside of awareness. Many of these findings will be covered in subsequent chapters. The combination of them has led many experts to begin questioning what consciousness is good for—if anything! The automatic system can learn, think, choose, and respond. It has ideas and emotions, or at least simple versions of them. It knows your "self" and other people. Even when people believe they are deciding something, often it can be shown that the automatic system has already decided. Their decisions are swayed by subliminal cues or other bits of information of which the person is unaware that have been processed automatically.

Many experts today believe that consciousness doesn't really do much of anything. Michael Gazzaniga (1998, 2003) concluded from his split-brain studies that consciousness is just a side effect of other processes and of thinking about the future, and that it doesn't serve any important function. Some psychologists think consciousness is simply a kind of emotional signal to call attention to our own actions so we don't confuse them with what other people have done (Wegner, 2002). Others have observed that the automatic system does more than we thought and the conscious system less, and maybe the field will soon conclude that the conscious system doesn't do anything at all (Bargh, 1982, 1994; Bargh, Chen, & Burrows, 1996; Bargh, Gollwitzer, Lee-Chai, Barndollar, & Trötschel, 2001). With all due respect to these experts, we disagree. We think that the conscious system was difficult and expensive (in terms of biological requirements) for nature to give us, so most likely there are some very profound advantages that make consciousness worth it. Yes, the automatic system does most of the work of the psyche, but the conscious system probably does something very important too. Most likely these special jobs involve complex kinds of thought that combine information and follow explicit rules, as in logical reasoning (Lieberman, Gaunt, Gilbert, & Trope, 2002).

Differences Between the Systems. For now, it is important to know that the two systems exist and to appreciate their established differences. These are summarized in ▶ **TABLE 2.1** (e.g., Bargh, 1994; Lieberman et al., 2002).

First, there is a difference in how much each system can do at the same time. The automatic system is like many different little machines doing many unrelated or loosely related things at once. The conscious system does one thing at a time. As you read, your automatic system converts the visual images of letters into words, converts the words into meanings, and links the information with all sorts of things that are already stored in memory. Meanwhile, you consciously have only one thought at a time.

The automatic system is quick and efficient. It performs tasks quite effectively and with relatively little effort. In contrast, the conscious system is slow and cumbersome. Return to the example of walking: Try the experiment of consciously controlling every muscle movement while you are walking. You can do it, but it is very slow and awkward. That is why the mind naturally tries to make everything automatic.

The conscious system often requires effort, while the automatic system doesn't. In fact, you have to deliberately start to think consciously about something, but the automatic system starts by itself and often cannot be stopped. If we show you a word with a missing letter, you probably cannot stop yourself from filling in the blank. Try to read these letters without thinking of a word: K*SS. Probably you can't. The automatic system is too quick and efficient. It gives you the answer before your conscious mind can even think to formulate the question.

All the differences mentioned so far favor the automatic system. If it were better at everything, however, we would have to conclude that the conscious system is just a poorer, dumber, less effective system all around, which would raise the question of why we have it at all. (And that's why some experts, like the ones quoted above, have begun to doubt openly that it has any value.) But the conscious system does have some advantages. First, the conscious system is much more flexible than the automatic system. The automatic system is like a well-programmed robot or computer. It performs standard, familiar tasks according to the program, and it does them very reliably, quickly, and efficiently. But when the automatic system confronts something novel and unfamiliar, it doesn't know how to deal with it. The conscious mind, slow and cumbersome as it is, is much better at confronting novel, unfamiliar circumstances and deciding how to react.

The advantage of the conscious system in dealing with novel circumstances is probably one crucial reason that human beings, as cultural animals, developed consciousness. Life in a cultural society is vastly more complicated, in terms of encountering new, unexpected, and unfamiliar dilemmas, than the lives of most other creatures. Imagine a robot that has been programmed to sort red beans from green beans. It will probably do this effectively and quickly, even performing much better than a human being. But then along comes a banana! The robot won't know what to do with a banana, unless it has been programmed for that eventuality too. Unlike a robot, a conscious human mind can deal with the banana even when it was expecting only red and green beans.

Another crucial advantage of the conscious system is that it is able to combine information in complex, rule-driven ways. An automatic system that has been well trained can estimate that, say, 6 times 53 is a few hundred, but only the conscious system can calculate

▶ **TABLE 2.1 The Duplex Mind: Conscious and Automatic Systems**

Conscious	Automatic
Slow	Fast
Controllable	Outside of conscious control
Guided by intention	Unintentional
Flexible	Inflexible
Good at combining information	Poor at combining information
Precise, rule-based calculations	Estimates
Can perform complex operations	Simple operations
Does one thing at a time	Can do many things at once
Reasoning	Intuition
Effortful	Effortless
Features full-blown emotions	Features quick feelings of like and dislike, good and bad
Depends on automatic system	Can be independent of conscious processing
"Figure it out"	"Go with your gut feeling"

that it is precisely 318. The conscious system alone can perform complex logical reasoning.

The influential social psychologist Daniel Kahneman (e.g., Kahneman & Frederick, 2002) prefers to describe the thinking styles of the two systems as reasoning versus intuition. The automatic system is intuitive, in the sense that it is guided by gut reactions and quick feelings rather than a process of carefully thinking through all the implications of a problem. When you face a decision and someone advises you to "go with your gut feeling," that person is essentially telling you to rely on your automatic system (and its intuitions) rather than trying to reason through the problem logically, as the conscious system will do. Often that is good advice, because the automatic system does produce quick and usually good answers. But the highest achievements and advances of culture depend on the application of careful reasoning, which is the province of the conscious system.

How They Work Together. The two parts of the duplex mind are not entirely independent of each other. In fact, they often work together (Strack & Deutsch, 2004). The automatic system serves the conscious system, in the sense that it operates behind the scenes to make conscious thought possible. You may think consciously that something you heard on the radio is illogical. But before that can happen, the automatic system has to have done a great deal of work: It processed the stream of sounds into

Go with your gut feeling, or figure out what is best?

comprehensible language, understood the gist of the message, and activated various other ideas in your memory that were associated with the core idea. The automatic system also works like an alarm system that signals to the conscious system that something is wrong and that careful, conscious thinking is needed.

For example, suppose you heard on the news that someone was seriously injured at a campus party last night, and the dean was recommending that all further parties be canceled. Your automatic system understands the reasoning: Party caused injury, injury is bad, so parties are bad, so the dean cancels all parties. But the automatic system also connects this news to your feelings, and you realize: Wait! I love parties! I don't want all parties to be canceled! This is about as far as the automatic system can process, but it sends out an alarm to the conscious system. Now you can reason through the situation consciously: One party caused an injury, but that doesn't reflect badly on all parties; there should be a way to reduce or avoid further injuries without canceling all parties. In that way, the two mental systems work together.

Conscious Override. Sometimes the two systems work against each other, however. One particularly important case is when the conscious system overrides the automatic impulse. You feel like doing something, but you restrain yourself. For example, if you are looking forward to having a donut, and you see someone else take the last donut just before you get to the serving tray, you may have a natural impulse to protest. Hey! Give me my donut! You might even feel like grabbing it out of the other person's hand. After all, most other animals would act that way if someone took their food. But human beings can restrain that impulse. Rarely do human beings come to blows over the last donut. Indeed, the point that people restrain themselves is an important key to the psychology of aggression. We shall see that a great many factors cause aggression: violent films, hot temperatures, frustration, and insults. Given that nearly everyone occasionally experiences frustration, wounded pride, media violence, and heat, you might think that human beings would be constantly violent. But in reality people are not usually aggressive or violent. Why not? People may have many angry impulses, but they restrain them. The conscious mind is often vital for overriding the impulses that the automatic system produces. As we shall see, this pattern is found in many spheres of social behavior, from dieting to prejudice.

Conscious overriding is vital to life in culture. Culture is full of rules about how to behave—norms, guidelines, laws, morals, and expectations. You can't just do whatever you feel like at any moment. Moreover, many situations are complicated and have hidden implications, so it is best to stop and think before acting. Imagine you are driving on a highway when another driver speeds up, passes you, and then slows

"Twenty preprogrammed hand gestures allow you to signal everything from a simple lane change to homicidal rage."

down to take the next exit. Your natural impulse might be to smash into the back of the other driver's car with your own car, to hold your horn down, or to "flip off" the other driver—but that might get you in trouble. It would be better for your conscious mind to override these impulses and exercise self-control over your anger.

THE LONG ROAD TO SOCIAL ACCEPTANCE

Living in a culture offers many advantages as compared with living in a merely social group. But it also makes much greater demands.

Consider what it takes to live in a North American city. If you're a bird, maybe you can just fly into town, find an empty tree, build a nest, and then hang around with some other birds until they let you stay. As a human, you need an apartment, which may take you a week of checking advertisements and going around to different addresses. (And to do that, you need to know how to read, how to use a map, and how to get and use a newspaper or the Internet.) You'll probably need to sign a lease promising to live there for a year. You need money to pay the rent, and probably that means you will need a job. A job typically requires credentials, such as education and training, and these may take years to obtain. A better job means more money, but it probably requires more training, and you have to perform well to keep the job. Finding a romantic partner is a much more complicated process in human beings than in other animals. You need to know where to meet people, how to act on a date, how to play the games and roles that are in fashion in this particular group.

This is one of the basic jobs of the human self: to garner acceptance. You need to figure out what other people prefer and expect, and then you need to change yourself to meet those expectations. The requirements for social acceptance are different in different cultures and eras. In the Victorian era (late 1800s), people who picked their noses or said four-letter words aloud were considered socially unacceptable, so most middle- and upper-class people learned to avoid doing those things. Nowadays saying four-letter words is more acceptable in many circles, whereas picking your nose is still not cool.

Outside the lab, people have to do many things to obtain social acceptance. It is not just a matter of etiquette. As noted above, people need to acquire skills and credentials, gain the discipline to hold down a job, attract and hold relationship partners, and so on.

BUILT TO RELATE

The long road that humans travel to social acceptance means that people have to do a great deal of

It is necessary to look through ads to be able to find an apartment.

work to get along with others. To do that, they must develop many skills and capabilities. One thing that sets humans apart from other animals is how many inner, psychological traits they have that help them get along. These include the understanding that other humans have inner states like theirs, the capacity for language, and the ability to imagine how others perceive them.

This brings up one very important and broadly helpful theme that we have already mentioned: What is inside people is there because of what happens between people. That is, *inner processes serve interpersonal functions*. The psychological traits people have are designed to enable humans to connect with each other.

When you first consider the matter, it seems the other way around: What is inside people determines what happens between them. Because we are capable of language, we talk to other people. Because we have emotional responses of love and affection, we become attached to others. There is some truth to this view, but only from a relatively narrow perspective. To understand human nature, it is important to recognize that evolution created humans with the capacity for language and the emotional capabilities for love and affection because these traits improved people's ability to connect with others.

Earlier in this chapter we discussed the social brain theory, which asserted that evolution made

Baloo

© Baloo -Rex May-/CartoonStock

intelligent brains not for understanding the physical environment but rather to increase the capability for having social relations. The intelligent brain is one of the defining traits of human beings. This was a first example of the pattern of inner processes serving interpersonal functions: The inner processes and structures (in this case, the intelligent brain) evolved for the sake of improving interpersonal relations.

There is increasing evidence that emotions also serve social functions. When people talk, even about seemingly trivial things, they end up sharing their feeling (Peters & Kashima, 2007). The discovery that they have similar emotional reactions creates a bond between them that contributes to a feeling of bonding and even to a willingness to trust each other with money.

Automatic processes (see the earlier section on the duplex mind) also serve interpersonal functions. When cues make people automatically think about a group of others, they respond in ways that suggest preparing to interact with that group. For example, when people think about a group they dislike, they automatically start feeling more aggressive, even if the other group is not aggressive. When they think about the elderly, they change their behavior to prepare for interacting with older people: If they have positive feelings toward the elderly, they become more similar and accommodating (e.g., they walk more slowly, enabling them to walk with old people); if their feelings toward this group are negative, they change in ways that make them less friendly to the elderly (they walk faster, making it harder for old people to keep up!) (Cesario, Plaks, & Higgins, 2006).

As with other themes, we should be careful not to overstate the case. Not all inner processes are there to serve interpersonal processes. Hunger and thirst, for example, are clearly there to prompt the animal or person to get enough food and water to sustain life. Hunger and thirst are thus inner processes that do not serve interpersonal functions. Still, many of the more advanced, complex, and interesting psychological phenomena do promote social interaction.

Thus, a social psychology approach to human nature will emphasize that many (though not all) inner processes exist for the sake of interpersonal interaction. In the next few chapters, we will see that the self, thinking, and emotion (among others) seem well designed to help people form and maintain relationships with others. Recall our discussion about trees earlier. Trees are neither social nor cultural. They do not need selves, nor the capacity to understand language, nor the knowledge that the inner states of other trees resemble their own. Trees were designed by nature to survive alone and get what they need from their physical surroundings. In contrast, humans were designed by nature to develop relationships and share information with each other. The human psyche is designed for social purposes, and especially for cultural ones, insofar as culture is a better way of being social.

NATURE SAYS GO, CULTURE SAYS STOP

What aspects of human behavior come from nature as opposed to culture? There are many different answers, but one broad pattern is a theme that we summarize as "nature says go, culture says stop." That is, people seem naturally to have impulses, wishes, and other automatic reactions that predispose them to act in certain ways. Culture serves not so much to create new wishes and desires as to teach or preach self-control and restraint.

Thus, people may naturally feel sexual desires and aggressive urges at many points; they do not seem to need to be taught by culture to have those feelings. In that sense, sex and aggression are natural. But culture does have considerable influence on both sex and aggression. This influence mainly takes the form of restraining behaviors. Culture is full of rules that restrict sex, as by designating certain sexual acts or pairings as unacceptable. Sexual morality is mostly a matter of saying which sexual acts are wrong; likewise, laws about sex mainly prohibit sex acts. (Imagine laws that required people to have sexual intercourse on particular occasions!) Likewise, aggression is subject to a broad variety of cultural restraints, including moral prohibitions and laws that forbid many aggressive acts.

Often, culture works by ideas. Many of those ideas tell people what not to do. Most laws and moral principles say what not to do rather than what one should do. The Ten Commandments of Judeo-Christian religion, for example, mostly begin "Thou shalt not . . ." and then mention some specific behavior. The only two that don't say "not" still imply it to some degree: Keeping the Sabbath holy is mostly a matter of not doing certain things (such as work or shopping) on the Sabbath, and honoring your parents is mostly a matter of refraining from disrespectful treatment.

Thus, the most famous list of moral rules in Western culture is basically a list of ideas (rules) about what not to do, probably because people naturally sometimes feel urges to do precisely those things, but the culture (including its religion) disapproves.

To be sure, it would be a gross oversimplification to say that the role of nature is *always* to create positive desires and impulses or that culture *only* says what not to do. There are some important exceptions. Disgust reactions, for example, are quite natural and say "no" in a big way. Likewise, people may start eating because official policy and the clock (representing culture) say it is lunchtime, and they may stop eating because their inner sensations (representing nature) signal them that their bellies are full. In this case, culture says start and nature says stop. People may start engaging in aggression because their government (culture) has declared war, and they may stop aggressing because bodily states (nature) of exhaustion or injury dictate that they cannot continue.

Still, "nature says go, culture says stop" is probably right more often than it is wrong, and it provides a helpful way to understand much of the interplay between nature and culture. Throughout this book we will see many examples in which impulses arise naturally and are restrained, with difficulty, by individuals who exert themselves to comply with cultural rules. Nature made us full of desires and impulses, and culture teaches us to restrain them for the sake of being able to live together in peace and harmony.

Self-control is one important psychological process that enables people to live in culture and follow cultural rules (e.g., Freud, 1930/1961). And most acts of self-control involve stopping oneself from thinking, feeling, or doing something (Baumeister, Heatherton, & Tice, 1994). With regard to spending money, eating and dieting, sexual behavior, drinking alcohol or taking drugs, and many similar behaviors, having good self-control means holding oneself back instead of acting on every impulse. Dieters need self-control to keep themselves from eating too much or eating the wrong kinds of food, for example. The desire to eat is natural; the restraints are cultural.

SELFISH IMPULSE VERSUS SOCIAL CONSCIENCE

Selfishness is a particularly important instance of the principle that nature says go and culture says stop. To put the matter in overly simple terms, nature has made us selfish, but culture needs us to resist and overcome selfish impulses.

Selfishness is natural. This is not to say that selfish behavior is good or appropriate, but only that nature programmed us to be selfish. This is probably rooted in the biological processes of natural selection. Natural selection favors traits that promote the survival

College students often manage to get along together even though they live in crowded dorm rooms.

and reproduction of the individual. Some biologists have occasionally proposed "group selection," suggesting that natural selection will promote traits that sacrifice the individual for the sake of the group, but most biologists have rejected those arguments (Ridley, 1993, 2004). (Some experts think group selection may occur when the individual and group interests are aligned.) Each animal looks out for its own welfare and perhaps that of its children. The natural tendency, reinforced by countless centuries of evolution, is to want what is best for oneself.

In contrast, culture often demands that what is best for society take precedence over the individual's wants and needs. In order to get along with others, people must take turns, respect each other's property, and stifle their anger or at least express it constructively. They may have to share their food and possessions, whether informally through acts of kindness or more systematically through taxes. Many will have to follow commands issued by authority figures.

Animals that live in social groups have to make some sacrifices for the sake of the group, but these may be minimal. Culture often imposes far greater requirements in terms of restraining selfishness. All cultures have systems of morality, and one of the main thrusts of morality is to do what is best for the community rather than what is best for the self. To return to the example of the Ten Commandments, those rules are divided between commands to uphold the religion (such as by not having other gods) and rules against behaviors that would undermine society (murder, theft, adultery, lying, coveting other people's things, and disrespecting one's parents).

Morality is often effective in small groups. In larger groups, law begins to take the place of morality, but it has the same overarching goal of restraining selfish

Digital Stock

Would you be more or less likely to avoid contact with this person?

actions in favor of what is best for the community. The difference seems to be that morality relies on a network of social relationships and therefore works best on people who know each other. The more that social life involves contacts between strangers, the more that laws are needed instead of just morals. Even in modern societies, small groups such as families usually rely on morals and informal rules, because these are sufficient in the context of the relationship. Far more people are willing to cheat, betray, or exploit a stranger than a member of their own immediate family. Guilt—an important emotion that pushes people to behave morally instead of selfishly—is far more commonly felt in connection with friends and relatives than strangers (e.g., Baumeister, Reis, & Delespaul, 1995; Tangney & Dearing, 2002).

Thus, self-interest is a major battleground between nature and culture. The self is filled with selfish impulses and with the means to restrain them, and many inner conflicts come down to that basic antagonism. That conflict, between selfish impulses and self-control, is probably the most basic conflict in the human psyche.

One place to understand this conflict is in how people react to someone who has a stigma—that is, a trait that others perceive as highly undesirable and that makes them want to avoid the person. Many people have an automatic reaction of wanting to avoid someone who has AIDS, or who has cancer, or who is blind or paralyzed, even if the person is not personally responsible for his or her problem. Researchers have found that the impulse to avoid

such people may be rooted in a natural fear of being contaminated by them (e.g., Rozin, Markwith, & McCauley, 1994). The automatic system does not necessarily adjust for whether the person's stigma is contagious or not, so people may irrationally and unfairly avoid people whose presence poses no danger. However, many people recognize consciously that these people do not deserve to be avoided, so the social conscience may motivate them to overcome their initial tendency to avoid the stigmatized person. The automatic reaction does not disappear, but given a moment, people can act on more socially desirable feelings, such as the wish to treat the stigmatized person as a normal human being (Pryor, Reeder, Yeadon, & Hesson-McInnis, 2004).

The capacity for consciously overriding impulses, described in the earlier section on the duplex mind, is often used in connection with the battle over self-interest. The natural and selfish impulses arise automatically. Morality, conscience, legal obedience, and other pathways to proper behavior often depend on conscious efforts to know and do the right thing.

TRADEOFFS: WHEN YOU CAN'T HAVE IT ALL

When there is no option that is clearly the best in every respect, choices have tradeoffs. A **tradeoff** is a choice in which taking or maximizing one benefit requires either accepting a cost or sacrificing another benefit. Every option you consider has both advantages and disadvantages. With cars, for example, buying the smaller car improves your gas mileage and is better for the environment but sacrifices safety or comfort. A human being is often faced with such complicated choices, and it is necessary to find some way to add up all the pluses and minuses in order to pick one option.

Tradeoffs are an important feature of human social life. Many decisions and dilemmas involve tradeoffs, so that there is no one right answer that will suit everyone. (In this way, tradeoffs also preserve diversity, because there is more than one way to be, with none being the best.) Solving one problem will sometimes create another.

Modern culture confronts individuals with a seemingly endless array of choices, and most of these present tradeoffs. Want to eat something delicious, or something less fattening? Want shoes that will be fashionable, or comfortable? Should you take an extra course and thereby learn more, or have a lower workload next semester? Follow your plan, or follow your heart?

One very important set of tradeoffs concerns time. Most commonly, the tradeoff requires choosing between something that has benefits right now versus something that has benefits in the future. Our

TRADEOFF a choice in which taking or maximizing one benefit requires either accepting a cost or sacrificing another benefit

shorthand term for this sort of tradeoff is "now versus tomorrow." Studies of delay of gratification (Mischel, 1974, 1996) often make the tradeoff between present and future explicit. In a typical study, a child is offered a choice between having one cookie right now—or three cookies if the child can wait for 20 minutes.

The ongoing controversy about drug use in sports involves a tradeoff, including a time dimension. Many athletes are tempted to try performance-enhancing drugs. Purists condemn these usages, likening drug use to cheating. But are sports different from everyday life? If you drink a cup of coffee to make yourself more alert for your psychology exam, are you cheating? Are people who use Prozac to make themselves cope better with life, or Viagra to make them perform better in bed, cheaters? And before long, gene splicing may be used to make people stronger, larger, faster, and better in other athletic realms—would those people (who benefited from events before they were born) be cheaters too?

One objection to letting athletes use performance-enhancing drugs is that these may be harmful. Some of them are. The tradeoff of now versus tomorrow is especially apparent in these cases, because the so-called sports dopers trade future health problems for current athletic success. Even there, different people will decide the tradeoff differently. The man who founded the National Academy of Sports Medicine once polled 200 Olympic-caliber American athletes about this question. He asked, if you could legally take a performance-enhancing drug that would guarantee that you would win every sports competition you entered for the next five years—but that would eventually kill you—would you take it? The overwhelming majority (though not all) said yes (Dion & Mellor, 2004).

Natural selection has not favored caring about the distant future. Our sensory organs tell us what is here right now. Our feelings and desires focus on the immediate present. The idea of sacrificing present joy for the sake of greater joy in the future would be foreign, difficult, even incomprehensible to most animals.

A dramatic demonstration of the difference emerged from a study with chimpanzees (Roberts, 2002). They were fed only once a day, always at the same time, and they were allowed to have all the food they wanted. Like humans and many other animals, chimps prefer to eat multiple times during the day, so they were always very hungry in the last couple hours before their next scheduled feeding. A sensible response would have been to keep some of the available food for later, especially for the hungry hours the next morning, but the animals never learned to do this. They would rejoice over the food when it came. They would eat their fill, and then they would ignore the rest, sometimes even engaging in food fights in which they would throw the unwanted food

at each other. Yet, despite repeated trials, they never learned to store food for later. Even the short span of 24 hours was apparently beyond their cognitive capacity for adjusting their behavior. In contrast, humans routinely acquire and store food for days, or even weeks and months.

Human beings are thus quite different from other animals. In particular, the conscious human mind can form ideas about the distant future, and current behavior can be changed on the basis of those ideas. Going to college is partly an exercise in delay of gratification for many students. A young person can earn money right away by getting a job right out of high school rather than going to college (which typically costs money rather than earning any). College students often have to live in crowded dormitories with rickety furniture and unappetizing food, whereas if they dropped out and got a job they might be able to rent a nicer apartment and eat better. In the long run, however, college pays off. The U.S. Census Bureau reported that people with advanced degrees earn, on average, four times as much as those with less than a high school diploma ($82,320 versus $20,873 in 2006). That's $62,000 more each year. If you compound that amount by a lifetime of work, the average person with an advanced degree will likely earn nearly $2 million more than a high school dropout during a 30-year career. Going to college thus sacrifices some immediate pleasures for the sake of a better future life.

The future is more important to cultural beings than to other animals, so the capacity to orient oneself toward the future rather than the present is probably a crucial skill for any cultural being to have. A person who always lived just for today, enjoying the current moment with no regard for the future, would not prosper in human society. Such a person would never pay bills, wash the laundry or dishes, brush or floss teeth. Such a person would probably eat candy and pastries rather than vegetables. Such a person would probably not go to college or hold down a job. Such a person would make no commitments that required sacrifices, such as to sustain a close relationship. Such a person would never save any money. Such a person would probably disregard any laws that were inconvenient.

That style of life is simply not suited for life in a cultural society. To live for any length of time in modern society, it is necessary to pay bills, take care of things, eat reasonably healthy food, obey the laws, exercise, and the like. Many of these acts entail some sacrifice in the short run. In the long run, however, the benefits that come from living in such a society make those sacrifices well worthwhile.

Facing up to tradeoffs is not easy. In fact, there is some research evidence that people dislike tradeoffs (Luce, 1998; Luce, Bettman, & Payne, 1997, 2001). When a decision has to be made, people prefer to

Political Tradeoffs

Tradeoffs are abundant in politics. Have you ever wondered why governments keep passing new laws, even though they hardly ever repeal any old ones? You would think that with the addition of more and more laws every year for hundreds of years, there would finally be enough. One explanation is that most laws are designed to remedy an existing problem, but sometimes they create new problems. Tradeoffs are responsible for some of the problems that arise.

As one famous example, in the 1990s the Ohio state legislature heard some sad stories about babies being born in prison (because their mothers were serving time). Taking pity on the babies, the government passed a new law to release pregnant women from prison. This solved one problem but created another, because all the women in Ohio prisons realized that they could get out of prison if they got pregnant, and many women would rather have a baby than be in prison. Female convicts began eagerly trying to have sex with male guards and lawyers. Some inmates would get a weekend pass to attend a relative's funeral—but would skip the funeral and spend the weekend having as much unprotected sex as possible. Thus, there was a tradeoff between preventing babies from being born in prison and encouraging more prisoners to get pregnant. In this case, the law was repealed.

One important political tradeoff links energy issues to environmental ones. Should American oil companies drill for oil in our national forests, where an accident might cause an oil spill that could destroy part of a beautiful forest and kill its wildlife? Many people want to protect the environment, yet they don't want to pay more for gasoline and electricity—and these goals are in conflict. Hence there is a tradeoff: The more you protect the environment, the more expensive power becomes. It is hard to strike exactly the right balance.

Another tradeoff connects taxes to government services. Everything the government does—maintain an army and police force, collect the garbage, provide public schools at whatever level of quality, deliver the mail, provide food for the poor—costs money, and the main method for governments to get money is to collect taxes. In general, higher taxes enable the government to provide more services. Here again is a tradeoff, because people do not want to pay high taxes, but they do want their government to provide good services.

To what extent do politicians recognize these tradeoffs? Social psychologist Phillip Tetlock (1981, 2000) analyzed the speeches of many politicians, with an eye toward whether they recognized that many problems have two sides. He noted, however, that politicians face another tradeoff in their own careers, because they have to get elected. If one politician says "Everything is expensive, and I can't give you better government services unless we raise taxes," whereas another says "I will give you better services *and* lower taxes," the second one may be more likely to win the election.

Tetlock found that politicians seem to shuffle back and forth as to whether they acknowledge tradeoffs. When running for election, they make simple promises and ignore the political realities of tradeoffs. A successful candidate might well promise cheaper energy *and* better protection for the environment, in order to win the most votes. Once elected, however, politicians

PhotoDisc

suddenly begin to recognize the complexity of tradeoffs, and their speeches often refer frankly to the difficulty of the choices, such as noting with regret that efforts to get cheaper oil may well require some sacrifices in environmental protection.

Is this change a matter of learning? After all, when one is just running for office and does not have any actual responsibilities of government, it may be possible to make all sorts of promises without fully realizing the tradeoffs involved. (Most politicians, like most people, really do want both cheaper energy and a cleaner environment.) Maybe they don't realize the tradeoffs until they actually hold office and have to face up to the difficult choices. But this is not what Tetlock concluded. He found that politicians acknowledge tradeoffs when they are in office—but only until their campaigns for reelection start. At that point, they go back to simple statements that promise all things, disregarding tradeoffs. Tetlock concluded that politicians are dealing with the tradeoff built into the election process: to win an election you must oversimplify the issues and ignore the implicit contradictions. ●

---

think that there is one best or right answer. They like to think that what they choose will bring the best all-around outcomes, and they dislike thinking that they have really lost out on some things in order to get other things. You may find that you don't like the tradeoffs we present throughout this book, because it is more comforting to think that there is always a single best answer. It is apparently normal to dislike the idea of tradeoffs, but don't let that prevent you from seeing how widespread and important they really are. The *Tradeoffs* box provides some examples of how political decisions often involve tradeoffs.

PUTTING PEOPLE FIRST

Can dogs hear better than people? If you have lived with a dog, you know they hear many things that people do not, such as very high or low tones, as well as very soft tones. One of your textbook authors is frequently teased by his wife that his dog is prone to barking at ghosts, because the dog will burst into barking for no reason that any person can discern. In that sense, dogs hear better than humans. On the other hand, dogs cannot distinguish between similar sounds. If your dog's name is Fido, he will probably also respond to "buy low," "hi ho," "my dough," and "Shiloh." In that sense, dogs don't hear as well as people.

The explanation is probably rooted in a basic tradeoff in perceptual systems, but it contains an important clue about human nature. Most sense organs (even artificial ones such as cameras) have a tradeoff between detection (how much they can see) and resolution (how clearly they see it). For most animals, detection is emphasized over resolution—they perceive something and respond long before they can tell precisely what it is. Humans have more emphasis on resolution, which means perceiving things precisely. Hence our ears cannot hear as wide a range of sounds, but we hear them much more distinctly.

More broadly, the sensory organs of most animals are aimed at detecting other species. This is crucial for survival. Animals must spot the predators who want to eat them (in order to run away in time) and the animals they eat (so they can pursue and catch them). The human sensory system is quite unusual in that it is not aimed mainly at other species. Human sense organs, especially eyes and ears, seem designed to help us perceive each other. We can pick our beloved's (or our enemy's) face out of a crowd or a choir up on stage, and we can hear tiny differences in spoken sounds.

Most likely, this unusual feature of human sense organs reflects a change in biological strategy. Nature selected humans to pursue survival and reproduction in a novel fashion. Instead of getting information from the environment, our sense organs are designed to help us get it from each other. And that's what culture is all about—humans getting information from each other in order to survive and reproduce. This is another theme of this book; we call it *putting people first*. And it doesn't stop with information. People get most of what they need from each other, instead of directly from the physical world around them.

Consider food. Many animals spend most of their waking hours looking for food and eating it. They search their environment for things to eat. Some animals search alone, and others search together, but in general they get their food directly from nature. Human food comes from nature too, but most people now get their food from other people. Over the past year, how much of what you ate did you get directly from nature, by picking it from plants or hunting and killing animals? Probably most, if not all, of what you ate came either from supermarkets, where the food prepared by others is sold, or in

PhotoDisc

Humans, hunting for food, wait patiently for their prey.

dining establishments such as restaurants and cafeterias, where food grown by some people is cooked and served by others. If all those institutions abruptly went out of business and people had to get their food directly from nature, most of us would not know how to go about it. Many people would go hungry.

To be sure, humans evolved under conditions different from modern life, and early humans did often get their food directly from the natural environment. But the modern world probably reflects the special aspects of the human psyche better than did the circumstances of prehistoric life. Humans are heavily interdependent and are quite good at developing cultural systems that allow them to benefit from each other's work. As people have learned to make culture work effectively, it is no longer necessary for everyone to hunt, fish, or grow food. Instead, you can become good at one very narrowly specialized task, such as repairing computers or selling shoes or caring for broken legs, and your work at this task gives you money with which you can buy the many different things you need and want.

What this tells us about the human psyche is that people have a deeply rooted tendency to look to each other first. When people have a problem or a need, they most often look to other people for help, relief, or satisfaction. Even when people just need information, they tend to get it from other people rather than directly from the world around them. Animals learn from their own experience. They deal with the physical world, and they are rewarded or punished depending on how things turn out. Humans, in contrast, rely much less on what they learn from their own direct experience with the physical world. People learn from each other and from the culture.

Evidence for this was provided by Van Beest and Williams (2006). In their studies, some participants gained money but were rejected and ostracized by others; other participants were accepted and included but lost money. The first group felt worse than the second. Money is an important means of getting what you need, but apparently people are more attuned to gaining social acceptance (even from complete strangers) than money.

The culture operates as a kind of "general store" of information. When people don't know what to do, they typically ask someone else who knows the culture's information. How do you get telephone service, or a new credit card? Is there sales tax on food? How early (before the scheduled start time) should one arrive for an airline flight, a bus trip, a dinner party, a baseball game, a physician's appointment? Can I get my money back for something, and if so, how? These answers are not the specific wisdom learned by specific individuals, but general rules for getting along in the culture, and any knowledgeable person can tell you the answers—after which you would be able to pass that information along to anyone else.

Putting people first builds on the earlier theme that people are "built to relate." Nature has constructed human beings to turn to each other for food, shelter, support, information, and other needs. The fact that so many inner processes serve interpersonal functions enables people to rely on each other and treat each other as vital resources.

The reliance on other people for information was shown in one of modern social psychology's first experimental investigations, the research on conformity by Solomon Asch (1955, 1956; see also Bond & Smith, 1996, on cultural differences). Asch presented research participants with a line-judging task, in which they simply had to say which of three lines was the best match to a specific line that was presented. The task was easy enough that everyone could get all the answers correct simply by looking at the lines. But Asch introduced a novel twist to this task. He ran the study in groups, and sometimes almost everyone in the group was secretly working with him. Only one person in the group was a real participant. When Asch gave a prearranged signal, all the confederates (the group members who were working with him and only pretending to be real participants) would give the wrong answer. Thus, the participant suddenly had to decide whether to give the answer that his or her eyes said was correct, or instead to go along with the group and give the answer that everyone else had given. If the human brain were designed mainly to learn from one's own direct experience, participants would still have given the right answer all the time. But they didn't. In a significant number of cases, participants went along with the group, giving the answer that they could see was wrong but that conformed to what everyone else was saying. Thus, sometimes people rely on other people more than on their own direct experience. In Asch's experiment, participants felt it was more important to be accepted by the group than to be correct on the line-judging task.

Recent work has confirmed the importance of getting information from others, with the twist that the effects depend on whether the other is similar to you. In experiments by Hilmert, Kulik, and Christenfeld (2006), participants heard another person express liking for some music. The participant's own evaluation of that same music was influenced by the other's views. If the other person had come across as similar to the participant in other musical opinions and personal background, then the participant liked the music more. If the other person was dissimilar, however, then his liking for the music made the participant dislike it. The implication is that we put people first—but especially people to whom we have some closeness or connection.

If your brain is like a personal computer, then culture is like the Internet. Hooking into the system greatly increases the power of what a single computer, and by analogy a single brain, can do. By belonging to culture, you can learn an immense amount of information, whereas if you had to learn from your own direct experiences, you would only have a tiny fraction of that knowledge. Our tendency to put people first is vital in enabling us to take advantage of the knowledge and wisdom that accumulates in the cultural general store.

This chapter has emphasized that human social behavior results from a mixture of nature and culture. Human beings are animals and, as such, have many of the same wants, needs, and behavior patterns that other animals have. According to the theory of evolution, human beings evolved from other animals. The special traits that make us human are thus mostly a result of gradual refinements of traits that animals had. Some notable biological traits differentiate humans from other animals: We have exceptionally large and capable brains, especially in proportion to body size. We walk upright. We can talk.

What makes us human is most apparent, however, in culture. The beginnings of culture can be found in other species, but these little bits of nonhuman culture exist mostly in small, isolated patterns of behavior that make only a relatively minor difference in the animals' life. In contrast, human life is deeply enmeshed in culture; indeed, it is hard to imagine what human life would be like without culture. Culture provides us with food and housing, with languages and things to talk about, with electricity and all the appliances that use it, with all our means of travel other than walking, with our forms of work and play, with science and religion, with medicine, with art and entertainment, and with all the ideas that give our lives meaning.

Cultures are diverse, but they also have many common themes. Phenomena such as language, cooking, clothing, and money are found all over the world, but not in other species. Human life would be vastly different without language,

cooking, clothing, and money, but it is only because of culture that we can have them.

Culture also creates problems that are special to humans. There cannot be crime without laws, nor bankruptcy without money, nor nuclear waste without nuclear technology. Only humans go to war, deliberately commit suicide, or take part in genocide. Culture is not all good. Still, its benefits far outweigh its costs. Culture has enabled human beings to thrive and multiply. Indeed, nearly all of the animals most closely related to humans (apes and other primates) live near the equator in tropical climates, but human beings have spread all over the globe and live comfortably in mountains and valleys, in sunny and wintry places, in deserts and other seemingly difficult places. Cultural learning (e.g., clothes, plumbing, indoor heating) makes this dispersion possible.

Perhaps most remarkably of all, culture has enabled human beings to increase their life span

substantially. Advances in public health and medical care now enable many people to live 80 years, more than double what our ancestors could expect. No other animals have been able to develop knowledge that extends their life span.

Many social psychologists have used the phrase "the social animal" to describe human beings, but many other animals are also social. What makes us human is the extent to which we are cultural animals. Culture is a better way of being social. For one thing, it allows humans to accumulate knowledge over time and across generations—something almost no other animals have been able to accomplish. Most social animals start over with each new generation, which must then solve the same problems of how to live comfortably. Each new generation of human beings, however, can learn from previous generations. (Otherwise, instead of reading this textbook, you'd be trying to master how to make fire and forage for food.)

The very fact that we can think about what makes us human is itself an important part of what makes us human. Human beings can think with language and meaning in a way that no other animal can. This makes our social lives much more complicated than they would otherwise be, but it also creates the richness of human life and experience. That is, it makes our social psychology more complicated to study and learn, but it also makes it vastly more interesting!

chapter summary

NATURE AND SOCIAL BEHAVIOR

- The power of socialization to change people is real, but limited.
- Nature is the physical world around us.
- Darwin's theory of evolution focuses on how change occurs in nature.

- Natural selection is a process whereby genetically based traits become more or less common in a population.
- "Survival of the fittest" means that animals compete with each other to survive.
- Reproductive success means creating offspring who will in turn create many offspring.
- A trait that increases an organism's survival rate or leads to better reproductive

success is likely to become more common in a population.
- Being social helps humans and other animals survive and reproduce.
- Larger brains evolved to enable animals to function well in complex social structures.
- The human brain evolved to capitalize on culture.

CULTURE AND HUMAN SOCIAL LIFE

- Culture is an information-based system in which many people work together to help satisfy their biological and social needs.
- A culture is what a group of people have in common, including shared beliefs, meanings, and values, as well as shared ways of doing things.
- Both nature and culture are important in shaping behavior.
- Humans, unlike most other creatures, base their actions on meaning and ideas.

- Nature has prepared humans to use ideas.
- Humans and some other animals are social. Humans are far more cultural than any other animal.
- Differences between social and cultural animals include the following:
  - Social animals work together; cultural animals also use extensive division of labor.
  - Social animals may learn things from one another; cultural animals deliberately share knowledge with the group.
  - Social animals may help kin; cultural animals have a broader sense of community and often help strangers.
  - Social animals mainly use aggression to resolve conflict; cultural animals have many alternatives, including moral principles, compromise, and the rule of law.

- Although cultures differ, differences are often merely matters of degree rather than opposites.

IMPORTANT FEATURES OF HUMAN SOCIAL LIFE

- The human mind is a duplex mind, meaning that it has both an automatic and a conscious system.
- The automatic system is especially useful for the simple tasks we perform, whereas the conscious system is useful for the more complex tasks.
- The automatic system is fast and relatively effortless, whereas the conscious system is slow and effortful.
- The automatic and conscious are not independent of one another. Sometimes they work together, and sometimes they work against each other.
- Living in a culture has many advantages, but it makes many demands.
- Inner processes often serve interpersonal functions. That is, the psychological traits people have enable them to connect better with others.
- In general (though not always), nature says go and culture says stop.
- Nature makes us selfish; culture requires us to resist selfish impulses.
- Most choices in life involve tradeoffs, both benefits and costs.

- An important aspect of many tradeoffs is short-term versus long-term gain.
- Humans get most of what they need from other people.
- Culture operates as a "general store" of information.
- Asch's study demonstrated that sometimes people rely more on information from other people than on their own senses.
- If the brain is like a personal computer, then culture is like the Internet. A computer can do a lot more when it is connected to the Internet than when it is a stand-alone machine.

WHAT MAKES US HUMAN? PUTTING THE CULTURAL ANIMAL IN PERSPECTIVE

- Although human beings evolved from other animals, humans have much larger brains than other animals, especially in proportion to body size.
- Big brains may have evolved to enable more complex social relationships.
- Another main difference between humans and other animals is culture. Culture allows humans to accumulate knowledge over time and across generations.
- Although culture is not all good, its advantages outweigh its disadvantages. For example, culture has enabled modern humans to more than double the life spans of our ancestors.

Key Terms

Automatic system 41
Conscious system 41
Cultural animal 32
Culture 35

Duplex mind 41
Mutation 30
Natural selection 29
Nature 28

Praxis 34
Psyche 27
Reproduction 30
Social animals 32

Survival 29
Theory of evolution 28
Tradeoff 48

[Quiz Yourself] Answers

1. Nature and Social Behavior
Answers: 1=d, 2=a, 3=a, 4=c

2. Culture and Human Social Life
Answers: 1=c, 2=d, 3=b, 4=d

3. Important Features of Human Social Life
Answers: 1=a, 2=b, 3=a, 4=b

Media Learning Resources

Make sure you check out the complete set of learning resources and study tools below. If your instructor did not order these items with your new book, go to www.ichapters.com to purchase Cengage Learning print and digital products.

Social Psychology and Human Nature BOOK COMPANION WEBSITE

www.cengage.com/psychology/baumeister Visit your book companion website, where you will find flash cards, practice quizzes, Internet links, and more to help you study.

CENGAGENOW™ JUST WHAT YOU NEED TO KNOW NOW!

Spend time on what you need to master rather than on information you have already learned. Take a pre-test for this chapter, and CengageNOW will generate a personalized study plan based on your results. The study plan will identify the topics you need to review and direct you to online resources to help you master those topics. You can then take a post-test to help you determine the concepts you have mastered and what you will still need to work on. Try it out! Go to www.cengage.com/login to sign in with an access code or to purchase access to this product.

CLASSIC AND CONTEMPORARY VIDEOS STUDENT CD-ROM

To see videos on the topics and experiments discussed in this chapter and to learn more about the research that social psychologists are doing today, go to the Student CD-ROM.

SOCIAL PSYCH LAB

These unique online labs give you the opportunity to become a participant in actual experiments, including re-creations of classic and contemporary research studies.

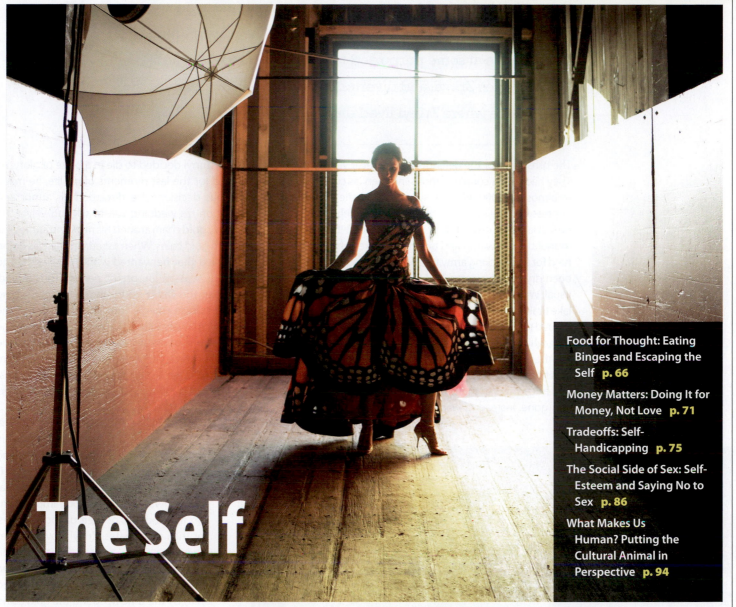

chapter 3

The Self

Food for Thought: Eating Binges and Escaping the Self p. 66

Money Matters: Doing It for Money, Not Love p. 71

Tradeoffs: Self-Handicapping p. 75

The Social Side of Sex: Self-Esteem and Saying No to Sex p. 86

What Makes Us Human? Putting the Cultural Animal in Perspective p. 94

Ryan McVay/Getty Images

WHAT IS THE SELF? p. 59
The Self's Main Jobs p. 59
Who Makes the Self: The Individual or Society? p. 60
Self-Awareness p. 64

WHERE SELF-KNOWLEDGE COMES FROM p. 67
Looking Outside: The Looking-Glass Self p. 68
Looking Inside: Introspection p. 69
Looking at Others: Social Comparison p. 70

Self-Perception p. 71
The Fluctuating Image(s) of Self p. 71
Why People Seek Self-Knowledge p. 73

SELF AND INFORMATION PROCESSING p. 77
Anything That Touches the Self . . . p. 77
Can the Self-Concept Change? p. 78

SELF-ESTEEM, SELF-DECEPTION, AND POSITIVE ILLUSIONS p. 81
Self-Esteem p. 81
Reality and Illusion p. 82
How People Fool Themselves p. 83
Benefits of Self-Esteem p. 84
Why Do We Care? p. 85
Is High Self-Esteem Always Good? p. 87
Pursuing Self-Esteem p. 88

SELF-PRESENTATION p. 89
Who's Looking? p. 90
Making an Impression p. 91
Self-Presentation and Risky Behavior p. 93

CHAPTER SUMMARY p. 94

In the late 1500s, near the height of the Ottoman Turkish empire, Sultan Suleiman the Magnificent set out with a giant army to conquer as much of Europe as he could. On the way to Vienna, he took offense at some purported remark by a Hungarian nobleman, Count Miklós Zrínyi, and diverted his entire force to conquer the small castle where Zrínyi lived on his lands (Turnbull, 2003). ‖‖‖

The prospects for the defenders were never very good. They had only a couple of thousand men, as compared to almost 100,000 with the sultan. The castle was not impressive (Suleiman himself called it a "molehill" when he first laid eyes on it). Its best feature was that it was surrounded by a swamp and an artificial lake, which were hard for an attacking army to cross, but the summer had been dry and this natural advantage was weaker than usual. When the Turks destroyed the dam, the artificial lake drained, leaving the castle exposed. The Turks bombarded the walls with their huge cannon and drilled tunnels, which they exploded to make the walls collapse.

After days of fighting, the defenders knew their cause was hopeless. Only 300 were left alive, their castle walls had huge holes in them, and most of their ammunition was gone. Instead of waiting for the Turks to storm in upon them, Zrínyi decided to die in a blaze of glory. As he prepared for the last moments of his life, he made some curious decisions. He discarded his armor and instead put on his wedding suit of silk and velvet. He hung a heavy gold chain around his neck and stuffed his pockets with gold coins. When asked why he was doing this, he replied that he wanted whoever killed him to know that he was an important person. Thus attired, he flung open the castle doors and led his remaining troops on a suicide charge right into the heart of the Turkish army. All were killed. (According to legend, the young wife of one of the soldiers remained in the castle until the Turks overran it, whereupon she threw a burning torch into the remaining ammunition supply, causing a terrible explosion that killed 3,000 Turkish soldiers along with herself.)

The striking thing about this story is the count's concern with self-presentation, which we shall see is the task of making good impressions on other people. It is easily understandable and rational that people want to make good impressions on their bosses, or their dating partners, or their teammates. Zrínyi, however, was trying to make a good impression on someone he did not yet know and who presumably would have already killed him by the time he found the gold coins. There is no practical value to being well regarded after you are dead, especially by the person who took your life. He's not going to be your buddy nor do you any favors. But it mattered to the count anyway.

Concern with making a good impression after you are dead may seem foolish, irrational, or even bizarre, but Count Zrínyi was far from alone in this respect. In fact, news reports in today's United States indicate that more and more people are stipulating plastic surgery to prepare their bodies for their funerals. They want to look their best at their last showing,

Zrínyi's Outburst, Johann Peter (1780–1856)/Magyar Nemzeti Galeria, Budapest, Hungary/The Bridgeman Figure Library

The monumental work *Zrínyi's Sortie*, dated 1825, by Peter Krafft (1780–1856). The scene is the sortie of Count Miklós Zrínyi and his men, heroic defenders of the castle of Szigetvár, against the besieging Turks in 1566, in which Zrínyi lost his life.

even though they will be dead and there must be better ways to spend money than for cosmetic operations on a corpse that is about to be buried or cremated!

As cultural beings, people have selves that are much more elaborate and complex than has been found anywhere else in the animal kingdom. The self is an important tool with which the human organism makes its way through human society and thereby manages to satisfy its needs. To be effective at this, the human self has taken shape in a way that it is marked by some deep, powerful drives. Among these drives is a strong concern with how one is perceived by others. This drive mostly serves the goals of survival and reproduction. However, many people care strongly about how others perceive them, even if those other people don't help them survive or reproduce. In some cases, people care about others who will kill them. We may care most about those we depend on, but the fact is that people have a deeply rooted tendency to care, broadly, about how others in general regard them. It's very hard not to care what other people think of you—at least some other people.

What Is the Self?

The self is peculiarly difficult to define. Everyone seems to know what it is and to use the term frequently (especially if you include words like "myself"), but hardly anyone can say exactly what it is. Some brain researchers have begun to say that the self is an illusion, mainly because they cannot find any specific spot in the brain that seems to correspond to the self, but in their everyday lives these researchers act as if they know exactly what the self is, and it is not an illusion. For example, they know the difference between what is their own and what is someone else's (wallet, apartment, feet, ideas, romantic partner). After all, if the self were merely an illusion, there would be no genuine difference between me and you, so how could we talk about whether that $20 bill is mine or yours?

Thus, nearly everyone has a basic understanding of what the self is, even if it is hard to put into words. To develop a more scientific understanding, let us begin by considering what its functions are, what its different main parts or aspects are, and where it comes from.

THE SELF'S MAIN JOBS

It may sound funny to ask "Why do we have selves?" Not having a self is not really an option! Everyone has a separate body, and selves begin with bodies, so there is no way for a human being to be completely without a self. Perhaps a more relevant question would concern the structure of the self: "Why are human selves put together the way they are?" One could also ask about their function: "What are selves for?" The structure and function questions are often related, because selves (like cars, tree leaves, forks, furnaces, and many other entities) are structured to serve a function. Moreover, as we saw in Chapter 2, many inner traits of human beings serve interpersonal functions. Much of the self is designed to enable you to relate to others, including claiming and sustaining a place in a cultural system that connects you to many other people.

Another theme of this book is the conflict between selfish impulses and social conscience. The self is right in the middle of this battle. On the one hand, selves sometimes naturally feel selfish (hence the very term *selfish*!), and in many situations they have strong impulses to do what is best for themselves. They are designed to know and do what is best for them. On the other hand, selfishness must be kept under control if society is to operate effectively, and selves often incorporate the morals and other values of the culture. Those morals mostly tell you to do what is best for the group instead of what is best for you personally or what you feel like doing. Hence the self must be able to understand these social morals and other values—plus be able to act on them, even when that requires overriding one's natural, selfish impulses.

The self has three main parts (▶ **FIGURE 3.1**), which correspond to several main things that the self does. The first part consists of **self-knowledge** (sometimes called **self-concept**). Human beings have self-

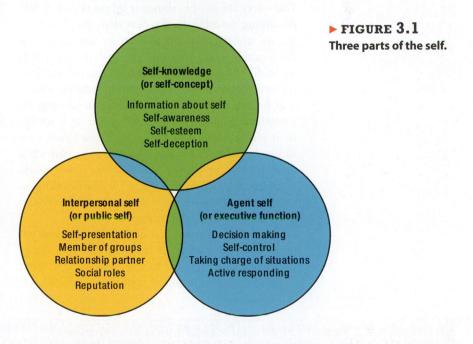

▶ **FIGURE 3.1**
Three parts of the self.

Self-knowledge (or self-concept)
Information about self
Self-awareness
Self-esteem
Self-deception

Interpersonal self (or public self)
Self-presentation
Member of groups
Relationship partner
Social roles
Reputation

Agent self (or executive function)
Decision making
Self-control
Taking charge of situations
Active responding

SELF-KNOWLEDGE (SELF-CONCEPT) a set of beliefs about oneself

awareness, and this awareness enables them to develop elaborate sets of beliefs about themselves. If someone says "Tell me something about yourself," you can probably furnish 15 or 20 specific answers without having to think very hard. Consider these experiences, all of which involve self-knowledge and self-awareness: You stop to think about what you would like to be doing in five years. You receive a grade on an exam and consider whether you are good at this particular subject. You check your hair in a mirror or your weight on a scale. You read your horoscope or the results of some medical tests. On a first date, your partner asks you about yourself, and you try to give honest answers that show the kind of person you are. You feel ashamed about something you did last week or last year, or you feel proud about something else you did. Such moments show the self reflecting on itself and on its store of information about itself.

The **interpersonal self**, or **public self**, is a second part of the self that helps the person connect socially to other people. Most people have a certain image that they try to convey to others. This public self bears some resemblance to the self-concept, but the two are not the same. Often, people work hard to present a particular image to others even if it is not exactly the full, precise truth as they know it. Consider some of the things people do to impress others. You dress up for a social event. You show your friends that you are easygoing and fun-loving. You convince your boss that you are serious, reliable, and work-oriented. You spend all day cleaning your home to get it ready for guests. You hold back from arguing for your religious or political views because you think the other people present might not approve of them. You worry about what someone thinks of you. When describing yourself on that first date, you leave out certain unflattering details, such as that nasty foot odor problem, or how you like to burp the words to "Auld Lang Syne." Furthermore, many emotions indicate concern over how one appears to others: You feel embarrassed because someone saw you do something stupid, or even just because your underwear was showing. You feel guilty if you forgot your romantic partner's birthday. You are delighted when your boss compliments you on your good work. These episodes reveal that the self is often working in complex ways to gain social acceptance and maintain good interpersonal relationships.

The third important part of the self, the **agent self** or **executive function**, is the part that gets things done. It enables the self to make choices and exert control, including both self-control and control over other people (and things). Sometimes you decide not to eat something because it is unhealthy or fattening. Sometimes you make a promise and later exert yourself to keep it. Sometimes you decide what courses to take or what job to take. Perhaps you cast a vote in an election. Perhaps you sign a lease for an apartment. Perhaps you make yourself go out jogging even though the weather is bad and you feel lazy. Perhaps you place a bet on a sports event. All these actions reveal the self as not just a knower but also as a doer.

In this chapter, we focus on the first two aspects of the self: self-knowledge and the interpersonal self. The next chapter will focus on the self in action.

WHO MAKES THE SELF: THE INDIVIDUAL OR SOCIETY?

Probably the best account of the origins of selfhood is that the self comes into being at the interface between the inner biological processes of the human body and the sociocultural network to which the person belongs (that is, the other people in the society, plus its "general store" of common beliefs and practices; e.g., James, 1892/1948). The importance of society is hard to deny; in fact, if you grew up on a deserted island and never met other human beings, you might hardly have a "self" at all in the usual sense. There would be no point in having a name, for example, if you never interacted with other people, nor would you have a reputation, an ethnic identity, or even a set of personal values. (At most you would have preferences, but they would not seem like your personal values if you never met anyone else who might be different.)

Then again, even without meeting other human beings, a person might still have a conception of self as a body separate from its environment. The difference between dropping a stone on your foot and dropping it on a tree root next to your foot is an important sign of self: Your foot is part of your self; the tree is not.

A True or Real Self? Many people like to think they have an inner "true" self. Most social scientists are skeptical of such notions. If the inner self is different from the way the person acts all the time, why is the inner one the "true" one? By what criterion could we say that someone's "true" self is shy if the person doesn't act shy most of the time? The idea of an inner "true" self different from behavior may have its origins in class prejudices (Sennett, 1974; Stone, 1977; Weintraub, 1978; see Baumeister, 1987). Back when social mobility began to increase, so that some aristocrats became poor while merchants became rich, the upper classes wanted to continue believing that they were inherently better than other people, even if the others had more money. The upper class could

---

INTERPERSONAL SELF (PUBLIC SELF) the image of the self that is conveyed to others

AGENT SELF (EXECUTIVE FUNCTION) the part of the self involved in control, including both control over other people and self-control

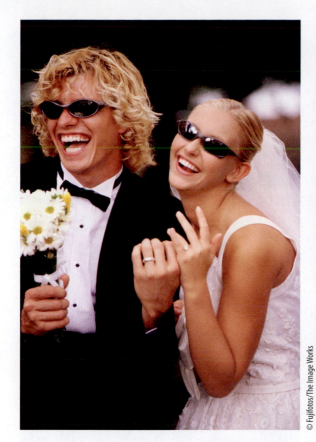

Different cultures have different wedding traditions.

not point to obvious differences in behavior, because in point of fact many aristocrats were drunken, conceited, stupid, lazy, sexually immoral, and in other respects deplorable. Hence, the upper class settled on the view that the superiority of the blue bloods lay in their inner traits that could not be directly seen.

Even if the inner "true" self is something of a fiction, people still believe in it, and these beliefs affect how they act. A classic article by sociologist Ralph Turner (1976) noted that different cultures (and different groups or historical eras within a culture) may differ in their ideas about the true self by placing emphasis on either of two main approaches: impulse and institution. **Self as impulse** refers to the person's inner thoughts and feelings. **Self as institution** refers to the way the person acts in public, especially in official roles. Many people recognize that they sometimes put on a public performance that differs from how they feel inside (Goffman, 1959). Turner's point was that cultures disagree as to whether the public actions or the inner feelings count as the more real or true side of the self. Suppose, for example, that a soldier is terrified in battle and wants to run and hide, but he steels himself and performs an act of heroism that helps win the battle. Which was the "real" man: the terrified coward or the brave hero?

Attitudes toward marriage may reflect different attitudes about the real self. In cultures that emphasize self as impulse, the actual wedding ceremony and its

legal or religious significance are secondary. Marriage is seen as a psychological union of two persons, and what matters is how they feel about each other. If they lose their love for each other, or become attracted to someone else, they may feel justified in abandoning their spouse because to do so is to be true to themselves. A marriage is thus only as good as the current emotional state of the partners. In contrast, a culture that emphasizes self as institution downplays the inner feelings and instead places great significance on role performance. A couple may have a good marriage even if they cease to love each other, so long as they remain true to their vows and act the way a proper husband and wife are supposed to act. The actual wedding ceremony counts much more in such societies than it does among the impulse-oriented societies, because it is at the wedding that the real self changes to become married in the eyes of society.

Culture and Interdependence. Selves are somewhat different across different cultures. The most studied set of such cultural differences involves independence versus interdependence. This dimension of difference entails different attitudes toward the self and different motivations as to what the self mainly

---

SELF AS IMPULSE a person's inner thoughts and feelings

SELF AS INSTITUTION the way a person acts in public, especially in official roles

tries to accomplish, and it results in different emphases about what the self is.

The idea that cultural styles of selfhood differ along the dimension of independence was introduced by Markus and Kitayama (1991; see also Triandis, 1989). Those two researchers, one American and one Japanese, proposed that Asians differ from North Americans and Europeans in how they think of themselves and how they seek to construct the self in relation to others. To avoid the overused term *self-concept* they introduced the term *self-construal*, which means a way of thinking about the self. An **independent self-construal** emphasizes what makes the self different and sets it apart from others. In contrast, an **interdependent self-construal** emphasizes what connects the self to other people and groups.

To appreciate the difference, it is useful to try a simple exercise such as asking yourself "Who or what am I?" and listing a dozen or more different answers off the top of your head. When you have done this, go through the list again and see how many of your answers express something unique or special about you (such as having an unusual skill or hobby) and how many express connection to others (such as belonging to a particular family, attending a particular university, or coming from a particular place). The relative amounts of those two types of answers indicate where you stand on independence (your unique traits) and interdependence.

It is not inherently better to be either independent or interdependent. Nor is everyone in one culture independent or interdependent. Still, Markus and Kitayama have contended (with support from subsequent work) that Easterners (e.g., people from Japan, China, Korea) tend to be more interdependent, whereas Westerners (e.g., people from the United States, Canada, Western Europe) tend to be more independent. Nor are these differences merely superficial ways of talking about the self. Instead, they represent deep-seated differences in what the person strives to become. The American ideal may be the self-made man or woman, who works alone to create or achieve something, possibly overcoming obstacles or other people's resistance in the process, and who eventually becomes a true individual in the sense of a unique person with highly special traits. In contrast, the Asian ideal of selfhood may be more the consummate team player who makes valuable contributions to the group, who does not let personal egotism stand in the way of doing what is best for the group, and who remains loyal to the group and

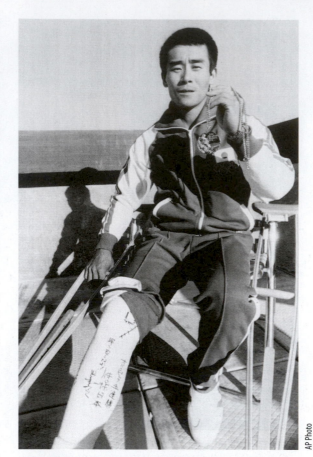

Shun Fujimoto, a member of the Japanese men's gymnastics team, completed the team competition at the 1976 Olympics despite a broken kneecap, collapsing in agony following his final dismount from the rings.

helps it overcome external threats. Asians see the self as deeply enmeshed in a web of personal, family, social, and cultural relationships, outside of which there is meaninglessness and loneliness. Americans see the self as following its own path to autonomy, self-sufficiency, and unique individuality.

A stunning story from the 1976 Olympics concerned a tight battle between the Japanese and the Soviet Russians for the men's team gymnastics medals (e.g., Clark, 1986). It came down to a performance on the rings by Shun Fujimoto in the last event. His performance was nearly perfect except for a slight stutter-step by one leg when he landed. His score was high enough that Japan won the gold medal by a very slight margin over the Russians.

What was remarkable about that story was that Shun had actually broken his kneecap in the previous event. The dismount made his injury even worse; it dislocated his broken kneecap and tore ligaments in his right leg. In other words, the most intense pain he could imagine was waiting for him at the end of his performance, and he still managed to concentrate on what he was doing and perform perfectly.

INDEPENDENT SELF-CONSTRUAL a self-concept that emphasizes what makes the self different and sets it apart from others

INTERDEPENDENT SELF-CONSTRUAL a self-concept that emphasizes what connects the self to other people and groups

When Americans hear Fujimoto's story, they probably understand it in terms of the independent self. They can imagine Shun wanting the glory of the gold medal, wanting to fulfill his dreams, and wanting to complete what he had worked for years to achieve. They think he would want to be admired for his heroic effort under intensely adverse circumstances.

But Asians probably see the story differently, with a more interdependent construal. It was not personal glory but obligation to the team that pushed him to take on that suffering. If he didn't compete, his team would lose the medal, and he didn't want to let them down. In fact, Shun concealed his injury from his teammates, in case their performances would be affected by worrying about him or expecting that the team might lose.

Social Roles. Let us return now to the question "What are selves for?" One answer, certainly, is that the self has to gain social acceptance. People are not designed to live by themselves. They need other people to accept them in order to have a job, to have friends and lovers, to have a family. The self is one tool people use to accomplish these goals. By learning how to act properly and how to conform to social rules and norms, people can improve their chances of social acceptance. In Chapter 2 we saw that human beings follow an especially long road to social acceptance. The self is constructed to help them on that road, which includes changing and adapting themselves so as to appeal to others.

Another important purpose of the self is to play **social roles**. A long tradition in psychology and sociology considers social behavior as resembling a play or a movie, in which different people play different roles (e.g., Biddle & Thomas, 1966; Goffman, 1959; Mead, 1934). Indeed some theorists, such as Erving Goffman (1959), have taken this view to an extreme and analyzed most human behavior and selfhood in terms of actors playing roles. A culture is a large system with many different roles, and everyone has to find a place in it (or several places). You cannot be a senator, or a nurse, or a parent, or a girlfriend, or a police officer unless you can reliably act in appropriate ways. Many roles, such as spouse or engineer, can only be adopted after you have taken a series of steps (such as having a wedding, or getting a college degree with a certain major); the self has to execute these steps just to get into the role. Then, after you have the role, you must perform the duties that define it. To succeed in traveling the long road to social acceptance, the person must have a self capable of all those jobs.

To be sure, humans are not the only creatures to have roles. For example, in ant colonies, ants have different roles, such as one or more fertile female "queens," some fertile male "drones," and many sterile female "workers," "soldiers," or other specialized groups. What is special about the human self is that it is flexible enough to take on new roles and to change roles. A single human being, for example, might over the course of a lifetime work at mowing lawns, writing for the school newspaper, managing the swim team, lifeguarding at several different pools, busing tables in the college dining hall, working with computers, managing others who work with computers, and so forth. Also, a person may perform similar jobs with several different organizations, such as a professor who moves from one university to another but teaches the same courses each time. In contrast, a worker ant almost always does the same job for its entire life and within the same colony of ants; it does not need a self that can adopt and shed different roles.

Where do these roles come from? Often they are part of the social system. If you live in a small peasant farming village, as most people in the history of the world have done, then many roles are not available to you. The limited opportunities in that village's social system mean that you could not be a

The woman in this picture has at least two roles: (a) she is a soldier, and (b) she is a mother.

SOCIAL ROLES the different roles a person plays, as in a play or a movie

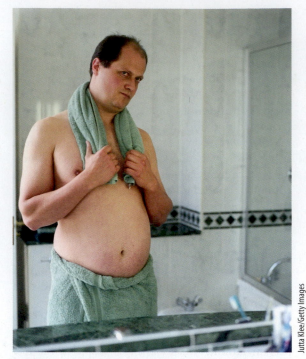

I see room for improvement.

studying the difference between being and not being self-aware. They developed several clever procedures to increase self-awareness, such as having people work while seated in front of a mirror, or telling people that they were being videotaped.

Researchers quickly found it necessary to distinguish at least two main kinds of self-awareness: public and private (e.g., Fenigstein, Scheier, & Buss, 1975; also Carver & Scheier, 1981). **Private self-awareness** refers to attending to your inner states, including emotions, thoughts, desires, and traits. It is a matter of looking inward. In contrast, **public self-awareness** means attending to how you are perceived by others, including what others might think of you. Public self-awareness looks outward to understand the self. Without public self-awareness, Count Zrínyi would not have dressed as he did on the last day of his life: He wore his wedding suit and gold because he was imagining how he would look to the enemy soldiers outside. Thus, instead of attending to his inner states directly, he thought about himself as seen through other people's eyes.

One thing researchers have found is that self-awareness usually involves evaluating the self, rather than just merely being aware of it. A person looks in the mirror and compares him- or herself against various standards. It is not just "Oh, there I am in the mirror. Is that what I look like? It doesn't matter." Rather, it's "Oh, my hair is a mess. This shirt looks good on me. I should lose a little weight." The essence of self-awareness is comparing oneself against these standards (good-looking hair, good clothing, fashionable slimness, respectively) and thereby coming up with good or bad evaluations about the self.

Standards. **Standards** are ideas (concepts) of how things might possibly be. Standards include ideals, norms, expectations, moral principles, laws, the way things were in the past, and what other people have done. Standards are an important example of one theme of this book—namely, the power of ideas to cause and shape behavior. The self is not good or bad in a vacuum, but only when compared to certain standards. Nearly all children start talking about standards (good, bad, nice) when they are around 2 years old, which is also the age at which their self-awareness blossoms (Kagan, 1981) and children begin to develop a concept of themselves as separate from their parents.

Self-awareness is often unpleasant, because people often compare themselves to high standards such as moral ideals for good behavior or a fashion model's good looks. There is some evidence, for example, that when girls and young women watch television shows featuring especially beautiful actresses and models, they feel less positive about themselves and become more likely to develop eating disorders (Becker,

basketball coach, for example, or a software consultant, or a movie star, because the only other people you ever meet are peasant farmers. Most roles are ways of relating to other people within a cultural system. If you lived alone in the forest, it would be silly to describe yourself as a police officer, a bartender, a schoolteacher, or vice president of telemarketing. A person's social identity thus shows the interplay of the individual organism and the larger cultural system: Society creates and defines the roles, and individual people seek them out, adopt them, and sometimes impose their own style on them. Without society, the self would not exist in full.

But let's start at the beginning. The self has its roots in the human capacity to turn attention back toward its source. Without self-awareness, selfhood and self-knowledge would be impossible. The next section will cover what social psychologists have learned about self-awareness.

SELF-AWARENESS

Self-awareness consists of attention directed at the self. Early in the 1970s, two social psychologists, Shelley Duval and Robert Wicklund (1972), began

---

SELF-AWARENESS attention directed at the self

PRIVATE SELF-AWARENESS looking inward on the private aspects of the self, including emotions, thoughts, desires, and traits

PUBLIC SELF-AWARENESS looking outward on the public aspects of the self that others can see and evaluate

STANDARDS ideas (concepts) of how things might possibly be

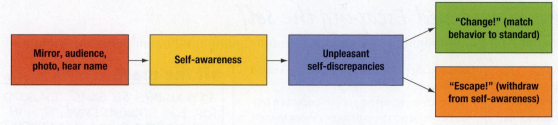

▶ **FIGURE 3.2** Self-awareness theory, proposed by Duval and Wicklund (1972), suggests that some situations, such as looking in a mirror, lead to self-awareness. Self-aware people feel bad because they notice any discrepancies between who they are and standards. They can either "change" by matching the behavior to the standard, or "escape" by trying to withdraw from the self-aware state.

Burwell, Herzog, Hamburg, & Gilman, 2002; Botta, 2000; Harrison, 2000, 2001, 2003; Lavine, Sweeney, & Wagner, 1999; Tiggemann & Pickering, 1996). But people feel good when they compare themselves to the "average person" or to specific people who are not doing as well, because one can usually surpass low standards (at least in one's own mind!).

When people are aware that they fall short of standards, the bad feeling leads to either of two reactions: change or escape (▶ **FIGURE 3.2**). One reaction is to try to remedy the problem, such as by improving oneself. This may be as simple as combing one's hair, or as complex as deciding to change basic aspects of one's life. Sometimes changing the standard is easier than changing the self. The other response is to try to avoid or reduce self-awareness, so as to escape from feeling bad.

Recent work suggests that a person's reactions to standards depends on how promising versus hopeless the prospect of meeting the standard seems (Silvia & Duval, 2001). When people think they can reach their goals or other standards in a reasonable time, self-awareness makes them try harder to do so. But if the goal looks unattainable or the person does not feel he or she is making satisfactory progress, then avoiding self-awareness looms as the more appealing solution.

Self-Awareness and Behavior. Self-awareness can make people behave better. Being self-aware makes you compare yourself to moral standards or other ideals. For example, in one study students took a test and had an opportunity to cheat on it. Students who took the test while sitting in front of a mirror were less likely to cheat than students who took the test without a mirror (Diener & Wallbom, 1976). Another study showed that people are less likely to eat fatty food when they are sitting in front of a mirror than when there is no mirror (Sentyrz & Bushman, 1998). Thus, again, self-awareness made people more attuned to societal standards and hence made them act in a more socially desirable manner. Other studies have shown that increasing self-awareness can

make people behave less aggressively, conform more to their sexual morals, and stay on their diets (Heatherton, Polivy, Herman, & Baumeister, 1993; Scheier, Fenigstein, & Buss, 1974; Smith, Gerrard, & Gibbons, 1997). Increased self-awareness makes people act more consistently with their attitudes about many different issues (Pryor, Gibbons, Wicklund, Fazio, & Hood, 1977); insofar as consistency is a good thing, those findings provide more evidence that self-awareness improves behavior.

The fact that self-awareness enables people to behave better according to cultural standards reflects the theme that inner processes serve interpersonal functions. Humans could not get along with each other so well if they did not have self-awareness. Self-awareness enables people to reflect on themselves and change themselves so as to become more attractive and socially desirable—precisely what is needed to improve their ability to get along.

Does self-awareness *always* make people behave better? Of course not. For example, terrorists might become more fanatical and more destructive as a result of being self-aware because their standard is to terrorize their enemy. But these exceptions are just that—exceptions. The general effect of high self-awareness is to make people more aware of positive, desirable standards and make them try harder to behave in a positive manner.

One class of largely destructive behaviors, however, does stem from high self-awareness. These behaviors arise when people are aware of themselves in some bad, upsetting aspect, and they cannot solve the problem. In those cases, they may attempt to escape from self-awareness by resorting to destructive or socially undesirable methods. The next section will look at this issue.

Escaping Self-Awareness. People seek to escape from self-awareness when it feels bad. In one study, people who performed actions contrary to their values and attitudes were told to take a seat in a waiting room afterward. Half the seats faced mirrors (which make a person self-conscious), whereas others faced

Eating Binges and Escaping the Self

Binge eating is a widespread problem, especially among adolescent and young adult females. Ironically, most of these young women are on a diet and trying to lose weight at the time, and the occasional eating binge thwarts their efforts to restrain their food consumption. Why would a woman who is on a carefully planned, calorie-counting diet suddenly one day eat most of the food in her refrigerator and cupboards?

One answer points to the importance of self-awareness. In this view, the woman may be beset with troubled thoughts and feelings that she is inadequate, unattractive, or otherwise unworthy. The process of eating enables her to escape from those thoughts and feelings. She forgets herself as she becomes absorbed in the activities of chewing, eating, and swallowing food.

Many chronic dieters are preoccupied with how others perceive them. They may think that other people are whispering about how fat they are, even if they are within the normal weight range. They also tend to be people with high standards and high expectations for themselves (including being ambitious students at good universities). If something goes wrong for them—whether an academic setback, such as a bad test grade, or a personal problem, such as a romantic rejection—this tendency to focus on the self can make them miserable. They find themselves thinking about all their own possible faults and shortcomings that could have caused the problem.

At such times, eating appeals because it provides a distraction from thoughts about the self. The troubling thoughts occur at a highly meaningful level: What's wrong with me? Will I ever be a success in my career? Will people want to love me? In contrast, eating focuses the mind at a low level of meaning: take a bite, notice the taste, chew, swallow. Low levels of meaning involve little or no emotion, just sensation. The worries and anxieties about whether you are good enough are replaced by a kind of emotional calm. Eating can thus help turn off bad emotions.

Although dieters are high in **public self-consciousness**, defined as thinking about how others perceive them, they are often low in private self-awareness of their inner states (e.g., Blanchard & Frost, 1983; Heatherton, Polivy, & Herman, 1989). This may be because dieting involves learning to ignore one's inner feelings of hunger. Ignoring hunger may be helpful to dieting, but a common side effect is that the person also loses awareness of inner signals of satiety (that is, of being "full" and having eaten enough). This can contribute to an eating binge, because the person keeps on eating even when the stomach is already full. The body sends out its usual "stop eating!" signal, but the mind has learned to ignore it along with other inner signals.

Normally, many dieters count every bite and calorie. This pattern of so-called monitoring

off the mark.com   by Mark Parisi

IT'S ALWAYS THE SAME...I'M GOOD FOR 364 STRAIGHT DAYS, THEN IN **ONE NIGHT** I BINGE ON A HUNDRED MILLION SERVINGS OF COOKIES AND MILK...

OVEREATERS ANONYMOUS

offthemark.com

Reprinted by permission of Atlantic Feature Syndicate/Mark Parisi.

helps keep track of food intake, so the dieter can carefully control how much she (or he) eats. This requires a watchful attitude toward the self. During an eating binge, however, self-awareness is often lost, and the person may lose track of how much she is eating. When you stop keeping track, it is hard to regulate. Even people who do not have eating disorders or dieting ambitions find that they eat more when they stop keeping track, such as when their attention is absorbed in a television show or party. ●

away from the mirrors. The people who had acted against their values generally chose to face away from the mirror (Greenberg & Musham, 1981). They wanted to avoid self-awareness in order not to be reminded that they had done something wrong. Other participants, who had not done anything wrong, were happy to sit facing the mirror.

Drinking alcohol is one of the most common methods of reducing self-awareness. Alcohol narrows attention, and this usually means directing it away from the self (although if you get drunk and just think about your problems, you may feel worse). Studies have confirmed that people who are drunk seem less aware of themselves—as shown, for example, in how much they talk about themselves (Hull, 1981; Hull, Levenson, Young, & Scher, 1983). Outside the lab, people drink when things have gone badly, because the alcohol helps them stop ruminating about "What is wrong with me?" Perhaps paradoxically, people also turn to alcohol when they feel good and want to celebrate. That's because people want to let down their inhibitions in order to have a good time, and self-awareness is central to most inhibitions (because self-awareness makes you compare yourself against morals and other standards of proper behavior).

People use other methods to escape self-awareness. Perhaps the most extreme and destructive of these is suicide. Attempts at suicide, even when unsuccessful, are often intended as ways to escape from a sense of self as being a terrible person, or a person who is responsible for some terrible event (Baumeister, 1990).

PUBLIC SELF-CONSCIOUSNESS thinking about how others perceive you

Not all escapes from self-awareness are destructive, but several of them are, possibly because people who are desperate to stop thinking bad thoughts about themselves don't worry about the harm their methods might cause. *Food for Thought* discusses how escaping self-awareness can contribute to eating binges.

One explanation for human self-awareness is that it is vital for **self-regulation**—the process by which the self controls and changes itself (Carver & Scheier, 1981). People deliberately try to alter their responses, such as trying to get out of a bad mood, or to keep their attention and thinking focused on some problem rather than letting their mind wander, or to resist temptation. It is no accident that self-awareness usually involves comparing oneself to meaningful standards, because that may be precisely what self-awareness is for. People can reflect on themselves, decide that they are not acting properly, and try to change. Understood in this way, self-awareness is part of the mechanism by which people can bring themselves into line with what other people, including their culture, want and expect. At a simple level, recognizing that your hair is a mess or your socks don't match may be an essential first step toward fixing the problem. (Chapter 4 will have more to say about self-regulation.)

Another explanation for human self-awareness is that we can adopt the perspective of other people and imagine how they see us. This reflects the "people first" theme that we introduced in Chapter 2: People are oriented toward other people. To get along, we look to others, and in particular we want to be accepted in social groups. Knowing how we appear to others is a great help toward making ourselves more appealing and acceptable to others. Self-awareness is helpful on the long road to social acceptance. It also indicates, again, that inner processes (in this case, self-awareness) serve interpersonal functions (to help people get along better with others).

At a more complex level, self-awareness can be an exercise in "What am I doing with my life?" Are you making progress toward your goals, such as receiving an education, getting a good job, or finding a suitable partner? People can feel good even though they have not reached their goals, as long as they are making progress toward them (Carver & Scheier, 1990). Self-awareness thus can help people manage their behavior over long periods of time so they can reach their goals.

Alcohol reduces self-awareness, thereby undermining inhibitions.

[**QUIZ YOURSELF**]

What Is the Self?

1. Self-knowledge is also known as _____.
   (a) self-awareness   (b) self-concept
   (c) self-regulation   (d) self-presentation

2. According to self-awareness theory, a self-aware state is _____.
   (a) pleasant
   (b) unpleasant
   (c) pleasant initially, then unpleasant later
   (d) neutral

3. Alcohol has been shown to _____ self-awareness.
   (a) decrease   (b) increase
   (c) not affect   (d) reverse

4. The presence of a mirror has been shown to _____ self-awareness.

   (a) decrease   (b) increase
   (c) not affect   (d) reverse

Where Self-Knowledge Comes From

"Tell me something about yourself." Such openings are common, and people will generally oblige by disclosing some information. But where do they get it? How do people amass so much knowledge about themselves? Do people know themselves accurately, or are they mistaken (or do they simply lie a lot)?

SELF-REGULATION the process people use to control and change their thoughts, feelings, and behaviors

Humans clearly have a self-concept, or at least a stock of self-knowledge, some of which is true and some of which is distorted. Social psychologists have labored for decades to develop and test theories about how people store this information about themselves.

The next sections examine various theories about the sources of self-knowledge. When reading them, please keep a couple of things in mind: People are not passive receptacles; they actively process information that comes in. Your friend, or your mother, or society may tell you that you are not artistically talented, but you may reject that message. Then again, if all of them tell you that all the time, you may be more inclined to believe it (and they may be right!). Another thing to keep in mind is that people do not get all their self-knowledge from the same source or process. Several of these theories may be simultaneously correct, or at least partly correct.

I'm sure everyone likes my hat.

LOOKING OUTSIDE: THE LOOKING-GLASS SELF

One influential theory is that people learn about themselves from others. Every day people interact with others, and through these interactions they learn how others perceive them. "Wow, you are really good at sports!" "You're beautiful!" "You are smart!" These and many similar comments help give people information about themselves. It may seem surprising that the theme of putting people first extends even to finding out about yourself, but in fact people do learn a great deal about themselves from social interactions, from what other people tell them, and from comparing themselves to other people. These interactions also help cultivate public self-awareness, which (as noted above) is our ability to imagine how others perceive us.

The term **looking-glass self** was coined by Charles Horton Cooley (1902) to refer to the idea that people learn about themselves from other people. Cooley proposed three components to the looking-glass self: (a) You imagine how you appear to others. (b) You imagine how others will judge you. (c) You develop an emotional response (such as pride or shame) as a result of imagining how others will judge you. It is as if other people hold up a mirror (a looking glass) in which you can see yourself. If you lived on a deserted island and never met anyone else, you would not know yourself nearly as well as you do growing up amid people.

The great American social philosopher George Herbert Mead (1934) elaborated on this notion to suggest that most self-knowledge comes from feedback received from other people, whether particular individuals or what he called the **generalized other** (a combination of other people's views). Essentially, other people tell us who and what we are.

The notion of the looking-glass self has been tested extensively. It is partly correct and partly incorrect. Certainly there is ample evidence that people do respond to the feedback they get from others. Then again, if the looking-glass self really were the main source of self-knowledge, then you would think there would be a pretty good match between how everybody thinks about someone and how the person thinks about him- or herself. But there isn't. Most research suggests that a person's self-concept is often quite different from what friends, family, and coworkers think of him or her (Shrauger & Schoeneman, 1979).

Why doesn't the looking-glass self work better? If we were to ask you to describe yourself, and then asked all your friends and acquaintances to describe you, why would there be so many differences? Social psychologists have found that there usually is a good match between a person's self-concept and how that person thinks he or she is regarded by others. The gap is between what someone's friends really think of him and what he thinks they think. For example, someone may think of herself as easy to get along with. If so, she probably thinks that everybody sees her as easy to get along with, but in reality other

---

LOOKING-GLASS SELF the idea that people learn about themselves by imagining how they appear to others

GENERALIZED OTHER a combination of other people's views that tells you who and what you are

people may think she is a difficult, high-maintenance sort of person.

A person may be mistaken about how other people regard him or her for two reasons. The first is that people do not always tell the truth. If you ask someone "Am I a pretty nice person, basically easy to get along with?" that person might just say "Sure!" without really meaning it. People are reluctant to communicate bad news (Tesser & Rosen, 1975), to criticize someone, to complain, and in other ways to tell people what is wrong with them. (This generalization is subject to cultural differences. In Israel, for example, people supposedly are much more willing to communicate objections and criticisms.) It is very hard to find out if you have bad breath, for example, because almost no one will want to tell you.

The second reason is that people are not always receptive to feedback from others. People may try to tell you that you are hard to get along with, but you may not accept what they say. (You might get angry, or argue that the person is wrong, or change the subject.) As the section on self-deception will show, people are very selective in how they process incoming information about themselves. This is perhaps the biggest fallacy in the notion of the looking-glass self: It seems to depict the person as a passive recipient of information, as if people simply believed whatever other people told them about themselves. In reality, people pick and choose, and sometimes they completely reject what others tell them.

It is no wonder that many people's self-concepts do not match what others think of them. With regard to your unappealing traits, there is a sort of conspiracy of silence: Others don't want to tell you, and you don't want to hear it.

LOOKING INSIDE: INTROSPECTION

One refreshingly simple explanation of the roots of self-knowledge is that people simply have direct knowledge of what they are like. They don't need to rely on what other people tell them; they just look inward, and they know the answer. **Introspection** refers to the process by which a person examines the contents of his or her mind and mental states. People seemingly can always tell what they are thinking and feeling, probably better than anyone else. The concept of "privileged access" refers to the power of introspection; that is, I have "privileged access" to my own feelings, which I can know directly but you (or anyone else) can only infer. You only know what I am feeling if I tell you, or if you are lucky enough or sharp enough to infer my feelings from observing me.

There is certainly something right in this. People do know their own thoughts and feelings in ways that others cannot match. Introspection is one source of self-knowledge. It has limits, though. One

DENNIS THE MENACE

Ketcham
7-8

©1991, North America Syndicate

Dennis the Menace used by permission of Hank Ketcham Enterprises and © North America Syndicate.

"MOM, WHAT DO I FEEL LIKE DOING?"

Young children believe that parents know them better than they know themselves.

is developmental. Many children think that their knowledge of their own inner states is no match for parental knowledge. In one study, children were asked, "Who knows best what kind of person you really are, deep down inside?" Privileged access would mean that everyone should say "I know myself best." But up until about the age of 11, children were more likely to say that their parents knew best (Rosenberg, 1979). The children thought that if they and their parents disagreed about some trait in the child, the parent would more likely be correct. This is remarkable: Children believe that their parents know them better than the children know themselves.

A more systematic and profound attack on introspection began with an influential article by Richard Nisbett and Timothy Wilson in 1977. They proposed that people do not really have much in the way of privileged access, and hence when they look inside they simply make mistakes, guess, or give what they assume are plausible or socially desirable answers. In a series of studies, Nisbett and Wilson and their colleagues showed that people often do not realize how their minds work. For example, in one study people had to choose which stockings to buy, and by scrambling the sequence the researchers were able to

---

INTROSPECTION the process by which a person examines the contents of his or her mind and mental states

show that most shoppers just chose whichever one they saw last. But they didn't realize what they were doing. Instead of saying "I just chose the last one," they said they chose based on color or softness (Nisbett & Wilson, 1977).

Another failure of introspection was shown in a study of how young men are affected by sexy car ads (Smith & Engel, 1968). The different ads emphasized each car's best features: One got good gas mileage, another had a good safety record, and so forth. One of the ads also featured a pretty young woman wearing only a dark sweater and black lace panties and holding a large spear. In different sessions, the attractive model was paired with different cars. The results showed that the men tended to choose whichever car was paired with the attractive woman. But when asked to explain their choice of car, the men never invoked the scantily clad, spear-carrying young woman; instead, they explained their choice on the basis of whatever was good about that car (e.g., "A good safety record is really important to me.")

Nisbett and Wilson's (1977) claim that people do not know their own minds met fierce resistance in some quarters. We noted in Chapter 1 that science tends to be self-correcting, so that the march of progress can gradually get closer and closer to the truth as new theories are tested and improved. In crucial respects, Nisbett and Wilson were right: People often do not know what goes on inside their minds. In other respects, however, they may have overstated the case. Sometimes people do know what they are thinking and feeling.

The difference lies partly in the duplex mind. As you may recall from Chapter 2, the duplex mind has two parts, one of which engages in automatic, nonconscious processing of information, while the other involves processes of which we are consciously aware. Introspection is a conscious process. The automatic system does a great deal of work that the conscious part of the mind does not know about or understand.

Is introspection valid? People can correctly know what they think and feel. On the other hand, they may not know why they are thinking or feeling something. Terry may be correct when he tells you that he did not like a novel that he read. You can believe his answer (assuming he is not deliberately lying) when he tells you whether he liked it or not. But his explanation of why he disliked it is less reliable. He may have disliked it for many reasons of which he is not aware.

LOOKING AT OTHERS: SOCIAL COMPARISON

Sometimes self-knowledge requires looking at other people. It may seem surprising that you learn about yourself by looking to others, but other people are vital to self-knowledge. In social comparison, you learn not the facts about yourself, but what value they have—in the context of what other people are like. Suppose, for example, that you score 126 on a test, or you discover that you can swim a mile in half an hour. Is that good or bad? By itself, neither. It is only good or bad in comparison to what others do.

The theory of **social comparison** (Festinger, 1954) laid out the power and the processes in which people learn about themselves by comparing themselves to others. Many facts about the self (such as swimming a mile in half an hour) don't carry much weight by themselves and only become meaningful in comparison to others. Social comparison is another instance (like the looking-glass self described earlier) of "putting people first"—we get the information we need, even about ourselves, by focusing on other people.

But to whom do you compare yourself? The most useful comparisons involve people in your same general category, whatever that might be. Comparing your swimming times to those of Michael Phelps, the legendary swimmer who won 14 Olympic gold medals, isn't going to be very enlightening, especially if you are a female, middle-aged, overweight swimmer who never learned how to do flip turns.

Michael Phelps is an upward comparison target for swimmers. If you compare yourself as a swimmer to him, you will probably feel bad.

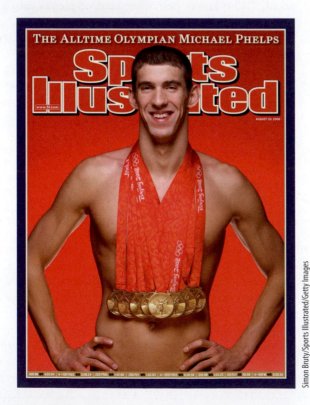

THE ALLTIME OLYMPIAN MICHAEL PHELPS

Simon Bruty/Sports Illustrated/Getty Images

SOCIAL COMPARISON examining the difference between oneself and another person

Sometimes people deliberately compare themselves to others who are better or worse. **Upward social comparisons**, involving people better than you, can inspire you to want to do better in order to reach their level. (However, they can also be discouraging.) **Downward social comparisons**, against people worse off than yourself, can make you feel good.

Sometimes people compare themselves to others who are close by, such as their friends and family members. Such comparisons can be hard on the relationship, especially for the one who doesn't come out looking good. It's fine for your sister or your husband to be a swimming champ if you aren't a competitive swimmer yourself; in fact, the other's success may reflect favorably on you. But if you are a serious swimmer and your partner consistently does better than you, you may be upset by this comparison, and that can drive you to put some distance between the two of you (Tesser, 1988).

SELF-PERCEPTION

Yet another theory about where self-knowledge comes from is that people learn about themselves in the same way they learn about others—by observing behavior and drawing conclusions. In a sense, this is the opposite of introspection theory, because it dismisses the whole "privileged access" issue. There is no special route to self-knowledge. You see what you do, and you draw conclusions about what you are like. This seemed like a radical theory to many social psychologists when it was proposed by social psychologist Daryl Bem in 1965. However, Bem's **self-perception theory** does not really claim that people have no privileged access to knowing their inner feelings and states. In fact, Bem proposed that when people did have such information, they might not rely on self-perception processes. But sometimes

looking inside is not adequate, and in those cases people are swayed by self-perception. For example, Lucy might say that she believes in God and thinks people ought to go to church, but somehow she never manages to get herself there. At some point she may notice this fact about herself and conclude that her religious convictions are perhaps somewhat weaker than she had always thought. If religion really mattered to her, she probably would manage to get to church once in a while. (Alternatively, she might decide that God doesn't really care whether she attends church or not.)

One important application of self-perception theory is the overjustification effect, described in *Money Matters*.

THE FLUCTUATING IMAGE(S) OF SELF

So far we have spoken about self-knowledge as the mass of information the person has and carries with him or her all the time. But social psychologists have discovered a smaller, in some ways more important, self-concept that changes much more easily and readily. Called the **phenomenal self** or the **working self-concept** (Jones & Gerard, 1967; Markus & Kunda, 1986), it is the image of self that is currently active in

---

UPWARD SOCIAL COMPARISON comparing yourself to people better than you

DOWNWARD SOCIAL COMPARISON comparing yourself to people worse off than you

SELF-PERCEPTION THEORY the theory that people observe their own behavior to infer what they are thinking and how they are feeling

PHENOMENAL SELF (WORKING SELF-CONCEPT) the image of self that is currently active in the person's thoughts

INTRINSIC MOTIVATION wanting to perform an activity for its own sake

EXTRINSIC MOTIVATION performing an activity because of something that results from it

OVERJUSTIFICATION EFFECT the tendency for intrinsic motivation to diminish for activities that have become associated with rewards

---

MONEY Matters

Doing It for Money, Not Love

One of the most important and dramatic instances of self-perception involves motivation. Early on, social psychologists learned to distinguish between intrinsic and extrinsic motivation (Deci, 1971). **Intrinsic motivation** refers to wanting to perform an activity for its own sake. The activity is an end in itself. Someone might be intrinsically motivated to paint, for example, because he enjoys the process of dabbing colors onto a canvas and takes satisfaction in creating a beautiful or striking picture.

Extrinsic motivation, in contrast, refers to performing an activity because of something that results from it. The activity is a means to some other end—it is pursued for what it accomplishes or leads to, rather than for the activity itself. A person who is extrinsically motivated to paint might paint in order to make money. This painter might be very motivated and might work very hard, even if she did not really like painting much at all. One test would be whether the person would choose to spend free time doing the activity, in the absence of external rewards

or incentives. An intrinsically motivated painter might well spend a free Sunday afternoon painting, but an extrinsically motivated painter would not (unless there was money or some other incentive).

Self-perception theory led to the prediction that extrinsic motivations would gradually win out over intrinsic ones when both were relevant. This is called the **overjustification effect**—the tendency for intrinsic motivation to diminish for activities that have become associated with rewards. Essentially, overjustification means that rewards transform play into work. Mark Twain understood this concept long before psychologists did. In *The Adventures of Tom Sawyer*, Twain wrote:

> There are wealthy gentlemen in England who drive four-horse passenger coaches twenty or thirty miles on a daily line, in the summer, because the privilege costs them considerable money; but if they were offered wages for the service that would turn it into work then they would resign.

Take the intrinsically motivated painter, and suppose that someone then began to pay him to paint. The painter would gradually see himself painting away and getting paid for it. And the logical inference would be that he is painting for the money—which implies that he doesn't really love to paint for its own sake. Accordingly, over time, being paid to paint would make the painter less and less intrinsically motivated to paint.

Extrinsic rewards can create confusion in people who are engaging in an activity they love to do. People begin to wonder why they are doing the activity, for enjoyment or for pay. Reggie Jackson, a baseball player whose salary at the time was $975,000 per year, was once asked why he played baseball. He said, "A lot of it is the money, but I'd be playing if I was making [only] $150,000." Bill Russell, the former basketball star, said, "I remember that the game lost some of its magical qualities for me once I thought seriously about playing for a living."

The overjustification effect has been confirmed in many studies (Deci, Koestner, & Ryan, 1999). If people get extrinsic rewards for doing something they intrinsically like to do, eventually the intrinsic motivation grows weaker and the person orients the activity more and more to its extrinsic rewards. In the first demonstrations of this pattern, students performed puzzles and were either paid or not paid for solving them (Deci, 1971). The researchers then left each student alone for a brief period and secretly observed whether the student continued to work on the puzzles (a sign of intrinsic motivation, because it indicated that the person enjoyed the puzzles enough to work on them when there was no reward). Students who had been paid showed a sharp drop in their interest in doing the puzzles once the pay stopped (see ▶ **FIGURE 3.3**). In contrast, students who had

Paying children to get good grades may undermine their intrinsic motivation for studying.

done the same number of puzzles but had never been paid continued to find them interesting. Thus, being paid made people think, "I only do these for money," and they no longer liked to do them for their own sake. Extrinsic motivation (money) had replaced intrinsic motivation (fun). Play had become work.

A crucial and revealing factor is whether the rewards are expected during the activity, as opposed to coming as a surprise afterward. You would only infer that somebody is painting for the sake of the money if the person knew in advance that painting would bring money. If the person painted and then received some money afterward, unexpectedly, you would not conclude that money was the driving force. The same logic applies to the self. When people perform an activity and anticipate they will be paid for it, their intrinsic interest in the task diminishes. In contrast, an unexpected reward does not alter their intrinsic motivation (Lepper, Greene, & Nisbett, 1973; Deci et al., 1999).

You might think that people would know directly whether they desire and enjoy some activity, and that extrinsic rewards would make little difference. (Recall the earlier discussion of introspection and "privileged access.") Certainly people do know to some extent what they want and what they like. But self-perception processes still have some influence. Thus, parents who want education to be intrinsically motivating to their children should think twice about

paying them for good grades. The money may cause confusion about why they are trying to get good grades: Is it because learning is fun, or is it because they receive money for good grades? Actually, there is some evidence that when rewards convey a clear message that "you're great!" they do not undermine intrinsic motivation (Rosenfeld, Folger, & Adelman, 1980), possibly because people like to be good at things. Moreover, sometimes people may say they like something but still not do it as frequently (Deci et al., 1999). ■

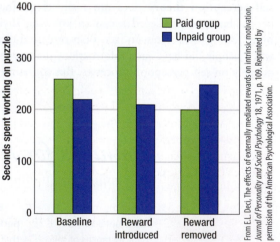

▶ **FIGURE 3.3** Average number of seconds participants in paid and unpaid groups spent working on a puzzle at baseline (before a reward was introduced to the paid group), when the reward was introduced, and after the reward was removed (Deci, 1971, p. 109).

the person's thoughts. Put another way, when you are self-aware, you are usually only aware of a small part of all the information you have about yourself. Each situation summons up only a few relevant aspects of the self, and these constitute the phenomenal self. The difference is comparable to that between all the information you have in your computer and what is currently displayed on the screen. The phenomenal self is what you see on the screen right now: It is only a small part of the total, but it is the part that you can use actively.

Different situations can call up different parts of self-knowledge into the phenomenal self. For one thing, whatever aspects of you stand out as unusual often become prominent in the phenomenal self. Thus, if you are the only woman in a roomful of men, you are probably quite aware of being a woman, whereas if you are among other women, your femaleness does not stand out so much and you may be less aware of it. Note that you are still a woman in either case, and of course you know it. The difference is merely what stands out in your mind (McGuire, McGuire, Child, & Fujioka 1978; McGuire, McGuire, Child, & Winton, 1979).

This sense of yourself as standing out is especially important when you are the only member of some category, such as a racial or ethnic group. If you are, say, the only African American on a committee, you may be acutely aware that other people think of you as African American, and you may identify more strongly than you would otherwise with being an African American. (Note that this is ironic, in a way. Some people might guess that you would identify yourself more as an African American if you were in a group that was composed entirely of African Americans.) Being the lone member of some category heightens self-awareness and can impair performance (Lord & Saenz, 1985). It can even make you feel that you are responsible for your group's reputation, which greatly increases the pressure. If you are the lone African American in the group and you perform badly, your performance may reflect on African Americans in general (Croizet, Désert, Dutrévis, & Leyens, 2001; Gonzales, Blanton, & Williams, 2002; Hyde & Kling, 2001; Steele, 1997, 1999; Steele & Aronson, 1995).

An important aspect of the self is being the same across time. Yet people think of themselves somewhat differently when focused on the present as opposed to the future (Wakslak, Nussbaum, Liberman, & Trope, 2008). When you think about yourself as you are today, the thought tends to be full of specific and concrete facts, such as being a student in this social psychology course and reading this textbook. In contrast, when you think about yourself in the future, such as a year or two from now, your ideas will tend to be more general and abstract, such as whether you will be engaged in studying and learning in general. Future versions of self have broader categories (a man, as opposed to a tall thin man with a beard; a sports fan, as opposed to a pro football fan who favors the San Diego Chargers), as compared to present concept of self. In general, the future self-concept is vague, simple, broad, and general, whereas the present self-concept tends to be much more clear-cut, complex, and specific.

WHY PEOPLE SEEK SELF-KNOWLEDGE

In the last section we considered some of the roots of self-knowledge. One additional root of self-knowledge is that people want to know themselves, so in many circumstances they actively seek out information about the self. They take personality tests (even magazine self-tests that have little or no scientific validity), consult horoscopes, spend years and thousands of dollars on psychoanalysis or other therapies that promises to improve self-knowledge, learn to meditate, and above all pay close attention to what others say about them. One former mayor of New York, Ed Koch, made a standard joke out of

Which people are most aware of their own race?

© 2004 Baby Blues Partnership. Reprinted by permission of King Features Syndicate.

the interest in self-knowledge by acknowledging that most people had an opinion about his performance as mayor. Whenever he met someone, instead of asking: "How're you doing?" as is customary, he would ask: "How'm I doing?"

Beginnings of Self-Knowledge. Human beings have a deep thirst for self-knowledge. Some people are more eager than others to learn about themselves, but hardly anyone is indifferent to self-knowledge. The evolutionary origins of the desire for self-knowledge are hard to establish, though one can easily propose many potential benefits that might come from knowing yourself. For example, creatures might have a better idea of which potential mates to pursue if they have a more accurate understanding of their own attractiveness (Kirkpatrick & Ellis, 2001). If you vastly overestimate your sex appeal, you might waste a great deal of time trying to hook up with people who are out of your league. Likewise, if someone challenges you, knowing your own strength and capabilities might dictate whether you choose to fight or back down, and mistakes could be costly.

The long road to social acceptance is one theme of this book, and self-knowledge can be helpful on that road. You need self-knowledge in order to fit in better with others. Will people like me? Am I similar to them? Such questions require self-knowledge. Moreover, as we have seen, cultural groups consist of different roles and different tasks, so it is valuable to know what your strengths and weaknesses are in order to know how best to fit in with the group. You don't want to demand to be the group's cook if you are terrible at cooking, because your bad food might make others dislike and reject you.

Three Reasons for Wanting Self-Knowledge. People want to learn about themselves, but they'd rather learn some things than others. Three main motives shape the quest for self-knowledge. These

three motives sometimes compete against each other, and different motives predominate in different people or different circumstances.

The first motive is the simple desire to learn the truth about oneself, whatever it is. This can be called the **appraisal motive**. It consists of a broad, open-minded curiosity, and its main preference is for information that is both important and reliable (Trope, 1983, 1986). For example, the appraisal motive may motivate people to start out with tasks of medium difficulty, because these offer the most information. If you start out with something that is very easy, then success does not give you much information about whether you have high or low ability, because anyone might succeed at an easy task. By the same token, if you start out with something that is very difficult, then failure does not give you much information about whether you have high or low ability, because anyone might fail at a difficult task.

The second motive, called the **self-enhancement motive**, is the desire to learn favorable or flattering things about the self. Unlike the appraisal motive, the self-enhancement motive can exert considerable bias, driving people to dismiss or ignore criticism while exaggerating or inflating any signs of their good qualities.

The third motive, the **consistency motive**, is a desire to get feedback that confirms what the person already believes about himself or herself. Once people have formed ideas about themselves, they are generally reluctant to revise those opinions. In this respect, self-knowledge is no different from knowledge about many aspects of the world: Once people have formed opinions or beliefs about almost anything, they are resistant to change. The consistency motive is also sometimes called the self-verification motive, which implies that people actively seek to "verify" their self-concepts by obtaining confirmation that what they think about themselves is correct (Swann, 1985, 1987).

To illustrate these three motives, suppose that you believe that you are not very good at sports. The appraisal motive would make you want to get more information about your sports abilities, regardless of what that information might say. The self-

---

APPRAISAL MOTIVE the simple desire to learn the truth about oneself, whatever it is
SELF-ENHANCEMENT MOTIVE the desire to learn favorable or flattering things about the self
CONSISTENCY MOTIVE a desire to get feedback that confirms what the person already believes about himself or herself

74 • **CHAPTER 3** THE SELF

enhancement motive might make you want to learn that you do have some talent at sports after all. (If you can't get such feedback, then the self-enhancement motive might drive you to avoid any more information about yourself at sports, and it might also push you to compensate for your athletic deficiencies by finding out that you are good at other things, such as music or cooking.) And the consistency motive would make you prefer to gain further evidence that you are bad at sports, because that is what you already think.

When Motives Compete. When such conflicts arise between motives, which one wins? Logic would suggest that the answer is based on what is most useful. Accurate information is almost always more useful than false information, because accurate information furnishes the best basis for making good choices. Hence, the appraisal motive should be the strongest.

It isn't, though. When Sedikides (1993) compared the three motives, the appraisal motive emerged as the weakest of the three. Self-enhancement was the strongest. People most want to hear good things about themselves. Their second preference is for confirmation of what they already think (consistency). They do also want accurate information, but the desire for the truth runs a distant third to the desires for favorable and consistent feedback.

Also, people sometimes have more than one reaction to feedback, especially if feeling and thinking pull in different ways. The self-enhancement motive has an especially strong emotional appeal, whereas the consistency motive has more of a cognitive appeal. People may be more willing to believe and accept consistent feedback in terms of their cognitive reactions, but emotionally they will yearn for and prefer flattering, positive feedback. If someone tells you that you are extremely talented, for example—more talented than you had believed—you may find that your logical mind is skeptical of this news, but emotionally you are happy to hear it (Jussim, HsiuJu, & Aiello, 1995; McFarlin & Blascovich, 1981; Shrauger, 1975; Swann, Griffin, Predmore, & Gaines, 1987).

One way of understanding this ranking of self-knowledge motives is to return to the "people first" theme. It is true that accurate knowledge would be the most useful for making decisions. But probably people want to be accepted by others more than they want a valid basis for making decisions. The human emotional system is set up to promote and reward any signs that the person is likely to be accepted by others. Hence, positive, flattering information is the most appealing, because others will like you most if you have good traits.

The fact that the self-enhancement motive is stronger than the appraisal motive means that people want to think well of themselves more than they want to know the truth. One implication is that sometimes people prefer to invalidate feedback, even in advance, if they think it might make them look bad. One of social psychology's best documented patterns of avoiding feedback that could make them look bad is self-handicapping, which is described in *Tradeoffs*.

Tradeoffs

Self-Handicapping

Why would someone get drunk before an important job interview? Why do some students stay out partying all night before an important test? Are underachievers all merely too lazy to get their work done?

An intriguing theory has suggested that some people's problems stem from a strategy called **self-handicapping** (Hirt, Deppe, & Gordon, 1991; Jones & Berglas, 1978; Smith, Snyder, & Perkins, 1983; Snyder & Higgins, 1990). Self-handicapping has been defined as putting obstacles in the way of one's own performance, so that anticipated or possible failure can be blamed on the obstacle instead of on lack of ability. The student who parties all night instead of studying before an exam may not get the best grade, but because that low grade can be blamed on not having studied, it does not signify that the student lacks intelligence.

Self-handicapping was first proposed as a possible explanation of alcohol abuse. Alcohol is widely (and correctly) seen as harmful to performance: Drunk people do not perform as well as sober ones. Hence, someone who fears that he or she will perform badly might find alcohol a convenient excuse.

The excuse appeals especially to someone who has already achieved a reputation for being smart or capable. (The importance of what other people think indicates that self-handicapping is primarily a self-presentational strategy, designed to control how one is perceived by others; Kolditz & Arkin,

© Michael Newman/PhotoEdit   © Gary Conner/PhotoEdit

Do some people turn to alcohol in order to provide themselves with a handy excuse for possible failure?

1982.) Many people who have a big success early in their careers worry that this was just a lucky break, and they fear that they will not be able to do as well again. For example, a rock band might have a big hit with their first recording, which launches them into fame and stardom, but they are afraid that their second recording will not be as good. Fans and critics may hail them as geniuses after the first success, but the band worries that the second album may make everyone reconsider and decide that the band is only a mediocre talent after all. Instead of letting that happen, some band members may develop a drug or alcohol problem. That way, if the second album is not as good, fans and critics can say "They are really talented, and it's too bad that the drug problem is keeping them from producing more great music." Their reputation as geniuses remains intact. Wouldn't you rather be known as a troubled genius than an earnest mediocrity?

Moreover, if the second performance is good, then people will assign extra credit, so the self-handicapper's reputation is even improved: "Look at what a great report she gave, even though she had been on a drinking binge all week. She must really be amazingly smart to do great work despite her drinking problem." Some people, such as those with high self-esteem, are drawn to this advantage, because it enriches one's credit for success (Tice, 1991).

In one series of experiments, participants were told that the purpose was to investigate whether some new drugs had temporary side effects on intelligent performance (Berglas & Jones, 1978). The experimenter explained that one drug temporarily made people smarter and the other made people temporarily less

intelligent (like alcohol). Participants then took a first IQ test. On this test, some people were given unsolvable multiple-choice questions, so they had to guess, but to their surprise the experimenter kept telling them their answers were correct. These participants experienced what is called noncontingent success: They were told they did well, but at some level they had to know that they had not really earned their good rating. In another condition, people were given easier problems and accurately told which ones they got correct (thus, contingent success). All participants were then told that their score was the highest that had been seen in the study so far.

Next, the experimenter asked the participant to choose one of the drugs, in preparation for a second IQ test (which would supposedly verify whether performance improved or got worse). One of the drugs (called Actavil) was supposed to increase intellectual performance, while the other drug (called Pandocrin) was supposed to decrease intellectual performance. Participants who had experienced the noncontingent success overwhelmingly chose the alcohol-like drug Pandocrin that would supposedly make them perform worse (see ▶ **FIGURE 3.4**). Why? They knew the experimenter thought they were brilliant, but they privately doubted they could do as well on the second test, so they wanted the drug that would give them an excuse for poor performance.

There was once a European chess champion named Deschappelles who won nearly all his

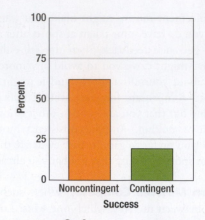

▶ **FIGURE 3.4** Percent of participants in the noncontingent and contingent success groups choosing the alcohol-like drug Pandocrin that supposedly decreased intellectual performance (Berglas & Jones, 1978).

matches. As he got old, however, he felt his mental powers waning, and he worried that smart young chess masters would defeat him. He used a self-handicapping strategy to preserve his reputation: He insisted that he would only play games in which his opponent got the first move (a major advantage in chess) and in which he gave up one of his pieces at the start of the game (another disadvantage for him) (Berglas & Baumeister, 1993). That way, if he lost, he would not lose respect, because the loss would be attributed to his disadvantages; when he won, people would marvel at his ability to overcome those handicaps. ●

Self-Knowledge and the Duplex Mind. The duplex mind is also relevant to the interplay between these conflicting motives. The automatic system tends to favor the self-enhancement motive. When people respond automatically to questions about themselves, they lean toward "everything good is me, and everything bad is not me." Under times of stress, or when people are preoccupied or distracted, this pattern of **automatic egotism** emerges (Paulhus & Levitt, 1987).

Often a conscious override is required in order to furnish a more balanced and consistent view of self. Modesty in particular often seems to require conscious, deliberate control, because people may have a first impulse to say they are wonderful, and they must overcome this impulse in order to offer a more humble account of themselves (Swann, Hixon, Stein-Seroussi, & Gilbert, 1990; Swann, Stein-Seroussi, & Giesler, 1992). It is a quick, automatic reaction to feel good about praise or to feel bad when criticized, but it takes a little more thought and effort to question the praise or to admit that the criticism may be valid. Thus, the different parts of the duplex mind may cultivate self-knowledge in different ways. The automatic system favors automatic egotism ("I'm good in general") while the conscious system can make corrections and strive toward a more balanced, accurate appraisal of the facts.

SELF-HANDICAPPING putting obstacles in the way of one's own performance so that anticipated or possible failure can be blamed on the obstacle instead of on lack of ability

AUTOMATIC EGOTISM response by the automatic system that "everything good is me, and everything bad is not me"

Where Self-Knowledge Comes From

1. The night before an important test, Boozer drinks all night instead of studying. This is an example of
_____.
   (a) self-awareness   (b) self-consciousness
   (c) self-fulfilling prophecy   (d) self-handicapping

2. "Do I like parades? Well, each year there have been several parades in town, and I haven't gone to one yet. I must not like parades." Which theory explains this internal dialogue?
   (a) Cognitive dissonance theory
   (b) Psychological reactance theory
   (c) Psychoanalytic theory
   (d) Self-perception theory

3. A teacher promises one of his preschool students a candy bar for finger painting, a task the student loves to do. The reward is likely to produce _____.
   (a) cognitive dissonance
   (b) downward social comparison
   (c) intrinsic motivation
   (d) the overjustification effect

4. The simple desire to learn the truth about oneself is called the _____ motive.
   (a) appraisal   (b) consistency
   (c) extrinsic   (d) self-enhancement

Self and Information Processing

ANYTHING THAT TOUCHES THE SELF . . .

Every day people process a great deal of information about their social worlds, and the self often exerts influence over how this information gets processed. For one thing, the self serves as a sign of importance: Anything that bears on the self is more likely to be important than things that do not touch the self. As a result, any link to the self makes the mind pay more attention and process more thoroughly.

One of the earliest and most basic effects of the self on information processing is the **self-reference effect**: Information bearing on the self is processed more thoroughly and more deeply, and hence remembered better, than other information. In the initial studies of this effect (Rogers, Kuiper, & Kirker, 1977), participants simply saw a series of words and were asked a question about each word. Sometimes these questions had nothing to do with the self, such as "Is this a long word?" and "Is it a meaningful word?" Other times, however, the question was "Does this word

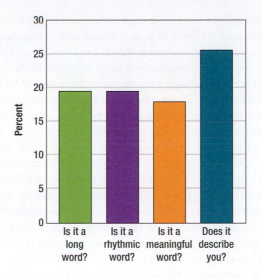

► FIGURE 3.5 The self-reference effect refers to the finding that information related to the self is more memorable than information related to something other than the self (Rogers, Kuiper, & Kirker, 1977).

describe you?" Later on, the researchers gave a surprise test to the participants, asking them to remember as many words on the list as they could. The rate of correct memory depended heavily on which question had been asked, and the questions about the self elicited the best memory (see ► **FIGURE 3.5**). For example, participants were more likely to remember the word *friendly* if they had been asked whether they were *friendly* than whether they knew what friendly meant or whether it was a long word (Rogers et al., 1977; Greenwald & Banaji, 1989; Higgins & Bargh, 1987; Klein & Kihlstrom, 1986; Symons & Johnson, 1997).

The implication was that simply thinking about a word in connection with the self led to better memory. In fact, even if participants answered "No" to the question about whether the word described them, they still remembered the word better than other words. The self apparently operates like a powerful hook, and whatever gets hung on it (even just for a moment) is more likely to be preserved.

A similar pattern has been called the **endowment effect**: Items gain in value to the person who owns them (Kahneman, Knetsch, & Thaler, 1990). If someone asks you how much you would pay for a souvenir mug, you might offer three dollars. If someone gives you the mug and then someone else wants to buy it from you, however, you would be prone to ask for more than three dollars. Somehow the mug became worth more to you during the time you owned it, even if that time was only a few minutes and you did not have any special experiences with

---

SELF-REFERENCE EFFECT the finding that information bearing on the self is processed more thoroughly and more deeply, and hence remembered better, than other information

ENDOWMENT EFFECT the finding that items gain in value to the person who owns them

it that might confer sentimental value. Simply being connected to the self gave it more value. Nor does this work only with cash value: People start to like things more when they own them (Beggan, 1992).

Likewise, things gain in value to the self who chooses them. In one famous demonstration, people either were given a lottery ticket or chose one themselves. Both tickets had identical chances of winning, and therefore objectively they had the same value (Langer, 1975). But when the researchers asked participants how much they would sell the ticket for, the price of the self-chosen tickets was consistently higher than the price of the randomly given tickets. Somehow the process of choosing the ticket oneself made it seem more valuable to the person who chose it.

Most people do not choose their names, but names are closely linked to the self. People develop affection for their names and for things that become connected to their names. One well-established finding is that people like the letters in their names more than they like other letters in the alphabet (Hoorens & Todorova, 1988; Jones, Pelham, Mirenberg, & Hetts, 2002; Nuttin, 1985, 1987; Prentice & Miller, 1992). In fact, not liking your own name is one sign of unconscious low self-esteem (Gebauer, Riketta, Broemer, & Maio, 2008).

The fact that people like the letters of their names may seem silly and trivial, but it can actually affect major life decisions (Gallucci, 2003; Pelham, Carvallo, DeHart, & Jones, 2003; Pelham, Mirenberg, & Jones, 2002). A person's choice of occupation and residence is sometimes swayed by this liking for one's own name. People named George or Georgia are more likely to decide to live in Georgia than in Virginia, whereas people named Virginia show the opposite preference. People named

Dennis or Denise are more likely than other people to become dentists; those named Larry or Laura are more likely to become lawyers. (And do you think it's just a coincidence that the Boy Scouts of America organization was founded by a man named Boyce?) You might think that that is a silly and shallow reason to choose one's occupation or home, and perhaps it is. People probably do not consciously think: "I would rather live in a place that is spelled with letters from my name." Rather, these effects (which are statistically significant, though quite small) probably arise because of the duplex mind. That is, the automatic system has some positive feelings connected with the name, and so it serves up a bit of positive feeling when those letters arise. When the person is trying to choose an occupation or a home, certain options just somehow "feel right," even though the person probably cannot consciously explain why. Becoming a dentist just intuitively feels a bit more appealing to someone named Dennis than to someone named Frank. This won't be enough to sway somebody who hates dentistry into choosing it as his life's work, but a few people who are on the borderline between dentistry and other choices might find themselves drawn to the field that sounds more like their name. (You may want to keep this effect in mind when naming your children!)

CAN THE SELF-CONCEPT CHANGE?

People usually believe that they have remained the same person over much of their lives. Your identity certainly changes, but it does so slowly. You have the same social security number, linked to the same tax status. Your name remains the same (even if you decide to change your last name when you marry, your first name is unaffected). You belong to the same family, though you may gradually add new members to this family (such as by marrying or having a baby). Once you start your career, you tend to stay in the same occupation for most of your life, and until recently it was common to spend one's entire career working for the same organization. Your gender remains the same in most cases, and you inhabit the same body for your entire life.

People do change, however. Children add new knowledge and skills as they grow up. Adults may take up new hobbies or break bad habits. Your body is continuous, but it changes too, first growing taller and stronger, then often growing fatter and less flexible, and finally developing wrinkles, shrinking, and acquiring other signs of old age.

Revising Self-Knowledge. Our concern here is with the possibilities of change in the self. When do people change so much that they also revise their self-concept? There are several plausible theories.

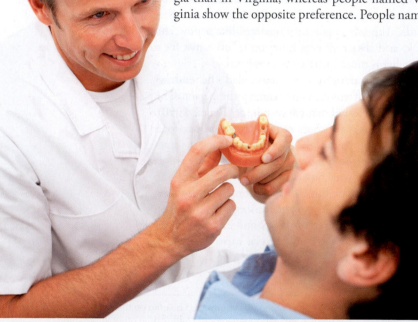

Dennis thought his career choice "just felt right somehow."

© Stockdisc Premium/Alamy

One is that you can simply decide to change how you think about yourself, and your actions will come around to reflect the new you (Jones, Rhodewalt, Berglas, & Skelton, 1981; Rhodewalt & Agustdottir, 1986). Another is the reverse: You can decide to change your behavior, and a change in self-concept will follow (see the material on cognitive dissonance in Chapter 7). Both are plausible, but neither gets at the full story.

The evidence suggests that one's social world is a powerful source of stability in the self. Other people expect you to remain pretty much the same. In part, this arises because people see other people in terms of stable traits, even though they do not see themselves that way (Jones & Nisbett, 1971). Seeing other people in terms of their personality traits reflects the assumption that people mostly remain the same over long periods of time, and indeed there is some evidence that in many respects personality traits do remain fairly stable over long stretches, even from childhood into adulthood (Backteman & Magnusson, 1981; Caspi & Roberts, 2001; Epstein, 1979; Eron & Huesmann, 1990).

The expectation that people stay the same can become a kind of pressure to remain constant. Many students notice this when they return home after a year or two at university, especially if they have not stayed in regular contact with everyone back home. They feel that their parents still treat them and regard them the way they were years earlier. Sometimes they find that their old friends from high school likewise seem to expect them to be the person they were back in high school.

Changing the Looking Glass. Research has confirmed that self-concept change is most common, and possibly easiest, when one's social environment changes (Harter, 1993). For example, self-esteem tends to stay relatively stable when one lives in the same social circle, and changes in self-esteem tend to accompany moving to a new school (especially going from high school to college) or a new home. One explanation is that people change gradually, but their social circle tends not to notice this and therefore pressures them to stay the same. When the person moves, the new social circle can see the new version of the person that has emerged from these gradual changes.

Earlier we discussed the concept of the looking-glass self. You know yourself by means of others. Hence changing your social circle is a promising way to change the self. Again, inner processes are tied to interpersonal relations, so when the social circle changes, the inner self may change too.

A similar conclusion emerged from studies on brainwashing. The techniques of brainwashing first attracted research attention during the Korean War, when Chinese communists sought to change the views of captured American soldiers. The Chinese had no grand theory about how to brainwash Americans, so they just experimented with different methods. At first they tried exposing the prisoners to all-day sessions of propaganda and indoctrination, telling them how great communism was and how bad American capitalism was. This did not work very well. Then the Chinese realized that the problem was not in what happened during the day. Rather, the problem was that every night the prisoners were sent back to the barracks with the other American prisoners, where each man's American identity reasserted itself. The Chinese found that brainwashing became much more successful and effective if they kept the prisoners separate from each other. That way, the American identity and American values were not bolstered by social contacts with other Americans, and the prisoners became much more malleable (Group for the Advancement of Psychiatry, 1957).

These findings about self-concept change support the view that what goes on inside the person is mainly there to serve interpersonal processes. Many people assume that the inner self is fixed, strong, and stable, and that what they do with other people is simply an expression of an inner "true" self. But that view appears to be mistaken. The important and powerful forces originate in the interactions and relationships between people, and what goes on inside the individual adapts to those interpersonal processes. This is yet another instance of our theme that inner processes serve interpersonal functions.

Promoting Change. When people want to change, therefore, it is important to use the social environment rather than fight against it. When people seek to change some aspect of themselves, such as trying to quit smoking or become more physically fit, they do best if they enlist the support of other people in their lives. It is hard to quit smoking if your spouse smokes and wants you to smoke with him or her. In contrast, if your spouse wants you to quit smoking, he or she will probably support your efforts to change, and your chances of success are improved (Heatherton & Nichols, 1994).

Indeed, one effective strategy for change is to persuade everyone else that you have changed. Once they expect you to act in a new and different way, you are more likely to stick to that new line of behavior. Thinking of yourself in the different way is not enough; it is more important and more powerful to get others to think of you in that way. (This also confirms our theme of putting people first: You use other people to help you to change.) In one experiment, people were induced to think of themselves in a new way, either introverted or extraverted. This was accomplished by asking people loaded questions

Preacher Pat Robertson experienced a self-concept change. Initially he felt that God wanted him to stay out of politics, but later he became extensively involved in politics and even campaigned for president of the United States.

AP Photo/Peter Southwick

their lives to fit the new version. For example, the preacher Pat Robertson published an autobiography, in which he mentioned that God had instructed him to stay away from politics. Later, Robertson decided to run for president. A new, updated version of his autobiography appeared, conveniently omitting the earlier message from God about keeping out of politics. The new version said that God wanted Robertson to run for office.

Such revisions of memory have been studied by social psychologists, most notably Michael Ross (1989). Ross and his colleagues have concluded that most of the time people want to believe they remain the same, but sometimes they also want to believe that they have changed, and they shuffle and edit the facts in their memory to fit whichever belief is more relevant. Thus, if people change their attitudes, they may forget what they used to believe, so that they think the new attitude does not reflect a change—rather, they say, "I thought so all along." In contrast, if they want to believe they have changed when they haven't, they may retroactively distort how they used to be. In one memorable demonstration, researchers looked at study skills enhancement programs at universities, which are designed to teach students how to study better. Most universities have such programs, but objective evidence suggests that they do not really accomplish much in the way of making people into better students or enabling them to get better grades. Students who take these programs, however, want to believe that they have improved. They persuade themselves that the program has worked by revising their memory of how bad they were before (Conway & Ross, 1984). For example, if a student's study skills rated a 5 out of 10 before the program, and the program accomplished nothing, the student would rate a 5 after it as well—but she might tell herself afterward that she really had been "more like a 3" before the program, so she can believe that she really did improve.

One of the most elegant demonstrations of how memory distorts the facts to fit the self-concept involved a study of women's menstrual periods (Ross, 1989). An initial survey revealed that some women thought their periods were generally quite unpleasant, whereas others thought theirs were mild and innocuous. The researchers asked the women to record their feelings and sensations on a daily basis through a couple of periods. After a month or more, the women were asked to rate how bad those periods had been. By comparing the daily ratings with the retrospective (a month later) ratings, the researchers could see how memory was distorted. Each woman's beliefs about her general reactions biased her recall. That is, the women who thought their periods were generally bad tended to recall the periods as having been worse than they had said at the time. Conversely,

(e.g., "What do you dislike about loud parties?"; Fazio, Effrein, & Falender, 1981). Some participants in the experiment answered these questions when sitting alone in a room, talking to a tape recorder, with a guarantee that their responses would be anonymous. These participants showed no sign of self-concept change. In contrast, other participants answered the same questions by speaking face-to-face with another person. These participants did change, not only in how they later saw themselves, but even in how introverted or extraverted they acted with a new, different person (Schlenker, Dlugolecki, & Doherty, 1994; Tice, 1992). The interpersonal context was necessary for changing the inner self.

Thus, one route to self-concept change involves internalizing your recent behavior. First you act in a certain way, and then gradually you come to think of yourself as being the kind of person who acts that way. Other people play a crucial role as well; acting that way by yourself, in secret, does not seem to produce much effect on the self-concept. In contrast, getting others to see you as that kind of person is helpful toward making you believe that you are that kind of person. Again, self and identity require social validation, a theme to which we will return later in the chapter in the section on self-presentation.

New Self, New Story. Once the self-concept has changed, people tend to revise their stories about

the women who thought their periods were generally not so bad recalled their periods as milder than they had rated them when they were occurring. We constantly revise our memories based on beliefs we hold about ourselves.

[QUIZ YOURSELF]

Self and Information Processing

1. The finding that we recall information better when it is relevant to the self is called the _____.
   (a) distinctiveness effect
   (b) hindsight bias
   (c) self-importance bias
   (d) self-reference effect

2. When she visited San Francisco, Letitia bought several handcrafted necklaces for $10 each. When she got home, her sister offered to buy one for $10, but Letitia refused. She wanted $15 for it instead. This example illustrates the _____ effect.
   (a) distinctiveness
   (b) endowment
   (c) intrinsic
   (d) overjustification

3. All other things being equal, which profession is Tex most likely to choose?
   (a) Bus driver
   (b) Car salesperson
   (c) Taxi driver
   (d) All of the above are equally likely.

4. When a bad event happens to a person, if it is extremely unpleasant people remember it as being _____, and if it was mildly unpleasant people remember it as being _____.
   (a) better than it was; better than it was
   (b) better than it was; worse than it was
   (c) worse than it was; better than it was
   (d) worse than it was; worse than it was

Self-Esteem, Self-Deception, and Positive Illusions

SELF-ESTEEM

Self-esteem refers to how favorably someone evaluates himself or herself. People with high self-esteem hold very favorable views, which usually means they consider themselves to be competent, likable, attractive, and morally good people. In principle, low self-esteem would be the opposite; that is, you might think that people with low self-esteem would regard themselves as incompetent, ugly, unlikable, and morally wicked. In practice, however, few people regard themselves in such strongly negative terms. A more common form of low self-esteem is simply the absence of strong positive views about the self. Thus, the person with high self-esteem says "I am great," but the person with low self-esteem says "I am so-so" rather than "I am terrible."

People with high self-esteem are not hard to understand. They think they have good traits, and they want others to share that view; they are willing to take chances and try new things because they think they will succeed. People with low self-esteem are the greater puzzle. What do they want, and what is it like to be one of them? There have been many different theories and assumptions about low self-esteem, but research is converging to show which of them are correct. Here are some of the main conclusions about people with low self-esteem:

- They do not want to fail. (This is contrary to some early theories, including those based on consistency, which assumed that people with low self-esteem would seek to confirm their bad impressions of themselves.) Indeed, people with low self-esteem have the same goals and strivings that people with high self-esteem have, such as to be successful and to get others to like them. The difference is mainly that people with low self-esteem are less confident that they can achieve these positive goals (McFarlin & Blascovich, 1981).

- Their ideas about themselves are conflicted and uncertain, a pattern called "self-concept confusion." When asked questions about themselves, people with low self-esteem are more likely than other people to say they do not know or are not sure; more likely to give contradictory answers, such as being both "calm" and "nervous"; and more likely to describe themselves differently on different days (Campbell, 1990).

- They focus on self-protection instead of self-enhancement. (**Self-protection** means trying to avoid loss of esteem.) People with low self-esteem go through life looking to avoid failure, embarrassment, rejection, and other misfortunes, even if this means not taking chances or pursuing opportunities (Baumeister, Hutton, & Tice, 1989).

- They are more prone to emotional highs and lows. Events affect them more strongly than other people, and so they are more vulnerable to mood swings and other emotional overreactions (Campbell, Chew, & Scratchley, 1991).

In recent decades, many psychologists have turned their attention to self-esteem, both as a research area and as a practical enterprise. The practitioners' focus

---

SELF-ESTEEM how favorably someone evaluates himself or herself
SELF-PROTECTION trying to avoid loss of esteem

WILEY@NON-SEQUITUR.COM DIST. BY UNIVERSAL PRESS SYND. WWW.UCOMICS.COM

Many people believe that low self-esteem lies at the root of many social and psychological problems.

is on how to increase self-esteem. They believe that low self-esteem lies at the root of many social and psychological problems and that American society as a whole can benefit from widespread efforts to boost nearly everyone's self-esteem (Branden, 1994).

Is the United States really suffering from an epidemic of low self-esteem? Evidence since the 1970s suggests otherwise; in fact, average self-esteem scores have been rising (Twenge, 2006; Twenge & Campbell, 2001). If anything, self-esteem in the United States is unrealistically high.

One of the first illustrations came in a simple little survey that asked people to rate their driving ability as above average, average, or below average. Almost all (90%) of the people said they were above average (Svenson, 1981). Statistically, one would expect only about half the people to be above average (and about half below it, of course). This finding of 90% above average was at first regarded as a strange and isolated curiosity, but soon similar results began to accumulate from other studies. In a large survey of a million high school students (College Board, 1976–1977; Gilovich, 1991), only 2% said they were below average in leadership ability (70% said they were above average). Even more strikingly, not one in a million claimed to be below average in the ability to get along with others, whereas 25% claimed to be in the top 1%!

What about particular groups, such as women and African Americans, who are sometimes thought to suffer from low self-esteem? In fact, their self-esteem is often pretty healthy too, despite various alarmist claims that it is low. Women's self-esteem is only slightly below that of men (Kling, Hyde, Showers, & Buswell, 1999). The difference is largest during adolescence, and it seems to be large not because the self-esteem of adolescent girls is especially low but because many teenage boys are very egotistical. Women and girls tend to be critical of their bodies, whereas boys and men think their bodies are just fine, and this discrepancy probably accounts for most if not all of the gender difference in self-esteem. (There is no sign that women regard themselves as less intelligent than men, for example, or less able to get along with others.) Meanwhile, African Americans actually have somewhat higher self-esteem than other Americans, though again the difference is not very large (Crocker & Major, 1989; Gray-Little & Hafdahl, 2000; Twenge & Crocker, 2002). Their high self-esteem makes African Americans somewhat unusual, because other minority groups average lower than European Americans in self-esteem (Twenge & Crocker, 2002). Still, no group really scores very low in self-esteem; the differences are just a matter of whether the group regards itself as significantly above average, or closer to average.

REALITY AND ILLUSION

The preceding section focused on self-esteem, which entails how well a person thinks or feels about self. Whether those feelings are accurate is another matter. Are self-concepts accurate, or filled with illusion?

In the 1960s, clinical psychologists noticed that depression is linked to low self-esteem and began to theorize that depressed people have a distorted perception of the world. They began studying the cognitive strategies of depressed people to see how those distortions arose (Beck, 1976, 1988; Beck & Burns, 1978; Beck, Rush, Shaw, & Emery, 1979; Clark, Beck, & Brown, 1989; Ottaviani & Beck, 1987; Shaw & Beck, 1977). For example, do depressed people ignore their own successes and good traits, while exaggerating their faults and failures? Some researchers began to conduct careful studies on how depressed people perceived and interpreted events.

These studies eventually produced a very surprising result. Depressed people don't seem to distort things very much; rather, normal (nondepressed) people are the ones who distort. Depressed people seem to be pretty equal in taking the blame for failure and the credit for success, whereas normal people reject blame for failure while claiming plenty of credit for success. Depressed people are pretty accurate about estimating how much control they have over events, whereas normal people overestimate control (Alloy & Abramson, 1979). Depressed people are pretty accurate at guessing who likes them and who doesn't, whereas normal people overestimate how favorably other people regard them (Lewinsohn, Mischel, Chaplin, & Barton, 1980). Instead of trying to understand how depressed people have learned to distort their thinking in a bad way, it seemed imperative to learn how normal people distort their thinking in a positive way. Somehow depressed people—unlike happy, healthy people—simply fail to put a positive spin on the events in their lives.

In 1988, social psychologists Shelley Taylor and Jonathon Brown provided an influential summary of the ways in which well-adjusted, mentally healthy people distort their perception of events. They listed three "positive illusions" that characterize the thought processes of these normal people:

- People overestimate their good qualities (and underestimate their faults). Normal people think they are smarter, more attractive, more likable, more virtuous, easier to get along with, and in other ways better than they actually are. This explains the "above average effect" already noted, by which most people claim to be better than the average person.

- People overestimate their perceived control over events. Normal people tend to think they are largely in control of events in their lives and that what happens to them is generally the result of their own actions. They believe they have the power to make their lives better and to prevent many misfortunes and problems from occurring.

- People are unrealistically optimistic. They think their own personal chances of getting a good job, having a gifted child, acquiring a great deal of money, and experiencing other positive events are better than the chances of the average person like themselves. Conversely, they think their chances of being unemployed, getting a divorce, having a retarded child, losing a lot of money, being severely injured in an accident, and experiencing other misfortunes are lower than the average person's chances. Each person tends to see his or her own future as somewhat brighter than other people's.

Don't people get into trouble because of these illusions? You might think that these illusions would create a broad overconfidence that could cause people to make poor decisions, such as overcommitting themselves, taking foolish chances, or investing money unwisely. They may sometimes have that effect, but apparently people have a remarkable capacity to set their illusions aside and be realistic when they have to make a decision. People have a special mind-set that goes with making choices (Gollwitzer & Kinney, 1989; Taylor & Gollwitzer, 1995). Once the decision is made, people then go right back to their optimistic and confident outlook.

Positive illusions flourish partly because of wishful thinking, also called self-deception. The next section will consider some ways people manage this.

HOW PEOPLE FOOL THEMSELVES

How do people sustain these positive illusions? Don't everyday experiences burst their bubble and force them to face reality? Someone who believes falsely that he is a genius at math might sign up for an advanced math class, for example, and getting a C or D would seemingly dispel any such illusions of mathematical brilliance. The fact that people seem able to keep these positive illusions intact for long periods of time has prompted social psychologists to examine **self-deception strategies**, the mental tricks people use to help them believe things that are false. Normally, of course, these are false beliefs that the person wants to be true.

If people's self-concepts were more affected by their failures than by their successes, then most people would probably consider themselves below average! But we have seen that the opposite is true. Self-deception is a pattern of cognitive tricks and strategies that people use to dismiss or diminish the impact of failures and other kinds of bad feedback. The power of bad feedback can be offset by these mental tricks as long as people use them in a biased fashion, so that successes and good feedback are accepted while failures and bad ones are questioned, discredited, and forgotten.

One self-deception strategy is called the **self-serving bias** (Gonzales, Pederson, Manning, & Wette, 1990; Weary, 1980; Zuckerman, 1979). This is a common method of interpreting events (and hence an important part of attribution theory—a broad attempt to explain how people interpret all sorts of social events and outcomes—to be discussed in Chapter 5). Essentially, the person claims credit for success but denies blame for failure. Getting a good grade on a test, for example, is taken as a sign that "I'm really smart and good at this." Getting a bad grade is more likely to be chalked up to external factors, such as not having had a good night's sleep, not having studied the right things, or bad luck. (Also recall the *Tradeoffs* box on self-handicapping, which helps make sure that the self gets credit for success but no blame for failure.)

A related strategy is to be more skeptical and critical of bad feedback than good feedback. In several studies, researchers had students take a test and then told them at random that they had done either very well or very poorly on the test. Even though they

---

SELF-DECEPTION STRATEGIES mental tricks people use to help them believe things that are false
SELF-SERVING BIAS a pattern in which people claim credit for success but deny blame for failure

© Cleve Bryant/PhotoEdit

If nobody else can do this, I must be pretty special.

had taken exactly the same test, the people who were told they had done well rated the test as fair and effective, but the people who were told they had done badly thought the test was unfair and poorly designed (Kunda, 1990; Pyszczynski, Greenberg, & Holt, 1985; Wyer & Frey, 1983). Such tactics enable people to avoid having to revise their self-concepts in light of failure, enabling them to keep their positive illusions intact.

The basic mental processes of attention and memory can also help by being selective. Many people end up remembering good things better than bad things, partly because they spend more time thinking about them and mentally replaying them (Baumeister & Cairns, 1992; Crary, 1966; Kuiper & Derry, 1982; Mischel, Ebbesen, & Zeiss, 1976). Although occasionally failures or criticism stick in one's mind, people usually try not to dwell on them, whereas they enjoy reliving their triumphs and great moments. Selectively focusing on good things can help counteract the power of bad things.

Controlling what you pay attention to has been called the "junk mail theory of self-deception" (Greenwald, 1988). You can often recognize a piece of junk mail just by looking at the envelope, so you can throw it away without having to open it and read the contents. In similar fashion, when bad or unwelcome news comes your way, you can often just recognize it as bad from the first and hence not spend much time absorbing it. In this way, you reduce its impact and make it easier to forget.

Another strategy makes use of the fact that good and bad are usually relative, as our earlier discussion of social comparison showed. Being able to run a mile in 7 minutes, for example, is neither good nor bad in itself; the evaluation depends on whom you are comparing yourself against. Compared to the speed of expert runners, a 7-minute mile is pathetically slow, but compared to overweight middle-aged bank tellers it is probably terrific. People can turn this to their advantage by choosing their comparison group carefully. People give the most attention to those who are just slightly worse than themselves, because those comparisons make them feel good (Crocker & Major, 1989; Taylor, 1983; Wills, 1981). The Japanese have an expression "Others' misfortunes taste like honey."

In a similar vein, people skew their impressions of other people so as to convince themselves that their good traits are unusual whereas their faults are commonly found in many other people (Campbell, 1986; Marks, 1984; Suls & Wan, 1987). For example, if you are musically talented but have trouble meeting deadlines, you may find yourself thinking that musical talent is rare but procrastination (putting things off, being late, missing deadlines) is common. That makes your fault seem minimal, whereas your good quality makes you special. People are especially inclined to engage in such distortions regarding traits that are central to their self-concepts, and people with high self-esteem are more prone to these distortions than people with low self-esteem. (Probably their high self-esteem is partly sustained by these tricks.)

Yet another strategy relies on the fact that many definitions of good traits are slippery, so people can choose a definition that makes them look good (Dunning & McElwee, 1995; Dunning, Meyerowitz, & Holzberg, 1989; Dunning, Perie, & Story, 1991; Dunning & Perretta, 2002). Most people want to be a good romantic partner, for example, but what exactly defines a good romantic partner? One person can think she is a good romantic partner because she is thoughtful, another can think the same because he is a good listener, and others might think they qualify because they are funny, or easy to get along with, or good in bed, or trustworthy, or able to hold their temper. Such shifting criteria may help explain how everyone can regard himself or herself as above average.

BENEFITS OF SELF-ESTEEM

In recent decades, American society has devoted plenty of effort to boosting self-esteem, especially among schoolchildren and other groups considered to need a boost. This was based on the hope that many benefits would flow from high self-esteem. Would high self-esteem cause people to do better in school? Do you have to love yourself before you can love someone else? Will high self-esteem prevent prejudice, violence, drug addiction, and other ills?

Many results have been disappointing. People with high self-esteem do report that they are smarter, are more successful, have more friends, enjoy better relationships, and are better-looking than other people, but objective measures say they aren't. Often high self-esteem amounts to nothing more than being "a legend in your own mind." For example, several studies have shown that people with high self-esteem claim to be especially intelligent, but on an actual IQ test they are no smarter than people with low self-esteem (Gabriel, Critelli, & Ee, 1994). Likewise, they say they are better-looking than other people, but when researchers get people to judge how good-looking people are from photos, the people with high self-esteem get no higher ratings than anyone else (Bowles, 1999; Diener, Wolsic, & Fujita, 1995; Gabriel et al., 1994; Miller & Downey, 1999). They think they are better-looking, but no one else can tell the difference.

Students with high self-esteem do have slightly higher grades than people with low self-esteem, but high self-esteem does not lead to good grades (Bachman & O'Malley, 1977, 1986; Baumeister, Campbell, Krueger, & Vohs, 2003; Forsyth & Kerr, 1999; Maruyama, Rubin, & Kingsbury, 1981; Pottebaum, Keith, & Ehly, 1986; Rosenberg, Schooler, & Schoenbach, 1989; Scheirer & Kraut, 1979; Skaalvik & Hagtvet, 1990; Wylie, 1979). If anything, it is the other way around: Getting good grades and doing well in school lead to high self-esteem. As we saw in Chapter 1, the fact that there is a correlation makes it hard to tell which causes which. Self-esteem and good grades are correlated (though weakly), but studies that track people across time have indicated that self-esteem is not the cause, but the result, of the good grades. To some extent, other factors, such as coming from a good family, cause both the high self-esteem and the good grades.

In terms of getting along with others, people with high self-esteem believe that they make a great impression on others and are well liked, but in fact there is no difference in how other people evaluate them (Adams, Ryan, Ketsetzis, & Keating, 2000; Battistich, Solomon, & Delucchi, 1993; Baumeister et al., 2003; Bishop & Inderbitzen, 1995; Brockner & Lloyd, 1986; Buhrmester, Furman, Wittenberg, & Reis, 1988; Campbell & Fehr, 1990; Glendenning & Inglis, 1999; Keefe & Berndt, 1996). If anything, sometimes people with high self-esteem are obnoxious and turn people off by thinking they are superior (Heatherton & Vohs, 2000; see also Colvin, Block, & Funder, 1995).

Sexual activity is another important interpersonal process. To learn how it is related to self-esteem, read *The Social Side of Sex.*

High self-esteem has two main benefits (Baumeister et al., 2003). The first is initiative. High self-esteem fosters confidence that you can do the right thing and should act on your best judgment. People with high self-esteem are more willing than other people to speak up in groups or committees. They are more willing to approach people and strike up new friendships. They are more willing to go against other people's advice and do what they think is best. They resist influence better. They are also more adventurous when it comes to experimenting with sex, drugs, and other activities. This is sadly contrary to the goals of researchers and therapists who hoped that high self-esteem would enable young persons to resist such temptations.

The second advantage of high self-esteem is that it feels good. High self-esteem operates like a stock of good feelings that the person can draw on. When life dumps misfortune on your head, such as when you experience failure or trauma, you can bounce back better if you have high self-esteem, because this is a resource that helps you overcome the bad feelings. People with low self-esteem lack this resource, and therefore misfortune hits them harder. If at first they don't succeed, people with high self-esteem are willing to try again harder, whereas people with low self-esteem are more likely to give up. Most broadly, people with high self-esteem are happier than people with low self-esteem (e.g., Diener & Diener, 1995).

Initiative and good feelings are certainly positive benefits, though they are far less than many self-esteem researchers had hoped. Self-esteem is not the solution to a broad range of psychological and social problems, but it does at least help in those regards.

WHY DO WE CARE?

People are often quite motivated to protect and increase their self-esteem. Indeed, we shall see that many patterns of thinking and acting that social psychologists have demonstrated are based on the desire to maintain one's self-esteem. But why? The preceding section indicated that high self-esteem does not really confer a great many advantages in an objective sense. Why do people care so much about self-esteem if all it does is boost initiative and feel good?

One influential answer is relevant to this book's theme that inner processes serve interpersonal relations. Maybe thinking well of yourself doesn't really matter very much (especially by the basic biological outcome criteria of improving survival or reproduction), but gaining social acceptance does. In this view, self-esteem is essentially a measure of how socially acceptable you are. It is noteworthy that self-esteem is mainly based on the reasons that groups use to accept or reject possible members: attractiveness, competence, likability, and morality. Many groups and people avoid and reject people who are

Self-Esteem and Saying No to Sex

Is there a link between self-esteem and sexual activity? There are multiple reasons for suggesting that there might be. For one thing, people with low self-esteem have been found to be more vulnerable to social influence than people with high self-esteem, a pattern that social psychologists began to uncover in the 1950s (Brockner, 1983; Janis, 1954; Janis & Field, 1959). This led many experts to hope that increasing self-esteem among young people would enable them to resist peer pressures to participate in sex at a young age. In particular, they thought that girls with low self-esteem might be talked into sex before they were ready.

Stockbyte/Getty Images

© David Young-Wolff/PhotoEdit

High self-esteem does not prevent pregnancy.

However, the evidence does not show that high self-esteem helps youngsters resist having sex. In one large and well-designed study, self-esteem was measured among more than 1,000 children at age 11; 10 years later, they were asked whether they had engaged in sexual intercourse by the age of 15. Among the men, there was no relationship between self-esteem and early sex. Among the women, there was a relationship—but in the opposite direction from what had been predicted. Girls with higher self-esteem at age 11 were more likely (rather than less likely) than others to have sex by the age of 15 (Paul, Fitzjohn, Herbison, & Dickson, 2000). Other studies have failed to find any relationship at all, however (Langer & Tubman, 1997; McGee & Williams, 2000).

Most people in our society consider children age 15 or younger to be too young to be having sex, and research suggests that most people begin having sex in their late teen years. People who remain virgins until around the age of 20 are therefore of interest. Is there any link between self-esteem and virginity? The answer is yes, but the link differs by gender.

For many women, apparently, virginity is a positive status, and they may take pride in it. Among men, however, virginity has less of a positive aspect, and many male virgins feel ashamed of their virginity. They may feel that they have failed to appeal to women. This is especially true if the men reach an age where they believe most of their peers are having sex and have regular girlfriends. Hence there is some link between virginity and low self-esteem in men but not in women (Sprecher & Regan, 1996; Walsh, 1991b).

For both genders, but especially for women, decisions about whether to have sex are complicated by the potential for pregnancy. Fear of getting pregnant has historically been an important factor holding women back from sexual activity. In this regard, however, high self-esteem seems to be a risk factor, because women with high self-esteem tend to downplay or ignore risks. High self-esteem is often marked by a sense of being special or better than others, and it contributes to a feeling that "bad things will not happen to me." In one study, women wrote down a list of their sexual activities, including whether they took precautions against pregnancy. Then they rated their chances of having an unwanted pregnancy. Women with high self-esteem had essentially the same sex lives and took the same chances as women with low self-esteem, but those with high self-esteem regarded themselves as safer (Smith et al., 1997). The researchers concluded that high self-esteem causes women to underestimate the dangers of sex. ■

unattractive, incompetent, disliked, and dishonest or otherwise immoral. Research has shown that increases in self-esteem come from increases in social acceptance, whereas rejection can threaten or lower your self-esteem (Leary, Tambor, Terdal, & Downs, 1995; also Leary & Baumeister, 2000).

This view of self-esteem as linked to social acceptance has been called sociometer theory. A **sociometer** is a measure of how desirable one would be to other people as a relationship partner, team member, employee, colleague, or in some other way. In this sense, self-esteem is a sociometer, because it measures the traits you have according to how much they

qualify you for social acceptance. Sociometer theory can explain why people are so concerned with self-esteem: It helps people navigate the long road to social acceptance. Mark Leary, the author of sociometer theory, compares self-esteem to the gas gauge on a car. A gas gauge may seem trivial, because it doesn't make the car go forward. But the gas gauge tells you about something that is important—namely, whether there is enough fuel in the car. Just as drivers act out of concern to keep their gas gauge above zero, so people seem constantly to act so as to preserve their self-esteem.

Sociometer theory is not the only possible explanation for why people might care about self-esteem. Another, simpler theory is that self-esteem feels good (as noted in the previous section), and because people want to feel good, they want to maintain their

SOCIOMETER a measure of how desirable one would be to other people

Reprinted by permission of Creator's Syndicate, Inc.

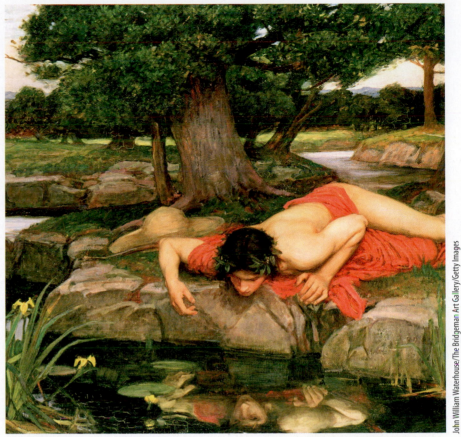

John William Waterhouse/The Bridgeman Art Gallery/Getty Images

self-esteem. A more complex variation on that theory invokes the theory of terror management, which holds that fear of death is at the root of all human striving. Terror management theorists assert that having high self-esteem helps shield people from fear of death, so people seek out self-esteem as a way of avoiding a recognition that they are going to die (Greenberg, Solomon, & Pyszczynski, 1997). Another common view is that self-esteem is based mainly on feeling competent rather than on social acceptance. However, recent evidence suggests that feeling accepted has a bigger impact on self-esteem than does feeling competent (Koch & Shepperd, 2008).

IS HIGH SELF-ESTEEM ALWAYS GOOD?

Focusing mainly on the benefits of high self-esteem might create the impression that high self-esteem is always a good thing. Alas, the benefits of high self-esteem may be balanced by drawbacks, as is the case with many tradeoffs.

The negative aspects of high self-esteem may be especially apparent in the form of narcissism, a trait that is linked to high self-esteem but that captures its worst aspects. The trait of narcissism is based on the Greek myth of Narcissus, a young man who fell in love with his own reflection in the water and did nothing but stare at it until he died. In psychology, **narcissism** refers to excessive self-love and a selfish orientation. Narcissists think very well of themselves and, as a result, are willing to take advantage of others. Among American college students, levels of narcissism have been increasing over time (Twenge, Konrath, Foster, Campbell, & Bushman, 2008). This self-centered generation has been dubbed "Generation Me" (Twenge, 2006).

Narcissism is not the same as high self-esteem, but the two are related. Probably the simplest way to understand the link is to think of narcissism as a subset of high self-esteem. That is, nearly all narcissists have high self-esteem, but many people have high self-esteem without being narcissists. To be sure, there has been some controversy about the self-esteem of narcissists. They often act superior to other people and seem to think they deserve to be treated better than others, but clinical psychologists used to think (and some still think) that this egotistical behavior is a disguise that conceals secret feelings of insecurity and low self-esteem. However, research has not been very successful at finding that narcissists really have low self-esteem; indeed, narcissists seem to be confident if not downright conceited through and through. The only area in which they do not seem to rate themselves especially high concerns getting other people to like them, which narcissists are relatively indifferent about. Admiration is more important to them than liking, and they want and expect others to admire them (Morf & Rhodewalt, 2001).

Narcissists tend to be more aggressive and violent than other people, especially when they suffer a blow to their egos (Bushman & Baumeister, 1998, 2002; Bushman, Bonacci, Van Dijk, & Baumeister, 2003).

The trait of narcissism is based on the Greek myth of Narcissus, a young man who fell in love with his own reflection in the water. As illustrated in the painting, narcissists are in love with themselves.

NARCISSISM excessive self-love and a selfish orientation

The self-esteem movement had hoped that raising self-esteem would reduce aggression, but there is no evidence that this is the case.

High self-esteem (and not just narcissism) is also associated with higher prejudice (Aberson, Healy, & Romero, 2000; Crocker & Schwartz, 1985). People who think well of themselves also tend to think their group is better than other groups, and they discriminate more heavily than other people in favor of their own group.

Narcissists also make poor relationship partners in many respects (Buss & Shackelford, 1997; Campbell, 1999, 2005; Campbell & Foster, 2002; Campbell, Foster, & Finkel, 2002). Narcissists typically approach relationships with the attitude "What's in it for me?" and hence do not really try to build a lasting intimacy with another person. They try to associate with glamorous people because they think these others will make them seem glamorous too. They adopt a "game-playing" approach to relationships that helps them maintain power and autonomy without giving much of themselves to the other person. They are also prone to infidelity; if a seemingly more desirable partner comes along, the narcissist will not have many qualms about dumping his or her current partner and hooking up with the new one. More broadly, narcissists are not as loyal to their partners as other people. They are prone to take advantage of their partners when they get the chance. Also, narcissists often think they deserve someone better, so even if they have a good relationship they may still keep an eye out in case a more attractive or desirable partner comes along. Loving someone who loves himself (or herself) is no picnic, because he will readily dump you in favor of someone else (see Campbell, 2005).

As we can see, most of the drawbacks of high self-esteem pertain to the person's relations with others. In tradeoff terms, high self-esteem has both costs and benefits, but they are not distributed fairly. The benefits of someone's high self-esteem mostly go to the person himself or herself, whereas the costs of someone's high self-esteem mostly fall on other people.

The previous section noted that people with high self-esteem have more initiative than those with low self-esteem. In general, initiative may be a good thing, but it certainly can contribute to antisocial actions as well. Research on bullies, for example, began with the old idea that bullies secretly suffer from low self-esteem, but this proved false. The most careful studies have found that bullies have high self-esteem, as do the people who help bullies by joining in to torment their victims; but people who stand up to bullies and resist them, including coming to the aid of victims, also have high self-esteem (Olweus, 1994; Salmivalli, Kaukiainen, Kaistaniemi, & Lagerspetz, 1999). This pattern captures both sides of initiative. People who think well of themselves have more initiative and use it either for bad purposes (bullying others) or for

good ones (resisting bullies and protecting victims). Low self-esteem was found mainly among the victims; in fact, the victim role is often a passive one, defined by the absence of initiative.

Persistence in the face of failure also takes initiative (and possibly some resource of good feelings to help overcome discouragement—remember that good feelings were the other benefit of high self-esteem). Many studies have found that people with high self-esteem are more likely than those with low self-esteem to keep trying despite an initial failure (Perez, 1973; Shrauger & Sorman, 1977). In general, we assume that this is a good thing, because the chances of eventual success are greater if you keep trying than if you give up. Then again, some endeavors are truly hopeless, lost causes, and continuing to try simply means greater failure. Think of a football coach who keeps calling for a play that never works because the other team knows how to defend against it; or an investor who keeps putting money into a stock that keeps losing; or a scientist who keeps trying to prove a theory that is truly wrong. People with high self-esteem are prone to make that kind of error too. Their persistence in the face of failure can be either a good or a bad thing (Janoff-Bulman & Brickman, 1982; McFarlin, 1985; McFarlin, Baumeister, & Blascovich, 1984; Sandelands, Brockner, & Glynn, 1988). In general, though, people with high self-esteem do seem to manage these situations better and make better use of information about when to persist as opposed to when to move on and try something else (Di Paula & Campbell, 2002; McFarlin, 1985).

PURSUING SELF-ESTEEM

Self-esteem does not just happen. Many people actively pursue self-esteem. Typically they choose some sphere or dimension (such as schoolwork, popularity, or sports) as important to them, invest themselves in it, and try to succeed at it.

Although most people in our culture pursue self-esteem, they go about it in different ways. People who already have high self-esteem pursue it by seeking to dominate others and to increase their competence at valued abilities. People with low self-esteem pursue it by seeking acceptance and validation from others, and especially by avoiding failures (Crocker & Park, 2004).

There is increasing evidence that pursuing self-esteem as an end in itself can have harmful consequences (Crocker & Park, 2004). Pursuing self-esteem can compromise the pursuit of competence, as when people choose easy tasks so they can be sure of succeeding. It impairs autonomy, because seekers of self-esteem often do whatever others will approve rather than what they themselves might want to do. The pursuit of self-esteem creates feelings of pressure to live up to others' expectations, and therefore it weakens people's intrinsic motivation (their interest in doing something for its own sake). It impairs learning, because when self-esteem is on the line people react to setbacks or criticism as threatening events rather than as helpful feedback. It can damage relationships, because self-esteem seekers compete against their relationship partners and thereby sometimes undermine intimacy and mutuality. They may also withdraw from partners who are too successful, because they feel that they are losing in comparison (see also Tesser, 1988). Last, the pursuit of self-esteem can be harmful to health, both because it increases stress and because it can lead to unhealthy coping behaviors, such as drinking and smoking, to deal with bad feelings associated with having one's self-esteem on the line.

When people stake their self-esteem on succeeding in some domain, then failure in that domain produces strong negative reactions, including increased anxiety and other negative emotions, as well as drops in self-esteem. If anything, the drops that go with such failures are bigger than the increases that come from success (Crocker, Sommers, & Luhtanen, 2002).

[**QUIZ YOURSELF**]

Self-Esteem, Self-Deception, and Positive Illusions

1. A person's overall self-evaluation or sense of self-worth constitutes his or her _____.
   (a) possible self   (b) self-awareness
   (c) self-efficacy   (d) self-esteem

2. Depressed people _____ how favorably other people regard them, whereas normal people _____ how favorably other people regard them.
   (a) estimate accurately; overestimate
   (b) estimate accurately; underestimate
   (c) underestimate; estimate accurately
   (d) underestimate; overestimate

3. Which of the following is a positive illusion that people hold?
   (a) People overestimate their strengths and underestimate their faults.
   (b) People overestimate their perceived control over events.
   (c) People are unrealistically optimistic.
   (d) All of the above.

4. When Frank does well on a test, he claims responsibility for the success, but when he does poorly on a test, he denies responsibility and blames his professor for writing a difficult test with ambiguous items. This is an example of _____.
   (a) a positive illusion
   (b) the overjustification effect
   (c) the self-reference effect
   (d) the self-serving bias

Self-Presentation

Self-esteem, or egotism, is a common explanation for behavior. Supposedly people do many things—work hard, get in a fight, compete, show off, enjoy compliments, and more—to bolster or protect their self-esteem. Yet why would people care so much about self-esteem? Why would the human psyche be designed to try to prove itself better than other people? Cultural animals do need to care, and care very much, about what *other* people think of them. Could it be that much of what is commonly regarded as egotism, as trying to think well of oneself, is at heart a concern with how others think of you?

Undeniably, people do want to think well of themselves. The self-deception strategies we listed earlier generally work so as to enable people to hold favorable views of themselves. (Although the line between fooling others and fooling yourself turns out to be much fuzzier than one might think.) Although people do want to preserve their self-esteem, on closer inspection it often turns out that they are most concerned with having other people view them favorably (Baumeister, 1982; Goffman, 1959; Schlenker, 1980). It's fine to like yourself, but what matters more is whether other people like you. In fact, if nobody else likes you, it is difficult to like yourself!

Many research studies do not make much of a distinction between private self-esteem and public

THE FAR SIDE® BY GARY LARSON

© 1991 FarWorks, Inc. All Rights Reserved/Dist. by Creators Syndicate

esteem, but those that do distinguish them often find that the concern with public esteem is greater. As the comedian Billy Crystal used to say, "It is more important to look good than to feel good!" This chapter opened with the story of Count Zrínyi, who wanted very much to make a good impression on whoever was going to kill him. Clearly feeling good wasn't the goal, because he would be dead. Looking good still mattered.

Probably the concern with looking good to others arises from the basic facts of human nature. Human beings achieve their biological goals of survival and reproduction by means of belonging to social and cultural groups. Getting other people to like you or respect you is very helpful for getting into these groups and staying there. We have said that one theme of human life is the long road to social acceptance. A big part of this road is making good impressions on other people and keeping a good reputation. That is what self-presentation is all about.

Self-presentation is defined as any behavior that seeks to convey some image of self or some information about the self to other people. Any behavior that is intended (even unconsciously) to make an impression on others is included. Self-presentation thus encompasses a wide range of actions, from explicit statements about the self (e.g., "You can trust me"), to how you dress or what car you drive, to making excuses or threats, to trying to hide your fear or anger so that other people will think you are cool.

WHO'S LOOKING?

A great many behavior patterns studied by social psychologists turn out to depend on self-presentation. This has been shown by comparing how people behave in public conditions, when others are present and one's behavior is identified, with private behavior, when one's actions will remain secret and confidential. If you mainly care about self-esteem, your behavior will be the same regardless of whether someone else is watching. But if you are concerned about what others think (that is, you are concerned with or motivated by self-presentation), then you will act differently when you are alone than when others are there.

For example, in Chapter 7 you will see that people often change their attitudes to be consistent with their behavior, especially if they have done something out of the ordinary or contrary to their usual beliefs. This pattern occurs mainly when other people are watching; it is much weaker if the behavior is done privately (Baumeister & Tice, 1984; Tedeschi, Schlenker, & Bonoma, 1971). Likewise, when people receive evaluations of their personality or their work, these evaluations have much more impact if they are public (that is, if other people know about them) than if they are private. Criticism received privately can easily be ignored or forgotten, whereas criticism that is heard by multiple other people must be dealt with. Even if you think the criticism is completely wrong, you cannot just dismiss it or ignore it if other people know about it. That criticism might cause other people to change their impression of you or treat you differently (Baumeister & Cairns, 1992; Baumeister & Jones, 1978; Greenberg & Pyszczynski, 1985).

Self-presentation creeps into many behaviors that might not at first seem to have an interpersonal aspect. For example, washing one's hands after using the restroom may seem like a simple matter of personal hygiene. But researchers who have secretly observed how people behave in public restrooms found that washing one's hands is affected by whether other people are watching. Women who used the toilet would usually wash their hands afterward if someone else was in the restroom, but if they believed themselves to be alone, they were more likely to skip washing (Munger & Harris, 1989).

Dieting is also guided by self-presentation. Despite all the talk of how healthy it is to be slim and fit, the strongest motive to lose weight is to make oneself attractive to others. As one expert researcher commented, "No one would diet on a deserted island!" (Heatherton, personal communication, 1993).

Even people with severe mental illnesses such as schizophrenia are well attuned to the importance of self-presentation. In a famous study, inmates at a mental hospital were told to report to the head psychiatrist for an interview (Braginski, Braginski, & Ring, 1969). On the way, by random assignment, they were told one of two purposes for the interview. Some were told that the purpose of the interview was to evaluate them for possible release from the hospital. You might think that mental patients would be anxious to be released into the outside world, but in fact many have anxieties and fears about that and prefer their safe, structured life in the mental hospital. When the interview began, these patients presented themselves as having serious problems and difficulties, presumably so that the psychiatrist would abandon any plan to release them into the world.

Other patients were told that the purpose of the interview was to decide whether to move them to a locked ward, where more dangerous patients were kept, and where consequently there were fewer comforts and freedoms. These patients presented themselves in the interview as being relatively sane and normal, so as to discourage any thoughts of moving them to the

SELF-PRESENTATION any behavior that seeks to convey some image of self or some information about the self to other people

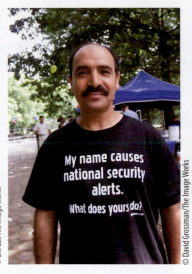

© Brand X Pictures/Alamy   © Bill Lai/The Image Works   © David Grossman/The Image Works   © Jeff Greenberg/PhotoEdit

What kinds of impression are these people trying to make, using their clothing?

locked ward. Thus, the level of psychopathology (craziness, to put it crudely) displayed by mental patients is at least partly self-presentation. It goes up and down in order to make the desired impression.

When social psychologists first began to recognize the importance of self-presentation, they regarded it as a form of hypocrisy—acting or pretending to be something other than what one is, possibly for bad reasons such as to manipulate others or to feed one's egotism. However, the field gradually recognized that making a good impression and keeping a good reputation constitute a basic and important aspect of human social life. It is not limited to a few phony or hypocritical individuals who seek to convey false impressions. Rather, nearly everyone strives for a good self-presentation as a way of obtaining social acceptance (Goffman, 1959; Schlenker, 1980). Through self-presentation, people can increase their chances of being accepted by others and can claim a valued identity within the social system, thereby enabling them to maintain their place in the group.

MAKING AN IMPRESSION

What makes for a good self-presentation? In many ways, the answers are obvious: One has to show oneself to have good traits and not bad ones. Presenting oneself as competent, friendly, honest, kind, loyal, strong, warm, helpful, and so on, makes for a good self-presentation (Schlenker, 1980). The main problem with defining what makes a good self-presentation arises when the values of the self-presenter and the audience diverge. Then the self-presenter faces a tradeoff between being true to his or her own values and making a good impression on the interaction partner (also called the audience). What the person

does depends on a variety of factors, including the importance of one's relationship to the audience and the importance of the issue to the self.

It is perhaps not surprising that people often present themselves along the lines favored by their audience. After all, people want to be liked, and conforming to others' values and expectations is a common strategy for achieving that. What is more surprising is that sometimes people deliberately present themselves in ways that they know their audience will not approve. This isn't the same as being more concerned with private reality than public appearance, because if someone really didn't care what others thought, that person wouldn't bother telling them they disagreed with them. But sometimes people deliberately make others see them in ways that the others don't approve.

If people are playing to the audience but not giving the audience what it wants, they must have some other motive for how they present themselves. This clues us in to a second important function of self-presentation: claiming identity.

A dramatic single instance of refusing to present oneself in a way the audience would approve occurred in the library at Columbine High School on the terrible day that two students brought guns and began shooting their fellow students. Cassie Bernall was in the library during the shootings, on her knees praying out loud. One of the gunmen asked if anyone there believed in God. Witnesses said that Cassie Bernall told him, "Yes, I believe in God." He shot her to death ("Faith, Heroics," 1999). Although some details of the story are disputed, it does seem that there was pressure on her to deny her religious faith, which she resisted at the cost of her life. Throughout history, many individuals have been pressured to renounce or reject their faith, and many have died for refusing to give the answers that others wanted to hear. Notice, again, that if she really didn't care about how other people saw her, she could easily have lied and denied her faith. She insisted on making a public statement of what she believed in, and that got her killed.

Claiming Identity. People aspire to many identities. A person may wish to be recognized as an artist, a talented athlete, an honest businessperson, a defender of certain values. In general, it is not enough simply to persuade yourself that you hold such an identity. Rather, the claims require social validation: Other people must come to perceive you as holding that identity. In an important sense, you cannot be a great artist, or a sports star, or a brilliant student if you are the only one who believes that you are. It becomes necessary to persuade others to see you in that light. This is the grander task of self-presentation: obtaining social validation for your identity claims.

People do use self-presentation to advance their claims to identity. In some studies, participants were made to feel either secure or insecure about their claims. For example, among participants who aspired to become expert guitarists, some were told that their personality profiles differed markedly from those of expert guitarists, which conveyed the message that the participant was not on his or her way to becoming one of those experts (Wicklund & Gollwitzer, 1982). Others were told that they fit the profile precisely, which made them feel as if they were doing well on their project of becoming an expert guitarist. They were then asked whether they would like to give guitar lessons to beginners, and if so how many. The people who had been made to feel insecure about their claims to becoming expert guitarists wanted to teach many more lessons than the people who were told they were already looking like expert guitarists. The insecure ones wanted to bolster their claims to being a guitarist by teaching guitar to others, because these others would view them as good guitarists.

Sometimes, the goal of claiming an identity can motivate a person to engage in self-presentation in a way the audience will not like. This is why people sometimes end up arguing about politics, rather than simply agreeing with what the other person says. They identify with their own political views strongly enough that they would rather stand up for what they believe in than make a good, congenial impression on someone who holds different values. The story about Cassie Bernall and religious faith is another example of this.

Tradeoff: Favorability Versus Plausibility. By and large, people seek to make good impressions, and so they present themselves favorably. A favorable or self-enhancing way of describing oneself prevails in most social psychology studies (Schlenker, 1975). Naturally, people do not go to extremes of claiming to be superstars or geniuses, but they tend to present themselves in the best possible light, within the range of what is plausible. One authority on self-presentation has described this as a tradeoff between favorability and plausibility. In plain terms, people present themselves as favorably as they think they can get away with! They may claim to be smart and attractive, but if they think other people will find out that their claims are exaggerated, then they tone down those claims (Schlenker, 1975, 1980). This tendency toward favorable self-presentations dovetails well with the "automatic egotism" described earlier in this chapter: People automatically tend to furnish a very positive image of themselves, unless circumstances dictate otherwise (Paulhus & Levitt, 1987).

What About Modesty? The tendency toward favorable self-presentation seems well designed to help people make a good first impression on other people. Not surprisingly, it is less needed and hence less common within established relationships. When people are among friends, they often stop boasting or presenting themselves in the best possible light. If anything, modesty seems more natural and common among friends, and it may even be the default or automatic response (Tice, Butler, Muraven, & Stillwell, 1995). There are several reasons for this, one of which is that your friends are probably familiar with your faults and failures. If you claim to be better than you are, they may be quick to point out that you are twisting the facts.

Possibly a deeper reason for the prevalence of modesty within long-term relationships and friendships is that it helps people get along better. Most religions have embraced humility as a virtue and regarded pride as either a sin or an obstacle to salvation. One purported secular goal of religion is to promote group harmony, and people probably can get along with humble, modest individuals better than they get along with puffed-up, conceited narcissists. Groups often must divide up resources that vary in quality, such as who gets the best piece of meat or who gets the better place to sleep. Humility and modesty make such divisions easier: "No, you choose." People who think highly of themselves are more likely to think that they deserve the best, and if a group has several such people, the argument can turn nasty.

There is some evidence that self-enhancement is especially strong in individualistic cultures that place a high emphasis on individual achievement and merit. In contrast, collectivistic cultures that emphasize group harmony above individual rights are less oriented toward self-enhancement (Heine, Lehman, Markus,

Looking cool, but at what cost?

& Kitayama, 1999). One team of experts has argued, for example, that the Japanese do not go around trying to prove their individual superiority over others; rather, they seek to improve themselves so as to become better members of their social group. If self-enhancement is found in such cultures, it often takes the form of trying to present oneself as a worthy member of the group or as belonging to a highly valued group (Sedikides, Gaertner, & Toguchi, 2003). Thus, though Japanese may not strive to prove themselves superior to other Japanese individually, many of them do believe that Japanese culture and people together are good and in many ways superior to others.

SELF-PRESENTATION AND RISKY BEHAVIOR

Self-presentation is so important to people that they will sometimes risk illness, injury, or even death in order to make a good impression (Leary, Tchividjian, & Kraxberger, 1994). Many people try to get a suntan because they believe it makes them look attractive and sexy, but sunbathing exposes the skin to dangerous radiation that can (and often does) cause skin cancer. Many young people smoke in an effort to look cool, adult, and sophisticated in front of others. Likewise, adolescent drinking is often driven by the belief that drinkers are perceived as tougher, more adult-like, and more rebellious than nondrinkers. Some people fear that others will think badly of them if they purchase condoms or if they suggest using condoms, so they engage in unprotected sex, thereby risking sexually transmitted infections (including AIDS). Some people drive fast or refuse to wear seat belts in order to project an image of bravery. Others resist wearing helmets when riding motorcycles or bicycles or playing sports.

The fact that people will take such risks with their health in order to make a good impression on others indicates that, at some level, gaining social acceptance is felt as an even stronger and more urgent motive

than the motivation to stay alive and healthy. Self-presentation can be stronger than self-preservation (as suggested by Billy Crystal's remark, quoted earlier, about looking good versus feeling good!). This is yet another sign that the human psyche is designed to gain and keep a place in a social group.

[**QUIZ YOURSELF**]

Self-Presentation

1. The comedian Billy Crystal used to say, "It is more important to look good than to feel good!" This concern with looking good to others is called _____.

   (a) self-awareness   (b) self-concept
   (c) self-handicapping   (d) self-presentation

2. John is a young gang member who wants to look tough to his fellow gang members. This concern about looking tough is called _____.

   (a) self-awareness   (b) self-consciousness
   (c) self-esteem   (d) self-presentation

3. Self-presentation concerns often influence people to engage in _____ actions than they would otherwise engage in.

   (a) less conservative   (b) less risky
   (c) more conservative   (d) more risky

4. People tend to furnish a very positive image of themselves, unless circumstances dictate otherwise. This tendency is called _____.

   (a) automatic egotism
   (b) private self-awareness
   (c) public self-presentation
   (d) self-handicapping

No other animal has a self that can begin to approach the human self in complexity and sophistication. Many of the features that make human beings special can be found in the self.

What is special about the human self begins with self-awareness and self-concept. Self-awareness is quite limited in most other species; indeed, very few animals can even recognize themselves in a mirror. In contrast, people have a remarkable ability to be aware of themselves, to think about themselves, and to change themselves. Self-awareness has at least two crucial dimensions, public and private, and these are useful for different things. Private self-awareness is useful for evaluating oneself, especially toward goals of self-improvement and self-regulation. Public self-awareness is vital for the task of gaining social acceptance, because it enables people to anticipate how others will perceive them.

In humans, self-awareness is more than the name implies (i.e., it is more than just paying attention to self). Self-awareness enables people to compare themselves to standards in a way that other animals cannot. They can evaluate whether they are conforming to cultural standards (such as morals and laws), personal standards (such as goals and ambitions), and perhaps others. This ability makes it possible for people to strive to improve and to behave morally. It also produces some distinctively human problems, such as eating disorders and suicide. Regardless, standards are important. They reveal one theme of this book: that human behavior is deeply shaped and guided by ideas. Many people deliberately try to become better people according to moral or cultural ideas. Nothing like it has been identified in any other species.

Self-awareness makes self-knowledge possible. Using language, people can express and remember many things about themselves. This process enables self-knowledge to become efficient, useful, and far-reaching. People develop elaborate theories about themselves. Turn on the television and watch any talk show: Even the most boring and shallow people seem to find endless things to say about themselves.

Know thyself! The quest for self-knowledge is another unique part of being human. Most people are eager to learn about themselves. The various motives for self-knowledge (self-enhancement, consistency, and appraisal) are centrally important among human beings but essentially unknown in other animals. Along with these motives go the concern with self-esteem and the cultivation of positive illusions. Self-deception may also be uniquely human. Some animals occasionally deceive each other, but as far as we can tell, only humans lie to themselves.

Another remarkable and distinctive feature of the human self is its ability to take and leave roles. Almost like a professional actor, the human self can take up a role, perform it well, then stop and move into a different role that requires acting differently. The self can switch roles during the day as it moves from one situation to another (e.g., from office to home or to a bar with friends). The self can also make more lasting changes, such as when a person gets a promotion or a new job. This ability of the human self to change with changing roles, along the way changing how it thinks and behaves, is vital for cultural beings. Successful cultures are large social systems with many different roles. The human self probably evolved to be able to play different roles.

Intrinsic motivation is found in most animal species, but extrinsic motivation is more specific to humans. One common form of extrinsic motivation involves doing something for money, and of course only humans have money. Extrinsic motivation is important for culture, because people will do things for the sake of cultural rewards (including money, prestige, status, and fame). These rewards are often vital for inducing people to do things that enable the culture to function properly. Few people have an intrinsic desire to collect garbage, pay taxes, or go to court, but many people do these things because of extrinsic motivation, and the culture operates more effectively when they do. Extrinsic rewards are the start of economic (money) relations, because they motivate people to produce more than they need themselves so they can trade some to others and thus get other things they want.

Humans know the difference between inner states and outward appearances (though not all cultures may be as sensitive to this difference as modern, Western ones). People engage in self-presentation, sometimes to make the optimal impression on the audience and sometimes to cement their claims to a particular social identity, gaining validation from having other people accept them in that role. Sometimes people engage in deceptive self-presentation, trying to present themselves as better than they really are. In general, the desire to communicate information about oneself to others is an important aspect of human life.

In short, the self is something that humans know about and care about in ways that would be impossible for most other animals. Humans strive to learn about themselves, to change themselves to fit cultural and other standards, and to get others to regard them favorably. The self is a vital tool for gaining social acceptance and for participating in culture, in ways that only human beings do.

chapter summary

WHAT IS THE SELF?

- The three main parts of the self are:
  - Self-knowledge or self-concept
  - The interpersonal self or public self
  - The agent or executive function

- The main purposes of the self include gaining social acceptance and playing social roles.
- Asians understand the self as interdependent

(connected to others in a web of social relations), whereas Americans lean toward an independent self-construal (seeing the self as a separate, special or unique, self-contained unit).

- Self-awareness is attention directed at the self, and usually involves evaluating the self.
- Private self-awareness refers to attending to one's inner states; public self-awareness means attending to how one is perceived by others.
- Self-awareness is often unpleasant, because people often compare themselves to high standards.
- Being self-aware can make people behave better.
- Human self-awareness is far more extensive and complex than what is found in any other species.
- Self-awareness is vital for self-regulation and adopting others' perspectives.

WHERE SELF-KNOWLEDGE COMES FROM

- The looking-glass self refers to the idea that we learn about ourselves from how others judge us.
- People often do not realize how their minds work.
- The overjustification effect is the tendency for intrinsic motivation to diminish for activities that have become associated with external rewards.
- The phenomenal self or the working self-concept is the part of self-knowledge that is currently active in the person's thoughts.
- Three motivations for wanting self-knowledge are the appraisal motive, the self-enhancement motive, and the consistency motive.
- Self-handicapping involves putting obstacles in the way of one's own performance, so that if one fails, the failure can be blamed on the obstacle, and if one succeeds, one looks especially competent.

SELF AND INFORMATION PROCESSING

- The self-reference effect refers to the finding that information bearing on the self is processed more thoroughly and more deeply, and hence remembered better, than other information.
- Self-concept is likely to change to be consistent with the public self, and with what people want to believe about themselves.

SELF-ESTEEM, SELF-DECEPTION, AND POSITIVE ILLUSIONS

- In many important respects, nondepressed people see the world in a distorted, biased fashion, whereas depressed people can see reality more accurately.
- The self-serving bias leads people to claim credit for success but deny blame for failure.
- People with high self-esteem think they are great, but most people with low self-esteem think they are only mediocre (rather than awful).
- People with low self-esteem do not want to fail, are uncertain about their self-knowledge, focus on self-protection rather than self-enhancement, and are prone to emotional highs and lows.
- Basking in reflected glory refers to people's tendency to want to associate with winners.

- High self-esteem feels good and fosters initiative, but does not confer many advantages in an objective sense.
- The sociometer theory suggests that self-esteem is a measure of how socially acceptable you think you are.
- High self-esteem and narcissism are associated with some negative qualities that pertain to relations with others, such as prejudice and aggression.
- Pursuing self-esteem as an end in itself can have harmful consequences.

SELF-PRESENTATION

- Most people are more concerned with looking good to others than with private self-esteem.
- Self-presentation is any behavior that seeks to convey some image of self or some information about the self to other people, or that seeks to make an impression on others.
- Nearly everyone strives for a good self-presentation as a way of obtaining social acceptance.
- Self-presentation is so important to people that they sometimes engage in risky or dangerous behavior in order to make a good impression.

WHAT MAKES US HUMAN? PUTTING THE CULTURAL ANIMAL IN PERSPECTIVE

- What is special about the human self begins with self-awareness and self-concept.
- The self is a vital and distinctively human tool for gaining social acceptance and for participating in culture.

Key Terms

Agent self (executive function) 60
Appraisal motive 74
Automatic egotism 76
Consistency motive 74
Downward social comparison 71
Endowment effect 77
Extrinsic motivation 71
Generalized other 68
Independent self-construal 62

Interdependent self-construal 62
Interpersonal self (public self) 60
Intrinsic motivation 71
Introspection 69
Looking-glass self 68
Narcissism 87
Overjustification effect 71
Phenomenal self (working self-concept) 71
Private self-awareness 64

Public self-awareness 64
Public self-consciousness 66
Self as impulse 61
Self as institution 61
Self-awareness 64
Self-deception strategies 83
Self-enhancement motive 74
Self-esteem 81
Self-handicapping 75
Self-knowledge (self-concept) 59
Self-perception theory 71

Self-presentation 90
Self-protection 81
Self-reference effect 77
Self-regulation 67
Self-serving bias 83
Social comparison 70
Social roles 63
Sociometer 86
Standards 64
Upward social comparison 71

[Quiz Yourself] Answers

1. What Is the Self?
Answers: 1=b, 2=b, 3=a, 4=b

2. Where Self-Knowledge Comes From
Answers: 1=d, 2=d, 3=d, 4=a

3. Self and Information Processing
Answers: 1=d, 2=b, 3=c, 4=c

4. Self-Esteem, Self-Deception, and Positive Illusions
Answers: 1=d, 2=a, 3=d, 4=d

5. Self-Presentation
Answers: 1=d, 2=d, 3=d, 4=a

Media Learning Resources

Make sure you check out the complete set of learning resources and study tools below. If your instructor did not order these items with your new book, go to www.ichapters.com to purchase Cengage Learning print and digital products.

Social Psychology and Human Nature BOOK COMPANION WEBSITE

www.cengage.com/psychology/baumeister Visit your book companion website, where you will find flash cards, practice quizzes, Internet links, and more to help you study.

CENGAGENOW™ JUST WHAT YOU NEED TO KNOW NOW!

Spend time on what you need to master rather than on information you have already learned. Take a pre-test for this chapter, and CengageNOW will generate a personalized study plan based on your results. The study plan will identify the topics you need to review and direct you to online resources to help you master those topics. You can then take a post-test to help you determine the concepts you have mastered and what you will still need to work on. Try it out! Go to www.cengage.com/login to sign in with an access code or to purchase access to this product.

CLASSIC AND CONTEMPORARY VIDEOS STUDENT CD-ROM

To see videos on the topics and experiments discussed in this chapter and to learn more about the research that social psychologists are doing today, go to the Student CD-ROM.

SOCIAL PSYCH LAB

These unique online labs give you the opportunity to become a participant in actual experiments, including re-creations of classic and contemporary research studies.

chapter 4

Choices and Actions: The Self in Control

Money Matters: How Money Can Trick You Into Making Bad Decisions **p. 101**

The Social Side of Sex: Gender, Sex, and Decisions **p. 102**

Food for Thought: Dieting as Self-Regulation **p. 116**

Tradeoffs: Now Versus Tomorrow: Delay of Gratification **p. 120**

What Makes Us Human? Putting the Cultural Animal in Perspective **p. 122**

WHAT YOU DO, AND WHAT IT MEANS p. 99
Making Choices **p. 100**
Why People Don't Choose **p. 103**
Choice and Change **p. 104**

FREEDOM OF ACTION p. 106
More or Less Free **p. 106**
Free Action Comes From Inside **p. 106**

Having an Out, Versus No Escape **p. 107**

GOALS, PLANS, INTENTIONS p. 108
Setting and Pursuing Goals **p. 108**
Hierarchy of Goals **p. 109**
Multiple Goals and Goal Shielding **p. 110**
Reaching Goals: What's the Plan? **p. 111**
Common Mistakes in Planning **p. 112**

SELF-REGULATION p. 113

IRRATIONALITY AND SELF-DESTRUCTION p. 117
Self-Defeating Acts: Being Your Own Worst Enemy **p. 118**
Suicide **p. 119**

CHAPTER SUMMARY p. 122

Terrorists have long chosen airplanes as targets for their violent acts. One of the most dramatic was the destruction of Korean Airlines Flight 858 in November 29, 1987. Unlike many such events, this act of terror has been recounted in detail by the perpetrator, a young woman named Kim Hyun Hee, in her book *The Tears of My Soul*. ||||

Kim Hyun Hee grew up in North Korea, a totalitarian communist state where all information is tightly controlled by the government. She learned in school that her country (though in fact a starving nation and an international outcast) was the greatest country in the world and blessed with a godlike leader, Kim Il-sung. By virtue of her hard work and her father's connections, she was able to attend the country's only major university, and her good record there earned her an invitation to become a special agent for the Korean foreign intelligence service.

One great day she was summoned to meet the director, who told her that she had been assigned to carry out a mission ordered by the Great Leader himself, the most important mission ever attempted by their organization and one that would decide North Korea's national destiny. He explained that she and a comrade would blow up a South Korean commercial airplane. This allegedly would cause the upcoming 1988 Olympics (scheduled for Seoul, South Korea) to be canceled, which in turn would lead to the unification of Korea under the communist government. She said she never understood how destroying a plane and killing some tourists would bring about the country's unification, but she did not question this, and she accepted it on faith.

Being assigned such a historic mission was a great honor to her. The director explained that if she succeeded, she would become a national hero, and she and her family would benefit greatly.

At the time, she never thought about the moral issue of killing so many people. "The act of sabotage was a purely technical operation," she recalled later; her attention was focused on the concrete details, rather than guilt or compassion for her victims or even idealistic reflections on her nation's destiny. Her contacts met her at the airport and gave her the parts to the bomb, which she assembled while sitting on the toilet in the women's restroom. She boarded the plane and stowed the bomb (hidden in a briefcase) in the overhead compartment. At a stopover she got off the plane, leaving the bomb there. Later that day, she heard on the news that the plane had exploded, and she mainly felt relief that she had succeeded, plus some pride at having done her part for her country.

She was supposed to make her way home, but she was captured by police. She began to suffer some distress over what she had done. She thought about the happy tourists on the plane, flying home and then abruptly killed. She began to have nightmares, such as that her family members were on the plane and she was shouting at them to get off but they would not listen. For the first time, she was tormented day and night by overwhelming feelings of guilt. She confessed, was sentenced to death, and then was pardoned by the South Korean authorities.

This extraordinary story reveals several important themes about human action:

- Hee's behavior was guided by the values and systems of her culture: Blowing up an airplane was not her idea, but she accepted it and carried it out on faith that it would benefit her nation.

- She trusted that her leaders were good people and knew what they were doing, and she obeyed them without question. She did not notice the moral dilemma in advance and thought only of doing her duty.

- The plans were overly optimistic.

Kim Hyun Hee, author of *The Tears of My Soul*.

Courtesy of Kimsoft

- By herself, she could have achieved very little, but she worked as part of a team.

- Her action followed carefully made plans, with minor adjustments during the mission.

- During the mission, she focused herself on the steps and details, never really questioning whether the project was a good idea in the first place. She focused on how, not why.

- Her nightmares focused on the panicky feeling of being unable to help her family escape.

- During the mission, she thought neither of moral issues nor of national destiny, instead focusing narrowly on the details; only afterward did she start to be troubled with guilt

- Her behavior was directed toward several goals at different levels; whether you label it a success or a failure depends on which goal you invoke. The mission was a success on its own terms, insofar as the airplane was destroyed and the passengers killed; Hee's capture was the only part that didn't go according to plan. Yet in the broader context

it was a total failure. The 1988 Olympics were held in South Korea as scheduled, and of course the grand goal of uniting the two Koreas under communist rule was not achieved. From the perspective of fulfilling the national destiny, she killed all those people for nothing.

The episode was largely self-defeating for her, insofar as she ended up in prison and (temporarily) sentenced to death. But she did not intend to bring herself to that negative outcome. Instead, she was pursuing highly favorable goals both for herself and her country. Her quest for good backfired.

This chapter focuses on making choices and acting on them. The human self—who and what you are—is defined by the choices you make, but the self is also there precisely to help make choices. Indeed, probably the brain itself evolved to help animals make the choices they faced, and the human brain is so large partly to enable humans to cope with all the complex and difficult choices they have. In this chapter we look at how people make choices and why they sometimes make stupid or destructive ones. ■

What You Do, and What It Means

It is possible to talk about animal behavior without asking what the acts or circumstances "mean" to the animal. Indeed, Skinnerian behaviorism (an approach that emphasized learning from reward and punishment as the main cause of behavior, and that dominated psychology in the 1950s and 1960s) did precisely that, with considerable success. Skinnerian behaviorism, however, failed to provide a satisfactory account of human behavior, precisely because of its failure to deal with meaning. As we saw in Chapter 2, human behavior is often guided by ideas, which is to say that it depends on meanings. A bear may go up the hill or not, but the bear's decision is not based on concepts or ideas such as laws, plans, religious duties, flexible schedules, or promises. In contrast, much of human behavior cannot be understood without such considerations.

Culture is a network of meaning, and human beings who live in culture act based on meaning; this is what makes them different from other animals. This is not to say that the psychologists who studied animals were wasting their time. Many of the principles that apply to animal behavior also apply to human behavior. But to explain human behavior, one needs more, and one especially needs meaning.

The importance of ideas—what you do depends partly on what it means—reflects the broad theme

that inner processes serve interpersonal functions. Meaning depends on language and is therefore learned only through culture. For example, some religions condemn eating beef, others eating pork, others eating all meat; these rules are all learned from the culture, and only humans (with our inner capacity for understanding meaning) can alter their eating habits based on such rules. To go hungry instead of eating forbidden food reflects another theme, of letting social conscience override selfish impulses.

Thinking enables people to make use of meaning. Many psychologists study thinking for its own sake. Thinking probably evolved to help creatures make better choices for guiding their behavior (though this cannot be proven at present). William James, the father of American psychology, once wrote that "thinking is for doing" (James, 1890), and modern social psychologists have shared that view (Fiske, 1992). One of the most basic uses of thought is to perform actions mentally before doing them physically. You can imagine yourself running a race, or asking someone for a date, or giving a talk in front of an audience, and these imaginary exercises seem to pave the way for really doing them.

How well does it work? As people imagine something, it

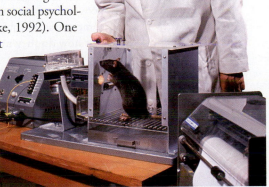

B. F. Skinner and his box. But what does it mean to you?

comes to seem more plausible and likely to them (Anderson, 1983; Anderson & Sechler, 1986; Carroll, 1978; Gregory, Cialdini, & Carpenter, 1982; Hirt & Sherman, 1985; Sherman, Zehner, Johnson, & Hirt, 1983). Salespeople make use of this process: Imagine yourself owning this car, they say, and the more you imagine it, the more likely you are to buy it.

In one carefully controlled study, some students were told to imagine themselves studying hard for an upcoming exam and doing well on it. These people got significantly higher grades than any other group—an average of 10 points better than the control group. (The control group just kept track of how much they studied without imagining any part of the future.) The ones who imagined themselves studying hard in fact did study longer and harder, which no doubt helped them achieve those high grades. In a different condition, students imagined having done well on the exam, including a vivid scene of looking at the posted grades, following the line across from their number to see a high score, and walking away with a big smile. These people did only slightly (2 points) better than the control group (Taylor & Pham, 1996). Apparently just imagining a good outcome isn't as effective as imagining yourself doing all the hard work to produce the success. But all in all, imagination has the power to help make things come true.

MAKING CHOICES

Human life is filled with choices. A trip to the grocery store would be a mind-numbing experience if you really confronted all the possible choices, and every year there seem to be more choices to make. One researcher noted that the average American supermarket in 1976 carried 9,000 different products, whereas 15 years later that figure had risen to 30,000 (Waldman, 1992)! Similar patterns can be found everywhere: more television channels, more hairstyles, more churches and religious denominations, more ways to invest your money, more kinds of blue jeans. The progress of culture seems to offer people more and more choices, and there must be some attraction, because people want more choices. But how do they make them?

Two Steps of Choosing. Social psychologists have uncovered several key features of the process of choosing. It helps to recognize that most people handle choosing in two steps (Kahneman & Tversky, 1979). The first step involves whittling the full range of choices down to a limited few. Out of the many dozens of possible cars you might buy (or of the millions of people you might marry!), you discard most of them and zero in on a few options. This step can be done rather quickly. It entails some risk that a potentially good choice will be rejected without careful consideration, but it is the only way that the human mind can deal with a large set of possible choices.

The second step involves more careful comparison of the highlighted options. Once the list of possible cars is down to four or five, you can test-drive them all and look at relevant information about each one. Most research focuses on this second step of decision making, because typically researchers study how someone chooses among a few major options, instead of focusing on how someone reduces a large set of choices down to a few. The prevailing assumption is that people perform some sort of mental cost–benefit analysis for each option, looking at the potential good and bad sides, and then add these up and pick the option that comes out best. Although this would seem to be the most rational thing to do, people are often less than fully rational, and their decisions are subject to biases, errors, and other influences. See *Money Matters* to learn how money can trick you into making bad decisions.

Influences on Choice. Here are some of the major patterns that guide people's choices:

1. **Risk aversion**. People are more affected by possible losses than by possible gains. In a simple demonstration, participants were asked whether they would take a perfectly fair bet on a coin flip, such that they would win or lose $10. Most people didn't want to bet, presumably because the prospect of losing $10 outweighs the prospect of winning the same amount, even though the odds are exactly equal (Kahneman & Tversky, 1984; Tversky & Kahneman, 1983).

   Another study looked at rational versus irrational (foolish) bets. Rational bets are ones that conform to what expert statistical risk appraisal would dictate. (For example, a 50% chance to win $20 is better than a 1% chance of winning $100. You evaluate the bet by multiplying the probability times the outcome: $1/2 \times \$20 = \$10$, whereas $1/100 \times \$100 = \$1$.) Researchers found that people were often rational, but when they were not, their irrational behavior was geared toward avoiding losses more often than pursuing gains (Atthowe, 1960). That is, people seemed more worried about the prospect of losing $10 than they were attracted by the possibility of winning $10.

2. **Temporal discounting**. A second influence is that what happens right now weighs more heavily

---

RISK AVERSION in decision making, the greater weight given to possible losses than possible gains

TEMPORAL DISCOUNTING in decision making, the greater weight given to the present over the future

How Money Can Trick You Into Making Bad Decisions

Suppose you have two job offers. One pays $50,000 per year and seems like it would be reasonably relaxed. The other will be stressful but pays better, at $63,000. Which do you choose?

Or suppose that after you get your job you are choosing between two apartments. They are about the same size and quality. One costs more but would enable you to walk to work. The cheaper one would require you to drive about half an hour each way. Which do you choose?

Many people would make these choices based on money—but this would make them less happy in the long run (Hsee & Zhang, 2004). This is not because money is irrelevant to happiness. Having more money is better! But there is a particular illusion that is created by the numerical value of money.

Look again at the differences between the options in these examples. The money difference is quantitative: a matter of degree. The other difference is qualitative: Some feature (e.g., walking to work) is present or absent. People tend to overestimate the impact of quantitative differences on happiness, relative to qualitative differences.

The reason for this is rooted in the difference between how one thinks while deciding versus how one experiences life. When you are deciding, you compare the two options (such as the two apartments). You think about them both at the same time. But once you live in one of them, you cease to think about the other one, by and large. The fact that you saved a certain amount of money by renting the cheaper apartment will vanish from your daily awareness. But whether you can walk to work or must drive half an hour in rush-hour traffic will affect you nearly every day. Even though you stop comparing it to what your life would have been like in the other option, that feature remains to intrude on your daily experience.

The difference between comparing multiple options and experiencing a single one was shown in a different way in another study (Bazerman, Loewenstein, & White, 1992). Participants considered two different ways of resolving a dispute with a neighbor. In one solution, the participant received $600 and the neighbor received $800. In the other solution, the participant and the neighbor each got $500. When participants had both options to compare, they preferred the first one, because it gave them more money ($600 vs. $500). However, when participants predicted their reaction to only one of the options (i.e., some participants considered only the first solution and others only the second solution), the first solution received less favorable ratings than the second, because they got less than the neighbor ($600 vs. $800).

In another study (Hsee, 1996), participants imagined shopping for a music dictionary in a used bookstore and were supposed to say how much they would be willing to pay, from $10 to $50. Some saw descriptions of two dictionaries, while others only saw a description of one dictionary. One dictionary had 10,000 entries and was in perfect condition. The other had 20,000 entries and was in perfect condition except for a torn cover. When comparing the two, people were willing to pay more for the one with the torn cover (because it had so much more information). Among participants who saw only one option, however, the torn cover reduced what people were willing to pay, because they were not able to appreciate the difference in amount of information between 10,000 versus 20,000 entries.

Thus, when choosing between options, people tend to focus on quantitative differences. But after you have made your choice, you live with what you chose, and the unchosen option is probably gone from your life. Remember to focus on what you will live with, not just what scores higher on paper when you compare. ■

PhotoDisc

---

than what might happen in the future. Would you rather have $1,000 today, or $1,200 two weeks from today? The logical choice would be the delayed one, because there is very little chance that you could invest the money wisely enough to turn $1,000 into $1,200 in two weeks, so if you take the delayed reward you will end up with more money. Most people, however, choose the immediate reward. For example, people who buy lottery tickets often choose the single check (immediate) payment option, which means they get all the money at once if they win—even though they might get more total money if they accept the winnings in more and smaller check amounts.

The discounting of the future can be seen in many contexts beyond money. For one such example that mixes sex and money, see *The Social Side of Sex*.

3. **The certainty effect**. Some features of a decision involve possibilities and odds, whereas others are certain. In buying a car, the likelihood that it will need repairs at a certain cost or frequency or that it will safeguard you in a collision are examples of things that might or might not happen, whereas you can be sure of the color and style you are getting. People tend to place undue weight on things that are certain. This is not to say that they completely ignore safety or repair records and just buy cars based on color, but they do end up relying on color a little more than they mean to do. This tendency to place too much emphasis on definite outcomes is called the **certainty effect** (Kahneman & Tversky, 1979).

CERTAINTY EFFECT in decision making, the greater weight given to definite outcomes than to probabilities

Gender, Sex, and Decisions

Someone of your preferred gender smiles at you and seems to be flirting a bit. There might be a chance to have sex later today. Then again, perhaps the person is just being friendly, and by making romantic or sexual advances you might end up embarrassing yourself and damaging the relationship. Do you make the advances?

The data suggest that the answer may depend on your gender. Men seem much more likely than women to chase after every potential (or even sometimes illusory) chance for sex. The reason for this difference may lie in the fact that evolution has prepared men and women to use different guidelines for making sexual decisions.

One general explanation, called **error management theory** (Haselton & Buss, 2000), is that both men and women make decisions so as to minimize the most costly type of error, but men's worst error is not the same as women's. The difference is rooted in a long evolutionary history, during which most males failed to reproduce at all, whereas most females did reproduce. Hence for females the goal is to get the best possible mate, and having sex too readily can defeat that goal. For a woman, to be on the safe side is to say no to sex a little longer, if only to make sure that her partner provides further proof that he is a good man and is devoted to her. In contrast, many male animals will have few or no opportunities to reproduce at all, and so in order to pass along their genes they should take advantage of every chance. It would be folly to pass up a chance for sex today if that opportunity might not be available tomorrow. These differences are increased by the differences in what the body

does to make a baby. If a woman gets pregnant by one man today, and a better partner comes along next week, her body is already committed to the (less attractive) pregnancy, so again it behooves her to wait until she is certain she has the best mate. In contrast, if a man makes one woman pregnant today and then a better partner comes along the following week, he is physically capable of impregnating her as well.

A recent study of temporal discounting showed how these sexual impulses can influence even decisions that do not, on the surface, have anything to do with sex. Participants in this study had to make choices between sooner smaller rewards (e.g., $5 tomorrow) and larger later ones (e.g., $10 a month from now—a typical tradeoff between present versus future). After they had made one round of choices, they were exposed to one of four types of stimuli. Some saw 12 pictures of attractive members of the opposite sex. Others saw 12 photos of relatively unattractive members of the opposite sex. Others saw 12 beautiful cars, and a final group saw 12 relatively ugly cars. Then they chose again between sooner smaller and

larger later rewards. Only one group showed a substantial shift toward the sooner smaller rewards: men who had looked at the beautiful women. The men in the other three conditions, and the women in all conditions, were relatively unaffected (Wilson & Daly, 2003).

Why? Again, evolution has selected men to leap at every mating chance. Apparently the sight of a pretty woman puts men into a mindset that emphasizes the present and discounts or ignores the future. A pretty woman can induce a man to spend much of his money right away, even at considerable cost to his future financial circumstances. She doesn't even have to try very hard. This study suggests that simply seeing her is enough to cause the man to forget about long-term financial prudence and focus on the here and now. ■

Digital Vision

For example, suppose you are playing Russian roulette. (A gun has some bullets in it while some of the chambers are empty, and when you play the game you point it at your head and pull the trigger once.) How much would you pay to remove one bullet, assuming either that (a) there are four bullets in the six chambers and two empties, or (b) there is only one bullet and five empties. Reducing

the number of bullets from four to three is exactly the same improvement in your chances of surviving the game as is reducing it from one to zero, but most people say they would pay significantly more to eliminate the only bullet (Kahneman & Tversky, 1979). This shows the certainty effect: They want to know they are completely safe.

4. **Keeping options open**. Some people prefer to postpone hard decisions and keep their options open as long as possible. In one study of online shoppers, some were offered a selection of bargains

---

ERROR MANAGEMENT THEORY the idea that both men and women seek to minimize the most costly type of error, but that men's and women's goals, and hence worst errors, differ

that were only available right away, whereas others had the additional option of coming back later to choose among the same options and bargains. Those who had to buy right away often did so. Those who could put off the decision generally decided to wait, indicating a preference for keeping one's options available until later. Unfortunately for the sellers, the customers who decided to postpone the decision hardly ever returned to make a purchase. It is not surprising that many salespeople make offers that expire immediately.

For some students, keeping a double major is a way of postponing a decision about their future. A double major requires students to divide their time and efforts, so they cannot be as successful at either subject as a single-major student would be, but some people pay this price in order to preserve their options (Shin & Ariely, 2004).

WHY PEOPLE DON'T CHOOSE

Postponing decisions may be part of a broader pattern called decision avoidance. In a review article titled "The Psychology of Doing Nothing," Christopher Anderson (2003) considered different forms this avoidance can take. One, called the **status quo bias**, is a simple preference to keep things the way they are instead of change. Would you want to exchange your home, your romantic partner, your course schedule, for another? The new one is unknown and might have unforeseen problems. People often stick with what they have, even when the alternatives seem better.

Another pattern that leads to doing nothing, called the **omission bias**, is taking whatever course of action does not require you to do anything (also called the default option). For example, when you complete a free registration to gain access to a website, often you must mark a particular box if you do not want to receive junk mail and advertisements. Why don't they leave it blank and let you just check it if you want to receive those mailings and ads? Because they want as many people as possible on their mailing list, and they know that many people will not do anything. In principle, it is just as easy for them to make "don't send mail" the default option as to make it "send mail." The omission bias means that many people will do nothing—they will leave the default in place—so they will get more people on their mailing list by making the default option "send mail" rather than "don't send."

One general theme behind decision avoidance is anticipated regret (Anderson, 2003). People avoid making choices and taking actions that they fear they will regret later on. Apparently people anticipate less regret over doing nothing than over doing something. They also know the status quo better than the alternatives, so there is a greater risk of regret if you decide to change than if you stand pat.

Another theme is that some decisions become too difficult. An influential study showed that people who visited a table with a display of jams were less likely to buy any of them if the table had 24 different varieties than if it had just 6 (Iyengar & Lepper, 2000). Some theorists have proposed that modern life offers too many choices (e.g., Schwartz, 2004).

Yet subsequent work has not found that people always recoil from too many choices. People like to have many options. Across many different circumstances, there is no general pattern that having more options leads to more avoidance of decisions (Scheibehenne, Greifeneder, & Todd, 2008). Sometimes having too few choices makes people reluctant to choose; for example, many people refuse to buy when they only see one option, even if it seems like an acceptable one (Mochon, 2008). Hence it is necessary for researchers to dig a bit deeper to see when this does or does not happen.

There are basically two reasons for failing to make a selection from a group of options, whether it is a matter of picking a spouse or a toothbrush or a car

---

STATUS QUO BIAS the preference to keep things the way they are rather than change
OMISSION BIAS the tendency to take whatever course of action does not require you to do anything (also called the default option)

SUDDENLY I HAVE AN URGE TO JUGGLE MACHETES...

ABSOLUTELY NO MACHETE JUGGLING

THE ESSENCE OF HUMAN NATURE

5-22 WILEY

©1997 Wiley Miller/ dist. by Washington Post Writers Group

E-mail: wileytoon@aol.com http://www.washingtonpost.com/wiley

to, you will experience reactance, which is an angry, disappointed feeling.

Reactance produces three main consequences (Brehm, 1966). First, it makes you want the forbidden option more and/or makes it seem more attractive. (If you weren't sure you wanted to see the concert, being told that you can't see it may increase your desire to see it and make you think it is likely to be a really good one.) Second, reactance may make you take steps to try to reclaim the lost option, often described as "reasserting your freedom." (You may try to sneak into the concert after all.) Third, you may feel or act aggressively toward the person who has restricted your freedom.

Many studies have supported reactance theory (Brehm & Brehm, 1981). Two-year-olds who are told not to play with a particular toy suddenly find that toy more appealing and are more likely to sneak over to it when they think no one is watching. Students who are told they can have their choice of five posters, but then are told that one of them (chosen at random, or even the one that was initially their third choice) is not available, suddenly like that one more and want it more. Labels designed to warn consumers about potentially objectionable material in TV programs, films, video games, and music often have the opposite effect of making people more interested in the "forbidden" media (Bushman & Cantor, 2003). Most ominously, men who have formed unrealistic expectations of having sex with a particular woman may become angry and even coercive if the woman rejects their advances (Baumeister, Catanese, & Wallace, 2002; Bushman, Bonacci, Van Dijk, & Baumeister, 2003).

The findings on reactance bring up the broader issues of free will and freedom of action. Regardless of whether someone believes in free will as a genuine phenomenon, there is little disputing the fact that people are sensitive to how much freedom of choice they have. Reactance theory emphasizes that people are motivated to gain and preserve choices. Having some of their choices taken away by someone else or some external event produces a very negative reaction in most people.

(White, Reisen, & Hoffrage, 2008). One is that none of the options seems good enough. The other is that it is hard to tell which one is the best. These two reasons have opposite relationships to the assortment of options. As there are more and more options, it is less and less plausible that none is good enough—but it gets harder and harder to be sure you've chosen the best one. You might test-drive two cars and decide that neither is good enough, but after you've tried two dozen cars, you should have found at least some satisfactory ones. But of course it's harder to pick the best of 24 than the better of 2.

Reactance. The interest in preserving options is the core of an important psychological theory that has held up well over several decades. Called **reactance theory**, it was first proposed by social psychologist Jack Brehm (1966; see also Brehm, 1972; Brehm & Brehm, 1981; Wicklund, 1974; Wortman & Brehm, 1975). The central point of reactance theory is that people desire to have freedom of choice and therefore have a negative, aversive reaction to having some of their choices or options taken away by other people or by external forces. The term reactance refers specifically to the negative feelings people have when their freedom is reduced. For example, if someone tells you that you cannot see a concert that you have been looking forward

CHOICE AND CHANGE

Making choices is a major part of life. Animals make simple choices in simple ways, but human beings have a far more complex inner capacity for making choices—which is good, because humans face very complex choices. Human choice is also much more momentous than what most animals do. Think of all the choices you make: what courses to take, whom to date and marry, whom to vote for, how to handle your money, what to do on a Sunday afternoon.

REACTANCE THEORY the idea that people are distressed by loss of freedom or options and seek to reclaim or reassert them

Understanding choice and decision making is a vital part of any effort to understand human life.

The essence of the idea of freedom is that you can do more than one thing (hence the need to choose among them). This is relevant even to very basic questions such as whether you can choose to change yourself. Some people think their traits are constant and stable, so there is little point in trying to change. Others think they can change. For example, some observers have noted that professional (baseball) athletes tend to have different attitudes in the United States and Japan (Heine, Lehman, Markus, & Kitayama, 1999). In general, the American athletes think in terms of innate talent, and hence simply performing up to their ability, whereas the Japanese athletes think of sport in terms of continual improvement through hard work.

That difference in thinking is not confined to athletes. Researcher Carol Dweck (1996) has shown that ordinary people and even children can be found exhibiting either style. She uses the term **entity theorists** to refer to people who regard traits as fixed, stable things (entities), as opposed to **incremental theorists** who believe that traits are subject to change and improvement. Entity theorists prefer to do things at which they are good, in order that success can gain them credit and admiration. They dislike criticism or bad feedback intensely (partly because they tend to think that bad traits are permanent). In contrast, incremental theorists are more likely to enjoy learning and challenges; they don't mind criticism or initial failure as much, because they expect to improve. Entity theorists often choose the easiest task, because they want guaranteed success, whereas incremental theorists prefer harder, more challenging tasks where they can learn (Dweck & Leggett, 1988). When students move to a new, more challenging environment, such as from elementary school to middle school, or from high school to college, the entity theorists are often discouraged and overwhelmed, and their performance goes down, whereas the incremental theorists keep striving to improve and often show gains in performance (Henderson & Dweck, 1990). Likewise, in lab studies, failure tends to be devastating to entity theorists and even to produce a kind of **learned helplessness** (they quit trying and give up) because they think the failure is proof that they are incompetent losers. In contrast, when incremental theorists fail, they simply try harder to improve (Zhao & Dweck, 1994; cited in Dweck, 1996).

Ultimately, the difference is between thinking that people are the way they are, period, versus thinking that people are constantly subject to change. People apply these different outlooks both to themselves and to others. Thus, entity theorists tend to interpret other people's behavior as reflecting their traits, whereas incremental theorists interpret them as caused by temporary states and external factors (Dweck, 1996). (See Chapter 5 for a detailed discussion of the difference between internal and external attributions.)

Hideo Nomo played for the Kintetsu Buffaloes, a Japanese professional baseball team, from 1990 to 1994. He signed with the Los Angeles Dodgers in 1995 as the first Japanese player in Major League baseball and won the Rookie of the Year award the same year.

Streeter Lecka/Getty Images

[**QUIZ YOURSELF**]

What You Do, and What It Means

1. Suppose you show up for a paid experiment and receive $10. The researcher says you can double your earnings if the outcome of a coin toss is a head, or lose your earnings if the outcome of a coin toss is a tail. Research shows that most people would __b__ .

   (a) flip the coin and try to get $20
   (b) not flip the coin and keep their $10
   (c) There is a 50/50 chance that people will flip the coin because the potential gain equals the potential loss.
   (d) The research evidence is mixed.

ENTITY THEORISTS those who believe that traits are fixed, stable things (entities) and thus people should not be expected to change

INCREMENTAL THEORISTS those who believe that traits are subject to change and improvement

LEARNED HELPLESSNESS belief that one's actions will not bring about desired outcomes, leading one to give up and quit trying

Freedom of Action

The question of whether people have free will has been debated for centuries, and its importance has been recognized in such fields as theology (religious doctrines), morality, and philosophy (e.g., Kant, 1797/1967). Psychologists are divided on the issue. Many believe that psychology must explain all behavior in terms of causes, and if a behavior is caused, then it is not truly or fully free. Others emphasize the fact that people make choices and could have chosen differently under other circumstances, and in that sense they believe people do have freedom.

Whether to believe in free will is more than just a philosophical debate. In fact, research suggests that belief in free will is valuable for society. When experimental manipulations induced people to reject their belief in free will, they became more willing to cheat on a test and steal money (Vohs & Schooler, 2008). Similar manipulations showed that disbelieving in free will causes people to become more aggressive and less helpful toward others (Baumeister, Masicampo, & DeWall, in press). These findings say nothing about whether free will really exists—but the belief in it helps cultural animals act in more prosocial ways, thereby helping the social system function better.

MORE OR LESS FREE

Whatever the ultimate decision is about free will, there is little disputing that people perceive that they make some choices and that some of these are freer than others. In particular, people have the subjective experience that sometimes they are constrained by external factors, whereas other times they can freely choose what they think is best. In other words, although absolute freedom is debatable, relative freedom is an important feature of social behavior. Among humans, greater freedom is marked by greater behavioral flexibility, controlled processes (as opposed to automatic ones), and self-regulation.

In order to live within a culture and human society, humans need a fairly complex and flexible decision-making apparatus. Most animals face choices to some degree, but these are limited in scope and meaning. An animal may have to choose which direction to walk in seeking food, or where to sleep, or whether to fight over some territory or resource. These are important decisions, but they are not nearly as complicated as the choices faced by human beings in our society, such as what college major or occupation to pursue, whether to lie about past sexual experiences, how much effort and time to spend trying to fix one's car before giving up and getting a new one, how much money to offer for a painting or a house, and whether to yield to family pressures about religious matters. Remember, inner processes serve interpersonal events—so the complex demands of living in human society call for an elaborate inner system for making decisions.

As cultural animals, humans rely on meaning to make their choices, and meaning generally offers multiple ways of understanding and deciding. Unlike most other animals, human beings can decide based on abstract rules, moral and ethical principles, laws, plans, contracts, agreements, and the like. This capacity for thinking about a decision or situation in multiple ways requires a flexible capacity for making those decisions.

FREE ACTION COMES FROM INSIDE

Self-determination theory is an important perspective on freedom of action. It builds on the research on intrinsic versus extrinsic motivation discussed in Chapter 3. Not all motivations are equal. As the authors of this theory, Ed Deci and Richard Ryan (1985, 2000; Ryan & Deci, 2000), point out, people may be motivated to perform well out of a deep passion for excellence or because of a bribe; they may be motivated to behave honestly out of an inner moral sense or because they fear others are watching them; they may be motivated to work hard because they love what they are doing or because they feel pressure to meet a looming deadline. As those three pairs of motivations indicate, people may be motivated

SELF-DETERMINATION THEORY the theory that people need to feel at least some degree of autonomy and internal motivation

by something originating inside them or by some external pressure or force. Doing things to satisfy external pressures is felt to be less free than acting from one's inner promptings. A central point of self-determination theory is that people have an innate need for autonomy, which means that at least some of their activities must be motivated by their inner drives and choices, rather than by external factors.

Believing you are acting autonomously and from intrinsic motivation has many benefits. People who act on that belief derive more satisfaction, are more interested in and excited about what they are doing, have greater confidence, and often perform better, persist longer, and show greater creativity. Autonomous action also contributes to vitality, self-esteem, and general well-being (akin to happiness) (deCharms, 1968; Deci, 1975; Deci, Koestner, & Ryan, 1999; Fisher, 1978; Ryan, 1982; Ryan & Deci, 2000). They are less prone to fall victim to passivity, alienation, and mental illness. For example, some teachers encourage their students to develop their own interests, make decisions, and in other respects exercise autonomy, whereas other teachers try to control their students. The students of the autonomy-supporting teachers end up more interested in their work, more curious to learn, and more eager for challenges, and they end up learning more (Amabile, 1996; Deci, Nezlek, & Sheinman, 1981; Deci et al., 1999; Flink, Boggiano, & Barrett, 1990; Grolnick & Ryan, 1987; Ryan & Deci, 2000; Ryan & Grolnick, 1986; Utman, 1997).

All these studies suggest that different levels of freedom of action have important implications for how people fare. Perhaps most important, when people reach the goals associated with their own autonomous or intrinsic desires, they feel happier and healthier, whereas reaching goals linked to extrinsic motivations is much less able to produce such benefits (e.g., Kasser & Ryan, 2001; Deci et al., 1999; Sheldon & Kasser, 1998).

HAVING AN OUT, VERSUS NO ESCAPE

One of the most profound illustrations that perceived freedom produces benefits is the **panic button effect**: Believing that one has an escape option can reduce stress, even if one never makes use of this option. In an early demonstration of this effect, participants were exposed to highly aversive noise stress—blasts of loud noise, delivered at random, unpredictable intervals for irregular lengths of time—while they were trying to solve puzzles. This noise stress had been previously shown to make it harder for people to perform their tasks; even afterward, when they sat in a quiet room, people who had been through the noise stress performed worse at a variety of tasks, indicating less concentration, less persistence, and lower frustration tolerance. In this experiment

(Glass, Singer, & Friedman, 1969), all participants were exposed to the same noise stress, and all of them had a button on the table in front of them. In reality, the button was not connected to anything and pressing it would have no effect. To some participants, however, the experimenter said that the button would turn off the noise. He said the participant could eliminate the noise if it became too stressful or hard to bear, though he said it would spoil the experiment if the participant pressed it, and he asked the participant not to use the button if possible. No one ever pressed the button. Yet the participants who had this "panic button" available to them did not show all the problems and impairments that the stress had caused. Even though they did not make use of the button to escape the stress, they derived considerable comfort just from knowing it was there.

Thus, even the false belief that one can exert control over events makes them more bearable. Does your neighbor's loud music keep you awake late at night? It may bother you less if you think that you could ask the neighbor to turn it down than if you think you have no choice but to listen to it. Do you suffer when you spend a Friday night alone once in a while? You may feel less lonely if you think you could find some friends or companions than if you think you have no such options. Indeed, at a broader level, many people believe in free will, and that belief could stem in part from the panic button effect. Believing you have free will means you think you have some control over your life, which may reduce stress.

PANIC BUTTON EFFECT a reduction in stress or suffering due to a belief that one has the option of escaping or controlling the situation, even if one doesn't exercise it

Goals, Plans, Intentions

A goal without a plan is just a wish.

—Antoine de Saint-Exupery (1900–1944), French writer and aviator, author of *The Little Prince*

We have already argued that ideas and meanings are centrally important to human action. Meaning connects things; thus, an action is meaningful to the extent that it is connected to other things or events. One important type of meaning links an action to a goal. Your current action, such as looking at this page, derives meaning from various future events that are presumably your goals, including learning something about social psychology, doing well in the course, getting an education, earning a degree, and preparing for a career. Without those or similar goals, you might still look at this page, but to do so would be relatively pointless and meaningless.

A **goal** is an idea of some desired future state (Oettingen & Gollwitzer, 2001). Goals, in turn, are the (meaningful) link between values and action (Locke & Kristof, 1996; Locke & Latham, 1990). That is, most people hold certain values, such as family, friends, religion, honesty, success, and health, but these broad and general preferences must be translated into something much more specific in order to serve as guides for behavior. A goal tells you how to pursue and uphold your values.

Goals can also be called personal projects (Little, 1989) or personal strivings (Emmons, 1989). Most people have more than one goal or project in their life toward which they work and strive at any given time. In fact, when people are asked to list their goals and similar personal projects, the average list contains 15 items (Little, 1989). Thus, the typical human life nowadays is characterized by a variety of different goals, some of which may be completely unrelated to others, and some of which may even be in conflict (e.g., if they make competing demands on a limited stock of time or money).

Experts disagree as to how goal-oriented other animals are; hence they disagree about how unique the goal pursuit of human beings is. The experts who believe that animals do pursue goals, in the sense of having mental ideas about future states and trying to make them come true, generally still concede that human beings do this far better and more extensively than other creatures. Animal goals mostly involve the immediate situation and an outcome that is already almost visible, such as climbing a tree or chasing a smaller animal (Tomasello & Call, 1997; see also Roberts, 2002). In contrast, human beings pursue goals that may be weeks, years, even decades away, such as in studying and working to become a successful lawyer. (Your textbook authors spent five years writing the first edition of this book!)

SETTING AND PURSUING GOALS

Where do goals come from? Almost certainly a person's goals reflect the influence of both inner processes and cultural factors. Perhaps the best way to think of this is that the culture sets out a variety of possible goals, and people choose among them depending on their personal wants and needs and also on their immediate circumstances. For example, throughout much of history the goals available to men and women were often quite different; women were barred from many professions, and men were not permitted to be homemakers. Modern Western society has in theory opened up a much wider range of options to both men and women, though both social and personal factors still steer men and women into some different goals and jobs. For example, pressure to earn enough to support a family causes many more men than women to take jobs that may be stressful, unpleasant, or physically dangerous as long as they offer high pay. In such cases, the man's goal of making enough money to attract a mate and support a family causes him to select some goals over other possible goals, such as having a pleasant job and reducing his risk of dying on the job (Farrell, 1993). Women, in contrast, tend to be less guided by materialistic and financial motives in choosing their careers; they give more emphasis to goals of fulfillment, safety, and flexibility (e.g., Kasser & Ryan, 1993). Again, these differences almost certainly reflect the influence of both individual preferences and cultural realities.

Pursuing goals involves at least two major steps, which involve different mental states. The first step includes setting goals (which may involve choosing among competing goals—you can't do everything at once), evaluating how difficult or feasible a goal is, and deciding how much you want to pursue it. The second step is pursuing the goal, which may include planning what to do and carrying out those behaviors (Gollwitzer, 1996; Locke & Kristof, 1995; Locke & Latham, 1990). Let us consider these two mental states in turn (see ▶ **TABLE 4.1**).

Setting goals is a time for being realistic. You may be choosing among different possible goals to pursue, or you may simply be deciding whether to commit yourself to a particular goal or not. People in this state are thoughtful and generally seek all sorts of information (both good and bad) about the goals they are contemplating. In this state, the "positive illusions" that characterize a great deal of normal thinking (see Chapter 3) are typically set aside,

GOAL an idea of some desired future state

and people instead tend to be quite accurate about their own capabilities and their chances of successfully achieving the goal (Gollwitzer & Kinney, 1989; Taylor & Gollwitzer, 1995).

A very different mind-set accompanies pursuing goals. The time for realism is past; instead, optimism and positive illusions help build confidence and foster better performance. The person zeroes in on the one goal and loses interest in information about other goals. Questions of whether and why to pursue the goal are set aside, in favor of questions about how to achieve it. The goal dominates information processing, such as by drawing attention to opportunities and obstacles, driving the person to develop workable and detailed plans, and stimulating the person to persist and keep trying even in the face of setbacks or interruptions.

Another benefit of goals is that they can bring the person back to resume an activity after an interruption (Gollwitzer, 1996). To get a good grade in a course, for example, you have to perform many activities that are spaced out in time, such as attending class, studying, and reviewing notes, over a period of several months. The goal (the mental idea of doing well in the class) can be important in helping you turn your efforts to pursuing the relevant activities. Even when you are enjoying watching a television show or practicing your athletic skills, you may stop those activities to attend class or study. Hardly any other animal is capable of making such decisions to stop one activity in order to resume pursuit of a previously pursued goal. Moreover, people who are most successful in life are those who are good at resuming activities after interruptions, because most major successes in life require the person to work on them on many different days, interspersed with other activities such as eating and sleeping.

Both the conscious and automatic systems help in the pursuit of goals. The conscious system does much of the goal setting, especially if the decision about whether to pursue a goal is complicated. The conscious system may also help provide the initiative to resume goals that have been interrupted. Also, crucially, if one step toward a goal is blocked, the conscious system may be helpful in devising an alternate strategy or route to reach the ultimate goal. The automatic system also contributes in an interesting way. Most people experience the so-called **Zeigarnik effect**, which is a tendency to experience automatic, intrusive thoughts about a goal that one has pursued but whose pursuit has been interrupted. (This is the duplex mind at work: The automatic system signals the conscious mind, which may have moved on to other pursuits, that a previous goal was left uncompleted.) That is, if you start working toward a goal and fail to get there, thoughts about the goal will keep popping into your mind while you are doing

▶ **TABLE 4.1** Mind-Sets and Goals

	MIND-SET	
	Goal Setting	**Goal Pursuit/Striving**
Function	Deciding what to do	Deciding how to do it, and doing it
Attitude	Open-minded	Closed-minded
Mental focus	Feasibility and desirability	Means and obstacles
Core question	Why should I do it?	How do I do it?
Style of thought	Realistic thinking	Optimistic thinking

other things, as if to remind you to get back on track to finish reaching that goal. Because most human activities naturally form themselves into units so that completing them is a goal, any sort of interruption can produce a Zeigarnik effect. One commonplace experience is that if the radio is turned off in the middle of a song that you like (or even one you don't like), you may have that song running through your mind for the rest of the day.

People perform better if they have goals, but some goals are more helpful than others. In general, it is most helpful to have specific goals and goals that are difficult but reachable (Locke & Kristof, 1996; Locke & Latham, 1990). A broad goal such as "getting an education" does not necessarily improve performance very much; specific goals such as "getting a good grade on my next test" are more helpful. People who shoot for high goals generally do better than those who set easy goals for themselves, unless the goals are so high as to be unrealistic, in which case they are discouraging.

HIERARCHY OF GOALS

Goals are not necessarily independent; in fact, most people have interlinked sets of goals. People usually have a hierarchy of goals, with short-term or proximal goals that operate as stepping-stones toward long-term or distal goals. For example, a high school student might decide she wants to be the chief executive officer (CEO) of a major corporation, which would be a distal goal, but if she had only that goal she would be unlikely to get very far. To become a CEO, you need to take many steps, such as getting an education, getting an entry-level job at a corporation, gaining experience, and working your way up through the ranks by way of a series of promotions (▶ **FIGURE 4.1**). It would be silly to drop out of high school and just look through the want ads in

---

ZEIGARNIK EFFECT a tendency to experience automatic, intrusive thoughts about a goal whose pursuit has been interrupted

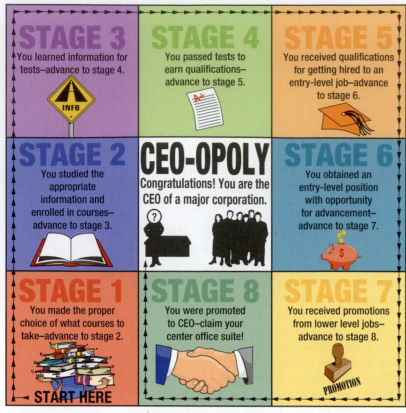

STAGE 3
You learned information for tests–advance to stage 4.

STAGE 4
You passed tests to earn qualifications–advance to stage 5.

STAGE 5
You received qualifications for getting hired to an entry-level job–advance to stage 6.

STAGE 2
You studied the appropriate information and enrolled in courses–advance to stage 3.

CEO-OPOLY
Congratulations! You are the CEO of a major corporation.

STAGE 6
You obtained an entry-level position with opportunity for advancement–advance to stage 7.

STAGE 1
You made the proper choice of what courses to take–advance to stage 2.

START HERE

STAGE 8
You were promoted to CEO–claim your center office suite!

STAGE 7
You received promotions from lower level jobs–advance to stage 8.

PROMOTION

▶ **FIGURE 4.1** A hierarchy of goals.

the newspaper for job openings as CEO of a major corporation, but if you only had the big, distal goal of becoming a CEO, without the proximal goals that lead up to it, you might not know any better (Bandura & Schunk, 1981). The person who has a hierarchy of goals, with many steps leading up to the ultimate distal goal, is far more likely to be successful.

The duplex mind is relevant to goal hierarchies. The automatic system can keep track of the goals and initiate behavior to pursue each step along the way. The conscious system may be useful, however, when an intermediate goal is blocked. Consciousness is a flexible system for processing information, and it can find a substitute goal when the overarching or ultimate goal is blocked. In the previous example, if you had a plan for becoming CEO but discovered that your corporation never hired a CEO from among its own vice presidents, then you might use your conscious information-processing system to figure out that once you became vice president you would need to look elsewhere (i.e., other corporations) for openings as a CEO, or else you would have to move laterally as vice president in order to have a chance to come back as CEO. The automatic system is much less effective at such flexible thinking; if its plan were

blocked, it might be at a loss to find an alternative pathway to the ultimate goal.

We have noted the problems that might arise if you have only distal, ultimate goals without forming a hierarchy of proximal goals. Conversely, there are also problems for people who have only proximal (short-term) goals without the distal (long-term) ones (Bandura & Schunk, 1981). These people essentially go through life dealing with one issue or problem at a time but without a sense of where they should be going in the long run. They may be good at paying the bills, doing their assigned tasks, and responding to immediate needs or problems in their relationships, but where they end up in life is likely to be the result of a series of accidents and may not necessarily be to their liking. Having only proximal goals is not much better than having only distal goals. To live your life effectively within human society and culture, it is important to have both distal and proximal goals (preferably interlinked). In other words, the most effective approach is to have an idea of where you would like to be in five or ten years (even if you change this goal, it is still important to have one) as well as some ideas of what you need to do this week, this month, and this year in order to get there.

MULTIPLE GOALS AND GOAL SHIELDING

Nearly everyone has many different goals. That presents a problem, however: How do you decide which to work on? Indeed, how do you prevent worries about unmet goals to distract you when you are working toward another goal? For example, just because you are working on a term paper or problem set, your other goals of finding a romantic partner, getting fit, and saving money do not magically disappear—but if you think about them, you won't get your paper finished.

In a sense, the different goals compete inside your mind. Each tries to get you to think about it and work toward it. Not only does the mind have to have a way to set priorities and pursue the top goals; it also needs to keep the others from interfering and distracting you from what you are doing. This process of **goal shielding** sometimes has to keep more important goals at bay. To continue the previous example, you may regard finding someone to marry as more important than doing your homework, but if you spend all your time and energy on your love life, you won't get your homework done. Therefore your mind has to shut out thoughts about your love life while you do the homework.

Goal shielding seems to occur naturally, even automatically (Shah, Friedman, & Kruglanski, 2002). When a person starts working toward one goal, the mind automatically shuts other goals away from consciousness. The more committed a person

GOAL SHIELDING when the activation of a focal goal the person is working on inhibits the accessibility of alternative goals

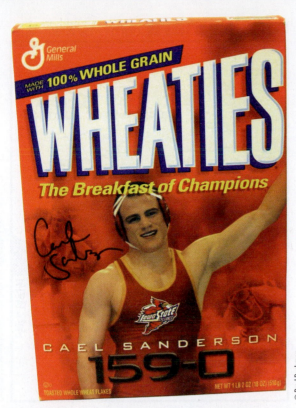

Cael Sanderson is currently the head wrestling coach at Penn State University. When he was a college student at Iowa State University, Sanderson was a student in Bushman's social psychology class.

doesn't happen to care about your schoolwork, then thinking of her won't make you study harder.

One of your textbook authors (Bushman) has a photo of Cael Sanderson in his office, because the photo inspires him to work hard and be his best. As a college student, Sanderson wrestled at Iowa State University, where he never lost a match (his record was 159–0). *Sports Illustrated* named his college career as the number 2 most outstanding achievement in college history. He was the first wrestler to appear on a *Wheaties* cereal box. He went on to win a gold medal in wrestling at the 2004 Olympics in Athens. Sanderson is currently the head wrestling coach at Iowa State University. When he was a college student, Sanderson was a student in Bushman's social psychology class—but now his picture serves to remind his former professor to strive for excellence!

Successful people actually seem to manage their social lives partly on the basis of these mental connections (Fitzsimons & Shah, 2008). When they have a goal, they automatically think more about people who will help them reach that goal or who at least support them in pursuing it. They draw closer to those helpful people and spend more time with them. It may seem unromantic to choose among your friends based on who is most helpful for reaching your goals, but probably that strategy contributes to success.

is to the current goal, the more effectively the mind shields this goal by blocking thoughts of other goals.

Different goals are also associated with different people in one's life. Hence being around certain people, or even thinking of them, can shift priorities among goals. Answering questions about a friend made people more helpful than answering questions about a coworker, presumably because the goal of helping is associated with friends more than with coworkers (Fitzsimons & Bargh, 2003). Thinking of one's mother primed goals of wanting to do well in school; as a result, thoughts of mother motivated people to try harder and perform better, even on laboratory tasks. And the closer people felt emotionally to their mother, the more strongly the thought of her made them want to do well (Shah, 2003).

Actually, mother may not always be the most effective person to stimulate goal pursuit, because people may associate multiple goals with their mothers. There are variations on the basic pattern that thinking of a person activates goals that you associate with that person (Shah, 2003). The more different goals associated with that person, the less any one of them is activated. And if the other person does not care about the goal, then thinking of him or her does not really get you working toward it. If your mother

REACHING GOALS: WHAT'S THE PLAN?

Once you have a goal, you can start to plan. Planning is beneficial because it focuses attention on how to reach the goal and typically offers specific guidelines for what to do. People who make specific plans are more likely to take steps toward their goals than people who fail to make plans; in fact, laboratory studies have indicated that making plans motivates people to get started working toward their goals (Gollwitzer, 1996). In one study, students agreed to furnish reports within 48 hours on how they spent their Christmas holidays. Some were asked to make specific plans as to when and where they would write the report; for others, it was left up to them to decide later on. The former were more than twice as likely as the latter to complete the reports on time (Gollwitzer, 1996). Thus, those who made specific plans were more likely to reach their goals than those who did not.

Plans have two main drawbacks. One is that if they are too detailed and rigid, they can be discouraging. In one study, students were encouraged to make either detailed daily plans for their studying, monthly plans, or no plans. The researchers expected the students with the daily plans to succeed the best, but they did not; those who planned by the month did best (Kirschenbaum, Humphrey,

& Malett, 1981; Kirschenbaum, Malett, Humphrey, & Tomarken, 1982). (Actually, among the best students, daily plans were very effective and sometimes surpassed the monthly plans. For everyone else, though, monthly plans worked best.)

Why? Trying to plan every day had several disadvantages. For one thing, making such detailed plans is tiresome and time-consuming, so many participants in the study soon stopped making plans altogether. Another, more important reason was that daily plans are too rigid and can be discouraging. They leave no scope for making changes and choices day by day, even if one figures out better ways to do things or encounters unexpected delays. People enjoy making some choices along the way, as opposed to having everything laid out precisely in advance. When things go wrong, a monthly plan can still be followed with some revisions, but the day-by-day plans are defeated, and the daily planners felt discouraged and frustrated as soon as they were behind schedule. Thus, plans and even specific plans are good, but too much detail and a lack of flexibility can undermine them (Kirschenbaum et al., 1982).

The second drawback of plans is that they tend to be overly optimistic. When was the last time you heard a story on the news saying, "Construction of the new building has been completed eight months ahead of schedule, and the total cost was $12 million less than had been projected"? Instead, most projects come in late and over budget. As one famous example, the opera house in Sydney, Australia, now recognized

SLEEP

CALCULATE TRIGONOMETRIC EQUATIONS

DEVELOP THEOREMS

EAT

DO LONG DIVISION

SLEEP

FELICIA PLANS HER DAY.

Making daily plans is a bad idea (unless you're a cat).

as one of the world's most beautiful and impressive buildings, was started in 1957. The plans said it would cost $7 million and be completed early in 1963. By 1963 it was nowhere near finished and it was already over budget. The plans were cut back to save time and money, but even so it was not finished until 1973 (10 years late), and the cost had run to more than $100 million (Buehler, Griffin, & Ross, 1994)!

COMMON MISTAKES IN PLANNING

The tendency for plans to underestimate the time and cost probably reflects the optimistic mind-set that people adopt once they have chosen a goal. It is not limited to giant buildings, either. In one study, students were asked to estimate how long it would take them to finish their thesis, and to furnish both an optimistic estimate and a pessimistic one ("assuming everything went as poorly as it possibly could"). Fewer than a third finished by their best estimate. Even more surprisingly, fewer than half finished even by their most pessimistic estimate (Buehler et al., 1994). That is, even when they tried to foresee every possible problem and worst-case scenario, they were still too optimistic. This optimistic bias is related to the **planning fallacy** (Kahneman & Tversky, 1979), defined as the "belief that one's own project will proceed as planned, even while knowing that the vast majority of similar projects have run late" (Buehler et al., 1994).

© BL Images Ltd./Alamy

The Sydney Opera House: Spectacular architectural achievement or catastrophe of planning . . . or both?

PLANNING FALLACY the tendency for plans to be overly optimistic because the planner fails to allow for unexpected problems

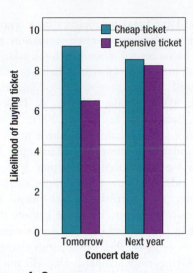

▶ **FIGURE 4.2 The high cost of tickets discouraged people from buying them for an imminent concert, but cost seemed irrelevant if the concert was a year away.**

Another sign that this tendency to make overly optimistic plans comes from people's positive illusions about themselves is that they are pretty accurate at predicting how other people will do. When research participants had to predict how long their roommates or friends would take to complete their projects, the predictions were remarkably accurate. Problems lie not with predicting in general, but with the distortions that arise when we think about ourselves. If you want a reliable estimate about how long it will take you to finish some project, don't trust your own judgment—ask someone else who knows you well!

Optimism seems to run wild when the perspective includes a long future; in the short run, people are more realistic. People make their short-run decisions based on what seems feasible, whereas long-range decisions are made with less concern for practical issues and more attention to how desirable something is. For example, would you rather do a difficult but interesting assignment or an easier but more boring one? If the assignment is due this week, students tend to choose the easy/boring one, whereas if the assignment is not due for a month or two, they pick the difficult/interesting one. In another study, the decision about whether to buy tickets for a show depended mainly on the quality of the show if the show was in the distant future, but if the show was soon, people's decisions depended more on the price of the ticket (see ▶ **FIGURE 4.2**; Liberman & Trope, 1998; Liberman, Sagristano, & Trope, 2002). As crunch time gets closer, people shift their decision criteria from broad, abstract values toward practical concerns. Thus, one of the biggest differences between long-term planning and dealing with present concerns is the greater pressure of practical constraints on the latter.

In general, people naturally feel more strongly about the present than about the distant future, so the here and now takes precedence over future considerations. But to be successful in life, it is usually necessary to consider the future. Overriding one's immediate wishes and feelings may thus be vital for long-term success. Such overriding requires a powerful ability, called self-regulation, that is far more developed in humans than in other species. Self-regulation, which is important for success in pursuing many goals, is examined in the next section.

[QUIZ YOURSELF]

Goals, Plans, Intentions

1. Goals are the meaningful link between _____.

   (a) beliefs and actions   (b) beliefs and emotions

   (c) values and actions   (d) values and emotions

2. Fatima seems obsessed with achieving the goal she is working toward. She can't seem to focus on anything else, even other goals. This is called _____.

   (a) goal shielding

   (b) the planning fallacy

   (c) psychological reactance

   (d) the Zeigarnik effect

3. Claudia is waiting in line to see a movie on the first day it is released. Just as she gets close to the ticket booth, the person in the booth announces that the movie is sold out. Rather than wait in line for the next show, Claudia leaves, but she spends the rest of the day thinking about the movie. This illustrates _____.

   (a) entity theory   (b) incremental theory

   (c) the planning fallacy   (d) the Zeigarnik effect

4. People are often overly optimistic about what they can accomplish. This is called the _____.

   (a) certainty effect   (b) optimistic bias effect

   (c) planning fallacy   (d) Zeigarnik effect

Self-Regulation

Self-regulation refers to the self's capacity to alter its own responses. It is quite similar to the everyday term "self-control." People regulate their thoughts, their emotions, their impulses and desires, and their task performance. Human beings have a much

SELF-REGULATION the self's capacity to alter its own responses; self-control

off the mark.com by Mark Parisi
offthemark.com

Journal Entry for Jan. 1
Sadly, I have already
broken one of my New Year's
resolutions and fear I may
soon break the other...

ATLANTIC FEATURE © 1996 MARK PARISI

Reprinted by permission of Atlantic Feature Syndicate/Mark Parisi.

greater capacity for self-regulation than most other creatures, and this is probably a crucial contributor to the human capacity to live in the complex social and cultural worlds we construct. Self-regulation enables people to be flexible, to adapt themselves to many different circumstances, rules, and demands. Self-regulation enables one's social conscience to prevail over selfish impulses, so that people can do what is right and good rather than just indulging their selfish inclinations. In this way, self-regulation enables people to live together and get along much better. This fits the general theme that inner processes serve interpersonal functions. Self-regulation enables people to keep their promises, obey rules, respect others, control their temper, and do other things that make for better interpersonal relations.

Self-regulation predicts success or failure in many different spheres. Most of the problems that afflict people in our society today have some component of inadequate self-regulation: drug and alcohol abuse, addiction, eating disorders, obesity, anxiety and anger control problems, unwanted pregnancy, unsafe sex and sexually transmitted diseases, gambling, overuse of credit cards, debt and bankruptcy, underachievement in school, poor physical fitness, violence and crime, and many more. People who are poor at self-control often end up rejected by their relationship partners, fired by their employers, or even

imprisoned for breaking society's laws. People who are good at self-control or self-regulation are more likely to be successful in work, school, relationships, and other important spheres of behavior (Baumeister, Stillwell, & Heatherton, 1994; Mischel, Shoda, & Peake, 1988; Shoda, Mischel, & Peake, 1990; Tangney, Baumeister, & Boone, 2004).

Effective self-regulation has three main components: standards, monitoring, and strength. The term *standards* was introduced in Chapter 3; it refers to concepts (ideas) of how things might or should be. In Chapter 3 we focused on how people compare themselves to standards, but there is more to it than that. When people find they do not measure up to their ideals or goals, they often try to change themselves. Having clear standards that do not conflict is important for successful self-regulation. If you don't know how you want to be, it is very difficult to change yourself toward that goal.

Standards can be supplied by the culture; thus, they represent an important way in which culture can influence behavior. Culture can tell people what is the right or good way to act. Part of the long road to social acceptance involves learning what the standards are—what is fashionable, acceptable, cool, or morally proper. Many youngsters find the early teen years (middle or junior high school) to be especially difficult and unhappy, because social life is changing and it is hard to learn the new standards amid a changing peer group.

Many standards, especially the ones learned from culture, involve what not to do: Don't lie, cheat, steal, spit on the floor, say forbidden words, cut in line, betray a friend, talk back to your teacher, drive when drunk, and so forth. Eight of the Ten Commandments in Judeo-Christian religion specifically say what not to do, and even the other two (honoring parents and keeping the Sabbath day holy) implicitly refer to things that should not be done. As we have repeatedly seen, nature says go and culture says stop. The culture's "stop" rules are standards, and self-regulation is required to implement them.

The second component of self-control is **monitoring**—keeping track of the behaviors or responses you want to regulate. Indeed, some experts believe that the central purpose of self-awareness (focusing attention on the self) is to promote self-regulation, because as you watch yourself you can monitor how well you are changing to reach your goals or other standards (Carver & Scheier, 1981, 1982). Without self-awareness, self-regulation would be difficult, if not impossible.

The way people monitor themselves is typically summarized as a feedback loop (see ▶ **FIGURE 4.3**). An easy-to-remember acronym is **TOTE**, which stands for **T**est, **O**perate, **T**est, and **E**xit (Carver & Scheier, 1981, 1982). The first test is a comparison

MONITORING keeping track of behaviors or responses to be regulated
TOTE the self-regulation feedback loop of Test, Operate, Test, Exit

of self against the standard. For example, if you have resolved to be nicer to your romantic partner, you may occasionally stop to consider how nice you have been toward that person today. If the test reveals a discrepancy—that is, you are not being as nice as you would like—then you move along to the "operate" phase, in which you exert conscious control to change yourself to become nicer. You might remind yourself to say nice things, or perhaps purchase a small gift to express your appreciation to your partner. At some point in the "operate" phase, you may test the self again. Am I being nice enough now? If the answer is no, then more operations (more changes to the self) are required. Eventually, perhaps, the answer is "yes," indicating that you have met the standard, and at this point you can complete the loop by exiting it.

The concept of feedback loops is borrowed from cybernetic theory, developed during and after World War II to help guide missiles toward their targets despite winds and other difficulties (Powers, 1973). Its most familiar illustration is the thermostat that helps regulate the temperature in a room: The test involves evaluating whether the current temperature is close to the level at which the thermostat has been set, and the "operate" phase involves turning on the heater or air conditioning unit; when another test reveals that the temperature has reached the desired level, the heater or air conditioner is shut off and the loop is exited.

Monitoring is a key ingredient in self-regulation and often presents the best opportunity for immediate improvement in self-regulation. If you want to keep to an exercise program, write on the calendar each day whether you had a workout. If you want to save money, make a list of what you spend your money on each day, and keep closer track of how much you earn and how much you save.

Dieting furnishes a good example of the importance of monitoring. If you are not dieting, you likely pay little or no attention to how much you eat—you may simply eat your fill. Dieters, in contrast, soon

Culture often tells us those things we cannot do, as displayed in this German sign.

begin to keep a close watch on how much they eat and how fattening these foods are (hence the familiar expression "counting calories"). When dieters eat in settings that undermine monitoring, they eat more. In particular, eating while watching television has long been known to increase calorie intake, mainly because people focus their attention on the television program and not on monitoring how much they consume (Leon & Chamberlain, 1973). Likewise, people overeat at parties, where their attention is focused on the other people and activities rather than on how much they eat (Logue, 1991).

An important study linked eating binges to failures in monitoring (Polivy, 1976). For this purpose, some dieters were induced to break their diet for the day of the experiment, while other dieters kept on their diets. Then both groups, plus a sample of nondieters, ate a snack of as many tiny sandwiches as they wanted. Afterward, the researchers asked everyone to estimate how much she or he had eaten. The nondieters were pretty accurate, as were the dieters whose diets had remained intact. But the dieters who had broken their diets made wildly inaccurate estimates of how many tiny sandwiches they had consumed. Apparently once their diet was broken, they stopped keeping track, which then enabled them to eat a great deal without realizing it.

Many factors interfere with monitoring and thereby undermine self-regulation, including emotional distress and being distracted, but probably the most widely recognized and important factor is alcohol intoxication. One effect of alcohol, even in mild doses, is to reduce attention to self (Hull, 1981), and as we have seen, without monitoring

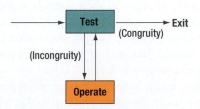

▶ **FIGURE 4.3** TOTE (Test, Operate, Test, Exit) model (Carver & Scheier, 1981, 1982). **The first test is a comparison of self against the standard. In the "operate" phase, you try to match behavior to the standard. Test again to see if the match is close enough to reduce anxiety. If it is not close enough, keep trying. If it is close enough, stop changing behavior (exit).**

Food for Thought

Dieting as Self-Regulation

Many people, though hardly any other animals, seek to control and restrain their eating and will therefore refrain from eating some tempting food even when it is readily available to them. Partly this reflects the progress of culture at providing food. Like most other animals, humans evolved under conditions of periodic scarcities of food, so nature designed us to keep and store food as much as possible. Now that much of the world lives amid ample available food, the body's natural tendency to store fat has turned from a life-saving asset to a life-endangering liability. In 2003, experts calculated that for the first time, more humans worldwide suffer from obesity than are in danger of starving. The problem is too much food, not too little.

Dieting—restricting one's food intake—is the standard response, but it requires self-regulation in order to override the natural desire to eat. To understand dieting as self-regulation, we suggest you imagine yourself going on a diet. What can self-regulation theory tell you about how to succeed? Consider the three main ingredients of self-regulation.

The first is a commitment to standards. A standard would be your goal in terms of weight (or perhaps body measurements such as waist size, or even percentage of body fat). It is helpful to have a realistic idea of what you should weigh. This is a high-level goal that may preside over the whole dieting process (which may take months).

It is helpful to set lower-level goals, such as losing a pound or two each week. Many dieters also find it helpful to set standards for food intake, such as not eating more than 1,500 calories per day.

The second ingredient is monitoring. This means keeping track of what you eat, how many calories you consume, and perhaps how much you weigh. External monitoring helps: Rather than relying on memory, keep a journal or diary that records what you eat each day. Also avoid eating in front of the television and other distractions, so you can be aware of how much you eat. If you don't keep track, you are not likely to succeed. Research shows that when dieters break their diets, they often stop keeping track and hence lose any sense of how much they are eating. This can produce an eating binge: You know you are eating too much, but you don't really know how much. The importance of monitoring means that it is important to eat under circumstances in which keeping track of food is possible.

Monitoring weight is another key aspect of dieting. Here the conventional wisdom suggested an exception to the rule to monitor closely. Folk wisdom said that weighing yourself every day can be discouraging because weight fluctuates, so weighing yourself once a week was supposed to be best. But several well-controlled studies have now shown that self-regulation theory is right after all: People who weigh themselves every day are most successful at losing

off the mark.com   by Mark Parisi

TODAY'S SPECIAL IS THE "RESOLUTION BUSTER"...A FATTY STEAK SMOTHERED IN FRENCH FRIES, MARINATED IN HARD LIQUOR, STUFFED WITH CHOCOLATE CAKE AND TOPPED WITH A CIGARETTE...

offthemark.com   1-3

MarkParisi@aol.com
ATLANTIC FEATURE SYND. ©2001 MARK PARISI

Reprinted by permission of Atlantic Feature Syndicate/Mark Parisi.

weight and at keeping it off (Wing, Tate, Gorin, Raynor, Fava, & Machan, 2007).

The third ingredient is willpower, or the capacity for change. The self's strength is used for many different activities, and it can be depleted if there are many other demands. An ideal time for dieting is a period of low stress or pressure, stable relationships, and few demands for major decisions. When your willpower has been depleted by coping with stress or deadlines, making hard decisions, resisting temptation, or other efforts to change the self, you will have less strength available for effective dieting. ●

(attending to) yourself, it is very difficult to self-regulate effectively. Hence people who have consumed alcohol tend to be worse at self-regulating in almost every sphere of behavior that has been studied. Intoxicated persons eat more, perform more violent and aggressive acts, spend more money, smoke more cigarettes, and engage in more inappropriate sexual behavior—and, yes, drinking alcohol even leads to drinking more alcohol when drinkers stop keeping track of how much they drink (Abraham & Beumont, 1982; Ashton & Stepney, 1982; Baumeister et al., 1994; Bushman & Cooper, 1990; Steele & Southwick, 1985).

The third ingredient of self-regulation is the **capacity for change**. This refers to what goes on in

the "operate" phase, during which people actually carry out the changes to their states or responses so as to bring them into line with the standards. This capacity corresponds to the popular notion of "willpower," and in fact it does seem to operate like a strength or energy.

Willpower can become depleted when people use it. In one study (Baumeister, Bratslavsky, Muraven, & Tice, 1998), participants arrived having skipped a meal, so most were hungry. The researchers baked fresh chocolate chip cookies in the laboratory, which filled the room with a delicious and tempting aroma. Each participant was seated at a table in front of a stack of these cookies and delectable chocolates, as well as a bowl of radishes. In the important condition, the experimenter told each participant "You have been assigned to the radish condition," which

CAPACITY FOR CHANGE the active phase of self-regulation; willpower

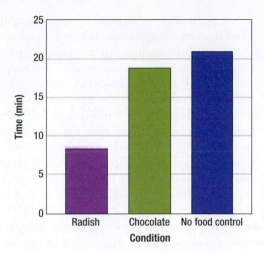

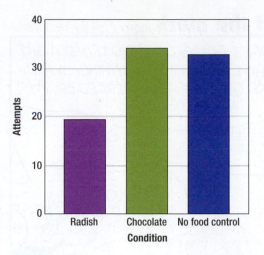

▶ **FIGURE 4.4** People who exercised self-control by eating radishes instead of chocolate gave up more easily on difficult tasks (Baumeister, Bratslavsky, Muraven, & Tice, 1998).

meant eating only radishes. The experimenter then left the participant alone for 5 minutes to eat. This task required considerable willpower to resist the tempting chocolates and cookies and to eat only the radishes as instructed. In other conditions, participants were permitted to eat cookies and chocolate instead of radishes, or no food was present at all. After this, the participants were set to work on some difficult (actually unsolvable) problems, and the researchers measured how long people kept trying before they gave up, because willpower is also needed to keep trying when you feel discouraged and want to quit. Consistent with the theory that willpower gets used up, the participants in the radish condition quit sooner than participants in the other two conditions. Thus, resisting temptation (in the form of chocolates and cookies) used up some willpower, so those participants had less left over to help them keep working on the frustrating puzzles. The results are depicted in ▶ **FIGURE 4.4**.

A more appealing interpretation of these results would be that eating chocolate made people stronger and more effective. Unfortunately for that view, the participants who ate chocolate were no different from the control participants who ate nothing at all. It was resisting temptation, rather than indulging in chocolate, that was responsible for the experimental results (Baumeister et al., 1998). Thus, willpower can be important for regulating one's eating; in fact, dieting is one of the most common behaviors that depends on self-regulation. To learn more about self-regulation in dieting, see *Food for Thought*.

How does one acquire or increase willpower? There is some evidence that willpower resembles a muscle (Baumeister, 2002): Regular exercise makes you stronger, even though the muscle is temporarily "tired" after a workout. When people perform regular self-control exercises, they show gradual improvements in their capacity for self-control, even on novel tasks. Such exercises may include trying to improve your posture, keeping track of what you eat,

trying to speak in complete sentences, and using your nondominant hand (your left hand if you're right-handed) to brush your teeth or open doors. Over the long run, these exercises will strengthen your capacity for self-regulation. Just don't perform them right before you are going to need your willpower, because that would be like lifting weights just before you have to carry furniture.

[**QUIZ YOURSELF**]

Self-Regulation

1. Self-regulation is most similar to which of the following concepts?
   (a) Self-awareness   (b) Self-consciousness
   (c) Self-control   (d) Self-esteem

2. Which of the following refers to a concept or idea of how things could be?
   (a) Capacity for change (b) Self-consciousness
   (c) Self-monitoring   (d) Standards

3. Which common household device best illustrates a feedback loop?
   (a) Dishwasher (b) Thermostat
   (c) Toilet   (d) Vacuum

4. What body part does willpower most resemble?
   (a) Bone   (b) Eye
   (c) Muscle (d) Stomach

Irrationality and Self-Destruction

Self-regulation, discussed in the previous section, can help people do what is rational, in the sense of what will produce the best results for them in the long run. We turn now from rational behavior and enlightened self-interest to their opposite: irrational and self-destructive behavior.

off the mark.com   by Mark Parisi

ACK! I GUESS I OVERDID IT LAST NIGHT. I HOPE I DIDN'T DO ANYTHING STUPID... LIKE GET MY TONGUE PIERCED OR MY ARM TATTOOED...

ATLANTIC FEATURE © 1998 MARK PARISI   offthemark.com

Reprinted by permission of Atlantic Feature Syndicate/Mark Parisi.

SELF-DEFEATING ACTS: BEING YOUR OWN WORST ENEMY

"She has self-destructive tendencies." "The other team didn't beat us, we beat ourselves." "I think he has some kind of death wish." How often have you heard such expressions? They refer to the common belief that people sometimes do things to bring failure, suffering, or misfortune upon themselves. The psychological term for such actions is **self-defeating behavior**. In everyday language, when people say what someone did was "stupid," they usually mean that it was self-defeating. The "stupid" actions are those that bring about some result contrary to what the person sought, especially if the person might or should have known better.

Self-defeating behavior is paradoxical. Why would self-destructive behavior ever occur? If rational behavior means doing what serves one's enlightened self-interest, how could rational beings do things that are harmful or detrimental to the self? Self-defeating behavior seems to be irrational in the extreme.

Yet there is no denying that people do plenty of self-defeating things. Many smoke cigarettes, thereby giving themselves lung cancer and other diseases. They eat unhealthy foods, thereby shortening their lives. They engage in risky sex, thereby increasing their chances of getting diseases or creating an unwanted pregnancy. They waste their money or gamble it away. They fail to take their medicine or follow physicians' orders, thereby preventing themselves from regaining health. The list goes on and on.

Most theories assume that psychological processes are designed to increase safety, security, and happiness, and ultimately to increase survival and reproduction. Self-defeating behavior is the opposite. It challenges psychological theory to explain how self-defeating behavior can be reconciled with the general assumption that people behave in adaptive, rational, self-benefiting ways. Many theories have been proposed, including Freud's (1920/1964) famous conclusion that people have an innate "death drive" that impels them to pursue their own downfall and death. A more recent version of this theory holds that many people, especially women, suffer from a "fear of success." The fear-of-success theory was proposed by Matina Horner (1972), herself the president of one of the most prestigious women's colleges (Radcliffe), who said that many young women believed that if they became too successful in their work they would end up lonely, rejected, and unable to find romantic partners. Because of this fear of success, she theorized, many women sabotage, or at least curtail, their careers.

After many decades of research, social psychologists have begun to establish the main facts about self-defeating behavior. A first conclusion is that people almost never directly seek failure, suffering, or misfortune. Freud's theory of a death drive is apparently wrong. People may perform self-destructive acts, but they do not do them out of self-destructive intentions. Likewise, carefully controlled studies have discredited the "fear of success" theory (Hyland, 1989). There is no sign that either men or women deliberately sabotage their careers or their work because they consciously (or unconsciously) fear what success will mean for them.

Instead, there appear to be two main reasons for self-defeating behavior. One of these involves tradeoffs: Sometimes good and bad outcomes are linked, and in order to get the desired, good outcome people accept the bad one too. The example of cigarette smoking illustrates this pattern. Yes, smoking causes cancer and other diseases, but hardly anyone decides to smoke in order to get cancer. People smoke for the pleasures and rewards of smoking, including the immediate and pleasant sensations caused by nicotine, and possibly the benefits of impressing others that one is sexy, cool, or mature. They accept some increased risk of lung cancer in order to reap the benefits.

A vivid self-defeating tradeoff was covered in Chapter 3 in *Tradeoffs: Self-Handicapping*. In self-handicapping, you will recall, people create obstacles to their own performance so as to furnish themselves with an excuse for possible failure. The self-handicapper thus sacrifices real chances at success in exchange for protection from the implications of failure (Jones & Berglas, 1978). If you are drunk when

---

SELF-DEFEATING BEHAVIOR any action by which people bring failure, suffering, or misfortune on themselves

taking a test, you will likely perform worse than if you were sober—but you are safe from being proven incompetent, because even if you perform badly on the test, people will attribute the failure to the alcohol rather than to low ability.

Self-defeating tradeoffs are especially likely when the reward is immediate and the cost is delayed. We noted in Chapter 2 that this was one common kind of tradeoff (now versus the future). Cigarettes offer immediate pleasure, whereas the cancer and death they may bring lie in the distant future. Many self-defeating acts have this characteristic of sacrificing the future for the sake of the present. Regarding the capacity to give up immediate pleasures for the sake of long-term or delayed benefits, see *Tradeoffs*.

The second pathway to self-defeating behavior involves faulty knowledge and a reliance on strategies that don't work. As with tradeoffs, the person is usually pursuing something positive and good, but the self-defeater chooses a strategy that backfires. Often people do not adequately understand what is effective in the world, either because they do not understand the world or they do not understand themselves correctly. For example, some people procrastinate because they believe that "I do my best work under pressure" (Ferrari, Johnson, & McCown, 1995)—that work left till the last minute will actually end up being better. This is generally false: Leaving things until the last minute generally makes it harder to do an adequate job, and procrastinators end up getting lower grades than others. Thus, they think that putting things off will help them do better work, but actually it makes them do poorer work. Students who procrastinate get lower grades than other students (Tice & Baumeister, 1997). When people are tested under identical laboratory conditions, chronic procrastinators perform worse than others, not better (Ferrari, 2001). In short, the claim that "I do my best work under pressure" is a false rationalization for almost everyone, and it is particularly false for procrastinators.

SUICIDE

Suicide has fascinated psychologists and other social scientists for more than a century. At first blush, suicide is the extreme of irrational, self-destructive behavior, because it brings a permanent end to the person's chances for happiness or success. People who believe that humans are created by a divine power generally regard suicide as a major sin because it thwarts their god's wishes. People who believe in evolution cannot understand how natural selection would produce an impulse to end one's own life, because it goes against the most basic urges toward survival and reproduction. (At most, they might think that sacrificing oneself for one's children might make biological sense, but that would only explain

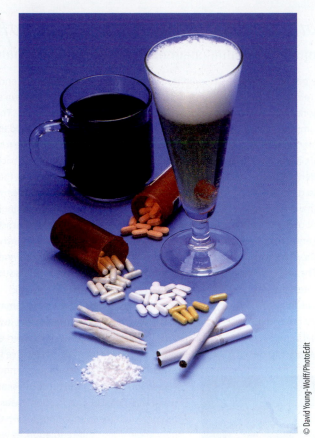

Many self-defeating behaviors trade off long-term costs for short-term pleasures or benefits.

a tiny minority of suicides.) Suicide is essentially unknown among nonhuman animals. Basically, humans are the only creatures who deliberately kill themselves, and many millions have done so (Joiner, 2005). How can this be explained?

Suicide often involves a tradeoff, which as we have seen is one major pathway to self-destructive behavior. Indeed, it often fits the now-versus-future pattern that we have seen as a common tradeoff in human decision making. Suicidal people are often in life circumstances that are acutely unpleasant to them, and their overriding wish is to escape from their emotional distress and feelings of personal worthlessness. They feel miserable and want those feelings to stop. To them, death may seem appealing, not as punishment or violence or suffering (as some theories have proposed) but simply as oblivion. They believe that death will bring peace and an end to their distress and suffering, which looks like an improvement to them. They are willing to trade away their future and all its potential joys in order to gain this immediate relief.

Suicide starts with some discrepancy between expectations (or other standards) and reality. Ironically, suicide rates are often highest in favorable circumstances, such as in rich countries, in places with good climates, or during the fine months of

Tradeoffs

Now Versus Tomorrow: Delay of Gratification

Some people spend their money on fun today, rather than save for a rainy day. Some people skimp on medical or dental care in favor of things they would rather do. Some people pursue sexual pleasure without worrying about future consequences. In these and other ways, people come to grief. What these self-defeating behaviors have in common is emphasizing the present over the future. However, human beings thrive and prosper best when they can sacrifice some short-term rewards for the sake of a better future. The ability to make those immediate sacrifices for later rewards is called the **capacity to delay gratification**.

During the 1960s, Walter Mischel and his colleagues developed a clever laboratory method for testing children's capacity to delay

The ability to delay gratification as a child is a good predictor of success later in life (Mischel, Shoda, & Peake, 1988).

gratification (Mischel, 1996; Mischel & Mendoza-Denton, 2002). Each child would be shown some treat, such as a cookie or a marshmallow. The experimenter would explain to each child that the experimenter was going to leave the room but the child could summon him or her back by ringing a bell on the table. As soon as the child did this, the child would receive the treat. However, if the child could refrain from ringing the bell and just wait until the adult returned, the child would get a bigger reward (e.g., three cookies instead of one). Some children were able to wait and get the larger reward; others succumbed to temptation and rang the bell.

Mischel's task is a classic tradeoff dilemma: whether to take the smaller reward right away or wait for the larger one. As we have seen elsewhere in this book, many tradeoffs involve time, especially pitting something right now versus something in the future. Research using this "delay of gratification" measure has provided the foundations for what we now know about self-regulation, as well as shedding valuable light on self-defeating behavior.

Seeing either the large or the small reward undermined the capacity to hold out. Apparently, seeing what you want stimulates a greater desire for it. Temptation is best resisted by avoiding the sight or thought of it. Many of the children sitting in the room with the bell and the marshmallows came up with this strategy

themselves: They would cover their eyes so as not to see the rewards (and be tempted by them), sing, turn around, make up little games, or even take a nap during the waiting period.

Even going to college is an exercise in delay of gratification. Most college students could earn more money, live in a nicer apartment, eat better food, and get a better car and clothes if they dropped out and got a job. College often requires living near the poverty line for several years, but its long-term payoffs are immense: As we saw in Chapter 2, a person with an advanced degree is likely to earn nearly $2 million more than a high school dropout over the course of a 30-year career.

The benefits of being able to delay gratification also emerged in Mischel's subsequent research. He followed up with many of the children years after they had participated in his experiments. Very few psychological traits seem to remain stable from early childhood into adulthood, and fewer yet have been shown to predict success or failure in life. The children who were good at delaying gratification when they were just 4 years old, however, grew into adults who were more popular with friends and family and more successful in universities and jobs than those who had not been able to resist taking the quick marshmallow in his lab (Mischel et al., 1998; Shoda et al., 1990). Thus, as they moved through life, being able to resist the impulse to take the immediate payoff really did seem to bring them greater rewards in the long run! ●

late spring and summer. To be miserable when all around you life seems great for everyone else can be deeply disturbing. Often the suicidal process is set in motion by a significant change for the worse, so that the present seems to fall short of what one has come to expect. For example, rich and poor people commit suicide at about the same rates, but changing from rich to poor produces a big increase in suicide rates. Put another way, suicide does not result from being poor all your life but rather from becoming poor when you are accustomed to being rich. Suicidal college students actually have higher grade point averages than other students—except in their most recent semester, when their grades dipped below average, which probably made them feel

that they were falling below what they had come to expect of themselves. Suicidal college students often have parents who expect them to perform well, and the students sometimes feel they cannot meet their parents' expectations (Davis, 1983; Farberow, 1975; Hendin, 1982; Maris, 1969, 1981; Rothberg & Jones, 1987).

Self-awareness is high among suicidal people; indeed, the human capacity for self-awareness may help explain why nonhuman animals do not kill themselves. In the section on self-awareness in Chapter 3, we saw that people sometimes seek to escape from self-awareness when contemplating the self is unpleasant. Suicidal people have often reached this point where self-awareness is acutely painful, and the attempt at suicide may be a desperate, extreme effort to stop ruminating about themselves (Baumeister,

CAPACITY TO DELAY GRATIFICATION the ability to make immediate sacrifices for later rewards

1990). In the weeks leading up to a suicide attempt, the person is typically full of thoughts of being a failure, a worthless individual, and an immoral person. Many suicidal individuals are acutely aware of being a burden to others, and they hate that feeling. Some feel cut off from others, and this too is profoundly upsetting.

You might think that suicidal people would be full of emotional distress, such as anxiety, regret, and guilt, but most studies have found the opposite: Suicidal people tend to be emotionally numb. Apparently, their problems are so upsetting that they respond by shutting down emotionally. They try to avoid thinking about the future or the past, and avoid all sorts of abstract, meaningful, or emotional material, focusing instead on the concrete here and now. In the movies, suicide notes are often philosophical: "I've had a good run, but I don't find my life worth living any further; please teach my son to be a good man." In reality, suicide notes tend to be mundane and concrete, such as "I paid the electric bill; tell Fred he can have my CDs" (Gottschalk & Gleser, 1960; Hendin, 1982; Henken, 1976; Shneidman, 1981).

The human mind cannot easily stop thinking meaningfully, and these unfortunate people find that they cannot really keep their thoughts and feelings at bay. Suicide starts to look appealing because it is a way to put an end to the distressing thoughts about how bad the self is. Although suicide trades away one's future for the sake of relief in the here and now, the suicidal person often does not reflect on that, because he or she is narrowly focused on the present and not thinking about the future. It is not so much a rejection of one's entire life as an attempt to escape from this week's numbing misery. If you are ever confronted with a friend or relative who is suicidal, besides getting professional help, one emphasis should be to help that person refocus on long-term goals and the pleasures and fulfillments that can still be found in the distant future, regardless of how miserable the immediate future may seem.

Another factor that pushes people toward suicide is burdensomeness (Joiner, 2005). That is, people commit suicide when they believe themselves to be a burden on others. For example, imagine a man who has long supported his family and after losing his job finds that he has to rely on others to support him. He may become acutely aware that the people he loves would be better off without him (or at least he may mistakenly think that is so). Therefore, he commits suicide as an (again, possibly misguided) act of kindness toward them, relieving them of the burden. Such feelings of guilt may be linked to human nature as cultural animals. People depend on each other and feel bad when they cannot provide for others or reciprocate what others do for them.

No single theory can account for all suicides. The desire to escape from misery may be the most common, but there are other pathways to suicide. Chapter 3 opened with the story of the Hungarian count who defied the powerful sultan and died in a suicidal charge. In that story, at least according to unverifiable legend, the young bride of one of the Christian defenders committed suicide by throwing a torch into the weapons stock, killing herself along with several thousand Turkish soldiers. She gave her own life for the sake of the cause in which she believed. In the same manner, this chapter opened with the story of a female terrorist who was prepared to give her own life, and nearly had to do so, in order to destroy a plane full of South Korean tourists. She believed, falsely as it turned out, that killing those people would prevent South Korea from holding the Olympics and would lead to the reunification of her country.

Suicide bombers have been in the news in recent years. The most dramatic were the Arabs who hijacked several airline flights and crashed them into the World Trade Center and the Pentagon in September 2001. Since then, numerous suicide bombers have given their lives to kill other people in various countries in the Middle East and occasionally elsewhere. These people sacrifice their lives to advance a cause, not to escape from a personal hell. Such self-sacrifice represents a commitment to cultural meanings that can override the basic biological drives toward survival and reproduction. Even if one regards them as misguided, futile, or evil, they show how cultural meanings can override biological impulses and cause people to put cultural goals above their own self-interest. Only cultural animals become suicide bombers.

[QUIZ YOURSELF]

Irrationality and Self-Destruction

1. In everyday terms, self-defeating behavior is defined as _____ behavior.
   (a) experimental   (b) intelligent
   (c) stupid   (d) taboo

2. The two main reasons for self-defeating behavior are _____.
   (a) death drive; fear of failure
   (b) faulty knowledge; tradeoffs
   (c) fear of failure; tradeoffs
   (d) faulty knowledge; fear of failure

3. What creatures intentionally kill themselves (i.e., commit suicide)?
   (a) Chimps   (b) Gorillas
   (c) Humans   (d) All of the above

4. Suicidal people are _____.
   (a) low in self-awareness
   (b) high in self-awareness
   (c) high in self-handicapping
   (d) focused on future consequences

Behavior is found in all animals, all the time. What sets humans apart (among other things that will be discussed in other chapters) is an elaborate inner system for controlling behavior. Meaningful thought enables human beings to make choices in novel ways and to link their here-and-now actions to far distant realities. Other animals, in contrast, just follow their instincts and respond to the here and now.

Only humans vote in elections, pay taxes, hold wedding ceremonies, make blueprints for the buildings they construct, resort to judges and lawsuits to resolve disputes, create and attend schools and colleges, pray, plan their battles, or celebrate events that occurred before they were born. Animals have sex, but only humans distinguish between meaningless and meaningful sexual relationships. Animals play, but only humans keep score, have referees, and distinguish between meaningful and meaningless games (as in whether the game has playoff implications).

Animals may have a limited understanding of what is happening now, but only humans seem to enrich their understanding of the present by thoughtful links to events in the distant past and future. Indeed, human goals often link what one does now to possible outcomes that lie years away. Thus, human action is not just a here-and-now response but is often designed to help bring about something far off, such as graduation or marriage or retirement. It can also be linked to things that have happened elsewhere or long ago, such as when people celebrate

Independence Day or a religious holiday. Moreover, people often follow abstract rules made in distant places by people they will never meet. Most Americans pay income tax, for example, though few have any direct contact with the people who make the tax laws.

Consciousness enables people to use complex reasoning processes to make their decisions. They can think about multiple options and do cost–benefit analyses to decide the best course of action.

Self-regulation is not uniquely human, but it seems far better developed among humans than among other species. Our capacity for self-control makes many aspects of human culture possible, because it enables us to change ourselves. We can adjust to new norms and opportunities, to changing fads and fashions, to religious doctrines, to new roles and rules. Self-regulation is the key to morality and virtuous behavior, for without the ability to alter one's actions based on general rules, there would be no point in having moral rules. Humans also use self-regulation in ways that other animals don't. Football players abruptly stop trying to knock their opponents

down when the ball goes out of bounds. Some hungry people pass up delicious and available food just because they are on a diet or because of religious symbolism.

The capacity for self-directed action has its dark side—namely, irrationality. Just as people are capable of altering their behavior on the basis of rational, enlightened plans, they are also capable of altering it to follow foolish and even self-destructive plans. The brilliance of human innovation is one of the wonders of the world, but humans have also done stupid and costly things on a scale that no other creatures can match. Humans are also alone in the animal kingdom in the occasional willingness of individuals to commit suicide.

Despite these occasional problems and misfortunes, however, human behavior is remarkably special. Perhaps the single greatest advance is freedom: By using meaningful thought, reasoning, and self-regulation, people have been able to free their actions from simply responding to their immediate surroundings. People have choices and make choices, and although choosing is sometimes stressful, people generally benefit from this freedom. When people rise up in revolutions or demonstrations, it is almost always to demand greater freedom, not less freedom. The spread of democracy and liberty thus continues in culture what nature and evolution began—namely, progress toward giving individuals greater freedom.

chapter summary

WHAT YOU DO, AND WHAT IT MEANS

- Human behavior depends on meaning.
- Inner processes such as thoughts, feelings, and motivations serve interpersonal functions.
- Imagining something makes it more likely to happen.
- Making a choice is typically a two-step process, involving whittling many choices down to a few and then doing a careful comparison of those few.
- Risk aversion refers to the finding that people are more affected by possible losses than by possible gains.
- Temporal discounting refers to the finding that the present is more important than the future in decision making. The farther in the future something lies, the less influence it has on the decision.

- In an evolutionary perspective, the most costly type of sexual error for a woman was to reproduce with a nonoptimal male, while the most costly sexual error for a man was to miss an opportunity to have sex and thus possibly to reproduce.

- The certainty effect refers to the tendency to place more emphasis on definite outcomes than on odds and probabilities.
- People may prefer to postpone hard decisions and keep their options open as long as possible.
- The status quo bias is a preference to keep things the way they are rather than change.
- The omission bias (sometimes called the default option) denotes taking whatever course of action does not require you to do anything.
- People often avoid making decisions because they fear they will later regret their choice.
- Reactance occurs when a freedom or a choice is removed, making the person want the lost option more and perhaps take steps to reclaim it.
- People can think of their traits as fixed and stable (entity theorists) or as subject to change and improvement (incremental theorists).
- Learned helplessness occurs when people think they will fail so they quit trying to succeed.

FREEDOM OF ACTION
- Belief in free will leads people to act in more prosocial ways.
- Although other animals may have free will, among humans free will has greater behavioral flexibility and can be regulated more easily.
- Humans rely on meaning to make their choices.
- Self-determination theory emphasizes that people need to feel that some of their behavior is caused by their own free will.
- The panic button effect refers to the finding that believing there is an escape option can reduce stress, even if the option is never used.

GOALS, PLANS, INTENTIONS

- Goals are ideas of some desired future state; they are the meaningful link between values and action.
- Goals tell you what to do in order to pursue and uphold your values, and setting and pursuing goals is a vital job of the self.
- Setting goals includes choosing among possible goals and evaluating their feasibility and desirability.
- Pursuing goals includes planning and carrying out the behaviors to reach goals.
- Both conscious and automatic systems help in the pursuit of goals.
- The Zeigarnik effect states that people remember uncompleted or interrupted tasks better than completed ones.
- People have goal hierarchies; some goals are long term and some are short term.
- Goal shielding is the process of keeping others from interfering with your goals.
- People's plans tend to be overly optimistic, especially over a long time span.

SELF-REGULATION
- Self-regulation, or self-control, refers to the self's capacity to alter its own responses; it is essential for cultural animals to adapt to many different demands.
- The three components of self-regulation are standards (concepts of how things should be), monitoring (keeping track of behaviors), and willpower/capacity for change (bringing behavior into line with standards).

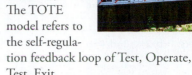

- The TOTE model refers to the self-regulation feedback loop of Test, Operate, Test, Exit.
- Willpower is like a muscle, getting depleted after it is used, but getting stronger with exercise.

IRRATIONALITY AND SELF-DESTRUCTION
- Self-defeating behavior is defined as any action by which people bring failure, suffering, or misfortune on themselves.
- People engage in self-defeating behavior because they are making tradeoffs or because they are using ineffective strategies, but not usually because they are directly seeking failure.
- The capacity to delay gratification is the ability to make short-term sacrifices in order to get long-term rewards.
- Suicidal people focus on the immediate present at a time when present circumstances may be changing for the worse.

WHAT MAKES US HUMAN? PUTTING THE CULTURAL ANIMAL IN PERSPECTIVE
- Cultural animals differ from other animals in their elaborate inner systems for controlling behavior.

Key Terms

Capacity for change 116
Capacity to delay gratification 120
Certainty effect 101
Entity theorists 105
Error management theory 102

Goal 108
Goal shielding 110
Incremental theorists 105
Learned helplessness 105
Monitoring 114
Omission bias 103
Panic button effect 107

Planning fallacy 112
Reactance theory 104
Risk aversion 100
Self-defeating behavior 118
Self-determination theory 106
Self-regulation 113

Status quo bias 103
Temporal discounting 100
TOTE 114
Zeigarnik effect 109

[Quiz Yourself] Answers

1. What You Do, and What It Means
Answers: 1=b, 2=d, 3=d, 4=c

2. Freedom of Action
Answers: 1=b, 2=c, 3=d, 4=b

3. Goals, Plans, Intentions
Answers: 1=c, 2=a, 3=d, 4=c

4. Self-Regulation
Answers: 1=c, 2=d, 3=b, 4=c

5. Irrationality and Self-Destruction
Answers: 1=c, 2=b, 3=c, 4=b

Media Learning Resources

Make sure you check out the complete set of learning resources and study tools below. If your instructor did not order these items with your new book, go to www.ichapters.com to purchase Cengage Learning print and digital products.

Social Psychology and Human Nature
BOOK COMPANION WEBSITE
www.cengage.com/psychology/baumeister
Visit your book companion website, where you will find flash cards, practice quizzes, Internet links, and more to help you study.

CENGAGENOW™ JUST WHAT YOU NEED TO KNOW NOW!
Spend time on what you need to master rather than on information you have already learned. Take a pre-test for this chapter, and CengageNOW will generate a personalized study plan based on your results. The study plan will identify the topics you need to review and direct you to online resources to help you master those topics. You can then take a post-test to help you determine the concepts you have mastered and what you will still need to work on. Try it out! Go to www.cengage.com/login to sign in with an access code or to purchase access to this product.

CLASSIC AND CONTEMPORARY VIDEOS STUDENT CD-ROM
To see videos on the topics and experiments discussed in this chapter and to learn more about the research that social psychologists are doing today, go to the Student CD-ROM.

SOCIAL PSYCH LAB
These unique online labs give you the opportunity to become a participant in actual experiments, including re-creations of classic and contemporary research studies.

chapter 5

Social Cognition

Food for Thought: It's the Thought That Counts (or Doesn't Count!) the Calories **p. 134**

Money Matters: The Price of Being Mrs. Hisname **p. 142**

The Social Side of Sex: Counting Sex Partners **p. 146**

What Makes Us Human? Putting the Cultural Animal in Perspective **p. 155**

Burke/Triolo Productions/Getty Images

WHAT IS SOCIAL COGNITION? p. 127
Thinking About People: A Special Case? **p. 127**
Why People Think, and Why They Don't **p. 128**
Automatic and Controlled Thinking **p. 129**
Thought Suppression and Ironic Processes **p. 134**

ATTRIBUTIONS: WHY DID THAT HAPPEN? p. 135
It's Not My Fault: Explaining Success and Failure **p. 136**

You Looking at Me? The Actor/ Observer Bias **p. 137**
The Attribution Cube and Making Excuses **p. 139**

HEURISTICS: MENTAL SHORTCUTS p. 141
Representativeness Heuristic **p. 141**
Availability Heuristic **p. 142**
Simulation Heuristic **p. 143**
Anchoring and Adjustment Heuristic **p. 144**

ERRORS AND BIASES p. 145
Confirmation Bias **p. 147**
Conjunction Fallacy **p. 147**
Illusory Correlation **p. 148**
Base Rate Fallacy **p. 148**
Gambler's Fallacy and the Hot Hand **p. 149**
False Consensus Effect **p. 149**
False Uniqueness Effect **p. 150**
Statistical Regression **p. 150**
Illusion of Control **p. 151**
Magical Thinking **p. 151**
Counterfactual Thinking **p. 152**

ARE PEOPLE REALLY IDIOTS? p. 154
How Serious Are the Errors? **p. 154**
Reducing Cognitive Errors **p. 154**

CHAPTER SUMMARY p. 156

Carolyn Briggs grew up in a small Midwestern town. She was small and shy. In high school she had a boyfriend named Eric. They fell into a pattern of getting drunk together on dates, and this combination of fun, intimacy, and rebellion led her to start having sex with him. |||||

He was in a rock band that he believed would someday make him a star, and she would travel with the band to their gigs, listen, watch, and sometimes dance. They enjoyed making fun of people, such as the so-called Jesus Freaks who would sometimes attend the concerts and try to convert the fans to their Christian beliefs.

When Carolyn got pregnant, Eric married her, even though this meant downplaying the rock band and taking a hard, low-paying job in a factory. They lived in a trailer park. Money was tight, and sex was rare and boring. When some of her high school friends visited and talked about taking Christ into their lives, Carolyn was no longer so quick to dismiss them. They seemed happy. She talked about this with her husband, and somewhat to her surprise he seemed interested. They bought a paperback modern version of the Bible at a

supermarket, even though the cost of $12 seemed very high and she was embarrassed to have the salesgirl see her buying a Bible. They started reading the Bible together each night. Sometimes Eric got tears in his eyes as he read, and Carolyn loved this.

This was the beginning of a deep involvement in fundamentalist Christian religion that was the center of her life for about 20 years, until she changed her views and rejected much of this faith and lifestyle, as she describes in her memoir *This Dark World*. At first the new life was enthralling. She stopped swearing and drinking almost overnight. She and her husband spoke about little except their baby and God. He quit the rock band for good and instead began playing Christian music with church groups. She reinterpreted her earlier life as one of sin and confusion, but she also found signs of salvation: Once when she was a child her family had nearly died from a carbon monoxide leak, but they were saved by a neighbor who broke down the door. This seemed now to her to have been a sign that Jesus would eventually break down her barriers and save her soul.

One night not long after her conversion there was a tornado warning, but she and her husband agreed that God would take care of them. It is very dangerous to stay in a trailer during a tornado, yet they stayed home and made popcorn instead of heading for a basement shelter. They told themselves it was their duty to live by faith instead of by human understanding. When other trailers in their park were blown over while theirs was not, they felt their faith had been vindicated because God had indeed saved them from the storm.

When Eric started to make a little more money, they spent it heavily on religious activities. They began to order Bibles by the hundreds and pass them out wherever they could, tossing them to hitchhikers or leaving them with the tip at restaurants. They sought out the most passionate, fundamentalist churches to join, and they openly scorned the faith and practice of "ordinary" Christians as laughably inadequate. (Later, Carolyn looked back on these sentiments as a mixture of pride, self-deception, and rationalization.) She was filled with love for Christ and for the small circle of intense believers among her friends. This was matched by hatred for

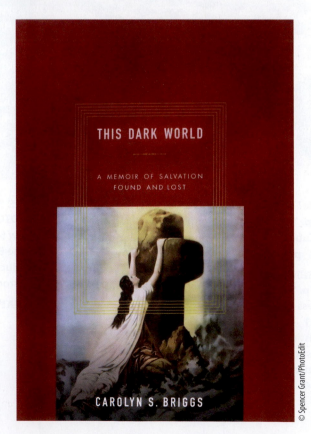

Carolyn Briggs, author of *This Dark World* (2003), converted into and then out of Christian fundamentalism.

THIS DARK WORLD

A MEMOIR OF SALVATION
FOUND AND LOST

CAROLYN S. BRIGGS

© Spencer Grant/PhotoEdit

others outside the circle. "Not only did we hate abortion, we hated homosexuality, we hated Hollywood, we hated the politics of the left. We hated. We hated" (p. 263). When her daughter was 14, Carolyn tried to make her swear she would remain a virgin until her wedding day. After a struggle, the girl gave in and promised she would. Afterward Carolyn felt guilty and cried.

At times Carolyn struggled with doubts, but she consciously decided not to dwell on inconsistencies in the religious teachings, and she rebuked herself for a lack of faith. Sometimes the idea of living by religious beliefs struck her as absurd. To cement her faith, she burned all their nonreligious music albums and some books in the backyard. She struggled with the loss of sexual desire for her husband, who had never made love to any other woman and still considered marital intercourse to be a gift from God, while Carolyn herself wished in vain for some religious authority or power to offer her an escape.

Then, when she was almost 40, she went to graduate school. In her new environment, the religious life she had led began to seem misguided. She told her husband she wanted to move out, and he tearfully begged her to stay and promised to love her until he died. She left anyway. She wavered at times and thought she should go back to God and family, but ultimately she couldn't.

Carolyn's story shows the remarkable power and flexibility of human thought. In her adult life she converted into and then out of an overwhelmingly powerful system of belief that shaped how she understood her life. It guided the choices she made and the emotions she felt. It drastically changed the intimate relationship she had with God, her husband, and her child. In spite of all of its power, no objective events can prove the truth or falsehood of religious belief. Faith is a human cognitive phenomenon, regardless of whether the spiritual or religious doctrines are true or false. How can someone believe so intensely and then reject those same beliefs, especially without objective events to illuminate the way the world is? One partial answer is that cognition is linked to the social and cultural world, so people's beliefs are shaped by those around them. But this answer is not quite complete. The story also illustrates some of the cognitive biases and errors that people can make. In this chapter, we will examine many of the processes of social cognition, which involve how people think about the events of their lives. ■

What Is Social Cognition?

The rise of social cognition in the 1970s marked a fundamental and sweeping change in how social psychologists studied people. Before the 1970s, social psychology was dominated by the doctrine of behaviorism, which held that in order to be scientific, psychologists should only study visible behavior and not make inferences about what was happening inside the person, such as thoughts and feelings. Social psychologists began to realize, however, that it is impossible to understand people without examining how they think and feel. In the 1970s, social psychologists began to focus their studies on people's thoughts and feelings.

Methods and techniques were developed to allow the direct and indirect observation of mental processes so that these processes could be studied scientifically. Among the first mental processes that social psychologists studied were attitudes and the motivation to be consistent in one's attitudes (see Chapter 7). The development of attribution theory in the 1960s and 1970s was one of the most important steps in the scientific study of thinking in social psychology. Attribution theory focuses on how people interpret the causes of events, such as external pressures or internal traits. The term **social cognition** became widely used in the 1980s; it encompassed a broad movement to study any sort of thinking by people about people and about social relationships (Fiske & Taylor, 1991).

THINKING ABOUT PEOPLE: A SPECIAL CASE?

Social psychologists study how people think about people. Why this topic in particular? Why not study how people think about frogs, or household appliances, or money, or the weather? Cognitive psychologists might study these other topics, but social psychologists focus on people. Is there something special about thinking about people?

In short, yes. People think about other people more than any other topic, and probably more than about all other topics combined (Fiske & Taylor, 1991). As a brief test, try turning on the television and scanning the channels. True, some shows are devoted to the physical world, such as those on *Animal Planet* or *The Discovery Channel*. But most shows are about people and their relationships with others. The news may occasionally cover a hurricane, an earthquake, or a tornado, but even footage of these natural disasters tends to emphasize how people are affected by them. Most news is about people's activities.

SOCIAL COGNITION a movement in social psychology that began in the 1970s that focused on thoughts about people and about social relationships

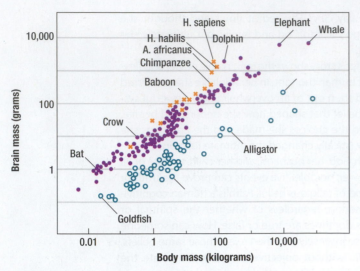

► **FIGURE 5.1** A plot of brain mass versus body mass for a variety of animals. The open circles represent fish and reptiles (including dinosaurs), the filled circles represent birds and mammals, and the x's represent primates (including humans and their immediate ancestors).

From "Cosmic Evolution-Epoch 7-Cultural Evolution." Fig. 7.13 located at http://www.tufts.edu/as/wright_center/cosmic_evolution. Copyright © 2005 by Eric J. Chasisson, Wright Center for Scientific Education. Reprinted by permission.

The fact that people think a lot about other people is relevant to several of our themes, such as "people first" (see Chapter 2). Remember, one standard theory is that the human brain evolved to solve problems in the physical environment, such making tools, finding shelter, and obtaining food. In fact, though, people spend relatively little time thinking about these things. Rather, people use their brains to think about each other, implying that humans evolved to rely on each other for information and help. The human mind is designed to participate in society, and this means its primary job is dealing with other people. Birds get their food from their environment, and so birds' brains are focused on trees and worms and predators. Most humans get their food by interacting with other people, and so people's brains are designed to think about other people.

People think so much about people because of the long road to social acceptance (see Chapter 2). We want to be included in social groups and relationships, but this takes a great deal of work. We need to think at great length about other people in order to be accepted by them. This is an ongoing project and process.

The emphasis on thinking about people shows that inner processes serve interpersonal functions (yet another theme from Chapter 2). Nature (evolution) gave us a powerful brain that can think elaborate thoughts, and this brain is used mainly for helping us relate to others—and not only for garnering social

acceptance. You need to understand your enemies and rivals almost as well as you know your friends and lovers.

WHY PEOPLE THINK, AND WHY THEY DON'T

Humans can do more and better thinking than any other animal on earth (Deacon, 1997; Heinz, Baron, & Frahm, 1988; Macphail, 1982). Human beings have a brain about the size of a large grapefruit, and it weighs about 3 pounds. Although some other animals have larger brains for their body size (e.g., small birds), much of their brain mass is devoted to motor functions (e.g., flying). If one compares the size of the cortex (the part of the brain involved in higher-order functions such as thinking) to the rest of the body, humans are at the top of the list (see ► **FIGURE 5.1**).

You might expect that because humans are well equipped to think, they would love to think and would spend all their free time doing it. This is certainly not the case. (If all thinking were fun, people would probably spend much of their free time doing math problems, but they don't.) Researchers have found that often people seem lazy or careless about their thinking. Social psychologists use the term **cognitive miser** to describe people's reluctance to do much extra thinking (Fiske & Taylor, 1984, 1991). Just as a miser tries to avoid spending money, the cognitive miser tries to avoid thinking too hard or too much. Of course, this isn't entirely a matter of

COGNITIVE MISER a term used to describe people's reluctance to do much extra thinking

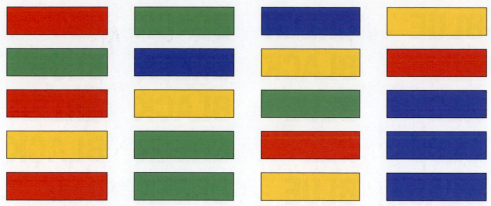

▶ **FIGURE 5.2** Stroop Test 1: Name the color of each rectangle out loud as quickly as you can.

laziness. Thinking takes effort. People's capacity to think, although greater than that of most animals, is limited, so people must conserve their thinking. There is ample evidence that when people's capacity for thinking is already preoccupied, they take even more shortcuts to reduce further the need for thought (e.g., Gilbert, Pelham, & Krull, 1988).

Some people seem to be such numskulls that you wonder whether they forgot they had a brain. For example, one young man went into a liquor store, pointed a gun at the clerk, and demanded all the cash in the register. When the bag was full, he demanded a bottle of whiskey too. The clerk refused to give up the whiskey, saying that he thought the robber was underage. After a brief argument, the robber showed the clerk his driver's license, thereby finally persuading the clerk to hand over the whiskey. Of course, the robber was arrested only two hours later, after the clerk called the police and gave them the robber's name and address!

Then again, people do think at great length about things that are interesting to them. The great genius Albert Einstein published an astonishing 258 articles during his lifetime, dealing with the most complicated issues in physics, and his thinking changed the way that scientists understand the world. Some people spend a great deal of effort thinking about their relationship partners (or how to get one). Some people think about particular events, such as the death of a loved one, for many years afterward. Some people think about baseball all the time and have a seemingly bottomless appetite for the latest game news, anecdotes, and statistics.

Not all thinking is equally difficult. As the theory of the duplex mind indicates, conscious thinking requires a lot more effort than automatic thinking. People generally prefer to conserve effort by relying on automatic modes of thought when they can. Unfortunately, the automatic system is not very good at some kinds of thinking, such as logical reasoning and mathematics. Therefore, the automatic mind develops various shortcuts, which give rough estimates or pretty good answers. Sometimes, though, people do find it necessary to employ the full power of conscious thought and analysis.

AUTOMATIC AND CONTROLLED THINKING

Humans have a duplex mind, as this book has emphasized (see Chapter 2). Some thinking proceeds by automatic means, whereas other thinking relies on conscious control. To illustrate this point, try the **Stroop test**. In ▶ **FIGURE 5.2**, you see several rectangles containing different colors. Say the name of the color in each rectangle out loud as quickly as you can. Go one row at a time, from left to right. If you have a watch, time how long it takes you to do the test. In ▶ **FIGURE 5.3**, you see several words written in different ink colors. Say the name of the ink color for each word as quickly as you can, ignoring what the word says. Go one row at a time, from left to right. In ▶ **FIGURE 5.4**, do the same thing—say the ink color, ignoring what the word says. For example, if the word **RED** is printed in blue ink, you should say "Blue."

The **Stroop effect** was first described by James Ridley Stroop in 1935. If you are like most people, it took you longer if the word and ink color didn't match (incongruent) than if they did match (congruent). In the incongruent test (when the word and ink color don't match), the automatic response is to say the word rather than the ink color. It takes conscious effort to override the automatic response and say the

---

STROOP TEST a standard measure of effortful control over responses, requiring participants to identify the color of a word (which may name a different color)

STROOP EFFECT in the Stroop test, the finding that people have difficulty overriding the automatic tendency to read the word rather than name the ink color

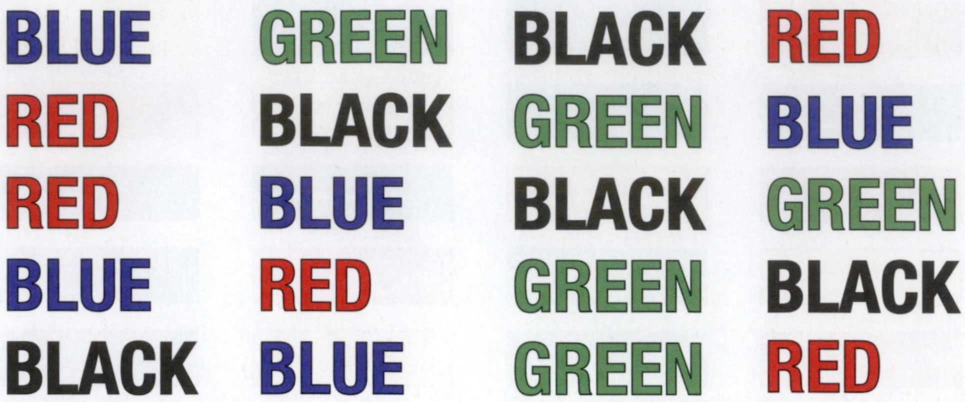

BLUE   GREEN   BLACK   RED

RED   BLACK   GREEN   BLUE

RED   BLUE   BLACK   GREEN

BLUE   RED   GREEN   BLACK

BLACK   BLUE   GREEN   RED

▶ **FIGURE 5.3** Stroop Test 2: Name the color of each word as quickly as you can, ignoring what the word says.

RED   BLUE   GREEN   BLACK

BLACK   BLUE   RED   GREEN

BLUE   BLACK   GREEN   RED

GREEN   BLUE   BLACK   RED

BLUE   BLACK   RED   GREEN

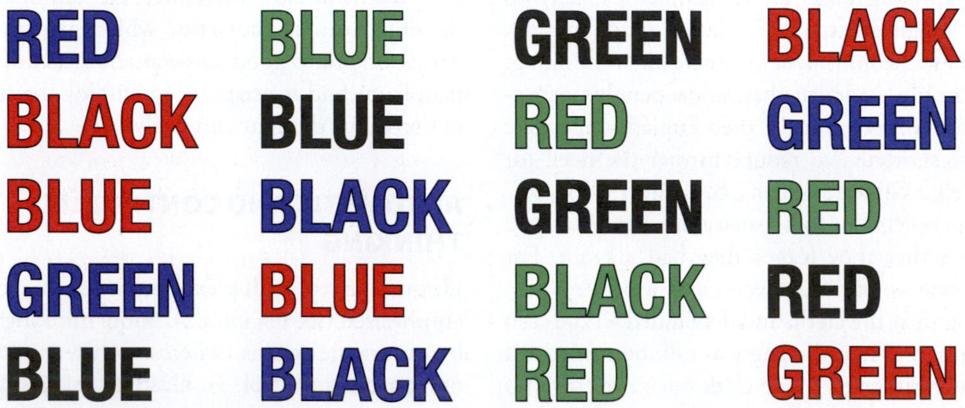

▶ **FIGURE 5.4** Stroop Test 3: As in Test 2, name the color of each word as quickly as you can, ignoring what the word says.

ink color instead. One of your textbook authors tried the Stroop test on a 3-year-old boy. He said, "This is easy!" (Because he couldn't read, he did not have to contend with the automatic response of the meaning of the printed word and therefore could just say the color of the ink.)

How do we know whether some thought is automatic or controlled? There is no one single test, because there are several dimensions to automatic thought. Unfortunately, this makes the definitions of automatic versus controlled processes somewhat complicated, because some thought or response may fit one criterion but not the others. Most phenomena are complex and exist on continuums rather than in black or white categories.

At least five elements distinguish automatic from controlled processes: *awareness, intention, control, effort,* and *efficiency.* When people are engaging in automatic thinking, they are not even aware that they are thinking. A good example is driving. People

who have been driving a long time don't have to think about how to do it; they just drive. If road conditions become bad, however, controlled thinking overrides automatic thinking. If it starts to rain or snow, people turn on their windshield wipers, think about whether the roads are slippery, pay more attention to other drivers, and so on. Second, automatic thinking is not guided by intention; it may just happen whether you intend it to or not. (Indeed, as the Stroop effect shows, automatic thoughts can intrude on your thinking even when you intend to think something else.) Automatic thoughts are not subject to deliberate control, so it can be difficult or even impossible to avoid having certain thoughts that have been cued. Automatic thoughts do not involve effort, whereas controlled thoughts often involve mental exertion and can feel taxing and tiring. Last, automatic thoughts are highly efficient, unlike controlled thoughts (which are often slow and cumbersome).

Automatic thinking involves little effort because it relies on knowledge structures. **Knowledge structures** are organized packets of information that are

KNOWLEDGE STRUCTURES organized packets of information that are stored in memory

stored in memory. These knowledge structures form when a set of related concepts is frequently brought to mind, or activated. When people think about a concept, it becomes active in memory. Related concepts also become activated. Over time, as related concepts are frequently activated together, the set of related concepts becomes so strongly linked that activation of one part of the set automatically activates the whole set. Once activated, these knowledge structures simply run their course, like an airplane set on autopilot. The result is automatic thinking.

Schemas. Schemas are knowledge structures that represent substantial information about a concept, its attributes, and its relationships to other concepts. The concept, for example, could be the self, another person, a social category (e.g., politicians), or an object. A schema for dancing, for example, would include movement, rhythm, repetition, and coordination, as well as connections to music, shoes, romance, fashion, art, and perhaps embarrassment. A schema for bears might include fur, claws, danger, climbing trees, hibernating, and growling, as well as relationships to honey, zoos, various football teams (e.g., Chicago Bears), stuffed toys ("teddy" bears), and drops in stock prices (a "bear market").

Schemas make the complex world much easier to understand. They help organize information by connecting beliefs that are related to each other. They help the mind form expectancies. Hence if someone asks you to go dancing, you know that person is probably not just telling you to go outside and move around, but perhaps initiating a romantic date, and you should wear nice shoes and be prepared for music.

One type of event that sparks conscious thinking is a violation of expectancies. In general, people seem to go through their daily lives with a solid idea of what is supposed to happen. When life conforms to what they expect, they don't generally find it necessary to think much about it. When events depart sharply from what people have learned to expect, they may stop and analyze what happened. This is a very useful pattern. People develop an understanding of their social world, and their expectancies and schemas are part of this understanding. Schemas are developed through your experiences, and they guide the way you process information. Getting through daily life is much easier if you have schemas and know what to expect. Events that violate your expectancies show that something might be wrong with how you understand the world, so it is worth pausing to analyze the situation. In a club, you ask someone to dance, and the person sometimes nods and accompanies you to the dance floor, or sometimes politely rejects you; all is as expected, with no need to analyze. But if your invitation to

dance is met with a big laugh or a hurried departure, you might stop to wonder what went wrong: Are you not allowed to ask people to dance? Is there something wrong with the way you look? Do you smell bad?

Scripts. Scripts are knowledge structures that contain information about how people (or other objects) behave under varying circumstances. In a sense, scripts are schemas about certain kinds of events. Scripts include many types of information such as motives, intentions, goals, situations that enable (or inhibit) certain behaviors, and the causal sequence of events, as well as the specific behaviors themselves. In films and plays, scripts tell actors what to say and do. In social psychology, scripts define situations and guide behavior: The person first selects a script to represent the situation and then assumes a role in the script. Scripts can be learned by direct experience or by observing others (e.g., parents, siblings, peers, mass media characters).

People learn schemas and scripts that influence how they perceive, interpret, judge, and respond to events in their lives. These various knowledge structures develop over time, beginning in early childhood. The pervasiveness, interconnectedness, and accessibility of any learned knowledge structure is largely determined by the frequency with which it is encountered, imagined, and used. With great frequency even complex knowledge structures can become automatized—so overlearned that they are applied automatically with little effort or awareness.

Priming. Memory is filled with concepts. Related concepts are linked together in memory (e.g., the concepts *orange* and *juice*). When one concept becomes activated in memory by thinking about it, related concepts become activated too. **Priming** means activating a concept in the mind. William James, philosopher and psychologist, described priming as the "wakening of associations." Once a concept has been primed, it can influence the way we interpret new information. For example, numerous studies have shown that people are faster at classifying a target word (e.g., *nurse*) when it is preceded by a related word (e.g., *doctor*) than when it is preceded by an unrelated word (e.g., *butter*) (Meyer & Schvaneveldt, 1971; Neely, 1991). Thus, a prime is a stimulus that activates further processing of the same or related stimuli. The prime doesn't have to be conscious. A casino in Windsor, Ontario, was fined

---

SCHEMAS knowledge structures that represent substantial information about a concept, its attributes, and its relationships to other concepts
SCRIPTS knowledge structures that define situations and guide behavior
PRIMING planting or activating an idea in someone's mind

5. Person enters a restaurant

1. Hostess greets person

6. Person looks at menu

8. Person eats food

4. Person orders food

3. Person pays for food

2. Hostess seats person

7. Person leaves restaurant

© Michael Newmann/PhotoEdit (all frames)

One example of a script is a restaurant script (Schank & Abelson, 1977). Try putting the frames in the correct order. The answer is printed below the frames. The fact that you can do this illustrates that scripts exist.

Answer: The order of the frames is 5, 1, 2, 6, 4, 8, 3, 7.

because their electronic slot machines flashed the subliminal message "win" to customers. The idea was that priming the concept "win" would make customers more optimistic so that they would shovel more coins into slot machines.

The power of priming to activate concepts, which then hang around in the mind and can influence subsequent thinking, was demonstrated in an early study by Higgins, Rholes, and Jones (1977). Participants were asked to identify colors while reading words. By random assignment, some participants read the words *reckless*, *conceited*, *aloof*, and *stubborn*, while others read the words *adventurous*, *self-confident*, *independent*, and *persistent*. The words did not seem at all important to the study. Then all participants were told that the experiment was finished, but they were asked to do a brief task for another, separate experiment. In that supposedly different experiment, they read a paragraph about a man named Donald who was a skydiver, a powerboat racer, and a demolition derby driver, and they were asked to describe the impression they had of Donald. It turned out that the words participants had read earlier influenced their opinions of him. Those who had read the words

reckless, *conceited*, *aloof*, and *stubborn* were more likely to view Donald as having those traits than were participants who had read the other words. That is, the first task had "primed" participants with the ideas of recklessness, stubbornness, and so forth, and once these ideas were activated, they influenced subsequent thinking.

Research has often used priming as a technique to trigger automatic processes. In one study (Bargh, Chen, & Burrows, 1996), participants first unscrambled sentences by choosing four out of five words to make a grammatically correct sentence. They were told to do this as quickly as possible. In the rude priming version, one of the five words was rude (e.g., *they/her/bother/see/usually*). In the polite priming version, one of the five words was polite (e.g., *they/her/respect/see/usually*). In the neutral priming version, the polite or rude word was replaced by a neutral word (e.g., *they/her/send/see/usually*). Participants were told that after they completed the task, they should come out into the hallway and find the experimenter. The experimenter waited for the participant, while pretending to explain the sentence task to a confederate. The confederate pretended to have a difficult time understanding the task. The experimenter refused to acknowledge the participant, who was waiting patiently for instructions on what to do next. The dependent variable in the study was whether participants interrupted the experimenter within a 10-minute period. Of course, it is rude to interrupt somebody who is speaking to another person. As can be seen in ▶ **FIGURE 5.5**, participants primed with rude words were much more likely to interrupt the experimenter than were participants primed with polite words. Thus, priming activated the idea of being rude (or polite), which then hung around in the mind and influenced behavior in a seemingly unrelated context.

Framing. Politicians call it "spin," but social psychologists call it "framing." **Framing** refers to how information is presented to others. Would you rather eat a hamburger that is 10% fat or 90% lean? The fat content is the same in both hamburgers, but the 90% lean one sounds much more appetizing. Research has shown that people spend a lot more money when they are told the money is a "bonus" than when they are told it is a "rebate" (Epley & Gneezy, 2007; Epley, Mak, & Idson, 2006). A rebate is the return of a loss of one's own money, so people are less likely to spend it. In 2008, President George W. Bush gave American families a "tax rebate" to stimulate the economy. Bush should have pitched this as a "tax bonus" if he wanted Americans to spend the money.

Is this a photo of an American soldier rescuing an Iraqi child, or is it a photo of an Iraqi child orphaned by American guns? It depends on your frame.

REUTERS/Damir Sagolj/Landov

Social psychologists have become very interested in the framing of health messages—whether they are more effective if they are framed in terms of gains or losses. A **gain-framed appeal** focuses on how doing something will make you healthier; a **loss-framed appeal** focuses on the downside, such as the potential for greater illness. An example of a gain-framed appeal is: "Flossing your teeth daily removes particles of food in the mouth, avoiding bacteria, which promotes fresh breath." An example of a loss-framed appeal is: "If you do not floss your teeth daily, particles of food remain in the mouth, collecting bacteria, which causes bad breath." Research has shown that gain-framed appeals are more effective when targeting behaviors that prevent the onset of disease, whereas loss-framed appeals are more effective when targeting behaviors that detect diseases that people may already have but not be aware of (Rothman, Bartels, Wlaschin, & Salovey, 2006). The media can also frame stories in different ways (Entman, 1993). For example, consider the photo of an American soldier holding an Iraqi child. The American media might use gain-framing: an American soldier rescuing a child during the Iraq war. The Arab media might favor loss-framing: this child has been orphaned by American guns.

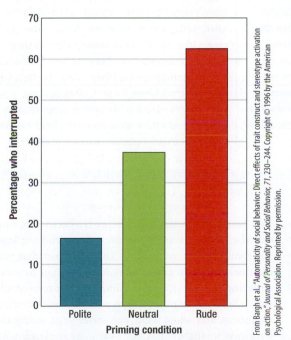

From Bargh et al., "Automaticity of social behavior: Direct effects of trait construct and stereotype activation on action," *Journal of Personality and Social Behavior, 71*, 230–244. Copyright © 1996 by the American Psychological Association. Reprinted by permission.

▶ **FIGURE 5.5** In one study (Bargh et al., 1996), participants primed with rude words were much more likely to interrupt the experimenter than were participants in the polite condition.

FRAMING whether messages stress potential gains (positively framed) or potential losses (negatively framed)

GAIN-FRAMED APPEAL focuses on the positive, such as how your teeth will be stronger and healthier if you brush and floss them every day

LOSS-FRAMED APPEAL focuses on the negative, such as the potential for getting cavities if you do not brush and floss your teeth every day

It's the Thought That Counts (or Doesn't Count!) the Calories

How much will someone eat? It depends partly on how hungry the person is. Someone who has not eaten anything for hours will eat more than someone who has just eaten a big meal. At least, that would make sense.

Not everyone follows that pattern, and some people even do the opposite. In one research paradigm, participants come to the lab after not having had anything to eat for several hours (e.g., Herman & Mack, 1975). By random assignment, participants are initially given nothing to eat, one milkshake, or two milkshakes. Afterward, participants are given three large containers of ice cream (chocolate, strawberry, and vanilla) to taste and rate. In reality, the researchers simply want to find out how much ice cream people will eat, as a function of whether they are already full (milkshake conditions) or hungry (no-milkshake condition).

Dieters react differently from nondieters in this situation. Nondieters do what you probably expect. Those who just consumed the milkshakes eat less ice cream, just enough to enable them to answer the questions on the rating sheet, whereas those who did not get any milkshake tend to chow down on the ice cream.

Dieters, however, show the opposite pattern (▶ FIGURE 5.6). That is, dieters who had not been given any milkshakes to consume were very restrained in tasting the ice cream. But dieters who had been assigned to drink milkshakes actually ate significantly more ice cream than the others. Researchers dubbed this tendency **counterregulation**—or, more informally, the "what the heck" effect—because the dieters seem to be thinking, "My diet is already blown for the day by drinking those milkshakes, so what the heck, I might as well enjoy some ice cream too!" (Herman & Mack, 1975).

The fact that the "what the heck" effect is driven by peculiar cognitions, rather than any bodily need for food, was demonstrated in a remarkable series of studies (Knight & Boland, 1981). Apparently whether the dieters think their diet is blown for the day depends more on how they think about certain foods than on the actual number of calories consumed. In one study, some dieters were given a snack of cottage cheese with fruit cocktail, which sounds like diet food but actually contained 580 calories. Others ate a small portion of ice cream that amounted to only 290 calories. Contrary to the actual caloric content, the ones who ate ice cream acted as if their diets were blown and ate more. Those who ate the cottage cheese and fruit cocktail acted as if their diets were still intact, even though their snack had contained twice as many calories as the ice cream. In another study, dieters had either a high-calorie or a low-calorie salad, or a high-calorie or low-calorie ice cream treat. Regardless of calories, those who ate the ice cream showed the "what the heck" effect, whereas those who had eaten the salads did not. The researchers tried another study in which they told participants precisely how many calories were in the assigned food, and even told them that they would eat this later on. Even under these conditions, dieters who expected to eat ice cream reacted as if their diets were blown, whereas those who expected to eat salad acted as if their diet were intact, regardless of the caloric content.

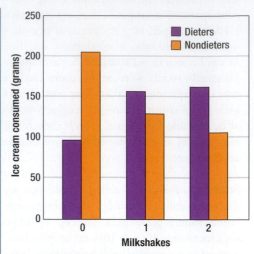

▶ **FIGURE 5.6** Nondieters who had had a milkshake ate less ice cream; dieters who had had milkshakes ate more ice cream (Herman & Mack, 1975)!

None of this makes rational sense. Even if you violate your diet for the day, you should avoid eating more fattening foods. Not only do dieters act as if one lapse ruins their diet for the day and it doesn't matter how much they eat thereafter, they also seem to make those decisions based on rigid ways of thinking about foods, regardless of how many calories the foods contain. Even when the salad contains twice as many calories as the ice cream treat, they act as if salad is good for diets. Trying to suppress thoughts of desired food does not help people restrain their eating (Soetens, Braet, Dejonckheere, & Roets, 2006; Soetens, Braet, & Moens, 2008). Thought suppression only makes people think more about the food they are trying not to think about—a rebound effect. ●

THOUGHT SUPPRESSION AND IRONIC PROCESSES

Most people have had thoughts they would like to erase from their minds. When people want to suppress a thought, their mind sets up two processes. One process keeps a lookout for anything that might remind the person of the unwanted thought. It is an automatic process that checks all incoming information for danger. The other is a controlled process that redirects attention away from the unpleasant thought. For example, if you are upset that you did not do well on a chemistry test and want to avoid worrying about it, your mind may automatically watch for anything that might remind you of tests or chemistry, and when some cue arises (e.g., seeing the person who sits in front of you in that class), your conscious mind quickly turns attention elsewhere (e.g., you don't say hello to that person). The problem with the controlled system is that whenever conscious control is relaxed, the automatic system is still

COUNTERREGULATION the "what the heck" effect that occurs when people indulge in a behavior they are trying to regulate after an initial regulation failure

watching for cues and may therefore flood the mind with them (Wegner, 1994).

As a child, the Russian writer Leo Tolstoy (1828–1910) was once challenged by his older brother Nikolenka to remain standing in a corner until he could stop thinking of a white bear (Biryukov, 1911). Poor Leo could think of nothing else. He quickly learned how difficult it is to control thoughts. Dan Wegner and his colleagues have replicated the informal experiment conducted by young Leo Tolstoy in more formal laboratory settings (Wegner, 1989; Wegner, Schneider, Carter, & White, 1987; Wenzlaff & Wegner, 2000). Regardless of the setting, the results are the same: People who are told not to think of a white bear cannot rid their minds of the white, furry creatures. People who are trying to overcome vices are better off not suppressing unwanted thoughts of the things they crave. For example, trying not to think about cigarettes only makes it more difficult for smokers to quit (Toll, Sobell, Wagner, & Sobell, 2001). The paradoxical effects of thought suppression have been linked to a variety of psychological disorders, especially anxiety disorders (e.g., phobias, obsessive-compulsive disorders, panic disorder, posttraumatic stress disorder; Najmi & Wegner, 2008). Even in dreams, suppressed thoughts are more likely to come to mind (Schmidt & Gendolla, 2008; Wegner, Wenzlaff, & Kozak, 2004). One review of all previous studies on the topic concluded that suppressing unwanted thoughts often backfires (Abramowitz, Tolin, & Street, 2001).

If suppressing thoughts does not work, what does work? Research has shown that distraction and even rumination are more effective than suppression (Lin & Wicker, 2007). Mental control is a form of self-regulation, discussed in detail in Chapter 4. *Food for Thought* describes how difficult it is for dieters to control their thoughts and consequently their eating habits.

[QUIZ YOURSELF]

What Is Social Cognition?

1. Organized beliefs we have about stimuli in our social world are known as _____.
   (a) automatic processes   (b) controlled processes
   (c) schemas   (d) self-concepts

2. What topic do people spend the greatest amount of time thinking about?
   (a) Food   (b) Money
   (c) People   (d) Weather

3. Which of the following is *not* one of the elements that distinguishes automatic from controlled processes?
   (a) Awareness   (b) Efficiency
   (c) Effort   (d) Relevance

4. During their first year of medical school, many medical students begin to think that they and other people they know are suffering from serious illness. This phenomenon, known as the medical student syndrome, is probably due to _____.
   (a) counterfactual thinking
   (b) false consensus
   (c) false uniqueness
   (d) priming

Attributions: Why Did That Happen?

Why did he do that? Why did she say that? Is she angry? Is he a fool? Is this job too hard for me? Does this good news mean that I am smarter than other people, or just lucky? People ask and answer these questions in their own minds all the time. Making the correct inferences is important, but not easy. There is no perfect way to go from what we actually see (such as someone's actions) to drawing firm conclusions about what that person is like inside (such as stable personality traits).

Attributions are the inferences people make about events in their lives. Indeed, the study of attributions was a revolutionary step in the history of social psychology, because it led social psychologists to abandon once and for all the behaviorist tradition that said psychology should only study observable, objective behavior and not talk about thoughts or other inner processes. Attributions opened the way for the study of thoughts and other cognitive processes.

Social psychologists began to study attributions because they are a crucial form of information processing that helps determine behavior. Two people may get identical bad grades on a test, but one of them works harder and does better the next time around, whereas the other gives up and drops out of the course. The attributions they make may help explain the difference. One student looked at the bad grade and thought, "I didn't study hard enough," so that person studied harder and improved. The other student looked at the same grade but thought, "I'm no good at this," or "This is too hard for me," or "This teacher sucks!" Such conclusions do not spur people to try harder, because they imply that all such effort is doomed to failure. Instead, they give up.

Fritz Heider analyzed what he called the "common sense psychology" by which people explain everyday events (Heider, 1958). Although there may be several

---

ATTRIBUTIONS the causal explanations people give for their own and others' behaviors, and for events in general

If Calvin fails, he wants to make an external attribution for the failure, whereas his teacher wants Calvin to make an internal attribution.

different explanations for behavior, Heider said most explanations fall into one of two major categories: (a) internal factors such as ability, attitudes, personality, mood, and effort; and (b) external factors such as the task, other people, or luck. For example, research has shown that when students perform poorly in the classroom, teachers make internal attributions (e.g., the student failed because he or she didn't study hard enough), whereas students tend to make external attributions (e.g., the test was ambiguous; see Burger, Cooper, & Good, 1982). The internal–external distinction has continued to emerge as a crucial dimension of attributions across several generations of researchers.

IT'S NOT MY FAULT: EXPLAINING SUCCESS AND FAILURE

One early thrust of attribution theory was to map out how people interpret success and failure. Heider's distinction between internal and external causes is certainly important. Success may be due to internal factors of the person such as effort, or could be due to external factors such as luck. Bernard Weiner (1972), another important attribution theorist, proposed a two-dimensional theory of attributions for success and failure. The first dimension was internal

versus external; the second dimension was stable versus unstable.

This two-dimensional map of attributions is illustrated in ▶ **FIGURE** 5.7. The four possible combinations of internal–external and stable–unstable yield the four main types of attributions that people make when they see themselves or someone else perform. Let us briefly consider each.

Internal, stable attributions involve ability. People may think their success reflects intelligence or talent. Conversely, they may decide that they failed at something because they lack the relevant ability. Ability attributions are very important because they invoke relatively permanent aspects of the self. People are motivated to conclude that they have high ability (e.g., Obach, 2003; Platt, 1988).

Internal, unstable attributions involve effort. Effort is unstable because it can change. If you think someone succeeded because she worked very hard, there is little guarantee that she would do well again (because she might not work as hard the next time). Then again, attributing failure to low effort can be very motivating, because people may think that they might succeed if they tried harder. There are cultural differences on this dimension. People from collectivist cultures emphasize effort, whereas people from individualistic cultures emphasize ability (e.g. Armbrister, 2002; Holloway, Kashiwagi, Hess, & Azuuma, 1986).

External, stable attributions point to the difficulty of the task. Success simply indicates the task was easy, whereas failure indicates it was hard. Most other people are likely to get the same result, because the crucial cause lies in the task, not in the person doing it.

Last, external and unstable attributions involve luck. If you attribute someone's success or failure to luck, there is very little credit or blame due to the person, nor is there any reason to expect the same result the next time.

Attributions are not made in a vacuum. Among other factors, people want to take credit for success

	Internal	External
Stable	Ability	Task difficulty
Unstable	Effort	Luck

▶ **FIGURE** 5.7 **Two-dimensional attribution theory (proposed by Weiner, 1972), illustrating the four possible combinations of internal–external and stable–unstable types.**

but deny blame for failure. This tendency is called the **self-serving bias**. Many studies of attribution have confirmed the widespread operation of the self-serving bias (Campbell & Sedikides, 1999). That is, across many different contexts and settings, people prefer to attribute their successes to ability and effort but tend to attribute their failures to bad luck or task difficulty (Zuckerman, 1979).

The self-serving bias occurs for several reasons. The main reason is simply that interpreting events in that way makes people feel good. They can maintain their high opinion of themselves by discounting their failures and maximizing the glory of their successes. However, evidence suggests that the self-serving bias is especially strong when people are explaining their successes and failures to others (Bradley, 1978; Tetlock, 1980). This would imply that they care more about what others think of them than about how they think of themselves. In other words, the self-serving bias is an important feature of self-presentation, described in Chapter 3 as people's efforts to control the impressions they make on others. (In a sense, self-presentation is about trying to influence the attributions that other people make about you.)

The self-presentational nature of the self-serving bias reflects another theme of this book, which is that inner processes serve interpersonal ends. People learn to think in ways that will help them get along better with others. If others see you as an incompetent loser, your chances of being accepted by others (e.g., hired for a good job) are low. Hence people want to maximize their credit for success while avoiding having their failures reflect badly on themselves.

Related to the self-serving bias is the tendency for individuals to overestimate how much they contributed to a group project. If you ask individuals in a group what percentage they contributed to the project, and add up the percentages, the sum is almost always greater than 100 percent (Ross & Sicoly, 1979). Part of the explanation for this effect is that individuals tend to view the other group members as a collective rather than as individuals. When individuals "unpack" the collaborations of the other group members, this bias is reduced (Savitsky, Van Boven, Epley, & Wight, 2005; Van Boven & Epley, 2003).

YOU LOOKING AT ME? THE ACTOR/OBSERVER BIAS

Suppose you go to a store and see a man shouting at the salesclerk. You might be tempted to conclude that the shouting person is a grumpy, obnoxious fellow. After all, obnoxious people certainly are more likely to shout at people in stores than are agreeable, easygoing, nice people.

Then again, the shouting man might see things very differently. If you asked him "Why are you

Bruce Bennett/Getty Images

In many fights and brawls, each side claims that the other side started it.

shouting?" he would be unlikely to give the answer "Because I am an obnoxious person!" More likely, he would say that the store clerk has treated him badly, and perhaps he has experienced a series of frustrations all day long.

In this example, we saw how you can reach very different conclusions (attributions) about the same behavior. The difference reflects one of the most durable patterns of attribution, called the **actor/observer bias** (Jones & Nisbett, 1971). It is relevant to any situation in which one person (the observer) is watching someone else's (the actor's) behavior. The bias occurs along the same basic dimension of attribution that we have already seen emerge repeatedly—namely, internal versus external. The actor/observer bias can be defined this way: Actors tend to attribute their own behavior to the situation (external), whereas observers tend to attribute actors' behavior to the actors (internal). Put more simply, actors tend to make external attributions, whereas observers make internal attributions.

The actor/observer bias can produce many misunderstandings and disagreements. Indeed, in an argument, it may be common for both sides to see themselves as responding to what the other does. "He started it!" is a common complaint, often heard on both sides, because each side attributes its own behavior to the situation but others' behavior to their traits and other dispositions. It seems natural to infer

---

SELF-SERVING BIAS the tendency to take credit for success but deny blame for failure
ACTOR/OBSERVER BIAS the tendency for actors to make external attributions and observers to make internal attributions

that *they* are fighting because they are mean, whereas *we* are fighting because they attacked us. Or, in the simpler words of pro hockey player Barry Beck on a brawl that broke out in one game, "We have only one person to blame, and that's each other!"

Some psychologists have focused on the observer side of the actor/observer bias, labeling it the **fundamental attribution error** (also sometimes called **correspondence bias**). When the error involves making an internal attribution about whole groups of people instead of specific individuals it is called the **ultimate attribution error** (Pettigrew, 1979). People have a bias to attribute another person's behavior to internal or dispositional causes (e.g., personality traits, attitudes) to a much greater extent than they should. People fail to take full notice and consideration of the external factors (e.g., the situation, constraints of the social environment) that are operating on the person. This is especially salient to social psychologists, who have traditionally studied how situations cause behavior—they think that the average person fails to appreciate how strong situational causes can be. This bias is found in individuals from both collectivist and individualist cultures (Krull, Loy, & Lin, 1999).

Indeed, it may be that the main thing people do when they observe another person's behavior is decide whether to make an internal attribution. In a sense, internal attributions are the main goal of the attribution process.

For example, is the person who commits an act of aggression a beast? Is the person who donates money to charity an altruist? To answer this kind of question, people make inferences on the basis of factors such as choice. Behavior that is freely chosen is more informative about a person than is behavior that is coerced. In one classic study (Jones & Harris, 1967), participants read a speech, ostensibly written by a college student, that either favored or opposed Fidel Castro, the former communist leader of Cuba. The participants were instructed to try to figure out the true attitude of the essay writer. Half of the participants were told that the student who wrote the essay had freely chosen to take this position. The other participants were told that the student was assigned the position by a professor. The study results are depicted in ▶ **FIGURE 5.8**. When asked to estimate the student's true attitude, participants were more likely to assume that there was a correspondence between his or her essay (behavior) and attitude (disposition)

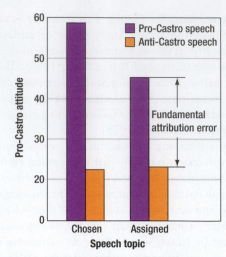

▶ **FIGURE 5.8** Participants in the Jones and Harris (1967) study thought that students who wrote a pro-Castro speech had pro-Castro attitudes, even if the speech topic was assigned to them. This is an example of the fundamental attribution error (also called correspondence bias).

when the student had a choice than when the student had no choice.

However, crucially, the participants in that study were willing to make internal attributions even when they were told the essay writer had had no choice. Logically, you cannot infer anything about someone's true opinion if the person's behavior was forced by the situation. This is the fundamental attribution error in action: People discounted the situational pressures to write a pro-Castro essay and concluded that the writer must have pro-Castro opinions.

There are at least four explanations for the fundamental attribution error. First, behavior is more noticeable than situational factors, which are often hidden. Second, people assign insufficient weight to situational causes even when they are made aware of them. Third, people are cognitive misers; they often take quick and easy answers rather than thinking long and hard about things. It takes considerably less cognitive effort to make internal attributions than to make external attributions by thinking about all the external factors that might be operating on the person. Fourth, language is richer in trait-like terms to explain behavior than in situational terms.

Try this simple exercise: First, write down as many terms as you can think of to describe an individual's personality or inner disposition. Next, write down as many terms as you can think of to describe the situational factors that could influence a person. There are thousands of trait adjectives for explaining behavior in terms of dispositional qualities (e.g., intelligent, outgoing, funny, introverted, mean, nice, creative,

FUNDAMENTAL ATTRIBUTION ERROR (CORRESPONDENCE BIAS) the tendency for observers to attribute other people's behavior to internal or dispositional causes and to downplay situational causes

ULTIMATE ATTRIBUTION ERROR the tendency for observers to make internal attributions (fundamental attribution error) about whole groups of people

dull, crazy, logical, flexible, patient, emotional), whereas there are relatively few terms for explaining behavior in situational terms (e.g., role, status, pressure, circumstance).

Recent work has begun to question the very existence of the actor/observer bias, however, especially when one sorts it out from the self-serving bias. Combining results from many different studies, Malle (2006) concluded that there was no consistent tendency for observers to make more dispositional attributions than actors. Still, there are genuine differences between how actors and observers explain actions (Malle, Knobe, & Nelson, 2007). Actors are more likely than observers to state reasons for how they acted ("I bought a motorcycle to save gas" vs. "He bought a motorcycle because he can't afford high gas prices"). Actors are also more likely to explain their acts by citing their beliefs, whereas observers point to the actors' desires: "I come here for lunch because they make the best hamburgers" vs. "He comes here for lunch because he likes the hamburgers."

Thus, the difference between drawing conclusions about self and drawing conclusions about others remains important. People judge others by their actions but judge themselves by their (generally good) intentions (Kruger & Gilovich, 2004). They can discount their own bad actions by saying "I didn't mean to do that," thus giving themselves a break that they do not give to others.

Taking this a step further, Pronin, Berger, and Molouki (2007) showed that people regard others as conforming but do not regard themselves as conformists to the same degree, again because they rely on introspection. That is, if they see another person purchasing the same kind of car or shirt or grill that neighbors have already bought, they assume that the other person is conforming. When they themselves purchase the same item under the same circumstances, they do not perceive themselves as conforming. Rather, they look inside and perceive that they thought it was a good buy or something that seemed useful to them for personal reasons. For example, in one study, students rated their own reasons for purchasing an iPod as having much less to do with social influence and conformity, as compared to other students who had bought an iPod.

In another study, students read about campus issues and were given (false and random) information about what a panel of students had decided. The students generally went along with the panel's recommendations, but they denied doing so out of conformity. However, they thought that other students would go along because of conformity. People do not see in themselves any desire to conform to others, so they do not chalk up their own behavior to conformity. The catch is that conformity pressures and processes may be mostly outside of consciousness, so people do not realize that they are conforming. They can see conformity in others but not in themselves. As Pronin and her colleagues (2007) put it, the result is that the individual thinks he or she is "alone in a crowd of sheep": Everyone else is conforming, but I am not.

THE ATTRIBUTION CUBE AND MAKING EXCUSES

Suppose you see a man named Joe kicking a dog named Fido. Is Joe a vicious person who abuses animals, or is Fido a vicious dog that attacks people? Social psychologist Harold Kelley proposed an attribution theory to answer questions like this. According to Kelley (1967), people make attributions by using the **covariation principle**—that for something to be the cause of a behavior, it must be present when the behavior occurs and absent when the behavior does not occur. Kelley proposed that people use three types of covariation information. The first type of information is **consensus**. It makes sense to ask whether other people would do the same thing if they were in the same situation. To obtain consensus information, ask the question "Do others behave similarly in this situation?" If the answer is yes, consensus is high. If not, consensus is low. The second type of information is **consistency**. To obtain consistency information, ask the question "Does the person usually behave this way in this situation?" If the answer is yes, consistency is high. If the answer is no, consistency is low. The third type of information is **distinctiveness**. To obtain distinctiveness information, ask the question "Does the person behave differently in different situations?" If the answer is yes, distinctiveness is high. If the answer is no, distinctiveness is low.

Kelley's theory is sometimes called the **attribution cube** because it uses three types of information to make attributions (see ▶ **TABLE 5.1**). People generally make an external attribution when consensus, consistency, and distinctiveness are all high. People generally make an internal attribution when consistency is high, but distinctiveness and consensus are

---

COVARIATION PRINCIPLE for something to be the cause of a behavior, it must be present when the behavior occurs and absent when the behavior does not occur

CONSENSUS in attribution theory, whether other people would do the same thing in the same situation

CONSISTENCY in attribution theory, whether the person typically behaves this way in this situation

DISTINCTIVENESS in attribution theory, whether the person would behave differently in a different situation

ATTRIBUTION CUBE an attribution theory that uses three types of information: consensus, consistency, and distinctiveness

► **TABLE 5.1** Kelley's Attribution Cube
Attributions are based on three dimensions (hence the term cube): consensus, consistency, and distinctiveness.

Consensus	Consistency	Distinctiveness	Attribution
High (Everyone kicks Fido)	High (Joe always kicks Fido)	High (Joe doesn't kick any other dogs, only Fido)	External (Fido is a vicious dog)
Low (Only Joe kicks Fido)	High (Joe always kicks Fido)	Low (Joe kicks all dogs)	Internal (Joe is a vicious person who kicks dogs)
Low (Only Joe kicks Fido)	Low (Joe sometimes kicks Fido)	High (Joe doesn't kick any other dogs, only Fido)	Ambiguous (Not sure whether it is something about Joe or something about Fido)

low. Other combinations of consensus, consistency, and distinctiveness lead to ambiguous attributions.

Consider again our example of Joe kicking Fido. To obtain consensus information, ask the question "Does everyone kick Fido?" To obtain consistency information, ask the question "Does Joe always kick Fido?" To obtain distinctiveness information, ask the question "Does Joe kick all dogs, or just Fido?" If consensus, consistency, and distinctiveness are all high (everyone kicks Fido; Joe always kicks Fido; Joe doesn't kick any other dogs, only Fido), then we make an external attribution (e.g., Fido is a vicious dog). If consistency is high (Joe always kicks Fido) but consensus and distinctiveness are low (only Joe kicks Fido; Joe kicks all dogs), we make an internal attribution (e.g., Joe is a vicious person who kicks dogs).

One good way to remember Kelley's theory is by considering an important interpersonal application of it—namely, making excuses (Snyder, Higgins, & Stucky, 1983). A good excuse is essentially an external attribution. People look for excuses when they have done something bad or wrong but do not want other people to conclude that the bad action reflects that they are a bad person. Based on the three types of information in Kelley's theory, there are three main types of excuses.

Suppose, for example, that you invite your boss over to dinner. Just as you are serving the meal, you attempt to fill her water glass and instead accidentally pour water all over her. You don't want her to make the attribution that you are a clumsy oaf who cannot be trusted with responsibility, or (worse yet) that you deliberately wanted to douse her fancy dress with ice water. So you might make any of three sorts of excuses. First, you might raise consensus: "Everybody spills water sometimes; it could happen to anyone." Second, you could lower consistency: "I don't usually spill things." Third, you could raise

distinctiveness: "Sorry about the water, but at least I got the red wine, gravy, and soup on the table without pouring them on your dress!"

[**QUIZ YOURSELF**]

Attributions: Why Did That Happen?

1. You and I work on a joint project, and it succeeds. In describing our relative contributions to the project, you assume that your contribution is greater than mine, but I assume that my contribution is greater than yours. This illustrates the _____.
   (a) actor/observer bias
   (b) false consensus effect
   (c) fundamental attribution error
   (d) self-serving bias

2. Hans sees Franz trip while walking down an outside flight of steps during the winter. "What a klutz," thinks Hans. Fifteen minutes later, Hans trips on the same flight of stairs. "Very icy today," thinks Hans. Hans' thinking illustrates the _____.
   (a) actor/observer bias
   (b) covariation principle
   (c) false consensus effect
   (d) Stroop test

3. Jose reads Sarina's essay that strongly supports capital punishment. Jose knows that Sarina had been assigned the task of writing the essay favoring capital punishment by her debate teacher. Jose is likely to _____.
   (a) believe that Sarina opposes capital punishment
   (b) believe that Sarina does, at least to some extent, favor capital punishment
   (c) believe that Sarina's position on capital punishment is neutral
   (d) reach no conclusion about Sarina's real position on capital punishment

Heuristics: Mental Shortcuts

Everything should be made as simple as possible, but not simpler.

—Albert Einstein

People have to make judgments and inferences about uncertain outcomes all the time, and they do it using limited information. What is the likelihood I will get a speeding ticket if I drive 10 miles per hour over the posted speed limit? What is the likelihood of my professor giving an unannounced quiz today in class? What is the likelihood that I will get a high-paying job if I major in psychology? What is the likelihood that this person will say yes if I ask him or her out on a date? What is the likelihood of divorce if I marry this person? What is the likelihood of getting lung cancer if I smoke cigarettes? What is the likelihood of getting pregnant or catching a sexually transmitted disease if I have unprotected sex with my partner?

As we have seen, controlled conscious thinking is difficult and requires effort, so most people prefer to rely on automatic processing when they can. Usually the automatic system works very well. The automatic system, however, is not smart enough to perform all the complex operations of reasoning; instead, it relies on shortcuts. These mental shortcuts, called **heuristics**, provide quick estimates (though sometimes inaccurate ones) for decisions about uncertain events. Heuristics greatly simplify our lives and usually lead to correct decisions, although sometimes they lead to errors. Research by Daniel Kahneman on heuristics even won the 2002 Nobel Prize in economics "for having integrated insights from psychological research into economic science, especially

concerning human judgment and decision-making under uncertainty" (*Nobel Prize*, 2008). Although people use several heuristics, we will feature the four most common ones: (a) representativeness, (b) availability, (c) simulation, and (d) anchoring and adjustment (Fiske, 2004). Other shortcuts will be discussed later. For example, stereotypes, sometimes considered to be heuristics, will be covered in Chapter 13 on prejudice and intergroup relations.

REPRESENTATIVENESS HEURISTIC

The **representativeness heuristic** is the tendency to judge the frequency or likelihood of an event by the extent to which it resembles the typical case. For example, in a series of 10 coin tosses, most people judge the series HHTTHTHTTH to be more likely than the series HHHHHHHHHH (where H is heads and T is tails), even though both series are equally likely. The reason is that the first series looks more random than the second series. It "represents" our idea of what a random series should look like.

We often think food that is labeled 100% natural is healthy. Often this is the case, but not always. Consider, for example, a surprising finding from a study on breakfast cereals conducted by *Consumer Reports*, a highly respected source of consumer information. In the study, rats were fed an exclusive diet of water and breakfast cereal for about 4 months. Rats that ate Lucky Charms grew and remained quite healthy, whereas rats that ate Quaker's 100% Natural Granola did not grow and got sick. Quaker's 100% Natural Granola seems to be representative of healthy food, but it is not. It turns out that Quaker 100% Natural Granola is packed full of saturated fats. In fact, a cup of the cereal contains about as much saturated fat as a half a rack of greasy beef ribs. In contrast, Lucky Charms contains no saturated fat. Although saturated fat is 100% natural, it is not good for your body (or for a rat's body).

Heavy reliance on the representativeness heuristic leads people to ignore other factors that influence the actual frequencies and likelihoods, such as rules of chance, independence, and base rate information. Consider the following example:

Tom is a 41-year-old who reads nonfiction books, listens to National Public Radio, and plays tennis in his spare time. Which is more likely?
a. Tom is an Ivy League professor.
b. Tom is a truck driver.

HEURISTICS mental shortcuts that provide quick estimates about the likelihood of uncertain events
REPRESENTATIVENESS HEURISTIC the tendency to judge the frequency or likelihood of an event by the extent to which it resembles the typical case

The Price of Being Mrs. Hisname

Person perception starts with first impressions, and one of the first things one learns about a person is his or her name. If people don't like their names, they can change them, but it costs time and money. Many people do face at least one choice point about changing their name. When a woman marries, she typically

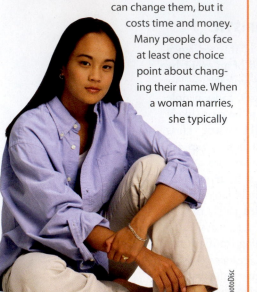

PhotoDisc

can choose between keeping the name she has had all her life, changing her last name to that of her new husband, or taking both her name and her husband's name ("hyphenating" the name). (Husbands are also allowed to change their last names, but very few do.) About three quarters (75%) of women in Western countries change their name.

Changing one's name has psychological consequences. As we have seen, most people are emotionally attached to their names, to the extent that they prefer the letters in their name over other letters in the alphabet (Nuttin, 1985). Yet the overwhelming majority of women elect to change their last names.

Name changers are perceived differently than name keepers, and the difference translates into significant amounts of money, as recent studies have shown (Noordewier, Van Horen, Ruys, & Stapel, 2009). A large European sociological study found that women who take their husband's name earn only about 76% as much as women who keep their birth name.

Why? Person perception factors may be crucial. Participants in one study judged job applications that made it clear that a woman had the same name as her partner, a different name, or a hyphenated name (Noordewier et al., 2008). The woman who kept her own name was judged to be more intelligent and ambitious than the woman who had changed or hyphenated her name, even if the rest of the application was identical. Women who took their husband's name were judged as more caring and emotional (but less intelligent and ambitious). Participants also estimated that the women who shared their husband's name earned less than those who had kept their own separate name when they married. On this, they were correct. But those expectations may in turn be one of the reasons behind the pay difference.

Why do some women resist the trend and keep their own names? Women who keep their original name when they marry differ from women who change names in several ways: The ones who keep their own name are younger, more likely to have a college education, less likely to have children, and more feminist in their attitudes (Hoffnung, 2006; Twenge, 1997). ■

Most people answer (a) because Tom seems like a typical Ivy League professor. People fail to consider, however, that there are a lot more truck drivers than there are Ivy League professors. Thus, in making that judgment, people rely on one kind of information (representativeness, which means how well Tom resembles the category of professors) instead of another (how many people there are in the category). The representativeness heuristic is related to the base rate fallacy described later in this chapter.

In some cultures, women who do not change their last name to the name of their husband are considered different from (unrepresentative of) other women. Are there financial consequences associated with women changing their names? See *Money Matters* to find out.

AVAILABILITY HEURISTIC

The **availability heuristic** is the tendency to judge the frequency or likelihood of an event by the ease with which relevant instances come to mind. The ease with which relevant instances come to mind is influenced not only by the actual frequency but also by factors such as how salient or noticeable the event is, how recent the event is, and whether attention was paid to the event. For example, after the movie *Jaws* came out, many people refused to swim in the ocean (and even in fresh water!) because they could not stop thinking about the great white shark in that movie that ate so many unsuspecting swimmers.

Thus, people overestimate the frequency of dramatic deaths and underestimate the frequency of less dramatic deaths (Fischhoff, Lichtenstein, Slovic, Derby, & Keeney, 1981). For example, airplane crash deaths are much more dramatic than are deaths caused by tobacco use, and they get a lot more attention from the mass media, which makes them stand out in memory (high availability). As a result, people think they are common. In fact, three jumbo jets full of passengers crashing every day for a year would not equal the number of deaths per year caused by tobacco use. Tobacco kills more than 435,000 people a year (Mokdad, Marks, Stroup, & Gerberding,

---

AVAILABILITY HEURISTIC the tendency to judge the frequency or likelihood of an event by the ease with which relevant instances come to mind

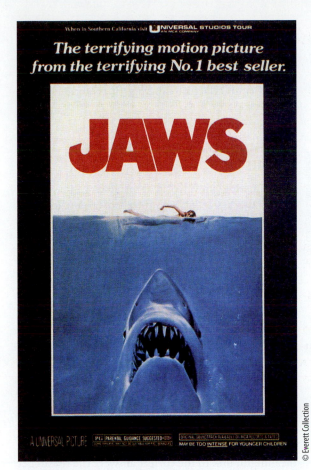

The terrifying motion picture from the terrifying No. 1 best seller.

JAWS

A UNIVERSAL PICTURE

"Just try to forget me, if you can!"

		Dream recalled	
		Yes	No
"Key" event happened	Yes	Available	Unavailable
	No	Unavailable	Unavailable

▶ **FIGURE 5.9** The availability heuristic provides one explanation of ESP beliefs. People remember salient events, but forget nonsalient events.

2004). It also takes tobacco a long time to kill a person, so deaths due to tobacco aren't as salient as deaths due to airplane crashes.

The availability heuristic might also help explain extrasensory perception (ESP) beliefs. Have you had a dream and later found that the dream came true? This has happened to most people. It might be because this event is more salient than the other possible events, as is shown in ▶ **FIGURE 5.9**.

It takes a skilled observer to notice when an expected event does not occur. For example, consider an incident in the story "Silver Blaze" from Sir Arthur Conan Doyle's (1894/1974) *The Memoirs of Sherlock Holmes*. Colonel Ross owned a horse named Silver Blaze, the favorite for the Wessex Cup. Silver Blaze had mysteriously disappeared, and the horse's trainer, John Staker, had been murdered. Inspector Gregory asked Sherlock Holmes to help investigate the case. During the investigation, Colonel Ross asked Sherlock Holmes, "Is there anything else to which you wish to draw my attention?" Holmes replied, "Yes, to the curious incident of the dog in the nighttime." Ross answered, "But the dog did nothing in the nighttime!" Holmes responded, "That is the curious incident." The dog was kept in the same stable

as Silver Blaze. Three boys were also in the stable; two slept in the loft while the third kept watch. The stable boy who kept watch had been drugged with opium. Holmes explained, "Though someone had been in and had fetched out a horse, he had not barked enough to arouse the two lads in the loft. Obviously the midnight visitor was someone whom the dog knew well." From this, the famous detective was able to figure out that it was the trainer who had taken the horse that night.

SIMULATION HEURISTIC

The **simulation heuristic** is the tendency to judge the frequency or likelihood of an event by the ease with which you can imagine (or mentally simulate) it. More easily imagined events are judged to be more likely than other events. Emotional reactions to events are intensified when people can easily imagine that they could have turned out differently.

Consider the following hypothetical example (Kahneman & Tversky, 1982):

> Mr. Crane and Mr. Tees were scheduled to leave the airport on different flights, at the same time. They traveled from town in the same limousine, were caught in a traffic jam, and arrived at the airport thirty minutes after the scheduled departure time of their flights. Mr. Crane is told that his flight left on time. Mr. Tees is told that his flight was delayed and just left five minutes ago. Who is more upset, Mr. Crane or Mr. Tees?

Most people think Mr. Tees would be more upset than Mr. Crane. The reason is that it is easier for people to imagine how Mr. Tees could have made his flight (e.g., if only the plane had waited a little

SIMULATION HEURISTIC the tendency to judge the frequency or likelihood of an event by the ease with which you can imagine (or mentally simulate) it

Can you tell who was the silver medalist by only looking at their facial expressions?

© Xing Guangli/Xh/Xinhua Press/Corbis

Satisfaction depends on thoughts about what might have been.

The simulation heuristic addresses these "if only" thoughts, also called counterfactual thoughts. We discuss counterfactual thinking in more detail later in this chapter.

ANCHORING AND ADJUSTMENT HEURISTIC

In estimating how frequent or likely an event is, people use a starting point (called an anchor) and then make adjustments up and down from this starting point. This mental shortcut or heuristic is called **anchoring and adjustment**. For example, if one party in a negotiation starts by suggesting a price or condition, then the other party is likely to base its counteroffer on this anchor. People use anchors even if they know they are just random numbers. Crucially, most research finds that people remain close, typically too close, to the anchor (Slovic & Lichtenstein, 1971). The anchor has far more impact than it deserves.

Participants in one study had to estimate what percentage of the United Nations was comprised of African countries (Tversky & Kahneman, 1974). Before they made their estimate, they were given an anchor that was ostensibly random and had no meaningful link to the correct answer. The researcher spun a *Wheel of Fortune* type wheel that contained the numbers 0–100. The wheel was rigged so that it stopped on 10 for half the participants and on 65 for the other half. These numbers were the anchors. Participants were asked if the percentage of African countries was higher or lower than the number on the wheel. Thus, some participants made their estimate after saying "more than 10%" while the rest made estimates after saying "less than 65%." The estimating task was the same for both groups, so in theory they should have made similar estimates, but both

longer, if only the traffic jam had cleared a few minutes earlier). Mr. Crane had no chance of making his flight even if one of those things had been different.

In another study (Medvec, Madey, & Gilovich, 1995), researchers videotaped television coverage of the 1992 Summer Olympic Games. They showed participants the immediate reactions of bronze and silver medalists at the end of the competition, and on the podium when they received their awards. Participants rated the bronze medalists to be happier than the silver medalists! Why? Although the silver medalists received a higher award than the bronze medalists, it was easier for them to imagine winning the gold medal. For the bronze medal winners, it was a close call to be on the podium with a medal at all. If a few small things had been different, they might have finished in fourth place and received no medal.

ANCHORING AND ADJUSTMENT the tendency to judge the frequency or likelihood of an event by using a starting point (called an anchor) and then making adjustments up or down

▶ **TABLE 5.2** The Most Common Mental Shortcuts (or Heuristics) That People Use

Heuristic	Definition	Example
Representativeness	The tendency to judge the frequency or likelihood of an event by the extent to which it "resembles" the typical case	In a series of 10 coin tosses, most people judge the series HHTTHTHTTH to be more likely than the series HHHHHHHHHH (where H is heads and T is tails), even though both are equally likely.
Availability	The tendency to judge the frequency or likelihood of an event by the ease with which relevant instances come to mind	People overestimate the frequency of dramatic deaths (e.g., dying in an airplane crash) and underestimate the frequency of less dramatic deaths (e.g., dying from lung cancer).
Simulation	The tendency to judge the frequency or likelihood of an event by the ease with which you can imagine (or mentally simulate) an event	In the Olympics, bronze medalists appear to be happier than silver medalists, because it is easier for a silver medalist to imagine being a gold medalist.
Anchoring and adjustment	The tendency to judge the frequency or likelihood of an event by using a starting point (called an anchor) and then making adjustments up and down from this starting point	If one party in a negotiation starts by suggesting a price or condition, then the other party is likely to base its counteroffer on this anchor.

groups stuck close to their anchor. The average estimate of participants who had been given the random number 10 was 25%, whereas the average estimate of those given the random number 65 was 45%. This study illustrates that people are influenced by an initial anchor value even though it may be unreliable (indeed, it was seemingly chosen at random).

► **TABLE 5.2** summarizes the definitions and examples of the four heuristics we have discussed. The next section discusses the most common cognitive errors people make.

AFP/AFP/Getty Images

"It was easier when you went to school, Dad. That was before the information age."

[QUIZ YOURSELF]

Heuristics: Mental Shortcuts

1. The strategy of judging the likelihood of things by how well they match particular prototypes constitutes the _____ heuristic.

    (a) availability   (b) matching

    (c) representativeness   (d) vividness

2. People's greater fear of flying than of driving can probably best be explained by the _____ heuristic.

    (a) anchoring and adjustment

    (b) availability

    (c) representativeness

    (d) simulation

3. "If only I hadn't driven home from work using a different route," thinks Minh, "then my car would not have been hit in the rear by that other driver!" Minh's statement most clearly reflects _____.

    (a) the availability heuristic

    (b) self-serving bias

    (c) counterfactual thinking

    (d) the self-fulfilling prophecy

4. Masako asked two friends to estimate the number of people living in Tokyo. The correct answer, according to the 2000 census, was just over 12 million. She asked the first friend whether it was more or less than 8 million. She asked the second friend whether it was more or less than 16 million. The first friend guessed 9 million people, whereas the second friend guessed 15 million people. The difference in estimates can best be explained using the _____ heuristic.

    (a) anchoring and adjustment

    (b) availability

    (c) representativeness

    (d) simulation

Errors and Biases

Our age has been described as the information age. For example, the number of TV channels has increased from three or four to hundreds. The Internet has made information more accessible than ever before. This increase in information has not had much impact on other animals, such as snails or squirrels, but it has had a tremendous impact on humans.

One resulting danger is **information overload**, defined as "the state of having too much information to make a decision or remain informed about a topic" (worldiq.com, 2008). Information overload can result from a high rate of new information being added (too much to keep up with), contradictions in available information, a low signal-to-noise ratio (too much irrelevant information compared to the amount of relevant information), and the lack of an efficient method for comparing and processing different types of information (worldiq.com, 2008). In one study (Lee & Lee, 2004), participants selected a CD player from a web page. The researchers manipulated the number of CD players available (18 or 27), and the number of attributes of the CD player (9 or 18), such as bass enhancement, type of warranty, and the ability to burn discs. As the number of alternatives and features available increased, consumers quickly became overwhelmed, dissatisfied, and confused by the number of choices involved.

One theme of this book is the duplex mind. The human mind has two main systems: the automatic system and the conscious system. The automatic

---

INFORMATION OVERLOAD having too much information to comprehend or integrate

the SOCIAL Side of SEX

Counting Sex Partners

At some point in the development of most intimate relationships, the two individuals ask each other how many people they have previously had sex with. A simple question with a simple answer, right? Hardly. In fact, even when people give supposedly honest answers to physicians or researchers, the answers are subject to distortion from a variety of sources (see Laumann, Gagnon, Michael, & Michaels, 1994; Morokoff, 1986; Wiederman, 1993).

One sign of distortion is that in all surveys, men report many more sex partners than women. For example, in 2004, ABC News conducted a national poll and reported on the show *PrimeTime Live* that the average American man has had sex with 20 partners but the average American woman has had only 6 partners (Sawyer, 2004). Similar results, though usually with lower numbers, have been reported in all other studies (e.g., Janus & Janus, 1993; Laumann et al., 1994). These inequalities are logically impossible. If we count only heterosexual behavior, and if there are roughly the same number of men as women, then the average numbers of sex partners must be equal. Every time a man has sex with a new woman, the woman also has sex with a new man. How can the numbers be so different? And same-sex behavior is not enough to explain the gap. If the ABC News numbers were correct, then the average American man would have had sex with 6 women and 14 men! Most evidence indicates that same-gender sex is much rarer than that (Laumann et al., 1994).

Most experts suspect that tallies of sex partners are affected by motivation. Men want to claim to have had many sex partners, because that indicates that they are handsome, charming, and virile. Women, however, want to claim relatively few partners, because women value being choosy and look down on others who have had many partners (Baumeister & Vohs, 2004; Buss & Schmitt, 1993; Miller & Fishkin, 1997). Still, how do these motivations translate into different tallies of sex partners?

One possible answer is that people lie. Men might invent more partners than they have had, and women might deny or conveniently forget some of their past sexual experiences. This is not a full explanation. The gender difference in sex partners is found even on anonymous surveys, in which people would have little to gain by lying and would supposedly not be embarrassed by the truth. Still, there are some signs of it. When researchers hooked people up to lie detectors, they changed their answers to the question about how many sex partners they had. Women, in particular, reported more partners when they were connected to lie detectors than when they could just write a number on a questionnaire (Alexander & Fisher, 2003).

Another possible answer is that differences are due to sex with prostitutes or homosexual activity. Few surveys include prostitutes, so these women (some of whom have had sex with thousands of men) could skew the data. These sex acts would be counted by the men but not by the women in the research sample (because prostitutes were not sampled). These do contribute something to the finding that men have more sex partners than women. However, some researchers have calculated that there is not nearly enough prostitution to account for the large gender difference in tallies of partners (Einon, 1994; Phillis & Gromko, 1985). The same goes for homosexual activity. True, gay males typically have more partners than gay females, but gay males are a relatively small segment of the population. Even when data are restricted to heterosexual and non-prostitute sex, men report more partners than women (Phillis & Gromko, 1985).

Research on social cognition has identified two processes that help produce the difference. One is a difference in how people count. People who have had more than about half a dozen partners do not always keep an exact count.

PhotoDisc

When asked how many partners they have had, they can either try to make a mental list, or they can estimate. Apparently, women usually answer by making a mental list, but this procedure is prone to underestimating (because it is easy to forget something that may have happened once or twice some years ago). In contrast, men tend to estimate, and estimating tends to produce inflated numbers (because men round up: a true figure of 22 might produce an estimated answer of "about 25"). Accordingly, when men and women try to give honest answers, they may still furnish systematically distorted numbers (Brown & Sinclair, 1999; Sinclair & Brown, 1999; Wiederman, 1997).

The other process involves shifting criteria. What exactly counts as sex? Research has shown that men are more likely than women to include borderline cases such as oral sex (Sanders & Reinisch, 1999). There is no truly correct answer, so, as social cognition researchers have found in many spheres, people use criteria that suit them and make them feel good (e.g., Dunning, 1999). Women want to report relatively few sex partners, so if they only had oral sex with someone they feel justified in saying they did not have sex. Men want to have higher tallies, so they think it is reasonable to include oral sex and other such cases. No doubt some people do lie about their sexual histories. But even when they try to tell the truth, they may furnish heavily biased answers. Moreover, these answers are distorted in the directions that give people the answers they prefer. ■

system helps people deal with information overload. The job of the automatic system is to make quick, fairly accurate judgments and decisions, whereas the conscious system works more slowly and thoroughly to make more precise judgments and decisions. Because most people are cognitive misers and do not like to expend mental effort, they rely heavily on the automatic system. The automatic system takes shortcuts, such as by using heuristics. Even though the automatic system is very good at helping people make fast decisions (it can do it in milliseconds!), it is not very good at making calculations, such as probabilities. Thus, the automatic system is prone to make several kinds of cognitive errors.

When it comes to the topic of sex partners, the quick answers differ considerably for men and women. For example, many studies have found dramatic but logically implausible differences in how men and women answer the question of how many sex partners they have had. Read *The Social Side of Sex* to find out more.

People generally have access to two types of information: (a) statistical information from a large number of people, and (b) case history information from a small number of people (could be even one person). Although people would make much better decisions if they paid the most attention to statistical information, they generally pay the most attention to case history information (Fiske & Taylor, 1991). For example, when buying a new car people are more influenced by what a few friends tell them about a car (case history information) than they are by what hundreds of people say about the car in *Consumer Reports* (statistical information). Even if the car has an outstanding repair record and is rated very highly by consumers, they won't buy it if their friend owned a similar car once and said it was a "lemon." In this section we describe some of the common cognitive errors and biases that affect people's decisions.

CONFIRMATION BIAS

Jonathan Cainer was born in the U.K. in 1958 (Smith, 2004). He dropped out of school when he was 15 years old, pumped gas at a service station, and played in a band called Strange Cloud. In the early 1980s he moved to the United States and became a manager at a nightclub in Los Angeles. There he met a psychic poet named Charles John Quatro, who told him he would someday write an astrology column read by millions. Cainer returned to the U.K. and enrolled at the Faculty of Astrological Studies in London. Today he does indeed write an astrology newspaper column that is read by more than 12 million people.

Are you impressed by the accuracy of Quatro's prediction regarding Cainer's future as an astrology columnist? We can predict your answer to this question, even though we have never met you (and we are not psychics). If you believe in astrology, we predict that you will be impressed. If you don't believe in astrology, we predict that you will not be impressed. Were we correct? Told you so!

This example illustrates the **confirmation bias** (Baggini, 2004), defined as the tendency to notice

information that confirms one's beliefs, and to ignore information that disconfirms one's beliefs. Philosopher Francis Bacon wrote in his book *Novum Organum* (1620) that "it is the peculiar and perpetual error of the human understanding to be more moved and excited by affirmatives than by negatives." Beliefs in paranormal phenomena such as telepathy can be explained by the confirmation bias (Rudski, 2002). The confirmation bias isn't limited to paranormal beliefs, however. This bias extends to a wide variety of beliefs (Nickerson, 1998). In the story that began this chapter, Carolyn and Eric stayed in their trailer during a hurricane, and they interpreted the fact that their trailer was not destroyed as confirming their faith that divine powers were watching over them. Other people who were skeptical of religious faith might have interpreted the fact that their trailer was blown off its base as a sign that no divine power was watching over them.

CONJUNCTION FALLACY

Consider the following hypothetical case (Tversky & Kahneman, 1983):

> Linda is 31, single, outspoken, and very bright. She majored in philosophy in college. As a student, she was deeply concerned with discrimination and other social issues, and she participated in anti-nuclear demonstrations. Which is *more* likely?
> **a.** Linda is a bank teller.
> **b.** Linda is a bank teller and active in the feminist movement.

Most people (87%) answered (b) even though this answer is mathematically impossible. Answer (b) can never be more likely than answer (a). Answer (b) can at best be equal to answer (a), but only if *all* bank tellers are active in the feminist movement. Because only some bank tellers are active in the feminist movement, answer (a) is more likely.

This cognitive error, called the **conjunction fallacy**, is the tendency for people to see an event as more likely as it becomes more specific because it is joined with elements that seem similar to events that are likely. However, the actual likelihood of an event being true *declines* when it becomes more specific because additional elements must also be true in order for the overall event to be true. The representativeness heuristic provides one possible explanation for the conjunction error.

CONFIRMATION BIAS the tendency to notice and search for information that confirms one's beliefs and to ignore information that disconfirms one's beliefs

CONJUNCTION FALLACY the tendency to see an event as more likely as it becomes more specific because it is joined with elements that seem similar to events that are likely

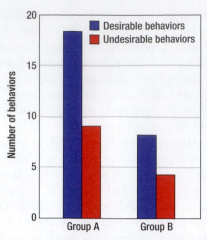

▶ **FIGURE 5.10** Actual correlation in Hamilton and Gifford (1976) study. Two-thirds of the behaviors were performed by Group A members (the majority), and two-thirds of the behaviors were desirable for both groups.

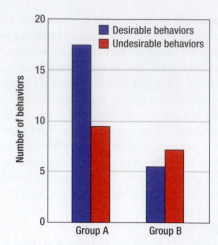

▶ **FIGURE 5.11** Illusory correlation in Hamilton and Gifford (1976) study. Even though two-thirds of the behaviors committed by Group B members were desirable, participants "recalled" Group B members committing more undesirable behaviors than desirable behaviors.

ILLUSORY CORRELATION

An **illusory correlation** occurs when people overestimate the link between variables that are related only slightly or not at all (e.g., Golding & Rorer, 1972). For example, people overestimate the frequency of undesirable behavior by minority group members. One explanation for this tendency is that minority group status and undesirable behaviors are both relatively rare. Because people are sensitive to rare events, the occurrence of two rare events together is especially noticeable.

In one study (Hamilton & Gifford, 1976), participants read a series of sentences describing a desirable or an undesirable behavior from a person belonging to group A or B (e.g., "John, a member of Group A, visited a sick friend in the hospital." "Allen, a member of Group B, dented the fender of a parked car and didn't leave his name."). Overall, two-thirds of the behaviors were desirable for both groups, and two-thirds involved a member of Group A—the majority (see ▶ **FIGURE 5.10**). Participants then estimated the number of desirable and undesirable behaviors performed by members of each group. The ratio of desirable to undesirable behaviors was the same for the two groups, so the estimates should have been the same for the two groups, but they were

not. Participants overestimated the number of undesirable behaviors performed by Group B (minority) members; in fact, they estimated more undesirable behaviors than desirable behaviors from Group B members (see ▶ **FIGURE 5.11**). Illusory correlations can even occur after exposure to only one unusual behavior performed by only one member of an unfamiliar group (e.g., Ben, a Jehovah's Witness, owns a pet sloth), called **one-shot illusory correlations** (Risen, Gilovich, & Dunning, 2004).

The mass media contribute to these illusory correlations. For example, if a mentally ill person shoots a famous person (e.g., Mark Chapman shoots Beatles guitarist John Lennon; John Hinckley Jr. shoots former U.S. President Ronald Reagan), the media draw attention to the mental status of the assassin. Assassinations and mental hospitalizations are both relatively rare, making the combination especially noticeable. Such media reporting adds to the illusion of a correlation between mental illness and violent behavior.

BASE RATE FALLACY

Another cognitive error is the **base rate fallacy**—the tendency to ignore or underuse base rate information (information about most people) and instead to be influenced by the distinctive features of the case being judged. Many cognitive errors are the result of people not paying attention to base rates. Consider the following example (Kahneman, Slovic, & Tversky, 1982):

A town has two hospitals. In the larger hospital, about 45 babies are born every day;

ILLUSORY CORRELATION the tendency to overestimate the link between variables that are related only slightly or not at all

ONE-SHOT ILLUSORY CORRELATION an illusory correlation that occurs after exposure to only one unusual behavior performed by only one member of an unfamiliar group

BASE RATE FALLACY the tendency to ignore or underuse base rate information and instead to be influenced by the distinctive features of the case being judged

in the smaller hospital, about 15 babies are born every day. In one year, each hospital recorded the number of days on which more than 60% of the babies born were boys. Which hospital recorded more such days?

a. The large hospital
b. The small hospital
c. About the same number of days (within 5% of each other)

Most people answer (c). People don't consider the fact that variability decreases as sample size increases. Think about flipping a coin 10 times and getting 6 heads versus flipping a coin 1,000 times and getting 600 heads. You are much more likely to get 6 heads in 10 flips than to get 600 heads in 1,000 flips. Tournaments that eliminate teams after a single loss, such as the World Cup soccer tournament or the NCAA college basketball tournament, allow underdogs a better chance to win, as compared to tournaments like the NBA (National Basketball Association) play-offs, in which each round is a series of games. In a single game, the weaker team might get lucky and win. Across many games, the better team will tend to win more often.

Soccer is especially vulnerable to the effects of small samples, because soccer games tend to have low scores such as 1–0. Thus, there may be only one goal scored in the entire championship contest, and that goal decides the winner. In contrast, a seven-game World Series of baseball may easily contain 40 to 50 points scored, and a seven-game basketball series will typically have more than 1,000 points, which makes it quite difficult for a relatively inferior team to beat the odds and win.

GAMBLER'S FALLACY AND THE HOT HAND

Suppose you flip a coin 10 times. You flip 9 heads in a row. Is your next flip more likely to be:

a. Heads
b. Tails
c. Heads and tails are equally likely.

Hot hand players answer (a) because they think they have a "hot" hand and their luck will continue. **Gambler's fallacy** players answer (b) because they think their luck will change and that a tails is "due." These biases may both stem from the same source—the representativeness heuristic. The correct answer is (c). If people think about it, they would agree that heads and tails are equally likely on any given flip. They might also agree that the outcome of any flip does not depend on the outcome of the previous flip.

To test these biases in the real world, researchers conducted a study in a casino in Reno, Nevada

© Mike Finn-Kelcey/Reuters/Corbis

One goal, one game: In 2004, underdog Greece surprised the world by winning the European championship in the world's most popular sport, soccer. Greece got there by beating the two hardest opponents, the tournament favorite Czechs in the semifinal game and the home team Portugal in the final, both by 1–0 scores. The Greeks might not have made it past the supposedly stronger teams if they had had to play seven-game series, but when the title is decided by one goal in one game, anything can happen.

(Sundali & Croson, 2006). Participants were videotaped while playing roulette. Because there are 38 numbers on a roulette wheel, 1/38 or 2.6% of the bets should fall on each number. The researchers could look at how each person bet over time. Most players exhibited both biases. Gambler's fallacy players were also more likely to be hot hand players. A statistician once said that gambling is a tax on the math incompetent. The tax is especially high for gambler's fallacy and hot hand players.

FALSE CONSENSUS EFFECT

People tend to overestimate the number of people who share their opinions, attitudes, values, and beliefs. This tendency is called the **false consensus effect** (Krueger & Clement, 1994; Marks & Miller, 1987). An early demonstration asked students whether they would walk around campus carrying a sign that said "Eat at Joe's" (Ross, Greene, & House,

---

HOT HAND the tendency for gamblers who get lucky to think they have a "hot" hand and their luck will continue

GAMBLER'S FALLACY the tendency to believe that a particular chance event is affected by previous events and that chance events will "even out" in the short run

FALSE CONSENSUS EFFECT the tendency to overestimate the number of other people who share one's opinions, attitudes, values, and beliefs

1977). Later they were asked how many other people they thought would be willing to carry such a sign. Those who agreed to carry the sign said that 62% of other people would also agree to carry the sign. Those who refused to carry the sign said that only 33% of other people would carry the sign. Obviously both can't be right, and one or both groups tended to overestimate the proportion of people who would respond the same way they themselves had.

The availability heuristic provides one possible explanation of the false consensus effect. When asked to predict what other people are like, people use the information that is most readily available—information about themselves and their friends. Because people tend to associate with similar others, this available information might lead people to overestimate the percentage of people who are similar to themselves. Another explanation is that people want to believe their views and actions are the correct ones, so they assume others would concur. Yet another explanation is that people use their own reaction as an "anchor" (remember the anchoring and adjustment heuristic?) and adjust it when having to furnish a broad prediction about people in general; as usual, they tend to remain too close to the anchor.

FALSE UNIQUENESS EFFECT

People tend to underestimate the number of people who share their most prized characteristics and abilities. This tendency is called the **false uniqueness effect** (Goethals, Messick, & Allison, 1991). It also is called the **better-than-average effect** and the **Lake Wobegon effect**. In Lake Wobegon, Minnesota, a fictional town invented by humorist Garrison Keillor (1985), "all the women are strong, all the men are good-looking, and all the children are above average." For example, religious people believe that other people are more likely to believe in paranormal phenomena but are less likely to hold religious beliefs than they are (Bosveld, Koomen, & Van der Pligt, 1996; Dudley, 1999). Similarly, people who engage in desirable health-protective behaviors (e.g., regular exercise, regular checkups, eating healthy foods), underestimate the number of other people who engage in similar behaviors (Suls, Wan, & Sanders, 1988). It appears that people overestimate consensus when it comes to their undesirable characteristics (false consensus) but underestimate consensus when it comes to their desirable characteristics (false uniqueness). As

off the mark.com by Mark Parisi

WHOA! WHAT ARE THE ODDS OF **THAT**?! WINNING THE LOTTERY **AND** GETTING HIT BY LIGHTNING...

Reprinted by permission of Atlantic Feature Syndicate/Mark Parisi.

noted in the previous section, they also overestimate consensus for their opinions and preferences.

This mixture of overestimating and underestimating can be remembered easily by noting that all distortions are in the direction most helpful for self-esteem. That is, you can feel good about yourself if your opinions are correct, and one sign of correctness is that most people agree with you (so you overestimate consensus for opinions). You can feel good about yourself if your faults are ones that many people have (so overestimate consensus regarding faults). And you can feel especially good about yourself if your talents and virtues are rare and exceptional ones that few people can match (so underestimate consensus regarding good characteristics). Probably this pattern is no accident. As we saw in Chapter 3, people like to think well of themselves, and many patterns of bias and distortion help them achieve and maintain their favorable self-views.

STATISTICAL REGRESSION

In the 19th century, Sir Francis Galton (1822–1911) introduced the concept of **statistical regression** (also called **regression to the mean**), which refers to the statistical tendency for extreme scores or extreme behavior to return toward the average. In his study of men's heights, Galton found that the tallest men usually had sons shorter than themselves, whereas the shortest men usually had sons taller than themselves. In both cases, the height of the children was less extreme than the height of the fathers.

FALSE UNIQUENESS EFFECT (BETTER-THAN-AVERAGE EFFECT, LAKE WOBEGON EFFECT) the tendency to underestimate the number of other people who share one's most prized characteristics and abilities

STATISTICAL REGRESSION (REGRESSION TO THE MEAN) the statistical tendency for extreme scores or extreme behavior to be followed by others that are less extreme and closer to average

To make it onto the cover of a major sports magazine, such as *Sports Illustrated*, an athlete or team must perform exceptionally well in addition to being lucky. However, appearing on the cover of *Sports Illustrated* got the reputation of being a jinx because athletes consistently performed worse afterward. For example, the Kansas City Chiefs football team lost to the Cincinnati Bengals on November 17, 2003, right after the team's previously undefeated season had been celebrated on the cover of that magazine. This loss has been blamed on the "*Sports Illustrated* jinx." The belief in the *Sports Illustrated* jinx is so strong that some athletes have even refused to appear on the cover (Ruscio, 2002). Many people attribute the subsequent poor performance to internal factors rather than to chance (e.g., after appearing on the cover of *Sports Illustrated*, athletes feel so much pressure that they choke). But the *Sports Illustrated* jinx can also be explained by the concept of regression to the mean (Gilovich, 1991). The magazine puts a team or athlete on the cover after an exceptionally good performance, and regression to the mean dictates that in most cases the next performance won't be as great, just as really short men don't usually have sons who are even shorter. If the magazine instead used cover photos featuring teams that had performed unbelievably badly that week, the magazine would get a reputation as a miracle worker for improving a team's luck and performance! But that too would be just a misunderstanding of regression to the mean.

In summary, the key to regression to the mean is that when one selects an instance (or a group) for extreme performance, it is almost always true that one will have selected a more extreme instance than is warranted. When events deviate from the average, people are more likely to think about the bad exceptions than about the good exceptions.

ILLUSION OF CONTROL

During a summer drought, retired farmer Elmer Carlson arranged a rain dance by 16 Hopis in Audubon, Iowa. The next day an inch of rain fell. "The miracles are still here, we just need to ask for them," explained Carlson. The belief that people can control totally chance situations is called the **illusion of control** (Langer, 1975; Langer & Roth, 1975). For example, gamblers in casinos who are playing craps often roll the dice harder for high numbers and softer for low numbers. People like to be in control of their own fate. The illusion of control may influence people to take more risks. For example, one study showed that traders working in investment banks who had an illusion of control took more risks and lost more money than other traders (Fenton-O'Creevy, Nicholson, Soane, & Willman, 2003).

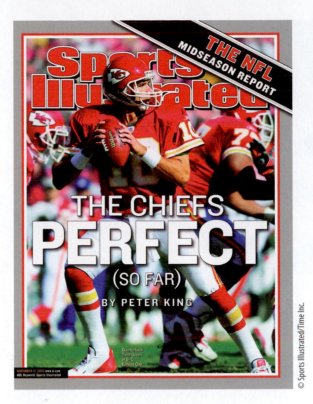

Appearing on the cover of *Sports Illustrated* has been considered a jinx, because athletic performance generally decreases after such exposure. However, the "*Sports Illustrated* jinx" is probably best explained by the concept of statistical regression.

MAGICAL THINKING

Magical thinking is thinking based on assumptions that don't hold up to rational scrutiny (Rozin & Nemeroff, 1990). One irrational assumption is that two objects that touch each other pass properties to one another. For example, people are afraid of wearing a sweater worn by an AIDS patient, though in reality there is no danger of getting AIDS from a garment. A second irrational assumption is that things that resemble each other share basic properties. For example, people are afraid of eating chocolate shaped

ILLUSION OF CONTROL the false belief that one can influence certain events, especially random or chance ones

MAGICAL THINKING thinking based on assumptions that don't hold up to rational scrutiny

Would you like to eat soup from this mini toilet bowl? Although many people would find it disgusting, restaurant diners in Taiwan don't seem to mind.

like a spider. A third irrational assumption is that thoughts can influence the physical world. For example, college students are afraid that thinking about a professor calling on you in class makes it happen. The concept of **contamination** is related to the first two assumptions (Rozin, 1987). When people think their food is contaminated (e.g., by insects or human hair), they become disgusted. These disgust responses have been found in many cultures, including Israeli, Japanese, Greek, and Hopi (Rozin, McCauley, & Imada, 1997). Disgust is a natural response that seems designed to help people avoid disease (Oaten, Stevenson, & Case, 2009). But that reaction gets applied even when it is irrelevant. You will not get sick from eating chocolate shaped like a spider or like dog feces. The unconscious mind does not seem to understand this and acts as if contamination can occur via any sort of association.

COUNTERFACTUAL THINKING

Counterfactual means "contrary to the facts." **Counterfactual thinking** involves imagining alternatives to past or present factual events or circumstances (Epstude & Roese, 2008; Kahneman & Miller, 1986; Kahneman & Tversky, 1982; Roese, 1997; Roese &

Olson, 1995). Counterfactual thinking is familiar to everyone, even if they have not heard the term before. We have all thought about "what might have been," if people had only behaved differently. What if you had studied harder in high school? What if your parents had never met? What if the other candidate had won the election? Douglas Hofstadter, cognitive science professor at Indiana University and author of the Pulitzer Prize–winning *Gödel, Escher, Bach: An Eternal Golden Braid*, wrote, "Think how immeasurably poorer our mental lives would be if we didn't have this creative capacity for slipping out of the midst of reality into soft 'what ifs'!" (Hofstadter, 1979).

Counterfactual thinking influences how students take tests (Krueger, Wirtz, & Miller, 2005). When taking multiple-choice tests, many students choose what they initially think is the correct answer. After thinking about it more, however, they begin to doubt their so-called first instinct and think that another answer is even better. Are students better off staying with their first choice, or should they switch their answer? About 75% of students think it is better to stick with their initial answer. Most college professors also believe that students should stick with their initial answer. Some test preparation guides also give the same advice: "Exercise great caution if you decide to change your answer. Experience indicates that many students who change answers change to the wrong answer" (Brownstein, Wolf, & Green, 2000, p. 6). However, virtually all studies show that students are better off switching answers (see Krueger et al., 2005, for a review). Krueger and his colleagues have dubbed this tendency the **first instinct fallacy**. It is defined as the false belief that it is better not to change one's first answer even if one starts to think that a different answer is correct.

So why do many students, professors, and test guide writers succumb to this fallacy? Research on counterfactual thinking can shed light on this issue. Assume that you got the answer wrong in the end and therefore engaged in counterfactual thinking about what you might have done to get it right. You'd probably feel the most regret if you had first written down the correct answer and then changed it to a wrong one. You'd feel less regret if you had first written the wrong answer and then refused to change it, because in that scenario you had never put down the right answer. Having first written the correct answer and then erased it makes you feel that you were so close to getting it correct that changing was a terrible mistake.

Counterfactual thinking can envision outcomes that were either better or worse than what actually happened. **Upward counterfactuals** involve alternatives that are better than actuality, whereas **downward counterfactuals** are alternatives that are worse than actuality (Markman, Gavanski, Sherman, & McMullen, 1993; McMullen, Markman, & Gavanski, 1995).

CONTAMINATION when something becomes impure or unclean

COUNTERFACTUAL THINKING imagining alternatives to past or present events or circumstances

FIRST INSTINCT FALLACY the false belief that it is better not to change one's first answer on a test even if one starts to think that a different answer is correct

UPWARD COUNTERFACTUALS imagining alternatives that are better than actuality

DOWNWARD COUNTERFACTUALS imagining alternatives that are worse than actuality

► **TABLE 5.3 Common Cognitive Errors**

Error or Bias	Definition	Example
Confirmation bias	The tendency to notice information that confirms one's beliefs and to ignore information that disconfirms one's beliefs	If you believe in astrology, looking for evidence that your horoscope is true and ignoring evidence that is inconsistent with your horoscope
Conjunction fallacy	The tendency to see an event as more likely as it becomes more specific because it is joined with elements that seem similar to events that are likely	If a man has a conservative ideology, thinking it is less likely that he is a businessman than a Republican and a businessman
Illusory correlation	The tendency to overestimate the link between variables that are related only slightly or not at all	Believing that professional black athletes are dangerous (even if Mike Tyson bites off ears!)
Base rate fallacy	The tendency to ignore or underuse base rate information and instead to be influenced by the distinctive features of the case being judged	Thinking that it is equally likely to have 60% of births be male in a small or a large hospital
Gambler's fallacy	The tendency to believe that a particular chance event is affected by previous events, and that chance events will "even out" in the short run	Believing that one is more likely to get a heads on a coin toss after the sequence TTTTTTTTT than after the sequence THHTTHTHT
False consensus effect	The tendency for people to overestimate the number of other people who share their opinions, attitudes, values, and beliefs	Believing that most people have the same religious beliefs as you do
False uniqueness effect	The tendency for people to underestimate the number of other people who share their most prized characteristics and abilities	People who exercise regularly underestimating the number of other people who also exercise regularly
Statistical regression	The statistical tendency for extreme scores or extreme behavior to return toward the average	The *Sports Illustrated* jinx, in which athletic performance usually declines after appearing on the cover of *Sports Illustrated*
Illusion of control	The belief that one can control totally chance situations	When gamblers throw dice softly for low numbers and throw dice hard for high numbers
Magical thinking	Thinking based on assumptions that don't hold up to rational scrutiny	Being afraid to eat chocolate shaped like bugs
Counterfactual thinking	Imagining alternatives to past or present factual events or circumstances	After getting in a car wreck, thinking "what if" I had gone home using a different route

For example, when Fatima looks back on her honeymoon, she can think it could have gone better (e.g., "We should have gone to a more exotic place!") or that it could have been worse (e.g., "Good thing we didn't get robbed!"). People make far more upward than downward counterfactuals, which is probably a good thing because it causes people to consider how to make things better in the future (Roese & Olson, 1997). For example, if Eduardo looks back on his exam and regrets not studying harder so he could have earned a higher grade, he will probably study harder next time. In contrast, if Eduardo looks back on his exam with relief that he did not fail it, he probably will not study harder next time.

Downward counterfactuals have their uses, of course. In particular, they help people feel better in the aftermath of misfortune (e.g., Taylor, 1983). When something bad happens, people say, "It could have been worse," and contemplating those even more terrible counterfactuals is comforting.

Ultimately, counterfactual thinking is probably one of the crucial traits that has helped people create and sustain the marvels of human society and culture. Most animals can barely perceive and understand their immediate surroundings, but people can dream of how it can be different. Democracy, women's liberation, and wireless technology did not exist in nature, but human beings were able to look at life as it was and imagine how it could be different, and these imaginings helped them change the world for the better.

The concepts of counterfactual thinking and regret are sometimes used interchangeably. The two concepts are related, but they are not the same thing (Gilovich & Medvec, 1995). One important difference is that regrets are feelings, whereas counterfactuals are thoughts. **Regret** involves feeling sorry for misfortunes, limitations, losses, transgressions, shortcomings, or mistakes (Landman, 1993).

The various cognitive errors discussed in this section are summarized in ► **TABLE 5.3**.

REGRET feeling sorry for one's misfortunes, limitations, losses, transgressions, shortcomings, or mistakes

Are People Really Idiots?

Some scientists claim that hydrogen, because it is so plentiful, is the basic building block of the universe. I dispute that. I say there is more stupidity than hydrogen, and *that* is the basic building block of the universe.
—Frank Zappa, musician and songwriter

Sometimes social cognition researchers are accused of perpetuating the idea that people are basically stupid. This is because researchers show that people make so many cognitive errors. Would nature have selected complete idiots to reproduce and pass on their genes to subsequent generations? We doubt it. Contrary to what Frank Zappa suggests, people are not basically stupid. The kinds of errors people make are not

random—they are quite predictable. People don't use logic when it comes to estimating the likelihood of uncertain events. They use "psycho-logic" instead. Because people are cognitive misers, they want quick and dirty answers to problems of uncertainty. They don't want to compute probabilities in their heads or on their calculators. That is why people use heuristics. More often than not, heuristics provide the correct answers, or at least answers that are good enough. The automatic system is also incredibly fast, capable of making decisions in milliseconds. People can even process information outside of conscious awareness.

HOW SERIOUS ARE THE ERRORS?

When heuristics do result in errors, how bad are the errors? Social cognition researcher Susan Fiske (2004) has pointed out that the errors might not be as bad as we think they are. Some errors are trivial, such as when someone buys the wrong brand of salsa or cereal. Other errors are self-correcting over time. For example, people overestimate how informative an extreme initial performance is of a person's actual abilities. After listening to a brilliant violin solo, an audience member might conclude that the musician is a gifted violinist (even if subsequent solos are less brilliant). Or after watching a basketball player miss an important free throw, an audience member might conclude that the player typically chokes under pressure (even if he later hits some important free throws). People fail to consider the impact of regression to the mean on performances that follow extreme initial performances. Over time, however, these positive and negative errors even out and correct each other. Eventually, an observer can come to realize what a person's true abilities are. It is possible that some errors may only occur in the social psychological laboratory—not in the real world. Other errors are corrected socially, such as when people give us feedback on what we did wrong. Still other errors can cancel each other out, if they occur in random combinations.

Evolutionary psychologists have argued that when it comes to the really important decisions, those involving survival and reproduction, people make relatively few stupid decisions (e.g., Cosmides, 1989; Cosmides & Tooby, 1992; Fiddick, Cosmides, & Tooby, 2000). Perhaps this is because they use the conscious system rather than the unconscious system when it comes to making important decisions. The quick and approximate answers provided by the unconscious system are not good enough, and people expend the mental energy required to make these important decisions.

REDUCING COGNITIVE ERRORS

Even if the errors aren't all that serious, who wants to make errors? Social psychologists have tried to identify factors that reduce cognitive errors. People can be taught to use relevant statistical probabilities rather than ignore them (Case, Fantino, & Goodie, 1999). Graduate training in disciplines that teach statistical reasoning can improve decision-making ability. For example, graduate students in psychology and medicine do better on statistical, methodological, and conditional reasoning problems than do students in law and chemistry, who do not learn about statistical reasoning (Lehman, Lempert, & Nisbett, 1988). Even crash courses on statistical reasoning are helpful in reducing cognitive errors (e.g., Lopes, 1987; Williams, 1992).

Making the information easier to process can also improve decision-making ability and reduce cognitive errors. For example, easy-to-understand food labels can help consumers make better food choices (Russo, Staelin, Nolan, Russell, & Metcalf, 1986).

One of the most effective ways of **debiasing** people from the tendency to make cognitive errors is to get them to use controlled processing (such as conscious reasoning) rather than automatic processing. Some examples include encouraging people to consider multiple alternatives (e.g., Hirt, Kardes, & Markman, 2004; Hirt & Markman, 1995; Sanna & Schwarz, 2003); to rely less on memory (e.g., Arkes, 1991; Williams, 1992); to use explicit decision rules (Arkes, 1991; Williams, 1992); to search for disconfirmatory information (e.g., Kray & Galinsky, 2003); and to use meta-cognition (e.g., Croskerry, 2003). **Meta-cognition** literally means "thinking about thinking." It is a reflective approach to problem solving that involves stepping back from the immediate problem to examine and reflect on the thinking process (Croskerry, 2003). Examples include quizzing oneself to evaluate one's understanding of what one has read in a textbook, planning how to approach a math exam, and evaluating progress toward achieving a learning goal (e.g., memorizing the periodic table of the elements for your chemistry class).

[**QUIZ YOURSELF**]

Are People Really Idiots?

1. What system is mainly responsible for the cognitive errors that people make?
   (a) Automatic system   (b) Controlled system
   (c) Primary system   (d) Secondary system

2. People make fewer cognitive errors when they are making decisions about _____.
   (a) trivial matters (e.g., what brand of toothpaste to buy)
   (b) important matters (e.g., what major to select in college)
   (c) very serious matters (e.g., survival and reproduction)
   (d) None of the above; cognitive errors are the same for the three types of matters.

3. Which type of graduate training that teaches statistical reasoning is most effective in reducing cognitive errors?
   (a) Business   (b) Chemistry
   (c) Law   (d) Psychology

4. The analysis of cognitions is called _____.
   (a) counterfactual thinking
   (b) explicit decision rules
   (c) meta-cognition
   (d) statistical reasoning

DEBIASING reducing errors and biases by getting people to use controlled processing rather than automatic processing

META-COGNITION reflecting on one's own thought processes

| **WHAT MAKES US HUMAN?** | Putting the Cultural Animal in Perspective |

The special or unique features of human psychology are readily visible in this chapter. Experts debate the question "Do animals think?" (that is, nonhuman animals), but the debate usually focuses on whether the very simple cognitive activities of animals, such as forming an expectancy and perceiving that it is violated, qualify as thinking. Only a few overly sentimental pet owners believe that animals can formulate complex thoughts or understand long sentences—let alone begin to match the higher flights of human thought, such as in philosophical or religious contemplation, theories of physics and chemistry, poetry, epic narratives, or even arguments about why a football game turned out as it did. Only humans think in those ways.

The remarkable power of human thought is seen not just in the use of symbolism, but in the combining of symbols. People use language to do most of their thinking, and human thought typically combines many small concepts into complex ideas, stories, or theories. A dog can learn several dozen one-word commands, but only humans can string together a long set of words to make sentences, paragraphs, long stories, speeches, or a book like this.

The capacity to use language opens up new worlds of thought, as it lets people explore the linkages of meaning. People can do mathematical and financial calculations, conduct cost–benefit analyses, and reason logically. Without language, other animals can engage in only the very simplest, most trivial versions of those forms of thought, or none at all.

The duplex mind is another distinctive feature of human thinking. Automatic processing is probably something both humans and animals have, but the powers of the conscious mind are more uniquely human. Only humans can perform the rule-based, systematic, precise thinking that the conscious system does, such as mathematical calculations, logical reasoning, and detailed cost–benefit comparisons of multiple options when facing a decision.

The simple fact is that most complex patterns of thought are uniquely human. Humans can analyze a complex situation and make attributions about why something happened (and they can also debate with each other about those attributions, to reach a consensual explanation). Only humans use heuristics. False consensus and false uniqueness biases are limited to humans.

Only humans engage in counterfactual thinking, which can be extremely helpful in enabling people to change their behavior in the future. Only humans suffer agonies of rumination and regret about what might have been, but that same power of counterfactual thinking has been a crucial aid to human progress. Over the centuries, people have looked around them at the state of the world and imagined how it could be better. Nature did not give us schools, written language, dental care, recorded music, airplane travel, or the justice system, but counterfactual thinking has enabled people to dream of such improvements—and then to help them become reality.

We saw in Chapter 3 that humans have a much more complex conception of self than other animals. This complex knowledge structure influences thought in many ways. Only humans will show self-serving biases or actor/observer differences, and only humans can learn to correct for these biases.

The remarkable power of human thought creates both unique errors and unique capabilities to find the truth. In other words, the special properties of the human mind lead to both right and wrong answers that other animals wouldn't get. Only humans can succumb to the base rate fallacy, because only humans can use base rates at all, so only humans can learn to use them correctly. Only humans fall prey to the regression fallacy, but only humans can develop an accurate understanding of regression to the mean and can therefore learn to avoid the mistake.

In short, most of the material in this chapter would be absent in a book on the psychology of other animals, because human cognition is generally unlike what is found in other species. This sweeping difference is quite unlike what we will see in the next chapter on emotion. That is because advanced cognitive processes are relatively new in evolution and specific to human beings, whereas emotion goes far back in evolutionary time. Thus, many animals have emotional reactions and expressions that resemble human ones in crucial respects. Even so, the fact that we can think about our emotions (and their causes) is likely to change them, as we shall see. For humans and human social life, thinking changes almost everything.

chapter summary

WHAT IS SOCIAL COGNITION?

- Social cognition is the study of any sort of thinking by people about people and about social relationships.
- People think about other people more than any other topic, and probably more than about all other topics combined.
- The human mind is designed to participate in society, and this means its primary job is dealing with other people.
- People think about other people in order to be accepted by them, or to compete with or avoid them.
- The term *cognitive miser* refers to people's reluctance to do much extra thinking.
- People generally prefer to conserve effort by relying on automatic modes of thought when they can.
- Knowledge structures are organized packets of information that are stored in memory.
- Schemas are knowledge structures that represent substantial information about a concept, its attributes, and its relationships to other concepts.

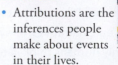

- A violation of expectancies sparks conscious thinking.
- Scripts are knowledge structures that contain information about how people (or other objects) behave under varying circumstances; scripts define situations and guide behavior.
- At least three main types of goals guide how people think:
  - Find the right answer to some problem or question.
  - Reach a particular, preferred conclusion.
  - Reach a pretty good answer or decision quickly.
- In the Stroop effect, the automatic response is to say the word rather than the ink color.

- The four elements that distinguish automatic from controlled processes are intention, effort, control, and efficiency.
- Priming is the tendency for frequently or recently activated concepts to come to mind more easily.
- Framing is how something is presented.
- Trying to suppress a thought can have the paradoxical effect of increasing the thought.
- In the counterregulation or "what the heck" effect, dieters eat more if they believe they have broken their diets than if they are hungry.

ATTRIBUTIONS: WHY DID THAT HAPPEN?

- Attributions are the inferences people make about events in their lives.
- Internal, stable attributions involve ability; internal, unstable attributions involve

effort; external, stable attributions point to the difficulty of the task; and external, unstable attributions involve luck.

- The self-serving bias suggests that people want to take credit for success but deny blame for failure.
- The actor/observer bias states that actors tend to make external attributions, whereas observers make internal attributions.
- The fundamental attribution error (also sometimes called correspondence bias) refers to the finding that people have a bias to attribute another person's behavior to internal or dispositional causes.
- The covariation principle states that for something to be the cause of a behavior, it must be present when the behavior occurs and absent when the behavior does not occur.
- The three types of covariation information are
  - Consensus
  - Consistency
  - Distinctiveness

HEURISTICS: MENTAL SHORTCUTS

- Heuristics are mental shortcuts or rules of thumb.
- The representativeness heuristic is the tendency to judge the frequency or likelihood of an event by the extent to which it resembles the typical case.
- The availability heuristic is the tendency to judge the frequency or likelihood of an event by the ease with which relevant instances come to mind.
- The simulation heuristic is the tendency to judge the frequency or likelihood of an event by the ease with which you can imagine (or mentally simulate) an event.
- The anchoring and adjustment heuristic suggests that when people estimate how frequent or likely an event is, they use a starting point (called an anchor) and then make adjustments up and down from this starting point.

ERRORS AND BIASES

- Information overload is the state of having too much information to make a decision or remain informed about a topic.
- Estimation and shifting criteria can result in biased counts of sexual partners.
- People generally have access to two types of information:
  - Statistical information from a large number of people
  - Case history information from a small number of people
- People generally pay the most attention to case history information.
- Confirmation bias is the tendency to notice information that confirms one's beliefs and to ignore information that disconfirms one's beliefs.
- An illusory correlation occurs when people overestimate the link between variables that are related only slightly or not at all. It can occur even after one exposure, called one-shot illusory correlations.
- The mass media contribute to illusory correlations by focusing on rare events.
- The base rate fallacy is the tendency to ignore or underuse base rate information and instead to be influenced by the distinctive features of the case being judged.
- The gambler's fallacy is the belief that a particular chance event is affected by previous events.
- The false consensus effect is the tendency to overestimate the number of people who share one's opinions, attitudes, values, or beliefs.
- The false uniqueness effect (also called the better-than-average effect and the Lake Wobegon effect) describes the finding that people tend to underestimate the number of people who share their most prized characteristics and abilities.
- Statistical regression (also called regression to the mean) refers to the statistical tendency for extreme scores or extreme behavior to return toward the average.

- One major evolutionary purpose of thinking is to decide how to respond when one's goals are blocked.
- The belief that people can control totally chance situations is called the illusion of control.
- The concept of contamination is related to
  - The irrational assumption that two objects that touch each other pass properties to one another
  - The irrational assumption that things that resemble each other share basic properties
- Counterfactual thinking involves imagining alternatives to past or present factual events or circumstances.
- Upward counterfactuals posit alternatives that are better than actuality, whereas downward counterfactuals posit alternatives that are worse than actuality.
- Regret involves feeling sorry for misfortunes, limitations, losses, transgressions, shortcomings, or mistakes.
- Regrets are feelings, whereas counterfactuals are thoughts.

ARE PEOPLE REALLY IDIOTS?

- More often than not, heuristics provide the correct answers, or at least answers that are good enough.
- Relying less on memory, considering multiple alternatives, using metacognition, searching for disconfirmatory information, and using explicit decision rules are all techniques that can reduce cognitive errors.

WHAT MAKES US HUMAN? PUTTING THE CULTURAL ANIMAL IN PERSPECTIVE

- The remarkable power of human thought creates both unique errors and unique capabilities to find the truth.

Key Terms

Actor/observer bias 137
Anchoring and adjustment 144
Attribution cube 139
Attributions 135
Availability heuristic 142
Base rate fallacy 148
Cognitive miser 128
Confirmation bias 147
Conjunction fallacy 147
Consensus 139
Consistency 139
Contamination 152
Counterfactual thinking 152
Counterregulation 134

Covariation principle 139
Debiasing 155
Distinctiveness 139
Downward counterfactuals 152
False consensus effect 149
False uniqueness effect (better-than-average effect, Lake Wobegon effect) 150
First instinct fallacy 152
Framing 133
Fundamental attribution error (correspondence bias) 138

Gain-framed appeal 133
Gambler's fallacy 149
Heuristics 141
Hot hand 149
Illusion of control 151
Illusory correlation 148
Information overload 145
Knowledge structures 130
Loss-framed appeal 133
Magical thinking 151
Meta-cognition 155
One-shot illusory correlation 148
Priming 131
Regret 153

Representativeness heuristic 141
Schemas 131
Scripts 131
Self-serving bias 137
Simulation heuristic 143
Social cognition 127
Statistical regression (regression to the mean) 150
Stroop effect 129
Stroop test 129
Ultimate attribution error 138
Upward counterfactuals 152

[Quiz Yourself] Answers

1. What Is Social Cognition?
Answers: 1=c, 2=c, 3=d, 4=d

2. Attributions: Why Did That Happen?
Answers: 1=d, 2=a, 3=b, 4=a, 5=a

3. Heuristics: Mental Shortcuts
Answers: 1=c, 2=b, 3=c, 4=a

4. Errors and Biases
Answers: 1=c, 2=c, 3=d, 4=d

5. Are People Really Idiots?
Answers: 1=a, 2=c, 3=d, 4=c

Media Learning Resources

Make sure you check out the complete set of learning resources and study tools below. If your instructor did not order these items with your new book, go to www.ichapters.com to purchase Cengage Learning print and digital products.

Social Psychology and Human Nature BOOK COMPANION WEBSITE

www.cengage.com/psychology/baumeister
Visit your book companion website, where you will find flash cards, practice quizzes, Internet links, and more to help you study.

CENGAGENOW JUST WHAT YOU NEED TO KNOW NOW!

Spend time on what you need to master rather than on information you have already learned. Take a pre-test for this chapter, and CengageNOW will generate a personalized study plan based on your results. The study plan will identify the topics you need to review and direct you to online resources to help you master those topics. You can then take a post-test to help you determine the concepts you have mastered and what you will still need to work on. Try it out! Go to www.cengage.com/login to sign in with an access code or to purchase access to this product.

CLASSIC AND CONTEMPORARY VIDEOS STUDENT CD-ROM

To see videos on the topics and experiments discussed in this chapter and to learn more about the research that social psychologists are doing today, go to the Student CD-ROM.

SOCIAL PSYCH LAB

These unique online labs give you the opportunity to become a participant in actual experiments, including re-creations of classic and contemporary research studies.

chapter 6

Emotion and Affect

The Social Side of Sex:
Can People Be Wrong
About Whether They Are
Sexually Aroused? **p. 165**

Tradeoffs: Affect Intensity,
or the Joys of Feeling
Nothing **p. 171**

Food for Thought: Mood
and Food **p. 179**

Money Matters: Emotions
and Prices **p. 182**

What Makes Us
Human? Putting the
Cultural Animal in
Perspective **p. 192**

Scott Barbour/Getty Images

WHAT IS EMOTION? **p. 161**
Conscious Emotion Versus
   Automatic Affect **p. 162**

**EMOTIONAL
   AROUSAL** **p. 162**
James–Lange Theory of
   Emotion **p. 162**
Cannon–Bard Theory of
   Emotion **p. 163**
Schachter–Singer Theory of
   Emotion **p. 164**
Misattribution
   of Arousal **p. 164**

**SOME IMPORTANT
   EMOTIONS** **p. 167**
Happiness **p. 167**
Anger **p. 171**
Guilt and Shame **p. 174**

**WHY DO WE HAVE
   EMOTIONS?** **p. 177**
Emotions Promote
   Belongingness **p. 177**
Emotions Cause Behavior—
   Sort Of **p. 178**
Emotions Guide Thinking and
   Learning **p. 178**

(Anticipated) Emotions Guide
   Decisions and Choices **p. 180**
Emotions Help and Hurt
   Decision Making **p. 181**
Positive Emotions Counteract
   Negative Emotions **p. 181**
Other Benefits of Positive
   Emotions **p. 182**

**GROUP DIFFERENCES IN
   EMOTION** **p. 183**
Are Emotions Different Across
   Cultures? **p. 183**
Are Women More Emotional
   Than Men? **p. 185**

**AROUSAL,
   ATTENTION, AND
   PERFORMANCE** **p. 186**

**EMOTIONAL
   INTELLIGENCE
   (EQ)** **p. 188**

**AFFECT
   REGULATION** **p. 189**
How to Cheer Up **p. 189**
Affect Regulation Goals **p. 190**
Gender Differences in Emotion
   Control Strategies **p. 190**
Is It Safe? **p. 191**

CHAPTER SUMMARY **p. 193**

Spam or junk e-mail messages are the plague of the digital age. Filters don't seem to work either. We all get plenty of spam each day, and we waste a lot of time deleting these junk e-mail messages.

The flood of spam is enough to make anyone fuming mad! Or is it? People respond to spam very differently. Consider two real people who appeared in the news for how they responded to spam. The first story is about Charles Booher, a 44-year-old Silicon Valley computer programmer (Tanner, 2003). Booher was arrested for threatening to torture and kill employees of the company who bombarded his computer with spam ads promising to enlarge his penis. According to prosecutors, Booher threatened to mail a "package full of Anthrax spores" to the company; to "disable" an employee with a bullet and torture him with a power drill and ice pick; and to hunt down and castrate the employees unless they removed him from their e-mail list. Booher used intimidating return e-mail addresses including Satan@ hell.org. He admitted that he had behaved badly, but said that he did so because the company had rendered his computer almost unusable for about two months by

a barrage of pop-up advertising and e-mail messages. Booher was arrested for the threats he made, but was released on $75,000 bond.

The second story is about a 26-year-old musician from Ottawa, Canada, named Brad Turcotte (Whyte, 2003). Like the rest of us, Turcotte is bombarded with spam e-mail. He said, "I was just staring at my inbox one day and looking at all these ridiculous subject lines"— such as Feel Better Now, Look and Feel Years Younger, and Do You Measure Up, to name but a few—"and I started thinking that some of these were pretty surreal and bizarre. And at the same time, I had been having trouble coming up with titles for some of my songs, so I started thinking that maybe there was something here." As a one-man band called *Brad Sucks*, Brad Turcotte wrote and recorded a song called "Look and Feel Years Younger." He recruited other musicians through the Internet to write additional songs, and assembled a CD of 14 songs titled Outside the Inbox. He sells the CDs on the Internet, and so far he has sold hundreds of CDs and hundreds of thousands of downloads. "I was surprised that so many people caught on to it," he said. "I thought it might just be a fun, goofy thing to do. It only occurred to me afterwards, oh, right, everyone gets this. Everyone in the world. How could I forget?"

Both men had the same problem and the same negative emotional reaction, but they coped with it very differently. Neither could get rid of the anger or irritation by simply deciding to feel better, so they both ended up having to do something. In one case the anger led to violent, possibly dangerous responses, but in the other it led to positive, creative responses. Emotional states are often so compelling that we struggle to feel good—these struggles range from the creative to the criminal.

Emotions make life rich and colorful, and they influence how people act, though not always in a good way (e.g., crimes of passion!). They still pose something of a mystery. Why do people have emotions? Why is the emotion system set up the way it is? We will try to answer these important questions in this chapter.

One clue is that emotions are mostly outside our conscious control, even though we may feel them

off the mark.com   by Mark Parisi

ATLANTIC FEATURE © 2002 MARK PARISI

@✿#!!
SPAM...

ANTLER ENLARGEMENT
WANT BIGGER ANTLERS?
ENLARGE YOUR ANTLERS
ANTLER SIZE MATTERS
IMPROVE YOUR MATING SEAS[O]

DELETE

MARK PARISI/ offthemark.com

1. I Got Your Letter (Verbose)
2. Do You Measure Up (adf)
3. Feel Better Now (Blind Mime)
4. You Are Being Watched (Son of Supercar)
5. Erik, Someone Wants To Date You (15-16 puzzle)
6. Urgent Business Relationship (MC Frontalot)
7. Look And Feel Years Younger (Brad Sucks)
8. Don't Worry Where Your Keys Are At (MemorailRT)

outside the inbox
songs inspired by spam

A compilation of songs inspired by and titled after the subject lines of mass-email.

9. Urgent Business Confidential (Uncle Azathoth)
10. Where Is The Best Place (Donkey T)
11. Your Medication (Sex Piano)
12. A Quick, Simple Form (Glenn Case)
13. psiloveyou (Jack Shite)
14. My Parents Are Gone For The Weekend... (Justin Bacon)

www.bradsucks.net/outsidetheinbox/

After being bombarded with lots of spam e-mail, Brad Turcotte organized a compilation CD called _Outside the Inbox_, in which he and other musicians wrote songs based on the subject lines of spam e-mail, such as "Look and Feel Years Younger."

consciously. (That's why neither Booher nor Turcotte could just shrug off their anger and feel good.) Emotions provide a feedback system. They bring us information about the world and about our activities in it. They reward and punish us, so we learn to set up our lives in ways that avoid bad emotions and maximize good emotions. Consider guilt as an example. Guilt helps us know we did something wrong. To avoid guilt, people may change their behavior in advance: They may try to keep their promises, obey the rules, treat other people kindly, and so on. If people could escape guilt just by deciding not to feel guilty, there would be less need to behave well in order to avoid guilt. If you could control your emotions, then anytime you started to feel guilty, you could just turn those feelings off and everything would be fine (at least as far as how you feel is concerned). Guilt can give us feedback and guide our behavior, but only if it and similar emotions are outside of our conscious control. ■

What Is Emotion?

Everyone knows what an emotion is, until asked to give a definition.
   —Beverly Fehr and James Russell
      (1984, p. 484)

It turns out to be fiendishly difficult to provide a definition of emotion, or even to provide several definitions of distinct concepts related to emotion. Some psychologists use the terms _emotion, affect,_ and _mood_ interchangeably, whereas others treat the terms as distinct concepts. The most common definitions emphasize **emotion** as a full-blown, conscious state that includes an evaluative reaction to some event. Emotion is thus a reaction to something, and the person who has the emotion knows it. You may feel angry because someone insulted you or happy because you got an "A" on your social psychology test. In contrast, **mood** is sometimes defined as a feeling state that is not clearly linked to some event. You may not know why you are in a good or bad mood, but you do know that you feel happy or sad. The third concept, **affect** (pronounced 'AF-ekt; note that this word is a noun, not a verb, which is pronounced ə-'fekt) is sometimes defined as a result of mapping all emotions onto a single good–bad dimension. Positive affect encompasses all good emotions, such as joy, bliss, love, and contentment. Negative affect encompasses all bad emotions, such as anger, anxiety, fear, jealousy, and grief. Most researchers argue that positive and negative affect are separate dimensions, not opposite ends of the same dimension (e.g., Cacioppo & Gardner, 1999; Watson & Clark, 1991, 1992; Watson & Tellegen, 1985). Other writers use affect to refer to emotion-type reactions that can occur regardless of consciousness. It makes no sense to say that someone is happy but doesn't know it; in that sense, the conscious feeling is the essence of the emotion. Still, some affective reactions can occur without consciousness. You can have a quick positive or negative feeling about something as simple as a word without being fully conscious of it.

EMOTION a conscious evaluative reaction to some event
MOOD a feeling state that is not clearly linked to some event
AFFECT the automatic response that something is good or bad

CONSCIOUS EMOTION VERSUS AUTOMATIC AFFECT

Regardless of how people use the terms *emotion*, *mood*, and *affect*, two quite different phenomena need to be distinguished. These correspond roughly to the two chambers of the duplex mind. One is **conscious emotion**, which is felt as a powerful, single (unified) feeling state. The other is **automatic affect**: responses of liking or disliking, of good and bad feelings toward something. These may be mixed (unlike the unity of conscious emotion) and may occur outside of consciousness.

We will use the term *emotion* to refer to the conscious reaction, often including a bodily response, to something. In contrast, we use the term *affect* to refer to the automatic response that something is good or bad (liking versus disliking). Affective reactions to things that are "good" and "bad" are automatic and very fast, occurring in the first microseconds of thought. As soon as you know what something is, you start to know whether you like or dislike it (Goleman, 1995a). This initial evaluation even occurs for things people have never encountered before, such as nonsense words like "juvalamu" (Bargh, Chaiken, Raymond, & Hymes, 1996). In contrast, full-blown emotion takes time.

There is no point in trying to decide whether automatic affect or conscious emotion is more important. Both are important, and it would be a mistake to assume that everything we learn about one of them applies to the other as well.

Emotions have both mental and physical aspects. In the next section we explore the physical aspects of emotional arousal.

[QUIZ YOURSELF]

What Is Emotion?

1. Conscious is to unconscious as _____ is to _____.
 (a) affect; emotion
 (b) emotion; affect
 (c) affect; mood
 (d) mood; affect

2. Affect is generally mapped onto _____ dimensions.
 (a) good and bad
 (b) masculine and feminine
 (c) specific and universal
 (d) strong and weak

3. Affective reactions to things that are "good" and "bad" generally occur in the first _____ of thought.
 (a) microseconds
 (b) seconds
 (c) minutes
 (d) hours

4. Fatima feels deep sadness because her dog died. What term most accurately describes what Fatima is feeling?
 (a) Affect
 (b) Emotion
 (c) Mood
 (d) All of the above

Emotional Arousal

One reason that people are fascinated by emotions is that they bridge the mind and the body. Emotions have both mental aspects (such as subjective feelings and interpretations) and physical aspects (such as a racing heartbeat or tears). The challenge is to say how the mental and physical aspects of emotion are linked together. One important area of connection involves the bodily response of arousal, which is linked to most conscious emotions, though not necessarily to automatic affect. **Arousal** is a physiological response that occurs within the body, including a faster heartbeat and faster or heavier breathing. We will say more about it as we cover the competing theories of emotion.

JAMES–LANGE THEORY OF EMOTION

In 1884, American psychologist William James and Danish psychologist Carl Lange proposed a theory linking the mental and physical aspects of emotion (James, 1884). Their theory, called the **James–Lange theory of emotion**, was described by James (1890) as follows:

> My theory . . . is that *the bodily changes follow directly the perception of the exciting fact, and that our feeling of the same changes as they occur is the emotion.* Common sense says: we lose our fortune, are sorry and weep; we meet a bear, are frightened and run; we are insulted by a rival, are angry and strike. The hypothesis here to be defended says that this order of sequence is incorrect, . . . we feel sorry because we cry, angry because we strike, afraid because we tremble, and not that we cry, strike, or tremble, because we are sorry, angry, or fearful, as the case may be. (p. 190, italics in original)

James and Lange proposed that the bodily processes of emotion come first, and then the mind's perception of these bodily reactions creates the subjective feeling of emotion (see ▶ **FIGURE 6.1**). When something happens, your body and brain supposedly

---

CONSCIOUS EMOTION a powerful and clearly unified feeling state, such as anger or joy

AUTOMATIC AFFECT a quick response of liking or disliking toward something

AROUSAL a physiological reaction, including faster heartbeat and faster or heavier breathing, linked to most conscious emotions

JAMES–LANGE THEORY OF EMOTION the proposition that the bodily processes of emotion come first and the mind's perception of these bodily reactions then creates the subjective feeling of emotion

perceive it and respond to it, and these physiological events form the basis for the emotion you feel.

Researchers tried for many years to prove the James–Lange theory, but they were largely unsuccessful. One important aspect of the theory is that different emotions must arise from different bodily responses. Data from many studies suggested, however, that the body's response seemed to be very similar for all different emotions. Whatever emotion the person felt, the body just showed a standard arousal pattern. Even tears, for example, are not limited to sadness, because people sometimes cry when they are happy or angry or afraid, and many others do not cry when they are sad. Tears, therefore, are not just a sign of sadness, but more likely a sign of intense feeling.

The James–Lange theory did, however, inspire the more contemporary facial feedback hypothesis (e.g., Tomkins, 1962; Izard, 1971, 1990). According to the **facial feedback hypothesis**, feedback from the face muscles evokes or magnifies emotions. Several studies have found support for this hypothesis. One of the cleverest manipulations of facial feedback consisted of having participants hold a pen in either their lips or their teeth while rating cartoons (Strack, Martin, & Stepper, 1988). This sounds like a trivial difference, but try it: When you hold the pen between your teeth, your face is forced into something like a smile, whereas when you hold it between your lips, your face resembles a frown. The facial feedback hypothesis holds that if you are smiling, you will enjoy things more than if you are frowning, and this is what the study found. Participants who held the pen in their teeth thought the cartoons were funnier than did participants who held the pen in their lips. Thus, if you put on a happy face, you will be happier and enjoy external events more.

CANNON–BARD THEORY OF EMOTION

Walter Cannon, a Harvard physiologist, and his colleague Philip Bard proposed an alternate theory of emotion (Bard, 1934; Cannon, 1927). The thalamus plays a central role in their theory. The thalamus (see ▶ **FIGURE 6.2**) is the part of the brain that is like a relay station for nerve impulses. Information from the emotional stimulus goes to the thalamus. From the thalamus, the information is relayed both to the cerebral cortex, which produces the experience of emotion, and to the hypothalamus and autonomic nervous system, which produces the increase in physiological arousal (see ▶ **FIGURE 6.3**). Suppose that you are walking down a dark alley in a dangerous part of town late one night, and you hear footsteps behind you. According to the **Cannon–Bard theory of emotion**, the thalamus will send two messages at the same time: one message that produces the emotional experience "fear," and one message

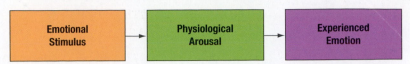

▶ **FIGURE 6.1** The James–Lange theory of emotion: An emotional stimulus (e.g., hearing footsteps behind you in a dark alley) produces physiological arousal (e.g., increased heart rate), which then produces an experienced emotion (e.g., fear).

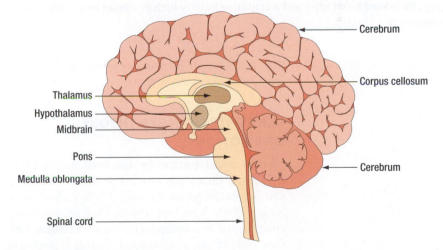

© David Young-Wolff/PhotoEdit   © David Young-Wolff/PhotoEdit

In research studies, people who held a pen with their teeth smiled and felt happier, whereas people who held the pen with their lips frowned and felt sadder.

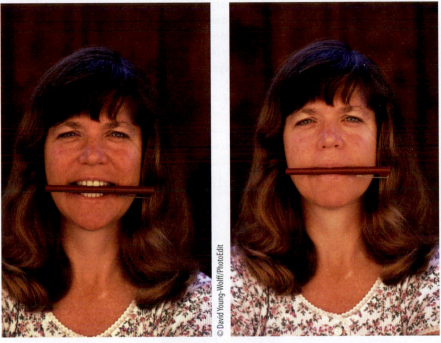

▶ **FIGURE 6.2** Diagram of the human brain.

FACIAL FEEDBACK HYPOTHESIS the idea that feedback from the face muscles evokes or magnifies emotions

CANNON–BARD THEORY OF EMOTION the proposition that emotional stimuli activate the thalamus, which then activates both the cortex, producing an experienced emotion, and the hypothalamus and autonomic nervous system, producing physiological arousal

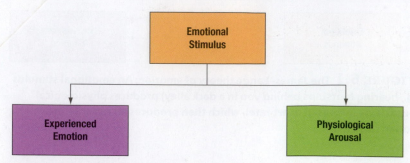

▶ **FIGURE 6.3** The Cannon–Bard theory of emotion: An emotional stimulus (e.g., hearing footsteps behind you in a dark alley) activates the thalamus. The thalamus sends two messages at the same time: one message to the cortex, which produces an experienced emotion (e.g., fear), and one message to the hypothalamus and autonomic nervous system, which produces physiological arousal (e.g., increased heart rate).

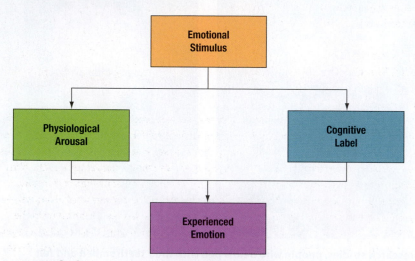

▶ **FIGURE 6.4** The Schachter–Singer theory of emotion: An emotional stimulus (e.g., hearing footsteps behind you in a dark alley) produces physiological arousal (e.g., increased heart rate) and a cognitive label, which produces an experienced emotion (e.g., fear).

that produces an increase in physiological arousal (e.g., heart rate, breathing rate).

SCHACHTER–SINGER THEORY OF EMOTION

Modern social psychology has been greatly influenced by a theory put forward by Stanley Schachter and Jerome Singer in the early 1960s (Schachter & Singer, 1962; Schachter, 1964). They proposed that emotion has two components (see ▶ **FIGURE 6.4**). One component, physiological arousal, is similar in all emotions. The other component, the cognitive label, is different for each emotion. The arousal is the mix of feelings you get when your sympathetic

SCHACHTER–SINGER THEORY OF EMOTION the idea that emotion has two components: a bodily state of arousal and a cognitive label that specifies the emotion
EXCITATION TRANSFER the idea that arousal from one event can transfer to a later event

nervous system is activated: the heart beats faster, more blood flows to the muscles and brain, the bronchioles in the lungs dilate so that more oxygen goes into the blood, and so on. The feeling of nervousness, such as when you are ready for a big test or a major public performance, is what it is like to have arousal by itself. Nervousness is thus a kind of generic emotional state (emotion without the label).

In the **Schachter–Singer theory of emotion**, emotion is something like a television program. The arousal is the on/off switch and volume control: It determines that there is going to be an emotion, and how strong it will be. The cognitive label is like the channel switch: It dictates which emotion will be felt.

A key issue in all these theories (James–Lange, Cannon–Bard, and Schachter–Singer) is how the mind deals with the body's arousal state. Sometimes the mind might not realize that the body is aroused, or why. *The Social Side of Sex* discusses this problem in connection with a particularly interesting form of arousal—sexual arousal. Read the box to find out more about how sexual arousal is related to emotions!

MISATTRIBUTION OF AROUSAL

The intriguing thing about the Schachter–Singer theory is that it allows for arousal states to be mislabeled or relabeled. That is, an arousal may arise for one reason but get another label, thereby producing a different reaction. For example, someone may not realize that what he or she is drinking has caffeine (e.g., if you think that you have decaffeinated tea when in reality it has caffeine; some aspirin products also contain caffeine), which may create an arousal state. The mind then searches for a label to make sense of the emotional state. If something frustrating happens, someone who has this extra, unexplained arousal may get much angrier than he or she would otherwise. This process is called **excitation transfer** (e.g., Zillmann, 1979): The arousal from the first event (drinking caffeinated tea) transfers to the second event (frustration).

There have been several important experimental demonstrations of mislabeling or relabeling arousal. In Schachter and Singer's (1962) original studies, participants were told that the researchers were studying the "effects of vitamin injections on visual skills." By the flip of a coin, participants received an injection of either adrenaline (epinephrine) or a placebo (saline solution, which has no effects; it was included just to control for any effects of having someone stick a needle into your arm). Adrenaline is a stimulant that causes your heart rate, blood pressure, and breathing rate to increase. Participants who received the adrenaline shot were either informed or not informed

Can People Be Wrong About Whether They Are Sexually Aroused?

Sexual arousal is one form of arousal. You might think it is simpler and clearer than emotional arousal because emotional arousal can be associated with such a wide spectrum of emotions, whereas sexual arousal is specific and focused. Yet sexual arousal has its ambiguities too.

One source of ambiguity is that the brain and the genitals are not always on the same page. Sexual stimulation may affect the brain, or the genitals, or neither, or both. There is some sign that the disconnect between the brain and the genitals is larger among women than men. That is, the link between self-reported arousal (that is, whether people think they are sexually turned on) and physiological measures of sexual arousal in the genitals are correlated about .60 in men but only about .25 in women (Chivers, Seto, Laan, Lalumière, & Grimbos, in press). Remember, correlations range in size from +/−1 (a perfect, exact match) to 0 (completely unrelated, no connection at all).

There is plenty of room for divergence in both genders, especially if the person's attitudes prescribe certain reactions that differ from what the body finds exciting. In one classic study (Adams, Wright, & Lohr, 1996), men's feelings about homosexuality were surveyed, and researchers chose men who were the most tolerant of gay sex and others who were most

strongly opposed to it. Then all the participants watched some films of homosexual men having sex with each other. The researchers measured both the feelings the men had while watching these films and their physiological response. The latter test used a device (called the penile plethysmograph) that wraps a rubber band around the penis to measure whether it starts to get an erection.

The two measures yielded opposite findings. The men who had said they were most strongly opposed to homosexuality reported that they did not like the gay films at all and that they were not turned on. The physiological data, however, showed that those men were the ones most aroused by those films. This finding lends support to the view that homophobia or anti-gay prejudice is strongest among men who may themselves have homosexual tendencies but find these unacceptable. They react against their own homosexual feelings by claiming to hate gay sex and to find it disgusting.

A comparable finding emerged from research on sex guilt in women (Morokoff, 1985). In this

PhotoDisc

work, women watched sexually explicit film clips. Women with high levels of sex guilt reported on questionnaires that they did not enjoy the films, and they rated their sexual arousal to the films as lower than any other women in the study. However, physiological measures of arousal—which assess the degree of lubrication in the vagina (measured using a device called a vaginal photoplethysmograph)—indicated that these women were actually more aroused than the other women in the study. Those who claim to be turned off by erotic films are actually likely to be turned on by them. ■

about the "side effects" of the drug (e.g., it causes heart pounding, trembling hands, etc.). Everyone was told that the injection contained the vitamins, but of course there were no actual vitamins.

Next, participants were exposed to a confederate who acted either happy and joyous (by playing with paper, rubber bands, pencils, folders, and hula hoops) or angry and resentful (with the aid of a questionnaire that asked many nosy, offensive questions, such as "Which member of your immediate family does not bathe or wash regularly?"). The researchers secretly observed to see whether the participant would join in and show similar emotion. The strongest emotional reactions were found among the people who had both received the stimulant, rather than the placebo, and been told that the injection would not have any side effects. If they received the stimulant and were told that it was a stimulant, then they

attributed their arousal state to the injection rather than to the situation, so they did not label it as an emotional state.

Perhaps the best-known demonstration of mislabeling arousal was a study done in Vancouver, Canada, where people can cross a scenic but scary bridge hanging by cords over a deep gorge. According to the authors (Dutton & Aron, 1974), the bridge has many features that might be arousing, such as "(a) a tendency to tilt, sway, and wobble, creating the impression that one is about to fall over the side; (b) very low handrails of wire cable which contribute to this impression; and (c) a 230-foot drop to rocks and shallow rapids below the bridge" (p. 511). The "control condition" bridge located further upriver was made of heavy cedar wood, did not tilt or sway, had sturdy handrails, and was only a few feet above a small stream. The researchers stationed an attractive woman on the

Capilano Canyon Suspension Bridge in North Vancouver, British Columbia. The bridge is 450 feet long, 5 feet wide, and hangs 230 feet above a rocky gorge. Men who had crossed this bridge were more likely to call a female research assistant than were men who had crossed a low, stable bridge (Dutton & Aron, 1974).

bridge, and she approached men who were crossing the bridge to ask them to complete a short questionnaire. After participants completed the questionnaire, the attractive female offered to explain the study in more detail when she had more time. She tore off a corner of a sheet of paper, wrote down her name and phone number, and invited each participant to call her if he wanted to talk further. The researchers kept track of whether the men actually called her.

The reasoning was that crossing the bridge would create an arousal state of fear, and then a conversation with a beautiful woman would lead them to label their fear-based arousal as attraction to her. Sure enough, the men who had crossed the suspension bridge were more likely to call the female researcher than were men who had crossed the stable bridge (even though it was the same woman). The researchers proposed that fear can be converted into love.

Perhaps you can use excitation transfer theory to improve your love life! Take your lover on an exciting date, such as to an amusement park or an action-packed movie, and then kiss him or her. According to excitation transfer theory, the arousal from the amusement ride or movie will transfer to raise your date's attraction to you.

Is the bodily arousal state really the same in all emotions? Subsequent research suggested that there is not just one single state underlying all emotions. More plausibly, there are at least two basic arousal states that feel quite different. One of these is pleasant and the other unpleasant. Many research studies have been done with neutral states, such as someone

receiving caffeine or another stimulant, and it does seem that these states can be converted into almost any emotion, good or bad. However, emotional arousal that comes from actual events, generated by the body in response to experience rather than chemically induced, is usually already either good or bad. "Good" arousal cannot be converted into "bad" arousal, nor can "bad" arousal be converted into "good" arousal (Marshall & Zimbardo, 1979; Maslach, 1979). Some studies have explicitly shown that when people experience pleasant arousal, they will not misattribute that state as an unpleasant emotion, or vice versa (Zanna, Higgins, & Taves, 1976).

Indeed, the only study that seems to suggest a successful conversion of a bad emotion into a good one is the Vancouver suspension bridge study described earlier (Dutton & Aron, 1974), and even this study is ambiguous. Remember, the key measure of attraction was whether the men called the woman, and this did not occur until much later. There is no way of knowing when they decided they liked the woman enough to call her—on the bridge, just after the bridge, or even the next day when remembering the experience. The notion that fear converted into love may be a misinterpretation of that study—maybe it was the relief or elation or bravado they felt after crossing the bridge that was converted into love. If so, then the results indicated converting one positive emotion into another, which would be more in line with subsequent findings.

If there are two types of naturally occurring arousal states—one good and one bad—the explanation of why real, everyday emotions can't be converted may lie with automatic affect. Remember, conscious emotion takes time to build, but automatic affect arises quickly. If an arousal starts to build to form the basis for a conscious emotional reaction, it will be shaped by the automatic reaction, so it too will feel good or bad. Hence, it will be hard to relabel a bad emotion as a good one, or vice versa. Converting one positive emotion into a different positive one, such as turning joy into pride, will be much easier. A warning to the wise: Always watch out for emotional overreactions fueled by caffeine!

3. Tyrone had a stressful day at the office, so he stopped at the gym on the way home to work out. Even after he gets home, Tyrone still feels wound up. When his wife remarks in passing that he forgot to take out the trash, Tyrone responds by yelling and cursing at his wife. Tyrone's overreaction to his wife's comment illustrates _____.
   (a) catharsis   (b) disinhibition
   (c) desensitization (d) excitation transfer

4. How many basic arousal states are there?
   (a) One   (b) Two
   (c) Three   (d) Four

Some Important Emotions

In this section we describe four important emotions: happiness, anger, guilt, and shame. In reading about each of these emotions, it is helpful to think back to one of this textbook's most important themes—namely, that inner processes serve interpersonal functions. To be sure, some emotions may serve more basic biological needs, especially survival and reproduction. But even there, people mainly achieve survival and reproduction by forming and maintaining good relationships with other people. Hence, for example, we should not ask, "How could feeling guilty ever benefit the person who feels that way?" Instead, it will be more enlightening to ask, "How does feeling guilty help a person maintain good relationships with others?"

HAPPINESS

One of the most compelling works of fiction to emerge from the Cold War is *One Day in the Life of Ivan Denisovich* by Alexander Solzhenitsyn. The main character has been sent to a prison labor camp in Siberia for 10 years, and he knows there is no guarantee that he will actually be released when his time is up. The situation is bleak. No family or loved ones ever visit him, and he is only allowed two letters per year. He has to work hard outdoors in freezing temperatures, with worn-out clothes that leave his fingers and toes constantly numb. No entertainment, not even anything to read. Sleeping on a rock-hard bed in a room full of other prisoners. Never a glimpse of a woman. Hardly any chance of escape, and anyone who did manage to escape would probably just freeze to death in the vast empty land. Yet on the last page of the book, the hero looks back on his day (remember, the whole book covers just one ordinary day in the middle of his 10-year prison sentence) and reflects that he was pretty lucky—it was "almost a happy day." He falls into a contented sleep.

How could someone have an "almost happy day" in a Siberian prison camp? The writer's goal was to draw attention to the millions of Russians who suffered terribly in the prison camp system. This is what made the story brilliant: Instead of describing a day that was totally awful, the author presented a relatively "good day" in such a miserable setting. The story shows the power of comparisons and expectations. If you expect the worst—and as a Siberian prisoner you would soon come to expect that—then anything slightly better than the very worst can seem quite good by contrast. The good events that surpassed his expectations seem pathetic to most of us. His dinner was two bowls of bad oatmeal, instead of one; he had avoided the worst work assignments; he had managed to get a little tobacco (the camp's only luxury); and he had found a small piece of metal, not useful for anything he could readily imagine, but maybe someday it might come in handy in some unknown way.

Defining Happiness. What is happiness, and how can it be reached? The term *happiness* is used at several different levels. One form of happiness is probably shared by human beings and many animals, and it refers simply to feeling good right now. When you get something to eat, or you warm up in the sun after being cold, you feel good, and you react with happy feelings.

Other forms of happiness are unique to human beings, in part because they involve a broader time span and the meaningful integration of multiple experiences. Thus, someone might be a happy person because he enjoys many positive emotional experiences, or because she hardly ever feels bad emotions. Indeed, one measure of happiness is **affect balance**: the frequency of positive emotions minus the frequency of negative emotions.

The most complex form of happiness is sometimes called **life satisfaction**. It involves not only evaluating how your life is generally, but also comparing it to some standard. Probably most animals can feel good or bad, but only humans have life satisfaction, because only humans can think meaningfully about their life as a whole and decide whether it lives up to their hopes and goals. Life satisfaction has a much broader time span than current emotion and affect balance.

Objective Roots of Happiness. What would make you happy? Most people answer this question by referring to objective circumstances. They think they would be happy if they had something along

---

AFFECT BALANCE the frequency of positive emotions minus the frequency of negative emotions
LIFE SATISFACTION an evaluation of how one's life is generally, and how it compares to some standard

Honey, are you happy we had kids?

these lines: plenty of money, a good job, a happy marriage or at least a good relationship, perhaps children, good health, and a nice place to live. These are called objective predictors, because they refer to objective aspects of one's life. With one exception, they are correct, because people who do have those things are happier than people who do not have them. Note that most of those objective predictors involve succeeding by biological and cultural standards. Thus, if people strive to feel good, they will do things that the culture values (such as marrying and succeeding at a good job), and if everyone were to do those things, the culture would thrive and flourish.

The one odd exception is having children. Couples who have children are less happy than couples who do not have children (e.g., Twenge, Campbell, & Foster, 2003). The drop in happiness has been shown repeatedly, with many different research samples and methods. It goes against intuitive beliefs, and in fact most parents expect that having children will increase their happiness. What's more, they continue to believe that having children has made them happier, even though the research clearly shows otherwise. Most likely this is because parenthood is riddled with self-deception and illusion. Parents do not want to believe that they made a big mistake by having children, and they also want to rationalize the efforts and sacrifices they have made. Having children is, however, a powerful source of meaning in life (Baumeister, 1991), so that even if becoming a parent does not increase happiness (in fact it lowers it), it does make life richer and more meaningful.

Culture plays a big role in all this. Nearly all cultures encourage people to have children, and toward that end they help promote the idea (even when false) that having children will make you happy. If enough people expect to become happy by having babies, the culture will increase in population, which cultures have generally found to be advantageous. Cultures that do not produce new generations will not survive, so nearly all successful cultures encourage reproduction. Moreover, cultures compete against others, and at some very basic level, those that have more people will triumph over those with fewer. It is not surprising that most cultures glorify parenthood, or at least motherhood, and bestow social approval on those who reproduce most. For a while, the Soviet Union gave medals to women who had the most children. This may seem odd, but it is merely a more explicit form of the approval that is found all over the world. Most likely it was motivated by urgent pragmatic forces: The Soviet Union suffered more deaths than any other country during World War II, so replenishing the population was more urgently needed there than in other countries. Giving medals to mothers was simply a logical extension of a basic value that almost all cultures embrace.

The fact that having children reduces happiness may actually be a fairly recent, modern phenomenon (e.g., Baumeister, 1991). Throughout most of history, most people were farmers, and they lived in societies that offered no social security systems, pensions, or other means of support. When you grew too old to work the farm, you would starve, unless you had children to take over the farm and support you. Childlessness was a disaster for a married couple, in terms of their practical and economic prospects. Only when the family changed from an economic unit to a haven of intimate relationships did the impact of parenthood shift to become more negative.

Many readers are worried when they read that having children is likely to reduce their happiness. Don't be! Most people want to have children, and do, and end up glad they did, even though along the way they are less happy than they would otherwise have been. The human mind is very good at forgetting bad things and emphasizing good ones. Also, if you want to reduce the negative effect on happiness, you can take several steps. The first is to have a stable relationship so as not to suffer the added stresses of being a single parent. The second is to prolong the "newlywed" phase of life between marriage and birth of first child, rather than rushing into parenthood. That phase may allow the relationship to become stronger, enabling it to better withstand the stresses of parenthood. (Also, many studies have confirmed that the interval between the wedding day and the birth of the first child is one of life's happiest times, especially for women; e.g., Campbell, 1981). Third, save up some money, which can be used to cover new expenses and thereby reduce some of the financial stresses that parenthood puts on the couple.

After World War II in the former Soviet Union, women who had lots of children were given medals.

The surprising thing about the objective predictors of happiness, however, is that the effects are weak. Yes, people with plenty of money are happier than people who don't have much money, but the difference is quite small. Apparently money can buy happiness, but not very much of it. There is only one objective circumstance that has been shown to make a big difference in happiness, and that involves social connections. People who are alone in the world are much less happy than people who have strong, rich social networks. (This strong link shows once again that inner processes, in this case happiness, are linked to interpersonal relationships, in this case forming and maintaining good connections to other people. The human emotional system is set up so that it is very hard for a person to be happy while alone in life.) For all other circumstances, even including health, injury, money, and career, the differences are small. If you think that reaching your goals will make you happy, you are likely to be disappointed, even though technically you are right. In general, that is, people who meet their goals are briefly happy, but then they go back to where they were before. People who reach their career goal may experience some

temporary happiness, but they do not live happily ever after. Most things wear off pretty soon.

The Hedonic Treadmill. The tendency for objective changes to wear off led some social psychologists to speak of the **hedonic treadmill** (Brickman & Campbell, 1971; Brickman, Coates, & Janoff-Bulman, 1978; Diener, Lucas, & Scollon, 2006; Kahneman, 1999; Kahneman, Knetsch, & Thaler, 1990; Kahneman, Wakker, & Sarin, 1997). Like a person on a treadmill, you may take big steps forward but end up in the same place. A big success at work or in romance will bring joy for a while, but then the person goes back to being as happy or unhappy as before. That doesn't mean that everyone goes back to the same level. Happy people go back to being happy, and unhappy ones go back to their former level of unhappiness (Diener et al., 2006).

In one of the most dramatic illustrations of the hedonic treadmill, researchers studied people who had won the state lottery (thereby gaining hundreds of thousands of dollars) and other people who had been severely paralyzed in an accident (Brickman et al., 1978). Such events are among the most extremely good or bad things that can happen to someone. At first, of course, the lottery winners were very happy, whereas the accident victims were very unhappy. A year afterward, however, the effects had largely worn off. Winning the lottery was wonderful, but the winners seemed to have lost their ability to appreciate everyday pleasures such as a friendly conversation or a sunset. Additionally, sudden wealth brought a number of problems: Annoying, needy relatives came out of the woodwork, tax problems brought new headaches, and the like. In general, a year after the big event the differences in happiness were not very noticeable.

It appeared that people got over big good events faster than they got over big bad events. People did not recover emotionally from being paralyzed as fast or as thoroughly as they got over the joy of winning the state lottery. Two large studies that tracked people across many years found that the hedonic treadmill does not work very well when life gets worse (Lucas, 2007). That is, people who acquired a disability during the study became less happy than they had been and tended to stay that way.

Subjective Roots of Happiness. If objective circumstances do not cause happiness, then what does? Happiness appears to lie more in our outlook and personality than in our circumstances. In a sense, some people are "born happy" whereas others remain grumpy and miserable no matter what

---

HEDONIC TREADMILL a theory proposing that people stay at about the same level of happiness regardless of what happens to them

happens. Longitudinal research has looked at a long list of objective predictors of happiness and, as usual, found that they had significant but very weak relationships to happiness (see Costa & McCrae, 1980, 1984; Costa, McCrae, & Zonderman, 1987). (Statistical significance means only that the relationship is not zero.) The advantage of this work was that it had also assessed the same people 10 years previously. Much can change in 10 years, including most of one's objective circumstances. Ten years from now you will probably have a different job, a different home, different friends, different hobbies, a different amount of money, possibly some different family members. And yet: The strongest predictor of each person's happiness turned out to be how happy the person had been 10 years before (Costa et al., 1987). It is not perfect, of course. Some people do change for the better or worse over long periods of time, but they are the exception. In general, people who are happy now will be happy in the future, while those who are grumpy or depressed or irritable now will continue to be so. Major events bring joy or sorrow, but these feelings wear off, and people go back to their own baseline. If you want to be married to a happy person in 10 years, find someone who is happy today (and preferably someone who was happy before meeting you!). Statistically, that person is your best bet for someone who will be happy in the future.

One reason happiness often remains the same across time is that happiness is rooted in one's outlook and approach to life. The importance of one's outlook is evident in the difference between subjective and objective predictors of happiness. In general, subjective predictors are much stronger. Subjective refers to how you feel about something, whereas objective refers to the something. Thus, how much money you make (objectively) has only a weak relationship to happiness, but how you feel about your income (subjectively) is a strong predictor of happiness. How healthy you are (objectively), measured by how often you got sick this year, has only a weak relationship to your happiness, but how satisfied you are with your health (subjectively) is stronger. Being married has only a weak impact on happiness, but being happily married is a strong factor.

Increasing Happiness. Recently, the "positive psychology" movement has begun to look for actions or exercises that can increase happiness. Some findings are promising. Several psychological patterns have been shown to increase happiness, such as forgiving others, being grateful for blessings, practicing religious beliefs, and being optimistic (Brown & Ryan, 2003; McCullough, 2008; McCullough, Emmons, & Tsang, 2002; McCullough, Rachal, Sandage, Worthington, Brown, & Hight, 1998; Ryff, 1995; Sheldon & Lyubomirsky, 2004; Thrash & Elliot, 2003).

These seem to have in common the idea of focusing one's attention on positive things. For example, one exercise you might try if you want to raise your happiness is to sit down once or twice a week and make a list of the good things that have happened to you. Research studies have confirmed that people who do this end up happier than control participants who do not (Lyubomirsky, 2001).

Regardless of what causes happiness, happy people are healthy people. For example, consider the results from a fascinating study of Catholic nuns (Danner, Snowdon, & Friesen, 2001). On September 22, 1930, the Mother Superior of the North American sisters sent a letter requesting that each Catholic nun "write a short sketch of [her] life. This account should not contain more than two to three hundred words and should be written on a single sheet of paper . . . include place of birth, parentage, interesting and edifying events of childhood, schools attended, influences that led to the convent, religious life, and outstanding events." More than 60 years later, these 180 sketches were scored for positive emotions. The researchers found that nuns who expressed high positive emotions lived about 10 years longer than the nuns who expressed low positive emotion! Positive emotions are apparently good for your health, though the results are correlational, so we cannot be sure whether the positive emotion is a sign or a cause of health.

It may well be that positive emotions have direct effects on the body that improve health, such as boosting the immune system. It may also be that happiness is linked to good social relations, as we have seen, and perhaps good social relations promote health whereas being alone in the world weakens bodily health. The link between health and belongingness could also go in either direction or both. Maybe people are drawn to associate with someone who is happy while avoiding sad or grumpy types (thus happiness affects belongingness). Or maybe having good social relations makes people happy whereas being alone reduces happiness (thus belongingness affects happiness). Maybe both are correct. There is even another possibility, which is that some underlying trait predisposes people to get along with others and to be happy.

In sum, happiness is linked to a variety of good outcomes, including health and success in life, but it is not yet clear what causes what. Further research will untangle these possible explanations. For now, it seems plausible that all the possible causal relationships are correct to some extent.

Some people often experience intense emotions, both positive and negative, whereas others rarely feel intense emotions of any sort. *Tradeoffs* describes the tradeoff of feeling versus not feeling intense emotions.

Affect Intensity, or the Joys of Feeling Nothing

Nearly everyone wants to be happy, and the emotional formula for happiness seems simple: You want to have plenty of good feelings and as few bad ones as possible. Unfortunately, life doesn't always cooperate. Over the last couple of decades, researchers have begun to recognize that some people

Dennis Flaherty/Getty Images

have many intense experiences, both good and bad, while others have relatively few.

One of the most systematic treatments of this difference is based on the Affect Intensity Measure (AIM; Larsen & Diener, 1987). Some sample items from the scale are: "When I'm happy, I feel like I'm bursting with joy" and "When I am nervous, I get shaky all over." People who score low on the scale have relatively few emotional reactions, and these tend to be rather subdued. In contrast, people who score high have strong emotions to all sorts of events. Consistent with traditional stereotypes, one study (Sheldon, 1994) found that advanced art college students had higher scores on the AIM than did advanced science college students. That is, future artists generally live with plenty of extreme emotions, whereas future scientists generally have more subdued emotional lives.

Which is better? Affect intensity appears to be a genuine tradeoff. People who score low on the AIM can go through life on a fairly even keel. They don't become too bothered about problems and stresses, but then again they don't feel swept away with passionate joy very often either. In contrast, life is an emotional rollercoaster for people with high affect intensity. Thus, you get both the good and the bad, or neither.

The quality of your life circumstances may dictate which is prefer-

able. If your life is in a positive groove, well under control, so that most experiences are good, then you may well get more meaningful enjoyment if you have high affective intensity. In contrast, if your life is filled with unpredictable, uncontrollable events, some of which are very bad, you may well prefer to have low affect intensity. You don't want to take the good with the bad if there is too much bad.

This tradeoff can affect the most intense and personal of relationships. People who have been hurt in love may become reluctant to let themselves fall in love again. Historians have even suggested that in past centuries, people were reluctant to love their children, because the high rate of child mortality would lead to heartbreak (Aries, 1962; Stone, 1977). If a woman from a good family had a baby, she would often send it out to the country to be nursed, even though objectively its chances of survival were slightly lower there (because the country was poorer) than if the child stayed with her. Preventing the woman from nursing her own baby kept maternal feelings of love to a minimum, so the mother was less hurt if the baby died. Older children were often sent out to live in other people's households starting when they were 6 or 7, so parents might not develop the lasting emotional bond to their children that comes from living together year after year. Once public health improved, however, and most children could be expected to survive into adulthood, parents could afford the risk of loving their children more, and they began to keep their children with them until they were nearly grown up. ●

ANGER

Anger is an emotional response to a real or imagined threat or provocation. Anger can range in intensity from mild irritation to extreme rage. Anger is different from aggression. Anger is an internal emotion, whereas aggression is an external behavior. (Aggression will be covered in Chapter 10.) Many events make people angry. These events can be interpersonal such as a provocation or a blow to the ego, or they can be stressors such as frustration, physical pain, or discomfort caused by heat, crowding, noise, or foul odors (Berkowitz, 1993).

Emotions can be grouped on two important dimensions: (1) unpleasant versus pleasant and

(2) high versus low arousal. Using these two dimensions, emotions can be sorted into four categories, defined by crossing pleasant versus unpleasant with high versus low arousal (see ▶ **FIGURE 6.5**). Anger falls in the unpleasant, high arousal category, because anger both feels bad and energizes the person. Angry people are thus highly motivated to take action, because the unpleasantness makes them want to do something to bring about a change, and the high arousal contributes to initiative.

The tendency to take action does not mean that effective or desirable actions are chosen. In fact, angry

ANGER an emotional response to a real or imagined threat or provocation

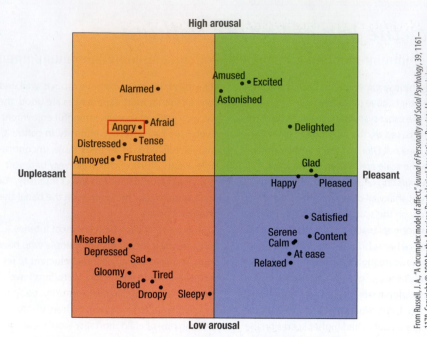

From Russell, J. A., "A circumplex model of affect," *Journal of Personality and Social Psychology*, 39, 1161–1178. Copyright © 1980 by the American Psychological Association. Reprinted by permission.

▶ **FIGURE 6.5** Emotions can be sorted into four categories, defined by crossing the pleasant versus unpleasant dimension with the high versus low arousal dimension (Russell, 1980).

people often make poor choices. Studies of risk taking show that angry people make some of the stupidest decisions, leaning in particular toward high-risk, high-payoff courses of action that often backfire and produce disastrous consequences (Leith & Baumeister, 1996). The self-destructive aspect of anger comes from this pattern of making risky, foolish choices. In fact, anger makes people downplay risks and overlook dangers (Lerner, Gonzalez, Small, & Fischhoff, 2003; Lerner & Keltner, 2001). Angry people actually become more optimistic; in this respect, angry and happy people resemble each other and differ from people who are sad or afraid (who tend toward pessimism) (Lerner et al., 2003).

The energizing aspect of anger contributes to making people feel strong and powerful (e.g., Lerner et al., 2003; Lerner & Keltner, 2001). Anger can thus be a powerful force in helping people stand up for what they believe is right. The American Revolution, the civil rights movement, the feminist movement, and other causes probably benefited from anger and the resultant willingness to take action. The other side of the energizing aspect of anger, however, is that people will also stand up and fight for things that may be trivial or ill advised, and they may choose their battles poorly. Angry people are impulsive and fail to consider the potential consequences of their actions (Scarpa & Raine, 2000).

Anger is widely recognized as a problem. It is one of the most heavily regulated emotions, in the sense that cultures have many different norms about anger.

Some of these norms conflict with each other. For example, norms say that sometimes it is justifiable to be angry, other times anger is wholly inappropriate, and yet other times there is an obligation to be angry (Averill, 1982). In another sense, however, anger is one of the least regulated emotions. When people are surveyed about how they control their emotions, they typically report that they have fewer and less effective techniques for controlling anger than for controlling other emotions (Tice & Baumeister, 1993).

Anger is quite different from contempt (Fischer & Roseman, 2007). Anger makes one want to argue or fight now, but the goal is to change the behavior of the other person, and in the long run anger often aims at reconciliation. Contempt, in contrast, leads to rejection and social exclusion of the other person. Thus, in a way, anger is more positively social, because it seeks to approach the other and bring about change in a way that the angry person hopes will benefit the relationship.

Causes of Anger. What makes people angry? People perceive their anger as a reaction to someone else's wrongdoing. Anger is greater if one sees the other person's behavior as (a) very harmful, (b) random or arbitrary, or (c) deliberately cruel. Many people hide their anger, especially at relationship partners. As a result, the partners don't know that what they do makes the other angry, so they are apt to do it again (Averill, 1982; Baumeister, Stillwell, & Wotman, 1990).

Anger seems maladaptive today—useless, counterproductive, harmful, divisive, and problematic. When people become angry, they do things they will regret later. They are impulsive, aggressive, and worse. Why would anger exist if it is harmful and maladaptive? It is reasonable to assume that it is (or was) adaptive, or else natural selection would likely have favored people who did not feel anger, and anger would gradually have disappeared from the human repertoire of emotions. In other words, despite all its faults and drawbacks, anger must have some positive value that helps the organism survive—or at least it must have had some positive value in the evolutionary past. Whether anger is suited to today's cultures and social circumstances is another question, however.

One line of explanation is that anger is adaptive because it motivates the person to act aggressively and assertively. The broader context is that emotions exist in order to motivate actions, and each emotion points toward a certain kind of act. Anger helps get people ready to defend themselves, assert their rights, pursue goals that might be blocked, and perform other beneficial acts.

A second line of explanation begins by objecting to the first: Why not go directly to the aggression? Why become angry first? Anger tips off your foes that you might attack them, allowing them to prepare themselves or even attack you preemptively. The second explanation is that anger helps reduce aggression. This may seem paradoxical, because studies show that people are more aggressive when they are angry than when they are not (Berkowitz, 1993). But that evidence could be misleading, because both anger and aggression occur in situations in which there is conflict, frustration, or provocation. If human beings had evolved to skip feeling anger and go directly to aggression, the absence of anger might not change the amount of aggression. Hence, in this second view, anger helps warn friends and family that something is wrong and aggression may be coming. This gives people time to resolve the conflict before it reaches the point of violence. Anger may therefore actually reduce aggression, compared to what the world would be like if people went directly into aggressive action as soon as they experienced conflict or frustration. For example, some powerful people manage to get their way with just a brief frown of displeasure or a slight raising of the voice: A hint of anger is enough to make other people scurry to do their bidding, and the powerful person hardly ever has to express a full-blown angry outburst, let alone engage in aggressive action.

Thus, anger may be social in an important sense, and in fact it may help enable people to live together. If anger is a warning sign of impending aggression, anger may help defuse conflict and prevent aggression. Yet as a sign of conflict and problem, anger may be antisocial. Moreover, the action-motivating function of anger may conflict with the social conflict-defusing aspect. Angry people may say or do things that make the problem worse. If one person wants to go out and the other wants to stay in, conflict is already there—but angry, insulting remarks will aggravate it and make it harder to reach a compromise. Research on negotiation has shown some social benefits of anger. When two people are negotiating and one shows anger, the other takes this as a sign to give in. It is a sign that the angry person will not compromise or make concessions, so one had best go along (Van Dijk, Van Kleef, Steinel, & Van Beest, 2008; see also Van Kleef, De Dreu, & Manstead, 2004a, 2004b). Anger is thus useful for a negotiator. To be sure, people dislike angry negotiators, so anger can backfire, especially if the non-angry negotiator has other options. That is, people will treat the angry person unfavorably if they can; but if they have to settle a negotiation, they concede more to the angry than to the non-angry person.

People seem aware that anger can be useful. Some people actually try to increase their angry feelings when they anticipate a social interaction in which anger might be useful, such as a difficult confrontation with a rival or enemy. Moreover, they are right:

Sometimes anger does improve performance in such difficult situations (Tamir, Mitchell, & Gross, 2008).

A final perspective on the causes of anger is the potential mismatch between people's natural reactions and the complexity of modern social life. Many emotional reactions developed during a time of simpler life circumstances. Anger might help you have the arousal to fight off a predatory animal, but it may be useless and even counterproductive to have the same feelings toward your computer when a file is accidentally deleted.

Hiding Versus Showing Anger. Because it is unpleasant, many people want to get rid of their anger when they experience it. There are three possible ways of dealing with anger. One standard approach that has been endorsed by many societies is never to show anger. (Nature supplies the impulse to be angry, but culture tells people to try to stop it.) It can end up prompting people to stuff their anger deep inside and repress it. There is some evidence that this is a costly strategy. Long-term concealed anger can be quite destructive to the person, increasing the risk of such illnesses as heart disease (e.g., Ellis, 1977). On the other hand, as we have seen, inner states follow outward expressions (as in the facial feedback hypothesis, discussed earlier), so if people generally act as if to show they are not angry, some anger may be diminished.

A second approach is to vent one's anger. This view treats anger as a kind of inner pressure or corrosive substance that builds up over time and does harm unless it is released. The **catharsis theory** falls in this category, because it holds that expressing anger (including verbal expression or even aggressive, violent action) produces a healthy release of emotion and is therefore good for the psyche. Catharsis theory, which can be traced back through Sigmund Freud to Aristotle, is elegant and appealing. Unfortunately, the facts and findings do not show that venting one's anger has positive value. On the contrary, it tends to make people more aggressive afterward and to exacerbate interpersonal conflicts (Geen & Quanty, 1977). Venting anger is also linked to higher risk of heart disease (for reviews, see Lewis & Bucher, 1992; Miller, Smith, Turner, Guijarro, & Hallet, 1996; Rosenman & Chesney, 1982). Even among people who believe in the value of venting and catharsis, and even when people enjoy their venting and feel some satisfaction from it, they are more likely to be aggressive after venting, even against innocent bystanders (Bushman, Baumeister, & Stack, 1999).

CATHARSIS THEORY the proposition that expressing negative emotions produces a healthy release of those emotions and is therefore good for the psyche

Ted Bundy in court. Bundy was a serial killer who murdered dozens of women. He was electrocuted in a Florida prison on January 24, 1989.

© Bettmann/Corbis

One variation of venting is intense physical exercise, such as running. When angry, some people go running or try some other form of physical exercise. Although exercise is good for your heart, it is not good for reducing anger (Bushman, 2002). The reason exercise doesn't work is that it increases rather than decreases arousal levels (recall the earlier section on arousal in emotion). Also, if someone provokes you after exercising, excitation transfer might occur (Zillmann, 1979). That is, the arousal from the exercise might transfer to the response to the provocation, producing an exaggerated and possibly more violent response.

In a nutshell, venting anger may be like using gasoline to put out a fire: It just feeds the flame. Venting keeps arousal levels high and keeps aggressive thoughts and angry feelings alive. Maybe you have heard of the joke, "How do you get to Carnegie Hall?" The answer is: "Practice! Practice! Practice!" Well, "How do you become an angry, aggressive person?" The answer is the same: "Practice! Practice! Practice!" Venting is just practicing how to behave more aggressively, by hitting, kicking, screaming, or shouting.

The third approach is to try to get rid of one's anger. This solution is important because the problems of both the other approaches (i.e., stuffing and venting) arise because the person stays angry.

The important thing is to stop feeling angry. All emotions, including anger, consist of bodily states (such as arousal) and mental meanings. To get rid of anger, you can work on either of those. Anger can be reduced by getting rid of the arousal state, such as by relaxing or by counting to 10 before responding. Anger can also be addressed by mental tactics, such as by reframing the problem or conflict, or by distracting oneself and turning one's attention to other, more pleasant topics. Certain behaviors can also help get rid of anger. For example, doing something such as petting a puppy, watching a comedy, making love, or performing a good deed can help, because those acts are incompatible with anger and the angry state becomes impossible to sustain (e.g., Baron, 1976).

GUILT AND SHAME

"[Guilt is] this mechanism we use to control people. It's an illusion. It's a kind of social control mechanism and it's very unhealthy. It does terrible things to our bodies. And there are much better ways to control our behavior than that rather extraordinary use of guilt." (Michaud & Aynesworth, 2000, p. 320)

What do you think of this view of guilt? Many people agree with it. Guilt does have a bad reputation in our culture. If you visit the "pop psychology" section in a public bookstore, you are likely to find several books telling you how to get rid of guilt. The underlying idea is that guilt is a useless (or even harmful) form of self-inflicted suffering. Most people seek to avoid guilt like the plague.

Then again, perhaps guilt deserves more credit than it gets. The previous quotation was actually from Ted Bundy, a notorious mass murderer who killed numerous young women. Perhaps if he had felt a little more guilt himself, he might have refrained from his criminal acts and some of those women would be alive today.

Research by social psychologists has gradually painted a picture of guilt that differs starkly from the negative view held by our culture (and by Ted Bundy). Guilt is actually quite good for society and for close relationships. You would not want to have a boss, a lover, a roommate, or a business partner who had no sense of guilt. Such people exist (they are called psychopaths), but they are often a disaster to those around them (Hare, 1998). They exploit and harm others, help themselves at the expense of others, and feel no remorse about those they hurt.

Guilt Versus Shame. What is guilt? **Guilt** is generally an emotional feeling that is bad, and it is usually associated with some implicit reproach that one has acted badly or wrongly. By and large, everyone occasionally does something wrong; the difference

GUILT an unpleasant moral emotion associated with a specific instance in which one has acted badly or wrongly

between people lies in whether they feel bad about it or not. Guilt is especially associated with acts that could damage a relationship about which one cares.

Guilt must be distinguished from **shame** (Tangney & Dearing, 2002). The difference lies in how widely the bad feeling is generalized. Guilt focuses narrowly on the action, whereas shame spreads to the whole person. Guilt says, "I did a bad thing." Shame says, "I am a bad person."

Research based on that distinction has repeatedly shown that shame is usually destructive whereas guilt is usually constructive. This may be worth keeping in mind when you deal with your assistants and workers, or your children, or your students (or even your romantic partners). How do you criticize them when they do something wrong? Calling their attention to what they did wrong may seem necessary, but phrasing your criticism in terms of being a bad person (e.g., "you rotten creep") is not nearly as constructive as allowing them to be a good person who did a bad thing. Thus, one should avoid making internal negative stable attributions about others (see Chapter 5). There is, after all, no remedy for being a bad person, so shame makes people want to withdraw and hide, or to lash out in anger. In contrast, guilt signifies a good person who did a bad thing, and there are plenty of ways that a good person can remedy an isolated bad act: apologize, make amends, reaffirm one's commitment to the relationship, promise not to repeat the misdeed, and so forth.

Effects of Guilt. Guilt motivates people to do good acts, such as apologizing. Apologies can help repair damage to relationships because they (a) convey the implicit agreement that the act was wrong, (b) suggest that the person will try not to do it again, and (c) counteract any implication that the bad action meant that the person does not care about the relationship. For example, if your partner cooks you a lovely dinner but you arrive an hour late and the food is spoiled, your partner may not care very much about the food itself, but the implication that you do not care about the relationship can be very upsetting. A convincing apology cannot revive the spoiled food, but it may prevent your partner from feeling that you do not care about the relationship (Baumeister, Stillwell, & Heatherton, 1994; Ohbuchi, Kameda, & Agarie, 1989; Tangney & Dearing, 2002; Tangney & Fischer, 1995).

Guilt also motivates people to make amends. When people feel guilty about something they have done, they try harder to perform positive or good actions. They are more likely to learn a lesson and try to behave better in the future. This too can help salvage a relationship from the damage done by some misbehavior. For example, in one study (McMillen & Austin, 1971), half the participants were induced to tell a lie. A previous participant (actually a

off the mark.com   by Mark Parisi

confederate) told them all about the study and what the correct answers to a test were before the experimenter arrived. Soon thereafter, the experimenter came and asked participants if they had heard anything at all about the study. All participants said no. Thus, half of the participants lied (because in fact they had heard about the study). After the study was over, the experimenter said that participants were free to go, but added that if they had extra time they could help him fill in bubble sheets for another study (an incredibly boring task). Participants who had not been induced to lie volunteered to help fill in bubble sheets for 2 minutes on average, whereas participants who had been induced to lie volunteered to help fill in bubble sheets for 63 minutes! The lying participants were apparently attempting to wipe away their guilt for lying to the experimenter by being more helpful. Guilt made them more willing to do something nice.

Many other social psychology studies have found that people behave in more socially desirable ways when they feel guilty (Cialdini, Darby, & Vincent, 1973; Harris, Benson, & Hall, 1975; Katzev, Edelsack, Reynolds, Steinmetz, Walker, & Wright, 1978). These research findings about the positive effects of guilt suggest that guilt is good for relationships, even though feeling guilty will be unpleasant. Sometimes, in order to make a relationship more successful, people must sacrifice their own selfish interests and do what is best for the other person. (Indeed, one theme of this book has been the need to rely on conscience and self-regulation to overcome selfish impulses in order for

---

SHAME a moral emotion that, like guilt, involves feeling bad but, unlike guilt, spreads to the whole person

civilized society and strong human relationships to survive.) Guilt is one force that pushes people toward making those relationship-enhancing sacrifices.

Guilt and Relationships. Some forms of guilt do not revolve around doing anything wrong. Sometimes people feel guilty simply because others have suffered more than they have. The term **survivor guilt** emerged after World War II based on observations of victims who had not suffered as much as others. Some people who survived the mass murder campaigns in concentration camps felt guilty for having survived when so many others died. Likewise, people who survived the atomic bombings of Hiroshima and Nagasaki felt guilty for having lived when so many others died. These people had not done anything wrong, but the phenomenon of survivor guilt shows that people are deeply sensitive to a sense of fairness and have some unease when life is "unfair" in their favor. (It is easy to be upset about unfairness when you are the one who got less than others; even some animals react to such unfairness, but they do not seem to mind when they get more than their share.) A more modern version of survivor guilt has been observed during economic recessions, when large firms must lay off many workers as in the current financial crisis. Those who remain often have some feelings of guilt for keeping their jobs when other deserving individuals have lost theirs (Brockner, Greenberg, Brockner, Bortz, Davy, & Carter, 1986).

All of this depicts guilt as a very interpersonal emotion, and it is. The stereotype of guilt depicts it as a solitary emotion, but even if someone feels guilty while alone, most likely the guilt is about something interpersonal. People mainly feel guilty about things they have done to others—hurting them, ignoring them, letting them down, or failing to meet their expectations. Moreover, they mainly feel guilty toward people they care about. Guilt is more linked to close relationships than other emotions. For example, people may often be afraid of total strangers, or annoyed by casual acquaintances, or frustrated by someone in a store or restaurant, but guilt is mainly felt toward family, good friends, and other loved ones (Baumeister, Reis, & Delespaul, 1995).

Many people count on guilt to push their loved ones to behave properly. Others try to help things along a bit. Guilt is one emotion that people actively try to make others feel. Some people become quite skilled at knowing what to say to make someone else feel guilty. As always, though, the guilt depends on the relationship, and a stranger may have a hard time making you feel guilty. The essence of most guilt-inducing strategies is "See how you are hurting me."

If you do not care about that person, you may not mind hurting him or her. In contrast, if the person is someone you love and care about, you will usually change your behavior to avoid hurting the person.

Guilt is thus an emotion well suited to cultural animals such as human beings. It depends on one's connections to others, and it makes people maintain better relationships with others. It also benefits a large system of interrelationships, which is what a culture is. And it encourages people to live up to cultural standards and rules (Baumeister et al., 1994).

SURVIVOR GUILT an unpleasant emotion associated with surviving a tragic event involving much loss of life

---

[**QUIZ YOURSELF**]

Some Important Emotions

1. One measure of happiness, affect balance, is equal to _____.
   (a) the frequency of positive emotions
   (b) the frequency of positive emotions divided by the frequency of negative emotions
   (c) the frequency of positive emotions minus the frequency of negative emotions
   (d) the frequency of positive emotions plus the frequency of negative emotions

2. Mimi just won the lottery in the state where she lives. What is her emotional response likely to be over time?
   (a) Mimi will be very happy at first, and will remain very happy.
   (b) Mimi will be very happy at first, but she will later return to her level of happiness before she won the lottery.
   (c) Mimi will be very happy at first, but she will later become very depressed after the good feeling wears off.
   (d) Mimi's initial and subsequent level of happiness will not change from what it was before she won the lottery.

3. Bill thinks that if he's irritated with his children, he'll feel better and be less inclined to hit them if he just yells and screams. Bill believes in the notion of _____.
   (a) catharsis
   (b) displacement
   (c) excitation transfer
   (d) negative reinforcement

4. Which statement best describes the research about guilt and shame?
   (a) Guilt and shame are both good for the individual and society.
   (b) Guilt and shame are both bad for the individual and society.
   (c) Guilt is bad and shame is good for the individual and society.
   (d) Guilt is good and shame is bad for the individual and society.

Why Do We Have Emotions?

If emotions are confusing, destructive reactions that make people do stupid things, then probably natural selection would have phased them out long ago, because people who had fewer and weaker emotions would fare better than people with plenty of strong emotions. People who lack emotions seem to have great difficulties in life (Damasio, 1994). It is true that sometimes emotions are confusing and cause people to do stupid, irrational, even self-destructive things. But all that tells us is that the benefits of emotion must be that much greater, because the benefits have to offset those costs.

One thing seems clear: Emotions comprise an important and powerful feedback system. Emotions tell us whether something is good or bad. You don't have much emotion over things you don't care about! Caring (motivation) is therefore one ingredient necessary for making emotion. As we go through life and things happen to us, emotions follow along afterward and help stamp in the strong sense that each event was good or bad. This is true for both automatic affect and conscious emotion. Whatever else emotions may do, they help formulate our reactions to whatever has just happened.

EMOTIONS PROMOTE BELONGINGNESS

Emotions help people get along better. This may seem surprising at first, because we are quick to notice when someone else's emotions make that person hard to get along with. Mostly, however, people's emotions promote their ties to others.

The best way to appreciate this is to look at the emotions people have when they either form or break a social bond with someone else. Forming social bonds is linked to positive emotions (Anderson, Russell, & Schumm, 1983; Baumeister & Leary, 1995; Belsky, 1985; Belsky, Lang, & Rovine, 1985; Belsky, Spanier, & Rovine, 1983; Bernard, 1982; Campbell, 1981; Campbell, Converse, & Rodgers, 1976; Glenn & McLanahan, 1982; Glenn & Weaver, 1978; Ruble, Fleming, Hackel, & Stangor, 1988; Spanier & Lewis, 1980; Twenge et al., 2003). People are happy at weddings (even if they cry!). They are usually delighted when they join a fraternity or sorority. They are excited or at least relieved when they get a job. Having children is revealing: People are usually all full of joyful smiles when they have children, even though in the long run being a parent leads to lower happiness in life, probably because of the stresses and demands of parenting.

Conversely, a host of bad emotions is linked to events that end, damage, or threaten relationships.

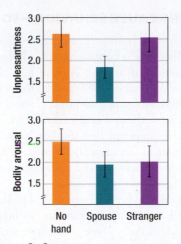

▶ **FIGURE 6.6** Holding someone's hand reduces how unpleasant stressful events are judged to be and even reduces bodily arousal, especially if the person is your spouse (Coan et al., 2006).

Having an enemy leads to fear or hate. Divorce and other forms of social rejection foster sadness, depression, and anger. Being treated badly or rejected unfairly causes anger. Doing something that hurts a loved one causes guilt. The threat that your partner might leave you for someone else causes jealousy. The prospect of being abandoned and alone causes anxiety. Losing a loved one causes grief.

Happy feelings often reflect healthy relationships (Gable & Reis, 2001), whereas hurt feelings often reflect damaged relationships (Leary & Springer, 2000). If you want to feel good and avoid emotional distress, the path is clear: Form and maintain good social relationships with other people! Social contact, especially with loved ones, can help people deal with stressful emotions. Women in one study waited to receive painful electric shocks (Coan, Schaefer, & Davidson, 2006). Stress responses (including brain scan measures) were greatly reduced if they were permitted to hold their husband's hand during the waiting period—especially if the marriage was a happy one. There was some benefit, though less, from holding a stranger's hand or holding hands with a husband in a not-so-happy marriage. Thus, a moment of physical contact with another person can reduce bad emotions caused by stress, and the greatest emotional boost comes from holding hands with someone you love. The results from this study are depicted in ▶ **FIGURE 6.6**.

The fact that emotions promote belongingness is yet another important instance of our general theme that what happens inside people serves what happens between people. Emotions (inner processes) help promote good interpersonal relations. People want to feel good and avoid bad emotions, and this desire impels them to try to form and maintain good relationships.

EMOTIONS CAUSE BEHAVIOR—SORT OF

Traditionally it has been assumed that emotions guide behavior. This view is consistent with what we know about physiological arousal. Arousal gets the body ready for action (Frijda, 1986; Frijda, Kuipers, & ter Schure, 1989). According to Frijda (1986), emotion does not exist without a readiness for action. Other theorists have proposed that implicit muscle movements are part of emotion (Berkowitz, 1993). That is, an emotion naturally and normally starts your body moving.

Then again, maybe emotions do not guide behavior. People have plenty of emotions without doing anything. Additionally, there is no single action associated with most emotions. Maybe fear prompts you to run away, but it is slow; if you depended on having full-blown fear, you would not escape fast enough. Maybe anger inspires you to fight, but most angry people don't fight. What is the behavior that is supposed to follow from guilt? From love? From joy?

The objection that emotion is too slow to guide behavior applies mainly to conscious emotion, of course. Automatic affect—the feeling of liking or disliking something—arises in a fraction of a second and therefore can be very helpful. When walking through a crowded room, you may meet someone unexpectedly, and you might have to decide whether to smile at that person or go the other way. The fast automatic reaction that tells you whether you like or dislike that person can be a big help. If you had to wait around for arousal to build and a full-fledged conscious emotion to occur, it would be too late to help you make that decision. *Food for Thought* talks about whether moods guide eating behavior.

When emotion causes behavior, it is often because the person wants to change or escape the emotional state. For example, researchers have long known that sad, depressed moods make people more helpful (e.g., Cialdini & Kendrick, 1976; Hornstein, 1982; Lerner, 1982; Reykowski, 1982). There are multiple reasons this could be true, such as that sadness makes people have more empathy for another person's suffering and need, or that sadness makes people less concerned about their own welfare. Then again, perhaps sadness makes people more concerned about themselves, in that they want to feel better. One team of researchers hit on an ingenious way to test this theory (Manucia, Baumann, & Cialdini, 1984). They put people in either a happy, sad, or neutral mood. They also gave everyone a pill. Some were told the pill had no side effects, but others were told that the pill would freeze or fix their emotional state for about an hour, which meant that whatever mood or emotion they currently had would continue for another hour. The point of this mood-freezing manipulation was that it made people think it was useless to try to feel better. The group of sad participants whose

pills supposedly had no side effects were more helpful than others, consistent with previous findings that sadness increases helping. But there was no rise in helpfulness among the mood-freeze participants. The researchers concluded that sad moods only lead to greater helping if people believe that helping will make them feel better. The emotion (sadness) does not directly cause behavior; rather, it makes people look for ways to escape the bad feeling.

There is another reason to suspect that the purpose of emotion is not directly causing behavior. When emotion does cause behavior, as in the so-called heat of passion, it often produces behaviors that are not wise or beneficial to the individual. For example, angry people often say and do things that they later regret, such as calling their boss an idiot (Van Dijk & Zeelenberg, 2002). Evolution favors traits that bring benefits and advantages. If emotions mainly caused foolish actions, then natural selection would have gradually phased emotion out of the human psyche. The irrationality of emotional actions is therefore a reason to suspect that the natural purpose of emotion lies elsewhere.

One seeming exception to the view that emotions do not cause behavior is communication. It seems that emotions are meant to be communicated and, in this sense, emotions do cause behavior. It may be natural to show one's feelings and artificial to hide them. Young children, for example, typically express their emotions freely and without reserve. As they grow up, they slowly learn to hide them sometimes, which is another sign that the influence of socialization is to restrain and conceal feelings rather than to instill them. Once again, nature says go and culture says stop!

EMOTIONS GUIDE THINKING AND LEARNING

As the previous section showed, emotion may or may not guide behavior directly. The link between emotion and behavior is far from clear, but emotion does influence thinking and learning. As we said earlier, emotions make up a feedback system that helps people process information about the world and their own actions in it. Emotions change the way people think and sometimes help them learn better.

A long-standing stereotype held that emotions undermine rational thinking and make people do foolish, crazy things. However, psychological studies have shown that people who lack emotions (often because of brain injuries or other problems) are not really better off. They have great difficulty adjusting to life and making decisions. Researcher Antonio Damasio (1994) described asking one such patient which of two dates would be better for his next appointment. The man spent most of an hour

Food for Thought

Mood and Food

People who feel bad often eat badly. For example, people who are depressed or lonely will eat so-called comfort foods that are typically rich in sugar, fat, and carbohydrates. Such foods are called "comfort foods" because they are often associated with childhood and home cooking (and thus the comfort of having a parent take care of you). They also provide a sense of well-being—at least until you start feeling guilty for eating them!

Many studies have linked food and mood. For example, in one study (Agras & Telch, 1998), participants were 60 obese women with binge-eating disorders. Binge eaters consume a large amount of food at one time. Sometimes they also feel out of control when eating. By the flip of a coin, half these women were assigned to fast for 14 hours, so they would be quite hungry, whereas the rest did not fast. All the women were then induced to have either a negative or a neutral mood, and then they were served a buffet meal (so they could eat as much as they wanted). How much the women ate depended on their mood but not on whether they had

fasted. In other words, being in a bad mood had a bigger effect on how much these women ate than how food deprived they were! The bad mood led to more eating, and eating seemed to help cheer the women up.

Other studies have reported similar results: Being in a bad mood leads to binge eating and a feeling of being out of control when eating (Agras & Telch, 1998; Telch & Agras, 1996). One study (Johnson, Schlundt, Barclay, Carr-Nangle, & Engler, 1995) compared binge-eating-disordered adults, nonclinical binge eaters, and adults who did not binge eat. All three groups overate in response to negative emotions. The effect of mood on food intake is not limited to people with eating disorders—it applies to all adults.

This doesn't mean that bad moods automatically or directly cause people to eat. Rather, eating seems to be a strategy for making yourself feel better. In one study, half the participants were told that eating would not change their mood. Then all were put into a sad, depressed mood by having them imagine they were the driver in a car accident that killed a child. Those

who had been told that eating wouldn't make them feel good did not eat any more than those in a neutral-mood control condition. Only those who thought eating might make them feel better indulged in heavy eating in response to the bad mood (Tice, Bratslavsky, & Baumeister, 2001). Thus, as noted in the text, it is wrong to say simply that emotion "causes" behavior. Emotional distress drives people to want to feel better, and they choose actions that they think will cheer them up. These findings are consistent with mood maintenance theory, which argues that people who are in a good mood try to maintain that good mood as long as they can (e.g., Handley, Lassiter, Nickell, & Herchenroeder, 2004). ●

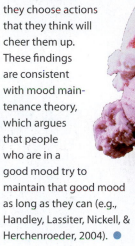

PhotoDisc

thinking of all the potential reasons to choose one or the other date, thus showing that he could analyze and think very logically, but he could not manage to choose between them. Finally Damasio just picked one date and the man immediately said "Fine!"

Research with such patients has also shown that emotions help people learn from their mistakes. Without emotions, people don't learn. In one study (Bechara, Damasio, Tranel, & Damasio, 1997), participants had to draw from various decks of cards. In some decks, the cards generally signaled that the participant would win a small amount of money. In other decks, the amounts of money were larger, but one could lose as well as win. Normal people with normal emotional responses would play the game by sampling each deck, and when they drew a card that cost them a large sum they would then avoid that deck for a while. The negative emotional reaction helped them learn to regard those decks as bad. The patients without emotion failed to learn. Even after they lost a big sum they would go right back to the same deck, often losing much more money in the process.

Thus, emotions help people learn. Bad emotions may help people think about their mistakes and learn

how to avoid repeating them. Sometimes this process is aided by counterfactual thinking, which Chapter 5 explained as a process of thinking about what might have been. Emotions make people engage in more counterfactual thinking (Roese & Olson, 1997), as in "I wish I hadn't said that," or "If I hadn't wasted time arguing on the phone, I would have gotten there on time," or "I should have asked that attractive person for his/her phone number."

Emotion can constitute valuable information that people learn about the world. According to the **affect-as-information hypothesis** (Clore, Gasper, & Garvin, 2001), people judge something as good or bad by asking themselves, "How do I feel about it?" If they feel good, they conclude that the thing is good. If they feel bad, then whatever they are dealing with must be bad. Research has shown that mood effects are eliminated when people misattribute their mood to an irrelevant source, such as the weather. In one study (Schwarz & Clore, 1983), researchers sampled phone numbers from the student directory, assigned them to sunny versus rainy conditions by the flip

AFFECT-AS-INFORMATION HYPOTHESIS the idea that people judge something as good or bad by asking themselves "How do I feel about it?"

of a coin, and waited for suitable days. The sunny days were the first two sunny spring days after a long period of gray overcast. For the first time in months, students went outside to play Frisbee. The rainy days were several days into a period of low-hanging clouds and rain. The interviewer pretended to call from out of town and asked a few questions about life satisfaction. The crucial manipulation was whether the interviewer first asked as an aside, "By the way, how's the weather down there?" This question was asked to draw students' attention to a plausible source of their present mood. Because the researchers weren't sure that this would work, they also included a condition in which the interviewer told students that the study was about "how the weather affects people's mood." The results showed that students were more satisfied with their lives on sunny days than on rainy days, but only when their attention was not drawn to the weather. Asking "How's the weather down there?" eliminated the effect of weather on people's life satisfaction.

When people are in an emotional state, they seem to see the world in a more emotional way, and this changes the way they process information. People put things in categories based more on their emotional tone than on their meaning. For example, does the word *joke* go more with *speech* or with *sunbeam*? People who are not having an emotion at the moment tend to group *joke* with *speech* because both involve talking (a logical grouping). In contrast, people who are happy or sad tend to group *joke* with *sunbeam* because both words have positive emotional meanings. Emotion thus attunes you to emotional connections out in the world (Niedenthal, Halberstadt, & Innes-Ker, 1999).

(ANTICIPATED) EMOTIONS GUIDE DECISIONS AND CHOICES

We said earlier that emotions are a feedback system, in the sense that they give us dramatic and powerful evaluations of whatever has just happened. In a sense, therefore, emotions focus on the recent past. Is that any help toward the future? One way they could help would be with learning, as noted above. Another, however, is that people can learn to anticipate how they will feel if something happens. As a result, they can begin to guide their behavior based on how they expect to feel. If emotion rewards and punishes behavior, then perhaps people decide how to act based on how they expect to feel afterward. They avoid acts that they expect will make them feel sad, angry, guilty, or embarrassed, and they favor acts that they think will make them feel happy, satisfied, or relieved.

Thus, *anticipated* emotion is important. Guilt is a good example: Guilt can really organize someone's life even if one hardly ever feels guilty. If guilt does its job, the person will anticipate and avoid acts that might lead to guilt. The person will end up behaving in a morally and socially desirable manner, and hence will almost never actually have to feel guilty.

Humans are the only animals that can travel mentally through time, preview a variety of different futures, and choose the one they think will bring them the greatest pleasure (or the least pain). **Affective forecasting** is the ability to predict one's emotional reactions to future events (Gilbert, Pinel, Wilson, Blumberg, & Wheatley, 1998). How do you think you would feel, and how long would this emotional state last, if (a) you won first prize in some athletic tournament, (b) you found out your romantic partner was having an affair with someone else, (c) you got a great job offer with a high starting salary, or (d) you were wrongly accused of cheating and had to withdraw from the university? Most people are fairly accurate at predicting which emotions they would feel, but they substantially overestimate how long they would feel that way. People also overestimate the intensity of their emotional reactions (Buehler & McFarland, 2001). The odds are that if any of these things did happen to you, you would get over it and return to your normal emotional state faster than you think. People are rarely happy or unhappy for as long as they expect to be. This error may occur because people focus too much attention on the event in question and not enough attention on other future events (Wilson, Wheatley, Meyers, Gilbert, & Axsom, 2000).

Is it a problem that our predictive powers are seriously flawed? It may be a blessing rather than a curse, according to social psychologist Dan Gilbert:

> Imagine a world in which some people realize that external events have much less impact than others believe they do. Those who make that realization might not be particularly motivated to change the external events. But one of the reasons we protect our children, for example, is that we believe we would be devastated if they were harmed or killed. So these predictions may be very effective in motivating us to do the things we as a society need to do, even though they might be inaccurate on an individual level. Anyone who wanted to cure affective forecasters of their inferential ills would be wise to measure both the costs and benefits of forecasting errors. (cited in Fiske, 2002)

Still, there may be some costs to predicting wrongly. Revenge, for example, is something people often pursue on the basis of affective forecasting errors (Carlsmith, Wilson, & Gilbert, 2008). People believe

---

AFFECTIVE FORECASTING the ability to predict one's emotional reactions to future events

that punishing someone who did something bad will bring them satisfaction and a feeling of closure. In reality, when people get revenge by punishing someone else, they continue to ruminate about the event and end up feeling worse than people who did not have the opportunity to take revenge. (The latter tend to move on and gradually forget about the issue.)

Anticipated emotion can be a powerful guide to behavior, though psychologists have only begun to study the ways in which this happens. Thus far, one of the most studied effects of anticipated emotion is anticipated regret. Mellers, Schwartz, Ho, and Ritov (1999) have argued that people make decisions more on the basis of how they expect to feel than on the basis of a fully logical, rational analysis of what will yield the greatest reward. Decision making shows a "status quo bias," which means that people tend to stick with what they have and be overly reluctant to make changes, even if changing would logically put them in a better position. Mellers et al. explain the status quo bias on the basis of anticipated regret: If you made the wrong decision, you would probably regret it more if you had made a change than if you had stuck with what you had.

Imagine this in the context of a romantic relationship: You have a reasonably good relationship, but someone else comes along who seems potentially an even better partner for you, though it is hard to be certain. According to the anticipated emotion theory, your decision will be based on considering how much you will regret either decision if it is wrong. If you stay with your pretty good partner even though the other partner could have been better, you may feel some regret. But you would feel even more regret if you dumped your pretty good partner and went off with the other one, and that turned out to have been a mistake. Anticipating the greater possible regret of making the second kind of mistake (dumping your current partner in favor of the new one) will bias the decision-making process toward staying with the status quo.

EMOTIONS HELP AND HURT DECISION MAKING

We have already seen that without emotions, people have trouble making up their minds. They can think through the good and bad features of different choices, but they have trouble settling on which one is best. Only recently has decision research started to take seriously the role of emotions in the choices and decisions people make (Connolly, 2002).

Evolution seems to have prepared humans and other primates to experience fear and anxiety in response to certain objects (e.g., snakes, spiders). Anxiety has been called "the shadow of intelligence" because it motivates people to plan ahead and avoid taking unnecessary risks (Barlow, 1988). According

to the **risk-as-feelings hypothesis** (Loewenstein, Weber, Hsee, & Welch, 2001), people react to risky situations based on how severe the worst outcome is and how likely it is to occur. They do this at a gut level. If their gut tells them the situation is too risky, they avoid it. (In terms of the duplex mind, gut reactions usually refer to the automatic system—in this case, automatic affective reactions.)

Strong conscious emotions can also influence people to engage in risky behavior and ignore future consequences. Sexual arousal often interferes with decision-making ability. For example, in one study (Blanton & Gerrard, 1997), men who saw sexually appealing photographs thought they were less likely to contract a sexually transmitted disease from a high-risk partner than did men who saw nonsexual photographs. Thus, their feeling of sexual arousal prevented them from appraising the danger accurately. Negative emotional responses to sex such as anxiety, guilt, and fear interfere with sexual behavior and also interfere with learning and retaining sexually relevant material, such as contraceptive information (Gerrard, Gibbons, & McCoy, 1993). Other negative emotions, such as depression, are associated with maladaptive decision making (Okwumabua & Duryea, 2003). To see how negative emotions affect how much money we spend, see *Money Matters*.

In summary, emotions call attention to good and bad outcomes but seem to make people disregard probabilities and odds. Anticipated emotions generally seem to help and inform decision making, but current emotional states can bias the process and lead to risky or foolish choices.

POSITIVE EMOTIONS COUNTERACT NEGATIVE EMOTIONS

Positive emotions are studied far less than negative emotions (Fredrickson, 2003). Compared to negative emotions, there are fewer positive emotions, and they are relatively undifferentiated. For example, it is difficult to distinguish joy, amusement, and serenity. In contrast, it is easier to distinguish anger, fear, and disgust.

What adaptive function do positive emotions serve? How did they help our ancestors survive? One possible answer is that positive emotions appear to solve problems of personal growth and development. Barbara Fredrickson has developed a **broaden-and-build theory** of positive emotions (e.g., Fredrickson, 1998, 2001, 2003). Positive emotions prepare an individual for later hard times. Positive emotions broaden and

---

RISK-AS-FEELINGS HYPOTHESIS the idea that people rely on emotional processes to evaluate risk, with the result that their judgments may be biased by emotional factors

BROADEN-AND-BUILD THEORY the proposition that positive emotions expand an individual's attention and mind-set

► **FIGURE 6.7**
Positive emotions broaden and expand an individual's attention and mind-set. These broadened mind-sets, in turn, build an individual's physical, intellectual, and social resources (Fredrickson, 2003).

Intellectual resources
• Develop problem-solving skills
• Learn new information

Physical resources
• Develop coordination
• Develop strength and cardiovascular health

Social resources
• Solidify bonds
• Make new bonds

Psychological resources
• Develop resilience and optimism
• Develop sense of identity and goal orientation

From B.L. Fredrickson, "The value of positive emotions," *American Scientist,* 91, 330-335. Reprinted by permission.

expand an individual's attention and mind-set. For example, joy broadens by creating the urge to play, push the limits, and become creative (Ellsworth & Smith, 1988; Frijda, 1986). These broadened mind-sets, in turn, build an individual's physical, intellectual, and social resources (see ► **FIGURE 6.7**).

Some research has shown that positive events are strongly related to positive emotions but not negative emotions, whereas negative events are strongly related to negative emotions but not positive emotions (Gable, Reis, & Elliot, 2000). However, in some studies, bad events affected both good and bad emotions, whereas good events mainly affected good emotions (David, Green, Martin, & Suls, 1997; Major, Zubek, Cooper, Cozzarelli, & Richards, 1997). In any case, this line of thought suggests that the value of positive emotions is found mainly in connection with positive events. Against that view, however, Fredrickson's work suggests that much of the value of positive emotions may lie in their power to overcome or prevent bad emotions.

OTHER BENEFITS OF POSITIVE EMOTIONS

Being in a good mood helps flexibility, creativity, and problem-solving ability. For example, in one study (Estrada, Isen, & Young, 1997), researchers put physicians in a good mood by giving them some candy. Physicians in the control group received no candy. Both groups of physicians were given a case of a patient with liver disease, and researchers timed how long it took them to diagnose the case. Physicians who received the candy were 19% faster and showed fewer distortions and more flexible thinking in comparison to physicians who received no candy. The results could not be due to a "sugar high" because the physicians were told to eat the candy after the study was over, and all of them waited.

Being in a bad mood does not help flexibility and creativity. For example, participants who thought about the French documentary *Night and Fog*, which is about the World War II concentration camps, did not perform better than individuals in a neutral mood (Isen, 2000). Thus, the effects are probably not due to mere arousal, because both positive and negative moods can increase arousal.

People in a positive mood also perform better, are more persistent, try harder, and are more motivated than people in a neutral mood (Erez & Isen, 2002). People are more motivated to perform tasks they enjoy doing, and being in a good mood makes tasks more enjoyable.

Being in a good mood can also serve a protective function. People in a good mood tend to avoid risks, such as in gambling (e.g., Isen & Patrick, 1983). People in a good mood want to remain in a good mood, and they would feel bad if they gambled away their earnings.

[QUIZ YOURSELF]

Why Do We Have Emotions?

1. _____ emotions are generally associated with forming social bonds, whereas _____ emotions are generally associated with breaking social bonds.
   (a) Unpleasant; pleasant
   (b) Pleasant; unpleasant
   (c) High arousal; low arousal
   (d) Low arousal; high arousal

2. According to the affect-as-information hypothesis, people judge something as good or bad by asking themselves which of the following questions?
   (a) "How do I feel about it?"
   (b) "What do I think about it?"
   (c) "When does it affect me most?"
   (d) All of the above

3. People generally _____ how long they will feel a particular emotion.
   (a) underestimate
   (b) accurately estimate
   (c) overestimate
   (d) All of the above, depending on whether the emotion is pleasant or unpleasant

4. Which of the following emotions motivates people to plan ahead and avoid taking unnecessary risks?
   (a) Anger   (b) Anxiety
   (c) Happiness   (d) Sadness

Group Differences in Emotion

ARE EMOTIONS DIFFERENT ACROSS CULTURES?

Do people in different cultures have different emotional lives? For many years experts assumed that the answer was yes. They thought that cultural differences would lead to huge differences in inner lives, so that you could not begin to understand how someone from another culture might feel. This view has lost ground, however, and some experts now agree that most emotions may be quite similar across cultural boundaries.

Paul Ekman and his colleagues have identified six basic emotions that can be reliably distinguished from facial expressions (see photographs): anger, surprise, disgust, happiness (or joy), fear, and sadness. These six basic emotions can be identified in many different cultures. A meta-analysis (Elfenbein & Ambady, 2002; also see Ekman et al., 1987) showed that people living in 37 countries on five continents could reliably recognize these six basic emotions from photos of facial expressions. These findings suggest that, based on facial cues, people have similar emotions everywhere and can recognize and understand one another despite their very different cultural backgrounds.

What about cultural differences in the expression of emotion? Differences in emotional expression are complex, and it is difficult to make global generalizations (Ellsworth, 1994; Mesquita & Frijda, 1992; Scherer & Wallbott, 1994). However, some consistent findings have emerged. Asian Americans generally place a greater emphasis on emotional moderation than European Americans. One study (Tsai, Chentsova-Dutton, Freire-Bebeau, & Przymus, 2002) examined facial and physiological responding to the six basic emotions in Asian Americans and European Americans. The study found many more similarities than differences. One exception was that during happiness, fewer Asian Americans than European Americans showed non-Duchenne smiles (the sort of smile you make to be polite, when you aren't really bursting with joy). Duchenne smiles (suggesting genuine inner joy) involve raising the corner of the lips and contracting the muscles around the eyes, a process that raises the cheeks or opens the mouth (e.g., Messinger, Fogel, & Dickson, 1999, 2001). Another study (Mesquita, 2003) compared emotions in collectivist and individualist contexts. In comparison to people from individualistic cultures, those from collectivist cultures experienced emotions that were based on assessments of social worth, were based more on

Six basic emotions that are recognized across many cultures (Ekman et al., 1987; Elfenbein & Ambady, 2002).

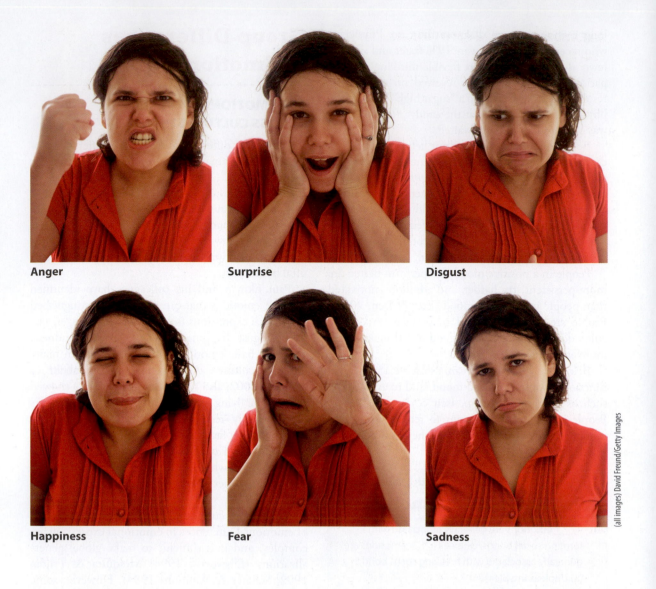

Anger   Surprise   Disgust

Happiness   Fear   Sadness

(all images) David Freund/Getty Images

the outer world than on the inner world, and were based more on self–other relationships than on the self.

James Russell, a longtime critic of the facial expression–emotion link, has critiqued Ekman's findings (Russell, 1994, 1995). Russell argues that Ekman's findings are based on carefully posed faces, whereas photos of spontaneous emotions are less easily recognized. Could it be that everyone can recognize posed facial expressions of emotion but not naturally occurring expressions during actual emotion? One reason for this might be that culture teaches people to conceal their emotions. One theme of this book is that nature says go whereas culture says stop. People don't need culture to teach them how to feel and show emotion. Culture does, however, teach people to hide their feelings, at least sometimes. Many people like children because they show their feelings so freely, but that may be merely because the children have not yet been socialized to hide their feelings. Adults who show all their feelings all the time risk being taken advantage of by others, as well as being

mocked or simply disliked. Because most adults have learned not to reveal all their emotions, their facial expressions during actual emotional reactions may be harder to read (especially by people from a different culture) than the expressions of people who are trying to make a particular emotional face, as in Ekman's research.

What should we make of the conflict between Ekman and Russell? Even if the cross-cultural recognition of emotional expressions were entirely limited to carefully posed faces, that universality would still be important. The fact that people can recognize the emotional expressions of someone from a different culture, even sometimes, shows that there is at least some natural way in which people everywhere are tuned in to the same basic emotions. If Russell is correct that members of different cultures learn to conceal or express their emotions differently, this is important too, but it does not contradict the underlying similarity. The emotional lives and expressions of adult human beings are a product of both nature and culture.

ARE WOMEN MORE EMOTIONAL THAN MEN?

A long-standing stereotype depicts women as more emotional than men. Women are supposed to be more readily overcome with feelings and to be more guided by them, in contrast to men, who make decisions based on cool, rational deliberation. Is this stereotype accurate?

A large-scale study by Larson and Pleck (1999) had adult married men and women carry beepers around. Whenever they heard a beep, they were supposed to stop what they were doing and fill out a quick rating of their current mood and emotional state. The researchers obtained thousands of emotion reports of what men and women felt as they went about their daily activities. The result? No gender differences. Men and women were remarkably alike in the degree to which they reported feelings at any point on the emotional continuum—strong bad emotions, strong good ones, mild bad, mild good, neutral. "There was simply no evidence that the husbands were less emotional than their wives," concluded the researchers (Larson & Pleck, 1999). They also tried breaking down the data into specific emotions, such as anger, guilt, nervousness, anxiety. Still nothing. Men and women had nearly identical reported emotional lives.

It wasn't just that the study was unable to find any differences. When the researchers looked at how people felt apart from emotions, some gender differences did emerge. Men were more likely to report feeling competitive, strong, awkward, and self-conscious, and women more often reported feeling tired. (Those feelings aren't what people normally call emotions.) The study was able to detect gender differences in some *feelings*—but in *emotions* there were apparently no differences to detect.

Could the lack of difference be hidden by where people spend their time? One group of researchers (Larson, Richards, & Perry-Jenkins, 1994) tried studying emotion separately at home and at work. Some gender differences emerged, but in the direction opposite to the stereotype of females being more emotional than males. With regard to negative emotions in particular, men reported more of these at work than women; indeed, men reported anger at work twice as often as women. Nevertheless, the researchers found little evidence that men and women differ greatly or that women are more emotional.

Other research with similar methods has obtained similar findings: Daily emotional experience is essentially the same regardless of gender (Larson & Pleck, 1999). Adolescent boys do report extreme positive feelings a little less often than girls, although there is no difference in negative emotions such as

Odd Anderson/ AFP/Getty Images

Duchenne smiles involve raising the corner of the lips and contracting the muscles around the eyes, which raises the cheeks or opens the mouth. In this photo, Venus Williams (left), winner of the 2005 Wimbledon Women's Singles, has a Duchenne smile, whereas runner-up Lindsay Davenport seems to be forcing a smile.

anger (Larson & Pleck, 1999). In laboratory studies, women sometimes report stronger emotional reactions (LaFrance & Banaji, 1992), although this outcome could be affected by social norms that put pressure on men to underreport emotional reactions. Lab studies that use physiological measures do not find women to show stronger reactions; if anything, those measures suggest that men sometimes have stronger emotional reactions than women (LaFrance & Banaji, 1992).

Observations on small children fit the view of greater emotionality in males. As far back as 1931, research showed that little boys have more frequent angry outbursts and temper tantrums than girls (Goodenough, 1931). Studies of infants either find no difference in emotionality or find that baby boys are more emotionally intense than baby girls (Brody, 1996; Buss, 1989; Rothbart, 1989). Observations of boys' play indicate that they seek out exciting, arousing themes but try to learn to manage fear and other emotions (Gottman, 1994). In games, boys put an emphasis on keeping their emotions under control so that feelings do not disrupt the game. Disputes are settled by appealing to abstract rules or, if necessary, replaying the disputed event, whereas girls' games are likely to end when emotion erupts. Partly for this reason, boys' games last longer than girls' games. Boys may find it more difficult than girls to calm themselves down when upset, so they work harder to avoid emotion in the first place. This pattern appears to be maintained in marital interactions: When married couples argue, husbands show stronger and longer-lasting physiological arousal than wives. As a result, husbands tend to avoid marital conflicts, whereas wives are more willing to argue and confront their spouse with problems (Gottman, 1994).

All these findings begin to suggest a very different conclusion: Men may be slightly *more* emotional than women, whereas women feel more willing to report their emotions and claim to have stronger feelings. Social norms may put pressure on men to stifle their emotions and not admit to having strong feelings, but the greater emotionality of women may be an illusion. Similar patterns are found in empathy research: On self-report measures, women claim to have more empathy than men, but when research uses objective measures of understanding the emotional states of others, no gender difference is found (Eisenberg & Lennon, 1983).

Love might be an exception: Men should be willing to admit being in love, and women are supposedly romantic and eager to find love. The view that women love more than men is contradicted by the evidence, however. Men fall in love faster than women, and women fall out of love faster than men (Hill, Rubin, & Peplau, 1976; Huston, Surra, Fitzgerald, & Cate, 1981; Kanin, Davidson, & Scheck, 1970). Men have more experiences of loving someone who does not love them back, whereas women have more experiences of receiving love but not reciprocating it (Baumeister, Wotman, & Stillwell, 1993). When a love relationship breaks up, men suffer more intense emotional distress than women (Hill et al., 1976).

In short, the traditional stereotype of female emotionality is wrong. Perhaps there is an understandable basis for it. Western society and culture have certainly put more pressure on men than on women to restrain their emotions and to refrain from expressing feelings. Hence as people observed each other, they would have seen women showing a great deal more emotion than men, which could produce the stereotype. Additionally, women have generally been stereotyped as being unable to handle responsibility and as being weak-willed—all of which would encourage a culture to stereotype women as emotional in order to justify denying them power.

Based on the research findings, one could even speculate that men are innately more emotional than women. The findings of greater male emotionality in love and work, plus during infancy, fit this pattern. Possibly male emotion has presented problems for society, as when male emotion leads to violence, risk taking, intoxication, and other potential problems. Holding up an ideal of men as cool, rational, and unemotional may be a way for society to keep the dangers of male emotion under control.

The general conclusion is that men and women have fairly similar emotional lives. They go through similar ranges of feeling in their daily lives. Slight differences can be found in special contexts—men get angry at work more often or fall in love faster than women—but these small average differences are overshadowed by the larger differences within gender. There are some signs that men's emotions last longer than women's. The apparent lack of gender differences in observed emotion may conceal a pattern such that boys and men are actually by nature more emotional but, as a result of this emotionality (and inability to get over the emotion), develop ways of avoiding emotionally intense situations and emotional provocations.

[QUIZ YOURSELF]

Group Differences in Emotion

1. How many "basic" facial emotions have been observed across dozens of different cultures?
   (a) Two   (b) Four
   (c) Six   (d) Eight

2. Which of the following lists contains only "basic" facial emotions (i.e., biologically determined, culturally universal in expression)?
   (a) Anger, disappointment, disgust
   (b) Fear, hope, surprise
   (c) Happiness, indifference, sadness
   (d) Happiness, sadness, surprise

3. Which group of Americans places the greatest emphasis on emotional moderation?
   (a) African Americans
   (b) European Americans
   (c) Asian Americans
   (d) Hispanic Americans

4. Which of the following is the conclusion of research evidence regarding emotional expression in males and females?
   (a) Females are more emotional than males.
   (b) Males are more emotional than females.
   (c) Males and females don't differ much in how emotional they are.
   (d) None of the above

Arousal, Attention, and Performance

We noted earlier that emotion contains arousal. Many people believe that emotional arousal is harmful—that it is better to calm down, especially when one is trying to make a logical decision or perform effectively in a crisis. Yet the arousal that goes with emotion seems designed by nature to make a person perform better, not worse. For example, when the person is aroused, more oxygen is sent to the brain and muscles than otherwise. So, is emotional arousal good or bad?

One answer is that the relationship between arousal and performance is an inverted U-shaped curve. That is, increasing arousal first makes for better performance, then for worse. Put another way, some arousal is better than none, but too much arousal can hurt performance. This view was proposed back in 1908 by Yerkes and Dodson (1908), based on studies with rats. ▶ **FIGURE 6.8** illustrates this **Yerkes–Dodson law**. The curve is lower for complex tasks than for difficult tasks because performance is generally lower for difficult tasks. In both cases, though, the link between arousal and performance resembles an inverted (upside-down) U, going up and then back down.

Arousal also seems good for narrowing and focusing attention. This is probably why people drink coffee or tea when they work: They want to be alert and focused, and consuming a drink that arouses them will produce that state. A famous theory by psychologist J. A. Easterbrook (1959) proposed that one major effect of arousal is to narrow attention, and this can explain both slopes of the inverted U-shaped curve that Yerkes and Dodson proposed. Easterbrook's main idea was that arousal makes the mind eliminate information and focus more narrowly. When people have very low arousal, they do not perform very well because the mind is deluged with all sorts of information (including much that is unhelpful or irrelevant, such as noise outside when you are studying), so it has a difficult time focusing on the task at hand. As arousal increases, the mind begins to screen out irrelevant information, which helps it focus better on the task at hand, and performance improves. At some point, corresponding to the peak on the curve and the best possible performance, the mind is processing all the information relevant to the task and nothing else. That's when you do your best work.

However, as arousal increases beyond that point, the mind continues to focus ever more narrowly—and this further narrowing requires that it throw out helpful, task-relevant information (because all the irrelevant information has already been screened out, so only the good stuff is left). Hence highly aroused people will be intensely, narrowly focused on what they are doing, but they may miss crucial information that is relevant or helpful. As a result, they end up performing worse than people with a moderate level of arousal.

The effects of stress on thinking appear to go along with Easterbrook's theory (Chajut & Algom, 2003). Under stress, people focus more narrowly on the task at hand, so up to a point, stress makes people perform

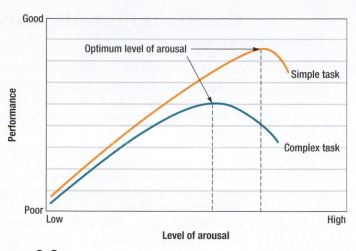

▶ **FIGURE 6.8** According to the Yerkes–Dodson law, some arousal is better than none, but too much can hurt performance (Yerkes & Dodson, 1908).

better—but beyond that point, stress makes people ignore relevant information. Research using multiple-choice tests has shown how this can happen. Under stress, people just scan the multiple answers until they find one that seems correct, and they pick that one, sometimes without considering all the options. Thus, if answer B sounds good, they might choose it without even considering answer D. This gets them done faster, but they may make more mistakes, especially if D was really a better answer than B (Keinan, 1987; Keinan, Friedland, & Ben-Porath, 1987).

YERKES–DODSON LAW the proposition that some arousal is better than none, but too much can hurt performance

Emotional Intelligence (EQ)

Many people with IQs of 160 work for people with IQs of 100, if the former have poor interpersonal intelligence and the latter have a high one.

—Howard Gardner

In the summer of 1987, Peter Salovey asked his friend John Mayer to help him paint the living room of his new house (Paul, 1999). Neither of them was a professional painter. Both were psychology professors who had done research on emotions. Generally, intellect and emotions are viewed as opposites. While painting, Salovey and Mayer wondered if there were points of intersection between the fields of emotion and intelligence. "Maybe it was the paint fumes," Mayer joked.

Three years later, they published an article on the topic of emotional intelligence (Salovey & Mayer, 1990). They defined **emotional intelligence** as "the ability to perceive emotions, to access and generate emotions so as to assist thought, to understand emotions and emotional knowledge, and to reflectively regulate emotions so as to promote emotional and intellectual growth" (Mayer & Salovey, 1997). Emotional intelligence is denoted by EQ rather than IQ.

The topic of emotional intelligence is widely popular in business circles. For example, when the *Harvard Business Review* published an article on the topic in 1998, it attracted more readers than any article published in the previous 40 years (Cherniss, 2000). When the CEO of Johnson & Johnson read that article, he was so impressed that he sent copies to the 400 top executives in the company worldwide (Cherniss, 2000).

In collaboration with their colleague David Caruso, John Mayer and Peter Salovey developed a scale to measure emotional intelligence called the Mayer-Salovey-Caruso Emotional Intelligence Test (MSCEIT; Brackett & Salovey, 2004; Mayer, Salovey, & Caruso, 2002; Mayer, Salovey, Caruso, & Sitarenios, 2003). The scale contains 141 items that measure four branches of emotional intelligence.

The first branch, Perceiving Emotions, is defined as the ability to recognize how you and those around you are feeling. It also involves perceiving emotions in objects, art, stories, music, and other stimuli. The second branch, Facilitating Thought, is defined as the ability to generate an emotion and then reason with this emotion. A sample item from this branch is given in ▶ **FIGURE 6.9**. The third branch, Understanding Emotions, is defined as the ability to understand complex emotions and how emotions can transition from one stage to another. The fourth branch, Managing Emotions, is defined as the ability to be open to feelings, and to modulate them in oneself and others so as to promote personal understanding and growth.

According to Mayer and Salovey, the branches are arranged from basic processes to more higher-ordered processes. The Managing Emotions aspect of emotional intelligence may be especially important. Recent work has found that people high on emotional intelligence are better than others at affective forecasting and less susceptible to common errors. That is, they predict their future emotions more accurately than other people. Scoring high on Managing Emotions was particularly conducive to being able to predict future emotions correctly (Dunn, Brackett, Ashton-James, Schneiderman, & Salovey, 2007).

Some evidence indicates that emotional intelligence may lead to success. For example, in one study (Lopes, Brackett, Nezlek, Schütz, Sellin, & Salovey, 2004), employees of a Fortune 400 insurance company who had previously recorded high emotional intelligence scores received greater merit increases, held higher company rank, and received higher ratings from peers and supervisors than did employees with low scores. The concept of emotional intelligence reached a much wider, popular audience through a 1995 trade book by Daniel Goleman, who used the concept in a much broader way to include more material. Goleman (1995b) equated emotional intelligence with "maturity" and "character," and he suggested that emotional intelligence (EQ) was a better predictor of success than IQ, though this was his own conclusion rather than a clear finding from scientific studies. Most likely, both "normal" intelligence and emotional intelligence have value for promoting success in life, and either one may be more useful in a particular field.

What mood(s) might be helpful to feel when searching a spreadsheet for errors?

	Not Useful				Useful
a. tension	1	2	3	4	5
b. rage	1	2	3	4	5
c. joy	1	2	3	4	5

▶ **FIGURE 6.9** Sample item from the Facilitating Thought branch of the Mayer-Salovey-Caruso Emotional Intelligence Test (MSCEIT).

From MSCEIT by John D. Mayer, Peter Saloway, and David R. Caruso. Copyright © Multi-Health Systems, Inc. Reprinted by permission.

EMOTIONAL INTELLIGENCE (EQ) the ability to perceive, access and generate, understand, and reflectively regulate emotions

Affect Regulation

One reason that emotional intelligence is beneficial is that it can help people control and regulate their feelings. When emotions run out of control, they can wreak havoc on inner and interpersonal processes. Indeed, so-called mental illness is often marked by severe emotional problems, and some experts have concluded that people who are poor at controlling their own emotional reactions are more likely to fall victim to such mental illnesses (Bradley, 1990; Greenspan & Porges, 1984; Van Praag, 1990).

Indeed, the importance of how people handle their emotional states was evident in the pair of stories with which we began this chapter. These concerned two men who were both upset about junk e-mail, but who regulated their emotions differently. One man (Charles Booher) responded with angry messages and threats, with the result that he was arrested. The other man (Brad Turcotte) used music and humor to transform the upsetting e-mail into a creative product that would entertain himself and other people.

Chapter 4 presented research on self-regulation, and we saw that the ability to self-regulate is important and valuable in many spheres of life. People do regularly seek to control their thoughts, desires, and actions. They often try to control emotions too, but there is an added difficulty: For the most part, emotions cannot be directly controlled. That is, if you are feeling bad, you cannot just decide to be happy and succeed by a simple act of will, in the same sense that you can drag yourself out of bed when you don't feel like getting up. Emotion control is a special case of self-regulation, and generally people have to rely on indirect strategies.

HOW TO CHEER UP

Thayer, Newman, and McClain (1994) undertook an ambitious attempt to map out people's affect regulation strategies. They used a series of questionnaire studies to find out what strategies people use to cope with a bad mood and make themselves feel better. Their list of strategies points to the different ways that emotion and mood can be altered.

One strategy is simply to do things that produce good feelings. People may cheer themselves up by eating something tasty, having sex, listening to music, or shopping (especially buying oneself a gift; Cohen & Andrade, 2004; Mick & DeMoss, 1990). A strategy that overlaps with this one involves simply doing something to take one's mind off the problem, such as watching television, changing one's location, avoiding the source of the problem, or taking a shower. Note that neither of these strategies addresses the original problem or source of bad feelings; instead, people seek to create a positive, pleasant state to replace the unhappy one.

Earlier in this chapter we saw that physical arousal is an important part of emotion. Hence for many people, raising or lowering their arousal is a promising strategy for affect regulation (Thayer et al., 1994). Arousal control strategies include exercise, drinking coffee or other caffeine, drinking alcohol, taking a nap, and using relaxation techniques. Exercise may be an especially interesting strategy because it first increases arousal but later, as one gets tired, reduces it.

Seeking social support is another common strategy for controlling emotion. People may call their friends when they feel bad. Others go out and actively seek others' company. This fits our theme of putting people first: Even to deal with their own problem emotions, people turn to other people. When you are upset about almost anything, you can go spend time with people who like you, and the odds are good that you will end up feeling better. Note that this does not solve the original problem that made you feel bad, but it does help you stop feeling bad.

A very different set of affect regulation strategies is based on trying to deal directly with the problem (the one that gave rise to the bad feelings) in some way. Many people report trying to reframe the problem, as by putting it into perspective or trying to see a conflict from the other person's side. Some try to use humor to make light of the problem and cheer themselves up. Others seek to vent their feelings, as by pounding a pillow, screaming, or crying (venting might feel good, but it usually just makes things worse). Religious activities such as praying help some people cope with their troubles; indeed, some studies have found religious activities rated as among the most effective strategies for regulating affect (e.g., Rippere, 1977).

To be sure, many of the strategies may work by more than one means. Exercise might bring both distraction and arousal control. Making jokes may be a way of spending time with others and reframing the problem as less serious than it seemed at first. Having sex may generate good feelings, distract one from the problem, and create a state of tiredness. If you're upset about having lost $100 because of a stupid purchasing decision, then making jokes or having sex or playing racquetball does not change the original problem in the least, but it could make you feel better.

Not all strategies are equally effective. Thayer et al. (1994) reported that the data are very complex, but if people had to choose one strategy as most effective, it might be exercise. Listening to music was also rated very highly as effective for changing a bad mood, as was seeking out social support. At the other extreme, watching television and trying to be alone were rated among the least successful ways of coping with a bad mood.

AFFECT REGULATION GOALS

In principle, affect regulation can have at least six different goals: One can seek to get into, get out of, or prolong a good mood, and the same three options apply to a bad mood (Tice & Bratslavsky, 2000). At first you might wonder why anyone would ever want to get out of a good mood or into a bad one, but in some situations it is inappropriate or even counterproductive to seem (or feel) overly happy. A physician may be in a terrifically happy mood one day, for example, but if he has to tell a patient that her illness is incurable and that she will die soon, a beaming smile may seem out of place. Likewise, an activist who has to present a case of injustice may find that an angry mood will be more effective than a cheerful, happy-go-lucky one.

In particular, people often seek to cultivate neutral moods prior to social interactions. In a series of laboratory studies (Erber, Wegner, & Therriault, 1994), researchers first induced good or bad moods by exposing participants to music, and then allowed them to select either cheerful or depressing reading material. Some participants expected to meet and talk with someone new; these participants chose reading material *opposite* to their current mood—happy people chose sad readings, and sad people chose happy ones—presumably as a way to bring them out of their current feeling and bring them into

a cool, neutral mood. (In contrast, people who did not anticipate an interaction chose mood-congruent readings—happy people chose happy readings, and sad people chose sad ones.) The implication is that people get ready for social interaction with a new partner by trying to get out of either a good or bad mood and into a neutral state.

Further work has shown that how people regulate their emotional states prior to social interaction is often very specific to the context (Erber & Erber, 2000). People who expect to interact with a depressed person often seek out positive stimuli that will make them even happier—possibly because they expect (rightly) that it will be depressing to talk to a depressed person and they want to fortify themselves with an extra good mood to help them resist being brought down. People who are going to interact with a close relationship partner do not seem to change their moods, possibly because they intend to share their good or bad feelings with the partner. In any case, it is clearly wrong to assume that all affect regulation is aimed at trying to feel better right away.

Sometimes people even seek to cultivate anger. People in one study preferred to listen to angry music rather than other types of music when they expected a social interaction that would require confrontation and assertion (Tamir et al. 2008; see ▶ FIGURE 6.10a). (In contrast, participants anticipating a cooperative or constructive social interaction chose other types of music.) Thus, people seemed to anticipate that anger might be a useful emotion in the upcoming interaction, so they chose stimuli to help them get and stay mad. What's more, it worked! The angrier participants performed better in the confrontational situation. The results are depicted in Figure 6.10b.

Thus, people seem to seek out emotions partly on the basis of what will be useful and helpful in their social interactions. This desire to be effective competes with the desire to feel good, of course. Many strategies of emotion regulation are simply aimed at the goal of getting out of a bad mood or into a good one (e.g., Larsen, 2000; Thayer et al., 1994).

GENDER DIFFERENCES IN EMOTION CONTROL STRATEGIES

Men and women may cope with bad moods in some different ways, although in general we support the view that men and women are more similar than different (Hyde, 2005). One general theory is that when feeling depressed, women frequently respond with rumination, as in thinking about the problem, whereas men more commonly try to distract themselves with other thoughts or activities (e.g., Nolen-Hoeksema, 1991). This may contribute to the higher rate of depression among women, because ruminating about why you are depressed is more likely to prolong the bad feelings than shifting your attention onto something more cheerful, such as a sports event or hobby. Men often seek to keep themselves busy doing some task or chore, which not only may take their mind off their troubles but may also furnish some good feelings of success and efficacy if they can achieve something useful.

Another difference can be found in what people consume. Women are more likely than men to turn to food when they feel bad (Forster & Jeffery, 1986; Grunberg & Straub, 1992). In contrast, men turn to alcohol and drugs to cope with the same feelings (Berkowitz & Perkins, 1987; Dube, Kumar, Kumar, & Gupta, 1978; Engs & Hanson, 1990; Richman & Flaherty, 1986). In a nutshell, women eat and men drink to regulate their moods.

There are other gender differences in mood regulation strategies (see Thayer et al., 1994). When seeking to feel better, men are more likely than women to use humor to make light of the problem (a tendency that some women may find annoying if they do not think the problem is funny!). Men are also more prone to report that sexual activity is a good way to improve their emotional state. In contrast, women are more likely to go shopping or to call someone to talk about the issue. Of course, as we saw in the earlier section on gender and emotion, men and women are far more similar than different in their overall experiences with emotion.

IS IT SAFE?

Is affect regulation a good idea? This chapter has emphasized that people have emotions for good reasons; if you prevent your emotions from functioning in their normal and natural manner, you may deprive yourself of their valuable guidance. We saw that people who lack emotions often have difficulty finding their way through life. On the other hand, we have seen that poor emotion regulation can also point the way to mental illness and other problems. How can this seeming contradiction be resolved?

You would not want to live without emotions entirely. Then again, emotions are an imperfect system. Sometimes, undoubtedly, emotions overreact to a situation; in particular, they may last past the point at which they have served their function. One expert described emotion regulation as "the ability to hang up the phone after getting the message" (Larsen, 2000, p. 129), and this seems a very apt characterization. Once emotions have done their job, it may be useful to be able to control them. In any case, culture teaches people that displays of emotion are inappropriate on many occasions. To be a successful member of almost any human society requires the ability to regulate one's emotional reactions to some degree.

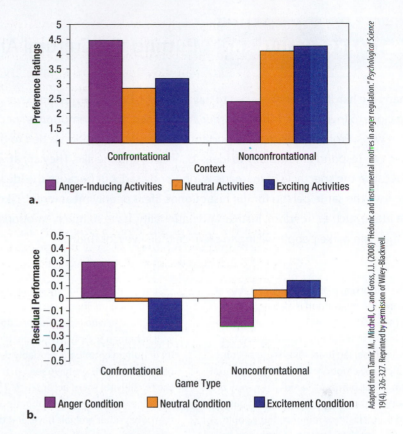

Adapted from Tamir, M., Mitchell, C., and Gross, J.J. (2008) "Hedonic and instrumental motives in anger regulation." *Psychological Science* 19(4), 326–327. Reprinted by permission of Wiley-Blackwell.

▶ **FIGURE 6.10** (a) **Preferences for anger-inducing, neutral, and exciting activities (i.e., listening to music and recalling events) when anticipating performing confrontational and nonconfrontational tasks. (b) Residual performance in the confrontational and nonconfrontational computer games, as a function of music condition.** (Tamir et al., 2008; pp. 326–327).

[QUIZ YOURSELF]

Affect Regulation

1. There is a(n) _____ relationship between emotional control and mental health.
(a) inverted-U
(b) negative
(c) null
(d) positive

2. What is the most effective strategy for improving a bad mood?
(a) Exercise
(b) Trying to be alone
(c) Watching television
(d) All of the above are equally effective for improving a bad mood.

3. Before interacting with someone who is depressed, what type of stimuli do people seek out?
(a) Angry
(b) Frightening
(c) Happy
(d) Sad

4. To regulate their moods, women tend to _____, whereas men tend to _____.
(a) eat; drink
(b) ruminate; distract themselves
(c) not use humor; use humor
(d) All of the above

Humans are hardly the only species to have feelings. Fear, rage, joy, and even something close to love can be found in other animals. But human emotion is special in certain ways. Probably the most important is that human emotion is tied to meaning. People can respond emotionally to ideas, concepts, and the like. They cry at weddings, not because the spectacle of marriage is inherently sad, but because the idea of pledging to love the same person for the rest of one's life is deeply meaningful. Likewise, some ideas, such as freedom, justice, and nationality, have so much emotional power that they can make people willing to sacrifice their lives for them.

The importance of meaning, and thus of ideas, in human emotion is also reflected in Schachter and Singer's (1962) theory, which emphasizes that a bodily reaction needs a cognitive label (an idea) in order to become a full-fledged emotion. Ideas are also central to human happiness. An animal is happy or unhappy depending mainly on what has happened in the last few minutes, but people can reflect on their lives as a whole and be satisfied or discontented. The power of ideas also enables people to suffer (or benefit) from misattribution of arousal, because the use of cognitive labels for inner states creates the possibility of switching labels or attaching a mistaken label. One emotion can be converted into another, as in the study in which fear and relief (from the suspension bridge) were converted into romantic attraction. Ideas can transform emotions, even after the bodily response is already in full gear.

Ideas also give human beings a larger range of subtle emotional differences than is found in most other species. As we said, many animals show fear, rage, and joy, but human beings have hundreds of different words for emotional states. Humans probably have so many different words for emotion because there are so many subtle differences in their emotional states. Being able to process so many subtly different ideas enables human emotion to be fine-tuned into many more subtly different grades of feeling.

Emotions are probably a vital help to people in navigating the long road to social acceptance. People who lack emotions do not fare well in human society. The distinctive complexity of human emotion is probably tied to some of the other tools we have seen that humans use to cultivate social acceptance. The human self, for example, is more elaborate and complex than what other animals have, and the complex self brings with it self-conscious emotions that inform and aid its activities. As an important example, the distinction between guilt and shame (doing a bad thing versus being a bad person) is probably beyond what most animals could understand; humans may be the only creatures who make use of that distinction.

Emotion is also linked to cognition (another tool used by humans on the road to social acceptance) in many and complex ways. We have already suggested that the human capacity for meaningful thought produces many more shades of emotional experience than would otherwise be possible, including many subtle distinctions between similar emotions (again, think of guilt versus shame). Humans are able to rely on anticipated emotion in their decision making, and even if their affective forecasting is sometimes off base, it can still inform and help human decision making in ways that would be impossible for almost any other creature.

The cognitive capabilities of human beings enable them to learn about their emotions too.

Emotional intelligence is a concept that may be largely useless in discussing most other animals, but many people develop an emotional intelligence that can sometimes be more useful than other forms of intelligence. Emotional intelligence—using the ideas associated with emotions—enables people to function and succeed better amid the complexities of human society and culture.

Emotional intelligence includes the power to regulate one's emotions (as in trying to control one's emotional state), and humans have cultivated that power much more than other animals. People learn how to conceal their emotions, which may be an important manifestation of the general principle that nature says go (that is, the same kinds of events produce the same emotions in all cultures) while culture says stop (people learn to hide or express their emotions differently depending on cultural norms and rules). Emotion regulation itself—such as in trying to stop feeling angry or to cheer up—shows how people deliberately exert control over their inner states. The very pursuit of happiness is also something that makes us human, because it depends on several unique human abilities, such as the ability to think about a different emotional state from what one is currently feeling, to form a goal of moving from one state to another, to integrate inner states across time (remember, only humans can understand happiness in terms of broad satisfaction with one's life in general), and to save up information about how to move from one state into a happier one.

Ultimately, emotions make human life more meaningful and satisfying. A human life without emotion would be handicapped because a person without emotions would be without an important tool, but there is more to it than that: A life without emotion would be empty and dull. Human beings care about their emotional lives in ways that other animals almost certainly don't.

chapter summary

WHAT IS EMOTION?

- Emotions are mostly outside our conscious control, even though we may feel them consciously.
- An emotion is a conscious reaction to something; a mood is a feeling state that is not clearly linked to some event; affect is the automatic response that something is good or bad (liking versus disliking).
- Positive affect encompasses all good emotions, such as joy, bliss, love, and contentment; negative affect encompasses all bad emotions, such as anger, anxiety, fear, jealousy, and grief.

EMOTIONAL AROUSAL

- Emotions have both mental aspects (such as subjective feelings and interpretations) and physical ones (such as a racing heartbeat or tears).
- James and Lange proposed that the bodily processes of emotion come first, and then the mind's perception of these bodily reactions creates the subjective feeling of emotion. Proponents of the James–Lange theory of emotion failed to find specific arousal patterns for different emotions.
- According to the facial feedback hypothesis, feedback from the face muscles evokes or magnifies emotions.
- Cannon and Bard proposed that the thalamus sends two messages at the same time in response to an emotional stimulus. One message is sent to the cortex, which produces an experienced emotion (e.g., fear). The other message is sent to the hypothalamus and autonomic nervous system, producing physiological arousal (e.g., increased heart rate).
- Schachter and Singer proposed that emotion has two components. One, the bodily state of arousal, is the same in all emotions. The other, the cognitive label, is different for each emotion.
- Sexual stimulation may affect the brain, the genitals, neither, or both.

- In excitation transfer, the arousal from one event transfers to a subsequent event.

SOME IMPORTANT EMOTIONS

- Affect balance is the frequency of positive emotions minus the frequency of negative emotions.
- Couples who have children are less happy than couples who do not have children.
- People who are alone in the world are much less happy than people who have strong, rich social networks.
- The hedonic treadmill describes the tendency to revert to one's usual level of happiness soon after an emotional event.
- Happiness is rooted in one's outlook and approach to life, as well as in one's genes.
- Forgiving others, being grateful for blessings, practicing religious beliefs, sharing good feelings, and being optimistic can all increase happiness.
- Happiness is linked to a variety of good outcomes, including health and success in life.
- Anger is an emotional response to a real or imagined threat or provocation.
- The catharsis theory holds that expressing anger produces a healthy release of emotion and is therefore good for the psyche, but research demonstrates that catharsis increases anger and aggression and has negative health consequences.
- Shame is usually destructive, whereas guilt is usually constructive.
- Guilt motivates people to do good acts and make amends to repair damage to relationships.

WHY DO WE HAVE EMOTIONS?

- At least two basic arousal patterns— pleasant and unpleasant—underlie emotions.
- Emotions comprise an important and powerful feedback system, telling us whether something is good or bad.
- Positive emotions are linked to forming social bonds, whereas bad emotions are linked to various events that end, damage, or threaten relationships.
- Emotion rarely causes behavior directly.
- People who lack emotions have great difficulty adjusting to life and making decisions.
- Emotions help people learn from their mistakes. Without emotions, people don't learn.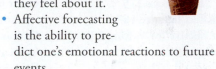
- According to the affect-as-information hypothesis, people judge something as good or bad by asking themselves how they feel about it.
- Affective forecasting is the ability to predict one's emotional reactions to future events.
- According to the risk-as-feelings hypothesis, people react to risky situations based on how severe the situation is and how likely it is to occur.
- Strong conscious emotions can also influence people to engage in risky behavior and ignore future consequences. Emotions call attention to good and bad outcomes but seem to make people disregard probabilities and odds.
- The broaden-and-build theory of positive emotions suggests that positive emotions expand an individual's attention and mind-set, which in turn, builds an individual's resources.
- Positive moods can increase flexibility, creativity, and problem-solving ability. People in a good mood perform better, are more persistent, try harder, and are more motivated than people in a neutral mood.
- Good moods can serve a protective function because individuals in a good mood tend to avoid taking risks.

GROUP DIFFERENCES IN EMOTION

- Six basic emotions have been observed in numerous cultures: anger, surprise, disgust, happiness, fear, and sadness. People of different cultures can reliably recognize posed facial expressions of these emotions.

- Men and women have similar emotional lives. Men may be slightly more emotional than women, but women may feel more willing to report their emotions and claim to have stronger feelings.
- Men fall in love faster than women, and women fall out of love faster than men.

AROUSAL, ATTENTION, AND PERFORMANCE

- Arousal serves to narrow and focus attention. Some arousal is better than none, but too much arousal can hurt performance.

EMOTIONAL INTELLIGENCE (EQ)

- Emotional intelligence is the ability to perceive emotions, to access and generate emotions so as to assist thought, to understand emotions and emotional knowledge, and to reflectively regulate emotions so as to promote emotional and intellectual growth.

AFFECT REGULATION

- People attempt to regulate their emotions by doing things that feel good, distracting themselves from negative emotions, controlling their arousal, seeking social support, or dealing with the emotion-causing issue directly.

WHAT MAKES US HUMAN? PUTTING THE CULTURAL ANIMAL IN PERSPECTIVE

- In humans, emotion is tied to meaning.

Key Terms

Affect 161
Affect-as-information hypothesis 179
Affect balance 167
Affective forecasting 180
Anger 171
Arousal 162
Automatic affect 162

Broaden-and-build theory 181
Cannon–Bard theory of emotion 163
Catharsis theory 173
Conscious emotion 162
Emotion 161
Emotional intelligence (EQ) 188

Excitation transfer 164
Facial feedback hypothesis 163
Guilt 174
Hedonic treadmill 169
James–Lange theory of emotion 162
Life satisfaction 167
Mood 161

Risk-as-feelings hypothesis 181
Schachter–Singer theory of emotion 164
Shame 175
Survivor guilt 176
Yerkes–Dodson law 187

[Quiz Yourself] Answers

1. What Is Emotion?
Answers: 1=b, 2=a, 3=a, 4=b

2. Emotional Arousal
Answers: 1=b, 2=c, 3=d, 4=b

3. Some Important Emotions
Answers: 1=c, 2=b, 3=a, 4=d

4. Why Do We Have Emotions?
Answers: 1=b, 2=a, 3=c, 4=b

5. Group Differences in Emotion
Answers: 1=c, 2=d, 3=c, 4=c

6. Arousal, Attention, and Performance
Answers: 1=b, 2=c, 3=d, 4=d

7. Emotional Intelligence (EQ)
Answers: 1=b, 2=b, 3=c, 4=b

8. Affect Regulation
Answers: 1=d, 2=a, 3=c, 4=d

Media Learning Resources

Make sure you check out the complete set of learning resources and study tools below. If your instructor did not order these items with your new book, go to www.ichapters.com to purchase Cengage Learning print and digital products.

Social Psychology and Human Nature
BOOK COMPANION WEBSITE

www.cengage.com/psychology/baumeister
Visit your book companion website, where you will find flash cards, practice quizzes, Internet links, and more to help you study.

CENGAGENOW JUST WHAT YOU NEED TO KNOW NOW!

Spend time on what you need to master rather than on information you have already learned. Take a pre-test for this chapter, and CengageNOW will generate a personalized study plan based on your results. The study plan will identify the topics you need to review and direct you to online resources to help you master those topics. You can then take a post-test to help you determine the concepts you have mastered and what you will still need to work on. Try it out! Go to www.cengage.com/login to sign in with an access code or to purchase access to this product.

CLASSIC AND CONTEMPORARY VIDEOS STUDENT CD-ROM

To see videos on the topics and experiments discussed in this chapter and to learn more about the research that social psychologists are doing today, go to the Student CD-ROM.

SOCIAL PSYCH LAB

These unique online labs give you the opportunity to become a participant in actual experiments, including re-creations of classic and contemporary research studies.

chapter 7

Attitudes, Beliefs, and Consistency

Money Matters: Would You Sell Your Soul For $1? p. 208

Food for Thought: Would You Eat a Bug or a Worm? p. 209

The Social Side of Sex: A–B Inconsistency and Erotic Plasticity p. 213

What Makes Us Human? Putting the Cultural Animal in Perspective p. 219

Janek Skarzynski/AFP/Getty Images

WHAT ARE ATTITUDES AND WHY DO PEOPLE HAVE THEM? p. 200
Attitudes Versus Beliefs p. 200
Dual Attitudes p. 200
Why People Have Attitudes p. 201

HOW ATTITUDES ARE FORMED p. 202
Formation of Attitudes p. 202
Polarization p. 205

CONSISTENCY p. 206
Heider's P-O-X Theory p. 206

Cognitive Dissonance and Attitude Change p. 206
Justifying Effort p. 207
Justifying Choices p. 208
Advances in Dissonance Theory p. 210
Is the Drive for Consistency Rooted in Nature or Nurture? p. 211

DO ATTITUDES REALLY PREDICT BEHAVIORS? p. 211
Attacking Attitudes p. 212

Defending Attitudes p. 212
Conclusion: Attitudes in Action p. 213

BELIEFS AND BELIEVING p. 214
Believing Versus Doubting p. 214
Belief Perseverance p. 215
Belief and Coping p. 215
Religious Belief p. 217
Irrational Belief p. 218

CHAPTER SUMMARY p. 220

Jack Kevorkian was born in 1928 in Pontiac, Michigan, the son of immigrants from Armenia who had fled to escape genocide during World War II. He was a brilliant child. School bored him. Once during sixth grade he was sent to the principal's office for throwing spitballs. The principal recognized that school was not sufficiently challenging and sent the boy immediately off to junior high school. Kevorkian also rejected the Orthodox Christian faith he had been taught. ‖‖‖

As a boy, Kevorkian wanted to become a sportscaster, but his family pushed him to do something more serious. He went to medical school. A memorable encounter with a middle-aged woman suffering intensely from incurable cancer left a deep impression on him. He thought that prolonging her life merely prolonged her suffering, and he felt that compassion for her dictated that she deserved a physician who would help her die if that is what she wanted to do. "From that moment on, I was sure that doctor-assisted euthanasia and suicide are and always were ethical, no matter what anyone else says or thinks," as he wrote later in his 1991 book *Prescription: Medicine.*

Death fascinated him. At the hospital where he worked, he tried to take photographs of the eyes of patients just before and just after they died. These efforts earned him the nickname "Doctor Death," which would later take on a different meaning. He accepted the nickname and even wore a black armband when he rushed through the building trying to set up his camera in time to record a death. The results of his efforts were published in a leading medical journal. Soon after that he began experimenting with transfusing blood from corpses to live patients.

Still the brilliant student, he mastered several foreign languages and began reading their medical journals. In one journal he came across evidence that the ancient Greeks had conducted medical experiments on condemned criminals. Intrigued, he visited Death Row at a nearby prison, and some of the convicted criminals said they would consent to being research subjects. He gave a speech at a medical conference advocating doing research on criminals (if they consented) during their executions, to improve medical understanding of the death process and other issues. The speech attracted some publicity. An animal rights group came out in favor, saying that this research would save the lives of lab rats and guinea pigs. Kevorkian's views embarrassed officials at the University of Michigan, where he was in residence as a physician, and they asked him to either cease his campaign or leave. He left.

In 1987 he started advertising in Detroit newspapers as a physician consultant for "death counseling." In 1988 he published an article with the title "The Last Fearsome Taboo: Medical Aspects of Planned Death." The article proposed a system of suicide clinics. People would be allowed to die as they chose, with their deaths planned in consultation with their doctors. Medical research could also be conducted in these clinics, allowing for the advancement of knowledge.

In 1988 Kevorkian built his first "suicide machine." It consisted of a gas mask attached to a canister of carbon monoxide. He made it from scrap parts from garage sales and hardware stores for about $30. He used it for the first time two years later. The first user was Janet Adkins, a 54-year-old woman who had Alzheimer's disease. She sat in Kevorkian's Volkswagen van. He helped her put the mask over her face, but she pushed the button that turned on the machine and terminated her life. Kevorkian was charged with murder, but a judge dis-

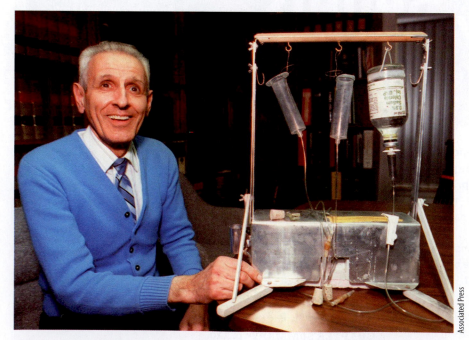

Jack Kevorkian and his suicide machine.

missed the case. Another judge, however, banned him from assisting in any more suicides.

Kevorkian defied the ban and helped more people commit suicide. The legal system struggled with how to deal with him. More murder charges were brought—but then dismissed. Some of the judges ruled that assisted suicide is a constitutional right, implying that Kevorkian's activities were legally acceptable. The authorities tried other tactics. His license to practice medicine was revoked. His home state of Michigan passed a law explicitly making it illegal to assist in suicide. But he continued to help people use his suicide machine. Typically they were old people with incurable and painful illnesses. More than 130 patients (or should they be called victims?) found death with his assistance. Kevorkian also gradually embraced his role as martyr for a cause. To court publicity, he refused to make bail and went on hunger strikes in jail. Once he showed up in court wearing a ball and chain and a homemade contraption resembling the stocks that colonial Puritans had used to punish and humiliate those who broke the rules in their community. His cause attracted some support. A group of other physicians declared support for assisted suicide, Oregon passed a "Death with Dignity Act," and there were scattered court rulings in favor of assisted suicide. A law to make physician-assisted suicide explicitly legal found its way onto the Michigan ballot, but voters rejected it.

Kevorkian is also an artist and jazz musician. In 1997 he released a CD titled *The Kevorkian Suite: A Very Still Life*, in which he played the flute and organ. The other musicians on the CD were from the Morpheus Quintet. In the liner notes, Kevorkian stated that Johann Sebastian Bach was his greatest musical hero. He also wrote that he was a big fan of jazz artists Benny Goodman and Artie Shaw. The CD cover contained an original painting by Kevorkian titled "A Very Still Life."

On September 17, 1998, Kevorkian administered a lethal injection to Thomas Youk, who was suffering from Lou Gehrig's disease (officially known as amyotrophic lateral sclerosis, a disease in which the brain can no longer control muscle movements because the motor neurons die). A videotape of the assisted suicide was shown on the CBS program *60 Minutes*. A jury found Kevorkian guilty of second-degree murder in the death of Youk. In his closing argument, the prosecutor described Kevorkian as a "medical hit man in the night with his bag of poison." The judge would not allow Thomas Youk's widow or brother to testify, calling their views irrelevant to a murder case. The judge sentenced Kevorkian to 10 to 25 years in prison for the killing of Youk, stating, "No one, sir, is above the law. No one. You had the audacity to go on national television, show the world what you did and dare the legal system to stop you. Well, sir, consider yourself stopped."

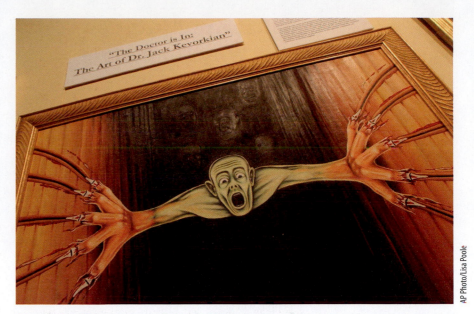

Oil painting titled "Nearer My God to Thee," by Jack Kevorkian.

Although the Youk family could not testify in court, they strongly defended Kevorkian's actions. Youk's widow, Melody, said her husband could control only his thumb and the first two fingers of one hand, and was losing his ability to speak and to digest food. Youk's brother, Terry, said, "The truth is my brother made that choice. He initiated the contact and Doctor Kevorkian fulfilled his wishes." Was Dr. Jack Kevorkian a murderer or a savior? The court considered him a murderer; the family of the deceased considered him a savior (Betzold, 1993; "Jury Deliberates in Kevorkian Murder Trial," 1999; "Kevorkian Gets 10 to 25 Years in Prison," 1999).

On June 1, 2007, Michigan's Governor Jennifer Granholm paroled Jack Kevorkian based on his good behavior in prison. On January 15, 2008, Kevorkian gave a speech to about 5,000 people at the University of Florida. He said that assisted suicide needs to be "a medical service" for willing patients. "My aim in helping the patient was not to cause death. My aim was to end suffering. It's got to be decriminalized," he said (Stripling, 2008).

This story about Dr. Jack Kevorkian anticipates several themes of this chapter. Attitudes exist in substantial part to help guide behavior, yet often it may seem that people act in ways contrary to their attitudes. When those seeming inconsistencies are examined more closely, however, consistency is often lurking nearby. Although Kevorkian was a doctor, and doctors are supposed to help people live rather than die, Kevorkian has consistently argued that people have a right to die and that physicians should help. Moreover, the story illustrates one of this book's themes—that inner structures serve interpersonal processes. ◼

What Are Attitudes and Why Do People Have Them?

The concept of the attitude is probably the most distinctive and indispensable concept in contemporary American social psychology.
—Gordon W. Allport, 1935

Why are attitudes so important? And why specifically to social psychology? Some attitudes seem trivial, but others are clearly important. Dr. Kevorkian went to prison because of his attitudes and the actions based on them. Throughout history, many people have suffered similar fates, and worse, for their attitudes. Attitudes are ideas—ideas that often determine how people will act.

ATTITUDES VERSUS BELIEFS

Attitudes differ from beliefs. **Beliefs** are pieces of information (facts or opinions) about something. **Attitudes** are global evaluations toward some object or issue (e.g., you like or dislike something, you are in favor of or opposed to some position) (Eagly & Chaiken, 1998). If you think that a certain person is president or that it is cloudy outside, that's a belief. Whether you like this person as president, or the clouds, is your attitude. Logically, attitudes are for choosing, whereas beliefs are for explaining. Beliefs and attitudes both serve interpersonal functions. People need to influence how others choose, and people also need to explain things to others.

DUAL ATTITUDES

"She says she likes jazz, but somehow she never seems to listen to it, and in fact when it comes on the radio she usually changes the station!" **Dual attitudes** are defined as different evaluations of the same attitude object: an implicit attitude and an explicit attitude (Wilson, Lindsey, & Schooler, 2000). This dual model of attitudes fits the duplex mind theme of this book. It is based on the notion that a person can have different, competing attitudes in the conscious as opposed to the automatic parts of the mind. **Implicit attitudes** are automatic and non-conscious evaluative responses. In contrast, **explicit attitudes** are controlled and conscious evaluative

responses. Implicit and explicit attitudes may conflict. Unconsciously you may like something that you consciously dislike (e.g., jazz music). In the United States few people from any ethnic group admit to holding racial prejudices, and most sincerely espouse the ideals of racial equality, yet many people show negative automatic responses toward other races (Fazio, Jackson, Dunton, & Williams, 1995; Greenwald, McGhee, & Schwartz, 1998).

The differences between explicit and implicit attitudes have led some researchers to propose that the two attitudes can be unrelated to each other and can serve different functions. Rather than experiencing conflict from holding discrepant dual attitudes, most people simply do not realize that they have an inner conflict. They think their only attitude is the conscious one, because that is what comes to mind when they think about the issue consciously. Russian novelist and philosopher Fyodor Dostoyevsky (1864/1961) wrote:

> Every man has reminiscences which he would not tell to everyone but only his friends. He has other matters in his mind which he would not reveal even to his friends, but only to himself, and that in secret. But there are other things which a man is afraid to tell even to himself, and every decent man has a number of such things stored away in his mind. (p. 33)

This quotation highlights two important facts about attitudes. First, there are some private attitudes that we would rather not share with others. Second, we may not be aware of all our own attitudes.

There are several different measures of implicit attitudes. Most involve measuring reaction times to stimuli. One popular measure is the Implicit Association Test (IAT), which measures attitudes and beliefs that people are either unwilling or unable to report. For example, one IAT examines implicit attitudes toward the elderly. The test shows that most Americans have an automatic preference for young over old people. First, participants report their explicit attitudes toward young and old people. For example, one question asks, "Which statement best describes you?"

> I strongly prefer *young people* to *old people*.
> I moderately prefer *young people* to *old people*.
> I like *young people* and *old people* equally.
> I moderately prefer *old people* to *young people*.
> I strongly prefer *old people* to *young people*.

Next, participants complete the implicit measure of attitudes. They classify words or images into categories as quickly as possible while making as few mistakes as possible. For the first test, they press one button if the words or images are "young or good" and they press another button if the words or images are "old or bad." The "good" words are *joy, love, peace,*

BELIEFS pieces of information about something; facts or opinions

ATTITUDES global evaluations toward some object or issue

DUAL ATTITUDES different evaluations of the same attitude object, implicit versus explicit

IMPLICIT ATTITUDES automatic and nonconscious evaluative responses

EXPLICIT ATTITUDES controlled and conscious evaluative responses

wonderful, *pleasure*, *glorious*, *laughter*, and *happy*. The "bad" words are *agony*, *terrible*, *horrible*, *nasty*, *evil*, *awful*, *failure*, and *hurt*. The images are faces of young and old people. For the second test, the pairings are reversed (i.e., "young or bad" versus "old or good"). Most people respond more slowly to the second test than to the first. Remarkably, this preference for young faces is just as strong in participants over 60 as in participants under 20! Thus, both young and old like young people better than old people. The authors of the IAT suggest that the preference occurs because the elderly are a stigmatized group.

The influential sociologist Erving Goffman (1963) used the term **stigma** to refer to an attribute that is "deeply discrediting" (p. 3). Other stigmatized groups include sick people, poor people, obese people, and mentally ill people (see Chapter 13 for more details). The people who developed the IAT claim that it is an indirect measure of prejudice. Other versions of the IAT use black and white faces, Arab and European faces, and fat and thin faces, instead of old and young faces.

People may feel that their group is better than other groups, but they may be reluctant to admit it so openly for fear of rejection by others. One study involving Greek and non-Greek college students examined attitudes toward sorority and fraternity members (Wells & Corts, 2008). The researchers paired names of sororities and fraternities (e.g., *Delta Omega Nu*) or names of academic and service groups (e.g., *Habitat for Humanity*) with "good" (e.g., *wonderful*) or "bad" words (e.g., *horrible*). As can be seen in ▶ **FIGURE 7.1**, Greek students were faster than non-Greek students in responding to sororities and fraternities paired with "good" words, whereas non-Greeks were faster than Greeks in responding to sororities and fraternities paired with "bad." Thus although Greeks and non-Greeks might not publicly admit their biases toward their own group, the IAT was able to detect these biases.

Critics suggest that the IAT is tainted by other factors, such as cognitive control capabilities (Gehring, Karpinski, & Hilton, 2003). Why might people respond faster when "old" is paired with "bad" than with "good"? Possibly because they think old people are bad. Alternately, "old" might be associated with "bad" because the media contain more bad information about old people than about young people. In other words, the IAT might measure personal attitudes, or perceived societal views, or some combination.

WHY PEOPLE HAVE ATTITUDES

Most animals don't need very many attitudes. They know what they like to eat (what tastes good), what fellow animals they like or dislike, and where they

Old or Bad

Young or Good

In the Implicit Association Test (IAT), participants press one computer key if the photo or word is "old or bad," and they press a different computer key if the photo or word is "young or good." Then the labels are reversed to "old or good" and "young or bad." Most people have faster reaction times when "old" is paired with "bad" and "young" is paired with "good" than when "old" is paired with "good" and "young" is paired with "bad."

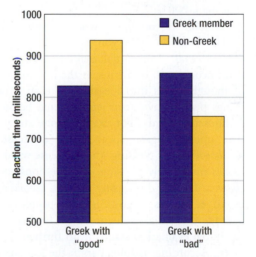

▶ **FIGURE 7.1**
Greek students were faster than non-Greek students in responding to sororities and fraternities paired with "good" words, whereas non-Greeks were faster than Greeks in responding to sororities and fraternities paired with "bad" words. (Based on data from Wells & Corts, 2008.)

like to sleep. Their world is not very complex, and a few simple attitudes can serve them well.

In contrast, human life is now highly complex, and people need to have a broad assortment of attitudes. People are asked to vote on many issues and candidates in elections. When shopping, they are presented with literally thousands of different choices within one supermarket or department store. Even if they know they want a particular product, such as a pair of gloves, they face a vast array of potential choices, and having some attitudes (e.g., mittens are

STIGMA an attribute that is perceived by others as broadly negative

better than gloves because they are warmer, or gloves are better than mittens because the fingers are more usable; leather is fashionable, but harder to maintain, plus some animal had to die; brown gloves might clash with my blue coat) can help. Attitudes are necessary and adaptive for humans. They help us adjust to new situations, seeking out those things in our environment that reward us and avoiding those things that punish us. Attitudes can even be a matter of life or death, influencing whether people take health risks or engage in healthy preventive behaviors.

Attitudes are mainly used to sort things into "good" and "bad" categories. The world is full of information (see Chapter 5), but just figuring things out and understanding them isn't enough. You can only make your way through a complicated world if you can sort things into good and bad. Sure enough, good and bad are among the most basic categories of thought. Although these categories are abstract, children understand them very early in life, especially the category "bad." In one study of children 2 to 6 years old, bad pictures were more readily identified than good pictures at all ages beyond 2 years, 5 months (Rhine, Hill, & Wandruff, 1967). This probably reflects one of the most basic psychological principles: bad is stronger than good (Baumeister, Bratslavsky, Finkenauer, & Vohs, 2001; Rozin & Royzman, 2001).

As soon as you know what something is, you start to know whether you like or dislike it (Goleman, 1995a). This initial evaluation is immediate and unconscious, occurring in the first microsecond of thought. This initial evaluation even occurs for things people have never encountered before, such as nonsense words. For example, one study found that among English speakers the nonsense word *juvalamu* is very pleasing, the nonsense word *bargulum* is moderately pleasing, and the nonsense word *chakaka* is very displeasing (Bargh, Chaiken, Raymond, & Hymes, 1996). Although people can easily override the initial evaluation with further thought, the initial evaluation stands if no further thought is given. According to John Bargh, the lead author on the study (and no doubt the inspiration for the word *bargulum*!), "We have yet to find something the mind regards with complete impartiality, without at least a mild judgment of liking or disliking" (cited in Goleman, 1995a). Put another way, people have attitudes about everything.

Attitudes are tremendously helpful in making choices. Perhaps it doesn't matter which person you think ought to be chosen to win the prize on *American Idol*. When you have to choose what courses to take next semester, however, you will find that attitudes come in very handy. Without attitudes, you face a bewildering array of options, all respectable intellectual endeavors, all taught by presumably competent faculty, all offering useful knowledge or at least something interesting. How can you choose, unless you have attitudes that say this course will be more interesting, or that one will be more useful to your chosen career, and that other one is likely to be dreadfully boring?

Previous research has shown that possessing an attitude increases the ease, speed, and quality of decision making (Fazio, Blascovich, & Driscoll, 1992). Thus, attitudes appear to have great functional value. In one study (Fazio & Powell, 1997), first-year college students completed measures of negative life events and health at two points in time. Students who entered college knowing their likes and dislikes on academically relevant issues experienced better physical and mental health in the new college setting than did other students. Attitudes are good for your health!

[QUIZ YOURSELF]

What Are Attitudes and Why Do People Have Them?

1. Which concept can be defined as pieces of information (facts or opinions) about something?
   (a) Attitudes   (b) Beliefs
   (c) Intentions   (d) Values

2. Which concept can be defined as a global evaluation?
   (a) Attitude   (b) Belief
   (c) Intention   (d) Value

3. Conscious is to unconscious as _____ is to _____.
   (a) explicit attitude; implicit attitude
   (b) implicit attitude; explicit attitude
   (c) primacy effect; recency effect
   (d) recency effect; primacy effect

4. Dual attitudes refer to _____ and _____ attitudes.
   (a) implicit; explicit
   (b) new; old
   (c) private; public
   (d) rewarded; unrewarded

How Attitudes Are Formed

FORMATION OF ATTITUDES

Several explanations have been offered for how attitudes are formed. We shall look at relatively simple explanations (mere exposure, classical conditioning) and also at more complicated explanations (operant conditioning, social learning).

Mere Exposure Effect. Most people have heard the aphorism "Familiarity breeds contempt." It is false. (Winston Churchill is said to have once rebutted the assertion that familiarity breeds contempt by pointing out that without a certain amount of familiarity, it is impossible to breed anything!) More than 200 studies have shown that "Familiarity breeds liking" (Bornstein, 1989). The **mere exposure effect** is the tendency for novel stimuli to be liked more after the individual has been repeatedly exposed to them. In 1968, social psychologist Robert Zajonc proposed that "mere repeated exposure of the individual to a stimulus is a sufficient condition for the enhancement of his attitude toward it" (p. 1). In plainer terms, just seeing something over and over is enough to make you like it. There is one qualification. If you initially dislike something, being exposed to it repeatedly will not make you like it more. In fact, it will make you like it less (e.g., Cacioppo & Petty, 1989; Klinger & Greenwald, 1994). For example, if you hear a song on the radio that you hate, the more you hear it, the more you will hate it.

To test his mere exposure hypothesis, Zajonc (1968) conducted three studies. Participants were exposed to Turkish words, Chinese-like characters, and yearbook photographs. The more frequently participants saw each stimulus, the more they liked it (see ▶ **FIGURE 7.2**). This mere exposure effect also occurs with animals other than humans, including crickets (Harrison & Fiscaro, 1974) and chickens (Zajonc, Reimer, & Hausser, 1973).

The mere exposure effect can also influence attitudes toward oneself. In one study, female college students chose a close female friend to participate in the study (Mita, Dermer, & Knight, 1977). The researchers took a photograph of the student and made two prints from it—a true print and a mirror (reversed) print. Participants liked the mirror print better than the true print, whereas their friends liked the true print better than the mirror print. Why? Both groups liked what they had been exposed to most frequently. People most commonly see themselves in a reversed image, as when they look in the mirror. In contrast, your friends mostly see your true image, because they look directly at you rather than seeing you in a mirror.

Classical Conditioning. Research has shown that both explicit and implicit attitudes can be formed through classical conditioning (Olson & Fazio, 2001). Ivan Pavlov, a Nobel Prize–winning Russian scientist, developed the theory of classical conditioning and demonstrated it in his experiments with dogs. Meat powder (**unconditioned stimulus**) makes the dog's mouth water (**unconditioned response**). The first time a researcher rings a bell (**neutral stimulus**), the dog's mouth does not water. However,

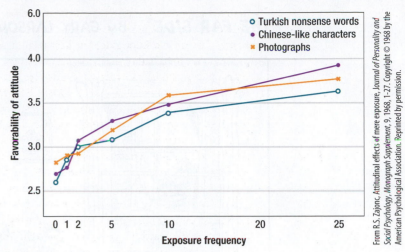

▶ **FIGURE 7.2** Relation between frequency of mere exposure to Turkish words, Chinese-like characters, and photographs and attitudes toward these stimuli (Zajonc, 1968).

From R.S. Zajonc, *Attitudinal effects of mere exposure, Journal of Personality and Social Psychology, Monograph Supplement, 9*, 1968, 1–27. Copyright © 1968 by the American Psychological Association. Reprinted by permission.

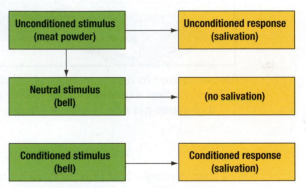

▶ **FIGURE 7.3** Ivan Pavlov proposed classical conditioning theory.

if the researcher rings the bell every time the dog gets meat powder, the dog begins to expect that every time it hears the bell it will be fed, and the bell becomes a **conditioned stimulus**. Eventually, the sound of the bell alone will make the dog's mouth water (**conditioned response**), even with no food around (see ▶ **FIGURE 7.3**). This principle is one of the foundations of the psychology of learning, and social psychologists have proposed that it could explain the formation of attitudes in humans. In a sense, Pavlov's

MERE EXPOSURE EFFECT the tendency for people to come to like things simply because they see or encounter them repeatedly

CLASSICAL CONDITIONING a type of learning in which, through repeated pairings, a neutral stimulus comes to evoke a conditioned response

UNCONDITIONED STIMULUS a stimulus (e.g., meat powder) that naturally evokes a particular response (salivation)

UNCONDITIONED RESPONSE a naturally occurring response (e.g., salivation)

NEUTRAL STIMULUS a stimulus (e.g., Pavlov's bell) that initially evokes no response

CONDITIONED STIMULUS a neutral stimulus that, through repeated pairings with an unconditioned stimulus, comes to evoke a conditioned response

CONDITIONED RESPONSE a response that, through repeated pairings, is evoked by a formerly neutral stimulus

THE FAR SIDE® By GARY LARSON

Unbeknownst to most students of psychology, Pavlov's first experiment was to ring a bell and cause his dog to attack Freud's cat.

dog developed a positive attitude toward the sound of the bell, where it had not had any attitude before, simply because the dog's positive attitude toward meat gradually became linked to the sound of the bell.

In a classic study (Staats & Staats, 1958), the word *Dutch* was systematically paired with positive words (e.g., *vacation*, *gift*), whereas the word *Swedish* was paired with negative words (e.g., *bitter*, *failure*). When tested afterwards, participants rated Dutch more positively than Swedish. The pairing was reversed for a second group of participants, and they rated Swedish more positively than Dutch. Classical conditioning may help explain the development of prejudice against social groups that are frequently associated with negative information in the media (Jonas, Eagly, & Stroebe, 1995), such as Arabs being associated with terrorism.

Advertisers use classical conditioning to their advantage by linking their products with famous or attractive people. For example, the shoe company Nike is named after the Greek goddess of victory. Famous athletes such as Michael Jordan and Tiger Woods have also endorsed Nike shoes. That's also why advertisers may cancel their contracts with famous people whose public perception abruptly changes. When football star Michael Vick was convicted of dog fighting and came to be seen as cruel to animals, sponsors stopped using him in their ad campaigns. It doesn't mean that the sponsors had opinions about the legality of his activities. They were simply invoking the principles of classical conditioning. They didn't want their product associated with someone the public disliked.

Operant Conditioning. Attitudes can also be formed through **operant conditioning** (also called **instrumental conditioning**). In this type of conditioning, developed by behaviorists such as Edward Thorndike and B. F. Skinner, participants are more likely to repeat behaviors that have been rewarded and less likely to repeat behaviors that have been punished. For example, if parents or teachers praise a child for doing well on math problems, then the child may develop a more positive attitude toward math. In one study (Bostrom, Vlandis, & Rosenbaum, 1961), students received either an "A" or a "D" (the grade was actually decided by the flip of a coin) on an essay they wrote (e.g., on socialized medicine). Even though the grades were randomly determined, students who received an "A" reported more favorable attitudes toward the topic than did students who received a "D." (Don't worry; your social psychology instructor won't be assigning grades in your class that way!)

Social Learning. By the early 1960s it became clear that conditioning by itself could not explain complex social behaviors. Social psychologist Albert Bandura theorized that the more powerful learning processes in understanding social behavior involved **social learning** (also called **observational learning**, **imitation**, or **vicarious learning**; e.g., Bandura, Ross, & Ross, 1961, 1963; Bandura, 1977). According to social learning theory, people learn how to behave by observing and imitating others. In several classic experiments, Bandura showed that young children imitated specific aggressive acts they observed in aggressive models, e.g., hitting a "Bobo" doll that they had seen an actor hit. Furthermore, he developed the concept of vicarious learning of aggression by showing that children were especially likely to imitate models that had been rewarded for behaving aggressively (Bandura, 1965; Bandura et al., 1963). Bandura argued that this imitation was the key to social learning. The idea is that people do not just imitate the specific social behaviors they see,

OPERANT CONDITIONING (INSTRUMENTAL CONDITIONING) a type of learning in which people are more likely to repeat behaviors that have been rewarded and less likely to repeat behaviors that have been punished

SOCIAL LEARNING (OBSERVATIONAL LEARNING, IMITATION, VICARIOUS LEARNING) a type of learning in which people are more likely to imitate behaviors if they have seen others rewarded for performing them, and less likely to imitate behaviors if they have seen others punished for performing them

but they make cognitive inferences based on their observations, and these inferences lead to generalizations in behavior. What is important is how the child interprets social events, and how competent the child feels in responding in different ways (Bandura, 1986). These cognitions provide a basis for stability of behavior tendencies across a variety of situations. Watching one parent hit the other parent may not only increase a child's likelihood of hitting. It may also increase the child's belief that hitting is OK when someone provokes you. Once again, the capacity to learn from others is important for enabling humans to be cultural beings.

Of course, social learning theory can also explain how attitudes are developed. For example, many teens learn what attitudes are acceptable by watching whether other teens are rewarded or punished for endorsing certain music, clothing styles, hairstyles, and convictions (Fiske, 2004).

POLARIZATION

Sometimes our attitudes about something can become stronger or weaker simply by thinking more about it. When we think about something, we may generate information that we did not consider when we formed our initial attitudes. Research suggests that as people reflect on their attitudes they become more extreme, an effect known as **attitude polarization** (Miller, McHoskey, Bane, & Dowd, 1993; Tesser, 1976; Wilson, Dunn, Kraft, & Lisle, 1989; Wilson, Hodges, & LaFleur, 1995). Even just thinking about an issue can move a person toward holding a more extreme attitude.

In addition, people who hold strong attitudes on certain issues are likely to evaluate relevant evidence in a biased manner. They tend to accept at face value evidence that confirms what they already believe, whereas they tend to be more critical of evidence that goes against their beliefs. Thus, even if people see an equal amount of confirming and disconfirming evidence (so that logically their attitude should not change), they become even more convinced of their initial attitudes and adopt them more strongly. The attitude polarization effect is especially likely to occur in people who have strong initial attitudes (Miller et al., 1993). In a famous study by Lord, Ross, and Lepper (1979), proponents and opponents of the death penalty read studies about the death penalty. The results showed that both groups were biased in favor of studies that matched their initial opinion on the death penalty. As a result, their attitudes became more polarized—the proponents became more in favor of the death penalty, whereas the opponents became more opposed to it. Attitude polarization occurs partly because people are reluctant to admit they are wrong. As they think more about an issue,

they tend to convince themselves that they were right all along.

Other studies show that people are more accepting of evidence presented by ingroup members (members of one's own group) than by outgroup members (members of a different group) (Mackie & Cooper, 1984). People are especially skeptical of evidence presented by outgroup members who are different from themselves. This reflects another theme we have seen repeatedly in this text: putting people first. People rely on others for information, and they especially rely on people who are similar to themselves. If people are biased to accept information from ingroup members, then most groups will tend to hold fairly similar opinions on many issues. This may make it easier for the group to work together. Alternatively, it may foster poor decision making. These issues are discussed in more detail in Chapter 14.

Many viewers' attitudes about musical performances have been shaped by watching the judges on the TV program *American Idol*.

M. Becker/American Idol 2009/Getty Images for Fox

[QUIZ YOURSELF]

How Attitudes Are Formed

1. Alissa heard a new song on the radio. A company used the same song in its advertising jingle, and the song was played over and over, so she was repeatedly exposed to the song. Alissa's attitude toward the song is likely to _____.
   (a) become ambivalent
   (b) become more negative
   (c) become more positive
   (d) remain the same

ATTITUDE POLARIZATION the finding that people's attitudes become more extreme as they reflect on them

2. If the word *pink* is followed by negative words and frowns from his mother, the toddler learns to respond negatively to the word *pink*. This is an example of _____.
   (a) classical conditioning   (b) operant conditioning
   (c) social learning   (d) verbal learning

3. Juan wasn't sure whether he was in favor of capital punishment or not. However, after receiving an "A" on a speech paper denouncing capital punishment, he decides that capital punishment is ineffective and inhumane. This is an example of _____.
   (a) classical conditioning   (b) operant conditioning
   (c) social learning   (d) verbal learning

4. After 3-year-old Davis sees his dad shaving, he covers his own face with shaving cream. This is an example of _____.
   (a) classical conditioning   (b) operant conditioning
   (c) social learning   (d) verbal learning

Consistency

Inconsistency does not much trouble dogs or bugs, but people feel some inner pressure to resolve it. To reduce their feelings of inconsistency, people may have to seek out new information or reinterpret old information, realign or even abandon cherished beliefs, or change patterns of behavior. People seem to strive for consistency. Indeed, the story about Jack Kevorkian that opened this chapter was full of consistency: He maintained his belief that it was right to assist suicides over many years, though this consistency cost him greatly and even landed him in prison. People don't like it when their beliefs, attitudes, and behaviors are inconsistent. (Nor do they approve of inconsistency in others!) This drive for

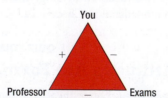

▶ **FIGURE 7.4** **You like your social psychology professor (+), but you hate exams (–), as does your professor (–). This cognitive structure is balanced because when the signs are multiplied, the result is positive (a negative times a negative times a positive equals a positive).**

BALANCE THEORY (P-O-X THEORY) the idea that relationships among one person (P), the other person (O), and an attitude object (X) may be either balanced or unbalanced

COGNITIVE DISSONANCE THEORY the theory that inconsistencies produce psychological discomfort, leading people to rationalize their behavior or change their attitudes

consistency is a central component of several theories in social psychology.

Most consistency theories have three things in common. First, they specify the conditions that are required for consistency and inconsistency of cognitions. Second, they assume that inconsistency is unpleasant and therefore motivates people to restore consistency. Third, they specify the conditions that are needed to restore consistency. In general, people choose the path of least resistance to restore consistency. Because attitudes are easier to change than behaviors, people often change their attitudes. We review the most influential consistency theories below. We then show how the duplex mind copes with inconsistency.

HEIDER'S P-O-X THEORY

In 1946, social psychologist Fritz Heider proposed **balance theory**. Balance theory is sometimes called **P-O-X theory** because it focuses on situations containing three elements (triads): the person (P), the other person (O), and the attitude object (X). Heider proposed that a person's understanding of the relationships among P, O, and X was either "balanced" or "unbalanced." *Balanced* is the term for consistency. (For example, the principle that "my enemy's enemy is my friend" is balanced, because there is something consistent about liking the person who has attacked your enemy.) A sign, + or –, is assigned to each relationship. To determine whether balance exists, simply multiply the signs together. If the outcome is positive, the cognitive structure is balanced (consistent). If the outcome is negative, it is unbalanced. For example, in ▶ **FIGURE 7.4**, you like your social psychology professor, but you and your professor both hate exams (you hate taking them and your professor hates writing and grading them). If you multiply the signs together, the outcome is positive, so the structure is balanced.

Balance theory states that balanced states are preferred over unbalanced states, and that unbalanced states motivate people to change them to balanced states.

COGNITIVE DISSONANCE AND ATTITUDE CHANGE

One of the most important applications of consistency to social phenomena is called **cognitive dissonance theory**. According to this theory, discrepancies between attitudes and behaviors produce psychological discomfort (cognitive dissonance). It is a theory about how people rationalize their behavior so as to bring their attitudes into line with their actions. We will examine the topic of persuasion in more detail in Chapter 8, but dissonance theory is an important special case of attitude change, because it centers on having people change their own attitudes.

The origins of cognitive dissonance theory lay in some confusing findings that emerged from persuasion research during its first flowering in the 1950s. At that time, psychology was dominated by operant conditioning theory (see "Formation of Attitudes" section earlier in this chapter), which was based on the simple idea that when people are rewarded, they will do more of whatever led to the reward. Applied to persuasion, operant conditioning theory held that the best way to get people to change their attitudes was to get them to act in the desired manner and then reward them for doing so. If you want people to like pumpernickel bread, get them to say they like it and then pay them big bucks for saying so. It sounded reasonable, but it never seemed to work very well. If anything, the people who said it for less money seemed to end up believing it more—opposite to operant conditioning theory.

Along came social psychologist Leon Festinger, who proposed that inconsistencies produce an unpleasant mental state called "cognitive dissonance." He said that people want to maintain consistency, so when they catch themselves being inconsistent they feel bad. The reason that paying somebody big bucks to claim to like pumpernickel bread didn't produce any actual liking was that the money resolved the inconsistency: "I don't really like it, but if you pay me a lot to say I like it, I'll say so." The more interesting case, thought Festinger, was when the pay was minimal: "I didn't think I liked pumpernickel bread, but I said I like it, and I was willing to say so without getting much money. I'm not a liar. I must really like it after all." *Money Matters* describes how one classic experiment provided evidence for this theory.

JUSTIFYING EFFORT

A second memorable study of cognitive dissonance, published the same year (Aronson & Mills, 1959), introduced the idea of **effort justification**. According to cognitive dissonance theory, people want to convince themselves that all their hard work and effort are worthwhile. (We saw how much Dr. Kevorkian suffered for his beliefs; perhaps that suffering cemented his belief in how right he was.) This particular study was stimulated by controversies on college campuses surrounding "hazing" initiations at fraternities and sororities. People who wanted to join those organizations often had to go through embarrassing or painful initiation rituals, such as being spanked or performing demeaning tasks for the older members of the organization. College administrators often sought to clamp down on these practices, but fraternity and sorority members said that these experiences helped forge strong ties to the group.

To reduce dissonance, people like to justify the effort they put into a task.

Dissonance researchers thought that perhaps the students were right.

The experiment by Aronson and Mills (1959) was disguised as a group discussion on sex, which back in the 1950s was pretty racy stuff. The participants were all college women who had signed up to join one of these groups. When the participant arrived, the experimenter (a man) said that the group had met several times already, and one problem had surfaced, which was that some people were too embarrassed to talk about sex. Did the participant think she could? All the women said yes. In the control condition, the experimenter said okay, she could join the group. But in the other conditions, he said that she would have to pass an embarrassment test. Some participants were given a mild test, in which they merely had to say a few words such as *virgin* and *prostitute* out loud to the male experimenter. Others, however, were given a more severe initiation in which they had to recite obscene words and read sexually explicit passages from paperback novels out loud to the male experimenter. For most participants, this was an embarrassing and unpleasant experience.

At the end of the test, the experimenter told each participant that she had passed and could join the interesting group. The supposedly interesting group turned out to consist of several biology graduate students droning on pointlessly about secondary sexual characteristics of insects such as cockroaches. The measure was how well the participant liked what she heard and how much she liked the group. The women

---

EFFORT JUSTIFICATION the finding that when people suffer or work hard or make sacrifices, they will try to convince themselves that it is worthwhile

Would You Sell Your Soul For $1?

In 1959, Leon Festinger and his colleague J. Merrill Carlsmith published a classic experiment to demonstrate how dissonance worked. It involved getting people to say things they did not really believe by paying them. The core question was how much pay would produce the most attitude change. Traditional reinforcement theory assumed that the more pay they received (the bigger the reward), the more people would come to believe what they said. Dissonance theory offered the opposite prediction: Small pay would produce the most attitude change.

Each participant came for a study called "Measures of Performance." The experimenter said it had to do with performing routine tasks, such as those found in factories. The experiment itself was excruciatingly boring. The participant spent the first half hour taking 12 little wooden spools off a tray one at a time, then putting them back on the tray, then off again, over and over and over. The second half hour was no better: The participant had to turn 48 square pegs a quarter turn clockwise, then again, and again, and again. Finally, when the participant was probably about bored to tears, the experimenter said that the study was over but then explained that there were some hidden wrinkles to the experiment— it was really about trying to motivate people to perform these routine, repetitious tasks. To do that, he employed a confederate who pretended to be a previous participant in the study and who would tell real participants that the task was fun, exciting, interesting, fascinating, and great. The

experimenter said the study's purpose was to see whether people who heard these glowing tributes performed better than others.

Then came the crucial part. The experimenter said that another participant was scheduled to arrive in a few minutes, and the confederate who was supposed to be there had called to cancel. The experimenter asked the participant to "fill in" and perform the confederate's job, which just entailed telling the next participant that the experiment was really interesting. Obviously this was false—the participant knew how deadly boring the task was—but the participant didn't want to refuse the request and so agreed to do what the experimenter asked. The experimenter paid the participant either $1 or $20 for performing this service. (Participants in the control group skipped this part of the experiment; they were not asked to lie and were paid nothing.) The next participant (who was actually a confederate) came in, the participant told this person that the task was really interesting, the confederate expressed some skepticism, the participant insisted, and the confederate finally agreed.

Later, in a different room, another researcher asked the participant to rate how much he or she had enjoyed the experiment. The results are shown in ▶ **FIGURE 7.5**. Participants had essentially lied for either $1 or $20, and they had a chance to undo the lie by convincing themselves that they did find the experiment enjoyable. Those who had been paid $20 did not say the task was enjoyable; their ratings were no different from those of participants who had not been asked to lie. They had experienced no

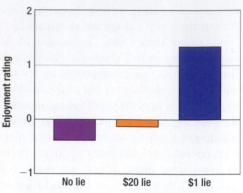

▶ **FIGURE 7.5** Participants in the Festinger and Carlsmith (1959) study who had been paid $1 to lie about how enjoyable the experiment was rated it as more enjoyable than did those in the other two groups, which were not significantly different from each other.

dissonance: They were willing to tell a lie for $20 (especially in the name of science; and $20 was worth a lot in 1959). But those who had been paid only $1 still had some dissonance, and they changed their attitudes. They said the task really had been interesting. It was a way of rationalizing their behavior so as to resolve the inconsistency: They could reassure themselves that they had not actually lied.

Thus, people are willing to do questionable things for large sums of money. But when they perform the same actions for a small amount of money, people feel a need to rationalize those actions, so they change their attitudes. ■

---

who had had no test or only a mild test didn't like it very much and said they didn't like the discussion or the group. But the women who had gone through the stressful, unpleasant initiation (the highly embarrassing test) rated the discussion and group much more favorably. As the fraternity members were saying, people who suffered more to get into a group ended up liking the group more. That was the only way to convince themselves that their suffering had been worthwhile. The mind's own drive for consistency is behind the process.

Thus, dissonance makes people seek to justify and rationalize any suffering or effort they have made. Perhaps surprisingly, dissonance reduction processes

can make people accept their suffering and even choose to continue it. *Food for Thought* describes how people will sometimes choose to suffer as a consequence of expecting to suffer, even if the choice is as unappealing as eating a worm!

JUSTIFYING CHOICES

The next big advance in cognitive dissonance theory was centered around something that, as we saw in Chapter 4, is very important to people: having a choice. (We also noted earlier in this chapter that attitudes are most helpful for choosing—so it would be useful and adaptive to review and revise attitudes

Food for Thought

Would You Eat a Bug or a Worm?

Would you eat a worm? Television reality shows like *Survivor* and *Fear Factor* typically include an episode in which people are asked to eat a variety of bugs, worms, and other foods that may be regarded as delicacies in some parts of the world but that strike most Americans as gross and unappealing, if not downright disgusting.

Yet social psychologists have found in multiple studies that if they set up the situational factors correctly, people—even modern American college students—will eat worms or bugs. This isn't because students think eating worms is about the same as eating dorm food! On the contrary, most start off with substantially negative attitudes toward eating such foods, but their attitudes can change.

One of the most thorough and revealing studies of worm eating looked at the underlying attitudes and beliefs that had to change (Comer & Laird, 1975). On the first day of the study, participants filled out questionnaires. On the second day, each participant was ushered into a laboratory room and told the task would be performed there. In one condition, participants were told the task would involve weight discrimination—whether they could tell which of two lumps of metal is heavier. The lab

was set up with a scale, some metal weights, and some paper. Other participants were told their assigned task would be to eat a worm. The lab was set up with a plate containing a (dead) worm, as well as a fork, a napkin, and a glass of water. The participant was left alone for a while, to allow time to get used to the idea. Then came more questionnaires, so the researchers could track people's thoughts.

After a time the experimenter returned and said he had made a mistake. Instead of being assigned the one task, the participant was supposed to be allowed to choose whether to do the worm-eating task or the weight discrimination task. Among the participants who had been told they were assigned to the weight discrimination task and then were given the chance to eat a worm instead, all (100%) said something to the effect of "No thanks!" All these participants stuck with the emotionally neutral weight discrimination task.

Among those who had expected to eat the worm and then were given the chance to do the weight discrimination task, however, most (80%) stuck with the worm. This may seem surprising, but the questionnaire data revealed that changed attitudes helped mediate the

choice. Most of these people had changed their views by increasing their belief that (a) I am brave, (b) I deserve to suffer, or (c) eating a worm isn't so bad. The people who failed to change any of these beliefs made up the 20% who jumped at the chance to do the weight discrimination task instead.

Thus, this study shows that sometimes people will choose to suffer as a consequence of expecting to suffer—but only if they have coped by changing some of their relevant beliefs and attitudes. ●

© Anders Ryman/Corbis

when making choices.) If you perform an action but do not have any choice, you don't have to rationalize it. In these studies (Linder, Cooper, & Jones, 1967), students were encouraged to write an essay saying that various controversial speakers should be banned from college campuses, which was contrary to what most students believed (they supported free speech and their own freedom to listen). Some were told that this was their assigned task in the experiment. Others were told "We would really appreciate it if you would do this, but it's entirely up to you to decide." Most people willingly agreed to the experimenter's request. Only the people in the latter (high-choice) condition experienced dissonance and changed their attitudes toward greater agreement with their essays.

People also experience dissonance when they make difficult choices. For example, should you major in A or B? Should you attend college A or B? Should you accept the job offer from company A or

B? Every decision involves tradeoffs (see Chapter 2), but people like to reduce their dissonance by justifying their choices. This type of dissonance is called **post-decision dissonance**. It is typically reduced by increasing the attractiveness of the chosen alternative and decreasing the attractiveness of the rejected alternatives.

Although choices seem to be good, too many of them may be bad. Too many choices can provide information overload and overwhelm people (see Chapter 5). Often people end up more unhappy as the number of choices expands. Barry Schwartz and his colleagues have described what they call the **tyranny of choice** (e.g., Schwartz, 2004; Schwartz,

POST-DECISION DISSONANCE cognitive dissonance experienced after making a difficult choice, typically reduced by increasing the attractiveness of the chosen alternative and decreasing the attractiveness of rejected alternatives

TYRANNY OF CHOICE the idea that although some choice is better than none, more choice is not always better than less choice

▶ TABLE 7.1 Maximization Scale (Schwartz, 2004)

Please rate each item on a scale from 1 ("completely disagree") to 7 ("completely agree").
1. When I watch TV, I channel surf, often scanning through the available options even while attempting to watch one program.
2. When I am in the car listening to the radio, I often check other stations to see if something better is playing, even if I'm relatively satisfied with what I'm listening to.
3. I treat relationships like clothing: I expect to try a lot on before I get the perfect fit.
4. No matter how satisfied I am with my job, it's only right for me to be on the lookout for better opportunities.
5. I often fantasize about living in ways that are quite different from my actual life.
6. I'm a big fan of lists that attempt to rank things (the best movies, the best singers, the best athletes, the best novels, etc.).
7. I often find it difficult to shop for a gift for a friend.
8. When shopping, I have a hard time finding clothing that I really love.
9. Renting videos is really difficult. I'm always struggling to pick the best one.
10. I find that writing is very difficult, even if it's just writing a letter to a friend, because it's so hard to word things just right. I often do several drafts of even simple things.
11. No matter what I do, I have the highest standards for myself.
12. I never settle for second best.
13. Whenever I'm faced with a choice, I try to imagine what all the other possibilities are, even ones that aren't present at the moment.
In large samples of college students, average scores ranged from 4.25 to 4.57. How does your score compare?

There are so many different socks to choose from. If they all were the same, they would always match!

Ward, Monterosso, Lyubomirsky, White, & Lehman, 2002). They developed a scale (see ▶ **TABLE 7.1**) to distinguish between two types of people: "maximizers," who always try to make the best possible choice, and "satisficers," who just try to make a "good enough choice" (even if there is a better choice they could have made). Their studies show that maximizers engage in more product comparisons (both before and after they make purchasing decisions), and they take longer to decide what to buy. When satisficers find an item that meets their standards, they stop looking. But maximizers never stop looking. They exert enormous effort reading labels, checking out consumer magazines, and trying new (and maybe "improved") products. Even though it is difficult (if not downright impossible) to check out every option, maximizers try to do just that. Even after making a decision, maximizers are not happy. They are nagged by the feeling that there is probably something better out there somewhere. Unfortunately, with this approach to life, maximizers are less satisfied with life, are less optimistic, and are more depressed than other people.

ADVANCES IN DISSONANCE THEORY

Another step forward came when researchers began to ask themselves what dissonance felt like. Was it an arousal state—that is, a bodily reaction in which the heart beats faster and in other respects the person seems more tense and nervous? In other words, does dissonance resemble an emotional reaction? A series of studies indicated that the answer is yes. When people performed actions contrary to their attitudes, they often felt acutely uncomfortable. If this feeling was blocked, they did not change their attitude. If they had this feeling but thought it was due to something else (specifically, a pill they had been given, along with instructions that the pill would make them feel tense and aroused), they did not change their attitudes (Zanna & Cooper, 1974; Zanna, Higgins, & Taves, 1976). Only people who felt discomfort and attributed it to their inconsistent behavior were driven to rationalize what they had done by changing their attitudes to match their actions. Dissonance is marked not only by arousal, but by an unpleasant arousal. It feels bad.

Another advance in dissonance theory linked the reaction to the interpersonal sphere. People may have some desire to be consistent in the privacy of their minds, but they have a much stronger desire to be seen by other people as consistent. We live in a social world in which people expect each other to be consistent. People who say one thing one day and something else another day are criticized as liars, hypocrites, gullible weaklings, untrustworthy or unreliable chameleons, and worse. It is important to act consistently when in the presence of others. This interpersonal dimension invokes the importance of self-presentation, discussed in Chapter 3: What is inside is often driven by what happens between people. Consistency may be yet another case in which inner processes serve interpersonal relations. On the long road to social acceptance, people learn that others expect them to be consistent and may reject them if they are not.

© Ty Milford/Masterfile

Many studies have shown the importance of self-presentation (that is, the effort to make a good impression or keep a good reputation) in cognitive dissonance. For example, when people act in ways that are contrary to their attitudes, the effects depend on who is looking. Writing an essay that violates your beliefs has little effect if it is done privately and anonymously, whereas if you have to put your name on it, you are more likely to feel dissonance and to change your attitude to match what you wrote. Recording some comments on an audiotape produces little dissonance, but saying the same thing on videotape (in which your face identifies you) produces dissonance and motivates attitude change. Telling someone that a task was interesting doesn't seem to have an effect if that person doesn't listen or doesn't believe you, but if you actually convince someone, then you feel a much greater need to convince yourself too. In the opening example of Dr. Kevorkian, consider how difficult it would have been for him to change his mind after he had become internationally famous for advocating doctor-assisted suicide.

IS THE DRIVE FOR CONSISTENCY ROOTED IN NATURE OR NURTURE?

Social psychologists have debated for decades the question of whether consistency is rooted in nature or nurture. Cultural variation would be one indication that it is learned. There is some evidence that the same basic drive for consistency can be found in very different cultures (Kitayama & Markus, 1999), but making choices does not seem to cause dissonance processes among East Asians the way it does for North Americans (Heine & Lehman, 1997; Hoshino-Browne, Zanna, Spencer, Zanna, Kitayama, & Lackenbauer, 2005; Kitayama, Snibbe, Markus, & Suzuki, 2004). On the other hand, the influence of social pressures toward consistency probably strengthens the drive. Either way, the root probably lies in the fact that groups of people can get along better if the people understand each other, and understanding each other is easier if people are somewhat consistent. People expect and pressure each other to be consistent, and people respond to these pressures and expectations by seeking to be consistent. Quite possibly the drive for consistency is rooted in our biological nature and strengthened by learning and socialization.

Most likely the drive toward consistency involves both parts of the duplex mind. The automatic system can learn to detect inconsistencies and send out alarm signals (distress, arousal). The conscious system then steps in and finds some resolution to the inconsistency by thinking about how to rationalize or rethink things. It is also possible that some modes of dissonance reduction are automatic.

Do Attitudes Really Predict Behaviors?

Psychology calls itself a behavioral science, which means that its main goal is predicting and explaining behavior. Attitudes are supposedly worth studying because they guide behavior. People act on the basis of what they like and dislike. Or do they? This is an important question, because if attitudes can't predict behavior, there would be little point in studying them.

Researchers have been examining the link between attitudes and behaviors for decades. An early sign that this link might be weak came before World War II. In the 1930s, many Americans did not like the Chinese for a variety of reasons, including a common perception that Chinese immigrants were taking American jobs. In 1934, a social psychologist named LaPiere (1934) and a young Chinese couple drove 10,000 miles across the country. They stopped at 184 restaurants and 66 hotels, auto camps, and tourist homes. They received service at all establishments, except for one dilapidated car camp where the owner refused to lodge them and called them "Japs." Six months later, LaPiere sent a questionnaire to the same establishments, asking whether they would accommodate Chinese guests. About 92% said they would *not* accommodate Chinese guests. This raised an early warning signal about attitudes: These business owners, at least, expressed attitudes that differed sharply from their actual behavior.

ATTACKING ATTITUDES

Most social psychologists had accepted Allport's assertion that the attitude is the most important concept in psychology. Accordingly, they were surprised when Alan Wicker wrote an article in 1969 arguing that attitudes were a trivial, peripheral phenomenon. After reviewing the results from 47 studies, Wicker concluded that attitudes did not cause behavior or even predict it very well. He went so far as to suggest that social psychology abandon the concept of attitude and that researchers go on to study more important things instead! He wrote, "Taken as a whole, these studies suggest that it is considerably more likely that attitudes will be unrelated or only slightly related to overt behaviors than that attitudes will be closely related to actions" (p. 65).

Once you set aside the assumption that people are generally consistent, it is not hard to find evidence that attitudes can differ from behavior. For example, a leader of an anti-pornography campaign was recently arrested with a prostitute. He had paid her for sex and was carrying a bottle of Viagra. To read about some interesting studies on attitude–behavior consistency in sexual behavior, see *The Social Side of Sex*.

DEFENDING ATTITUDES

Wicker's (1969) critique provoked a crisis in the field. Many social psychologists had spent their careers studying attitudes, and they were very disturbed to hear that attitudes were just little ideas flitting around inside people's minds that had no connection to what the people actually did. Attitude researchers circled the wagons to defend themselves, seeking ways to show how attitudes actually might have a closer link to behavior.

General Attitudes and Specific Behaviors. A first response in defense of attitudes was that the gap between general attitudes and specific behaviors was too big (Ajzen & Fishbein, 1977). Researchers might ask what someone's attitude was toward helping people and then measure whether the person was willing to donate blood. The problem is that someone might be in favor of helping people generally, but might be afraid of needles. In contrast, if researchers measured attitudes toward giving blood, these attitudes were much better predictors of whether the person would actually give blood. The solution, though it did help indicate that attitudes could predict behavior, sacrificed broad general attitudes and put a burden on researchers to measure a vast number of very specific attitudes rather than a few general ones.

Behavior Aggregation. Another solution to the problem of attitude–behavior inconsistency comes from aggregating behavior, which means combining across many different behaviors on different occasions (Rushton, Brainerd, & Pressley, 1983). A person's attitude toward helping others might fare better if we didn't measure behavior by a single test, such as giving blood. Instead, we could add up whether the person gives blood, plus whether the person donates money to charity, plus whether the person volunteers to work with the homeless, plus whether the person stops to help a handicapped person cross the street. A person with a more positive attitude toward helping others will perform more of these behaviors, and this could add up to a substantial difference, even though the general attitude's link to any single behavior may be weak or unreliable.

Broad Attitude in Context. A third solution is that general attitudes can help cause behavior, but only if they are prominent in the person's conscious mind and influence how the person thinks about the choices he or she faces (Fazio & Towles-Schwen, 1999). When asked to give blood, the person might say no despite having a favorable attitude toward helping others, because the person might not think of the question in terms of helping others. (The person might think of it in terms of being scared of needles, or of needing all his or her blood for a tennis match or hot date later that day!) If you first caused the person to reflect on his or her attitude toward helping others, then when the request for a blood donation came along, the person would see it as an opportunity to help, and hence the person's willingness to give blood would be shaped by that broad attitude. The broad attitude can influence specific behavior, but only if it has a chance to shape how the person interprets and construes the specifics of the here-and-now situation.

Attitude Accessibility. **Accessibility** refers to how easily the attitude comes to mind. Highly accessible attitudes can be quite influential because they come to mind very easily (Ajzen, 2001; Fazio, 1990). Obviously, an attitude that does not easily come to

ACCESSIBILITY how easily something comes to mind

the SOCIAL SIDE of SEX

A–B Inconsistency and Erotic Plasticity

As we have seen, attitude researchers have struggled with what they call the **A–B problem**, the problem of inconsistency between attitudes (A) and behaviors (B). In sex, there is ample room for contradictions between people's attitudes and their actual behaviors. One general prediction derives from the view that female sexuality is more open than male sexuality to influence from social, cultural, and situational factors (Baumeister, 2000). If that

PhotoDisc

is correct, then women should show lower attitude–behavior consistency than men, because women's sexual responses depend much more on the immediate situation and various other social influences. What a man wants may be the same regardless of context, but if the woman's sexual response depends on what it means and on other particulars, then her general attitude won't be as relevant as his.

Same-gender sexual activity is one place where attitudes and behaviors diverge. A major survey during the 1990s asked people both about their attitudes toward homosexual activity ("Do you like the idea of having sex with someone of your own gender?") and about their actual behavior ("Have you had sex with someone of your own gender during the past year?") For men, the two questions overlapped heavily: A large majority (85%) of those who favored homosexual activity had engaged in it during the past year. In contrast, attitudes and behaviors were much less consistent for women: Less than half of those who liked the idea had actually done it recently (Laumann, Gagnon, Michael, & Michaels, 1994).

The gender gap in consistency can be found in heterosexual behavior too. Multiple studies have looked at whether people engage in sexual activity of which they do not approve, and all have found that women do this far more than men (Antonovsky, Shoham, Kavenocki, Modan, & Lancet, 1978; Christensen & Carpenter, 1962; Croake & James, 1973).

Most people believe they should use condoms, especially when having sex with new or unfamiliar partners, but many

people fail to do so. The gap between pro-condom attitudes and non-condom-using behaviors is larger among women than men (which is ironic, given that a condom detracts from male enjoyment more than female enjoyment) (Herold & Mewhinney, 1993). Likewise, most people strongly favor being faithful to your partner if you have a committed relationship, but many people do occasionally indulge in kissing or sexual intercourse, or anything in between, with other partners. Again, women's behavior is more inconsistent than men's. In one study, men's attitudes regarding infidelity explained about 33% of their behavior, whereas women's attitudes explained only 11% (Hansen, 1987).

We saw that one solution to the A–B problem is for social psychologists to measure very specific attitudes. This doesn't resolve the gender problem, though. Several studies have measured whether people had sex on an occasion when they did not feel desire for sex. Both men and women do this (e.g., usually to please a partner who is feeling amorous), but more women than men do it (Beck, Bozman, & Qualtrough, 1991; O'Sullivan & Allgeier, 1998).

Apart from the special case of opportunity constraints, men's attitudes predict their sexual behavior much better than women's. The reason is not that women are generally inconsistent (indeed, there is no such general pattern outside of sexual activity). Rather, women's sexual responses are specific to the person, the situation, and what it all means, so their general attitudes are not highly relevant. In contrast, men tend to like and dislike the same things day in and day out, regardless of specific situations, so their general attitudes predict their behavior much better. ■

mind will have little opportunity to exert influence on thought, emotion, and behavior. One meta-analysis of 88 studies found that attitudes that are certain, stable, consistent, accessible, and based on direct experience are especially effective in predicting behavior (Kraus, 1995).

CONCLUSION: ATTITUDES IN ACTION

What, then, can we say about attitudes and behavior? Attitudes are essentially a matter of liking versus disliking things in the social world, and as such they are among the most basic and universal phenomena

that psychology studies. It is probably impossible for a human being to live without having attitudes. And, more to the point, when attitudes are lacking, it is difficult to know how to act. A central theme of this book is that inner processes serve interpersonal functions. Attitudes help us navigate through the complicated world of society and culture. Even just interacting with a group of peers would be difficult without attitudes. Attitudes tell you which people you like and which people you don't like, and shared

---

A–B PROBLEM the problem of inconsistency between attitudes (A) and behaviors (B)

attitudes about other objects (liking warm weather, disliking broccoli, liking a certain sports team, hating a particular music group) create bonds between people along with giving them much to talk about.

In retrospect, it seems a bit absurd that social psychologists questioned whether attitudes had any relationship to behavior. Why would the human mind be full of attitudes if they didn't affect behavior? Yet Wicker (1969) was correct in pointing out that the existing data at that time showed that people often acted in ways that went against what they had said their attitudes were. His challenge to social psychologists led to a productive rethinking of how to study attitudes and behaviors. Consistency is there to be found, but it is not as simple or as prevalent as many experts had assumed.

You can't always believe everything you read.

[**QUIZ YOURSELF**]

Do Attitudes Really Predict Behaviors?

1. In 1934, a social psychologist named LaPiere and a Chinese couple drove 10,000 miles across the country, stopping at numerous hotels and restaurants. The Chinese couple received service at all of the establishments except one. Six months later, LaPiere sent a questionnaire to the same establishments, asking whether they would accommodate Chinese guests. How many said they would accommodate Chinese guests?
   (a) More than 90%   (b) About 25% of them
   (c) About 75% of them   (d) Less than 10%

2. After reviewing the results from 47 studies, what did Wicker conclude in his 1969 article about the relationship between attitudes and behaviors?
   (a) It is almost perfect.
   (b) It is strong.
   (c) It is moderate in size.
   (d) It is so weak that the concept of attitudes should be abandoned.

3. According to Gordon Allport, what is the most important concept in psychology?
   (a) Aggression   (b) Attitudes
   (c) Discrimination   (d) Social influence

4. The best way to predict whether people will go see Rocky XXX is to assess their attitudes toward _____.
   (a) boxing   (b) films
   (c) previous Rocky films   (d) sports

Beliefs and Believing

Consistency is an important issue for beliefs just as much as for attitudes. You want your beliefs about the world to be consistent with the world.

BELIEVING VERSUS DOUBTING

"I understand what you're saying, but I don't believe it!" Clearly there is a big gap between understanding and believing. Or is there? Recent research has suggested that doubting/disbelieving is separate from understanding—but believing immediately, *automatically* accompanies understanding. Consider the title of one article on this pattern: "You Can't Not Believe Everything You Read" (Gilbert, Tafarodi, & Malone,1993)! As soon as you understand it, you believe it; only then, and only maybe, do you take a second step of changing your mind. If someone tells you the moon is made of green cheese, there is a brief moment when you believe it, even though you probably quickly change your opinion.

The difference is important. Believing and disbelieving are not on an equal par. If for some reason the mind is prevented from taking the second step of changing your mind, you might just go on believing that the moon is made of green cheese. People do not seem naturally able to take in information while withholding judgment as to whether it is correct or not.

The duplex mind may be implicated here. The automatic system automatically believes the information it is given. The conscious system can override this belief by deciding that it is false. If you only use automatic processing, you will believe lots of things that aren't true (Gilbert, 1991, 1993).

Children, for example, are notoriously gullible. If believing and disbelieving were equal acts that occurred at the same step, then children would first learn to understand without either believing or disbelieving anything, and then gradually learn to judge information as true or false. This is not what happens, though. Children first believe everything they are told, and only later learn to doubt and question (Gilbert, 1991). Likewise, in lab studies, people who are supplied with information while they are distracted (such as when the experimenter tells them to remember a phone number for later) end up believing things they are told more than people who are not distracted.

Out in the world, religious and political cults are sometimes accused of "brainwashing" their members into believing strange things. To strengthen belief in their ideas, they often make sure their converts are tired or distracted (even by physical pain, hunger, or discomfort) when the doctrines are presented. If you wanted people to understand your cult's ideas best, you would want them rested and alert when you presented your teachings, but if you want someone to believe everything, then you should present your ideas when the person is not at full mental power. Tired or distracted people do not make it to the second step (of doubt); they stop at the first step, which combines understanding and believing (Gilbert, 1991, 1993).

In short, when you understand something, believing it is automatic, whereas to doubt and question it may require controlled, conscious thought. The automatic system is fairly uncritical and accepts as true whatever it is told. The conscious mind can override this and change from belief to disbelief. But as we know, conscious activity requires time and effort, which people do not always have.

BELIEF PERSEVERANCE

Once beliefs form, they are resistant to change. This is true even of false beliefs that have been discredited. This effect is called **belief perseverance**. In an influential study by Ross, Lepper, and Hubbard (1975), participants were given 25 real and fictitious suicide notes and were told to identify the real ones. By the flip of a coin, participants were told either that they had correctly identified 24 of the 25 (success feedback) or that they had correctly identified 10 of the 25 (failure feedback). Both groups were told that the average was 16 correct. At the end of the study, all participants were told that the feedback they had received was bogus. Nevertheless, participants who had received success feedback thought they were more

accurate on the current test and that they would be more accurate on a future test than did participants who had received failure feedback. Participants thus continued to believe the feedback even though it had been discredited by the researcher.

A classic study about firefighters provided important evidence of belief perseverance (Anderson, Lepper, & Ross, 1980). Half the participants read cases suggesting that risk-taking people make better firefighters than cautious people, whereas the other half read cases suggesting that cautious people make better firefighters than risk-taking people. Both groups of participants were told to come up with theories explaining the cases they had read. Then participants were told that the study was over and that the cases they had read were bogus. However, participants did not abandon their firefighting theories, even though the evidence on which they were based had been discredited by the researcher.

The good news is that there is a remedy for belief perseverance. Explaining the opposite theory (e.g., why a cautious person might make a better firefighter than a risk-taking person) reduces or eliminates belief perseverance (Anderson & Sechler, 1986; Lord, Lepper, & Preston, 1984). If you want to understand things correctly, it is good to cultivate the habit of trying out the opposite theory to whatever theory you initially believe.

BELIEF AND COPING

Beliefs help people understand the world around them. This is especially apparent when people experience serious problems, such as misfortunes or disasters. The general term for how people attempt to deal with traumas and go back to functioning effectively in life is **coping**. The study of coping is an important opportunity for social psychologists to understand beliefs.

Something that puzzled psychologists for decades was that the psychological impact of trauma often went far beyond the physical or pragmatic harm. People are sometimes quite upset over having their apartment robbed, even though they may not have lost much of value and most of the loss is repaid by insurance. Some rape victims may be traumatized for years even though they suffer no lasting or permanent physical harm. How can these processes be understood? Bodily injury and money may be two components of trauma, but clearly there is something else.

BELIEF PERSEVERANCE the finding that once beliefs form, they are resistant to change, even if the information on which they are based is discredited

COPING the general term for how people attempt to deal with traumas and go back to functioning effectively in life

off the mark.com — by Mark Parisi

I CAN DEAL WITH IT... I'VE BEEN EATEN BY A SNAKE, BUT I'LL JUST GO ON WITH MY LIFE... I'M OKAY!

LEWIS TESTS THE LIMITS OF POSITIVE THINKING.

Coping is easier for some people than others.

One important answer is that a crime affects a victim's beliefs about the world. Social psychologist Ronnie Janoff-Bulman (1992) has called these beliefs **assumptive worlds**, a term that expresses the view that people live in social worlds based on their assumptions about how things operate. These include three main types of assumptions, all of which help people live healthy and happy lives, but any of which can be shattered when one is a victim of a crime:

1. **The world is benevolent**. Basically, people are nice, life is safe, and one can count on good things happening most of the time. The opposite belief is that the world is a dangerous place full of evil, untrustworthy people.

2. **The world is fair and just**. The world is fair, so people generally get what they deserve. If you follow the rules and treat others with fairness and kindness, you can expect to be treated that way yourself.

3. **I am a good person**. I am someone of value and therefore deserve good things to happen to me.

If someone steals your wallet, or vandalizes your car, or assaults you during a stroll in the park, this creates a problem because it violates those beliefs. As you try to explain to yourself how such a thing can happen, you may feel that you cannot continue to maintain those three beliefs as well as you did before. Ultimately, effective coping may involve figuring out how to explain the crime while still permitting yourself to continue believing that, by and large, the world is benevolent and fair and you are a good person who deserves good things.

This view of coping helps explain a surprising finding that emerged from one of Janoff-Bulman's early studies (Bulman & Wortman, 1977), which concluded that blaming oneself is often a good way to cope. That study interviewed individuals who had been paralyzed in serious accidents. All the victims had asked the question "Why me?" and nearly all had come up with an answer. To the researchers' surprise, it did not seem to matter what explanation they came up with—fate, God's will, their own mistakes, or other factors. The big difference was whether they did or did not have an explanation. Those who had found an explanation coped better than those who had not, as rated by hospital staff and others. This finding was surprising because most psychologists at the time assumed that blaming oneself for misfortune or trauma would be bad for the person. Therapists who heard a patient blame himself or herself would often rush in to insist that such an explanation was wrong, and the person should avoid self-blame. Yet self-blame seemed to work just fine in helping people cope. The researchers' explanation was that blaming oneself can actually help people achieve a sense of control. The paralyzed victims would say things like "It was my fault; I was driving too fast" or "I wanted to impress my friends, so I jumped, even though I knew it was risky." If people believe that their own foolish actions caused their misfortunes, it helps them feel that they can avoid future misfortunes by not repeating those mistakes. In contrast, people who cannot explain their misfortunes to themselves are more likely to think that something bad could happen to them again, regardless of what they do. They feel much more vulnerable and have a hard time getting over what happened.

Not all self-blame is good, of course. Janoff-Bulman thoughtfully distinguished between blaming oneself for one's actions, as opposed to blaming oneself for being a bad person. Someone who reacts to being robbed or injured by thinking "I am a worthless person and I deserve to have bad things happen to me" is not going to bounce back very effectively. It is much more helpful to think "I am basically a good and competent person, and I foolishly took a risk that brought this harm to me—so if I act more wisely in the future, I can avoid further problems."

The upshot is that mental processes play a central role in helping people cope with and recover from misfortunes. A broad theory of **cognitive coping** was put forward by Shelley Taylor (1983), who outlined

Reprinted by permission of Atlantic Feature Syndicate/Mark Parisi.

ASSUMPTIVE WORLDS the view that people live in social worlds based on certain beliefs (assumptions) about reality

COGNITIVE COPING the idea that beliefs play a central role in helping people cope with and recover from misfortunes

Victims of purse snatching and similar crimes are often more upset than the financial loss or inconvenience would warrant. Such events can change one's view of the world.

several kinds of beliefs that need to be bolstered or restored in the wake of trauma. Her original work focused on women who had breast cancer, but the ideas have been applied in many other contexts since then.

One important type of cognitive coping is based on the belief that whatever happened could have been worse, so at least the person was somewhat lucky. The technical term for this is **downward comparison** (Wills, 1981). People compare themselves and their situations to other people who are worse off, and this makes people feel better about themselves. For example, women whose breast cancer resulted in surgery to remove a lump from the breast compared themselves to others who had lost an entire breast. The reverse comparison was rare or absent: No women who lost an entire breast compared themselves with women who had only had the lumpectomy. In everyday life, many people seem to understand this principle, because "It could have been a lot worse" is a standard phrase that people say to someone to whom something bad has just happened.

Other beliefs in cognitive coping pertain to self-esteem and control. Victims of trauma and misfortune often need to find some way to restore their belief that they are good people and that they can exert control over what happens to them. Taylor observed that many women cultivated beliefs that they could control their cancer and prevent it from coming back, even though these beliefs often had little or no medical validity. The women thought that by eating certain foods or acting in a certain way (even by getting a divorce), they could keep themselves safe. These beliefs, although wrong according to medical knowledge (and many were later proven wrong, because the cancer did eventually come back), were a great source of comfort.

Still another type of helpful belief is that all things have some useful or higher purpose. The majority of women in Taylor's research sample reported positive changes in their lives that had come from having breast cancer. Many said they had learned to appreciate what was truly important in life, such as love and family, and had learned not to get upset over minor things. Religious beliefs are also helpful to people under these circumstances, because people can accept on faith that God has some purpose for letting these misfortunes occur to them, or even that their suffering has helped test and cement their faith. Others look to their own good deeds. A woman named Maureen Fischer suffered badly when her 3-year-old daughter died from a brain tumor, but she turned this tragedy into something good by raising money for and founding a hospitality lodge where families with very sick children could come for free vacations. In this way, her daughter's death helped her find a way to bring joy and comfort to many suffering families.

When people encounter disasters or suffering, their beliefs must help them get by, and sometimes these beliefs must change. Even so, consistency is important in dictating whether beliefs will be helpful or not. Some traumas seem to contradict beliefs—such as assumptions about the world being a safe, benevolent, and fair place—that people need in order to go on living. Coping requires finding a way to make the trauma seem compatible or even consistent with those beliefs. Other beliefs help frame the problem in a way that makes it more tolerable, such as believing that the misfortune could have been much worse, or believing that the bad event led to some good purpose.

RELIGIOUS BELIEF

Religion involves a very important category of beliefs. Science cannot generally say anything about

---

DOWNWARD COMPARISON comparing oneself to people who are worse off

Wildfire burns 500 acres and forces the evacuation of more than 50,000 homes in Santa Barbara, California.

Mark Ralston/AFP/Getty Images

whether religious beliefs are true or false. Regardless of objective truth, however, psychology can shed light on why some people accept religious beliefs while other people reject those same beliefs. It can also explore the benefits that people get from believing in religion, again regardless of whether those beliefs are true.

The appeal of religion throughout history has been partly its ability to explain the world, especially those things that cannot be explained by science. Religion can explain both large and small things. It can explain grand issues, such as where the sun, earth, and moon came from, where the person (or soul) existed before birth, and what happens after death; but religion can also explain smaller things, such as why your child got sick. Religion can also provide other benefits, including social support, a sense of meaning, purpose, and direction for one's life, and an environment that fosters the development of virtues such as honesty or integrity (Exline, 2002). Religious beliefs can help people cope with stress (e.g., Pargament, 1997; Smith, McCullough, & Poll, 2003). For example, people recover more quickly from being sexually assaulted if they use religion to cope with the traumatic event (Frazier, Tashiro, Berman, Steger, & Long, 2004). People who rely on religion to help them cope are also less likely to fall back on ineffective coping strategies, such as drinking alcohol (e.g., Bazargan, Sherkat, & Bazargan, 2004).

Research has shown that appealing to a superordinate (high, all-encompassing) principle is an effective way to reduce dissonance (Burris, Harmon-Jones, & Tarpley, 1997). For example, between 1831 and 1844, a preacher named William Miller launched the Great Second Advent Awakening, also known as the Millerite Movement (Knight, 1999). Based on his study of the biblical verse in Daniel 8:14, Miller calculated that Jesus Christ would return to earth sometime between March 21, 1843, and March 21, 1844. After those dates passed, Samuel Snow, a follower of Miller, used the biblical verse in Habakkuk 2:3 to extend the date to October 22, 1844. (Note how changing these details allowed people to maintain consistency in the overriding belief.) When that prophecy also failed, thousands of believers left the movement, calling the prophecy the Great Disappointment. Some of the followers, however, concluded that the prophecy predicted not that Jesus Christ would return to earth on October 22, 1844, but that a special ministry in heaven would be formed on that date. They continued to believe in Miller's teachings.

However, the road to religious belief sometimes contains stumbling blocks (for reviews, see Exline, 2002; Exline & Rose, 2005). At a cognitive level, people may have trouble dealing with inconsistent doctrines or resolving existential questions. At a more emotional level, some religious doctrines and practices can elicit feelings of fear and guilt. People may also experience feelings of anger or resentment toward God when tragedies occur in their lives. Religion offers great benefits to many believers, but maintaining faith is not always easy.

IRRATIONAL BELIEF

People believe lots of seemingly crazy things, even though there is no rational basis for these beliefs (Tobacyk & Milford, 1983). These include paranormal beliefs (about Bigfoot, UFOs, etc.), as well as beliefs that are logically and statistically flawed (e.g., the belief that one can control chance events, the belief that random events even out in the short run). We explored some of these irrational beliefs in Chapter 5. When it comes to irrational beliefs, the minuses probably outweigh the pluses. People who hold irrational beliefs are more anxious (Tobacyk & Downs, 1986), cope less well with terminal illnesses (Thompson, Norris, & Hanacek, 1993), are more likely to become depressed over time (Persons & Rao, 1985), and have lower levels of self-esteem (Daly & Burton, 1983). People who think they are lucky are more likely to gamble and may therefore squander their money trying to beat unbelievable odds or to recoup large amounts of money they have already lost.

How do gamblers sustain their optimism as their losses mount? After all, if you lose more than you win (as most gamblers do), you should logically conclude either that you aren't lucky or that gambling is a foolish thing to do with your money, so you should stop. An intriguing series of studies suggests that gamblers maintain their positive (irrational) beliefs by using a series of tricks. In particular, they convince themselves that many losses were "near wins," so they don't count those against themselves. Thus, if they bet on sports, they feel lucky and smart if they win the bet, and they feel unlucky or dumb if their team loses by a wide margin. But if they lose by a small margin, they tell themselves that they should have won. This permits them to remain confident that they will win in the future (Gilovich, 1983).

WHAT MAKES US HUMAN?   Putting the Cultural Animal in Perspective

Humans are not unique in having attitudes. Animals have attitudes, at least in the sense that they like and dislike certain things. But humans have far more attitudes than other animals, and the mental processes associated with them are probably far more complex. The way attitudes and beliefs operate is much more complicated among humans. For one thing, consistency pressures seem much more central in human than in animal functioning. It is doubtful that animals can really understand inconsistency beyond very simple events (e.g., expecting something and suddenly not finding it). There is little reason to think that animals engage in rationalization, whereas humans are quick to rationalize, especially when they experience cognitive dissonance. Likewise, balance theory and other attempts to maintain consistency among multiple beliefs are much more prominent in human than in animal psychology.

One reason for the greater human concern with consistency is that we use language in dealing with each other. Humans ask each other for explanations. If a person didn't like carrots, for example, and then one day her friends found her gobbling carrots by the handful, they would probably ask her to explain the inconsistency. Without language, other animals don't do that sort of thing, so they do not need to think about or prepare explanations for their inconsistent actions.

The way people think creates other special processes involving attitudes and beliefs. People can hold dual attitudes, in which their conscious attitude differs from their automatic response; animals that lack higher-level cognitions don't have that kind of inner conflict. We saw that simply thinking about an issue causes people's opinions to become polarized, but most animals would not be capable of that much thinking and hence wouldn't have to cope with its polarizing consequence. We also saw that doubting and questioning, and ultimately rejecting a belief as untrue, is often a second step in human thinking that may require conscious thought. Nonprimates probably lack the capacity to make true/false judgments. In practice, that probably means they believe everything that is presented to them. Much of the great progress in human culture, from science to philosophy, involves carefully considering multiple views and rejecting those that are found to be false. Without the capacity to judge something as false, animals have been unable to develop science or philosophy.

Humans also use attitudes and beliefs much more extensively than other animals in how they relate to the world around them. We develop elaborate sets of beliefs to help us understand the world. (Again, only humans have developed science, religion, and philosophy.) Beliefs have another benefit, in that they can help people cope with misfortune. To an animal, a bad event (such as an injury) is just a practical matter, but for humans bad events affect their beliefs about the world, and people can use or modify those beliefs to help themselves bounce back.

WHAT ARE ATTITUDES AND WHY DO PEOPLE HAVE THEM?

- Beliefs are pieces of information, facts or opinions; attitudes are broad evaluations (liking or disliking) toward some object or issue.
- Implicit attitudes are automatic, nonconscious, evaluative responses; explicit attitudes are controlled, conscious, evaluative responses.

- Dual attitudes refer to having different, competing attitudes, one conscious and the other in the nonconscious or automatic part of the mind.
- People may not be aware of all their own attitudes.
- The Implicit Association Test (IAT) is a measure of attitudes and beliefs, including some that people may be either unwilling or unable to report.
- The term *stigma* refers to an attribute that is perceived by others as having a broad, negative value.
- Attitudes help deal with the complex social world. People need far more attitudes than most animals.
- As soon as you know what something is, you start to know whether you like or dislike it (in the first microsecond of thought).
- To be impartial—as a judge or referee is supposed to—may require overcoming one's attitudes.
- Attitudes are tremendously helpful in making choices. Possessing an attitude increases the ease, speed, and quality of decision making.

HOW ATTITUDES ARE FORMED

- The mere exposure effect is the tendency for novel stimuli to be liked more after the individual has been repeatedly exposed to them. Familiarity breeds liking!
- Classical conditioning (also called Pavlovian conditioning) is the repeated pairing of an unconditioned stimulus with a conditioned stimulus, until the conditioned stimulus elicits a response similar to that elicited by the unconditioned stimulus.
- Classical conditioning may help explain the development of prejudiced attitudes against social groups that are frequently associated with negative information in the media.
- Advertisers use classical conditioning to direct attitudes by linking their products with famous or attractive people or with feeling good.
- Operant conditioning (also called instrumental conditioning) is a type of learning. People are more likely to repeat behaviors that have been rewarded and are less likely to repeat behaviors that have been punished.

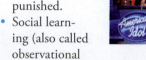

- Social learning (also called observational learning, imitation, or vicarious learning) is the type of learning in which people are more likely to imitate behaviors if they have seen others rewarded for performing those behaviors, and are less likely to imitate behaviors if they have seen others punished for performing them.
- Attitudes can be formed or changed through operant conditioning, classical conditioning, or observational learning.
- Attitude polarization is the tendency for attitudes to become more extreme as people think about or reflect on their attitudes, especially if they held strong attitudes to begin with.
- If people see an equal amount of confirming and disconfirming evidence, they become even more convinced of their initial attitudes and adopt them more strongly.
- People are more accepting of evidence presented by ingroup members and more skeptical of evidence presented by outgroup members.

CONSISTENCY

- To reduce their feelings of inconsistency, people may have to seek out new or reinterpret old information, realign or abandon cherished beliefs, or change patterns of behavior. People will generally choose the easiest of these (the path of least resistance), which often means changing their attitudes.
- Consistency theories have three parts:
  - They specify the conditions that are required for consistency and inconsistency of cognitions.
  - They assume that inconsistency is unpleasant and therefore motivates people to restore consistency.
  - They specify the conditions that are needed to restore consistency.
- Balance theory (or P-O-X theory) focuses on situations containing three elements (triads): one person (P), the other person (O), and an attitude object (X). Relationships among these three elements can be balanced (consistent) or unbalanced.
- Balance theory states that balanced (consistent) states are preferred over unbalanced states, and that unbalanced states motivate people to change them to balanced states (people prefer and seek consistency).
- According to cognitive dissonance theory, discrepancies between attitudes and behaviors produce psychological discomfort (cognitive dissonance), which causes people to rationalize their behavior so as to bring their attitudes into line with their actions.
- People who were paid a small amount to lie came to change their attitudes to believe their own lie; people who were paid a large amount to lie did not.
- Effort justification is the idea that people who expend a great deal of effort will want to convince themselves that their effort was worthwhile.

- People will sometimes choose to suffer as a consequence of expecting to suffer, if they have coped with their expectation by changing some of their relevant beliefs and attitudes.
- People who suffer more to get into a group end up liking the group more.
- Choice is necessary for dissonance and attitude change.
- Dissonance is marked by unpleasant arousal.
- People may have some desire to be consistent in the privacy of their minds, but they have a much stronger desire to be seen by other people as consistent.
- The drive for consistency may be rooted in our biological nature and strengthened by learning and socialization, and it may involve both parts of the duplex mind.

DO ATTITUDES REALLY PREDICT BEHAVIORS?

- The A–B problem is the problem of inconsistency between attitudes (A) and behaviors (B). The link between attitudes and behaviors is often weak.
- Men's general attitudes predict their sexual behavior much better than women's.
- Attitudes predict behavior best if any or all of the following conditions are met:
  - Attitude measures are very specific.
  - Behaviors are aggregated across time and different situations.

- Attitudes are consciously prominent and influence how the person thinks about the choices he or she faces.
- Attitudes are highly accessible (i.e., they come to mind easily).

BELIEFS AND BELIEVING

- The automatic system automatically believes; the conscious system can override this belief by deciding that it is false.
- Belief perseverance is the idea that once beliefs form, they are resistant to change.
- Explaining the opposite theory reduces or eliminates belief perseverance.
- *Coping* is the general term for how people attempt to deal with traumas and go back to functioning effectively in life.
- *Assumptive worlds* is a term for the view that people form a complex understanding of their world and live according to that. Their assumptions typically include the following, any of which can be violated by misfortune or trauma:
  - The world is benevolent.
  - The world is fair.
  - I am a good person.
- Blaming oneself can be a good way to cope, if one blames oneself for having made a mistake, as opposed to blaming oneself for being a bad person.
- Cognitive coping identifies several kinds of beliefs that need to be bolstered or

restored in the wake of trauma, including the following:
- Reevaluate the trauma using downward comparison, in which people compare themselves and their situations to other people who are worse off.
- Restore self-esteem.
- Restore belief in control.
- Find positive changes resulting from the trauma.
- Irrational beliefs are often maintained despite contradictory evidence.

WHAT MAKES US HUMAN? PUTTING THE CULTURAL ANIMAL IN PERSPECTIVE

- Although other animals have some attitudes (e.g., they have likes and dislikes), humans have many more attitudes.
- Humans also have far more complex attitudes than other animals do.
- Only humans rationalize their behaviors by changing their attitudes.
- Because humans have conscious thought, they can question, doubt, and reject a belief as untrue. Other animals lack this ability.
- Only humans develop elaborate sets of beliefs to help them understand the world.

Key Terms

A–B problem 213
Accessibility 212
Assumptive worlds 216
Attitude polarization 205
Attitudes 200
Balance theory (P-O-X theory) 206
Belief perseverance 215
Beliefs 200

Classical conditioning 203
Cognitive coping 216
Cognitive dissonance theory 206
Conditioned response 203
Conditioned stimulus 203
Coping 215
Downward comparison 217
Dual attitudes 200

Effort justification 207
Explicit attitudes 200
Implicit attitudes 200
Mere exposure effect 203
Neutral stimulus 203
Operant conditioning (instrumental conditioning) 204
Post-decision dissonance 209

Social learning (observational learning, imitation, vicarious learning) 204
Stigma 201
Tyranny of choice 209
Unconditioned response 203
Unconditioned stimulus 203

[Quiz Yourself] Answers

1. What Are Attitudes and Why Do People Have Them?
Answers: 1=b, 2=a, 3=a, 4=a

2. How Attitudes Are Formed
Answers: 1=c, 2=a, 3=b, 4=c

3. Consistency
Answers: 1=b, 2=b, 3=a, 4=c

4. Do Attitudes Really Predict Behaviors?
Answers: 1=d, 2=d, 3=b, 4=c

5. Beliefs and Believing
Answers: 1=a, 2=b, 3=d, 4=a

Media Learning Resources

Make sure you check out the complete set of learning resources and study tools below. If your instructor did not order these items with your new book, go to www.ichapters.com to purchase Cengage Learning print and digital products.

Social Psychology and Human Nature BOOK COMPANION WEBSITE

www.cengage.com/psychology/baumeister Visit your book companion website, where you will find flash cards, practice quizzes, Internet links, and more to help you study.

CENGAGENOW™ JUST WHAT YOU NEED TO KNOW NOW!

Spend time on what you need to master rather than on information you have already learned. Take a pre-test for this chapter, and CengageNOW will generate a personalized study plan based on your results. The study plan will identify the topics you need to review and direct you to online resources to help you master those topics. You can then take a post-test to help you determine the concepts you have mastered and what you will still need to work on. Try it out! Go to www.cengage .com/login to sign in with an access code or to purchase access to this product.

CLASSIC AND CONTEMPORARY VIDEOS STUDENT CD-ROM

To see videos on the topics and experiments discussed in this chapter and to learn more about the research that social psychologists are doing today, go to the Student CD-ROM.

SOCIAL PSYCH LAB

These unique online labs give you the opportunity to become a participant in actual experiments, including re-creations of classic and contemporary research studies.

chapter 8

Social Influence and Persuasion

Money Matters: Even a Penny Will Help   **p. 231**

Food for Thought: Convert Communicators and Health Messages   **p. 237**

The Social Side of Sex: Scared Into Safe Sex?   **p. 239**

Tradeoffs: Should Speakers Talk Fast or Slow?   **p. 247**

What Makes Us Human? Putting the Cultural Animal in Perspective   **p. 251**

Justin Sullivan/Getty Images

TWO TYPES OF SOCIAL INFLUENCE   p. 225
Being Liked: Normative Influence   **p. 225**
Being Correct: Informational Influence   **p. 227**

TECHNIQUES OF SOCIAL INFLUENCE   p. 228
Techniques Based on Commitment and Consistency   **p. 228**
Techniques Based on Reciprocation   **p. 231**

Techniques Based on Scarcity   **p. 233**
Techniques Based on Capturing and Disrupting Attention   **p. 234**

PERSUASION   p. 235
Who: The Source   **p. 235**
Says What: The Message   **p. 237**
To Whom: The Audience   **p. 242**
Two Routes to Persuasion   **p. 244**

RESISTING PERSUASION   p. 247

Attitude Inoculation   **p. 248**
Forewarned Is Forearmed   **p. 249**
Stockpile Resources   **p. 249**
Defenses Against Influence Techniques   **p. 250**

CHAPTER SUMMARY   p. 252

James Warren Jones was born in Crete, Indiana, during the height of the Great Depression, on May 13, 1931 (Hall, 1987). His father was not an important part of his life and was thought to be a member of the Ku Klux Klan. His mother essentially raised him alone. ‖‖‖

As a child, Jones was also influenced by a Pentecostal woman who lived in his neighborhood. As a teen, Jones became a devout member of the Church of the Nazarene. He earned degrees from Indiana University and Butler University.

In September 1954, Jones was invited to preach at an Assemblies of God Pentecostal church. Although the church liked Jones and wanted to hire him, they would not approve his request for an interracial congregation. Jones decided to form his own interracial church on April 4, 1955, which he called the Wings of Deliverance. The church's name was later changed to the People's Temple. In 1960, the People's Temple was officially made a member of the Christian Church (Disciples of Christ) denomination in Indianapolis, and Jones was ordained as a minister, even though he had no formal theological training.

In 1965, Jones moved his congregation to northern California, where he said racial equality could grow unhindered. Jones also thought California would be a safer place than Indiana if a nuclear war broke out (Levi, 1982). Seventy families, half black and half white, followed Jones to California (Hall, 1987). In California, the members of People's Temple lived a communal life. All items of value (income, real estate, insurance policies) were given to Jones, who liquidated and redistributed them equally among the members. Jones believed in catharsis (see Chapters 6 and 10), which involved public punishment for transgressions (Committee on Foreign Affairs, 1976). Guilt or innocence was determined by a vote of the congregation. Guilty children were often brutally spanked by Jones. Guilty adults were placed in a ring and forced to "box" with bigger and stronger congregation members. In California, the church grew to 20,000 members, and Jones amassed a fortune estimated at more than $15 million.

In 1977, paranoia and unfavorable press reports led Jones to move his congregation again, this time to 4,000 acres of dense jungle in Guyana, on the northern coast of South America. At first there were only 50 people in this new Jonestown, but the community grew to more than 900 residents. Conditions in the jungle were harsh.

People worked long hours, lived in dormitories, and mainly ate beans and rice (meat and vegetables were reserved for meals with visitors). Meanwhile, Jones worked far fewer hours and lived in his own private house with a well-stocked refrigerator. Jones claimed that he needed the refrigerator because he had a blood sugar problem.

Much of the religion that Jones practiced was borrowed from the Pentecostal movement. Jones claimed to have the power to "discern spirits," the power of healing, and the ability to see into the future (Reston, 1981). Jones also proclaimed himself to be the Second Coming of Christ.

Jones installed loudspeakers in Jonestown, and used them to indoctrinate his followers. He "read" the news to his followers, and frequently "portrayed the United States as beset by racial and economic problems" (Hall, 1987). Jones developed a belief called Translation, in which he and his followers would all die together and would move to another planet for a life of bliss and harmony. He used the loudspeakers to practice what he called White Nights. In the middle of the night, sirens blared over the loudspeakers, and the residents would gather in the central pavilion. Jones told them that attacks by mercenaries were imminent, that the end was near, and that they would need to make the ultimate sacrifice for "the Cause." They lined up and drank a liquid described as poison, expecting to die. When they did not die, Jones told them that they had passed the "loyalty test" (Levi, 1982). However, he told them that if ever the colony was actually threatened by mercenaries, "revolutionary suicide" would be real, and it would demonstrate their devotion to "the Cause." Jones used armed guards to fend off a mercenary invasion. The guards were also told to prevent residents from leaving Jonestown.

A few people did manage to leave Jonestown. Some of them formed a group called Concerned Relatives, which alleged that Jones had brainwashed his followers and was holding them in Guyana against their will (Moore, 1986). The group found a voice in Congress through California Congressman Leo Ryan. On November 14, 1978, Ryan, a small group of media

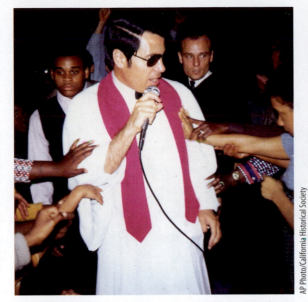 

Jim Jones (left). At Jonestown, 914 people committed suicide (right). Only a few fled into the jungle to escape.

representatives, and several members of Concerned Relatives departed for Jonestown (Hall, 1987). Ryan and his party interviewed several Jonestown residents, some of whom expressed a desire to leave. Jones told Ryan that the residents of Jonestown could come and go as they pleased. However, when Ryan attempted to take a group of 16 Jonestown residents back to the United States, armed guards opened fire on them, killing Ryan, three media representatives, and one Jonestown resident (Moore, 1985).

Fearing retribution, Jones summoned his followers to the central pavilion. He said the end was near and the time had come for them to commit "revolutionary suicide." One woman dissented, but her opinion was quickly suppressed (Moore, 1985). Jones ordered the residents to drink purple Kool-Aid laced with cyanide and a variety of sedatives and tranquilizers. The residents were organized into lines. First to drink were the infants and children; many mothers poured the poison down their children's throats (Hall, 1987). The final body count was 914 people, including 276 children. Jones himself died by shooting himself in the head rather than drinking the poisoned Kool-Aid. A few residents fled into the jungle and survived.

How could Jim Jones have influenced his followers to such a deep level that more than 900 of them committed revolutionary suicide? This chapter focuses on social influence. Social influence is rooted in social life. It enables us to coexist with others. As we have said throughout this book, humans depend on others for their survival and well-being. Because we survive via other people, we need to be able to influence other people to give us what we need and want.

The use of force is a simple way to influence others. Aggression can be regarded as a form of social influence (see Chapter 10). Although aggression works in the short run, it backfires in the long run. Aggression has many unintended consequences and side effects that limit its usefulness. In addition, cultures generally frown on aggression and seek to restrain it. Accordingly, people have developed other, nonaggressive ways to influence each other.

As social animals, people are exceptionally responsive to each other. As cultural animals, people rely on each other for information about the world and for guidance about how to act in uncertain situations. This dependency on others creates opportunities for social influence. ▪

Two Types of Social Influence

Social influence is a broad category. Social psychologists distinguish between two major forms of social influence: normative and informational (Deutsch & Gerard, 1955). Let us consider each of these in turn.

BEING LIKED: NORMATIVE INFLUENCE

Normative influence involves going along with the crowd in order to be liked and accepted. As we have seen throughout this book, humans have a fundamental need to belong to social groups. Being accepted and included improves one's chances for

NORMATIVE INFLUENCE going along with the crowd in order to be liked and accepted

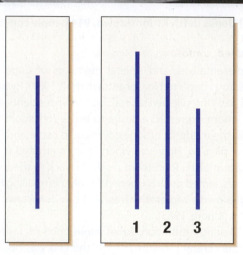

In the studies conducted by Asch (1955), participants chose line 1, 2, or 3 as matching the comparison line (shown in the box to the left of lines 1, 2, and 3). During the experiment, six of the seven people were confederates who gave the wrong answer (photo on right). Most participants went along with the group, even though the group gave an obviously wrong answer.

survival (and improves life in many other ways). However, there is a long road to acceptance within the group. To live together, people usually need to agree on common beliefs, values, attitudes, and behaviors that reduce ingroup threats and act for the common good. Therefore, people learn to conform to their group's rules. The more we see others behaving in a certain way or making particular decisions, the more we feel inclined to follow suit. This happens even when we are in a group of complete strangers: we will go along with the others to avoid looking like a fool.

The studies conducted by Solomon Asch (1955) illustrate the power of normative influence (see Chapters 1 and 9). Asch asked participants to judge which of three lines matched a comparison line. In some studies, the participant was asked last in a group of confederates, all of whom had been instructed to give the same wrong answer. Asch found that many participants went along with the confederates and gave the wrong answer, even though they could plainly see it was wrong, rather than deviate from the group. In some studies, Asch varied the discrepancy between the standard line and the comparison lines to discover the point at which the error made by the confederates was so glaring that no participants would conform. These manipulations did not eliminate the effect: Participants went along with the group even when the group made flagrant errors. To be accepted by the group was more important to participants than to be correct.

Several factors influence whether people will conform to group norms. In one study, Asch (1955) varied the number of unanimous confederates from 1 to 15. He found that conformity increases as group size increases up to a point, then levels off (see ▶ **FIGURE 8.1**).

In another study, one of the confederates was a "dissenter" who always gave the correct answer. The dissenter reduced conformity by about one-fourth. In addition, participants who gave the correct answer reported feelings of warmth and closeness toward the dissenter. Asch wondered whether the dissenter reduced conformity because he was accurate or because he deviated from the other confederates. So Asch conducted another study in which the dissenter disagreed with the other confederates but chose another incorrect answer. Half the time the dissenter made a moderate error, choosing a line that was incorrect but not too far off; the other half of the time the dissenter made an extreme error. The results showed that when the dissenter made a moderate error, conformity decreased by about one-third; when

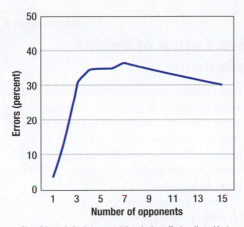

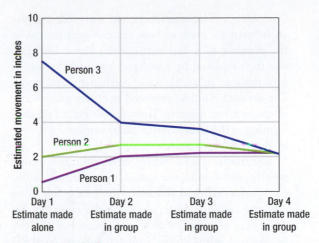

Size of the majority that opposed them had an effect on the subjects. With a single opponent, the subject erred only 3.6% of the time; with two opponents, he erred 13.6%; three, 31.8%; four, 35.1%; six, 35.2%; seven, 37.1%; nine, 35.1%; fifteen, 31.2%.

► **FIGURE 8.1** Effect of group size on conformity in the Asch (1955) experiment: As the number of confederates increased from one to four, conformity increased dramatically; as more confederates were added, conformity leveled off.

► **FIGURE 8.2** Sherif (1935) used the autokinetic effect to study the development of group norms. Over time, the judgments of the individual group members converged to the same estimate.

the participants did make errors, most were moderate rather than extreme. When the dissenter made an extreme error, conformity decreased by almost three-fourths! Furthermore, when participants did make errors—and this occurred on only 9% of trials—all of the errors were moderate, none extreme. Thus, the extreme dissenter had a remarkably freeing effect on participants. The implication is that people feel considerable pressure to conform to a group if everyone agrees, but if there is any sort of disagreement among group members, then people become willing to stand up for what they believe.

When people deviate from group norms, they may pay a heavy price, including social rejection (see Chapter 11 for more on the psychology of rejection). Social rejection can be painful. Asch found that people would agree with the group, even when they knew the group was wrong, rather than suffer social rejection. Other research has shown that people who deviate from the group do indeed run a heightened risk of being rejected. For example, in an early study conducted by Stanley Schachter (1951), groups of eight individuals discussed the case of a juvenile delinquent named Johnny Rocco. Each group consisted of five real participants and three confederates. One confederate, the "deviant," adopted the extreme position of punishing Rocco severely and did not deviate from this position during group discussion. A second confederate, the "slider," initially adopted the extreme position of punishing Rocco but then "slid" toward the position adopted by most group members. A third confederate, the "mode," adopted the position of most group members. At the end of the group discussion, the experimenter told everyone

that a smaller group was needed for the next group discussion, so that the group needed to vote one member out. Most groups voted out the deviant. A review of similar studies showed that groups are quick to reject deviants or nonconformists (Tata et al., 1996). Rejection is more likely when there are only one or two nonconformists than when there are many nonconformists (Tata et al., 1996).

BEING CORRECT: INFORMATIONAL INFLUENCE

If you look at a pinpoint of light in a dark room, the light appears to move even though it does not actually move at all. This illusion of movement, caused by very slight movements of the eye, is called the **autokinetic effect**.

Muzafer Sherif (1935) used the autokinetic effect to study the formation of group norms. **Group norms** are the beliefs or behaviors that a group of people accepts as normal. Sherif asked individual participants in a dark room to estimate how far the light moved. Their individual estimates ranged from about 1 inch to about 8 inches. They repeated this process on subsequent days, but in the presence of two other participants. As participants heard the estimates provided by others, their individual answers converged and became more similar (see ► **FIGURE 8.2**).

These social norms are not temporary, either; they can last at least one year (Rohrer, Baron, Hoffman, & Swander, 1954). These social norms can also be transmitted from one person to another. In another study that used the autokinetic effect (Jacobs &

AUTOKINETIC EFFECT illusion, caused by very slight movements of the eye, that a stationary point of light in a dark room is moving

GROUP NORMS the beliefs or behaviors that a group of people accepts as normal

Campbell, 1961), researchers had a confederate give an inflated estimate of how far the light moved in the presence of a real participant. The confederate was then replaced by a real participant, who was in turn replaced by another real participant, and so on. The inflated estimate persisted over five generations of research participants. Thus, people ended up conforming to the (false) norms set by someone who was by this point long gone.

The studies conducted by Sherif indicate a second type of social influence called informational influence. **Informational influence** involves going along with the crowd because you think the crowd knows more than you do (rather than because you want to be liked, as with normative social influence). It fits the "people first" theme we have seen throughout this book: People get valuable information from others, and sometimes they give more weight to what others think than to what their own eyes and ears tell them.

Two types of situations produce informational influence: (a) ambiguous situations, so that people do not know how to behave; and (b) crisis situations, so that people don't have time to think for themselves. In these situations, people conform to what others are doing because they assume that those others know what they are doing. Sometimes this assumption is wrong—others really do not know more than we do. In fact, others may assume that we know more than they do. In some cases, nobody knows anything, which is called a state of **pluralistic ignorance** (also see Chapter 9).

In short, there are two different motives to conform: normative and informational. A key difference is whether the conforming person comes to believe that others are right or believes they are wrong but conforms simply to avoid rejection, ridicule, hostility, or other kinds of punishment. Informational social influence helps produce **private acceptance**—a genuine inner belief that others are right. Normative social influence may elicit mere **public compliance**—outwardly going along with the group but maintaining a private, inner belief that the group is wrong. The Jonestown example contained both. Some people probably believed that Jones was a great religious leader with correct views, because they were surrounded by others who expressed those beliefs. Others went along under pressure of punishment and threat of death.

INFORMATIONAL INFLUENCE going along with the crowd because you think the crowd knows more than you do

PLURALISTIC IGNORANCE looking to others for cues about how to behave, while they are looking to you; collective misinterpretation

PRIVATE ACCEPTANCE a genuine inner belief that others are right

PUBLIC COMPLIANCE outwardly going along with the group but maintaining a private, inner belief that the group is wrong

Two Types of Social Influence

1. Lucyna initially believes that when she becomes angry it is helpful to yell and scream to vent her anger. This emotional cleansing is called catharsis. After listening to her professor's lecture on the research evidence contradicting catharsis, Lucyna no longer believes that venting works. This change in belief illustrates _____.
   (a) the autokinetic effect
   (b) informational influence
   (c) normative influence
   (d) public compliance

2. The autokinetic effect is a(n) _____.
   (a) false group consensus
   (b) group norm
   (c) illusion of perceived movement
   (d) influential bias in social influence

3. The type of conformity based on a fear of social rejection is called _____.
   (a) ingratiation   (b) modeling
   (c) private acceptance   (d) public compliance

4. Tyrone plans to vote for candidate Duck in the local elections. Before he votes, his friends explain why they're going to vote for candidate Goose. In the voting booth, Tyrone votes for candidate Goose. This is an example of _____.
   (a) private acceptance
   (b) psychological reactance
   (c) public compliance
   (d) reciprocity

Techniques of Social Influence

Social influence techniques can be organized according to four basic principles: (1) commitment and consistency, (2) reciprocation, (3) scarcity, and (4) capturing and disrupting attention.

TECHNIQUES BASED ON COMMITMENT AND CONSISTENCY

Several techniques of influence are based on the principle of commitment and consistency (Cialdini, 2001). Once people make a commitment, they feel both internal and external pressure to behave consistently with that commitment. If people don't behave consistently with their commitments, they experience a form of psychological discomfort called cognitive dissonance (see Chapter 7). Once people make a commitment, they feel obligated to follow through on it.

Foot-in-the-Door Technique. Cult recruiters don't just ask a complete stranger on the street, "Hey, you! Do you want to give us all your belongings and join our cult today?" It is revealing to learn how Jim Jones recruited followers (Ornstein, 1991). Members of the People's Temple would ask a passerby to help for just five minutes by stuffing and mailing a few envelopes. Jim Jones explained, "They came back for more. You know, once I get somebody, I can get them to do anything." Once a person became a member of the People's Temple, monetary contributions were voluntary. Next, Jones required a 10% contribution. After that, he required a 25% contribution. Finally, he required everything—a 100% contribution.

This technique is called the **foot-in-the-door technique**. It is based on the principle of starting with a small request in order to get eventual compliance with a larger request. The term refers to the efforts of door-to-door salespeople to get "one foot in the door" as a prerequisite to getting their whole body into the house. (The assumption was that the customer won't slam the door in your face as long as your foot is in the way.) Complying with small requests seems like no big deal, but it increases the likelihood of complying with larger requests later on. It is easier to comply the second time than the first time. If the increment in compliance requests is gradual, it may seem like a smaller request than if it is made in one giant leap.

In the first experimental study on the foot-in-the-door technique (Freedman & Fraser, 1966), a researcher posing as a volunteer worker went door to door and asked California homeowners if they would be willing to display a three-inch-square sign on their doors that said BE A SAFE DRIVER. Everyone agreed to this small request. Two weeks later, a different researcher asked the same homeowners if they would allow a very large, poorly lettered, sign reading DRIVE CAREFULLY to be installed on their front lawns. Nearly 80% agreed to the second, larger request. Meanwhile, other people were approached with the second request but not the first one. Of them, only 20% agreed to have the sign installed on their front lawns. Agreeing to the small request paved the way for consenting to the big one. Once people had committed themselves to safe driving in their neighborhood by putting a small sign on their door, they felt obligated to behave consistently with that commitment by placing a very large sign on their lawn. If a person makes a small commitment, a related larger one is more likely to follow.

"Would you like to super-size that?"

Car salespeople sometimes use the low-ball technique.

Low-Ball Technique. A second approach that shifts from a smaller request to a larger request is the **low-ball technique**. In this technique, the requester first gets a person to comply with a seemingly low-cost request and only later reveals hidden additional costs. Car salespeople sometimes try this technique on potential customers. You come into a car dealership and test drive a car you really want to buy. The salesperson quotes you an excellent price, you agree to the deal, and you sign an offer. The salesperson goes to talk to the sales manager, and then returns with some "bad news" (e.g., you will only get $400 on your trade-in, rather than the $2,000 you had been promised; the iPod player with 18 speakers costs extra, even though the salesperson had told you it came with the car; or perhaps the sales price you were offered was an error and must be raised $500). The original price is really a "low ball" that the salesperson threw at you.

In one test of the low-ball influence technique, college students were recruited to participate on "thinking processes" that was to be conducted at 7:00 in the morning (Cialdini, Cacioppo, Bassett, & Miller, 1978). Half of the students were thrown a low ball: The researcher asked if they would be interested in participating in a study on thinking processes *before* telling them they would have to be at the lab at 7 a.m. After they agreed to participate, the

---

FOOT-IN-THE-DOOR TECHNIQUE influence technique based on commitment, in which one starts with a small request in order to gain eventual compliance with a larger request

LOW-BALL TECHNIQUE influence technique based on commitment, in which one first gets a person to comply with a seemingly low-cost request and only later reveals hidden additional costs

researcher told them the bad news about the early scheduling. Even though the researcher gave them a chance to change their minds, 56% agreed to participate. In contrast, among students who were told of the starting time before they made a commitment, only 24% agreed to participate. Perhaps surprisingly, the low-balled subjects were also more likely than the others to actually show up for the study. Thus, the low-ball technique increased both promises to comply and actual compliance.

Although the low-ball technique is considered unscrupulous, it often works. Why? As with the foot-in-the-door technique, it is based on the principle of commitment and consistency. Commitments have a tendency to "grow their own legs" (Cialdini, 2001); that is, people often add new reasons and justifications to support their initial commitment. One lesson we learned from cognitive dissonance theory is that people like to justify their decisions (see Chapter 7). Your initial decision to buy the car was based on a single "leg"—the great initial offer the salesperson quoted you. But then other legs start growing. You like the color. It's fast. It smells good inside. The iPod player sounds great. And so on. The salesperson then throws a low ball that knocks over the leg that initially held up your decision to buy the car (the great initial offer), but the decision doesn't fall through because now all the new legs are holding it up. You fulfill your commitment and buy the car.

Bait-and-Switch Technique. Car salespeople also use a technique called **bait-and-switch**. The car dealership places an ad for a car at a great price, but when you get to the showroom the car is "sold out." The dealership placed the ad simply to get you into the showroom. Once you are there, they can try to sell you another car. You are baited with one car (usually a stripped-down model with no options, sold at an unbelievably low price), and then you are switched to another car (usually a fully loaded model that goes for a much higher price). The American Bar Association warns consumers about this technique; it is a form of fraud, and is not legal.

The bait-and-switch technique is used by businesses other than car sales. For example, you may go to a store because they advertised a product you want, but when you get to the store you discover that the product is sold out. Since you are already at the store, you decide to go shopping anyway. The ad served its purpose—it got you into the store.

The bait-and-switch technique, like the low-ball and foot-in-the-door techniques, is based on the principle of commitment and consistency (Cialdini, 2001). It gets people to make a psychological commitment, and then relies on consistency pressures to keep them loyal to this commitment even when the influencer changes the terms.

Labeling Technique. The **labeling technique** is another way to induce compliance. It involves assigning a label to an individual and then requesting a favor that is consistent with the label. Former Egyptian President Anwar Sadat used the labeling technique to persuade those he negotiated with (Cialdini, 2001). Before negotiations began, Sadat would tell his opponents that they and the citizens of their country were widely known for being cooperative and fair. In doing so, Sadat gave his opponents a label to live up to. According to former Secretary of State Henry Kissinger, Sadat was a successful negotiator because he understood how to get others to act on his behalf by giving them a reputation to uphold. The labeling technique is related to the self-fulfilling prophecy (see Chapter 13). People tend to live up to the label others give them.

Research has shown that the labeling technique can persuade both children and adults. Elementary school children who are told by an adult "You look to me like the kind of girl (or boy) who understands how important it is to write correctly" were more likely to choose a penmanship task several days later than were children who were not labeled (Cialdini, Eisenberg, Green, Rhoads, & Bator, 1998). Similarly, adults who were previously told that they were "above average citizens" were more likely to vote several days later than were adults previously told that they were "average citizens" (Tybout & Yalch, 1980).

The labeling technique is also based on the commitment and consistency principle. Whether positive labels are assigned by oneself or by others, people like to live up to them. Labeling also makes use of the importance of self-concepts (see Chapter 3). How people think about themselves can influence their behavior. Thus, if you want to influence that person's behavior, an effective technique is to get the person to think of himself or herself in a manner that will produce the desired result. A person who thinks of herself as helpful will often be more helpful than a person who doesn't.

Legitimization-of-Paltry-Favors Technique. Most people want to be viewed as helpful, even if the amount of help they give is trivial. In the **legitimization-of-paltry-favors technique**, the requester makes a small amount of aid acceptable. To

---

BAIT-AND-SWITCH influence technique based on commitment, in which one draws people in with an attractive offer that is unavailable and then switches them to a less attractive offer that is available

LABELING TECHNIQUE influence technique based on consistency, in which one assigns a label to an individual and then requests a favor that is consistent with the label

LEGITIMIZATION-OF-PALTRY-FAVORS TECHNIQUE influence technique in which a requester makes a small amount of aid acceptable

MONEY Matters

Even a Penny Will Help

Asking for donations is hard work, and one gets used to refusals. A clever technique developed by Cialdini and Shroeder (1976) found a way to make it harder for people to say no. In their study, some confederates simply asked for a donation to the American Cancer Society, while others added the phrase "Even a penny will help." Adding the latter phrase nearly doubled the rate at which people said yes and gave a donation.

Of course, getting donations of only a penny would not be really of much help to the American Cancer Society! But the researchers found that the average size of the donations did not change. Thus, the even-a-penny method produced many more donations of the same approximate size, resulting in a big increase in total amount.

Why? Most reasons people give for refusing resemble "I do not have enough money to donate," but such reasons do not work with the even-a-penny method. Everyone can afford to give a penny! To refuse a request when even a penny would be acceptable might make the refuser feel cheap and petty. Apparently, though, once people decide to go ahead and donate, they donate the amount they would normally give (rather than just giving a penny). ■

The door-in-the-face technique is often effective.

see how this can lead to persuasion, read the *Money Matters* box.

TECHNIQUES BASED ON RECIPROCATION

Reciprocity—if you take care of me, I will take care of you—is one of the foundations of culture. All cultures understand reciprocity and expect people to obey its norms. The appreciation of reciprocity is deeply rooted in human nature; one sign of this is that people feel guilty if someone does them a favor and they cannot repay it in some way. This sentiment is the foundation for some of the best moral behavior and good treatment of others. Unfortunately, it is also something that sneaky people can exploit to influence others.

Two influence techniques are based on reciprocation: (a) door-in-the-face and (b) that's-not-all (Cialdini, 2001).

Door-in-the-Face Technique. An effective way to get people to comply with a request is to start by making an inflated request (that will most likely be rejected) and then retreat to a smaller request. The smaller request, the one that was desired all along, is likely to be accepted because it appears to be a concession. This is called the **door-in-the-face technique** because the first refusal is like slamming a door in the face of the person making the request. In negotiations between labor and management, both sides often use this tactic. They initially make extreme demands that they do not expect to get. Later they retreat to more reasonable demands. Although the expression "door in the face" vividly describes the procedure, the key to compliance is not the initial refusal but rather reciprocity. After the first offer is refused, the salesperson or negotiator makes a more

DOOR-IN-THE-FACE TECHNIQUE influence technique based on reciprocity, in which one starts with an inflated request and then retreats to a smaller request that appears to be a concession

"How much would you pay for all the secrets of the universe? Wait, don't answer yet. You also get this six-quart covered combination spaghetti pot and clam steamer. <u>Now</u> how much would you pay?"

The that's-not-all technique is effective too.

reasonable offer, and people feel obliged to reciprocate this seemingly kind and generous behavior by becoming more agreeable themselves.

Salespeople sometimes use the door-in-the-face technique. If you were a pool table dealer, which would you advertise—the $329 model or the $3,000 model? This question was answered in a *Consumer Reports* article ("Quote," 1975). The article describes a two-week experiment by a business promotion manager at Brunswick. During the first week, customers were shown the low-end model and were then encouraged to consider more expensive models—the traditional trading-up approach. The average pool table sale during the first week was $550. During the second week, customers were first shown the $3,000 model regardless of what they wanted to see, and then were allowed to see the other models in declining order of price. The average pool table sale during the second week was more than $1,000.

To demonstrate the door-in-the-face method, researchers asked people if they would volunteer two hours per week for at least two years in a community mental health agency. They all said no. Next, they were asked if they would volunteer for two hours on a single occasion. About 76% of participants volunteered. In contrast, only 29% volunteered if they were just asked to work two hours on a single occasion (without the prior request for two years). Moreover, the door-in-the-face people were not simply agreeing

without meaning to follow through. Among all those who volunteered, 85% of participants in the door-in-the-face group showed up, whereas only 50% of participants in the control group showed up (Miller, Seligman, Clark, & Bush, 1976).

The door-in-the-face technique does not work, however, if the first request is so extreme that it is seen as unreasonable (Schwarzwald, Raz, & Zvibel, 1979). The door-in-the face technique also does not work if the first and second requests are made by different people (Cialdini, Vincent, Lewis, Catalan, Wheeler, & Darby, 1975). This probably reflects the importance of reciprocation. The key to getting someone to agree is to pretend you are doing the person a favor by reducing your request to a much more reasonable level, so the person will feel an obligation to agree to it. If the second offer or request comes from someone different, no sense of reciprocal obligation is created.

That's-Not-All Technique. The **that's-not-all technique**, like the door-in-the-face technique, begins with an inflated request. However, before the person can answer yes or no, the requester sweetens the deal by offering a discount or bonus. Perhaps you've seen this technique on television. First, the "regular" price is reduced, and then several additional bonuses are added.

A cupcake booth on a college campus was the setting for a field experimental test of the that's-not-all technique (Burger, 1986). Customers were randomly assigned to one of three conditions. In the that's-not-all group, one researcher told the customer that the cupcakes cost $1.25. At this point, a second researcher tapped the first researcher on the shoulder. Before the customer could say anything, the first researcher raised his hand and said, "Wait a second." After a brief conversation with the second researcher, the first researcher told the customer that he would lower the price to $1.00 because they were planning to close the booth soon. In the bargain group, the participant was told, "These are only $1.00 now. We were selling them for $1.25 earlier." In the control group, customers were simply told that the cupcakes cost $1.00. The results showed that more customers in the "that's-not-all" group bought cupcakes (55%) than in the bargain (25%) or control (20%) groups. Customers in the "that's-not-all" group most likely complied more because they felt as if the researcher were doing them a personal favor, whereas in the bargain group, the researcher did the same favor for everyone. People felt most obligated to reciprocate when they believed the seller was making an exception for them personally.

The that's-not-all technique, like the door-in-the-face technique, is based on reciprocal concessions and a sense of personal obligation. When a stranger

THAT'S-NOT-ALL TECHNIQUE influence technique based on reciprocity, in which one first makes an inflated request but, before the person can answer yes or no, sweetens the deal by offering a discount or bonus

Courtesy Everett Collection

For sale, secondhand white disco suit, one of a kind, only $145,000.

AP Photo/Elise Amendola

Would you pay $2,300 for a doll?

or interaction partner does something kind for you, you feel an obligation to do something nice or kind in return. A discount or bonus can increase compliance by sweetening the deal. Reciprocity is one of the most basic traits of human beings, because it goes to the essence of what a cultural animal is. It is in our genes to pay back what others do for us and to recognize when other people do—or do not—reciprocate. Thus, people can be readily exploited by unscrupulous salespeople who take advantage of their basic human tendency to reciprocate.

TECHNIQUES BASED ON SCARCITY

What is rare is a greater good than what is plentiful.

—Aristotle

According to the scarcity principle, rare opportunities are more valuable than plentiful opportunities.

For example, although Cabbage Patch dolls only cost about $20 in the store, some very rare ones can sell for more than $2,300! When people compete with each other for scarce items at an auction, the price can quickly skyrocket. For example, the white polyester suit John Travolta wore in the movie *Saturday Night Fever* sold for $145,000 at an auction. Quite similar suits could easily be purchased for a couple dollars at a second-hand store, but the fact that it had been worn by a star in a hit movie made this particular suit seem special, even unique. People quickly get caught up in competitive situations.

Scarcity is sometimes used as a heuristic cue in decision making—what is rare is good. The scarcity heuristic is illustrated by the results of a consumer preferences study (Worchel, Lee, & Adewole, 1975). Participants were each given a cookie to taste and rate. Some participants received the cookie from a jar containing 10 cookies, whereas others received the cookie from a jar containing 2 cookies. Even though the cookies came from the same *Nabisco* box, the people who took the cookie from the jar containing only 2 cookies rated it higher than did the people who took the cookie from the jar containing 10 cookies.

One reason why the scarcity principle works is because it takes more effort to obtain rare items than plentiful items. Often we have to compete with others for scarce opportunities. Perhaps that is why potential lovers and potential employees "play hard to get." They want others to think that they are a hot commodity with lots of options. If you don't agree to the person's request, you could lose a valuable partner or employee.

Another reason why the scarcity principle works is that people, especially those from individualistic cultures, highly value their freedom. As opportunities become scarce, we lose our freedom to obtain them. When our personal freedom is threatened, we experience an unpleasant emotional response called psychological reactance (see Chapter 4). This unpleasant emotion motivates us to obtain the scarce opportunity.

Various influence techniques are based on scarcity. One is the **limited-number technique**, saying that only a limited number of these products will be available. Another is the **fast-approaching-deadline technique**, saying that an item or a price is only available for a limited time. The point of both is that your chances to buy the product are limited, either by how few there are or by the time available.

TECHNIQUES BASED ON CAPTURING AND DISRUPTING ATTENTION

Other influence techniques try to capture the attention of the target of influence, or try to distract the target of influence. When influencers have strong arguments, they want to attract the attention of targets because they want people to think about the convincing arguments. When influencers have weak arguments, they want to disrupt the attention of targets so they won't think too deeply about the unconvincing arguments.

Pique Technique. Often when panhandlers approach us, they ask "Can you spare a quarter?" or "Can you spare any change?" People who live in large cities have heard these requests so many times that they often just ignore the panhandler and move on. Pedestrians have a refusal script in mind the instant they see a panhandler, such as "Sorry, I don't have any change." To be effective, the panhandler must disrupt this refusal script and capture the pedestrian's attention. The **pique technique** captures the pedestrian's attention by making the request novel. Instead of asking whether the pedestrian can spare any change, for example, the panhandler could ask whether the pedestrian can spare 17 cents.

In one study (Santos, Leve, & Pratkanis, 1994), confederates disguised as panhandlers asked pedestrians whether they had any change, or they asked them whether they had 17 cents. The results showed that 37% of pedestrians complied with the 17 cents request, whereas only 23% complied with the spare change request. It helps to grab people's attention before they tune out.

"Can you spare some change?" is not a very effective way for panhandlers to get money. They would be better off asking "Can you spare 17 cents?"

Disrupt-Then-Reframe. In the **disrupt-then-reframe technique**, a non sequitur or unexpected element is introduced to provide a momentary disruption. The disruption absorbs critical thinking functions and prevents individuals from processing the persuasive message. The requester then reframes the message in a positive light.

For example, researchers managed to disrupt attention by stating the price of Christmas cards in pennies (rather than dollars) before stating, "It's a bargain!" (Davis & Knowles, 1999). When homeowners were told that a package of eight cards cost $3.00, about 40% of the homeowners bought the cards. When homeowners were told the cards cost 300 pennies (the disruption), "which is a bargain" (the reframing), about 80% of the homeowners bought the cards. In another study (Knowles & Linn, 2004), people were more likely to buy cupcakes at a bake sale when they were called "halfcakes" rather than "cupcakes" before the seller declared "They're delicious!" To work, this technique requires both the disruption and the reframing, in that order. Distraction prevents people from processing persuasive messages at a deep level.

As you may have noticed, many influence and persuasion techniques are based on the duplex mind. In many cases, persuaders want to influence someone to do something that he or she would not sensibly do. The conscious, rational mind is therefore the enemy, and the persuaders seek to neutralize and bypass it by working with the automatic mind. For example, whether you want to buy a pastry shouldn't logically depend on whether it is labeled a "halfcake" or a "cupcake," and certainly your willingness to buy something ought to be the same regardless of whether its price is

LIMITED-NUMBER TECHNIQUE influence technique based on scarcity, in which one tells people that an item is in short supply

FAST-APPROACHING-DEADLINE TECHNIQUE influence technique based on scarcity, in which one tells people an item or a price is only available for a limited time

PIQUE TECHNIQUE influence technique in which one captures people's attention, as by making a novel request

DISRUPT-THEN-REFRAME TECHNIQUE influence technique in which one disrupts critical thinking by introducing an unexpected element, then reframes the message in a positive light

three dollars or 300 cents. But it takes conscious processing to recognize that those are the same and that one's willingness to buy should be the same. The automatic system is more susceptible to such tricks and biases, so persuaders prefer to work with it—and to keep the conscious mind from getting into the act.

[QUIZ YOURSELF]

Techniques of Social Influence

1. The technique in which an influencer prefaces the real request by first getting the person to agree to a smaller request is called the _____ technique.
   (a) door-in-the-face   (b) foot-in-the-door
   (c) low-ball   (d) pique

2. The class first asks their professor to cancel the next exam. The professor says "No way!" The class then asks the professor to postpone the exam one week. The professor says "Okay." This is an example of what technique?
   (a) Disrupt-then-reframe   (b) Door-in-the-face
   (c) Foot-in-the-door   (d) Low-ball

3. Mohamed accepts a job to shingle the roof of a house. He later learns that he also is expected to shingle the detached garage as part of the original agreement. This is an example of what technique?
   (a) Door-in-the-face
   (b) Legitimization-of-paltry-favors
   (c) Low-ball
   (d) That's-not-all

4. Which of the following is an explanation of the fast-approaching-deadline technique?
   (a) Capturing and disrupting attention
   (b) Commitment and consistency
   (c) Reciprocity
   (d) Scarcity

Persuasion

Persuasion is an attempt to change a person's attitude. It is a form of social influence. The scientific study of persuasion can be traced back to Carl Hovland, a social psychologist at Yale University. Hovland received a contract from the U.S. Army to study the morale of soldiers. President Franklin D. Roosevelt was worried that American soldiers would lose their will to fight Japan after defeating the German Nazis. White House adviser Lowell Mellett was told that the newly drafted soldiers "haven't the slightest enthusiasm for this war or this cause. They are not grouchy, they are not mutinous, they just don't give a tinker's dam" (*Why We Fight*, 2004). The Army Morale Branch tried to improve soldier morale, but failed due to the

"deadly effects of prepared lectures indifferently read to bored troops." The War Department hired Frank Capra, of Fox and Disney studios, to produce a series of films called *Why We Fight*. From 1942 to 1945, Hovland left Yale and went to Washington, D.C., to study the effects of these films on soldier morale (Hovland, Lumsdaine, & Sheffield, 1965). Hovland conducted more than 50 experiments on persuasion and found that although the films were successful in helping soldiers understand the factual basis of the war, they were unsuccessful at motivating soldiers to fight the war. Soldiers were no more eager to die for America after watching films than before.

After the war, Hovland returned to Yale University. The Rockefeller Foundation gave him a grant to continue his studies on persuasion and communication. Hovland and his colleagues conducted a systematic program of research that focused on "who says what to whom" (Hovland, Janis, & Kelley, 1953). The "who" component is the source of the message, such as a person who is making a speech. The "says what" component is the actual message, such as the speech. The "to whom" component is the audience, the people who hear the speech.

These three components of persuasion were proposed by Aristotle more than 2,000 years before Hovland was born. In *Rhetoric*, Aristotle specified three components of the persuasive process: the speaker, the subject of the speech, and the hearer to whom the speech is addressed (*Rhet*. I.3, 1358a37ff.). Aristotle also identified three elements necessary to persuade an audience: (a) emotional appeal (pathos), (b) intellectual appeal (logos), and (c) charisma (ethos). As we have seen, when social psychologists take up an idea, they often find they are not the first to have thought of it. But they can test and evaluate ideas using the experimental method and thereby make an important, original contribution to understanding. Aristotle was brilliant, but he conducted no experiments. Many seemingly brilliant ideas turn out to be wrong, and only careful testing can determine which ones are correct.

WHO: THE SOURCE

> Some people thinks the media puts too much pressure on women to look a certain way. But what about, maybe the media isn't putting enough pressure on, because there's still so many fatty boom-booms walking around?
> —Politically incorrect comedian Ali G, on the limited power of media influence

Perhaps the most important characteristics of the source of a message are credibility and likability. Let's look at both of these important characteristics.

PERSUASION an attempt to change a person's attitude

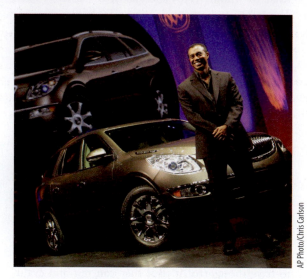

Tiger Woods is a credible source for golf clubs and balls, but not for cars.

Source Credibility. The **source** is the individual who delivers the message. A source can be credible or not credible. According to the Merriam-Webster dictionary, credibility is "the quality or power of inspiring belief." However, a source may inspire belief in some situations but not others. For example, as an expert and champion golfer, Tiger Woods is certainly a credible source for some products he endorses, such as Nike golf balls and clubs, but he is not a credible source for other products he endorses, such as Buick cars. Tiger Woods is not a mechanic or a professional racecar driver.

Speaker credibility was the topic of a famous early series of studies by Hovland and Weiss (1951). For example, participants read one speech advocating the development of atomic submarines. By random assignment, the speaker was said to be either a well-known physicist (Robert J. Oppenheimer) or a writer for *Pravda* (the newspaper of the Communist Party in the former Soviet Union). Participants reported their opinions about the topics in the speeches before, immediately after, and a month after reading the speeches. The results showed that immediately after reading the speech, highly credible sources produced more opinion change than did less credible sources. A month later, however, there was an increase for the less credible source and a decrease for the highly credible source. Therefore, in the long run, the overall amount of opinion change was about the same for the two sources. Hovland and Weiss called this the **sleeper effect**. Over time, people separated the message from the messenger. If they remembered the speech, they forgot who gave it. Subsequent research has shown that the sleeper effect is very reliable (Pratkanis, Greenwald, Leippe, & Baumgardner, 1988).

What makes a source credible? Hovland identified two characteristics: (a) **expertise**, which is how much the source knows; and (b) **trustworthiness**, which is whether the source will honestly tell you what he or she knows. Experts can influence us because we assume they know what they are talking about. But experts cannot be persuasive unless we trust them. A Gallup poll showed that the general public perceived car salespeople, insurance salespeople, advertisers, and lawyers as the least trustworthy people. Those considered most trustworthy were pharmacists, clergy, physicians, and professors. The difference between the two groups of people is that the first group has something to sell, and therefore something to gain—your money! In one study (Eagly & Chaiken, 1998), a physician from a drug company claiming that its company's drug was safe was less persuasive than the Food and Drug Administration (FDA) making the same claim. *Food for Thought* explains yet another way that communicators can be persuasive by being especially trustworthy.

Powerful speakers are also assumed to be credible (e.g., Erickson, Lind, Johnson, & O'Barr, 1978; Newcombe & Arnkoff, 1979). Powerless speech, such as speech containing disclaimers (e.g., "I'm not an expert, but . . ."), detracts from the speaker's credibility and therefore is less successful at exerting influence.

Although he didn't conduct any research on the topic, Aristotle recognized the importance of source credibility in persuasion. According to Aristotle, "The persuasion is accomplished by a character whenever the speech is held in such a way as to render the speaker worthy of credence." According to Aristotle, credible speakers display "(i) practical intelligence (*phronêsis*), (ii) a virtuous character,

---

SOURCE the individual who delivers a message

SLEEPER EFFECT the finding that, over time, people separate the message from the messenger

EXPERTISE how much a source knows

TRUSTWORTHINESS whether a source will honestly tell you what he or she knows

Food *for* Thought

Convert Communicators and Health Messages

Usually experts must be trustworthy to be credible. However, people can make up for their deficits in trustworthiness by arguing against their past transgressions. Such people are called **convert communicators**, and they can be quite persuasive (Levine & Valle, 1975). This tactic is especially effective when used by low-status communicators that audiences might otherwise ignore. Because of the commitment and consistency principle, we take notice when people argue against their previously held attitudes and behaviors. Drug addicts, alcoholics, and chain smokers may lack status and prestige, but they can still be very credible sources when they tell us how they overcame their undesirable behaviors.

For example, Subway ads often feature a man named Jared Fogle, who lost an amazing 235 pounds by eating low-calorie, low-fat Subway sandwiches instead of high-calorie, high-fat

Courtesy Subway Restaurants/Doctor's Associates, Inc.

Courtesy Subway Restaurants/Doctor's Associates, Inc.

foods. In less than a year, he went from 425 pounds to 190 pounds. Obese people may listen to Jared because he was probably heavier than they are now and they may be impressed by how much weight he lost.

Convert communicators are likable because they are similar to audience members. They also

Convert communicators who describe how they overcame obstacles can be very persuasive. For example, Jared Fogle lost 235 pounds in less than a year by eating low-calorie, low-fat Subway sandwiches instead of high-calorie, high-fat foods. The company took advantage of his credibility by featuring him in their advertisements.

show a sense of mastery because they were able to overcome their undesirable behavior, which enhances their credibility. For example, research has shown that a reformed alcoholic is a much more persuasive source than a lifelong teetotaler on the subject of the importance of abstaining from alcohol (Levine & Valle, 1975). ●

---

and (iii) good will" (*Rhet.* II.1, 1378a6ff.). Aristotle's list of characteristics resembles those proposed by Hovland's group. Practical intelligence is similar to expertise—expert sources are intelligent and know what they are talking about. "Virtuous character" and goodwill are similar to trustworthiness—trustworthy sources appear to be honest, virtuous, and good-willed. Aristotle argued that if the speaker displayed practical intelligence without virtuosity and goodwill, the audience would doubt the speaker's aims, but that if the speaker displayed all three characteristics, "it cannot rationally be doubted that his suggestions are credible." It is not necessary that the speaker actually possess any of these characteristics—only that the audience believe that the speaker has these characteristics.

Source Likability. We are also persuaded by sources we like. Two factors that influence whether we like someone are similarity and physical attractiveness. In a study that examined source similarity, students at the University of California, Santa Barbara, read a speech advocating the use of SAT scores in college admissions (Mackie, Worth, & Asuncion, 1990). The arguments for using SAT scores were either strong or weak. Strong arguments were persuasive when the delegate who wrote the speech was

a fellow student at the University of California, Santa Barbara, but not when the delegate was a student at the University of New Hampshire. (Weak arguments were not persuasive regardless of who wrote the speech.) Thus, overall, the similar source was more persuasive than the dissimilar source.

Physical attractiveness produces a positive reaction from others (see Chapter 11). We assume that attractive people also possess many other desirable traits—including traits that can influence how persuasive a person is, such as intelligence. This is called the **halo effect**. Attractive political candidates are more effective at persuading people to vote for them than are unattractive candidates, even though many voters deny the impact of attractiveness on electability (e.g., Budesheim & DePaola, 1994; Efran & Patterson, 1974).

SAYS WHAT: THE MESSAGE

Messages can vary on several dimensions. In this section we examine some of the most important.

CONVERT COMMUNICATORS people perceived as credible sources because they are arguing against their own previously held attitudes and behaviors

HALO EFFECT the assumption that because people have one desirable trait (e.g., attractiveness) people also possess many other desirable traits (e.g., intelligence)

Did physical attractiveness persuade voters to elect former Attorney General Jennifer Mulhern Granholm to be governor of Michigan?

Reason Versus Emotion. There are two approaches in presenting a persuasive message. One can present the cold, hard facts, or one can appeal to emotions. Which approach works best? Well-educated and analytical people are more responsive to arguments based on logic and reason (e.g., Hovland, Lumsdaine, & Sheffield, 1949).

Emotional responses can also be very effective. In *Rhetoric*, Aristotle wrote that the success of a persuasive message depends on the emotional state of the audience; "for we do not judge in the same way when we grieve and rejoice or when we are friendly and hostile" (cp. *Rhet.* II.1, 1378a1ff.). Research has

Humor can make the source more likable.

shown that people who are in a good mood are more receptive to persuasive messages than other people. One study found that persuasion was increased when college students ate peanuts and drank Pepsi while reading the messages (Janis, Kaye, & Kirschner, 1965).

One way to put an audience in a good mood is to use humor. About 40% of all ads employ humor (Unger, 1996). Research shows that people pay more attention to humorous messages than to serious messages (Duncan & Nelson, 1985). Humor can also make the source more likable (Gruner, 1985). On the downside, people may remember that a message was funny but forget what the message was about (Cantor & Venus, 1980).

Humor isn't the only emotional approach that speakers can use—fear is another option. Do scare tactics work to persuade people? If so, how much should you scare them? Just a little? Or should you scare the daylights out of them? Carl Hovland based his persuasion research on learning theory, which focuses on the link between the stimulus and the response. Hovland predicted that a frightening message (the stimulus) would increase arousal, attention, and comprehension of the message, which would result in attitude change (the response). Attitude change, in turn, should function as a reinforcement because it reduces the fear.

Hovland's colleagues Irving Janis and Seymour Feshbach (1953) conducted a study on the effect of fear appeals on attitudes toward dental health. All students heard the same essential information on tooth decay, but the speeches differed in the amount of fear they aroused. Students in the low fear group were warned of the results of not using the proper toothbrush; students in the high fear group watched a graphic film that showed the horrifying effect of tooth decay. Students reported their dental hygiene behaviors before and after hearing the speech. The results showed the most attitude change in the low fear group, and the least attitude change in the high fear group. The authors speculated that strong fear might cause defensive reactions in audience members, causing them to tune out the message. For another illustration of fear's effect on attitudes, see *The Social Side of Sex*.

In a later publication, Janis (1967) suggested that fear appeal and attitude change have an inverted U-shaped relationship. Attitude change is lowest for no fear and extremely high fear appeals, with the most attitude change occurring for moderate fear appeals. Subsequent research has shown that fear appeals are persuasive if they do not paralyze the audience with fear, if the audience is susceptible to the danger, and if the audience is told how to avoid the danger (e.g., Rogers, 1983). A meta-analysis of 105 studies involving about 18,000 participants

the SOCIAL SIDE of SEX

Scared Into Safe Sex?

The so-called sexual revolution of the 1960s produced a widespread increase in sexual activity in the 1970s. People began having sex at younger ages, more premarital and extramarital sex, and more sex partners. However, in the 1980s the AIDS epidemic burst into public consciousness. An incurable and fatal disease, AIDS made the free and easy sexual behavior of the 1970s seem dangerous and irresponsible.

Although some people did become more careful about their sex partners, it did not seem likely that entire nations would go back to the degree of sexual abstinence that had been the norm in the 1950s. (To be sure, attitudes about sex change more rapidly than realities, and many historians believe that both the sexual abstinence of the 1950s and the sexual freedom of the 1970s have been overstated.) Accordingly, there was a movement to influence people, perhaps especially young people, about the dangers of AIDS. But what sort of influence would be most effective?

One approach used messages that would generate the maximum amount of fear, such as by emphasizing that one careless sex act can lead to a painful, grisly death. Many organizations thought this was the best way to go. However, they had not turned to social psychologists to learn whether inspiring fear is a good way to change attitudes and behaviors. Social psychologists had repeatedly found that strong fear-inspiring messages often backfire, failing to yield

the desired changes in behavior (Hovland et al., 1953; Janis & Feshbach, 1953).

The specific effect of fear-inspiring anti-AIDS films was studied by Morris and Swann (1996). They reasoned that some people would find depictions of AIDS victims personally threatening and, as a result, would deny their fear and ignore the message. In several studies, the researchers showed emotionally powerful films about AIDS to sexually active college students. These films depicted young people discussing how they had gotten AIDS and how their lives had changed. The films were explicitly made to instill a sense of fear and vulnerability in young people so as to influence their sexual behavior toward more caution and restraint.

The films backfired. The sexually active young people who saw the films rejected the fear-inducing message. They rated their own risk of getting AIDS in the next five years as significantly lower than did a control sample of participants who had not seen any film. (Control participants in one study read pamphlets about AIDS prevention; in the other study they did not have any AIDS messages at all.) Thus, the film designed to make people worry more about their risk actually made them worry less.

Ironically, the films did succeed in increasing perceived risk among one group of people: Virgins (participants who had never had sex) who watched the same films rated their risk of AIDS as higher than virgins in the control conditions.

Strong fear appeals can often backfire.

At the end of the experimental session, the researchers offered all participants some informational pamphlets about AIDS to take home. These results confirmed the conclusion that some people were denying the reality of risk. Sexually active people who had watched the films took fewer pamphlets than control participants. Virgins who watched the film took more pamphlets than virgins in the control condition.

With sex, as with other behaviors, instilling fear is an unreliable mode of influence. People resist feeling bad, and they may resist the influence attempt that uses fear. Sexually active people do live with some risk of AIDS; in order to avoid facing that risk, they rejected the message and lowered their perception of danger. Only virgins, for whom AIDS is not a current danger, were able to attend to the fear-inducing message and respond with a plausibly increased awareness of risk. ■

---

found that fear appeals are especially effective if people feel vulnerable to the threat (De Hoog, Stroebe, & De Wit, 2007). The research on fear appeals is affecting public policy. For example, the Canadian government now requires cigarette makers to carry on 50% of each pack graphic images of the hazards of smoking. Research indicates that written warnings accompanied by pictures are 60 times more likely to inspire smokers to quit than are written warnings only (Newman, 2001). In this case, the target audience knows exactly how to avoid the danger—quit smoking. Even advertisers want to frighten us into buying their products. Who wants to get caught with bad breath, dandruff, and stinky armpits? Fear appeals can be persuasive, as long as people don't become too afraid.

Stealing Thunder. The message is what the source says. Because people expect communicators to argue for their own best interests, we are taken aback when they do the opposite and argue against their own self-interests. In the courtroom, this is called **stealing thunder**—the practice of revealing potentially incriminating evidence (thunder) first, so as to negate its impact. If attorneys can reveal the incriminating evidence first, instead of hoping the other side doesn't bring it up, then they can diminish its importance in the minds of the jury. Research has shown that this tactic is effective. A jury simulation study had participants read a transcript of an assault and battery

---

STEALING THUNDER revealing potentially incriminating evidence first to negate its impact

© Courtesy of The Centers for Disease Control and Prevention

When you're only No.2, you try harder. Or else.

Little fish have to keep moving all of the time. The big ones never stop picking on them.

Avis knows all about the problems of little fish.

We're only No.2 in rent a cars. We'd be swallowed up if we didn't try harder.

Avis can't afford to relax.

There's no rest for us.

We're always emptying ashtrays. Making sure gas tanks are full before we rent our cars. Seeing that the batteries are full of life. Checking our windshield wipers.

And the cars we rent out can't be anything less than spanking new Plymouths.

And since we're not the big fish, you won't feel like a sardine when you come to our counter.

We're not jammed with customers.

Advertisers can sometimes enhance sales by seeming to argue against their own self-interest. Consumers think the advertisers are more honest and are therefore more persuaded by the ad.

case; the incriminating evidence was the defendant's previous assault conviction (Williams, Bourgeois, & Croyle, 1993). They were randomly assigned to one of three groups. Participants pretending they were members of a jury (mock jurors) in the No Thunder group were not told of the defendant's previous conviction. Mock jurors in the Thunder group learned about the previous conviction from the prosecution. Mock jurors in the Stolen Thunder group learned about the previous conviction from the defense, but they were reminded that the previous conviction was not related to the present case. After reading the transcript, participants decided whether the defendant was guilty or not guilty. The results showed that the conviction rate was lower in the Stolen Thunder group than in the Thunder group. The lowest rate of conviction was in the No Thunder group, suggesting that information about a prior conviction is damaging (even if jurors are told to ignore it).

Advertisers also use the tactic of mentioning a minor flaw of their own product, before they go on to tout its positive features. For example, a rental car business boasts "Avis, We're Number 2," and a makeup manufacturer confesses "L'Oreal: Expensive."

Another factor in persuasion is how a message is conveyed. That is, does the presenter offer only one side of the argument, or are both sides given? One interesting example of one-sided versus two-sided messages can be found in political campaigns. One-sided messages are more effective when audience members are less educated or have already made up their minds on the issue.

Should a political candidate talk only about his or her own strengths, or also about the opponent's weaknesses? In politics, negative campaigning is defined as trying to depict one's opponent as bad. Instead of focusing on what is good about one's own candidate, a negative advertisement talks mainly about the other side and tries to turn voters against him or her. Polls indicate that many voters disapprove of negative campaigning, and many candidates say they will refrain from criticizing their opponents. Nonetheless, one has only to watch television in the later stages of almost any major campaign to see negative advertisements.

Why are negative ads so common? Do they really work? The results of social psychology research on negative campaigning have been mixed. In many cases, negative campaigning involves tradeoffs. One cost is that negative campaigning tends to produce lower evaluations of both candidates. In several laboratory studies, participants read campaign ads that were either positive or negative. When both sides used negative ads, the participants perceived both candidates more negatively (Budesheim, Houston, & DePaola, 1996). Negative ads also made participants less likely to say they would vote, at least if voting was difficult (e.g., because of bad weather) (Houston, Doan, & Roskos-Ewoldsen, 1999). Negative campaigning may be most effective as a desperation measure by a candidate who is far behind in the polls and is willing to try anything to make the election closer. Even if a race is pretty close, candidates may turn negative in an attempt to get ahead. For example, in the 2008 U.S. presidential election, Republican vice presidential candidate Sarah Palin accused Barack Obama of "palling around with terrorists" because of his association with Bill Ayers, a former leader of the antiwar group the Weathermen, which conducted a bombing campaign directed at U.S. government buildings during the late 1960s and early 1970s (Boyle, 2008). Ayers is now a Distinguished Professor at the University of Illinois at Chicago. Obama spokesman Bill Burton released a statement about the relationship between the two men: "Senator Obama strongly condemns the violent actions of the Weathermen group, as he does all acts of violence. But he was an eight-year-old child when Ayers and the Weathermen were active, and any attempt to connect Obama with events of almost forty years ago is ridiculous."

Negative campaigning does not really win very many votes, but perhaps that is not its goal—instead, the goal is to reduce the other side's votes. If voters

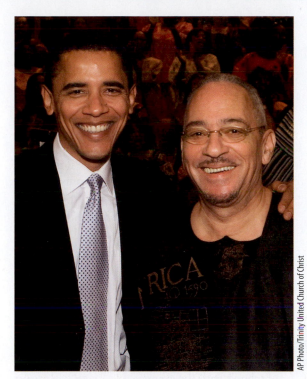

During the 2008 presidential election, both major political parties ran negative campaign advertisements, such as one that included Barack Obama's controversial reverend Jeremiah Wright.

for the other side stay home while one's own supporters are fanatical enough to vote despite an ugly, negative campaign, it might still work. Further research is needed before we can know whether the tradeoff yields more benefits than costs.

Repetition. Often persuasive messages, such as advertisements, are shown repeatedly. Does this help or hurt the message? Recall that the mere exposure effect is the tendency for novel stimuli to be liked more after the individual has been exposed to them repeatedly (see Chapter 7). Accumulated research confirms that repeated exposure to ads does influence memory for ads (Janiszewski, Noel, & Sawyer, 2003). The initial attitude toward the product makes a difference (e.g., Cacioppo & Petty, 1989). If the person has a neutral or positive response to the message initially, then repeated exposure can make the message more persuasive; if the person hates the message right off the bat, hearing it again and again will only make things worse.

Even if the audience initially likes the message, they don't want to hear it too many times, or advertisement wear-out might occur. **Advertisement wear-out** is defined as a "condition of inattention and possible irritation that occurs after an audience or target market has encountered a specific advertisement too many times" (*Dictionary of Marketing Terms*, 2004). A good example is the guy from Verizon asking, "Can you hear me now? Good." These advertisements depict the man asking the same question into his cell phone over and over. Fortunately, the company stopped airing these ads. Of course, it is possible that the advertising industry overstates the danger of wear-out, because the greater the perceived danger of wear-out, the faster companies buy new ad campaigns, and the more money advertisers make. Advertisers have to influence their clients as well as the people who watch their ads!

One good way to prevent advertisement wear-out is to use **repetition with variation**—repeat the same information, but in a varied format (e.g., Pratkanis & Aronson, 1992; Smith & Dorfman, 1975). A good example is the Energizer Bunny ads. These depict a toy bunny banging a drum as he marches

---

ADVERTISEMENT WEAR-OUT inattention and irritation that occurs after an audience has encountered the same advertisement too many times

REPETITION WITH VARIATION repeating the same information, but in a varied format

Advertising wear-out can occur when an ad is repeated too many times, such as with Verizon's "Can you hear me now?" guy.

across many different, often funny scenes, as if to show that his batteries will never wear out. In general, repetition increases persuasion if the audience initially has a neutral or positive opinion on the topic; it decreases persuasion if the audience initially has a negative opinion.

TO WHOM: THE AUDIENCE

In studying persuasion, one cannot ignore the characteristics of audience members, such as how intelligent they are. Some people are easier to persuade than others, and certain persuasion techniques work better on some people than on others.

Intelligence. The studies conducted by Hovland and his colleagues showed that more intelligent soldiers learned more from the films, analyzed the ideas more thoroughly, and were more persuaded by two-sided arguments than by one-sided ones (Hovland et al., 1949; Hovland & Weiss, 1951). Building on this research, Hovland's colleague William McGuire (1968) developed a model for persuasion that emphasized processes such as reception and yielding. **Receptivity** refers to whether you "get" the message (Did you pay attention to it? Do you understand it?). **Yielding** refers to whether you "accept" the message. McGuire found that audience members with high self-esteem were receptive to persuasive messages because they had confidence in their initial positions. However, they did not yield to the message because they were satisfied with their existing attitudes. He also found that audience members with high intelligence were receptive to persuasive messages because they had longer attention spans and were better able to comprehend arguments. However, they also did not yield because they had confidence in their existing attitudes. Later work has largely confirmed McGuire's model (Rhodes & Wood, 1992). Moderately intelligent people are easiest to persuade.

Need for Cognition. Most people are mentally lazy; they are cognitive misers (see Chapter 5). In contrast, people high in need for cognition like to think, analyze situations, and solve mental problems. **Need for cognition** is "the tendency for an individual to engage in and enjoy effortful thinking" (Cacioppo & Petty, 1982, p. 116). For example, people high in need for cognition may be more likely than others to watch the debates in a presidential election, because they like to think about the issues and candidates (Ahlering, 1987). Some sample items are "I like to have the responsibility of handling a situation that requires a lot of thinking" and "I prefer my life to be filled with puzzles that I must solve."

Research has shown that people high in need for cognition are more persuaded by strong arguments and are less persuaded by weak arguments than are people low in need for cognition (e.g., Cacioppo, Petty, & Morris, 1983). For example, some weak arguments for instituting qualifying exams for college students are:

- The risk of failing is a challenge most students would welcome.
- Graduate students have complained that because they have to take comprehensives, undergraduates should take them also.
- The exams would increase fear and anxiety enough to promote more studying.

Some strong arguments for instituting exams are:

- Average starting salaries are higher for graduates of schools with the exams.
- The quality of undergraduate teaching has improved at schools with the exams.
- Graduate and professional schools show a preference for undergraduates who have passed a comprehensive exam.

These arguments have been used in several studies on communication and persuasion (Petty & Cacioppo, 1986). Because they think more about the arguments, people with high need for cognition have attitudes that are more resistant to change (Haugtvedt & Petty, 1992).

Concern About Public Image. Some people, such as those high on the traits of self-monitoring (see Chapter 11) and public self-consciousness (see Chapter 3), are very concerned about their public image. Persuasive messages that focus on name brands and stylish products appeal to such people. In one study (Snyder & DeBono, 1985), people high in self-monitoring gave ads that focused on image (e.g., "Barclay . . . You can see the difference") higher ratings than ads that focused on quality (e.g., "Barclay . . . You can taste the difference"). Another study showed that people high in public self-consciousness were even concerned about the brand of peanut butter they ate (Bushman, 1993). Even though the jars contained the same peanut butter, individuals high in public self-consciousness gave the jar with the generic *Billy Boy* label very negative ratings and gave the jar with the *Smuckers* label very positive ratings. If people are concerned about the brand of peanut butter they buy, they are probably even more con-

---

RECEPTIVITY whether you "get" (pay attention to, understand) the message

YIELDING whether you "accept" the message

NEED FOR COGNITION a tendency to engage in and enjoy effortful thinking, analysis, and mental problem solving

cerned about the clothes they wear and the cars they drive.

Age. There is a U-shaped relationship between age and persuasion. The easiest people to persuade are young children. According to the **impressionable years hypothesis**, adolescents and young adults are also easily persuaded (Dawson & Prewitt, 1969). One study analyzed survey data from 2,500 American adults who participated in national elections between 1956 and 1980 (Krosnick & Alwin, 1989). Respondents reported their attitudes several times during four-year periods. The results showed that attitudes changed the most in 18- to 25-year-olds, followed by 26- to 33-year-olds. Attitudes changed very little in 34- to 83-year-olds. A more recent study took a closer look at attitudes in 8,500 American adults 60 to 80 years old (Visser & Krosnick, 1998). In this age range, attitudes changed most in the oldest adults. Thus, middle-aged people may be the most resistant to persuasion.

Once attitudes are formed in young adulthood, they remain fairly stable over time. In a classic study conducted by Theodore Newcomb (1943), women attending Bennington College in Vermont between 1935 and 1939 reported their political attitudes. These women came from politically conservative, wealthy families who could afford to send their daughters to a private college during the Great Depression. At Bennington, these women encountered faculty members and older students who were much more politically liberal than their parents were. After having been exposed to more liberal ideas at Bennington, these students consistently voted against their families' political ideology up to 25 years later (Newcomb, Koenig, Flacks, & Warwick, 1967), and even 50 years later (Alwin, Cohen, & Newcomb, 1991).

Cultural Differences. People from individualist cultures tend to place more emphasis on the individual, whereas people from collectivist cultures tend to place more emphasis on the group. Hang-Pil and Shavitt (1994) tested what types of advertisements appealed to members of these two cultures. Half of the participants were from the United States (individualist); the other half were from Korea (collectivist). One set of ads focused on the person (e.g., "Treat yourself to a breath-freshening experience"); the other set of advertisements focused on the group (e.g., "Share this breath-freshening experience"). The results showed that Americans were more persuaded by the individualistic ads, whereas Koreans were more persuaded by the collectivist ads. Another study showed that Americans had more favorable attitudes toward products that offered "separateness,"

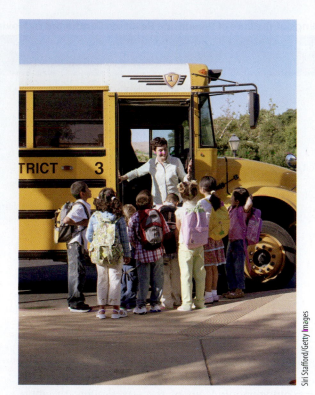

Siri Stafford/Getty Images

Children can be easily persuaded.

whereas Chinese had more favorable attitudes toward products that offered "togetherness" (Wang, Bristol, Mowen, & Chakraborty, 2000).

Overheard Messages. Other research has shown that if people think they are overhearing a message, it is more persuasive than if they see it as a sales pitch (Walster & Festinger, 1962). People are more persuaded by messages that do not seem to be designed to influence them. Advertisers sometimes use this "overheard communicator trick" to persuade consumers.

Research has shown that advertisements with omitted conclusions are more persuasive than advertisements with conclusions (Kardes, 1988). Consumers appear to be more strongly influenced by the advertised message if they draw the conclusion on their own.

When ads appear on television, most people leave the room, surf channels, or ignore the ads until the program returns. That is why advertisers sometimes use product placement, as when Lark cigarettes paid $350,000 to have James Bond smoke their cigarettes in *License to Kill*. One reason product placements work so well is that people don't realize that advertisers are trying to influence them, so they let down their guard. Product placement occurs in most

---

IMPRESSIONABLE YEARS HYPOTHESIS proposition that adolescents and young adults are more easily persuaded than their elders

What types of sources are most persuasive?	What types of messages are most persuasive?	Who is receptive to persuasive messages?
Highly credible sources	Logical messages—mainly with educated, analytical people	People who are in a good mood
Likable sources	Moderately fear-inducing messages	People of average intelligence
Convert communicators	Two-sided messages	People concerned about their public image (high self-monitoring, high public self-consciousness)
Sources who argue against their own self-interest	Moderately discrepant messages	Very young or very old people
	Messages that are repeated (but may backfire)	

forms of media, including video games. For example, product placement is very prominent in racing video games. Players recall the products placed immediately after the game and also months later (Nelson, 2002). "Overheard" messages can be quite persuasive.

Distraction. We saw earlier that distraction is sometimes helpful to influence because it gets the conscious mind out of the way (leaving the more gullible automatic system to deal with the message). Persuasion researchers such as Festinger and Maccoby (1964) have shown that distraction can help persuasion by preventing the conscious mind from thinking of counterarguments. In their study, college students read a persuasive message that argued against the Greek system on campus. Because these students belonged to Greek fraternities, they were not very receptive to the message. By the flip of a coin, half of the students were distracted by a cartoon while they read the message. The results showed that the cartoon distracted participants from counterarguing the message.

Distraction isn't always helpful. If you have a really good argument but the person listening is distracted, he or she won't understand how good your case is. ▶ **TABLE 8.1** summarizes the major results of persuasion studies conducted by Hovland, his colleagues, and other researchers.

TWO ROUTES TO PERSUASION

One theme of this book has been the duplex mind: The mind has two systems, one conscious (controlled) and the other unconscious (automatic). Influence attempts can operate using either system. That is, some forms of influence rely on appealing to conscious, rational, deliberate processing, whereas other forms rely on activating automatic responses. One appeals to enlightened self-interest; the other appeals to motivations or responses that may not be fully understood. "Illicit" or "tricky" forms of persuasion rely more on the latter. Both types of influence can be successful.

Social psychologists have avidly studied persuasion at least since the 1940s and have reported many findings, some of them seemingly contradictory or incompatible. For example, distraction sometimes increases and sometimes decreases persuasion. To resolve these problems, the **elaboration likelihood model**, or **ELM** for short (e.g., Petty & Cacioppo, 1986), and the **heuristic/systematic model** (e.g., Eagly & Chaiken,

ELABORATION LIKELIHOOD MODEL (ELM) theory that posits two routes to persuasion, via either conscious or automatic processing

HEURISTIC/SYSTEMATIC MODEL theory that posits two routes to persuasion, via either conscious or automatic processing

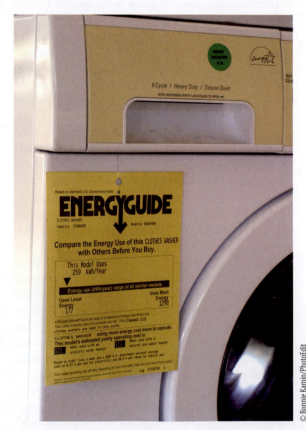

© Bonnie Kamin/PhotoEdit

Is this a persuasive message to consumers?

1998) have posited two routes to persuasion. (The two theories are quite similar, and experts use either set of terms.) One route involves conscious processing, whereas the other route involves automatic processing. These routes correspond with the duplex mind. We describe the ELM and refer to the heuristic/systematic model when the two models differ.

The route to persuasion that involves conscious processing is called the **central route** (or **systematic processing** in the heuristic/systematic model); it is depicted on the left side of ▶ **FIGURE 8.3**. Persuasion that occurs along the central route involves careful and thoughtful consideration of the content of the message. The route that involves automatic processing is called the **peripheral route** (or **heuristic processing** in the heuristic/systematic model); it is depicted on the right side of figure. Persuasion that occurs along the peripheral route involves the influence of some simple cue, such as how attractive the source is. We will start at the top of the figure and work our way down the left side before working our way down the right side.

First, the person encounters a persuasive message. The first question is whether the person is motivated to process the message. This is influenced by two factors: personal relevance and need for cognition. **Personal relevance** refers to whether people expect the issue "to have significant consequences for their own lives" (Apsler & Sears, 1968). The more personally relevant the issue, the more motivated people are to think about the persuasive message at a deep level. Some issues have personal relevance throughout our lives (e.g., the tax structure of the country we live in, the quality of water where we live); other issues have personal relevance for a certain period of time (e.g., raising college tuition, the price of textbooks); still others have personal relevance only under very transient conditions (e.g., dishwasher ads are personally relevant only when a person is shopping for a dishwasher). The other factor that influences motivation to process the persuasive message is need for cognition. As mentioned previously, people high in need for cognition like to think, and are therefore more likely than people low in need for cognition to think about the message at a deep level. Recent research shows that messages processed at a deep level are especially resistant to change (Blankenship & Wegener, 2008).

Just because people are motivated to process a message does not mean they will be able to process it. Two factors influence one's ability to process the message: distractions and knowledge. As mentioned previously, distraction disrupts the ability to think about a persuasive message. Participants in one study were exposed to ads for a variety of consumer products (Tsal, 1984). Half the participants were distracted by having them count the number of random clicks on a tape recording. Weak arguments were

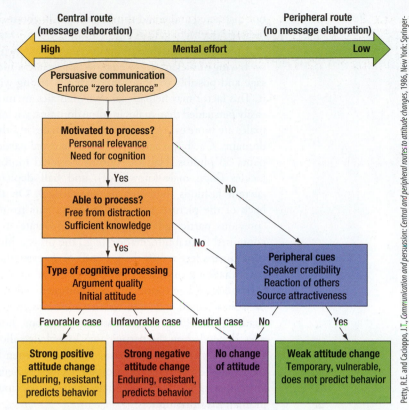

▶ **FIGURE 8.3** Elaboration likelihood model (ELM) of persuasion (Petty & Cacioppo, 1986).

Petty, R.E. and Cacioppo, J.T., Communication and persuasion: Central and peripheral routes to attitude changes, 1986, New York: Springer-Verlag. Reprinted with kind permission of the authors and Springer Science and Business Media.

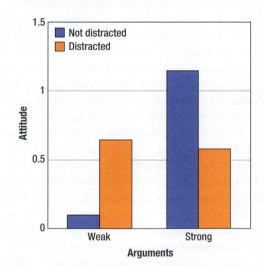

▶ **FIGURE 8.4** Distraction decreases our ability to think about a persuasive message. When the message arguments are weak, distraction increases the persuasiveness of the message. When the message arguments are strong, distraction decreases the persuasiveness of the message (Tsal, 1984; cited in Petty & Cacioppo, 1986).

more effective with distracted participants, probably because they were unable to think carefully about the message and discover its weaknesses (see left side of ▶ **FIGURE 8.4**). In contrast, strong arguments worked best on the central route—that is, when people were

CENTRAL ROUTE (SYSTEMATIC PROCESSING) the route to persuasion that involves careful and thoughtful consideration of the content of the message (conscious processing)

PERIPHERAL ROUTE (HEURISTIC PROCESSING) the route to persuasion that involves some simple cue, such as attractiveness of the source (automatic processing)

PERSONAL RELEVANCE degree to which people expect an issue to have significant consequences for their own lives not distracted and could think consciously about the message (see right side of Figure 8.4).

Conscious (central route) processing also depends on having sufficient knowledge to appreciate a message and possibly to understand what is wrong with it. This factor may help explain why females are more easily persuaded than males in some domains, whereas males are more easily persuaded than females in other domains. Cacioppo and Petty (1980) showed participants 36 photos. Half the photos depicted football tackles (high male knowledge), and half depicted current fashions (high female knowledge). On the back of the picture were written comments from a "previous participant" (actually a confederate) that contained factual information (e.g., the dress is blue, the runner's feet are off the ground) or an evaluation (e.g., that's a great tackle) that was either accurate or inaccurate. When comments were completely factual or were accurate, men and women were equally persuaded. The effects of inaccurate evaluations, however, depended on the participant's knowledge about the topic. Men were less persuaded than women by inaccurate evaluations of football tackles, whereas women were less persuaded than men by inaccurate evaluations of fashion.

If a person is motivated and able to process the message, the outcome of the processing that occurs depends on the quality of the arguments and the initial attitude. A persuasive message can be either strong or weak. When arguments are strong, thinking about them leads people to recognize their validity and to come up with further thoughts that support the message. In contrast, thinking about a message with weak arguments leads people to recognize its flaws and to come up with thoughts that argue against the message. Strong messages lead to strong positive attitude change, whereas weak messages can lead to attitude change in the opposite direction.

Of course, the person's initial attitude sets some limits on how much the attitude can change. If the person has a very strong initial attitude, even a very strong opposing message may fail to change it. Additionally, people process information in a biased way: They are much more critical of messages that go against their views than of messages that agree with their initial attitude (Lord, Ross, & Lepper, 1979). If people are not motivated or able to process a message, they may be persuaded by cues peripheral to the message. Some examples of peripheral cues are:

- Experts know best.
- The more arguments, the better.
- Good products are more expensive.
- What is beautiful is good.

In a study by Petty and Cacioppo (1979,), college students read a message about senior comprehensive exams. By the flip of a coin, students were assigned to high or low relevance groups. Students in the high relevance group were told that the exams would be instituted at their university within 2 years (Yikes! I have to take the test to graduate!). Students in the low relevance group were told that the exams would be instituted within 10 years (Who cares? I'll be gone by then!). The source of the message was either an expert (a university dean) or a nonexpert (a high school student) and had little or no impact on highly involved students. They had to take the exam regardless of the source of the message. Participants who were not highly involved, however, were influenced by the peripheral cue of source expertise.

In summary, there are two routes to attitude change. People who think about the message travel down the central route, whereas people who don't think about the message take the peripheral route. Attitude change that occurs via the peripheral route tends to be weak. It is temporary, vulnerable to change, and does not predict future behavior very well. Persuasion by the central route produces much more durable and powerful attitude change. But of course the central route is often the more difficult one to use, because you actually have to have strong, effective arguments.

Does talking fast make a speaker more credible? To find out, see *Tradeoffs*.

[QUIZ YOURSELF]

Persuasion

1. Pauline reads an article citing several reasons for having life insurance. When she notices that the article is really an insurance company advertisement, she decides that life insurance is a waste of money. When the topic of insurance comes up a few weeks later, Pauline thinks that life insurance is a good use of money. This change in attitude over time represents the _____ effect.
   (a) primacy   (b) reactance
   (c) recency   (d) sleeper

2. Maureen is very intelligent, Audrey is moderately intelligent, and Denise is not very intelligent. A two-sided persuasive message will probably be most effective on _____.
   (a) Audrey
   (b) Denise
   (c) Maureen
   (d) The three women should be equally affected.

3. While listening half-heartedly to a lecture, Jamaal hears his professor cite several reasons why playing violent video games increases aggression. Jamaal accepts these reasons solely because his professor has been correct before. In this example, Jamaal is using _____ processing.
   (a) alpha   (b) central route
   (c) omega   (d) peripheral route

Should Speakers Talk Fast or Slow?

People who are trying to persuade others, such as car salespeople and auctioneers, talk really fast. Is talking fast a good strategy or a bad one? Two early field experiments found that fast speakers were more persuasive than slow speakers (Miller, Maruyama, Beaber, & Valone, 1976). In the first study, participants were adults in public locations such as parks and shopping malls. A researcher posing as a radio announcer stopped people and asked them to evaluate the radio program for that day, which was on "The danger of drinking coffee." The message argued that coffee was bad because it contains caffeine, a poisonous drug that causes heart damage, migraine headaches, stomach ulcers, and a host of other problems. The speaker who delivered the message was either a "locksmith" (low-credibility source) or a biochemist (high-credibility source). The speech rate was either slow (102 words per minute) or fast (195 words per minute). Overall, the high-speed message was more persuasive than the low-speed message, and the high-credibility source was more persuasive than the low-credibility source.

In the second study, the researchers used an unfamiliar topic instead: "The Dangers of Hydroponically Grown Vegetables." The speech rate was slow (111 words per minute), moderate (140 words per minute), or fast (191 words per minute). The faster the speech, the more persuasive the message was judged to be. Fast speakers were also judged to be more intelligent, knowledgeable, and objective. The authors concluded, "Beware of the fast talker" (p. 621).

These early results show that speaking fast makes people think you are more credible. This is good if thinking is low (i.e., the credibility serves as a peripheral cue, using the terminology of the elaboration likelihood model of attitude change). But if thinking would have been high, then fast talking distracts people from processing the arguments. This could be bad if the arguments supporting the message are strong, but good if the arguments supporting the message are weak.

A study by Smith and Shaffer (1991) tested this hypothesis that fast talking can backfire. Researchers approached undergraduate students and had them listen to a message about a recently passed law that raised the legal age for purchasing and consuming alcoholic beverages from 19 to 21 years. (Before conducting the study, the researchers found out that almost all students were opposed to the new law; they wanted to be able to drink legally at age 19 rather than 21.) By the flip of a coin, students heard a speech in favor of the new law (counterattitudinal group) or a speech that opposed the new law (the proattitudinal group). The speech was delivered at a slow (144 words per minute), moderate (182 words per minute), or fast (214 words per minute) rate. As with earlier studies (Miller et al., 1976), Smith and Shaffer found that as speech rate increased, the perceived credibility of speakers also increased. The more important question is whether the speech influenced the students' attitudes. As can be seen in ▶ FIGURE 8.5, as speech rate increased, students showed more agreement with the counterattitudinal message but less agreement with the proattitudinal message. (Note that Figure 8.5 depicts a significant interaction between type of message and speed of speech; see Chapter 1 for a description of interactions.) Thus, people should talk fast if their arguments are weak, so people won't have time to think about the arguments. If their arguments are strong, people should talk more slowly, so people can think about and appreciate the arguments. ●

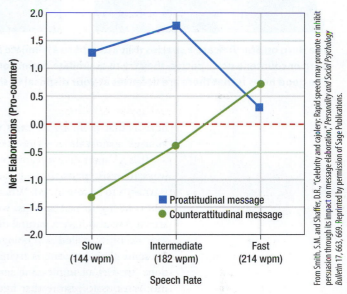

From Smith, S.M. and Shaffer, D.R., "Celebrity and cajolery: Rapid speech may promote or inhibit persuasion through its impact on message elaboration," *Personality and Social Psychology Bulletin* 17, 663, 669. Reprinted by permission of Sage Publications.

▶ **FIGURE 8.5** Speaking fast is good if the audience thinks your arguments are weak (because they won't have time to think about them), but bad if the audience thinks your arguments are strong (Smith & Shaffer, 1991).

---

4. Research shows that a person who is distracted from a message is more likely to be persuaded by that message. The elaboration likelihood model explains this by suggesting that _____.
   (a) distractions take up most of the person's peripheral processing ability
   (b) distractions serve as cues for rewards and punishments concerning being persuaded
   (c) a distracting attitude makes the source more likable
   (d) distractions prevent people from engaging in central route processing of information

Resisting Persuasion

The Borg ("Cyborg") are among the most evil villains in space encountered by *Star Trek* crew members. They are a species that looks half human, half machine. When the Borg encounter a new species, they say, "This is the Borg Collective. Prepare to be assimilated. We will add your biological and technological distinctiveness to our own. You will adapt to service us. Resistance is futile." Sometimes the people who want to influence us seem like the Borg trying to assimilate us—resistance seems futile. The good

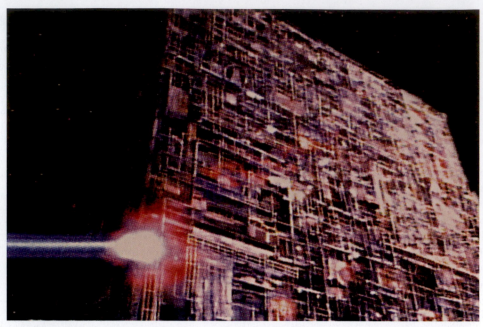

The Borg on *Star Trek* are a species that attempt to assimilate all other species (left). They live as a collective in a cube (right). When the Borg encounter a new species, they try to assimilate them. Sometimes the people who want to gain influence over us seem like the Borg. The good news is that there are defenses at your disposal to shield you against those who wield weapons of influence.

news is that there are defenses you can use to shield yourself against these weapons of influence.

This chapter has already presented some useful ways to resist persuasion. For example, to be fore-warned is to be forearmed. When we know that some-one is trying to persuade us, we can prepare for the attack. We also have a natural defense against persua-sive attempts, called psychological reactance: When we sense that someone is trying to restrict our free-dom, we feel an unpleasant emotional response that motivates us to restore that freedom. In this section we discuss some other shields that can be used to pro-tect us from those who wield weapons of influence.

ATTITUDE INOCULATION

People brought up in a germ-free environment are highly vulnerable to diseases because their bodies have not built up antibodies to attack them. Medicine has helped to solve this problem by inoculating people: Exposing people to weakened doses of viruses (as in a flu shot) helps make their immune systems stronger. McGuire and his colleagues transferred the concept of inoculation to the study of attitudes (McGuire, 1961, 1964; McGuire & Papageorgis, 1961; Papageorgis & McGuire, 1961). They argued that cultural truisms (e.g., "Smoking is bad for your health") should be especially vulnerable to counterarguments, because they exist in a kind of "germ-free" environ-ment in which their validity is never challenged. McGuire argued that in order to immunize people against persuasion, it is good to expose them to some of the counterarguments against these cultural

truisms and let them build up defenses against the counterarguments. Of course, being exposed to too many counterarguments, like too heavy a dose of the live virus, could have the opposite effect, reducing resistance rather than strengthening it.

Research has shown that inoculation works. In one study, high school students inoculated seventh- and eighth-graders against peer pressure to smoke. For example, the seventh- and eighth-graders were taught to respond to advertisements implying that liberated women smoke by saying "She is not really liberated if she is hooked on tobacco." They also role-played situations in which peers were trying to per-suade them to smoke. For example, after being called "chicken" for not taking a cigarette, they answered with statements like "I'd be a real chicken if I smoked just to impress you." Inoculated children were half as likely as uninoculated children at another junior high school to begin smoking (Perry, Killen, Slinkard, & McAlister, 1980; see also Chassin, Presson, Sherman, & Edwards, 1990; Falck & Craig, 1988).

Credit card debt is a growing problem worldwide, and college students aren't immune to it. Credit card companies often target college students because they are quick to use credit cards and slow to pay them back (because students don't have much money). A degree isn't the only thing students leave college with. Many also leave with a mountain of credit card debt. One student said, "My credit card prob-lems were a major added worry to everything else and . . . made my freshman year horrible" (Stanford, 1999, p. 13). Some students even get so discouraged with their credit card bills that they commit suicide

(Consumer Federation of America, 1999). Fortunately, college students can be inoculated against persuasive attempts to acquire and use credit cards (Compton & Pfau, 2004). Students in this study who were taught how to critically evaluate persuasive messages in credit card advertisements were able to resist these ads.

Social psychologists Zakary Tormala and Richard Petty (2002) proposed a theory of persuasion based on the statement "What doesn't kill me makes me stronger." These researchers found that when people resist persuasion, they become more confident in their initial attitudes. When people think they have successfully resisted persuasion, they decide that their initial attitude is correct and, therefore, feel more certain about it. This seems a logical conclusion because if their attitude were incorrect, they would have abandoned it and accepted the persuasive message. In summary, inoculating people by exposing them to weak arguments can protect them against stronger arguments.

FOREWARNED IS FOREARMED

Sneak attacks on attitudes can be devastating. If people know an attack is coming, however, they can prepare to defend themselves. High school students in a study were forewarned either 2 or 10 minutes in advance that they would hear a speech on "Why Teenagers Should Not Be Allowed to Drive" (not a very popular topic, as you might guess) (Freedman & Sears, 1965). The remaining students heard the same talk, but received no forewarning. The results showed that students who received no forewarning were persuaded the most, followed by those who received 2 minutes' warning, followed by those who received 10 minutes' warning. When people believe that someone is trying to persuade them (and take away their freedom of choice), they experience an unpleasant emotional response called psychological reactance, which motivates them to resist the persuasive attempt (see Chapter 4). Often people will

College students are bombarded by ads promoting credit cards, such as this one that has the school logo on it. Fortunately, students can be inoculated against these ads.

do exactly the opposite of what they are being persuaded to do; this is called **negative attitude change** or a **boomerang effect**. The parents of Romeo and Juliet in Shakespeare's play found this out when their efforts to end the romance only drove the young lovebirds closer together.

STOCKPILE RESOURCES

To deal with persuasion attempts, we should use all the resources at our disposal: physical, cognitive, and social. In the Iraq war, American soldiers used sleep deprivation and music to break Iraqi prisoners' resistance ("Sesame Street," 2003). The music included songs from the heavy metal group Metallica and from children's television programs (*Sesame Street*, *Barney*) because Iraqi prisoners hated this music. As discussed in the section on the mere exposure effect, repeated

NEGATIVE ATTITUDE CHANGE (BOOMERANG EFFECT) doing exactly the opposite of what one is being persuaded to do

In the Iraq war, U.S. interrogators sought to break the resistance of Iraqi prisoners by forcing them to listen to music from the heavy metal group Metallica (left) and from the public television show *Barney* (right).

exposure to a disliked stimulus (such as unpleasant music) makes people dislike the stimulus even more. As discussed in Chapter 6, unpleasant events put people in a bad mood. People don't like being in a bad mood, but it takes a lot of effort to repair a bad mood. If people use their cognitive resources to repair a bad mood, they have fewer resources available to fight off persuasive attempts.

Although using irritating music may be a new tactic, sleep deprivation is a very common tactic used on POWs during times of war. We all function much better after a good night's sleep. Gilbert (1991) has suggested that we may be more susceptible to persuasion tactics when we are tired. When we hear someone make a statement, we immediately accept the statement as being true, regardless of whether it is actually true. It is only with mental effort that we recognize the statement to be false and reject it. All of this happens in a fraction of a second. People usually have enough cognitive energy and motivation to mentally reject statements that sound false, but when people are tired, their mental energy levels drop, and they become more susceptible to false statements.

DEFENSES AGAINST INFLUENCE TECHNIQUES

Knowledge is power, and in this section we share some knowledge that will help you resist the most common persuasion techniques.

Defenses Against Techniques Based on Commitment and Consistency. Several influence techniques are based on the principle of commitment and consistency, including the foot-in-the-door technique, the low-ball technique, the bait-and-switch technique, the labeling technique, and the legitimization-of-paltry-favors technique. The commitment and consistency principle is a great time saver. If we had to weigh the pros and cons of each decision, we would soon become overwhelmed, and we would not be able to function. It is much easier to make a commitment once and then behave consistently with that commitment.

The power of the commitment and consistency principle comes from the sense of obligation it creates. When people freely make commitments, they feel obligated to behave consistently with those commitments. There are costs for behaving inconsistently: Inconsistency between one's attitudes and actions can result in cognitive dissonance, which is an unpleasant emotional response (see Chapter 7). If your inconsistent behaviors affect others, you may suffer social rejection and ostracism, which don't feel good either. However, you should *not* feel obligated to behave consistently with a commitment that you were tricked into making. If it is not clear whether you were tricked into making a commitment, ask

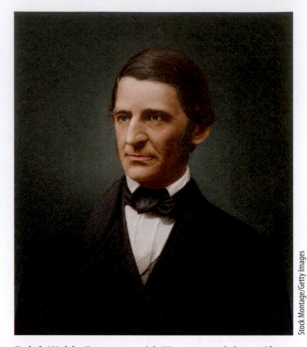

Ralph Waldo Emerson said, "Pay every debt, as if God wrote the bill."

yourself this question: "Knowing what I know now, if I could go back in time, would I make the same commitment?" (Cialdini, 2001). If the answer is "yes," behave consistently with the commitment. If the answer is "no," don't do it!

Another way to resist influence is to make a public commitment to your position (Myers, 2006). Commitments are much more binding when they are made in public than when they are made in private. For example, research has shown that straw polls of mock jurors can lead to more deadlocks (Davis et al., 1993). Standing up for your convictions in public makes you less susceptible to what others have to say.

Defenses Against Techniques Based on Reciprocation. Ralph Waldo Emerson said, "Pay every debt, as if God wrote the bill." He was advocating the value of the principle of reciprocation: People should feel obligated to repay favors and concessions. If people don't reciprocate, they feel guilty.

Generally, the principle of reciprocation is beneficial to society. It allows us to give, knowing that if we cast our bread upon the water it will come back to us, as the Judeo-Christian Bible advises (Ecclesiastes 11:1). The problem is that some people (those who want to persuade us) cast a crumb on the water and expect a loaf in return. For example, a charitable organization may give us inexpensive address labels and expect a large donation in return.

This chapter discussed two influence techniques based on reciprocal concessions: the door-in-the-face technique and the that's-not-all technique. How do we defend ourselves against people who use these techniques to manipulate us? Robert Cialdini (2001) recommends that we accept initial favors or concessions in good faith but be ready to define them as tricks if they prove to be tricks. Once they are defined as tricks, we will no longer feel obligated to reciprocate with a favor or concession. The reciprocation rule says that favors are to be repaid with favors. Tricks do not have to be repaid with favors!

Defenses Against Techniques Based on Scarcity.
The principle of scarcity generally serves people well. Scarce items usually are more valuable than plentiful items. In the influence business, however, people often use the scarcity principle to convince us that their products are scarce and that we should get them now, while we can.

We discussed two techniques based on scarcity: the limited-number technique and the fast-approaching-deadline technique. How do we defend ourselves against people who use these techniques to influence us? Easier said than done! Our natural response to scarcity is to panic. We want to seize the opportunity before it slips away. When our freedom is threatened, we experience psychological reactance. Unfortunately, this emotional response to scarcity interferes with our ability to think clearly. Cialdini (2001) recommends a two-stage process of resistance. First, we should use the tide of emotional arousal we feel in response to scarce items as a cue to stop short. We need to calm ourselves so we can think clearly and rationally. Second, we should ask why we want the item. Is it because it is scarce, or is it because of its own merits? "Because it is the last day of a sale" or "because it is the last one" is not a good reason for purchasing an item. We should buy something only if we really want it, not because it is scarce.

Defenses Against Techniques Based on Capturing and Disrupting Attention.
We also discussed the pique technique, which is based on capturing attention. The pique technique catches people off guard, so they comply without thinking. Thus, the antidote is to stop and think before acting.

Whether someone asks you for a quarter or for 17 cents should not determine whether you comply.

Finally, we discussed the disrupt-then-reframe technique, which is based on disrupting attention. As mentioned previously, distraction increases persuasion for weak messages and decreases persuasion for strong messages. The key, therefore, is to eliminate the distraction so we can process the message at a deep level.

[QUIZ YOURSELF]

Resisting Persuasion

1. When I am driving my car and someone tailgates me to make me go faster, I slow down. This is an example of _____.
   (a) cognitive dissonance
   (b) door-in-the-face
   (c) low-balling
   (d) psychological reactance

2. Knowing in advance that we are a target of a persuasive message is called _____.
   (a) cognitive dissonance
   (b) elaboration
   (c) forewarning
   (d) psychological reactance

3. The theory that exposure to weak versions of a persuasive message increases later resistance to that message is called _____.
   (a) attitude inoculation
   (b) negative attitude change
   (c) psychological reactance
   (d) the sleeper effect

4. Cialdini says that we should accept initial favors or concessions in good faith, but be ready to define them as tricks if they prove to be tricks. This defense is most effective for techniques based on the _____ principle.
   (a) capturing and disrupting attention
   (b) commitment and consistency
   (c) reciprocation
   (d) scarcity

WHAT MAKES US HUMAN? Putting the Cultural Animal in Perspective

All social animals rely on others for some of what they want and need, so they face the same basic problems of needing to influence others, at least sometimes. The need to exert social influence is not limited to human beings. But some methods of influence, and of resisting influence, are distinctly human.

The duplex mind is rather distinctively human, so only humans have two routes to persuasion. In particular, human beings have a special capacity for cognitive reasoning and thinking, so the central, or systematic, route to persuasion works better with humans than with any other animal. People can respond to a persuasion attempt by elaborating on it and thinking about it in ways that no other creatures do. For example, when trying to persuade a dog, a duck, or a dolphin to do something, there is not much to be gained by appealing to reason or morality.

The extent to which people think about what others tell them, thereby elaborating on and embellishing a simple persuasive message, also reflects the extensive makeup of the human self. We have seen that many characteristics of the recipient (e.g., intelligence) affect the impact of the persuasive message. Such inner traits and processes probably play a much bigger role in human influence than in influence in other species.

The self is also highly relevant to the labeling technique. As we saw, getting people to label themselves as being a certain kind of person is an effective way to change their behavior. People have elaborate self-concepts that can be swayed in this way. With most other animals, the scope for influence by labeling the self-concept would be much smaller.

As cultural beings, humans are characterized by a social life filled with elaborate norms and implicit rules. Many persuasion techniques make use of these norms and rules. Humans everywhere recognize the norm of reciprocity, based on an abstract concept of fairness, and they accept obligations to reciprocate what is done for them. As we have seen, several influence techniques capitalize on norms of fairness and reciprocity.

Another special dimension of the complexity of human social life is our ability to anticipate and care about how others perceive us, and to alter our behavior to make an impression. The distinction between private acceptance and public compliance is crucial to understanding human influence, but it is mostly irrelevant to understanding influence among other animals. Humans have a much more elaborate inner self and a more advanced understanding of the difference between inner sentiments and overt, expressive acts than other creatures. In plainer terms, only humans respond to social pressure by saying things they don't mean, or by going along with the crowd while keeping doubts to themselves.

The moral rules that are common to human cultures also capitalize on the human capacity for feeling guilty over violations of interpersonal norms, and persuaders can play on people's guilt to influence them. The door-in-the-face and foot-in-the-door techniques, for example, may well operate by making the person start to feel guilty.

We saw that humor can be a factor in persuasion, as indicated by the fact that so many advertisements try to be funny. There is as yet no sign that nonhuman animals have a sense of humor, so humor would only be useful in persuading people.

Although we have focused on special opportunities to influence people, there is another side: People are uniquely able to resist influence and persuasion. Most of the means of resisting influence involve use of conscious control over responses (wait until your emotional reaction has subsided before making a decision), shifting among perspectives (consider an alternative view), and conscious reasoning (evaluate the message logically). These capacities are pretty much absent outside of our species. People, therefore, have special powers and weapons that enable them to avoid being swayed.

chapter summary

TWO TYPES OF SOCIAL INFLUENCE

- Normative influence involves going along with the crowd in order to be liked and accepted.
- People from collectivist countries are more likely to be influenced by group norms than are people from individualist countries.
- Conformity increases as group size increases (up to a point, then it levels off).
- People will conform to a group in which everyone agrees, but if there is any sort of disagreement among group members, then people become willing to stand up for what they believe and go against the majority.
- People who deviate from a group are often rejected by the group.
- Group norms are the beliefs or behaviors a group of people accepts as normal.

- Informational influence involves going along with the crowd because you think the crowd knows more than you do, such as when
  - The situation is ambiguous, so people do not know how to behave.
  - There is a crisis and people don't have time to think for themselves.

TECHNIQUES OF SOCIAL INFLUENCE

- The foot-in-the-door technique gets someone to comply with a large request by first making a small request.
- The low-ball technique involves shifting from a smaller request to a larger request after the person has committed to the small request.
- The bait-and-switch technique involves making a great offer and then switching to a less desirable offer.
- The labeling technique involves assigning a label to an individual and then requesting a favor that is consistent with that label.

- The legitimization-of-paltry-favors technique involves asking for a very small contribution in order to get a larger contribution.
- The door-in-the-face technique involves making an inflated request (that will most likely be rejected) and then retreating to a smaller request. (It only works if the first request is not too extreme and if the same person makes both requests.)
- The that's-not-all technique begins with an inflated request but is quickly followed by a discount or bonus.
- According to the scarcity principle, rare opportunities are more valuable than plentiful opportunities.
- With the limited-number technique, the customer is told that items exist in a limited supply.

- With the fast-approaching-deadline technique, the customer is told that items can only be obtained for a limited time.
- When our personal freedom is threatened, we experience an unpleasant emotional response called psychological reactance, which motivates us to do what is forbidden.
- The pique technique captures the target's attention by making the request novel to increase the chances of compliance with the persuasive request.
- In the disrupt-then-reframe technique, a non sequitur or unexpected element is introduced to provide a momentary disruption that interrupts critical thinking and increases the chances of compliance with the persuasive request.

PERSUASION

- Persuasion is an attempt to change a person's attitude.
- According to the sleeper effect, over time people separate the message from the messenger.
- Two characteristics can influence source credibility:
  - Expertise—how much the source knows
  - Trustworthiness—how honest the source is
- Fast talkers are assumed to be more credible and intelligent than slow talkers (as long as the speech is not too fast to be comprehended).
- Powerful speakers are believed to be credible.
- Powerless speech includes compound requests and disclaimers.
- Convert communicators make up for their deficits in trustworthiness by arguing against their past transgressions.
  - They can be very persuasive.
  - They are likable because they are similar to audience members.
  - They show a sense of mastery because they were able to overcome their undesirable behavior.
- Similarity and physical attractiveness increase liking and therefore increase persuasion.

- People who are in a good mood are more receptive to persuasive messages.
- Instilling fear is an unreliable mode of influence; moderate fear appeals are more persuasive than high or low fear appeals.
- Stealing thunder is the practice of revealing potentially incriminating evidence to negate its impact. It works because it makes the source appear more honest and credible.
- One-sided persuasive messages work best when the audience is not able to process the message thoroughly; two-sided messages work best when the audience can process the message thoroughly.
- Message discrepancy is the difference between the initial attitude of the audience and the content of the speaker's message.
- Repetition polarizes initial responses to the persuasive message, although advertising wear-out can occur when an ad is repeated too many times.
- Audience members with moderate levels of self-esteem and intelligence are most affected by persuasive messages.
- Need for cognition is the tendency for an individual to engage in and enjoy effortful thinking.
- People high in need for cognition are more persuaded by strong arguments and are less persuaded by weak arguments than are people low in need for cognition.
- Overheard messages are more persuasive than direct attempts to change attitudes.
- If the message is weak, distraction makes the message more effective, but if the message is strong, then distraction makes the message less effective.
- The elaboration likelihood model (ELM) and the heuristic/systematic model are similar. They describe two routes to persuasion: one involving conscious processing and one involving automatic processing.
- The route that involves conscious processing is called the central route or systematic processing. The route that involves automatic processing is called the peripheral route or heuristic processing.
- Personal relevance is the degree to which people expect an issue to have significant consequences for their own lives.

- Two factors influence our ability to process a message: whether we are free from distractions and whether we have sufficient knowledge.
- Peripheral cues such as source expertise have no effect on people who are motivated to process a persuasive message, but can have an effect on people who are not motivated to process the message.

RESISTING PERSUASION

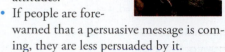

- In order to immunize people against persuasion, it is good to expose them to some of the counterarguments and let them build up defenses against the counterarguments.
- When people resist persuasion, they become more confident in their initial attitudes.
- If people are forewarned that a persuasive message is coming, they are less persuaded by it.
- The boomerang effect (negative attitude change) results from psychological reactance to the persuasive attempt; the result is an attitude opposite to the persuasive message.

WHAT MAKES US HUMAN? PUTTING THE CULTURAL ANIMAL IN PERSPECTIVE

- The duplex mind is only found in humans, so only humans have two routes to persuasion.
- Inner traits and processes play a much bigger role in human influence than in influence in nonhuman animals.
- Many persuasion techniques rely on norms and implicit rules. Humans have far more elaborate norms and implicit rules than nonhuman animals.
- Probably only humans feel guilty if they break norms and rules.
- The distinction between private acceptance and public compliance play a much bigger role in human influence than in influence in nonhuman animals.
- Humor can be a factor in persuasion, but nonhuman animals probably do not have a sense of humor.
- Probably only humans can resist influence and persuasion.

Key Terms

Advertisement wear-out 241
Autokinetic effect 227
Bait-and-switch 230
Central route (systematic processing) 245
Convert communicators 237
Disrupt-then-reframe technique 234
Door-in-the-face technique 231
Elaboration likelihood model (ELM) 244
Expertise 236

Fast-approaching-deadline technique 234
Foot-in-the-door technique 229
Group norms 227
Halo effect 237
Heuristic/systematic model 244
Impressionable years hypothesis 243
Informational influence 228
Labeling technique 230

Legitimization-of-paltry-favors technique 230
Limited-number technique 234
Low-ball technique 229
Need for cognition 242
Negative attitude change (boomerang effect) 249
Normative influence 225
Peripheral route (heuristic processing) 245
Personal relevance 245
Persuasion 235

Pique technique 234
Pluralistic ignorance 228
Private acceptance 228
Public compliance 228
Receptivity 242
Repetition with variation 241
Sleeper effect 236
Source 236
Stealing thunder 239
That's-not-all technique 232
Trustworthiness 236
Yielding 242

[Quiz Yourself] Answers

1. Two Types of Social Influence
Answers: 1=b, 2=c, 3=d, 4=a

2. Techniques of Social Influence
Answers: 1=b, 2=b, 3=c, 4=d

3. Persuasion
Answers: 1=d, 2=c, 3=d, 4=d

4. Resisting Persuasion
Answers: 1=d, 2=c, 3=a, 4=c

Media Learning Resources

Make sure you check out the complete set of learning resources and study tools below. If your instructor did not order these items with your new book, go to www.ichapters.com to purchase Cengage Learning print and digital products.

Social Psychology and Human Nature BOOK COMPANION WEBSITE

www.cengage.com/psychology/baumeister
Visit your book companion website, where you will find flash cards, practice quizzes, Internet links, and more to help you study.

CENGAGENOW JUST WHAT YOU NEED TO KNOW NOW!

Spend time on what you need to master rather than on information you have already learned. Take a pre-test for this chapter, and CengageNOW will generate a personalized study plan based on your results. The study plan will identify the topics you need to review and direct you to online resources to help you master those topics. You can then take a post-test to help you determine the concepts you have mastered and what you will still need to work on. Try it out! Go to www.cengage.com/login to sign in with an access code or to purchase access to this product.

CLASSIC AND CONTEMPORARY VIDEOS STUDENT CD-ROM

To see videos on the topics and experiments discussed in this chapter and to learn more about the research that social psychologists are doing today, go to the Student CD-ROM.

SOCIAL PSYCH LAB

These unique online labs give you the opportunity to become a participant in actual experiments, including re-creations of classic and contemporary research studies.

chapter 9

Prosocial Behavior: Doing What's Best for Others

The
Lohier
Family Home

Sponsored by

The
Batchelor
Foundation

Habitat for Humanity®
of Greater Miami

Tradeoffs: The Prisoner's Dilemma   p. 262

Money Matters: Money, Prosocial Behavior, and Self-Sufficiency   p. 263

Food for Thought: Restaurants, Rules, and the Bad Taste of Nonconformity   p. 269

The Social Side of Sex: Helping, Sex, and Friends   p. 276

What Makes Us Human? Putting the Cultural Animal in Perspective   p. 284

Doug Benz/Getty Images for WTA

WHAT IS PROSOCIAL BEHAVIOR?   p. 257
Born to Reciprocate   p. 259
Born to Be Fair   p. 259

COOPERATION, FORGIVENESS, OBEDIENCE, AND CONFORMITY   p. 261
Cooperation   p. 261
Forgiveness   p. 264
Obedience   p. 265
Conformity   p. 267

WHY DO PEOPLE HELP OTHERS?   p. 269
Evolutionary Benefits   p. 270
Two Motives for Helping: Altruism and Egoism   p. 271
Is Altruism Possible?   p. 273

WHO HELPS WHOM?   p. 274
Helpful Personality   p. 275
Similarity   p. 275
Gender   p. 275
Beautiful Victims   p. 275
Belief in a Just World   p. 276
Emotion and Mood   p. 277

BYSTANDER HELPING IN EMERGENCIES   p. 278
Five Steps to Helping   p. 278
Too Busy to Help?   p. 281

HOW CAN WE INCREASE HELPING?   p. 282
Getting Help in a Public Setting   p. 282
Educate Others   p. 282
Provide Helpful Models   p. 282
Teach Moral Inclusion   p. 283

CHAPTER SUMMARY   p. 285

> **He who saves one life, it is as if he saves the world entire.**
>
> —Jewish Talmud ‖‖‖

During World War II, members of the German Nazi Party killed millions of civilian Jews. More than 99% of Polish Jewish children were killed. Yet one member of the Nazi Party is buried in a cemetery on Mount Zion in Jerusalem. The Council of the Yad Vashem planted a carob tree on the Avenue of the Righteous in honor of this Nazi, with a plaque calling him a Righteous Gentile—a title reserved for "Extending help in saving a life; endangering one's own life; absence of reward, monetary and otherwise, and similar considerations which make the rescuer's deeds stand out above and beyond what can be termed ordinary help" (Gutman, 1995). Who was this Nazi? His name was Oskar Schindler.

Oskar Schindler was born April 28, 1908, in what is now the Czech Republic. His father and mother, Hans and Louisa Schindler, were devout (and wealthy) Catholics. However, their strict religious teachings did not seem to affect their son. At a young age, Oskar became a gambler, drinker, and womanizer, and he retained these habits throughout his life. At age 20, Oskar married Emilie Pelzl, but he continued to have affairs with other women, thereby fathering at least two children. By societal standards, he was certainly not a saint.

Nor was he a brilliant businessman; the Schindler family business went bankrupt in 1935. After that low point, Oskar Schindler sought work in nearby Poland. When Nazi Germany invaded Poland, he joined the Nazi Party to get some of the economic and political benefits given to card-carrying Nazis. In 1939 he followed the occupying forces to Krakow, the capital of German-occupied Poland, where he bought a factory that made mess kits and field kitchenware for the German army. He used cheap Jewish labor from the Krakow ghetto as workers in his factory. Others called his factory workers *Schindlerjuden* (Schindler Jews); Schindler called them "my children."

Although Schindler was busy in the factory during the day, at night he entertained Nazi Schützstaffel (SS) officers to get on their good side, and it worked. For example, during an inspection of Schindler's factory, an SS officer told an elderly Jew named Lamus, "Slip your pants down to your ankles and start walking." Lamus did what he was told. "You are interfering with all my discipline here," Schindler said. "The morale of my workers will suffer. Production for *das Vaterland* (the father country) will be affected." The officer took out his gun. "A bottle of schnapps if you don't shoot him," Schindler said. Grinning, the officer put the gun away and went to Schindler's office to collect his liquor (Gutman, 1995).

In the summer of 1942, Schindler witnessed a German raid on the Jewish ghetto. The Jews that remained alive were sent on a train to a concentration camp to be killed. Schindler was very moved by what he saw, and said, "I was now resolved to do everything in my power to defeat the system" (Gutman, 1995). For example, he convinced a German general that the nearby Plaszow camp could be used for war production. The general agreed, and Plaszow was officially transformed into a war-essential "concentration camp." Schindler made a list of all the workers he would need for his camp.

By the spring of 1944, the Germans retreated on the Eastern Front and ordered that all camps be emptied. Schindler knew that if his workers were moved to another camp they would be killed. He bribed, pleaded, and worked desperately to save his workers. Finally,

Oskar Schindler (third from left) with German army officers.

Schindler was authorized to move 1,000 workers from the Plaszow camp to a factory in Brnenec. The other 25,000 people at Plaszow were sent to the gas chambers and furnaces at Auschwitz.

Ostensibly the new factory was producing parts for V2 bombs, but Schindler told the workers to produce only defective parts so the bombs wouldn't kill anyone. Jews escaping from the transports fled to Schindler's factory. Schindler even asked the Gestapo to send him all intercepted Jewish fugitives "in the interest of continued war production" (Gutman, 1995). Almost 100 additional people were saved in this way. Schindler spent all of his money and traded all of his possessions (and his wife's jewelry!) for food, clothing, medicine, and liquor (to bribe SS officers). Because the workers dreaded the SS visits that might come late at night, Oskar and Emilie Schindler slept in a small room in the factory.

Late one evening, Schindler received a phone call from the railway station asking whether he would accept two railway cars full of Jews that no other concentration camp would accept. The cars had been frozen shut at a temperature of 5 °F (−15° C) and contained almost a hundred sick men who had been locked inside for 10 days. Schindler quickly agreed to accept the Jews as workers in his factory. Thirteen of the men were already dead. For many days and nights, Oskar and Emilie Schindler nursed the rest back to health. Only three more men died. The Jews who died were given a proper (secret) Jewish burial, paid for by Schindler.

World War II ended in Europe on May 8, 1945. In the early morning of May 9, 1945, Oskar and Emilie fled to Austria's U.S. Zone (dressed in prison garb, under the "protection" of eight *Schindlerjuden*, and with a letter in Hebrew testifying to their life-saving actions). Before they left, Schindler received a ring made from Jews' gold fillings as a gift from his grateful "children." The ring was inscribed with the Talmudic verse: "He who saves one life, it is as if he saved the world entire." After the war, a survivor asked Schindler whatever happened to his gold ring. "Schnapps," Schindler replied. He was still no conventional saint!

Oskar Schindler's grave. The Hebrew inscription reads: "A Righteous Man Among the Gentiles." The German inscription reads: "The Unforgettable Savior of the Lives of 1200 Hunted Jews."

On October 9, 1974, Oskar Schindler died of liver failure in Frankfurt, Germany, at age 66 (too much Schnapps!). His wish to be buried in Israel was honored. He was buried at the Catholic cemetery on Mount Zion in Jerusalem. On his tombstone are written the following words in Hebrew: "A Righteous Man Among the Gentiles." The German inscription reads: "The Unforgettable Savior of the Lives of 1200 Hunted Jews."

Death was the punishment for helping Jews during the Holocaust. Perhaps that is why less than 1% of the non-Jewish population in Nazi-occupied Europe attempted to save any Jews. Yet Schindler spent millions of dollars and risked his life to save a group of people whom the Nazis called "vermin" and "rats." In this chapter we will examine why humans behave in helpful and cooperative ways, even when, as the Schindler story shows, it may not be in their own self-interest to do so. ■

What Is Prosocial Behavior?

Prosocial behavior is defined as doing something that is good for other people or for society as a whole. Prosocial behavior includes behavior that respects others or allows society to operate. Culture is a whole that is more than the sum of its parts, but only if people cooperate and follow the rules will culture be able to yield its benefits. In a nutshell, prosocial behavior builds relationships. It is the opposite of antisocial behavior, which means doing something bad for others or for society. Antisocial behavior usually destroys relationships (see Chapter 10).

Social psychologists have had a peculiar love/hate relationship with prosocial behavior. Most social psychology textbooks feature helping as the main prosocial behavior, while belittling others. When they discuss conformity, obedience, and other forms of following the rules, textbooks have often been sharply critical, suggesting that these are bad things. It is true

PROSOCIAL BEHAVIOR doing something that is good for other people or for society as a whole

that obedience and conformity can be bad—mindless obedience to a demented leader (e.g., Hitler) can produce all sorts of terrible consequences. For the most part, however, obedience and conformity are good things. Society would collapse if people didn't follow most of the rules most of the time. For example, consider what would happen if people decided to ignore traffic rules, such as "Stop," "Wrong Way," "Yield," and "Speed Limit" signs. Traffic accidents and fatalities would increase sharply! Likewise, imagine what would happen if most people just took things from stores without paying, or ignored the tax laws, or if restaurants and grocery stores disobeyed health regulations and sold rotten food.

Obeying the rules, conforming to socially accepted standards of proper behavior, and cooperating with others are important forms of prosocial behavior. Helping—which most social psychology textbooks treat as the quintessential form of prosocial behavior—is actually something of an "extra" or a luxury. Heroic acts like those of Oskar Schindler are impressive and memorable, but rare. Society and culture can still bring immense benefits if people do not perform altruistic, self-sacrificing acts of helping. If no one obeys the rules, however, society will fall apart and chaos will reign. Following rules is essential. Helping is less essential, though certainly helping makes the world a much nicer place, and some forms of helping (such as what parents do for their small children) are probably vital for the survival of the species.

We rely on other people to follow their own self-interest while obeying the rules. They sell us their food in exchange for our money, which is good for them and for us. No helping or self-sacrifice on their part is necessary, but it is vital that they obey the rules by not selling us spoiled meat or doing something else fraudulent.

Imagine two societies, one in which people are happy and healthy, and another in which people are fearful, poor, and desperate. What might account for the difference? The happy society probably has people who cooperate with each other, respect each other, follow the rules, and contribute to the general welfare. The unhappy society is likely full of people who break the rules; its social life is marked by crime, corruption, distrust, betrayal, and wide-ranging general insecurity.

A society in which people respect and follow the rules is said to have an effective **rule of law**. If there are no laws, or laws exist but are widely ignored and disobeyed, the rule of law is said to be lacking. The rule of law may occasionally seem a problem, such as when you get a speeding ticket, but in reality the rule of law is usually a huge boost to the quality of life. If you lived in a society where the rule of law had broken down, or had not yet appeared, you would find life hard and dangerous. Indeed, researchers have found a positive correlation between happiness and rule of law, across a number of different societies (Veenhoven, 2004).

Fairness and justice are also important factors in predicting prosocial behavior. If employees perceive the company they work for to be fair and just, they are more likely to be good "company citizens" (Lee, 1995). For example, they are more likely to voluntarily help others in the workplace and more likely to promote the excellence of their employer, without any promise of reward for these behaviors. This pattern of doing what's best for the organization, without necessarily gaining selfish benefits, has been called the "good soldier" syndrome (Organ, 1988). The crucial point is that people behave better when they think the rules are fair.

Much prosocial behavior is stimulated by others, such as when someone acts more properly because other people are watching. Dogs will stay off the furniture and out of the trash when their owners are present, but they blithely break those rules when alone. Humans may have more of a conscience, but they also still respond to the presence or absence of others. Public circumstances generally promote prosocial behavior. Participants in one study sat alone in a room and followed tape-recorded instructions (Satow, 1975). Half believed that they were being observed via a one-way mirror (public condition), whereas others believed that no one was watching (private condition). At the end of the study, the tape-recorded instructions invited the participant to make a donation by leaving some change in the jar on the table. The results showed that donations were seven times higher in the public condition than in the private condition. Apparently, one important reason

Others will see how much you contribute.

© Steve Skjold/Almay

RULE OF LAW when members of a society respect and follow its rules for generous helping is to make (or sustain) a good impression on the people who are watching.

One purpose of prosocial behavior, especially at cost to self, is to get oneself accepted into the group, so doing prosocial things without recognition is less beneficial. Self-interest dictates acting prosocially if it helps one belong to the group. That is probably why prosocial behavior increases when others are watching. Other studies have shown that favors increase compliance in both private and public settings, but compliance is greater in public settings (Whatley, Webster, Smith, & Rhodes, 1999).

It may seem cynical to say that people's prosocial actions are motivated by wanting to make a good impression, but one can see this pattern in a positive light. One theme of this book has been that people travel a long road to social acceptance. People do many things to get others to like them, and prosocial behavior is no exception.

BORN TO RECIPROCATE

Reciprocity is defined as the obligation to return in kind what another has done for us. Folk wisdom recognizes reciprocity with such sayings as "You scratch my back, and I'll scratch yours." Reciprocity norms are found in all cultures in the world (Triandis, 1978). If I do something for you, and you don't do anything back for me, I'm likely to be upset or offended, and next time around I may not do something for you. If you do something for me, and I don't reciprocate, I'm likely to feel guilty about it. Reciprocity is also found in animals other than humans. For example, social grooming (cleaning fur) is reciprocated in many species.

The reciprocity norm is so powerful that it even applies to situations in which you do not ask for the favor. Phil Kunz, a sociology professor at Brigham Young University in Provo, Utah, sent 578 Christmas cards to a sample of complete strangers living in Chicago (Kunz & Woolcott, 1976). When somebody sends you a card, you feel obligated to send one back. Does this apply even to complete strangers? Apparently so, because Dr. Kunz received a total of 117 cards from people who had no idea who he was. He also received several unexpected long-distance telephone calls from people who had received one of his Christmas cards. Although most of the cards just contained signatures, a significant number of them contained handwritten notes, long letters, and pictures of family and pets. Only 6 of the 117 people who sent Kunz cards said they couldn't remember him.

Most often people consider reciprocity to be direct—you help someone who may help you later. However, scientists have argued that some reciprocity may be indirect—help someone and receive help from someone else, even strangers who know you only through reputation (Ferriere, 1998). Helping

off the mark.com — by Mark Parisi

I'M A LOUSY TIPPER AND I'D LIKE YOUR RUDEST WAITRESS SO I WON'T FEEL GUILTY ABOUT IT...

Reprinted by permission of Atlantic Feature Syndicate/Mark Parisi.

someone or refusing to help has an impact on one's reputation within the group. We all know people who are consistently helpful, and others who are not.

Does reciprocity apply to seeking help as well as giving help? Often you might need or want help, but you might not always accept help and certainly might not always seek it out. People's willingness to request or accept help often depends on whether they think they will be able to pay it back (i.e., reciprocity). If they don't think they can pay the helper back, they are less willing to let someone help them (Fisher & Nadler, 1976). This is especially a problem among the elderly because their declining health and income are barriers to reciprocating (Dowd, 1975). As a result, they may refuse to ask for help even when they need it, simply because they believe they will not be able to pay it back.

People often have an acute sense of fairness when they are on the receiving end of someone else's generosity or benevolence, and they prefer to accept help when they think they can pay the person back. We discuss this sense of fairness in the next section.

BORN TO BE FAIR

The central theme of this book is that human beings are cultural animals, that the impulse to belong to culture is in our genes. Fairness is part of culture. Fairness starts with reciprocity. **Norms** are standards

RECIPROCITY the obligation to return in kind what another has done for us

NORMS standards established by society to tell its members what types of behavior are typical or expected

established by society to tell its members what types of behavior are typical or expected. Norms that promote fairness can have an important influence on whether people contribute to the common good (Biel, Eek, & Gärling, 1999). Two such norms are equity and equality. **Equity** means that each person receives benefits in proportion to what he or she has contributed (e.g., the person who does the most work gets the highest pay). **Equality** means that everyone gets the same amount. Both kinds of fairness are used and understood much more widely by humans than by any other animal.

According to some evolutionary theories, an individual's ability to reproduce largely depends on his or her position within the social group (Buss, 1999). In order to maintain fitness-enhancing relationships, the individual must continually invest time, energy, and resources in building good relationships with others in the social group. To take without giving something back runs the risk that others might resent you and might ultimately reject or exclude you from the group. After all, hardly any groups can afford to have lots of members (other than babies, perhaps) who take and take without contributing anything. It will be hard to pass on your genes to the next generation when the people you want to mate with shun you.

People are designed by nature (so to speak) to belong to a system based on fairness and social exchange. As one sign of the importance of fairness to human nature, the feeling that one has no value to others—that you are a taker rather than a giver—is a major cause of depression (Allen & Badcock, 2003). To be sure, there are plenty of obnoxious people who take more than they give, but most of them don't see themselves that way. People who do see themselves as taking more than they give may become depressed. To avoid depression, people may seek to contribute their fair share.

Some suicides may reflect the same concern with being fair and reciprocal. We saw in Chapter 4 that human beings differ from most other animals in that they commit suicide. One reason some people commit suicide is that they think they are a burden on other people—that others do things for them that they cannot reciprocate, so the others would be better off if they were dead (Filiberti et al., 2001; Joiner et al., 2002). Of course, people are not better off when someone commits suicide. Suicide has numerous negative effects on those left behind. Not only

do the survivors miss the dead person, they may even blame themselves for the suicide.

The concern with fairness makes people feel bad when they don't contribute their fair share, but it can also affect people who think that their good performance makes others feel bad. When we outperform others, we may have mixed emotions. On the one hand, we may feel a sense of pride and pleasure because we have surpassed the competition. On the other hand, we may feel fear and anxiety because those we have outperformed might reject us or retaliate. Interpersonal concern about the consequences of outperforming others has been called **sensitivity about being the target of a threatening upward comparison** (Exline & Lobel, 1999). Outperformers often become distressed when they believe that others are envious that they did not perform as well.

Is reciprocity unique to humans? More simply, do animals understand "fairness"? A study of monkeys provides a fascinating answer (de Waal & Davis, 2003). The researchers trained monkeys to fetch rocks. Each monkey was rewarded with a slice of cucumber for each rock collected. The monkeys could see each other getting these rewards, and they soon learned to keep bringing rocks to get cucumber slices. Then, however, the researchers randomly gave some monkeys a grape for their rock. To a monkey, a grape is a much better treat than a slice of cucumber. The monkeys who got the grapes were very happy about this. The other monkeys were mad, however. They acted as if it were unfair that they only got the cucumber slice for the same act that earned other monkeys a grape. The ones who didn't get the grapes protested, such as by refusing to bring more rocks ("going on strike") or by angrily flinging the cucumber slice away. This study attracted international media attention, with the implication being that monkeys understand fairness and object to unfairness.

Do they really? Perhaps the study was overinterpreted. Yes, a monkey is smart enough to protest when it is treated unfairly. But if unfairness per se is the problem, then the monkeys who received the grapes should have protested too. They didn't. Researchers who study fairness distinguish between two kinds of unfairness, namely being **underbenefited** (getting less than you deserve) and being **overbenefited** (getting more than you deserve). Monkeys and several other animals seem to have an acute sense of when they are underbenefited. Only humans seem to worry about being overbenefited. A full-blown sense of fairness, one that encompasses both aspects, is found only among humans. For people to be truly fair, they must object to being overbenefited as well as to being underbenefited (even if the latter objection is stronger).

People do feel guilty when they are overbenefited. In lab studies, people feel guilty if they receive a

---

EQUITY the idea that each person receives benefits in proportion to what he or she contributes

EQUALITY the idea that everyone gets the same amount, regardless of what he or she contributes

SENSITIVITY ABOUT BEING THE TARGET OF A THREATENING UPWARD COMPARISON interpersonal concern about the consequences of outperforming others

UNDERBENEFITED getting less than you deserve

OVERBENEFITED getting more than you deserve

larger reward than others for performing the same amount or same quality of work (Austin, McGinn, & Susmilch, 1980). Getting less than your fair share provokes anger and resentment, but getting more than your fair share produces guilt (Hassebrauck, 1986).

People who harm others (perhaps without meaning to do so) prefer to do something nice for the person they harm, and they prefer the nice act to exactly match the harm they did, so that fairness and equity are restored (Berscheid & Walster, 1967). They act as if the harm they did creates a debt to that person, and they desire to "pay it back" so as to get the relationship back on an even, fair footing.

The term **survivor guilt** was coined to refer to the observation that some people felt bad for having lived through terrible experiences in which many others died, such as the atomic bombing of Hiroshima, Japan, or the death camps in Nazi-occupied Europe (Lifton, 1967; Niederland, 1961). People especially felt guilty about family members and other relationship partners who died while they survived. Some gay men who survived AIDS likewise reported feeling guilty at being spared at random from the disease that killed so many of their friends and lovers (Wayment, Silver, & Kemeny, 1995). In business, when corporations are forced to fire many employees as part of downsizing, the ones who keep their jobs often feel guilty toward friends and colleagues who have lost theirs (Brockner, Davy, & Carter, 1985). All these findings suggest that the human psyche has a deep sensitivity to unfairness, and that people (unlike almost any other animals) feel bad even if the unfairness is in their favor.

Cooperation, Forgiveness, Obedience, and Conformity

COOPERATION

Cooperation is a vital and relatively simple form of prosocial behavior. **Cooperation** is based on reciprocity: You do your part, and someone else does his or her part, and together you work toward common goals. Cooperating is vital for social groups to succeed, especially if they are to flourish in the sense of the whole being more than the sum of its parts.

Psychologists have studied cooperation by using the **prisoner's dilemma**, which forces people to choose between a cooperative act and another act that combines being competitive, exploitative, and defensive. The prisoner's dilemma, a widely studied tradeoff, is discussed in detail in *Tradeoffs*.

Political scientist Robert Axelrod once held a computer tournament designed to investigate the prisoner's dilemma situation using the payoff matrix shown in ▶ **TABLE 9.1**. Contestants in the tournament submitted computer programs that would compete in a prisoner's dilemma game for 200 rounds. These followed many different strategies, such as being antagonistic every round, cooperating every round, or deciding each move at random.

▶ **TABLE 9.1** Prisoner's Dilemma: Computer Tournament

	Player 1 (Antagonistic)	Player 2 (Cooperative)
Player 2 (Antagonistic)	Both get 1 point	Player 1 gets 0 points Player 2 gets 5 points
Player 2 (Cooperative)	Player 2 gets 0 points Player 1 gets 5 points	Both get 3 point

SURVIVOR GUILT feeling bad for having lived through a terrible experience in which many others died

COOPERATION when each person does his or her part, and together they work toward a common goal

PRISONER'S DILEMMA a game that forces people to choose between cooperation and competition

The Prisoner's Dilemma

The prisoner's dilemma is a classic tradeoff that many psychologists have adapted for use in research. The dilemma arises in a story about two criminals, whom we will call Bart and Mack. They are arrested on suspicion of having committed armed robbery, and sure enough they are found to be carrying concealed weapons, but the police do not have enough evidence to link them to the robbery. Accordingly, the police question them separately. Both men are invited to confess to the crime and hence betray the other. What happens to either of them depends on how both of them react.

One possibility is that neither man confesses to the crime. This is the prosocial option (well, prosocial when crime isn't involved!): They cooperate with each other and reject the police's deals. If this happens, they can only be convicted of the minor charge of carrying concealed weapons. Both men will get a light jail sentence.

Another possibility is that one man will confess and the other will not. If Bart confesses and Mack holds out, then the police will let Bart turn state's evidence. In reward for his testimony against Mack, Bart can go free (the best possible outcome for Bart); the police will be able to get Mack convicted of the robbery, and he will get a long prison sentence (the worst possible outcome for Mack). Of course, the outcomes are reversed if Bart holds out and Mack confesses.

The last possibility is that both confess. The police then do not have to give anyone a free pass, because both men have incriminated

themselves. Both will go to prison for moderately long sentences, though perhaps not as long as the sentence that one gets if the other betrays him.

The dilemma is thus whether to confess and betray your partner, or to hold out and cooperate with him. In a broader sense, it is a choice between a cooperative response and an antagonistic response. Confessing betrays your partner for your own benefit, and it also protects you in case your partner seeks to betray you. Cooperating (refusing to confess) involves taking a risk that could bring a good outcome for both people, but leaves you vulnerable to the longest sentence if your partner chooses to confess. Put another way, both men are better off if both cooperate and refuse to confess, because they both get light sentences (see ▶ **TABLE 9.2**). However, you can get the best outcome for yourself by confessing while your partner holds out, so many people will be tempted to try that route.

Yet another way of understanding the tradeoff is that it is between what is best for one person versus what is best for everyone. What is best for you is to confess, because you either get off totally free (if your partner holds out) or get a medium rather than a long sentence (if you both betray each other). But the best outcome for both men is achieved if both refuse to confess. This is the dilemma of human cultural life in a

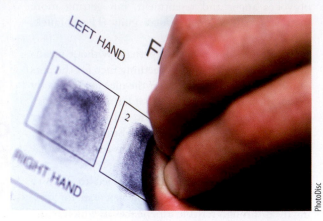

PhotoDisc

nutshell: whether to selfishly pursue your own impulses, regardless of the rules and other people's welfare, or instead to do what is best for all.

The prisoner's dilemma is called a **non-zero-sum game**, a term from game theory with important implications for social life. **Zero-sum games** are those in which the winnings and losings add up to zero. Poker is zero-sum, because a certain amount of money changes hands, but there is no net change in the amount; what some people lose is precisely equal to what the others win. Likewise, tennis and chess are zero-sum, in the sense that one player wins (+1) and the other loses (−1), so the sum is zero. But in prisoner's dilemma, both players can win, or both can lose. If more of human social life can be put on a non-zero-sum basis, so that everyone can win or gain something, life might be better overall (Wright, 2000). Put more simply, when social interactions are zero-sum, my gain is your loss, so you and I are inevitably working against each other. Non-zero-sum interactions offer the possibility that we can both win, such as if we cooperate to help each other or solve each other's problems. Competing and fighting are often zero-sum, because one side wins at the other's expense. Love, however, is often non-zero-sum, because two people who love each other both gain benefits from the relationship and are better off. ●

▶ **TABLE 9.2 Prisoner's Dilemma: Original Story Version: What Would You Choose?**

	Mack Confesses	Mack Stays Loyal
Bart Confesses	Medium prison terms for both	Bart goes free; long prison term for Mack
Bart Stays Loyal	Mack goes free; long prison term for Bart	Light prison sentences for both

The strategy that gained the most points for the player was tit-for-tat (Axelrod, 1980): Just do whatever the other player did last time. If the other player cooperated, then you should cooperate too. If the other player defected, then you should too.

Obviously tit-for-tat is closely based on reciprocation, and it is no accident that reciprocation works so well: It promotes cooperation when the other person is cooperative, but it also protects you from being taken advantage of when the other person is competitive.

Undoubtedly some people are more cooperative than others. One difference lies in how people

NON-ZERO-SUM GAME an interaction in which both participants can win (or lose)
ZERO-SUM GAME a situation in which one person's gain is another's loss

MONEY Matters

Money, Prosocial Behavior, and Self-Sufficiency

Human beings derive many benefits from cooperation, helping, forgiveness, and other prosocial acts. Money, however, can enable people to purchase many of the same benefits. Money may therefore make people less prone to engage in prosocial behavior.

The idea that money promotes self-sufficiency was put forward and tested in a clever and well-designed set of experiments (Vohs, Mead, & Goode, 2006). They started with a common observation. When one doesn't have much money (such as when one is a student!) and has to move to a new apartment, one depends on the help of friends. Perhaps you buy pizza and beer for the group, and everyone helps carry your boxes and furniture to the new place. In contrast, when people have plenty of money, they hire professional movers instead of needing their friends to do the work.

The findings showed that the effects of money on self-sufficiency come from merely making people think about money. The manipulations included sitting participants in front of a computer that had a screen saver display with dollar bills (as compared to a blank screen or a display of fish), having participants unscramble groups of words to make sentences that referred to money (as opposed to neutral topics), and even simply displaying a stack of play money to participants. People who had been reminded of money were less likely than others to give help to someone in the experiment, even when that person specifically asked for help. They were even less likely to help a confederate who spilled a box of pencils and had to pick them up.

It wasn't just that money made people self-ish or self-centered, however. In other studies in the same investigation, participants found themselves in difficulty, such as when they were assigned to work on puzzles that were quite difficult. They were told they could ask for help if they needed it. Participants who had been primed with the idea of money were less likely than others to ask for help and were slower to ask for help if they did ask.

Thus, money seemed to increase self-sufficiency: It made people less likely to give

"BUT WE CAN CONSOLE OURSELVES THAT MONEY IS THE ROOT OF ALL EVIL."

© Harley Schwadron/CartoonStock

help or to ask for help. In a final study, participants were asked whether they wanted to work together with someone or alone. Those who had been primed with money were more likely than others to choose to work alone.

Money is a purely cultural phenomenon, but cultural attitudes toward money have always resulted in mixed feelings (e.g., regarding the love of money as the "root of all evil"). The self-sufficiency findings suggest why that may be. Money provides benefits, but it also seems to pull people apart and reduce their prosocial inclinations. ■

---

interpret the situation. Cooperators see the prisoner's dilemma and related situations as an issue of good versus bad behavior (with cooperation being good). Competitors see it as weak versus strong, with cooperation being weak (Beggan, Messick, & Allison, 1988; Liebrand, Wilke, & Wolters, 1986). It is hardly surprising that people are more prone to cooperate if they think of cooperation as a sign of moral goodness than as a sign of weakness.

What happens when people with different approaches are matched in the prisoner's dilemma game? Sadly, the results show a familiar pattern: bad is stronger than good (Kelley & Stahelski, 1970; Miller & Holmes, 1975; Misra & Kalro, 1979). When both players favor cooperation, not surprisingly, they both tend to cooperate (and do pretty well). When both lean toward competition, then the game soon degenerates into everyone choosing the competitive response on every trial, and no one ends up doing well. When there is one of each, the game likewise degenerates into mutual exploitation and defensiveness. Thus, two virtuous people can do well by each other, but if either one plays selfishly, trust and cooperation are soon destroyed. This is an important and profound insight into how people relate to each other. If both people want to cooperate, they can succeed in doing so, for mutual benefit. If either one is not cooperative, then cooperation is typically doomed. Cooperation is a fragile tendency, easily destroyed. This probably reflects the facts of evolution: Across most species, competition is the norm and cooperation is rare. For example, research has shown that pigeons usually defect during a tit-for-tat condition of a prisoner's dilemma game even though it means earning only one-third of the food that they could have earned if they had cooperated (Green, Price, & Hamburger, 1995). The pigeons choose smaller but more immediate rewards rather than larger but delayed rewards. Humans are much better at cooperating than most other animals, but this should be regarded as small progress in overcoming the natural competitive tendencies that are still alive and well (and strong) in humans too.

Successful cooperation also seems to depend on communication. If communication is difficult, there is less cooperation (Steinfatt, 1973). Communication allows for the emergence of cooperation (Miller, Butts, & Rodes, 2002). Cooperation drops sharply when partners avoid discussion during a prisoner's dilemma game (Kiesler, Sproull, & Waters, 1996). Can money reduce cooperation and helping? To find out, see *Money Matters*.

"FORGIVE YOU?... SURE I'LL FORGIVE YOU...
THE MOMENT I SEE SOMETHING I REALLY
WANT ON THE SHOPPING CHANNEL."

© Edgar Argo/CartoonStock

FORGIVENESS

Forgiveness is an important category of prosocial behavior (e.g., Exline, Worthington, Hill, &
McCullough, 2003). **Forgiveness** is complicated to
define, but in general it refers to ceasing to feel angry
toward and ceasing to seek retribution against someone who has wronged you. According to theories
of fairness, reciprocity, and equity, if someone does
something bad to you, that person owes you a kind
of debt—an obligation to do something positive for
you to offset the bad deed. Forgiveness in that context involves releasing the person from this obligation, just as one might cancel a monetary debt. This
does not mean that you condone what the person
did. It just means that you won't hold it against him
or her.

As we have seen, human beings have longer-
lasting relationships than most other animals, and
forgiveness is an important contributor to this. When
people hurt, disappoint, or betray each other, the bad
feelings can damage the relationship and drive the
people to leave it. Forgiveness can help heal the relationship and enable people to go on living or working together (McCullough, Pargament, & Thoresen,
2000). The more strongly someone is committed to a
particular relationship, the more likely he or she is to
forgive an offense by the other partner (Finkel, Rusbult, Kumashiro, & Hannon, 2002).

Forgiveness is an important part of a successful romantic or marital relationship, as is increasingly recognized by both researchers and spouses
themselves (Fenell, 1993; Fincham, Hall, & Beach,

2005). Couples that forgive each other have higher
levels of relationship satisfaction (e.g., Kachadourian,
Fincham, & Davila, 2004, 2005). But what causes
what? Researchers have recently begun tracking
couples over time, to see which comes first (Paleari,
Regalia, & Fincham, 2005). Partners who forgave
each other for doing something wrong were happier
than other couples six months later. In contrast, earlier satisfaction with the relationship did not predict
later forgiveness. This pattern of findings indicates
that forgiveness leads to better relationships, not vice
versa.

The benefits of forgiveness have been well documented in research, even attracting attention from
the positive psychology movement. It is fairly obvious that being forgiven is beneficial to the person
who did something wrong, because the person no
longer needs to feel guilty or owes a debt to the one
who has been hurt. Perhaps more surprisingly, forgiveness also has great benefits for the forgivers. They
report better physical and mental health than victims
who hold grudges (Coyle & Enright, 1997; Freedman & Enright, 1996; Witvliet, Ludwig, & van der
Laan, 2001).

The downside of forgiveness may be that it invites
people to offend again. So far, research has suggested
that this is not typical. If anything, it seems that
offenders are glad to be forgiven and often feel grateful, which may motivate them to perform more good
deeds. In a study by Kelln and Ellard (1999; see also
Wallace, Exline, & Baumeister, 2008), participants
were led to believe they had accidentally broken
some laboratory equipment. They received a message
of forgiveness, or retribution, or both, or neither.
Later, the experimenter asked for a favor. Those who
had been forgiven were most willing to do the favor.
Thus, instead of inviting repeat offenses, forgiveness
led to more prosocial behavior.

How does forgiveness lead to more satisfying relationships? One answer is that when someone refuses
to forgive a loved one for doing something wrong,
this tends to come up again in future conflicts, making them harder to resolve (Fincham, Beach, &
Davila, 2004). "It's just like when you forgot my
birthday last year!" When each new conflict prompts
the couple to bring up unforgiven old grudges, minor
arguments quickly become major fights, and this sets
the couple on the downward spiral that is typical of
unhappy, problem-filled relationships (see Chapter
12). Forgiveness can help prevent this destructive
pattern from starting.

Forgiveness is linked to seeing the other person's
perspective and hence avoiding some cognitive biases
that can drive people apart. When any two people
have a conflict, especially if one does something to
hurt the other, people tend to perceive and understand it in biased ways. The victim tends to emphasize

---

FORGIVENESS ceasing to feel angry toward or seek retribution against someone who has
wronged you

In a 1981 internationally notorious hate crime, Mehmet Ali Agca shot Pope John Paul II four times. While still in the hospital, the pope publicly forgave the man who had tried to kill him. He even visited the man in prison. Although he was an old man when he was shot, the pope recovered from his wounds and went on to live a very active life for many years. Religious people tend to be more forgiving than others, and forgiving is good for the health of the forgiver.

all the bad consequences ("That really hurt my feelings"), while the perpetrator may focus on external factors that reduce his or her blame ("I couldn't help it"). Hence they don't understand or sympathize with each other. People in highly satisfying dating relationships don't show those biases (Kearns & Fincham, 2005). Instead, they see the other person's point of view better ("I know you couldn't help it"). Couples who think that way are more willing to forgive each other and hence better able to recover from a misdeed. Forgiveness helps couples get past even such relationship-threatening events as sexual infidelity, enabling the relationship to survive and recover (Hall & Fincham, 2006).

Why don't people forgive? Research has identified several major barriers that reduce willingness to forgive. One fairly obvious factor is the severity of the offense: The worse the person treated you, the harder it is to forgive (Exline et al., 2003). Another is a low level of commitment to the relationship (Finkel et al., 2002). In a sense, forgiving is making a generous offer to renounce anger and claims for retribution as a way of helping to repair and strengthen the relationship, and people are more willing to do this for relationships that are very important to them. Apologies also help elicit forgiveness. When someone has wronged you but is sincerely remorseful and expresses an apology, you are much more willing to forgive than when no such apology or remorse is expressed (e.g., Darby & Schlenker, 1982; Gonzales, Haugen, & Manning, 1994). Inner processes also can lead toward or away from forgiveness. In particular, how the person thinks about the transgression can be decisive. If you think that you might easily

have performed a similar offense, you become more willing to forgive (Exline, Baumeister, Zell, Kraft, & Witvliet, 2008). In contrast, ruminating about what someone did to you can increase anger, which in turn makes forgiveness less likely (McCullough, Bono, & Root, 2007).

Some persons are also more forgiving than others. Religious people forgive more readily than non-religious people (e.g., Tsang, McCullough, & Hoyt, 2005), in part because religions generally promote and encourage values that help people live together, and in fact some religions prominently extol forgiving as an important virtue. (For example, the most famous and widely repeated prayer in the Christian religion couples a request for forgiveness with a promise to forgive others: "And forgive us our debts, as we forgive our debtors" (Matthew 6:12).) In contrast, narcissistic individuals are often "too proud to let go" when they have been offended (Exline, Baumeister, Bushman, Campbell, & Finkel, 2004). These conceited and self-centered individuals have a broad belief that they deserve special, preferential treatment, and they are outraged when someone offends them. They are easily offended and generally think they deserve some major compensation before they will consider forgiving.

OBEDIENCE

Obedience to orders can be prosocial, and in many respects it is highly desirable that people carry out the orders of their superiors. Large groups such as

OBEDIENCE following orders from an authority figure

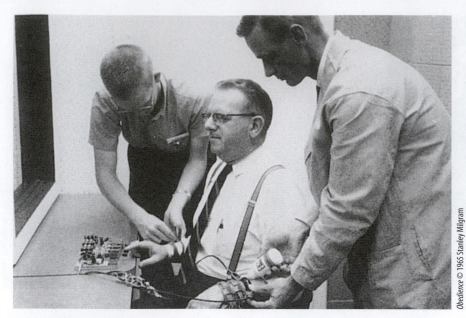

Conducting the Milgram study, the experimenter attaches shock electrodes to the wrists of the "learner" (actually a confederate) while the "teacher" (the real participant) helps out.

Obedience © 1965 Stanley Milgram

military units, corporations, and sports teams cannot function effectively without some degree of obedience. If people refuse to follow the leader's directions, the group degenerates into an ineffective collection of individuals.

Social psychologists have generally taken a dim view of obedience. This attitude can be traced to one of the classic studies in the field. In 1963, Stanley Milgram published a report called "Behavioral Study of Obedience." His research interest, like that of many psychologists at the time, was shaped by the disturbing events of World War II, including large-scale massacres of civilians by Nazi German troops. After the war, the international outcry against these atrocities presented an ongoing challenge to social science to account for how seemingly ordinary, decent, well-intentioned individuals could do such things. Many of the killers defended themselves by saying "I was only following orders." The odds are that if someone asked you whether you might have helped kill Jews, homosexuals, Roma (gypsies), communists, and other defenseless civilians if you had lived in Nazi Germany, you would say no. Most people would say that they would have behaved more like Oskar Schindler than like the Nazi soldiers (see the story at the beginning of this chapter). But would they really?

Milgram set up a study to see whether Americans would in fact follow orders that might injure or possibly kill someone. Participants were recruited for a study on learning, and when they arrived they were told that they would play the role of a teacher who would deliver electric shocks as punishment for mistakes made by a learner. They met the learner:

a mild-mannered, middle-aged man who was actually a confederate. The man mentioned that he had a heart condition.

The experimenter showed the participant an impressive-looking shock delivery apparatus, which had a row of switches with labels running from "Mild shock" up to "Danger: Severe shock" and then even "XXX." The experimenter said that each time the learner made a mistake, the participant should flick a switch, starting from the mildest shock (15 volts) and working upward toward the most severe shock (450 volts), in 15-volt increments. The experimenter said that although the shocks were painful, they would not be lethal.

They started the exercise, and the learner kept making mistakes. The participant sat by the experimenter, who instructed him or her to deliver shocks. Although the learner was in another room, the participant could still hear him. (Subsequent studies showed that people were less willing to deliver severe shocks if the learner was in the same room with them, as opposed to being out of sight.) If the participant hesitated, the experimenter had a standard series of prods that commanded the participant to continue. To make it harder to continue, the learner followed a script that included groaning, screaming in pain, banging on the wall, and shouting that he had a heart condition, that his heart was starting to bother him, and that he did not want to continue the study. Eventually the learner stopped responding at all, so for all the participant knew, the learner had passed out or died. The experimenter, however, said to treat no response as a mistake and therefore to continue delivering higher shocks.

Before he ran the study, Milgram surveyed a group of psychiatrists for predictions as to what would happen. How many participants would go all the way and deliver the most severe shock of 450 volts? The psychiatrists had faith that the participants would resist authority, and they predicted that only 1 in 1,000 would be willing to deliver the most severe shocks. In the actual study, the majority of participants (62.5%) went all the way up to the maximum shock (see ▶ **FIGURE 9.1**)! To be sure, this wasn't easy for them: Many showed acute signs of distress, such as sweating, making sounds, and sometimes having fits of nervous laughter that seemed out of control. But they still did what they were told.

Social psychologist Jerry Burger recently replicated Milgram's findings and found nearly identical results, although he had to stop at 150 volts for ethical reasons ("People," 2008). Even after hearing cries of pain, 70% of participants kept shocking (Milgram found that 80% of participants kept shocking after 150 volts).

Much has been said and written about Milgram's studies (including some serious debates as to whether it is ethical for researchers to put their participants through such experiences). The intellectual community was deeply shocked (no pun intended) to learn how far American citizens, despite the moral lessons of Nazi Germany, would obey orders to hurt another person.

Milgram's research has given obedience a bad name. His study was published in the early 1960s, and the rest of that decade saw a broad countercultural movement in which many young and some older people became hostile to authority and asserted that disobedience was a positive good, a right, and even an obligation. Bumper stickers such as "Question Authority!" abounded.

Yet, again, obedience can usually be a good thing. As we have already noted, very few organizations can function properly without obedience. Even families would fall apart if children refused to obey their parents' rules. Milgram's study focused on a peculiar situation in which obedience has morally bad outcomes, but this is exceptional. In most situations, obedience produces good outcomes. For example, how could a football team win a game if the pass receivers refused to obey the quarterback's play calling, or indeed if they disobeyed the orders of the referees? What would happen if people refused to obey traffic signals?

The fact that people obeyed Milgram's instructions may reveal an important fact about human nature, and one that depicts it as less morally bankrupt than is often said. People are naturally inclined to belong to groups, to seek social acceptance, and to put other people first. When a seemingly legitimate authority figure gives them commands, they tend to obey. This tendency does contain some danger, such as when a misguided, power-hungry, or irresponsible leader gives immoral commands. But the willingness to obey authority figures is probably an important and positive aspect of human psychology that enables people to live effectively in large groups (and hence in culture). Obedience is ultimately prosocial behavior, because it supports group life and helps cultures to succeed. Milgram's studies provide cautionary evidence that obedience can be abused and can, under extraordinary circumstances, lead to immoral actions. But those circumstances are rare exceptions, and they should not blind us to the (mostly) prosocial benefits of obedience.

In a sense, participants who refused to obey the authority figure in a Milgram study were still obeying some rules—typically moral rules. Human cultural life sometimes contains conflicting rules, and sometimes people obey the wrong ones. If your professor tells you that obedience is bad, then try this: During the next exam, discuss the questions in a loud voice with the students seated near you, and if the professor objects, bring up the Milgram study's ostensible

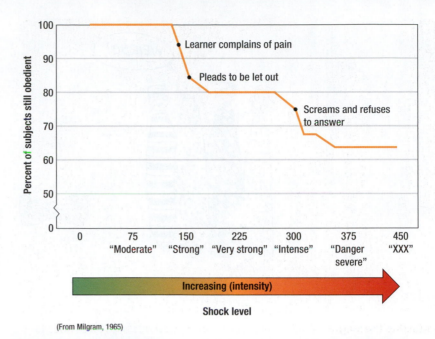

(From Milgram, 1965)

▶ **FIGURE 9.1** Results from the Milgram experiment, showing that most participants (62.5%) would deliver severe shocks to someone even if it harmed that person.

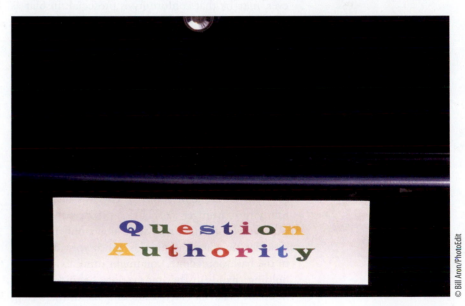

In the 1960s bumper stickers like this appeared everywhere.

lesson that obedience to authority is bad. You're likely to see the professor suddenly change her or his tune about the value of obeying rules! (Don't actually try this. You might get expelled from your university!)

CONFORMITY

Conformity is going along with the crowd (see Chapter 8). Like obedience, conformity has had a bad reputation among social psychologists, and

CONFORMITY going along with the crowd

WEIRDO!

Most women wash their hands after using a public restroom—but only if they think someone else is watching!

this stems in part from influential early studies that depicted people doing foolish, irrational, or bad things in order to conform. The broader point, however, may be that conformity is prosocial, insofar as the studies show how people put other people first and exhibit a strong desire to get along with others. If people put themselves first, by being selfish, prosocial behavior decreases (Silfver, Helkama, Lönnqvist, & Verkasalo, 2008).

People conform to the behavior of others more, and in general conform to social norms more, when others are watching (Insko, Smith, Alicke, Wade, & Taylor, 1985). For example, do people wash their hands after using the toilet in a public restroom? One study found that most women (77%) did—but only if they thought someone else was in the restroom too (Munger & Harris, 1989). Among the women who thought they were alone, only a minority (39%) washed their hands. (So if your date goes to the bathroom alone, you might think twice about holding hands!) The motivation behind socially desirable behavior (such as washing hands after using the toilet) can be to gain acceptance and approval from others.

Recent research shows that the presence of conformists dramatically increases the group size for which cooperation can be sustained (Guzmán, Rodríguez-Sickert, & Rowthorn, 2007). In other words, tendency toward conformity enables people to function better in larger groups. Larger groups are good for culture because larger groups produce more culture (e.g., art, music, science) than smaller groups.

To learn more about conformity and restaurants, see *Food for Thought*. It includes information that might change the way you order your food for years to come.

Cooperation, Forgiveness, Obedience, and Conformity

1. Psychiatrists predicted that _____ participants would go all the way in Milgram's experiment, giving the maximum shock level (450 volts) to the confederate.

(a) 1 in 10   (b) 1 in 50
(c) 1 in 100   (d) 1 in 1,000

2. A hockey coach orders a player to injure an opposing team's star player. Although the player is personally opposed to intentionally injuring other players, he follows the coach's order. This illustrates _____.

(a) conformity   (b) compliance
(c) cooperation   (d) obedience

3. The results from Milgram's experiments are generally taken to show that _____.
(a) males are more physically aggressive than females
(b) people can be sadistic
(c) people often are resistant to situational pressures
(d) situational pressures can overwhelm individual differences

Food for Thought

Restaurants, Rules, and the Bad Taste of Nonconformity

Earlier in this chapter we suggested that conforming to rules is an important form of prosocial behavior, without which society would disintegrate into chaos. The Outback Steakhouse restaurant has for years advertised "No Rules" as its slogan. Do they really mean no rules apply? If you and six friends ate an ample meal there and then refused to pay, citing "no rules" as your justification, would the restaurant managers approve? Or how about if you grabbed food off the plates of other diners, or decided to run naked through their kitchen (violating Food and Drug Administration rules, which are in force regardless of the restaurant's advertising slogans or policies). If you were to try any or all of these behaviors at the nearest Outback Steakhouse, you'll quickly discover that they have plenty of rules after all.

Not all restaurant behavior involves conforming. In fact, psychologists have recently documented a curious pattern of deliberate nonconformity among restaurant diners. The surprising thing, though, is that it often leaves people less satisfied with their meal than they might otherwise have been.

"I'll have the chicken."

"Hey, I was going to order the chicken! But that's OK, I'll order something else."

Have you ever heard such an exchange? When people eat together in a restaurant, they often act as if there were only one of each item on the menu and feel some obligation not to order the same food that someone else in the party has already ordered. Of course, there is no need to order different things. The restaurant almost certainly has enough chicken for everyone who wants it. Nonetheless, people seem to order different things.

A careful research project by Ariely and Levav (2000) confirmed that people do in fact order different foods. In their first study, they tracked the orders of hundreds of diners at a restaurant, to see how often people ordered the same versus different entrees. They then used a computer simulation to form other groups at random, for comparison purposes. This comparison showed that people who are together ordered different foods more often than they would by chance.

In a second experiment, they let people order from a menu of different beers. By random assignment, some of the groups had to order in secret, while the others ordered aloud in the usual manner. When diners didn't know what the others were having, they often ordered the same beer, but when they heard someone else order a particular beer, they switched to order something different.

Perhaps surprisingly, this impulse to order something different makes people less satisfied with their food or drink. The researchers found that when diners ordered in secret (and therefore often ordered the same thing), they were pretty happy with what they had. When they ordered aloud, the person who ordered first

PhotoDisc

(and therefore got what he or she wanted) was also pretty happy. But things weren't so good for the people who ordered later and often made a point of not ordering the same item that the first person had ordered. Those individuals were less satisfied with what they got.

It's not entirely clear why people feel the urge to order something different. Perhaps they just think that conformity is bad, so they try to avoid conforming to what someone else has done. But conformity is not really so bad. The people who order the same item, when it is their first choice, end up enjoying it more than the ones who switch to a second choice just to be different.

Apparently, the best practice is just to order your first choice, even if somebody else has already ordered it. Your second choice really won't taste as good, on average. Instead of trying to be different and nonconforming, just order what you would like best! ●

---

4. The tendency for people to go along with the crowd is called _____.
   (a) compliance   (b) conformity
   (c) cooperation   (d) obedience

Why Do People Help Others?

In a 1964 interview, Oskar Schindler was asked why he helped the Jews. He answered:

> The persecution of Jews in occupied Poland meant that we could see horror emerging gradually in many ways. In 1939, they were forced to wear Jewish stars, and people were herded and shut up into ghettos. Then, in the years '41 and '42 there was plenty of public evidence of pure sadism. With people behaving like pigs, I felt the Jews were being destroyed. I had to help them. There was no choice.

Several Schindlerjuden ("Schindler Jews") survivors were asked the same question about Oskar Schindler's motives for helping them. Here are some of their responses (cited in Aberly, 2004):

> He was an adventurer. He was like an actor who always wanted to be center stage. He got into a play and he could not get out of it.
> —Johnathan Dresner

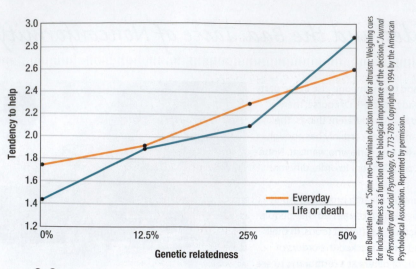

From Burnstein et al., "Some neo-Darwinian decision rules for altruism: Weighing cues for inclusive fitness as a function of the biological importance of the decision," *Journal of Personality and Social Psychology, 67,* 773–789. Copyright © 1994 by the American Psychological Association. Reprinted by permission.

▶ **FIGURE 9.2** As genetic relatedness increases, helping also increases, in both everyday situations and life-or-death situations (Burnstein et al., 1994).

Schindler was a drunkard. Schindler was a womanizer. His relations with his wife were bad. He often had not one but several girlfriends. Everything he did put him in jeopardy. If Schindler had been a normal man, he would not have done what he did.

—Mosche Bejski

We owe our lives to him. But I wouldn't glorify a German because of what he did for us.

—Danka Dresner

I couldn't make him out . . . I think he felt sorry for me.

—Helen Rosenzweig

I don't know what his motives were, even though I knew him very well. I asked him and I never got a clear answer. But I don't give a damn. What's important is that he saved our lives.

—Ludwik Feigenbaum

People might have several different motives for helping. The Jews who were saved by Schindler during World War II attributed to him several different motives. Some thought he was selfish, some thought he was altruistic and heroic, and some thought he was crazy. In this section we explore some of the possible reasons why people help others.

EVOLUTIONARY BENEFITS

It is clear that receiving help increases the likelihood of passing one's genes on to the next generation, but what about giving help? In the animal world, the costs of helping are easy to spot. A hungry animal that gives its food to another has less left for itself. Selfish animals that don't share are less likely to starve. Hence evolution should generally favor selfish, unhelpful creatures. Indeed, Richard Dawkins (1976/1989) wrote a book titled *The Selfish Gene.* According to Dawkins, genes are selfish in that they build "survival machines" to increase the number of copies of themselves. The helpfulness of people like Schindler likewise carries risks; he would probably have been imprisoned and executed if he had been caught.

One way that evolution might support some helping is between parents and children. Parents who helped their children more would be more successful at passing on their genes. Although evolution favors helping one's children, children have less at stake in the survival of their parents' genes. Thus, parents should be more devoted to their children, and more willing to make sacrifices to benefit them, than children should be to their parents. In general, we should help people who have our genes, a theory known as **kin selection** (Darwin, 1859/n.d.; Hamilton, 1964). For example, you should be more likely to help a sibling (who shares 1/2 of your genes) than a nephew (who shares 1/4 of your genes) or a cousin (who shares 1/8 of your genes). There is plenty of research evidence that people do help their family members and close relatives more than they help other people. In both life-or-death and everyday situations, we are more likely to help others who share our genes (Burnstein, Crandall, & Kitayama, 1994). However, life-or-death helping is affected more strongly by genetic relatedness than is everyday helping (see ▶ **FIGURE 9.2**).

Research has shown that genetically identical twins (who share 100% of their genes) help each other significantly more than fraternal twins (who share 50% of their genes) (Segal, 1984). Likewise, survivors of a fire at a vacation complex said that when they realized the complex was on fire, they were much more likely to search for family members than for friends (Sime, 1983).

Thus, the natural patterns of helping (that favor family and other kin) are still there in human nature. However, people do help strangers and non-kin much more than other animals do. People are not just like other animals, but they are not completely different either. Humans are cultural animals, selected by nature to participate with nonrelatives in a larger society. Our natural inclinations to help kin have been amplified via emotional responses to translate into more far-reaching actions.

Empathy is an especially important emotion when it comes to understanding why people help. Dramatic evidence for this was provided in a study

KIN SELECTION the evolutionary tendency to help people who have our genes

Research indicates that we are more likely to help others who have our genes.

that this is something that sets humans apart from even their closest animal relatives.

TWO MOTIVES FOR HELPING: ALTRUISM AND EGOISM

The 19th-century philosopher Auguste Comte (1875) described two forms of helping based on very different motives. One form he called **egoistic helping**, in which the helper wants something in return for offering help. The helper's goal is to increase his or her own welfare. The other form he called **altruistic helping**, in which the helper expects nothing in return for offering help. The helper's goal in this case is to increase another's welfare.

These two different types of helping are produced by two different types of motives (see ▶ **FIGURE 9.3**). Altruistic helping is motivated by **empathy**, an emotional response that corresponds to the feelings of the other person. When people see a person in distress, they usually feel that person's distress; when they see a person who is sad, they feel that person's sadness. The sharing of feelings makes people want to help the sufferer to feel better.

The ability to experience another person's pain is characteristic of empathy. One study (Singer, Seymour, O'Doherty, Kaube, Dolan, & Frith, 2004) used functional magnetic resonance imaging (fMRI) to assess brain activity while participants experienced a painful shock (represented by green in Figure 9.4). They then compared it to the brain activity while participants watched a loved one experience a painful shock (represented by red in ▶ **FIGURE 9.4**).

The researchers used couples as participants because couples are likely to feel empathy for each other. The study found that the brain's reaction was about the same for receiving shocks as for watching

of 18-month-old toddlers (Warneken & Tomasello, 2006). When the adult researcher dropped something, the human toddlers immediately tried to help, such as by crawling over to where it was, picking it up, and giving it to him. (The babies also seemed to understand and empathize with the adult's mental state. If the researcher simply threw something on the floor, the babies didn't help retrieve it. They only helped if the adult seemed to want help.) The researchers then repeated this experiment with chimpanzees. The chimps were much less helpful, even though the human researcher was a familiar friend. This work suggests that humans are hardwired to cooperate and help each other from early in life, and

---

EGOISTIC HELPING when a helper seeks to increase his or her own welfare by helping another
ALTRUISTIC HELPING when a helper seeks to increase another's welfare and expects nothing in return
EMPATHY reacting to another person's emotional state by experiencing the same emotional state

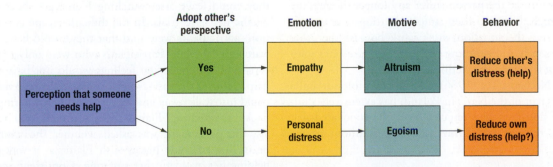

▶ **FIGURE 9.3** Two routes to helping: The top route is motivated by altruism, whereas the bottom route is motivated by egoism.

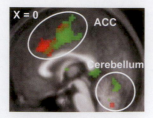

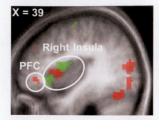

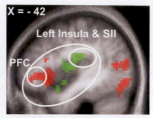

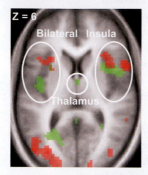

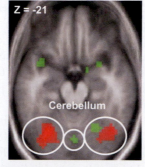

Reprinted with permission from: Singer T., Seymour B., O'Doherty J., Kaube H., Dolan R.J., Frith C.D. "Empathy for pain involves the affective but not the sensory components of pain" *Science*, Vol. 303, p. 1157–1162, February 2004.

▶ **FIGURE 9.4** Pain-related activation associated with either experiencing pain oneself (green) or observing one's partner feeling pain (red) (Singer et al., 2004).

needy that overshadowed all other attributes except their dependence on aid." Schindler said about the Jews he helped: "I had to help them. There was no choice." On the face of it, the statement is wrong: Of course he had a choice. But in another sense, he felt he didn't. He cared about the Jews as fellow human beings, and he felt their suffering. Turning his back or shutting his eyes would not have been enough to make him forget their suffering, so he felt he had to help them.

Stanislaw Dobrowolski, the director of a council to save Polish Jews in Nazi-occupied Krakow, dismissed Schindler's altruistic motives altogether (cited in Aberly, 2004). In his view, Schindler's heroism was more about his own ego trip than about any altruistic concern to reduce the suffering of others.

Untangling these different motives for helping has been an ongoing challenge for social psychologists. One study (Batson, Duncan, Ackerman, Buckley, & Birch, 1981) was presented to participants as a test of the effects of stress on task performance. Through a rigged lottery, the "other participant" (actually a confederate named Elaine) was assigned to perform 10 trials of a task while receiving random electric shocks (the stressor) on each trial. The real participant watched Elaine over a closed-circuit TV. Before the study began, the participant overheard a conversation in which Elaine told the experimenter that she was afraid of receiving the shocks because as a child she had been thrown from a horse into an electric fence. Ever since that experience, she had been terrified of electricity. The experimenter apologized, but said Elaine would have to receive the shocks anyway because she had lost the coin toss.

To manipulate empathy, the researchers told half of the participants that Elaine's values and interests were very similar to their own (high-empathy condition). People feel more empathy toward someone they believe is similar to themselves. The other participants were told that Elaine's values and interests were quite different (low-empathy condition). To test for egoistic motives for helping, the researchers also manipulated how difficult it was to escape. In the easy-escape condition, participants were told that they could leave after watching Elaine get shocked on the first two trials. In the difficult-escape condition, participants were told that they would have to watch all 10 trials. Participants who were only concerned about their own feelings would not have to help Elaine in the easy-escape condition. Instead they could just walk away and forget about her suffering.

After watching Elaine suffer through two trials, the participant was asked whether she would be willing to trade places with Elaine as a way of helping her avoid further suffering. Consistent with empathy–altruism theory, almost all the participants in the high-empathy group traded places with Elaine,

one's lover receive shocks. Brain activation also correlated with individual empathy scores—the more empathic people said they were, the more brain activity they experienced while watching their partner suffer.

According to the **empathy–altruism hypothesis** (Batson, Batson, Slingsby, Harrell, Peekna, & Todd, 1991), empathy motivates people to reduce other people's distress, as by helping or comforting them. How can we tell the difference between egoistic and altruistic motives? When empathy is low, people can reduce their own distress either by helping the person in need or by escaping the situation so they don't have to see the person suffer any longer. If empathy is high, however, then simply shutting your eyes or leaving the situation won't work because the other person is still suffering. In that case, the only solution is to help the victim feel better.

Nechama Tec (1986), a sociology professor and a survivor of the Nazis in Poland, has extensively studied non-Jews who rescued Jews. She concluded that the rescuers had "universalistic perceptions of the

EMPATHY–ALTRUISM HYPOTHESIS the idea that empathy motivates people to reduce other people's distress, as by helping or comforting

regardless of whether it was easy or difficult to escape (see ▶ **FIGURE 9.5**). In the low-empathy group, participants left if it was easy for them to escape the unpleasant task of watching Elaine suffer. If it was difficult to escape, more than half of them traded places with Elaine (rather than watch her suffer longer).

The Batson et al. (1981) study provided evidence for both kinds of helping. In the low-empathy condition, people helped only to make themselves feel good. If they could walk away and ignore the victim's suffering, many chose that path. In contrast, people who felt high empathy helped regardless of whether they were allowed to escape. High-empathy helping is centered on the victim's needs, not on one's own prospects for feeling good.

There are two alternative hypotheses to the empathy–altruism hypothesis in which helping is triggered by empathy but may still reflect selfish motives (Batson et al., 1988). According to the **empathy–specific reward hypothesis**, empathy triggers the need for social reward (e.g., praise, honor, pride) that can be gained by helping. According to the **empathy–specific punishment hypothesis**, empathy triggers the fear of social punishment (e.g., guilt, shame, censure) that can be avoided by helping. Both of these hypotheses can easily explain the results from the Batson et al. (1981) study described above. Batson and his colleagues (1988), however, conducted five additional studies and found support for the empathy–altruism hypothesis but not for the empathy–reward or empathy–specific punishment hypotheses.

There is another alternative hypothesis to the empathy–altruism hypothesis. When people see someone suffering, they feel bad too. According to the **negative state relief hypothesis** (Cialdini, Darby, & Vincent, 1973), people help others in order to relieve their own distress. This view holds that people help mainly to make themselves feel better. However, a meta-analytic review of the literature found little support for the negative state relief hypothesis (Carlson & Miller, 1987).

IS ALTRUISM POSSIBLE?

As they conducted research on whether helping is driven by empathy and sympathy for victims or by the selfish desire to feel better, social psychologists gradually became involved in a centuries-old debate about whether people are basically good or evil—or, more to the point, basically good or selfish. Many philosophers have asked whether people really perform morally good actions such as altruistic helping if they are motivated by a desire to feel good. In a nutshell, the argument is this: If you donate money to charity or help a needy victim because it makes you feel good to do so, aren't you really just being

▶ **FIGURE 9.5** In the Batson et al. (1981) study, people in the high-empathy group helped regardless of whether escape was easy or difficult. In the low-empathy group, people helped mainly when they could not escape.

selfish and self-serving? Ultimately the question becomes: Is genuine altruism even possible?

Social psychologists have split on this debate. Nobody disputes that some helping is egoistical, in the sense that people sometimes help in order to gain benefits for themselves such as improved mood or a good reputation. They disagree as to whether egoism is the only motive. Some point out that people will help even when they could feel better by other, simpler means, such as by escaping the situation (as in the previous study with Elaine). They also think it is sad to dismiss so much genuine helping as mere selfishness—after all, helping someone for selfish reasons deserves to be recognized as something more positive and socially desirable than hurting someone for selfish reasons! If we dismiss Schindler's actions as those of a self-centered glory hound, do we not make the world an uglier, less heroic place—and possibly discourage others from taking such heroic risks in the future? Others have argued, however, that even empathic helping is a way to make oneself feel better. The debate goes on today.

Our view is that the debate cannot be resolved because it puts the question the wrong way. It may well be true that people feel better when they help and that these good feelings promote helping. But instead of supporting a negative conclusion about people—that people are always basically selfish—this should foster a more positive, optimistic view. Isn't it great that natural selection selected human beings to be able to get pleasure from helping others?

EMPATHY–SPECIFIC REWARD HYPOTHESIS the idea that empathy triggers the need for social reward (e.g., praise, honor, pride) that can be gained by helping

EMPATHY–SPECIFIC PUNISHMENT HYPOTHESIS the idea that empathy triggers the fear of social punishment (e.g., guilt, shame, censure) that can be avoided by helping

NEGATIVE STATE RELIEF HYPOTHESIS the idea that people help others in order to relieve their own distress

Although people assume that altruistic helping exists, it might not.

The conflict between selfish impulses and social conscience has been one theme of this book. Often people have to be socialized to resist selfish impulses so as to do what is best for society and culture (Baumeister, 2005). Children must be taught to share, to take turns, and to respect the property of others, for example. The fact that nature has enabled people to feel empathy for the suffering of others and to feel good when they lend help is one (very welcome and constructive) way to avoid that conflict. The social conscience is there to make people do what is best for others, and for society at large, even when doing so means overriding selfish impulses. The fact that people can get satisfaction from helping others makes it easier for the social conscience to accomplish this. If no one ever got any satisfaction from doing good deeds, there would probably be far fewer good deeds.

Selfishness may be part of human nature, but so is helpfulness. Human beings help their children and kin, their friends, and sometimes even total strangers. It is unfair to call them selfish just because this helping is often motivated by the fact that helping feels good. The innately prepared pleasure we get from helping is one important element in the basic goodness of human nature (see also Peterson & Seligman, 2004; Snyder & Lopez, 2002).

Are some people more likely to help than others? If so, who are they? We discuss this topic in the next section.

[QUIZ YOURSELF]

Why Do People Help Others?

1. Jean Luc's house is on fire. His grandparents, wife, children, and cousins are in the house. Based on kin selection theory, whom should he save first?
   (a) His children   (b) His cousins
   (c) His grandparents   (d) His wife

2. Eliza trips, falls, and begins to cry. When Mariah sees Eliza crying in pain, she starts to cry too. Mariah's response is called _____.
   (a) altruism   (b) egoism
   (c) empathy   (d) reactance

3. After seeing a victim of misfortune, empathy motivates us to _____.
   (a) gain the approval of bystanders
   (b) gain the approval of the victim
   (c) reduce our own discomfort
   (d) reduce the discomfort of the victim

4. After seeing a victim of misfortune, personal distress motivates us to _____.
   (a) gain the approval of bystanders
   (b) gain the approval of the victim
   (c) reduce our own discomfort
   (d) reduce the discomfort of the victim

Who Helps Whom?

Before we look at specific factors that differentiate who helps whom, let us consider the big picture. One thing that is special and remarkable about humans is their willingness to help others, even unrelated others. Imagine that you were offered a chance to get some nice reward for yourself, maybe money or good food. You could either get it just for yourself, or you could get a duplicate of your reward delivered to someone you had known for 15 years (and still get your own full reward). Which would you choose? Most people would eagerly choose to benefit a friend or acquaintance, especially if they could do so without cost to themselves.

Yet when this exact experiment was tried on chimps, the results were quite different. Chimps are closely related to human beings, but they did not show any interest in helping their longtime (15-year) acquaintances. They took the reward for themselves, but they did not do the kind favor for others (Silk et al., 2005). Thus, the basic motive to bring help and benefits to others who aren't blood relatives appears to be something that sets human beings apart from our closest animal relatives.

HELPFUL PERSONALITY

Eva Fogelman studied the family backgrounds of rescuers of Jews and found some common denominators: "a nurturing, loving home: an altruistic parent or beloved caretaker who served as a role model for altruistic behavior; a tolerance for people who were different" (cited in Robinson, 1995). Similarly, Oliner and Oliner (1988; also Midlarsky, Jones, & Corley, 2005) studied 231 Gentiles who rescued Jews in Nazi Europe and 126 nonrescuers matched on age, gender, education, and geographic location during the war. Rescuers had higher ethical values, had stronger beliefs in equity, had greater empathy, and were more likely to see all people as equal.

In a typical questionnaire measure of altruistic personality (Rushton, Fulker, Neale, Nias, & Eysenck, 1986), respondents are asked to indicate the frequency with which they have engaged in specific prosocial behaviors within the past year, such as helping or offering to help others (e.g., "I have donated blood") and giving to charity (e.g., "I have given money, goods, or clothes to a charity"). This scale, called the Self Report Altruism Scale, has been shown to correlate with peer ratings of altruism, completion of an organ donor card, and paper-and-pencil measures of prosocial orientation (Rushton, Chrisjohn, & Fekken, 1981). The altruistic personality also appears to have a genetic component (Rushton et al., 1986).

SIMILARITY

Research has shown that people are more likely to help someone who is similar to them than someone who is different. The similarity bias especially works for outward symbols that are readily identifiable, such as apparel. For example, in one study (Emswiller, Deaux, & Willits, 1971), hippies were more likely to help other hippies than non-hippies.

GENDER

Research indicates that males are more helpful than females in the broader public sphere, toward strangers, and in emergency settings (Eagly & Crowley, 1986). For example, since 1904 the Carnegie Hero Fund Commission has given awards to "heroes," defined as "a civilian who voluntarily risks his or her own life, knowingly, to an extraordinary degree while saving or attempting to save the life of another person" (Carnegie Hero Fund Commission, 2002).

More than 90% of the individuals who have received Carnegie medals have been men. Females are more helpful in the family sphere, in close relationships, and in situations that require repeated contact over a long period of time such as in volunteering (e.g., Aries & Johnson, 1983). Females tend to feel more sympathy and empathy for people who need help than do males (Eisenberg & Lennon, 1983; Hoffman, 1977).

When it comes to receiving help, females are more likely to receive help than are males, regardless of whether the helper is male or female. If a car has a flat tire, for example, people are more likely to stop and help if the owner is female than if the owner is male (e.g., Penner, Dertke, & Achenbach, 1973; Pomazal & Clore, 1973).

Males and females also differ in the types of help they offer their friends and relatives in sexual relationships. Read *The Social Side of Sex* to find out how.

BEAUTIFUL VICTIMS

One of the most robust findings in the helping literature is that people are more likely to help attractive individuals than unattractive individuals. This holds true for male and female helpers and for males and females in need of help. This finding has been shown in both laboratory and field settings (e.g., Harrell, 1978). It has been shown in emergency situations and in nonemergency situations. In one study (Benson, Karabenick, & Lerner, 1976), for example, people using phone booths at airports found a completed application form in the booth, a photograph of the applicant, and an addressed, stamped envelope. Half of the photos depicted an attractive applicant; the other half depicted an unattractive applicant. Callers were much more likely to mail applications for attractive applicants than for unattractive applicants. In another study (West & Brown, 1975), male college students walking by the student health center were approached by a woman who said she

Women, especially beautiful women, are most likely to receive help.

the SOCIAL SIDE of SEX

Helping, Sex, and Friends

A sexual relationship may seem like a private matter between two people, but in fact people depend on help from their friends and relatives in multiple ways. Just meeting sex partners is often a matter of relying on one's network. One landmark study of sexual practices found that less than half the people met their sex partners or marriage partners by introducing themselves, such as by approaching someone at a bar (Laumann, Gagnon, Michael, & Michaels, 1994). (Also, self-introductions were most likely to lead to short-term affairs rather than long-term relationships.) In contrast, many people were introduced to their lovers by friends, coworkers, or relatives. Family members were responsible for bringing together relatively few sex partners, but the likelihood of those relationships lasting was especially high, probably because your family knows you and will only introduce you to someone who is likely to be a good match. If your mother or brother introduces you to someone, it is probably not for the sake of casual sex but rather someone with whom you might have a long-term relationship.

Helping is also apparent in how people act on spring break, which for many college students is a brief, exciting time of intense partying and sexual opportunity. A team of researchers followed a sample of Canadian students who traveled to Florida for one spring break (Maticka-Tyndale, Herold, & Mewhinney, 1998). They found

that most traveled in same-sex groups. On the way down, many of these groups made pacts or other agreements to help each other during the week. These agreements differed by gender. The men generally promised to help each other find a partner to have sex with. They would agree that they all wanted to have sex and that they would support each other's efforts. If they were sharing a room, they would make plans as to how to keep it discreetly available in case one of them wanted to bring a woman there for sex. (For example, the others might agree to stay out late or even sleep on the beach if someone was having sex in the hotel room.) The women, in contrast, made agreements to help each other avoid having sex. They usually agreed that their goal was to refrain from sex, unless one happened to find true love. They promised each other, for example, that if one of them got drunk and was being "hit on" (that is, targeted with romantic or sexual advances) by a particular man, the others would swoop in and bring her safely away. If they were sharing a room, they might promise not to leave one of them alone in it with a man. Thus, males and females differ dramatically in how they help their friends in sexual situations.

Why? The most likely explanation is rooted in the social exchange theory of sex (see Chapter 12; also Baumeister & Vohs, 2004). In that view, society treats sex as something that men want from women, so men give women other resources (love, commitment, respect, attention,

Paul Viant/Getty Images

money) in exchange. Spring break sex is typically "free" sex that is not accompanied by commitment or other resources. From the exchange perspective, free sex signifies a good deal for men and a bad one for women. That is why men will try to support and help each other to engage in free sex, whereas women will try to support and help each other to avoid that sort of sex. ■

---

desperately needed money for a tetanus shot. Male students were more likely to give the woman money if she was attractive than if she was unattractive.

BELIEF IN A JUST WORLD

When the British marched a group of German civilians around the Belsen concentration camp at the end of World War II to show them what their soldiers had done, one civilian said, "What terrible criminals these prisoners must have been to receive such treatment" (Hewstone, 1990). This statement was not made by a guard who was trying to justify his behavior; it was made by an innocent civilian. Why was

this person blaming the victim? One possible explanation is that the person believed that the world is a just place where people get what they deserve and deserve what they get, a phenomenon referred to as **belief in a just world** (Furnham, 2003; Lerner & Miller, 1978; Lerner & Simmons, 1966).

One unfortunate consequence of belief in a just world is that it leads people to blame the victim. They assume that those who suffer a bad fate had it coming to them. For example, people assume that rape victims must have behaved or dressed provocatively, that poor people are lazy, and that sick people are responsible for their illness. On the other hand, "blaming the victim" has become such a taboo and condemned response in the social sciences that many people today will refuse to blame a victim even when the victim does bear some of the blame. Research on violence

BELIEF IN A JUST WORLD the assumption that life is essentially fair, that people generally get what they deserve and deserve what they get

and aggression has frequently shown, for example, that many violent acts stem from incidents in which both people provoked or attacked each other. Two patrons in a bar may start by exchanging insults, move along to shoving and hitting, and end up in a violent fight in which one is injured or killed. The killer is certainly to blame, but the so-called victim also deserves some blame under those circumstances. Victims generally deserve sympathy, and some are indeed entirely free from blame, but other victims do share responsibility for what happened to them.

People who believe the world is just will help others, but only if they think those people deserve the help (Zuckerman, 1975). People who believe in a just world are not helpful toward victims who are perceived to be responsible for their own predicament (DePalma, Madey, Tillman, & Wheeler, 1999). People who believe most strongly in a just world express more negative attitudes toward helping the elderly, because they believe that the elderly are responsible for meeting their own social, economic, and health needs (MacLean & Chown, 1988).

Belief in a just world can sometimes promote helping because the helper desires to deserve good outcomes. Again, the essence of believing in a just world is that people deserve what they get and get what they deserve. By extension, if you help others, you are a good and deserving person, so you can expect good things to happen to you. This can take on an almost superstitious aspect, as when people perform good or helpful acts in the expectation that they will be rewarded later.

Students sometimes show this sort of superstitious helping. Students at one college were asked to volunteer to do a good deed, such as serving as a reader for blind students or doing extra psychology experiments (Zuckerman, 1975). During the routine parts of the semester, helping was fairly low, and it made no difference whether the students had high or low belief in a just world. However, when the request came just before exam time, the students who believed in a just world were significantly more willing to help. Presumably they thought at some level that their good deeds would be rewarded by better luck and a better grade on the exam. If good things happen to good people, then it may help to do good deeds so as to become a good person.

EMOTION AND MOOD

In general, positive feelings increase helping. Research has shown that helping is increased by all kinds of pleasant situations, such as sunny weather (Cunningham, 1979), eating a cookie (Isen & Levin, 1972), and imagining a Hawaiian vacation (Rosenhan, Salovey, & Hargis, 1981). One possible explanation for this phenomenon is that people want

The big fishes (such as rich, powerful individuals) believe the world is a just place where people get what they deserve and deserve what they get.

to maintain their good mood, and acting helpfully toward another person may allow them to sustain their good feelings (see Chapter 6).

On the other hand, bad emotions can sometimes increase helping. One way to resolve these findings is to suggest that some negative emotions may promote helping more than others. (Thus, perhaps guilt motivates helping, whereas shame or anger makes people unhelpful.) Another possibility is that the same emotion can have different effects. Focusing on yourself versus the victim can make a big difference, for example, even when the emotion is the same.

> [QUIZ YOURSELF]
>
> ## Who Helps Whom?
>
> 1. The trait that produces helping across a wide variety of settings is called the _____ personality.
>   (a) altruistic
>   (b) egoistic
>   (c) narcissistic
>   (d) overbenefited
>
> 2. When it comes to receiving help, males are more likely to help _____ and females are more likely to help _____.
>   (a) females; females
>   (b) females; males
>   (c) males; females
>   (d) males; males
>
> 3. People are especially inclined to help someone who is _____.
>   (a) altruistic
>   (b) authoritarian
>   (c) low in status
>   (d) physically attractive
>
> 4. People are especially likely to feel unsympathetic to a victim of misfortune if they _____.
>   (a) are in a good mood
>   (b) believe in a just world
>   (c) feel overbenefited
>   (d) feel underbenefited

On March 13, 1964, Kitty Genovese was attacked by a knife-wielding rapist outside her apartment in Queens, New York, while several of her neighbors watched from their windows.

Crossing the village, Mowaka is overpowered by army ants. (Later, bystanders were all quoted as saying they were horrified, but "didn't want to get involved.")

Bystander Helping in Emergencies

On March 13, 1964, a young woman named Kitty Genovese was attacked by a knife-wielding rapist outside her apartment in Queens, New York. News reports said her screams for help aroused 38 of her neighbors. Many watched from their windows while, for 35 minutes, she tried to escape. None called the police or sought to help in any other manner. In fact, her attacker left her twice and then returned each time; if someone had come to help her into the building during those intervals, she would have lived. Some of the witnesses didn't help because they thought it was a lover's quarrel. The *New York Times* newspaper article that described the event was titled "Thirty-Eight Who Saw Murder Didn't Call the Police."

The incident made the national news and ignited a storm of controversy. How could people just sit by and let a woman be murdered? Talking heads weighed in with their theories about urban decay, alienation, and other roots of the seemingly heartless indifference of the onlookers. Although the facts of this case have been disputed (e.g., Manning, Levine, & Collins, 2007), it led to a long line of social psychology studies on why bystanders might fail to help a victim in an emergency.

Most of the intellectuals who appeared on the news to discuss the Genovese murder assumed that the reasons for failing to help lay within the person. In a sense, they made what Chapter 5 described as the "fundamental attribution error": They underestimated the importance of situational factors. Even so, no news reporters could induce any of the bystanders to say "I really didn't care whether that young woman lived or died." It fell to social psychologists to show that the special power of such emergency situations could explain what came to be known as the **bystander effect**: People are less likely to offer help when they are in the presence of others than when they are alone.

FIVE STEPS TO HELPING

Two social psychologists, John Darley and Bibb Latane, whose offices were a few miles from the site of the Genovese murder, took the lead in studying the bystander effect. Gradually they came to recognize an absurd aspect of the controversy: the assumption that helping would be the normal, natural response. Instead, they proposed that there are at least five steps to helping in an emergency situation (see ▶ **FIGURE 9.6**). These amounted to five possible reasons that people would not help. A victim would only get help if the bystander resolved all five of these

BYSTANDER EFFECT the finding that people are less likely to offer help when they are in a group than when they are alone

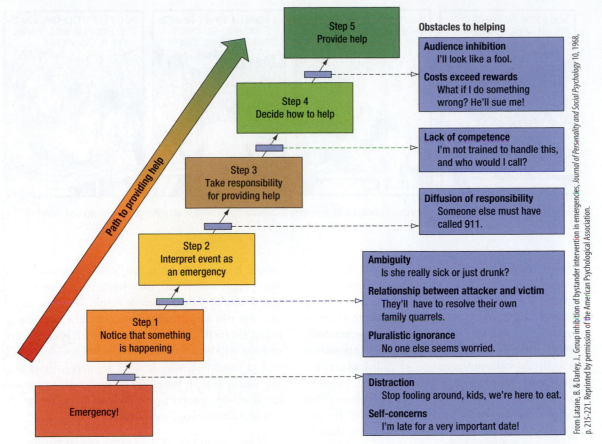

From Latane, B. & Darley, J., Group inhibition of bystander intervention in emergencies, *Journal of Personality and Social Psychology* 10, 1968, p. 215-221. Reprinted by permission of the American Psychological Association.

▶ **FIGURE 9.6** Five steps to helping and the obstacles encountered at each step (Latane & Darley, 1968).

steps in the optimal way. Crucially, the presence of a crowd can interfere with helping at each step.

Step 1: Notice That Something Is Happening.

The first step is to notice that something is happening. One obstacle to noticing the incident is being distracted: People who are busy or preoccupied are less likely to notice what is happening around them. Of course, we are more distracted when others are around. In one study (Latane & Darley, 1968), male college students completed a questionnaire in a room, either alone or with two strangers. While they were working, smoke started pouring into the room through a wall vent. Students who were alone noticed the smoke right away. In contrast, those in groups took about four times as long to notice the smoke. The difference (between 5 and 20 seconds, in this case) may be crucial in some emergency situations, such as a fire.

Step 2: Interpret Meaning of Event.

Once you have noticed something is happening, the second step is to interpret the meaning of the event. Is it an emergency or not? Few people encounter emergencies on a regular basis, and emergencies do not usually come with obvious labels. How someone interprets these ambiguous situations can be decisive. For example, you notice a man stagger down the street and then slump onto the ground. Is he having a heart attack, so that your timely intervention might be needed to save his life? Or is he merely drunk, so that if you rush over to him your reward might be nothing more than having him puke on your shoes?

Sometimes it is hard to tell whether an event is an emergency. In 1993 in the UK, a 2-year-old boy named James Bulger was dragged out of a shopping mall, kicking and screaming, by two 10-year-old boys. The older boys dragged Bulger two and a half miles from the shopping mall to a railroad track, where they beat him to death. Sixty-one people said they had seen the boys dragging Bulger out of the mall, but none intervened. As one witness said, he thought the boys were "older brothers taking a little one home."

When it is easy to tell, people are more likely to intervene. To show the power of interpretations (Shotland & Straw, 1976), researchers staged a physical fight between a man and a woman. Bystanders offered help 65% of the time when she shouted "Get away from me; I don't know you." Bystanders offered help only 19% of the time when she shouted "Get away from me; I don't know why I ever married you." Perhaps they interpreted the event as a marital spat rather than as an emergency. Some of the bystanders who witnessed the Kitty Genovese murder thought it was only a lover's quarrel.

Pluralistic ignorance in the classroom can interfere with learning. Pluralistic ignorance in an emergency setting can interfere with helping.

What are the obstacles to helping at this step? People often look to others for clues about how to behave. We think that others might know something that we don't know. If others do not react to an event, we conclude that it is not an emergency because otherwise they would be reacting. This phenomenon of collective misinterpretation is called **pluralistic ignorance**. We forget that others, in turn, might be looking to us for clues about how to behave. They assume that we know more than they do. Because everybody assumes that others know more than he or she does, when in reality nobody knows anything, nobody reacts. Everybody is certain that nothing is wrong, when actually the event is an emergency!

Pluralistic ignorance is not restricted to emergency situations. Have you ever sat through a class feeling completely lost and confused about the material being presented? You want to ask a question, but you're too embarrassed to ask it. No one else is saying anything, so you assume that everybody else understands the material. In fact, the other students are probably just as confused as you are. Pluralistic ignorance in the classroom can prevent learning, just as in an emergency situation it can prevent helping. Others often don't know as much as we give them credit for.

Step 3: Take Responsibility for Providing Help.
The third step is taking responsibility for providing help. You might notice that something is happening and decide that it is an emergency, but that is not enough. If you are to help, you must be willing to take responsibility for helping. The obstacle to this step of helping is called **diffusion of responsibility**. With several potential helpers around, the personal responsibility of each bystander is reduced. If you are the only person present, 100% of the responsibility for providing help rests on your shoulders; if two

people are present, each has 50% responsibility; if four people are present, each has 25% responsibility; and so on. In crowds, people think, "Perhaps someone else will help; perhaps someone else has already called for help." With everyone thinking that someone else will help or has helped, nobody helps.

Eva Fogelman, who studied rescuers of Jews during World War II, found that a bystander was much less likely to intervene on behalf of Jews if he or she was in a crowd. Fogelman wrote,

> It appears to be a human proclivity to assume that someone else, the person beside you in a crowd, will be the one to intervene. It is not my responsibility, a bystander explains. Someone else will take care of it. Thus, by way of a "diffusion of responsibility," a bystander's conscience is assuaged, permitting the bystander to carry on his or her way." (cited in Robinson, 1995)

The importance of diffusion of responsibility was demonstrated in lab experiments by Darley and Latané (1968). Participants believed they were taking part in a group discussion over an intercom system. During the session, another participant (actually a prerecorded voice) apparently started having a seizure and called for help. Participants who thought they were part of a six-person group generally did not help, because they thought someone else would do so. In contrast, if the participant thought he or she was the only one who knew about the victim's seizure, the participant helped almost every time.

Step 4: Know How to Help.
The fourth step is deciding how to help. Having assumed the responsibility to help, the person must now figure out what to do. An obstacle to offering direct help is the feeling of lack of competence—people don't feel qualified to help, or they think that somebody else is more qualified to help than they are. Researchers have shown that there is no effect for those who feel competent to intervene directly. For example, female participants

PLURALISTIC IGNORANCE looking to others for cues about how to behave, while they are looking to you; collective misinterpretation

DIFFUSION OF RESPONSIBILITY the reduction in feeling responsible that occurs when others are present

in a study by Cramer, McMaster, Bartell, and Dragna (1988) were either registered nurses or general education students. On their way to the lab, each one passed by a workman (actually a confederate) who was standing on a ladder, fixing a light fixture. In the lab, participants worked on a task either alone or with a confederate who was pretending to be another participant and whose instructions were to sit still and do nothing during the upcoming accident. In the hall, participants heard the ladder fall over, they heard a thud, and then they heard the workman groaning in pain. The vast majority of nurses helped, regardless of whether they were working alone or with a passive bystander. For them, lack of competence was no obstacle to helping. General education students were much more likely to help if they were working alone than if they were working with a passive bystander.

People who don't feel competent to offer direct help can still offer indirect help, which involves calling someone else to help. In the age of cell phones, offering indirect help is quite easy, and it may often be the wisest and safest course of action. Physical injuries are best handled by people with medical training, such as ambulance workers. Dangerous situations are best handled by people with proper training, such as police officers. Stalled motorist problems are best handled by people with proper training, such as the highway patrol. Calling others for help is still being helpful. Before cell phones, however, people faced much more difficult choices: either try to help in person or do nothing at all.

Step 5: Provide Help. The fifth and final step is to take action by offering help. There are obstacles to helping at this step also. One obstacle is called **audience inhibition**—people don't want to feel like a fool in front of others if they offer help and the person does not want help. People also might not help if the costs outweigh the benefits (see ▶ **TABLE 9.3**; e.g., Piliavin, Piliavin, & Rodin, 1975).

TOO BUSY TO HELP?

One of the more moving and memorable stories from the Judeo-Christian Bible has come to be known as the "Parable of the Good Samaritan." It goes like this:

A certain man went down from Jerusalem to Jericho, and fell among thieves, which stripped him of his raiment, and wounded him, and departed, leaving him half dead. And by chance there came down a certain priest that way: and when he saw him, he passed by on the other side. And likewise a Levite, when he was at the place, came and looked on him, and passed by on the other side. But a certain Samaritan, as he journeyed, came where he was: and when he saw him, he had compassion on him. And went to

▶ **TABLE 9.3** Some Costs and Benefits of Helping

	Helping	Not Helping
Costs	Lose time	Guilt
	Injury	Social disapproval
	Legal liability	Legal liability
	Worsen situation	
Benefits	Self-praise	Avoid risk of injury
	Reward	Avoid risks of helping
	Social approval	

him, and bound up his wounds, pouring in oil and wine, and set him on his own beast, and brought him to an inn, and took care of him. And on the morrow when he departed, he took out two pence, and gave them to the host, and said unto him, Take care of him; and whatsoever thou spendest more, when I come again, I will repay thee. (Luke 10:30–35)

Would the parable of the Good Samaritan actually prompt bystanders to help in an emergency? To find out, researchers recruited students at the Princeton Theological Seminary who were studying to be ministers (Darley & Batson, 1973). Half of them came to the psychology building expecting to give a talk about the Good Samaritan parable, so that the issue of helping needy victims should have been prominent in their minds. The remaining students were told to give a talk on job opportunities for seminary students.

Does being in a hurry make bystanders less likely to help in an emergency? To find out, students were also divided into low, moderate, and high "hurry" conditions. When they arrived at the lab for their appointment, they were told that their talk would be given in an auditorium in another building, and they were sent on their way. Those in the low-hurry condition were told that they were ahead of schedule and had plenty of time. Those in the moderate-hurry condition were told that they were right on schedule. Those in the high-hurry condition were told that they were late and that their audience was waiting for them. On the way to give their speech, all participants passed a man (actually a confederate) who was slumped in a doorway, coughing and groaning. The measure of helping was whether students stopped to help the man.

The topic of the speech—and thus whether they were thinking about career prospects or about the Bible's most famous story of bystander helping—had no effect on helping. Several seminary students going to give a talk on the parable of the Good Samaritan

AUDIENCE INHIBITION failure to help in front of others for fear of feeling like a fool if one's offer of help is rejected

literally stepped over the victim, as they hurried on their way! Time pressures, however, had a significant effect on helping. Participants in the low-hurry condition were more than six times more likely to help than were participants in the high-hurry condition. The more time people had, the more likely they were to help.

How Can We Increase Helping?

GETTING HELP IN A PUBLIC SETTING

People aren't cold and uncaring when it comes to helping others. They are just uncertain about what to do. If you need help in an emergency setting, your best bet is to reduce the uncertainties of those around you concerning your condition and their responsibilities (Cialdini, 1993, p. 113). If you need

emergency help when in a crowd of people, pick a face out of the crowd. Stare, speak, and point directly at that person. Say, "You, sir, in the blue sweatshirt, I need help. Call an ambulance now."

With that one statement you have reduced all the obstacles that might prevent or delay help.

- He notices you. (reduces distraction)
- He understands that help is needed. (reduces pluralistic ignorance)
- He understands that he, not someone else, is responsible for providing help. (reduces diffusion of responsibility)
- He understands exactly how to provide help. (reduces concerns about lack of competence)
- He should not be inhibited by an audience. (reduces audience inhibition)

Decades of research have shown that if you follow this advice, you will maximize the likelihood of receiving help in a public setting.

EDUCATE OTHERS

Once people understand the situational factors that interfere with helping in emergency situations, they should be more likely to help. Students in one experiment (Beaman, Barnes, & Klentz, 1978) heard a lecture on why bystanders often don't help. Other students heard a different lecture or no lecture at all. As part of a different study in a different location, students found themselves walking with an unresponsive confederate past someone sprawled beneath a bicycle. The group that heard the lecture was much more likely to help (67% vs. 27%). The researchers replicated the study by separating the lecture and the opportunity to help by two weeks. Two weeks later, when encountering a person slumped over, the group that had heard the lecture was still much more likely to help (43% vs. 25%).

PROVIDE HELPFUL MODELS

> Example is not the main thing in influencing others. It is the only thing.
> —Albert Schweitzer: humanitarian, theologian, missionary, organist, and medical doctor

If unresponsive models interfere with helping, as often occurs in public when bystanders fail to offer help, can helpful models increase helping? The answer is a resounding yes. Fourth- and fifth-graders in a classic study by Rosenhand and White (1967) played a bowling game in which gift certificates could be earned. The gift certificates could be traded for candy and toys. Near the bowling game was a box labeled "Trenton Orphans Fund." The box also contained pictures of orphans in ragged clothing. Half the students were exposed to a helpful adult model,

Prosocial television programming increases helpful behavior in children.

© Kay Nietfeld/dpa/Corbis

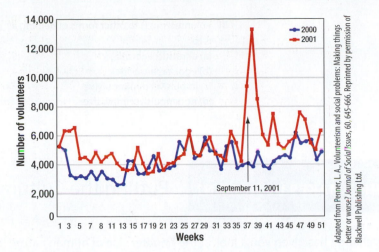

Adapted from Penner, L. A., Volunteerism and social problems: Making things better or worse? *Journal of Social Issues*, 60, 645-666. Reprinted by permission of Blackwell Publishing Ltd.

▶ **FIGURE 9.7** Volunteer rates increased sharply just after September 11, 2001; no comparable increase occurred in 2000 (adapted from Penner, 2004).

and half were not. Each time the adult model won gift certificates, he put half of them in the orphan box and said, "If you would like to give some of your gift certificates to them you can, but you do not have to." Students who were not exposed to the model were told the same thing. The students were then left alone to play the game. The results showed that 48% of students who were exposed to the adult model helped the orphans, whereas 0% of students who were not exposed to the adult model helped the orphans. If the researchers had included a child model condition, donations might have been even higher than for the adult model condition, because people are more influenced by similar others.

The models don't need to be live either. Filmed models are also effective. Research has shown that prosocial television programs such as *Lassie*, *Mr. Rogers' Neighborhood*, *Barney*, and *Sesame Street* increase helpful behavior in children (Hearold, 1986).

Another way to model helpful behavior is to be a volunteer. More than 55% of Americans over 18 volunteer to do some prosocial helping (Penner, 2002). Americans volunteer an average of 19 billion work hours each year, and they contribute $226 billion each year (Penner, 2002). **Volunteering** is a planned, long-term, nonimpulsive decision. Significant events can have a large effect on volunteer rates. For example, the number of people who volunteered more than tripled the week after the September 11 terrorist bombing (Penner, 2004; see ▶ **FIGURE 9.7**).

However, the rate of volunteering returned to normal levels three weeks later.

TEACH MORAL INCLUSION

Often people sort others into "us" (people who belong to the same group or category as we do, called ingroup members) and "them" (people who belong to a different group or category than we do, called outgroup members). (Chapter 13 describes the distinction between ingroups and outgroups in more detail.) One way to increase helping is to make everybody on this planet a member of your "ingroup." People, regardless of how they differ from us (e.g., ethnic background, gender, sexual orientation), are still part of the human family and on that basis may still be worthy of our help.

[**QUIZ YOURSELF**]

How Can We Increase Helping?

1. At which stage do potential helpers weigh the costs of helping versus not helping before making their decisions?
   (a) Assuming responsibility to help
   (b) Providing help
   (c) Interpreting the situation as an emergency
   (d) Noticing the emergency

2. TV programs such as *Barney*, *Lassie*, and *Mr. Rogers' Neighborhood* have been shown to _____ helpful behavior in children.
   (a) decrease
   (b) increase
   (c) have no effect on
   (d) Not enough research has been conducted to answer this question.

VOLUNTEERING a planned, long-term, nonimpulsive decision to help others

3. Volunteerism is to other forms of helping as _____ is to _____.
(a) altruistic; egoistic
(b) egoistic; altruistic
(c) impulsive; nonimpulsive
(d) nonimpulsive; impulsive

4. Treating everyone as a member of your ingroup is known as _____.
(a) diffusion of responsibility
(b) moral inclusion
(c) kin selection
(d) pluralistic ignorance

WHAT MAKES US HUMAN?	Putting the Cultural Animal in Perspective

This chapter has given you a look at the brighter side of human nature (but get ready for the darker side in the next chapter!). Prosocial behavior shows people doing things that bring benefits to others and help their culture and society to operate successfully. Traditionally, social psychologists have emphasized helping, but there are many other important forms of prosocial behavior. We may be inspired by the heroic acts of people like Oskar Schindler, but society's successful functioning depends less on that sort of occasional, spectacular heroism than on everyday prosocial behavior like following rules, cooperating, reciprocating, forgiving, taking turns, and obeying legitimate authority. If most people do those things most of the time, the cultural system can succeed in making everyone better off. Recent centuries of human history have gradually seen power shift from individuals (such as kings who could command or decree whatever they wanted) to the rule of law, and in the process life has gotten safer and happier for most people. Even today, happiness levels are higher in countries with a strong rule of law than in those that lack the rule of law (Veenhoven, 2004).

Perhaps the most sweeping and important difference in prosocial behavior between humans and other animals is that humans will do prosocial things for others who are not family members. As with most animals, human helping gives first priority to family members and loved ones, but human beings will also do nice things for total strangers. Sharing your food with your mother or your son does not indicate anything special about your humanity—many other animals would do the same. But donating money or blood to benefit people you will never meet is distinctively, and remarkably, human. In fact, we saw that 18-month-old human toddlers will even help non-kin voluntarily, and that they are more helpful than older chimps in similar situations. Nature seems to have prepared people to understand and care about each other and to offer help when possible.

Some animals can learn to follow rules, but usually these are very specific rules, made and enforced by another (typically bigger) animal whose presence is often essential for enforcing the rules. Rule following took a big leap with human evolution. People can follow laws, moral principles, and other rules even when they are alone, and they can apply them to novel situations, making following rules a vital form of prosocial behavior. Following rules even without someone watching your every move is an important basis for human culture.

Obedience is related to following rules. Again, many animals can learn to obey specific commands. Only humans expect each other to tell the difference between legitimate and wrongful authority and to obey only the former. Even the military has come around (after atrocities such as the My Lai massacre during the Vietnam War and the Abu Ghraib prison abuses during the Iraq War) to advocating that soldiers have a duty to disobey orders that are improper. Studies such as Milgram's (1963) have shown that it is hard for people to disobey direct orders from seemingly legitimate authority figures, but it can be done. The human being is (sometimes, at least) an autonomous, thinking, moral agent, even when receiving orders.

Conformity is simpler and cruder than following rules, because all it requires is the ability to see what others are doing and the desire to do the same. Many animals exhibit a herd instinct sort of conformity, in which they unthinkingly copy the behavior of others. Unlike other animals, people exchange information with each other and rely on what others tell them to learn about the world.

Likewise, the beginnings of reciprocity can be seen among animals, but typically this involves sharing with kin. Unlike most animals, humans can reciprocate with strangers. Cooperation, too, is more advanced in humans than in many other species. Some animals seem to cooperate, in that they do complementary things, but mostly these are fixed action patterns. Humans can decide to cooperate or not, and often they decide to cooperate.

Reciprocity and cooperation indicate some understanding of fairness. (If you don't pay it back, you're not being fair.) Some other animals have a crude understanding of fairness, but mostly they are upset when they are underbenefited. Humans often feel guilty or uncomfortable when they are overbenefited too.

Last, empathy may be more centrally important to human helping than to the prosocial behavior of other animals. People are much better than most other creatures at understanding what someone else is feeling, and this capacity to appreciate someone else's pain and suffering is an important factor in promoting helping behavior.

WHAT IS PROSOCIAL BEHAVIOR?

- Prosocial behavior involves doing good for others or society; it builds relationships and allows society to function.
- Obeying rules, conforming to norms, cooperating, and helping are all forms of prosocial behavior.
- Public circumstances generally promote prosocial behavior. That is, people behave better when others are watching and know who they are.
- Reciprocity is the obligation to return in kind what another has done for us.
- Equity means that each person receives benefits in proportion to what he or she did. Equality means that everyone gets the same amount, regardless of performance.
- A full sense of fairness, recognizing both underbenefits and overbenefits, is important in humans but probably absent in other animals.

COOPERATION, FORGIVENESS, OBEDIENCE, AND CONFORMITY

- Prisoner's dilemma is a game that consists of tradeoffs between cooperation and competition.
- Zero-sum games are those in which the winnings and losings add up to zero, so that one's gain is another's loss.
- If one member of a pair is not cooperative, then cooperation is typically doomed.
- Communication improves the chances of cooperation.
- Forgiveness helps repair relationships and provides health benefits to both the forgiver and the forgiven person.
- Forgiveness is more likely when the offense or hurt was minor and when the offending person apologizes. People who are religious, are committed to the relationship, and are not self-centered or narcissistic are more willing to forgive than other people.

- A majority of participants in Milgram's experiments delivered extreme shocks to a screaming victim in obedience to an authority figure.
- Although mindless obedience can be bad, in most cases society is better off if people obey society's rules.
- Conformity means going along with the crowd. It can be good or bad.
- Conformity and obedience can be prosocial behaviors, in that they make it easier to get along with others and for society to function.

WHY DO PEOPLE HELP OTHERS?

- The evolutionary theory of kin selection suggests that we prefer to help others who are related to us.
- Altruistic helping is motivated by empathy, an emotional response that corresponds to the feelings of the other person, because it motivates people to reduce others' distress.
- Egoistic helping is motivated by the desire to reduce one's own distress, according to negative state relief theory.

WHO HELPS WHOM?

- Many people get pleasure from helping others.
- People are more likely to help similar others than dissimilar others.
- Males are more helpful than females in the broader public sphere, toward strangers, and in emergencies, whereas females are more helpful in the family sphere, in close relationships, and in volunteering.
- Females are more likely to receive help than are males, regardless of whether the helper is male or female.
- People are more likely to help attractive individuals than unattractive individuals.
- Belief in a just world refers to the finding that people believe that the world is mostly fair and that people usually get what they deserve.
- People who believe the world is just will help others, but only if they think those people deserve the help.

- Positive moods generally increase helping, but some bad moods, such as guilt, can also promote helping.

BYSTANDER HELPING IN EMERGENCIES

- The bystander effect is the finding that people are less likely to offer help when they are in a group than when they are alone.
- The five steps to helping during an emergency are:
  - Notice that something is happening.
  - Interpret the event as an emergency.
  - Take responsibility for providing help.
  - Know what to do.
  - Take action and provide help.
- Pluralistic ignorance involves thinking others know something that we don't know, even if others don't know it either.
- Diffusion of responsibility refers to the reduction in helping that occurs when multiple bystanders all assume that others will take the responsibility of helping.
- People who are in a hurry help less than those who aren't, even if those in a hurry are thinking about the Good Samaritan.

HOW CAN WE INCREASE HELPING?

- Helping can be increased by:
  - Reducing uncertainties
  - Educating others about bystander indifference
  - Providing helpful models
  - Teaching moral inclusion (making others a part of the ingroup)

WHAT MAKES US HUMAN? PUTTING THE CULTURAL ANIMAL IN PERSPECTIVE

- Humans, unlike other animals, frequently act in a prosocial manner toward others who are not family members.
- Rule following, obedience, and conformity are often depicted as negative acts, but for the most part are prosocial acts.

Key Terms

Altruistic helping 271
Audience inhibition 281
Belief in a just world 276
Bystander effect 278
Conformity 267
Cooperation 261
Diffusion of
    responsibility 280
Egoistic helping 271
Empathy 271

Empathy–altruism
    hypothesis 272
Empathy–specific
    punishment
    hypothesis 273
Empathy–specific reward
    hypothesis 273
Equality 260
Equity 260
Forgiveness 264

Kin selection 270
Negative state relief
    hypothesis 273
Non-zero-sum game 262
Norms 259
Obedience 265
Overbenefited 260
Pluralistic ignorance 280
Prisoner's dilemma 261
Prosocial behavior 257

Reciprocity 259
Rule of law 258
Sensitivity about being the
    target of a threatening
    upward comparison 260
Survivor guilt 261
Underbenefited 260
Volunteering 283
Zero-sum game 262

[Quiz Yourself] Answers

1. What Is Prosocial Behavior?
Answers: 1=b, 2=b, 3=a, 4=d

2. Cooperation, Forgiveness, Obedience, and Conformity
Answers: 1=d, 2=d, 3=d, 4=b

3. Why Do People Help Others?
Answers: 1=a, 2=c, 3=d, 4=c

4. Who Helps Whom?
Answers: 1=a, 2=a, 3=d, 4=b

5. Bystander Helping in Emergencies
Answers: 1=a, 2=d, 3=a, 4=a

6. How Can We Increase Helping?
Answers: 1=b, 2=b, 3=d, 4=b

Media Learning Resources

Make sure you check out the complete set of learning resources and study tools below. If your instructor did not order these items with your new book, go to www.ichapters.com to purchase Cengage Learning print and digital products.

Social Psychology and Human Nature BOOK COMPANION WEBSITE

www.cengage.com/psychology/baumeister
Visit your book companion website, where you will find flash cards, practice quizzes, Internet links, and more to help you study.

CENGAGENOW™ JUST WHAT YOU NEED TO KNOW NOW!

Spend time on what you need to master rather than on information you have already learned. Take a pre-test for this chapter, and CengageNOW will generate a personalized study plan based on your results. The study plan will identify the topics you need to review and direct you to online resources to help you master those topics. You can then take a post-test to help you determine the concepts you have mastered and what you will still need to work on. Try it out! Go to www.cengage.com/login to sign in with an access code or to purchase access to this product.

CLASSIC AND CONTEMPORARY VIDEOS STUDENT CD-ROM

To see videos on the topics and experiments discussed in this chapter and to learn more about the research that social psychologists are doing today, go to the Student CD-ROM.

SOCIAL PSYCH LAB

These unique online labs give you the opportunity to become a participant in actual experiments, including re-creations of classic and contemporary research studies.

chapter 10

© Siephoto/Masterfile

Aggression and Antisocial Behavior

Tradeoffs: Is Military Action an Effective Way to Fight Terrorism? p. 292

The Social Side of Sex: Sexual Aggression p. 302

Food for Thought: Is There a Link Between Diet and Violence? p. 309

What Makes Us Human? Putting the Cultural Animal in Perspective p. 319

DEFINING AGGRESSION AND ANTISOCIAL BEHAVIOR p. 289
Is the World More or Less Violent Now Than in the Past? p. 292

IS AGGRESSION INNATE OR LEARNED? p. 294
Instinct Theories p. 294
Learning Theories p. 295
Nature *and* Nurture p. 296

INNER CAUSES OF AGGRESSION p. 297
Frustration p. 297
Being in a Bad Mood p. 298
Hostile Cognitive Biases p. 299
Age and Aggression p. 299
Gender and Aggression p. 300

INTERPERSONAL CAUSES OF AGGRESSION p. 301
Selfishness and Influence p. 301
Domestic and Relationship Violence: Hurting Those We Love p. 301

EXTERNAL CAUSES OF AGGRESSION p. 303
Weapons Effect p. 303
Mass Media p. 304
Unpleasant Environments p. 306
Chemical Influences p. 306

SELF AND CULTURE p. 309
Norms and Values p. 309
Self-Control p. 310
Wounded Pride p. 311
Culture of Honor p. 312

OTHER ANTISOCIAL BEHAVIOR p. 314
Lying p. 314
Detecting Liars p. 314
Cheating p. 315
Stealing p. 316
Littering p. 317

CHAPTER SUMMARY p. 319

Rwanda, a country located in east-central Africa, was originally home to the Hutus (see "Rwanda," 2004; "Timeline," 2008). About 600 years ago, the Tutsis, a tall warrior people that lived in Ethiopia, invaded and conquered the area and installed a king with almost godlike powers. |||||

Although the Hutus greatly outnumbered the Tutsis, they agreed to raise crops for the Tutsis in exchange for protection from hostile intruders. In 1890, Rwanda became part of German East Africa. In 1916, during World War I, Belgium invaded the German territories, and after the war Rwanda came under Belgian rule as a League of Nations mandate.

Traditionally, the differences between Hutus and Tutsis were occupational rather than ethnic. The Hutus had the low-status farming jobs, whereas the Tutsis had the high-status cattle herding jobs. In terms of appearance, the Hutus were supposedly short and square whereas the Tutsis were supposedly tall and thin. That may have been true 600 years ago, but today it is not possible to tell them apart. The two groups not only look the same, they also speak the same language, inhabit the same parts of the country, follow the same traditions, and intermarry.

The Belgians considered the Tutsis as superior to the Hutus and even produced identity cards classifying the two groups according to their ethnic background. Tutsis (of course) agreed with the Belgians, and enjoyed better jobs, educational opportunities, and living conditions for decades. Resentment among the Hutus against the Tutsis gradually built up, culminating in a series of riots in 1959 that overthrew the ruling Tutsi king. During these riots, more than 20,000 Tutsis were killed, and many more fled to nearby countries. When Belgium relinquished power and granted independence in 1962, the Hutus took control of the country; many Tutsis left Rwanda and went to live in neighboring Burundi.

With the Hutus in power, the Tutsis were used as the scapegoats for every problem the country faced. Hate media fueled the fire. For example, a 1992 leaflet picturing a machete asked the question: "What shall we do to complete the social revolution of 1959?" In 1993, Burundi president Melchior Ndadaye, a Hutu, was assassinated by hardline Tutsi soldiers. The media used the assassination to incite anger against Tutsis. The media falsely reported that the president had been tortured and castrated. (In precolonial times, some Tutsi kings had castrated defeated enemy rulers.)

On 6 April 1994, Rwandan president Juvenal Habyarimana, a Hutu, was killed when his plane was shot down above the airport. Nobody was sure who shot down the plane, but the Tutsis were blamed. Encouraged by media propaganda, a genocide began. Radio broadcasts called for a "final war" to "exterminate the (Tutsi) cockroaches." The UN commander in charge of peacekeeping operations at the time, General Romeo Dallaire, said: "Simply jamming [the] broadcasts and replacing them with messages of peace and reconciliation would have had a significant impact on the course of events" (Smith, 2003).

Not all broadcasters participated in the propaganda. Thomas Kamilindi, a Hutu, resigned from a state-run radio station because he refused to broadcast hate propaganda. Kamilindi was called a "dog" and was almost killed for "sympathizing" with the Tutsis. A commander who happened to pass by just as a soldier pointed a gun at Kamilindi's head saved him. Kamilindi's 5-year-old daughter was murdered while she was visiting her Tutsi maternal grandparents.

In just 100 days, about 800,000 Tutsi and Hutu sympathizers were killed. They were killed with guns, machetes, sticks, and stones. Hutus were given incentives for killing Tutsis, such as money, food, and even the dead Tutsis' houses and property.

Hate media were also used to incite rape and sexual assault against Tutsi women. For example, leaflets contained statements such as "You Tutsi women think that you are too good for us" and "Let us see what a Tutsi woman tastes like." A 1996 United Nations report stated that "rape was the rule and its absence the exception." The report also stated that "rape was systematic and was used as a 'weapon' by the perpetrators of the massacres." The report estimated that between 250,000 and 500,000 Tutsi women and girls had been raped, and that many had been raped by men who knew they were HIV positive (de Brouwer, 2005).

The international community largely ignored the genocide. UN troops withdrew after the murder of 10 soldiers. The U.S. government was reluctant to involve itself in the "local conflict" in Rwanda and refused to label the killings as "genocide," a decision that former President Bill Clinton later came to regret. In a TV interview Clinton stated that he believes if he had sent 5,000 U.S. peacekeepers, more than 500,000 lives could have been saved ("Triumph of Evil," 1995).

There were some bright spots in this story. Hotel manager Paul Rusesabagina sheltered 1,268 Tutsis and Hutu sympathizers while mobs cried for their blood outside his hotel ("Paul Rusesabagina," 2006). This real-life story formed the basis for the 2004 movie *Hotel Rwanda*.

The end of the story had a twist that continues to be important today. A Tutsi army invaded and conquered the country, causing flight and consternation among the Hutus, just as the UN intervened to restore order. The UN found itself in the uncomfortable position of protecting Hutu killers from the Tutsi avengers. Some Hutu groups crossed the border into the Congo, where they operated somewhat freely, including by robbing, killing, and raping Congolese citizens. The new Tutsi government sponsored forces that went into the Congo and sought to kill the Hutu forces. Meanwhile, the new government uncomfortably sought peace and reconciliation, including by forbidding anyone to distinguish between who was Hutu and who was Tutsi. People were only permitted to identify with being Rwandan.

The genocide in Rwanda illustrates several important points about violence and aggression. It illustrates the role of the mass media in aggression. It illustrates that frustrated people can sometimes lash out at the source of their frustration in violent ways. It illustrates that aggressors often dehumanize their victims, such as by calling them cockroaches or dogs. It illustrates that females can become the vulnerable targets of male aggression. On the other hand, it also illustrates that people can resist situational forces that increase aggression. Thomas Kamilindi quit his job and refused to broadcast hate messages. Paul Rusesabagina, a Hutu, refused to let the Hutu soldiers kill the Tutsis taking refuge in the hotel he was managing.

Early psychological theories (such as Freud's) depicted aggression as the outburst of powerful inner forces. More recent theories have considered aggression as a kind of strategic behavior that people use to

Some of the victims of the 1994 massacre in Rwanda.

AP Photo/Brennan Linsley

influence others, get what they want, and defend certain ideas that they see as under attack (Baumeister, 1997; Tedeschi & Felson, 1994). Understanding aggression is important not only to social psychologists but also to society at large. One can adopt either a pessimistic or an optimistic view of aggression in human life. On the pessimistic side, there is a great deal of aggression, and it is sad to think how much avoidable suffering it causes all over the world. On the optimistic side, there are many situations that could lead to aggression, but aggression arises in only a few of them, so somehow most people manage to inhibit their aggressive tendencies most of the time. ■

Defining Aggression and Antisocial Behavior

On June 30, 2004, a 42-year-old German computer technician named Armin Meiwes was sent to prison for killing and eating Bernd Juergen Brandes in March 2001. His victim, also in his 40s, had responded to Meiwes' Internet advertisement seeking a thin and healthy man "for slaughter." Brandes bought a one-

way ticket to the defendant's home village and spent an evening with him before volunteering to be killed. The two had sex and hours of sadomasochistic interactions before Meiwes stabbed Brandes to death. Meiwes ate the flesh of Brandes over several months, defrosting cuts from his freezer. He told the court that it was the realization of a boyhood fantasy he had about killing and eating classmates. Investigators said that Meiwes had Internet contact with hundreds of other people who shared his fantasy. Rock artist

© Uwe Zucchi/Pool/Reuters/Corbis

© Police Handout/Reuters/Corbis

Armin Meiwes (left) killed and ate Bernd Juergen Brandes (right), who responded to an Internet ad seeking a man "for slaughter." Meiwes had a "slaughtering room" in his house in Rotenburg, Germany.

Marilyn Manson said Meiwes inspired the title of his 2007 CD, *Eat Me, Drink Me*.

On 10 May 2006, Meiwes was sentenced to life in prison. Since entering prison, Meiwes has become a vegetarian and has joined a prisoners' group favoring Green Party politics. Meiwes plans to write his memoirs in order to persuade other people with similar fantasies to seek professional help before it is too late. He has also helped investigators analyze evidence from other cannibal murders.

Was this bizarre and gruesome act committed against Brandes an act of aggression? Not according to most social psychological definitions of aggression! Most social psychologists define human **aggression** as any behavior intended to harm another person who does not want to be harmed (Baron & Richardson, 1994). This definition includes three important features. First, aggression is a behavior—you can see it. Aggression is not an emotion, such as anger (see Chapter 6 for a discussion of emotions). Aggression is not a thought, such as mentally rehearsing a murder (see Chapter 5 for a discussion of cognitions). Second, aggression is intentional (not accidental), and the intent is to harm. For example, a dentist might intentionally drill a patient's teeth (which hurts!), but the goal is to help rather than hurt the patient.

Third, the definition stipulates that the victim wants to avoid the harm. Thus, again, the dental patient is excluded, because she or he is not seeking to avoid the harm (in fact, the patient probably booked the appointment weeks in advance and paid to have the dental work done). Suicide and sadomasochistic sex play are also not included, because again the victim actively seeks to be harmed. In the case of Meiwes, the victim volunteered for slaughter, so Meiwes' killing does not count as aggression.

Note that behaviors that are intended to harm others are still acts of aggression even if they don't actually harm them. For example, if a person shoots a gun at you but misses, it is still an act of aggression. In December 2008, President George W. Bush made a farewell visit to Iraq. The event was marred, however, when Iraqi journalist Muntadar al-Zaidi threw his shoes at Bush during a press conference ("Shoes," 2008). When he threw the first shoe, Mr. Zaidi shouted, "This is a goodbye kiss from the Iraqi people, dog." When he threw the second shoe, Mr. Zaidi shouted, "This is for the widows and orphans and all those killed in Iraq." Showing the soles of shoes to someone is a sign of contempt in Arab culture. Bush narrowly dodged both shoes.

Security personnel quickly wrestled Mr. Zaidi to the ground and arrested him. The next day, thousands of Iraqis took to the streets to demand the release of Mr. Zaidi. In Iran, protestors held their own shoe-throwing rally in support of Mr. Zaidi (Vennard, 2008). The protesters waved their shoes in the air, and then threw them at posters of Mr. Bush. Similar protests were held in other parts of the region. The Turkish firm that made the shoes was forced to hire an additional 100 employees because the demand was so high for the type of shoes Mr. Zaidi threw at Mr. Bush. The shoe was called "Model 271," but it was renamed the "Bush shoe." In the city of Tikrit, Iraq (Sadam Hussein's hometown), an artist made a sculpture of the shoe thrown at Bush and put it on the grounds of an orphanage, but the local authorities made them remove it. Mr. Zaidi was originally sentenced to three years in jail, but the sentence was later reduced to one year. In this case, Mr. Zaidi committed an act of aggression because he intended to verbally and physically harm Mr. Bush.

It is useful to distinguish among various forms and functions of aggression. By forms we mean how the aggressive act is expressed, such as physically (e.g., hitting, kicking, stabbing, shooting) or verbally (e.g., yelling, screaming, swearing, name calling). In displaced aggression, a substitute aggression target is used (e.g., Marcus-Newhall, Pedersen, Carlson, & Miller, 2000). For example, a woman is berated by her boss at work but does not retaliate. When she gets home, she kicks her dog or yells at a family member instead.

Different forms of aggression can be expressed directly or indirectly. In **direct aggression**, the victim is physically present; in **indirect aggression**, the

---

AGGRESSION any behavior intended to harm another person who is motivated to avoid the harm

DIRECT AGGRESSION any behavior that intentionally harms another person who is physically present

INDIRECT AGGRESSION any behavior that intentionally harms another person who is physically absent

During George W. Bush's farewell visit to Iraq as U.S. president, an Iraqi journalist threw his shoes at Bush (a sign of contempt in Arab culture) and called him a "dog" for killing thousands of civilians, leaving the country full of widows and orphans. An artist erected a statue of the shoe thrown at Bush on the grounds of an orphanage, but local authorities removed it.

victim is absent. For example, physical aggression can be direct (e.g., hitting a person in the face) or indirect (e.g., burning his house down while he is on holiday). Likewise, verbal aggression can be direct (e.g., screaming in a person's face) or indirect (e.g., spreading rumors behind her back). Males are more likely than females to use direct aggression, whereas females are more likely than males to use indirect aggression (e.g., Lagerspetz, Bjorkqvist, & Peltonen, 1988).

Aggressive acts may also differ in their function or motivation. Consider two examples. In the first, a husband finds his wife and her lover together in bed. He grabs his rifle from the closet and shoots and kills them both. In the second, a "hitman" uses a rifle to kill another person for money. The form of aggression is the same (shooting and killing victims with a rifle), but the motives are quite different. In the first example, the husband is motivated by anger. He is enraged when he finds his wife making love to another man, so he shoots them both. In the second example, the "hitman" is primarily motivated by money. The "hitman" probably does not hate his victim. He might not even know his victim, but he kills the person anyway for the money.

To capture different functions or motives for aggression, psychologists make a distinction between **reactive aggression** (also called hostile, affective, angry, impulsive, or retaliatory aggression) and **proactive aggression** (also called instrumental aggression; e.g., Buss, 1961; Dodge & Coie, 1987; Feshbach, 1964). Reactive aggression is "hot," impulsive, angry behavior that is motivated by a desire to harm someone. Proactive aggression is

"cold," premeditated, calculated behavior that is motivated by some other goal (obtaining money, restoring one's image, restoring justice). Some social psychologists have argued that it is difficult (if not impossible) to distinguish between reactive and proactive aggression because they are highly correlated and because motives are often mixed (Bushman & Anderson, 2001). For example, what if the husband who finds his wife making love to another man instigates a deadly plan to slowly poison both individuals. Would this be reactive or proactive aggression?

Violence is aggression that has as its goal extreme physical harm, such as injury or death. For example, one child pushing another off a tricycle is an act of aggression but is not an act of violence. One person intentionally hitting, kicking, shooting, or stabbing another person is an act of violence. The Federal Bureau of Investigation (FBI) classifies four crimes as "violent": homicide, aggravated assault, forcible rape, and robbery. Thus, all violent acts are aggressive acts, but not all aggressive acts are violent. Only the ones that try to cause extreme physical harm are violent.

Antisocial behavior is a term that research psychologists have used in casual and somewhat inconsistent ways (though clinicians have a more precise definition). In general, it seems to refer to behavior

---

REACTIVE AGGRESSION "hot," impulsive, angry behavior that is motivated by a desire to harm someone

PROACTIVE AGGRESSION "cold," premeditated, calculated harmful behavior that is a means to some practical or material end

VIOLENCE aggression that has as its goal extreme physical harm, such as injury or death

ANTISOCIAL BEHAVIOR behavior that either damages interpersonal relationships or is culturally undesirable

Is Military Action an Effective Way to Fight Terrorism?

Many countries resort to military action to stop terrorism. For example, in response to Palestinian suicide bombings, Israel has assassinated militant leaders, detained thousands of suspects, and launched preemptive military strikes to undermine the infrastructure of terrorist groups. But even Israel's top generals and intelligence chiefs have acknowledged that although effective in the short term, this policy has the long-term effect of radicalizing the population and creating a new pool of terrorist recruits (Moore, 2003).

After the terrorist attacks of September 11, 2001, the Bush administration declared a war on terror designed to root out terrorist networks "of global reach" (Bush, 2001). The United States attacked Afghanistan, which was harboring the notorious Osama bin Laden, while military units and intelligence operatives rounded up or eliminated suspected terrorists around the world. Next, the United States invaded Iraq. In the short term, these actions badly damaged al-Qaeda and its affiliates and also removed the potential threat posed by Iraqi leader Saddam Hussein (Record, 2003). In the long term, however, they radicalized a new generation of *jihadis*. (In Islam,

a *jihad* is a holy struggle or war. The greater jihad is the holy war over sin; the lesser jihad is the holy war against infidels or unbelievers.) They produced a decentralized global terrorist infrastructure even more difficult to fight, transformed Iraq into a new rallying point for anti-American militants, and resulted in a dramatic increase in terrorist acts around the world (Chipman, 2003; Cronin, 2003). Even a classified U.S. intelligence report concluded that the Iraq war had increased (rather than decreased) the threat of terrorism worldwide ("Iraq war," 2006). At the same time, even moderate Muslims were alienated, and anti-American attitudes in the Muslim world reached all-time lows (U.S. approval ratings of close to 0% in some countries; Zogby & Zogby, 2004).

According to Hani Sibai, director of the Al Maqrizi Center for Historical Studies, "Iraq is currently a battlefield and a fertile soil for every Islamic movement that views jihad as a priority." According to Sabi, very few of the individuals involved in the Iraqi jihad are members of al-Qaeda. "Even if the U.S. forces capture all leaders

Wathiq Khuzaie/Getty Images

of Al Qaeda or kill them all, the idea of expelling the occupiers and nonbelievers from the Arabian Peninsula and all the countries of Islam will not die" (Stern, 2004).

According to data from the Rand Corporation (cited in Stern, 2004), worldwide terrorist attacks were almost twice as high in the two years following September 11, 2001, as in the two years preceding it. Thus, although military action decreases terrorist attacks in the short term (as by removing some terrorists and disrupting communications), it may increase terrorist attacks in the long term because it recruits many more terrorists to the cause. ●

---

that either damages interpersonal relationships or is culturally undesirable. Aggression is often equated with antisocial behavior (e.g., American Psychiatric Association, 1994; Paik & Comstock, 1994). Others have pointed out, however, that aggression is often a social as well as an antisocial strategy, in that it is a way that people seek to manage their social lives, such as by influencing the behavior of others to get their way (Tedeschi & Felson, 1994). Littering, cheating, and lying, on the other hand, are behaviors that qualify as antisocial but may or may not be aggressive.

IS THE WORLD MORE OR LESS VIOLENT NOW THAN IN THE PAST?

The world seems more violent today than ever before, with international and civil wars being waged around the world. Yet quantitative studies of body counts, such as the proportion of prehistoric skeletons with axe and arrowhead wounds, suggest that prehistoric societies were far more violent than our own (Pinker,

2007). Although one can kill a lot more people with a bomb than with an axe, the death rates per battle were much higher in the past. Estimates show that if the wars of the 20th century had killed the same proportion of the population as ancient tribal wars, then the death toll would have been 20 times higher than it actually was—2 billion rather than 100 million (Pinker, 2007).

More recent data confirm that violence is decreasing over time. European murder rates have decreased dramatically since the Middle Ages (e.g., Eisner, 2001; Gurr, 1981). For example, estimated murders in England dropped from 24 per 100,000 in the 14th century to 0.6 per 100,000 by the early 1960s. The major decline in violence seems to have occurred in the 17th century during the "Age of Reason," beginning in the Netherlands and England and then spreading to other European countries (Pinker, 2007).

The *Human Security Brief 2007* (2008) shows that global violence has been falling steadily since the middle of the 20th century. For example, the number

Although modern weapons can kill a lot more people than ancient weapons, the world is actually a more peaceful place today than in the past.

of battle deaths in interstate wars has declined from more than 65,000 per year in the 1950s to fewer than 2,000 per year in the 2000s. There have also been global declines in the number of armed conflicts and combat deaths, the number of military coups, and the number of deadly violence campaigns waged against civilians.

A number of other observations are consistent with the idea that human society is becoming less violent over time. Pinker (2007, p. 18) notes: "Cruelty as entertainment, human sacrifice to indulge superstition, slavery as a labor-saving device, conquest as the mission statement of government, genocide as a means of acquiring real estate, torture and mutilation as routine punishment, . . .—all were common features of life for most of human history. But, today, they are rare to nonexistent in the West, far less common elsewhere than they used to be, concealed when they do occur, and widely condemned when they are brought to light." To your textbook authors, this sounds like genuine progress!

In today's digital age we certainly are more informed about wars and other acts of violence than in past ages. "If it bleeds, it leads" seems to be the rule used to determine what news stories to focus on. Because violent images are more available to us now than ever before, we might assume that violence levels are also higher (see discussion of availability heuristic in Chapter 5). However, it seems that over time this planet is actually becoming a more peaceful place to live. One reason is that aggression may be becoming less effective: Although aggression may

work in the short run, it does not seem to work in the long run (see *Tradeoffs*).

The fact that aggression and violence are decreasing over time is consistent with one of the book's key themes: nature says yes whereas culture says no. One of the main goals of culture is to reduce and replace aggression. When two social animals want the same thing, aggression is the main way of settling who gets it. Culture offers other, better ways of settling conflicts: property rights, money, courts of law, compromise, religious and moral rules, and the like. The main exception has been rivalries between cultures, which sometimes are settled with aggression. Even so, culture has sought to reduce these conflicts, such as with the Geneva Convention and other rules of war that constrain violence. World organizations such as the United Nations also try to reduce aggression between countries.

[QUIZ YOURSELF]

Defining Aggression and Antisocial Behavior

1. Which of the following would be considered aggression?
   (a) A baseball batter's line drive accidentally hits the pitcher in the knee.
   (b) A girl attempts to punch her little brother, but misses.
   (c) A depressed man commits suicide.
   (d) All of the above

Is Aggression Innate or Learned?

The 19th and 20th centuries saw many attempts to improve society. The hope was to design a perfect society so that people could live together in peace, love, and harmony. Communism was based on these ideals, and indeed many Western intellectuals in the early part of the 20th century supported the Soviet Union because they thought it endorsed the Christian ideals they had learned in Sunday school: sharing, equality, tolerance, and the like (Crossman, 1987). Some went so far as to say that Jesus and his disciples were the first communists, because they took care of each other, shared all their possessions freely with each other, and made decisions collectively. Communism was only one of the plans for making the perfect society. Democracy, fascism, and other systems also aimed at creating a society in which people could all live together in friendly or loving harmony.

Aggression gradually emerged as the crux of the problem, however. If aggression only stems from frustration, exploitation, and injustice, then if one designed a perfect society, there would be no aggression. For example, if people were only aggressive because of injustice, then eliminating injustice would eliminate aggression. Even frustration might in theory be eliminated, and much aggression along with it. (But don't count on it!)

On the other hand, if people are naturally, innately aggressive, then no amount of social engineering will

Sigmund Freud believed that human motivational forces are based on instinct.

Time Life Pictures/Mansell/Time Life Pictures/Getty Images

be able to get rid of it. No matter how well a society is designed, people will still be aggressive. Perfect social harmony will prove elusive. If people are inherently aggressive, then aggression will always be with us, and society or culture needs to find ways of living with it, such as by passing laws to punish wrongful aggression.

INSTINCT THEORIES

First given scientific prominence by Charles Darwin (1871/1948), the instinct theory of aggression viewed aggressive behavior as an evolutionary adaptation that had enabled animals and then humans to survive better. This instinct presumably developed during the course of evolution because it promoted survival of the species. Because fighting is closely linked to mating, the aggressive instinct helped ensure that only the strongest individuals would pass on their genes to future generations.

Sigmund Freud argued that human motivational forces, such as sex and aggression, are based on instincts. An **instinct** is an innate (inborn, biologically programmed) tendency to seek a particular goal, such as food, water, or sex. In his early writings, Freud proposed the drive for sensory and sexual gratification as the primary human instinct. He called this constructive, life-giving instinct **eros**.

INSTINCT an innate (inborn, biologically programmed) tendency to seek a particular goal, such as food, water, or sex

EROS in Freudian theory, the constructive, life-giving instinct

After witnessing the horrific carnage of World War I, however, Freud concluded that a single life force could not be responsible for so much violence. He proposed, therefore, that humans also have a destructive, death instinct, which he called **thanatos**.

Freud's views undoubtedly influenced Konrad Lorenz (1966), whose instinct theory of aggression posited a buildup of aggressive urges (like hydraulic pressure inside a closed environment) that, if not released through some other activity, would inevitably lead to aggression. Although little empirical evidence has ever been found to support this "hydraulic" model of aggression, the theory that aggression results from the buildup of an internal drive or tension that must be released still has a profound influence on clinical psychology. It motivates popular venting and cathartic therapies even though numerous studies have found no significant evidence supporting the hydraulic model (for reviews, see Berkowitz, 1993; Geen & Quanty, 1977; Scott, 1958).

Empirical evidence supporting the existence of innate, relatively automatic aggressive responses has been demonstrated for many species (e.g., Lorenz, 1966). For example, in the male Stickleback fish, a red object triggers attack 100% of the time (Timbergen, 1952). However, no parallel innate aggressive response has been demonstrated in humans (Hinde, 1970).

You can probably appreciate the implications. If people have an innate need to attack and destroy something, then no society can really get rid of aggression. At best, society can provide safe targets for the innate drive to aggress. On the other hand, if aggression is merely a response to frustration, injustice, or other circumstances, then it might be possible to eliminate aggression by designing society so as not to provide the circumstances that cause it. The instinct theories of aggression were pessimistic on this: No matter how well society is designed, people will still have a drive to inflict harm.

LEARNING THEORIES

According to social learning theory (Bandura, 1973, 1983; Mischel, 1973; Mischel & Shoda, 1995), aggression is not an innate drive like hunger in search of gratification. People learn aggressive behaviors the same way they learn other social behaviors—by direct experience and by observing others. In social learning theory, the shift is from internal causes to external ones. When people observe and copy the behavior of others, this is called **modeling**. Modeling can weaken or strengthen aggressive responding. If the model is rewarded for behaving aggressively, further aggression (both by the model and by the observer) becomes more likely. If the model is punished for behaving aggressively, further aggression becomes less likely.

To demonstrate the social learning of aggression, Bandura and his colleagues allowed preschool children to watch either an aggressive adult role model, a nonaggressive model, or no model (Bandura, Ross, & Ross, 1961, 1963). The aggressive model abused a large, inflatable clown called a Bobo doll. The model laid the Bobo doll on its side, sat on it, punched it repeatedly in the nose, and said "Sock him in the nose." The model then beat the doll on the head with a mallet and said "Hit him down." The model tossed the doll up in the air and said "Throw him in the air." The model kicked the doll about the room, saying "Kick him" and "Pow."

In contrast, the nonaggressive model played with Tinker Toys the entire time, so children in that condition saw no aggressive activity. After 10 minutes, the experimenter entered the room, informed the child that he or she would now go to another game room, and said good-bye to the model. The other room contained both aggressive toys (a Bobo doll, a mallet and pegboard, dart guns, and a tetherball with a face painted on it) and some nonaggressive toys (a tea set, crayons and paper, a ball, dolls, teddy bears, cars and trucks, and plastic farm animals). The point of the study was to see whether children attacked the Bobo doll or played in some nonaggressive manner. The children who had watched the aggressive model showed the highest levels of aggression (see ▶ **FIGURE 10.1**).

To be sure, these studies do not meet our definition of human aggression, because the target of the aggressive act was a Bobo doll rather than a real

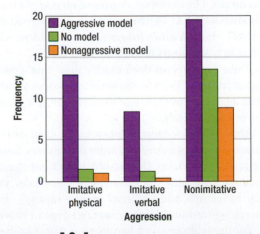

▶ **FIGURE 10.1** Results from a Bobo doll study conducted by Bandura and his colleagues (1961). Children exposed to aggressive models behaved more aggressively than did children exposed to nonaggressive models or no models.

THANATOS in Freudian theory, the destructive, death instinct
MODELING observing and copying or imitating the behavior of others

Bandura and colleagues (1963) found that children readily imitated filmed aggressive adult models.

person. However, many other studies have shown that aggressive models can influence people of all ages to behave more aggressively toward human targets. In one study (Liebert & Baron, 1972), children could help or hurt another child's chance of winning a prize by pressing either a green "HELP" button or a red "HURT" button. Participants were told that when they pressed the "HURT" button, a handle that the other child was turning would get really hot and burn him. In reality, of course, there was no child in the other room, and no one got hurt. Children who had watched a violent film pressed the "HURT" button down longer than did children who had watched a nonviolent film.

These experiments don't exactly show that aggression is learned. They do, however, show that inhibitions against aggression can be overcome if a model acts out aggressively.

Although all creatures are innately disposed to learn some things better and faster than others, learning is still important. The impulse to lash out against someone who hurts or threatens or humiliates you may be natural and universal (nature says go), but the rules governing action or restraint depend heavily on culture (culture says when to stop). Some anthropologists and others believe that without cultural encouragement, there would be no aggression (e.g., Alland, 1972), but the majority of social scientists (and your textbook authors) disagree, partly because aggression has been found everywhere. The nonviolent human being is the product of culture. Without culture, there would be even more aggression than there is, especially within each social group.

Aggressive instincts can also be modified. Cats prey on rats instinctively. But an early experiment showed that when kittens and rats were raised together, none of the kittens killed rats (Kuo, 1930). When kittens were raised in isolation, 54% of them killed rats. When kittens were raised by a mother who killed rats, 85% of the kittens killed rats. Thus, it is "natural" for learning to change and shape aggressive patterns. In the same way, presumably, cultural socialization can subdue or encourage aggressive impulses and actions.

NATURE *AND* NURTURE

Many experts on aggression (and your textbook authors) favor a middle ground in this nature-versus-nurture dispute. Both learning and instinct are relevant (e.g., Baron & Richardson, 1994; Berkowitz, 1993).

As already noted, learning clearly plays a role. People can learn how to behave aggressively. Even more important and more commonly, they learn how to restrain aggression. People learn and mostly obey complicated rules about aggression. Some of the most remarkable evidence of this can be seen in American football games. The defensive players have to charge at the quarterback as ferociously as they can, eager to slam into him and knock him to the ground. But they have to be able to stop this attempted aggression at a split-second's notice when the quarterback steps out of bounds, or he throws the ball, or the referee blows the whistle.

As for nature, it is hard to dispute that aggression is found all over the world, and indeed some of its patterns are universal. For example, in all known societies, most of the violence is perpetrated by young adult men (e.g., U.S. Federal Bureau of Investigation, 2008). In no society do the majority of violent criminals turn out to be middle-aged women, for example.

Most likely, the Freudian theory of innate aggression needs a major overhaul. Freud and others thought aggression was like hunger: The need bubbles up from inside and has to be satisfied in some way. In that view, the aggressive drive is independent of circumstances. In contrast, perhaps natural selection has led to aggressive impulses as a way to respond to certain (social) events, such as someone else's getting something you want. To appreciate the difference, imagine what life would be like if you always got everything you wanted. According to the Freudian view, you would still have aggressive impulses, because the aggressive drive would still bubble up and make you want to hit people or smash things. In contrast, if aggression is merely an innate response to not getting what you want, you might in principle never have an aggressive impulse if you always got everything you wanted.

Humans don't have to learn to behave aggressively. Rather, aggression seems to come naturally. They learn how to control their aggressive impulses. Thus, it may be natural to feel aggressive impulses in response to certain provocations. But cultural beings learn to bring those natural impulses under control so as to follow the rules. This fits the theme that nature says go, whereas culture says stop. All known human societies have rules against aggression, though they may consider some aggression acceptable. For human beings who live in culture, aggression is subject to rules and limits.

[QUIZ YOURSELF]

Is Aggression Innate or Learned?

1. In Freud's theory, life-giving instinct is to death instinct as _____ is to _____.
   (a) eros; thanatos   (b) thanatos; eros
   (c) id; superego   (d) superego; id

2. Learning is to instinct as _____ is to _____.
   (a) external forces; internal forces
   (b) internal forces; external forces
   (c) Sigmund Freud; Konrad Lorenz
   (d) Konrad Lorenz; Sigmund Freud

3. Abdul believes that children are aggressive because they imitate what they see family members and media characters do. Abdul's beliefs are consistent with _____ theory.
   (a) Freudian   (b) frustration
   (c) instinct   (d) social learning

4. The wide variation in homicide rates across different countries illustrates the effect of _____ on violence and aggression.
   (a) aggressive cues   (b) frustration
   (c) nature   (d) nurture

Mauricio Duenas/AFP/Getty Images

Aggressive instincts can be modified so that even cats and rats can live together peacefully.

Inner Causes of Aggression

FRUSTRATION

In 1939 a group of psychologists from Yale University published a book titled *Frustration and Aggression* (Dollard, Doob, Miller, Mowrer, & Sears, 1939). In this book, they proposed the **frustration-aggression hypothesis**, which they summarized on the first page of their book with these two bold statements: (a) "the occurrence of aggressive behavior always presupposes the existence of frustration," and (b) "the existence of frustration always leads to some form of aggression." (Note the strong use of "always" in both sentences; social psychologists today hardly ever dare say "always" or "never"!) They defined **frustration** as blocking or interfering with a goal. The Yale group formulated the frustration-aggression hypothesis based on the early writings of Sigmund Freud (1917/1961). Freud believed that people are primarily motivated to seek pleasure and avoid pain. People were presumed to be frustrated when their pleasure-seeking or pain-avoiding behavior was

---

FRUSTRATION-AGGRESSION HYPOTHESIS proposal that "the occurrence of aggressive behavior always presupposes the existence of frustration," and "the existence of frustration always leads to some form of aggression."

FRUSTRATION blockage of or interference with a personal goal

blocked. Freud regarded aggression as the "primordial reaction" to frustration. (As we saw earlier, Freud eventually revised his theory to include an aggressive instinct, but the Yale group favored his earlier theory.)

Neal Miller (1941), one of the original authors of *Frustration and Aggression*, was quick to revise the second statement of the frustration-aggression hypothesis. He recommended that the statement be changed to "Frustration produces instigations to a number of different types of response, one of which is an instigation to some form of aggression" (p. 338). Miller continued to hold that the first statement of the hypothesis (aggression is *always* preceded by frustration) was true.

Most experts today think Miller and his colleagues went too far by saying "always." There can be aggression without frustration, and frustration without aggression. Still, there is no denying the basic truth that aggression is increased by frustration.

The Rwanda genocide was triggered in part by frustration on the part of Hutus that the Tutsis were so much better off than they were, even though the Tutsis were the minority group. They were also sick and tired of having a Tutsi king. Of course, frustration does not justify the Hutus' slaughtering the Tutsis.

BEING IN A BAD MOOD

Angry, frustrated, distraught, upset people have long been regarded as being prone to aggressive behavior. As the previous section showed, psychologists have long believed that frustration causes aggression, and the data have confirmed that—but it is not the whole story, because some aggression is not caused by frustration. More recently, Leonard Berkowitz (1989) proposed that all states of negative affect—not just

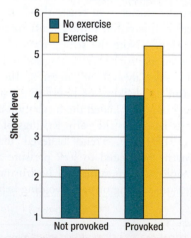

▶ **FIGURE 10.2 Arousal from physical exercise can transfer to a provocation and increase aggression (Zillmann, Katcher, & Milavsky, 1972).**

frustration—deserve to be recognized as causes of aggression. To be sure, not all varieties of negative affect have been tested for aggression-enhancing effects, but it is clear that some of them are quite capable of increasing aggression. When researchers want to elicit high levels of aggression in the laboratory, they typically start by inducing some aversive emotional state, such as anger or indignation.

Why do unpleasant moods increase aggression? One possible explanation is that angry people aggress in the hope that doing so will enable them to feel better. Research has consistently shown that people who feel bad often try to remedy or repair their moods (Morris & Reilly, 1987). Because many people believe that venting is a healthy way to reduce anger and aggression (see Chapter 6), they might vent by lashing out at others to improve their mood. Studies by Bushman, Baumeister, and Phillips (2001) replicated the standard finding that anger increases aggression—but also found a revealing exception. When participants believed that their angry mood would not change for the next hour no matter what they did (ostensibly because of side effects of a pill they had taken), anger did not lead to aggression. The implication is that anger does not *directly* or *inevitably* cause aggression. Rather, angry people attack others because they believe that lashing out will help get rid of their anger and enable them to feel better.

As we saw in Chapter 6, many emotions are characterized by a bodily state called arousal, which is a feeling of excitement or tenseness. Moreover, we saw that arousal caused by one event can sometimes be transferred to something else, thereby increasing one's reaction to it. Aggression can be increased by this "excitation transfer." That is, arousal deriving from nonaggressive sources (such as physical exercise or an erotic nonviolent movie) can be mistaken for anger and can therefore increase aggression.

In a revealing study by Zillmann, Katcher, and Milavsky (1972), half the participants exercised by riding a stationary bike. The other half did not exercise. Then participants were provoked (insulted) or not provoked by a confederate. Participants were then given an opportunity to punish the confederate by shocking him. The results showed that unprovoked participants were not very aggressive, regardless of whether they had ridden the bike or not. Provoked participants, however, were more aggressive if they had ridden the bike than if they had not (see ▶ **FIGURE 10.2**). Thus, the maximal aggression came from the combination of a provocation and some leftover bodily arousal.

The fact that aversive emotional states lead to aggression has been asserted for decades and is supported by many research findings. However, it is important to point out that being in a bad mood is neither a necessary nor a sufficient condition for aggression. There is negative affect without aggression, and vice versa.

HOSTILE COGNITIVE BIASES

As we noted in Chapter 5, the attributions we make for another person's behavior can have a strong influence on our own behavior. Perceptions are more important than reality in predicting responses to social situations. People are much more likely to behave aggressively when they perceive ambiguous behaviors from others as stemming from hostile intentions than when they perceive the same behaviors as coming from other intentions. When an ambiguous event occurs, do we give others the benefit of the doubt, or do we assume they are out to get us? This is a question of attributions. Some people assume that others are out to attack them, even if they are not; that is, they attribute hostile intent to other people.

The **hostile attribution bias** is the tendency to perceive ambiguous actions by others as hostile. For example, if a person bumps into you, a hostile attribution would be that the person did it on purpose to hurt you. A meta-analysis of 41 studies involving more than 6,000 participants showed a strong relationship between hostile attribution of intent and aggressive behavior (Orobio de Castro, Veerman, Koops, Bosch, & Monshouwer, 2002). This relationship holds for both children and adults (e.g., Epps & Kendall, 1995). If you think they meant to hurt you, then you want to hurt them.

Two other related biases have been proposed: the hostile perception bias and the hostile expectation bias. The **hostile perception bias** is the tendency to perceive social interactions in general as being aggressive. Whereas the hostile attribution bias pertains specifically to whether someone is attacking you, the hostile perception bias might involve seeing two other people having a conversation and inferring that they are arguing or getting ready to fight. Research has shown that this bias is more prevalent in aggressive individuals than in nonaggressive individuals (Dill, Anderson, Anderson, & Deuser, 1997). Aggressive people see the world as an aggressive place.

The **hostile expectation bias** is the tendency to expect others to react to potential conflicts with aggression. Individuals who are characteristically aggressive are more likely than nonaggressive individuals to expect others to behave in an aggressive manner (Dill et al., 1997). For example, if you bump into another person, a hostile expectation would be that the person will assume that you did it on purpose and will attack you in return. In summary, aggressive people have inner biases that make them (a) expect others to react aggressively, (b) view ambiguous acts

Some people have a hostile attribution bias—they interpret the ambiguous actions of others as hostile actions.

as aggressive, and (c) assume that when someone does something to hurt or offend them, it was deliberately and intentionally designed to have that hurtful effect.

Such biases are an impediment to peace and harmony in our social world. If more people could give each other the benefit of the doubt more often, the world would be a less violent place. We live in a world in which some people think everyone is on the verge of fighting or battling against everyone else.

AGE AND AGGRESSION

Children do not commit many violent crimes, especially as compared to young men; this may mean that the biological impulses to behave aggressively only emerge around puberty. This is true in many species, where young adult males compete with each other, sometimes aggressively, to gain status and thereby attract females for mating. Then again, perhaps it is just that children can't do much damage, being smaller, weaker, and more subject to external control. Most 3-year-olds aren't out roaming the streets after

HOSTILE ATTRIBUTION BIAS the tendency to perceive ambiguous actions by others as aggressive

HOSTILE PERCEPTION BIAS the tendency to perceive social interactions in general as being aggressive

HOSTILE EXPECTATION BIAS the tendency to assume that people will react to potential conflicts with aggression

Aggressiveness peaks at age 2. Fortunately, it is curtailed by nap times, curfews, limited strength, and general incompetence.

© Mary Kate Denny/PhotoEdit

dark, so it may be hard for them to commit violent crimes even if they were so inclined. (It's past their bedtime!) Yet Richard Tremblay (2000) has provided evidence that the world's most aggressive human beings are very young children. His research team observed toddlers in day-care settings and recorded that about 25% of interactions involve some kind of physical aggression (e.g., a child pushes another child out of the way and takes her toy). No adult group, not even violent youth gangs or hardened criminals, resorts to aggression 25% of the time. (Remember our definitions, though: most toddler aggression isn't severe enough to qualify as violence.)

The high level of aggression among toddlers again fits the theme that nature says go and culture says stop. Human children naturally rely on physical aggression to resolve their disputes, including influencing other toddlers to get what they want. Toddlers may resort to aggression 25% of the time, but as they grow up, they learn to inhibit aggression. Talk to them, sue them, or whatever, but don't hit them!

Although most people become less aggressive over time, a subset of people become *more* aggressive over time. The most dangerous years for this subset of individuals (and for society) are late adolescence and early adulthood. This is because aggressive acts become more extreme (e.g., weapons are used more frequently). Official records show that violent criminal offending is highest for both males and females between ages 15 and 30 and declines significantly after that (although the rates are much higher for males than for females). For example, the average age of murderers is about 27 years old (U.S. Federal Bureau of Investigation, 2008).

GENDER AND AGGRESSION

Psychological studies show that when male rats are under stress, they respond by either fighting or running away, called the **fight or flight syndrome** (Taylor, Klein, Lewis, Gruenewald, Gurung, & Updegraff, 2000). In contrast, female rats respond to stress by nurturing others and making friends, called the **tend and befriend syndrome** (Taylor et al., 2000). The effect also occurs in humans.

Gender differences in aggression are very noticeable by the preschool years, with boys showing higher levels of physical aggression than girls (Loeber & Hay, 1997). In later elementary grades and in adolescence, gender differences increase. Indirect aggression becomes much greater for girls than boys; physical aggression becomes much greater for boys than girls; and verbal aggression is about the same for girls and boys (Crick & Grotpeter, 1995; Lagerspetz et al., 1988; Vaillancourt, 2005). These gender differences culminate in dramatic differences in physically violent behavior in young adulthood, reflected in huge gender differences in murder rates. There is no known society in which women commit most of the violent crimes (Steffensmeier & Allan, 1996); gender differences in violence are universal.

Nevertheless, this should not lead one to believe that females are never physically aggressive. Females do display physical aggression in social interactions, particularly when they are provoked by other females (Collins, Quigley, & Leonard, 2007). When it comes to heterosexual domestic relationships, women are slightly *more* likely than men to use physical aggression against their partners (e.g., Archer, 2000; Straus, 1997)! However men are more likely than women to inflict serious injuries and death on their partners. Laboratory studies with college students often yield higher aggression by men, but provocation apparently has a greater effect on aggression than does biological sex. Sex differences in aggression practically disappear under high provocation (Bettencourt & Miller, 1996). Again, though, men inflict more harm than women, perhaps because nature has endowed men with greater strength and capacity to cause injury.

FIGHT OR FLIGHT SYNDROME a response to stress that involves aggressing against others or running away

TEND AND BEFRIEND SYNDROME a response to stress that involves nurturing others and making friends

Interpersonal Causes of Aggression

SELFISHNESS AND INFLUENCE

Two social psychologists put forward a broad theory of aggression arguing that aggression should be understood as a form of social influence (Tedeschi & Felson, 1994). Instead of a learned response, or a reaction to frustration, or an eruption of innate drives, they suggested, aggression is mainly a way by which people try to alter the behavior of others so as to enable the aggressors to get what they want. This theory highlights the social rather than the antisocial nature of aggression, because it depicts aggression as a way in which people relate to others.

Creatures that don't take care of themselves tend not to survive and reproduce, so evolution has made most animals (including humans) selfish (Dawkins, 1976/1989). Humans can rise above their selfishness, but the selfish core is still there. Social life inevitably breeds some degree of conflict between selfish beings, such as when two people want the same food or the same mate, when both want to have the warmer or dryer place to sleep, or even when both want to watch different television programs! Aggression is one means that social animals use to resolve some of these disputes.

When do people resort to aggression to get what they want? Tedeschi and Felson (1994) cited several factors. The more they want the reward (think of saving the life of someone you love), the more willing people are to use violence to get it. People are more likely to resort to aggression when they believe it will bring success, such as if the other person seems unlikely to retaliate. (If the other person is bigger and stronger than you, then aggression does not seem a promising way to get what you want.) Some people regard physical violence as immoral and will not engage in it under almost any circumstances, whereas others are far less inhibited.

Blaming someone for unfair actions can lead to aggressive retaliation. The most commonly cited unfair things that people do include disloyalty, disregarding the feelings of others, hostility, breaking promises and other agreements, selfishness, rudeness, lateness, and vicious gossip (Messick, Bloom, Boldizar, & Samuelson, 1985; Mikula, Petri, & Tanzer, 1989). People use many means to strike back or punish someone who has wronged them, ranging from directly hitting the person, to spreading nasty rumors, to committing property crimes such as burglary or vandalism. In fact, one study of arson (setting fires) in Houston concluded that three out of every five arsons were done as a way of getting revenge for some perceived unjust mistreatment (Pettiway, 1987). People set fires to punish a bar or restaurant that had thrown them out, to get back at an ex-lover, or in retaliation for similar grievances.

In short, aggression is a strategy that many social animals (including humans) use to help them get what they want. To learn about one particular case—namely, sexual aggression—see *The Social Side of Sex*. Human culture may invoke laws and moral principles to try to get people to resolve their disputes using peaceful means, and most people probably agree that nonviolent means are better, but every day, all over the world, many people find themselves resorting to violence to get something or just to get even.

DOMESTIC AND RELATIONSHIP VIOLENCE: HURTING THOSE WE LOVE

Domestic violence (also called **family violence** or **intimate-partner violence**) is violence that occurs within the home, between people who have a close relationship with each other. Examples of domestic violence include a husband beating his wife, a mother hurting her child, a parent sexually molesting a child, brothers and sisters hitting each other, a child witnessing parents fighting, and an adult striking an elderly parent. If anything, aggression is highest between siblings, as compared to all other relationships (Wiehe, 1991). In 1984, the U.S. Surgeon General declared domestic violence to be the

---

DOMESTIC VIOLENCE (FAMILY VIOLENCE, INTIMATE-PARTNER VIOLENCE) violence that occurs within the home or family, between people who have a close relationship with each other

the SOCIAL SIDE of SEX

Sexual Aggression

We have seen that many people use aggression to get what they want from others, and one thing that people sometimes want—and use force to get—is sex. Most cultures recognize the problem that some men force women to have sex against their will. The opposite problem, of women forcing men to have sex, has generally been ignored, though surveys suggest it also occurs (e.g., Anderson & Struckman-Johnson, 1998). Still, when women force men to have sex, the traumatic consequences appear to be much less than what female rape victims suffer (Anderson & Struckman-Johnson, 1998). Sometimes, too, men force other men to have sex, and women force other women. Male coercion of females is generally considered to be the most serious social problem, however.

Defining rape or sexual coercion is a difficult issue that has compounded the problem of understanding, because sexual coercion consists of multiple phenomena that almost certainly have different causes. Some researchers have favored broad, loose definitions of sexual coercion, using one big category that includes everything from being attacked, beaten, and forced into intercourse by a stranger to the case of a young man who kisses a woman against her will. Efforts to understand the causes of sexual coercion depend heavily on such definitions. Because there are far more cases resembling the stolen kiss than the forcible stranger rape, the stolen kiss data can crowd out the violent stranger rapes. The National Health and Social Life Survey (NHSLS; Laumann, Gagnon, Michael, & Michaels, 1994) concluded that between 15% and 22% of women had been forced into some sexual activity against their will, but only 1% were forced by strangers. The majority of victims, in fact, said the person who forced them was someone they were in love with at the time.

Even if a woman is in love with the man who forced her, or has consented to kissing or petting with him, or even if she has previously (or subsequently) consented to sex with that man, that does not make any kind of forced sexual activity any less of a crime. A woman (or a man, for that matter) always has the right to refuse sexual advances at any time, and it is both highly immoral and illegal to continue to demand sex when one's partner has indicated an unwillingness to go any further. It is upsetting and even traumatic to be subjected to unwanted sexual advances, whether one knows the attacker or not. However, researchers who use broad definitions of sexual coercion and then combine all acts when evaluating the harm done to victims may seriously underestimate the negative effects of some of the most atrocious acts of sexual violence.

How the victims fare depends on which definition of rape is used. Victims of violent rape, especially by strangers, often suffer lasting problems, including fear and anxiety, depression, and sexual problems (e.g., Meyer & Taylor, 1986; Rynd, 1988). Many blame themselves. Some withdraw from other people and become socially isolated. In contrast, when looser definitions of sexual coercion were used in other studies, the results suggested much less lasting trauma. Often the man apologized and the woman simply forgave him and went on to consider him a friend (Murnen, Perot, & Byrne, 1989). O'Sullivan, Byers, and Finkelman (1998) found that three out of five rape victims said they had had consensual sex with the rapist on a previous occasion, and two out of five had some consensual activity (such as making out or oral sex) on the same day as the rape. Koss (1988) found that two out of five rape victims would consent to having sex with the rapist on a later occasion. Almost certainly these data are not based on violent stranger rapes—they refer instead to acquaintance and date rape patterns, which are different in some ways (though still immoral).

The old stereotype of the rapist was either a woman-hater or a man who lacked social skills and could not get sex via romance and persuasion and therefore resorted to violence.

PhotoDisc

Research, including studies on date rapists, has painted a very different picture (for reviews, see Baumeister, Catanese, & Wallace, 2002; Felson, 2002). Sexually coercive men generally have other sex partners and indeed may have more sex than noncoercive men. A sexually coercive man generally does not hate women, but he may devalue them, may have little empathy for their concerns or suffering, and is likely to feel that women have hurt or betrayed him in the past. His peer group places high emphasis on sexual conquests, and he wants to have some to boast about. He is therefore motivated to downplay his use of force or coercion and claim instead that he had consensual sex (because it bolsters his ego and reputation). In fact, he probably prefers not to use force, but he is willing to use any means he can, including trickery, false promises, untrue declarations of love, and force, to get sex. He has high sexual motivation and enjoys impersonal, uncommitted sex. If his crime was date rape, it was often preceded by some consensual activity such as oral sex; when the woman wanted to stop, he forced her to continue. He thinks very highly of himself and may well have narcissistic personality patterns, including the sense that he deserves special rewards such as sexual favors (Bushman, Bonacci, Van Dijk, & Baumeister, 2003). He may think the woman owes him sex and that he is only using a bit of force to claim what he deserves. Therefore, he may not even admit to himself that what he is doing is immoral and illegal. ■

number one health risk in the United States. Domestic violence is the leading cause of injuries to women ages 15–44, more common than muggings, auto accidents, and cancer deaths combined. Women in noncommitted relationships are especially at risk. The risk of domestic violence for women who are separated, divorced, cohabiting with a partner, or never married is three times higher than the risk for married women (Zalar, Harris, Kyriacou, Anglin, & Minow, 2000).

Women aren't the only victims of domestic violence. Women actually attack their relationship partners slightly more often than men do, although women don't cause as much harm (Archer, 2000). The average husband is taller, stronger, and heavier than his wife, so if they get into a physical fight, she is much more likely to be injured or killed than he is. Male victimization is also underreported. Domestic violence also occurs in homosexual relationships (Miller, Greene, Causby, White, & Lockhart, 2001; Pitt, 2000), and again, women are as violent as men, if not more so.

Physically weaker family members, such as children or elderly parents, are especially at risk of becoming domestic violence victims because they cannot fight back. Research shows that abusive spouses also tend to be abusive parents (Ross, 1996). Parents who were abused as children are significantly more likely than others to abuse their own children (Caesar, 1988; Cappell & Heiner, 1990). (One should not overstate this relationship, as is commonly done. By far, most victims of abuse do not become abusers themselves.)

Domestic violence is not a recent phenomenon; it has a long history. Gradually, culture is intervening to prohibit and punish it. This indicates the slow process of culture entering more and more previously private spheres to exert control over aggression. The American Puritan tradition regarded the nuclear family as sacrosanct and held that no one should intervene in how parents raise their children, but modern American culture is increasingly rejecting that view to insist that parents refrain from aggressive and violent treatment. According to a 2008 report from Save the Children organization, the corporal punishment of children (including spanking) is illegal in 24 countries. Nature may say to hit, but more and more cultures are saying to stop.

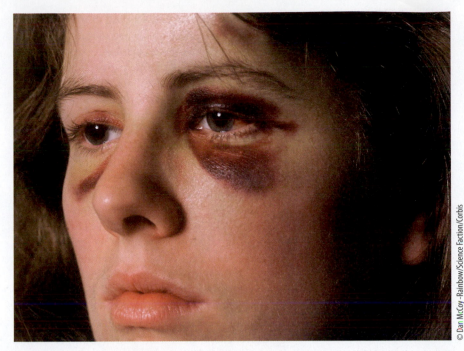
Sometimes people hurt the ones they love the most.

3. Which of the following statements is false?
   (a) Women attack their relationship partners more often than men do.
   (b) In an attack, men cause more damage than women do.
   (c) The average husband is taller, stronger, and heavier than his wife.
   (d) All of the above are true.

4. What is the leading cause of injuries to women ages 15–44 years old?
   (a) Auto accidents   (b) Home accidents
   (c) Domestic violence   (d) Muggings

External Causes of Aggression

WEAPONS EFFECT

> Guns not only permit violence, they can stimulate it as well. The finger pulls the trigger, but the trigger may also be pulling the finger.
>
> —Leonard Berkowitz, Emeritus Professor of Psychology, University of Wisconsin

Obviously, using a weapon can increase aggression and violence, but can just seeing a weapon increase aggression? In 1967, Leonard Berkowitz and Anthony LePage conducted a study to find out. Angry participants were seated at a table that had a shotgun and a revolver on it—or, in the control

[QUIZ YOURSELF]

Interpersonal Causes of Aggression

1. What theory of aggression posits that people use aggression to restore justice?
   (a) Frustration-aggression theory
   (b) Instinct theory
   (c) Social influence theory
   (d) Social learning theory

2. Which group of people is especially at risk for domestic violence?
   (a) Men in committed relationships
   (b) Men in noncommitted relationships
   (c) Women in committed relationships
   (d) Women in noncommitted relationships

condition, badminton racquets and shuttlecocks. The items on the table were described as part of another experiment that the researcher had supposedly forgotten to put away. The participant was supposed to decide what level of electric shock to deliver to a confederate, and the electric shocks were used to measure aggression. The experimenter told participants to ignore the items, but apparently they could not. Participants who saw the guns were more aggressive than were participants who saw the sports items. Several other studies have replicated this effect, which has been dubbed the **weapons effect**.

Some studies have tested the weapons effect outside of the lab. In a field study (Turner, Layton, & Simons, 1975), a confederate driving a pickup truck purposely remained stalled at a traffic light to see whether the motorists trapped behind him would honk their horns (the measure of aggression). The truck contained either a military rifle in a gun rack and a bumper sticker that said VENGEANCE (two aggressive cues), or a rifle and a bumper sticker that said FRIEND (one aggressive cue), or no rifle and no bumper sticker (no aggressive cues). The more aggressive cues the blocked motorists saw, the more likely they were to honk their horns (see ▶ **FIGURE 10.3**). What is amazing about this study is that you would have to be pretty stupid to honk your horn at a driver with a military rifle in his truck and a VENGEANCE sticker on his bumper! It is certainly much safer to honk at someone who is not driving around with weapons and violent bumper stickers. These findings again bring up the duplex mind. Horn honking was probably not a product of logical, conscious thought. Most likely, it was mediated by the automatic system. The aggressive cues activated aggressive tendencies via a nonconscious, automatic response, making people react more aggressively than they would have otherwise (Anderson, Benjamin, & Bartholow, 1998). A meta-analysis (Carlson, Marcus-Newhall, & Miller, 1990) of 56 published studies confirmed that the mere sight of weapons increases aggression in both angry and nonangry individuals.

A fast-food restaurant called "Buns and Guns" in war-torn Beirut serves Lebanese food with a bang. The restaurant is decorated with realistic-looking weapons, ammunition, and camouflage netting. The motto is "A sandwich can kill you." Chicken on a skewer is called "rocket-propelled grenade," and pita bread is called "terrorist bread." The owner, Yousef Ibrahim, said, "They accuse us of terrorism, so let's serve terrorist bread, why not? The important thing is that they laugh" ("Lebanese," 2008). If Ibrahim had taken social psychology and learned about the

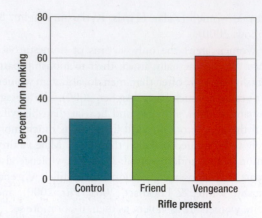

▶ **FIGURE 10.3** Motorists are more likely to honk at another driver in the presence of aggressive cues, such as a rifle and a VENGEANCE bumper sticker (Turner et al., 1975).

weapons effect, he would know that it is more likely that customers will fight and argue in his restaurant than laugh.

MASS MEDIA

As we saw in the opening story about the genocide in Rwanda, the mass media can reduce inhibitions that restrain aggression. Social scientists have extensively studied the effects on aggression of exposure to violent media.

After reviewing all the scientific evidence, the United States Surgeon General said, "It is clear to me that the causal relationship between televised violence and antisocial behavior is sufficient to warrant appropriate and immediate remedial action. . . . There comes a time when the data are sufficient to justify action. That time has come." This statement was issued decades ago—in 1972 (Steinfeld, 1972). Since then, the evidence has grown stronger. A meta-analytic review of 431 studies involving more than 68,000 participants showed that violent media exposure increases aggressive behavior, angry feelings, aggressive thoughts, and physiological arousal (e.g., heart rate), and decreases helping behavior (Bushman & Huesmann, 2006). Laboratory experiments have shown that exposure to violent media *causes* people to behave more aggressively immediately afterwards. Of course, violent media are not the only cause of aggression, nor even the most important cause, but they are definitely not a trivial cause. Longitudinal studies have shown that violent media effects persist over time. In a 15-year longitudinal study (Huesmann, Moise, Podolski, & Eron, 2003) involving 329 participants, heavy viewers of violent TV shows in first and third grade were three times more likely than others to be convicted of criminal behavior by the time they were in their 20s. They were also more

---

WEAPONS EFFECT the increase in aggression that occurs as a result of the mere presence of a weapon

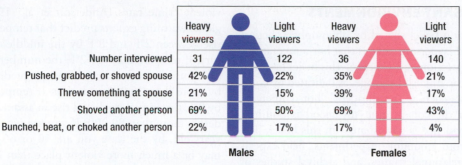

	Heavy viewers	Light viewers	Heavy viewers	Light viewers
Number interviewed	31	122	36	140
Pushed, grabbed, or shoved spouse	42%	22%	35%	21%
Threw something at spouse	21%	15%	39%	17%
Shoved another person	69%	50%	69%	43%
Bunched, beat, or choked another person	22%	17%	17%	4%
	Males		**Females**	

▶ **FIGURE 10.4** Women as well as men who were heavy childhood viewers of violent TV shows were much more likely to have abused their spouses and assaulted another adult at least once in the last year, according to self-reports, other-reports, and police records (Huesmann et al., 2003).

From Huesmann et al., "Longitudinal relations between childhood exposure to media violence and adult aggression and violence: 1977–1992, *Developmental Psychology, 39,* 201–221. Copyright © 2003 by the American Psychological Association. Reprinted by permission.

likely to abuse their spouses and assault other people (see ▶ **FIGURE 10.4**).

The Surgeon General's report focused on TV rather than video game violence. But there are at least three reasons to believe that violent video games might be even worse than television violence. First, video game play is active, whereas watching TV is passive. People learn better when they are actively involved. Suppose you wanted to learn how to fly an airplane. What would be the best method to use: read a book, watch a TV program, or use a video game flight simulator? Second, players of violent video games are more likely than others to identify with a violent character. If the game involves a first-person shooter, players have the same visual perspective as the killer. If the game is third person, the player controls the actions of the violent character from a more distant visual perspective. In either case, the player is linked to a violent character. In a violent TV program, viewers might or might not identify with a violent character.

Third, violent games directly reward violent behavior by awarding points or allowing players to advance to the next game level. In some games, players are rewarded through verbal praise, such as hearing the words "Nice shot!" after killing an enemy. It is well known that rewarding behavior increases its frequency. (Would people go to work if their employers did not pay them?) In TV programs, reward is not directly tied to the viewer's behavior. A recent study provided the first evidence that violent games produce stronger effects than television (Polman, Orobio de Castro, & van Aken, 2008). In this study, some participants played violent games while others watched the games being played. The effects on aggression were stronger for boys who played video games than for boys who watched others play the games.

One type of media deserves special mention: violent media that contain sex, such as rape depictions.

As we saw in the opening story, hate media may have contributed to the rape and sexual assault of women and girls during the 1994 genocide in Rwanda. Several social psychological experiments have examined the impact of violent sexual media on aggression against women. In one experiment (Donnerstein & Berkowitz, 1981), college men watched one of four film clips: (1) a nonviolent non-sexually-explicit clip, (2) a nonviolent sexually explicit clip of a couple enjoying making love, (3) a violent sexual clip of a man raping a woman who resisted the rape, or (4) a violent sexual clip of a man raping a woman who initially resisted the rape but then seemed to enjoy it. Afterwards, participants were insulted by either a male or a female confederate and were then given the chance to punish the confederate using electric shocks. The results showed that men who viewed a rape scene were more aggressive than men who did not view a rape scene, especially when the aggression target was the female provoker. Men who saw the clip showing the woman who enjoyed being raped had the highest levels of aggression. Nonviolent sex did not increase aggression. In fact, the men who viewed nonviolent sex were *less* aggressive toward the female provoker than toward the male provoker. Thus, media depictions of pure sex reduced aggression, but films showing some kinds of violent sex led to more aggression.

There are also long-term effects of viewing violent sexual media, such as desensitization to the pain and suffering experienced by women who have been the victims of sexual assault. Research has shown that even several days after watching violent sex scenes in "slasher" films, men still displayed an increased tolerance for aggression directed toward women (Malamuth & Check, 1981; Mullin & Linz, 1995). A few field studies have also shown a link between viewing violent pornography and sexual aggression (Kingston, Fedoroff, Firestone, Curry, & Bradford, 2008).

UNPLEASANT ENVIRONMENTS

One common belief shared by philosophers, fiction writers, and laypersons alike is that hot temperatures increase aggression and violence. This belief has even crept into the English language, as indicated by common phrases such as "hot-headed," "hot-tempered," "hot under the collar," and "my blood is boiling." Research evidence is consistent with this belief. The evidence from laboratory experiments, field experiments, correlational studies, and archival studies of violent crimes indicates that hotter temperatures are associated with higher levels of aggression and violence (Anderson, Anderson, Dorr, DeNeve, & Flanagan, 2000). Studies that compare the violence rates of regions that differ in climate have generally found that hotter regions have higher violent crime rates (Anderson & Anderson, 1996). Time period studies generally have found higher violence rates in hot years, hot seasons, hot months, and hot days (Anderson, Bushman, & Groom, 1997; Leffingwell, 1892). Anderson and colleagues (1997) analyzed temperature and crime rate data in the United States over a 45-year period. They found that murder and assault rates were higher during hotter years than during cooler years, and were higher during hotter summers than during cooler summers. Nonviolent crimes were not affected by temperature. Field and archival studies have found similar results. For example, in baseball games, the hotter the temperature, the more common it is for the pitcher to hit the batter with a pitched ball (see ▶ FIGURE 10.5) (Reifman, Larrick, & Fein, 1991).

When people think of the consequences of global warming (the observation that the weather all over the world is getting a little hotter year by year), they focus mainly on the impact on agricultural crops and flooding. However, there may also be an impact on

violent crime rates (Anderson et al., 1997). Most global warming experts predict that temperatures will rise between 2°F and 8°F by the middle of this century. If temperatures rise 2°F, the number of assaults and murders in the United States is predicted to rise by more than 25,000 each year. If temperatures rise by 8°F, the annual predicted rise in assaults and murders is more than 80,000. If you are now around 20 years old, by the time you are 50 or 60, the world may be a much more violent place than it is now, if temperatures continue to rise.

Other unpleasant environmental events can also increase aggression. Numerous studies have shown that loud noises can increase aggression (Geen & McCown, 1984; Geen & Powers, 1971; Moore & Underwood, 1979), including traffic noise (Gaur, 1988). Noise can also increase aggression in nonhuman species, such as mice and rats (Renzi, 1990; Sheard, Astrachan, & Davis, 1975). Foul odors (Rotton, 1979), secondhand smoke (Jones & Bogat, 1978), and air pollution (Rotton & Frey, 1985) also can increase aggression. Crowding can increase aggression in unpleasant environments, such as in psychiatric wards (e.g., Nijman & Rector, 1999; Palmstierna, Huitfeldt, & Wistedt, 1991) and prisons (e.g., Lawrence & Andrews, 2004). All these unpleasant environmental factors increase aggression because they make people feel bad and grumpy (Berkowitz, 1993).

CHEMICAL INFLUENCES

Numerous chemicals have been shown to influence aggression. In this section we discuss the role of chemicals in violence and aggression.

Testosterone. Aggression increases testosterone as much as testosterone increases aggression. **Testosterone** is the male sex hormone. It is a simple chemical arrangement of carbon rings, a derivative of the cholesterol molecule (Mitchell, 1998). Both males and females have testosterone, but males have much more of it. Levels peak during puberty and begin to decline around age 23.

Testosterone has been linked to aggression. Robert Sapolsky (1998), author of *The Trouble with Testosterone*, wrote: "Remove the source of testosterone in species after species and levels of aggression typically plummet. Reinstate normal testosterone levels afterward with injections of synthetic testosterone, and aggression returns." For example, rats that received testosterone injections for 12 weeks responded with more aggression when their tails were pinched than did rats that received placebo injections (McGinnis, Lumia, Breuer, & Possidente, 2002). A meta-analysis of 54 studies found that testosterone also increases aggression in humans (Book, Starzyk, & Quinsey, 2001). Violent male prisoners have higher levels of

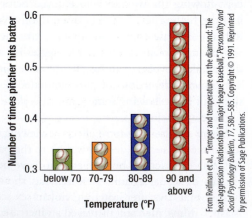

From Reifman et al., "Temper and temperature on the diamond: The heat-aggression relationship in major league baseball," *Personality and Social Psychology Bulletin, 17*, 580–585. Copyright © 1991. Reprinted by permission of Sage Publications.

▶ **FIGURE 10.5** The hotter the temperature, the more common it is for the pitcher to hit the batter with a pitched ball (Reifman et al., 1991).

TESTOSTERONE the male sex hormone, high levels of which have been linked to aggression and violence in both animals and humans

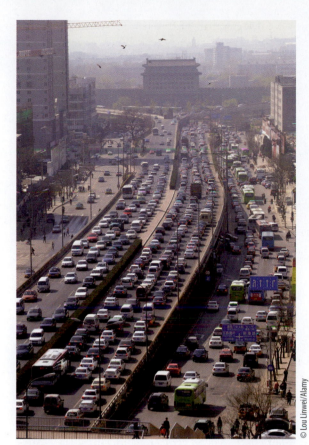
Traffic noise and pollution can increase aggression.

testosterone than other males do (e.g., Dabbs, Carr, Frady, & Riad, 1995). (For more information, see *Tradeoffs* about testosterone in Chapter 11.) However, in correlational studies it is also possible that aggression increases testosterone, or that some third factor increases both aggression and testosterone. For example, aggressive cues such as guns can increase both testosterone and aggression levels (Klinesmith, Kasser, & McAndrew, 2006).

Serotonin. In our brains, information is communicated between neurons (nerve cells) by the movement of chemicals across a small gap called the synapse. The chemical messengers are called neurotransmitters. **Serotonin** is one of these neurotransmitters. Its chemical name is 5-hydroxytryptamine, or 5-HT. It has been called the "feel good" neurotransmitter.

Low levels of serotonin have been linked to aggression and violence in both animals and humans (e.g., Ailman, 1994; Grossman, 1995; Nelson & Chiavegatto, 2001; Berman, Tracy, & Coccaro, 1997). In experiments involving animals and humans, decreasing serotonin levels increases aggression levels, which shows a causal link between serotonin and aggression (Kantak, Hegstrand, & Eichelman, 1981; Berman, McCloskey, Fanning, Schumacher, & Coccaro, 2009). Low serotonin appears to produce an inability to inhibit impulsive responses to unpleasant events

such as provocation (Soubrie, 1986). For example, criminals convicted of impulsive violent crimes have lower serotonin levels than criminals convicted of premeditated crimes (Linnoila, Virkkunnen, Scheinin, Nuttila, Rimon, & Goodwin, 1983).

Alcohol. Alcohol has long been associated with violent and aggressive behavior. There is ample evidence of a correlation between alcohol and aggression. More than 50% of people who commit violent crimes were intoxicated when the crimes occurred (e.g., Greenberg, 1981; Innes, 1988; Pernanen, 1991). A meta-analytic review (Lipsey, Wilson, Cohen, & Derzon, 1997) of 130 studies found that alcohol was positively correlated with both criminal and domestic violence. But as we learned in Chapter 1, correlation does not necessarily imply causation. It is difficult to draw causal conclusions about the relation between alcohol and aggression from correlational studies (Brain, 1986). For example, the aggressor may misreport alcohol ingestion as an excuse or to avoid punishment.

The experimental method avoids these and many other pitfalls because the researcher controls the occurrence of events and randomly assigns participants to groups. Meta-analytic reviews of experimental studies come to the same conclusion: alcohol increases aggression (e.g., Bushman & Cooper, 1990; Ito, Miller, & Pollock, 1996; Lipsey et al., 1997). In fact, sometimes alcohol is deliberately used to promote aggression. The military historian John Keegan (1993) noted that it has been standard practice for many centuries to issue soldiers some alcohol before they went into battle, both to reduce fear and to increase aggression.

Does all of this mean that aggression is somehow contained in alcohol? No. Alcohol increases rather than causes violent or aggressive tendencies. Factors that normally increase aggression, such as provocation, frustration, aggressive cues, and violent media, have a stronger effect on intoxicated people than on sober people (Bushman, 1997). Put another way, alcohol mainly seems to increase aggression in combination with other factors. If someone insults or attacks you, your response will be more violent if you are drunk than sober. When there is no provocation, however, the effect of alcohol on aggression may be negligible. Plenty of people enjoy an occasional drink without turning violent.

There are several possible explanations for why alcohol increases aggressive tendencies. One explanation is that alcohol reduces inhibitions (Graham, 1980). Normally people have strong inhibitions against behaving aggressively, and alcohol reduces these inhibitions—it paralyzes the brakes. One interesting theory provides a plausible explanation of

---

SEROTONIN the "feel good" neurotransmitter, low levels of which have been linked to aggression and violence in both animals and humans

how alcohol might paralyze the brakes (Gailliot & Baumeister, 2007). The brain's activities rely almost exclusively on glucose for energy. Self-control takes a lot of energy, and acts of self-control deplete relatively large amounts of glucose. Alcohol reduces glucose throughout the brain and body and also impairs many forms of self-control, including the self-control needed to restrain aggressive impulses. Another explanation is that alcohol has a "myopic" or narrowing effect on attention (Steele & Josephs, 1990). This causes people to focus attention only on the most salient features of a situation (e.g., provocation) and not pay attention to more subtle features. Several experiments have found support for the myopia theory (e.g., Denson, Aviles, Pollock, Earleywine, Vasquez, & Miller, 2008; Giancola & Corman, 2007).

A third explanation is that alcohol increases aggression by decreasing self-awareness (Hull, 1981). As was noted in Chapter 3, people become more aware of their internal standards when attention is focused on the self. Most people have internal standards against behaving aggressively, but alcohol reduces people's ability to focus on these internal standards. A fourth explanation is that alcohol disrupts executive functions (Giancola, 2000), the cognitive abilities that help us plan, organize, reason, and achieve goals. A fifth explanation is that alcohol increases aggression because people expect it to do so. In many cultures, drinking occasions are culturally agreed-on "time-out" periods when people are not held responsible for their actions. Those who behave aggressively while intoxicated can therefore blame the bottle for their actions.

In one recent study (Bègue, Subra, Arvers, Muller, Bricout, & Zorman, 2009), males in France from the general population were told that they were participating in a taste test study conducted by a bogus private corporation. Participants were given a low alcohol dose (target BAC of 0.05%) or a high alcohol dose (target BAC of 0.1%). Within each group, participants were told that they had received a low, moderate, or high alcohol dose. As part of the study, participants also had to taste mashed potatoes that a confederate seasoned with salt and hot sauce. The rude confederate yelled at the researcher, violently kicked the leg of the participant's chair, and said, "Just wait 'til you taste your mashed potatoes, it'll blow your head off!" The measure of aggression was the amount of salt and hot sauce the participant then put on the confederate's mashed potatoes. The results showed that what participants were told about the amount of alcohol they received had a bigger effect on their aggression than what they actually received. Participants who were told they had received a high dose of alcohol spiked the confederate's mashed potatoes with the most salt and hot sauce, followed

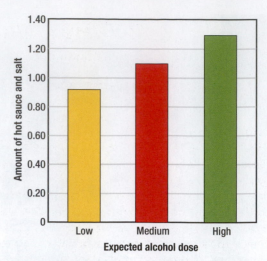

▶ **FIGURE 10.6 People who thought they had received a high dose of alcohol were the most aggressive. They "spiked" their partner's mashed potatoes with a large dose of salt and hot sauce (Bègue et al., 2009).**

by those who were told they had received a moderate alcohol dose, followed by those who were told they had received a low alcohol dose (see ▶ **FIGURE 10.6**). Thus, one reason that alcohol contributes to aggression is that people assume it will do so, regardless of the true alcohol content of what they drink.

If what you drink can affect aggression, what about what you eat? *Food for Thought* summarizes some intriguing findings about this link.

Is There a Link Between Diet and Violence?

Food for Thought

In his memoirs about his life as a violent youth gang member in Los Angeles, "Monster" Kody Scott (Shakur, 1993) reflected that whenever he started to spend a serious amount of time with his gang, he often began to feel grumpy and irritable after a few days. He thought this might have something to do with what he ate at those times. Most gang members do not go home for dinner to eat a balanced meal with plenty of vegetables, vitamins, protein, fiber, and other nutritious foods. Instead, they eat erratically, often late at night, and almost exclusively from fast-food outlets that serve fatty, sweet, and fried foods. Scott thought that subsisting on junk food for weeks at a time might contribute to the readiness of gang members to react violently when provoked.

Is this plausible? Is there a link between diet and violence rates? During the early 1980s, a criminologist named Stephen Schoenthaler instituted dietary changes in a dozen juvenile correctional institutions. He simply removed two types of foods from their diets: fried foods (e.g., hamburgers, sausages, French fries) and sugary foods (e.g., cookies, milkshakes, soft drinks). His data, which involved 8,076 juvenile delinquents, showed that removing these unhealthy foods led to a 47% reduction in antisocial behavior, including assaults, insubordination, suicide attempts, and rule violations. Schoenthaler notes, "the more violent the bad behavior [before dietary interventions began], the more the improvement" ("New Studies," 2004).

Vitamin supplements also reduce antisocial behavior in juvenile delinquents. In a typical study, Schoenthaler gave a vitamin supplement to 71 inmates of a state juvenile detention facility. He compared antisocial behavior when prisoners were getting the supplement versus when they were getting a placebo. The result was a startling improvement in behavior with the supplement. Total violence fell by two-thirds. Escape attempts and going AWOL (absent without official leave) plummeted from 79 incidents to 13. Property crimes dropped by half.

The vitamin supplement results obtained for juvenile delinquents have also been obtained for adult prisoners. Researchers in the United Kingdom gave 231 young adult prisoners either a placebo or a vitamin supplement (Gesch, Hammond, Hampson, Eves, & Crowder, 2002). Prisoners receiving vitamin supplements for a minimum of two weeks were involved in 35% fewer violent and antisocial infractions than those who received a placebo. The lead author

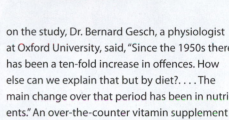

Mike Kemp/Getty Images

on the study, Dr. Bernard Gesch, a physiologist at Oxford University, said, "Since the 1950s there has been a ten-fold increase in offences. How else can we explain that but by diet?. . . . The main change over that period has been in nutrients." An over-the-counter vitamin supplement seems like an inexpensive way to reduce antisocial behavior.

So perhaps Scott was right: Junk food can help make someone into a violent "monster." Much more research is needed, but at present the link between diet and violence appears to be real and significant (for a review see Benton, 2007). Obviously, no one is suggesting that gang violence would disappear if only we could get a few young men to eat more fruits and vegetables. But it is very plausible that some diets make people more irritable than others, and that rates of violence can be affected by diet. ●

Self and Culture

In this section we discuss the role of culture and self-views in aggression and violence.

NORMS AND VALUES

Amok is one of the few Malay words used in the English language. The term, which dates back to 1665, means "a murderous or violently uncontrollable frenzy that occurs chiefly among Malays" (*Merriam-Webster Dictionary*). **Running amok**, roughly translated, means going berserk. Historically, the typical pattern was that a young Malay man who had suffered some loss of face or other setback would run amok, heedlessly performing violent acts (and sometimes not-so-coincidentally damaging the property of the people who had done him wrong). The Malays believed that these responses were normal and natural and that it was impossible for young men to restrain their wild, aggressive actions under those circumstances. However, when the British colonial administration disapproved of the practice and began to hold the young men responsible for their actions and to punish them for the harm they did, most Malays stopped running amok (Carr & Tann, 1976).

The history of "running amok" thus reveals some important points about aggression. First, it shows the influence of culture: The violence was accepted by one culture and prohibited by another. When the local culture changed, the practice died out. Second, it shows that cultures can promote violence without placing a positive value on it. There is no sign that the Malays approved of running amok or thought it was a good, socially desirable form of action, but positive value wasn't necessary. All that was needed was for the culture to believe that it was normal for people to lose control under some circumstances and

RUNNING AMOK according to Malaysian culture, refers to behavior of a young man who becomes "uncontrollably" violent after receiving a blow to his ego

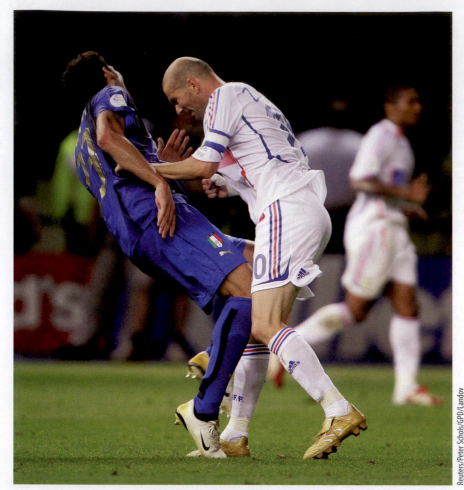

In the 2006 World Cup final, France's soccer captain Zinedine Zidane became angry, lost control, and head-butted Italy defender Marco Materazzi. Zidane has said he attacked Materazzi because he insulted his mother and sister. Zidane got a red card and was ejected from the game. Without their captain, France lost to Italy by 5–3 in a penalty shootout.

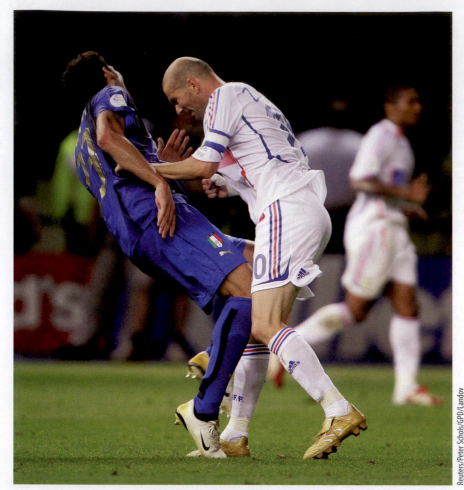
Reuters/Peter Schols/GPD/Landov

they don't positively encourage it. For example, if a man catches his wife having sex with another man, many cultures forgive him for violence, up to and including killing one or both of them. Still, this is not the same as regarding killing them as a good thing. Nowhere are men given medals or prizes for killing their unfaithful wives and their lovers. When nature supplies the impulse to behave violently, culture sometimes tells people to stop; when culture falls silent, tolerating or condoning violence, then aggression will rise. Cultures can become more violent without positively encouraging violence. All that is necessary is to stop saying no.

SELF-CONTROL

In 1990, two criminologists published a book called *A General Theory of Crime* (Gottfredson & Hirschi, 1990). Such a flamboyant title was bound to stir controversy. After all, there are many crimes and many causes, so the idea of putting forward a single theory was pretty bold. What would their theory feature? Poverty? Frustration? Genetics? Violent media? Bad parenting? As it turned out, their main theory boiled down to poor self-control. Research has shown that poor self-control is one of the "strongest known correlates of crime" (Pratt & Cullen, 2000, p. 952). And poor self-control is a better predictor of violent crimes than of nonviolent crimes (Henry, Caspi, Moffitt, & Silva, 1996). Self-control is covered in detail in Chapter 4; we discuss it only briefly here. The concept of self-control is related to other factors in aggression that we have already discussed. For example, intoxicated people have less control over their aggressive behavior than do sober people. Children 1–3 years old have difficulty controlling their behavior, and they are also quite aggressive. People with strong self-control are generally not violent.

The emphasis on poor self-control as a cause of crime is consistent with some themes of this book. We have seen that the conflict between selfish impulses and social conscience crops up over and over. Most crime is selfish, because it seeks to benefit the individual at others' expense. Society mostly tries to socialize people to restrain aggressive and criminal impulses; indeed, by definition, culture and society try to get people to obey the norms and rules of good, law-abiding behavior. (Even criminal parents do not usually teach or encourage their children to commit crimes, contrary to one stereotype.)

Gottfredson and Hirschi provided plenty of data to back up their theory. For one thing, criminals seem to be impulsive individuals who don't show much respect for rules in general. In the movies, criminals often specialize in one specific kind of crime, almost like any other job. But in reality, most criminals are arrested multiple times—for different crimes. If self-

act violently as a result. Third, it shows that when people believe their aggression is beyond control, they are often mistaken: The supposedly "uncontrollable" pattern of running amok died out when the British cracked down on it. The influence of culture was thus mediated through self-control.

Some cultures or subcultures place positive value on fighting and aggression, at least in the sense of giving more respect to men who fight well. But researchers have not been successful at showing that people value fighting and violence. Even in youth gangs, most people say they don't like or approve of the violence (e.g., Jankowski, 1991). Violence is nowhere regarded as a positive good or end in itself. More often, violence may receive grudging acceptance as a necessary evil.

The link between culture and violence brings us back to the theme that nature says go and culture says stop. Some cultures condone losing control and engaging in violence under some circumstances, but control is a general capacity for bringing one's behavior into line with rules and standards, most criminals lack it.

Another sign is that the lives of criminals show low self-control even in behaviors that are not against the law. They are more likely than law-abiding citizens to smoke cigarettes, to be involved in traffic accidents, to be involved in unplanned pregnancies, to fail to show up for work or school regularly, and the like.

Indeed, social psychology has found many causes of violence, including frustration, anger or insult, alcohol intoxication, violence in the media, and hot temperatures. Yet this raises the question of why there isn't more violence than there is. After all, who hasn't experienced frustration, anger, insult, alcohol, media violence, or hot weather in the past year? Despite these common experiences, most people do not hurt or kill anyone. These factors may give rise to violent impulses, but mostly people restrain themselves. Violence starts when self-control stops.

WOUNDED PRIDE

For years, most social psychologists accepted the view that most aggression derived from low self-esteem. From murderers to playground bullies, violent individuals were assumed to have low opinions of themselves. Research, however, has contradicted that view (e.g., Baumeister, Smart, & Boden, 1996). If anything, violent individuals typically think they are better than others and have grandiose or inflated opinions of their own worth. For example, Adolf Hitler and his Nazi accomplices probably did not have low self-esteem. They thought they were the "Master Race," superior to everyone else. Aggression often starts when someone comes along and questions or challenges those favorable self-views. Wounded pride seems to be the most apt descriptor of how self-views are linked to aggression.

This is not to say that high self-esteem causes aggression. Indeed, most people with high self-esteem are not aggressive. But violent individuals typically have the trait of narcissism, which includes thinking oneself superior or special, feeling entitled to preferential treatment, being willing to exploit others, having low empathy with "lesser" human beings, and entertaining grandiose fantasies or other ideas about oneself as a great person (see Morf & Rhodewalt, 2001). The term *narcissism* comes from the Greek myth about a handsome man who falls in love with his own reflection in the water.

The Narcissistic Personality Inventory is a self-report scale that measures narcissism (Raskin & Terry, 1988). Several studies have shown that people who score high on the Narcissistic Personality Inventory respond with high levels of aggression when they receive a blow to their ego (e.g., Bushman &

▶ **TABLE 10.1** Comparison of narcissistic responses to items on the Narcissistic Personality Inventory and statements made by Eric Harris and Dylan Klebold, the two Columbine High School students who murdered 13 and wounded 23 others before killing themselves (Twenge & Campbell, 2003).

Narcissistic Personality Inventory Item	Quotation from Columbine Killer
I insist upon getting the respect that is due to me.	"Isn't it fun to get the respect that we're going to deserve?"—Eric Harris
I wish someone would someday write my biography.	"Directors will be fighting over this story."—Dylan Klebold "Tarantino . . . Spielberg."—Eric Harris
I can make anyone believe anything I want them to.	"I could convince them that I'm going to climb Mount Everest, or I have a twin brother growing out of my back. I can make you believe anything."—Eric Harris

Baumeister, 1998). Violent prisoners also have much higher narcissism scores than nonviolent people (Bushman & Baumeister, 2002). It may be revealing that some items in this scale are remarkably similar to statements made by Eric Harris and Dylan Klebold, the two Columbine High School students who murdered 13 and wounded 23 others before killing themselves (see ▶ **TABLE 10.1**; Twenge & Campbell, 2003).

The wounded pride idea was perhaps first shown in social psychology by Brown (1968). His participants (all male) played a trucking game in which both players earned money but one could exploit the other. The confederate first exploited the participant, and later the participant had a chance to get revenge but at significant cost to himself. In between, participants got feedback from an audience. When the participant received positive feedback, he was not inclined to seek revenge for having been exploited. When the audience told him he looked like a sucker, however, he would typically seek revenge regardless of what it cost him.

The wounded pride factor has found its way into so much aggression research that it is often scarcely noticed. Most laboratory studies on aggression include some kind of provocation in the form of an insult delivered to the participant by the person toward whom the participant will later be able to aggress. Without such an insult, most studies find hardly any aggression. Essentially, most studies of aggression simply show that other factors can increase or decrease the effect of wounded pride. Without an insult, alcohol and violent movies typically do not produce a significant increase in aggression. Even the contribution of narcissism depends on the insult. When narcissists receive praise, they are no more aggressive than anybody else (Bushman & Baumeister, 1998).

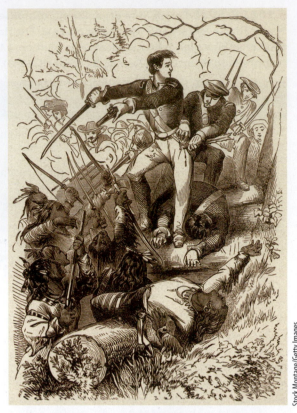

Sam Houston at San Jacinto; painting in the Texas State Capitol by Harry Arthur McArdle (1836–1908).

Both nature and culture may contribute to the importance of wounded pride in causing violence. In nature, many (mainly male) animals compete for status, and some fighting is required to reach and keep a high rank. Fighting is often a response to a challenge to one's favorable position. In humans, this translates into thinking you have to defend your good name or good opinion of yourself by lashing out at anyone who tries to attack it. As for culture, the concept of "honor" has often required violent action to maintain it, as the next section explains.

CULTURE OF HONOR

Sam Houston had to have his mother's permission to join the army in the 1812 war because he was not yet 21 years old. His mother, Elizabeth Houston, agreed to let him join, but before he left, she gave him two gifts (Day & Ullom, 1947). One was a gold ring, with the word *honor* inscribed inside; Houston wore this ring until his death. The other gift was a musket, which his mother gave him with the following admonition:

My son, take this musket and never disgrace it; for remember, I had rather all my sons

should fill one honorable grave, than that one of them should turn his back to save his life. Go, and remember, too, that while the door of my cottage is open to brave men, it is eternally shut against cowards.

Houston was born in Virginia in 1793 and moved to Tennessee after his father died in 1807. In 1832 he moved to Texas, and he went on to become one of the heroes of that state. In fact, he was in command of the Texas soldiers who won their independence by defeating the Mexican army, shouting "Remember the Alamo!" Texas later became the southern tip of the United States, and one of its largest cities was named for Sam Houston.

The southern United States has long been associated with higher levels of violent attitudes and behaviors than the northern United States. In comparison to northern states, southern states have more homicides per capita, have fewer restrictions on gun ownership, allow people to shoot assailants and burglars without retreating first, are more accepting of corporal punishment of children at home and in schools, and are more supportive of any wars involving U.S. troops (Cohen & Nisbett, 1997). Even the names of places and businesses are more violent in the South and West than in the North (Kelly, 1999). An analysis of place names (e.g., lakes, summits, parks, cities, towns) in the United States found that 80% of the places with violent names were located in the South and West. Some examples are Gun Point, Florida; War, West Virginia; and Rifle, Colorado. Similarly, 68% of the businesses in the United States with violent names (e.g., "War Taxi" and "Rifle Realty," and even "Shotgun Willy's Daycare Center" and "Shotgun Willies Strip Club"!) were located in the South and West.

Social psychologists Dov Cohen and Richard Nisbett (1997) hypothesized that these regional differences are caused by a southern **culture of honor**, which calls for a violent response to threats to one's honor. This culture apparently dates back to the Europeans who first came to the United States. The northern United States was settled by English and Dutch farmers, whereas the South was settled by Scottish and Irish herders. Sam Houston was of Scottish-Irish descent. A thief could become rich quickly by stealing another person's herd. The same was not true of agricultural crops in the North; it is difficult to quickly steal 50 acres of corn. Herdsmen had to be ready to protect their herds with a violent response. A man who did not respond in this way would be branded as an easy mark. A similar culture of violence exists in the western United States, the so-called Wild West, where one could also lose one's wealth quickly by not protecting one's herd. (Cowboys herded cows, hence the name.) This

CULTURE OF HONOR a society that places high value on individual respect, strength, and virtue, and accepts and justifies violent action in response to threats to one's honor

violent culture isn't confined to the southern and western United States. Cultural anthropologists have observed that herding cultures throughout the world tend to be more violent than farming ones (Campbell, 1965; Edgerton, 1971; Peristiany, 1965).

To test the culture of honor idea experimentally, Cohen, Nisbett, Bowdle, and Schwarz (1996) asked male college students to deliver some materials to the office at the end of a narrow hallway and then return to the lab. Between the participant and the office was a confederate working at a file cabinet by a door labeled "Photo Lab." To allow the participant to pass, the confederate had to push the file drawer in. Seconds later, the participant walked back down the hall and found the confederate working at the file cabinet again. The confederate slammed the file drawer shut, bumped into the participant with his shoulder, and called the participant a derogatory name referring to an unflattering part of the body. The confederate then walked back into the "Photo Lab." Two observers who were stationed in the hall, ostensibly doing homework, rated the participant's emotional reactions. Participants in the control group completed the same procedures without being bumped. The results showed that participants from the North were more amused and less angry by being bumped than were participants from the South. Some southern men actually seemed ready to have a fistfight (which was why the experimental script called for the confederate to disappear behind the locked door to the Photo Lab!).

The southern and western United States are not the only places where cultures of honor exist. Another example is ethnic Albania. The following quotation is from the Kanun, which describes the laws that govern customs and practices in Albania:

> An offence to honor is never forgiven. The person dishonored has every right to avenge his honor; no pledge is given, no appeal is made to the Elders, no judgment is needed, no fine is taken. The strong man collects the fine himself. A man who has been dishonored is considered dead according to the Kanun.

Humiliation appears to be the primary cause of violence and aggression in cultures of honor (William, 1993). **Humiliation** is a state of disgrace or loss of self-respect (or of respect from others). It is related to the concept of shame that was discussed in Chapter 6. Recall that feelings of shame frequently lead to violent and aggressive behavior. In cultures of honor, there is nothing worse than being humiliated, and the appropriate response to humiliation is swift and intense retaliation.

Humiliation may also be an important cause of terrorism (Atran, 2003). To many people in the Middle East, having the United States and its allies occupy their countries is humiliating. This occupation may encourage suicide bombings and other acts of terrorism. Interviews with terrorists led Stern (2004) to conclude that the primary motivation for terrorism is "overwhelming feelings of humiliation." For example, the founder of the Muslim Jambaz Force said, "Muslims have been overpowered by the West. Our ego hurts. We are not able to live up to our own standards for ourselves." Osama bin Laden's deputy, Ayman Zawahiri, told Islam youth to carry arms and defend their religion with pride and dignity rather than submit to the humiliation of Western globalization. According to Stern, "Holy wars take off when there is a large supply of young men who feel humiliated and deprived; when leaders emerge who know how to capitalize on those feelings; and when a segment of society is willing to fund them."

In fact, the Holocaust, genocide, ethnic cleansing, terrorism, and suicide bombings may all have their roots in humiliation (e.g., Lindner, 2002). For example, World War II was triggered, at least in part, by the humiliation that the Versailles Treaty inflicted on Germany after World War I. Hitler attacked his neighbors to retaliate for past humiliations inflicted on Germany. Hitler may have perpetrated the Holocaust to avert future humiliation that he feared from "World Jewry" (Lindner, 2002). After World War II, the Marshall Plan was designed to bring dignity and respect rather than humiliation to Germany. Instead of starting World War III, Germany has become a cooperative and peaceful member of the European family.

HUMILIATION a state of disgrace or loss of self-respect (or of respect from others)

Humans aren't the only ones who lie. Koko the gorilla bit a researcher and then lied about it.

Other Antisocial Behavior

Aggression and violence aren't the only forms of antisocial behaviors (although they are the forms social psychologists have studied the most). In this section we examine four other common forms of antisocial behavior: lying, cheating, stealing, and littering.

LYING

> I was not lying. I said things that later on seemed to be untrue.
> —Richard Nixon, discussing Watergate

Lying is not telling the truth. Humans aren't the only ones who do it. Some other animals do it too. For example, Stanford researchers taught a gorilla named Koko more than 1,000 signs based on American Sign Language (Patterson & Linden, 1981). When Koko was five, she was playing a game of chase with one of the researchers and bit him. Using sign language, the researcher asked, "What did you do?" Koko answered, "Not teeth." The researcher said, "Koko, you lied." Koko then admitted, "Bad again Koko bad again." Koko had lied, she knew it, and she knew it was wrong. Although some animals do lie, humans do it more than other animals—at least once a day (DePaulo, Kashy, Kirkendol, Wyer, & Epstein, 1996). Most animals are incapable of lying, and those who do lie do not seem to grasp the self-

serving benefits of lying nearly as well as dishonest humans.

Sometimes the stakes for lying are low, such as being embarrassed if one is caught. At other times the stakes are very high, such as lying to a spouse about infidelity or lying to a country about the reasons for going to war. When it comes to getting a job, people often lie about their qualifications and skills to increase the chance that they will be hired (Weiss & Feldman, 2006).

The cliché "All's fair in love and war" suggests that it is okay to lie to gain advantages in these high-stakes situations. Social psychologists have done a lot more research on lying for love than on lying for war, and they have found that people are quick to tell lies if it will improve their love (or sex) lives. Both men and women are willing to lie to increase their chances of going out with an attractive partner (Rowatt, Cunningham, & Druen, 1999). Lying is less common for very high stakes issues in sexual relationships, such as whether the person has AIDS (Williams, 2001). Lying in romantic relationships tends to be reciprocal—if one partner lies, the other lies too (Cole, 2001). As expected, lying is associated with less commitment to the relationship.

Some people are good at lying and some people are bad. Actors are especially good at lying (Siegman & Reynolds, 1983).

DETECTING LIARS

Is it possible to reliably detect lying? "Liar, liar, pants on fire!" is a phrase that children like to use when they think another child is lying. It would be much easier to identify liars if their pants were on fire. Because pants don't spontaneously combust when people lie, more subtle cues must be used. Sometimes outside information is available, such as when facts or a witness directly contradict the lie. When outside information is unavailable, people often rely on verbal and nonverbal cues, what the legal profession calls *demeanor*. In one study, more than 500 participants were shown videotapes of college women who either lied or did not lie (Ekman & O'Sullivan, 1991). The women in the videotapes were told to describe the positive feelings they felt while watching a film. Half the women saw a nature film and were therefore telling the truth. The other women saw a very gruesome and upsetting film, and they were therefore lying when they claimed to feel good. The participants were law enforcement personnel, including members of the U.S. Secret Service, Central Intelligence Agency (CIA), Federal Bureau of Investigation (FBI), National Security Agency, Drug Enforcement Agency, and California police and judges, as well as psychiatrists, college students, and working adults. The results showed that only the

---

LYING not telling the truth

In the movie *Meet the Parents*, Robert De Niro (an ex–CIA agent) gives his daughter's boyfriend (played by Ben Stiller) a lie detector test, asking him all sorts of invasive personal questions.

© Universal/Courtesy Everett Collection

Lie to Me is a TV drama inspired by a real-life specialist who can read clues in the face, body, and voice to expose the truth in criminal investigations. Although a few people may be able to do this, they are not as reliable as one would like. The average person has great difficulty detecting lies.

CHEATING

A thing worth having is a thing worth cheating for.

—W. C. Fields (1880–1946)

Cheating is widely recognized as an antisocial, undesirable behavior, yet it is widespread. It occurs among some athletes, who take performance-enhancing drugs to increase their competitiveness (Honour, 2004). It occurs in many students, who cheat in school to get ahead (Athanasou & Olasehinde, 2002). Although most students acknowledge that cheating is wrong, more than 75% admit to having cheated in high school or college (Davis, Grover, Becker, & McGregor, 1992). It is much easier to cheat in the digital age, too. The Internet makes term paper access remarkably easy, allowing many students to plagiarize part or all of their written school assignments (e.g., Park, 2003). Some schools are cracking down on cheaters. At the University of California at Davis, for example, students receive No. 2 pencils with their exams that read, "Fill in your own bubble or be in trouble" (Altschuler, 2001). Other professors use plagiarism-checking websites to screen student papers.

Who Cheats? People who cheat tend to have lower academic ability than those who don't cheat (Pino & Smith, 2003). For example, one study found that cheating was negatively correlated with scores on arithmetic tests (Hill, 1934). Perhaps intelligent people don't need to rely on others to pass tests. They figure it out for themselves.

As with many undesirable social behaviors, self-control seems to be an important predictor of cheating. Students who have low self-control are more likely to cheat than those with high self-control (e.g., Bichler & Tibbetts, 2003; Jensen, Arnett, Feldman, & Cauffman, 2002). Cynical people are more likely to cheat than noncynical people (Treynor, in press). People are also more likely to cheat if they believe that human behavior is not subject to free will (Vohs & Schooler, 2008).

Reducing Cheating. As we learned in Chapter 3 on the self, increasing self-awareness can decrease antisocial behaviors. In one study, students who were sitting in front of a mirror were less likely to cheat on a test than were students who were not sitting in front of a mirror (Diener & Wallbom, 1976). Arousal can

secret service personnel detected lying at better than chance levels. In general, people are not very good at detecting liars (Bond & DePaulo, 2008).

People also pay attention to other cues, even if they are not diagnostic. If you engage in weird behaviors (e.g., raise a shoulder to your ear, extend an arm to the ceiling), people will think you are lying even if you are not (Bond, Omar, Pitre, Lashley, Skaggs, & Kirk, 1992).

Textual analysis programs can detect lying at slightly better than chance levels, correctly detecting liars at least 60% of the time (Newman, Pennebaker, Berry, & Richards, 2003). When liars tell stories, the stories are not complex, they contain fewer self- and other-references, and they contain more negative emotion words.

Sometimes a mechanical device known as a polygraph (popularly called a lie detector) is used to "detect" lies. A polygraph measures physiological responses such as blood pressure, pulse, respiration, and skin conductivity while the subject is asked and answers a series of questions, on the theory that false answers will produce distinctive measurements. The problem with lie detector tests is that they can make it look as though someone is lying, even if the person is telling the truth. In a 1998 Supreme Court case, *United States v. Scheffer*, the majority stated: "There is simply no consensus that polygraph evidence is reliable. . . . Unlike other expert witnesses who testify about factual matters outside the jurors' knowledge, such as the analysis of fingerprints, ballistics, or DNA found at a crime scene, a polygraph expert can supply the jury only with another opinion."

off the mark.com   by Mark Parisi

YOUR TERM PAPER ON "THE GROWING PROBLEM OF PLAGIARISM IN SOCIETY" IS EYE-OPENING...ESPECIALLY SINCE IT'S THE THIRD TIME I'VE SEEN IT...

© 2003 MARK PARISI DIST. BY UFS., INC.   offthemark.com

decrease cheating if people misattribute their arousal as guilt. Participants in one study were told that the researchers were studying the effects of a vitamin supplement on vision (Dienstbier & Munter, 1971). Half of the participants were told that one side effect of the pill was that it would increase arousal. The other half were told that the pill had no side effects. All participants were given a vocabulary test, supposedly predictive of college success. Participants were given an opportunity to cheat on the test by changing answers. Cheating was much more common among participants who expected the pill to increase arousal (49%) than among participants who did not expect the pill to have side effects (27%). Participants who considered cheating presumably experienced some arousal. Participants who expected side effects from the pill attributed the arousal to the pill, and many of them went ahead to cheat. In contrast, participants who expected no side effects attributed the arousal to fear or guilt, so they refrained from cheating. Again, guilt is an important emotion for promoting desirable, legitimate, noncheating behavior (see Chapter 6).

STEALING

According to the U.S. Department of Commerce, employee theft costs American business more than $50 billion a year (Mather, 2004). The U.S. Chamber of Commerce estimates that 75% of all employees steal at least once, and that 50% of those employees steal repeatedly. Consider the following letter that a woman wrote to her employer (Mather, 2004):

To whom it may concern, I must admit that I have been part of the problem with the missing inventory. Three other people and I (I do not want to name names) have been taking items from here for the past couple of years. At first we did it because it was easy and I figured no one would miss anything.

The several-page letter then went on to list tens of thousands of dollars of theft. The letter concluded:

I really want to say that I am sorry and that I will not do it again. This is completely out of character for me. I am a wife, mother and grandmother and do not need the money. Please give me another chance.

The employer was shocked to see who signed the letter. "I can't believe it was [name], she was the perfect employee. Never took a sick day, no vacations, here early. There were absolutely no warning signs of this" (Mather, 2004). Although crimes such as burglary and robbery tend to be reported to police, other crimes such as employee theft, customer theft, and credit card fraud tend not to be reported to the police (Taylor, 2003).

Social psychologists have studied stealing and other antisocial behaviors and the factors that contribute to them. One such factor is the presence of others. The presence of others increases arousal (see Chapter 14 on groups). When people are in large groups, they become anonymous and lose their sense of individuality, a state called **deindividuation**. People in a deindividuated state are especially likely to engage in antisocial behaviors, such as theft.

In a well-known study by Diener, Fraser, Beaman, and Kelem, (1976), children who were trick-or-treating on Halloween were greeted by an experimenter who said, "You may take one of the candies. I have to go back to my work in another room." Some children go trick-or-treating alone, and some go in groups. By the flip of a coin, half of the children were assigned to an identifiable group, and half were assigned to an anonymous group. The experimenter asked each child in the identifiable group what his or her name was and where he or she lived. The experimenter then carefully repeated each child's name and address to let the child know that he or she could be identified. The experimenter did not identify the children in the anonymous group. A hidden observer recorded whether each child took more than one piece of candy from a large bowl. The results showed that children were most likely to steal candy when they were in a group and when the experimenter could not identify them (see ▶ **FIGURE 10.7**).

DEINDIVIDUATION a sense of anonymity and loss of individuality, as in a large group, making people especially likely to engage in antisocial behaviors such as theft

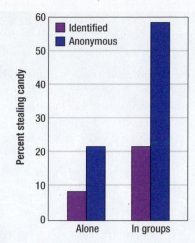

▶ **FIGURE 10.7** Children were most likely to steal candy when they were in a group and were not identifiable.

The Texas Department of Transportation launched a campaign to combat litter with the motto "Don't Mess With Texas."

LITTERING

Litter is a big problem in many places. For example, each year 140 million cigarette butts are tossed out on Texas highways. Although convicts pick up some of the litter, hired crews (paid with taxpayer dollars) pick up 90% of it. To fight the problem, the Texas Department of Transportation launched a campaign with the motto "Don't Mess With Texas." This advertising campaign played on the pride of Texans in their home state—they love their state so much that they should not ruin it with litter. (The slogan was also designed to seem aggressive and macho, so as to appeal to the young men who were perceived as the source of much littering and who might not respond as well to a seemingly effeminate slogan such as "Please Be Clean." "Don't Mess With Texas" is well suited to a culture of honor state!)

When everybody else seems to be littering, individuals are more likely to litter too (e.g., Krauss, Freedman, & Whitcup, 1978; Reiter & Samuel, 1980). Males litter more than females, and young people more than older people (Krauss et al., 1978).

Litter is not only unattractive, but it can also cause health problems to humans and animals. How can litter be reduced? One way is through antilittering norms. **Norms** are social standards that prescribe what people ought to do. Litter can be reduced by antilittering norms, especially **injunctive norms** that specify what most others approve or disapprove of (Cialdini, Reno, & Kallgren, 1990; Kallgren, Reno, & Cialdini, 2000; Reno, Cialdini, & Kallgren, 1993). In contrast, **descriptive norms**, which specify what most people do, are not effective at reducing littering (Cialdini et al., 1990; Kallgren et al., 2000; Reno et al., 1993). Messages that explicitly command people not to litter are less effective than messages that appeal to social norms (Reich & Robertson,

1979). This may be due to psychological reactance—the unpleasant emotional response people experience when someone is trying to restrict their freedom to engage in a behavior. Such threats frequently backfire (see Chapter 4 for a more detailed description of psychological reactance).

One reason norms might work is because people feel guilty if they don't follow them. As we learned in Chapter 6 on emotions, guilt can have a positive impact on people's behavior, including reducing litter. After a littering campaign, people said they would feel more guilty if they littered (Grasmick, Bursik, & Kinsey, 1991).

Other factors can help too. Research has shown that recycling can substantially reduce litter (Reams, Geaghan, & Gendron, 1996). Paying a deposit on cans and bottles reduces that type of litter, although it has little impact on other types of litter (e.g., Trinkaus, 1984). Placing trash cans along streets also helps reduce litter (Finnie, 1973). Thus, making it convenient or rewarding for people to get rid of trash is effective.

A recent article published in the prestigious magazine *Science* describes six studies that examined a number of antisocial behaviors (Keizer, Lindenberg, & Steg, 2008). All six studies tested the so-called Broken Windows Theory (Wilson & Kelling, 1982), which proposes that signs of disorder such as broken windows, litter, and graffiti induce other antisocial behaviors. The studies took place in the Netherlands, where bicycles are the major means of transportation.

NORMS social standards that prescribe what people ought to do
INJUNCTIVE NORMS norms that specify what most others approve or disapprove of
DESCRIPTIVE NORMS norms that specify what most people do

People were more likely to litter when they saw graffiti (Photo B) than when they saw no graffiti (Photo A).

In Study 1, bicycles were parked in an alley containing a No Graffiti sign. Participants in the disorder condition saw graffiti painted in the alley, whereas participants in the order condition saw no graffiti (see the photos on this page). Attached to each bike's handlebars was a flyer that read "We wish everybody happy holidays," signed with the name of a bogus sportswear shop. The results showed that participants were more likely to litter by throwing the flyers on the ground if the alley had graffiti (69%) than if the alley had no graffiti (33%). Thus, a cluttered environment caused people to increase their littering.

In Study 2, participants saw a no trespassing sign on a fence, which required them to take a 200-meter detour (more than 218 yards). The fence also contained a sign that prohibited locking bikes to the fence. In the disorder condition, four bikes were locked to the fence. In the order condition, no bikes were locked to the fence. Participants were much more likely to trespass when they saw bikes illegally locked to the fence (82%) than when they saw no bikes locked to the fence (27%). In Study 3, shoppers were more likely to litter (by tossing a flyer placed under their windshield wiper on the ground) if the parking lot was full of shopping carts containing "Please return your shopping cart" stickers (58%) than if there were no shopping carts in the parking lot (30%). (To discourage shoppers from returning the carts in the disorder condition, the researchers smeared Vaseline all over the handlebars of the carts!) In the Netherlands, setting off fireworks is against the law (enforced by a €60 fine, about $85 at the time). In Study 4, participants were more likely to litter a flyer attached to their bicycles if they heard fireworks (80%) then if they heard no fireworks (52%). In Studies 5 and 6, money was visible in a plastic window of a package placed in a mailbox. Participants were more likely to steal the money if the mailbox was covered with graffiti (27% vs. 13%) and if there was litter placed around the mailbox (25% vs. 13%). The results of these studies are consistent with Broken Windows Theory: Signs of disorder induced antisocial behaviors such as littering, trespassing, and stealing. Seeing signs of disorder may reduce the power of injunctive norms that discourage antisocial behavior.

Aggression provides a curious perspective on what makes us human. In some ways, humans are far more aggressive than our biological relatives. Most fighting between animals stops far short of serious injury or death, whereas humans kill each other. Only humans have invented tools to increase aggression, and these (from spears and guns to nuclear weapons) have greatly escalated the harm people do to each other. Only humans have been able to accumulate knowledge across generations (a hallmark of culture) so as to create weapons of mass destruction that are capable of destroying entire nations and possibly even wiping out the entire human population of the planet.

Only humans kill for ideas, such as religion or honor or political ideals. Only humans commit genocide, defined as the attempt to kill everyone in a particular racial or ethnic category. Only humans declare war on other groups, maintain military establishments to prepare for war in time of peace, and bestow honors on the individuals who kill their enemies most brilliantly or effectively. Only humans deliberately create chemical substances (such as alcohol) that make them more violent.

Still, human culture is unique in its devices for restraining aggression. Only humans commit crimes, in part because only humans can enact laws that define socially undesirable acts as crimes. The long history of culture is in part a story of placing ever more careful and thorough restraints on aggression, ranging from ancient moral laws ("Thou shalt not kill") to laws that forbid parents from spanking their children or prohibit people from sending hostile e-mail messages. Only humans have police forces that deter and punish criminals—though, again, the police must often use violence to stop violence. This is the paradox of culture: Step by step, it has created the technology to do more harm while also creating laws and other devices to reduce and prevent harm, another example of a tradeoff (involving very high stakes). Yet the level of violence and aggression in the world has decreased over time.

The elaborate mental apparatus that people have has transformed aggression too. Factors such as the hostile attributional bias are probably unique to humans, because only humans make inferences about someone else's intentions. A hostile attributional bias is a way of interpreting the behavior of others—"I think you intended to hurt me!"—that increases the likelihood of an aggressive response. Animals know whether they were hurt or not, but they probably do not have much capacity to choose an aggressive or a nonaggressive reaction based on whether they think the hurt was inflicted intentionally or accidentally.

Aggression is not the only kind of antisocial behavior. The same paradox can be seen in other behaviors. Culture creates new opportunities for antisocial behavior, such as insurance fraud, insider trading, overcharging, and all sorts of scams. At the same time, culture seeks to promote and reward behavior that follows the rules. Insider trading was unknown in biblical times, but so were the laws against it.

The impulses to commit aggression and other antisocial acts are deeply rooted in the social nature of human beings. Social animals are generally selfish, and because they get what they want from other animals, they are often tempted to exploit or hurt others. The human capacity for self-control is probably much more extensive than what other animals have, and it is responsible for the fact that people mostly refrain from acting on their violent and antisocial impulses.

chapter summary

DEFINING AGGRESSION AND ANTISOCIAL BEHAVIOR

- Aggression is any behavior that intentionally harms another person who is motivated to avoid the harm. Violence is aggression that has extreme harm as its goal.
- Antisocial behavior refers to behavior that either damages interpersonal relations or is culturally undesirable.
- Aggressive acts frequently fail to produce the intended, desired consequences and often bring about serious unintended consequences, mostly antisocial ones.
- Aggression is universal, but cultural rules restrict and govern aggression in different ways.
- Aggression evolved to help social animals deal with their social lives, but culture, as a better way of being social, offers new, nonviolent ways of resolving conflicts and problems.

IS AGGRESSION INNATE OR LEARNED?

- Freud (and others) proposed that people have an innate instinct that causes them to behave aggressively.
- According to social learning theory, aggression is not an innate drive but rather a learned behavior.
- When people observe and copy the behavior of others, this is called modeling.

- Inhibitions against aggression can be overcome if a model acts out aggressively.
- Learning and cultural socialization can subdue or encourage innate aggressive impulses and aggressive action.
- Aggression is a product of both nature and learning.

INNER CAUSES OF AGGRESSION

- The original frustration-aggression hypothesis states that the occurrence of aggressive behavior always presupposes the existence of frustration and the existence of frustration always leads to some form of aggression.
- There can be aggression without frustration, and frustration without aggression, but aggression is increased by frustration.
- Unpleasant moods increase aggression, but being in a bad mood is neither a necessary nor a sufficient condition for aggression.
- Anger does not directly or inevitably cause aggression, but the belief that aggression will help get rid of anger does increase aggression.
- The hostile attribution bias is the tendency to perceive ambiguous actions by others as intentionally hostile.
- The hostile perception bias is the tendency to perceive social interactions in general as being aggressive.
- The hostile expectation bias is the tendency to expect others to react to potential conflicts with aggression.
- About 25% of toddler interactions in day-care settings involve some kind of physical aggression.
- In all known societies, young men just past the age of

puberty commit most of the violent crimes and acts.

INTERPERSONAL CAUSES OF AGGRESSION

- Domestic violence (also called family violence or intimate-partner violence) is violence that

occurs within the home, between people who have a close relationship with each other (such as parents and children, spouses, and siblings).
- The sibling relationship is the most violent relationship in the world.
- In 1984, the U.S. Surgeon General declared domestic violence to be the number one health risk in the United States.
- Women attack their relationship partners slightly more often than men do, but women don't cause as much harm.

EXTERNAL CAUSES OF AGGRESSION

- People behave more aggressively in the mere presence of a weapon.
- Exposure to violent media increases aggression.
- Hotter temperatures are associated with higher levels of aggression and violence.
- Unpleasant environmental events, such as noise, crowding, foul odors, air pollution, and secondhand smoke, can increase aggression.
- Increases in testosterone, junk food, and alcohol lead to increased aggression. Decreases in serotonin and increases in vitamins reduce aggression.

SELF AND CULTURE

- Running amok, roughly translated, means going berserk. Cultural changes in running amok show that when people believe their aggression is beyond control,

they are often mistaken.
- Poor self-control is an important cause of crime.

- Violent individuals, rather than having low self-esteem, typically think themselves better than other people and have grandiose or inflated opinions of their own worth.
- The term *narcissism* describes the condition of thinking oneself superior or special, feeling entitled to preferential treatment, being willing to exploit others, having low empathy with "lesser" human beings, and entertaining grandiose fantasies or other ideas about oneself as a great person.
- Much aggression involves wounded pride, so narcissists are especially likely to become aggressive.
- The southern United States has a culture of honor, which accepts and even calls for violent responses to threats to one's honor.
- Humiliation (a state of disgrace or loss of respect) appears to be a primary cause of violence and aggression in cultures of honor.

OTHER ANTISOCIAL BEHAVIOR

- Lying, cheating, stealing, and littering are forms of antisocial behavior.
- Deindividuated people are more likely to steal than people who can be readily identified.
- Norms are social standards that prescribe what people ought to do.
- Injunctive norms specify what most others approve or disapprove.

WHAT MAKES US HUMAN? PUTTING THE CULTURAL ANIMAL IN PERSPECTIVE

- Human cultures mostly attempt to restrain violence and aggression.

Key Terms

Aggression 290
Antisocial behavior 291
Culture of honor 312
Deindividuation 316
Descriptive norms 317
Direct aggression 290
Domestic violence (family violence, intimate-partner violence) 301

Eros 294
Fight or flight syndrome 300
Frustration 297
Frustration-aggression hypothesis 297
Hostile attribution bias 299
Hostile expectation bias 299
Hostile perception bias 299
Humiliation 313

Indirect aggression 290
Injunctive norms 317
Instinct 294
Lying 314
Modeling 295
Norms 317
Proactive aggression 291
Reactive aggression 291
Running amok 309

Serotonin 307
Tend and befriend syndrome 300
Testosterone 306
Thanatos 295
Violence 291
Weapons effect 304

[Quiz Yourself] Answers

1. Defining Aggression and Antisocial Behavior
Answers: 1=b, 2=d, 3=c, 4=c

2. Is Aggression Innate or Learned?
Answers: 1=a, 2=a, 3=d, 4=d

3. Inner Causes of Aggression
Answers: 1=d, 2=a, 3=a, 4=b

4. Interpersonal Causes of Aggression
Answers: 1=c, 2=d, 3=d, 4=c

5. External Causes of Aggression
Answers: 1=b, 2=c, 3=c, 4=c

6. Self and Culture
Answers: 1=c, 2=d, 3=a, 4=c

7. Other Antisocial Behavior
Answers: 1=c, 2=b, 3=b, 4=a

Media Learning Resources

Make sure you check out the complete set of learning resources and study tools below. If your instructor did not order these items with your new book, go to www.ichapters.com to purchase Cengage Learning print and digital products.

Social Psychology and Human Nature BOOK COMPANION WEBSITE
www.cengage.com/psychology/baumeister
Visit your book companion website, where you will find flash cards, practice quizzes, Internet links, and more to help you study.

CENGAGENOW™ JUST WHAT YOU NEED TO KNOW NOW!
Spend time on what you need to master rather than on information you have already learned. Take a pre-test for this chapter, and CengageNOW will generate a personalized study plan based on your results. The study plan will identify the topics you need to review and direct you to online resources to help you master those topics. You can then take a post-test to help you determine the concepts you have mastered and what you will still need to work on. Try it out! Go to www.cengage.com/login to sign in with an access code or to purchase access to this product.

CLASSIC AND CONTEMPORARY VIDEOS STUDENT CD-ROM
To see videos on the topics and experiments discussed in this chapter and to learn more about the research that social psychologists are doing today, go to the Student CD-ROM.

SOCIAL PSYCH LAB
These unique online labs give you the opportunity to become a participant in actual experiments, including re-creations of classic and contemporary research studies.

chapter 11

Attraction and Exclusion

Amana Images/Getty Images

Tradeoffs: Testosterone—
A Blessing and
a Curse p. 326

Money Matters: Is
Manhood Measured in
Dollars or Inches? p. 335

The Social Side of Sex:
What Is Beauty? p. 337

Food for Thought: Social
Rejection and the Jar of
Cookies p. 340

What Makes Us
Human? Putting the
Cultural Animal in
Perspective p. 347

THE NEED TO
  BELONG p. 325
Belongingness as a Basic
  Need p. 325
Two Ingredients to
  Belongingness p. 328
Not Belonging Is Bad
  for You p. 329
Best Friends, Lovers,
  and . . . p. 329

ATTRACTION: WHO LIKES
  WHOM? p. 329
Similarity, Complementarity,
  Oppositeness p. 330

Social Rewards: You Make Me
  Feel Good p. 331
Tit for Tat: Reciprocity and
  Liking p. 332
You Again: Mere
  Exposure p. 333
Looking Good p. 335

REJECTION p. 338
Effects of Rejection: Inner
  Reactions p. 339
Behavioral Effects of
  Rejection p. 341
Loneliness p. 342

What Leads to Social
  Rejection? p. 343
Romantic Rejection and
  Unrequited Love p. 345

CHAPTER SUMMARY p. 348

She told the producers of the show that she wanted to meet and marry a man with good inner qualities. She went so far as to say that she cared little about physical attractiveness and was much more concerned with personality and other inner traits. Perhaps she sincerely thought that good looks and other superficial traits were not her concern, but when the show's bus opened and a series of very ordinary looking men came up to meet her, she struggled to hide her dismay, and hidden cameras later captured her complaining about the men's lack of physical charms. Some of the men were obese, others were bald, and few were genuinely handsome.

The men had been told that the woman was looking for personality rather than good looks, so they felt hopeful about being the one she would select, even though they agreed that she was quite beautiful herself. They were soon disappointed. As one disgruntled man pointed out, by the second day of eliminations, she had eliminated every man weighing over 200 pounds. Meanwhile, one man clearly regarded himself as better looking than everyone else, and this narcissistic fellow engaged in a variety of bullying and putdowns that made most characters regard him as a jerk, but Melana went out of her way to convince herself that he was not a jerk. On the round on which she sent all the tubby and balding men home, she was seen lying on the floor with the narcissistic fellow with their arms around each other, kissing passionately.

Late in the game, after Melana had whittled the set of eligible men down to a handful of candidates, the producers surprised everyone by adding several new male suitors—this time all young and handsome, if rather shallow in some ways. This was the test to see how good looks would fare against the inner qualities she had presumably found among the average ones. After that point, whenever Melana had to choose someone for a date, she invariably chose one of the handsome young fellows. (She did say she already knew the original men and needed dates with the new guys to give them a fair chance.) More men were sent home, until she was down to the final two. One was the last of the original "average Joes"; the other was a handsome newcomer. On final dates, she discovered that Adam, the last of the average Joes, was not so average: He was in fact a millionaire who owned several luxury homes, had part-ownership in a bar, and had a successful career as an investor. He noticed that she suddenly warmed to him, becoming more flirtatious and affectionate toward him when he revealed his assets. Perhaps it was too late, however. She chose the other finalist: Jason, a handsome but shallow waiter who at age 26 was still living with his parents.

Melana would not be the first person to choose physical attractiveness over other traits. What made her story so dramatic was that she had initially insisted that she was not interested in surface appearance and instead wanted inner qualities in a man. Her emphasis on looks even led her to disregard other qualities that also contribute to a couple's well-being—namely, career success and wealth.

Like most reality shows, *Average Joe* was about acceptance and rejection. The show revolved around a large group of people who were rejected one by one, or sometimes in groups, until at last the "winner" was

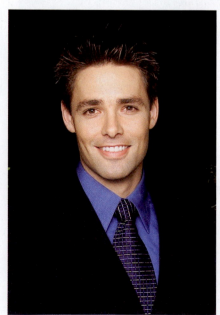

Photos of Jason and Melana.

© NBC/Courtesy: Everett Collection, Frederick M. Brown/Getty Images the person who staved off rejection the longest (think *Survivor*, *Big Brother*, *The Bachelor*, *The Bachelorette*, *The Apprentice*, and others). The woman in *Average Joe* could only accept one man, presumably as a husband or long-term relationship partner, and along the way she had to reject everyone else.

Like reality television (though perhaps the resemblance ends there!), this chapter is about attraction, social acceptance, and rejection. **Attraction** refers to anything that draws two or more people together, making them want to be together and possibly to form a lasting relationship. In social psychology it is especially used to refer to what makes people like (or start to love) each other. **Social acceptance** means that other people have come to like you, respect you, approve of you, and in general regard you in ways that will lead them to include you in their groups and relationships. **Rejection**, also known as **social exclusion**, is the opposite of acceptance: It means that others exclude you, so that you are not able to form or keep a social bond with them.

The quest for social acceptance is not limited to human beings. All social animals need to be accepted. Likewise, social rejection is a problem and a source of distress for many social animals as well as for human beings. The basic patterns we shall see in this chapter—attraction based on similarity or good looks, rejection of those who are different—are more linked to the social than the cultural aspect of human nature.

It is not surprising that people have developed many ways to make themselves attractive to others. One cautionary note, which we suspect Melana Scantlin may someday recognize, is that the traits that make someone most attractive upon first meeting are not always the same traits that make for a successful relationship. Testosterone levels are an important factor in this sort of tradeoff, as the *Tradeoffs* box explains. ◾

The Need to Belong

Why is social attraction important? Forming bonds is a big part of human life. Social animals (including plenty of nonhuman ones) survive and reproduce mainly by way of their relationships with others. In order to survive, it is vital to form and maintain some relationships. Forming relationships involves securing acceptance, which often depends on getting others to feel and think positively about you. That (along with the flip side, rejection) is the focus of this chapter. Sustaining long-term close relationships will be the focus of the next chapter.

BELONGINGNESS AS A BASIC NEED

People survive and reproduce better if they have relationships, but that doesn't mean they only want relationships for those reasons. Most likely, the "need to belong" is a powerful drive within the human psyche, and it affects people who are neither worried about survival nor urgently interested in reproduction. In our evolutionary past, the people who had a stronger need to belong probably fared better than other people, so that today's humans are mainly descended from ancestors who had a strong need to belong (see Bowlby, 1969, 1973; also Baumeister & Leary, 1995). This book's theme of "putting people first" is probably linked to the need to belong. Human beings relate to their physical environment by relating to other people first. We get even our basic food and shelter from other people, rather than directly from nature. People who didn't care about being with other people probably didn't live as well as those who formed strong social networks, and the need to belong helps make people want to form those networks. To enjoy the benefits of culture, people have to have an inner drive to connect with other people.

The universality of the need to belong was once aptly summarized by social psychologist Warren Jones (1989), who was presenting an overview of his research program on loneliness: "In two decades of studying loneliness, I have met many people who say they have no friends. I have never met anyone who didn't want to have any friends." Converging evidence from other sources casts doubt on the stereotype that some people are by nature loners or are indifferent to human social contact. True, some people may want many friends whereas others are content with just a few, but everybody needs somebody. Even religious hermits, who supposedly live alone in nature, typically rely heavily on one or two people who visit them regularly (e.g., in their cave) and supply much-needed human contact. Full deprivation of interpersonal contact is extremely stressful for everyone. It is said that prisoners at San Quentin who were sentenced to solitary confinement and no communication with each other resorted to desperate measures just to achieve some connection with other humans: Many of the men learned to speak down into their toilets, so the sound could pass through the pipes into other cells. They generally did not know who they were talking with, probably

---

ATTRACTION anything that draws two or more people together, making them want to be together and possibly to form a lasting relationship

SOCIAL ACCEPTANCE a situation in which other people have come to like you, respect you, approve of you, and include you in their groups and relationships

REJECTION (SOCIAL EXCLUSION) being prevented by others from forming or keeping a social bond with them; the opposite of acceptance

Tradeoffs

Testosterone—A Blessing and a Curse

Testosterone is a hormone associated with masculinity. Both men and women have it, though men have 9 or 10 times as much as women. (Women are somewhat more sensitive to it, though men are still more affected by testosterone overall, because they have so much more.) Most people, both men and women, tend to admire manly traits (especially in men), and they look upon testosterone as a good thing.

The researcher Jim Dabbs, one of psychology's leading experts on testosterone, reported that as he became known for this research, he received many inquiries from individuals about whether it was possible to increase their testosterone level. No one ever asked him about how to reduce it! Such one-sided interest suggests that people think very favorably of testosterone and will do almost anything for more of it. People don't seem to appreciate the tradeoffs, which come through much more clearly in Dabbs's (2000) book on the hormone. In reality, testosterone is a very mixed blessing, both for the individual who has it and for others connected with that person. High-testosterone men are more exciting but less reliable. They are restless in many ways, shown by their frequent interest in exploring new places and meeting new people, but this also makes them less prone to stay at home and take care of their families (see ▶ **FIGURE 11.1**).

Nature seems to have recognized that testosterone is better suited for finding mates than for maintaining stable families, and it has made

some remarkable adjustments (Dabbs, 2000). First, testosterone reaches its peak in young men around the age of 20 and declines steadily after that, so that it is highest during the years of single male competition but lower over the more family-centered years that typically follow. Second, when a young man becomes a father, his testosterone level typically drops. In fact, in one experiment, men who were soon to become fathers held a baby doll wrapped in a blanket that had previously been around a real baby (and therefore still had some baby smell), and after just a half hour these men experienced a significant decrease in their testosterone levels (Storey, Walsh, Quinton, & Wynne-Edward, 2000).

Testosterone makes one more willing to take risks (Dabbs, 2000). The tradeoffs there are obvious. High-testosterone men are more likely to perform heroic acts—and criminal ones, both of which involve risk-taking. Competition also involves risk, and high-testosterone individuals are much more eager than others to compete in all sorts of spheres. If you don't compete, you can't win, but you can't lose either. The low-testosterone man may prefer to sit safely and comfortably on the sidelines, but the one with high testosterone wants to jump into the fray and test his mettle.

Testosterone seems to help promote high sex drive, in both men and women. Transsexuals who get testosterone shots (which help turn a woman into a man) report that they have more feelings of sexual desire and sexual interest (Van Goozen, Cohen-Kettenis, Gooren, Frijda, & Can de Poll, 1995). Those who get testosterone blockers, which reduce the effect of testosterone, report a drop in sex drive. Among typical heterosexual individuals, higher levels of testosterone in both men and women are linked to higher sex drives in many studies, though some studies find no differences (for review, see Baumeister, Catanese, & Vohs, 2001). One study showed that males who simply came into contact with a female confederate while waiting in line for an experiment had higher testosterone levels than men who

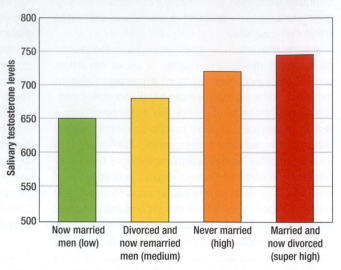

▶ **FIGURE 11.1** These data link low testosterone to a stable marriage; higher levels go with single status and divorce.

came in contact with a male confederate (Roney, Mahler, & Maestripieri, 2003). Whenever a relation is found, however, it links high testosterone to more desire.

As we saw in Chapter 10, high-testosterone men are also more violent than others. The aggressive and sexual passions that come with high testosterone are accompanied by a corresponding lesser interest in simpler, gentler pleasures. Men with low testosterone are kinder, more trustworthy, and more affectionate.

High testosterone may lead to an exciting life, but a difficult one. The fascination with sex and violence can produce risky activities and problems. Probably such individuals have more active sex lives, but they also have shorter lives (Worthman, 1999). So all those people clamoring to raise their testosterone levels should be careful what they wish for! ●

Bold adventures, passionate romances, but early graves.

People will do almost anything for more testosterone.

could not communicate very effectively, and might not have much to talk about—and the prospect of talking with your head stuck inside your toilet would be off-putting to many—but it was worth it to them just to hear another voice and know that theirs was heard. If the only road to social acceptance requires putting your head into a toilet, many people will do it.

Talking into toilets may seem bizarre to you, or outside your realm of experience. More commonly, you probably know people who rely on the Internet for much of their social life and social contact. The Internet allows people to interact with strangers and feel as though they can form social connections without much risk or anxiety (McKenna & Bargh, 1998, 1999, 2000). Some people manage to satisfy the need to belong by spending time in Internet chat rooms, where they may have intimate conversations with other people. Some who suffer from social anxiety or have feelings that society rejects and stigmatizes—so that opening up face-to-face with people they know is threatening, even dangerous—find they can communicate about their inner selves with complete strangers under the safe protection of anonymity that the Internet offers.

Talking into toilets is just one extreme and vivid instance of how hard people will work to connect with others. The long road to social acceptance has been a repeated theme of this book, and this chapter will show the variety of ways in which people strive to gain acceptance—and the variety of ways they suffer when they fail to connect with others. Nobody wants to end up all alone in the world; in fact, most human beings could hardly survive by themselves. As this chapter will show, people work long and hard to secure acceptance by others and to avoid rejection.

Social animals probably developed a kind of "herd instinct" long ago, but the human need to belong goes beyond that. A herd is a large collection of animals that all do pretty much the same thing. In contrast, human social life is more complicated, in that individuals may play distinct roles and have all sorts of specific, individual relationships with other members of the group. There is some evidence that the animal species most closely related to human beings have more complex social lives than other kinds of animals, in part because they can understand relations among others. One monkey can recognize that two other monkeys have an alliance, or that they might form one, or that they are enemies who may be prone to fight against each other, and the monkey might adjust its own behavior toward these others accordingly. Humans do the same. In fact, one thought-provoking theory has proposed that the driving force behind the evolution of intelligence and the brain was social: Animals developed larger, smarter brains in order to keep track of more

Prisoners in San Quentin who were sentenced to solitary confinement and no communication with each other resorted to desperate measures such as talking to each other through toilets just to achieve some connection with other humans.

relationships and more complicated social networks (Dunbar, 1998).

The **need to belong** is defined as the desire to form and maintain close, lasting relationships with some other individuals (Ainsworth, 1989; Axelrod & Hamilton, 1981; Barash, 1977; Baumeister & Leary, 1995; Bowlby, 1969; Buss, 1990, 1991; Hogan, Jones, & Cheek, 1985). Without this motive, people might just live alone; they would certainly be willing to abandon a partner as soon as he or she became annoying. The need to belong drives people to affiliate, commit, and remain together, and it makes them reluctant to live alone. People usually form relationships easily and readily, such as with neighbors and work colleagues. They are reluctant to let relationships end, even if they do not see any clear purpose in continuing the relationship. For example, when workers at a corporation go through a training group exercise in which they meet regularly for a set period of time, the group typically resists its impending breakup, such as by promising to remain in touch with each other and even planning reunions (Egan, 1970; Lacoursiere, 1980; Lieberman, Yalom, & Miles, 1973). The group's purpose will be over, and in fact most of these planned reunions never take place, but nobody wants to admit that the interpersonal connections are coming to an end. By the same token, when people break off a romantic relationship, they usually say they want to preserve some

NEED TO BELONG the desire to form and maintain close, lasting relationships with other individuals

parts of their intimate connection despite terminating the romantic connection. "Let's just be friends" is the common breakup line, though in reality most ex-lovers do not sustain close friendships with each other (Baumeister & Wotman, 1992). Promising to remain friends is usually just a way to avoid the fact that a social bond is being broken.

Indeed, people are often reluctant to put an end even to bad relationships. People remain in relationships even with violent, abusive partners. This has been an enduring puzzle to psychologists and a source of vexation to therapists (Andrews, 1989; Barnett & Gotlib, 1988; Coyne, 1976; Coyne, Kahn, & Gotlib, 1987; Hooley, Orley, & Teasdale, 1986; Howes & Hokanson, 1979; Marks & Hammen, 1982; Strube, 1988; Swann & Predmore, 1985; Swann, Wenzlaff, Krull, & Pelham, 1992; Weissman & Paykel, 1974). A breathtaking variety of theories have been put forward to explain why women stay with men who humiliate or beat them, though it has been hard to prove any one of these theories correct, and many views (such as that some women have a masochistic desire to be beaten and abused) have been discredited. The broadest and simplest explanation is that breaking off relationships goes against the basic tendencies of human nature. We are designed to connect, not to separate, and even if the relationship is bad, there is a deeply rooted impulse not to terminate it. (In Chapter 12, we will cover more material about why people stay in bad relationships, especially in the section on the investment model.)

TWO INGREDIENTS TO BELONGINGNESS

What exactly do people want? The need to belong has two parts (Baumeister & Leary, 1995). First, people want some kind of regular social contacts. Of course, not all interactions are equally satisfying. Aversive social contacts, such as fighting and arguing, do not satisfy the need to belong. Positive social contacts are better, though neutral ones, such as watching television together or simply having breakfast together, are also satisfying. Second, people want the stable framework of some ongoing relationship in which the people share a mutual concern for each other.

Having either of these without the other produces partial satisfaction. For example, people who have many encounters with other people but without the relationship framework are better off than people who are fully isolated, but they are not fully satisfied either. Imagine being a tollbooth collector who interacts with people all day long but never sees anyone for more than a minute or two and mostly just says the same few words over and over. The same goes for telemarketers, who may speak to many people on the phone but without any real

FOR THE LAST TIME, NO!

The need to belong is an important need!

connection. Prostitutes have rather intimate interactions with many individuals, but again without the context of an ongoing relationship these are not satisfying (Adler, 1980; McLeod, 1982; Symanski, 1980). Conversely, people who have the stable context without the frequent interactions also suffer from the lack of face-to-face contact, even while they may treasure the relationship. Long-distance relationships or so-called commuter marriages reveal this pattern: The partners place great value on the bond they have with their far-off lover, but they yearn to spend more time together (Bunker, Zubek, Vanderslice, & Rice, 1992; Gerstel & Gross, 1982, 1984; Govaerts & Dixon, 1988; Harrison & Connors, 1984; Winfield, 1985).

People may want to belong, but most do not seek to make new friends endlessly. Some people want more friends than others, but most people seem to think that having about four to six close relationships is enough (Caldwell & Peplau, 1982; Wheeler & Nezlek, 1977). That is, if you have about five people who care about you, whose company you enjoy, and with whom you can spend time on a regular basis, you probably feel fairly satisfied with your social life. (Having at least one of those relationships be a romantic pairing may also be important to most adults.) If you have fewer than that, you may be on the lookout for more. Few people seem eager to have more. In one survey (Reis, 1990), the majority of college students rated "having a few close friends" as extremely important, whereas "having lots of casual friends" was relatively unimportant.

Another sign is how people act in people-rich settings such as universities. There are so many people at a university that, in principle, you could interact with someone new every day. As you may notice, that's not how people actually conduct their social lives. Most students form a social circle of about half a dozen other people and devote their time and energy to interacting with the members of this circle rather than to constantly seeking new friends (Wheeler & Nezlek, 1977).

NOT BELONGING IS BAD FOR YOU

The need to belong is called a need, rather than merely a want, because when it is thwarted people suffer more than just being unhappy. (A want is something that we can live without; a need is something that we have to have in order to be healthy.) Failure to satisfy the need to belong leads to significant health problems, up to and including a higher risk of death. Death rates from all kinds of diseases are higher among people without social connections than among those with social connections (Lynch, 1979). People who are alone in the world have more physical and mental health problems than people who belong to a good social network (Bhatti, Derezote, Kim, & Specht, 1989; Cacioppo, Hawkley, Berntson, et al., 2002; Cacioppo, Hawkley, Crawford, et al., 2002; DeLongis, Folkman, & Lazarus, 1988; Goodwin, Hunt, Key, & Samet, 1987; Hawkley, Burleson, Berntson, & Cacioppo, 2003; Herlitz et al., 1998; Kiecolt-Glaser, Garner, Speicher, Penn, Holliday, & Glaser, 1984; Kiecolt-Glaser, Fisher, Ogrocki, Stout, Speicher, & Glaser, 1987; see Uchino, Cacioppo, & Kiecolt-Glaser, 1996, for a review). Loneliness is hard on the body, impairing its natural powers including the immune system and its ability to recover from sickness or injury (Cacioppo & Hawkley, 2005).

BEST FRIENDS, LOVERS, AND . . .

Are close friends and romantic relationships the main or only way to satisfy the need to belong? In principle, there is another option, especially for cultural animals such as human beings: One can "belong" to a group or organization. Some people may find those social connections satisfying even if they do not form close friendships there (Gardner, Pickett, & Knowles, 2005). As we shall see later in this chapter, some people can satisfy their wish for belongingness and keep loneliness at bay by feeling connected to a group or organization (even a university, or a professional sports team of which they are only fans). This seems to work better for men than for women (Gardner et al., 2002).

Attraction: Who Likes Whom?

Social psychologists have labored long and hard to study the start of possible friendships and other forms of liking. Two people who are just meeting may come to like each other, or they may not. Which way they go depends on a variety of factors. Social psychology's task has been to identify those factors.

Some social psychologists, such as the influential researcher Edward E. Jones (1964), approached the question of attraction by studying what people actively do to try to make someone like them. (The term **ingratiation** is used for this, although ingratiation also has the connotation of being something a bit sneaky or manipulative.) This is a useful complement to the simple studies of who-likes-whom. Imagine you met someone and wanted to get that person to like you, either as a friend or as a romantic partner. What would you do? Jones found that people seem to have an intuitive knowledge of what fosters attraction, and they use that knowledge to get other people to like them. We will see several examples in the coming sections.

Not much will prove surprising in these research findings. People like good-looking, friendly people who are similar to themselves in important ways, and

INGRATIATION what people actively do to try to make someone like them

they like people who are nice to them. That much is hardly surprising. Still, let us review the main conclusions.

SIMILARITY, COMPLEMENTARITY, OPPOSITENESS

Two old clichés make opposite predictions about who likes whom. "Birds of a feather flock together" suggests that people mainly like others who resemble themselves, whereas "Opposites attract" points to the contrary conclusion—that people are drawn to people dissimilar to themselves. Note that in such circumstances, whatever result social psychologists produce will look in retrospect like common sense. (This is why you shouldn't rely only on common sense when taking your social psychology exams! See Chapter 1 for a discussion on the weaknesses of common sense.)

In any case, decades of research by social psychologists have produced a clear and definitive winner in this battle of the clichés. Opposites do not attract very often. The birds of a feather are the ones who end up flocking together and staying together. In social psychology's terms, similarity is a common and significant cause of attraction (Byrne, 1971).

Most likely, you can see this yourself. Classify yourself on several major dimensions along which people differ. Choose ones that matter to you—perhaps age, race, level of education, liberal/conservative, religious or not, athletic or not, rich or poor. Then classify your several closest friends. The odds are that you and your close friends will fall in similar categories far more often than in different ones. People who want to influence us are well aware of this principle; sometimes they try to get us to like them by claiming that they are similar to us.

The appeal of similarity was illustrated in an amusing way by a news story (Green, 2005). A man and a woman made contact via the Internet and began to exchange emails. They discovered they had a great deal in common, and they became attracted to each other. They "dated" for about six months via e-mail messages, though they did not reveal their names. The woman was also older than she had led the man to believe, so when he asked for her picture, she sent him a photo from a magazine. As their emotions grew stronger, the man pressured the woman to meet him for a romantic rendezvous. She finally relented and agreed to meet him on a dark beach. He went there, heart pounding, and saw a woman waiting for

him as promised, wearing white shorts and a pink tank top. He spoke to her and she turned around, and they both got a shock: She was his mother! Obviously, nobody wants to date his own mother (especially because she was still married to his father, who became a laughingstock when the story hit the news and who took a very dim view of the whole episode), but family members generally are quite similar to each other, so it is not surprising that when their identities were concealed they had many similarities that produced the attraction.

Similarity can promote liking in many spheres. Having friends who like to do the same things you like to do can be important. After all, if none of your friends likes to play tennis, how are you going to find someone to play with? Some people compartmentalize their social lives more than others. People who are high in **self-monitoring** (Gangestad & Snyder, 2000; Lennox & Wolfe, 1984; Snyder, 1974; Snyder & Gangestad, 1986) seek to maximize each social situation, whereas those low in that trait pay more attention to permanent connections and feelings rather than fluctuating ones. Hence the high self-monitor tennis player would prefer to play tennis with the best (or most evenly matched) tennis player in his or her circle of friends, whereas the low self-monitor would prefer to play tennis with his or her best friend, regardless of tennis ability.

Some of the most striking effects of similarity are found in marriage, even though marriage, which usually binds together two people of opposite genders, is often assumed to be one of the spheres where opposite or at least complementary (thus different) traits promote attraction. In fact, most spouses are similar in many basic respects. For example, husband and wife tend to have similar levels of intelligence (Jensen, 1977). (When you get married, don't call your spouse an idiot, because your spouse's IQ probably is close to your own!) Married partners are also similar on other dimensions, including physical attractiveness, education, and socioeconomic status (Murstein & Christy, 1976). Similarity contributes not only to the initial attraction but to the development of close bonds. Couples who are more similar to each other in attractiveness are more likely to progress toward more loving and committed relationships (see ▶ **FIGURE 11.2**; White, 1980).

The **matching hypothesis** states that people tend to pair up with others who are equally attractive (Feingold, 1988; McKillip & Reidel, 1983; Walster, Aronson, Abrahams, & Rottmann, 1966). This is especially true among lovers, but it also is true among friends. It occurs in same-sex and in opposite-sex relationships.

Why does similarity promote attraction? The pattern seems widespread and probably very deeply rooted in the psyche, so explanations should probably

---

SELF-MONITORING the ability to change one's behavior for different situations

MATCHING HYPOTHESIS the proposition that people tend to pair up with others who are equally attractive

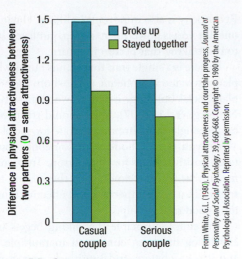

From White, G.L. (1980). Physical attractiveness and courtship progress, *Journal of Personality and Social Psychology, 39*, 660–668. Copyright © 1980 by the American Psychological Association. Reprinted by permission.

▶ **FIGURE 11.2 Dissimilarity in physical attractiveness increases the risk of breaking up (White, 1980).**

invoke simple, basic tendencies. If human beings were naturally selected "for" culture, and we evolved under conditions of competing cultures, there would be an advantage to those people who attached themselves strongly to similar others. People who were drawn more to the different, the exotic, the foreign, might detach from their group and join another, but this would be risky. Newcomers aren't trusted as much as long-familiar mates (Fukuyama, 1999). Hence people who preferred to form bonds with people very different from themselves might tend to leave behind fewer offspring than people who attached themselves to others like themselves.

There is some evidence that matching is driven more by rejecting dissimilar others than by liking similar others (Rosenbaum, 1986). In fact, as people get to know each other and find out about dissimilarities, liking goes down. Norton, Frost, and Ariely (2007) showed that most people believe that the more they know about someone, the more they like that person—but in reality, they tend to like someone less as they learn more. They start off assuming the other person will be similar. But once they find some dissimilarities, these seem to multiply, so that new evidence confirms dissimilarity and reduces liking. In an online dating study, these researchers found, sure enough, that after the date was over they knew more about the person but liked him or her less than previously.

The attraction to similar others is probably social rather than cultural (see Chapter 2 for a discussion of the distinction between social and cultural animals). That is, it is not something that originates with human beings living in culture, but rather something that originated among animals that formed into groups to help each other live better. Groups composed of similar animals would probably help each other live better. If anything, culture has created more value in diversity and complementarity, because cultural systems can take advantage of different roles and different talents.

Thus, as culture progresses and forms large, complex, interacting groups, there may be more need for complementarity. The movement toward diversity in organizations and the workplace may reflect an attempt to capitalize on the value of being different (see Chapter 14). But when people pick their friends and lovers, they still tend to look for those who are similar to themselves.

SOCIAL REWARDS: YOU MAKE ME FEEL GOOD

For several decades, psychological theory was dominated by **reinforcement theory**, which held that people and animals will perform behaviors that have been rewarded more than other behaviors. Applied to the issue of interpersonal attraction, this theory predicted that people would mainly like others who are rewarding to them—those who benefit them or make them feel good.

Two themes of ingratiation research confirm the importance of interpersonal rewards (Jones & Wortman, 1973). A first broad strategy for getting someone to like you is to do favors for that person. By definition, favors bring benefits to the recipient, and so favors make the person feel positively toward the person who did the favor. A man who wants a woman to like him will often do a broad variety of favors for her, such as sending her flowers, buying her dinner, and giving her gifts. Now and then people will recognize a favor as manipulative and resent it (Brehm & Cole, 1966), but in general favors are a good way to promote liking.

The second broad strategy involves praise. Most people feel good when they receive a compliment, so if you want someone to like you, you will probably be tempted to give that person plenty of compliments. Telling people what you like about them and what you see as their best traits is by and large a good way to go through life, because it both reinforces the traits you approve of and makes people like you. The only limitation is that if people see the praise as manipulative or insincere they may discount it. Otherwise, however, praising people is a reliable way to get them to like you (Jones & Wortman, 1973).

Consider Joe Girard, for example (Cialdini, 2001). Joe makes a living selling cars in Detroit, Michigan. He is so successful at his job that he is even listed in

---

REINFORCEMENT THEORY the proposition that people and animals will perform behaviors that have been rewarded more than they will perform other behaviors

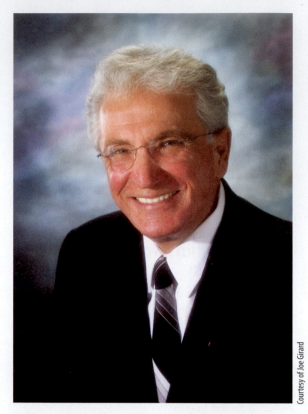

Courtesy of Joe Girard

Each month Joe Girard sends each of his former customers (more than 13,000 of them!) a postcard that says: "I like you! Joe Girard." This may be one reason why Joe Girard is listed in the *Guinness Book of World Records* as the "Greatest Car Salesman."

the *Guinness Book of World Records* as the "Greatest Car Salesman." He earns more than $200,000 a year selling cars! Every day he works, Joe sells an average of five cars and trucks. Joe was once asked the secret of his success. His response was: "Finding the salesman you like, plus the price. Put them together, and you get a deal." Joe does something else that might help his sales. Each month Joe sends each of his 13,000 former customers a postcard in the mail. The postcard contains only five words: "I like you! Joe Girard." Praise can even help you sell cars.

Why do rewards promote liking? This is no big mystery. Rewards mean getting what you want. Any organism should learn to like people, places, animals, or things that provide it with what it wants and needs. This may be as simple as classical conditioning: You learn to associate feeling good with being with someone, so naturally you like that person more.

TIT FOR TAT: RECIPROCITY AND LIKING

Chapter 9 emphasized that reciprocity is important for culture and therefore for human beings. Culture depends on reciprocity: If I do something for you, you should do something for me in return.

Reciprocity is also important in liking. Having someone like you is powerful at a deep, gut level: It is hard to resist liking that person in return.

If there is a single trait that stands out as what people most value in someone with whom they contemplate social bonding, it is trustworthiness (Cottrell, Neuberg, & Li, 2007). Why should trustworthiness be the single most important trait for social appeal? When you form a bond with someone, you expect to do positive things for that person. Trustworthiness means that you can expect the other person to reciprocate. That is an important and effective foundation for a good relationship.

The simple principle that liking begets (reciprocal) liking has been confirmed in multiple studies, and it is so obvious and intuitively correct that few studies now bother to focus on it. Still, whenever participants receive feedback that someone else likes them, they almost invariably feel a surge of affection for that person. The power of reciprocal liking seems to be universal. Thus, even research that finds differences between cultures in how people think about friendships and how they attract new friends still finds the common principle: If someone likes you, it is hard to resist liking that person in return (Fiske & Yamamoto, 2005).

Reciprocation can take other forms and in that respect can imply similarity. In nonverbal behavior, reciprocity can take the form of mimicking. In one well-known study (Chartrand & Bargh, 1999), participants interacted with a confederate whom they wanted to like them. Sometimes the confederate touched his or her face during the conversation, and other times the confederate wiggled his or her foot. Without realizing what they were doing, participants mimicked these behaviors themselves. A follow-up study showed that mimicry is often successful as a means of increasing liking. Participants talked to a confederate who had been trained to mimic the participant's nonverbal behavior (or not). When the confederate performed the same nonverbal behaviors as the participant—for example, wiggling her foot in response to seeing the participant wiggle her foot—the participant ended up liking the confederate more (Lakin & Chartrand, 2005).

We started this chapter by describing the *Average Joe* television reality show that featured Melana Scantlin. The sequel, *Average Joe: Hawaii*, had another beautiful woman courted by a bevy of ordinary-looking men. In this series, one of the nerdy-looking men adopted an unusual strategy, which was to declare himself wildly in love with the woman early in the game. It is a risky strategy, at least assuming that the declarations of love were truthful, because to fall in love with someone far more attractive than yourself (not to mention someone who was being courted by a couple of dozen other men!) makes you highly vulnerable to heartbreak. In this case, however, it had a powerful impact. The gorgeous young woman responded to the nerdy man's love for her, and she repeatedly selected him to continue in the game, even after the producers introduced a row of handsome young alternative suitors. The thoroughly smitten young man made it into the final round of two men, although she, like Melana Scantlin in the first game, ultimately chose the shallow but handsome fellow over the passionately devoted but average-looking guy. (Then the handsome guy dumped her.) Still, he had gone much farther than he otherwise could have, simply by loving the woman unreservedly. It was hard for her to resist the fact that he loved her so much.

Reciprocation of liking may have a hugely powerful effect in everyday friendships. Its impact is more of a problem in romance, however. The difference may lie in the simple truth that you can have many friends but usually only one love relationship, in most cultures.

Research on one-sided, unrequited love has confirmed that people are positively attracted when they learn that someone else likes them, but if they do not want to reciprocate those feelings, they soon start to find the other person's attraction to them to be a burden or problem. If you were to find out that someone has a crush on you, your first reaction would

I'm starting to like you more and more.

almost certainly be positive—it is good to be loved. But if you did not really want that person as your partner, soon you would feel uncomfortable around him or her. Initially it is flattering to learn that someone likes you, but if you do not want to marry that person, your later reaction is a struggle with guilt and a search for ways to let the person down easily (Baumeister, Wotman, & Stillwell, 1993).

Reciprocity brings us back to the broad theme of humans as cultural animals. If people liked those who liked them, this reciprocity would make people better suited to culture. Creatures who mainly liked those who disliked them would have a difficult time forming the network of relationships that makes culture possible. You are safer and better off among people who like you than among people who don't care about you one way or the other. Putting people first, to mention another theme of this book, seems to work best when it involves people who like us and are similar to us.

YOU AGAIN: MERE EXPOSURE

What we have seen so far is hardly surprising. People like those who are similar to them, who like them back, and who make them feel good. But another pattern is less intuitively obvious. Apparently people sometimes like others based on nothing more than familiarity. That is, they grow to like people whom they encounter on a regular basis. This **propinquity** effect is robust and reliable. A classic study by Festinger, Schachter, and Back (1950) tracked friendship

It's hard to say no to someone who really loves you.

PROPINQUITY being near someone on a regular basis

formation in a dormitory, and it found that people made friends (as well as enemies) most frequently among the people who lived close to them.

Chapter 7 on attitudes described the mere exposure effect: People come to hold more positive attitudes toward familiar stimuli than toward novel, unfamiliar ones. Merely seeing or encountering something or someone on a regular basis increases liking.

An extension of the mere exposure effect involves shared experiences. For example, many years from now in some far-off place you may meet a stranger and discover during the conversation that the two of you attended the same college or came from the same home town or had the same kind of pet. Logically, there is little reason that this should promote liking, but the odds are that you and this other person will begin to have friendly feelings toward each other based on this shared experience.

People seem to develop positive feelings toward someone even if the shared experiences were bad. Laboratory participants who are strangers and have no common bond except that they experience electric shock together end up liking each other more (Latane, Eckman, & Joy, 1966)! A similar conclusion emerges from research on combat veterans. Going through combat is mostly a highly stressful, dangerous, sad, and terrifying experience, marked by loud noise, confusion, death and injury to friends, and uncertainty about one's own survival. Yet military groups who experience combat seem to bond to each other from the experience. One sign is that military reunions are better attended by groups who went through combat than by groups who did not share battlefield experience (Elder & Clipp, 1988).

Why do familiarity and shared experiences promote liking? The effect of familiarity and shared experiences goes beyond simple explanations in terms of conditioning (positive associations). Most likely it is very deeply rooted in the psyche, which means its roots are far back in our evolutionary history. One should perhaps ask why even very simple animals would become fond of familiar stimuli or familiar other animals. A tendency to grow fond of the familiar would help stamp in the preference for a stable environment (so animals might learn to like their homes). It would certainly promote stable social bonds. Imagine, for example, that nature programmed animals in the opposite way, so that familiarity led to contempt or some other form of disliking. How would families stay together? How would friendships, alliances, or other partnerships survive? If you always preferred a stranger to someone you knew, social life would be in constant turmoil. In contrast, if you automatically grew to like

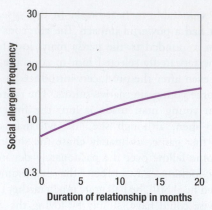

▶ **FIGURE 11.3 The longer the relationship continues, the more people are bothered by their partner's minor annoying habits, and the more negative emotion they have in response to them.**

the people you saw regularly, you would instinctively prefer them to strangers, and groups would form and stabilize easily. Given the advantages of stable groups (e.g., people know each other, know how to work together, how to make decisions together, how to adjust to each other), it is not surprising that nature favored animals that grew to like (rather than dislike) each other on the basis of familiarity.

As with all these patterns, it is important not to overstate them. Of course we do not grow to love everyone we see on a regular basis. Some people are a pain in the neck, and seeing them every day will not make them seem like adorable sweethearts. There is even an interesting pattern of research suggesting that a partner's annoying habits grow more annoying with repeated exposure (see ▶ **FIGURE 11.3**). This is called the **social allergy effect**, based on the analogy to ordinary allergies, which grow worse over time. If you have a slight allergy to cats and you move in with a romantic partner who has a cat, your cat allergy is likely to grow more severe as you are exposed to the cat more frequently. In the same way, early in a relationship you may be only slightly bothered by how your partner chews with her mouth open, or picks his toenails while watching television, or keeps repeating some stupid phrase such as "like, wow"— but this slight irritation will most likely grow more bothersome over time (Barbee, Lawrence, & Cunningham, 1998; Cunningham, 2009; Cunningham, Barbee, & Druen, 1997; Cunningham, Barbee, & Mandal, in press). In short, familiarity and repeated exposure can sometimes make bad things worse. But the most common consequence is that people grow to like people (and places and things) that become familiar to them.

This increase in liking caused by familiarity, like nearly every social psychology effect, involves a shift in the odds rather than a black-and-white absolute difference. In this case, seeing someone regularly

SOCIAL ALLERGY EFFECT the idea that a partner's annoying habits become more annoying over time

MONEY Matters

Is Manhood Measured in Dollars or Inches?

What is the measure of a man? Women have long known that physical dimensions are a key component of their attractiveness, and women's concern with losing weight and being thin is at least partly rooted in the competition to be desirable to men. One relevant measure is the ratio of waist size to hip size. Research by Singh (1993) and others has found that men are more attracted to women with a ratio of about 0.7, and they have clear preferences when they judge a woman only by her silhouette. A low ratio like 0.7 is compatible with the so-called hourglass figure that men find desirable. If the ratio is higher, as it is for women with bigger bellies, attraction is less.

In an effort to see whether women would judge men by equally simple (some might say shallow!) criteria, Singh (1995) prepared silhouette drawings of men with varying waist-to-hip ratios and asked women to rate them for attractiveness. Sure enough, women did have a slight preference for a certain body shape in men, with a waist-to-hip ratio of around 0.9 and normal overall weight. Of course, this doesn't necessarily mean very much, because that was all the information the women had on which to judge the men, and the effect was small.

In his final study, therefore, Singh added a second variable: how much money the man earned. Waist-to-hip ratio still mattered, a little, but the amount of money the man made was much more important, especially when women were judging him as a partner for a long-term relationship or marriage. Women much preferred the men with high incomes over the low-paid ones. Dollars mattered more than inches, though for maximum appeal, both the right body and a high income were needed.

Of course, waistline is not the only part of a man that can be measured in inches. Being tall matters, and there is in fact some tradeoff between money and height, according to research with an online dating service by Hitsch, Hortaçsu, and Ariely (2006). Women's choices depended on both men's height and their salaries. Taller was better, but money could compensate. Thus, a man who was 5 feet 8 inches tall could get as many dates as a man who was six feet tall, provided that the shorter man made more money—precisely, $146,000 per year more! For a 5 foot 2 inch man to do as well as a six-footer, he would need to earn an extra $277,000.

The news for short men is not all bad, however. Women may express some preference for dating tall men, but when they meet them they do not find them any more attractive. Moreover, short men report having had just as many dates as tall men, so obviously they find ways of overcoming any prejudice against them (Sheppard & Strathman, 1989). ■

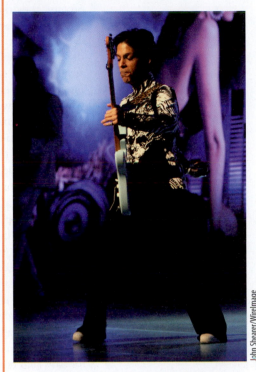

John Shearer/WireImage

At 5' 2 1/2" (1.59 meters) tall, dollars matter more than inches.

---

and becoming familiar with that person leads to a slight increase in the odds that you will end up liking that person. The mere exposure effect is probably an important part of the propinquity effect, noted earlier. We like those who live near us because we see them frequently.

LOOKING GOOD

In the Melana Scantlin story that started the chapter, a beautiful and desirable woman chose a physically attractive man over one with substance and success. Such a choice is not uncommon. When all else is equal, most people show a substantial preference for attractive over unattractive others. Even when all else is not equal, physical good looks count for a lot and can trump other good points.

Some of the advantages of good looks fall into the stereotype that has been called the **what is beautiful is good effect**. That is, people assume that physically attractive people will be superior to others on many other traits. These traits include happiness, sexual warmth, popularity, and even intelligence and success (Eagly, Ashmore, Makhijani, & Longo, 1991; Feingold, 1992; Jackson, Hunter, & Hodge, 1995). To be sure, not all good traits are assumed to be linked to attractiveness. Beautiful women and handsome men are not assumed to be more honest than others, for example. There is also some evidence of cultural variation. Koreans, for example, place more value than North Americans on honesty and compassionate concern for others, and Koreans also are more likely to think that attractive people will be higher than average on those traits (Wheeler & Kim, 1997).

Good looks can outweigh other factors in attraction. (To see one how one group of researchers tried to put a dollar value on physical attributes, read *Money Matters*.) Indeed, this fact produced one of

---

WHAT IS BEAUTIFUL IS GOOD EFFECT the assumption that physically attractive people will be superior to others on many other traits

the most famous disappointments in social psychology's research on attraction. A group of researchers set up a campus dating service to test their various theories about interpersonal liking (Walster et al., 1966). They collected all sorts of information about the students in their pool; then they matched them at random and sent them out on dates. The researchers favored theories emphasizing similarity and reciprocity: they thought people who were most similar to each other on various attributes would enjoy their dates the most. This was not what happened. Instead, the main conclusion was that the dating partner's attractiveness was the strongest predictor of how much people enjoyed the date: The more attractive your partner was, the better you liked him or her. The fancy theories about matching and similarity and reciprocity couldn't shine through the overwhelming preference for the best-looking partners.

It is perhaps understandable that people want their dating partners and romantic partners to be physically attractive (see *The Social Side of Sex*). But good looks are valued in many other, nonromantic settings as well. Attractive children are more popular among other children than their less attractive peers, and teachers like them more too (Clifford & Walster, 1973; Dion, 1973; Dion, Berscheid, & Walster, 1972). There is even some evidence that 3-month-old babies prefer to look at more attractive faces (Langlois, Roggman, Casey, & Ritter, 1987). Good-looking people do better in job interviews, including for jobs that are not based on looks (Cash & Janda, 1984; Mack & Rainey, 1990). We saw in the chapter on prosocial behavior that attractive people sometimes get more help in emergency situations (West & Brown, 1975).

For men, modern clothing is linked more to displaying wealth and status than showing off the body as a sex object. Women in one study were asked to rate how attractive they found men as potential husbands, dates, or lovers, based on seeing photographs of them (Grammer, Fink, Moller, & Thornhill, 2003). The researchers had actually taken two photos of each man. In one photo, the man wore classy and expensive clothes, including a navy blue blazer, nice tie, and Rolex watch. For the other photo, each man put on a Burger King server outfit, complete with hat. Women expressed very little desire to meet, date, sleep with, or marry the men they saw wearing Burger King outfits, probably because those outfits are associated with low status and not much money. The very same men attracted much more interest when dressed up in classy, expensive clothes.

Body shape is another component of attractiveness and sex appeal. A so-called hourglass figure composed of a narrow waist with wider hips and shoulders is most appealing in both men and women, though naturally the widest shoulders are seen as more attractive in a man than a woman. There is some cultural variation as to what figure is seen as ideal, and in particular plump women are regarded as more attractive by some cultures than by others, though being hugely obese is not regarded as lovely by almost any culture. Even within a culture, standards of beauty change. For example, the weight of *Playboy* centerfolds and Miss America Pageant contestants and winners has decreased substantially since 1960 (Garner, Garfinkel, Schwartz, & Thompson, 1980).

The sources of cultural variation in ideal body weight are not fully known, although one factor may be whether food is scarce. That is, in a culture where there is often not enough to eat, a plump woman is probably rich and healthy, whereas a skinny woman is more in danger of starving or might have a disease. Men in such cultures might prefer slightly larger women because their bodies will be better able to support a baby. Of course, the men don't necessarily think about whether the woman can nurse a baby. It is just that the men who for whatever reason were attracted to the plumper women were more successful at passing on their genes, whereas the men who liked the skinniest women produced fewer surviving babies.

The preference for slender versus fuller figures seems to change fairly easily. In fact, men can change their preferences even within the same day! One study stopped Princeton students going to dinner or coming back from it to furnish ratings of attractiveness of women from photos. The hungry men (before dinner) preferred plumper women than the men who were full from dinner (Nelson & Morrison, 2005).

So far we have focused on what makes people attractive and attracted to each other. In the next section we turn to the other side of the coin: social rejection and exclusion.

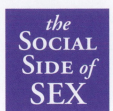
What Is Beauty?

Most people can agree fairly well on who is beautiful and who isn't, but it is much harder to say why someone is beautiful. Also, people agree more about women than about men, possibly because physical attractiveness counts more for women than for men (Buss, 1994). In lab studies by Maner, Gailliot, and DeWall (2007), both men and women automatically looked more at beautiful women (more than handsome men) in a group of faces. Probably the reasons differed. The men see beautiful women as potential mates. The women see them as potential rivals and want to check out the competition. (Did it ever strike you as odd that men's magazines are filled with pictures of beautiful women—but so are women's magazines?)

Evolutionary psychologists generally think that female beauty is linked to signs of being a good mate and potential partner, which especially means being young and healthy. If cultural variation in beauty were random, you might expect that gray hair and wrinkled skin would be regarded as beautiful in some cultures, but no known culture treats old-looking women as more beautiful than younger-looking ones. A clear complexion is nearly always prized, possibly because it was a sign of health: Many infectious diseases such as pox left permanent marks on the skin, so clear skin would be one sign of a healthy mate. Today's men and women are descended from male ancestors who chose young and healthy-looking women.

Symmetry is a surprisingly powerful source of beauty. That is, people whose faces and bodies are exactly the same on both sides are regarded as more attractive than people whose right side is different from their left side. Symmetry is a sign of two important things: being healthy and having good genes. Faults or defects in someone's genes produce discrepancies between the left and right sides. The most symmetrical person presumably has the fewest genetic defects.

One of the most remarkable demonstrations of the power of symmetry began by measuring a series of body parts (such as earlobes and little fingers) of young adult men, to see how closely they matched. Then the researchers asked each man to sleep in a T-shirt some night when he did not use deodorant or cologne. Each man brought the T-shirt to the lab and left it there. A sample of young women then sniffed each T-shirt and rated how good it smelled (of course without knowing which men had worn them). They also informed the researchers of when they had had their last period. The most symmetrical men's T-shirts were rated as smelling the best, and this effect was mainly found among the women who were at the point in the menstrual cycle at which they would be most fertile. Thus, when women are most prone to get pregnant, they are most drawn to the bodily smell of men who were most symmetrical and hence would probably have the best genes (Thornhill & Gangestad, 1999).

Another demonstration of the importance of symmetry was done by doubling images. That is, researchers took facial photos of people, then cut each photo down the middle, threw out one side at random, and filled in the blank with the mirror image of the other side. For example, they might create a photo of you by taking the left side of your face, making a mirror image of it, and attaching the mirror image (as the right side) to the real left side. The result was faces that looked much like the original people but were more exactly symmetrical. Participants consistently rated these reworked images as more attractive than the original faces. Thus, increasing the symmetry of a face made it seem more attractive.

Another source of beauty is typicality. That is, people who look different from others are generally regarded as less attractive. This theory was proposed two centuries ago by the German philosopher Immanuel Kant (1790/1924), who thought that the mind reviews all the faces it has ever seen, forms a sort of average or composite,

© Corbis

Which photo is more attractive? The one on the left shows the actual face; the one on the right was made by duplicating the left side on the right, so that the face is perfectly symmetrical. Most people find the symmetrical picture to be more attractive than the true picture.

and regards that as the most attractive. Recent advances in computer technology finally made it possible to test his theory by morphing faces together to make up an average. In a landmark study, researchers started with 16 different faces that varied in attractiveness. Then they combined pairs of faces using computer imaging software, so that they made 8 new faces, each of which was an "average" of two of the original faces. They then merged these again by pairs, and again, ultimately creating a single image that was the average of all 16. Participants consistently rated the original, actual faces as less attractive than the 2-face composites; the 4-face composites got even higher ratings; and the images that had been made by averaging all 16 faces were rated as the most beautiful (Langlois et al., 1987).

Further work has shown that the ultimate, most attractive faces are not really averages of everyone, but rather averages of the faces that are high on the other indices of beauty, such as youth and health. That is, a face that averages across the entire life span, including a baby, a little girl, an adolescent, a young adult, a middle-aged woman, and an old woman, is not as attractive as a face that is made by averaging a group of young adult women. ■

Rejection

One day a young man named Kip Williams was walking through a park, and unexpectedly he saw a Frisbee spinning toward him. He caught it and looked about for its source. Two other guys waved to him, and he threw it back to them. Everyone smiled, and the three of them threw the Frisbee around for a few minutes. Then, oddly, the other two stopped throwing him the Frisbee and ignored him. He stood there for a few minutes, his smile gradually fading, until he realized that they weren't going to include him anymore. Feeling surprisingly sick and sad, he turned and slunk away.

In most cases that would have been the end of the story, but Williams went on to become a social psychologist. He remembered the experience and his strong feelings. After all, why should he have expected the others to keep him in their game forever, and why should he even care? He hadn't gone to the park expecting to play Frisbee; he didn't know the guys, so they didn't owe him anything; and he didn't lose anything of importance or value—yet somehow at a gut level he had been quite upset by the way the two fellows had excluded him. He turned his attention to the study of what happens when someone is rejected, excluded, or ignored.

Ostracism refers to being excluded, rejected, and ignored by others. The term comes from ancient Greece. One custom in Athens was that if a person behaved offensively or too aggressively, someone would write that person's name on a piece of broken pottery and put it in one of the large containers allocated in public places. These pieces of pottery, called *ostraka* (from which the word *ostracism* is derived) were collected and tallied, and if one person was named 6,000 times, the entire community agreed to

Lt. Henry Flipper was the first African American to graduate from West Point, in 1877. He was ostracized the entire time he was a student at West Point.

give that person the silent treatment for 10 years: no one would speak to or interact with that person.

Nowadays the term *ostracism* is used for smaller-scale practices of ignoring, as when a person refuses to speak to his or her spouse for a period of time. The close-knit Amish community will sometimes ostracize someone who is regarded as having violated the community's rules, such as by cheating someone, breaking religious rules, or misbehaving sexually. The silence is sometimes also used in military groups, such as if someone is believed to have cheated or broken the military code of honor. In such cases, no one speaks to the person or even acknowledges his existence. No one looks at you or responds to anything you say. Lt. Henry Flipper, the first black man to go to West Point, had to endure that treatment for his entire four years of college, because the other cadets believed that it was inappropriate for an African American to study there to become an officer in the army (Williams, 2001).

We opened this section with the brief story about Kip Williams being ostracized by strangers for a few minutes. Such experiences may be unpleasant, but when one is ostracized by people about whom

OSTRACISM being excluded, rejected, and ignored by others one cares deeply, or over a long period of time, the impact is almost certainly considerably worse (Williams, 2001). The fact that some people (like Williams himself in the Frisbee story) feel bad after even a few minutes of ostracism attests to the power and importance that the human psyche attaches to being socially accepted. To be ostracized for months at a time by a spouse or parent can be devastating.

Much ostracism is informal, and some targets do not even know why they are being ostracized. One woman reported in an interview that her father had ostracized her off and on since she was 12, and she was now 40. Despairing of ever having a warm connection to her family again, she moved halfway around the world. Eventually her siblings contacted her and told her that her father was expected to die soon. This was one last chance to make up, so she made the long flight home, booked into a hotel, and finally went to the hospital. Even then she was torn between the desire to connect and the fear of being rejected again. She stood outside her father's hospital room struggling within herself as to what to say and whether to go in. Summoning all her courage, she finally walked in and looked at the now frail but still recognizable man lying on the bed. He was surprised to see her. "Oh Daddy, please don't leave me," she said. The old man's eyes filled with tears, but then he turned his face to the wall and never said a word to her. That was the last time she ever saw him. (As the researcher, Williams found these stories so hard to bear that he had to hire research assistants to take over the rest of the interviews.)

EFFECTS OF REJECTION: INNER REACTIONS

Nobody thinks it's fun to be rejected, to be thrown out of a group, or to have your heart broken. The inner states that arise in response to rejection are almost uniformly negative. People who are repeatedly or continually ostracized by others over a long period of time report a broad variety of problems: pain, illness, depression, suicidal thoughts, eating disorders, helplessness, promiscuity (Williams, 2001; Williams & Zadro, 2005). Their self-esteem suffers, and they feel worthless. Some of them say life seems meaningless and pointless (Williams, 2001; Williams & Zadro, 2005).

Being rejected repeatedly can cause people to develop expectations that other people will reject them too. This forms the basis of a personality trait called **rejection sensitivity**. Sometimes these expectations make people so hypersensitive to possible rejection that they become reluctant to open up or get close to others for fear of being hurt. This can set up a vicious circle in which rejection sensitivity causes people to push others away (so as to reduce the risk of getting hurt), which then damages relationships, causing more rejection and increasing the sensitivity (Downey & Romero-Canyas, 2005; Sommer & Rubin, 2005).

The common experience "you hurt my feelings" is usually tied to an implicit message that "you don't care about our relationship" (Leary, Springer, Negel, Ansell, & Evans, 1998). Anything a person does or says that suggests the person doesn't care about you as much as you care about him or her, or doesn't care about the relationship as much as you do, can hurt your feelings. Obviously, rejection almost always involves the sense that the rejecter doesn't care about the relationship, so hurt feelings are common. Perhaps surprisingly, it doesn't seem to matter much whether people actively try to reject you or do it more casually or thoughtlessly. Your feelings may be deeply hurt even if the other person never intended to hurt you and never thought about you at all, such as if your lover forgot your birthday. Instead, the amount of hurt feelings depends on how much you care about the relationship and how clear a sign you received that the other person doesn't care as much (Leary, 2005).

Not all rejection produces an immediate wave of emotional distress, however. In fact, the initial reaction to rejection is often closer to numbness, "feeling nothing," than anxiety or sadness (Twenge, Catanese, & Baumeister, 2003). This is possibly rooted in biology: the body reacts to the pain of social rejection with the same response it uses to physical pain, and severe pain often deadens the body to all feeling (MacDonald & Leary, 2005; Panksepp, 1998, Panksepp, Herman, Conner, Bishop, & Scott, 1978; Panksepp, Najam, & Soares, 1980; Panksepp, Vilberg, Bean, Coy, & Kastin, 1978; see also DeWall & Baumeister, 2006). People who suffer terrible physical injuries, such as a broken bone or severe wound, may become numb, and sometimes athletes who are injured during a game don't fully feel the pain until the game is over. This could help explain why rejected people sometimes do antisocial things that might alienate other people further: They have become numb to the pain of social exclusion and hence don't realize that what they are doing might drive people away.

The numb or stunned feeling that comes from a strong (and especially an unexpected) rejection can interfere with normal psychological functioning. Rejection interferes with cognitive processing: In simple terms, rejection makes people temporarily stupid. They are less effective at processing complex information such as reasoning (Baumeister, Twenge,

---

REJECTION SENSITIVITY a tendency to expect rejection from others and to become hypersensitive to possible rejection

Food for Thought

Social Rejection and the Jar of Cookies

|||||||||||||||||||||||||||||||||||||||||||||||||||||||||||||||||||||||||||||||||||||||||||||||||||||||||||||||||||||||||||||

The love of your life, or at least the person you thought was the love of your life, storms out the door, saying "I don't ever want to see you again!" and calling you a variety of names like loser, creep, and hopelessly inept lover. According to one stereotype, you might go home and eat an entire cheesecake, or a whole gallon of ice cream.

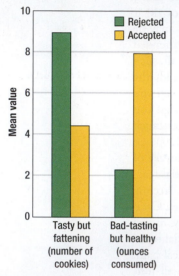

▶ **FIGURE 11.4 Rejection weakens self-control: Rejected persons ate more cookies but drank less.**

What does research say? The stereotype is actually fairly accurate. Social anxiety and fears of rejection are linked to eating binges and eating disorders (Blanchard & Frost, 1983; Chiodo, 1987; Gross & Rosen, 1988; Strober & Humphrey, 1987). In lab studies, rejected people are more prone to eat fattening or junk food (Twenge, Catanese, & Baumeister, 2002). This fits the more general pattern that rejection impairs self-regulation. People may want to eat cake, ice cream, or French fries much of the time, but usually they restrain these impulses because they know such foods are bad for them. After experiencing a rejection, however, the restraints are undermined. In one study, rejected people ate nearly twice as many cookies as people who had been accepted by a group (Baumeister et al., 2005). They also rated the cookies as tasting better, though the increased eating was statistically independent of the taste ratings, and some people ate more cookies even though they didn't find the taste particularly appealing. ("I didn't like the cookies, but I couldn't stop eating them!" said one participant who had been rejected by the group.)

The results seem to reflect a breakdown in control rather than an increase in hunger. If the food doesn't taste good but is good for you, rejection produces the opposite pattern (of reduced consumption). Rejected participants in one study were exhorted (both verbally and with a cash incentive) to consume a healthy but very bad-tasting beverage consisting of unsweetened Kool-Aid mixed with both water and vinegar. The brew resembled some medicines and health drinks that taste bad but are worth consuming for their health benefits. (Vinegar is actually good for you.) Participants who had just experienced social acceptance or had received neutral feedback made themselves consume about 8 ounces of the gross-tasting drink, but rejected people averaged only about 2 ounces (Baumeister et al., 2005; see ▶ **FIGURE 11.4**).

What these results have in common with the cookie-eating study is self-regulation. People need self-regulation to prevent themselves from eating junk foods, just as they need it to make themselves consume things they don't like but are good for them. On both counts, rejected people fared worse.

The bottom line is that rejected people do not self-regulate their eating as well as other people. They eat more junk food, and they consume less of what is good for them. ●

PhotoDisc

& Nuss, 2002). Rejection also undermines self-regulation: In the aftermath of rejection, people become more impulsive, more inclined to do something they will regret later (but that may seem appealing now) (Baumeister, DeWall, Ciarocco, & Twenge, 2005). Rejected people may, for example, blow their diets by eating a giant cake or a large serving of ice cream, or they may waste a large amount of money. See *Food for Thought* for some experimental findings on rejection and eating.

The conflict between social conscience and selfish impulse is an important theme of social psychology. Apparently, most people resolve this in favor of doing the sort of proper, generous, unselfish actions that society approves—but mainly if they enjoy and anticipate social acceptance. Rejection appears to change how people approach that conflict, making them more prone to favor the selfish impulse. Acting in a socially conscientious manner (such as waiting in line, paying taxes, or refraining from littering) often requires some degree of effort and sacrifice, and those sacrifices are compensated by the rewards of social acceptance. Accordingly, if people reject you, you may feel less inclined to make those efforts and sacrifices.

One more constructive response to rejection is to become more attuned to social cues and information about other people. Rejection makes people start to look about, cautiously, for new potential friends (Maner, DeWall, Baumeister, & Schaller, 2007). Participants in one experiment were rejected (or not) and then were permitted to read other people's diaries. The rejected people showed an increase in attention to the interpersonal events in the diaries, such as whether the diary writer had a date or played tennis with someone else (Gardner, Pickett,

& Brewer, 2000). When rejected people think they might have a chance to form a bond with someone or even to get back together with the person who rejected them, they focus their attention on this possibility and think at length about their possible relationship partners. Indeed, being able to think about people who do love you may shelter you from the pain of being rejected by someone else. Participants in another study who brought along a photograph of someone who loved them fared better and felt better after being rejected in the lab than did people who had no photos, and also better than someone who had brought photos of a favorite celebrity (Gardner et al., 2005).

BEHAVIORAL EFFECTS OF REJECTION

How should rejected people act? Conroy's novel *The Prince of Tides* tells the story of a young man from farm country who went to a major state university in a big city. At the end of fraternity rush, he was stunned to learn that not a single fraternity offered him a bid. By chance he met a young woman who was in a similar predicament; the two formed a bond, eventually falling in love and marrying. They decided that if they were not to spend all their time at parties and other Greek life functions, they would devote themselves to their studies, and they achieved top grades (in fact the woman graduated first in her class). They also resolved to help others: The man became a teacher and the woman a physician. This story shows an ideal, exemplary response to rejection, marked by forming new social bonds, improving intellectual work, and engaging in prosocial behavior.

Social psychology studies have painted a very different picture of how people react to rejection, however. As we saw earlier in this chapter, rejected participants show decreases rather than increases in intelligent thought, and indeed IQ test performance often drops substantially among people who have just been rejected. Instead of seeking to form new social bonds, rejected people often treat new interaction partners with skepticism, aloofness, avoidance, or even outright hostility (Twenge, Baumeister, Tice, & Stucke, 2001). Instead of devoting themselves to others, rejected people are typically less generous, less cooperative, and less helpful than others, and they are more willing to cheat or break rules of good behavior (Twenge, Ciarocco, Cuervo, Bartels, & Baumeister, 2004). They act in shortsighted, impulsive, even self-destructive ways (Twenge et al., 2002).

Repeated experiences of rejection or social exclusion (being left out of social groups) can create aggressive tendencies. One study surveyed high school students about various groups in their school, such as "jocks," "potheads," and popular kids. Students

School shooters are typically rejected teens who feel like social outcasts.

reported that they frequently imagined attacking, beating, shooting, and otherwise harming people in groups that had rejected or humiliated them (Gaertner & Iuzzini, 2005).

School violence grabbed America's attention in the 1990s. The media publicized a series of incidents in which students took guns or other weapons to school and killed other students. Sometimes these were precisely targeted, such as when one killed his ex-girlfriend's new boyfriend. Others seemed more random, such as when a student opened fire in a cafeteria where 400 students were dining, and the widely spraying bullets killed several students and wounded quite a few more.

What drove these students to lethal violence? One common theme was feeling socially excluded. It was never the most popular, well-loved students who brought guns to school and opened fire; rather, it was those who felt picked on, excluded, and rejected by others. A careful investigation of 15 of these incidents concluded that at least 13 of them involved young men who were going through long and painful experiences of being rejected by others (Leary, Kowalski, Smith, & Phillips, 2003).

Aggression and rejection are linked in multiple ways. Aggression can lead to rejection. For example, young children in particular tend to exclude and avoid other children who start fights or engage in bullying (though as the students reach adolescence, this pattern of rejection diminishes, and aggressive adolescents are sometimes accepted by others; Juvonen & Gross, 2005). In lab studies, students who receive an experience of being rejected by others tend to show high levels of aggression toward someone who offends or provokes them—and, ominously, they

You can be lonely even when surrounded by people.

are also more aggressive than average toward neutral people who haven't done anything bad to them (Twenge et al., 2001).

There are a few glimmers of hope. In particular, if the rejected person has some prospect of being accepted or included, either back into the group that excluded him or her or into a new group, then the rejected person's behavior is more positive and prosocial. If someone comes along and is kind to the rejected person, such as by praising the person or being nice in other ways, the rejected person may respond favorably, as by refraining from aggression, by cooperating, or by conforming (Ouwerkerk, Kerr, Gallucci, & Van Lange, 2005; Williams & Zadro, 2005). Rejected people who have a chance to form a new friendship may engage in positive nonverbal behaviors, such as mimicking the nonverbal behavior of the new person (Lakin & Chartrand, 2005); as we have seen, nonverbal mimicry is a positive behavior that helps people come to like each other.

LONELINESS

Loneliness is the painful feeling of wanting more human contact or connection than you have. The

stereotype of the lonely person is a socially inept loser who doesn't know how to get along with others, who perhaps has little to offer other people, who has few or no friends, and who spends much of the time alone, perhaps envying other people who have friends and lovers—but recent research has begun to paint a very different picture. There are very few differences between lonely and nonlonely people. They do not differ in intelligence or attractiveness. They spend about the same amount of time interacting with other people. Thus, lonely does not mean alone: Loneliness is essentially independent of the quantity of relationships or social interaction (Wheeler, Reis, & Nezlek, 1983).

Not all lonely people are the same, either. Researchers have recognized variations in loneliness. It may be quite common for people to feel a temporary loneliness when they move to a new place and are separated from their friends and family. In many cases those feelings go away as soon as the person starts making friends at the new home. Other people, however, suffer from chronic loneliness that may last for months or years. In general, when researchers speak of lonely people, they are referring to people who suffer chronic loneliness that has lasted for a substantial period of time and is not showing signs of letting up.

By and large, the lonely do not lack social skills, though they somehow fail to use them as much as others (they can get along well with others but they don't; Cacioppo & Hawkley, 2005). The main deficiency that has been established is that lonely people are poorer at figuring out other people's emotional states (Pickett & Gardner, 2005). This lack of emotional sensitivity could be either a cause of loneliness (because it makes it harder to attract and keep friends), or possibly a result, or perhaps both.

These findings indicate that loneliness is much more complex than simply a failure to find other people to be with. You can be lonely living in a densely populated city like New York. You can even be lonely when married, though married people are on average a bit less likely to be lonely than single people (Peplau & Perlman, 1982; Russell, Peplau, & Cutrona, 1980). Being far from home is one strong predictor of loneliness (Cacioppo et al., 2000), which is probably one reason that in many cultures people live their entire lives close to their place of birth and are reluctant to relocate, even for a seemingly great career opportunity.

The long road to social acceptance is a theme to which we have returned repeatedly, and apparently some people find the road too long and difficult— but they pay a price for not making the full effort. Staying close to family is one strategy that seems to shorten the road, in the sense that if your family lives nearby, you have easier and readier access to

LONELINESS the painful feeling of wanting more human contact or connection than you have

some forms of social acceptance than if you live far away.

Loneliness originates in a gap between the amount or quality of social relationships that you have and the amount or quality that you want. In principle this can be because you want a normal amount but have less than that—or because you have a normal amount but want a great deal more (Gardner et al., 2005).

In theory, loneliness can also be an issue of either the quality or the quantity of relationships. You might be lonely because you don't have enough contact with others, or because the time you spend with others does not satisfy your needs. In practice, the data suggest that most loneliness stems from a lack of close, satisfying relationships. Lonely people may spend plenty of time with other people, but just talking to many different people is not good enough, and they may suffer if they do not feel that enough people care about them and want to maintain a long-term, close relationship. Put another way, loneliness is typically rooted in the quality rather than the quantity of social interaction (Cacioppo & Hawkley, 2005): Lonely people spend plenty of time with others, but they do not come away from these interactions feeling satisfied. To be sure, most research on loneliness has focused on people who live in large cities or universities, and people who are lonely when there are many others around are probably suffering from a lack of quality rather than quantity. Living far from others, such as if you worked as a forest ranger in the Arctic, might produce loneliness for lack of quantity of interaction. Still, in the modern world, most loneliness is linked to quality rather than quantity of interaction.

Relationships to large groups or organizations are relevant for men, though apparently not for women. That is, a man who has few or no close friends but feels strongly connected to his corporation or university or sports team will probably not suffer from loneliness, but a woman in the same circumstance will typically still feel lonely (Gardner et al., 2004).

Some people can even stave off loneliness by forming attachments to celebrities or people they see on television. Women who watch many situation comedies feel less lonely than other women who have the same number of friends and lovers but do not watch so many shows (Kanazawa, 2002). Apparently the televised characters come to feel like friends and family to them, especially if they watch the same shows regularly and develop feelings about the characters.

Other people fight off loneliness by forming quasi-relationships with nonhuman entities. For example, they might bond with a dog or cat, or treat a potted plant like a person. Some people even name their cars and treat them like family members (Gardner et al., 2005). A vivid depiction of such a strategy

© Thomas Northcut/Getty Images

A relationship with your dog can stave off loneliness.

was provided in the movie *Castaway*, in which Tom Hanks played a Federal Express worker who was stranded on a desert island for many months with no human contact at all. To keep himself sane and stave off loneliness, he painted a face on a volleyball that washed up on the island with him, named the ball "Wilson," and talked to it as if it were a close human friend. In fact, he almost risked his life to "rescue" Wilson when the ball floated away from his raft.

Loneliness takes its toll on the body. Lonely people sleep as much as nonlonely people, but the sleep is not as good or as refreshing, and they may end up feeling chronically tired. Loneliness also seems to be bad for one's physical health. Lonely people take longer than others to recover from stress, illness, or injury (Cacioppo & Hawkley, 2005). The poor health stems from several factors, including sleep problems. A good sleep is very healthy, but the poor sleep of lonely people prevents their body from getting the rest it needs. They spend the same amount of time in bed as others, but the lonely person is more prone to lie there awake or to wake up during the night (Cacioppo, Hawkley, Berntson, et al., 2002, Cacioppo, Hawkley, Crawford, et al., 2002).

WHAT LEADS TO SOCIAL REJECTION?

We have seen that being rejected or socially excluded is generally painful and harmful. Why do people inflict such rejection on each other? Several lines of research are starting to furnish answers.

Children are rejected by their peers for three main reasons (Juvonen & Gross, 2005). First, aggressive children are rejected, possibly because children do not like violence and will avoid bullies and others whom they regard as dangerous. Second, some children withdraw from contact with others, and they in turn are rejected by others. The avoidance of withdrawn, isolated children escalates into adolescence, thereby creating a particular problem for people who move toward adulthood becoming more and more disconnected from social groups.

Third, and related to the other two, deviance leads to rejection. Children who are different in any obvious fashion are more likely to be rejected. Children reject others who look different, act differently, or otherwise seem different. Being handicapped, belonging to a racial minority, speaking differently, not knowing the locally favored style of music or clothing, not watching the same television shows or listening to the same music, having an unusual family arrangement (e.g., living with grandmother rather than parents, or having two daddies or two mommies), or speaking with an accent—any of these can cause a child to be rejected by others. Even being clearly less intelligent or more intelligent than most of the other kids in the class can elicit rejection. This does not mean that

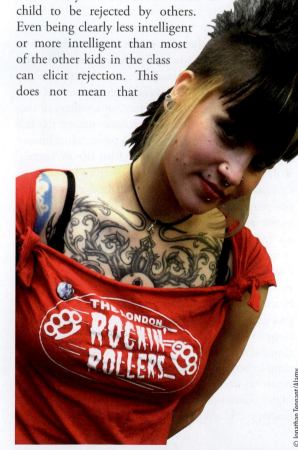

Even adults are often threatened by people who look "different."

© Jonathan Tennant/Alamy

the children make a deliberate or conscious decision that they do not approve of someone's personality or lifestyle. In terms of the duplex mind, the reaction against those who are different is probably automatic, and the reaction that leads children to reject others is probably rooted in automatic processes.

Among adults, the simplest and most general explanation for rejection is deviance (Wright, Giammarino, & Parad, 1986). Groups reject others who are different in important or meaningful ways from the rest of the group. Indeed, groups seem to find deviants threatening, and they are more bothered by a nonconformist or poor performer who is in the group than by one who is outside the group (Hogg, 2005). This is important evidence of the importance of group solidarity. Someone who is different from your group, but is not part of your group, doesn't threaten the unity of your group. In contrast, someone who is different to the same degree but still belongs to your group undermines group unity. Groups reject insiders more than outsiders for the same degree of deviance (Marques & Yzerbyt, 1988).

Bad performance by a member of your own group is rated more negatively than an identically bad performance by someone who is not in the ingroup (Marques & Paez, 1994, Marques, Abrams, Páez, & Hogg, 2001). Conversely, good performance by a member of the ingroup is rated more positively than identically good performance by someone outside the ingroup. Apparently, groups want their members to be successful, and they will reject members who are prone to failure.

Much deviance involves breaking the rules. Deviants don't do what they are expected or supposed to do. As we saw in the chapter on prosocial behavior, groups can only operate successfully if most people follow most of the rules most of the time, so each act of deviance presents some problem or threat to the success of the group. Deviants therefore undermine the quality of life for the rest of the group. If no one ever steals, for example, you don't need to worry about being robbed, so you don't need to lock your doors, buy security systems, pay for insurance, and take other precautions. The Qur'an (the holy book of Islam) prescribes that societies should cut off the hands of thieves, even someone who just steals a piece of fruit. This strikes many people in other cultures as unfair and excessive, but most likely the underlying sentiment is that the thief isn't just taking someone's piece of fruit—he or she is undermining the trust and security that everyone else would otherwise enjoy. A severe punishment might be justified if it would actually prevent people from doing things that spoil group life for everyone else. In other words, we miss the point if we view Islamic law as cruel or overly punitive for cutting off someone's hand as punishment for stealing a piece of fruit: The hand is cut off because stealing in general undermines trust and degrades the whole fabric of social relationships.

A further reason that groups may reject deviants lies in the so-called **bad apple effect** (Colman, 1982). This effect is named after the cliché that one bad apple can spoil the whole barrel, because the rot that infects one apple can spread to other apples. Applied to social behavior, the implication is that one person who breaks the rules can inspire other people to follow his or her example. As the example of stealing illustrated, the issue from the point of view of society as a whole is that if some people get away with stealing, then others may be tempted to steal also, and chaos can result. Sadly, bad apples seem to inspire more copycats than good apples: People are more easily swayed to follow the example of deviant misbehavior than of virtuous, exemplary, or heroic action (Ouwerkerk et al., 2005). Thus, if you break the group's rules, the group may believe it is best to reject or expel you, lest others follow your bad example.

The threat of being expelled or rejected does seem to be an important force in producing good behavior. When participants were expelled from a group after they had followed the example of a bad apple—and then were reinstated in the group, ostensibly due to an accident or technical problem—they subsequently behaved much better and more prosocially than others, generally following the example of the good rather than the bad apples (Ouwerkerk et al., 2005). Even the threat of being expelled is sometimes enough to discourage people from following bad apples (Kerr et al., in press). This is probably an important explanation for why rejection is so powerful and important in life. Human groups need people to follow rules and conform to shared values, and the threat of rejection is a strong force encouraging them to do so.

The link between rejection and deviance has been confirmed in research on families. A large survey (Fitness, 2005) asked people what were the worst things that family members do to each other, and how these behaviors related to being rejected by the family. The most commonly cited bad behaviors were seen as justifying expelling someone from the family; most of these behaviors involved violating the basic rules or expectations that govern how family members are supposed to treat each other. These included rejection, abandonment, disloyalty, sexual abuse, becoming (or marrying) a loser or criminal, and betrayal.

This research was not meant to pass moral judgment on whether such behaviors justify expulsion from the family. The point is simply that the threat of expulsion discourages people from doing those things to their loved ones. The net result is that family members treat each other better, and the family bonds remain stronger. The (very real) pain of rejection serves the function of holding families and other groups together.

ROMANTIC REJECTION AND UNREQUITED LOVE

Most people experience romantic rejection at some point. They wanted someone for a romantic partner, but that person failed to match those feelings and declined any offers of a relationship. These failed romances can occasionally develop into serious problems, ranging from suicidal despair to violent stalking.

One impressive early paper on romantic rejection used attribution theory to understand the reasons women gave for refusing an offer of a date (Folkes, 1982). As we saw in Chapter 5, attributions can be sorted along three dimensions: internal/ external, stable/unstable, and global/specific. The reasons the women privately held for refusing dates tended to be internal to the man, stable, and global: There was something seriously wrong with him, as she saw it (internal). Also, his deficit was viewed as relatively permanent (stable) and was viewed as extending to many areas of his life (global). But the reasons women told the men were external, unstable, and specific. Thus, when a man she didn't fancy asked her for a date on Friday, she might say that she couldn't go out with him that night because her parents were coming to visit. This reason is external (it has nothing to do with him), unstable (it pertains only to that particular night, or perhaps that weekend), and highly specific. People are often surprised when the romance-seekers they reject come around again and keep trying, but trying again would seem natural under those circumstances. She can't go out with him this Friday because her parents are coming to visit—so why not ask her out for next Friday? In contrast, if she said "I can't go out with you because you're not very good-looking, you don't have enough money, you're not smart enough for me, and you smell bad," he would probably be much less likely to respond with "OK, then how about next Friday?" All the reasons for her refusing the offer for this Friday would also apply to next Friday.

Unrequited love is defined as a situation in which one person loves another but the other does not

---

BAD APPLE EFFECT the idea that one person who breaks the rules can inspire other people to break the rules also

UNREQUITED LOVE a situation in which one person loves another but the other does not return that love

off the mark.com   by Mark Parisi

THIS JUDGE IS KNOWN FOR HIS STRICT RESTRAINING ORDERS...

offthemark.com   ©2008 MARK PARISI DIST. BY UFS INC.

Restraining orders for stalkers can sometimes be strict. Don't stalk!

return that love. It is a common experience among adolescents and young adults, and most single people have at least one experience a year in which they have a crush on someone who does not have similar feelings toward them, or (conversely) in which they do not reciprocate someone else's feelings of romantic attraction toward them. The two roles are quite different and go with very different types of feelings. Most men and women have experience in both roles, though men have more experiences of being the rejected lovers, and women are more often in the rejecting role (Baumeister et al., 1993; Hill, Blakemore, & Drumm, 1997).

The rejected lovers experience a kind of emotional roller-coaster, in which they alternate between hopeful, exciting, passionate feelings and insecure despair. They suffer intensely, but they are also drawn to the good parts, and they tend to look back on a failed love with some bittersweet affection. In contrast, the rejecters tend to think there was nothing good about the episode, and they are more likely to wish the whole thing had never happened (Baumeister & Wotman, 1992; Baumeister et al., 1993).

Rejection is felt as a blow to one's self-esteem. Broken-hearted lovers often wonder if something is wrong with them, or if they somehow did something

STALKING persisting in romantic, courtship, or other behaviors that frighten and harass the rejecter in a relationship

wrong that prevented the other from becoming romantically attracted to them. They try to find some way to bolster their self-esteem, and nothing seems to work quite so well as finding a new lover.

Broken-hearted lovers may engage in stalking behaviors toward the rejecter. **Stalking** refers to persisting in romantic or courtship behavior (e.g., repeated phone calls) or other behaviors that frighten and harass the rejecter in the relationship (Bjerregaard, 2000; Cupach & Spitzberg, 2000; Davis & Frieze, 2000). Although unrequited love is something that both genders experience, women are disproportionately the victims of stalkers. Data from the National Violence Against Women (NVAW) Survey showed that women report being stalked in the context of current or former romantic partners (marriage, cohabitation, or dating), whereas men rarely reported being stalked in the context of a current or former romantic relationship (Tjaden & Thoennes, 1998). Male and female victims of stalking reported feeling that their safety was being threatened and carried weapons to protect themselves far more than nonvictims (45% vs. 29%) Thus, the sting of unrequited love may lead rejected people to stalk their rejecters, and this tendency is particularly strong among rejected men.

For the rejecters, the problem is not self-esteem but guilt. As the concept of a need to belong implies, people are designed to form and maintain relationships, not to reject them, and most people find that refusing someone's offer of love is difficult. They feel guilty for hurting the other person, and to minimize feelings of guilt they strive to convince themselves that they never led the other person on, so that the other person's love and resultant suffering were not their fault. Guilt is a central part of the difficulty of rejecting someone, and this difficulty is probably linked to a basic fact about human nature: Humans are programmed to form and maintain social bonds, and breaking them goes against the grain. Even if you don't want someone's love, it is difficult and sometimes painful to refuse it.

The message of rejection is difficult for both persons. The rejecter feels guilty and wants to avoid hurting the other person's feelings. The person who is about to be rejected is often eager to grasp at straws and seize on any sign of possible encouragement. It is therefore no wonder that the message often does not get communicated very well: The one doesn't want to say it, and the other doesn't want to hear it.

As we have seen, the road to social acceptance is often long. Rarely does it seem longer or harder than in unrequited love. Loving someone who does not return your feelings can be extremely discouraging and painful. And even rejecting someone's love is not usually easy.

Reprinted by permission of Atlantic Feature Syndicate/Mark Parisi.

WHAT MAKES US HUMAN?   Putting the Cultural Animal in Perspective

Much of what we have seen in this chapter is not unique to human beings. Many social animals seek social acceptance and try to avoid being rejected. Good-looking, rewarding, similar animals are attractive. Deviants are vulnerable to rejection. Most social animals (and that category includes nearly all the close biological relatives of humankind) want to be allowed to belong to a group and want to avoid being rejected or excluded.

There are, however, some special features, or at least twists, to the human quest for belongingness. The basic need to belong may be the same in humans as in other animals, but some of the processes are different. People use language to form and maintain relationships, and this enables them to disclose much more information about themselves. People can be similar or dissimilar on many dimensions that other animals cannot process: religion, favorite sports team, zodiac sign, political opinions, and many more. More broadly, humans traverse a long road to social acceptance, which means they have to spend a large and ongoing amount of time and energy to secure and maintain their place in the social group. A bird or frog can gain access to the group simply by being there and joining in, but humans who seek social acceptance need money, skills, the right clothes, an understanding of complex social norms, and much else.

Human social systems are more complex than those of other creatures, so there is more emphasis on being special or unique. We have seen that being similar is important for attraction, in humans as in other animals, but culture also places value on diversity. A culture is a system, and a system made up of all identical parts is not much of a system. Whether you are finding a niche in your career or persuading a loved one to choose you instead of a romantic rival, you may often feel some pressure to establish yourself as different or special. Put very simply, if you can do something useful that no one else in your small group can do (find a particular food, make fire, install plumbing, fix computers, prepare income tax returns, kick long field goals), you are safe: They cannot afford to exclude you. The strategy of promoting social acceptance via unique abilities is largely unknown outside of human beings, but it is very important in our human social life. Put more simply, most social animals seek acceptance via similarity, and humans do too, but only humans cultivate social acceptance by trying to be special or different.

Another striking difference is that human relationships are not just between the two people involved: They often require some validation or recognition by the culture. Animals have families, but these do not have legal status. If the father becomes separated from his offspring, he is not required—except among humans—to pay child support year after year. Both humans and animals experience romantic attraction and sexual mating, but only humans formalize the bond with a wedding license and a ceremony, so that every member of the large social group recognizes the bond and knows what it means. Animals can break up just by wandering off, whereas married humans require a divorce court. In the same vein, many animals neglect or even abuse their young, but only humans have formal systems to stop this, such as police or legal intervention. Animals may sometimes work together to build something, but only humans sign contracts or incorporate their partnerships or sue each other when the project fails.

Divorce courts, police interventions, and lawsuits may seem like an unpleasant aspect of human relationships. What have we done to ourselves? Yet these institutions represent something very positive: Human society has sought to protect people from betrayal and abuse by their relationship partners. Culture recognizes, validates, and encourages relationships, and ultimately it reduces some of the risk and suffering that go with the process of connecting with someone. If two animals work together to get some food and then the bigger one takes it all, the smaller one is simply out of luck. The more vulnerable human being, however, may go to court or try some other cultural recourse, and because the system is there, the stronger one is less likely to cheat or betray in the first place. In such ways, culture makes relationships stronger and better.

chapter summary

THE NEED TO BELONG

- Social acceptance means getting others to like you, respect you, approve of you, and in general want to have some kind of relationship with you.
- Rejection, also known as social exclusion, means that others exclude you, so that you are not able to form or keep a social bond with them.
- Testosterone, a hormone associated with masculinity, is a mixed blessing, both for the individual who has it and for others connected with that person; it is better suited to finding mates than to maintaining stable families.
- The need to belong, defined as the desire to form and maintain close, lasting relationships, is a powerful drive within the human psyche.
- According to social brain theory, the driving force behind the evolution of intelligence and the brain was the need to understand others so as to form and maintain social relationships.
- People usually form relationships easily and readily but are reluctant to let relationships end.
- The need to belong has two parts:
  - Regular social contact with others
  - Close, stable, mutually intimate contact
- Failure to satisfy the need to belong leads to significant health problems, up to and including a higher risk of death.

ATTRACTION: WHO LIKES WHOM?

- Ingratiation is actively to try to make someone like you.
- Similarity is a common and significant cause of attraction.
- People prepare for social interaction by shifting to become more similar to the people they expect to interact with.

- People with the trait of high self-monitoring seek to maximize each social situation, whereas those low in that trait pay more attention to permanent connections and feelings rather than fluctuating ones.
- The matching hypothesis states that people tend to pair up with others who are equally attractive.
- As culture progresses and forms large, complex, interacting groups, there may be more need for complementarity, but when people pick their friends and lovers, they still tend to look for those who are similar to themselves.
- In general, favors are a good way to promote liking.
- Praising people is a reliable way to get them to like you.
- Liking begets (reciprocal) liking.
- Mimicry is often successful as a means of increasing liking.
- Propinquity (being near someone on a regular basis) causes attraction, but it also can to lead to conflict and friction.
- Familiarity breeds liking.
- The social allergy effect refers to the finding that a partner's annoying habits grow more annoying with repeated exposure.
- When all else is equal, most people show a substantial preference for attractive over unattractive others.
- The what is beautiful is good effect suggests that people assume that physically attractive people will be superior to others on many other traits.
- Attractive children are more popular with other children than their less attractive peers, and teachers like them more too.
- Evolutionary psychologists generally think that beauty is linked to signs of being a good mate and potential partner,

which especially means being young and healthy.
- Symmetry is a powerful source of beauty.
- Average faces are more attractive than individual faces.
- Women are more attracted to men who look rich and successful.

REJECTION

- Ostracism refers to being excluded, rejected, and ignored by others.
- Being rejected repeatedly can cause people to develop expectations that others will reject them, resulting in a personality trait called rejection sensitivity.
- "You hurt my feelings" is usually tied to an implicit message that "you don't care about our relationship."
- The initial reaction to rejection is often closer to numbness than to anxiety or sadness. It can interfere with normal psychological and cognitive functioning.
- Rejection undermines self-regulation and often makes people behave selfishly rather than acting in a socially conscientious manner.
- Repeated experiences of rejection or social exclusion can create aggressive tendencies.
- Aggression can lead to rejection.
- Loneliness is the painful feeling of wanting more human contact or connection (either more quantity or quality of relationships) than you have.
- There are very few differences between lonely and nonlonely people, with the major exception that lonely people are poorer at figuring out other people's emotional states.
- Loneliness is bad for physical health.
- Children are rejected by their peers for three main reasons:
  - Because they are aggressive or violent

- Because they are withdrawn or socially isolated
- Because they are different from other children in some way
- Among adults, the simplest and most general explanation for rejection is deviance.
- Groups reject insiders more than outsiders for the same degree of deviance.

- The bad apple effect suggests that one person who breaks the rules can inspire other people to follow his or her example.
- Humans are programmed to form and maintain social bonds; breaking them goes against the grain and makes the rejecter feel guilty.

WHAT MAKES US HUMAN? PUTTING THE CULTURAL ANIMAL IN PERSPECTIVE

- Human social systems are more complex than those of other creatures, so there is more emphasis on each individual being special or unique.
- Human relationships often require some validation or recognition by the culture.

Key Terms

Attraction 325
Bad apple effect 345
Ingratiation 329
Loneliness 342
Matching hypothesis 330

Need to belong 327
Ostracism 338
Propinquity 333
Reinforcement theory 331

Rejection (social exclusion) 325
Rejection sensitivity 339
Self-monitoring 330
Social acceptance 325

Social allergy effect 334
Stalking 346
Unrequited love 345
What is beautiful is good effect 335

[Quiz Yourself] Answers

1. The Need to Belong
Answers: 1=b, 2=d, 3=c, 4=b

2. Attraction: Who Likes Whom?
Answers: 1=b, 2=c, 3=b, 4=b

3. Rejection
Answers: 1=c, 2=c, 3=b, 4=a

Media Learning Resources

Make sure you check out the complete set of learning resources and study tools below. If your instructor did not order these items with your new book, go to www.ichapters.com to purchase Cengage Learning print and digital products.

Social Psychology and Human Nature BOOK COMPANION WEBSITE

www.cengage.com/psychology/baumeister
Visit your book companion website, where you will find flash cards, practice quizzes, Internet links, and more to help you study.

CENGAGENOW™ JUST WHAT YOU NEED TO KNOW NOW!

Spend time on what you need to master rather than on information you have already learned. Take a pre-test for this chapter, and CengageNOW will generate a personalized study plan based on your results. The study plan will identify the topics you need to review and direct you to online resources to help you master those topics. You can then take a post-test to help you determine the concepts you have mastered and what you will still need to work on. Try it out! Go to www.cengage.com/login to sign in with an access code or to purchase access to this product.

CLASSIC AND CONTEMPORARY VIDEOS STUDENT CD-ROM

To see videos on the topics and experiments discussed in this chapter and to learn more about the research that social psychologists are doing today, go to the Student CD-ROM.

SOCIAL PSYCH LAB

These unique online labs give you the opportunity to become a participant in actual experiments, including re-creations of classic and contemporary research studies.

chapter 12

Close Relationships: Passion, Intimacy, and Sexuality

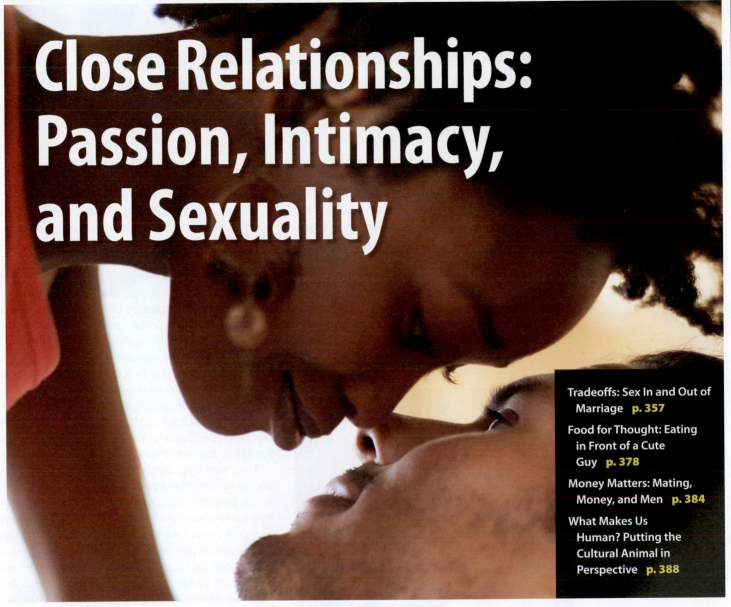

© Corbis Super RF/Alamy

Tradeoffs: Sex In and Out of Marriage **p. 357**

Food for Thought: Eating in Front of a Cute Guy **p. 378**

Money Matters: Mating, Money, and Men **p. 384**

What Makes Us Human? Putting the Cultural Animal in Perspective **p. 388**

WHAT IS LOVE? p. 354
Passionate and Companionate Love **p. 354**
Love and Culture **p. 355**
Love Across Time **p. 356**
Sternberg's Triangle **p. 358**

DIFFERENT TYPES OF RELATIONSHIPS p. 359
Exchange Versus Communal **p. 359**
Attachment **p. 361**
Loving People Who Love Themselves **p. 364**

MAINTAINING RELATIONSHIPS p. 365
I Love You More Each Day (?) **p. 366**
Investing in Relationships That Last **p. 366**
Thinking Styles of Couples **p. 367**
Being Yourself: Is Honesty the Best Policy? **p. 369**

SEXUALITY p. 372
Theories of Sexuality **p. 372**
Sex and Gender **p. 374**

Homosexuality **p. 377**
Extradyadic Sex **p. 379**
Jealousy and Possessiveness **p. 381**
Culture, Female Sexuality, and the Double Standard **p. 386**

CHAPTER SUMMARY p. 389

Their own marriage crumbled, and years later Diana said she never forgot the sound of her mother's footsteps crunching on the gravel driveway as she left their home on the day of their divorce in 1969. In 1975 her father became the Earl of Spencer, which automatically elevated his family (including Diana) into the aristocracy. At school, Diana was a mediocre student but a good athlete. She did not go on to college. Instead she worked at a series of dull jobs.

In 1977 Diana and her older sister Sarah were invited to a party, where they met Charles, the Prince of Wales. Sarah was originally regarded as the more promising girlfriend for him, and he dated her for a while, but soon Charles found himself attracted to the blossoming young beauty Diana. By 1980 they were seeing each other frequently, and the attraction was mutual.

The match seemed improbable, which lent the entire episode the aura of a fairy tale. On their wedding day, he was 32 years old, while she was still 19. He was in line to become king of England, while she was working as a kindergarten assistant. The public continued to see him as a somewhat odd-looking and awkward fellow, while Diana was soon accepted as one of the world's great beauties, and her wardrobe became a source of fascination and imitation throughout the world. Their first public appearances were marked by an easygoing rapport between them and by a seemingly obvious pleasure in each other's company. When their engagement was announced, reporters asked them whether they were in love, and both said "Yes!" though Charles added "whatever love means" (a line that certainly won him no points as a dashing, romantic suitor!).

Their wedding, shortly before Diana's 20th birthday, was an international event. An estimated 600,000 people lined the streets to watch the wedding party go from Buckingham Palace to St. Paul's Cathedral. Millions of people around the world watched it on television. Diana later said that on that day she was "so in love with my husband that I couldn't take my eyes off him" and that she felt herself the luckiest girl in the world. And even if the prince did look a bit odd, the lavishly spectacular wedding seemed a perfect ending for a fairy tale in which an ordinary schoolgirl grew up, fell in love with a (sort of) handsome prince, married him in the so-called wedding of the century, thence to settle down and wait until they would someday become king and queen. In reality, the fairy tale was not over but would take a non-fairy-tale turn in the coming months.

Diana quickly became pregnant and produced a son who also would become heir to the throne, and two years later the couple had another son. The public took Princess Di into its heart, and she responded by trying to be perfect in her role. She supported charity causes, visited hospitals, and did other good deeds, all the while trying to raise her royal sons properly. Everything seemed perfect.

Prince Charles and Princess Diana on the balcony of Buckingham Palace on their wedding day, July 29, 1981.

AP Photo/Tim Graham Picture Library

But things were not perfect, and indeed the marriage went downhill, first secretly, then more publicly. Her husband, Charles, did not come to love her as she wanted. Indeed, when they first got engaged, he privately told a friend he did not love her yet (though he expected that he would soon). More problematically, he retained strong ties to his mistress, Camilla Parker Bowles, even inviting her to the wedding, and continued his sexual affair with her after the wedding. Camilla Parker Bowles was also married at the time and had two children of her own. Diana later said in a BBC interview, "There were three of us in the marriage. It was a bit crowded." Her assessment won her widespread sympathy, though some subsequent reports have claimed that her comment was not entirely honest because at that time there was a fourth person in the marriage too—namely, Diana's lover.

Apparently, once the princess concluded that she was not getting the love she wanted from her husband, she sought it elsewhere. She had an affair with a handsome riding instructor on the palace staff. He fell hard for her. After five years, she broke it off. (The head of palace security took the riding instructor aside and told him how to deal with the breakup: "Well, look, you know, if it's over, consider yourself to have been in a very privileged position. Really, that's the end of it. Live with that memory.") She was hurt when he wrote a book about his affair with her.

Another affair, this time with an art dealer, also ended badly when the man broke up with her and went back to his wife. The man started receiving nuisance hangup calls, and after several hundred of these he went to the police, who traced the calls to the princess. (In some contexts, such behavior can be considered stalking, though no one is likely to prosecute a royal princess for it.) Another affair with a professional athlete also led to a highly publicized blowup.

These were hard times for Diana. She developed psychological symptoms, including eating disorders and self-mutilation (cutting herself). She worried that the royal family was plotting to ruin her image and even to kill her. She was intensely lonely and depressed. She heard her separation from Charles announced on the radio and thought "the fairy tale [has] come to an end." Four years later, in 1996, they were officially divorced.

In 1997, she thought she had finally found a new love to satisfy her. She told a friend, "I'm no longer lonely. I know what love is now." There were several men in her life, and there is some dispute as to which relationship she meant. We may never know, because on the last day of August she was killed in a car crash near Paris. Her death provoked an international outpouring of grief, including huge demonstrations of affection in London and elsewhere. The authorities were shocked by how many people came to express their grief and how many people's lives she had seemingly touched in some way. It is estimated that 6 million people crowded the streets

Prince Charles and his lover Camilla Parker Bowles who later became his second wife.

of London for her funeral procession. A giant crowd listened via loudspeakers outside the funeral ceremony, and their applause was so loud that the people indoors were disturbed to hear it.

The public reaction to her death was so strong that the authorities planned a ceremony a year later to commemorate its anniversary. Turnout was much lower than expected. Apparently the public had gotten over its grief. The love of the public is short-lived, resembling passion more than intimacy or commitment. (There was, however, a revival of affection for Diana in 2005, when Charles announced his intention to marry his longtime mistress Camilla. Diana's fans protested the marriage.)

Love and other close, intimate relationships make up a major part of life. Most people in North America today, and probably most people in most other modern cultures, believe that to miss out on love and intimacy would be to live a poorer, emptier life, compared to people who experience those things. In Chapter 11 we saw that having social bonds is linked to better mental and physical health on all sorts of measures. Many of those advantages have been specifically linked to marriage: People who marry live longer and healthier lives than people who never marry, and people who stay married live longer and better than those who divorce (Horowitz, White, & Howell-White, 1996; Hu & Goldman, 1990; also see Johnson, McGue, Krueger, & Bouchard, 2004).

Some qualifications are needed, before you start thinking "I'd better marry somebody, anybody, as soon as possible!" Unhappy marriages produce considerable stress and other bad effects that can nullify the advantages of marriage and in some cases leave people worse off married than alone (e.g., Coyne & DeLongis, 1986; DeLongis, Folkman, & Lazarus, 1988; Kiecolt-Glaser, Fisher, Ogrocki, Stout, Speicher, & Glaser, 1987; Myers, 1992). Thus, not just marriage but happy marriage may be the most important thing. There may also be a gender difference, though more data are needed. To men, the big difference is being married versus not married, but for women, the quality of the relationship (happy versus unhappy) seems more powerful (Kiecolt-Glaser & Newton, 2001).

In Chapter 1 we discussed how the conclusions from research depend on the methods. The data on the advantages of marriage have some built-in ambiguities because of the research methods. We saw in Chapter 1 that research cannot easily establish causality unless it uses random assignment to conditions, and of course no researchers can randomly assign people to be married versus single. It is possible that people who are healthier and saner to start with are more likely to marry, so their better health might not be a result of the marriage. Research has shown that there are some inborn, genetic factors that steer some people toward marriage and others toward remaining single (Johnson et al., 2004). That is, married people are genetically different from lifelong single people, on average, and some of those differences could contribute to the differences in health and longevity. For example, a person born with a genetic problem that caused many health problems over the years might find it harder than a healthy person to marry (because people prefer to marry healthy, attractive partners) and also might be more likely to die at a young age (because of the health problems).

Then again, some of the differences in outcomes are probably caused by the benefits of marriage. For example, Catholic priests do not live as long or as healthy lives as do Protestant ministers (Bernard, 1982). It does not seem likely that genetic traits steer men into Catholic versus Protestant faith—so the difference in how long they live is more likely due to the fact that only the Protestant clergy marry. ■

What Is Love?

"I'm a 17-year-old girl and I think I'm in love, but my parents say I don't know what real love is. What is love and how can I tell if I'm really in love?" (Reinisch, 1990, p. 89). Thus wrote a young woman to the Kinsey Institute, asking an earnest and personal question—and one that most people have struggled with at some point.

No simple answer can be given. Part of the problem is that there is more than one kind of love, so more than one phenomenon needs to be explained. The same person might feel different kinds of love toward several different people, even at the same point in his or her life. Most American adults say "I love you" into the telephone to their mothers on Mother's Day, for example, but what they mean by those three words is probably (hopefully!) quite different than when they say "I love you" while kissing and hugging the person to whom they are engaged to be married.

PASSIONATE AND COMPANIONATE LOVE

An important distinction between two main kinds of love has emerged from many years of research (see Hatfield & Rapson, 1987). The experts called the two kinds of love "passionate" and "companionate." By **passionate love**, they mean having strong feelings of longing, desire, and excitement toward a special person. Passionate love (also called **romantic love**) makes people want to spend as much time as possible together, to touch each other and engage in other physical intimacies (often including sex), to think about each other and feel joy merely upon seeing each other, and to exhibit other patterns that suggest strong emotions.

In contrast, **companionate love** (sometimes called **affectionate love**) is less strongly emotional; it tends to be calmer and more serene. Companionate love means perceiving the other person as your soulmate or special partner. It signifies a high level of mutual understanding and caring and in many cases a commitment to make the relationship succeed. As the term implies, companionate love is what makes people want to remain each other's good companions. Someone high in companionate love is likely to say things like "My wife is my best friend." That kind of love is not the same as what usually motivates people to start a new sexual relationship, but it may be essential to a successful long-term marriage.

There is probably a physiological, even biochemical, difference between the two kinds of love. People who feel passionately in love have high levels of phenylethylamine (PEA), a neurotransmitter that enables information to travel from one brain cell to another (Liebowitz, 1983; Walsh, 1991a). This chemical produces strong emotional feelings, including those "tingling" sensations of excitement and euphoria that you get when the person you love walks into the room or holds your hand. It also helps produce high

---

PASSIONATE LOVE (ROMANTIC LOVE) strong feelings of longing, desire, and excitement toward a special person

COMPANIONATE LOVE (AFFECTIONATE LOVE) mutual understanding and caring to make the relationship succeed

intensity and frequency of sexual desire. The emotional churning and the sense of being in an altered state (sometimes compared to being high on drugs) is very likely linked to some chemical in the body, and PEA is a leading candidate, although further research is needed, and passionate love may affect more than one chemical. In any case, companionate love does not seem to be characterized by these elevated levels of PEA.

LOVE AND CULTURE

The PEA response suggests that passionate love involves something more basic than cultural learning, although undoubtedly culture can work with or against the biochemical responses to love objects. The question of whether romantic love is universal or is simply a product of Western culture has been fiercely debated. Some authorities (e.g., de Rougemont, 1956) have argued that romantic love is a cultural construction, possibly introduced into Western culture by the Crusaders or troubadours, who brought it from the Middle East and elaborated it into its mythological status at the royal courts of Europe (where most marriages were arranged for political reasons, so passionate love flourished in extramarital affairs), and then embraced as one of the culture's main goals and values during the so-called Romantic Period (roughly 1775–1850). From the social constructionist view, cultural values and meanings have shaped personal feelings and changed the way people run their lives, and the cultural construction of love is an important case in point.

More recent cross-cultural work, however, has begun to suggest that passionate love is not merely a product of Western culture. In 1995, anthropologist William Jankowiak published a painstaking, influential book titled *Romantic Passion: A Universal Experience?* His answer was yes. Careful anthropological investigations led him to the conclusion that romantic love is indeed found everywhere (that is, in the vast majority of cultures he surveyed around the world, though not in every single one). This is not to suggest that culture plays no role. The forms and expressions of romantic passion vary significantly, as does the culture's attitude toward passionate love. Modern Western culture (whose influence is certainly spreading through many parts of the world) has come to regard passionate love as an important part of life, so that if you never experience it, you will have missed out on a major form of fulfillment. Possibly, people in other cultures feel love as we do but do not place the same value on it and do not feel that a life without passionate love is by definition a lesser life.

In fact, passionate love may seem like a form of temporary insanity. Thus, although most cultures

Stockbyte Platinum/Alamy

© Kevin Dodge/Masterfile

Love changes over the years.

have recognized the existence of passionate love, different cultures and even different eras in Western culture have held very different attitudes toward it. The historian Lawrence Stone (1977) concluded that in bygone centuries in Europe, people regarded passionate love as a form of mental imbalance that made people feel and act in strange, even crazy ways. They did not think that passionate love was a good

Romantic love is not just an invention of Western culture.

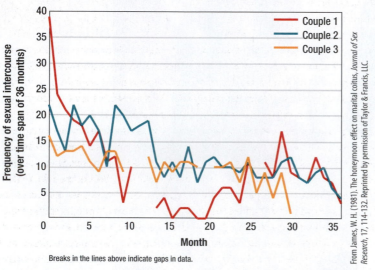

From James, W. H. (1981). The honeymoon effect on marital coitus. *Journal of Sex Research, 17*, 114–132. Reprinted by permission of Taylor & Francis, LLC.

Breaks in the lines above indicate gaps in data.

▶ **FIGURE 12.1** For most couples, sex is most frequent during the first month and first year after their wedding and declines after that. From James (1981).

reason to marry someone; indeed, proposing marriage while in love would strike them as similar to making any major life decision while drunk or on drugs! And they certainly didn't think that passionate love made a good basis for marriage. Companionate love seemed a much better bet.

Passionate love may therefore be found among humans everywhere, but how they experience it and how they regard it may depend on their culture. People are hooked into their cultural system, and the system can influence how they love.

LOVE ACROSS TIME

Companionate love may be harder to create than passionate love, which often arises spontaneously and

without people trying to fall in love. Companionate love is what makes a good marriage or a stable, trustworthy, lasting relationship, but it takes sustained work and effort to build trust, intimacy, and other foundations of companionate love. Passionate love may be the most effective emotion for starting a relationship; companionate love may be the most effective emotion for making it succeed and survive in the long run.

One reason for skepticism about passionate love as the basis for marriage is that it tends to be temporary (e.g., Acker & Davis, 1992). This is hard for most people to appreciate, especially young people who may not yet have spent many years in the same romantic relationship and who think that their passionate feelings are sure to be permanent. But most people experience passionate love for a relatively brief period in a relationship—a year, perhaps, or two or three at most, if one is very lucky. If the relationship continues, it tends to rely more on companionate love. A successful long-term relationship thus depends on making an effective transition from one kind of love to the other.

A behavioral sign of the decrease in passion can be found in data about frequency of sexual intercourse. Many studies have found that as time goes by, the average married couple has sex less and less often (Blumstein & Schwartz, 1983; Greenblat, 1983; Griffit, 1981; James, 1981; Laumann, Gagnon, Michael, & Michaels, 1994; Udry, 1980). Newlyweds generally live up to the stereotype of passionate young lovers who have relatively frequent sex. But this does not last. James (1981) found that the frequency of sexual intercourse declined by about half after the first year of marriage, from about 18 times per month during the first year to about 9 times per month in the second year. It continued to decrease more slowly after that (see ▶ **FIGURE 12.1**). Likewise, studies that follow married couples over many years find that they start off having sex relatively often, but that this frequent rate decreases sharply at first and then continues to go down as the couple grows old together (Ard, 1977). However, the decline in frequency of sex is not entirely due to aging. If a couple has a long marriage, their frequency of sex goes down, but if they then divorce and remarry, they typically show a big increase in sexual frequency with their new partners (Call, Sprecher, & Schwartz, 1995). To learn more about the relationship between marriage and sex, see *Tradeoffs*.

The biochemical rush associated with high levels of PEA (if that is indeed the chemical dimension of love) is thus not destined to be permanent. It is probably a feature linked to new love and the forming of a new relationship bond. Unfortunately, many people probably mistake its normal and natural decline for a sign that they are no longer in love. They stop feeling

Sex In and Out of Marriage

It often seems as if married and single people envy each other. Single people think it must be wonderful to have a loving, devoted sex partner who sleeps with you every night, and they anticipate that getting married finally brings on a lifetime of great sex. Married people imagine that single life is full of sexual adventure and novelty, trying new acts and new partners anytime one wants instead of going to bed with the same old person according to the same old routine.

There are of course many reasons to marry (or not to marry), but we focus here on the links between marriage and sex, as indicated by the National Health and Social Life Survey (Laumann et al., 1994). The data suggest, first, that neither of the stereotypes invoked in the preceding paragraph is entirely correct. Frequent passionate sex, as seen in movies and novels, appears to be fairly unusual, and only a tiny fraction (8%) of married or single people have sex more than three times per week. Married people do have more sex than single people, or at least more than single people who are not cohabiting with a romantic partner. Living together without marriage is marked by the highest rates of sexual activity, though living together may not be the cause; unmarried cohabitation is mainly found among young people early in a relationship, and such individuals may have more sexual desire than others. Cohabitors also do not have many of the distractions of married life, such as small children, who can interfere with time and energy (and even privacy!) needed for sex. If you compare married people and single cohabitors of the same age, the frequency of sex is pretty similar,

although the married people still have sex somewhat less often.

Thus, married people have more sex, in terms of quantity—but what about quality? Quality of sex is harder to measure, but one index might be how long people spend on a given sex act. By this measure, it looks as though single people have better sex. Married sex is more likely than unmarried sex to be finished in less than 15 minutes. Single persons are more likely than married ones to spend more than an hour on a single sexual event. Single people are also more likely than married ones to say that their most recent sex act included some activity beyond basic genital intercourse, which is another sign that they put effort and imagination into sex.

Not all signs of quality favor the single. When asked whether their most recent sex partner brought them physical or emotional satisfaction, married people are more likely than single ones to say yes. (Orgasm rates were nearly identical, however.) This may be partly because the marriage relationship contains love (and hence emotional satisfaction), and partly because a married spouse knows how to please you better than someone who is unfamiliar with your body. Single people are more likely than married ones to report consuming alcohol before sex, and alcohol does interfere with sexual responsiveness. Then again, at least the single people who drink before sex share the enjoyment of drinking; married people are prone to drink alone before sex, if at all.

One last and probably unsurprising difference is that single people have more sex partners than married ones. Though not all married people are faithful, most are, so marriage really does seem

PhotoDisc

to entail settling down with one regular sex partner. Single people are more likely than married ones to have had several sex partners in the past year—then again, they are also more likely to have had none at all.

The relationship between marriage and sex thus appears to be a tradeoff. Married people have more frequent sex. Single people have more partners. Married people benefit from a partner who knows their responses and who loves them. Single people spend more time and energy on each sex act and try more things. For many single people, life alternates between periods of exciting sex with a new partner and periods of no sex with any partner. For many married people, sex conforms to a stable and regular pattern of familiar activities, once or twice a week. ●

---

swept away, and in particular their feelings of sexual desire for each other may dwindle to the individuals' normal, baseline levels, but the two people may mistake this process to mean that they have lost interest in each other or, even more ominously, that the other person has ceased to love them.

The story of Princess Diana and Prince Charles, with which this chapter began, is instructive about the difference between passionate and companionate love. The start of their romance captured the world's imagination because it seemingly embodied the vital features of passionate love: a beautiful woman, a royal prince, blossoming attraction culminating in a spectacular

wedding and then the birth of two handsome sons. Apparently, though, Charles and Diana failed to make the transition to companionate love, and their years together were not marked by intimacy, mutual devotion, and becoming each other's best friend. When passionate love fails to convert into companionate love (regardless of whether that is actually what transpired between Diana and Charles), the story line is likely to be one of a wonderful, romantic beginning followed by a downward spiral of stress, disappointment, estrangement, and ultimate failure. Fortunately, many people avoid that fate and do sustain a happy marriage for a long time or even a lifetime.

▶ **FIGURE 12.2** The triangle on the left represents a relationship that is high in intimacy and passion, but low in commitment. The triangle on the right represents a relationship that is high in intimacy and commitment but low in passion.

STERNBERG'S TRIANGLE

A more elaborate theory of the nature of love has been proposed by Robert Sternberg (1986). Instead of speaking of two different kinds of love, Sternberg proposed that love is composed of three different ingredients (see ▶ **FIGURE 12.2**). The first of these is **passion**, which he explained in terms of feelings of romantic attraction, physical attraction to the other person, and sexual interest. Passion is largely an emotional state and is characterized by high bodily arousal: When you feel passion, your heart beats more rapidly than usual, you become excited and alert, and you may also feel sexual arousal. Passion makes people want to be together and in many cases makes them want to kiss, hold hands, and perhaps have sex.

The second ingredient in Sternberg's scheme is **intimacy**. Intimacy, in his view, is the common core of all love relationships. It refers to feeling close to the other person. Empathy is important in intimacy; indeed, intimacy includes a sense of understanding the partner and being understood by him or her. Intimacy also entails a mutual concern for each other's welfare and happiness. When two people have a high degree of intimacy, they have a basic feeling of caring and concern about one another, they want each other to be happy and healthy, and they may often seek to do things that will benefit each other. Intimate partners try to take care of each other, and they emphasize communication about their lives, feelings, and problems.

The third ingredient is decision and **commitment**. Sternberg observed that when many people speak of love, they refer more to a conscious decision than to a feeling state. Emotions come and go, but commitments based on decisions remain constant unless

PASSION an emotional state characterized by high bodily arousal, such as increased heart rate and blood pressure

INTIMACY a feeling of closeness, mutual understanding, and mutual concern for each other's welfare and happiness

COMMITMENT a conscious decision that remains constant

off the mark.com — by Mark Parisi

HOW ABOUT IF I JUST WRITE YOUR NAME IN SUNSCREEN AND GET A BAD SUNBURN INSTEAD?

TATTOOS

OPEN

MARK PARISI 8-20

offthemark.com

ATLANTIC FEATURE © 1993 MARK PARISI
Reprinted by permission of Atlantic Feature Syndicate/Mark Parisi.

This man does not seem committed to his partner.

they are deliberately revoked. For example, if you ask someone whether she loves her husband or her children, she may say "Of course!" without having to think about it. If love referred only to passion, she would have to stop and examine her emotions at that moment to see whether she actually felt passionate attraction toward the other person. But if love means commitment, and she has made that commitment, then she can say "Of course!" without requiring a survey of her current inner feelings.

Passion, intimacy, and commitment are not three different "kinds" of love. Instead, Sternberg proposed that any given love relationship can mix those three ingredients in any combination. Some love relationships might have high intimacy, high commitment, but low passion. Others might have plenty of passion and commitment but little intimacy. Can you think of examples of those types? The first (high intimacy and commitment but low passion) might describe a marriage that is still strong after many decades. The second might describe a "whirlwind romance" in which two people fall madly in love and marry quickly, before they have gotten to know each other very well.

An ideal love might contain substantial measures of all three ingredients. If none of the three is present, Sternberg would say, there is no love. In his research, he concluded that intimacy is the most common ingredient; relatively few relationships utterly lack

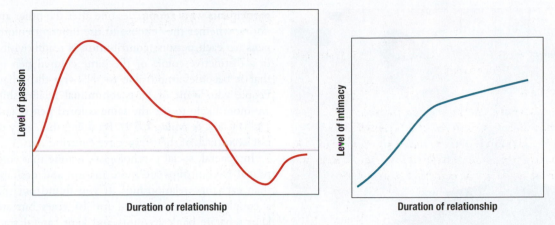

▶ **FIGURE 12.3** Passion and intimacy have different time courses over a relationship. Passion increases dramatically and then tends to decline steadily over time, whereas intimacy starts low and tends to increase over time.

intimacy. Still, the feeling called "love at first sight" usually involves low intimacy; you hardly know the person yet, and passion is the main ingredient.

The three ingredients typically have different time courses. Passion can arise quickly but, as already noted, also tends to diminish after a while. Intimacy, in contrast, arises more slowly but can continue increasing for a long time (Acker & Davis, 1992; Baumeister & Bratslavsky, 1999). One theme of this book is the long road to social acceptance, and nowhere is the length of this road more obvious than in the slow, long-term development of an intimate relationship. The bond of intimacy continues to solidify for years. Last, decisions and commitments are typically made at particular points in time (such as agreeing to stop dating other people or proposing marriage).

The shift from passionate to companionate love is explained by Sternberg's theory in terms of a change in the mixture of love's three ingredients (see ▶ **FIGURE 12.3**). Companionate love emphasizes intimacy and commitment, whereas passionate love consists mainly of passion (obviously). Commitment may help solidify the trust and mutual concern that contribute to companionate love. Thus, in his account, a typical long-term sexual relationship might start out consisting mainly of passion, but over time the intimacy grows stronger as passion grows weaker, and at some point a decision is made to solidify a long-range commitment. Commitment can help keep the couple together during periods of conflict or dissatisfaction, which many couples experience sooner or later. If the commitment is not made, or if intimacy does not grow, then the relationship is likely to break up after the early stage. The couple may still experience a great deal of passion, but once the passion dies down, there may be little to replace it, and there will be little to keep them together.

[**QUIZ YOURSELF**]

What Is Love?

1. Passionate love is an aspect of _____.
  (a) Eastern culture
  (b) Western culture
  (c) both Eastern and Western cultures
  (d) neither Eastern nor Western cultures

2. Passionate love is to companionate love as _____ love is to _____ love.
  (a) affectionate; romantic   (b) committed; intimate
  (c) married; single   (d) romantic; affectionate

3. People who feel passionately in love have high levels of _____.
  (a) acetylcholine   (b) dopamine
  (c) epinephrine   (d) phenylethylamine

4. In the triangle theory of love, what does companionate love stem from?
  (a) Commitment   (b) Intimacy
  (c) Passion   (d) Both (a) and (b)

Different Types of Relationships

Not all people are the same, nor are all relationships the same. Let us consider some of the basic differences in how people relate to each other.

EXCHANGE VERSUS COMMUNAL

There are at least two different basic types of relationship. These can be called exchange and communal relationships (Clark, 1984; Clark & Mills, 1979).

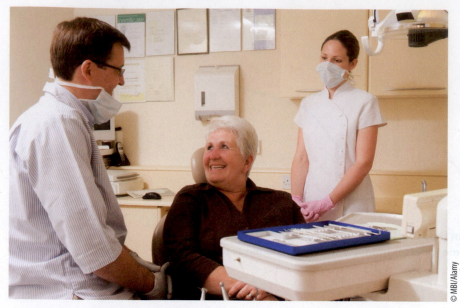

This dentist and his client may enjoy seeing each other, but their relationship is based on the exchange of a service for money.

Exchange relationships are based on reciprocity and fairness; each person does something for the other mainly in the expectation of getting some direct benefit in return. **Communal relationships**, in contrast, are based on mutual love and concern; in this type of relationship, people do things for each other without expecting to be repaid. The relationship between a family dentist and a regular customer would be one example of a long-term exchange relationship: The dentist and client may be friendly to each other and even enjoy seeing each other, but the basis of their interaction is still the exchange of dental care for money. In contrast, a long-term communal relationship might exist between two sisters, who help each other out during difficult times by giving emotional support and even money without expecting that the other will pay it back.

One difference between communal and exchange relationships is whether the people keep track. Thus, some couples that live together keep track of who pays which bills, who buys the groceries, and so forth, to make sure that everything is equal. Other couples live together in a more communal fashion, putting all their money into a joint bank account and letting either one spend it without having to check with the other. Even in terms of chores and doing favors for each other, some couples keep careful track, while others don't. In the lab, researchers have measured communal versus exchange orientation by having

participants work on puzzles one after the other and noting whether they choose to use different colored pens (so each person's contribution is readily visible in a distinctive color) or the same colored pen (so that it becomes impossible to tell who did what). People who want or have communal relationships are more likely to use the same colored pen (Clark, 1984; Clark & Mills, 1979). By doing that, they do not keep track of their respective contributions.

In general, social psychologists assume that communal relationships are more mature and desirable than exchange relationships. If you found out that a couple had been married for 10 years but still kept separate bank accounts and kept careful track of who paid for what, you would probably think something was wrong with the relationship, and you might question their commitment to each other. In fact, couples who pool their money in a communal fashion while living together are more likely to remain together and to get married than cohabiting couples who keep their relationship on an exchange basis by maintaining separate accounts (Blumstein & Schwartz, 1983).

This bias in favor of communal relationships, however, is specific to close or intimate relationships. Across the broader society, exchange relationships seem much more powerful for driving progress and increasing wealth (e.g., Seabright, 2004). There are communal societies in which possessions are shared freely by all, but these tend to be simple, even relatively primitive cultures. The rich and flourishing cultures have all apparently become that way by taking advantage of social and economic exchange, because the rewards for success encourage achievement and risk taking. Thus, ultimately, there may be a tradeoff between the two types of relationship. Exchange relationships promote achievement, increase wealth, and ultimately drive progress, whereas communal relationships make people feel safe and secure and provide a haven where others care for you regardless of how much you achieve. This tradeoff may explain why most people in modern societies ultimately try to have some of both. They spend their working lives in a network of exchange relationships, where their salary and other rewards are directly proportional to what they accomplish and they do things for others specifically in order to get money or other rewards in return. Meanwhile, they try to set up their families on a communal basis, where people care for each other without keeping track of who contributed what and everyone shares with everyone else.

In any case, communal interactions are healthier and more mature in close relationships. People in communal close relationships help each other more than do people in exchange close relationships (Clark, Ouellette, Powell, & Milberg, 1987). They feel better about helping each other (Williamson &

EXCHANGE RELATIONSHIPS relationships based on reciprocity and fairness, in which people expect something in return

COMMUNAL RELATIONSHIPS relationships based on mutual love and concern, without expectation of repayment

Clark, 1989) and are more responsive to each other's emotional states (Clark et al., 1987). They keep track of each other's needs, rather than what the other does for them, and this attention to the other's needs reflects an ongoing concern to take care of each other (Clark et al., 1987; Clark, Mills, & Corcoran, 1989). Communal relationships also promote a greater sense of unity and shared identity, so the relationship feels more solid.

The underlying reality may be that communal and exchange relationships are based on different rules. Exchange relationships are based on reciprocity. In exchange relationships, you should only allow someone to do something for you if you are ready to repay that favor. Fairness and even exchange are uppermost concerns. In contrast, communal relationships are based on the norm of mutual concern. You can let the other person do things for you without any immediate idea of how to repay it, just as you would be willing to do a great deal for your partner without expecting anything in return. Instead of equality and repayment, the underlying rules involve caring for the other person and being available and ready to provide support, help, and other resources whenever the person needs you.

ATTACHMENT

During the dark days of World War II, London, England, endured daily bombings by the German air force. London was the nation's capital and it was necessary for many people to remain at work there, but many parents decided to send their children to live out in the country, where the danger from bombs was much less. Although this practice promoted safety, it required many small children to be separated from their parents for significant periods of time. A British psychologist, John Bowlby, observed how the children dealt with these separations, and on this basis he began to formulate a theory about different styles of attachment. This theory was revived by relationships researchers in the 1980s and has become an influential, powerful way of understanding all close relationships (especially romantic ones).

Like many psychologists of his era, Bowlby was influenced by both Freudian and learning psychology, and these views treated adult behavior as shaped by early childhood experiences. Bowlby thought that how adults relate to others—romantic partners, work colleagues and bosses, even organizations—would essentially copy or repeat the style of interaction they had learned in childhood. He saw some children deal with separation from parents by clinging and crying and refusing to let go; others pretended they didn't like their parents and didn't care whether they were there or not; still others seemed to deal with the separation in a sad but accepting manner. He thought

Relationship questionnaire

_____ A. I am somewhat uncomfortable being close to others; I find it difficult to trust them completely, difficult to allow myself to depend on them. I am nervous when anyone gets too close, and often, others want me to be more intimate than I feel comfortable being.

_____ B. I find it relatively easy to get close to others and am comfortable depending on them and having them depend on me. I don't worry about being abandoned or about someone getting too close to me.

_____ C. I find that others are reluctant to get as close as I would like. I often worry that my partner doesn't really love me or won't want to stay with me. I want to get very close to my partner, and this sometimes scares people away.

▶ **FIGURE 12.4 Three attachment styles (anxious, secure, and avoidant) from one-item measure by Hazan and Shaver (1987).**

that these early experiences would shape how the children would later carry on their adult relationships. Bowlby's descriptions of the styles of interaction have influenced subsequent work, but today the weight of opinion does not favor the view that adult styles of interaction are strongly shaped by early childhood experiences. Many people change and develop new styles of relating long after early childhood. (Also, when research findings do indicate that a person has remained the same from childhood into adulthood, researchers today note that this could reflect some underlying genetic trait rather than the causal influence of childhood experiences.)

Types of Attachment. The original theory identified three types of attachment. Bowlby's observations were extended by Phillip Shaver and his colleagues (Bartholomew & Shaver, 1998; Cooper, Shaver, & Collins, 1999; Hazan & Shaver, 1987) to describe adult relationships, including love and romantic relationships. Shaver's group found that people could classify themselves reliably. It wasn't even necessary to use a long, fancy questionnaire; a single item (see ▶ **FIGURE 12.4**) was enough to sort people into categories. The categories range along a continuum from pulling close to pushing away. At one extreme lie the clinging types who want to be as close as possible, who ideally would like to experience a complete merger with someone else, and whose problems stem from the fact that others don't want to be as close as they do. This style of attachment is called _anxious/ambivalent_. At the other extreme lie the _avoidant_ individuals, who are uncomfortable when others want to get too close and who try to maintain some distance between themselves and relationship partners.

In the middle, between the anxious and avoidant styles, lie the secure individuals. _Secure attachment_ is characterized by a comfortable balance: the person is happy to become close and intimate with others and does not worry inordinately about being abandoned or hurt. Earlier, we noted that the difference between communal and exchange relationships is a kind of tradeoff, that both have advantages in appropriate contexts. In that sense, neither communal nor exchange is inherently better than the other. All attachment styles are not equal, however. In almost all published studies, the secure attachment style produces the best outcomes.

The best that can be said for the other attachment styles is that they provide some limited kind of defense mechanisms or ways of coping with painful relationships. In fact, the avoidant attachment style is thought to start when parents (especially mothers) reject or neglect their babies, fail to express affection and other emotions, avoid physical contact, and fail to provide comfort when the babies are upset (Ainsworth, Blehar, Waters, & Wall, 1978). An upset baby whose mother fails to provide comfort may learn to turn off the desire to be close to the mother as a way of preventing itself from feeling worse (Edelstein & Shaver, 2004).

Two Dimensions of Attachment? As the study of attachment styles evolved, researchers gradually moved from the single dimension (running from anxious/ambivalent to secure to avoidant) in favor of a two-dimensional **attachment theory** (Bartholomew & Horowitz, 1991; Brennan, Clark, & Shaver, 1998; Collins & Feeney, 2000; Edelstein & Shaver, 2004). The two dimensions are now called *anxiety* and *avoidance*. A simple way to remember them is that one dimension (anxiety) refers to attitudes toward the self and the other dimension (avoidance) refers to attitudes toward the other person. Though both of these dimensions should be understood as a continuum, we can use a simple high-versus-low split on each dimension to create vivid images of four different attachment styles (see ▶ **FIGURE 12.5**). Thus, the new theory offers four styles, instead of the three in the earlier version, mainly by splitting the "avoidant" category into two.

The first of the four styles is, again, **secure attachment**. Securely attached people are low on anxiety and low on avoidance (or, to put it another way, they have favorable attitudes toward both self and others). They are good at close relationships. They trust their partners, share their feelings, provide support and comfort (and happily receive these as well), and enjoy their relationships. Their relationships tend to be stronger, more durable, more satisfying, and more intimate than those of people in the other categories (Collins & Feeney, 2000, 2004).

The second category is called **preoccupied attachment**, though some experts still prefer the original term **anxious/ambivalent**. People in this category are low on avoidance, reflecting the fact that they want and enjoy closeness to the other person, but they tend to have high anxiety and a more negative attitude toward themselves. These individuals want to merge and cling but worry that their relationship partners will abandon them, possibly because they think their partners will discover their faults and flaws (Bartholomew & Horowitz, 1991; Collins & Feeney, 2004; Collins & Read, 1990; Hazan & Shaver, 1987; Simpson, 1990). Preoccupied individuals tend to see partners as inconsistent, unreliable, and reluctant to commit. They seek more and more closeness, and their frequent efforts to force others to remain close to them can cause their partners to perceive them as overly controlling (or even "suffocating"). Preoccupied individuals may provide large amounts of comfort, support, and care to others, but sometimes they provide too much or give more than is wanted, partly because they provide care more to satisfy their own need to connect than out of any genuine sensitivity to their partner's needs (Feeney, 1996; Feeney & Collins, 2001; Kunce & Shaver, 1994).

In the third type, **dismissing avoidant attachment**, people see themselves as worthy, adequate individuals (thus low anxiety) but seek to prevent relationships from becoming too close (Bartholomew, 1990; Collins & Feeney, 2004). They view

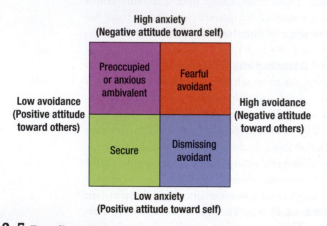

▶ **FIGURE 12.5** Two dimensions of attachment: anxiety and avoidance.

ATTACHMENT THEORY a theory that classifies people into four attachment styles (secure, preoccupied, dismissing avoidant, and fearful avoidant) based on two dimensions (anxiety and avoidance)

SECURE ATTACHMENT style of attachment in which people are low on anxiety and low on avoidance; they trust their partners, share their feelings, provide and receive support and comfort, and enjoy their relationships

PREOCCUPIED (ANXIOUS/AMBIVALENT) ATTACHMENT style of attachment in which people are low on avoidance but high on anxiety; they want and enjoy closeness but worry that their relationship partners will abandon them

DISMISSING AVOIDANT ATTACHMENT style of attachment in which people are low on anxiety but high on avoidance; they tend to view partners as unreliable, unavailable, and uncaring

partners as unreliable, unavailable, and uncaring. They seek to rely on themselves rather than on others. Their relationships are marked by more distance, lower commitment, and lower enjoyment than those of secure or preoccupied individuals. Their partners sometimes see them as withdrawn or aloof and as reluctant to open up (that is, they are slow to disclose personal feelings and experiences). They provide less care and support to their loved ones than do secure or preoccupied people.

Fourth, **fearful avoidant attachment** is characterized by both high anxiety and high avoidance. These people have low opinions of themselves and keep others from becoming close. They view potential relationship partners as untrustworthy, uncaring, and otherwise unavailable. They worry that they are unlovable. Given their issues with both self and others, this worry may not be entirely unfounded!

How firm are these styles? Although each person may have a habitual attachment style, anyone can occasionally have a relationship with a different style, partly because of the partner's influence (Baldwin, 1992). You might normally be secure, for example, but you might find yourself preoccupied in a particular relationship, especially if the partner treats you in an erratic or anxiety-producing manner.

In many ways, the avoidant individuals (both dismissing and fearful) present the biggest theoretical puzzle (Collins & Feeney, 2004; Edelstein & Shaver, 2004). We have said that the need to belong and the desire for close relationships is common to all human beings, yet at least on the surface avoidant people seem to push others away rather than keep them close. But the seeming contradiction is misleading. Avoidant individuals desire and seek out connections with others. Their problem is that they worry that if they give in to these wishes and become close to others, they will be hurt. Thus, the fear of closeness lies alongside the need to belong, and the two urges can come into conflict. Quite possibly their fear of closeness originates in previous experiences, whether very early in life such as having had a distant or rejecting mother, or as a result of early romantic experiences that ended in pain and suffering. Put another way, avoidant individuals have the same basic need to belong as other people, but they seem to learn to turn it off or disconnect it to avoid being hurt. Outwardly they may act as if they are indifferent to closeness with others, but secretly they often suffer a great deal during separations (e.g., Spangler & Grossman, 1993; Sroufe & Waters, 1977).

Avoidant individuals thus perform a delicate balancing act. They want contact and relatedness with other people, but they seek to avoid becoming too close. In a sense, they want human connection and companionship but without allowing too much intimacy. Some deal with this by keeping multiple

For some avoidant individuals, the fear of closeness can be traced back to early childhood, such as when parents ignore or reject their child.

relationships going at the same time, so that if one partner starts to get too close, they can shift emphasis to another. Others manage the problem by frequently introducing conflict into a relationship, such as by getting into fights and arguments over seemingly minor things. That way they can stay connected to someone but prevent the relationship from becoming too close. Others simply set up their social lives so that they keep interactions relatively short, thus preventing intimacy from developing (Tidwell, Reis, & Shaver, 1996).

Attachment and Sex. The differences between the attachment styles can also be seen in people's sex lives. Not surprisingly, secure individuals generally have good sex lives with fewer problems than others. In contrast, preoccupied individuals may use sex to pull others close to them. They (especially preoccupied women) are more prone than others to have sex when they do not want to do so, because they fear that if they say no they may lose some degree of connection, or because they hope that having sex will make their partner love them more. Likewise, they engage in more risky sex, again because they are afraid to say

FEARFUL AVOIDANT ATTACHMENT style of attachment in which people have both high anxiety and high avoidance; they have low opinions of themselves and keep others from getting close

no. As a result, they have more lifetime sexual partners than others and also have more problems such as unwanted pregnancy (Bogaert & Sadava, 2002; Cooper et al., 1998; Impett & Peplau, 2002).

Avoidant individuals have the same dilemma with sex as with belongingness: They have the same desire for it as other people do, but they resist intimacy. Some (perhaps especially women) may end up avoiding sex because they fear the intimacy it will promote. Others separate sex and love, having one-night stands or extramarital affairs in which the chances of lasting, intimate love are low (Brennan & Shaver, 1995; Collins & Feeney, 2004). They can even use sex as a strategy for balancing distance against intimacy. Thus, we know a man who dated an avoidant woman for several years. The relationship became sexual quite rapidly, but the couple spent far more time having sex than sharing personal feelings or experiences. After two years, the woman was finally able to bring herself to say "I love you" to the man—and then a week later she started a sexual relationship with someone else. Most likely she had resisted recognizing her growing love, as any avoidant person would. When she finally confronted it, she quickly found herself wanting to sabotage the rising intimacy by having sex with another partner, which had the predictable effect of keeping the first lover from growing too close to her.

LOVING PEOPLE WHO LOVE THEMSELVES

"First you must love yourself, and only then are you ready to love someone else"—this is a popular belief in our culture. It is variously attributed to the psychological thinkers Erik Erikson, Carl Rogers, and Abraham Maslow, but it is probably a misreading of their works. Erikson (1950) said that people must resolve their identity crisis and know who they are before they are ready to start working on intimacy. He didn't say you had to love yourself—merely know yourself (and it is even questionable whether knowing yourself is a prerequisite for having a good relationship). Rogers (1961) focused on self-actualization (the global process of cultivating your talents and becoming a better person all around) rather than self-love. He also thought that people needed to receive unconditional love before they were ready to reach self-actualization. This is in a sense the opposite of the idea that self-love comes first; instead, being loved comes first, self-esteem later. Maslow (1968) likewise proposed that belongingness and love needs were more basic than self-esteem needs; his views, too, run contrary to the theory that self-esteem comes first, love later.

Still, those theories are no more than theories. What do the facts and findings say about loving yourself and loving others? The evidence is at best weak and inconsistent in terms of showing that loving yourself contributes to loving others. In some cases, people who love themselves lavishly are less likely to love anyone else.

Let us begin with self-esteem. People with low self-esteem engage in a variety of behaviors that can undermine a relationship (Murray, Bellavia, Rose, & Griffin, 2003; Murray, Rose, Bellavia, Holmes, & Kusche, 2002). They are skeptical or distrustful when their partners express love or support, and sometimes they act as if they expect their partners to dump them. Still, these problematic behaviors do not seem to translate into breaking up faster. One possible reason is that people with high self-esteem do other, different things that are bad for relationships. When there are problems or conflicts in a relationship, people with high self-esteem are quicker to decide "I don't have to put up with this!" and to contemplate ending the relationship (Rusbult, Morrow, & Johnson, 1987; Sommer, Williams, Ciarocco, & Baumeister, 2001). Probably the different levels of self-esteem contribute to those different reactions. People with low self-esteem doubt that they are lovable, so they expect others to leave them. People with high self-esteem think they are lovable, so they think they can find a new partner relatively easily. The net result may be that high- and low-self-esteem people break up at about the same rate, but for different reasons. The other side of the coin is that people of all levels of self-esteem can have lasting, successful relationships.

The risk that self-love can present to relationship harmony is magnified if one looks at narcissism (see also Chapter 10), which is a personality type based on very high self-love. Narcissists have high self-esteem and a strong though somewhat unstable self-love, but these qualities do not make for good relationships; indeed, their selfishness and other qualities may harm relationships. They approach relationships in a game-playing spirit of having fun or as a pragmatic way of getting what they want (including sex) (Campbell & Foster, 2002). They seek out successful, beautiful, admired people to date, because they think they are similar to them, and they believe that the glamour or prestige of their partners makes them look good (Campbell, 1999).

Getting along with a narcissist is no picnic! Narcissists tend to hog the credit when things go well but blame their partners when things go badly (Campbell, Reeder, Sedikides, & Elliot, 2000; Farwell & Wohlwend-Lloyd, 1998; Morf & Rhodewalt, 2001; Schütz, 2000, 2001), which can certainly put a strain on a relationship. In an observational study in which couples discussed problems that threatened their self-esteem, narcissists had fewer positive interactions with their spouses than other people did (Schütz, 1999).

off the mark.com
by Mark Parisi

ARG! HOW CAN WE HAVE A DECENT CONVERSATION WHEN YOU'RE SO FULL OF YOURSELF?!

offthemark.com   ATLANTIC FEATURE © 1995 MARK PARISI

Reprinted by permission of Atlantic Feature Syndicate/Mark Parisi.

Being in a relationship with a narcissist is no picnic. Because they are so full of themselves, they don't think about others.

Ultimately, narcissists tend to be less committed to love relationships than other people are (Campbell & Foster, 2002). Narcissists tend to keep one eye on the relationship but another eye out to see whether a better partner might come along. Narcissists think they are superior beings and overestimate how attractive they are; as a result, they think they can and should have the most desirable romantic partners. A narcissist may love you for the time being, but he or she will dump you as soon as a better prospect comes along.

If self-love leads to loving others, narcissists should be the best lovers, because they love themselves the most. The evidence suggests the opposite, however: In narcissists, at least, loving yourself detracts from loving others. Narcissists are interested in others mainly as a way of boosting their own inflated views of themselves. Hence their relationships tend to be prone to breakup. This may help explain why marriages among celebrities often end in divorce: Being a celebrity tends to push people to become more narcissistic (partly because they are widely admired and highly paid), and this leads to relationship problems, especially when new partners are constantly and readily available.

Although narcissism is one problematic extreme, some less extreme versions of self-love and self-esteem may be helpful for relationships. A more minimal form of self-love is **self-acceptance**, which means simply regarding yourself as being a reasonably good person as you are. The same study that found narcissism to be linked to fewer positive interactions with the spouse found that self-acceptance was linked to more positive interactions (Schütz, 1999). These findings suggest that having a very negative, critical attitude toward yourself can interfere with the capacity to love. The best summary of current knowledge on this issue is to say that either extreme of self-love or self-hate is likely to be detrimental to intimacy. Conversely, someone with a simple and secure appreciation of self, without being conceited or overblown, may be the best romantic partner.

[QUIZ YOURSELF]

Different Types of Relationships

1. Exchange relationship is to communal relationship as _____ is to _____.
(a) concern; reciprocity   (b) passion; concern
(c) reciprocity; concern   (d) reciprocity; passion

2. What attachment style is associated with high levels of anxiety and high levels of avoidance?
(a) Dismissing avoidant   (b) Fearful avoidant
(c) Preoccupied   (d) Secure

3. Individuals who see themselves as worthy and adequate but seek to prevent relationships from becoming too close have what type of attachment style?
(a) Dismissing avoidant   (b) Fearful avoidant
(c) Preoccupied   (d) Secure

4. What personality trait is associated with a grandiose, inflated view of the self?
(a) Narcissism   (b) Self-acceptance
(c) Self-efficacy   (d) Self-esteem

Maintaining Relationships

Information is available everywhere about how people form relationships. Countless books, movies, and studies look at how people become attracted to each other and reach the point of making a commitment to carry on an intimate relationship. Most people have some idea about how to do this. In contrast, how people manage to keep a relationship going, sometimes for 40 or 50 years, seems a mystery. Social psychology is only gradually beginning to provide answers to the question of how people keep their relationships alive and well.

SELF-ACCEPTANCE regarding yourself as being a reasonably good person as you are

In reality, the relationship is not improving steadily.

What goes on between partners in a long-term relationship? How do they keep it going? What causes some relationships to succeed while others fail? These processes have fascinated social psychologists in recent decades. Indeed, the effort to study them required the field to change, because a long-term relationship cannot be created in a one-hour laboratory experiment, which had been the preferred research method of social psychologists. Because people spend most of their lives and most of their social interactions with people they have some sort of relationship with, a social psychology that failed to understand close relationships was by definition missing out on crucial aspects of social life. Let us consider some of what has been learned.

Whether relationships continue depends partly on how people deal with temptation, especially the temptation to seek other possible partners. Miller (1997) had people in dating relationships look at photos of attractive members of the opposite sex and recorded how long they looked at them. He contacted the participants months later to see whether they were still together with the same relationship partner. The longer they had looked, the more likely they were to break up. Apparently, exposing yourself to temptation (even just by looking at photos of attractive members of the opposite sex) is one sign that the person may be drifting toward breaking up.

There is some evidence that men and women respond to relationship threats and temptations in different ways. In a series of studies (Lydon, Menzies-Toman, Burton, & Bell, 2008), people who were in committed relationships were introduced to an attractive single person (or, in other studies, imagined this experience). Women reacted to meeting a desirable man by increasing their commitment to their current partner, such as by tolerating his faults more, thinking more positively about him, or increasing

her level of commitment to him. Men, on the other hand, reacted to meeting an attractive single woman by reducing their commitment to their current partner and becoming more critical of her. The implication is that meeting a tempting new partner makes men entertain the possibility of a new relationship instead of the one they have, whereas women try to defend their current relationship.

I LOVE YOU MORE EACH DAY (?)

Many people in happy marriages say that their relationships continue to grow and improve over the years. People striving to have good and lasting relationships want to know what secrets or actions enable this to happen. If you form a relationship when you are falling in love, everything seems wonderful and perfect. How can things continue to get even better than that?

The data suggest a very different picture. People may say and even believe their relationships are getting better, but usually they are mistaken. Sprecher (1999) had people report on their relationship quality year after year, and also report on changes. People in happy relationships consistently said their relationship was better each year. But if you compared how they rated it this year with how they rated it last year, there was no change. The ever-improving relationship is largely a myth. Good relationships essentially stay the same over long periods of time.

The only alternative to staying the same is to get worse. Many longitudinal studies that track couples over years find essentially two outcomes: Some stay the same, and others get worse (e.g., Levenson & Gottman, 1983; Sprecher, 1999). Relationships start off good, and either they stay good or they go downhill. The problem of how to have a good long-term relationship is therefore not finding a way to make it better and better; rather, the crucial thing is to avoid the downward spiral. Moreover, once relationships begin to deteriorate, it is apparently difficult and unusual to stop this process. The most important challenge is therefore to prevent the downward spiral from starting.

INVESTING IN RELATIONSHIPS THAT LAST

The question "Why do people stay with their long-term relationship partners?" was the focus of years of research by relationships expert Caryl Rusbult (1983). She began by noting the simpleminded answer: People stay with relationships when they are happy and satisfied. This is not wrong, but it is not a full explanation. People who were satisfied with their relationships were more likely than unsatisfied partners to stay together, but the statistical link was surprisingly weak—which meant that there must be some other factors at work.

Eventually Rusbult and her colleagues developed a theory called the **investment model**, with three factors. The first factor, sure enough, is satisfaction. Do you like your partner? Are you glad you have this particular relationship? Do you enjoy spending time together? Does your partner please and satisfy you? If your answers are yes, the relationship is more likely to survive. This is hardly surprising.

The second factor is the quality of available alternatives. Maybe your relationship is not really satisfying, but you don't see anyone else on the horizon who might be better. In that case, you might remain in an unsatisfying relationship. Conversely, your relationship may be pretty good and satisfying, but if someone clearly better than your partner comes along and makes you an offer, you may be tempted to leave. Here, Rusbult's theory makes the important point that a decision on whether to stay or leave a particular relationship doesn't depend only on how you evaluate that relationship. The decision also depends on whether you could do better with someone else.

The third factor is how much the individual has invested in the relationship. Rusbult notes that many investments are "sunk costs," which means that the person has put time, effort, emotion, and other resources into a relationship and cannot get them back out. If you have struggled for two years to get your partner to understand your feelings or respect your needs, and you then break up and start over with someone else, all that struggle is lost. You may have to repeat it all with your new partner. A couple that has spent 20 years together, amassing savings, coordinating careers, raising children, and the like, may be resistant to change simply because they have invested so much in the relationship and do not want to lose it. Even if another attractive partner comes along, they may cling to the relationship that they have worked hard to build. When an old married person dies, friends sometimes tell the widow or widower, "You don't get over it; you get used to it." The implication is that the lost partner is not replaceable. Even if you remarry, you cannot rebuild what you may have shared with someone for many decades of your adult life.

Each of these three factors alone has a weak (though significant) ability to predict whether couples stay together or break apart. Putting them together provides a very strong (statistically) basis for prediction. If you are satisfied with the relationship, don't see appealing alternatives, and have invested a great deal in the relationship, you will almost certainly remain committed to it. Charles and Diana, whose relationship story opened this chapter, were clearly not satisfied and had plenty of alternatives,

Commitment to one's relationship is weaker when many high-quality alternative partners are available.

and these facts probably helped cause their relationship to break up even though they had invested a fair amount (public statements, time, money, love, plus the raising of children) in it.

The investment theory can even explain some of the phenomena that have puzzled psychologists for decades, including why people (especially women) remain in relationships with physically violent, abusive partners (e.g., Rusbult & Martz, 1995). Logically, one would think that if your partner hits, hurts, or abuses you, you should immediately get out of that relationship and find someone else. Satisfaction is generally not very high in abusive relationships. But many abuse victims do not believe they have alternatives. Some believe they are not attractive enough to find someone else (a belief that the abusive spouse sometimes encourages). At the same time, many abuse victims invest a great deal in making the relationship work, often over long-term cycles in which brief episodes of violent abuse are followed by repentance, making up, sharing feelings, and promising to do better in the future. The victim may be reluctant to chuck aside all that has been achieved and take a chance on a new partner who may be no better.

THINKING STYLES OF COUPLES

Certainly people do some things that help their relationships succeed. High on the list are ways in which the couple deals with problems and conflicts. If you live with someone for many years, there is a

---

INVESTMENT MODEL theory that uses three factors—satisfaction, alternatives, and investments—to explain why people stay with their long-term relationship partners

high likelihood that sooner or later the person will be unpleasant or difficult, at least occasionally. It is also likely that conflicts will arise when the two of you want different things, such as spending a vacation at the beach or visiting one person's parents, or when you disagree about money.

Some research has compared happy couples with couples whose relationships are in trouble. Seeing how those two types of couples differ, especially in how they deal with problems and conflicts, can shed light on what makes some couples happier than others.

Some of the crucial differences between happy and unhappy couples are based on the attributions they make. (As we saw in Chapter 5, attributions are inferences about the causes of events.) In strong, happy relationships, partners seem willing to give the partner the benefit of the doubt most of the time. For example, Holtzworth-Munroe and Jacobson (1985) asked people how they would respond when the partner did something unpleasant, as opposed to doing something nice. The happy couples said they would probably attribute the partner's unpleasant behavior to some external factor, such as thinking that the person must be under stress at work. In contrast, when the partner does something pleasant, the member of a happy couple was likely to view this as further proof of what a good person the partner is. In short, good acts were attributed to the partner's inner qualities, while bad acts were dismissed as due to external factors. The researchers called this pattern (internal attributions for good behavior, external for bad) the **relationship-enhancing style of attribution**. It strengthens the relationship by making the partners see each other in a positive light.

The unhappy couples interpreted events along the opposite lines. If the partner did something nice, they tended to think it was due to external factors. For example, if the husband brought the wife flowers, she might think, "He must have just gotten those on sale" or even "He did something wrong and is trying to cover it up." If the partner did something bad, the person would think, "Well, that's just typical!" and see it as a reflection of the kind of person the partner was. Thus, bad acts were attributed to the partner's inner qualities, whereas good acts were dismissed as due to external factors. The researchers called this pattern the **distress-maintaining style of attribution**.

These styles of thinking explain why it is often so difficult to save a relationship that is in trouble, even with the aid of professional marriage therapists.

What attribution does she make for his gift? "He must love me very much." "He must have done something wrong and wants to pacify me." "He must have gotten those on sale." "He's such a sweetheart." "He probably wants something from me."

Getting people to change their actions and treat each other better is certainly an important first step, but once the distress-maintaining attributional pattern is in place, good actions tend to be discounted. You may decide to try to be nicer to your partner in order to try to strengthen the relationship, but your partner is likely to dismiss your positive acts. Meanwhile, even if you are trying to be good, you may occasionally slip up and say or do something unkind—in which case your distress-maintaining partner is likely to see this as the "real" you emerging again. You can't win, at least as long as your partner follows the distress-maintaining style of thinking.

Other important thought processes include how people look at the relationship itself. Happy couples tend to exaggerate how wonderful the relationship is. When problems arise, they may see them as isolated incidents. In this way, they sustain a view that the

---

RELATIONSHIP-ENHANCING STYLE OF ATTRIBUTION tendency of happy couples to attribute their partner's good acts to internal factors and bad acts to external factors

DISTRESS-MAINTAINING STYLE OF ATTRIBUTION tendency of unhappy couples to attribute their partner's good acts to external factors and bad acts to internal factors

relationship is great. MacDonald and Ross (1999) found that people's ratings of their dating relationships were more positive and optimistic than were the ratings of those same relationships by the young lovers' parents and roommates. (The roommates' predictions about whether the relationship would last were the most accurate!) Vaughan (1986) found that when couples start to move toward breaking up, there is often a reassessment, in which they go back and reinterpret past events as far less wonderful and positive than they seemed at the time. For example, many happy couples maintain a highly romanticized story of how they first met, suggesting that they discovered that they were truly meant for each other and that they really turned each other on because they had a terrific rapport. When the same couple is preparing for breakup or divorce, they create a new version of the story of how they first met, suggesting that it was just an accident, that they happened to be lonely or sexually desperate and were willing to strike up a romance with anybody who happened to be there, or that the attraction was based on false impressions.

Another important process is devaluing alternatives. Johnson and Rusbult (1989) had people who were in relationships rate the attractiveness of several potential dating partners. The people in the most committed relationships gave these potential partners low ratings, especially when the other person was attractive and would actually have been available as a possible dating partner. These circumstances were considered to be the most threatening, and so the devaluing of alternatives was probably a defensive response against the danger of becoming interested in someone else. Sure enough, in another study those same researchers found that people who failed to devalue alternatives were more likely to break up than people who did. In other words, people in lasting relationships did not find other people appealing, whereas people in doomed relationships (the ones that later broke up) found other people appealing and even increased their attraction to them over time. Recall that when Miller (1997) let people look at attractive photos of opposite-sex individuals for as long as they wanted, the duration of looking predicted whether they broke up with their current partner: Those who looked longest were most likely to break up.

In another study (Simpson, Gangestad, & Lerma, 1990), young, heterosexual participants who were in relationships rated photos of young opposite-sex persons as less attractive than did people who are not in relationships. The two groups did not differ in how they rated young same-sex individuals or older opposite-sex individuals—neither of which constituted a potential threat to their current dating relationship. Thus, only the potential alternative partners were

Honesty sometimes is not the best policy, even if you are George Washington and "cannot tell a lie."

devalued. The implication is that closing your mind to other potential partners is one way to help keep your relationship safe.

BEING YOURSELF: IS HONESTY THE BEST POLICY?

Listen to the discussions on television about what is best for long-term relationship success, and one common theme is honesty. The prevailing wisdom is that honesty is crucial, even essential, for relationship success. You have to be able to be yourself and show yourself as you really are, and your partner has to honestly accept this.

Then again, when you are shopping with your romantic partner and she or he asks "Does this garment make me look fat?" should you honestly say "Yes, but no more than most of your other clothes"? Honesty may be overrated. After all, people who are wildly, passionately in love often idealize and overestimate their partners—is that necessarily a bad thing? Why does love make us see each other as better than we are, if seeing each other accurately is best for relationship success?

There are in fact two very different views about honesty's role in successful relationships. One holds that honesty is the best policy: It is best if two people understand each other fully and correctly, communicate all their feelings, and accept each other for who they are. The other is that the people should idealize each other and see each other in a positively biased fashion.

During passionate love, two people generally take a very positive, even distorted view of each other. Friends will say, "What does he see in her?" or "I can't believe she thinks he's so brilliant." Moreover, the lovers tend to encourage and help each other to see each other in this idealized fashion. On dates, they wear their best clothes and are on their best behavior: thoughtful, charming, considerate, and proper. A woman might be careful that her new boyfriend only sees her when her hair is combed and she is wearing makeup. A man may clean up his language and monitor the opinions he expresses so as to make a good impression.

Because of these practices, people fall in love with an idealized version of each other. Such illusions may be difficult to sustain over the long run. Still, does that mean people should rush into honesty? Perhaps. You probably do want to be known and loved for who you really are. You might feel insecure if your partner has never seen the "real" you and instead has only known you on your best behavior. You may feel that if the other person ever found out what you are really like, he or she would reject and abandon you. The love between Charles and Diana may have started off with both people idealizing each other, but when the fairy tale ended and reality set in, the problems began.

The question then becomes, should you try to preserve your partner's idealized version of you for as long as possible? Or should you reveal your true self, with all your flaws and failings, and seek to be accepted that way?

Research has provided conflicting answers. Work by William Swann and his colleagues (e.g., Swann, 1985, 1987; see also Chapter 3) sought to show that people desire others to see them as they see themselves. (Admittedly, most people see themselves in a positively distorted fashion, so this is not the same as all-out honesty.) These researchers found that different rules apply in dating as opposed to marriage. When dating, people were most intimate with partners who viewed them most favorably. Within marriage, however, people were most intimate with partners who saw them as they saw themselves. In fact, people with low self-esteem were more intimate with partners who viewed them relatively less favorably than with partners who thought highly of them (Swann, De La Ronde, & Hixon, 1994).

In contrast, studies by Murray and Holmes (1993, 1994; Holmes, 2004; Murray, Holmes, & Griffin, 1996) support the idealization view. In their studies, couples were assessed on how much they idealized each other, as well as on relationship satisfaction. The researchers then followed up with the couples after many months to see whether they were still

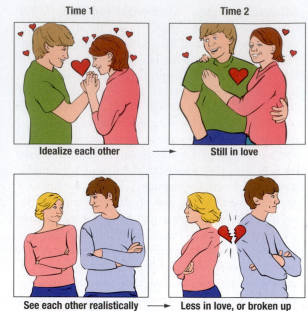

▶ FIGURE 12.6 Idealize each other and you will stay together longer.

dating and, if so, how they were doing. They found that people who saw each other in the most positive fashion had the happiest relationships—and the most durable ones (that is, least likely to break up). Moreover, the idealization seemed to be the crucial cause. Having a very positive view of the other person at Time 1 led to a happier relationship at (later) Time 2, but a happy relationship at Time 1 did not predict a positive opinion of the partner at Time 2 (see ▶ **FIGURE 12.6**). This finding is consistent with the relationship-enhancing style of thought discussed in the previous section: People who downplay their partners' bad points and emphasize their partners' good points have the happiest relationships.

One resolution of these seemingly discrepant findings has to do with what aspects of self are being measured (Swann, 1998). Swann's studies measured very specific features of the self, whereas Murray and Holmes measured global, overall appreciation. It is therefore plausible that both findings are correct. People may want their partner to see them accurately in the little things but to hold a broadly positive view of them in the vague, general sense. It is better for your partner to know accurately whether you are good at fixing the car, balancing the checkbook, being on time for a date, or acting in a charming and respectful manner in front of your partner's parents. If your partner vastly overestimates you on any of those, there may be trouble! But at the same time, you probably want your partner to think that you are a wonderful person in general. If your partner has a somewhat inflated view of what a nice person you are, how intelligent you are, or how physically

This Victorian couple may not look like they are madly in love, but their marriage probably lasted longer than most marriages today.

pretentious. In those marriages, husband and wife would dress up for dinner together. They sometimes addressed each other in relatively formal terms. They did not necessarily pour out all their inner feelings to each other but kept some distance. They tried to keep up good, proper behavior even when alone together. In a sense, they remained on their best behavior, so that 5 or 25 years into a marriage they still acted almost as if they were still courting. To the modern sensibility, these practices seem like a silly way to go about having a close relationship with someone. The modern mind thinks that people should share everything about themselves.

But perhaps the Victorian practices deserve to be reconsidered. In fact, the middle-class Victorians had the longest lasting marriages in Western history, on average (Macfarlane, 1986; Shorter, 1975; Stone, 1977). How can you make a relationship tolerable for 40 years? Perhaps the Victorians had a valid solution: Be on your best behavior. The research by Murray and her colleagues lends support to this view. Rather than requiring your partner to see you at your worst, such as sitting on the couch in dirty underwear and scratching yourself, or pouring forth all sorts of neurotically insecure thoughts, you want to help your partner continue to idealize you. On a first date, most people dress and act carefully so as to make the best impression they can. Perhaps if they continued to do this through many years of committed relationship and marriage, they would get better results.

attractive you are, this may help the relationship to survive.

Another, perhaps deeper way to reconcile these findings is that people want selective confirmation of how they think of themselves—neither total honesty nor total illusion. They want their partners to see them at their best, which is a real and valid part of who they are, as opposed to seeing either the full nasty truth or a fictional version that is unrealistically perfect. The most attractive, brilliant, and charming, but still genuine, version of yourself is the one you'd like your partner to believe is the real you. The relationship-enhancing style of thought focuses on your partner's best traits and ignores the bad ones, but it does not fabricate nonexistent good traits.

It is therefore probably a good idea to stay on your best behavior for a relatively long period of time. Relationships do benefit when the people can sustain highly favorable views of each other. You want to allow your partner to see you at your best and to keep up a somewhat idealized view of the kind of person you are.

The marriages among the middle class during the Victorian period (late 19th century, before World War I) are often mocked these days as phony and

---

[QUIZ YOURSELF]

Maintaining Relationships

1. Over the years, people in happy relationships say that their relationship _____; in fact, it _____.
   (a) is improving; does improve
   (b) is improving; stays the same
   (c) stays the same; does stay the same
   (d) stays the same; improves

2. People want their partner to see them _____ in the little things and to see them _____ in general.
   (a) accurately; accurately   (b) accurately; positively
   (c) positively; accurately   (d) positively; positively

3. People who have a distress-maintaining attributional style make _____ attributions if their partner does something good, and _____ if their partner does something bad.
   (a) external; external   (b) external; internal
   (c) internal; external   (d) internal; internal

4. In order to have a happy long-term relationship with a significant other, it helps to have a _____ view of one's partner.
   (a) negative   (b) neutral
   (c) positive   (d) realistic

Associated Press

Constructionist theories emphasize that sexual attitudes and behaviors are shaped by cultural influences.

Sexuality

Are love and sex the same thing? Undoubtedly they overlap in many cases and are often intertwined. But a recent social theory proposes that they have two separate biological bases, which can sometimes result in confusion.

This theory was put forward by Diamond (2003b, 2004) based on her studies of female sexuality through time. Diamond's basic point is that humans form relationships based on two separate systems, which can reinforce each other or be in conflict. One of these is the attachment system (see the earlier section on attachment theory). This is an urge to connect and form close social bonds with a few individuals. The other system is the sex drive, based on the principles of mating. Diamond says that evolution probably shaped the sex drive to focus on the opposite gender (because only heterosexual sex can create children). The attachment drive, in contrast, is probably gender neutral. Most children (boys and girls) form their first attachment to their mother, and later develop close friendships or attachments to other people, often primarily of their own gender.

SOCIAL CONSTRUCTIONIST THEORIES theories asserting that attitudes and behaviors, including sexual desire and sexual behavior, are strongly shaped by culture and socialization

If attachment and sexuality remained completely separate, there might be no problem, but in reality human beings mix intimacy with sex. The natural sex drive might dictate an initial preference for opposite-gender sex partners, but the attachment drive can promote intimacy between people of the same gender, and sometimes this can result in sexual attraction too.

A curious pattern that Diamond observed in her data led her to conclude that attachment and sex were somewhat separate, independent systems that can produce these surprising effects. She found that many women identified themselves as heterosexual but then found themselves having a homosexual (lesbian) relationship. At that point, these women might identify themselves as lesbians. Crucially, however, the lesbian orientation often did not outlast the relationship: If the woman broke up with her girlfriend, she would not go looking for another woman, but instead would often find a man as her next romantic partner. Her affair with another woman was thus not a sign of a deep, fixed, unchangeably lesbian orientation. Instead, it was a result of her love and intimacy with a particular human being who happened to be a woman. She might have lesbian love with her, but when the relationship ended, she would revert to the standard heterosexual preference, and her next partner would be a man.

Diamond (2003a) concluded that if there is a "gay gene," love is not on it. Love comes from the attachment drive, and that drive is independent of gender. You can love both your mother and your father, both your son and your daughter, both your best male and best female friend. A gay gene (if it exists, which is controversial) would stipulate sexual orientation, so it might dictate which gender you would want to have sex with, but it would not limit your ability to experience love and intimacy with either gender. Attachment can lead to sexual desire, and sexual intimacy can promote attachment, so the two are not entirely independent—which is why sometimes people find themselves attracted to someone of the "wrong" gender, however they have defined it.

THEORIES OF SEXUALITY

There are several basic theoretical approaches to sex. Especially popular and influential during the 1970s were **social constructionist theories**, which asserted that cultural forces and socialization shape how people assign meaning to their lives, with the result that sexual attitudes and behaviors vary widely based on culture (see DeLamater & Hyde, 1998; Staples, 1973). It is no accident that this view was most influential during the peak years of the "sexual revolution" (1960s to 1970s). The sexual revolution had changed sexual attitudes and behaviors so rapidly in such a short time that it seemed as though almost any further changes would be possible. To regard patterns of sexual desires as innately programmed seemed incompatible with how much change had occurred in a decade.

The social constructionist approach to sex acknowledges that there may be some biological foundations to sex, but most forms of sexual desire are seen as the result of cultural conditioning. Who wants to do what to whom (sexually) is seen as a result of social and political influences, including upbringing and media influence. Gender differences in sexuality are seen as highly changeable roles that are created by society to serve political or other goals. Feminist theory, which also reached a peak at this time, allied itself closely with the social constructionist approach to sex. In that view, women's sexuality was shaped by how men had long sought to control and oppress women; again, cultural influences (in this case, the influence of male-dominated culture on women) were seen as decisive (e.g., Kitzinger, 1987).

Evolutionary theory emerged in the 1970s and 1980s to provide a radically different view of sex. **Evolutionary theory** asserts that the sex drive has been shaped by natural selection and that its forms therefore tend to be innate (e.g., Symons, 1979, 1995). Those patterns of sexual desire that led prehistoric men and women to have the most children would win in the evolutionary competition, with the result that people today are mainly descended from people who had those patterns of desire. For example, many prehistoric men might have been attracted to old women instead of young women, but old women usually do not have babies. The men who married old women would therefore not pass on their genes. As a result, today's men would all be descended from men who preferred younger women (Buss, 1994).

The evolutionary approach sees gender differences as rooted in biology and hence as less flexible and less influenced by politics and culture than is suggested by the social constructionist view. One basis for gender differences lies in different reproductive strategies. People today are descended from those ancestors who raised the most children, but what succeeded best for one gender may not be the same as what worked best for the other. A woman can have only a few babies in her lifetime; each one occupies her body for at least nine months and typically makes demands on her time and energy for years. Hence a woman would by nature be cautious about sex and mating, because each pregnancy is a huge investment for her. A man, on the other hand, can make a baby with only a few minutes of pleasure. Biologically, he could walk away and never expend any more time, effort, or other resources on that baby, yet still have passed along his genes. Hence brief, casual, one-time sexual encounters will be more appealing to men than to women (Trivers, 1972).

off the mark .com   by Mark Parisi

I KNOW YOU'D LIKE TO PASS ON YOUR GENES, TROY, BUT I WON'T BE YOUR ACCOMPLICE...

offthemark.com

Men can also be much less choosy than women about their partners, for the same reason. After all, the quality of your offspring depends on both your genes and those of your partner. If a woman gets pregnant by a low-quality man and then a better man comes along, she cannot make another baby for many months (by which time the better mate may be long gone). Hence the most effective strategy for women would involve being cautious and choosy before consenting to sex. In contrast, if a man gets a low-quality woman pregnant and then a better partner comes along, he can make a baby with the new woman almost immediately. Having sex with low-quality partners is thus more costly for women than for men (Symons, 1979; Buss & Schmitt, 1993). As one sign of this, when researchers ask people what is the minimum IQ you would want to have in a sex partner, women give higher numbers than men (Buss & Schmitt, 1993).

The same logic would predict differences in the number of sex partners desired. A woman can get pregnant only about once a year regardless of how many men she has sex with, whereas a man can make many different babies if he has sex with many different women. Moreover, for a woman, getting pregnant is not the only or main issue; she also wants a man to help provide for her and her children. (For example, if she has two children and is pregnant

---

EVOLUTIONARY THEORY theory of sexuality asserting that the sex drive has been shaped by natural selection and that its forms thus tend to be innate

A woman pays a higher biological price than a man for making a poor choice of sex partners, and so it behooves women to be more cautious than men about sex.

with a third, she may find it hard to get food for her family by herself, especially if getting food requires chasing animals or climbing trees.) Hence she may want to form a close relationship with a man whom she can trust to stick around and provide for her. A woman with one intimate partner is more likely to receive male care over a long term than a woman who changes partners frequently. Nature may therefore have shaped women to desire sex mainly in the context of committed, lasting relationships. Men, in contrast, can be successful at passing on their genes by having sex with many different partners.

A third theoretical perspective on sexuality is based on **social exchange theory**, which seeks to understand social behavior by analyzing the costs and benefits of interacting with each other (Blau, 1964; Homans, 1950, 1961; Sprecher, 1998). In this view, sex is a resource that women have and men want. Men therefore have to give women other resources in exchange for sex (Baumeister & Vohs,

2004; Symons, 1979). These resources may include money, attention, respect, love, and commitment. Male sexuality is not seen as having much value for social exchange, whereas most cultures place a high value on female sexuality. Most cultures do not place as much value on virginity or marital fidelity in men as in women. (Indeed, some commentators think that the marriage of Charles and Diana was partly shaped by pressure on Charles to marry a virgin, on the assumption that a future king should not marry someone who has already had other sex partners. It is doubtful that a female heir to the throne would be under similar pressure to marry a male virgin.) Likewise, in the extreme, women can sell sex for money—prostitution has been found all over the world in many different cultures—whereas that option is not widely available to men (except for a small number who, like women, cater to male customers).

Social exchange theory provides an economic perspective on sex. In essence, women's sexuality is the supply, and men's sexuality creates the demand. Moreover, people are hooked into the system, in the sense that their sexual decisions are affected by what other people in their peer group or community are doing. The "price" of sex, which is to say how much the man must invest before the woman consents to sex, may vary according to the standard laws of supply and demand. You may have noticed the difference if you have attended a school or college where one gender far outnumbers the other: The minority gender has much more influence. When men outnumber women (so that the supply of sex is lower than demand), the price is high: People have relatively little premarital or extramarital sex, and men must usually make a serious commitment before they can have sex. If a man doesn't want to make the commitment, he has few alternatives available and will probably just not have much sex. In contrast, when women outnumber men (such as after a major war, or in some low-income groups where many men have been lost to violence, prison, suicide, or outmigration), the price of sex drops, and women cannot usually demand much from the man in exchange for sex. If she refuses sex, he can just move on and get it from someone else.

SEX AND GENDER

Stereotypes about gender and sexuality include the following: (a) Men want sex more than women. (b) Men separate love and sex more than women. (c) Women's sexuality is more natural, whereas men's sexuality reflects more cultural influence. (d) Women serve as "gatekeepers" who restrict the total amount of sex and decide whether and when sex will happen. Two of these are correct, and two are incorrect; can you pick which ones are which?

SOCIAL EXCHANGE THEORY theory that seeks to understand social behavior by analyzing the costs and benefits of interacting with each other; it assumes that sex is a resource that women have and men want

The first stereotype asserts that there is a gender difference in strength of sex drive. During the 1970s, sex was seen as an unmitigated good; to say that men had a stronger sex drive implied that they were somehow better than women. However, the notion that more sex is always better was soon discredited as AIDS, unwanted pregnancies, and other problems surfaced. So it is perhaps possible now to take a fresh look at whether there is a gender difference in sex drive without worrying that some possible conclusions will be politically incorrect.

Nearly all the evidence supports the view that men have a stronger sex drive than women (see ▶ **FIGURE 12.7**). What behaviors do you think would reveal the strength of sex drive? Almost any form of overtly sexual behavior you might suggest is something men do more than women. Men think about sex more often, are aroused more often, desire sex more often, desire more sex partners, and desire more different kinds of sex acts than women. Men initiate sex more and refuse sex less than women. Men take more risks and expend more resources to get sex. Men want sex earlier in the relationship, want it more often during the relationship, and even want it more in old age. Men have more positive attitudes about their own genitals than do women, and they also have more positive attitudes about their partner's genitals than do women. Men find it harder to live without sex. (For example, some religious callings require people to give up sex, but all evidence suggests that men fail at this far more commonly than women.) And men rate their sex drives as stronger than women rate theirs. Essentially, every measure and every study point to greater sexual motivation among men (Ard, 1977; Beck, Bozman, & Qualtrough, 1991; Buss & Schmitt, 1993; Buzwell & Rosenthal, 1996; Cohen & Shotland, 1996; Knoth, Boyd, & Singer, 1988; Laumann et al., 1994; Leiblum & Rosen, 1988; Leitenberg & Henning, 1995; McCabe, 1987; Miller & Fishkin, 1997; Murphy, 1992; Oliver & Hyde, 1993; O'Sullivan & Byers, 1996; Reinholtz & Muehlenhard, 1995; Sprecher & Regan, 1996; for a review, see Baumeister, Catanese, & Vohs, 2001).

One of the largest and most consistent gender differences is in the desire for casual, uncommitted sex (Oliver & Hyde, 1993), which is probably based in a simple desire to have sex with different partners. The term **Coolidge effect** was coined to refer to the sexually arousing power of a new partner. Specifically, a male animal would have sex and researchers would measure how long it took until he could become aroused again, as a function of having either the same partner or a new partner willing to copulate with him (e.g., Wilson, Kuehn, & Beach, 1963). Males typically were more rapidly and more aroused by the new partner than by the familiar one (Francoeur, Perper, Scherzer, Sellmer, & Cornog, 1991, p. 130).

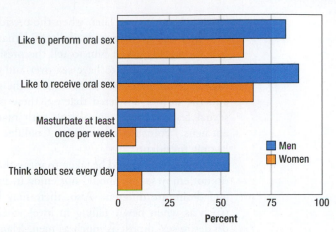

▶ **FIGURE 12.7** More men than women report high sexual desire on almost every measure, but some differences are bigger than others.

The term *Coolidge effect* is based on an amusing story about former U.S. President Calvin Coolidge, who was known for being a man of very few words. Once he and the First Lady toured a farm and were shown around separately. The First Lady noticed that the chicken area had many females but only one male. She inquired about this seeming imbalance, and the farmer assured her that the cock was in fact able to perform sexually dozens of times every night. "Please point that out to Mr. Coolidge," she told the

President Calvin Coolidge and his wife Grace.

COOLIDGE EFFECT the sexually arousing power of a new partner (greater than the appeal of a familiar partner)

farmer. A short time later, when the president came to this area, the farmer dutifully said that his wife had specifically asked him to tell the president that the rooster was able to have sex over and over each night. "Same hen every time?" asked the president, and the farmer answered that no, these prodigious sexual feats involved copulating with many different hens. "Point that out to Mrs. Coolidge," said the laconic president.

None of this should be taken to mean that women do not enjoy sex, or should not enjoy it. Enjoyment and desire are different. Also, there may be phases (such as when newly falling in love) when women do desire sex almost as much as men. Many couples find that their sexual desires seem to match almost perfectly when they are falling in love, and they get married expecting a lifelong rich sexual relationship—but when the passionate phase wears off, they revert to their different baselines, and the husband usually wants sex more than the wife.

The second stereotype was that men can separate sex and love more than women. This stereotype probably arose from a valid observation, which was that men are much more interested than women in having sex without love. (The evolutionary theory, described above, offers a strong explanation for why this should be true; see also Oliver & Hyde, 1993.) Men do surpass women in seeking and enjoying sex without love.

On the other hand, love and sex can be separated in the opposite manner—enjoying love without sex—and it appears that women find this more acceptable. Thus, as to which gender can separate love from sex better, we have a seeming standoff: Men accept sex without love, whereas women accept love without sex. (Both genders, however, probably find love combined with sex to be the best.) To resolve this standoff, one national survey asked people whether they agreed with the statement "Love and sex are two different things" (Janus & Janus, 1994). More women than men agreed with this statement. In that sense, women separate sex and love more than men. Hence the stereotype that men separate love from sex more easily than women is wrong.

The third stereotype has depicted women as closer to nature and men as closer to culture. This is relevant to the clash of theories we noted earlier: Is the sex drive mainly determined by culture, politics, and socialization, or by genes, hormones, and innate biological motivations? The answer does differ by gender—but in the way opposite to the stereotype.

To be sure, both nature and culture have an influence on every human being's sexuality. The balance between nature and culture can be expressed in terms of **erotic plasticity**, defined as the degree to which the sex drive can be shaped and altered by social, cultural, and situational forces. High plasticity indicates that culture can shape the person's sex drive to a great extent, whereas a more "natural" and inflexible sex drive would have low plasticity.

Considerable evidence shows that women have higher erotic plasticity than men (Baumeister, 2000). (It is not necessarily better or worse to have high plasticity.)

Adult women often go through many changes in their sexual feelings and desires, whereas men remain much more constant through life (e.g., Kinsey, Pomeroy, Martin, & Gebhard, 1953). Even switching back and forth between heterosexual and homosexual forms of sexuality is more common among women than men (e.g., Savin-Williams, 1990; Whisman, 1996). A man's sexual desires at age 20 are probably the same ones he will have at age 60, except for the natural diminishment due to aging. In contrast, a woman may have changed her desires and feelings several times along the way (Adams & Turner, 1985; Ard, 1977). Another sign is that many social and cultural factors have a stronger influence on female than male sexuality. For example, highly educated women have quite different sex lives than uneducated women, and highly religious women have very different sex lives than nonreligious women—but for men, the corresponding differences are much smaller (Adams & Turner, 1985; Laumann et al., 1994). Thus, two powerful cultural forces (religion and education) affect female sexuality more strongly than male sexuality.

The difference in plasticity suggests a fairly basic difference in how the sex drive operates. We have seen that culture influences what things mean. Women's sexual responses typically depend on what sex means: who the partner is, what sex might signify about the relationship, what other couples are doing at similar stages, how she feels about the sexual partner, and what her sexual activity might signify about her as a person. Male sexuality seems much more to be a bodily, physical response. For example, a man who likes oral sex might well enjoy it whenever and wherever (and with whomever) the opportunity arises, but a woman who likes oral sex will only want it under certain circumstances and in contexts that carry the right meanings.

In short, the third stereotype is wrong, even specifically backwards. Male sexuality is closer to nature and less affected by culture; women's sexuality is less biological and more closely tied to social and cultural meanings.

The fourth stereotype depicted women as the gatekeepers who restrict sex and decide whether and when it will happen. This is correct. Because men are not very choosy or cautious about sex, they are

EROTIC PLASTICITY the degree to which the sex drive can be shaped and altered by social, cultural, and situational forces

usually willing to have it under a wide variety of circumstances. Women are much more selective and hence become the ones who make the decision. Many findings confirm that women are the sexual gatekeepers. For example, a study of couples in various relationship stages (McCabe, 1987) considered the category of "reluctant virgins"—people who had a dating partner and wanted to be having sex but were not having it because their partner did not consent. This category was filled almost entirely with men. The implication is that men were ready for sex fairly early, but whether sex happened depended on the woman's choice.

One revealing study by Cohen and Shotland (1996) surveyed dating couples at Pennsylvania State University. They asked how many dates participants thought there should be before sex. They also asked each participant to estimate how many dates other people thought there should be before sex. There was a surprising difference: Nearly everyone thought that other people were leaping into bed faster than they themselves were. (For example, women thought that they would have sex after an average of 18 dates, but women typically estimated that other women would have sex after about 13 dates). Crucially, the researchers compared when the individual wanted to start having sex and when the couple actually did start having sex. The correlation between what men wanted and what happened was not significantly different from zero. In other words, when the man wanted to have sex was essentially irrelevant to whether or when the couple actually did have sex. In contrast, there was a very high correlation between the woman's preferences and the couple's activities. Thus, a couple starts having sex when the woman thinks it is appropriate; usually the man has been ready and waiting for some time.

Many dates involve eating together, and it is fair to assume that eating together usually precedes having sex together. To learn more about the effects of dieting on sex, read *Food for Thought*.

HOMOSEXUALITY

All these findings apply mainly to heterosexual relationships. In many respects, homosexual romance, sex, and love are quite similar to what happens between heterosexuals (for example, the desire for multiple partners is more common among male than female homosexuals; Bell & Weinberg, 1978), but there are some special aspects. For one, there are no clearly defined gender roles, so homosexuals may feel freer to negotiate their roles in romance and sex without conforming to how society has trained people to act. Of course, this can also make things a bit more awkward, precisely because one does not have a culturally determined script. For example, if

I'm ready when you're ready.

you are a heterosexual, you probably know how to act on a date with someone of the opposite sex, but if you were on a date with a member of your own sex, there are fewer standard rules to say who should pay the bill, who should hold the door for whom, and so forth.

The basic fact that homosexuality exists all over the world and survives generation after generation poses a fundamental challenge to some of the major theories discussed so far. If sexuality is a product of cultural conditioning, how can homosexuality continue to exist? Most cultures have condemned homosexuality to varying degrees, and dominant cultures have often taken a fairly extreme position that homosexuality is sinful, illegal, and socially undesirable. If cultural socialization shapes sexuality, why is anyone a homosexual? On the other hand, if the sex drive is shaped by evolution based on natural selection and success at reproduction, then again homosexuality should have vanished long ago, because homosexual sex does not produce children. How would a "gay gene" be passed along to future generations, if gay sex does not produce children?

At present there are no satisfactory answers. One intriguing theory, put forward by social psychologist Daryl Bem (1996, 1998), is known as EBE, for "exotic becomes erotic." It is based on Schachter's (1964) theory of emotion, discussed in Chapter 6, which holds that emotions arise when people have a bodily response of arousal and then put a label on it. Bem proposed that there is not a specific gene for homosexuality, but there are genetic contributions to temperament. Heterosexual development proceeds because boys and girls are temperamentally different and therefore play mainly with their own gender

Eating in Front of a Cute Guy

In the movie (and novel) *Gone With the Wind*, the heroine, Scarlett O'Hara, prepares for a dinner party by eating a meal at home. Asked about the seeming absurdity of eating just before dinner, she explains her behavior in self-presentational terms: A lady is expected to eat very little, so even though she is going to a dinner party, she will make the best impression if she hardly eats anything there. And because she is a hungry human being, the best way for her to refrain from eating the delicious food at the party is to be satiated before she goes!

Research has confirmed that people, perhaps especially women, eat sparingly in the presence of an attractive member of the opposite sex. In a laboratory study by Pliner and Chaiken (1990), college students ate a meal in the presence of an attractive male or female confederate. Both men and women ate less in the presence of an opposite-gender than a same-sex confederate. Moreover, the reduced eating was correlated with the motive to gain social approval by doing what is socially desirable, for both men and women. For women, additionally, the restraint on eating was linked to the wish to seem feminine. Thus, female eating in particular is tied to the pressures to please others and live up to cultural ideals of femininity.

The importance of making a good impression on a potential dating partner was confirmed in other work. Mori, Chaiken, and Pliner (1987) gave

participants the opportunity to eat snack foods (peanuts and M&M candies) while engaged in a get-acquainted conversation with a confederate. The confederate was either male or female. Half the time the confederate was presented as a desirable and interesting person, but half the time the confederate came across as something of a narrow-minded loser who had no hobbies or interests other than watching television, who had no career goals other than making money, and who claimed to already be in a romantic relationship. Female participants ate by far the least when in the presence of the attractive, desirable, and available man; they ate more in the presence of a woman or an unattractive man. Thus, they seemed to restrain their eating for self-presentational reasons, mainly to make a good impression on a potential dating partner. The results were less clear-cut for male participants. They ate less in the presence of a woman than in the presence of a man, but the woman's availability and desirability did not seem to affect their eating. Men's restraint may be a matter of politeness and general norms that are activated by any woman, rather than a particular effort to make a good impression.

Thus, restraining one's food intake may be more important to women seeking to make a good impression on a potential dating partner than it is to men. This was confirmed in another study, in which female participants were given feedback suggesting that they had scored as either masculine or feminine in terms of their

PhotoDisc

interests and personality. When women received private feedback that they were feminine, they ate less, consistent with the view that femininity operates as a cue to refrain from eating. But in another condition, the women were told that their male partners had seen their masculine/ feminine scores. The women who thought their partner knew they had scored as "masculine" ate the lowest amount of any group in the experiment. Presumably they sought to reestablish their feminine image by eating lightly, thereby conforming to the cultural ideal of femininity. ●

during childhood. To boys, therefore, other boys are familiar, whereas girls are different and "exotic." In adolescence, the boy may start to spend time around girls and will find himself nervous and otherwise aroused because they are different. He then learns to label this as sexual arousal. For heterosexual girls, the reverse applies: Boys seem different and exotic, so being around them is more arousing, and this arousal becomes labeled as romantic and sexual attraction.

Homosexuals, in Bem's theory, follow a similar process, except that during childhood they typically play with the other gender rather than their own. Some boys are temperamentally suited to prefer quiet play with girls rather than rough-and-tumble play with boys. When these boys reach adolescence, girls seem familiar, whereas other boys seem exotic. The

nervousness arising from boys then gets labeled as sexual arousal. The reverse applies to girls, though as Bem (1998) noted, girls are more likely than boys to grow up having regular contact with and playmates of both genders. (Bem suggested that women may be more bisexual than men precisely because they grow up around both boys and girls.)

At least one crucial step in Bem's theory—the labeling of nervousness as sexual arousal, leading to homosexual self-identification—has not yet been supported (or contradicted, for that matter) by data, probably because it is unethical to do properly controlled experiments that might transform someone into a homosexual. Bem's theory fit well with the research findings available at the time he developed it (the 1990s), but at present it still rests partly on speculation. And if Bem's theory does not turn out to be correct, then researchers must keep on looking for the mysterious combination of nature (genes, hormones) and social experiences that leads to homosexuality. Almost certainly there will be a combination of nature and nurture. For example, if one identical twin is gay, then the odds are about 50% that the other twin is gay (Bailey & Pillard, 1995). This is far above chance, which indicates that genes have something to do with it. But it is far short of a full explanation: If identical twins share 100% of their genes, then they should share 100% of genetic traits (such as eye color), whereas homosexuality is only shared at 50%. Social influences and personal experiences must explain the 50% of cases in which one twin is gay and the other is not.

Another reason to be cautious about Bem's theory is that it says that attraction is based on being different. We saw in Chapter 11 that friendship and other forms of attraction are more commonly based on similarity than difference (that is, "opposites attract" is not usually correct). It is possible that sexual desire is different, and indeed sexual attraction to the opposite gender is more common than attraction to one's own gender. Sexual desire may therefore be a special case. Still, more research is needed before psychology can claim to have a solid understanding of these matters.

EXTRADYADIC SEX

In the course of long relationships, many couples have some conflicts about sex. One person may want to try some sex act that the other doesn't, or one may simply want sex more than the other. In theory, the logical solution might be to find another partner. After all, if your husband doesn't want to play tennis with you, you just find another tennis partner and tell your husband about it later. Alas, that approach doesn't seem to work so well with sex.

In most long-term romantic relationships, the two partners expect each other to refrain from having sex with anyone else. When one person violates that expectation, the other is likely to be upset, and the relationship may be damaged or may even break up. This chapter began with the story of Charles and Diana, and though their marriage may have had multiple problems, it seems likely that the frequent infidelities by both of them contributed to their difficulties and eventual divorce. Even the term *infidelity* conveys a value judgment of disapproval (which is why many researchers prefer more neutral terms such as extramarital sex or **extradyadic sex**, which includes unmarried dating partners who occasionally have sex with someone other than each other).

Some couples have an "open" relationship, by which they mean that they are permitted to have sex with other people. There was a stage during the sexual revolution of the 1970s during which many people aspired to have such relationships and even to participate openly in sex with other people. Under those circumstances, extramarital sex was not regarded as being unfaithful.

Rare or Common? Different surveys have reported different rates of extramarital sex. Some conclude that nearly half of married people eventually stray (e.g., Thompson, 1983); other studies conclude that extramarital sex is quite rare. There are several reasons for the different numbers, but two of them are important. First, there probably have been changes in the rate of extramarital sex. It may have been more common and more tolerated in the 1970s than afterward, especially when the herpes and AIDS epidemics became widely known. (The high rates found by Thompson, 1983, essentially summarized statistics from the 1970s, before the dangers of herpes and AIDS were recognized.) Second, different studies use different sampling methods, and people who volunteer to answer a survey about sex are more likely to report extensive sexual experience than people who do not volunteer (Morokoff, 1986; Wiederman, 1993, 2004).

The most reliable numbers suggest that there is far less extramarital sex (indeed far less sex altogether) than you might think from movies, novels, and TV shows such as *Desperate Housewives*. According to the National Health and Social Life Survey (NHSLS), more than 75% of husbands and 90% of wives claim to have been completely faithful over the entire period of their marriage (Laumann et al., 1994). Using another well-constructed national sample, Wiederman (1997) concluded that 23% of men and 12% of women have ever engaged in extramarital sex (including in a previous marriage). Even if these numbers are precisely accurate, the actual rates of infidelity may end up being a little higher, because some people who have not yet had an affair will eventually do so. Still, that is not likely to make a huge difference, so one must assume that monogamy and fidelity are the norm. Estimates that half of married men have affairs (e.g., Thompson, 1983) are probably not accurate. The truth is closer to 1 out of 3 or 4 husbands, and 1 out of 9 or 10 wives, has sex with someone other than the spouse while married. Moreover, many of these are one-time occurrences in the course of a long marriage. In any given year, more than 90% of husbands and wives remain sexually faithful to their spouses.

EXTRADYADIC SEX having sex with someone other than one's regular relationship partner, such as a spouse or boy/girlfriend

Men are often surprised to learn they are not related to their children.

AP Photo/Chicago Sun-Times, Robert A. Davis

Attitudes About Extradyadic Sex. Tolerance for extramarital sex remains fairly low. More than 90% of both men and women consistently say that extramarital sex is wrong (either "always wrong" or "almost always wrong"; Laumann et al., 1994). In the same survey, only 1% said that having sex with someone other than your spouse is "not wrong at all." To be sure, there is a range of opinion. Well-educated people are more tolerant of extramarital sex than less educated people, men are more tolerant than women, and happily married people are less tolerant than unhappily married ones (Reiss, Anderson, & Sponaugle, 1980).

Extradyadic Sex and Breakups. Another consistent finding is that extramarital sex is a risk factor for breaking up. That is, people who remain faithful are more likely to stay together than people who have sex with other partners (Laumann et al., 1994). This is true even for couples who have an "open marriage" or other understanding that permits extramarital sex (Blumstein & Schwartz, 1983). For example, using data from a major national survey, Wiederman (1997) crossed the question "Have you ever had extramarital sex?" with the question "Have you ever gotten a divorce?" and found a significant relationship. Among men who had had extramarital sex, 38% had gotten a divorce too, whereas only 15% of fully faithful husbands had divorced. Among women, the corresponding numbers were 20% and 8%. Thus, having extramarital sex was associated with more than double the divorce rate, as compared to fidelity.

One cannot leap to the conclusion, however, that extramarital sex causes divorce. After all, researchers cannot randomly assign people to have or not have extramarital sex, which is the sort of research design needed for firm conclusions about causality (see Chapter 1). Some people may be deeply unhappy about their marriage and have an affair as a result of their dissatisfaction. The affair could therefore be a symptom rather than a cause of the marital unhappiness, and perhaps those people would have gotten a divorce even if they had not had an affair.

People express different opinions about the link between extramarital sex and breaking up. Many people seem to judge themselves differently from their partners. People often view their own infidelities (if they have committed them) as a result rather than a cause of the problems in their relationships (Spanier & Margolis, 1983). Their partner's infidelities, however, are seen as an important cause leading directly to the relationship problems and even to the breakup. This finding probably reflects a self-serving bias (discussed in Chapter 5): People see their own misbehavior as being caused by external factors and not producing bad consequences, but see their

To be sure, all these data are based on self-reports (what people are willing to tell an interviewer or report on a questionnaire), and it is hard to rule out the possibility that people claim to be more faithful than they are. In recent years, DNA tests have begun to confirm that many children (between 5% and 15%, according to most experts on paternity testing) are not biologically related to the man they believe is their father, presumably because the mother conceived the child through extramarital sex (Abraham, 2002). If that many women actually have children as a result of secret affairs, then the total amount of extramarital sex by women is probably much higher than we have assumed, and higher than many women are admitting. There may be plenty of desperate housewives after all!

Evolutionary psychologists (e.g., Buss, 1994) have pointed out that having such affairs and duping the husband into raising the children as if they were his own is a strategy that makes good sense from the (admittedly amoral) standpoint of passing on one's genes. Highly successful and attractive men may have the best genes, and so a woman can make the best offspring by conceiving a child with such a man, even if he is not willing to marry her. To receive long-term financial support and care, she may need to marry a different man who might not have such good genes, but if he believes her children are his, he will take good care of them and provide for them. It does appear to be true that millions of men in North America and Western Europe have been fooled into raising children not their own (Abraham, 2002). Some experts have proposed that for a woman to dupe a man into raising children who were secretly conceived via extramarital sex is more immoral than rape (Abraham, 2002).

partner's actions in a less favorable light; in short, they would prefer to blame the divorce on their partner's actions than on their own. Still, these data do suggest that the causal arrow can point in either direction: marital problems can lead to infidelity, or vice versa. In a famous television interview, Princess Diana attributed her marital problems to Charles's infidelities, but she neglected to mention her own. If she was like most people, she was quick to say that her partner's sexual activities with others had damaged the marriage, whereas her own outside sexual activities were merely a result of the problems in the marriage—in effect, blaming him but not herself for similar actions.

We also should not overstate the link. Affairs do not lead inevitably to breaking up. In fact, as Lawson (1988) found, only a small minority of extramarital affairs lead to divorce. Infidelity is a risk factor, but the risk remains fairly small. Still, the affair is often a bigger risk than people think. Lawson (1988) found that many people in her sample began their extramarital affairs with the firm belief that they could control the new sexual involvement and that their marriage would not be affected. Often they were wrong. In particular, many people find themselves falling in love with their extramarital sex partners, especially when they have sex repeatedly or on a regular basis over a period of months. The strong emotional involvement often develops into a threat to the marriage, indeed more than the sex itself. Even if the marriage survives, it may be damaged or shaken by one person's love for someone else.

These patterns fit several themes. We saw earlier in this chapter that looking at tempting alternative partners can lead to breaking up one's current relationship, and now we see that having sex or romance with other partners likewise puts the relationship at risk. Avoiding those temptations is thus one constructive strategy to help preserve a relationship. One theme of this book is that nature says go and culture says stop. It is apparently natural to feel tempted from time to time to admire or even pursue alternative partners, but people can learn to resist and overcome these temptations. Another theme is the importance of self-regulation for overriding antisocial impulses. Being happily married or attached does not mean that the automatic system is indifferent to other possible partners. Self-regulation (here, in the form of stopping oneself from pursuing other partners) is a big part of the work that goes into making a relationship succeed.

Extradyadic Activity in Dating Relationships.

Infidelity has also been studied in dating relationships. Hansen (1987) defined "extradyadic relations" as erotic kissing, petting, or intercourse with someone other than your steady dating partner, and he found that 71% of men and 57% of women had experienced this (either by doing it or having their partner do it). Despite the high frequency of experiences, most people expressed low tolerance and a negative attitude toward such activity. Many people disapproved of such activities but occasionally engaged in them anyway. The self-serving bias was apparent there too. Hansen found that people rated their own extradyadic relations as less bad than their partner's. When asked how much the extradyadic relations had caused pain and suffering, only 9% of men and 14% of women said their own infidelity had hurt their partner a great deal. In contrast, 45% of men and 30% of women said their partner's infidelity had hurt them a great deal. As in the Spanier and Margolis (1983) findings, people seem more willing to make excuses for their own misbehavior than for their partner's!

There are several possible reasons for the fact that people say their own infidelities were less harmful than their partners' infidelities. One may be simple knowledge. If you think your partner never knew anything about your own infidelity, then you might think that he or she was not hurt by it. In contrast, if you say your partner's infidelity hurt you, then you do know about it. It seems likely that the attributional bias of making more excuses for your own misbehavior than for your partner's misbehavior is the main cause of the differential self-blame, but differential knowledge (such that a person is not harmed by infidelities about which he or she does not know) could also be a contributing factor.

JEALOUSY AND POSSESSIVENESS

In medieval Europe, there were relatively few police and courts, and the system of law enforcement was not equal to the task of maintaining order. If people misbehaved or committed crimes, it often fell to the community itself to take action. One common form of punishment for less serious crimes and offenses was called the charivari (French word) or shivaree (English word) (Shorter, 1975). The whole village would gather together at some crucial place, such as outside the house of the offender. They would bring pots and other items and bang them together to make a loud noise. They would also shout or chant insulting remarks and might make embarrassing sounds. The point was to humiliate the offender.

The charivari was used to punish adultery. If a wife had sex with a man other than her husband, and enough people found out, the village would stage a charivari. Ironically, though, the charivari was not generally used to punish the adulterous woman or her lover. Instead, the village would punish the husband. The implication was that he had not satisfied his wife sexually or exerted sufficient control over her

In medieval Europe, charivari was the punishment for less serious crimes.

People often become jealous when they find their partner is having an affair with someone else (or even if they think their partner is having an affair).

behavior, so he needed to be punished. Apparently, if a man's wife had sex with another man, it was the husband's fault (Shorter, 1975).

The husband's humiliation, whether implicitly felt in the mere shame of his wife's infidelity, or explicitly recognized through the charivari, suggests an important link between jealousy and pride or self-esteem. When two people decide to have an extra-marital affair, they often think mainly of themselves, and they may not intend any harm to their spouses. But if the affair comes to light, the spouses will have a variety of negative reactions, and these are often linked to a feeling of humiliation. Finding out that your spouse or romantic partner has been unfaithful is often a serious blow to your pride. Sure enough, people married to unfaithful partners have lower self-esteem than people married to faithful partners (Shackelford, 2001).

Jealousy is a common response to partner infidelity, and many people feel jealous over even fairly minor signs that the partner might be interested in someone else, such as a flirtatious conversation at a party. Researchers distinguish jealousy from envy on the basis that jealousy is a fear of losing something that you have, whereas envy is a desire for something you do not have (Pines & Aronson, 1983).

Cultural Perspective. Some experts believe that jealousy is a product of social roles and expectations. In particular, some argue that Western societies have made men believe that women are their property, so men are jealous and sexually possessive of women. If only the culture taught people differently, the emotion of jealousy might disappear, according to this view.

Support for the cultural theory of jealousy came most famously from the anthropologist Margaret Mead's (1928) work *Coming of Age in Samoa*, though subsequent researchers have questioned her methods and conclusions and have even suggested that the handful of Samoans she interviewed were joking. Mead claimed that the Samoans did not have sexual jealousy or possessiveness. They allow their partners to share intimate interactions with others. Similar observations have been made about Native American (Eskimo) cultures, in which male houseguests sometimes have sex with the hostess, with her husband's permission.

More recent work, however, has questioned those seemingly idyllic, nonpossessive attitudes. Ira Reiss (1986a, 1986b) concluded that sexual jealousy is found in all cultures and societies, although its forms, rules, and expressions may vary from one to another. Eskimos do in fact have considerable sexual jealousy. The occasional sharing of a wife's sexual favors occurs only under certain circumstances, including consent by everyone involved and usually a desire to form a closer relationship between the two families. Hupka (1981) conducted a cross-cultural study of 92 different societies and cultures, and he found sexual jealousy in all of them, although again there were variations in how it was dealt with. In some, for example, a husband was permitted to beat or even kill his wife if he caught her having sex with another man, whereas other cultures prohibited such violent responses. Buunk and Hupka (1987) found that different countries focused jealousy on different acts—for example, kissing someone other than your spouse elicits jealousy in some but is permitted in others—but again jealousy was found everywhere, and the various cultures were more similar than different.

These findings suggest that society can modify and channel jealousy but cannot effectively eliminate it. Apparently, some degree of sexual possessiveness is deeply rooted in human nature. It is apparently normal and natural to feel jealous if you find your partner has had sexual relations with someone else.

Evolutionary Perspective. The apparent universality of jealousy suggests that we should look to biological and evolutionary patterns to help explain it. Buss (1994) and his colleagues have argued that there are strong evolutionary reasons for jealousy, but these reasons differ somewhat for men as opposed to women. These differences can be traced to the differences in male versus female reproductive systems. Both men and women supposedly want to pass on their genes, but the possibilities and dangers differ.

Men know that their wives can only have a few children, and normally just one at a time. Hence a major threat to the man's reproductive goal is the possibility that another man might make his wife pregnant. Throughout most of history, it was impossible for men to know whether the children borne by their female partners were in fact the men's own offspring, so there was a constant danger of ending up having to raise another man's child. The only solution was to keep strict control over the wife's sexual behavior. In various cultures, some men have kept their wives locked up and guarded, such as in a harem. Other men insisted that their wives wear iron chastity belts, which were originally designed as protection against rape but soon were adapted to help men retain confidence in their wives' fidelity. Such practices are largely absent in the modern Western world, though some men (and a few women) use threatened or actual physical violence to pressure their partners into remaining faithful. Because suspicions of jealousy can be unfounded, this violence sometimes hurts innocent victims. Even if the partner has been unfaithful (and, as noted above, DNA tests suggest that paternity uncertainty is still an important issue; Abraham, 2002), perpetrating or threatening physical violence against a romantic partner is immoral and illegal.

For women, the threat is different. If a woman's husband has sex with another woman, he has only expended a small quantity of sperm, and there is plenty more where that came from! The sperm itself

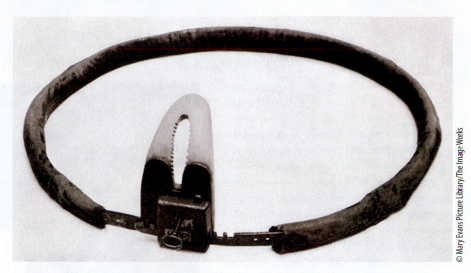

In the past some men required their wives to use chastity belts to make sure they didn't have sex with another man.

is thus no great loss, and a single sex act does not therefore constitute much of a threat. On the other hand, the woman may depend on the man to provide her with food and other resources, as well as provide for her children. If he becomes involved with another woman, he may bestow some of his resources on her, which would leave the wife and her children in a poorer position. Men are well aware that women seek men who have resources, and this influences their behavior (see *Money Matters*). Hence the greatest threat to the woman is the possibility that the man will become emotionally involved with someone else and therefore withhold these crucial resources.

This evolutionary theory about gender differences in sexual possessiveness was put to a test by Buss, Larsen, Westen, and Semmelroth (1992). They asked students a difficult question: Would it be worse for the person you love to have a one-time sexual encounter with another person without any emotional involvement, or for the person you love to have a lasting, emotionally intimate relationship with a member of your gender—but one that did not include sexual intercourse?

To be sure, neither men nor women were very happy with either possible scenario. But when forced to choose, they could do so—and their choices differed by gender. The majority of men (60%) objected more strongly to the sexual infidelity. In contrast, the women objected more to the emotional infidelity (only 17% objected more to the sexual infidelity). These findings fit the evolutionary view: Male possessiveness focuses heavily on the sex act and is less concerned with intimate conversations, whereas female possessiveness emphasizes the emotional relationship and is less concerned with the sex act itself.

As is often the case, subsequent work has made the picture more complicated. In particular, men are

Mating, Money, and Men

Women are attracted to men partly on the basis of thinking men will be generous providers. At some level, men seem to know this. Thoughts of women, sexuality, and mating change the way that men handle money.

One classic tradeoff involves now versus later. With money, people sometimes must choose between taking some money now versus getting a larger amount later. In research, as in life, the choice is often such that waiting for the larger amount will bring the best outcome in the long run, but when people feel money pressure in the heat of the moment, they will accept less in order to have it immediately. Research by Van den Bergh, Dewitte, and Warlop (2008) showed that after men looked at sexy pictures or handled brassieres, they were more inclined to take the money now rather than waiting for more money later.

The importance of sexual attraction was shown by Wilson and Daly (2003), who had participants choose between receiving a modest amount of money (e.g., $15) right away and receiving a larger sum (e.g., $50) several weeks later. Most people in most conditions were willing to wait for the larger reward, but men who had looked at pictures of attractive women shifted toward taking the money right away. No such shift was found if the men looked at

PhotoDisc

pictures of unattractive women, or pictures of attractive or unattractive cars. Women looking at pictures of men likewise were unaffected. Thus, the urgency to have money now stems from male desire for attractive females.

The so-called ultimatum game (a popular research method) involves having one person decide how to divide payment between self and another person. The other person can then either accept the deal or refuse it, and if he or she refuses, neither person gets anything. The second person, "the responder," is thus sometimes faced with a choice between money and pride. For example, if both persons worked on the task, and the divider offers to split a $10 payment by keeping $8 and giving the responder only $2, the responder faces an unpleasant choice. The $2 is unfair and a bit humiliating, but then again it is arguably better to take $2 than nothing. In general, men tend to refuse such unfair offers in order to preserve their pride. But if the previous part of the experiment had involved having the men look at pictures of women in bikinis and lingerie, the men tend to swallow their pride and take the money (Van den Bergh et al., 2008).

The underlying principle appears to be that when men are thinking about wooing women, they realize that money is important to have, because women choose men on that basis. An early investigation by Roney (2003) showed that after men had looked at pictures of attractive women, they placed higher value on money and expressed greater ambition to become financially successful in life, as compared to men who looked at photos of older, relatively unattractive women. Similar effects were found just by having men fill out the questionnaires in the presence of attractive women, as opposed to being in the presence of only other men. Thus, attraction to women makes men want money. ■

---

often upset over both sexual and emotional relationships that link their wives or girlfriends with another man (Buunk, Angleitner, Oubaid, & Buss, 1996; DeSteno, Bartlett, Braverman, & Salovey, 2002; Harris, 2000). Also, some subjects assume that one form of infidelity will lead to the other, so the difference between sexual and emotional infidelity may not be as simple as the hypothetical dilemma posed by the experimenters makes it seem (DeSteno et al., 2002). Nonetheless, there is reason to think that men and women do experience jealousy somewhat differently on average and may worry about different aspects of what their partners do with other lovers.

Causes of Jealousy. Jealousy thus seems to be a product of both the person and the situation. This impression is confirmed if we ask about the accuracy of people's jealous suspicions. To be sure, there are some cases of false jealousy; in particular, abusive individuals who have jealous rages and become

physically violent toward their partners often are acting on suspicions that are completely unfounded (e.g., Gondolf, 1985; Renzetti, 1992). But many jealous suspicions are accurate.

In one large-scale investigation (Blumstein & Schwartz, 1983), researchers interviewed both husband and wife separately and then compared notes. Thus, they could ask the husband whether he believed his wife had ever been unfaithful and then check his response against his wife's actual (confidential) answer as to whether she had in fact strayed. They found that most suspicions of infidelity were justified. Only about 10% of wives' suspicions and 13% of husbands' suspicions were mistaken. Thus, paranoid (false) jealousy is fairly rare, although it does exist. In marriage, at least, people who suspect their spouses of being unfaithful are usually correct. (The rates of unfounded suspicion were higher among couples who were living together without being married. For both men and women, slightly more than

20% of the people who suspected their cohabiting partners had been unfaithful were wrong.)

This is not to say that the partner always knows. There were many cases in which the partner falsely believed that the spouse had been faithful. Across various categories, these amounted to between 20% and 30% of unfaithful partners (Blumstein & Schwartz, 1983). Among college dating couples, Seal (1997) found that a large number were unaware of their partners' genuine infidelities. Thus, a sizable minority of people manage to keep their affairs secret from their partners. But among spouses who suspected infidelity, most were correct. In any case, the evidence suggests that most but not all jealous suspicions have some valid basis.

Jealousy and Type of Interloper.
The identity of the interloper (that is, the third person who has sex with one member of a romantic couple) also has an impact on how jealous people get. A common reaction to learning of a partner's infidelity is to disparage the interloper: "If you had to have an affair, did you have to choose such a loser/slut/jerk/idiot/pig?" (Lawson, 1988). But there is something irrational about such reactions. After all, would you prefer your partner to have sex with someone who is not a suitable partner (and hence no competition to you)—or with somebody who is terrific? Remember, jealousy is essentially a response to a threat to your romantic attachment, so the less of a threat the interloper is, the less jealous you should feel. A loser won't steal your partner away, but a desirable, eligible person might.

This reasoning led Salovey and his colleagues (DeSteno & Salovey, 1996; Salovey & Rodin, 1991) to predict that people's jealousy would depend on how their own traits stacked up against those of the interloper. Their results fit very well with the view of jealousy as responding to threat. Even if the other person was reasonably talented, people were less jealous as long as those talents did not resemble their own. The worst jealousy occurred when the partner became involved with someone whose abilities exceeded their own, in the same area. Thus, if you are a student in medical school, and your partner sleeps with an athlete, you may be unhappy about it, but your jealousy may remain at only a moderate level. Your jealousy would be much worse if your partner slept with someone who (like you) is also a medical student, and it will be worst of all if that other person has better grades than you or already has a medical degree. Similarly, if you are an athlete, then you'll be more jealous about your partner having sex with another athlete than with a medical student, and if the interloper's athletic skills surpass your own you will be extremely jealous.

Even the gender of the other person is important. Wiederman and LaMar (1998) found that men are less jealous and upset if their girlfriend has sex with a woman than with a man. Probably this is because they believe that another man might steal the girlfriend away, whereas a woman would not be able to do so. Ironically, however, the same researchers found that women were less upset if their boyfriend had sex with another woman than with a man. In other words, both men and woman seem to object more strongly to a male interloper than to a female interloper. Women are regarded as less threatening. This fits the economic (exchange) theory of sexuality discussed earlier: In sex, women give something of value, whereas men take.

Social Reality.
Thus far, however, we have not mentioned what may be the biggest factor of all in determining jealousy: the number of other people who know about the extradyadic sex (Pines & Aronson, 1983). If you learn that your partner has had a highly discreet, secret affair, you may well be upset, but your jealousy will not reach the highest levels. The worst situation is apparently to realize that you are the last person in your social network to learn about your partner's affair. By the time you find out, most of your friends already know about it, as do various other people. In simple terms, the more other people know about your partner's affair, the more upset and jealous you are likely to be.

Why does it matter so much what other people think? Probably this brings us back to the issue of self-esteem and pride. Your partner's affair makes you look bad. It makes you look like an incompetent lover who is unable to control your partner or keep him or her satisfied. This is why other people's knowledge becomes so important. The more other people know about the affair, the more they know something that reflects badly on you. The textbook theme of "putting people first" entails that people care about what others think, and that applies very strongly to sex.

Researchers sometimes use the term **social reality** to refer to public awareness of some event (Wicklund & Gollwitzer, 1982). If something happens but nobody knows about it, it does not have much social reality (although it has objective reality). It is therefore possible to go on with life afterward and more or less pretend that the whole episode never happened. In contrast, if other people know about it, it is harder to ignore it or put it behind you.

Social reality is thus an important determinant of jealousy. If many other people know about your partner's infidelity, you may find it difficult to continue with the relationship. You have to face them, after all, and you may wonder when you go out with your

---

SOCIAL REALITY beliefs held in common by several or many people; public awareness

partner whether other people are looking at the two of you and thinking about your partner's infidelity.

The extreme of this problem was probably faced by Hillary Rodham Clinton in 1998. Her husband, President Bill Clinton, had been accused of extramarital affairs, but as long as these were only rumors she could discount them as having no social reality. In fact, she had insisted on national television that these accusations stemmed from "a vast right-wing conspiracy" of people trying to discredit her husband by spreading false rumors. When President Clinton admitted to having had an affair, and when details of the sexual escapades were published and read by millions of Americans, the event gained considerable social reality, and his wife could no longer pretend they were false. It must have been difficult for her to proceed with her public appearances while everyone was thinking about her husband's sexual shenanigans with a much younger woman.

CULTURE, FEMALE SEXUALITY, AND THE DOUBLE STANDARD

All known cultures seek to regulate sex in some ways. The reason is not hard to guess. Unregulated sexual behavior produces all sorts of social turmoil and disruption: jealous partners committing acts of violence, marriages collapsing, unwanted babies, epidemics of sexually transmitted diseases. Bailey and Aunger (1995) studied one African society that was very permissive with regard to sex, so that premarital and extramarital sex was common, and though many individuals derived excitement and enjoyment from these activities, the social costs were huge. In particular, sexually transmitted diseases rendered around 40% of the woman unable to bear children—which was both a lasting source of heartbreak to these unfortunate individuals (and their husbands) and a significant disruption in how society would pass along resources from one generation to the next.

In sex, nature certainly says "go" whereas culture has often pleaded "stop!" These pleas have generally been directed more at women than at men, resulting in a widespread pattern called the cultural suppression of female sexuality. Why women? Different explanations have been put forward. One follows from what was said earlier about female erotic plasticity: Women's sexuality responds to cultural influences better than men's, so if a culture wants to control sexuality, it will be more successful focusing on women.

Another, more common explanation is that the cultural suppression of female sexuality is rooted in men's wish to control women. A related explanation has to do with **paternity uncertainty**—the fact that a man cannot be sure that the children born to his female partner are his. To be sure, recent advances in DNA testing have finally made it possible for a man to be certain. Research with these techniques has consistently found that a great many women trick their husbands into supporting children fathered by an illicit lover, a fact that some feminists (e.g., Ehrenreich, 1999) have regarded with pride, though it has also spawned a men's rights movement that seeks to release divorced men from paying child support for children who are not genetically related to them. According to the paternity uncertainty view, men try to stifle female sexuality in order to make their wives less interested in having sex with other partners. This interpretation does not have much direct evidence, however.

Much discussion of the cultural suppression of female sexuality has focused on the so-called double standard of sexual morality. The **double standard** is defined as a pattern of moral judgment that says specific sexual behaviors (especially premarital sex) are acceptable for men but immoral for women. By the conventional view, this double standard is a mechanism by which men seek to control women's sexuality.

The view of the double standard as reflecting male control of women received a severe blow in one of the most comprehensive and influential reviews of published research on sexuality (Oliver & Hyde, 1993). In every study that had found evidence of a double standard, women supported it more than men. Apparently, women are the ones who condemn other women while permitting men to do similar things. For example, a large national survey in 1965 (before the sexual revolution had gotten far) asked whether a woman who engaged in premarital sex was immoral (King, Balswick, & Robinson, 1977). "Yes" answers were received from 42% of men but from 91% of women (we will discuss this difference further in a few paragraphs). Thus, women condemned other women much more harshly than men condemned them. Subsequent work confirmed this in another way. Millhausen and Herold (1999) asked female college students whether they themselves believed in the double standard (nearly all said no) and whether they thought others believed it (most said yes)—and if so, who these others were. Far more said the condemnation of women came from other women than from men. (The rest said it came from both genders equally.)

In retrospect, evidence for the double standard has always been much weaker than is often assumed. Millhausen and Herold (1999) were not the only

---

PATERNITY UNCERTAINTY the fact that a man cannot be sure that the children born to his female partner are his

DOUBLE STANDARD condemning women more than men for the same sexual behavior (e.g., premarital sex)

ones to find that few people expressed support for it. In a series of careful studies, Sprecher (1989) tried multiple ways of measuring it and found either no double standard or even a **reverse double standard**—that people condemned men more than women for the same sexual behavior.

A methodological error in past work had created a false impression of widespread belief in a double standard. The error was rooted in the fact that women are generally less permissive than men about sexual morality in general. For example, national surveys from the 1930s to the 1950s asked people whether premarital sex was acceptable for everyone, acceptable for no one, or acceptable for men but not for women (Smith, 1994). Only the last option indicates a true double standard, and only a tiny fraction of respondents endorsed it. But there was a gender difference: Women tended to say premarital sex was acceptable for no one, whereas men tended to say it was acceptable for everyone. Careless researchers were misled into thinking that there was widespread support for a double standard. They confused "being rated acceptable *by* men" as meaning "being rated acceptable *for* men." In reality, most men and most women made judgments that showed no double standard.

Thus, the double standard is weaker than assumed and, more surprisingly, is supported by women more than men. Moreover, the importance of women and the female community in restraining sex is not limited to these few moral judgments. In fact, the cultural control of female sexuality comes primarily from women, and the pressures on women to restrain their sexual activities come from other women. Thus, it is women who punish the sexually active woman or girl with gossip and a bad reputation, who promote religious or moral injunctions to refrain from sex, who tell girls about the dangers of sex and pregnancy, and who in some cultures support and carry out surgical procedures that impair the woman's physical capacity to enjoy sex (Boddy, 1989; Coleman, 1961; Du Bois-Reymond & Ravesloot, 1996; Hicks, 1996; Kahn, Smith, & Roberts, 1984; Lightfoot-Klein, 1989; Shandall, 1967, 1979; for a review, see Baumeister & Twenge, 2002).

Why would women seek to restrain each other's sexuality? The answer is probably based neither on pathology nor on self-destructive motives, but rather may lie in a simple and rational response to women's situation. The social exchange theory of sex (described above) offers a clear explanation. For most of history, women have lacked opportunities to acquire wealth, education, power, and other resources to provide themselves with a good life. A woman's sexuality has often been the main resource she had with which to bargain (by making a favorable marriage) for access to the good life. It was therefore important for each woman to maintain as high an exchange value as

possible for her sexuality. As with any resource, the price depends on supply and demand; restricting the supply raises the price. To the extent that the community of women could restrain each other's sexuality, they all stood to benefit from the higher value.

When men can get sex without offering much in return, women derive relatively little benefit from their sexual favors. In contrast, when sex is not readily available, men may offer women a great deal in return for sex, including love and commitment, long-term financial partnerships, and other resources. Such offerings have been crucial to women's well-being in cultures and historical periods in which women were prevented from providing for themselves in other ways. Rather than being passive dupes or victims of culture, women appear to have responded in rational ways so as to make the best of their circumstances. Putting pressure on each other to restrain sexual behavior has sometimes been in women's best interests.

[**QUIZ YOURSELF**]

Sexuality

1. Which theory proposes that sexual attitudes and behaviors are the result of cultural forces and socialization?
   (a) Attachment theory
   (b) Evolutionary theory
   (c) Social construction theory
   (d) Social exchange theory

2. When men outnumber women, the price of sex _____.
   (a) decreases
   (b) increases
   (c) increases then decreases
   (d) stays the same

3. Bjorn loves his wife, but he discovers that she has been unfaithful to him. To make matters worse, everyone knows she has been unfaithful to him. The common knowledge that Bjorn's wife has been unfaithful to him is called _____.
   (a) double standard
   (b) reverse double standard
   (c) social construction
   (d) social reality

4. Waldo believes that premarital sex is acceptable for men but unacceptable for women. This belief illustrates _____.
   (a) double standard
   (b) erotic plasticity
   (c) reverse double standard
   (d) social construction

REVERSE DOUBLE STANDARD condemning men more than women for the same sexual behavior (e.g., premarital sex)

Sexual attraction and mating are found throughout nature, but they take on new and added dimensions among human beings. For one thing, long-term monogamous mating is much more common among human beings than among other species, especially apes and other primates. The ability to stay sexually faithful to one partner for decades appears to be quite specific to humans (Barash & Lipton, 2002; Smuts, 1996).

Culture helps. The view that humans are "naturally" monogamous is contradicted by data indicating that polygamy has been common in many societies and cultures. Only after some historical struggles did most modern cultures ban polygamy and insist that you can only marry one spouse at a time. Were people not thus influenced by culture, monogamy would be less common.

The effect of human culture on love and mating can perhaps be most plainly seen in divorce. If two animals have a sexual relationship that fails to satisfy them, especially if they frequently annoy and aggravate each other, they can dissolve their relationship just by walking away. Human beings require the culture's permission, which often entails hiring lawyers and negotiating for months over what will happen to their jointly owned property and their children.

The cultural control of close relationships extends far beyond divorce, of course. Many laws regulate what goes on in the family, affecting everything from hitting family members to bequeathing them money. Culture also shapes relationships via informal influence, such as how relationships and sex are depicted in the mass media, which in turn helps shape how people treat each other. No other species has ever changed or reinvented its gender roles to the extent that human beings have done. In general, these changes have been positive: Unlike some animals, for example, humans are culturally discouraged from eating or beating their offspring.

Sex itself has been profoundly affected by culture. Formal laws have prohibited various sex acts (for example, oral and anal sex have been illegal in many cultures) and various kinds of sex partners (same-gender partners, relatives, or underage children). The mixture of economic, moral, and religious factors that created the cultural control of female sexuality is almost impossible to imagine in any other species. Patterns of sexual activity changed in many ways during the 20th century, with its so-called sexual revolution(s), including vast increases in premarital sex and oral sex. Among the many factors contributing to these changes were the improvements in birth control technology. Only cultural (human) animals have been able to invent new ways of controlling pregnancy and to change their sexual norms on that basis.

Perhaps the biggest difference is in human intimacy. Having mastered language, people have been able to create complex, intricate selves. Forming a close relationship often begins with a great deal of talking, by which people reveal and disclose their inner selves to each other. Indeed, one theory of language has proposed that the reason humans evolved to use language was to promote close relationships (Dunbar, 1996), because talking enabled people to get to know each other and stay connected much more efficiently than the methods used by other primates. It is almost impossible to imagine a human marriage or other close relationship without language and conversation. The slow building of intimacy by talking to each other for years is an important aspect of the long road that people follow to form bonds with each other.

The seemingly endless human fascination with love and sex has also produced a steady stream of cultural activity to depict and celebrate them. The basic inclinations toward sex and mating may be rooted in biology and shared across many species, but in human art they are transformed into something grander and more meaningful. Most of the music you hear consists of songs about love. Most books and movies have some coverage of love, not even counting the pornography industry that finds a ready market for simple depictions of sex. In fact, if you took away love (including sex) and violence (including crime), it is hard to imagine the American film industry surviving at all! Poetry too has long favored themes of love and romance, whereas no baboons or turtles write love sonnets to their sweethearts. Attractive nude young women have been favorite subjects for painters and sculptors. In short, much of human culture is about close relationships, love, and sexuality.

One of the most interesting and curious facts about human sex is that most people use a face-to-face position for intercourse. Most other mammals, including the great apes who are believed to be humans' closest biological relatives, rely on having the male enter the female from behind. Why are humans different? Possibly the more upright human posture for walking contributed by changing the direction of the internal organs. There may be a more social explanation, however, and one that points to something special and wonderful about human nature. The face-to-face position enables lovers to look into each other's eyes, kiss each other on the lips, and say sweet things to each other during sex. In that way, it is more compatible with promoting intimacy and sharing deep feelings of love. Quite possibly the earliest humans who began to make love in this position found that they were able to transform sex into a more meaningful act and one that would, by increasing love and intimacy, help build stronger families—and so perhaps their offspring fared better than people who still favored the older, animal positions for sex. If so, then the combination of love, intimacy, and sex is a crucial part of what makes us human.

- Good relationships are good for you. Married people (especially happily married people) live longer, healthier lives than single or divorced people.

WHAT IS LOVE?

- Passionate love (also called romantic love) refers to having strong feelings of longing, desire, and excitement toward a special person.
- Companionate love (sometimes called affectionate love) refers to a high level of mutual understanding, caring, and commitment to make the relationship succeed.

- Passionate love is found all over the world, but the forms and expressions of romantic passion vary significantly from one culture to another.
- Companionate love is important for a long, happy marriage or a stable, trustworthy, lasting relationship.
- Married people have sex more often and more satisfyingly, but single people spend more time at each sexual episode and have more different partners.
- Sternberg proposed that love is composed of passion, intimacy, and commitment, and that these three ingredients can vary in strength in different relationships.

DIFFERENT TYPES OF RELATIONSHIPS

- Exchange relationships are based on reciprocity and fairness.
- Communal relationships are based on love and concern for each other, without expectation of direct, equal repayment.
- Communal relationships are more desirable in intimate relationships, but exchange relationships are more powerful for driving progress and increasing wealth in larger groups.
- The four kinds or styles of attachment are
  - Secure attachment, characterized by comfort with intimacy and no excessive fears of abandonment

- Dismissing avoidant attachment, characterized by avoidance of intimacy and discomfort with close relationships while viewing partners as unreliable, unavailable, and uncaring
- Fearful avoidant attachment, characterized by avoidance of intimacy and discomfort with close relationships while viewing the self as unlovable
- Preoccupied (or anxious/ambivalent) attachment, characterized by excessive desire for closeness to the point of desiring to merge with the partner, and worry about abandonment

- Self-love and narcissism may not be beneficial to good relationships, but self-acceptance may help one get along with others.

MAINTAINING RELATIONSHIPS

- People in good relationships often think their relationships are getting better and better, but research suggests they actually stay at the same (good) level.
- The three factors of the investment model are
  - Satisfaction with the partner
  - Quality of alternative partners
  - Investment (sunk costs) in the relationship
- The relationship-enhancing style of attribution involves attributing good acts to the partner's inner qualities and attributing bad acts to external factors. The distress-maintaining style of attribution is just the opposite.
- People in love generally hold idealized versions of each other.
- Relationships can thrive when couples remain on their best behavior with each other.

SEXUALITY

- Diamond's work suggests that attachment/love and sex are two separate psychological systems in humans, so love and sex don't always match.
- Social constructionist theories of sex assert that sexual attitudes and behaviors vary widely based on culture and learning. These theories seek to understand how personal experiences and cultural influences shape sexual desire and behavior.
- Evolutionary theory emphasizes that the sex drive was shaped by natural selection. Evolutionary psychologists seek to understand innate patterns of sexual desire and behavior.
- The social exchange theory views sex as a resource that women have and that men want and are willing to exchange other resources for.
- On average, men have a stronger sex drive than women.
- The stereotype that men separate love from sex more easily than women is wrong.
- Women show more erotic plasticity than men, meaning that women's sex drive can be shaped and altered by social, cultural, and situational forces, whereas men are more driven by innate, biological needs.
- Women act as the gatekeepers who restrict sex and decide whether and when it will happen.
- The most reliable data suggest that infidelity is fairly rare in modern Western marriage.
- Extramarital sex is a risk factor for divorce. Whether it is a symptom or cause is disputed.
- Sexual jealousy is found in all cultures and societies, although its forms, rules, and expressions may vary from one to another, suggesting that some degree of sexual possessiveness is deeply rooted in human nature.

- Jealousy can focus on either a sexual or an emotional connection to an outsider. Men may focus more strongly on the sexual aspect than women.
- The more other people know about your partner's infidelity, the more upset and jealous you are likely to be.
- All known cultures seek to regulate sex in some ways.
- Paternity uncertainty refers to the fact that a man cannot be sure that the children born to his female partner are his (at least until recent advances in DNA testing).
- The sexual double standard is defined as a pattern of moral judgment that says specific sexual behaviors are acceptable for men but immoral for women. It is supported more by women than by men.
- Across different cultures, it has sometimes been in women's best interests to put pressure on each other to restrain sexual behavior.

WHAT MAKES US HUMAN? PUTTING THE CULTURAL ANIMAL IN PERSPECTIVE

- Long-term monogamous mating is much more common among human beings than among other species.

Key Terms

Attachment theory 362
Commitment 358
Communal relationships 360
Companionate love (affectionate love) 354
Coolidge effect 375
Dismissing avoidant attachment 362

Distress-maintaining style of attribution 368
Double standard 386
Erotic plasticity 376
Evolutionary theory 373
Exchange relationships 360
Extradyadic sex 379
Fearful avoidant attachment 363

Intimacy 358
Investment model 367
Passion 358
Passionate love (romantic love) 354
Paternity uncertainty 386
Preoccupied (anxious/ ambivalent) attachment 362

Relationship-enhancing style of attribution 368
Reverse double standard 387
Secure attachment 362
Self-acceptance 365
Social constructionist theories 372
Social exchange theory 374
Social reality 385

[Quiz Yourself] Answers

1. What Is Love?
Answers: 1=c, 2=d, 3=d, 4=d

2. Different Types of Relationships
Answers: 1=c, 2=b, 3=a, 4=a

3. Maintaining Relationships
Answers: 1=b, 2=b, 3=b, 4=c

4. Sexuality
Answers: 1=c, 2=b, 3=d, 4=a

Media Learning Resources

Make sure you check out the complete set of learning resources and study tools below. If your instructor did not order these items with your new book, go to www.ichapters.com to purchase Cengage Learning print and digital products.

Social Psychology and Human Nature BOOK COMPANION WEBSITE
www.cengage.com/psychology/baumeister Visit your book companion website, where you will find flash cards, practice quizzes, Internet links, and more to help you study.

CENGAGENOW JUST WHAT YOU NEED TO KNOW NOW!
Spend time on what you need to master rather than on information you have already learned. Take a pre-test for this chapter, and CengageNOW will generate a personalized study plan based on your results. The study plan will identify the topics you need to review and direct you to online resources to help you master those topics. You can then take a post-test to help you determine the concepts you have mastered and what you will still need to work on. Try it out! Go to www.cengage.com/login to sign in with an access code or to purchase access to this product.

CLASSIC AND CONTEMPORARY VIDEOS STUDENT CD-ROM
To see videos on the topics and experiments discussed in this chapter and to learn more about the research that social psychologists are doing today, go to the Student CD-ROM.

SOCIAL PSYCH LAB
These unique online labs give you the opportunity to become a participant in actual experiments, including re-creations of classic and contemporary research studies.

chapter 13

Prejudice and Intergroup Relations

Money Matters: Racial Discrimination in Sports—Paying More to Win **p. 394**

Food for Thought: Prejudice Against the Obese **p. 399**

The Social Side of Sex: Roots of Antigay Prejudice **p. 401**

Tradeoffs: Competition Versus Cooperation **p. 405**

What Makes Us Human? Putting the Cultural Animal in Perspective **p. 425**

Trae Patton/© NBC/Courtesy Everett Collection

ABCS OF INTERGROUP RELATIONSHIPS: PREJUDICE, DISCRIMINATION, AND STEREOTYPES p. 393
Common Prejudices and Targets p. 396

WHY PREJUDICE EXISTS p. 402
Us Versus Them: Groups in Competition p. 403
Ignorance? The Contact Hypothesis p. 406

Rationalizations for Oppression p. 407
Stereotypes as Heuristics p. 407
Prejudice and Self-Esteem p. 408

CONTENT OF PREJUDICE AND STEREOTYPES p. 409
Are Stereotypes Always Wrong, Mostly Wrong, or Mostly Right? p. 409
Are Stereotypes Always Negative? p. 410

INNER PROCESSES p. 411

OVERCOMING STEREOTYPES, REDUCING PREJUDICE p. 414
Conscious Override p. 414
Contact p. 418
Superordinate Goals p. 418

IMPACT OF PREJUDICE ON TARGETS p. 418
Self-Fulfilling and Self-Defeating Prophecies p. 419
Stigma and Self-Protection p. 421

Stereotype Threat **p. 422**

CHAPTER SUMMARY p. 425

What if the government forcibly removed a family member from your home and shipped him or her more than 1,000 miles (1,600 km) away to live in a settlement camp? That is precisely what some white Australians did to Aboriginal and half-caste (half white, half Aborigine) children until as late as the 1970s. |||||

Cliff engravings suggest that Aborigines had lived in Australia for more than 45,000 years before white people arrived. When the British occupation of Australia began in 1788, Aboriginal resistance was immediate, but the British made it clear that they intended to stay. In 1824, white settlers in Tasmania were given authority from the government to shoot Aborigines. In 1830, the Aboriginal people of Tasmania were forcibly resettled on Flinders Island, where conditions were so bad that many died. Later the community was moved to Cape Barren Island. Some white Australians wanted to rid themselves of an "unwanted third race" of "half-caste" children. The half-caste population was growing rapidly, because far more white men than women came to Australia (in part because the British sent mostly male convicted prisoners to Australia as a penal colony), and many of these white men married or mated with Aboriginal women.

In 1905, the Chief Protector was made the legal guardian of every Aboriginal and half-caste child, regardless of whether the child's parents were living. Settlement camps were established across the continent to keep the half-caste children from contact with the rest of Australian society. The government was afraid that if half-caste children remained with their mothers they would marry Aboriginals. If the half-castes were taken from their homes as children and reared in settlement camps, they would marry other half-castes, quarter-castes, or whites. It is estimated that between 10% and 30% of Aboriginal and half-caste children were forcibly removed from their homes and relocated in settlement camps between 1910 and 1970 (Australian Human Rights and Equal Opportunity Commission, 1997). One child described how it happened:

> They put us in the police ute [car] and said they were taking us to Broome [a city in Western Australia]. They put the mums in there as well. But when we'd gone about ten miles they stopped, and threw the mothers out of the car. We jumped on our mothers' backs, crying, trying not to be left behind. But

the policeman pulled us off and threw us back in the car. They pushed the mothers away and drove off, while our mothers were chasing the car, running and crying after us. We were screaming in the back of that car.

Chief Protector Cook said:

> Children are removed from the evil influence of the aboriginal camp with its lack of moral training and its risk of serious organic infectious disease. They are properly fed, clothed and educated as white children, they are subjected to constant medical supervision and in receipt of domestic and vocational training.

Xavier Herbert, Acting Superintendent of the Darwin Half-Caste Home, disagreed that the children were "properly fed":

> The porridge, cooked the day before, already was sour and roped from the mould in it, and when doused with the thin milk, gave up the corpses of weevils by the score. The bread was even worse, stringy grey wrapped about congealed glue, the whole cased in charcoal.

Some children were also told that their mothers were "sluts" and alcoholics and did not love them anymore. This resettlement policy produced what has become known as the "stolen generations."

In 1996, New South Wales Premier Bob Carr apologized in Parliament for how the Aborigines had been treated. That same year, Doris Pilkington published a book titled *Follow the Rabbit-Proof Fence*. The book is named after a fence that was constructed to keep rabbits from destroying the western farmlands. (The rabbit story is another interesting indication of cultural clash. There were no rabbits in Australia when whites arrived, but at some point the settlers brought some from Europe to raise for food. Some escaped, and because

Australia had no animals that ate rabbits, they multiplied out of control and threatened to eat everything in sight. The rabbit-proof fence was thus itself a symbol of the damage wrought by the white conquest of Australia.) The fence ran from north to south across almost the whole continent of Australia. In 1931, three children escaped the Moore River Native Settlement and followed the fence 1,500 miles (2,400 km) to their home in Jigalong. One of the girls was Doris Pilkington's mother, Molly Craig, who was 14 years old at the time. The other two girls were Daisy, her 8-year-old half-sister, and Gracie Fields, her 10-year-old cousin. Gracie was recaptured, but Molly and Daisy eventually made it home.

Molly later married an Aborigine man and had two daughters, Doris and Annabelle. Molly and her two daughters were taken to the Moore River Native Settlement, but Molly escaped and walked back to Jigalong again, this time with her two daughters; she carried the infant Annabelle the entire way. The authorities caught them and took Annabelle away, and Molly never saw her again. Annabelle was told that she was an orphan and that she was white. She was sent to another institution, because her skin color was light. Doris was transferred to a Christian mission, where she was told that her people were devil-worshippers. Doris was 25 before she saw her parents again. Annabelle still refuses

From left to right, **Gracie Fields (Laura Monaghan), Daisy Craig (Tianna Sansbury), and Molly Craig (Everlyn Sampi)** from the 2002 movie *Rabbit-Proof Fence*, a true story about three half-caste girls who were taken from their families and put in a settlement camp. The girls escaped the settlement camp and followed a fence 1,500 miles (2,400 km) to their home.

Reuters/HO/Landov

to acknowledge her mother, sister, and Aborigine heritage. Molly Craig died on January 13, 2004, at the age of 87 in Jigalong. ■

ABCs of Intergroup Relationships: Prejudice, Discrimination, and Stereotypes

The *Follow the Rabbit-Proof Fence* story illustrates the concept of prejudice. **Prejudice** is a negative attitude or feeling toward an individual based solely on that individual's membership in a certain group. More specifically, it illustrates **racism**, defined as prejudiced attitudes toward a particular race. Racism today is more subtle than in the past, and often takes the form of what is called **aversive racism** (Gaertner & Dovidio, 1986). Aversive racists simultaneously hold egalitarian values and negative (aversive or unpleasant) feelings toward minorities. They believe in racial equality and equal opportunity, but they also feel uncomfortable around minorities and try to avoid them when possible. For example, when European Americans are talking to African Americans, they may sit farther away, maintain less eye contact, talk in a less friendly manner, and end discussions sooner than they do when talking to other whites

(Pettigrew, 1985). Of course, not everyone who is uncomfortable when talking to strangers is a racist.

Prejudiced feelings sometimes lead people to discriminate against others. **Discrimination** refers to unequal treatment of different people based on the groups or categories to which they belong. An example of discrimination against Native Americans would be the practice of keeping them on reservations instead of letting them live wherever they want. Sometimes discrimination can occur without prejudiced feelings. For example, suppose that a state police force sets a requirement that its officers must all be at least six feet (1.83 m) tall, because it believes that "height equals might" and that criminals won't take short officers seriously. This height requirement would discriminate against women, Hispanics, and Asians because they are generally shorter than six feet tall. To read about discrimination in paying athletes of different races, see the *Money Matters* box.

PREJUDICE a negative feeling toward an individual based solely on his or her membership in a particular group

RACISM prejudiced attitudes toward a particular race

AVERSIVE RACISM simultaneously holding egalitarian values and negative feelings toward minorities

DISCRIMINATION unequal treatment of different people based on the groups or categories to which they belong

Racial Discrimination in Sports—Paying More to Win

Many people argue that racial integration and diversity produce value for organizations. The evidence behind this claim has been mixed at best. But recent analyses of the economics of sports have begun to show that racial discrimination is in fact costly for some teams.

One of the best studies on the cost of discrimination in sports involved English football (soccer) teams (Szymanski, 2000). These teams provided a useful test because teams were relatively free to hire athletes as they saw fit, which included the option of discriminating by race. There were also no salary caps, revenue sharing, and other financial regulations that distort the economic marketplace. In the 1970s, black players began to enter the major league, and some teams hired them eagerly while others chose not to do so. Given the relatively free market for talent, the result was that black players got lower salaries than white players, regardless of ability.

(This is because a player can get a higher salary when more teams want to bid for his services.)

Another way of putting this is that black players cost less than white players, at any level of ability. It does not matter whether white or black players are better overall. All that matters is that, whatever your talent level, your salary would be lower if you were black, so the team that hires you instead of a white player in effect gets a bargain: a better player for the same money.

In general, teams with higher payrolls get better players and therefore win more games. But when the researcher analyzed teams for the number of black players they had, he found that using more black players allowed teams to win more games for the same amount of money. A team that had no black players would have to

David Madison/Getty Images

pay 5% more overall in player salaries to achieve the same win–loss record as a team that did have black players.

Thus, organizations do pay a price for racial discrimination. Hiring the best talent you can get regardless of race is the most effective strategy. To refuse to hire based on race means paying more or winning less, or both. ■

Stereotypes are beliefs that associate groups of people with certain traits. Stereotypes refer to what we believe or think about various groups. They can be good or bad. For example, one might stereotype older people as wise or as slow. Fat people have been stereotyped as jolly or as lacking in self-control. Stereotypes are sometimes difficult to change. One reason is that people tend to throw exceptions to the rule into a separate category, called a **subtype** (Richards & Hewstone, 2001). For example, if a man meets a woman who doesn't fit the stereotype of the warm and nurturing woman, he can either discard or modify his stereotype of women, or he can put her into a subtype, such as "career woman" (Altermatt & DeWall, 2003).

Prejudice, discrimination, and stereotypes are the ABCs of intergroup relationships. The **A**ffective component is prejudice, the **B**ehavioral component is discrimination, and the **C**ognitive component is stereotyping.

The human mind seems naturally inclined to sort objects into groups rather than thinking about each object separately. This process of **categorization** makes it much easier to make sense of a complicated world. The process of sorting people into groups on the basis of characteristics they have in common (such as race, gender, age, religion, or sexual orientation) is called **social categorization**. As we saw in Chapter 5, people tend to be "cognitive misers," which means they generally think in easy, simple ways that minimize mental effort. Categorizing people is an easy and efficient way of simplifying the world and reducing mental effort. When people form an impression of a person, they typically use what personal information they have about the individual, but invoking stereotypes is a relatively easy way to fill in gaps in this knowledge.

Modern objections to stereotyping and prejudice go far beyond the chance of an inaccurate prediction, of course. Today, people object to stereotyping and prejudice even if there might be considerable accuracy to many stereotypes. The view that prejudice and stereotyping are morally wrong is a product of modern Western culture. Several centuries ago, Western culture shifted to the view that each person had a right to be judged as an individual, regardless of his or her category. Prior to that, there was greater acceptance of judging people based on categories and groups. Even legal judgment followed such principles. For example, if a man rebelled against the local

---

STEREOTYPES beliefs that associate groups of people with certain traits

SUBTYPES categories that people use for individuals who do not fit a general stereotype

CATEGORIZATION the natural tendency of humans to sort objects into groups

SOCIAL CATEGORIZATION the process of sorting people into groups on the basis of characteristics they have in common (e.g., race, gender, age, religion, sexual orientation)

ruler, the ruler might have the man's entire extended family imprisoned or executed (e.g., Stone, 1977). Nowadays, punishing the whole family for one individual's crime would seem unjust and unfair.

Biased judgments based on stereotypes and prejudices are not only unfair and immoral; in some cases, they can have lethal consequences. For example, if a police officer possessed the stereotypic expectation that black people are more likely to be violent and aggressive than white people, it could influence split-second decisions whether to shoot black suspects, with tragic consequences. Indeed, recent work using computer simulations (similar to video games) has found that people, whether police officers or college students, are more likely to mistakenly shoot at unarmed black suspects than unarmed white suspects (e.g., Correll, Park, Judd, & Wittenbrink, 2002; Greenwald, Oakes, & Hoffman, 2003; Payne, 2001; Plant & Peruche, 2005; Butz, Plant, & Doerr, 2007). That is, when a research participant sees an ambiguous scene with a possibly dangerous man who may or may not be armed, the participant is more likely to shoot at the man if he is black than if he is white (even if he is not actually armed). Perhaps ironically, the bias is not confined to European American research participants: African Americans are also more likely to shoot at the possibly threatening man if he is black than if he is white.

One big difference between sorting people and sorting things is the level of emotional involvement. For example, when sorting people into heterosexual, bisexual, or homosexual categories, the sorter belongs to one of the categories and feels emotionally attached to it. In contrast, someone who sorts fruits into apples and oranges is probably not emotionally attached to these categories. **Outgroup members** ("them") are people who belong to a different group or category than we do. **Ingroup members** ("us") are people who belong to the same group or category as we do.

Most people assume that outgroup members are more similar to each other than ingroup members are to each other. This false assumption, known as the **outgroup homogeneity bias**, is reflected in statements such as "They're all alike" and "If you've seen one, you've seen them all!" In fact, one of the earliest studies of outgroup homogeneity used campus fraternities at a university. The researchers found that students believed that the members of their own fraternity had many different traits, values, and activities, but that members of other fraternities were much more similar to each other (Linville & Jones, 1980).

In fact, people see outgroup members as even looking similar to one another. Have you ever felt embarrassed because of confusing two people of a different racial group than your own? If so, you're

Does Hillary Clinton fit the stereotype of the warm and nurturing woman? If not, people may throw her into a subtype such as "career woman."

When viewing an ambiguous scene with a possibly dangerous man who may or may not be armed, participants are more likely to shoot at the man if he is black than if he is white.

not alone. Research has shown that eyewitnesses are more accurate at identifying people of their own racial group than at identifying people of a different racial group (e.g., Devine & Malpass, 1985; Meissner & Brigham, 2001). However, when outgroup

---

OUTGROUP MEMBERS people who belong to a different group or category than we do
INGROUP MEMBERS people who belong to the same group or category as we do
OUTGROUP HOMOGENEITY BIAS the assumption that outgroup members are more similar to one another than ingroup members are to one another

"Sorry, we're all cat people. The dog people are in that boat over there."

members are angry, the opposite is true (Ackerman et al., 2006). Angry outgroup members are easier to distinguish than are angry ingroup members. This finding reflects the importance of keeping track of dangerous people. Angry members of another group may pose a major threat, so the human mind automatically pays close attention to them and makes a strong mental note of who those people are.

Outgroup homogeneity bias has a simple explanation: We don't have as much exposure to outgroup members as we do to ingroup members. Thus, we don't have much chance to learn about how outgroup members differ from one another. This lack of exposure can have several negative consequences such as prejudice.

COMMON PREJUDICES AND TARGETS

> "If we were to wake up some morning and find that everyone was the same race, creed and color, we would find some other cause for prejudice by noon."
>
> —George Aiken, former Governor and U.S. Senator from Vermont

Prejudice comes in many varieties. Most arise from external characteristics that are readily visible, such as race, gender, weight, or clothing (e.g., turbans worn by some Muslim men and head scarves worn by some Muslim women; small hats called yarmulkes or kippas worn by some Jewish men). Probably the most widely discussed prejudice in modern North America is racial prejudice (racism), followed by gender prejudice (sexism). Racial prejudice has been an important social problem, particularly prejudices held by European Americans about African Americans. In some respects, however, European American prejudice against African Americans is quite different from most cases of prejudice. Because society has sought for decades to reduce or erase this type of prejudice, even people who hold such prejudices feel conflicted about them and may seek to conceal them. Sexist prejudice, particularly men's attitudes toward women, has also been recognized as an important social problem.

Most people claim not to be prejudiced, but then again perhaps they just think that is the right thing to say. Sometimes behavior differs from expressed attitudes. One study of online dating found that half the white women and 80% of the white men said that race didn't matter to them—hence they would be willing to date anyone from any race (Levitt & Dubner, 2005). But if you look at how those people responded to other ads, race did seem to matter. The white women who said race did not matter to them sent 97% of their responses to white men. Likewise, the white men who were supposedly open to any race sent 90% of their responses to white women. Thus, these people claimed not to care about race, but when actually contacting someone to date they showed a strong preference for their own race.

While people may at least strive to conceal if not overcome their racial and gender prejudices, other prejudices are often held with much less inner conflict or debate, such as against Arabs and Muslims, obese individuals, and homosexuals.

Arabs and Muslims. Fill in the blank: Islamic _____. For many people living in the Western world, the words that come to mind are negative, violent ones such as "extremist," "fundamentalist," "insurgent," "militant," "jihadist," "mujahideen," or "terrorist." Adherents of the religion of Islam are called Muslims. The word Muslim means "one who submits to Allah (God)." There are about 2 billion Muslims in the world ("Muslim Population," 2009). Islam began on the Arabian peninsula in the seventh century, and most Arabs today are Muslims; however, a majority of the world's Muslims are not Arabs.

Prejudice and discrimination against Arabs and Muslims living in the United States has increased dramatically since the September 11, 2001, terrorist attacks (Hendricks, Ortiz, Sugie, & Miller, 2007). For example, they have been removed from airplanes without probable cause, out of fear they might be terrorists. In 2004, Yusuf Islam (formerly known as singer Cat Stevens) was not allowed to enter the United States because he was on a "terrorist watch list." Former Homeland Security Secretary Tom Ridge accused him of having some unspecified relationship with terrorist activity. This is the same (dangerous?) guy who wrote the song *Peace Train*:

Cause out on the edge of darkness, there rides
a peace train
Oh peace train take this country, come take
me home again

Women in head scarves have been jeered and insulted. Mosques have been sprayed with graffiti and bullets. Highly visible forms of discrimination (e.g., vandalism, assault) are relatively rare; pleas from the government, civil liberties groups, and others imply that such acts are socially and legally unacceptable. Less visible forms of discrimination, however, persist. For example, in the year following the September 11 attacks, the Equal Opportunity Employment Commission received 706 complaints of workplace discrimination against Arab Americans, 383 more than in the year before the attacks (Equal Opportunity Employment Commission, 2002). In workplace discrimination cases, it is often unclear whether the disputed action (e.g., job termination) is motivated by prejudice or other causes (e.g., poor job performance).

One study focused on less visible forms of discrimination against Arabs (Bushman & Bonacci, 2004). The researchers used a modern variation of Stanley Milgram's (1977) "lost letter" technique to examine prejudice toward socially undesirable groups (Stern & Faber, 1997). Milgram dropped self-addressed, stamped envelopes around a college campus and counted the number of lost letters that were mailed. People mailed more letters addressed to socially desirable groups (e.g., a medical research group) than to socially undesirable groups (e.g., a communist organization). In the Bushman and Bonacci (2004) study, white participants received a "lost e-mail" message addressed to a person with an Arab surname (e.g., Mohammed or Fatima Hameed) or a European American surname (e.g., Peter or Julianne Brice). The e-mail stated that the intended recipient either had or had not won a prestigious four-year college scholarship. The e-mail requested a reply within 48 hours. Thus, if the participant did not forward the e-mail, the student would not be able to benefit from a scholarship worth tens of thousands of dollars. Participants had all completed a measure of prejudiced attitudes toward Arabs a few weeks before they received the e-mail message. The scale had items such as "I can hardly imagine myself voting for an Arab-American who is running for an important political office." As can be seen in ▶ **FIGURE 13.1**, prejudiced participants were 12% less likely to return a lost e-mail reporting that someone named Hameed had won a scholarship than they were to return a similar message delivering good news to someone named Brice. Conversely, highly prejudiced people were 19% more likely to return a lost e-mail stating that someone named Hameed had

In 2004, Yusuf Islam (left photo), formerly known as singer Cat Stevens (right photo) was not allowed to enter the United States because he was on a "terrorist watch list." Former Homeland Security Secretary Tom Ridge accused him of having some unspecified relationship with terrorist activity.

Since September 11, 2001, discrimination against Arabs has increased in the United States.

not won the scholarship than they were to return a message saying that someone named Brice had not won (returning a message bearing bad news could hurt the intended recipient). People with low prejudice scores, on the other hand, were just as likely to return a positive lost e-mail intended for recipients with an Arabic surname as a European surname, and they were likely to treat negative messages in the same equitable way.

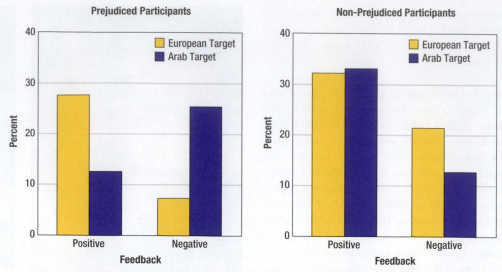

Prejudiced Participants

Percent

(y-axis: 0, 10, 20, 30, 40)

- European Target
- Arab Target

Positive   Negative

Feedback

Non-Prejudiced Participants

Percent

(y-axis: 0, 10, 20, 30, 40)

- European Target
- Arab Target

Positive   Negative

Feedback

▶ **FIGURE 13.1** Prejudiced participants who received a lost e-mail announcing a person had won a scholarship were less likely to return it if it was addressed to a recipient with an Arabic name than if it was addressed to a recipient with a European name. The opposite was true if the e-mail announced that the person had not won the scholarship. Non-prejudiced people were not affected by the name of the person who was supposed to receive the e-mail. Source: Based on data from Bushman and Bonacci (2004).

In another study, white participants were to shoot at a target in a video game if he had a gun, and to not shoot if he had no gun (Unkelbach, Forgas, & Denson, 2008). The researchers manipulated whether the target wore Muslim headgear (turban/hijab) or not. Participants were more likely to shoot at the target if he wore Muslim headgear, regardless of whether he had a gun or not.

Dutch participants in one study saw a news program either about Islamic terrorist acts or about the Olympic Games (Das, Bushman, Bezemer, Kerkhof, & Vermeulen, 2009). Because the news media frequently link Muslims with terrorism, it was thought that the effects of terrorism news might carry over to the population of Muslims as a whole, even if most Muslims are as appalled by terrorist acts as non-Muslims are. Participants then rated their attitudes toward Arab integration into Dutch society. In the middle of the data collection, the well-known Dutch filmmaker Theo van Gogh (great-grandson of the brother of famous Dutch painter Vincent van Gogh) was murdered by Mohammed Bouyeri while

Theo van Gogh (left) was brutally murdered by an Islamic extremist after he made a controversial film about the abuse of Muslim women. In the week following van Gogh's murder, numerous anti-Muslim acts occurred in the Netherlands, such as this school bombing in Eindhoven (right).

Food for Thought

Prejudice Against the Obese

In the United States, diet and activity level are the second leading cause of death behind tobacco, and the gap is shrinking over time. Diet and activity are associated with almost every health risk known. However, obesity has other negative effects besides health risks, the biggest of which is the stigma associated with being fat. Anti-fat attitudes are strong, and they begin as early as preschool (Cramer & Steinwert, 1998). Five-year-old children say they would rather lose an arm than be fat (Kolata, 1992). Even the nurses and doctors who treat them have strong negative attitudes and reactions toward obese patients (Bejciy-Spring, 2008). The stigma is strong despite the fact that so many people are fat. In the United States, about two out of every three adults are considered either overweight or obese (Centers for Disease Control, 2007).

Research has shown that compared to normal weight people, overweight people are considered to be less intelligent, less hardworking, less attractive, less popular, less successful, less strong-willed, and less trustworthy (Harris, Harris, & Bochner, 1982; Hebl & Heatherton, 1997; Larwood & Gattiker, 1995; Lerner, 1969; Staffieri, 1967). Obese people are also assumed to be less conscientious, less agreeable, less emotionally stable, and less extraverted than normal weight individuals, even though these stereotypes are false (Roehling, Roehling, & Odland, 2008). College students said they would rather marry a cocaine user, shoplifter, embezzler, or blind person than an obese person (Tiggemann & Rothblum, 1988).

The stigma associated with obesity is also contagious. Participants in one study indicated whether they thought male job applicants should be hired (Hebl & Mannix, 2003). Half the participants saw a photo of the applicant sitting next to a normal-sized woman, whereas the other half saw the same applicant sitting next to an obese woman. The woman was actually the same person, but in the obese condition she wore an obese prosthesis (a "fat suit") to make her look fat. The results showed that the applicants were rated more negatively if they were shown sitting next to an obese woman. This effect is called **stigma by association**.

Being fat can even cost you money, especially if you are a woman (Jones, 2004). Obese women earn about 6% less than other women, and obese men about 3% less than other men. The

Digital Vision/Getty Images

cumulative effect can be significant. An obese worker who is paid $1.25 less an hour over a 40-year career will end up making $100,000 less before taxes.

Unlike many unfortunate fates that may befall a person, obesity is considered by many people to be self-inflicted (Clayson & Klassen, 1989; DeJong, 1980, 1993). Thus, people are likely to blame fat people for their plight (Crandall, 1994). Obesity has many costs indeed! ●

---

riding his bike in Amsterdam. Bouyeri shot Van Gogh repeatedly with an automatic handgun, stabbed him with a butcher's knife, slit his throat in a ritualistic manner, and then tried to behead him. When this failed, he nailed two letters to Van Gogh's body with a knife. One of the letters called for jihad and the fall of the United States and Europe ("'Islamist' Held," 2004). Van Gogh was murdered just two months after the release of his highly controversial film about the abuse of Muslim women. The film, titled *Submission*, focuses on Muslim women who have been beaten and raped by their abusive husbands. On their half-naked bodies are written Qur'an verses that describe the physical punishments permitted for women who do not obey their husbands. The Netherlands has generally been considered to be one of the most tolerant countries in the world. After Van Gogh's murder, it was not very tolerant of its Muslim population, mainly immigrants from Morocco and Turkey. In the week following his murder, several Islamic schools and mosques were bombed, burned, and vandalized in the Netherlands ("Dutch Muslim School Hit by Bomb," 2004; "Dutch Islamic School Set Ablaze,"

2004). The researchers included Van Gogh's murder as a naturally occurring factor in their study. The results showed that terrorism news and Van Gogh's murder increased negative attitudes about the integration of Arabs into Dutch society. Other research has shown that the more participants are exposed to news, the more prejudiced they are against Arabs and Muslims (Persson & Musher-Eizenman, 2005).

People Who Are Overweight. Another highly visible characteristic of individuals subject to prejudicial attitudes is obesity. Although some clothes may be "revealing" or "slimming," it is difficult to hide one's weight. Unlike racist and sexist attitudes, many people will openly admit and even act upon their negative attitudes toward obese people (see *Food for Thought*).

Homosexuals. Although a person's sexual orientation is not as readily visible as his or her race, gender, or weight, antigay prejudices are often quite strong,

STIGMA BY ASSOCIATION rejection of those who associate with stigmatized others

On October 6, 1998, Matthew Shepard, a gay 22-year-old student at the University of Wyoming in Laramie, was taken from a bar, beaten, and left for dead. Shepard was found 18 hours later, and died five days later from his injuries.

leading sometimes to violence and discrimination. For example, on October 6, 1998, Matthew Shepard was sitting in a bar, having a beer (Brooke, 1998). Shepard was a 22-year-old political science student at the University of Wyoming, and the bar was known as a favorite hangout for gay people. Aaron McKinney, 22, and Russell Henderson, 21, entered the bar and walked up to Shepard. One witness recalled what happened: "He indicated he was gay, and they said they were gay, too." The bartender said Shepard "definitely wasn't drunk when he came in, and he wasn't drunk when he went out." McKinney and Henderson drove Shepard to an open field, pistol-whipped him with a .357 magnum handgun, burned him, tied him to a fence, and left him for dead in the near freezing temperatures. They also stole his wallet and shoes. Shepard's friends said he did not know the two men who assaulted him.

Eighteen hours later, Shepard was found by two passing motorcyclists who thought at first he was a scarecrow because of the way he was positioned on the fence. Shepard was flown by helicopter to a hospital. Five days later, he died. Just hours after his death, two gay organizations received identical messages applauding the killing of Matthew Shepard. The messages closed with the words, "I hope it happens more often." Rev. Fred Phelps of the Wesboro Baptist Church in Topeka, Kansas, started organizing a protest over Shepard's funeral. Phelps sent out faxes urging people to protest the funeral by carrying signs containing messages such as *NO TEARS FOR QUEERS, FAG MATT IN HELL*, and *GOD HATES FAGS*. Phelps

also started a website with the domain name www.godhatesfags.com. (In fact, the very term *fag* reflects antigay sentiment. It is derived from the word *faggot*, a bundle of wood to be set on fire; in the past homosexuals were sometimes burned at the stake.)

Although the case of Matthew Shepard is extreme, it is not an isolated incident. For example, in a survey of almost 4,000 students at 58 Massachusetts high schools, 31% of gay respondents said they had been threatened or injured at school in the past year, which is about five times greater than the percentage for heterosexual respondents (Brooke, 1998).

Many people who would never admit to holding a negative stereotype about another race will freely and openly say that they think homosexuals are bad (e.g., Herek, 2000). Researchers have begun to study homophobia in laboratory studies. Phobias are excessive fears, so **homophobia** is an excessive fear of homosexuals or homosexual behavior. In one study (Bernat, Calhoun, Adams, & Zeichner, 2001), heterosexual male college students first completed a scale designed to measure homophobic attitudes (e.g., "Gay people make me nervous" and "I would hit a homosexual for coming on to me"). The researchers selected men who had either high or low scores on the homophobia scale. Participants watched a male homosexual erotic videotape and reported their emotional reactions afterwards. Homophobic participants reported feeling more anxious and angry after watching the homosexual erotic videotape than did nonhomophobic participants. Next, participants were given an opportunity to shock another man (actually a confederate) on a task. The level of shock given was used to measure aggression. By the flip of a coin, the male confederate was described as either gay

HOMOPHOBIA excessive fear of homosexuals or homosexual behavior

Roots of Antigay Prejudice

Why are people prejudiced against homosexuals? As noted in the text, the prejudice is strong, and many consider it normal and natural to abhor sexual deviance. Some people invoke religious or biblical statements condemning homosexuality, but most likely those statements are a result rather than an original cause of antigay bias. Other people think it is simple to say that homosexuality is unnatural, but in fact homosexual activity is found in other species besides humans (e.g., beetles, birds, dolphins, fruit bats, orangutans, sheep; Owen, 2004). Homosexuality is also found all over the world among humans, so nature, at least, does not regard homosexuality as unnatural.

There are some curious facts about antigay prejudice. It is stronger among men than women

Some female Japanese macaques, like these two in Kyoto, prefer to be with females, even when males are present in their group.

(Herek & Capitanio, 1996), even though men are more likely than women to take part in homosexual activity and to be homosexuals (Laumann, Gagnon, Michael, & Michaels, 1994). Then again, the apparently greater tolerance among women could be due to the fact that when people answer questions about homosexuality, they think mainly of male homosexuality. To correct for this methodological problem, Whitley (1988) asked people separate questions about attitudes toward male versus female homosexuality; he found that both men and women were more intolerant of homosexuality in their own gender (see also Herek & Capitanio, 1999).

Simple logic might dictate the opposite. After all, if you were the only heterosexual man in your town (because all the others were gay), you would be in a great position to choose the most desirable women for yourself. Put another way, every man who turns out to be gay reduces the competition for the number of available women. Conversely, when people of the opposite sex turn out to be gay, a heterosexual's odds of finding an ideal mate are reduced. Heterosexuals ought logically to be delighted to learn that members of their own gender are gay and ought to be more opposed to homosexuality in the opposite gender. But that's not what the data say.

At present, the most likely explanation is that people's attitudes are mainly rooted in fear that they themselves will be the target of romantic or sexual advances from homosexuals. People do not want to be in the position of having to reject homosexual overtures (see Whitley, 1988). That may be why they are more strongly opposed to homosexuality in their own gender.

Many people believe homosexuality is unnatural, but in fact homosexual activity has been found all over the world in humans and in nonhuman species.

A further dimension may be that they fear that they might have a positive response to homosexual advances. We saw in Chapter 6 that the men who expressed the strongest antigay views were also the most sexually aroused by watching gay pornography, though the men were reluctant to admit it, and their arousal was only verified by measuring their erectile responses (Adams, Wright, & Lohr, 1996). The fear of one's own possible reactions might explain why people often treat homosexuals with such strong reactions of disgust and hatred, as if the homosexuals represented a dangerous threat. ■

(involved in a "committed gay relationship with his partner, Steve, for two years") or straight (involved in a "committed dating relationship with his girlfriend for two years"). Homophobic participants gave the homosexual confederate more intense and longer shocks than did nonhomophobic participants; the groups did not differ in their aggression toward the heterosexual confederate. (For information on the roots of antigay prejudice, see *The Social Side of Sex*.)

People are especially likely to feel prejudice toward gay people if they believe that homosexuality is a lifestyle choice rather than a biological predisposition

(Wood & Bartkowski, 2004). Opposition to gay rights is most pronounced among people with conservative political and religious beliefs (Wood & Bartkowski, 2004), who appear to be disgusted by homosexuality (Olatunji, 2008). There are also cultural differences in tolerance toward homosexuality. For example, Dutch children living with lesbian parents are more open about growing up in a lesbian family, are less homophobic, and have fewer emotional and behavioral problems than American children in similar families (Bos, Gartrell, Van Balen, Peyser, & Sandfort, 2008).

Other potential targets of prejudice include the elderly, Jews (whom we discuss in a later section), and people with stigmas. **Stigmas** include characteristics of individuals that are considered socially unacceptable. Besides overweight, other stigmas include mental illness, sickness, poverty, and physical blemishes.

Why Prejudice Exists

Why does prejudice exist? One view holds that prejudice is a product of a wicked culture. By this view, children start off innocent, trusting, and accepting of all others, but they are taught through socializing agents (including parents and the mass media) to dislike and reject certain groups.

There is certainly something correct in the view that stereotypes and prejudices are learned through socialization. Stereotypes often contain specific information about specific groups, and this information must be learned (as opposed to being innate

off the mark.com   by Mark Parisi

WE DON'T KNOW WHAT TO MAKE OF THIS, MR. STEIER, BUT WE FIND OURSELVES WISHING YOU'D PUT A SHIRT ON...

MARK PARISI/ 3-26   MarkParisi@aol.com   offthemark.com   ©2004 MARK PARISI DIST. BY UFS, INC.

Reprinted by permission of Atlantic Feature Syndicate/Mark Parisi.

Individuals with stigmas are often the targets of prejudice and discrimination.

knowledge). On the other hand, the tendency to hold stereotypes and prejudices may be innate. Even children do not turn out on close inspection to be sweet, accepting, and tolerant. As we saw in Chapter 11, children everywhere seem instantly ready to reject anyone who is different in any way. Although the predisposition to categorize by stereotypes may be natural, the content of stereotypes is certainly learned through socialization.

At present, your textbook authors have reluctantly come to the conclusion that prejudice is natural. As we shall see in the later section on overcoming prejudice, it seems that people automatically and normally know stereotypes and think of them, whereas they have to exert themselves to override them. More important perhaps, prejudices are found all over the world; we know of no culture in which gender stereotypes are unknown, or where members of rival groups view each other with only respect and admiration. That doesn't make prejudice right or acceptable, but as social scientists we should not be surprised to find it.

The conclusion is that the tendency to align with similar others and square off against different others, including forming negative stereotypes of them and discriminating against them, is deeply rooted in the human psyche. Some social psychologists noted early on that if two groups were involved in a laboratory study, and the experimenter allowed one person to decide how much to pay each participant, the person would usually give more money to members of

---

STIGMAS characteristics of individuals that are considered socially unacceptable (e.g., being overweight, mentally ill, sick, poor, or physically scarred)

his or her own group than to members of the other group, even if the groups were chosen completely at random (e.g., Billig & Tajfel, 1973; Brewer, 1979; Brewer & Silver, 1978; Tajfel & Billig, 1974; Tajfel, Billig, Bundy, & Flament, 1971). Various theories were proposed to explain this finding. Was it because people felt similar to members of their own group? Was it because they had grown to like them? Was it because they had had conflict with the outgroup? Was it because they expected members of their own group to repay the good treatment later on?

A European research team led by Henri Tajfel decided to conduct a program of studies that would determine what caused these patterns of **ingroup favoritism** (preferential treatment of, or more favorable attitudes toward, people in one's own group, as compared to people in other groups). They formed an experimental plan: They would start out with groups that were so meaningless that people would not show any ingroup favoritism; then they would gradually add in other variables (such as the presumption that the group members were similar to each other, or had to depend on each other, or had common goals) and see at what point the ingroup favoritism started.

But the plan failed—for a very revealing reason. It failed because the research team could never get to the starting point. They were unable to make a group that seemed so arbitrary or trivial that no ingroup favoritism was found. If the experimenters did nothing more than flip a coin to assign participants to a "red team" and a "blue team" (see Locksley, Ortiz, & Hepburn, 1980), the red team members soon began to think that the blue team members were stupid or obnoxious or immoral, and they would favor other red team members if they could. This automatic preference for members of one's own group even in the absence of pragmatic benefit or personal relationship is called the **minimal group effect**.

These findings suggest that people are normally and naturally ready to go along with dividing the world up into "us" and "them" and to adopt a negative stance toward "them." Prejudice and discrimination follow naturally from this tendency. As we said, the content of stereotypes may be learned, but the readiness to hold stereotypes is deeply rooted and not easily overcome.

Prejudice may be yet another sphere in which nature says go whereas culture sometimes says stop. Nature has prepared human beings to divide the world into "us" and "them" and to hold prejudices against "them." Culture sometimes strives to teach people to overcome their prejudices. Modern diverse cultures in particular struggle to get people to set aside their prejudices and treat each other with fairness and tolerance, but the struggle is not an easy one, and total success has proven elusive. Of course,

culture does not always say stop. As we noted earlier, the content of stereotypes is almost always learned, and people learn from their culture what members of other groups are supposedly like. That goes for stereotypes that are fairly accurate and ones that are wildly distorted.

US VERSUS THEM: GROUPS IN COMPETITION

In the 1950s, Muzafer Sherif conducted a study at Robber's Cave State Park in Oklahoma (Sherif & Sherif, 1953). The park, named after a cave that was once supposedly inhabited by robbers, was located in a remote area far from external influences. Participants were 22 white, middle-class, 11-year-old boys who thought they were going on a summer camp experience. Little did they know that the camp was being run by a social psychologist! Sherif divided the boys into two groups of 11 that were approximately equal in athletic ability and camping experience. He then transported the two groups to the park in separate buses and assigned them to cabins located in different areas of the park. The study was conducted in three stages, with each stage lasting about one week.

During the first stage, the two groups of boys had no contact with each other. The boys in each group cooperated in activities such as swimming, pitching tents, preparing meals, and hiking. During this stage, the boys in each group became good friends. One group called itself the Rattlers; the other group called itself the Eagles. Both groups made flags and stenciled the group names on their T-shirts.

During the second stage, the boys met each other and competed in contests such as baseball and tug-of-war. The stakes were high, because the winners took home valuable prizes including trophies, medals, cash, and pocketknives. The two groups began eating together in a common mess hall, where the prizes were on display for all to see. The contests produced strong feelings of prejudice toward the other group. At first it was limited to name-calling, such as calling the other boys "pigs," "sissies," "cheaters," and "stinkers." Before long, however, the boys started committing physical acts of aggression. Following their first loss at a baseball game, the Eagles burned the Rattlers' flag, and the Eagles' leader proclaimed "You can tell those guys I did it . . . I'll fight 'em." The next day, the Rattlers burned the Eagles' flag in retaliation. When the Eagles won a tug-of-war by sitting down and digging in their heels, the Rattlers accused them of cheating and that night invaded their cabin,

---

INGROUP FAVORITISM preferential treatment of, or more favorable attitudes toward, people in one's own group

MINIMAL GROUP EFFECT the finding that people show favoritism toward ingroup members even when group membership is randomly determined

overturning beds, tearing out mosquito netting, and causing extensive damage. The next morning, the Eagles took revenge on the Rattlers' cabin, and then began to store rocks to throw at the Rattlers if they retaliated. The Eagles eventually won the tournament and took home the valuable prizes. No consolation prizes were given to the losers. The defeated Rattlers immediately raided the Eagles' cabin and stole the prizes, which provoked further fighting. Things became so bad that the camp counselors were forced to intervene. At the end of the second stage, it was fair to say that the opposing groups of boys hated each other. It had taken only a week and a few competitions to transform groups of 11-year-old campers into violent haters.

During the third stage, the researchers tried to reduce the hostility between groups. They soon found out that creating hostility between groups was much easier than reducing it (another sign that people are predisposed to develop negative feelings toward outgroups). First, the researchers tried telling each group good things about the boys in the other group. This attempt failed miserably. Neither group believed the propaganda. Next, the psychologists tried noncompetitive contact, such as having the boys watch movies together, eat meals together, and shoot off fireworks together on the Fourth of July. This didn't work either. It just gave the boys another chance to fight. For example, when the boys ate together, they ended up having food fights.

Finally, the researchers tried to induce cooperation by having the boys work together toward shared goals, called **superordinate goals**. The researchers rigged some urgent problems that the boys could solve only by working together. First, the camp's water supply failed. The camp staff blamed the problem on "vandals." The Eagles and Rattlers inspected the water lines separately but found no problems. They came together at the source of water, a large tank that was practically full, where they discovered a sack stuffed inside the water faucet. The boys worked together on the faucet for more than 45 minutes. Finally they fixed it, and the two groups rejoiced together. The second superordinate goal involved showing a feature-length movie. The staff called the boys together and said they could get one of two films, *Treasure Island* or *Kidnapped*. Both groups yelled approval of these films. After some discussion, one Rattler said, "Everyone who wants *Treasure*

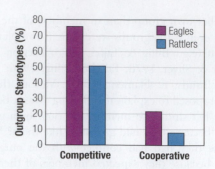

▶ **FIGURE 13.2** Percentage of outgroup members classified negatively after competition and after cooperation.

Island raise their hands." Most of the boys voted for this film. The staff said that the film would cost $15 (a serious amount of money in those days), and the camp could not afford to pay the whole amount. After some more discussion, the boys arrived at a solution—each group would pay $3.50 and the camp would pay the remaining $8.00. The boys even decided to eat dinner together.

By the end of the third stage, negative stereotypes of outgroup members had decreased dramatically (see ▶ **FIGURE 13.2**). At breakfast and lunch the last day of camp, many boys sat next to boys in the other group. The boys agreed that they wanted to return to Oklahoma City all together on one bus, instead of going home in separate buses. When the staff agreed to the request, some of the boys actually cheered. The Rattlers even agreed to use the $5 they had won in a contest to buy malts for all the boys at a rest stop.

Several theories have been proposed to explain prejudice, such as the prejudice that existed between the Eagles and Rattlers. **Realistic conflict theory** provides one explanation of prejudice (Sherif, 1966). According to this theory, competition over scarce resources leads to intergroup hostility and conflict. A common example is a situation in which jobs are scarce and an established group blames immigrants for "taking the food out of our children's mouths." By **competition** we mean that some people attain their goals only if other people do not (Johnson & Johnson, 1983). By **cooperation** we mean that people work together with others to help all of them achieve their goals (Johnson & Johnson, 1983). In the Robber's Cave study, competition over valued prizes such as cash and pocketknives led to an all-out feud between two groups of ordinary 11-year-old boys. The two groups of boys didn't even differ on any visible dimension, such as racial or ethnic background. In everyday life, where it is easier to distinguish "us" from "them" on the basis of obvious physical traits, prejudice and hostility may arise even more swiftly.

According to realistic conflict theory, groups should have the most negative attitudes toward their

---

SUPERORDINATE GOALS goals that can be achieved only by cooperating and working with others

REALISTIC CONFLICT THEORY the idea that competition over scarce resources leads to intergroup hostility and conflict

COMPETITION situation in which people can attain their goals only if others do not

COOPERATION situation in which people must work together with others to help all achieve their goals

Tradeoffs

Competition Versus Cooperation

Many people in the United States and other Western societies perceive the world as a dog-eat-dog place in which people compete to survive and prosper. Not all societies adopt this view of competition. In his analysis of 25 cooperative, peaceful societies, Bruce Bonta (1997) found that competition did not exist in 23 of the 25 societies. In these 23 societies, even the games children play lack competition. For example, the !Kung children of Namibia and Botswana in southern Africa love to play a game called *zeni*. The children use a stick to throw into the air a weight that is attached by a thong to a feather. Then they use the stick to try to catch the object. Although the children exhibit widely different skill levels, they do not compete against each other. They just play the game for fun (Draper, 1976).

The Piaroa of Venezuela are intensely opposed to competition and even put it in the same category as cannibalism (Overing, 1986). The Chewong of the Malay Peninsula are so opposed to competition that they don't even have a word for it in their language (Howell, 1989). The Tristan Islanders had virtually no knowledge of competition until 1961, when they were forced to relocate to Great Britain for two years after a volcano erupted on their island. The Tristan Islanders did not fit in well with the highly competitive English society (Keir, 1966). The Ifaluk, who live on a small Pacific atoll in the Federated States of Micronesia, value most highly a person who is *maluwelu* (calm, quiet, respectful, obedient, kind, gentle). The word *maluwelu* is also used to describe a lagoon when the wind is calm. They strongly devalue traits such as showing off, being disrespectful, and displaying personal possessions (Bonta, 1997). The Birhor, a tribal society of central India, do not compete for scarce resources and rarely accumulate possessions (Adhikary, 1984).

Competition was found in 2 of the 25 peaceful societies, but it was limited to competition in business dealings. More than 100 years ago, the Fipa of western Tanzania transformed their society from one based on violence and war to one based on nonviolence and peace. The Fipa are very competitive in their business dealings, but the competition is constructive and peaceful (Willis, 1989). The other competitive peaceful society is the Jains of India. The Jains believe in *ahimas* (nonviolence), and they take vows to avoid any socially harmful acts, including stealing and telling lies. Yet they are quite competitive in the business world. An analysis of these studies does not prove that competition leads to violence, but it does show that cultures have the power to say "stop" even though our natural tendency is to compete for limited resources.

However, there might be a tradeoff to embracing cooperation and shunning competition.

The 25 societies that Bonta (1997) studied are not very successful or powerful, in either economic or political terms. Competition may produce prejudice, hostility, and aggression, but it also produces progress and advancement. Communism sought to eliminate competition (at least based on greed) by eliminating private ownership and private property, but without incentives it was an economic failure. The effect can be summed up in one of the stock phrases that Soviet-bloc workers used to say before the collapse of European communism: "They pretend to pay us, and we pretend to work." Many small European countries competed for centuries for local power, at great cost in warfare and suffering, but as a result European military skills so far surpassed those of the rest of the world that Europeans were able to conquer and colonize most other peoples they encountered. Indeed, according to some analyses, the competition among many small, neighboring countries was a central fact that enabled Europe to surpass and overpower other cultures that had once been clearly more powerful (McNeill, 1982). Competition has costs, but it also offers gains. ●

The !Kung children of Namibia and Botswana play a noncompetitive game called *zeni*.

Dancers from Ifaluk, one of the 25 peaceful, cooperative societies studied by Bruce Bonta (1997).

rivals, and these attitudes should be strongest, when resources are scarce and groups must compete for them. (You need food, water, and air to live, but few groups fight over air, because there is plenty for everyone. In contrast, fighting over food has a long history, and some predictions are that as the world's supply of fresh water begins to run short over the course of this century, conflicts over water will increase.) Competition is not a part of every society. *Tradeoffs* describes 25 peaceful, cooperative, noncompetitive societies.

One could argue that realistic conflict theory is just frustration/aggression theory (see Chapter 10) applied to group conflict. Competition is a zero-sum game in which one side's gain is the other side's frustration.

Evolution may have had a hand in instilling the human readiness to form groups and hold prejudices against rival groups. Hunter/gatherer groups lived under conditions of fairly scarce resources, which is why they roamed over large areas. If two groups tried to spend the summer in the same area, there might not be enough food for both groups, so one group would have to leave. The groups would therefore be natural enemies. If one group contained people who readily formed prejudices against the others and acted quickly to drive the others out, whereas the other group failed to develop such attitudes, the more prejudiced group would very likely win the competition for scarce resources.

Most discussions of prejudice and stereotyping today focus on unfavorable treatment of the outgroup, but that is simply the other side of the coin of preferential or favorable treatment of the ingroup. For example, if a wealthy African American businessman gives a large sum of money to make scholarships available for African American students, is he discriminating against nonblacks (who are not eligible for his money) or helping members of his own group? Both are correct. When we understand prejudice as doing positive, favorable deeds for members of one's own group, it is easier to see how this could be favored in evolution and become part of human nature. Imagine human beings who didn't do anything special or nice for members of their own families or for the people with whom they lived and worked. Such people might well have lost out in natural selection, if pitted against groups in which most members helped and supported one another.

The challenges of living in a diverse society have sensitized modern individuals to the problems created by prejudices. People from different groups seem ready to distrust each other and develop negative views of each other. It is important to remember that humans evolved under conditions in which they interacted mainly with members of their own group, not other groups. (In other words, diverse societies are a fairly modern invention.) Groups whose members wanted to help and support one another probably flourished better than groups who didn't. But in modern life people have to live in harmony with people who belong to very different groups. This is not what we evolved for, but it is the reality of modern life.

Numerous studies have shown that groups are more influenced by competition than individuals are, a finding that has been dubbed the **discontinuity effect** (Schopler & Insko, 1992). The discontinuity effect appears to be motivated by fear and greed (Insko, Schopler, Hoyle, & Dardis, 1990; Schopler, Insko, Drigotas, & Graetz, 1993). People don't trust the members of other groups, so they grab as many resources as they can. If the outgroup is cooperative, they will take advantage of it. However, intergroup competitiveness is not inevitable. For example, it can be reduced by having people think about the long-term effects of their actions (Insko et al., 1998). It can also be reduced by making group members identifiable (Schopler, Insko, Drigotas, & Wieselquist, 1995). Recall from Chapter 10 that when people become deindividuated they are more likely to steal and engage in other antisocial behaviors, such as acts of violence and aggression.

The crucial implication of the discontinuity effect is that groups won't usually get along as well as individuals. To illustrate, imagine two people from different races—white, black, Asian, or other—who have a dispute; they sit down, one-to-one, and try to resolve the issue. What are the odds that they can work it out? Now imagine that the dispute is between groups—six people of one race and six of the other. What are the odds that these groups can reach an acceptable compromise? The discontinuity effect holds that the two groups will be less likely to find a mutually agreeable compromise than the two individuals. One Asian and one African can perhaps find a mutually satisfactory compromise; six Asians talking to six Africans might not. This is not a reflection on the particular races but rather on universal human nature.

IGNORANCE? THE CONTACT HYPOTHESIS

Another view is that prejudice stems from ignorance. According to this view, people who have very little contact with other groups have no information about them, so they try to fill the gap by forming stereotypes. If people could resolve ignorance by having more interactions and getting more firsthand information about outgroups, prejudice would diminish or even disappear.

More than 50 years ago, Gordon Allport (1954) proposed the **contact hypothesis**, which states that regular interaction between members of different groups reduces prejudice, providing that it occurs under favorable conditions. According to this hypothesis, negative prejudices arise and survive because the two groups don't have much contact with each other. Bringing conflicting groups together supposedly reduces prejudicial feelings as members

---

DISCONTINUITY EFFECT the finding that groups are more extreme, and often more hostile, than individuals

CONTACT HYPOTHESIS the idea that regular interaction between members of different groups reduces prejudice, providing that it occurs under favorable conditions

of different groups come to know and understand one another. For example, integrating children of different racial backgrounds should reduce prejudice as these students interact with one another and learn more about each other.

Research has shown some support for the contact hypothesis, provided that the contact is pleasant and positive and other conditions are met (Pettigrew & Tropp, 2005). (When the contact is not so mutually satisfying, the result can be an increase in hostility and prejudice.) For example, in a recent field experiment (Shook & Fazio, 2008), white college students were assigned white or black dorm roommates by the flip of a coin. Although students in interracial dorm rooms reported being less satisfied with each other than did roommates in same-race dorm rooms, prejudiced attitudes decreased over time among students in interracial rooms but not among students in same-race rooms. A recent six-month longitudinal study of 1,655 secondary school students from Belgium, England, and Germany showed a reciprocal relationship between contact and prejudice (Binder et al., 2009). Not only did contact reduce prejudice, but prejudiced people also avoid contact with minority group members.

RATIONALIZATIONS FOR OPPRESSION

Some social psychologists have sought to explain prejudice and stereotyping on the basis of the political goals of the powerful group (e.g., Sidanius & Pratto, 1999). They propose, for example, that European Americans constructed stereotypes of African Americans as inferior beings to justify keeping them in an inferior position in society. Likewise, some feminists have suggested that men invented stereotypes of women simply to rationalize men's continued oppression of women. For example, the view that women were unsuited for higher education (even to the extent of bizarre medical theories proposing that if a woman studied too much, her uterus would come loose and wander aimlessly around inside her body) might have been invented so that men could justify refusing to admit women to universities. Traditional female stereotypes can be used to justify the oppression of women (e.g., Jost & Kay, 2005).

The fact that stereotypes can justify social inequality does not mean that stereotypes were deliberately invented as part of a conspiracy to oppress certain people. Rather, it suggests that people in positions of relative power and wealth find stereotypes to be an appealing way of explaining their superiority.

STEREOTYPES AS HEURISTICS

The previous section presented stereotypes as a kind of conspiracy, claiming that people deliberately

Over time, roommates of different races become less prejudiced.

© Tom Stewart/Corbis

invented stereotypes for devious, manipulative ends. A simpler and less insidious view is that people often rely on stereotypes as mental shortcuts, just as they simplify the world in countless other ways. In Chapter 5, we saw that people use a variety of heuristics to help them understand the world in clear, simple ways. Stereotypes may be heuristics too. Gordon Allport (1954) described stereotyping as "the law of least effort." It is difficult and tiring to get to know each individual on his or her own merits, starting with a completely open mind, and to form a valid, carefully tested impression of each person. It is much easier to go through life prejudging people and assuming they will fit general stereotypes based on quickly recognizable categories: Men are competitive or untrustworthy, African Americans are good at music and sports, women are gentle or moody, Europeans are classy but arrogant, Latinos are fun-loving and passionate but are usually late for appointments, and so forth. Such generalizations appeal to the lazy mind or cognitive miser.

Research has shown that stereotypes are energy-saving devices. In one study (Macrae, Milne, & Bodenhausen, 1994), participants performed two tasks at the same time. In one task they were to form an impression of another person using a list of traits. Half of the participants saw only the name of the person they were to form an impression of (e.g., John), whereas the other half also saw a stereotypic label (e.g., John—skinhead). Underneath the name was a list of 10 traits, of which half were consistent with the stereotype (e.g., for skinheads, rebellious, aggressive, dishonest, untrustworthy, dangerous) and half were not (e.g., lucky, observant, modest, optimistic, curious). The other task involved listening to a prose

▶ TABLE 13.1 Explanations for Why Prejudice Exists

Explanation	Definition	Example
Competition	According to realistic conflict theory, competition over scarce resources leads to intergroup hostility and conflict.	Competition over good housing, schools, and jobs can lead to hostility toward outgroup members.
Ignorance	People who have very little contact with other groups have no information about them, so they try to fill the gap by forming stereotypes.	People who have little contact with Muslims may assume that they all support the jihad against the West.
Rationalizations for oppression	To retain their status, powerful groups justify and rationalize prejudice against less powerful groups.	Some feminists have suggested that men invented stereotypes of women simply to rationalize continued oppression of women.
Stereotypes as heuristics	To simplify their world, people often rely on stereotypes as mental shortcuts or heuristics.	Rather than collect information about each African American individually, it requires less mental effort to stereotype them all as good at music and sports.
Prejudice boosts self-esteem	People can feel better about themselves if they consider their own group superior and all other groups inferior.	People might feel better about themselves if they think their own religion is the only true one and all others are false.

passage and trying to remember what they heard. Participants' performance on both tasks was tested. Participants who saw a stereotype label recalled twice as many stereotypical traits as did participants who did not see the label. They also remembered more information about the prose passage. Thus, when people were encouraged to use stereotypes, they actually had better memory for the prose information because they were able to save mental energy by stereotyping the skinheads. Similar effects were obtained in a follow-up study even when the stereotype labels were presented subliminally. Using stereotypes enabled people to process more information, consistent with the view that stereotypes are useful tools that enable people to understand others more easily (and, in these cases, more accurately too). In simple terms, we use stereotypes because it simplifies the process of thinking about other people.

People use stereotypes when their ability to judge is diminished. One clever study sorted participants into "morning people," who like to wake up early but get sleepy early in the evening, versus "night people," who have energy long after dark but find it hard to drag themselves out of bed in the morning (Bodenhausen, 1990). Each group was tested for how much it used stereotype thinking in the morning versus evening. Morning people are more prone to use stereotypes at night (when they are tired) than in the morning (when they are alert). Night people do the opposite: They rely on stereotypes more in the morning than the evening. These findings fit the broader point that people use stereotypes to conserve effort and energy.

People learn the content of stereotypes mainly from other people in their group. That is because people spend much more time with ingroup members than with outgroup members. This fits one of the themes of this book—"putting people first." People rely on other people for information about the world, rather than learning about the world through direct experience. If you have a stereotype about Russians, you probably learned it from your non-Russian friends rather than from direct observation of Russians.

PREJUDICE AND SELF-ESTEEM

We have seen that most stereotypes are negative and that most prejudices depict outgroups as inferior or as having bad traits. Several reasons for this have been suggested. One simple motivational explanation for the negative tone of most stereotypes is that people use them to boost self-esteem. The basic idea is that most people want to have high self-esteem, which is one of the most common assumptions underlying a great deal of research in social psychology. High self-esteem feels good. Applied to prejudice, the idea is that by regarding members of other groups as inferior, people enhance their self-esteem by virtue of belonging to their own group. Put another way, if all the other groups are inferior, then your own group must be superior—so you must be pretty good to belong to it. In this way, prejudice can be self-affirming. By using stereotypes to justify and act on prejudices, people can claim for themselves a feeling of mastery and self-worth (Fein & Spencer, 1997). For a summary of why prejudice exists, see ▶ **TABLE 13.1**.

Why Prejudice Exists

1. If some participants are randomly assigned to a "blue group" and others are assigned to a "maize group," the "blue group" members will think they are superior to the "maize group" members, whereas the "maize group" members will think they are superior to the "blue group" members. What is this phenomenon called?
   (a) Discontinuity effect
   (b) Minimal group effect
   (c) Outgroup favoritism
   (d) Outgroup homogeneity bias

2. The Robber's Cave study provides _____.
   (a) evidence that stereotypes once formed can almost never be changed
   (b) evidence that competition is necessary to the creation of intergroup conflict
   (c) evidence that mere contact will greatly reduce intergroup hostility
   (d) None of the above

3. According to the discontinuity effect, _____.
   (a) both groups and individuals are influenced by competition
   (b) groups are more influenced by competition than individuals are
   (c) individuals are more influenced by competition than groups are
   (d) neither groups nor individuals are influenced by competition

4. What condition is required for the contact hypothesis to be confirmed?
   (a) Contact only works among people of equal status.
   (b) Contact only works when outgroup members are perceived as typical members of their group.
   (c) Contact only works when the contact occurs daily.
   (d) Contact seems to work regardless of whether certain conditions are met.

Content of Prejudice and Stereotypes

In this section we examine the content of prejudice and stereotypes. One might say that people today have a stereotype about stereotypes, which is that stereotypes are typically both wrong and negative. Is that stereotype accurate?

ARE STEREOTYPES ALWAYS WRONG, MOSTLY WRONG, OR MOSTLY RIGHT?

Earlier we covered the theory that stereotypes are heuristics. As we saw in Chapter 5, people use heuristics and other shortcuts in their thinking to conserve mental effort and time. Heuristics can lead to errors, but heuristics survive because they often produce the right answer. This has led some researchers to wonder whether some stereotypes have some element of accuracy. For example, you might have the stereotype that men are taller than women, and so when meeting a married couple you would generally expect the husband to be taller than the wife. Sometimes you would be wrong, because some women are taller than their husbands. Still, you would be right most of the time.

That, after all, is how heuristics work. They take an approach that is true most of the time and follow it as if it were always true. Janet Swim (1994) investigated gender stereotypes to see how big the kernel of truth was. Her findings were disturbing to some, because they suggested that people's stereotypes are accurate in both content and degree. She had her participants say on what traits men and women differed, and how big they thought the difference was. When she compared these estimates against published studies on actual gender differences, she found that the stereotypes were mostly quite accurate. That is, not only were her participants correct about what traits were different between men and women—they were also pretty accurate at estimating the size of the differences.

A thorough tour of evidence about stereotype accuracy and inaccuracy was taken by Jussim and colleagues (in press). Overall, the picture they found was one of remarkable accuracy, with some notable exceptions. Most studies found that people's judgments about racial and ethnic differences averaged within 20% of the objective facts. Hence severe inaccuracies were not common. They found the same general level of accuracy for gender stereotypes (like the Swim study described above).

On the other hand, political stereotypes were consistently inaccurate: Democrats and Republicans do not perceive each other very accurately (Judd & Park, 1993). Also, a survey by Terracciano and colleagues (2005) found that stereotypes about personality traits based on countries were not very accurate. For example, if we were to ask you what sort of personality is typical among Germans, or French, or Brazilians, you might be able to come up with an answer, but it is not likely to be very accurate.

Moreover, even the evidence of accuracy in general does not translate into everyone being correct. We said that Jussim and colleagues found that the average level of accuracy was high, but they also noted that in every study there were plenty of individuals who expressed wildly inaccurate stereotypes.

The high level of accuracy in modern stereotypes may also indicate that stereotyping has changed. Most participants in these studies were modern

ARE STEREOTYPES ALWAYS NEGATIVE?

Are stereotypes always negative? No, of course not. Many people hold the stereotype that Asian Americans are good at math, or engineering, or schoolwork in general, or that African Americans have superior talents in a variety of culturally valued spheres such as music and sports. A once-popular stereotype that fat people were jolly contributed to how Santa Claus became depicted. If Santa were invented today, he would almost certainly be fashionably slim and debonair! Conversely, if a new character were introduced today as a fat old man with a long beard and a silly red pantsuit, he probably would be a bad guy or troublemaker.

Bad stereotypes generally present more of a cultural problem than good ones, because they entail prejudging a person in a bad way. But good stereotypes can also be harmful, although the harm may not be as readily apparent. Consider, for example, the difference between hostile sexism and benevolent sexism (Glick & Fiske, 1996). Hostile sexism is exemplified by what feminists label as "male chauvinist pigs" who view women in a derogatory manner. Some sample items from the scale used to measure hostile sexism are "Once a woman gets a man to commit to her, she usually tries to put him on a tight leash" and "Women are too easily offended" (Glick & Fiske, 1996, p. 512). Benevolent sexism is exemplified by chivalrous men who open doors for women and insist on paying for dinner. Benevolent sexism seems to paint a favorable view of women, but it is also grounded in gender stereotypes. Some sample items from the scale used to measure benevolent sexism are "A good woman should be set on a pedestal by her man" and "Many women have a quality of purity that few men possess" (Glick & Fiske, 1996, p. 512). The two forms of sexism tend to be correlated.

Research has shown that benevolent sexism is worse than hostile sexism for women's cognitive performance (Dardenne, Dumont, & Bollier, 2007). The authors of this research even called benevolent sexism an "insidious danger." In other words, according to these researchers, opening doors for women is worse than insulting them. In addition, women who have benevolent sexist attitudes are more likely to perceive safety restrictions (e.g., not driving alone on a long trip) as justified and for their own good (Moya, Glick, Expósito, de Lemus, & Hart, 2007).

Benevolent sexism may be more harmful than hostile sexism because some women may accept it or even enjoy it. In some parts of the world, such as the southern United States, benevolent sexism is even considered to be romantic. Some people with strong opinions on these matters consider it bad for women to let men hold doors or coats for them or perform other courtesies, because these attitudes

The perception that African Americans are superior musicians is a stereotype, but not a negative one.

university students, who have been taught to be careful about using stereotypes and avoiding unfair prejudice. Seventy years ago, German Nazis stereotyped Jews as greedy, ruthless individuals conspiring to destroy their country as a step toward world domination—a mistaken notion that contributed to horrific mass murder.

Another question regarding the accuracy of stereotypes is what happens when people judge a particular other person. Meta-analyses that combine the results of many different studies have generally concluded that there is a genuine effect of stereotypes on judgment of individual persons, but it is a pretty small one (Jussim et al., in press). In contrast, when judging an individual person, people rely quite heavily on information specific to the person (Kunda & Thagard, 1996). In other words, when people meet someone and form an impression of that person, they mostly rely on whatever they learn about that individual, and they may fill in the gaps with stereotypes to a small extent.

Prejudice has multiple roots. To the extent that prejudices are held as a heuristic way of understanding the social world, people may try to hold fairly accurate stereotypes. In contrast, to the extent that people hold prejudices in order to bolster their own self-esteem at the expense of others, or to rationalize the status quo and justify their oppression of disadvantaged minorities, stereotypes may be exaggerated or even entirely fabricated and hence have little or no factual basis.

A man opening a door for a woman may seem polite, but it is a form of sexism. If a man opens the door for another person regardless of whether that person is male or female, it is not sexism.

reflect sexism. Even saying "ladies first" would be considered oppressive.

Inner Processes

Inner processes (e.g., emotions) can also contribute to prejudice and stereotyping. Stereotypes can form simply on the basis of **salience**—a psychological term roughly meaning "obviousness" (e.g., Hamilton, Dugan, & Trolier, 1985; Hamilton & Gifford, 1976). We described one of these studies in Chapter 5 when we discussed illusory correlations (Hamilton & Gifford, 1976). That is, simply standing out can contribute to stereotyping. If you were, say, the first blond person to arrive on an island, people would pay extra attention to what you did, and if you did something memorable (say, you did something to disgrace a local church), people would remember that "blond people are against religion," and the next blonds to arrive would have to cope with that stereotype.

The research findings based on salience are interesting because they show how stereotypes can form from purely cognitive (mental) processes, without any influence of emotion or motivation. When motivation enters the picture, it can greatly increase the likelihood of prejudice. One classic formulation of motivated prejudice is scapegoat theory. **Scapegoat theory** proposes that people blame their problems and misfortunes on outgroups, which contributes to negative attitudes toward these outgroups. This process is linked to attribution theory, discussed in Chapter 5, which looks at how people infer the causes of events. One theme introduced there was the **self-serving bias**: People like to take credit for success but refuse blame for problems and failures. When times are bad, people prefer to blame others (scapegoats) rather than their own bad judgment or incompetence.

Scapegoating creates friction in any diverse society. Throughout Western history, the Jews have suffered repeatedly as a result of being blamed for the

SALIENCE being obvious or standing out
SCAPEGOAT THEORY the idea that blaming problems and misfortunes on outgroups contributes to negative attitudes toward these outgroups
SELF-SERVING BIAS the tendency for people to take credit for success but refuse blame for problems and failures

problems of Christian societies. Jews were blamed for the death of Jesus, even though it was the Romans who actually performed the execution. Modern Romans, however, were European and Christian, so the Christian community in Europe preferred to put the blame on the Jewish outgroup rather than on members of their own ingroup.

Even in the 20th century, Jews were scapegoats. Germans were shocked and baffled by their country's abrupt surrender in World War I (which, thanks in part to battlefield standstills and government propaganda, they had thought they were winning all along). When the Nazis accused the Jews of having stabbed the German war effort in the back, many Germans found this theory more believable and appealing than blaming their own leaders and politicians, and the wide acceptance of this theory helped fuel the hostility toward Jews that enabled the murderous Holocaust.

Social psychologists conducted a famous test of scapegoat theory using race relations in the United States. Hovland and Sears (1940) correlated the market price of cotton with the frequency of interracial lynching incidents in the southern United States over a period of 49 years, 1882 to 1930. Lynching is execution by a vigilante mob. Typically, a group of people will hang or otherwise kill someone who has been accused of a crime but not legally convicted, and of course such killings are themselves both illegal and immoral. The researchers chose the price of cotton because many white families in the South made their living by growing cotton. Since the amount they could grow in a given year stayed about the same (given how much land they owned), a drop in cotton prices meant a big drop in income and hence financial problems for many. Hovland and Sears reasoned that when people were thus poorer than usual, they would want to blame their troubles on an outgroup, and they thought African Americans would make a convenient scapegoat. Hence, they reasoned, illegal violence against African Americans (as measured by lynching) would go up when cotton prices went down. The data confirmed this hypothesis. Subsequent work with more elaborate statistical methods reconfirmed this hypothesis (Hepworth & West, 1988).

To be sure, the correlation between cotton prices and interracial lynching is not necessarily a pattern of scapegoating. It might be explained on other, related grounds, such as frustration (resulting from low cotton prices and less money) leading to aggression. Still, whatever the inner processes, it does suggest that harsh times cause people to behave more aggressively toward outgroups.

Students judge female university instructors as less competent than male instructors after receiving negative evaluations from them but not after receiving positive evaluations from them.

Research indicates that conflict and stress tend to bring out stereotypes. The subtitle of one of these studies is "She's fine if she praised me but incompetent if she criticized me" (Sinclair & Kunda, 2000). In these studies, college students evaluated female university instructors as less competent than male instructors after receiving negative evaluations from them but not after receiving positive evaluations from them. The stereotype that women are less competent than men was not used by students who were praised by a woman or by students who watched someone else receive praise or criticism from a woman.

Similar findings have been reported for racial stereotypes. People are more likely to use racial stereotypes when there is a disagreement or conflict than when everyone agrees (e.g. Sinclair & Kunda, 1999). For example, white participants in one study read about a court case, gave their verdict, and then observed a videotape of a black or white fellow juror who either agreed or disagreed with the participant's verdict (Kunda, Davies, Adams, & Spencer, 2002). Participants then completed a task in which they had to decide, as quickly as possible, whether a string of letters was a real word or not (this task is called a **lexical decision task**). Half of the letter strings were real words, and half were random letters. Half of the words were black stereotypic words (e.g., *athletic*, *rap*,

---

LEXICAL DECISION TASK deciding as quickly as possible whether a string of letters is a real word or not

crime, poor, drugs), and half were neutral words (e.g., *jeans, clerk, parade, soap*). The results showed faster reaction times to black stereotypical words when black fellow jurors disagreed with participants. Thus, stereotypes may lay buried and forgotten much of the time, but when a black person disagrees with a white person, the stereotypes start leaping to mind.

Emotional stress can activate stereotypes and lead to distortions in how people see the world. One team of researchers collected facial photos of people of different races, including whites, Arabs, and blacks (Maner et al., 2005). The photos were carefully chosen to have no particular expressions, and participants who were themselves in a calm or neutral state rated them all that way. However, in one experimental condition participants first viewed scenes from a horror movie that induced fearful states. When these participants looked at the same faces, they saw the faces of people from other races as angry and threatening, though they did not show any change in how they perceived the faces of people from their own race. Moreover, these effects occurred mainly among people who held stereotypes of the other races as dangerous and threatening. For example, white people who regarded Arabs as dangerous tended to see the blank Arab faces as angry and threatening (when the white perceivers were already afraid). But white people who did not hold that stereotype of Arabs did not shift in how they perceived the Arab faces.

How does prejudice operate? One simple theory is that people simply prejudge others based on their assumptions. That is, if you held the typical stereotype of Germans, then whenever you met a German you would assume that he or she would be hardworking, grumpy, efficient, and aggressive. You would treat that person in that way regardless of the person's actual traits.

Some stereotypes may operate that way, but social psychology research has suggested that the actual process is often more subtle and complex. Some research shows that people use their stereotypes more as hypotheses to be tested than as rules that can be applied in all cases. In an influential experiment (Darley & Gross, 1983), students were exposed to background information about a schoolgirl named Hannah. Some participants saw a videotape that depicted her as from a rich, privileged family, whereas others saw a videotape that depicted her as from a poor, working-class family. The participants were then asked to guess how well she was doing in school. The typical prejudice and stereotype would predict that the girl from the upper-class background would be doing better in school than the girl from the working-class background, but the researchers found no such difference. Participants were not willing to leap from knowing her background to making predictions or assumptions about her intellectual ability.

However, other participants saw a second videotape. In this second tape, Hannah was taking an oral test in school. There was only one version of this videotape, and it depicted Hannah's performance as inconsistent. Sometimes she seemed to perform quite well, but at other points she seemed bored by the test and not able to furnish the proper answers.

You might think that seeing someone take a test of intellectual ability would eliminate the effect of stereotypes, but in fact the Hannah experiment found exactly the opposite. The stereotypes based on family background emerged only among people who saw Hannah taking the test. The mechanism was probably one of **confirmation bias**, which we saw in Chapter 5 is a tendency to focus more on evidence that supports (confirms) one's expectations than on evidence that contradicts them. The participants who believed Hannah came from a rich family paid more attention to the parts of the test on which she was doing well, and so concluded that their expectations (that rich children do better in school) were confirmed. Meanwhile, the participants who believed she came from a poor family focused on the parts of the test on which she did poorly; they too concluded that their expectations (that poor children do worse in school) were confirmed.

The participants did not truly prejudge Hannah. Their prejudices did not lead to firm assumptions about how smart she would be; instead, the prejudices functioned more like expectations, which they then sought to test against Hannah's behavior. Unfortunately, perhaps, they ended up viewing her behavior in a biased manner, so their ultimate impression of her was biased.

[QUIZ YOURSELF]

Inner Processes

1. The psychological term for obviousness is _____.
   (a) heterogeneous   (b) homogeneous
   (c) nonsalience   (d) salience

2. What theory proposes that people blame their problems and misfortunes on outgroups?
   (a) Catharsis theory
   (b) Realistic conflict theory
   (c) Relative deprivation theory
   (d) Scapegoat theory

3. In a famous 1940 study, Hovland and Sears found that as cotton prices decreased, the number of lynchings _____.
   (a) decreased
   (b) increased
   (c) increased and then decreased
   (d) was not affected

CONFIRMATION BIAS the tendency to focus more on evidence that supports one's expectations than on evidence that contradicts them

Overcoming Stereotypes, Reducing Prejudice

"The greatest and noblest pleasure which men can have in this world is to discover new truths; and the next is to shake off old prejudices."
—Frederick the Great, 18th-century King of Prussia (and namesake of one of your textbook authors)

How prejudiced are Americans today? One view that can be heard on many talk shows that focus on race relations is that the United States is a deeply prejudiced, racist society. A contrary view is this:

The sociological truths are that America, while still flawed in its race relations, is now the least racist white-majority society in the world; has a better record of legal protection of minorities than any other society, white or black; offers more opportunities to a greater number of black persons than any other society, including all those of Africa. (quoted by Krauthammer, 1997, p. 2-E)

This comment may sound as though it came from someone unfamiliar with American problems or unsympathetic to African Americans, but in fact the source was Orlando Patterson, a highly respected black scholar who was chair of the African-American Studies program at Harvard University.

Which view is correct? Both could be. It depends on what the standard is. Compared to our American ideals of full tolerance and equality, there is still far too much prejudice, as the first characterization suggests. Compared to most other societies in the history of the world, however, the United States is remarkably tolerant, equal, and supportive, as Patterson's comment expresses.

It is undeniable that prejudice exists in the United States today. Contrary to what some people have claimed, the race problem still exists even though the nation now has a black president—Barack Obama. Indeed, to eliminate prejudice completely seems an impossible ideal. Still, modern Americans have come far in overcoming many prejudices and stereotypes. Most people now believe that prejudices based on race and gender are unfair and even immoral, and if people do know those stereotypes, they may try not to let them cloud their judgment of individuals. In most societies in world history, a person's race and gender would steer the person toward one sort of life, with one set of opportunities and not others, but modern American society has come remarkably far in removing those obstacles. Though the society was formed by white men, and the government still is disproportionately composed of white men, the laws and court rulings issued by those men have changed society so that African Americans, women, and other categories of people can run for president (and win), serve on the Supreme Court, rise to the top of universities and corporations, represent their country in international diplomacy, and in other ways have access to the best positions and rewards the culture has to offer.

None of this should be taken to imply that prejudice has been conquered or that cruel, immoral, and sometimes vicious acts of prejudice and discrimination have ceased. Prejudice is still a force in the United States; its influence ranges from hate crimes to demeaning ethnic jokes. The point is merely that American society has made considerable progress in fighting against some important kinds of prejudice, especially those based on race and sex.

CONSCIOUS OVERRIDE

If prejudice is natural, and culture sometimes wants to say "stop" to prejudice, those who hold prejudiced

It is true that the United States has elected its first black president, Barack Obama. It is not true, however, that racism is no longer a problem in the United States.

Mark Wilson/Getty Images

views must consciously override the response. The battle against prejudice is fought between the two halves of the duplex mind. The automatic system may often sustain prejudices, for many of the reasons we have already noted: Stereotypes simplify the world and help people make snap judgments; thus, they appeal to the automatic system (which is usually looking for ways to process information quickly). The conscious system can strive to overcome those prejudices and stereotypes so as to support equality and avoid prejudging individuals.

Numerous studies have shown that people harbor prejudiced attitudes toward particular social groups at the implicit or unconscious level, even though they honestly report having no prejudiced attitudes at the explicit or conscious level (e.g. Fazio, Jackson, Dunton, & Williams, 1995; Fazio & Olson, 2003; Greenwald, McGhee, & Schwartz, 1998; Payne, 2001; also see Chapter 7). Implicit prejudiced attitudes have been found to do a good job in predicting behavior, especially spontaneous behaviors (Rydell & McConnell, 2006). In one study, implicit racist attitudes did a better job of predicting workplace discrimination in hiring practices than did explicit attitudes (Ziegert & Hanges, 2005). In another study, implicit attitudes about alcohol did a better job of predicting drinking behavior than did explicit attitudes (Payne, Govorun, & Arbuckle, 2008). Because people are reluctant to admit that they have racist attitudes or drinking problems, these explicit measures are not very good predictors of behavior.

Intriguing evidence about this inner struggle to overcome prejudice was provided by Richeson and Shelton (2003; also Richeson, Trawalter, & Shelton, 2005), who studied the aftereffects of talking with someone of a different race. As we saw in Chapter 4, self-regulation operates like a muscle that gets tired after use. Participants in their study showed just such tiredness: They performed worse than other participants (who spoke to someone of their own race) on a standard test of self-regulation (the Stroop task, which requires people to override their first impulse in order to give the correct response; see Chapter 5). The effect was strongest for participants who had the strongest prejudices. Thus, when people talk to someone from another race, they have to regulate themselves carefully in order to hide their prejudices and to make sure they do not say anything that could be interpreted as offensive or biased. This extra effort takes its toll, leaving people less able to self-regulate afterward. People do exert themselves consciously to overcome and hide their prejudices, even though the effort may be costly.

Of course, in many cases the conscious mind is quite comfortable hanging onto its prejudices and does not try to override the prejudicial reaction of the automatic system. The difference can perhaps be appreciated by comparing anti-black and anti-obese prejudices in the United States today. Most Americans regard racial prejudice as immoral and will consciously strive to avoid thinking or expressing negative stereotypes of African Americans. In contrast, many people are content to think and express negative stereotypes of obese people; they do not consciously try to override the automatic reaction (possibly unless they are talking to an obese person).

Mental Processes of Nonprejudiced People. The view that overcoming prejudice is based on conflict between conscious and automatic responses emerged from a famous series of studies by social psychologist Patricia Devine (1989). She initially sought to find which mental processes underlay prejudice, and she approached the problem by seeking to ascertain what was different between prejudiced and nonprejudiced people. She used a questionnaire to classify people as either prejudiced or nonprejudiced, choosing people who were at both extremes. Then she gave them a series of tests to see where the difference lay.

Her first hypothesis was that the difference lay in knowledge of stereotypes: Maybe nonprejudiced people are not familiar with the stereotypes. Upon testing both groups, however, she found that they had equal knowledge of the content of stereotypes.

Her second hypothesis was that the difference lay in whether the stereotype is activated (i.e., whether it springs to mind) when one encounters a member of the group. Nonprejudiced people might know the stereotype of African Americans, for example, but not think of the stereotype when they encounter an individual African American. This too proved to be wrong: Both prejudiced and nonprejudiced people do think of the stereotype when they encounter someone from the stereotyped group. This suggested that the automatic system was at work, automatically retrieving the prejudicial information when it recognized a member of the category.

Her third hypothesis, therefore, was that the automatic system operates in similar ways in both prejudiced and nonprejudiced people, but nonprejudiced people employ their conscious processing to override the stereotype and replace prejudiced thoughts with thoughts more in line with their values of tolerance, fairness, and equality. This proved correct. Nonprejudiced people still know and think of stereotypes, but they override them. This fits our theme that nature says go and culture says stop: It is normal and natural to have some degree of prejudice, but the conscious mind can learn to overcome these reactions and treat people in a fair and tolerant manner.

Discrimination in Reverse. Research has shown that when people are accused of prejudice, they often exert themselves to prove the opposite. Indeed, one possible illustration of this was relevant to the 2008 presidential election. The Democratic primary featured a struggle between a woman, Hillary Clinton, and a black man, Barack Obama, either of whom would have been the first person in that category to become president. Clinton was heavily favored early in the race, partly on the basis of her campaign organization. Some commentators also thought she had an advantage insofar as there are plenty of women but relatively few black men, which might translate into more votes for Clinton. However, other observers noted that America has far more people seeking to prove that they have no racial prejudice against blacks than to prove they have no sexist prejudice against women, which would therefore translate into more votes for Obama (who eventually won the race).

In an early laboratory study (Dutton & Lake, 1973), white participants who had evaluated themselves as relatively unprejudiced were either accused or not accused by the experimenter of being racist. After leaving the study, participants encountered a black or white panhandler (actually a confederate) who asked for money. The black panhandler received more money from participants who had been accused of being racist than from other participants (not accused of racism). The white panhandler received an equal amount of money from the two groups of participants. Thus, white people gave more money to the black confederate to contradict the characterization of themselves as prejudiced.

In another study (Dutton, 1971), black couples and white couples (actually confederates) visited 40 different Canadian restaurants that had advertised dress code regulations, including jacket and tie for male diners. The male partner in each couple violated the dress code by wearing a turtleneck sweater instead of a shirt and tie; thus, according to restaurant policy, the restaurant could refuse service to them. When a black couple entered the restaurant first, they were served 75% of the time; when a white couple entered first, they were served only 30% of the time. The restaurant personnel may have had no conscious prejudices, but they subtly showed a reverse discrimination pattern. They treated the black couple more favorably in order to avoid the appearance of being biased.

There was a revealing twist in the restaurant study's data. About 45 minutes after the first couple arrived, the second couple from the other race arrived, and they too violated the dress code. In general, the second couple was treated the same as the first. Thus, the restaurant owners were not discriminating against white people in any obvious way, because each one treated the white and the black couples the same. However, the decision how to react depended on which couple arrived first, and this initial decision showed the reverse discrimination pattern. If the black couple arrived first, then they were seated despite breaking the rules; if later a white couple also broke the rules, they too were seated. If the white couple arrived first, they were usually turned away, and once the restaurant staff had refused service to the white couple, they felt justified in turning away the black couple on the same basis.

Thus, people overcome prejudice by making conscious efforts to be fair and equal in how they treat others. Many people try extra hard to avoid anything that could be interpreted as showing racial or gender prejudice. People may not try as hard to overcome and override prejudices against gay people, obese people, and others. But the progress in overcoming racial and gender prejudice shows the way toward possibly reducing these other prejudices as well, so that North American society can live up to its ideals of judging each person as an individual rather than prejudging him or her as a member of a group or category.

Motives for Overcoming Prejudice. The previous sections have suggested two different reasons for wanting to overcome prejudice. One is a possibly heartfelt dedication to equality and a corresponding belief that prejudice is morally wrong. The other is an appreciation that expressing prejudice could provoke social disapproval. For example, most European Americans report that they do not want to respond with prejudice toward African Americans, but is this a sincere desire to promote equality or merely a strategic reluctance to say things that might make some people angry?

Both motives are real, but different people may emphasize one or the other (or neither), according to Plant and Devine (1998). These social psychologists developed a measure that can help classify people's responses according to these two motives. The measure assesses Internal Motivation to Respond Without Prejudice, which is understood as a motivation based on a strong inner belief that prejudice is wrong. It also assesses External Motivation to Respond Without Prejudice, which is essentially a sense that it is socially unwise to express opinions that others will regard as socially undesirable or politically incorrect. ▶ **FIGURE 13.3** contains the items for both these scales. The scales can also be modified to assess motives to avoid prejudice against gay people, obese people, Arabs, or any other group. The internal and external motivations to avoid prejudice are not mutually exclusive. Some people have both, and others have neither.

People's source of motivation to respond without prejudice (i.e., the *reason* why they are motivated) has important implications for behavior. For example,

Internal Motivation to Respond Without Prejudice

1. I attempt to act in nonprejudiced ways toward Black people because it is personally important to me.

2. According to my personal values, using stereotypes about Black people is OK (reverse scored.)

3. I am personally motivated by my beliefs to be nonprejudiced toward Black people.

4. Because of my personal values, I believe that using stereotypes about Black people is wrong.

5. Being nonprejudiced toward Black people is important to my self-concept.

External Motivation to Respond Without Prejudice

1. Because of today's PC (politically correct) standards, I try to appear nonprejudiced toward Black people.

2. I try to hide any negative thoughts about Black people in order to avoid negative reactions from others.

3. If I acted prejudiced toward Black people, I would be concerned that others would be angry with me.

4. I attempt to appear nonprejudiced toward Black people in order to avoid disapproval from others.

5. I try to act nonprejudiced toward Black people because of pressure from others.

Note: Answer each item on a scale running from 1=strongly disagree to 9=strongly agree. For #2 on the Internal Motivation scale, subtract your answer from 10. Then add across items, and divide by the number of items. The average score for college students is about 8 for the Internal Motivation scale and about 5 for the External Motivation scale. Source: Plant and Devine (1998).

▶ **FIGURE 13.3** Test yourself: What is your motivation to overcome prejudice?

Political correctness is the norm in the United States today.

people who are only externally motivated to respond without prejudice report low-prejudice attitudes and beliefs when they have to provide their responses out loud to an experimenter or another person. However, if they are allowed to write their answers on a questionnaire in an anonymous setting, they report attitudes that are more prejudiced. Thus, they shift their answers across settings depending on whether others will be privy to their responses. In contrast, people who are internally motivated to respond without prejudice report low-prejudice attitudes and beliefs regardless of how or to whom they provide their answers. Those neither internally nor externally motivated report moderately prejudiced attitudes regardless of the setting. (Very few present-day Americans consistently express strong racial prejudices.)

Although externally motivated people shift their responses to comply with social pressure to respond without prejudice, this public conformity comes at a price. White people who are primarily externally motivated to respond without prejudice become angry when they feel pressured to respond in a politically correct manner. When they are released from such pressure (i.e., when they are no longer under the watchful eye of a nonprejudiced audience), they respond with a backlash and actually express more prejudice than if they had not been pressured to respond without prejudice (Plant & Devine, 2001).

White people who are primarily internally motivated to avoid prejudice have more deeply internalized, well-practiced nonprejudiced reactions than the other groups. This inner commitment to overcome prejudice allows them to override and replace any unwanted biased responses, including even very subtle biases that can occur automatically and with hardly any conscious recognition, resulting in more effective control of prejudice (e.g., Amodio, Harmon-Jones, & Devine, 2003; Devine, Plant, Amodio, Harmon-Jones, & Vance, 2002).

CONTACT

As we learned earlier, prejudice can be reduced by contact (Binder et al., 2009; Pettigrew & Tropp, 2005; Shook & Fazio, 2008). Sometimes even vicarious contact can work, such as knowing that a good friend who is a member of your group has a close relationship with an outgroup member (e.g., Wright, Aron, McLaughlin-Volpe, & Ropp, 1997). Although overt expressions of prejudice can be reduced by direct educational and attitude-change techniques (see Chapter 8), more covert expressions of prejudice, such as deliberate avoidance or mild harassment, can be reduced by intergroup contact (Dovidio & Gaertner, 1999).

SUPERORDINATE GOALS

As Sherif discovered, cooperating to achieve common goals is one powerful antidote to intergroup conflict. When the Eagles and Rattlers worked together to achieve common goals, they stopped hating each other and even grew to like each other. Other studies have found similar results. In one study (Bay-Hinitz, Peterson, & Quilitch, 1994), researchers found that when children play cooperative games, their aggressive behavior decreases and their cooperative behavior increases. In contrast, when they play competitive games, their aggressive behavior increases and their cooperative behavior decreases.

One technique used to achieve a common goal is the jigsaw classroom. The **jigsaw classroom** is a cooperative learning technique developed by social psychologist Elliot Aronson to reduce feelings of prejudice (Aronson, 2000; Aronson, Blaney, Stephin, Sikes, & Snapp, 1978; Aronson & Patnoe, 1997). Just as each piece of a jigsaw puzzle is necessary to complete the puzzle, some contribution from each student in a jigsaw classroom is necessary to complete an assignment.

For example, after each person learns as much as possible about his or her assigned topic, students from different groups who were assigned the same topic meet together to become experts on their topic. Once each individual is up to speed, the jigsaw groups reconvene, and members share with each other what they have learned. Group members must work together as a team to accomplish a common goal.

Several studies have shown positive outcomes for jigsaw classrooms. Research shows that participation in jigsaw classrooms decreases racial prejudice and increases academic performance (Aronson & Osherow, 1980; Walker & Crogan, 1998). The jigsaw classroom has been successfully applied in places other than the United States, including Australia (Walker & Crogan, 1998) and Nigeria (Alebiosu, 2001).

Impact of Prejudice on Targets

We have now seen that prejudice is very common. Most cultures have stereotypes, at least of rival external groups. If two countries have recently fought against each other in a war, each will likely have some prejudices and stereotypes about the other, and most likely rather negative ones.

JIGSAW CLASSROOM a cooperative learning technique for reducing feelings of prejudice

In addition, diverse cultures typically have to contend with the fact that members of different groups or categories have stereotypes about the other groups. As one example, all societies have both men and women, and your textbook authors would be very surprised to find any society in which men and women do not hold some stereotypes about each other.

What effects do prejudices and stereotypes have on their targets? What is it like to grow up in a culture that regards you as unattractive, or incompetent, or dangerous? Or, for that matter, what is it like to live in a culture that expects you to be wise and kind?

Probably the most common reaction is that people dislike being stereotyped; they want to be known and judged as individuals. Being stereotyped in a negative manner is especially unpleasant. In one series of studies, women who used feminist doctrines to express negative stereotypes of men elicited reactions that sometimes took the form of sexual harassment (Maass, Cadinu, Guarnieri, & Grasselli, 2003). The experimenters instructed the men to select stimulus pictures to send to a woman via e-mail. Some of the available pictures were of nature and animals and were thus neutral, but others were sexually explicit and even pornographic images, and in all conditions the women had indicated that they found such pictures offensive. To expose someone to sexual materials against that person's explicit wishes is a form of sexual harassment. Men were most likely to choose such pictures if the woman had stereotyped men in a degrading or insulting manner. Though this finding does not excuse or justify sexual harassment, it does indicate that reactions to being stereotyped can be quite negative and even hostile or aggressive. When women express negative stereotypes of men, they fuel hostility between the genders; in the same way, expressing negative stereotypes of any group may make it harder for the different kinds of people to get along with each other.

SELF-FULFILLING AND SELF-DEFEATING PROPHECIES

In the 1970s, many Americans first encountered oil shortages and similar problems of scarcity. As a joke, the host of the *Tonight Show* (back then it was Johnny Carson) announced during his monologue that there was about to be a national shortage of toilet paper. He got a good laugh from the audience, but nationwide many people went out and bought extra toilet paper so they would be prepared for the national shortage. In reality no shortage had been forecast, but the mass buying created one. One woman discovered that her grandmother had stored hundreds of rolls of toilet paper in her closet. When she asked her grandmother why she had so much, she said, "Johnny said there is going to be a shortage." Not long after, Carson had to go on the air to declare that he had just been joking and there was no need to

worry about a shortage of toilet paper, and the panic buying subsided. Thus, the false expectation of an upcoming shortage made people react in ways that created a real, although temporary, shortage.

This toilet paper example illustrates a more general principle: Once we accept the expectations of others, we tend to behave in a manner that is consistent with those expectations, and as a result the expectations come true.

In 1948, Robert Merton, a sociology professor at Columbia University, introduced the concept of **self-fulfilling prophecy**, defined as a belief about the future that comes true in part because the belief causes it to come true (as with the toilet paper shortage). According to Merton, a self-fulfilling prophecy involves three stages. First, a person believes that a certain event will happen in the future. Second, this expectation, or prophecy, leads to a new behavior that the person would have not engaged in without the expectation. Third, the expected event takes place (partly as a result of the change in behavior), and the prophecy is fulfilled.

As a vivid example, Merton used the collapse of the Last National Bank, which was a stable and solvent financial institution in the early 1930s. First, people began to believe (incorrectly) that the Last National Bank was on the verge of bankruptcy. Second, the people who had accounts at the bank panicked and withdrew all their money. Third, the bank collapsed. The initial belief (that the bank was ready to collapse) was false, but once people withdrew all their money, the bank really did collapse.

Several studies have found results that are consistent with the self-fulfilling prophecy. In one famous

---

SELF-FULFILLING PROPHECY a prediction that ensures, by the behavior it generates, that it will come true

People with baby faces live up to an honesty stereotype.

research demonstration of this effect, participants were children from 18 classrooms. The researchers gave all participants an IQ test, then randomly chose 20% of the children from each room and told the teachers they were "intellectual bloomers." Teachers were told that these bloomers would show remarkable gains in IQ during the year. The results showed that by the end of the year the supposed "intellectual bloomers" really did bloom (Rosenthal & Jacobson, 1968). They improved their IQ scores by an average of 12 points, as compared with gains of 8 points among other students. Thus, teachers' expectations, which were initially false and baseless, became a reality, probably because the teachers focused more positive attention on the students who they expected would bloom (see also Smith, 1980).

A comprehensive literature review by Jussim and Harber (2005) found that although self-fulfilling prophecies do occur in the classroom, the effects are relatively small. Teacher expectations do predict student performance, but that is because teacher's expectations are often accurate, not because the expectations become self-fulfilling prophecies.

The concept of the self-fulfilling prophecy offers one way to predict the effects of stereotypes on their targets. People often live up or down to what is expected of them, especially if others treat them in certain ways based on those expectations. Applied to stereotypes, a self-fulfilling prophecy would mean that people would come to act like the stereotypes others hold of them. Research shows that students from stigmatized groups (e.g., minority students, students from lower social classes) are especially

vulnerable to self-fulfilling prophecies (Jussim & Harber, 2005).

Social psychologist Leslie Zebrowitz and her colleagues have conducted research showing that stereotypes about people with so-called "baby faces" (i.e., young-looking facial features) can create both self-fulfilling and self-defeating prophecies. Baby faces have characteristic features, such as large eyes, a round face, thin eyebrows, and a small nose bridge. Research has shown that people with such "baby faces" are assumed to be more childlike than people with more mature faces (Zebrowitz & Montepare, 1992; Zebrowitz-McArthur & Montepare, 1989). For example, people with baby faces are assumed to be more honest than others (hence the metaphor "wide-eyed innocence"). In contrast, the stereotypical criminal has small, beady, close-set eyes, a large jaw and puffy cheeks, a bent nose, and facial hair (which most babies don't have!). Research has shown that people with baby faces live up to the stereotype of being more honest than others (Zebrowitz, Voinescu, & Collins, 1996).

Stereotypes don't always produce self-fulfilling prophecies; sometimes they can create self-defeating prophecies. A **self-defeating prophecy** is a prediction that ensures, by the behavior it generates, that it will not come true. Having a baby face may be an asset to a female, but it might be a liability to a male, especially one who wants to be regarded as masculine and tough. Research shows that baby-faced boys, including a sample of juvenile delinquents, had higher grades than their mature-faced peers, refuting the stereotype of baby-faced people as being intellectually weak (Zebrowitz, Andreoletti, Collins, Lee, & Blumenthal, 1998). Lower-social-class boys with baby faces committed more crimes than their mature-faced peers, refuting the stereotype of baby-

---

SELF-DEFEATING PROPHECY a prediction that ensures, by the behavior it generates, that it will not come true

faced people as warm, submissive, and physically weak (Zebrowitz et al., 1998). In other words, when nature happens by chance to give a boy a babyish facial structure, he often tries harder to prove that he is no baby, either by excelling in school or by succeeding in crime and violence.

Most social scientists have long assumed that self-fulfilling prophecy effects would be the main, most powerful way that stereotypes affect their targets. They assumed that people could not entirely resist internalizing the stereotypes that society held of them. However, people often can and do resist. One of the most surprising contradictions to the self-fulfilling prophecy effect formed the basis for a new line of theory and research, discussed in the next section.

STIGMA AND SELF-PROTECTION

Throughout much of American history, the culture has held stereotypes of African Americans as inferior to European Americans in various ways. Some of these probably originated during the period of slavery. Black people were stereotyped as lazy, intellectually backward, and childlike. These stereotypes most likely reflected the fundamental attribution error (see Chapter 5), which attributes people's behavior to their inner traits even when it was really caused by external circumstances. All over the world, slaves have generally been lazy as far as their masters are concerned (Patterson, 1982), and why shouldn't they be? People rise above laziness in response to incentives that reward hard work, such as money, power, and status, but these were all denied to slaves. Likewise, American slaves had almost no opportunity for schooling or education, without which intellectual attainments are difficult if not impossible. Many aspects of the slave's role resemble the child's role: few rights, utter dependency on others, inability to make decisions about one's own life, and the inability to express any striving for long-term future goals. Any sensible person would behave that way in that situation, and it is unfortunate but perhaps understandable that observers made the mistake of seeing those behaviors as reflecting people's innate traits rather than situational forces.

What survived into the 20th century, long after slavery had been abolished, was a general perception of African Americans as inferior to European Americans. What were the consequences for African Americans born in that new era? Most social scientists assumed that African Americans could not help internalizing those negative views to some degree, just as with any self-fulfilling prophecy. The broadest result of American prejudices would therefore be that African Americans would have low self-esteem. To live in a culture that regards you and treats you as a second-class citizen would, seemingly inevitably, cause you to see yourself that way. The low self-

esteem could then perhaps explain many behavioral patterns that might be observed, from lower occupational attainment to crime and violence.

This line of thought was standard, but in the late 1980s it was turned upside down by a surprising finding. Two social psychologists, Jenny Crocker and Brenda Major (1989), reviewed dozens of studies and established a startling conclusion: African Americans on average do not suffer from low self-esteem. If anything, African Americans have higher self-esteem than European Americans. Subsequent work has verified this finding and shown that African Americans are actually somewhat unusual in this regard (e.g., Judd & Park, 1993). Most American minority groups do have somewhat lower self-esteem than mainstream European Americans, but African Americans continue to score consistently higher on self-esteem (Twenge & Crocker, 2002).

How could this be? No one disputed the fact that American society had held prejudices that regarded black people as inferior. How did they manage not only to resist internalizing the message, but to end up with higher self-esteem than other groups? Crocker and Major (1989) had three answers, each of which is rooted in cognitive strategies and processes similar to those covered in Chapter 5.

The first involved social comparison—specifically, the choice of comparison targets. To an animal living in the forest, success and failure can probably be measured directly in terms of getting something to eat, but to cultural beings, success and failure are relative. Your salary, for example, might be a measure of how well you are doing, but by itself it doesn't mean much. Salary is an index of success only in comparison to what other people are earning. Crocker and Major concluded that people compare themselves to people within their own group. The self-esteem of a minority group might therefore not suffer from the fact that its members earn less than members of other groups. The earnings of other groups are regarded as irrelevant. They mainly compare themselves against each other.

The second involves the criteria of self-worth. People judge themselves by many criteria. As we saw in Chapter 3 on the self, people often choose criteria on which they do well and avoid criteria that make them look bad. If you're good at basket weaving or meteorology, you may decide that those are important measures of self-worth, but if you are bad at them, you may decide that they are trivial and irrelevant. Groups, too, can reject or discount the standards that make them look bad, focusing instead on the things they do well. African Americans have been exceptionally successful in some of the most salient and highly respected spheres of American society (such as music and sports), and these successes can furnish a compelling basis for high self-esteem.

The third process involves attribution theory (again!). We noted earlier in this chapter that the

self-serving bias (making internal attributions for successes and external attributions for failures) can help explain the thinking and actions of people who hold stereotypes. It may also help explain the reactions of targets of prejudice. Crocker and Major (1989) proposed that some disadvantaged minority groups might protect their self-esteem by attributing their problems to other people's prejudices against them. Assume, for example, that most people's lives contain some successes and some failures, and that each individual's self-esteem will depend on how he or she adds those up. If you can use the self-serving bias to dismiss your failures as irrelevant to your worth, your self-esteem can be higher than if you blame yourself for your failures. Crocker and Major proposed that despite all its costs and harm, prejudice does offer one advantage to the target—an external attribution for failure. Targets of prejudice can blame their failures and problems on prejudice. As a result, they can base their self-esteem mainly on their successes, and their self-esteem will rise.

A subsequent experiment confirmed this pattern (Crocker, Voelkl, Testa, & Major, 1991). African American college students wrote an essay and received feedback that was critical and negative. This feedback came from a European American confederate pretending to be another participant.

Did the criticism cause a drop in self-esteem? It depended on attributions. Half the participants believed that the other participant knew who they were, including their race. These participants showed no drop in self-esteem, because they inferred that the

bad evaluation reflected the prejudices of the evaluator. Being criticized as a result of someone's prejudice should not lower one's self-esteem, of course, so the participants who made this attribution (that the bad evaluation was caused by prejudice) shrugged it off. In contrast, the other participants were told that the evaluator knew nothing about them. They could not dismiss the evaluation as a result of racial prejudice, because they thought the evaluator did not know their race. Their self-esteem did suffer (temporarily) as a result of the bad evaluation.

Thus, although both groups received exactly the same evaluation, only one group experienced a drop in self-esteem. Of course, neither group had any strong evidence about whether the evaluation was motivated by racial prejudice, and in reality the evaluation (exactly the same for everyone) was decided by the experimental procedure. All that differed was that one group was able to conclude that prejudice might be one possible cause of it, and they apparently used this possibility as a basis for dismissing the criticism and maintaining their self-esteem.

If nothing else, these findings show that people are not just passive recipients of social influence. Cultures tell some groups that they are inferior, but many members of those groups successfully reject such messages.

STEREOTYPE THREAT

We have seen that people do not like being stereotyped and often strive extra hard to show that

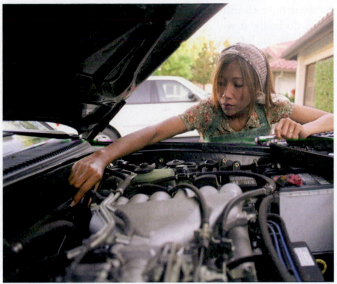

Can you identify the stereotype threats that these individuals face? In what way would failure be less bad if their genders were reversed?

they do not fit negative stereotypes of their group. Sometimes stereotypes can even create self-defeating prophecies, as in the case of baby-faced boys who want to be regarded as macho and tough (Zebrowitz et al., 1998). This observation has been elaborated in a profound way by several social psychologists, who noted that when a stereotype might apply, people fear that their behavior will confirm it. This fear is called **stereotype threat** (Steele & Aronson, 1995). When people fear that they will be negatively stereotyped, their performance suffers.

Stereotype threat may operate most powerfully when it is difficult to contradict. Thus, if your group is stereotyped as liking greasy food, you can relatively easily show that it does not apply to you, simply by choosing healthier foods when others are watching. In contrast, if your group is stereotyped as being bad at singing, you would have to sing well in order to contradict it, and singing well (especially when you are nervous because of stereotype threat!) may be quite difficult.

Intellectual performance is of particular interest, because of its importance in American culture and society. Girls score slightly lower than boys on math tests, even among gifted children (Benbow, Lubinski, Shea, & Eftekhari-Sanjani, 2000). The difference seems to be due to mathematical reasoning, because females can do simple arithmetical computations better than males. In a similar vein, African American students score lower on many tests than European American students (e.g., Gottfredson, 1997; Jencks & Phillips, 1998). Claude Steele and his colleagues wondered whether these gender and race differences might be partly due to stereotype threat, and they conducted a series of studies to test this hypothesis.

Several studies played on the stereotype that women perform worse than men on mathematical

tests (e.g., Spencer, Steele, & Quinn, 1999). When the math test was described as producing no gender differences, women performed as well as men. However, when the math test was described as producing gender differences, women performed worse than men. Women feared that if they did poorly, it would reinforce people's beliefs about female inferiority at math, and the resulting worry contributed to lowering their performance (Spencer et al., 1999). Even subtle cues can produce this effect, such as when the experimenter is male rather than female (Stone & McWhinnie, 2008). The effects are especially large if women are concerned that performing poorly will reflect badly on all women rather than on them personally (Wout, Danso, Jackson, & Spencer, 2008). The same thing happens to white men when the comparison group is Asian men (Aronson, Lustina, Good, Keough, Steele, & Brown, 1999).

Other studies by Steele's group took on the controversial issue of racial differences in intellectual performance (Steele & Aronson, 1995). Although IQ tests have been accused of racial bias, defenders of the tests have argued that they are designed to predict performance in school, and the tests (which predict the performance of white students quite accurately) often predict higher grades for black students than the students actually end up achieving. Could that discrepancy be due to stereotype threat? In an important study (Steele & Aronson, 1995), researchers told some participants that the test had been shown to have no racial bias and no racial differences. In that condition, African American participants performed as well as their SAT scores would predict. Other participants

---

STEREOTYPE THREAT the fear that one might confirm the stereotypes that others hold

received no such instruction, so the stereotype threat ("If I do badly, it will confirm people's stereotype of African Americans as intellectually inferior") remained an important force in the situation. In that situation, African Americans performed worse than others and worse than their SAT scores would predict. Other research has shown that under stereotype threat, African Americans experience an increase in blood pressure (Blascovich, Spencer, Quinn, & Steele, 2001). Eliminating the stereotype threat does not entirely eliminate the test-score gap between blacks and whites (Sackett, Hardison, & Cullen, 2004a, 2004b; Steele & Aronson, 2004), but it does eliminate the troubling pattern in which many students perform below what their tested SAT scores predict.

A meta-analysis found that stereotype threat does impair test performance for women and minorities (Nguyen & Ryan, 2008). Why does the impairment occur? Anxiety appears to be the culprit. Confirming negative stereotypes makes people anxious, and the more anxious people are, the more their performance suffers (e.g., Abrams, Crisp, Marques, Fagg, Bedford, & Provias, 2008; Brodish & Devine, 2009). When people become anxious, they try to calm down, but this takes a lot of effort and mental resources, which depletes people of the mental resources they need to perform well on the test (Johns, Inzlicht, & Schmader, 2008). Indeed, people who experience a stereotype threat show activity in the part of their brain involved in emotional processing rather than in the part of their brain involved in thinking and reasoning (Krendl, Richeson, Kelley, & Heatherton, 2008).

Fortunately, there is a silver lining on this dark cloud of stereotype threat. Recent research shows that people can be inoculated against stereotype threat. In one study, older people did better on a math test if they first interacted with their grandchildren than if they did not (Abrams et al., 2008, Study 1). Even imagining interacting with younger people improved performance (Abrams et al., 2008, Study 2). When older people interact with younger people, they feel less anxious about their test performance.

As Steele and other researchers frequently point out, nearly everyone is a member of some group that is sometimes the target of stereotyping. Stereotype threat can affect everyone. Minority groups sometimes hold the stereotype of European Americans as prejudiced, so in interracial interactions white people sometimes worry lest anything they say be interpreted as a sign of prejudice.

Indeed, this sort of stereotype threat makes interracial interactions more difficult for all concerned. Research on interactions between black and white people has found that both parties approached these interactions with heightened anxiety, for just these reasons. Black people worried that their white interaction partners would be biased against them, so they feared behaving in ways that might justify these prejudices. Meanwhile, the white participants worried that they would be perceived as prejudiced by their black interaction partners, and they too feared that they might do something to confirm those stereotypes (Plant, 2004; Shelton, 2003).

Stereotype threat should promote sympathy for minority groups, especially in difficult performance contexts. It is hard enough to perform well on your own, but it is that much more difficult to perform well while worrying that others will take failure as confirmation of negative stereotypes. No one likes to fail, and many people will avoid some risks in order to reduce the chances of failure. If failure reflects not only on you but also on an entire category of people to which you belong, the burden of failure is greatly increased, and it is not surprising that some people will withdraw in order to avoid such pressure.

Conflict between groups is not unique to humans. As cultural animals, however, humans surround group conflict with meanings, values, and other ideas. Having a hostile feeling toward a rival group may be something that many animals experience, but creating a negative stereotype of the other group is something that requires the powerful mental apparatus of the human mind.

Moreover, the content of stereotypes and prejudices is generally learned, and as we saw, it is not so much learned by direct experience as from other people similar to oneself. Deliberately passing social ideas to the young is something that sets humans apart, and in general it is one of the wonders of human nature—but humans also teach stereotypes and prejudices to their children. This is not to say that children are naturally inclined toward love and tolerance of everyone. Human children seem all too ready to reject anyone who is different, so they quickly and readily acquire negative views of other groups.

Culture increases the scope and importance of prejudices. If a fish were prejudiced toward another group of fish, it might avoid interacting with them, but this would not affect the other fish very much. Humans, in contrast, rely on each other and their social network for their livelihoods. Prejudice can interfere with someone's chances to get a particular job, live in a desirable home, hold political office, and choose a desired mate. Victims of discrimination lose out on many cultural rewards, from prestige and self-esteem to money. People may use prejudices and stereotypes to strengthen the bonds within their group. This shows once again the theme that inner processes serve interpersonal relations: People form and maintain stereotypes because those mental structures help them deal with the social world.

But there is another, more positive side to human nature. Unlike other animals, humans can rise above their prejudices and feelings. People can reinvent and restructure the society in which they live—indeed, the processes of social change seem to go on relentlessly, at least in the modern world. People can also change themselves, by questioning their values and pushing themselves to think, feel, and act differently.

Thus, only humans have been able to rise above their natural antagonisms and create a society in which people from different, even formerly competing, groups can live together in peace, tolerance, and harmony. In the past century, the United States (like many other countries) has seen dramatic improvements in the social respect and opportunities offered to women, and it has moved far toward racial equality and tolerance too. In many countries of the world, people from different groups that once hated, despised, and fought each other now live side by side and cooperate actively in a respectful, smoothly functioning system. The capacity for progress of this sort is one of the biggest advantages of human culture. The progress toward defeating prejudice and discrimination—though still incomplete and imperfect—is a very positive indication of what makes us human.

chapter summary

ABCS OF INTERGROUP RELATIONSHIPS: PREJUDICE, DISCRIMINATION, AND STEREOTYPES

- Prejudice is a negative feeling or attitude toward an individual based solely on his or her membership in a particular group.
- Discrimination refers to unequal treatment of different people based on the groups or categories to which they belong.
- Stereotypes are beliefs that associate groups of people with certain traits.
- The view that prejudice and stereotyping are morally wrong is a product of modern, Western culture. Many cultures tolerate stereotyping.

- Most stereotypes are negative, and most prejudices depict outgroups as inferior or as having bad traits.
- Outgroup members ("them") are people who belong to a different group or category than we do.
- Ingroup members ("us") are people who belong to the same group or category as we do.
- The outgroup homogeneity bias assumes that outgroup members are more similar to one another than ingroup members are to one another.
- Stigmas include characteristics of individuals that are considered socially unappealing, such as being overweight,

mentally ill, sick, or poor, or having a physical blemish.
- Stigma by association shows that people are discriminated against for merely being associated with a stigmatized person.
- Both men and women are more intolerant of homosexuality in their own gender than in the opposite gender.
- Although stereotypes often contain culturally specific information, the tendency to form stereotypes and prejudices may be innate.
- People automatically and

normally know stereotypes and think of them, whereas they have to exert themselves to override them.

WHY PREJUDICE EXISTS

- Ingroup favoritism is preferential treatment of, or more favorable attitudes toward, people in one's own group, as compared to people in other groups.
- Realistic conflict theory suggests that competition over scare resources leads to intergroup hostility and conflict; hostilities form when groups compete against each other.
- Some societies have little or no competition. These are typically peaceful, economically undeveloped groups.
- Competition has costs, but it also has benefits.
- Evolution may have had a hand in instilling the human readiness to form groups and hold prejudices against rival groups.
- The discontinuity effect suggests that groups are more prone to hostile competitiveness than individuals are.
- The contact hypothesis proposes that regular interaction between members of different groups reduces prejudice, providing that it occurs under favorable conditions.
- People often rely on stereotypes as heuristics (mental shortcuts).
- By using stereotypes to justify and act on prejudices, people can increase their feelings of self-worth.

CONTENT OF PREJUDICE AND STEREOTYPES

- Some stereotypes are accurate, others are wrong, and others are partly true but overgeneralized.

- Stereotypes can form from purely cognitive processes, without any influence of emotion or motivation. Still, emotion or motivation can greatly increase the likelihood of prejudice.

INNER PROCESSES

- Scapegoat theory proposes that people blame their problems and misfortunes on outgroups.
- Conflict and stress tend to bring out stereotypes and prejudice.
- People use their stereotypes more as hypotheses to be tested than as rules that can be applied in all cases.
- American society has made considerable progress in fighting against some important kinds of prejudice, especially those based on race and sex.

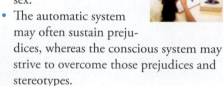

- The automatic system may often sustain prejudices, whereas the conscious system may strive to overcome those prejudices and stereotypes.
- When people are accused of prejudice, they often exert themselves to prove the opposite.

OVERCOMING STEREOTYPES, REDUCING PREJUDICE

- People overcome prejudice by making conscious efforts to be fair and equal.
- The internal (belief that prejudice is morally wrong) and external (desire to avoid social disapproval) motivations for avoiding prejudice are not mutually exclusive.

- The jigsaw classroom, developed to reduce prejudice, is a cooperative learning technique in which group members must work together as a team and share unique information to accomplish a common goal.

IMPACT OF PREJUDICE ON TARGETS

- The self-fulfilling prophecy effect proposes that people will come to act in accordance with the stereotypes that others hold of them.
- Stereotypes can also create a self-defeating prophecy, which ensures, by the behavior it generates, that it will not come true.

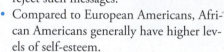

- Cultures may tell some groups that they are inferior, but many members of those groups successfully reject such messages.
- Compared to European Americans, African Americans generally have higher levels of self-esteem.
- Stereotype threat is the fear that a stereotype might apply and that one's behavior might confirm it.
- Stereotype threat makes interracial interactions anxiety provoking for both races, because both worry about confirming stereotypes about themselves.

WHAT MAKES US HUMAN? PUTTING THE CULTURAL ANIMAL IN PERSPECTIVE

- Unlike other animals, only humans have been able to rise above their natural antagonisms and create a society in which people from different, even formerly competing, groups can live together in peace, tolerance, and harmony.

Key Terms

Aversive racism 393
Categorization 394
Competition 404
Confirmation bias 413
Contact hypothesis 406
Cooperation 404
Discontinuity effect 406
Discrimination 393

Homophobia 400
Ingroup favoritism 403
Ingroup members 395
Jigsaw classroom 418
Lexical decision task 412
Minimal group effect 403
Outgroup homogeneity bias 395

Outgroup members 395
Prejudice 393
Racism 393
Realistic conflict theory 404
Salience 411
Scapegoat theory 411
Self-defeating prophecy 420
Self-fulfilling prophecy 419

Self-serving bias 411
Social categorization 394
Stereotype threat 423
Stereotypes 394
Stigma by association 399
Stigmas 402
Subtype 394
Superordinate goals 404

[Quiz Yourself] Answers

1. ABCs of Intergroup Relationships: Prejudice, Discrimination, and Stereotypes
Answers: 1=a, 2=c, 3=b, 4=b

2. Why Prejudice Exists
Answers: 1=b, 2=b, 3=b, 4=d

3. Content of Prejudice and Stereotypes
Answers: 1=a, 2=a, 3=a, 4=c

4. Inner Processes
Answers: 1=d, 2=d, 3=b, 4=a

5. Overcoming Stereotypes, Reducing Prejudice
Answers: 1=a, 2=b, 3=c, 4=c

6. Impact of Prejudice on Targets
Answers: 1=d, 2=a, 3=c, 4=a

Media Learning Resources

Make sure you check out the complete set of learning resources and study tools below. If your instructor did not order these items with your new book, go to www.ichapters.com to purchase Cengage Learning print and digital products.

Social Psychology and Human Nature
BOOK COMPANION WEBSITE
www.cengage.com/psychology/baumeister
Visit your book companion website, where you will find flash cards, practice quizzes, Internet links, and more to help you study.

CENGAGENOW™ JUST WHAT YOU NEED TO KNOW NOW!
Spend time on what you need to master rather than on information you have already learned. Take a pre-test for this chapter, and CengageNOW will generate a personalized study plan based on your results. The study plan will identify the topics you need to review and direct you to online resources to help you master those topics. You can then take a post-test to help you determine the concepts you have mastered and what you will still need to work on. Try it out! Go to www.cengage .com/login to sign in with an access code or to purchase access to this product.

CLASSIC AND CONTEMPORARY VIDEOS STUDENT CD-ROM
To see videos on the topics and experiments discussed in this chapter and to learn more about the research that social psychologists are doing today, go to the Student CD-ROM.

SOCIAL PSYCH LAB
These unique online labs give you the opportunity to become a participant in actual experiments, including re-creations of classic and contemporary research studies.

chapter 14

Groups

Tradeoffs: Diversity in Groups **p. 432**

Food for Thought: Is Binge Eating Socially Contagious? **p. 439**

Money Matters: Money, Power, and Laughter **p. 454**

What Makes Us Human? Putting the Cultural Animal in Perspective **p. 457**

Heikki Saukkomaa/AFP/Getty Images

WHAT GROUPS ARE AND DO p. 432

GROUPS, ROLES, AND SELVES p. 434

GROUP ACTION p. 436
Social Facilitation **p. 436**
Social Loafing **p. 439**
Punishing Cheaters and Free Riders **p. 441**
Deindividuation and Mob Violence **p. 441**
Shared Resources and the Commons Dilemma **p. 442**

HOW GROUPS THINK p. 443
Brainstorming, and the Wisdom of Groups **p. 443**
Why Do People Love Teams? **p. 445**
Transactive Memory: Here, You Remember This **p. 445**
Groupthink **p. 446**
Foolish Committees **p. 447**
Group Polarization and the "Risky Shift" **p. 447**

POWER AND LEADERSHIP p. 449
Leadership **p. 449**
Toxic Leaders **p. 450**
What Is Power? **p. 452**
Effects of Power on Leaders **p. 453**
Effects of Power on Followers **p. 456**
Legitimate Leadership **p. 456**

CHAPTER SUMMARY p. 457

In 1863 a well-to-do Michigan farming family gave birth to a son. As a boy, Henry never took to farming, instead showing an abiding interest in mechanical things. He became popular in his neighborhood for fixing people's watches. At age 16 he took a job as an apprentice machinist. Eventually he joined the Edison Engineering Company and at the age of 30 was their chief engineer. ‖‖‖

Local travel at the time depended on horses, but clever young men around the country were experimenting with ways to make self-propelled ("auto-mobile") vehicles. Henry began to tinker with internal combustion engines and began to work on a car (calling it the "Quadricycle," to link it with the popular bicycle). His neighbors had taken to calling him "Crazy Henry" because he spent his evenings and weekends shut up in his garage with his contraption. But they were impressed when late one night he got the car moving. According to legend, it smashed a hole in the side of the garage and drove around the neighborhood with Henry at the wheel.

The car market didn't seem very large. In the year 1900, barely 1 in 10,000 Americans owned an automobile. Nobody expected cars would someday swarm everywhere. Cars were in the news, though. A Vermont man, accompanied by a mechanic and a dog named Bud (all three wearing goggles) made the first coast-to-coast car trip in 65 days, after which they were hailed as national heroes.

Henry went to work for the fledgling Detroit Automobile Company. In two years, it didn't even manage to sell six cars. The company went bankrupt, and Henry was fired. Unemployed, he entered some automobile races and won them. This attention attracted some new financial backers. In 1903 Henry and some other men started the Ford Motor Company, with himself as vice president and chief engineer. A quiet banker named Gray was the first president, but Ford's racing fame dictated that they name the firm after him. The manufacturing system involved having two or three men work together to make a car. Obviously these men had to have enormous skill and knowledge, which made their work relatively expensive. The company was initially only able to make three cars per day, using parts made by other companies. Henry cast about for ways to make the production more efficient. In 1907 Henry said that his goal was to create "a motor car for the great multitude."

Up until this point, cars were rare and expensive machines, usually custom-made toys for the rich. More than 240 companies had been formed to build automobiles, so the prospects for great success by any one were not good. It wasn't even clear that gasoline-powered engines would become the norm. In 1906, a steam-powered car (the Stanley Steamer) set the car speed record by going 127 miles per hour.

A big opportunity and challenge arose when the Ford company developed the Model T. This was the first practical car that ordinary people could afford. Henry threw out the tradition of custom-built cars and made them all exactly the same, even offering only one color. (Henry's remark, "The customer can have any color he wants so long as it's black," became famous.) The design of the Model T did not change from the first one built in 1908 until the final, 15-millionth one in 1927.

Four years after the first Model T was made, three out of every four cars in America were Model Ts. Even in 1918, half of all cars sold in the United States would be Model T Fords. But this escalating demand called for a much more efficient (and cheaper) system for making these cars.

Ford's solution to this problem is the reason we are featuring this story in the chapter on groups. Ford broke up the manufacture of the car into 84 steps and assigned each one to a different worker. Thus, instead of two or three master craftsmen making each car, a great many men worked on each car. Each man, rather than knowing how to build an entire car, could specialize in

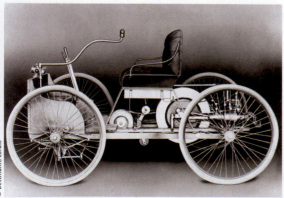

Henry Ford and his Quadricycle (1896).

© Bettmann/Corbis

© Corbis

just one small job. At first, Ford tried a system in which the cars being built were set up on a row of sawhorses. Each worker would do his part on the first vehicle and then move on to the next one. Runners brought parts for each job and left them next to each car. This cut production time down to about 17 hours per car, and Ford workers were soon producing 26,000 cars a month. But there were constant problems. The parts didn't all arrive at the same pace, so many workers had to stand around and wait before they could do their next task. In addition, a fair amount of time was lost as the workers moved around.

The biggest breakthrough came in 1913, with what became known as the assembly line. (Earlier versions had been tried, dating back to 1901.) Instead of having workers move from one car to another, with parts having to be delivered to constantly changing locations, Ford decided that each worker could stay in one place with a pile of ready parts. The cars would move along a conveyer belt. The initial experiment was done using ropes and pulleys to pull the cars along the belt, but the success of this plan quickly led to using a continuous chain pulled by a motor. Once this plan was adopted and a few bugs worked out, the time to make a new car dropped to 93 minutes. At the height of production, a new car rolled off the assembly line every 24 seconds. The car's price dropped as low as $99, though this did not include tires, lights, or a top.

By dividing the task into many parts, Ford found that he could hire workers without expecting them to master a great deal of information about manufacturing cars. It takes a long time for a person to learn how to build an entire car; learning to do one small task might take only a few days. The assembly line was a tremendous success, and Ford became the largest car manufacturer in the world.

There was a problem, however: Many workers disliked the repetitious, boring, low-paid work. Many quit, and Ford was constantly hiring and training new workers. Henry came up with another stroke of genius to solve this problem. He would resist the temptation to pay the workers the minimum amount. He announced a new minimum wage of $5 per day, more than double the average at the time. This made him seem a hero to the working class, a role he accepted. "A business that makes nothing but money is a poor kind of business," he said in a later interview. Other capitalists called Ford "a traitor to his class," complaining that he was raising expectations and the cost of labor everywhere, but he ignored their complaints. Ordinary people flocked to work for him—and, with their higher wages, began buying Model T cars themselves. Business boomed. Ford reaped other benefits, including improved loyalty of his employees, and he saved money on training. Later he boasted that paying $5 a day was one of the smartest cost-cutting moves he had ever made (Gross, 1996).

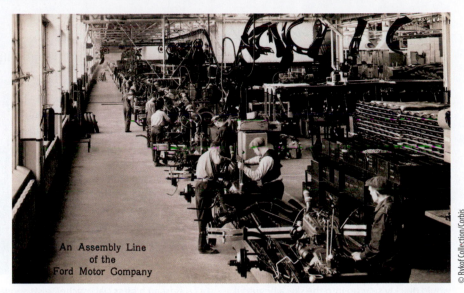

An Assembly Line of the Ford Motor Company

© Bykof Collection/Corbis

In 1913 Henry Ford introduced the assembly line into his factory, which greatly improved productivity rates.

Can groups outperform individuals? Of course a group of 10 people can probably accomplish more than one person, but can a 10-person group outperform 10 people working alone? Culture enables human beings to form groups that can do things that no groups of other animals can, like build and operate a fishing boat, or publish a newspaper, or install artificial heat in everyone's home. To be sure, sometimes a group is less than the sum of its parts. But culture makes it possible (not guaranteed, but possible) for the group to become more than the sum of its parts, as illustrated in this story about Henry Ford.

What does this story exemplify about the social psychology of groups? A strong and persevering leader, experimenting with new ideas and methods, and good organization can breed success, of course. And by sharing rewards with his followers, Ford increased their loyalty, which also helped the group.

But most of all, the assembly line took division of labor to a new level. When ants or wolves hunt, they do so in a kind of swarm in which most individuals perform the same act. The individual acts are interchangeable. On the Ford moving assembly line, in contrast, each person performed a different job requiring some limited but specific knowledge or skill. Using this method, a group of people, each having minimal knowledge and skill, could produce something magnificent. The group was far more than the sum of its members. This is one important key to how human beings can use the power of culture to make groups that can achieve far more than collections of individuals operating alone. Interactive, complementary roles can make up a powerful system. ■

Diversity in Groups

The novelist Jerzy Kosinski filled his novels with vivid, moving stories from his personal life, which included many hardships. Kosinski himself eventually committed suicide. The title of his novel *The Painted Bird* refers to a story in which a character would capture a black bird and then, holding the blindfolded bird in one hand, dab it with different colors of paint until the bird was a collage of all colors of the rainbow. When no black feathers remained visible, he would remove the hood and release the frightened animal. The bird would quickly soar up into the sky, a beautiful spectacle of flying colors. Soon another black bird would come by and strike at it, however, and then another and another, until the painted bird disappeared in a mass of black birds that tore it to pieces.

The story captures a sad truth of nature: Often animals that look different from the others are targeted for rejection and outright violence. Animals do not seem to value diversity in their groups. They are not even content with excluding those who are different, but often actively destroy them.

American society has committed itself to promoting diversity, and there is much talk everywhere about how groups and institutions (work groups, universities, sports teams, and the like) will perform better if they are diverse. But is diversity always better? Is it safe for Americans to assume that they will always be able to outperform other, less diverse societies, such as the Japanese? There may be both costs and benefits to diversity. Homogeneous (that is, nondiverse) groups may have some advantages too, along with their drawbacks. Many advocates of diversity oppose women's colleges or African American schools (because they exclude male or nonblack students), but such institutions have provided good educations for many students, and a cautious scientist would not insist that more diverse school populations always produce better results. (Of course, some people might oppose same-sex colleges on moral grounds even if they do provide a first-rate education.)

DigitalVision

Research by social psychologists suggests that diversity involves tradeoffs (see Levine & Moreland, 1998, for a review). On the plus side, diverse groups can be more flexible and creative than groups marked by greater similarity among the members. Greater diversity can bring together more perspectives and possibly more information. Surowiecki (2004) concluded that groups can be smarter than the smartest individuals, but only if different people contribute different information to the mix. Diverse groups, by definition, have a better chance of bringing together different information than similar groups.

Recent research has confirmed that a group's collective wisdom can exceed the sum of its individual members, but only if the individual members have diverse and different views (Page, 2008). In fact, a group of diverse individuals can make better decisions than a group of similar individuals that are much smarter. The reason is that the errors of diverse people tend to cancel each other out, so when you average them you get the best answer. In contrast, similar individuals tend to make the same types of errors, so when you average them you really don't gain much.

On the minus side, diversity can make it harder for people to cooperate and work together. The different backgrounds can result in poor communication and misunderstandings. Often diverse groups perform less well than other groups. The difficulty in getting very different people to work together can result in frustration, resentment, low morale, and even feelings of alienation from (or reduced commitment to) the group (Levine & Moreland, 1998).

This tradeoff helps explain one seeming paradox that will be seen throughout this chapter. Groups perform best if people are individually identified and perform their separate, distinct roles. Yet groups have all sorts of pressures that push everyone to be and become the same. Why are there such widespread conformity pressures in so many groups, if diversity is superior? The tentative answer for now is that diversity can produce benefits, but it has costs as well. Indeed, the advantages of groups may be specific to cultural animals, because they involve sharing information and role differentiation. ●

What Groups Are and Do

A **group** is a collection of people, usually people who are doing or being something together. But that is hardly a satisfactory definition. Groups can be defined in different ways. What makes a collection of people a group? Can two people (a "dyad") be a group? Do the members of a group have to know each other or interact?

Probably the most appropriate answer is that some groups seem more like groups than others. One could say that Canadians are a group, but that is a very large and diverse group, and most of the members don't know each other. Forty strangers on a bus don't make much of a group. Forty people waiting in line for football tickets may be a bit more like a group, given their common goal and perhaps their shared loyalty to their team. Forty people working together on an assembly line or football team make a much more coherent group. Yes, a dyad can be a group, but it is perhaps a special kind of group, and the processes and dynamics of a dyad (e.g., two

GROUP a collection of at least two people who are doing or being something together

people in a romantic relationship) are probably different from what goes on in a larger group. For one thing, two people can really relate as equals and make their decisions jointly so that each is satisfied, but a group of 100 probably cannot make decisions in that way; they will need either a leader who makes decisions or a democratic voting system that lets the preferences of the majority determine the decision.

What makes a group feel united? As we said, a football team is more like a group than 40 strangers on a bus, for several reasons (see Campbell, 1958; Lickel, Hamilton, Wieczorkowska, Lewis, Sherman, & Uhles, 2000). They have a common identity, exemplified by the team name, whereas the strangers on the bus do not. The team members interact frequently with one another, unlike the strangers on the bus who often sit silently and don't talk to each other. The team members depend on one another, whereas the bus passengers do not. The team members work together toward common goals, again unlike the bus riders. The team members have common beliefs, values, and practices, such as about the importance of football, and they are similar in other respects such as athleticism and gender, whereas the bus riders share only their faith that the bus will take them to their different destinations. The team members share emotionally powerful experiences, such as in winning or losing big games, whereas the bus riders do not. In fact, if something emotionally powerful were to happen to the bus, such as being hijacked or having an accident, the riders might start to act and feel more like a group. One example is United Airlines flight 93 that was hijacked by terrorists. Several passengers and crew made telephone calls aboard the flight, learned about the terrorist attacks on the World Trade Center and the Pentagon and tried to regain control of the plane. The plane crashed in a field near Shanksville, Pennsylvania, about 150 miles (240 km) northwest of Washington, D.C., killing all on board including 40 passengers and crew and four hijackers. An analysis of the flight recorders revealed that passengers and crew prevented the aircraft from reaching the hijackers' intended target, thought to be either the White House or United States Capitol.

Thus, one factor is whether the members of a group feel similar to each other. For this reason, more diverse groups may find it harder to come together as a group, compared to groups that start off being similar. Then again, diversity brings other benefits; to appreciate these, see *Tradeoffs* on diversity.

Most likely another factor is the presence of an outgroup, especially a rival or enemy. Sports teams are often cohesive groups, not simply because they wear uniforms of the same color, but because they frequently have to work together for the common good against a common opponent. A team that merely practiced, without ever playing against an opponent, would probably not feel so unified. It is quite possible

Sara Wolfram/Getty Images

Conflict between groups helps solidify feelings of belonging to a group.

that the deeply rooted human impulse to form social groups was partly stimulated by competition among groups. If a lone person wanted something—the fruit on a particular tree, for example—and a group also wanted it, the group would almost always win. Over evolutionary history, loners would therefore be losers, whereas the people who passed on their genes toward future generations would be the ones who formed groups (see Hoyle, Pinkley, & Insko, 1989).

What, then, do groups accomplish? Answers to this can be found at both the social and cultural level. Social animals tend to live in groups, because groups provide several clear benefits. They promote safety, they find and share food, and they can do tasks that no one individual can do alone.

Human groups are not just social but also cultural, and culture greatly increases what groups can do (see Baumeister, 2005). Cultural groups preserve information in the group and pass it along to future generations, greatly increasing the benefit of being able to absorb and communicate information. Cultural groups also benefit from role differentiation. Everyone specializes at something, in effect becoming an expert at his or her role, and the result is that all of the jobs are performed by experts.

Ford's assembly line exemplifies these advantages of groups. Knowledge about how to make cars was accumulated and preserved by the group, enabling it to be gradually improved. The first assembly line had the workers move along the line, rather than the cars. The second, improved version had the cars move down the line, pulled along by ropes. The third version had a motorized conveyor belt move the cars along. Furthermore, the company used information and reasoning to reorganize itself to make the assembly system better. And the essence of the assembly line is division of labor. Instead of having two or three men make the entire car, the new system used many workers, each of whom specialized in a few simple tasks. The result was repeated improvements in the ability to make more cars better, faster, and cheaper.

[QUIZ YOURSELF]

What Groups Are and Do

1. Which of the following is probably not a group?
   (a) Three children playing hide-and-go-seek
   (b) Three neighbors having a barbecue
   (c) Three strangers quietly waiting for a bus
   (d) Three students working together on a class project

2. In one high school class, the teacher lets students select their own groups to work on an important class project. As expected, similar students group themselves together. In another class, the teacher randomly divides students into groups, so dissimilar students are often grouped together. Which is likely to be the main advantage of the dissimilar groups over the homogeneous (similar) ones?
   (a) The dissimilar (heterogeneous) groups will be more cooperative.
   (b) The dissimilar groups will be more efficient.
   (c) The dissimilar groups will generate a greater variety of information.
   (d) The dissimilar groups will have higher morale.

3. Which of the following greatly increased the production of automobiles in Henry Ford's plants?
   (a) The added health benefits workers received
   (b) The assembly line
   (c) The higher pay workers received
   (d) The longer work week

4. Which of the following is an advantage of a group?
   (a) Groups can provide safety in numbers.
   (b) Groups can help each other find food.
   (c) Groups can make difficult tasks easier to perform.
   (d) All of the above

Groups, Roles, and Selves

No snowflake in an avalanche ever feels responsible.
—Stanislaus Lezczynski, King of Poland (1704–1709, 1733–1735)

A vital and distinctive feature of human groups is that many of them are made up of distinct, well-defined, individual roles. Each person has a different job to do, and each person can specialize and become an expert at that job. The different jobs complement each other, so the joint effort improves total performance. The assembly line thus reveals a crucial advantage that cultural groups have over merely social groups, such as wolves or bees. Complementary roles produce better results than simply having everyone chip in and do the same thing.

The advantages of specialized roles were recognized long before Henry Ford invented the assembly line. In medieval farming villages, for example, it was probably good to have a blacksmith. But if everyone tried to be a blacksmith, the village would starve. The same goes for musicians, artists, and priests. When human groups advanced to the point that they did not need every person to be producing as much food as possible all the time, they became able to support musicians, artists, and priests. But if everyone in a tribe or village wanted to be a musician, the group would be unable to survive. Today, the same goes for teachers, police officers, physicians, plumbers, fortune-tellers, prostitutes, computer repair technicians, comedians, airline flight attendants, and barbers. Human roles only work in the context of a large system when most other people do something else.

Identifying individual people with their unique roles within the group is an important key to the success of human groups. In this chapter, we will see repeatedly that groups do better when people are individually identified and perform their unique roles. In contrast, when people blend together into a group and lose their unique place, such as by submerging their identities into the group, the groups perform less well and sometimes produce downright ugly results.

Social psychologists have coined the term **deindividuation** to refer to loss of self-awareness and of individual accountability in a group. The term, from the same root as "individual," implies a loss of individuality. You might assume that deindividuation would be a good thing. Being anonymous is an important source of protection of individual rights and freedoms. That, after all, is why most important votes are taken by secret ballot, so that people do not feel pressure to vote a certain way and can instead make decisions based on their own inner reasoning and conscience. To the extent that this is the general pattern, you might expect that individual behavior would be better when people are deindividuated, because people could do what they think is right rather than succumb to group pressure.

The reality is more problematic, however. Deindividuated people often behave badly. In the chapter on antisocial behavior, we saw that trick-or-treaters took more Halloween candy when they were deindividuated by costumes that concealed their faces than

DEINDIVIDUATION the loss of self-awareness and of individual accountability in a group

Movements such as National Socialism (Nazism) submerge individual identity into the group. The results have often been destructive, for themselves and others.

when they were identified (Diener, Fraser, Beaman, & Kelem, 1976). In other studies, deindividuated participants showed much higher levels of aggression toward people they did not like, such as giving them intense electric shocks (Zimbardo, 1970). We shall see repeatedly in this chapter that group processes can produce costly and destructive results when people submerge their individual identities in the group.

Although this conclusion has emerged in a halting way from laboratory findings, it was also spectacularly confirmed by some of the major historical movements of the 20th century. For example, the essence of fascist movements was that the individual should be submerged in the group, and the individual's self-interest should be subordinated to the best interests of the group. The most successful (at least for a while) fascists were the German Nazis, who did achieve some impressive successes in rebuilding a shattered, starving nation and fighting a war against the combined great powers of the world, but whose inner dynamics degenerated into a level of shocking cruelty and evil that went beyond what had been seen in other places—and that ultimately resulted in the sweeping destruction of their own country. Their experiment with deindividuation was thus a disaster for all concerned.

Before closing this section, it is important to appreciate a few other important points about role differentiation. First, in a culture, the roles are defined by the system; they exist independently of the individual. The United States has one president, 100 senators, and nine Supreme Court justices. A select few individuals occupy those roles today, but after all those men and women are dead and gone, those roles will still exist and be occupied by other

individuals. The system creates the role, and different human beings occupy it, each one coming and going. When you get a job, it will most likely be a position that someone else had before you and someone else will have after you.

The split between people and roles means that people have to have selves that are flexible enough to adopt (and occasionally drop) roles. Ants, for example, benefit from a social system that has several different roles, but each ant is programmed by nature for only one role, and ants do not change jobs very often. In human society, new roles become available all the time. Individual humans often have careers that involve a series of different jobs and different roles.

Belonging to a human cultural group thus involves two separate demands. One is to find common values and other sources of similarity that can cement one's allegiance to the group. The other is to find some special or even unique role within the group.

The tension between trying to be similar to everyone in the group and trying to be different from others has been the thrust of **optimal distinctiveness theory**, an important theory put forth by social psychologist Marilynn Brewer and her colleagues (e.g., Brewer, 1993, 1999; Leonardelli & Brewer, 2001; Pickett, Silver, & Brewer, 2002). Brewer observed that human behavior in groups is marked by an unending tension between trying to be similar and trying to be different. When people feel very similar to others, they try to be different. When they feel different, they try to be more similar.

OPTIMAL DISTINCTIVENESS THEORY proposition that when people feel very similar to others in a group, they seek a way to be different, and when they feel different, they try to be more similar

Most individuals have
multiple roles.

In one test of the theory, Lau (1989) examined
whether African Americans in various situations identified themselves as feeling close to African Americans
in general. For example, do you think a black woman
would identify most strongly with her racial group if
she lived in a predominantly white area, a predominantly black area, or an area with about equal numbers
of blacks and whites? Lau found such group identity
to be strongest among African Americans who lived
in areas in which 40–70% of the population was also
African American. Living in such an area created the
optimal, medium level of distinctiveness.

[QUIZ YOURSELF]

Groups, Roles, and Selves

1. When Devan is at a hockey game, he often gets
   swept away in the excitement. He is no longer
   self-conscious and, as a result, often does and says
   things that he later regrets. Hockey games seem to
   create in Devan a state of _____.
   (a) catharsis   (b) deindividuation
   (c) excitation transfer   (d) pluralistic ignorance

2. Circumstances that increase _____ will decrease
   _____.
   (a) anonymity; empathy
   (b) anonymity; diffusion of responsibility
   (c) self-awareness; deindividuation
   (d) self-awareness; empathy

3. What type of movement suggests that self-interest
   should be subordinated to the best interests of the
   group?
   (a) Fascism   (b) Anarchy
   (c) Capitalism   (d) Democracy

4. When people feel very similar to others, they try
   to be _____; when people feel very different from
   others, they try to be _____.
   (a) different; different   (b) different; similar
   (c) similar; different   (d) similar; similar

Group Action

Many people do many things in groups. The effect of
working in a group (as compared to working alone)
is variable: Sometimes the group produces improvement, other times disaster. Social psychologists have
spent years mapping out these effects.

One theme we have already suggested is that the
effects of groups are often negative when people are
submerged in the group. In contrast, when people
retain their individual identities and feel personally accountable for their actions, many of the bad
effects of groups are prevented or reduced, and the
positive effects of groups are more common. Identifying people and holding them accountable for
their actions produces better outcomes. To be sure,
accountability is not a cure-all for the broad range
of lapses, mistakes, and mental biases people show
in groups. But when people believe they may have
to justify their actions and decisions to other people,
they tend to be more careful and thorough in their
thinking, including using all the information available to them and thinking about how they would
respond to possible criticisms (Lerner & Tetlock,
1999). People cooperate more with others when they
are individually identified, whereas the anonymity of
groups produces more greed, fear, and other dangerous reactions (Schopler, Insko, Drigotas, Wieselquist,
Pemberton, & Cox, 1995).

SOCIAL FACILITATION

Many experts regard Triplett's (1897–1898) work as
the first social psychology experiments (see Chapter
1). While watching bicycle races, he noticed that
cyclists who raced alone against the clock generally were slower than those who raced against competitors. This observation led to his experiment. He
conducted research by telling participants to wind
fishing reels as fast as they could. Those who did this
task alone were slower than those who did it when
someone else was competing against them. Triplett
thought that the presence of others stimulated a
competitive instinct, causing people to work harder.

Later generations of social psychologists began to
pursue this work, but by this time the notion of a
"competitive instinct" had gone out of fashion as a
viable explanation. Competition was not really necessary, anyway. Some people performed better merely

On complex tasks, the presence of others decreases task performance.

because there were observers present, as opposed to competitors (Cottrell, Wack, Sekerak, & Rittle, 1968; Seta & Seta, 1995). This finding led to the tentative conclusion that **evaluation apprehension** (concern about how others are evaluating you) is the driving factor. People increase effort when others are present because they want the others to evaluate them favorably.

Another problem is that the presence of others doesn't always make people perform better. Have you ever given a speech or performance in front of a large audience? Many people find the audience unnerving and make mistakes (e.g., Beilock & Carr, 2001; Butler & Baumeister, 1998; Wallace & Baumeister, 2002; Wright & Jackson, 1991; Wright & Voher, 1995). If an audience merely stimulated a competitive instinct, people would never "choke under pressure."

These diverse, seemingly conflicting sets of observations were integrated into an exciting theory proposed by social psychologist Robert Zajonc (1965). His theory was rooted in observations of animal learning (e.g., Spence, 1956). Zajonc proposed that being in the presence of other people (or, for animals, other members of the same species) is arousing: It makes one breathe faster, makes the heart beat faster, sends adrenaline through the system, and so forth. One well-known effect of arousal is to increase the **dominant response**, which is defined as the most common response in that situation. Thus, whatever you are normally inclined to do, you will be even more strongly inclined to do when in the presence of others. The essence of Zajonc's **social facilitation theory** (see ▶ **FIGURE 14.1**) is that the presence of others increases the dominant response tendency. For example, if you usually (though not always) choose hamburgers over hot dogs, then choosing hamburgers is your dominant response when you are asked to choose between them. When others are present, you will be especially likely to choose a hamburger.

The dominant response theory can explain both the good and the bad effects of the presence of

others—both the faster cycling times in the presence of competition and the mistakes the amateur pianist makes when playing for an audience. For familiar, easy, and well-learned behaviors, the dominant response is to perform well, and performance increases when others are watching. For difficult, unfamiliar tasks, the dominant response is to perform less well, so mistakes become more common when others are watching.

The social facilitation theory has been confirmed by many studies (Bond & Titus, 1983). In fact, one investigation even found it among cockroaches (Zajonc, Heingartner, & Herman, 1969). A simple maze (▶ **FIGURE 14.2a**) required cockroaches to run straight ahead when a light was turned on to escape the light (hopefully you don't know this

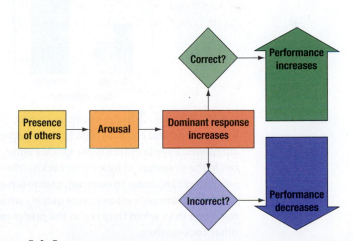

▶ **FIGURE 14.1** Robert Zajonc's theory of social facilitation: The presence of others increases arousal. Arousal increases whatever response is dominant. If the dominant response is correct, performance increases. If the dominant response is incorrect, performance decreases.

EVALUATION APPREHENSION concern about how others are evaluating your performance
DOMINANT RESPONSE the most common response in a given situation
SOCIAL FACILITATION THEORY proposition that the presence of others increases the dominant response tendency

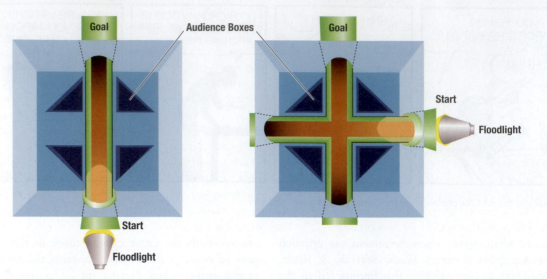

(a) Simple maze

Goal

Audience Boxes

Start

Floodlight

(b) Complex maze

Goal

Start

Floodlight

▶ **FIGURE 14.2** (a) In the simple maze, the dominant response is to run straight ahead, which is also the correct response. (b) In the more complex maze, the dominant response is to run straight ahead, which is the incorrect response (the correct response is to turn right). In the social conditions, there was a cockroach in each audience box. In the alone conditions, the audience boxes were empty. Source: Zajonc et al. (1969).

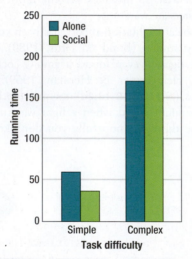

▶ **FIGURE 14.3** In the study by Zajonc, Heingartner, and Herman (1969), cockroaches completed simple mazes more quickly when they ran in the presence of four other cockroaches than when they ran alone. In contrast, cockroaches completed complex mazes more quickly when they ran alone than when they ran in the presence of four other cockroaches.

from personal experience, but cockroaches hate the light and scurry for the darkness whenever a light is turned on). In a more complex maze (Figure 14.2b), the cockroach had to make a right turn. When four other cockroaches were standing nearby (in the audience boxes), the cockroach went through the simple maze faster than when it was alone (see ▶ **FIGURE 14.3**). On the difficult maze, however, cockroaches

were slower in the presence of peers than when alone. Cockroaches probably do not suffer evaluation apprehension or other complex human motives, so this finding was best explained in the simple, basic terms of social facilitation.

Social facilitation theory has many applications to the real world. For example, many modern offices have more public shared space (such as large rooms where everyone is present) rather than private offices. Is this a good design decision? It depends. If the employees are working on simple or well-learned tasks, then this design works well because the presence of others should increase their performance. On the other hand, if the employees are working on complex or creative tasks, the design is bad because the presence of others is likely to decrease their performance. The Ford assembly line worked well in part because the tasks were simple, so the dominant response was to perform them correctly.

More recent work has concluded that social facilitation effects depend on three processes (Aiello & Douthitt, 2001). Bodily arousal confers more energy and increases the dominant response. Evaluation apprehension makes people strive to make a good impression (but also creates worries). And some degree of distraction occurs, insofar as people start paying attention to each other rather than the task. The last fits the "putting people first" orientation we have seen over and over in this textbook.

The presence of others can also influence food consumption, as described in *Food for Thought.*

To be sure, evaluation apprehension does affect performance among humans, and it may intensify

Food *for* Thought

Is Binge Eating Socially Contagious?

Binge eating has become a prominent problem in recent decades, especially among young women. It is defined by alternating periods of uncontrolled, lavish eating and of severe restraint marked sometimes by fasting or even purging through induced vomiting or taking laxatives. It is associated with the clinical diagnosis of bulimia. These patterns were rarely noted or observed prior to the 1960s, but they have quickly become a serious problem. Recent estimates suggest that between one out of twenty and one out of five female college students engages in this behavior.

How could a pattern of problem behavior change so quickly from relatively unknown to widespread? Part of the answer lies in group processes. Crandall (1988) studied college sororities and found that binge eating patterns seemed to be contagious, in the sense that they spread through the group. Crandall observed that binge eating was most commonly noted when groups of young women, all about the same age, interacted regularly. Young women who joined sororities would adopt the behavior patterns of the group—sometimes including binge eating.

In fact, binge eating was associated with popularity in the sororities. There were two different patterns. In one, the more a young woman engaged in binge eating, the more popular she was. This suggests that women perceived binge eating as a pathway to social success. It also indicates that binge eating carried no social penalty. On the contrary, apparently the group rewarded binge eating, as the women who engaged in it most frequently were most highly regarded by the other group members.

The other pattern was only slightly less worrisome. In one sorority, there were apparent norms for the optimal amount of binge eating. The most popular women were those who were closest to these norms. Thus, there was apparently at least some disapproval directed toward the most extreme binge eaters. Still, women who failed to engage in binge eating also paid a price in terms of lower popularity.

The second pattern, indicating social norms for binge eating, is consistent with the idea that women picked up the habit from their friends. Sure enough, Crandall's research found that a woman's tendency toward binge eating had typically become quite similar to that of her friends by the end of the academic year. In other words, members of the group became more like their friends over time. Because the members of the sorority typically engaged in binge eating, new members adopted this pattern as they made friends. ●

Evaluation apprehension is bad for the appetite.

---

the effects of others' presence. An evaluative observer has a stronger effect than a blindfolded bystander (Cottrell et al., 1968). The possibility of evaluation seems to inspire certain kinds of people to do their best. In particular, **narcissists** are individuals who regard themselves as better than others and are constantly trying to win the admiration of others. These glory hounds perform best when others are watching or when there are important rewards riding on the outcome of their performance, whereas they tend to slack off when there is no opportunity to bring credit to themselves (Wallace & Baumeister, 2002). This pattern, however, can elicit resentment from other group members, who recognize that the narcissist is not a team player but rather is looking for individual honors.

SOCIAL LOAFING

The preceding section showed that the presence of others can make people perform better, especially on easy and familiar tasks. But wait: Around the same time that Triplett was noticing that cyclists rode faster when there were other cyclists, a French engineer named Max Ringelmann was coming to a very different conclusion (see Chapter 1). Ringelmann observed farm workers, and he saw that as new men were added, the total output didn't seem to increase as much as it should. He conducted experiments in which men pulled carts either alone or together. In theory, two men should pull twice as hard (200%) as one (and if social facilitation theory is at work here, two men should pull more than twice as hard!)—but in fact two men pulled only 186% as hard. When there were four men, the drop in total effort was even bigger. In eight-man teams, each man was not even pulling half as hard as the lone men. Here was a clear example of a human group being less than the sum of its parts: Somehow the men didn't seem to work as hard in a team as they did when alone (Ringelmann, 1913, published in French; cited in Kravitz & Martin, 1986). What went wrong?

NARCISSISTS individuals who regard themselves as better than others and are constantly trying to win the admiration of others

Although it looks as though these people are pulling the rope as hard as they can, research shows that they would pull harder if they were pulling alone.

Several factors reduce an individual's productivity when working in a group, such as difficulty coordinating efforts with others. But subsequent research confirmed a pattern that came to be known as **social loafing**: People reduce effort when working in a group, compared to when working alone (Latane, Williams, & Harkins, 1979). In lab studies, for example, participants were assigned to make as much noise as possible by clapping and shouting. Recordings verified that they were louder (indicating greater effort) when working alone than in a group. Three people, each cheering alone, made about as much total noise as six people cheering together.

The pattern of social loafing has also been called the **free rider problem** (e.g., Kerr & Bruun, 1983). This term is probably derived from trams, subways, and buses in Europe, which rely on the honor system for payment: People are supposed to buy a ticket and punch it or scan a debit card when they climb on board. The money from these tickets pays for the transportation system. But some people simply get on and ride without paying. They thus take free rides, letting others provide the money that keeps the system going.

Free riders presumably know they are cheating the system and taking advantage of others. In lab studies, most social loafers say they are working as hard as they can, even though the experimental results prove that they aren't. Apparently, many people are not aware that they are socially loafing, or at least they are reluctant to admit it (Karau & Williams, 1993).

Why does social loafing occur? One important factor is the feeling of being submerged in the group, and therefore not being individually accountable. When the contributions of individual group members are identified, so that everyone (or at least the leader) knows who did what, social loafing is greatly reduced (Kerr & Bruun, 1981; Williams, Harkins, & Latane, 1981). People are less likely to steal free rides on the subway if they will be identified than if they think they can do it anonymously. Likewise, people work harder for their team or group if they believe that others will know if they slack off (Karau & Williams, 1993).

The importance of individual identification exemplifies the theme we have already noted: Groups produce more negative effects when individual identities are submerged in the group. During the 1980s and 1990s, "accountability" became a major buzzword in American businesses. Accountability meant that each person was held individually responsible for his or her decisions and job performance. The drive for accountability was fueled in part by the growing recognition that a lack of individual accountability contributes to social loafing.

The difference between feeling individually accountable versus submerged in the group probably holds the key to the apparent contradiction between Ringelmann and Triplett. Remember, Triplett found that people performed better when others were present, whereas Ringelmann found the opposite. But in Triplett's studies, performers were individually identified; in fact, they were often competing against one another. In Ringelmann's observations, the men were yoked together pulling carts, and no one could know how hard any individual man pulled. Competition and accountability lead to greater effort, but submersion in the group leads to social loafing.

A related cause of social loafing is the desire not to be a sucker (Kerr, 1983). Once members of a group begin to suspect that others are loafing, they loaf too, because they do not want to do all the work on behalf of others. If you and a friend had to paint the garage, and your friend spent most of the time taking calls on her cell phone while you did most of the painting, you might well feel that you had been foolish to do more than your fair share of the work, especially if credit (and pay) was shared equally between the two of you. This pattern has also been called the **bad apple effect** (Kerr et al., in press; Kurzban & Leary, 2001; see Ouwerkerk, Van Lange, Gallucci, & Kerr, 2005), based on the folk observation that one bad apple can spoil all the other apples. One loafer can thus cause other workers to loaf as well.

Again, individual identification helps overcome the tendency to loaf. People are less prone to copy a social loafer if they believe they will get credit or blame for their own work. When people believe their

SOCIAL LOAFING (FREE RIDER PROBLEM) the finding that people reduce effort when working in a group, compared to when working alone
BAD APPLE EFFECT the idea that one social loafer can cause other people to loaf as well

© Fancy Collection/SuperStock

If he does all the work will she share in the credit?

own contribution to the group is unique, especially if it is also important and meaningful, they are less likely to loaf (Kerr & Bruun, 1983).

How is social loafing to be reconciled with social facilitation? The pattern of social facilitation is deeply rooted in nature and indeed is found in other species. Nature, apparently, has prepared people to become excited when others are around, and this can make for better performance. Social loafing and especially the bad apple effect appear to be much more distinctively human, insofar as people must often force themselves to do work that they dislike. Only humans worry about being a sucker, and perhaps only humans can reason through to the conclusion that they might as well enjoy the same benefit as others for half the effort, if they can get away with it.

PUNISHING CHEATERS AND FREE RIDERS

Social psychologists have been using game-based methods to study people's motives for several decades, and recently economists have begun to adopt similar research methods. One recent finding is that when participants recognize that other players are showing signs of social loafing or free riding, they will punish them—even if it costs the participant money to punish the free rider (Fehr & Gächter, 2002).

This pattern is shocking to many economists. Certainly free riders can gradually undermine the system for everyone, but economists generally assume that rational human beings will maximize their own payoffs. Why would they give up some of their own money to punish a free rider, rather than just doing the best they can for themselves and leaving the free rider problem to others? Economists even came up with a name for this—**altruistic punishment** (Fehr & Gächter, 2002). It is altruistic in the sense that the individual sacrifices his or her own gain for the betterment of all, by punishing people who cheat the system. This might be compared to a bystander who risks injury in order to stop a crime, such as by attacking the criminal.

The irrationality of altruistic punishment suggests that it may involve something very deeply rooted in the psyche, which fits the theme of this book that natural selection has favored humans who are able to participate in a cultural society. One trait that would fit that description very well would be a deeply rooted impulse to punish people who cheat or beat the system. Culture depends on a system, and those who cheat the system can ruin it for everyone. Altruistic punishers may suffer in the short run, but in the long run they are likely to benefit. A group of people who are all willing to punish cheaters and free riders will have a safer, fairer system—and hence may survive and reproduce better—than a group of people who don't guard their culture against cheating and free riding.

DEINDIVIDUATION AND MOB VIOLENCE

Earlier in this chapter, we introduced another form of being submerged in the group: deindividuation. The term signifies a loss of individuality, and research has come to define it as a loss of individual accountability and reduction of self-awareness, mainly due to the presence of others (Diener et al., 1976; Festinger, Pepitone, & Newcomb, 1952; Zimbardo, 1970). Social psychologists quickly reached the (preliminary) conclusion that deindividuation makes people more willing to act on their own impulses, which can increase antisocial behavior (see Chapter 10). We have seen that in many situations nature says go, whereas culture says stop. Apparently, one way that culture says "stop" is by holding people individually accountable for their actions, and when people become anonymous and not identifiable, they are less likely to heed the culture's pleas to stop. It is in a sense ironic that merging into the group can make people behave less in accordance with cultural values,

---

ALTRUISTIC PUNISHMENT the finding that people will sometimes sacrifice their own gain for the betterment of all, by punishing people who cheat the system

May I please see some ID?

SHARED RESOURCES AND THE COMMONS DILEMMA

Land, food, money, tools, jewels, and other resources can be held in two ways. One is private property, in which a single person owns the resource. The other is to have resources shared by the group, so that people take what they need and leave the rest to others. The march of human history has seen a dramatic shift in ownership patterns. The earliest humans seem to have had relatively few possessions, and much of what they had was shared communally by the family, tribe, or other group. Modern Western civilizations, in contrast, have adopted private ownership of most goods, though communal ownership is still sometimes seen within families (e.g., any member of the family is permitted to take and eat food from the family refrigerator).

Private ownership has severe social costs. One is inequality. Estimates suggest, for example, that the top 10% of wealthy Americans own 83% of the valuable resources (Schaefer, 2003). The results are even more dramatic if one considers the top 0.5% of wealthy Americans own 44% of the valuable resources (Schaefer, 2003). Another possible inequality can occur when ambitious and greedy private owners take advantage of others to increase their share. Religious orders in many parts of the world have insisted that clergy and other people who devote their lives to spiritual striving renounce worldly possessions, sometimes taking a vow of poverty. In a very different manner, some social movements such as socialism and communism have advocated reducing or abolishing private property so that people will share ownership of valuable resources and not seek to exploit one another.

Yet joint, communal ownership has costs, too (thus indicating another tradeoff!). Resources that are not owned by anyone do not receive the preserving care that they get from individual owners. Communism became notorious for pollution and waste, because individuals had no incentive to take care of the publicly owned resources. On a smaller scale, you might notice that your friends who live in dorm rooms or rental properties do not take care of these dwellings as carefully as they do their rooms at home or as carefully as people who own their own dwelling.

Social psychologists became interested in the problems of communal resources under the name of the **commons dilemma**—the tendency for shared or jointly owned resources to be squandered and not used in an optimal or advantageous fashion. The term is derived from a work by Hardin (1968) on the "tragedy of the commons."

There are actually two kinds of conflict in the commons dilemma, both of which have been seen repeatedly in this book. The first is social conscience versus selfish impulse: People take things for themselves even when it hurts the group as a whole. The

because cultural values are group values. Thus, as people merge into the group, they sometimes feel freer to go against the group's values.

A review by Postmes and Spears (1998) concluded that the effects of deindividuation are somewhat erratic, which calls into question any general conclusion such as "deindividuated people are more violent." They found that whether members of the group were anonymous to one another didn't seem to matter much, but being anonymous to outsiders did make people more willing to violate norms, such as by stealing and cheating. Likewise, what mattered in terms of self-awareness was whether people were attuned to how other people regarded them, not whether they were privately thinking about themselves. Thus, deindividuation makes people more willing to behave badly insofar as they cease worrying about what others think of them.

Postmes and Spears (1998) concluded that accountability is the single biggest factor in predicting aggression. As we have said, people behave most in line with general social norms when they feel individually accountable for their acts. When not accountable, they will go along with what others are doing at the moment, even when these situational norms go against what is generally considered morally good. This is probably how looting happens during a riot: Most people believe stealing is wrong, but when one is submerged in the group and other members of the group are stealing, the individual goes along with the here-and-now group and steals too.

COMMONS DILEMMA the tendency for shared or jointly owned resources to be squandered and not used in an optimal or advantageous fashion

second involves time (again, the tradeoff of "now versus later"). To manage a resource for the long run, it is best to restrain oneself in the present. People could actually benefit their own selfish goals best if they would all simply go slowly, allowing the resource to replenish itself fully. But that is not what people do. They take most of the resource now, leaving little for later.

Communication helps. When people can communicate and urge each other to show restraint, they do not use up the resource as fast (e.g., Brechner, 1977). Unfortunately, they still tend to take too much, so the resource is still badly managed and ends up being depleted prematurely.

Another factor is the behavior of others. When people observe that others are greedily taking more for themselves rather than showing restraint in order to benefit everyone over the long term, they tend to copy this behavior. Earlier in this chapter we saw that the tendency to follow bad behavior is called the bad apple effect. When people observe others behaving well, they also tend to behave more favorably, but people copy bad behavior more quickly and readily than they copy good behavior.

[QUIZ YOURSELF]

Group Action

1. The presence of others helps individual performance on _____ tasks, and hurts individual performance on _____ tasks.
   (a) boring; interesting   (b) interesting; boring
   (c) easy; difficult   (d) difficult; easy

2. Professor Walleye Bass finds that having other faculty members observe his class improves his lectures. This improvement is the result of _____.
   (a) evaluation apprehension
   (b) mere presence
   (c) social loafing
   (d) None of the above

3. Easy identification of the contributions of group members _____.
   (a) decreases group efficiency
   (b) decreases evaluation apprehension
   (c) decreases social facilitation
   (d) decreases social loafing

4. Snap, Crackle, and Pop have a group project in their nutrition class. They write a paper on breakfast nutrition. Snap and Crackle do all the work, whereas Pop does little or no work. Because grades are assigned to groups of students, Snap, Crackle, and Pop all get "A"s. Pop's "A" grade illustrates _____.
   (a) a free ride
   (b) downward social comparison
   (c) the bad apple effect
   (d) upward social comparison

How Groups Think

Groups should seemingly be smarter than individuals. Folk wisdom says that two heads are better than one, so 10 heads ought to be better yet. The general principle is that groups are smarter than individuals. But are they? The following sections will reveal a mixture of answers.

Before we are too hard on groups, however, it is important to remember the idea that humans evolved to belong to cultural groups—groups that share and preserve information. It is normal and natural for people to share information and to look to others for information. Moreover, if information is to be shared through a group, there will be natural tendencies for human groups to think alike. Social psychologists have been good at finding absurd or destructive excesses of this tendency, such as when everyone in a group clings to a false belief. But these excesses are probably linked to basic tendencies that are neither absurd nor destructive. Groups do far more good than harm.

BRAINSTORMING, AND THE WISDOM OF GROUPS

Although fields such as advertising often borrow ideas from psychology, sometimes the advertising people get there first. Brainstorming is an idea that was developed by advertising executives in the 1950s to increase the creativity of their groups, and only after it had made its mark in ad groups did psychologists begin to conduct research on it. **Brainstorming** is a form of creative thinking in groups, using a procedure in which all group members are encouraged to generate as many ideas as possible without holding back or worrying about being wrong. They are also encouraged to build on each other's ideas. The core assumption is that creative people can feed off each other's thinking processes and creative energy, thereby coming up with more and better ideas than could the same number of people working alone.

The benefits of brainstorming have been gradually confirmed by careful research. Compared against the same number of people working alone, people working together in a brainstorming group session enjoy the process of generating ideas more than people who toil alone. When they finish the work, they evaluate it more favorably, rating it as more creative and successful. People who work alone but hear about brainstorming groups also immediately recognize the advantages of brainstorming and express the belief that they would do better if they were in

---

BRAINSTORMING a form of creative thinking in groups, using a procedure in which all group members are encouraged to generate as many ideas as possible

© Mike Baldwin / Cornered

"OK, let's hear it. But I'm warning you, it better not be another one of your half-baked ideas."

© Mike Baldwin/CartoonStock

a brainstorming group (Paulus, Dzindolet, Poletes, & Camacho, 1993; Stroebe, Diehl, & Abakoumkin, 1992).

But that's all. If you read the preceding paragraph carefully, you probably noticed that it didn't say that the brainstorming groups actually performed better—only that they thought they were better, and they had more fun. When researchers actually check the quality and quantity of ideas, the performance of brainstorming groups is quite disappointing. In a meta-analysis, Mullen, Johnson, and Salas (1991) combined the results of 18 separate studies and concluded that the output of brainstorming groups is substantially lower than that of people working separately. Eight people working individually produce more ideas than eight people brainstorming. Nor does brainstorming increase quality by sacrificing quantity; the quality of work coming out of the brainstorming groups is lower too. In short, brainstorming doesn't improve creative output—it reduces it.

The brainstorming research was disappointing but not surprising. There is a long tradition of groups being regarded as having negative traits: immoral, dangerous, stupid, impulsive, violent, and even beastly (e.g., Mackay, 1841/1932). The French writer Gustave le Bon (1908) wrote that when people come together in a group, they lose their ability to think as reasonable human beings and instead become dominated by the "group mind," which effectively moves them to a lower, more animalistic level of evolution.

Francis Galton (1822–1911), the pioneering scientist who stimulated much research in psychology, thought that most people were not very intelligent, and groups of people even less so. One day he attended a fair where there was a contest to guess the weight of a steer. The very large animal was there to be viewed, but the contest was made more difficult by the rule that the guess had to be how much the creature would weigh after being slaughtered and prepared for sale. People paid a small amount for a ticket, on which they would write their guesses, and the most accurate guess would win a prize. Some contestants were cattle farmers or butchers who might have had some knowledge of meat weights, but most others knew little about it and couldn't offer much more than a guess based on whim or a lucky number. After the contest, Galton obtained the 800 tickets and did some statistics on the guesses, hoping to provide more data on the foolishness and stupidity of the herd of common people (Surowiecki, 2004).

The correct answer was 1,198 pounds. When Galton compiled the 800 guesses, thinking they would be way off, he found their average to be 1,197. He was stunned. How could all those unintelligent, uninformed people produce an almost perfect answer?

This anecdote was used by James Surowiecki (2004) to open his book *The Wisdom of Crowds*. Surowiecki's work is an important counterweight to the long tradition of research indicating that groups produce stupid judgments. He has compiled an impressive list of patterns in which the collective wisdom turns out to be smarter than even the experts. For example, no expert on sports is consistently able to predict the outcome of sports events better than the final betting line, which is directly based on the bets of many individuals, even though those bets are distorted by wishful thinking, whims, guesses, and favorite colors. Likewise, almost no stockbroker can consistently pick winning stocks better than the market as a whole.

One of the most dramatic, if less scientific, illustrations of the power of collective wisdom comes from the television show *Who Wants to Be a Millionaire?* This is a game show (featured in the recent Academy-Award-winning movie *Slum Dog Millionaire*) in which contestants can win large sums of money by giving only correct answers to a series of questions. Each multiple-choice question has four possible answers. When stumped, the contestant can either call an expert (selected in advance, usually the smartest or most knowledgeable person the contestant knows) or poll the studio audience. Surowiecki went through the statistics on how these "lifelines" worked out. Calling an expert was pretty good, producing the correct answer about two-thirds (65%) of the time. But polling the studio audience yielded the right answer 91% of the time! Thus, a crowd of random people sitting in a television studio was more likely to get the right answer than a carefully chosen expert.

It is remarkable to think that large groups of people are smarter than the smartest individuals, but under the right circumstances they are. "It's as if we've been programmed to be collectively smart," said Surowiecki (2004, p. 11). But the conditions that enable crowds to achieve this high level of intelligent functioning are often violated, as we will see below in connection with groupthink and other group processes. These conditions include diversity of opinion and independence. That is, each person must be able to think for himself or herself, and each person must be able to get some information from his or her own perspective. If everyone is forced or pressured to think the same thing, or if their main information is seeing what everyone else does, watch out—group wisdom may degenerate into group stupidity.

Many people working independently, all getting their own bits of information, often produce a surprisingly accurate average. If someone can pull together that information, the group can be wise. But when groups fall into the trap of following each other or conforming to dominant views, their power is lost. These conclusions fit this book's theme of regarding humans as cultural animals. In order to perform effectively, people must operate as separate, independent members of a group, pooling and sharing their diverse information. Only then do people become "collectively smart," in Surowiecki's words.

You may notice a seeming contradiction. Groups can be smarter than individuals, but brainstorming groups don't perform as well as independent individuals. But brainstorming groups don't meet Surowiecki's criteria for success. Group members don't work independently and contribute their separate ideas—rather, they interact, which raises the likelihood that some will feel left out, will defer to the opinions of others, will be too shy to criticize the group, or in other ways will be held back from contributing what they can.

WHY DO PEOPLE LOVE TEAMS?

We have seen that groups often do not perform as well as a number of individuals working alone (though groups do usually outperform a single person). Why do people love the idea of working in groups? Why do American companies want everyone to be a "team player"? Why do they form teams?

The section on brainstorming suggested a partial answer. It noted that people believe teams will outperform the same number of people working individually (even though that belief usually turns out to be wrong). Maybe people are just stuck in a mistaken view of reality and make their decisions based on that mistake.

A more complex and reasonable answer was furnished by Allen and Hecht (2004). They reviewed a great many published studies and noted a consistent

In the television game show *Who Wants to Be a Millionaire?* people who are stumped get more questions correct when they poll the studio audience (91%) than when they ask an expert (65%). Surely the audience members aren't smarter than a preselected expert!

pattern. Many people, including business managers, believe that teams are highly effective for improving performance, but in reality the majority of teams don't live up to their reputation (either in the lab or in real business organizations). If performance were the only measure, then most corporations and other organizations should forget about teamwork and cultivate individual excellence. But performance is not the only measure, and working in teams has many side benefits. People enjoy their work more. Working in teams satisfies their need to belong. It enables them to feel confident, effective, and superior (if only because many members of teams think they are the star, or at least a crucial team member who deserves a large share of the credit for any success the team has). The enjoyment and other psychological benefits of teams may explain why people are so eager to form and join them, even if they really do not improve performance most of the time.

TRANSACTIVE MEMORY: HERE, YOU REMEMBER THIS

As we have seen, groups are most likely to be "collectively smart" if members' minds work independently. The best strategy may be for members to specialize as to who remembers what. In a world of information overload, there is simply too much for any one person to remember. Hence the solution: Different people should focus on different things.

The idea that information is dispersed through the group runs directly contrary to the old "group

Working in teams provides many psychological benefits.

better when they are trained together, in part because they can help slot people into particular roles for learning different things. That is, the group can speed its learning by figuring out who is good at what parts of the task. As a result, each person can concentrate on learning his or her specialty, rather than everyone trying to learn everything (Liang, Moreland, & Argote, 1995; Moreland, Argote, & Krishnan, 1996, 1998).

GROUPTHINK

Irving Janis (1972, 1982) introduced the term **groupthink** to social psychology. The term itself is borrowed from novelist George Orwell, who used it in his novel about totalitarianism called *1984*. The term refers to the tendency of group members to think alike. Janis used it specifically to mean a style of thought in which the group clings to a shared but flawed or mistaken view of the world rather than being open to learning the truth. In decision making, groupthink means that the group sticks to its preferred course of action, refusing to consider alternatives fairly and refusing to recognize the dangers or flaws in its plan.

The roots of groupthink probably lie in the desire to get along. Members of a group do not want to spend all their time arguing, nor do they want the other members to dislike them. They most enjoy being together and working together when they all agree. In principle, a group will have the most information if people bring diverse viewpoints and air conflicting opinions (as noted in the preceding section), but such discussions can be difficult and unpleasant. Hence people become reluctant to criticize the group, attack its basic beliefs, or question each other. This creates the illusion that everyone is in agreement.

Several aspects of a situation make groupthink more likely. First, the group tends to be fairly similar and cohesive to start with (and then becomes more so as a result of groupthink). That is, the members of the group share many views and ideas in common, and they tend to get along well with each other. Second, a strong, directive leader makes groupthink more likely. Third, the group may be isolated in some sense from others, so that it is not exposed to disturbing facts or contrary views. Fourth, the group may have high self-esteem, regarding itself as a superior, elite collection of people who do not need to worry about what outsiders think or want.

Social psychologists have identified several important signs that indicate when groupthink is occurring. First, there is pressure toward conformity. Groupthink originates in people's desire to get along and, toward that end, to hold the same views and opinions.

mind" theories, according to which thinking in groups is mainly a matter of having everyone think the same thing. This contradiction was noted by Wegner (1986; Wegner, Giuliano, & Hertel, 1985), who coined the term **transactive memory** to refer to a process by which members of a small group remember different kinds of information. For example, when the electricity goes out and you need a candle, it helps if you can remember where the candles are. But it is almost as good if you know that your roommate remembers where they are. You don't have to remember everything yourself.

What makes a group most effective is if group members know about what they know and can shift responsibility for remembering to the best-suited individuals (Hollingshead & Brandon, 2003). For example, a romantic couple moving in together might start off by having the woman do the cooking, because that fits traditional roles and assumptions, but as they get to know each other they might realize that the man is more interested in food and has a better memory for recipes, so they could reallocate the role to him. In studies by Hollingshead (1998), the best performance on group memory tasks was by intimate couples who worked face to face. They did better than pairs of strangers and better than couples who were not face to face. The crucial difference was that by looking at each other, they could tell which of them knew the answer best.

Transactive memory begins at the learning stage, not just at the remembering stage. Groups perform

---

TRANSACTIVE MEMORY a process by which members of a small group remember different kinds of information

GROUPTHINK the tendency of group members to think alike

A second sign is an appearance of unanimous agreement. Because dissent is suppressed, people get the impression that everyone in the group agrees with the group's plans or views. What is said in the group meetings consists mainly of expressions of support and agreement. The illusion of consensus is sometimes furthered by **self-censorship**, which means that individuals decide not to express their doubts or bring up information that goes against the group's plans and views. Thus, many individual members of the group may have doubts or know things that spell trouble for the group, but everyone thinks that no one else does, so each person decides not to rock the boat. This creates a vicious circle: Because no one is willing to express any doubts, the impression that no one (else) has any doubts becomes very strong.

An illusion of invulnerability is a third sign. When the experts all agree, it is easy to think that nothing can go wrong. Information about risks, costs, and dangers is suppressed, everyone expresses faith and optimism, and this creates the sense that the group can accomplish almost anything. Many of the worst disasters in history have arisen because this sort of illusion of invulnerability caused groups to make decisions without fully appreciating the flaws and dangers in their plan.

A sense of moral superiority is a fourth sign. Such groups regard themselves as good and virtuous. They hold high ideals and believe that they live up to them better than other people. This belief reinforces the patterns of self-censorship and pressure to conform that we have already noted.

A fifth sign is a tendency to underestimate opponents. Groupthink helps groups regard themselves as superior. The other side of the coin is that their opponents and enemies are regarded with disrespect, disdain, and contempt. Groups who are engaging in groupthink may refuse to negotiate with their enemies because they think they are evil. They do not fear their enemies because they regard them as weak. This can prove costly, because if you underestimate your enemies, your chances for success are much less than you think, and your plans will not go smoothly.

FOOLISH COMMITTEES

Most organizations rely on committees to study issues and make decisions. This approach is based on an eminently sensible principle: It may be hard for a single person to know all sides of an issue and all aspects of a problem. By bringing together a group of people with different knowledge and different viewpoints, the outcome can be improved. Ideally, each person contributes something different, the group members respect each other's opinions, and the committee can achieve a broad level of wisdom and understanding that is above and beyond what anyone working alone could accomplish.

But ask anyone with extensive experience whether committees generally achieve high levels of wisdom and understanding. Most likely, the answer will be a laugh or a roll of the eyes. What goes wrong?

Careful laboratory studies of group decisions have begun to reveal the problems that cause committees to fail to live up to their promise. One important factor is that members of a committee want to get along with each other, so they focus more on what they have in common than on their different perspectives. These pressures toward group harmony end up stifling the free exchange of information.

In one set of studies, Stasser and Titus (1985; see also 1987) told a group of participants to decide which of two job candidates should be hired. Each member of the group was given some information about the two candidates. There were seven reasons to hire Anderson and only four reasons to hire Baker, and the group had all of the reasons—so, logically, the committee should have chosen Anderson. Yet most groups ended up choosing Baker, who was objectively the poorer candidate.

The roots of the wrong decision lay in how the information was distributed. The researchers gave each member of the group the same four reasons for choosing Baker, but they gave each person only one of the reasons for choosing Anderson. Each person got a different reason for choosing Anderson, so if the committee members managed to pool their knowledge, they would realize that there were more reasons to hire Anderson. After all, that is how committees are supposed to work, by bringing together all the different information that the various members have.

But they didn't manage to pool their information. Instead of talking about all seven different reasons for hiring Anderson, they mainly talked about the four reasons for hiring Baker. That is, their group discussion focused on what they all knew in common, rather than on the unique information each person had.

Thus, a committee can end up being less than the sum of its parts, even in purely informational terms. Instead of bringing together different views and information, committees often narrow their focus to what they have in common. Information is lost rather than gained.

GROUP POLARIZATION AND THE "RISKY SHIFT"

As we saw in the last section, committees are often formed on the principle that many people working together can be smarter and make better decisions

---

SELF-CENSORSHIP choosing not to express doubts or other information that goes against a group's plans and views

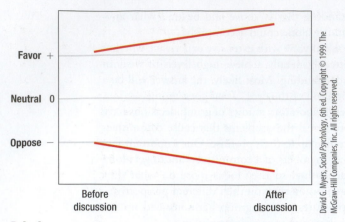

▶ **FIGURE 14.4** Group polarization occurs when group discussion leads people to become more extreme in the direction of their initial opinions.

than individuals working alone. Yet often the decisions of committees seem foolish. This has prompted research into how groups make decisions.

Early on, social psychologists stumbled onto a peculiar pattern in group decision making, which they dubbed the risky shift (Stoner, 1961; Wallach, Kogan, & Bem, 1962). The **risky shift** was defined as a tendency for groups to take greater risks than the same individuals (on average) would have decided to take individually. Somehow the process of talking about the dilemma moved the group toward a more extreme, risky view. (If you read the earlier section on groupthink, this result will not surprise you!)

Rather soon after the risky shift was discovered, exceptions began to appear. Sometimes the group would shift toward more cautious decisions, which was the opposite of a risky shift. (Some social psychologists began to speak of a "stingy shift" or a "conservative shift.") For a time, there were arguments and confusion, but the correct principle began to emerge with an important paper by Serge Moscovici and Marisa Zavalloni (1969). The effect of groups is not invariably either a risky or a stingy shift. Rather, the primary effect is to drive the group toward a greater extreme in whatever direction it was already headed. If the group leans initially toward risk, then group discussion will yield greater risk. If the group leans toward caution, discussion will make it all the more cautious.

The movement toward either extreme became known as the **group polarization effect**. (Polarization means moving away from the middle, toward either extreme.) It can be defined as a shift toward a more extreme position resulting from group discussion (illustrated in ▶ **FIGURE 14.4**).

RISKY SHIFT a tendency for groups to take greater risks than the same individuals (on average) would have decided to take individually

GROUP POLARIZATION EFFECT a shift toward a more extreme position resulting from group discussion

Group polarization depends on the fact that people in the group are fairly similar, so that they all initially lean in the same direction (e.g., they are all somewhat inclined to take a risk). This resembles what tends to happen in everyday life. Even when a large and diverse set of people are all thrown together, such as first-year students arriving at college, they soon sort themselves into groups of like-minded individuals. (As we saw in the chapter on attraction, similarity is a common and strong basis for forming friendships.) As a result, most people spend most of their time interacting with people who think and feel rather similarly. Hence when they discuss issues, they accentuate each other's beliefs and feelings, thereby contributing to group polarization.

[**QUIZ YOURSELF**]

How Groups Think

1. Which of the following is not an effect of brainstorming in groups?
   (a) People have more fun working in groups than alone.
   (b) People think that the quality and quantity of answers are better when they work in groups than when they work alone.
   (c) The quality and quantity of answers are better when people work in groups than when they work alone.
   (d) All of the above are effects of brainstorming in groups.

2. Samantha is considering a new product line to compete with the leading manufacturer in her business. Although her staff wonders privately if the new product is a good idea, they support her decision rather than undermine her authority. This is an example of _____.
   (a) deindividuation   (b) group polarization
   (c) groupthink   (d) risky shift

3. Which of the following is *not* a symptom of groupthink?
   (a) Conformity pressure
   (b) Overestimating opponents
   (c) Illusion of unanimity
   (d) Sense of moral superiority

4. The Department of Psychology is in the process of hiring a new faculty member. Although the individual members of the search committee tend to favor hiring Dr. Slight Favorite, most are still somewhat uncertain as to how they will finally vote. Friday afternoon they will discuss the candidate. What will be the most likely outcome of their deliberations?
   (a) They will decide to hire Dr. Slight Favorite.
   (b) They will decide not to hire Dr. Slight Favorite.
   (c) They will be deadlocked.
   (d) They will form another committee.

Power and Leadership

Being powerful is like being a lady. If you have to tell people you are, you aren't.
—Margaret Thatcher

Many groups strive for equality. In modern marriage, in particular, the ideal is that husband and wife own everything in common and make decisions equally, with respect and consideration for each other. In parallel, democracy is spreading through the world, with its similar emphasis on equality and joint decision making. In a democracy, each person's vote counts the same, and millions of votes may be counted in order to decide something important.

In practice, however, equality is not very efficient for making decisions, and it may have other drawbacks. Instead of full equality, most groups have leaders. Large groups don't just have leaders, they typically have a hierarchy of power, ranging from a leader at the top, down through several ranks of others who have some authority but must respect what the top leader says, down to the lowest levels of people who take orders and directives but cannot give them. Try to imagine, for example, an army that did away with all ranks and ascribed equal authority to every soldier, so that the army would never take action unless everyone (or at least a majority) voted in favor. No armies actually operate like this—and probably for very good reasons! Such an army would probably never manage to decide to fight a battle. And if it did, it would probably be hopeless at deciding what tactics to use amid the chaos, noise, trauma, and confusion of battle. Bad commanders have caused many battles to be lost, but an army without commanders would be even worse off, and it would probably lose every time.

Social psychologists have made only halting progress toward understanding the important issues of power and leadership. The importance of power in society is not matched by the extent of knowledge from research laboratories. We can well hope that future editions of this textbook will contain many more findings and general principles. Still, let's examine some of what has been learned so far.

LEADERSHIP

Leadership is vitally important but poorly understood. Bad leaders can ruin countries, organizations, or military units. One team of researchers sought to determine how big an impact the chief executive officer (CEO) has on the performance of a company, as reflected in its profits. They concluded that the answer was about 14%, or one-seventh (Joyce, Nohria, & Roberson, 2003). That is a huge impact for one person to have. Another study concluded that high-performing executives added an average of $25 million to the value of their company, as compared with average performers (Barrick, Day, Lord, & Alexander, 1991).

The importance of leadership emerged from a wide-open study of corporate success called Good to Great (Collins, 2001). The research group scanned the Fortune 1000 to identify companies that had had 15 years of below-average performance followed by 15 years of above-average performance. They found 11 companies that had undergone this sort of sustained improvement, and then the research team tried to identify what these improving companies had in common. To the surprise of the researchers, the biggest common factor was leadership: All the companies had been transformed by a new CEO who took over the organization and improved its performance.

Moreover, two traits characterized the 11 CEOs who led their companies to lasting success. One was being modest and humble. This conclusion came as a shock at the time, because the business world had been much enamored of celebrity CEOs with flamboyant, self-promoting styles and probably streaks of narcissism. The other important trait was extreme persistence, also known as "fierce resolve" (Collins, 2001). These leaders made decisions and stuck with them, even if the early results were disappointing. Recall the story about Henry Ford that opened this chapter: His first two car companies were failures, and his first attempt at a low-cost Ford, the Model N, was not very successful, but he stayed the course and achieved legendary success with the Model T.

Additional evidence suggests that most good leaders are perceived as having several basic traits (Hogan & Kaiser, 2005; Kouzes & Posner, 2002; Lord, Foti, & DeVader, 1984). Good leaders are decisive; they make a decision and stick with it. They are competent at the group's tasks. (Among hunter-gatherer tribes, which were the norm for most human beings in prehistoric times, the headman was usually one of the best hunters in the group.) Good leaders are seen as having integrity; they are honest and have good moral character (or at least they are perceived that way). Last, they have vision—some concept of what the group can become or achieve—and they use this vision to motivate other people to set aside self-interest in order to work toward the group's goals.

Another useful way of thinking about leadership divides the leader role into two components: task orientation and relationship orientation (Yukl, 2006). Task orientation means getting the job done well, and it is no accident that the best workers are often promoted into leader roles. Task oriented leaders focus on planning, motivating, coordinating inputs from group members, setting goals, and providing feedback. Relationship orientation refers to maintaining good relationships among the group. Boosting morale, resolving conflicts, taking care of group

Robert Mugabe, President of Zimbabwe.

© Jon Hrusa/epa/Corbis

Assertiveness may be helpful for the task dimension but harmful for the interpersonal dimension. The best leaders seem to strike the right balance of being somewhat but not too assertive.

TOXIC LEADERS

Bad leaders can be disastrous. History has many examples of leaders who have brought ruin, misery, and death to their followers (recall the example of Jim Jones in Chapter 8). One leader who has gone from an international hero to a despised pariah is Robert Mugabe, and his story is sobering.

Mugabe was a leader of the black uprising in Rhodesia, a relatively rich country in southern Africa. When his revolution succeeded, he became the first president of his country, newly renamed Zimbabwe. Representatives from 96 countries attended the independence ceremony, in which Mugabe promised peace and reconciliation, even assuring the 200,000 white citizens that he would be their friend and ally. The country had been impoverished by the war, but it had tremendous natural resources, including rich farmland and diamond mines, as well as a strong industrial base. Zimbabwe was seen as the potential breadbasket of southern Africa, able to grow enough food to feed much of the rest of the continent.

Over time, Mugabe narrowed his goals and focused ever more on increasing and cementing his own power. In the process he turned the once prosperous country from a breadbasket to a basket case. His talk of making the country rich through capitalism was abandoned in favor of Marxist politics, which brought poverty. Racial reconciliation was abandoned when the black majority grew impatient with Mugabe's policies, and in a transparent bid for popular support he announced that the government would confiscate farms owned by white people and give them to poor black peasants. This drove most of the white people out of the country, taking knowledge and skills with them. Then, instead of giving the confiscated farms to poor and hungry black citizens, he gave the best to his cronies and loyalists, many of whom were already rich and few of whom knew anything about farming. Food production fell dramatically, and soon many Zimbabweans were starving. Instead of exporting food to other countries, as it had once done, Zimbabwe became dependent on donations of food from the outside world. Mugabe pressed ahead: "If I see anyone with cold feet," he said, "I'll put hot irons under them."

Zimbabwe could not even buy food because the economy was in a catastrophic state. Inflation reached such high levels that the money became virtually worthless. The majority of the workforce was unemployed. Meanwhile the corrupt government continued to pay lavish salaries to its leaders, along with other perks such as frequent brand-new

members, and promoting group spirit are important parts of this component. Many leaders are good at one or the other of these two components of leadership, but a high quality leader must be good at both.

Narcissists may not necessarily make great leaders, but that does not mean that there is no link between narcissism and leadership. Narcissists may be more likely than others to become group leaders, for better or worse. In lab studies by Brunell, Gentry, Campbell, Hoffman, Kuhnert, and DeMarree (2008), groups of four strangers were assembled with no leader and assigned to discuss a problem and make a recommendation. The researchers tracked who emerged as a leader in each group. In every study, people scoring high on the trait of narcissism were most likely to emerge as leaders. This appeared to be less a matter of seeking attention than of simply wanting to be in control and having the confidence to speak up frequently. Their confidence caused other group members to defer to them.

Speaking up and being assertive in other ways may help a person move into a leadership role, but it is not necessarily a recipe for successful leadership. In research with MBA (master's of business administration) students and with actual business managers, Ames and Flynn (2007) found that as assertiveness increased, leadership quality first increased—and then decreased. Assertiveness was defined as the tendency to speak up for, defend, and promote one's values and goals. Leaders who were low in assertiveness were seen as unable to motivate people and unable to get things done, so they were ineffective. At the other extreme, highly assertive leaders were viewed negatively in interpersonal terms (even if effective in some ways): unfriendly, bossy, manipulative, and generally not likable.

The mixed effects of assertiveness mesh well with the idea of the two components of leadership.

Mercedes cars. Although the government was clearly going broke, Mugabe sent his army into a seemingly pointless civil war in the Congo, on the other side of Africa, at the cost of a million U.S. dollars a day.

In 2002, Mugabe came up for reelection, and by now there was a serious chance that the disillusioned masses would vote him out. He rigged the election shamelessly, including sponsoring systematic violence against members of the opposition party (and throwing the opposing presidential candidate into prison on trumped-up charges of treason). Colin Powell, America's first black Secretary of State, observed that Mugabe had blatantly stolen his victory. At the next election, in 2007, Mugabe came in second in the first round and looked certain to lose the runoff, whereupon his supporters became so violent against the opposition party that Mugabe's election opponent withdrew from the race.

The starving masses waited in line for food handouts from foreign donors, but Mugabe's men refused to give food to anyone who could not produce a membership card in their party. Many of the world's governments protested against how Mugabe had stolen the election, but he dismissed their accusations as nothing more than racism and continued to cement his hold on power while driving his country into ever greater ruin. When the Archbishop Desmond Tutu, a highly respected black leader who had won the Nobel Peace Prize, dared to call Mugabe a tyrant, Mugabe denounced him as an "angry, evil, and embittered little bishop." Cruel words, perhaps, but his long-suffering countrymen have endured far worse under this president.

Bosses can also make bad leaders. There are plenty of bad bosses in American business. Many surveys have found that between two-thirds and three-quarters of workers say the worst aspect of their job is their immediate boss (Hogan & Kaiser, 2005). Perhaps such surveys bring out a tendency to complain, but other, more objective methods of assessing managerial performance yield an average estimate that about half the bosses in the United States are inept (DeVries & Kaiser, 2003).

What makes some leaders so disastrous for their followers? Research has begun to fill in the picture of what makes a bad boss. After surveying many findings, one research study identified four patterns (Leslie & Van Velsor, 1996). One was simply that the person was promoted above his or her abilities and never managed to adjust to the demands and responsibilities of the new job. A second pattern was failure to build a team, as by making poor hiring choices. This may sound obvious, but it is often difficult to choose the right people for the team, especially because almost everyone knows that during a job interview you should try to project an image as a cooperative, reliable, talented, and motivated worker. Most bad bosses know how to look good during the job interview. Too bad they can't act that way after they are hired!

The third pattern of bad bosses involved poor interpersonal skills that created conflicts between the leader and subordinates. For example, some leaders may be arrogant and thus offend their group by demanding outward shows of respect and deference. ("Because I said so, that's why!") Others are simply insensitive—they don't know or don't care about the people who work for them. And the fourth pattern involved interpersonal actions that undermined the group's ability to work together, such as betraying someone's trust, failing to keep promises, taking advantage of subordinates, or frequently changing his or her mind.

One admirable attempt to distinguish dangerous leaders from others was undertaken by Jack Mayer (1993). He observed that politicians do not differ in mental health from the rest of the population, so a certain number of mentally ill people (even clinically insane) will come to power here and there. The successful ones may be able to think effectively, but the madness will be found in their emotional lives.

In particular, the dangerous leaders suffer from "emotional disregard and disconnection from others" (Mayer, 1993, p. 337). This disconnection is not necessarily harmful in anyone, and even a leader with that characteristic will not necessarily turn to violence or evil, becoming instead a legalistic or technocratic ruler. However, when the emotional disconnection is combined with a proneness to violence, there is disaster in the making. Such a leader will be willing to undertake destructive projects, pursuing dreams of glory and grandeur (or even just vindictive grudges and hatreds) without worrying much about how his or her followers may be put at risk of intense suffering. Napoleon and Hitler are good examples. Although most histories focus on their conflicts with other nations and on the struggles and sufferings of their enemies and victims, it is instructive to recall what happened to their own followers. France was bled white by Napoleon's wars, and a generation had to cope with a lack of men who could serve as heirs, husbands, and fathers. Germany suffered even worse from Hitler's wars. Napoleon once responded to the news of the battlefield deaths of his own troops by saying that "soldiers are meant to be killed," a chilling comment that revealed how little emotional connection he felt with the agony and sacrifice of the young men who followed him.

Mayer went on to outline three main sets of criteria for dangerous leaders. First was the indifference toward people's suffering, along with devaluation of other people in general. This allows the leader to manipulate, exploit, and even kill without regret. Second, the dangerous leader is intolerant of criticism, and he or she will often take steps to suppress dissent. Stifling the free press and imprisoning

Myself, your glorious leader.

All in a day's work?

dissidents are often early signs of a dangerous leader. (Mugabe, for example, has repeatedly arrested journalists who criticize his regime, and his opponent in the 2002 election was arrested for treason and could have been condemned to death.) Third, a dangerous leader has a grandiose sense of national entitlement. This corresponds to the egotism that we have already seen in the chapter on aggression as characterizing violent and dangerous individuals.

WHAT IS POWER?

Power is an important aspect of leadership, insofar as leaders make decisions that affect the group. **Power** means one person's control over another person.

Power can seem addictive. People who get a taste of power often show patterns of seeking more power. The careers of many powerful individuals, from Napoleon to John D. Rockefeller, suggest a steady rise in their grasping for ever greater power, even though the amount of power they already have seems enough to satisfy any normal person's needs and indeed far exceeds what normal folks can even dream of attaining. Napoleon, for example, was already emperor of France and held power over conquered territories all around Europe, including Germany, Austria, and Poland. Why did he need to attack Russia too?

Although power is normally understood as an aspect of control, a famous essay by Hans Morgenthau (1962) proposed that it is linked to belongingness as well. Morgenthau compared power to love, although at first blush the two may seem totally different. Yet both power and love effectively merge separate individuals. The difference is that love entails a more or less equal and mutual union, whereas

People are often afraid to question the leader.

power effects a one-sided union in which the will of the powerful person is imposed on the subordinate. Morgenthau went on to point out that this unequal merging (unlike love) ultimately fails to save the powerful person from loneliness, because the self of the subordinate effectively disappears; even at the moment of peak domination, the powerful person finds himself or herself alone again after all. Morgenthau suggests that this dissatisfaction explains why powerful people seek even more power, thinking that this will help them escape from loneliness. It also explains why powerful people often insist on displays of love from their underlings ("our beloved leader"). Yet it continues to be lonely at the top.

POWER one person's control over another person

EFFECTS OF POWER ON LEADERS

The imbalance in power causes a variety of effects, many of which appear harmful. Lord Acton, a British nobleman, is often quoted as saying "Power tends to corrupt, and absolute power corrupts absolutely." David Kipnis (1972, 1976) studied the corrupting effects of power. He assigned participants to be managers over groups of workers. By random assignment, some of the managers had considerable power, such as the ability to give pay raises and bonuses, to deduct pay, to reassign workers, and even to fire them. The other, low-power managers had no such powers and simply had the title of manager. Both were supposed to get their workers to perform well. Kipnis collected a great deal of data on how things went in these two situations.

The managers without objective powers urged the workers to do better, praised them, proposed goals and targets, and gave advice. These tactics are quite reasonable ways to influence people, but the powerful managers spurned them. Instead they issued commands, made threats, and also made promises or offers of money (using the powers they held). The ones who were given power began to use it more and more over time. What they said was part of throwing their power around.

How do powerful people perceive their underlings? Kipnis (1972) also measured how the managers in his research rated their workers. The actual performance of the workers was carefully controlled by the experimenter so that it was identical in the two conditions (powerful versus not-so-powerful managers). Yet the managers perceived these objectively identical workers in quite different ways. The managers with more power evaluated the performance of their workers much more poorly than did the managers who lacked objective power. Powerful bosses gave their workers little credit for the work they did, preferring to see the workers as simply carrying out the commands of the manager. In this way the powerful managers took credit for what was accomplished without forming a favorable view of the employees. In contrast, the managers with less power believed that the workers' own motivation and efforts were mainly responsible for what was achieved, and they rated the workers more favorably overall. Having power makes you look down on others and underestimate their worth.

How do powerful people treat their followers? The prisoner's dilemma game (discussed in Chapter 9, on prosocial behavior) forces people to make a choice between two moves. One is cooperative; the other is exploitative, self-serving, and defensive. Lindskold and Aronoff (1980) used the game to see how powerful versus less powerful people treated each other. The highly powerful individuals favored self-serving responses rather than cooperative ones. Even when

off the mark.com   by Mark Parisi
offthemark.com

OF COURSE, CUPID WAS EVENTUALLY CORRUPTED BY HIS POWER

Reprinted by permission of Atlantic Feature Syndicate/Mark Parisi.

low-power people showed a consistent pattern of being willing to cooperate, high-power people would often continue to take advantage of them and pursue their individual goals. Highly powerful people seem to disregard and even prey on the weak. These patterns certainly support Lord Acton's comment that power tends to corrupt.

Then again, not all power corrupts, and some people wield it in positive ways. Social psychologists have searched for a more balanced theory about power that can recognize its benefits as well as its costs. One general theory of power has been put forward by Keltner, Gruenfeld, and Anderson (2003). They proposed that power has five crucial effects.

Emotion. Power feels good. People with power are more likely to feel positive, pleasant emotions and to express these good feelings. For example, people who report feeling more dominant and powerful in life, such as those in leadership roles, generally report more positive and happy emotions (Watson & Clark, 1997). People with little power are more prone to feel and express negative emotions such as guilt and depression.

Rewards Versus Punishments. Power makes people attend more to rewards than to punishments, whereas lack of power has the opposite effect. Essentially, power focuses its possessors on the possibility of getting what they want. It makes them more likely to pursue whatever rewards appeal to them, including money, sex, attention, food, possessions, and success. Put another way, they look for opportunities.

Money, Power, and Laughter

Who laughs more, rich and powerful people, or poor and dependent ones? Existing theories offer bases for predicting both answers. Rich and powerful people can do what they want, so perhaps they feel free to let go and laugh, while those low in power wait to see whether others laugh first. Alternatively, people low in power might laugh at the powerful person's jokes, as a way of ingratiating themselves.

To test these hypotheses, Stillman, Baumeister, and DeWall (2007) assigned participants to high- or low-power roles and then measured how much they laughed at someone's jokes. Power was manipulated by control over money: Participants were told that a cash prize would be given to someone and either they or someone else would have the final decision. Then they interacted with someone who managed to tell several jokes, including both funny and unfunny ones. The researchers secretly recorded how much the participant laughed.

Low power led to more laughing. Apparently, having someone else control your money makes you more prone to laugh—regardless of whether the jokes are funny or not. Indeed, the researchers had difficulty coding the laughter according to whether the jokes were funny or not, because low-power people seemed to laugh even at odd times when nothing funny had been said.

Was this laughter a ploy to ingratiate themselves with the powerful person? Not necessarily. In one of the studies, participants merely watched a video of someone talking, so that nobody would seemingly know whether they laughed or not. They still laughed more. They also laughed more when they were interacting with a coworker who had no more money or power than they did.

Laughter may well be a strategy for making friends, because people like people who laugh (e.g., Fraley & Aron, 2004; Sprecher & Regan, 2002). Apparently, people who lack money and power are eager to make friends with anyone (not just those who are powerful). They become more prone to laugh at anybody's jokes—even if the jokes aren't funny! ■

Lack of money is no laughing may matter, yet people without money seem to laugh more (see *Money Matters*).

Opportunistic Flexibility. Powerful people seem to think in terms of how they can use circumstances, benefit from them, or work with them. Powerful people change their behavior more across different situations than do powerless people (Guinote, 2008). You might think that low-power people bend to situations while high-power people remain true to their inner feelings, but the reverse seems to be true. Changing to fit the situation enables the powerful person to get the most out of it. For example, powerful people plan more leisure on weekends and more work during the week, compared to less powerful people. A low-power person might plan to spend a weekend reading a novel, for example, regardless of the season, but a powerful person will take more heed of the special opportunities of winter as opposed to summer (e.g., skiing, going to the beach).

Adapting one's plans and actions to get the most out of situational opportunities is not the same as being at the mercy of the situation. Even though powerful people may change how they act, they are not pushed around by the situation. As the title of a recent article states, "Power reduces the press [as in pressure] of the situation" (Galinsky,

Magee, Gruenfeld, Whitson, & Liljenquist, 2008). High- versus low-power participants in their studies responded in different ways to seemingly identical situations. High-power people perceived more choices, conformed less to the opinions expressed by others, and generated creative ideas that were farther apart from what other people had already put forward, as compared to people low in power. In contrast, people who lack power shift their attention more to threats and dangers. Instead of thinking about how to get what they want, they focus more on how to avoid losing what they have, and they are more prone to see ambiguous situations as dangerous or threatening.

The phrase "thinking outside the box" has become something of a cliché in recent years, but it is nonetheless relevant here. If we think of the situation as the "box," then power enables people to think outside the box, but that includes finding ways to use the box to their own best advantage. People low in power remain inside the box in their thinking, and hence they may never fully appreciate what the box could do for them.

The Duplex Mind. As we have seen in this book's repeated references to the duplex mind, mental processes can be sorted into conscious, controlled ones and relatively automatic ones. Keltner et al. (2003) propose that power makes people rely more on automatic processing, whereas people who lack power engage in more controlled thinking. The reason is probably that the greater vulnerability of people low in power makes them feel the need to think carefully before acting. People who are held accountable for their actions—which is typical of people with low power—think in more complex ways, such as considering both sides of an issue rather than simply emphasizing the side they favor (Lerner & Tetlock, 1999; Tetlock, 1992). Powerful people are rarely told by others that they are wrong, so they become lazy in their thinking, which is the specialty of the automatic system.

Approach Versus Inhibition. Last, power removes inhibitions against acting, whereas a lack of power makes people more inhibited. In a sense, this theme underlies all the others, because it inclines powerful people to act assertively to pursue the rewards they want (including using others to help them get what they want), which brings the positive feeling of pursuing and getting these rewards.

The approach or action orientation makes powerful people more likely than others to engage in socially inappropriate behavior. Powerful people sometimes get into trouble when they act on their impulses without thinking about possible consequences. President Clinton nearly lost his position as leader of the free world because he briefly fooled around with a young woman on his staff and then tried to cover it up. There is some evidence that sexual harassment occurs because powerful men automatically think of sex in connection with power (Bargh, Raymond, Pryor, & Strack, 1995). This automatic thinking, along with the tendency to act impulsively to pursue what one wants (and, perhaps crucially, the willingness to regard others as means toward one's own satisfaction), increases the likelihood of trying to pressure subordinates into granting sexual favors.

As we have seen, Henry Ford used his power to create a better system that enriched himself, his family, his workers, and his stockholders, and also enriched society by providing a convenient and appealing mode of travel. Other leaders have brought disaster to their followers. Is power ultimately good or bad? Perhaps neither, according to some recent social psychology studies. These studies suggest that power increases the tendency to take action, and this can be for good or ill.

A series of studies suggested that power leads to action even if the power is logically irrelevant to the action (Galinsky, Gruenfeld, & Magee, 2003). That is, power seems to create a state of mind that favors action. Lacking power, in contrast, brings a wait-and-see mental state marked by inhibition and inaction. In one of these studies, participants played the card game blackjack after being assigned the role of either manager or worker (builder) on a

Feeling powerful makes you more likely to ask for another card. (But it doesn't make you more likely to win!)

separate task. Although being manager had nothing to do with the blackjack game, the managers were more likely to follow the active strategy of taking an additional card, whereas the low-power participants tended to stick with the cards they had been dealt and not ask for a new one. In another study, mental states were manipulated by having people remember and write about prior experiences in which they had either held power over someone or been subjected to another person's power. They performed this task while seated in a room in which an annoying fan was blowing directly on them. People in the high-power condition (those who were writing about having power over someone else) were more likely than those in the low-power condition to get up and move the fan or turn it off.

One of these studies is particularly relevant to the question of whether power is used for good or bad ends (Galinsky et al., 2003). States of mind were manipulated again by having participants write about personal experiences of having power or being at the mercy of someone else's power. Half the participants played a commons dilemma game, in which people could passively allow the common good to remain large or could actively and selfishly take points for themselves. The other participants played a different kind of game in which the active response was to donate money for a public good, whereas the passive response was to keep one's own money and rely on others to be generous. In both games, the high-power participants took the active response, whereas the low-power participants tended to be more passive. Thus, power increased the tendency to take action both for selfish gain and for the benefit of others. Power doesn't always corrupt—sometimes it ennobles, too.

The idea that power can cut both ways was supported in a different way by Lee-Chai, Chen, and

Chartrand (2001). In their studies, they looked at some leaders who felt a communal bond with their followers and at other leaders who were out for themselves without caring so much about others. The leaders who had a communal bond with their followers typically wanted to use their power to improve the lot of their underlings; in fact, many of them felt an obligation to do so. As a result, these leaders used their power to take care of their followers. In contrast, leaders who were out for themselves used their power for their own good, often to the harm or detriment of their followers. Thus, again, power can be used to harm or to benefit those who are at the mercy of the powerful.

EFFECTS OF POWER ON FOLLOWERS

Let us turn attention now from those with power to their subordinates. Being in a subordinate position, according to our definition of power, means that another person can decide what happens to you and that you may be forced to do things you do not want to do. Not surprisingly, subordinates pay extra attention to the powerful person and try to understand him or her. Careful laboratory studies have shown that when people are dependent on someone else, they spend extra time thinking about that person, analyzing that person's behavior, and trying to figure out that person's traits and personality (Erber & Fiske, 1984).

When there is conflict, the person with less power is at an obvious disadvantage. Hence people with less power will be especially prone to foster peace and harmony. When subordinates ask for peace and cooperation, the powerful person may simply take this as a given and not be very responsive, whereas when the powerful person asks for peace and harmony, low-power people should be highly receptive. Some evidence for this was provided by laboratory studies with experimental games: Lab participants low in power responded very positively when the high-power person suggested cooperation and an end to conflict (Lindskold & Aronoff, 1980).

Another fascinating study showed that people low in power adapt to the expectations of high-power people, even without realizing it (Copeland, 1994). Participants in this study were given randomly assigned, bogus information about the ostensible personality traits of their interaction partners. Power was manipulated in terms of which person was permitted to make decisions about the next phase of the study. The two participants then had a 10-minute conversation, which was tape-recorded in such a way that each person was recorded on a separate channel. Judges who did not know the experimental manipulation then listened to what each person said and

rated whether the person showed those traits that the partner had been anticipating. Low-power individuals ended up acting the way their high-power partners expected, more than the reverse. Many were unaware that they changed their behavior, and some of the changes were to the individual's own disadvantage. Thus, when power is unequal, the lower-ranking person may unwittingly make a variety of changes in behavior as influenced by the unstated expectations of the person high in power, even if the low-power person might not want to make those changes.

LEGITIMATE LEADERSHIP

The maintenance of power often depends on legitimizing myths (Chen & Tyler, 2001). **Legitimizing myths** purport to explain and justify why people in power deserve to be in power. In an ostensible meritocracy, those in power have to contend that they have superior merit, such as by being smarter, more talented, or harder working than those who rank below them. After all, some degree of inequality is inevitable, and nearly all societies have power structures, so the crucial question is whether the inequality of power is fair and legitimate. The individuals or groups in power must typically find some reason that everyone will accept as establishing that their power is indeed fair and legitimate.

In short, the quest to bolster legitimacy is typically an ongoing problem for those in power. Even as they hold and exercise power, they must remain on the lookout for ideas or values that can be used to justify their position of power and their influence over others.

LEGITIMIZING MYTHS explanations used to justify why people in power deserve to be in power

> [QUIZ YOURSELF]
> # Power and Leadership
>
> 1. What two traits are possessed by CEOs who lead their companies to lasting success?
>   (a) Good looks and intelligence
>   (b) Humility and persistence
>   (c) Persistence and intelligence
>   (d) Narcissism and persistence
> 2. Powerful is to powerlessness as _____ is to _____.
>   (a) affect; cognition   (b) cognition; affect
>   (c) approach; inhibition (d) inhibition; approach
> 3. Research has shown that in the prisoner's dilemma game, more powerful people choose to _____ and less powerful people choose to _____.
>   (a) cooperate; cooperate (b) cooperate; defect
>   (c) defect; cooperate   (d) defect; defect
> 4. Research shows that power leads to _____.
>   (a) action   (b) competition
>   (c) cooperation   (d) inaction

Putting the Cultural Animal in Perspective

In this chapter we have glimpsed some of the best and the worst of human nature. Sometimes, as in violent lynch mobs and mass murder campaigns, groups bring out the worst in people and enable them to do things much more terrible than they would likely do alone. Other times, as on the assembly line, groups manage to achieve things that would be far beyond the powers of all the same group members acting individually.

One pattern we have seen is that submerging the individual in the group often leads to bad outcomes such as violence, groupthink, and the waste of resources in the commons dilemma, whereas keeping people individually identified and accountable helps to promote positive results. Humans are perhaps much better equipped than other animals to maintain separate, accountable identities, so humans can benefit from groups in ways that most other animals cannot.

Role differentiation and the division of labor help make human groups especially effective. People can take on and adapt to different roles, and they can design and function in a group that is a network of individually defined roles. Culture is especially powerful for creating such systems of interlocking, complementary roles. It is possible that human beings first created culture in order to enjoy some of these benefits of group systems. Groups of animals may have a couple of roles, such as male and female, or leader and follower, but human groups such as corporations and universities can consist of hundreds of different roles with separate jobs and distinct functions.

The distinctively human traits make some effects stronger than those found in animals. We saw that social facilitation occurs in animals (even cockroaches!), but among humans the impact of others is intensified by evaluation apprehension. People are better than animals at anticipating how others will evaluate them and at adjusting their behavior accordingly.

Communication is important to the success of many groups. As language users, people can communicate much more effectively than other animals. To be sure, this does not always lead to good results, because (as in groupthink) people can use their words to put pressure on others to conform to a faulty idea. By and large, though, good communication is central to the great success of human groups.

Power and leadership are found in the animal world, but they too take on new dimensions in human society. For one thing, the power of communication enables humans to preside over much larger groups. (Millions of U.S. citizens follow the laws made by their government, for example, even though they might never meet the president or any member of Congress face to face.)

More impressively, perhaps, humans have gradually developed means of transferring power without violence. Among most animals, power is held by the strongest male, who has his way with food and females until another male comes along and physically defeats him. Through most of human history, many rulers retained power until their death. A remarkable achievement of the modern era has been the democratic transfer of power, whereby the person or party that loses an election will peacefully turn over power to a new set of rulers. In some parts of the world, this has still never happened, but the tide of history seems to spread peaceful democratic transition to more and more places.

Restricting power has been one of the great achievements of human culture. As we saw, in groups of animals, the leader can do almost anything he (or less often she) wants. Humans have gradually learned to hold their leaders accountable. The progress of culture has included imposing more and more restrictions on power, so that even the topmost leaders can be arrested, put on trial, and removed from office against their will. Even in the family, the husband or father no longer holds the extreme power over his wife and children that was common in many earlier societies, a power that at times has extended to life and death. Humans use laws—which are among the most powerful elements of culture—to restrict and restrain the uses of power. In this way, abuses of power can be reduced, and life can become better for the vast majority of people.

chapter summary

WHAT GROUPS ARE AND DO

- Humans can use the power of culture to form groups that can achieve far more than collections of individuals operating alone.
- In human evolution, a tendency to form groups may have been beneficial because
  - There is safety in numbers.
  - Group members can help each other find food.
- Groups can accomplish tasks that would be too difficult for lone individuals.
- Cultural groups preserve information and pass it along to future generations.

- Cultural groups can use information, as well as reason from experience, to organize themselves.
- Cultural groups benefit from role differentiation and division of labor.

GROUPS, ROLES, AND SELVES

- Complementary roles (as in the role differentiation of cultural groups) produce

better results than simply having everyone do the same thing.

- Human roles work in the context of a large system in which most other people do something else.
- In fascist movements, the individual's self-interest is subordinated to the best interests of the group.
- Putting the best interests of the collective (that is, society as a whole) above those of the individual makes tyranny more likely.
- Culture creates roles that are independent of the individuals who occupy those roles.
- Human selves are flexible enough to take on (and occasionally drop) roles.
- Optimal distinctiveness theory refers to the tension between trying to be similar to everyone in the group and trying to be different from others.
- Identifying people in groups and holding them accountable for their actions produces better outcomes.

GROUP ACTION

- Zajonc's theory of social facilitation states that the presence of others increases arousal, which increases the dominant response tendency (the most common response in that situation).
- Social facilitation theory states that the presence of others can make people perform better, especially on easy and familiar tasks.
- The presence of others can change people's eating patterns.
- Narcissists are individuals who regard themselves as better than others and are constantly trying to win the admiration of others.

- Evaluation apprehension may intensify the effects of others' presence.
- Social loafing (also called the free rider problem) refers to the finding that people reduce effort when working in a group, compared to when working alone, especially if their work is not individually identifiable.
- The bad apple effect refers to the finding that one loafer can cause other workers to loaf as well.
- Deindividuation refers to a loss of self-awareness and of individual accountability in a group, which can lead to antisocial behavior.
- The commons dilemma is the tendency for shared or jointly owned resources to be squandered and not used in an optimal or advantageous fashion (the "tragedy of the commons").
- Communication, personality, mood, and the behavior of others all affect the tendency to overuse a common resource (the commons dilemma).

HOW GROUPS THINK

- Brainstorming involves encouraging group members to share and generate as many ideas as possible without holding back or worrying about being wrong; it produces less creative output but is liked better than working separately.
- Large groups of people can make better predictions than the smartest members of the group if people operate as separate, independent members and then pool and share their diverse information.
- Transactive memory refers to a process by which the members of a small group remember different kinds of information.
- Groupthink refers to the tendency of group members to think alike. It is especially likely if the group
  - Is similar and cohesive
  - Has a strong, directive leader
  - Is isolated from other ideas
  - Has high self-esteem
- Groupthink is marked by these symptoms:
  - Pressure toward conformity

- An appearance of unanimous agreement
- An illusion of invulnerability
- A sense of moral superiority
- Underestimation of opponents
- Groups tend to focus more on information held in common by all members than on unique information each person has.
- The risky shift is the tendency for groups to take greater risks than the same individuals (on average) would have decided to take individually.
- The group polarization effect is defined as a shift toward a more extreme position resulting from group discussion.

POWER AND LEADERSHIP

- Large groups typically have a hierarchy of power.
- Successful leaders are humble and extremely persistent.
- People who are perceived as good leaders have integrity, decisiveness, competence, and vision.
- Power refers to one person's control over another person's outcomes and behavior.
- Power has five crucial effects on the powerful: it feels good, it alters attention to rewards and punishments, it changes the relationships between people, it makes people rely more on automatic processing, and it removes inhibitions against taking action.
- People with less power are especially prone to fostering peace and harmony. They adapt to the expectations of high-power people, even without realizing it.
- Legitimizing myths purport to explain why those in power deserve to be in power.

WHAT MAKES US HUMAN? PUTTING THE CULTURAL ANIMAL IN PERSPECTIVE

- Submerging the individual in the group often leads to bad outcomes.
- Humans have gradually developed means of transferring power without violence.
- Restricting power has been one of the great achievements of human culture.

Key Terms

Altruistic punishment 441
Bad apple effect 440
Brainstorming 443
Commons dilemma 432
Deindividuation 434
Dominant response 437

Evaluation
  apprehension 437
Group 432
Group polarization
  effect 448
Groupthink 446

Legitimizing myths 456
Narcissists 439
Optimal distinctiveness
  theory 435
Power 452
Risky shift 448

Self-censorship 447
Social facilitation
  theory 437
Social loafing (free rider
  problem) 440
Transactive memory 446

[Quiz Yourself] Answers

1. What Groups Are and Do
Answers: 1=c, 2=c, 3=b, 4=d

2. Groups, Roles, and Selves
Answers: 1=b, 2=c, 3=a, 4=b

3. Group Action
Answers: 1=c, 2=a, 3=d, 4=a

4. How Groups Think
Answers: 1=c, 2=c, 3=b, 4=a

5. Power and Leadership
Answers: 1=b, 2=c, 3=c, 4=a

Media Learning Resources

Make sure you check out the complete set of learning resources and study tools below. If your instructor did not order these items with your new book, go to www.ichapters.com to purchase Cengage Learning print and digital products.

Social Psychology and Human Nature BOOK COMPANION WEBSITE

www.cengage.com/psychology/baumeister
Visit your book companion website, where you will find flash cards, practice quizzes, Internet links, and more to help you study.

CENGAGENOW™ JUST WHAT YOU NEED TO KNOW NOW!

Spend time on what you need to master rather than on information you have already learned. Take a pre-test for this chapter, and CengageNOW will generate a personalized study plan based on your results. The study plan will identify the topics you need to review and direct you to online resources to help you master those topics. You can then take a post-test to help you determine the concepts you have mastered and what you will still need to work on. Try it out! Go to www.cengage.com/login to sign in with an access code or to purchase access to this product.

CLASSIC AND CONTEMPORARY VIDEOS STUDENT CD-ROM

To see videos on the topics and experiments discussed in this chapter and to learn more about the research that social psychologists are doing today, go to the Student CD-ROM.

SOCIAL PSYCH LAB

These unique online labs give you the opportunity to become a participant in actual experiments, including re-creations of classic and contemporary research studies.

Glossary

||||||||||||||||||||||||||||||||||||||||||||||||||||||||||||||||||||||||||||||||||||||||||||||||||||||||||

A–B PROBLEM the problem of inconsistency between attitudes (A) and behaviors (B)

ABC TRIAD Affect (how people feel inside), **B**ehavior (what people do), **C**ognition (what people think about)

ACCESSIBILITY how easily something comes to mind

ACTOR/OBSERVER BIAS the tendency for actors to make external attributions and observers to make internal attributions

ADVERTISEMENT WEAR-OUT inattention and irritation that occurs after an audience has encountered the same advertisement too many times

AFFECT the automatic response that something is good or bad

AFFECT-AS-INFORMATION HYPOTHESIS the idea that people judge something as good or bad by asking themselves "How do I feel about it?"

AFFECT BALANCE the frequency of positive emotions minus the frequency of negative emotions

AFFECTIVE FORECASTING the ability to predict one's emotional reactions to future events

AGENT SELF (EXECUTIVE FUNCTION) the part of the self involved in control, including both control over other people and self-control

AGGRESSION any behavior intended to harm another person who is motivated to avoid the harm

ALTRUISTIC HELPING when a helper seeks to increase another's welfare and expects nothing in return

ALTRUISTIC PUNISHMENT the finding that people will sometimes sacrifice their own gain for the betterment of all, by punishing people who cheat the system

ANCHORING AND ADJUSTMENT the tendency to judge the frequency or likelihood of an event by using a starting point (called an anchor) and then making adjustments up or down

ANGER an emotional response to a real or imagined threat or provocation

ANTHROPOLOGY the study of human culture—the shared values, beliefs, and practices of a group of people

ANTISOCIAL BEHAVIOR behavior that either damages interpersonal relationships or is culturally undesirable

APPLIED RESEARCH research that focuses on solving particular practical problems

APPRAISAL MOTIVE the simple desire to learn the truth about oneself, whatever it is

AROUSAL a physiological reaction, including faster heartbeat and faster or heavier breathing, linked to most conscious emotions

ASSUMPTIVE WORLDS the view that people live in social worlds based on certain beliefs (assumptions) about reality

ATTACHMENT THEORY a theory that classifies people into four attachment styles (secure, preoccupied, dismissing avoidant, and fearful avoidant) based on two dimensions (anxiety and avoidance)

ATTITUDE POLARIZATION the finding that people's attitudes become more extreme as they reflect on them

ATTITUDES global evaluations toward some object or issue

ATTRACTION anything that draws two or more people together, making them want to be together and possibly to form a lasting relationship

ATTRIBUTION CUBE an attribution theory that uses three types of information: consensus, consistency, and distinctiveness

ATTRIBUTIONS the causal explanations people give for their own and others' behaviors, and for events in general

AUDIENCE INHIBITION failure to help in front of others for fear of feeling like a fool if one's offer of help is rejected

AUTOKINETIC EFFECT illusion, caused by very slight movements of the eye, that a stationary point of light in a dark room is moving

AUTOMATIC AFFECT a quick response of liking or disliking toward something

AUTOMATIC EGOTISM response by the automatic system that "everything good is me, and everything bad is not me"

AUTOMATIC SYSTEM the part of the mind outside of consciousness that performs simple operations

AVAILABILITY HEURISTIC the tendency to judge the frequency or likelihood of an event by the ease with which relevant instances come to mind

AVERSIVE RACISM simultaneously holding egalitarian values and negative feelings toward minorities

BAD APPLE EFFECT the idea that one person who breaks the rules (or one social loafer) can inspire other people to break the rules (or loaf) also

BAIT-AND-SWITCH influence technique based on commitment, in which one draws people in with an attractive offer that is unavailable and then switches them to a less attractive offer that is available

BALANCE THEORY (P-O-X THEORY) the idea that relationships among one person (P), the other person (O), and an attitude object (X) may be either balanced or unbalanced

BASE RATE FALLACY the tendency to ignore or underuse base rate information and instead to be influenced by the distinctive features of the case being judged

BEHAVIORISM theoretical approach that seeks to explain behavior in terms of learning principles, without reference to inner states, thoughts, or feelings

BELIEF IN A JUST WORLD the assumption that life is essentially fair, that people generally get what they deserve and deserve what they get

BELIEF PERSEVERANCE the finding that once beliefs form, they are resistant to change, even if the information on which they are based is discredited

BELIEFS pieces of information about something; facts or opinions

BETWEEN-SUBJECTS DESIGN an experiment in which each participant is exposed to only one level of the independent variable

BIOLOGICAL PSYCHOLOGY (PHYSIOLOGICAL PSYCHOLOGY, NEUROSCIENCE) the study of what happens in the brain, nervous system, and other aspects of the body

BRAINSTORMING a form of creative thinking in groups, using a procedure in which all group members are encouraged to generate as many ideas as possible

BROADEN-AND-BUILD THEORY the proposition that positive emotions expand an individual's attention and mind-set

BYSTANDER EFFECT the finding that people are less likely to offer help when they are in a group than when they are alone

CANNON–BARD THEORY OF EMOTION the proposition that emotional stimuli activate the thalamus, which then activates both the cortex, producing an experienced emotion, and the hypothalamus and autonomic nervous system, producing physiological arousal

CAPACITY FOR CHANGE the active phase of self-regulation; willpower

CAPACITY TO DELAY GRATIFICATION the ability to make immediate sacrifices for later rewards

CATEGORIZATION the natural tendency of humans to sort objects into groups

CATHARSIS THEORY the proposition that expressing negative emotions produces a healthy release of those emotions and is therefore good for the psyche

CENTRAL ROUTE (SYSTEMATIC PROCESSING) the route to persuasion that involves careful and thoughtful consideration of the content of the message (conscious processing)

CERTAINTY EFFECT in decision making, the greater weight given to definite outcomes than to probabilities

CLASSICAL CONDITIONING a type of learning in which, through repeated pairings, a neutral stimulus comes to evoke a conditioned response

CLINICAL PSYCHOLOGY branch of psychology that focuses on behavior disorders and other forms of mental illness, and how to treat them

COGNITIVE COPING the idea that beliefs play a central role in helping people cope with and recover from misfortunes

COGNITIVE DISSONANCE THEORY the theory that inconsistencies produce psychological discomfort, leading people to rationalize their behavior or change their attitudes

COGNITIVE MISER a term used to describe people's reluctance to do much extra thinking

COGNITIVE PSYCHOLOGY the study of thought processes, such as how memory works and what people notice

COMMITMENT a conscious decision that remains constant

COMMONS DILEMMA the tendency for shared or jointly owned resources to be squandered and not used in an optimal or advantageous fashion

COMMUNAL RELATIONSHIPS relationships based on mutual love and concern, without expectation of repayment

COMPANIONATE LOVE (AFFECTIONATE LOVE) mutual understanding and caring to make the relationship succeed

COMPETITION situation in which people can attain their goals only if others do not

CONDITIONED RESPONSE a response that, through repeated pairings, is evoked by a formerly neutral stimulus

CONDITIONED STIMULUS a neutral stimulus that, through repeated pairings with an unconditioned stimulus, comes to evoke a conditioned response

CONFEDERATE a research assistant pretending to be another participant in a study

CONFIRMATION BIAS the tendency to notice, search for, and focus on information that supports one's expectations or beliefs and to ignore information that contradicts them

CONFORMITY going along with the crowd

CONFOUNDING occurs when the effects of two variables cannot be separated

CONJUNCTION FALLACY the tendency to see an event as more likely as it becomes more specific because it is joined with elements that seem similar to events that are likely

CONSCIOUS EMOTION a powerful and clearly unified feeling state, such as anger or joy

CONSCIOUS SYSTEM the part of the mind that performs complex operations

CONSENSUS in attribution theory, whether other people would do the same thing in the same situation

CONSISTENCY in attribution theory, whether the person typically behaves this way in this situation

CONSISTENCY MOTIVE a desire to get feedback that confirms what the person already believes about himself or herself

CONSTRUCT VALIDITY OF THE CAUSE the extent to which the independent variable is a valid representation of the theoretical stimulus

CONSTRUCT VALIDITY OF THE EFFECT the extent to which the dependent variable is a valid representation of the theoretical response

CONTACT HYPOTHESIS the idea that regular interaction between members of different groups reduces prejudice, providing that it occurs under favorable conditions

CONTAMINATION when something becomes impure or unclean

CONVERT COMMUNICATORS people perceived as credible sources because they are arguing against their own previously held attitudes and behaviors

COOLIDGE EFFECT the sexually arousing power of a new partner (greater than the appeal of a familiar partner)

COOPERATION situation in which people work together with others to achieve a common goal

COPING the general term for how people attempt to deal with traumas and go back to functioning effectively in life

CORRELATION the relationship or association between two variables

CORRELATION COEFFICIENT (r) the statistical relationship or association between two variables

CORRELATIONAL APPROACH a nonexperimental method in which the researcher merely observes whether variables are associated or related

COUNTERFACTUAL THINKING imagining alternatives to past or present events or circumstances

COUNTERREGULATION the "what the heck" effect that occurs when people indulge in a behavior they are trying to regulate after an initial regulation failure

COVARIATION PRINCIPLE for something to be the cause of a behavior, it must be present when the behavior occurs and absent when the behavior does not occur

CULTURAL ANIMAL the view that evolution shaped the human psyche so as to enable humans to create and take part in culture

CULTURE an information-based system that includes shared ideas and common ways of doing things

CULTURE OF HONOR a society that places high value on individual respect, strength, and virtue, and accepts and justifies violent action in response to threats to one's honor

DEBIASING reducing errors and biases by getting people to use controlled processing rather than automatic processing

DEINDIVIDUATION a sense of anonymity and loss of individual accountability in a group, making people more likely to engage in antisocial behaviors such as theft

DEPENDENT VARIABLE the variable in a study that represents the result of the events and processes

DESCRIPTIVE NORMS norms that specify what most people do

DEVELOPMENTAL PSYCHOLOGY the study of how people change across their lives, from conception and birth to old age and death

DIFFUSION OF RESPONSIBILITY the reduction in feeling responsible that occurs when others are present

DIRECT AGGRESSION any behavior that intentionally harms another person who is physically present

DISCONTINUITY EFFECT the finding that groups are more extreme, and often more hostile, than individuals

DISCRIMINATION unequal treatment of different people based on the groups or categories to which they belong

DISMISSING AVOIDANT ATTACHMENT style of attachment in which people are low on anxiety but high on avoidance; they tend to view partners as unreliable, unavailable, and uncaring

DISRUPT-THEN-REFRAME TECHNIQUE influence technique in which one disrupts critical thinking by introducing an unexpected element, then reframes the message in a positive light

DISTINCTIVENESS in attribution theory, whether the person would behave differently in a different situation

DISTRESS-MAINTAINING STYLE OF ATTRIBUTION tendency of unhappy couples to attribute their partner's good acts to external factors and bad acts to internal factors

DOMESTIC VIOLENCE (FAMILY VIOLENCE, INTIMATE-PARTNER VIOLENCE) violence that occurs within the home or family, between people who have a close relationship with each other

DOMINANT RESPONSE the most common response in a given situation

DOOR-IN-THE-FACE TECHNIQUE influence technique based on reciprocity, in which one starts with an inflated request and then retreats to a smaller request that appears to be a concession

DOUBLE STANDARD condemning women more than men for the same sexual behavior (e.g., premarital sex)

DOWNWARD COUNTERFACTUALS imagining alternatives that are worse than actuality

DOWNWARD SOCIAL COMPARISON comparing oneself to people who are worse off

DUAL ATTITUDES different evaluations of the same attitude object, implicit versus explicit

DUPLEX MIND the idea that the mind has two different processing systems (conscious and automatic)

ECONOMICS the study of the production, distribution, and consumption of goods and services, and the study of money

EFFORT JUSTIFICATION the finding that when people suffer or work hard or make sacrifices, they will try to convince themselves that it is worthwhile

EGOISTIC HELPING when a helper seeks to increase his or her own welfare by helping another

ELABORATION LIKELIHOOD MODEL (ELM) theory that posits two routes to persuasion, via either conscious or automatic processing

EMOTION a conscious evaluative reaction to some event

EMOTIONAL INTELLIGENCE (EQ) the ability to perceive, access and generate, understand, and reflectively regulate emotions

EMPATHY reacting to another person's emotional state by experiencing the same emotional state

EMPATHY–ALTRUISM HYPOTHESIS the idea that empathy motivates people to reduce other people's distress, as by helping or comforting

EMPATHY–SPECIFIC PUNISHMENT HYPOTHESIS the idea that empathy triggers the fear of social punishment (e.g., guilt, shame, censure) that can be avoided by helping

EMPATHY–SPECIFIC REWARD HYPOTHESIS the idea that empathy triggers the need for social reward (e.g., praise, honor, pride) that can be gained by helping

ENDOWMENT EFFECT the finding that items gain in value to the person who owns them

ENTITY THEORISTS those who believe that traits are fixed, stable things (entities) and thus people should not be expected to change

EQUALITY the idea that everyone gets the same amount, regardless of what he or she contributes

EQUITY the idea that each person receives benefits in proportion to what he or she contributes

EROS in Freudian theory, the constructive, life-giving instinct

EROTIC PLASTICITY the degree to which the sex drive can be shaped and altered by social, cultural, and situational forces

ERROR MANAGEMENT THEORY the idea that both men and women seek to minimize the most costly type of error, but that men's and women's goals, and hence worst errors, differ

EVALUATION APPREHENSION concern about how others are evaluating your performance

EVOLUTIONARY THEORY theory of sexuality asserting that the sex drive has been shaped by natural selection and that its forms thus tend to be innate

EXCHANGE RELATIONSHIPS relationships based on reciprocity and fairness, in which people expect something in return

EXCITATION TRANSFER the idea that arousal from one event can transfer to a later event

EXPERIMENT a study in which the researcher manipulates an independent variable and randomly assigns people to groups (levels of the independent variable)

EXPERIMENTAL REALISM the extent to which study participants get so caught up in the procedures that they forget they are in an experiment

EXPERTISE how much a source knows

EXPLICIT ATTITUDES controlled and conscious evaluative responses

EXTERNAL VALIDITY the extent to which the findings from a study can be generalized to other people, other settings, and other time periods

EXTRADYADIC SEX having sex with someone other than one's regular relationship partner, such as a spouse or boy/girlfriend

EXTRINSIC MOTIVATION performing an activity because of something that results from it

FACIAL FEEDBACK HYPOTHESIS the idea that feedback from the face muscles evokes or magnifies emotions

FACTORIAL DESIGN an experiment that includes more than one independent variable or factor

FALSE CONSENSUS EFFECT the tendency to overestimate the number of other people who share one's opinions, attitudes, values, and beliefs

FALSE UNIQUENESS EFFECT (BETTER-THAN-AVERAGE EFFECT, LAKE WOBEGON EFFECT) the tendency to underestimate the number of other people who share one's most prized characteristics and abilities

FAST-APPROACHING-DEADLINE TECHNIQUE influence technique based on scarcity, in which one tells people an item or a price is only available for a limited time

FEARFUL AVOIDANT ATTACHMENT style of attachment in which people have both high anxiety and high avoidance; they have low opinions of themselves and keep others from getting close

FIELD EXPERIMENT an experiment conducted in a real-world setting

FIGHT OR FLIGHT SYNDROME a response to stress that involves aggressing against others or running away

FIRST INSTINCT FALLACY the false belief that it is better not to change one's first answer on a test even if one starts to think that a different answer is correct

FOOT-IN-THE-DOOR TECHNIQUE influence technique based on commitment, in which one starts with a small request in order to gain eventual compliance with a larger request

FORGIVENESS ceasing to feel angry toward or seek retribution against someone who has wronged you

FRAMING whether messages stress potential gains (positively framed) or potential losses (negatively framed)

FREUDIAN PSYCHOANALYSIS theoretical approach that seeks to explain behavior by looking at the deep unconscious forces inside the person

FRUSTRATION blockage of or interference with a personal goal

FRUSTRATION-AGGRESSION HYPOTHESIS proposal that "the occurrence of aggressive behavior always presupposes the existence of frustration," and "the existence of frustration always leads to some form of aggression."

FUNDAMENTAL ATTRIBUTION ERROR (CORRESPONDENCE BIAS) the tendency for observers to attribute other people's behavior to internal or dispositional causes and to downplay situational causes

GAIN-FRAMED APPEAL focuses on the positive, such as how your teeth will be stronger and healthier if you brush and floss them every day

GAMBLER'S FALLACY the tendency to believe that a particular chance event is affected by previous events and that chance events will "even out" in the short run

GENERALIZED OTHER a combination of other people's views that tells you who and what you are

GOAL an idea of some desired future state

GOAL SHIELDING when the activation of a focal goal the person is working on inhibits the accessibility of alternative goals

GROUP a collection of at least two people who are doing or being something together

GROUP NORMS the beliefs or behaviors that a group of people accepts as normal

GROUP POLARIZATION EFFECT a shift toward a more extreme position resulting from group discussion

GROUPTHINK the tendency of group members to think alike

GUILT an unpleasant moral emotion associated with a specific instance in which one has acted badly or wrongly

HALO EFFECT the assumption that because people have one desirable trait (e.g., attractiveness) people also possess many other desirable traits (e.g., intelligence)

HEDONIC TREADMILL a theory proposing that people stay at about the same level of happiness regardless of what happens to them

HEURISTIC/SYSTEMATIC MODEL theory that posits two routes to persuasion, via either conscious or automatic processing

HEURISTICS mental shortcuts that provide quick estimates about the likelihood of uncertain events

HISTORY the study of past events

HOMOPHOBIA excessive fear of homosexuals or homosexual behavior

HOSTILE ATTRIBUTION BIAS the tendency to perceive ambiguous actions by others as aggressive

HOSTILE EXPECTATION BIAS the tendency to assume that people will react to potential conflicts with aggression

HOSTILE PERCEPTION BIAS the tendency to perceive social interactions in general as being aggressive

HOT HAND the tendency for gamblers who get lucky to think they have a "hot" hand and their luck will continue

HUMILIATION a state of disgrace or loss of self-respect (or of respect from others)

HYPOTHESIS an idea about the possible nature of reality; a prediction tested in an experiment

ILLUSION OF CONTROL the false belief that one can influence certain events, especially random or chance ones

ILLUSORY CORRELATION the tendency to overestimate the link between variables that are related only slightly or not at all

IMPLICIT ATTITUDES automatic and nonconscious evaluative responses

IMPRESSIONABLE YEARS HYPOTHESIS proposition that adolescents and young adults are more easily persuaded than their elders

INCREMENTAL THEORISTS those who believe that traits are subject to change and improvement

INDEPENDENT SELF-CONSTRUAL a self-concept that emphasizes what makes the self different and sets it apart from others

INDEPENDENT VARIABLE the variable manipulated by the researcher that is assumed to lead to changes in the dependent variable

INDIRECT AGGRESSION any behavior that intentionally harms another person who is physically absent

INFORMATION OVERLOAD having too much information to comprehend or integrate

INFORMATIONAL INFLUENCE going along with the crowd because you think the crowd knows more than you do

INGRATIATION what people actively do to try to make someone like them

INGROUP FAVORITISM preferential treatment of, or more favorable attitudes toward, people in one's own group

INGROUP MEMBERS people who belong to the same group or category as we do

INJUNCTIVE NORMS norms that specify what most others approve or disapprove of

INSTINCT an innate (inborn, biologically programmed) tendency to seek a particular goal, such as food, water, or sex

INTERACTION refers to the joint effects of more than one independent variable on the dependent variable

INTERDEPENDENT SELF-CONSTRUAL a self-concept that emphasizes what connects the self to other people and groups

INTERNAL VALIDITY the extent to which changes in the independent variable caused changes in the dependent variable

INTERPERSONAL SELF (PUBLIC SELF) the image of the self that is conveyed to others

INTIMACY a feeling of closeness, mutual understanding, and mutual concern for each other's welfare and happiness

INTRINSIC MOTIVATION wanting to perform an activity for its own sake

INTROSPECTION the process by which a person examines the contents of his or her mind and mental states

INVESTMENT MODEL theory that uses three factors—satisfaction, alternatives, and investments—to explain why people stay with their long-term relationship partners

JAMES–LANGE THEORY OF EMOTION the proposition that the bodily processes of emotion come first and the mind's perception of these bodily reactions then creates the subjective feeling of emotion

JIGSAW CLASSROOM a cooperative learning technique for reducing feelings of prejudice

KIN SELECTION the evolutionary tendency to help people who have our genes

KNOWLEDGE STRUCTURES organized packets of information that are stored in memory

LABELING TECHNIQUE influence technique based on consistency, in which one assigns a label to an individual and then requests a favor that is consistent with the label

LEARNED HELPLESSNESS belief that one's actions will not bring about desired outcomes, leading one to give up and quit trying

LEGITIMIZATION-OF-PALTRY-FAVORS TECHNIQUE influence technique in which a requester makes a small amount of aid acceptable

LEGITIMIZING MYTHS explanations used to justify why people in power deserve to be in power

LEXICAL DECISION TASK deciding as quickly as possible whether a string of letters is a real word or not

LIFE SATISFACTION an evaluation of how one's life is generally, and how it compares to some standard

LIMITED-NUMBER TECHNIQUE influence technique based on scarcity, in which one tells people that an item is in short supply

LONELINESS the painful feeling of wanting more human contact or connection than you have

LOOKING-GLASS SELF the idea that people learn about themselves by imagining how they appear to others

LOSS-FRAMED APPEAL focuses on the negative, such as the potential for getting cavities if you do not brush and floss your teeth every day

LOW-BALL TECHNIQUE influence technique based on commitment, in which one first gets a person to comply with a seemingly low-cost request and only later reveals hidden additional costs

LYING not telling the truth

MAGICAL THINKING thinking based on assumptions that don't hold up to rational scrutiny

MAIN EFFECT the effect of a single independent variable on the dependent variable, ignoring the effects of other independent variables

MATCHING HYPOTHESIS the proposition that people tend to pair up with others who are equally attractive

MERE EXPOSURE EFFECT the tendency for people to come to like things simply because they see or encounter them repeatedly

META-ANALYSIS a quantitative literature review that combines the statistical results (e.g., correlation coefficients) from all studies conducted on a topic

META-COGNITION reflecting on one's own thought processes

MINIMAL GROUP EFFECT the finding that people show favoritism toward ingroup members even when group membership is randomly determined

MODELING observing and copying or imitating the behavior of others

MONITORING keeping track of behaviors or responses to be regulated

MOOD a feeling state that is not clearly linked to some event

MUNDANE REALISM the extent to which the setting of an experiment physically resembles the real world

MUTATION a new gene or combination of genes

NARCISSISM excessive self-love and a selfish orientation

NARCISSISTS individuals who regard themselves as better than others and are constantly trying to win the admiration of others

NATURAL SELECTION the process whereby those members of a species that survive and reproduce most effectively are the ones that pass along their genes to future generations

NATURE the physical world around us, including its laws and processes

NEED FOR COGNITION a tendency to engage in and enjoy effortful thinking, analysis, and mental problem solving

NEED TO BELONG the desire to form and maintain close, lasting relationships with other individuals

NEGATIVE ATTITUDE CHANGE (BOOMERANG EFFECT) doing exactly the opposite of what one is being persuaded to do

NEGATIVE STATE RELIEF HYPOTHESIS the idea that people help others in order to relieve their own distress

NEUTRAL STIMULUS a stimulus (e.g., Pavlov's bell) that initially evokes no response

NON-ZERO-SUM GAME an interaction in which both participants can win (or lose)

NORMATIVE INFLUENCE going along with the crowd in order to be liked and accepted

NORMS standards established by society that tell its members what types of behavior are typical or expected

OBEDIENCE following orders from an authority figure

OMISSION BIAS the tendency to take whatever course of action does not require you to do anything (also called the default option)

ONE-SHOT ILLUSORY CORRELATION an illusory correlation that occurs after exposure to only one unusual behavior performed by only one member of an unfamiliar group

OPERANT CONDITIONING (INSTRUMENTAL CONDITIONING) a type of learning in which people are more likely to repeat behaviors that have been rewarded and less likely to repeat behaviors that have been punished

OPERATIONAL DEFINITIONS observable operations, procedures, and measurements that are based on the independent and dependent variables

OPTIMAL DISTINCTIVENESS THEORY proposition that when people feel very similar to others in a group, they seek a way to be different, and when they feel different, they try to be more similar

OSTRACISM being excluded, rejected, and ignored by others

OUTGROUP HOMOGENEITY BIAS the assumption that outgroup members are more similar to one another than ingroup members are to one another

OUTGROUP MEMBERS people who belong to a different group or category than we do

OVERBENEFITED getting more than you deserve

OVERJUSTIFICATION EFFECT the tendency for intrinsic motivation to diminish for activities that have become associated with rewards

PANIC BUTTON EFFECT a reduction in stress or suffering due to a belief that one has the option of escaping or controlling the situation, even if one doesn't exercise it

PASSION an emotional state characterized by high bodily arousal, such as increased heart rate and blood pressure

PASSIONATE LOVE (ROMANTIC LOVE) strong feelings of longing, desire, and excitement toward a special person

PATERNITY UNCERTAINTY the fact that a man cannot be sure that the children born to his female partner are his

PERIPHERAL ROUTE (HEURISTIC PROCESSING) the route to persuasion that involves some simple cue, such as attractiveness of the source (automatic processing)

PERSONAL RELEVANCE degree to which people expect an issue to have significant consequences for their own lives

PERSONALITY PSYCHOLOGY the branch of psychology that focuses on important differences between individuals

PERSUASION an attempt to change a person's attitude

PHENOMENAL SELF (WORKING SELF-CONCEPT) the image of self that is currently active in the person's thoughts

PHILOSOPHY "love of wisdom"; the pursuit of knowledge about fundamental matters such as life, death, meaning, reality, and truth

PIQUE TECHNIQUE influence technique in which one captures people's attention, as by making a novel request

PLANNING FALLACY the tendency for plans to be overly optimistic because the planner fails to allow for unexpected problems

PLURALISTIC IGNORANCE looking to others for cues about how to behave, while they are looking to you; collective misinterpretation

POLITICAL SCIENCE the study of political organizations and institutions, especially governments

POST-DECISION DISSONANCE cognitive dissonance experienced after making a difficult choice, typically reduced by increasing the attractiveness of the chosen alternative and decreasing the attractiveness of rejected alternatives

POWER one person's control over another person

PRAXIS practical ways of doing things

PREJUDICE a negative feeling toward an individual based solely on his or her membership in a particular group

PREOCCUPIED (ANXIOUS/AMBIVALENT) ATTACHMENT style of attachment in which people are low on avoidance but high on anxiety; they want and enjoy closeness but worry that their relationship partners will abandon them

PRIMING planting or activating an idea in someone's mind

PRISONER'S DILEMMA a game that forces people to choose between cooperation and competition

PRIVATE ACCEPTANCE a genuine inner belief that others are right

PRIVATE SELF-AWARENESS looking inward on the private aspects of the self, including emotions, thoughts, desires, and traits

PROACTIVE AGGRESSION "cold," premeditated, calculated harmful behavior that is a means to some practical or material end

PROPINQUITY being near someone on a regular basis

PROSOCIAL BEHAVIOR doing something that is good for other people or for society as a whole

PSYCHE a broader term for mind, encompassing emotions, desires, perceptions, and all other psychological processes

PSYCHOLOGY the study of human behavior

PUBLIC COMPLIANCE outwardly going along with the group but maintaining a private, inner belief that the group is wrong

PUBLIC SELF-AWARENESS looking outward on the public aspects of the self that others can see and evaluate

PUBLIC SELF-CONSCIOUSNESS thinking about how others perceive you

QUASI-EXPERIMENT a type of study in which the researcher can manipulate an independent variable but cannot use random assignment

RACISM prejudiced attitudes toward a particular race

RANDOM ASSIGNMENT procedure whereby each study participant has an equal chance of being in each treatment group

REACTANCE an unpleasant emotional response that people often experience when someone is trying to restrict their freedom

REACTANCE THEORY the idea that people are distressed by loss of freedom or options and seek to reclaim or reassert them

REACTIVE AGGRESSION "hot," impulsive, angry behavior that is motivated by a desire to harm someone

REALISTIC CONFLICT THEORY the idea that competition over scarce resources leads to intergroup hostility and conflict

RECEPTIVITY whether you "get" (pay attention to, understand) the message

RECIPROCITY the obligation to return in kind what another has done for us

REGRET feeling sorry for one's misfortunes, limitations, losses, transgressions, shortcomings, or mistakes

REINFORCEMENT THEORY the proposition that people and animals will perform behaviors that have been rewarded more than they will perform other behaviors

REJECTION (SOCIAL EXCLUSION) being prevented by others from forming or keeping a social bond with them; the opposite of acceptance

REJECTION SENSITIVITY a tendency to expect rejection from others and to become hypersensitive to possible rejection

RELATIONSHIP-ENHANCING STYLE OF ATTRIBUTION tendency of happy couples to attribute their partner's good acts to internal factors and bad acts to external factors

REPETITION WITH VARIATION repeating the same information, but in a varied format

REPLICATION repeating a study to be sure similar results can be obtained

REPRESENTATIVENESS HEURISTIC the tendency to judge the frequency or likelihood of an event by the extent to which it resembles the typical case

REPRODUCTION producing babies that survive long enough to also reproduce

REVERSE DOUBLE STANDARD condemning men more than women for the same sexual behavior (e.g., premarital sex)

RISK AVERSION in decision making, the greater weight given to possible losses than possible gains

RISK-AS-FEELINGS HYPOTHESIS the idea that people rely on emotional processes to evaluate risk, with the result that their judgments may be biased by emotional factors

RISKY SHIFT a tendency for groups to take greater risks than the same individuals (on average) would have decided to take individually

RULE OF LAW when members of a society respect and follow its rules

RUNNING AMOK according to Malaysian culture, refers to behavior of a young man who becomes "uncontrollably" violent after receiving a blow to his ego

SALIENCE being obvious or standing out

SCAPEGOAT THEORY the idea that blaming problems and misfortunes on outgroups contributes to negative attitudes toward these outgroups

SCHACHTER–SINGER THEORY OF EMOTION the idea that emotion has two components: a bodily state of arousal and a cognitive label that specifies the emotion

SCHEMAS knowledge structures that represent substantial information about a concept, its attributes, and its relationships to other concepts

SCRIPTS knowledge structures that define situations and guide behavior

SECURE ATTACHMENT style of attachment in which people are low on anxiety and low on avoidance; they trust their partners, share their feelings, provide and receive support and comfort, and enjoy their relationships

SELF AS IMPULSE a person's inner thoughts and feelings

SELF AS INSTITUTION the way a person acts in public, especially in official roles

SELF-ACCEPTANCE regarding yourself as being a reasonably good person as you are

SELF-AWARENESS attention directed at the self

SELF-CENSORSHIP choosing not to express doubts or other information that goes against a group's plans and views

SELF-DECEPTION STRATEGIES mental tricks people use to help them believe things that are false

SELF-DEFEATING BEHAVIOR any action by which people bring failure, suffering, or misfortune on themselves

SELF-DEFEATING PROPHECY a prediction that ensures, by the behavior it generates, that it will not come true

SELF-DETERMINATION THEORY the theory that people need to feel at least some degree of autonomy and internal motivation

SELF-ENHANCEMENT MOTIVE the desire to learn favorable or flattering things about the self

SELF-ESTEEM how favorably someone evaluates himself or herself

SELF-FULFILLING PROPHECY a prediction that ensures, by the behavior it generates, that it will come true

SELF-HANDICAPPING putting obstacles in the way of one's own performance so that anticipated or possible failure can be blamed on the obstacle instead of on lack of ability

SELF-KNOWLEDGE (SELF-CONCEPT) a set of beliefs about oneself

SELF-MONITORING the ability to change one's behavior for different situations

SELF-PERCEPTION THEORY the theory that people observe their own behavior to infer what they are thinking and how they are feeling

SELF-PRESENTATION any behavior that seeks to convey some image of self or some information about the self to other people

SELF-PROTECTION trying to avoid loss of esteem

SELF-REFERENCE EFFECT the finding that information bearing on the self is processed more thoroughly and more deeply, and hence remembered better, than other information

SELF-REGULATION the self's capacity to alter its own responses; self-control

SELF-SERVING BIAS the tendency for people to take credit for success but deny blame for problems and failures

SENSITIVITY ABOUT BEING THE TARGET OF A THREATENING UPWARD COMPARISON interpersonal concern about the consequences of outperforming others

SEROTONIN the "feel good" neurotransmitter, low levels of which have been linked to aggression and violence in both animals and humans

SHAME a moral emotion that, like guilt, involves feeling bad but, unlike guilt, spreads to the whole person

SIMULATION HEURISTIC the tendency to judge the frequency or likelihood of an event by the ease with which you can imagine (or mentally simulate) it

SLEEPER EFFECT the finding that, over time, people separate the message from the messenger

SOCIAL ACCEPTANCE a situation in which other people have come to like you, respect you, approve of you, and include you in their groups and relationships

SOCIAL ALLERGY EFFECT the idea that a partner's annoying habits become more annoying over time

SOCIAL ANIMALS animals that seek connections to others and prefer to live, work, and play with other members of their species

SOCIAL CATEGORIZATION the process of sorting people into groups on the basis of characteristics they have in common (e.g., race, gender, age, religion, sexual orientation)

SOCIAL COGNITION a movement in social psychology that began in the 1970s that focused on thoughts about people and about social relationships

SOCIAL COMPARISON examining the difference between oneself and another person

SOCIAL CONSTRUCTIONIST THEORIES theories asserting that attitudes and behaviors, including sexual desire and sexual behavior, are strongly shaped by culture and socialization

SOCIAL EXCHANGE THEORY theory that seeks to understand social behavior by analyzing the costs and benefits of interacting with each other; it assumes that sex is a resource that women have and men want

SOCIAL FACILITATION THEORY proposition that the presence of others increases the dominant response tendency

SOCIAL LEARNING (OBSERVATIONAL LEARNING, IMITATION, VICARIOUS LEARNING) a type of learning in which people are more likely to imitate behaviors if they have seen others rewarded for performing them, and less likely to imitate behaviors if they have seen others punished for performing them

SOCIAL LOAFING (FREE RIDER PROBLEM) the finding that people reduce effort when working in a group, compared to when working alone

SOCIAL PSYCHOLOGY branch of psychology that seeks an understanding of how people affect and are affected by others

SOCIAL REALITY beliefs held in common by several or many people; public awareness

SOCIAL ROLES the different roles a person plays, as in a play or a movie

SOCIOLOGY the study of human societies and the groups that form those societies

SOCIOMETER a measure of how desirable one would be to other people

SOURCE the individual who delivers a message

STALKING persisting in romantic, courtship, or other behaviors that frighten and harass the rejecter in a relationship

STANDARDS ideas (concepts) of how things might possibly be

STATISTICAL REGRESSION (REGRESSION TO THE MEAN) the statistical tendency for extreme scores or extreme behavior to be followed by others that are less extreme and closer to average

STATUS QUO BIAS the preference to keep things the way they are rather than change

STEALING THUNDER revealing potentially incriminating evidence first to negate its impact

STEREOTYPE THREAT the fear that one might confirm the stereotypes that others hold

STEREOTYPES beliefs that associate groups of people with certain traits

STIGMA an attribute or characteristic that is perceived as negative or considered socially unacceptable (e.g., being overweight, mentally ill, sick, poor, or physically scarred)

STIGMA BY ASSOCIATION rejection of those who associate with stigmatized others

STROOP EFFECT in the Stroop test, the finding that people have difficulty overriding the automatic tendency to read the word rather than name the ink color

STROOP TEST a standard measure of effortful control over responses, requiring participants to identify the color of a word (which may name a different color)

SUBTYPES categories that people use for individuals who do not fit a general stereotype

SUPERORDINATE GOALS goals that can be achieved only by cooperating and working with others

SURVIVAL living longer

SURVIVOR GUILT feeling bad for having survived a terrible experience or tragic event in which many others died

TEMPORAL DISCOUNTING in decision making, the greater weight given to the present over the future

TEND AND BEFRIEND SYNDROME a response to stress that involves nurturing others and making friends

TESTOSTERONE the male sex hormone, high levels of which have been linked to aggression and violence in both animals and humans

THANATOS in Freudian theory, the destructive, death instinct

THAT'S-NOT-ALL TECHNIQUE influence technique based on reciprocity, in which one first makes an inflated request but, before the person can answer yes or no, sweetens the deal by offering a discount or bonus

THEORIES unobservable constructs that are linked together in some logical way

THEORY OF EVOLUTION a theory proposed by Charles Darwin to explain how change occurs in nature

TOTE the self-regulation feedback loop of Test, Operate, Test, Exit

TRADEOFF a choice in which taking or maximizing one benefit requires either accepting a cost or sacrificing another benefit

TRANSACTIVE MEMORY a process by which members of a small group remember different kinds of information

TRUSTWORTHINESS whether a source will honestly tell you what he or she knows

TYRANNY OF CHOICE the idea that although some choice is better than none, more choice is not always better than less choice

ULTIMATE ATTRIBUTION ERROR the tendency for observers to make internal attributions (fundamental attribution error) about whole groups of people

UNCONDITIONED RESPONSE a naturally occurring response (e.g., salivation)

UNCONDITIONED STIMULUS a stimulus (e.g., meat powder) that naturally evokes a particular response (salivation)

UNDERBENEFITED getting less than you deserve

UNREQUITED LOVE a situation in which one person loves another but the other does not return that love

UPWARD COUNTERFACTUALS imagining alternatives that are better than actuality

UPWARD SOCIAL COMPARISON comparing yourself to people better than you

VIOLENCE aggression that has as its goal extreme physical harm, such as injury or death

VOLUNTEERING a planned, long-term, nonimpulsive decision to help others

WEAPONS EFFECT the increase in aggression that occurs as a result of the mere presence of a weapon

WHAT IS BEAUTIFUL IS GOOD EFFECT the assumption that physically attractive people will be superior to others on many other traits

WITHIN-SUBJECTS DESIGN an experiment in which each participant is exposed to all levels of the independent variable

YERKES–DODSON LAW the proposition that some arousal is better than none, but too much can hurt performance

YIELDING whether you "accept" the message

ZEIGARNIK EFFECT a tendency to experience automatic, intrusive thoughts about a goal whose pursuit has been interrupted

ZERO-SUM GAME a situation in which one person's gain is another's loss

References

Aberly, A. N. (2004). Oskar Schindler: The man and the hero. Retrieved January 3, 2009, from http://remember.org/imagine/schindler.html

Aberson, C. L., Healy, M., & Romero, V. (2000). Ingroup bias and self-esteem: A meta-analysis. *Personality and Social Psychology Review, 4*, 157–173.

Abraham, C. (2002, December 14). Mommy's little secret. *The Globe and Mail* (Toronto), pp. F1, F6.

Abraham, S. F., & Beumont, P. J. V. (1982). How patients describe bulimia or binge eating. *Psychological Medicine, 12*, 625–635.

Abramowitz, J. S., Tolin, D. F., & Street, G. P. (2001). Paradoxical effects of thought suppression: A meta-analysis of controlled studies. *Clinical Psychology Review, 21*(5), 683–703.

Abrams, D., Crisp, R. J., Marques, S., Fagg, E., Bedford, L., & Provias, D. (2008). Threat inoculation: Experienced and imagined intergenerational contact prevents stereotype threat effects on older people's math performance. *Psychology and Aging, 23*, 934–939.

Acker, M., & Davis, M. H. (1992). Intimacy, passion and commitment in adult romantic relationships: A test of the Triangular Theory of Love. *Journal of Social and Personality Relationships, 9*, 21–50.

Ackerman, J. M., Shapiro, J. R., Neuberg, S. L., Kenrick, D. T., Schaller, M., Becker, D. V., et al. (2006). They all look the same to me (unless they're angry): From outgroup homogeneity to out-group heterogeneity. *Psychological Science, 17*(10), 836–840.

Adams, C. G., & Turner, B. F. (1985). Reported change in sexuality from young adulthood to old age. *Journal of Sex Research, 21*, 126–141.

Adams, G. R., Ryan, B. A., Ketsetzis, M., & Keating, L. (2000). Rule compliance and peer sociability: A study of family process, parent-child school-focused interactions and children's classroom behavior. *Journal of Family Psychology, 14*, 237–250.

Adams, H. E., Wright, L. W., Jr., & Lohr, B. A. (1996). Is homophobia associated with homosexual arousal? *Journal of Abnormal Psychology, 105*, 440–446.

Adhikary, A. K. (1984). *Society and world view of the Birhor: A nomadic hunting and gathering community of Orissa.* Calcutta: Anthropological Survey of India.

Adler, P. (1980). On becoming a prostitute. In E. Muga (Ed.), *Studies in prostitution* (pp. 22–26). Nairobi: Kenya Literature Bureau.

Agras, W. S., & Telch, C. F. (1998). The effects of caloric deprivation and negative affect on binge eating in obese binge-eating disordered women. *Behavior Therapy, 29*, 491–503.

Ahlering, R. F. (1987). Need for cognition, attitudes, and the 1984 Presidential election. *Journal of Research in Personality, 21*, 100–102.

Aiello, J. R., & Douthitt, E. A. (2001). Social facilitation: From Triplett to electronic performance monitoring. *Group Dynamics: Theory, Research, and Practice, 5*, 163–180.

Ailman, W. F. (1994). *The Stone Age present.* New York: Simon and Schuster.

Ainsworth, M. D. S. (1989). Attachments beyond infancy. *American Psychologist, 44*, 709–716.

Ainsworth, M. D. S., Blehar, M. C., Waters, E., & Wall, S. (1978). *Patterns of attachment: A psychological study of the strange situation.* Hillsdale, NJ: Erlbaum.

Ajzen, I. (2001). Nature and operation of attitudes. In T. Fiske, D. L. Schacter, & C. Zahn-Waxler (Eds.), *Annual review of psychology* (Vol. 52, pp. 27–58). Palo Alto, CA: Annual Reviews.

Ajzen, I., & Fishbein, M. (1977). Attitude-behavior relations: A theoretical analysis and review of empirical research. *Psychological Bulletin, 84*, 888–918.

Alebiosu, K. A. (2001). Cooperative learning and students' affective learning outcome in Nigerian chemistry classrooms. *IFE Psychologia, 9*, 135–142.

Alexander, M. G., & Fisher, T. D. (2003). Truth and consequences: Using the bogus pipeline to examine sex differences in self-reported sexuality. *Journal of Sex Research, 40*, 27–35.

Alland, A., Jr. (1972). *The human imperative.* New York: Columbia University Press.

Allen, N. B., & Badcock, P. B. T. (2003). The social risk hypothesis of depressed mood: Evolutionary, psychosocial, and neurobiological perspectives. *Psychological Bulletin, 129*, 887–913.

Allen, N. J., & Hecht, T. D. (2004). The "romance of teams": Toward an understanding of its psychological underpinnings and implications. *Journal of Occupational and Organizational Psychology, 77*, 439–461.

Alloy, L. B., & Abramson, L. Y. (1979). Judgment of contingency in depressed and nondepressed students: Sadder but wiser? *Journal of Experimental Psychology: General, 108*(4), 441–485.

Allport, G. W. (1954) *The nature of prejudice.* Reading, MA: Addison-Wesley.

Altermatt, T. W., & DeWall, C. N. (2003). Agency and virtue: Dimensions underlying subgroups of women. *Sex Roles, 49*, 631–641.

Altschuler, G. C. (2001, January 7). Battling the cheats. Retrieved October 17, 2004, from http://www.physics.ohio-state.edu/~wilkins/osu_and_ohio/essays/cheat-altschuler.html

Alwin, D. F., Cohen, R. L., & Newcomb, T. L. (1991). *Political attitudes over the life span.* Madison: University of Wisconsin Press.

Amabile, T. M. (1996) *Creativity in context.* Boulder, CO: Westview Press.

American Psychiatric Association. (1994). *Diagnostic and statistical manual of mental disorders* (4th ed.). Washington, DC: Author.

Ames, D. R., & Flynn, F. J. (2007). What breaks a leader: The curvilinear relation between assertiveness and leadership. *Journal of Personality and Social Psychology, 92*, 307–324.

Amodio, D. M., Harmon-Jones, E., & Devine, P. G., (2003). Individual differences in the activation and control of affective race bias as assessed by startle eyeblink response and self-report. *Journal of Personality and Social Psychology, 84*, 738–753.

Anderson, C. A. (1983). Imagination and expectation: The effect of imagining behavioral scripts on personal intentions. *Journal of Personality and Social Psychology, 45*, 293–305.

Anderson, C. A., & Anderson, K. B. (1996). Violent crime rate studies in philosophical context: A destructive testing approach to heat and southern culture of violence effects. *Journal of Personality and Social Psychology, 70*, 740–756.

Anderson, C. A., Anderson, K. B., Dorr, N., DeNeve, K. M., & Flanagan, M. (2000). Temperature and aggression. In M. Zanna (Ed.), *Advances in experimental social psychology* (Vol. 32, pp. 63–133). New York: Academic Press.

Anderson, C. A., Benjamin, A. J., Jr., & Bartholow, B. D. (1998). Does the gun pull the trigger? Automatic priming effects of weapon pictures and weapon names. *Psychological Science, 9*, 308–314.

Anderson, C. A., Bushman, B. J., & Groom, R. W. (1997). Hot years and serious and deadly assault: Empirical tests of the heat hypothesis. *Journal of Personality and Social Psychology, 73*, 1213–1223.

Anderson, C. A., & Dill, K. E. (2000). Video games and aggressive thoughts, feelings, and behavior in laboratory

and real life. *Journal of Personality and Social Psychology, 78*(4), 772–790.

Anderson, C. A., Lepper, M. R., & Ross, L. (1980). The perseverance of social theories: The role of explanation in the persistence of discredited information. *Journal of Personality and Social Psychology, 39*, 1037–1049.

Anderson, C. A., & Sechler, E. S. (1986). Effects of explanation and counterexplanation on the development and use of social theories. *Journal of Personality and Social Psychology, 20*, 24–34.

Anderson, C. J. (2003). The psychology of doing nothing: Forms of decision avoidance result from reason and emotion. *Psychological Bulletin, 129*, 139–167.

Anderson, P. B., & Struckman-Johnson, C. (Eds.). (1998). *Sexually aggressive women: Current perspectives and controversies.* New York: Guilford Press.

Anderson, S. A., Russell, C. S., & Schumm, W. R. (1983). Perceived marital quality and family life-cycle categories: A further analysis. *Journal of Marriage and the Family, 45*, 127–139.

Andrews, J. D. W. (1989). Psychotherapy of depression: A self-confirmation model. *Psychological Review, 96*, 576–607.

Antonovsky, H. F., Shoham, I., Kavenocki, S., Modan, B., & Lancet, M. (1978). Sexual attitude–behavior discrepancy among Israeli adolescent girls. *Journal of Sex Research, 14*, 260–272.

Apsler, R., & Sears, D. O. (1968). Warning, personal involvement, and attitude change. *Journal of Personality and Social Psychology, 9*, 162–168.

Archer, J. (2000). Sex differences in aggression between heterosexual partners: A meta-analytic review. *Psychological Bulletin, 126*, 651–680.

Ard, B. N. (1977). Sex in lasting marriages: A longitudinal study. *Journal of Sex Research, 13*, 274–285.

Ariely, D., & Levav, J. (2000). Sequential choice in group settings: Taking the road less traveled and less enjoyed. *Journal of Consumer Research, 27*, 279–290.

Aries, E. J., & Johnson, F. L. (1983). Close friendship in adulthood: Conversational content between same-sex friends. *Sex Roles, 9*, 1183–1196.

Aries, P. (1962). *Centuries of childhood: A social history of family life* (Trans. R. Baldick). New York: Random House.

Arkes, H. R. (1991). Costs and benefits of judgment errors: Implications for debiasing. *Psychological Bulletin, 110*, 486–498.

Armbrister, R. C. (2002). A cross-cultural comparison of student social attributions. *Psychology in the Schools, 39*, 39–49.

Aronson, E. (2000). *Nobody left to hate: Teaching compassion after Columbine.* New York: W. H. Freeman.

Aronson, E. (2007). *The social animal.* New York: Worth.

Aronson, E., Blaney, N., Stephin, C., Sikes, J., & Snapp, M. (1978). *The jigsaw classroom.* Beverly Hills, CA: Sage.

Aronson, E., & Carlsmith, J. M. (1968). Experimentation in social psychology. In G. Lindzey & E. Aronson (Eds.), *Handbook of social psychology* (2nd ed., Vol. 2, pp. 1–79). Reading, MA: Addison-Wesley.

Aronson, E., & Mills, J. (1959). The effect of severity of initiation on liking for a group. *Journal of Abnormal and Social Psychology, 59*, 177–181

Aronson, E., & Osherow, N. (1980). Cooperation, prosocial behavior, and academic performance: Experiments in the desegregated classroom. *Applied Social Psychology Annual, 1*, 163–196.

Aronson, E., & Patnoe, S. (1997). *The jigsaw classroom: Building cooperation in the classroom* (2nd ed.). New York: Addison Wesley Longman.

Aronson, J., Lustina, M. J., Good, C. Keough, K., Steele, C. M., & Brown, J. (1999). When White men can't do math: Necessary and sufficient factors in stereotype threat. *Journal of Experimental Social Psychology, 35,* 29–46.

Asch, S. E. (1955, November). Opinions and social pressure. *Scientific American,* 31–35.

Asch, S. E. (1956). Studies of independence and conformity: I. A minority of one against a unanimous majority. *Psychological Monographs, 70* (No. 416).

Ashton, H. & Stepney, R. (1982). *Smoking: Psychology and pharmacology.* London: Tavistock.

Athanasou, J. A., & Olasehinde, O. (2002). Male and female differences in self-report cheating. *Practical Assessment, Research and Evaluation, 8*(5). Retrieved October 18, 2004, from http://PAREonline.net/getvn .asp?v=8&n=5

Atran, S. (2003) Genesis of suicide terrorism. *Science, 299,* 1534–1539.

Atthowe, J. M. (1960). Types of conflict and their resolution: A reinterpretation. *Journal of Experimental Psychology, 59,* 1–9.

Austin, W., McGinn, N. C., & Susmilch, C. (1980). Internal standards revisited: Effects of social comparisons and expectancies on judgments of fairness and satisfaction. *Journal of Experimental Social Psychology, 16,* 426–441.

Australian Human Rights and Equal Opportunity Commission. (1997). *Bringing them home: The "Stolen Children" report.* Retrieved January 5, 2009, from http://www .humanrights.gov.au/Social_Justice/bth_report/index .html

Averill, J. R. (1982). *Anger and aggression: An essay on emotion.* New York: Springer-Verlag.

Axelrod, R. (1980). More effective choice in the prisoner's dilemma. *Journal of Conflict Resolution, 24,* 3–25

Axelrod, R., & Hamilton, W. D. (1981). The evolution of cooperation. *Science, 211,* 1390–1396.

Bachman, J. G., & O'Malley, P. M. (1977). Self-esteem in young men: A longitudinal analysis of the impact of educational and occupational attainment. *Journal of Personality and Social Psychology, 35,* 365–380.

Bachman, J. G., & O'Malley, P. M. (1986). Self-concepts, self-esteem, and educational experiences: The frog pond revisited (again). *Journal of Personality and Social Psychology, 50,* 35–46.

Backteman, G., & Magnusson, D. (1981). Longitudinal stability of personality characteristics. *Journal of Personality, 49,* 148–160.

Baggini, J. (2004). Bad moves: Confirmation bias. Retrieved October 25, 2004, from http://www .butterfliesandwheels.com/badmovesprint.php?num=42

Bailey D. S., Leonard K. E., Cranston J. W., & Taylor S. P. (1983). Effects of alcohol and self-awareness on human physical aggression. *Personality and Social Psychology Bulletin, 9,* 289–295.

Bailey, J. M., & Pillard, R. C. (1995). Genetics of human sexual orientation. *Annual Review of Sex Research, 6,* 126–150.

Bailey, R. C., & Aunger, R. V. (1995). Sexuality, infertility and sexually transmitted disease among farmers and foragers in central Africa. In P. Abramson & S. Pinkerton (Eds.), *Sexual nature/sexual culture* (pp. 195–222). Chicago: University of Chicago Press.

Baldwin, M. W. (1992). Relational schemas and the processing of social information. *Psychological Bulletin, 112,* 461–474.

Bandura, A. (1965). Influence of models' reinforcement contingencies on the acquisition of imitative responses. *Journal of Abnormal and Social Psychology, 66,* 575–582.

Bandura, A. (1973). *Aggression: A social learning theory analysis.* Englewood Cliffs, NJ: Prentice-Hall.

Bandura, A. (1977). *Social learning theory.* Englewood Cliffs, NJ: Prentice-Hall.

Bandura, A. (1983). Psychological mechanism of aggression. In R. G. Geen & E. I. Donnerstein (Eds.), *Aggression: Theoretical and empirical reviews* (Vol. 1, pp. 1–40). New York: Academic Press.

Bandura, A. (1986). *Social foundations of thought and action: A social-cognitive theory.* Englewood Cliffs, NJ: Prentice-Hall.

Bandura, A., Ross, D., & Ross, S. (1961). Transmission of aggression through imitation of aggressive models. *Journal of Abnormal and Social Psychology, 63,* 575–582.

Bandura, A., Ross, D., & Ross, S. (1963). Vicarious reinforcement and imitative learning. *Journal of Abnormal and Social Psychology, 67,* 601–607.

Bandura, A., & Schunk, D. H. (1981). Cultivating competence, self-efficacy, and intrinsic interest through proximal self-motivation. *Journal of Personality and Social Psychology, 41,* 586–598.

Barash, D. P. (1977). *Sociobiology and behavior.* New York: Elsevier.

Barash, D. P., & Lipton, J. E. (2002). *Myth of monogamy: Fidelity and infidelity in animals and people.* New York: W. H. Freeman.

Barbee, A. P., Lawrence, T., & Cunningham, M. R. (1998) When a friend is in need: Feelings about seeking, giving, and receiving social support. In P. Anderson & L. Guerro (Ed.), *Handbook of communication and emotion* (282–298). New York: Academic Press.

Bard, P. (1934). Emotion: 1. The neuro-humoral basis of emotional reactions. In C. Murchison (Ed.), *Handbook of general experimental psychology.* Worcester, MA: Clark University Press.

Bargh, J. A. (1982). Attention and automaticity in the processing of self-relevant information. *Journal of Personality and Social Psychology, 43,* 425–436.

Bargh, J. A. (1994). The four horsemen of automaticity: Awareness, intention, efficiency, and control in social cognition. In R. S. Wyer, Jr., & T. K. Srull (Eds.), *Handbook of social cognition* (pp. 1–40). Hillsdale, NJ: Erlbaum.

Bargh, J. A., Chaiken, S., Raymond, P., & Hymes, C. (1996). The automatic evaluation effect: Unconditional automatic attitude activation with a pronunciation task. *Journal of Experimental Social Psychology, 32,* 104–128.

Bargh, J. A., Chen, M., & Burrows, L. (1996). Automaticity of social behavior: Direct effects of trait construct and stereotype activation on action. *Journal of Personality and Social Psychology, 71,* 230–244.

Bargh, J. A., Gollwitzer, P. M., Lee-Chai, A., Barndollar, K., & Trötschel, R. (2001). The automated will: Nonconscious activation and pursuit of behavioral goals. *Journal of Personality and Social Psychology, 81,* 1014–1027.

Bargh, J. A., Raymond, P., Pryor, J. B., & Strack, F. (1995). The attractiveness of the underling: An automatic power–sex association and its consequences for sexual harassment. *Journal of Personality and Social Psychology, 68,* 768–781.

Barlow, D. H. (1988). *Anxiety and its disorders: The nature and treatment of anxiety and panic.* New York: Guilford Press.

Barnett, P. A., & Gotlib, I. H. (1988). Psychosocial functioning and depression: Distinguishing among antecedents, concomitants, and consequences. *Psychological Bulletin, 104,* 97–126.

Baron, R. A. (1976). The reduction of human aggression: A field study of the influence of incompatible reactions. *Journal of Applied Social Psychology, 6,* 260–274.

Baron, R. A., & Richardson, D. R. (1994). *Human aggression* (2nd ed.). New York: Plenum Press.

Barrick, M. R., Day, D. V., Lord, R. G., & Alexander, R. A. (1991). Assessing the utility of executive leadership. *Leadership Quarterly, 2,* 9–22.

Barry, H., III, & Paxson, L. M. (1971) Infancy and early childhood: Cross-cultural codes II. *Ethnology, 10,* 466–508.

Bartholomew, K. (1990). Avoidance of intimacy: An attachment perspective. *Journal of Social and Personal Relationships, 7,* 147–178.

Bartholomew, K., & Horowitz, L. M. (1991). Attachment styles among young adults: A test of a four-category model. *Journal of Personality and Social Psychology, 61,* 226–244.

Bartholomew, K., & Shaver, P. R. (1998). Measures of attachment: Do they converge? In J. A. Simpson & W. S. Rholes (Eds.), *Attachment theory and close relationships* (pp. 25–45). New York: Guilford Press.

Batson, C. D., Batson, J. G., Slingsby, J. K., Harrell, K. L., Peekna, H. M., & Todd, R. M. (1991). Empathic joy and the empathy–altruism hypothesis. *Journal of Personality and Social Psychology, 61,* 413–426.

Batson, C. D., Duncan, B. D., Ackerman, P., Buckley, T., & Birch, K. (1981). Is empathic emotion a source of altruism motivation? *Journal of Personality and Social Psychology, 40,* 290–302.

Batson, C. D., Dyck, J. L., Brandt, J. R., Batson, J. G., Powell, A. L., McMaster, M. R., & Griffitt, C. (1988). Five studies testing two new egoistic alternatives to the empathy–altruism hypothesis. *Journal of Personality and Social Psychology, 55*(1), 52–77.

Battistich, V., Solomon, D., & Delucchi, K. (1993). Interaction processes and student outcomes in cooperative learning groups. *The Elementary School Journal, 94,* 19–32.

Baumeister, R. F. (1982). A self-presentational view of social phenomena. *Psychological Bulletin, 91,* 3–26.

Baumeister, R. F. (1987) How the self became a problem: A psychological review of historical research. *Journal of Personality and Social Psychology, 52,* 163–176.

Baumeister, R. F. (1990). Suicide as escape from self. *Psychological Review, 97,* 90–113.

Baumeister, R. F. (1991). *Meanings of life.* New York: Guilford Press.

Baumeister, R. F. (1997). *Evil: Inside human cruelty and violence.* New York: W. H. Freeman.

Baumeister, R. F. (2000). Gender differences in erotic plasticity: The female sex drive as socially flexible and responsive. *Psychological Bulletin, 126,* 347–374.

Baumeister, R. F. (2002). Ego depletion and self-control failure: An energy model of the self's executive function. *Self and Identity, 1,* 129–136.

Baumeister, R. F. (2005). *The cultural animal: Human nature, meaning, and social life.* New York: Oxford University Press.

Baumeister, R. F. (2005). *The cultural animal: Human nature, meaning, and social life.* New York: Oxford University Press.

Baumeister, R. F., & Bratslavsky, E. (1999). Passion, intimacy, and time: Passionate love as a function of change in intimacy. *Personality and Social Psychology Review, 3,* 49–67.

Baumeister, R. F., Bratslavsky, E., Finkenauer, C., & Vohs, K. D. (2001). Bad is stronger than good. *Review of General Psychology, 5,* 323–370.

Baumeister, R. F., Bratslavsky, E., Finkenauer, C., & Vohs, K. D. (2001). Bad is stronger than good. *Review of General Psychology, 5,* 323–370.

Baumeister, R. F., Bratslavsky, E., Muraven, M., & Tice, D. M. (1998). Ego depletion: Is the active self a limited resource? *Journal of Personality and Social Psychology, 74,* 1252–1265.

Baumeister, R. F., & Cairns, K. J. (1992). Repression and self-presentation: When audiences interfere with self-deceptive strategies. *Journal of Personality and Social Psychology, 62,* 851–862.

Baumeister, R. F., Campbell, J. D., Krueger, J. I., & Vohs, K. D. (2003). Does high self-esteem cause better performance, interpersonal success, happiness, or healthier lifestyles? *Psychological Science in the Public Interest, 4,* 1–44.

Baumeister, R. F., Catanese, K. R., & Vohs, K. D. (2001). Is there a gender difference in strength of sex drive? Theoretical views, conceptual distinctions, and a review of relevant evidence. *Personality and Social Psychology Review, 5,* 242–273.

Baumeister, R. F., Catanese, K. R., & Wallace, H. M. (2002). Conquest by force: A narcissistic reactance theory of rape and sexual coercion. *Review of General Psychology, 6,* 92–135.

Baumeister, R. F., DeWall, C. N., Ciarocco, N. J., & Twenge, J. M. (2005). Social exclusion impairs self-regulation. *Journal of Personality and Social Psychology, 88,* 589–684.

Baumeister, R. F., Heatherton, T. F., & Tice, D. M. (1994). *Losing control: How and why people fail at self-regulation.* San Diego, CA: Academic Press.

Baumeister, R. F., Hutton, D. G., & Tice, D. M. (1989). Cognitive processes during deliberate self-presentation: How self-presenters alter and misinterpret the behavior of their interaction partners. *Journal of Experimental Social Psychology, 25,* 59–78.

Baumeister, R. F., & Jones, E. E. (1978). When self-presentation is constrained by the target's knowledge:

Consistency and compensation. *Journal of Personality and Social Psychology, 36,* 608–618.

Baumeister, R. F., & Leary, M. R. (1995). The need to belong: Desire for interpersonal attachments as a fundamental human motivation. *Psychological Bulletin, 117,* 497–529.

Baumeister, R. F., Masicampo, E. J., & DeWall, C. N. (in press). Prosocial benefits of feeling free: Disbelief in free will increases aggression and reduces helpfulness. *Personality and Social Psychology Bulletin.*

Baumeister, R. F., Reis, H. T., & Delespaul, P. A. E. G. (1995). Subjective and experiential correlates of guilt in everyday life. *Personality and Social Psychology Bulletin, 21,* 1256–1268.

Baumeister, R. F., Smart, L., & Boden, J. M. (1996). Relation of threatened egotism to violence and aggression: The dark side of high self-esteem. *Psychological Review, 103,* 5–33.

Baumeister, R. F., Stillwell, A. M., & Heatherton, T. F. (1994). Guilt: An interpersonal approach. *Psychological Bulletin, 115,* 243–267.

Baumeister, R. F., Stillwell, A. M., & Wotman, S. R. (1990). Victim and perpetrator accounts of interpersonal conflict: Autobiographical narratives about anger. *Journal of Personality and Social Psychology, 59,* 994–1005.

Baumeister, R. F., & Tice, D. M. (1984). Role of self-presentation and choice in cognitive dissonance under forced compliance: Necessary or sufficient causes? *Journal of Personality and Social Psychology, 46,* 5–13.

Baumeister, R. F., & Twenge, J. M. (2002). Cultural suppression of female sexuality. *Review of General Psychology, 6,* 166–203.

Baumeister, R. F., Twenge, J. M., & Nuss, C. K. (2002). Effects of social exclusion on cognitive processes: Anticipated aloneness reduces intelligent thought. *Journal of Personality and Social Psychology, 83,* 817–827.

Baumeister, R. F., & Vohs, K. D. (2004). Sexual economics: Sex as female resource for social exchange in heterosexual interactions. *Personality and Social Psychology Review, 8*(4), 339–363.

Baumeister, R. F., & Wotman, S. R. (1992). *Breaking hearts: The two sides of unrequited love.* New York: Guilford Press.

Baumeister, R. F., Wotman, S. R., & Stillwell, A. M. (1993). Unrequited love: On heartbreak, anger, guilt, scriptlessness, and humiliation. *Journal of Personality and Social Psychology, 64,* 377–394.

Bay-Hinitz, A. K., Peterson, R. F., & Quilitch, H. R. (1994). Cooperative games: A way to modify aggressive and cooperative behaviors in young children. *Journal of Applied Behavior Analysis, 27,* 435–446.

Bazargan, S., Sherkat, D. E., & Bazargan, M. (2004). Religion and alcohol use among African-American and Hispanic inner-city emergency care patients. *Journal for the Scientific Study of Religion, 43,* 419–428.

Bazerman, M. H., Loewenstein, G. F., & White, S. B. (1992). Reversals of preference in allocation decisions: Judging an alternative versus choosing among alternatives. *Administrative Science Quarterly, 37*(2), 220–240.

Beaman, A. L., Barnes, P. J., & Klentz, B. (1978). Increasing helping rates through information dissemination: Teaching pays. *Personality and Social Psychology Bulletin, 4,* 406–411.

Bechara, A., Damasio, H., Tranel, D. & Damasio, A. R. (1997). Deciding advantageously before knowing the advantageous strategy. *Science, 275,* 1293–1295.

Beck, A. T. (1976). *Cognitive therapy and the emotional disorders.* New York: Meridian.

Beck, A. T. (1988). *Cognitive therapy of depression: A personal reflection.* The Malcolm Millar Lecture in Psychotherapy. Aberdeen: Scottish Cultural Press.

Beck, A. T., & Burns, D. (1978). Cognitive therapy of depressed suicidal outpatients. In J. O. Cole, A. F. Schatzberg & S. H. Frazier (Eds.), *Depression: Biology, psychodynamics, and treatment* (pp. 199–211). New York: Plenum Press.

Beck, A. T., Rush, A. J., Shaw, B. F., & Emery, G. (1979). *Cognitive therapy of depression.* New York: Guilford Press.

Beck, J. G., Bozman, A. W., & Qualtrough, T. (1991). The experience of sexual desire: Psychological correlates in a college sample. *Journal of Sex Research, 28,* 443–456.

Becker, A. E., Burwell, R. A., Herzog, D. B., Hamburg, P., & Gilman, S. E. (2002). Eating behaviours and attitudes following prolonged exposure to television among ethnic Fijian adolescent girls. *British Journal of Psychiatry, 180,* 509–514.

Beggan, J. K. (1992). On the social nature of nonsocial perception: The mere ownership effect. *Journal of Personality and Social Psychology, 62,* 229–237.

Beggan, J. K., Messick, D. M., & Allison, S. T. (1988). Social values and egocentric bias: Two tests of the might over morality hypothesis. *Journal of Personality and Social Psychology, 55,* 606–611.

Bègue, L., Subra, B., Arvers, P., Muller, D., Bricout, V., & Zorman, M. (2009). The message, not the bottle: Extrapharmacological effects of alcohol on aggression. *Journal of Experimental Social Psychology, 45*(1), 137–142.

Beilock, S. L., & Carr, T. H. (2001). On the fragility of skilled performance: What governs choking under pressure? *Journal of Experimental Psychology: General, 130,* 701–725.

Bejciy-Spring, S. M. (2008). R-E-S-P-E-C-T: A model for the sensitive treatment of the bariatric patient. *Bariatric Nursing and Surgical Patient Care, 3*(1), 47–56.

Bell, A. P., & Weinberg, M. S. (1978). *Homosexualities: A study of diversity among men and women.* New York: Simon & Schuster.

Belsky, J. (1985). Exploring individual differences in marital change across the transition to parenthood: The role of violated expectations. *Journal of Marriage and the Family, 47,* 1037–1044.

Belsky, J., Lang, M. E., & Rovine, M. (1985). Stability and change in marriage across the transition to parenthood: A second study. *Journal of Marriage and the Family, 47,* 855–865.

Belsky, J., Spanier, G. B., & Rovine, M. (1983). Stability and change in marriage across the transition to parenthood. *Journal of Marriage and the Family, 45,* 567–577.

Bem, D. J. (1965). An experimental analysis of self-persuasion. *Journal of Experimental Social Psychology, 1,* 199–218.

Bem, D. J. (1996). Exotic becomes erotic: A developmental theory of sexual orientation. *Psychological Review, 103,* 320–335.

Bem, D. J. (1998). Is EBE theory supported by evidence? Is it androcentric? A reply to Peplau et al. (1998). *Psychological Review, 105,* 395–398.

Benbow, C. P., Lubinski, D., Shea, D. L., & Eftekhari-Sanjani, H. (2000). Sex differences in mathematical reasoning ability: Their status 20 years later. *Psychological Science, 11,* 474–480.

Benson, P. L., Karabenick, S. A., & Lerner, R. M. (1976). Pretty pleases: The effects of physical attractiveness, race, and sex on receiving help. *Journal of Experimental Social Psychology, 12,* 409–415.

Benton, D. (2007). The impact of diet on anti-social, violent and criminal behaviour. *Neuroscience and Biobehavioral Reviews, 31*(5), 752–774.

Berglas, S. C., & Baumeister, R. F. (1993). *Your own worst enemy: Understanding the paradox of self-defeating behavior.* New York: Basic Books.

Berglas, S., & Jones, E. E. (1978). Drug choice as a self-handicapping strategy in response to non-contingent success. *Journal of Personality and Social Psychology, 36,* 405–417.

Berkowitz, A. D., & Perkins, H. W. (1987). Recent research on gender differences in collegiate alcohol use. *Journal of American College Health, 36,* 123–129.

Berkowitz, L. (1989). Frustration-aggression hypothesis: Examination and reformulation. *Psychological Bulletin, 106,* 59–73.

Berkowitz, L. (1993). *Aggression: Its causes, consequences, and control.* New York: McGraw-Hill.

Berkowitz, L., & Donnerstein, E. (1982). External validity is more than skin deep. *American Psychologist, 37,* 245–257.

Berkowitz, L., & LePage, A. (1967). Weapons as aggression-eliciting stimuli. *Journal of Personality and Social Psychology, 7,* 202–207.

Berman, M. E., McCloskey, M. S., Fanning, J. R., Schumacher, J. A., & Coccaro, E. F. (2009). Serotonin augmentation reduces response to attack in aggressive individuals. *Psychological Science, 20*(6), 714–720.

Berman, M. E., Tracy, J. I., & Coccaro, E. F. (1997). The serotonin hypothesis of aggression revisited. *Clinical Psychology Review, 17,* 651–665.

Bernard, J. (1982). *The future of marriage.* New Haven, CT: Yale University Press.

Bernat, J. A., Calhoun, K. S., Adams, H. E., & Zeichner, A. (2001). Homophobia and physical aggression toward homosexual and heterosexual individuals. *Journal of Abnormal Psychology, 110,* 179–187.

Berscheid, E., & Walster, E. (1967). When does a harm-doer compensate a victim? *Journal of Personality and Social Psychology, 6,* 433–441.

Bettencourt, B. A., & Miller, N. (1996). Gender differences in aggression as a function of provocation: A meta-analysis. *Psychological Bulletin, 119,* 422–447.

Betzold, M. (1993). *Appointment with Dr. Death.* Momentum Books.

Bhatti, B., Derezotes, D., Kim, S., & Specht, H. (1989). The association between child maltreatment and self-esteem. In A. M. Mecca, N. J. Smelser, & J. Vasconcellos (Eds.), *The social importance of self-esteem* (pp. 24–71). Berkeley: University of California Press.

Bichler, G., & Tibbetts, S. G. (2003). Conditional covariation of binge drinking with predictors of college students cheating. *Psychological Reports, 93,* 735–749.

Biddle, B. J., & Thomas, E. J. (1966). *Role theory: Concepts and research.* New York: Wiley.

Biel, A., Eek, D., & Gärling, T. (1999). The importance of fairness for cooperation in public-goods dilemmas. In P. Juslin & H. Montgomery (Eds.), *Judgment and decision making: Neo-Brunswikian and process-tracing approaches* (pp. 245–259). Mahwah, NJ: Erlbaum.

Billig, M., & Tajfel, H. (1973). Social categorization and similarity in intergroup behaviour. *European Journal of Social Psychology, 3*(1), 27–52.

Binder, J., Zagefka, H., Brown, R., Funke, F., Kessler, T., Mummendey, A., et al. (2009). Does contact reduce prejudice or does prejudice reduce contact? A longitudinal test of the contact hypothesis among majority and minority groups in three European countries. *Journal of Personality and Social Psychology, 96*(4), 843–856.

Biryukov, P. (1911) *Leo Tolstoy: His life and work.* New York: Charles Scribner's Sons.

Bishop, J. A., & Inderbitzen, H. M. (1995). Peer acceptance and friendship: An investigation of their relation to self-esteem. *Journal of Early Adolescence, 15,* 476–489.

Bjerregaard, B. (2000). An empirical study of stalking victimization. *Violence and Victims, 15,* 389–406.

Blackwell, B., & Hutchins, I. (1994). *Delights of the garden.* New York: Doubleday

Blanchard, F. A., & Frost, R. O. (1983). Two factors of restraint: Concern for dieting and fluctuations. *Behavior Research and Therapy, 21,* 259–267.

Blankenship, K. L., & Wegener, D. T. (2008). Opening the mind to close it: Considering a message in light of important values increases message processing and later resistance to change. *Journal of Personality and Social Psychology, 94*(2), 196–213.

Blanton, H., & Gerrard, M. (1997). Effect of sexual motivation on men's risk perception for sexually transmitted disease: There must be 50 ways to justify a lover. *Health Psychology, 16,* 374–379.

Blascovich, J., Spencer, S. J., Quinn, D., & Steele, C. (2001). African Americans and high blood pressure: The role of stereotype threat. *Psychological Science, 12,* 225–229.

Blau, P. N. (1964). *Exchange and power in social life.* New York: Wiley.

Blumstein, P., & Schwartz, P. (1983). *American couples: Money, work, and sex.* New York: Morrow.

Boddy, J. (1989). *Wombs and alien spirits: Women, men and the Zar cult in northern Sudan.* Madison: University of Wisconsin Press.

Bodenhausen, G. V. (1990). Stereotypes as judgmental heuristics: Evidence of circadian variations in discrimination. *Psychological Science, 1,* 319–322.

Bogaert, A., & Sadava, S. (2002). Adult attachment and sexual behavior. *Personal Relationships, 9,* 191–204.

Bond, C. F., & Titus, L. J. (1983). Social facilitation: A meta-analysis of 241 studies. *Psychological Bulletin, 94,* 265–292.

Bond, C. F., Jr., & DePaulo, B. M. (2008). Individual differences in judging deception: Accuracy and bias. *Psychological Bulletin, 134*(4), 477–492.

Bond, C. F., Jr., Omar, A., Pitre, U., Lashley, B, R., Skaggs, L. M., & Kirk, C. T. (1992). Fishy-looking liars: Deception judgment from expectancy violation. *Journal of Personality and Social Psychology, 63*(6), 969–977.

Bond, R. A., & Smith, P. B. (1996). Culture and conformity: A meta-analysis of studies using Asch's (1952, 1956) line judgment task. *Psychological Bulletin, 119,* 111–137.

Bonta, B. D. (1997). Cooperation and competition in peaceful societies. *Psychological Bulletin, 121,* 299–320.

Book, A. S., Starzyk, K. B., & Qunisey, V. L. (2001). The relationship between testosterone and aggression: A meta-analysis. *Aggression and Violent Behavior, 6,* 579–599.

Bornstein, R. F. (1989). Exposure and affect: Overview and meta-analysis of research, 1968–1987. *Psychological Bulletin, 106,* 265–289.

Bos, H. M. W., Gartrell, N. K., Van Balen, F., Peyser, H., & Sandfort, T. G. M. (2008). Children in planned lesbian families: A cross-cultural comparison between the United States and the Netherlands. *American Journal of Orthopsychiatry, 78*(2), 211–219.

Bostrom, R. N., Vlandis, J. W., & Rosenbaum, M. E. (1961). Grades as reinforcing contingencies and attitude change. *Journal of Educational Psychology, 52*(2), 112–115.

Bosveld, W., Koomen, W., & Van der Pligt, J. (1996). Estimating group size: Effects of category membership, differential construal and selective exposure. *European Journal of Social Psychology, 26,* 523–535.

Botta, R. A. (2000). The mirror of television: A comparison of Black and White adolescents' body image. *Journal of Communication; 50,* 144–159.

Bowlby, J. (1969). *Attachment and loss: Vol. 1. Attachment.* New York: Basic Books.

Bowlby, J. (1973). *Attachment and loss: Vol. 2. Separation anxiety and anger.* New York: Basic Books.

Bowles, T. (1999). Focusing on time orientation to explain adolescent self concept and academic achievement: Part II. Testing a model. *Journal of Applied Health Behaviour, 1,* 1–8.

Boyd, R., & Richerson, P. J. (1985) *Culture and the evolutionary process.* Chicago: University of Chicago Press.

Boyle, J. (2008, October 5). Weathermen: Home-grown US radicals. Retrieved October 13, 2008, from http://news .bbc.co.uk/2/hi/americas/7653486.stm

Brackett, M. A., & Salovey, P. (2004). Measuring emotional intelligence with the Mayer-Salovey-Caruso emotional intelligence test (MSCEIT). In G. Geher (Ed.), *Measurement of emotional intelligence* (pp. 181–196). Hauppauge, NY: Nova Science.

Bradley, G. W. (1978). Self-serving biases in the attribution process: A reexamination of the fact or fiction question. *Journal of Personality and Social Psychology, 36,* 56–71.

Bradley, S. J. (1990). Affect regulation and psychopathology: Bridging the mind-body gap. *Canadian Journal of Psychiatry, 35,* 540–547.

Braginski, B.M., Braginski, D.D., & Ring, K. (1969). *Methods of madness: The mental hospital as a last resort.* NY: Holt, Rinehart & Winston.

Brain, P. F. (1986). Multidisciplinary examinations of the "causes" of crime: The case of the link between alcohol and violence. *Alcohol and Alcoholism, 21,* 237–240.

Branden, N. (1994). *The six pillars of self-esteem.* New York: Bantam Books.

Brechner, K. C. (1977). An experimental analysis of social traps. *Journal of Experimental Social Psychology, 13,* 552–564.

Brehm, J. W. (1966). *A theory of psychological reactance.* New York: Academic Press.

Brehm, J. W. (1972). *Responses to loss of freedom: A theory of psychological reactance.* Morristown, NJ: General Learning Press.

Brehm, J. W., & Cole, A. H. (1966). Effect of a favor which reduces freedom. *Journal of Personality and Social Psychology, 3,* 420–426.

Brehm, S. S., & Brehm, J. W. (1981). *Psychological reactance.* New York: Wiley.

Brennan, K. A., Clark, C. L., & Shaver, P. R. (1998). Self-report measures of adult attachment. In J. A. Simpson & W. S. Rholes (Eds.), *Attachment theory and close relationships* (pp. 46–76). New York: Guilford Press.

Brennan, K. A., & Shaver, P. R. (1995). Dimensions of adult attachment, affect regulation, and romantic relationship functioning. *Personality and Social Psychology Bulletin, 21,* 267–283.

Brewer, M. B. (1979). In-group bias in the minimal intergroup situation: A cognitive-motivational analysis. *Psychological Bulletin, 86,* 307–324.

Brewer, M. B. (1993). The role of distinctiveness in social identity and group behavior. In M. A. Hogg & D. Abrams (Eds.), *Group motivation: Social psychological perspectives* (pp. 1–16). Hertfordshire, UK: Harvester Wheatsheaf.

Brewer, M. B. (1999). Multiple identities and identity transition: Implications for Hong Kong. *International Journal of Intercultural Relations, 23,* 187–197.

Brewer, M. B., & Silver, M. (1978). Ingroup bias as a function of task characteristics. *European Journal of Social Psychology, 8*(3), 393–400.

Brickman, P., & Campbell, D. T. (1971). Hedonic relativism and planning the good society. In M. H. Apley (Ed.), *Adaptation-level theory: A symposium* (pp. 287–302.). New York: Academic Press.

Brickman, P., Coates, D., & Janoff-Bulman, R. (1978). Lottery winners and accident victims: Is happiness relative? *Journal of Personality and Social Psychology, 36,* 917–927.

Briggs, C. S. (2003). *This dark world: A memoir of salvation found and lost.* London: Bloomsbury.

Brockner, J. (1983). Low self-esteem and behavioral plasticity: Some implications. In L. Wheeler & P. Shaver (Eds.), *Review of personality and social psychology, Vol. 4* (pp. 237–271). Beverly Hills, CA: Sage.

Brockner, J., Davy, J., & Carter, C. (1985). Layoffs, self-esteem, and survivor guilt: Motivational, affective, and attitudinal consequences. *Organizational Behaviour and Human Decision Processes, 36,* 229–244.

Brockner, J., Greenberg, J., Brockner, A., Bortz, J., Davy, J., & Carter, C. (1986). Layoffs, equity theory, and work performance: Further evidence of the impact of survivor guilt. *Academy of Management Journal, 29,* 373–384.

Brockner, J., & Lloyd, K. (1986). Self-esteem and likability: Separating fact from fantasy. *Journal of Research in Personality, 20,* 496–508.

Brodish, A. B., & Devine, P. G. (2009). The role of performance-avoidance goals and worry in mediating the relationship between stereotype threat and performance. *Journal of Experimental Social Psychology, 45*(1), 180–185.

Brody, L. R. (1996). Gender, emotional expression, and parent-child boundaries. In R. D. Kavanaugh, B. Zimmerberg, & S. Fein (Eds.), *Emotion: Interdisciplinary perspectives* (pp. 139–170). Mahwah, NJ: Erlbaum.

Brooke, J. (October 10, 1998). Gay man beaten and left for dead; 2 are charged. *New York Times.* Retrieved April 29, 2009, from http://www.nytimes.com/ads/marketing/laramie/index.html

Brown, B. R. (1968). The effects of need to maintain face on interpersonal bargaining. *Journal of Experimental Social Psychology, 4,* 107–122.

Brown, K. W., & Ryan, R. M. (2003). The benefits of being present: Mindfulness and its role in psychological well-being. *Journal of Personality and Social Psychology, 84,* 822–848.

Brown, N. R., & Sinclair, R. C. (1999). Estimating number of lifetime sexual partners: Men and women do it differently. *Journal of Sex Research, 36,* 292–297.

Brownstein, S. C., Wolf, I. K., & Green, S. W. (2000). *Barron's how to prepare for the GRE: Graduate Record Examination.* Hauppauge, NY: Barrons Education Series.

Brunell, A. B., Gentry, W. A., Campbell, W. K., Hoffman, B. J., Kuhnert, K. W., & DeMarree, K. G. (2008). Leadership emergence: The case of the narcissistic leader. *Personality and Social Psychology Bulletin, 34,* 1663–1676.

Budesheim, T. L., & DePaola, S. J. (1994). Beauty or the beast? The effects of appearance, personality and issue information on evaluations of political candidates. *Personality and Social Psychology Bulletin, 20,* 339–348.

Budesheim, T. L., Houston, D. A., & DePaola, S. J. (1996). The persuasiveness of in-group and out-group political messages: The case of negative political campaigning. *Journal of Personality and Social Psychology, 70,* 523–534.

Buehler, R., Griffin, D., & Ross, M. (1994) Exploring the "planning fallacy": Why people underestimate their task completion times. *Journal of Personality and Social Psychology, 67,* 366–381.

Buehler, R., & McFarland, C. (2001). Intensity bias in affective forecasting: The role of temporal focus. *Personality and Social Psychology Bulletin, 27,* 1480–1493.

Buhrmester, D., Furman, W., Wittenberg, M.T., & Reis, H.T. (1988). Five domains of interpersonal competence in peer relationships. *Journal of Personality and Social Psychology, 55,* 991–1008.

Bulman, R. J., & Wortman, C. B. (1977). Attributions of blame and coping in the "real world": Severe accident victims react to their lot. *Journal of Personality and Social Psychology, 35,* 351–363.

Bunker, B. B., Zubek, J. M., Vanderslice, V. J., & Rice, R. W. (1992). Quality of life in dual-career families: Commuting versus single-residence couples. *Journal of Marriage and the Family, 54,* 399–407.

Burger, J. M. (1986). Increasing compliance by improving the deal: The that's-not-all technique. *Journal of Personality and Social Psychology, 51,* 277–283.

Burger, J. M., Cooper, H. M., & Good, T. L. (1982). Teacher attributions of student performance: Effects of outcome. *Personality and Social Psychology Bulletin, 8,* 685–690.

Burnstein, E., Crandall, C., & Kitayama, S. (1994). Some neo-Darwinian decision rules for altruism: Weighing cues for inclusive fitness as a function of the biological importance of the decision. *Journal of Personality and Social Psychology, 67,* 773–789.

Burris, C. T., Harmon-Jones, E., & Tarpley, W. R. (1997). "By faith alone": Religious agitation and cognitive dissonance. *Basic and Applied Social Psychology, 19,* 17–31.

Bush, G. W. (2001, September 20). *Address to a joint session of Congress and the American people.* Retrieved November 22, 2004, from http://www.whitehouse.gov/news/releases/2001/09/20010920-8.html

Bushman, B. J. (1993). What's in a name? The moderating role of public self-consciousness on the relation between brand label and brand preference. *Journal of Applied Psychology, 78,* 857–861.

Bushman, B. J. (1997). Effects of alcohol on human aggression: Validity of proposed explanations. In D. Fuller, R. Dietrich, & E. Gottheil (Eds.), *Recent developments in alcoholism: Alcohol and violence* (Vol. 13, pp. 227–243). New York: Plenum Press.

Bushman, B. J. (2002). Does venting anger feed or extinguish the flame? Catharsis, rumination, distraction, anger, and aggressive responding. *Personality and Social Psychology Bulletin, 28,* 724–731.

Bushman, B. J., & Anderson, C. A. (2001). Is it time to pull the plug on the hostile versus instrumental aggression dichotomy? *Psychological Review, 108,* 273–279.

Bushman, B. J., & Baumeister, R. F. (1998). Threatened egotism, narcissism, self-esteem, and direct and displaced aggression: Does self-love or self-hate lead to violence? *Journal of Personality and Social Psychology, 75,* 219–229.

Bushman, B. J., & Baumeister, R. F. (2002). Does self-love or self-hate lead to violence? *Journal of Research in Personality, 36,* 543–545.

Bushman, B. J., Baumeister, R. F., & Phillips, C. M. (2001). Do people aggress to improve their mood? Catharsis beliefs, affect regulation opportunity, and aggressive responding. *Journal of Personality and Social Psychology, 81,* 17–32.

Bushman, B. J., Baumeister, R. F., & Stack, A. D. (1999). Catharsis, aggression, and persuasive influence: Self-fulfilling or self-defeating prophecies? *Journal of Personality and Social Psychology, 76,* 367–376.

Bushman, B. J., & Bonacci, A. M. (2004). You've got mail: Using e-mail to examine the effect of prejudiced attitudes on discrimination against Arabs. *Journal of Experimental Social Psychology, 40,* 753–759.

Bushman, B. J., Bonacci, A. M., Van Dijk, M., & Baumeister, R. F. (2003). Narcissism, sexual refusal, and sexual aggression: Testing a narcissistic reactance model of sexual coercion. *Journal of Personality and Social Psychology, 84,* 1027–1040.

Bushman, B. J., Bonacci, A. M., Van Dijk, M., & Baumeister, R. F. (2003). Narcissism, sexual refusal, and sexual aggression: Testing a narcissistic reactance model of sexual coercion. *Journal of Personality and Social Psychology, 84,* 1027–1040.

Bushman, B. J., Bonacci, A. M., Van Dijk, M., & Baumeister, R. F. (2003). Narcissism, sexual refusal, and sexual aggression: Testing a narcissistic reactance model of sexual coercion. *Journal of Personality and Social Psychology, 84,* 1027–1040.

Bushman, B. J., & Cantor, J. (2003). Media ratings for violence and sex: Implications for policy makers and parents. *American Psychologist, 58,* 130–141.

Bushman, B. J., & Cooper, H. M. (1990). Effects of alcohol on human aggression: An integrative research review. *Psychological Bulletin, 107,* 341–354.

Bushman, B. J., & Hucsmann, L. R. (2006). Short-term and long-term effects of violent media on aggression in children and adults. *Archives of Pediatrics and Adolescent Medicine, 160,* 348–352.

Buss, A. H. (1961). *The psychology of aggression.* New York: Wiley.

Buss, A. H. (1989). Temperaments as personality traits. In G. A. Kohnstamm, J. E. Bates, & M. Rothbart (Eds.), *Temperament in childhood* (pp. 49–58). Chichester: Wiley.

Buss, D. M. (1990). The evolution of anxiety and social exclusion. *Journal of Social and Clinical Psychology, 9,* 196–210.

Buss, D. M. (1991). Evolutionary personality psychology. *Annual Review of Psychology, 42,* 459–491.

Buss, D. M. (1994). *The evolution of desire: Strategies of human mating.* New York: Basic Books.

Buss, D. M. (1999). *Evolutionary psychology: The new science of the mind.* New York: Allen & Bacon.

Buss, D. M., & Schmitt, D. P. (1993). Sexual strategies theory: An evolutionary perspective on human mating. *Psychological Review, 100,* 204–232.

Buss, D. M., & Shackelford, T. K. (1997). From vigilance to violence: Mate retention tactics in married couples. *Journal of Personality and Social Psychology, 72,* 346–361.

Buss, D. M., Larsen, R. J., Westen, D., & Semmelroth, J. (1992). Sex differences in jealousy: Evolution, physiology, and psychology. *Psychological Science, 3,* 251–255.

Butler, J. L., & Baumeister, R. F. (1998). The trouble with friendly faces: Skilled performance with a supportive audience. *Journal of Personality and Social Psychology, 75,* 1213–1230.

Butz, D. A., Plant, E. A., & Doerr, C. (2007). Liberty and justice for all? The implications of exposure to the United States flag for intergroup relations. *Personality and Social Psychology Bulletin, 33,* 396–408.

Buunk, B. P., Angleitner, A., Oubaid, V., & Buss, D. M. (1996). Sex differences in jealousy in evolutionary and cultural perspective: Tests from the Netherlands, Germany, and the United States. *Psychological Science, 7,* 1103–1116.

Buunk, B., P. & Hupka, R. B. (1987). Cross-cultural differences in the elicitation of sexual jealousy. *Journal of Sex Research, 23,* 12–22.

Buzwell, S., & Rosenthal, D. (1996). Constructing a sexual self: Adolescents' sexual self-perceptions and sexual risk-taking. *Journal of Research on Adolescence, 6,* 489–513.

Byrne, D. (1971). *The attraction paradigm.* New York: Academic Press.

Cacioppo, J. T., Ernst, J. M., Burleson, M. H., McClintock, M. K., Malarkey, W. B., Hawkley, L. C., et al. (2000). Lonely traits and concomitant physiological processes: The MacArthur Social Neuroscience Studies. *International Journal of Psychophysiology, 35,* 143–154.

Cacioppo, J. T., & Gardner, W. L. (1999). Emotion. *Annual Review of Psychology, 50,* 191–214.

Cacioppo, J. T., & Hawkley, L. C. (2005). People thinking about people: The vicious cycle of being a social outcast in one's own mind. In K. D. Williams, J. P. Forgas, & W. von Hippel (Eds.), *The social outcast: Ostracism, social exclusion, rejection, and bullying* (pp. 91–108). New York: Psychology Press.

Cacioppo, J. T., Hawkley, L. C., Berntson, G. G., Ernst, J. M., Gibbs, A. C., Stickgold, R., et al. (2002). Lonely days invade the nights: Social modulation of sleep efficiency. *Psychological Science, 13,* 385–388.

Cacioppo, J. T., Hawkley, L. C., Crawford, L. E., Ernst, J. M., Burleson, M. H., Kowalewski, R. B., et al. (2002). Loneliness and health: Potential mechanisms. *Psychosomatic Medicine, 64,* 407–417.

Cacioppo, J. T., & Petty, R. E. (1980). Sex differences in influenceability: Toward specifying the underlying processes. *Personality and Social Psychology Bulletin, 6(4),* 651–656.

Cacioppo, J. T., & Petty, R. E. (1982). The need for cognition. *Journal of Personality and Social Psychology, 42,* 116–131.

Cacioppo, J. T., & Petty, R. E. (1989). Effects of message repetition on argument processing, recall and persuasion. *Basic and Applied Social Psychology, 10,* 3–12.

Cacioppo, J. T., Petty, R. E., & Morris, K. J. (1983). Effects of need for cognition on message evaluation, recall, and persuasion. *Journal of Personality and Social Psychology, 45,* 805–818.

Caesar, P. L. (1988). Exposure to violence in the families-of-origin among wife-abusers and maritally nonviolent men. *Violence and Victims, 3,* 49–63.

Caldwell, M. A., & Peplau, L. A. (1982). Sex differences in same-sex friendships. *Sex Roles, 8,* 721–732.

Call, V., Sprecher, S., & Schwartz, P. (1995). The incidence and frequency of marital sex in a national sample. *Journal of Marriage and the Family, 57,* 639–650.

Campbell, A. (1981). *The sense of well-being in America.* New York: McGraw-Hill.

Campbell, A., Converse, P. E., & Rogers, W. L. (1976). *The quality of American life: Perceptions, evaluations, and satisfactions.* New York: Russell Sage.

Campbell, D. T. (1958). Common fate, similarity, and other indices of the status of aggregates of persons as social entities. *Behavioral Science, 3,* 14–25.

Campbell, J. D. (1986). Similarity and uniqueness: The effects of attribute type, relevance, and individual differences in self-esteem and depression. *Journal of Personality and Social Psychology, 50,* 281–294.

Campbell, J. D. (1990). Self-esteem and clarity of the self-concept. *Journal of Personality and Social Psychology, 59,* 538–549.

Campbell, J. D., Chew, B., & Scratchley, L. S. (1991). Cognitive and emotional reactions to daily events: The effects of self-esteem and self complexity. *Journal of Personality, 59,* 473–505.

Campbell, J. D., & Fehr, B. A. (1990). Self-esteem and perceptions of conveyed impressions: Is negative affectivity associated with greater realism? *Journal of Personality and Social Psychology, 58,* 122–133.

Campbell, J. K. (1965). Honour and the devil. In J. G. Peristiany (Ed.), *Honour and shame: The values of Mediterranean society* (pp. 112–175). London: Weidenfeld & Nicolson.

Campbell, W. K. (1999). Narcissism and romantic attraction. *Journal of Personality and Social Psychology, 77,* 1254–1270.

Campbell, W. K. (2005). *When you love a man who loves himself.* Naperville, IL: Sourcebooks.

Campbell, W. K., & Foster, C. A. (2002). Narcissism and commitment in romantic relationships: An Investment Model analysis. *Personality and Social Psychology Bulletin, 28,* 484–495.

Campbell, W. K., Foster, C. A., & Finkel, E. J. (2002). Does self-love lead to love for others? A story of narcissistic game playing. *Journal of Personality and Social Psychology, 83,* 340–354.

Campbell, W. K., Reeder, G. D., Sedikides, C., & Elliot, A. J. (2000). Narcissism and comparative self-enhancement strategies. *Journal of Research in Personality, 34,* 329–347.

Campbell, W. K., & Sedikides, C. (1999). Self-threat magnifies the self-serving bias: A meta-analytic integration. *Review of General Psychology, 3,* 23–43.

Cannon, W. B. (1927) The James-Lange theory of emotion: A critical examination and an alternative theory. *American Journal of Psychology, 39,* 10–124.

Cantor, J. R., & Venus, P. (1980). The effect of humor on recall of a radio advertisement. *Journal of Broadcasting, 24,* 13–22.

Cappell, C., & Heiner, R. B. (1990). The intergenerational transmission of family aggression. *Journal of Family Violence, 5,* 135–152.

Carlsmith, K. M., Wilson, T. D., & Gilbert, D. T. (2008). The paradoxical consequences of revenge. *Journal of Personality and Social Psychology, 95(6),* 1316–1324.

Carlson, M., Marcus-Newhall, A., & Miller, N. (1990). Effects of situational aggression cues: A quantitative review. *Journal of Personality and Social Psychology, 58,* 622–633.

Carlson, M., & Miller, N. (1987). Explanation of the relation between negative mood and helping. *Psychological Bulletin, 102,* 91–108.

Carnegie Hero Fund Commission. (2002). Requirements for a Carnegie Medal. Available at http://www.carnegiehero.org/nominate.php

Carr, J. E., & Tann, E. K. (1976) In search of the true Amok: Amok as viewed within Malay culture. *American Journal of Psychiatry, 133(11),* 1295–1299.

Carroll, J. S. (1978). The effect of imagining an event on expectations for the event: An interpretation in terms of the availability heuristic. *Journal of Experimental Social Psychology, 14,* 88–96.

Carver, C. S., & Scheier, M. F. (1981). *Attention and self-regulation: A control theory approach to human behavior.* New York: Springer Press.

Carver, C. S., & Scheier, M. F. (1982). Control theory: A useful conceptual framework for personality-social, clinical and health psychology. *Psychological Bulletin, 92,* 111–135.

Carver, C. S., & Scheier, M. F. (1990). Origins and functions of positive and negative affect: A control-process view. *Psychological Review, 97,* 19–35.

Case, D. A., Fantino, E., & Goodie, A. S. (1999). Base-rate training without case cues reduces base-rate neglect. *Psychonomic Bulletin and Review, 6(2),* 319–327.

Cash, T. F., & Janda, L. H. (1984). The eye of the beholder. *Psychology Today, 18,* 46–52.

Caspi, A., & Roberts, B. W. (2001). Personality development across the life course: The argument for change and continuity. *Psychological Inquiry, 12,* 49–66.

Centers for Disease Control. (2007). U.S. obesity trends 1985–2007. Retrieved November 24, 2008, from http://www.cdc.gov/nccdphp/dnpa/obesity/trend/maps

Cesario, J., Plaks, J. E., & Higgins, E. T. (2006). Automatic social behavior as motivated preparation to interact. *Journal of Personality and Social Psychology, 90,* 893–910.

Chajut, E., & Algom, D. (2003). Selective attention improves under stress: Implications for theories of social cognition. *Journal of Personality and Social Psychology, 85,* 231–248.

Chartrand, T. L., & Bargh, J. A. (1999). The chameleon effect: The perception-behavior link and social interaction. *Journal of Personality and Social Psychology, 76,* 893–910.

Chassin, L., Presson, C. C., Sherman, S. J., & Edwards, D. A. (1990). The natural history of cigarette smoking: Predicting young-adult smoking outcomes from adolescent smoking patterns. *Health Psychology, 9,* 701–716.

Chen, E. S., & Tyler, T. R. (2001). Cloaking power: Legitimizing myths and the psychology of the advantaged. In A. Y. Lee-Chai & J. Bargh (Eds.), *The use and abuse of power: Multiple perspectives on the causes of corruption* (pp. 241–261). Philadelphia: Psychology Press.

Cherniss, C. (2000, April 15). *Emotional intelligence: What it is and why it matters.* Paper presented at the Annual Meeting of the Society for Industrial and Organizational Psychology, New Orleans. Retrieved August 12, 2004, from http://www.eiconsortium.org/research/what_is_emotional_intelligence.htm

Chiodo, J. (1987). Bulimia: An individual behavioral analysis. *Journal of Behavior Therapy and Experimental Psychiatry, 18,* 41–49.

Chipman, J. (2003). *The military balance: Press conference.* London: International Institute for Strategic Studies.

Chivers, M. L., Seto, M. C., Laan, E., Lalumière, M. L, & Grimbos, T. (in press). Agreement of genital and subjective measures of sexual arousal: A meta-analysis. *Archives of Sexual Behavior.*

Christensen, H. T., & Carpenter, G. R. (1962). Value–behavior discrepancies regarding premarital coitus in three Western cultures. *American Sociological Review, 27,* 66–74.

Cialdini, R. B. (1993). *Influence: Science and practice* (3rd ed.). New York: HarperCollins.

Cialdini, R. B. (2001). *Influence: Science and practice* (4th ed.). Boston: Allyn and Bacon.

Cialdini, R. B., Cacioppo, J. T., Bassett, R., & Miller, J. A. (1978). Low-ball procedure for producing compliance: Commitment then cost. *Journal of Personality and Social Psychology, 36,* 463–476.

Cialdini, R. B., Darby, B. L., & Vincent, J. E. (1973). Transgression and altruism: A case for hedonism. *Journal of Experimental Social Psychology, 9,* 502–516.

Cialdini, R. B., Eisenberg, N., Green, B. L., Rhoads, K., & Bator, R. (1998). Undermining the undermining effect of reward on sustained interest: When unnecessary conditions are sufficient. *Journal of Applied Social Psychology, 28,* 249–263.

Cialdini, R. B., & Kendrick, D. T. (1976). Altruism as hedonism: A social development perspective on the relationship of negative mood state and helping. *Journal of Personality and Social Psychology, 34,* 907–914.

Cialdini, R. B., Reno, R. R., & Kallgren, C. A. (1990). A focus theory of normative conduct: Recycling the concept of norms to reduce littering in public places. *Journal of Personality and Social Psychology, 58,* 1015–1026.

Cialdini, R. B., & Schroeder, D. A. (1976). Increasing compliance by legitimizing paltry contributions: When even a penny helps. *Journal of Personality and Social Psychology, 34*(4), 599–604.

Cialdini, R. B., Vincent, J., Lewis, S., Catalan, J., Wheeler, D., & Darby, B. L. (1975). Reciprocal concessions procedure for inducing compliance: The door-in-the-face technique. *Journal of Personality and Social Psychology, 31,* 206–215.

Clark, D. (1986). *The missing link.* New York: Humansphere.

Clark, D. A., Beck, A. T., & Brown, G. (1989). Cognitive mediation in general psychiatric outpatients: A test of the content specificity hypothesis. *Journal of Personality and Social Psychology, 56,* 958–964.

Clark, M. S. (1984). Record keeping in two types of relationships. *Journal of Personality and Social Psychology, 47,* 549–557.

Clark, M. S., & Mills, J. (1979). Interpersonal attraction in exchange and communal relationships. *Journal of Personality and Social Psychology, 37,* 12–24.

Clark, M. S., Mills, J., & Corcoran, D. (1989). Keeping track of needs and inputs of friends and strangers. *Personality and Social Psychology Bulletin, 15,* 533–542.

Clark, M. S., Ouellette, R., Powell, M., & Milberg, S. (1987). Recipients' mood, relationship type, and helping. *Journal of Personality and Social Psychology, 53,* 94–103.

Claypool, H. M., Mackie, D. M., Garcia-Marques, T., McIntosh, A., & Udall, A. (2004). The effects of personal relevance and repetition on persuasive processing. *Social Cognition, 22,* 310–335.

Clayson, D. E., & Klassen, M. L. (1989). Perception of attractiveness by obesity and hair color. *Perceptual and Motor Skills, 68,* 199–202.

Clifford, M., & Walster, E. (1973). The effect of physical attractiveness on teacher expectations. *Sociology of Education, 46,* 248–258.

Clore, G. L., Gasper, K., & Garvin, E. (2001). Affect as information. In J. P. Forgas (Ed.), *Handbook of affect and social cognition* (pp. 122–144). Mahwah, NJ: Erlbaum.

Coan, J. A., Schaefer, H. S., & Davidson, R. J. (2006). Lending a hand: Social regulation of the neural response to threat. *Psychological Science, 17*(12), 1032–1039.

Cohen, D., & Nisbett, R. E. (1997). Field experiments examining the culture of honor: The role of institutions in perpetuating norms about violence. *Personality and Social Psychology Bulletin, 23,* 1188–1199.

Cohen, D., Nisbett, R. E., Bowdle, B. F., & Schwarz, N. (1996). Insult, aggression, and the Southern culture of honor: An "experimental ethnography." *Journal of Personality and Social Psychology, 70,* 945–960.

Cohen, J., & Andrade, E. B. (2004). Affect, intuition, and task-contingent affect regulation. *Journal of Consumer Research, 31,* 358–367.

Cohen, L. L., & Shotland, R. L. (1996). Timing of first sexual intercourse in a relationship: Expectations, experiences, and perceptions of others. *Journal of Sex Research, 33,* 291–299.

Colapinto, J. (2000). *As nature made him: The boy who was raised as a girl.* New York: HarperCollins.

Cole, R. (2001). Lying to the one you love: The use of deception in romantic relationships. *Journal of Social and Personal Relationships, 18*(1), 107–129.

Coleman, J. S. (1961). *The adolescent society.* New York: Free Press.

College Board. (1976–1977). *Student descriptive questionnaire.* Princeton, NJ: Educational Testing Service.

Collins, J. (2001). *Good to great.* New York: HarperCollins.

Collins, N. L., & Feeney, B. C. (2000). A safe haven: An attachment theory perspective on support-seeking and caregiving in adult romantic relationships. *Journal of Personality and Social Psychology, 58,* 644–663.

Collins, N. L., & Feeney, B. C. (2004). An attachment theory perspective on closeness and intimacy. In D. Mashek & A. Aron (Eds.), *Handbook of closeness and intimacy* (pp. 163–187). Mahwah, NJ: Erlbaum.

Collins, N. L., & Read, S. J. (1990). Adult attachment, working models and relationship quality in dating couples. *Journal of Personality and Social Psychology, 58,* 644–663.

Collins, R. L., Quigley, B., & Leonard, K. (2007). Women's physical aggression in bars: An event-based examination of precipitants and predictors of severity. *Aggressive Behavior, 33*(4), 304–313.

Colman, A. M. (1982). *Game theory and experimental games: The study of strategic interaction.* Oxford, UK: Pergamon Press.

Colvin, C. R., Block, J., & Funder, D. C. (1995). Overly positive evaluations and personality: Negative implications for mental health. *Journal of Personality and Social Psychology, 68,* 1152–1162.

Comer, R., & Laird, J. D. (1975) Choosing to suffer as a consequence of expecting to suffer: Why do people do it? *Journal of Personality and Social Psychology, 32,* 92–101.

Committee on Foreign Affairs. (1979). *The death of Representative Leo J. Ryan, Peoples Temple, and Jonestown: Understanding a tragedy.* U.S. House of Representatives, 96th Congress, First Session. Washington, DC: Government Printing Office.

Compton, J. A., & Pfau, M. (2004). Use of inoculation to foster resistance to credit card marketing targeting college students. *Journal of Applied Communication Research, 32*(4), 343–364.

Comte, I. A. (1875). *System of positive polity* (Vol. 1). London: Longmans, Green.

Connolly, T. (2002). Regret in decision making. *Current Directions in Psychological Science, 11,* 212–216.

Consumer Federation of America. (1999, June 8). Credit card debt imposes huge costs on many college students: Previous research understates extent of debt and related problems. Retrieved October 11, 2008, from www.consumerfederation.org/backpage/press.html

Conway, M., & Ross, M. (1984). Getting what you want by revising what you had. *Journal of Personality and Social Psychology, 47,* 738–748.

Cook, T. D., & Campbell, D. T. (1979). *Quasi-experimentation.* Boston: Houghton Mifflin.

Cooley, C. H. (1902). *Human nature and the social order.* New York: Charles Scribner's Sons.

Cooper, M. L., Shaver, P. R., & Collins, N. L. (1998). Attachment styles, emotion regulation, and adjustment in adolescence. *Journal of Personality and Social Psychology, 74,* 1380–1397.

Copeland, J. T. (1994). Prophecies of power: Motivational implications of social power for behavioral confirmation. *Journal of Personality and Social Psychology, 67,* 264–277.

Correll, J., Park, B., Judd, C. M., & Wittenbrink, B. (2002). The police officer's dilemma: Using ethnicity to disambiguate potentially threatening individuals. *Journal of Personality and Social Psychology, 86,* 1314–1329.

Cosmides, L. (1989). The logic of social exchange: Has natural selection shaped how humans reason? Studies with the Wason selection task. *Cognition, 31,* 187–276.

Cosmides, L., & Tooby, J. (1992). Cognitive adaptations for social exchange. In J. Barkow, L. Cosmides, & J. Tooby (Eds.), *The adapted mind: Evolutionary psychology and the generation of culture* (pp. 163–228). Oxford, UK: Oxford University Press.

Costa, P. T., & McCrae, R. R. (1980). Influence of extraversion and neuroticism on subjective well-being: Happy and unhappy people. *Journal of Personality and Social Psychology, 38,* 668–678.

Costa, P. T., & McCrae, R. R. (1984). Personality as a life-long determinant of well-being. In C. Z. Malatesta & C. E. Izard (Eds.), *Emotion in adult development* (pp. 141–157). Beverly Hills, CA: Sage.

Costa, P. T., McCrae, R. R., & Zonderman, A. B. (1987). Environmental and dispositional influences on well-being: Longitudinal follow-up of an American national sample. *British Journal of Psychology, 78,* 299–306.

Cottrell, C. A., Neuberg, S. L., & Li, N. P. (2007). What do people desire in others? A sociofunctional perspective on the importance of different valued characteristics. *Journal of Personality and Social Psychology, 92,* 208–231.

Cottrell, N. B., Wack, D. L., Sekerak, G. J, & Rittle, R. H. (1968). Social facilitation of dominant responses by the presence of an audience and the mere presence of others. *Journal of Personality and Social Psychology, 9,* 245–250.

Coyle, C. T., & Enright, R. D. (1997). Forgiveness intervention with post-abortion men. *Journal of Consulting and Clinical Psychology, 65,* 1042–1046.

Coyne, J. C. (1976). Toward an interactional description of depression. *Psychiatry, 39,* 28–40.

Coyne, J. C., & DeLongis, A. (1986). Going beyond social support: The role of social relationships in adaptation. *Journal of Consulting and Clinical Psychology, 54,* 454–460.

Coyne, J. C., Kahn, J., & Gotlib, I. H. (1987). Depression. In T. Jacob (Ed.), *Family interaction and psychopathology* (pp. 509–533). New York: Plenum Press.

Cramer, P., & Steinwert, T. (1998). Thin is good, fat is bad: How early does it begin? *Journal of Applied Developmental Psychology, 19,* 429–451.

Cramer, R. E., McMaster, M. R., Bartell, P. A., & Dragna, M. (1988). Subject competence and minimization of the bystander effect. *Journal of Applied Social Psychology, 18,* 1133–1148.

Crandall, C. S. (1988). Social contagion of binge eating. *Journal of Personality and Social Psychology, 55,* 588–598.

Crandall, C. S. (1994). Prejudice against fat people: Ideology and self-interest. *Journal of Personality and Social Psychology, 66,* 882–894.

Crary, W. G. (1966). Reactions to incongruent self-experiences. *Journal of Consulting Psychology, 30,* 246–252.

Crick, N. R., & Grotpeter, J. K. (1995). Relational aggression, gender, and social-psychological adjustment. *Child Development, 66,* 710–722.

Croake, J. W., & James, B. (1973). A four year comparison of premarital sexual attitudes. *Journal of Sex Research, 9,* 91–96.

Crocker, J., & Major, B. (1989). Social stigma and self-esteem: The self-protective properties of stigma. *Psychological Review, 96,* 608–630.

Crocker, J., & Park, L. E. (2004). The costly pursuit of self-esteem. *Psychological Bulletin, 130,* 392–414.

Crocker, J., & Schwartz, I. (1985). Prejudice and ingroup favoritism in a minimal intergroup situation: Effects of self-esteem. *Personality and Social Psychology Bulletin, 11,* 379–386.

Crocker, J., Sommers, S. R., & Luhtanen, R. K. (2002). Hopes dashed and dreams fulfilled: Contingencies of self-worth and admissions to graduate school. *Personality and Social Psychology Bulletin, 28,* 1275–1286.

Crocker, J., Voelkl, K., Testa, M., & Major, B. (1991). Social stigma: The affective consequences of attributional ambiguity. *Journal of Personality and Social Psychology, 60,* 218–228.

Croizet, J. C., Désert, M., Dutrévis, M., & Leyens, J. P. (2001). Stereotype threat, social class, gender, and academic under-achievement: When our reputation catches up to us and takes us over. *Social Psychology of Education, 4,* 295–310.

Cronin, A. K. (2003). *Terrorists and suicide attacks* (No. RL32058). Washington, DC: Congressional Research Service.

Croskerry, P. (2003). The importance of cognitive errors in diagnosis and strategies to minimize them. *Academic Medicine, 78,* 775–780.

Crossman, R. H. (1987). *The god that failed.* Washington, DC: Regnery Gateway. (Original work published 1949)

Cunningham, M. R. (1979). Weather, mood, and helping behavior: Quasi experiments with the Sunshine Samaritan. *Journal of Personality and Social Psychology, 37,* 1947–1956.

Cunningham, M. R. (2009) Social allergies. In H. Reis & S. Sprecher (Eds.), *Handbook of human relationships.* Thousand Oaks, CA: Sage.

Cunningham, M. R., Barbee, A. P., & Druen, P. B. (1997). Social antigens and allergies: The development of hypersensitivity in close relationships. In R. Kowalski (Ed.), *Aversive interpersonal behaviors* (pp. 190–215). New York: Plenum Press.

Cunningham, M. R., Barbee, A. P., & Mandal, E. (in press). Hurtful behaviors in the workplace. In R. Kowalski (Ed.), *Feeling hurt in close relationships.* Cambridge University Press.

Cupach, W. R., & Spitzberg, B. H. (2000). Obsessive relational intrusion: Incidence, perceived severity, and coping. *Violence and Victims, 15,* 357–372.

Dabbs, J. M. (2000). *Heroes, rogues, and lovers: Testosterone and behavior.* New York: McGraw-Hill.

Dabbs, J. M., Jr., Carr, T. S., Frady, R. L., & Riad, J. K. (1995). Testosterone, crime, and misbehavior among 692 male prison inmates. *Personality and Individual Differences, 18,* 627–633.

Daly, M. J., & Burton, R. L. (1983). Self-esteem and irrational beliefs: An exploratory investigation with implications for counseling. *Journal of Counseling Psychology, 30,* 361–366.

Damasio, A. R. (1994) *Descartes' error.* London: Picador.

Danner, D., Snowdon, D., & Friesen, W. (2001). Positive emotions in early life and longevity: Findings from the Nun Study. *Journal of Personality and Social Psychology, 80,* 804–813.

Darby, B. W., & Schlenker, B. R. (1982). Children's reactions to apologies. *Journal of Personality and Social Psychology, 43,* 742–753.

Dardenne, B., Dumont, M., & Bollier, T. (2007). Insidious dangers of benevolent sexism: Consequences for women's performance. *Journal of Personality and Social Psychology, 93*(5), 764–779.

Darley, J. M., & Batson, C. D. (1973). From Jerusalem to Jericho: A study of situational and dispositional variables in helping behavior. *Journal of Personality and Social Psychology, 27,* 100–108.

Darley, J. M., & Gross, P. H. (1983). A hypothesis-confirming bias in labeling effects. *Journal of Personality and Social Psychology, 44*(1), 20–33.

Darley, J. M., & Latane, B. (1968). Bystander intervention in emergencies: *Journal of Personality and Social Psychology, 8,* 377–383.

Darwin, C. (1859). *The origin of species by means of natural selection, or the preservation of favoured races in the struggle for life* (reprinted from the 6th ed.). New York: A. L. Burt.

Darwin, C. (1948). *Origin of species.* New York: Modern Library. (Original work published 1871)

Das, E., Bushman, B. J., Bezemer, M. D., Kerkhof, P., & Vermeulen, I. E. (2009). How terrorism news reports increase prejudice against outgroups: A terror management account. *Journal of Experimental Social Psychology, 45,* 453–459.

David, J. P., Green, P. J., Martin, R., & Suls, J. (1997). Differential roles of neuroticism, extraversion, and event desirability for mood in daily life: An integrative model of top-down and bottom-up influences. *Journal of Personality and Social Psychology, 73,* 149–159.

Davies, G. (2002). *A history of money from ancient times to the present day.* Cardiff: University of Wales Press.

Davis, B. P., & Knowles, E. S. (1999). A disrupt-then-reframe technique of social influence. *Journal of Personality and Social Psychology, 76,* 192–199.

Davis, J. H., Stasson, M. F., Parks, C. D., Hulbert, L., Kameda, T., Zimmerman, S. K., & Karou, O. (1993). Quantitative decisions by groups and individuals: Voting procedures and monetary awards by mock civil juries. *Journal of Experimental Social Psychology, 29,* 326–346.

Davis, K. E. & Frieze, I. H. (2000). Research on stalking: What do we know and where do we go? *Violence and Victims, 15,* 473–487.

Davis, P. A. (1983). *Suicidal adolescents.* Springfield, IL: C. C. Thomas.

Davis, S. F., Grover, C. A., Becker, A. H., & McGregor, L. N. (1992). Academic dishonesty: Prevalence, determinants, techniques, and punishments. *Teaching of Psychology, 19,* 16–20.

Dawkins, R. (1989). *The selfish gene.* New York: Oxford University Press. (Original work published 1976)

Dawson, R. E., & Prewitt, K. (1969). *Political socialization.* Boston: Little, Brown.

Day, D., & Ullom, H. H. (Eds.). (1947). *The autobiography of Sam Houston.* Norman: University of Oklahoma Press.

De Brouwer, A.-M. (2005). *Supranational criminal prosecution of sexual violence: The ICC and the practice of the ICTY and the ICTR.* Mortsel, Belgium: Intersentia.

De Hoog, N., Stroebe, W., & De Wit, J. B. F. (2007). The impact of vulnerability to and severity of a health risk on processing and acceptance of fear-arousing communications: A meta-analysis. *Review of General Psychology, 11*(3), 258–285

de Rougemont, D. (1956). *Love in the Western world.* New York: Schoeken.

de Waal, F. B. M. (2002). Evolutionary psychology: The wheat and the chaff. *Current Directions in Psychological Science, 11,* 187–191.

de Waal, F. B. M., & Davis, J. M. (2003). Capuchin cognitive ecology: Cooperation based on projected returns. *Neuropsychologia, 41,* 221–228.

Deacon, T. (1997). What makes the human brain different? *Annual Review of Anthropology, 26,* 337–357.

deCharms, R. (1968). *Personal causation.* New York: Academic Press.

Deci, E. L. (1971). The effects of externally mediated rewards on intrinsic motivation. *Journal of Personality and Social Psychology, 18,* 105–115.

Deci, E. L. (1975). *Intrinsic motivation.* New York: Plenum Press.

Deci, E. L., Koestner, R., & Ryan, R. M. (1999). A meta-analytic review of experiments examining the effects of extrinsic rewards on intrinsic motivation. *Psychological Bulletin, 125,* 627–668.

Deci, E. L., Nezlek, J., & Sheinman, L. (1981). Characteristics of the rewarder and the intrinsic motivation of the rewardee. *Journal of Personality and Social Psychology, 40,* 1–10.

Deci, E. L., & Ryan, R. M. (1985). *Intrinsic motivation and self-determination in human behavior.* New York: Plenum Press.

Deci, E. L., & Ryan, R. M. (2000). The "what" and "why" of goal pursuits: Human needs and the self-determination of behavior. *Psychological Inquiry, 11,* 227–268.

DeJong, W. (1980). The stigma of obesity: The consequences of naive assumptions concerning the causes of physical deviance. *Journal of Health and Social Behavior, 21*(1), 75–87.

DeJong, W. (1993). Obesity as a characterological stigma: The issue of responsibility and judgments of task performance. *Psychological Reports, 73,* 963–970.

DeLamater, J., & Hyde, J. S. (1998). Essentialism vs. social constructionism in the study of human sexuality. *Journal of Sex Research, 35,* 10–18.

DeLongis, A., Folkman, S., & Lazarus, R. (1988). The impact of daily stress on health and mood psychological and social resources as mediators. *Journal of Personality and Social Psychology, 54,* 486–495.

DeMeis, J., & Stearns, E. (1992). Relationship of school entrance age to academic and social performance. *Journal of Educational Research, 86,* 21–27.

Denson, T. F., Aviles, F. E., Pollock, V. E., Earleywine, M., Vasquez, E. A., & Miller, N. (2008). The effects of alcohol and the salience of aggressive cues on triggered displaced aggression. *Aggressive Behavior, 34*(1), 25–33.

DePalma, M. T., Madey, S. F., Tillman, T. C., & Wheeler, J. (1999). Perceived patient responsibility and belief in a just world affect helping. *Basic and Applied Social Psychology, 21,* 131–137.

DePaulo, B. M., Kashy, D. A., Kirkendol, S. E., Wyer, M. M., & Epstein, J. A. (1996). Lying in everyday life. *Journal of Personality and Social Psychology, 70*(5), 979–995.

DeSteno, D. A., Bartlett, M. Y., Braverman, J., & Salovey, P. (2002). Sex differences in jealousy: Evolutionary mechanisms or artifact of measurement? *Journal of Personality and Social Psychology, 83,* 1103–1116.

DeSteno, D. A., & Salovey, P. (1996). Evolutionary origins of sex differences in jealousy? Questioning the "fitness" of the model. *Psychological Science, 7,* 367–372.

Deutsch, M., & Gerard, H. B. (1955). A study of normative and informational social influences upon individual judgment. *Journal of Abnormal and Social Psychology, 51,* 629–636.

Devine, P. G. (1989). Stereotypes and prejudice: Their automatic and controlled components. *Journal of Personality and Social Psychology, 56,* 5–18.

Devine, P. G., & Malpass, R. S. (1985). Orienting strategies in differential face recognition. *Personality and Social Psychology Bulletin, 11*(1), 33–40.

Devine, P. G., Plant, E. A., Amodio, A. M., Harmon-Jones, E., & Vance, S. L. (2002). Exploring the relationship between implicit and explicit prejudice: The role of motivations to respond without prejudice. *Journal of Personality and Social Psychology, 82,* 835–848.

DeVries, D., & Kaiser, R. B. (2003, November). Going sour in the suite. Paper presented at the Maximizing Executive Effectiveness workshop, Miami, FL.

DeWall, C. N., & Baumeister, R. F. (2006). Alone but feeling no pain: Effects of social exclusion on physical pain tolerance and pain threshold, affective forecasting, and interpersonal empathy. *Journal of Personality and Social Psychology, 91,* 1–15.

Di Paula, A., & Campbell, J. D. (2002). Self-esteem and persistence in the face of failure. *Journal of Personality and Social Psychology, 83,* 711–724.

Diamond, L. M. (2003a). An attachment perspective on female sexual fluidity. Paper presented at the Women's Sexualities Conference: Historical, Interdisciplinary, and International Perspectives, sponsored by the Kinsey Institute for Research in Sex, Gender, and Reproduction, Bloomington, IN.

Diamond, L. M. (2003b). What does sexual orientation orient? A biobehavioral model distinguishing romantic love and sexual desire. *Psychological Review, 110,* 173–192.

Diamond, L. M. (2004). Emerging perspectives on distinctions between romantic love and sexual desire. *Current Directions in Psychological Science, 13,* 116–119.

Dickinson, D. J., & Larsen, J. D. (1963). The effects of chronological age in months on school achievement. *Journal of Educational Research, 56,* 492–493.

Dictionary of marketing terms. (2004). http://www.marketingpower.com/live/mg-dictionary-view3424.php

Diener, E., & Diener, M. (1995). Cross-cultural correlates of life satisfaction and self-esteem. *Journal of Personality and Social Psychology, 68,* 653–663.

Diener, E., Fraser, S. C., Beaman, A. L., & Kelem, R. T. (1976). Effects of deindividuation variables on stealing among Halloween trick-or-treaters. *Journal of Personality and Social Psychology, 33,* 178–183.

Diener, E., Lucas, R. E., & Scollon, C. N. (2006). Beyond the hedonic treadmill: Revisions to the adaptation theory of well-being. *American Psychologist, 61,* 305–314.

Diener, E., & Wallbom, M. (1976). Effects of self-awareness on antinormative behavior. *Journal of Research in Personality, 10,* 107–111.

Diener, E., Wolsic, B., & Fujita, F. (1995). Physical attractiveness and subjective well-being. *Journal of Personality and Social Psychology, 69,* 120–129.

Dienstbier, R. A., & Munter, P. O. (1971). Cheating as a function of the labeling of natural arousal. *Journal of Personality and Social Psychology, 17,* 208–213.

Dill, K. E., Anderson, C. A., Anderson, K. B., & Deuser, W. E. (1997). Effects of aggressive personality on social expectations and social perceptions. *Journal of Research in Personality, 31,* 272–292.

Dion, J., & Mellor, B. (2004, August). Is sport really good for you? *EnRoute,* pp. 33–34.

Dion, K. (1973). Young children's stereotyping of facial attractiveness. *Developmental Psychology, 9,* 183–188.

Dion, K. K., Berscheid, E., & Walster, F. H. (1972). What is beautiful is good. *Journal of Personality and Social Psychology, 24,* 285–290.

Dodge, K. A., & Coie, J. D. (1987). Social-information-processing factors in reactive and proactive aggression in children's peer groups. *Journal of Personality and Social Psychology, 53,* 1146–1158.

Dollard, J., Doob, L., Miller, N., Mowrer, O., & Sears, R. (1939). *Frustration and aggression.* New Haven, CT: Yale University Press.

Donnerstein, E., & Berkowitz, L. (1981). Victim reactions in aggressive erotic films as a factor in violence against women. *Journal of Personality and Social Psychology, 41,* 710–724.

Dostoevsky, F. (1961). *Notes from the underground.* Forgotten Books. (Original work published 1864)

Dovidio, J. F., & Gaertner, S. L. (1999). Reducing prejudice: Combating intergroup biases. *Current Directions in Psychological Science, 8,* 101–105.

Dowd, J. J. (1975). Aging as exchange: A preface to theory. *Journal of Gerontology, 30,* 584–594.

Downey, G., & Romero-Canyas, R. (2005). Rejection sensitivity as a predictor of affective and behavioral responses to interpersonal stress: A defensive motivational system. In K. D. Williams, J. P. Forgas, & W. von Hippel (Eds.), *The social outcast: Ostracism, social exclusion, rejection, and bullying.* New York: Psychology Press.

Doyle, A. C. (1974). *The memoirs of Sherlock Holmes.* London: J. Murray; Cape. (Original work published 1894)

Draper, P. (1976). Social and economic constraints on child life among the !Kung. In R. B. Lee & I. DeVore (Eds.), *Kalahari hunter-gatherers: Studies of the !Kung San and their neighbors* (pp. 199–217). Cambridge, MA: Harvard University Press.

Du Bois-Reymond, M., & Ravesloot, J. (1996). The roles of parents and peers in the sexual and relational socialization of adolescents. In K. Hurrelmann & S. Hamilton (Eds.), *Social problems and social contexts in adolescence* (pp. 175–197). New York: Aldine de Gruyter.

Dube, K. C., Kumar, A., Kumar, N., & Gupta, S. P. (1978). Prevalence and pattern of drug use amongst college students. *Acta Psychiatrica Scandinavica, 57,* 336–356.

Dudley, R. T. (1999). Self-other judgments of paranormal and religious belief. *Journal of Social Behavior and Personality, 14,* 309–314.

Dunbar, R. I. M. (1993). Coevolution of neocortical size, group size, and language in humans. *Behavioral and Brain Sciences, 16,* 681–694.

Dunbar, R. I. M. (1996). *Grooming, gossip, and the evolution of language.* Cambridge, MA: Harvard University Press.

Dunbar, R. I. M. (1998). The social brain hypothesis. *Evolutionary Anthropology, 6,* 178–190.

Duncan, C. P., & Nelson, J. E. (1985). Effects of humor in a radio advertising experiment. *Journal of Advertising, 14,* 33–40, 64.

Dunn, E. W., Brackett, M. A., Ashton-James, C., Schneiderman, E., & Salovey, P. (2007). On emotionally intelligent time travel: Individual differences in affective forecasting ability. *Personality and Social Psychology Bulletin, 33*(1), 85–93.

Dunning, D. (1999). A newer look: Motivated social cognition and the schematic representation of social concepts. *Psychological Inquiry, 10,* 1–11.

Dunning, D., & McElwee, R. O. (1995). Idiosyncratic trait definitions: Implications for self-description and social judgment. *Journal of Personality and Social Psychology, 68,* 936–946.

Dunning, D., Meyerowitz, J. A., & Holzberg, A. D. (1989). Ambiguity and self-evaluation: The role of idiosyncratic trait definitions in self-serving assessments of ability. *Journal of Personality and Social Psychology, 57,* 1082–1090.

Dunning, D., Perie, M., & Story, A. L. (1991). Self-serving prototypes of social categories. *Journal of Personality and Social Psychology, 61,* 957–968.

Dunning, D., & Perretta, S. (2002). Automaticity and eyewitness accuracy: A 10-to-12 second rule for distinguishing accurate from inaccurate positive identifications. *Journal of Applied Psychology, 87,* 951–962.

Dutch Islamic school set ablaze. (2004, November 9). *BBC News.* Retrieved January 26, 2005, from http://news.bbc.co.uk/1/hi/world/europe/3997943.stm

Dutch Muslim school hit by bomb. (2004, November 8). *BBC News.* Retrieved January 26, 2005, from http://news.bbc.co.uk/2/hi/europe/3991547.stm

Dutton, D. G. (1971). Reactions of restaurateurs to blacks and whites violating restaurant dress requirements. *Canadian Journal of Behavioural Science, 3,* 298–302.

Dutton, D. G., & Aron, A. P. (1974). Some evidence for heightened sexual attraction under conditions of high anxiety. *Journal of Personality and Social Psychology, 30,* 510–517.

Dutton, D. G., & Lake, R. A. (1973). Threat of own prejudice and reverse discrimination in interracial situations. *Journal of Personality and Social Psychology, 28,* 94–100.

Duval, S., & Wicklund, R. (1972). *A theory of objective self-awareness.* New York: Academic Press.

Dweck, C. S. (1996) Implicit theories as organizers of goals and behavior. In P. Gollwitzer & J. Bargh (Eds.), *The psychology of action: Linking cognition and motivation to behavior* (pp. 69–91). New York: Guilford Press.

Dweck, C. S., & Leggett, E. L. (1988). A social-cognitive approach to motivation and personality. *Psychological Review, 95,* 256–273.

Eagly, A. H., Ashmore, R. D., Makhijani, M. G., & Longo, L. C. (1991). What is beautiful is good, but. . .: A meta-analytic review of the physical attractiveness stereotype. *Psychological Bulletin, 110,* 109–128.

Eagly, A. H., & Chaiken, S. (1998). Attitude structure and function. In D. T. Gilbert, S. T. Fiske, & G. Lindzey (Eds.), *Handbook of social psychology* (4th ed., Vol. 1, pp. 269–322). New York: McGraw-Hill.

Eagly, A. H., & Crowley, M. (1986). Gender and helping behavior: A meta-analytic view of the social psychological literature. *Psychological Bulletin, 100,* 283–308.

Easterbrook, J. A. (1959). The effect of emotion on the utilization and the organization of behavior. *Psychological Review, 66,* 183–201.

Edelstein, R. S., & Shaver, P. R. (2004). Avoidant attachment: Exploration of an oxymoron. In D. Mashek & A. Aron (Eds.), *Handbook of closeness and intimacy* (pp. 397–412). Mahwah, NJ: Erlbaum.

Edgerton, R. (1971). *The individual in cultural adaptation.* Berkeley: University of California Press.

Efran, M. G., & Patterson, E. W. J. (1974). Voters vote beautiful: The effects of physical appearance on a national election. *Canadian Journal of Behavioral Science, 6,* 352–356.

Egan, G. (1970). *Encounter: Group processes for interpersonal growth.* Monterey, CA: Brooks/Cole.

Ehrenreich, B. (1999, March 8). The real truth about the female. *Time, 153*(9), 57–91.

Einon, D. (1994). Are men more promiscuous than women? *Ethology and Sociobiology, 15*(3), 131–143.

Eisenberg, N., & Lennon, R. (1983). Sex differences in empathy and related capacities. *Psychological Bulletin, 94,* 100–131.

Eisner, M. (2001). Modernization, self-control and lethal violence: The long-term dynamics of European homicide rates in theoretical perspective. *British Journal of Criminology, 41,* 618–638.

Ekman, P., Friesen, W. V., O'Sullivan, M., Chan, A., Diacoyanni-Tarlatzis, I., Heider, K., et al. (1987). Universals and cultural differences in the judgments of facial expressions of emotion. *Journal of Personality and Social Psychology, 53,* 712–717.

Ekman, P., & O'Sullivan, M. (1991). Who can catch a liar? *American Psychologist, 46*(9), 913–920.

Elder, G. H., Jr., & Clipp, E. C. (1988). Combat experience, comradeship, and psychological health. In J. P. Wilson, Z. Harel, & B. Kahana (Eds.), *Human adaptation to extreme stress: From the Holocaust to Vietnam* (pp. 131–156). New York: Plenum Press.

Elfenbein, H. A., & Ambady, N. (2002). On the universality and cultural specificity of emotion recognition: A meta-analysis. *Psychological Bulletin, 128,* 203–235.

Ellis, A. (1977). *How to live with—and without—anger.* New York: Reader's Digest Press.

Ellsworth, P. C. (1994). Sense, culture, and sensibility. In S. Kitayama & H. R. Markus (Eds.), *Emotion and culture.* Washington, DC: American Psychological Association.

Ellsworth, P. C., & Smith, C. A. (1988). Shades of joy: Patterns of appraisal differentiating pleasant emotions. *Cognition and Emotion, 2,* 301–331.

Emmons, R. A. (1989). The personal striving approach to personality. In L. Pervin (Ed.), *Goal concepts and personality and social cognition* (pp. 87–126). Hillsdale, NJ: Erlbaum.

Emswiller, T., Deaux, K., & Willits, J. E. (1971). Similarity, sex, and requests for small favors. *Journal of Applied Social Psychology, 1,* 284–291.

Engs, R. C., & Hanson, D. J. (1990). Gender differences in drinking patterns and problems among college students: A review of the literature. *Journal of Alcohol and Drug Education, 35,* 36–47.

Entman, R. M. (1993). Framing: Toward clarification of a fractured paradigm. *Journal of Communication, 43,* 51–58.

Epley, N., & Gneezy, A. (2007). The framing of financial windfalls and implications for public policy. *Journal of Socio-Economics, 36,* 36–47.

Epley, N., Mak, D., & Idson, L. C. (2006). Bonus or rebate? The impact of income framing on spending and saving. *Journal of Behavioral Decision Making, 19*(3), 213–227.

Epps, J., & Kendall, P. C. (1995). Hostile attribution bias in adults. *Cognitive Therapy and Research, 19,* 159–178.

Epstein, S. (1979). The stability of behavior: I. On predicting most of the people much of the time. *Journal of Personality and Social Psychology, 37,* 1097–1126.

Epstude, K., & Roese, N. J. (2008). The functional theory of counterfactual thinking. *Personality and Social Psychology Review, 12,* 168–192.

Equal Opportunity Employment Commission. (2001). Muslim/Arab employment discrimination charges since 9/11. Retrieved January 7, 2002, from http://www.eeoc.gov/origin/z-stats.html

Erber, R., & Erber, M. W. (2000). The self-regulation of moods: Second thoughts on the importance of happiness in everyday life. *Psychological Science, 11,* 142–148.

Erber, R., & Fiske, S. T. (1984). Outcome dependency and attention to inconsistent information. *Journal of Personality and Social Psychology, 47,* 709–726.

Erber, R., Wegner, D. M., & Therriault, N. (1996). On being cool and collected: Mood regulation in anticipation of social interaction. *Journal of Personality and Social Psychology, 70,* 757–766.

Erez, A., & Isen, A. M. (2002). The influence of positive affect on the components of expectancy motivation. *Journal of Applied Psychology, 87,* 1055–1067.

Erickson, B., Lind, E. A., Johnson, B. C., & O'Barr, W. M. (1978). Speech style and impression formation in a court setting: The effects of "powerful" and "powerless'" speech. *Journal of Experimental Social Psychology, 14,* 266–279.

Erikson, E. H. (1950). *Childhood and society.* New York: Norton.

Eron, L. D., & Huesmann, L. R. (1990). The stability of aggressive behavior—even into the third generation. In M. Lewis & S. M. Miller (Eds.), *Handbook of developmental psychopathology* (pp. 147–156). New York: Plenum Press.

Estrada, C. A., Isen, A. M., & Young, M. J. (1997). Positive affect facilitates integration of information and decreases anchoring in reasoning among physicians. *Organizational Behavior and Human Decision Processes, 72,* 117–135.

Exline, J. J. (2002). Stumbling blocks on the religious road: Fractured relationships, nagging vices, and the inner struggle to believe. *Psychological Inquiry, 13,* 182–189.

Exline, J. J., Baumeister, R. F., Bushman, B. J., Campbell, W. K., & Finkel, E. J. (2004). Too proud to let go: Narcissistic entitlement as a barrier to forgiveness. *Journal of Personality and Social Psychology, 87,* 894–912.

Exline, J. J., Baumeister, R. F., Zell, A. L., Kraft, A. J., & Witvliet, C. V. O. (2008). Not so innocent: Does seeing one's own capability for wrongdoing predict forgiveness? *Journal of Personality and Social Psychology, 94,* 495–515.

Exline, J. J., & Lobel, M. (1999). The perils of outperformance: Sensitivity about being the target of a threatening upward comparison. *Psychological Bulletin, 125,* 307–337.

Exline, J. J., & Rose, E. (2005). Religious and spiritual struggles. In R. F. Paloutzian & C. L. Park (Eds.), *Handbook of the psychology of religion* (pp. 315–330). New York: Guilford Press.

Exline, J. J., Worthington, E. L., Hill, P., & McCullough, M. E. (2003). Forgiveness and justice: A research agenda for social and personality psychology. *Personality and Social Psychology Review, 7,* 337–348.

Faith, heroics and bedtime snacks hailed at Columbine funerals. (1999, April 26). *CNN.* Retrieved December 26, 2004, from http://www.cnn.com/US/9904/26/school.shooting.funeral/

Falck, R., & Craig, R. (1988). Classroom-oriented primary prevention programming for drug abuse. *Journal of Psychoactive Drugs, 20,* 403–408.

Farberow, N. L. (1975). Cultural history of suicide. In N. L. Farberow (Ed.), *Suicide in different cultures* (pp. 1–16). Baltimore, MD: University Park Press.

Farrell, W. (1993). *The myth of male power.* New York: Berkley Books.

Farwell, L., & Wohlwend-Lloyd, R. (1998) Narcissistic processes: Optimistic expectations, favorable self-evaluations, and self-enhancing attributions. *Journal of Personality, 66,* 65–83.

Fazio, R. H. (1990). Multiple processes by which attitudes guide behavior: The MODE model as an integrative frame work. In P. Zanna (Ed.), *Advances in experimental social psychology* (Vol. 23, pp. 75–109). San Diego, CA: Academic Press.

Fazio, R. H., Blascovich, J., & Driscoll, D. M. (1992). On the functional value of attitudes: The influence of accessible attitudes on the ease and quality of decision making. *Personality and Social Psychology Bulletin, 18,* 388–401.

Fazio, R. H., Effrein, E. A., & Falender, V. J. (1981). Self-perceptions following social interaction. *Journal of Personality and Social Psychology, 41,* 232–242.

Fazio, R. H., Jackson, J. R., Dunton, B. C., & Williams, C. J. (1995). Variability in automatic activation as an unobtrusive measure of racial attitudes: A bona fide pipeline? *Journal of Personality and Social Psychology, 69,* 1013–1027.

Fazio, R. H., & Olson, M. A. (2003). Implicit measures in social cognition research: Their meaning and uses. *Annual Review of Psychology, 54,* 297–327.

Fazio, R. H., & Powell, M. C. (1997). On the value of knowing one's likes and dislikes: Attitude accessibility, stress, and health in college. *Psychological Science, 8,* 430–436.

Fazio, R. H., & Towles-Schwen, T. (1999). The MODE model of attitude–behavior processes. In S. Chaiken (Ed.), *Dual-process theories in social psychology* (pp. 97–116). New York: Guilford Press.

Feeney, B. C., & Collins, N. L. (2001). Predictors of caregiving in adult intimate relationships. *Journal of Personality and Social Psychology, 80,* 972–994.

Feeney, J. A. (1996). Attachment, caregiving, and marital satisfaction. *Personal Relationships, 3,* 401–416.

Fehr, B., & Russell, J. A. (1984). Concept of emotion viewed from a prototype perspective. *Journal of Experimental Psychology: General, 113,* 464–486.

Fehr, E., & Gächter, S. (2002). Altruistic punishment in humans. *Nature, 415*(6868), 137–140.

Fein, S., & Spencer, S. J. (1997). Prejudice as self-image maintenance: Affirming the self through derogating others. *Journal of Personality and Social Psychology, 73,* 31–44.

Feingold, A. (1988). Matching for attractiveness in romantic partners and same-sex friends: A meta-analysis and theoretical critique. *Psychological Bulletin, 104,* 226–235.

Feingold, A. (1992). Gender differences in mate selection preferences: A test of the parental investment model. *Psychological Bulletin, 112,* 125–139.

Felson, R. B. (2002). *Violence and gender reexamined.* Washington, DC: American Psychological Association.

Fenell, D. (1993). Characteristics of long-term first marriages. *Journal of Mental Health Counseling, 15,* 446–460.

Fenigstein, A., Scheier, M. F., & Buss, A. H. (1975). Public and private self-consciousness: Assessment and theory. *Journal of Consulting and Clinical Psychology, 43,* 522–527.

Fenton-O'Creevy, M., Nicholson, N., Soane, E., & Willman, P. (2003) Trading on illusions: Unrealistic perceptions of control and trading performance. *Journal of Occupational and Organizational Psychology, 76,* 53–68.

Ferrari, J. R. (2001). Procrastination as self-regulation failure of performance: Effects of cognitive load, self-awareness, and time limits on "working under pressure." *European Journal of Personality, 15,* 391–406.

Ferrari, J. R., Johnson, J. L., and McCown, W. G. (1995). *Procrastination and task avoidance: Theory, research, and treatment.* New York: Plenum Press.

Ferriere, R. (1998, June 11). Help and you shall be helped. *Nature, 393,* 517–519.

Feshbach, S. (1964). The function of aggression and the regulation of aggressive drive. *Psychological Review, 71,* 257–272.

Festinger, L. (1954). A theory of social comparison processes. *Human Relations, 7,* 117–140.

Festinger, L., & Carlsmith, J. M. (1959). Cognitive consequences of forced compliance. *Journal of Abnormal and Social Psychology, 58,* 203–210.

Festinger, L., & Maccoby, N. (1964). On resistance to persuasive communications. *Journal of Abnormal and Social Psychology, 68,* 359–366.

Festinger, L., Pepitone, A., & Newcomb, T. (1952). Some consequences of deindividuation in a group. *Journal of Abnormal and Social Psychology, 47,* 382–389.

Festinger, L., Schachter, S., & Back, K. W. (1950) *Social pressures in informal groups: A study of human factors in housing.* New York: Harper.

Fiddick, L., Cosmides, L., & Tooby, J. (2000). No interpretation without representation: The role of domain-specific representations and inferences in the Wason selection task. *Cognition, 77,* 1–79.

Filiberti, A., Ripamonti, C., Totis, A., Ventafridda, V., De Conno, F., Contiero, P., & Tamburini, M. (2001). Characteristics of terminal cancer patients who committed suicide during a home palliative care program. *Journal of Pain and Symptom Management, 22,* 544–553.

Fincham, F. D., Beach, S. R., & Davila, J. (2004). Forgiveness and conflict resolution in marriage. *Journal of Family Psychology, 18,* 72–81.

Fincham, F. D., Hall, J. H., & Beach, S. R. H. (2005). 'Til lack of forgiveness doth us part: Forgiveness in marriage. In E. L. Worthington (Ed.), *Handbook of forgiveness* (pp. 207–226). New York: Wiley.

Finkel, E. J., Rusbult, C. E., Kumashiro, M., & Hannon, P. (2002). Dealing with betrayal in close relationships: Does commitment promote forgiveness? *Journal of Personality and Social Psychology, 82,* 956–974.

Finnie, W. C. (1973). Field experiments and litter control. *Environment and Behavior, 5,* 123–143.

Fischer, A. H., & Roseman, I. J. (2007). Beat them or ban them: The characteristics and social functions of anger and contempt. *Journal of Personality and Social Psychology, 93*(1), 103–115.

Fischer, P., Greitemeyer, T., & Frey, D. (2008). Unemployment and aggression: The moderating role of self awareness on the effect of unemployment on aggression. *Aggressive Behavior, 34*(1), 34–45.

Fischhoff, B., Lichtenstein, S., Slovic, P., Derby, S. L., & Keeney, R. L. (1981). *Acceptable risk.* New York: Cambridge University Press.

Fisher, C. D. (1978). The effects of personal control, competence, and extrinsic reward systems on intrinsic motivation. *Organizational Behavior and Human Performance, 21,* 273–288.

Fisher, J. D., & Nadler, A. (1976). Effects of donor resources on recipient self-esteem and self-help. *Journal of Experimental Social Psychology, 12,* 139–150.

Fiske, S. (2002, November/December). Forecasting the future. *Psychology Today.* Retrieved January 30, 2009, from http://www.psychologytoday.com/articles/pto-20021125-000001.html

Fiske, S. T. (1992). Thinking is for doing: Portraits of social cognition from daguerreotype to laserphoto. *Journal of Personality and Social Psychology, 63,* 877–889.

Fiske, S. T. (2004). *Social beings: A core motives approach to social psychology.* New York: Wiley.

Fiske, S. T., & Taylor, S. E. (1984). *Social cognition.* New York: Random House.

Fiske, S. T., & Taylor, S. E. (1991). *Social cognition* (2nd ed.). New York: Random House.

Fiske, S. T., & Yamamoto, M. (2005). Coping with rejection: Core social motives, across cultures and individuals. In K. D. Williams, J. P. Forgas, & W. von Hippel (Eds.), *The social outcast: Ostracism, social exclusion, rejection, and bullying.* New York: Psychology Press.

Fitness, J. (2005). Bye, bye, black sheep: The causes and consequences of rejection in family relationships. In K. D. Williams, J. P. Forgas, & W. von Hippel (Eds.), *The social outcast: Ostracism, social exclusion, rejection, and bullying.* New York: Psychology Press.

Fitzsimons, G. M., & Bargh, J. A. (2003). Thinking of you: Nonconscious pursuit of interpersonal goals associated with relationship partners. *Journal of Personality and Social Psychology, 84,* 148–164.

Fitzsimons, G. M., & Shah, J. Y. (2008). How goal instrumentality shapes relationship evaluations. *Journal of Personality and Social Psychology, 95,* 319–337.

Flink, C., Boggiano, A. K. and Barrett, M. (1990). Controlling teaching strategies: Undermining children's self-determination and performance. *Journal of Personality and Social Psychology, 59*(5), 916–924.

Folkes, V. S. (1982). Communicating the reasons for social rejection. *Journal of Personality and Social Psychology, 18,* 235–252.

Forster, J. L. & Jeffery, R. W. (1986). Gender differences related to weight history, eating patterns, efficacy expectations, self-esteem, and weight loss among participants in a weight reduction program. *Addictive Behaviors, 11,* 141–147.

Forsyth, D. R., & Kerr, N. A. (1999, August). *Are adaptive illusions adaptive?* Poster presented at the annual meeting of the American Psychological Association, Boston, MA.

Fraley, B., & Aron, A. (2004). The effect of a shared humorous experience on closeness in initial encounters. *Personal Relationships, 11,* 61–78.

Francoeur, R. T., Perper, T., Scherzer, N. A., Sellmer, G. P., & Cornog, M. (1991). *A descriptive dictionary and atlas of sexology.* New York: Greenwood Press.

Frayser, S. G. (1985). *Varieties of sexual experience: An anthropological perspective on human sexuality.* New Haven, CT: HRAF Press.

Frazier, P., Tashiro, T., Berman, M., Steger, M., & Long, J. (2004), Correlates of levels and patterns of positive life changes following sexual assault. *Journal of Consulting and Clinical Psychology, 72,* 19–30.

Fredrickson, B. L. (1998). What good are positive emotions? *Review of General Psychology, 2,* 300–319.

Fredrickson, B. L. (2001). The role of positive emotions in positive psychology: The broaden-and-build theory of positive emotions. *American Psychologist, 56,* 218–226.

Fredrickson, B. L. (2003). The value of positive emotions. *American Scientist, 91,* 330–335.

Freedman, J. L., & Fraser, S. C. (1966). Compliance without pressure: The foot-in-the-door technique. *Journal of Personality and Social Psychology, 4,* 196–202.

Freedman, J. L., & Sears, D. O. (1965). Warning, distraction, and resistance to influence. *Journal of Personality and Social Psychology, 1*(3), 262–266.

Freedman, S. R., & Enright, R. D. (1996). Forgiveness as an intervention goal with incest survivors. *Journal of Consulting and Clinical Psychology, 64,* 983–992.

Freud, S. (1961). *Civilization and its discontents* (standard ed.). London: Norton. (Original work published 1930)

Freud, S. (1961). *Mourning and melancholia* (standard ed.). London: Norton. (Original work published 1917)

Freud, S. (1964). *Beyond the pleasure principle* (J. Strachey, Trans.). New York: Norton. (Original work published 1920)

Frey, R. G. (1983). *Rights, killing, and suffering: Moral vegetarianism and applied ethics.* Oxford, UK: Blackwell.

Friedman, L. M. (2002). *American law in the 20th century.* New Haven, CT: Yale University Press.

Frijda, N. H. (1986). *The emotions.* New York: Cambridge University Press.

Frijda, N. H., Kuipers, P., & ter Schure, E. (1989). Relations among emotion, appraisal, and emotional action readiness. *Journal of Personality and Social Psychology, 57,* 212–228.

Fukuyama, F. (1999). *Trust.* New York: Free Press.

Funder, D. C. (2001). Personality. *Annual Review of Psychology, 52,* 197–221.

Furnham, A. (2003). Belief in a just world: Research progress over the past decade. *Personality and Individual Differences, 34,* 795–817.

Gable, S. L., & Reis, H. T. (2001). Appetitive and aversive social interaction. In J. Harvey (Ed.), *Close romantic relationships: Maintenance and enhancement* (pp. 169–194). Mahwah, NJ: Erlbaum.

Gable, S. L., Reis, H. T., & Elliot, A. J. (2000). Behavioral activation and inhibition in everyday life. *Journal of Personality and Social Psychology, 78,* 1135–1149.

Gabriel, M. T., Critelli, J. W., & Ee, J. S. (1994). Narcissistic illusions in self-evaluations of intelligence and attractiveness. *Journal of Personality, 62,* 143–155.

Gaertner, L., & Iuzzini, J. (2005). Rejection and entitativity: A synergistic model of mass violence. In K. D. Williams, J. P. Forgas, & W. von Hippel (Eds.), *The social outcast: Ostracism, social exclusion, rejection, and bullying.* New York: Psychology Press.

Gaertner, S., L., & Dovidio, J. F. (1986). The aversive form of racism. In J. F. Dovidio & S. L. Gaertner (Eds.), *Prejudice, discrimination, and racism* (pp. 61–89). San Diego, CA: Academic Press.

Gailliot, M. T., & Baumeister, R. F. (2007). The physiology of willpower: Linking blood glucose to self-control. *Personality and Social Psychology Review, 11*(4), 303–327.

Galinsky, A. D., Gruenfeld, D. H., & Magee, J. C. (2003). From power to action. *Journal of Personality and Social Psychology, 85,* 453–466.

Galinsky, A. D., Magee, J. C., Gruenfeld, D. H., Whitson, J. A., & Liljenquist, K. A. (2008). Power reduces the press of the situation: Implications for creativity, conformity, and dissonance. *Journal of Personality and Social Psychology, 95,* 1450–1466.

Gallucci, M. (2003) I sell seashells by the seashore and my name is Jack: Comment on Pelham et al. (2002). *Journal of Personality and Social Psychology, 85,* 789–800.

Gangestad, S. W., & Snyder, M. (2000). Self-monitoring: Appraisal and reappraisal. *Psychological Bulletin, 126,* 530–555.

Garcia-Marques, T., & Mackie, D. M. (2001). The feeling of familiarity as a regulator of persuasive processing. *Social Cognition, 19,* 9–34.

Gardner, W. L., & Gabriel, S. (2004). Gender differences in relational and collective interdependence: Implications for self-views, social behavior, and subjective well-being. In A. Eagly, A. Beall, & R. Sternberg (Eds.), *The psychology of gender* (2nd ed., pp. 169–191). New York: Guilford Press.

Gardner, W. L., Pickett, C. L., & Brewer, M. B. (2000). Social exclusion and selective memory: How the need to belong influences memory for social events. *Personality and Social Psychology Bulletin, 26,* 486–496.

Gardner, W. L., Pickett, C. L., & Knowles, M. (2005). Social snacking and shielding: Using social symbols, selves, and surrogates in the service of belonging needs. In K. D. Williams, J. P. Forgas, & W. von Hippel (Eds.), *The social outcast: Ostracism, social exclusion, rejection, and bullying.* New York: Psychology Press.

Gardner, W., Seeley, E., Gabriel, S., Pennington, G., Solomon, J., Ernst, J., et al. (2002). The role of "his" and "her" forms of interdependence in everyday life: Gender, belonging, and social experience. Unpublished manuscript, Northwestern University.

Garner, D. M., Garfinkel, P. E., Schwartz, D., & Thompson, M. (1980). Cultural expectations of thinness in women. *Psychological Reports, 47,* 483–491.

Garnets, L. D. (1996). Life as a lesbian: What does gender have to do with it? In J. C. Chrisler, C. Golder, & P. D. Rozee (Eds.), *Lectures on the psychology of women* (pp. 137–151). New York: McGraw-Hill.

Gaur, S. D. (1988). Noise: Does it make you angry? *Indian Psychologist, 5,* 51–56.

Gazzaniga, M. S. (1998). *The mind's past.* Berkeley: University of California Press.

Gazzaniga, M. S. (2003, January). *The when, where, what, and why of conscious experience.* Paper presented at the 25th Annual National Institute on the Teaching of Psychology Convention, St. Petersburg Beach, FL.

Gebauer, J. E., Riketta, M., Broemer, P., & Maio, G. R. (2008). *Journal of Experimental Social Psychology, 44,* 1346–1354.

Geen, R. G., & McCown, E. J. (1984). Effects of noise and attack on aggression and physiological arousal. *Motivation and Emotion, 8,* 231–241.

Geen, R. G., & Powers, P. C. (1971). Shock and noise as instigating stimuli in human aggression. *Psychological Reports, 28,* 983–985

Geen, R. G., & Quanty, M. B. (1977). The catharsis of aggression: An evaluation of a hypothesis. In L. Berkowitz (Ed.), *Advances in experimental social psychology* (Vol. 10, pp. 1–37). New York: Academic Press.

Gehring, W. J., Karpinski, A., & Hilton, J. L. (2003). Thinking about interracial interactions. *Nature Neuroscience, 6,* 1241–1243.

Gerrard, M., Gibbons, F. X., & McCoy, S. B. (1993). Emotional inhibition of effective contraception. *Anxiety, Stress & Coping: An International Journal, 6,* 73–88.

Gerstel, N., & Gross, H. (1982). Commuter marriages: A review. *Marriage and Family Review, 5,* 71–93.

Gerstel, N., & Gross, H. (1984). *Commuter marriage: A study of work and family.* New York: Guilford Press.

Gesch, B. C., Hammond, S. M., Hampson, S. E., Eves, A., & Crowder, M. J. (2002). Influence of supplementary vitamins, minerals and essential fatty acids on the antisocial behaviour of young adult prisoners: Randomised, placebo-controlled trial. *British Journal of Psychiatry, 181,* 22–28.

Giancola, P. R. (2000). Executive functioning: A conceptual framework for alcohol-related aggression. *Experimental Clinical Psychopharmacology, 8,* 576–597.

Giancola, P. R., & Corman, M. D. (2007). Alcohol and aggression: A test of the attention-allocation model. *Psychological Science, 18*(7), 649–655.

Gilbert, D. T. (1991). How mental systems believe. *American Psychologist, 46,* 107–119.

Gilbert, D. T. (1993). The assent of man: Mental representation and the control of belief. In D. Wegner & J. Pennebaker (Eds.), *Handbook of mental control* (pp. 57–87). Englewood Cliffs, NJ: Prentice-Hall.

Gilbert, D. T., Pelham, B. W., & Krull, D. S. (1988). On cognitive business: When person perceivers meet persons perceived. *Journal of Personality and Social Psychology, 54,* 733–740.

Gilbert, D. T., Pinel, E. C., Wilson, T. D., Blumberg, S. J., & Wheatley, T. P. (1998). Immune neglect: A source of durability bias in affective forecasting. *Journal of Personality and Social Psychology, 75,* 617–638.

Gilbert, D. T., Tafarodi, R. W., & Malone, P. S. (1993). You can't not believe everything you read. *Journal of Personality and Social Psychology, 65,* 221–233.

Gilovich, T. (1983). Biased evaluation and persistence in gambling. *Journal of Social and Personal Psychology, 44,* 1110–1126.

Gilovich, T. (1991). *How we know what isn't so.* New York: Free Press.

Gilovich, T., & Medvec, V. H. (1995). The experience of regret: What, when, and why. *Psychological Review, 102,* 379–395.

Glass, D. C., Singer, J. E., & Friedman, L. N. (1969). Psychic cost of adaptation to an environmental stressor. *Journal of Personality and Social Psychology, 12,* 200–210.

Glendenning, A., & Inglis, D. (1999). Smoking behaviour in youth: The problem of low self-esteem? *Journal of Adolescence, 22,* 673–682.

Glenn, N. D., & McLanahan, S. (1982). Children and marital happiness: A further specification of the relationship. *Journal of Marriage and the Family, 44,* 63–72.

Glenn, N. D., & Weaver, C .N. (1978). A multivariate multisurvey study of marital happiness. *Journal of Marriage and the Family, 40,* 269–282.

Glick, P., & Fiske, S. T. (1996). The Ambivalent Sexism Inventory: Differentiating hostile and benevolent sexism. *Journal of Personality and Social Psychology, 70,* 491–512.

Goethals, G. R., Messick, D. M., & Allison, S. T. (1991). The uniqueness bias: Studies of constructive social comparison. In J. Suls & T. A. Wills (Eds.), *Social comparison: Contemporary theory and research.* Hillsdale, NJ: Erlbaum.

Goffman, E. (1959). *The presentation of self in everyday life.* New York: Doubleday Anchor.

Goffman, E. (1963). *Stigma: Notes on the management of a spoiled identity.* Englewood Cliffs, NJ: Prentice-Hall.

Golding, S. L., & Rorer, L. G. (1972). Illusory correlation and subjective judgment. *Journal of Abnormal Psychology, 80,* 249–260.

Goleman, D. (1995a, August 8). Brain may tag all perceptions with a value. *New York Times,* 1–10.

Goleman, D. (1995b). *Emotional intelligence.* New York: Bantam.

Gollwitzer, P. M. (1996). The volitional benefits of planning. In P. M. Gollwitzer & J. A. Bargh (Eds.), *The psychology of action: Linking cognition and motivation to behavior* (pp. 287–312). New York: Guilford Press.

Gollwitzer, P. M., & Kinney, R. F. (1989). Effects of deliberative and implemental mind-sets on the illusion of control. *Journal of Personality and Social Psychology, 56,* 531–542.

Gondolf, E. W. (1985). *Men who batter: An integrated approach for stopping wife abuse.* Holmes Beach, CA: Learning Publications.

Gonzales, M. H., Haugen, J. A., & Manning, D. J. (1994). Victims as "narrative critics": Factors influencing rejoinders and evaluative responses to offenders' accounts. *Personality and Social Psychology Bulletin, 20,* 691–704.

Gonzales, M., Pederson, J., Manning, D., & Wetter, D. (1990). Pardon my gaffe: Effects of sex, status, and consequence severity on accounts. *Journal of Personality and Social Psychology, 58,* 610–621.

Gonzales, P. M., Blanton, H., & Williams, K. J. (2002). The effects of stereotype threat and double-minority status on the test performance of Latino women. *Personality and Social Psychology Bulletin, 28*(5), 659–670.

Goodenough, F. L. (1931). *Anger in young children.* Minneapolis: University of Minnesota Press.

Goodwin, J. S., Hunt, W. C., Key, C. R., & Samet, J. M. (1987). The effect of marital status on stage, treatment, and survival of cancer patients. *Journal of the American Medical Association, 258,* 3125–3130.

Gottfredson, L. (Ed.). (1997). Intelligence and social policy. *Intelligence, 24,* 1–320.

Gottfredson, M. R., & Hirschi, T. (1990). *A general theory of crime.* Stanford, CA: Stanford University Press.

Gottman, J. M. (1994). *What predicts divorce?* Hillsdale, NJ: Erlbaum.

Gottschalk, L. A., & Gleser, G. C. (1960). An analysis of the verbal content of suicide notes. *British Journal of Medical Psychology, 33,* 195–204.

Govaerts, K., & Dixon, D. N. (1988). . . .Until careers do us part: Vocational and marital satisfaction in the dual-career commuter marriage. *International Journal for the Advancement of Counseling, 11,* 265–281.

Graham, K. (1980). Theories of intoxicated aggression. *Canadian Journal of Behavioral Science, 12,* 141–158.

Grammer, K., Fink, B., Moller, A. P., & Thornhill, R. (2003). Darwinian aesthetics: Sexual selection and the biology of beauty. *Biological Reviews, 78,* 385–407.

Grasmick, H. G., Bursik, R. J., & Kinsey, K. A. (1991). Shame and embarrassment as deterrents to noncompliance with the law: The case of an antilittering campaign. *Environment and Behavior, 23,* 233–251.

Gray-Little, B., & Hafdahl, A. R. (2000). Factors influencing racial comparisons of self-esteem: A quantitative synthesis. *Psychological Bulletin, 126,* 26–54.

Green, G. (2005, December 9). Man dates gal on Internet for six months—and it turns out she's his mother! Retrieved July 6, 2006, from http://entertainment.tv.yahoo.com/news/wwn

Green, L., Price, P. C., & Hamburger, M. E. (1995). Prisoner's dilemma and the pigeon: Control by immediate consequences. *Journal of the Experimental Analysis of Behavior, 64,* 1–17.

Greenberg, J., & Musham, C. (1981). Avoiding and seeking self-focused attention. *Journal of Research in Personality, 15,* 191–200.

Greenberg, J., & Pyszczynski, J. (1985). Compensatory self-inflation: A response to the threat to self-regard of public failure. *Journal of Personality and Social Psychology, 49,* 273–280.

Greenberg, J., Solomon, S., & Pyszczynski, T. (1997). Terror management theory of self-esteem and cultural worldviews: Empirical assessments and conceptual refinements. In M. P. Zanna (Ed.), *Advances in experimental social psychology* (Vol. 29, pp. 61–139). San Diego, CA: Academic Press.

Greenberg, S. W. (1981). Alcohol and crime: A methodological critique of the literature. In J. J. Collins (Ed.), *Drinking and crime: Perspectives on the relationships between alcohol consumption and criminal behavior.* New York: Guilford Press.

Greenblat, C. (1983). The salience of sexuality in the early years of marriage. *Journal of Marriage and the Family, 45,* 277–288.

Greenspan, S. I., & Porges, S. W. (1984). Psychopathology in infancy and early childhood: Clinical perspectives on the organization of sensory and affective-thematic experience. *Child Development, 55,* 49–70.

Greenwald, A. G. (1988). Self-knowledge and self-deception. In J. S. Lockard & D. L. Paulhus (Eds.), *Self-deception: An adaptive mechanism?* (pp. 113–131). Englewood Cliffs, NJ: Prentice-Hall.

Greenwald, A. G., & Banaji, M. R. (1989). The self as a memory system: Powerful, but ordinary. *Journal of Personality and Social Psychology, 57,* 41–54.

Greenwald, A. G., McGhee, D. E., & Schwartz, J. K. L. (1998). Measuring individual differences in implicit cognition: The implicit association test. *Journal of Personality and Social Psychology, 74,* 1464–1480.

Greenwald, A. G., Oakes, M. A., & Hoffman, H. G. (2003). Targets of discrimination: Effects of race on responses to weapons holders. *Journal of Experimental Social Psychology, 39,* 399–340.

Gregory, L. W., Cialdini, R. B., & Carpenter, K. M. (1982). Self-relevant scenarios as mediator of likelihood estimates and compliance: Does imagining make it so? *Journal of Personality and Social Psychology, 43,* 89–99.

Griffitt, W. (1981). Sexual intimacy in aging marital partners. In J. Marsh & S. Kiesler (Eds.), *Aging: Stability and change in the family* (pp. 301–315). New York: Academic Press.

Grolnick, W. S., & Ryan, R. M. (1987). Autonomy in children's learning: An experimental and individual differences investigation. *Journal of Personality and Social Psychology, 52,* 890–898.

Grondin, S., Deshaies, P., & Nault, L. P. (1984). Trimestres de naissance et participation au hockey et au volleyball. *La Revue Québécoise de l'Activité Physique, 2,* 97–103.

Gross, D. (1996). *Forbes greatest business stories of all time.* New York: Wiley.

Gross, J., & Rosen, J. C. (1988). Bulimia in adolescents: Prevalence and psychosocial correlates. *International Journal of Eating Disorders, 7,* 51–61.

Grossman, D. (1995). *On killing: The psychological cost of learning to kill in war and society.* New York: Little, Brown.

Group for the Advancement of Psychiatry. (1957). *Methods of forceful indoctrination: Observations and interviews.* New York: Author.

Grunberg, N. E., & Straub, R. O. (1992). The role of gender and taste class in the effects of stress on eating. *Health Psychology, 11,* 97–100.

Gruner, C. R. (1985). Advice to the beginning speaker on using humor: What the research tells us. *Communication Education, 34,* 142–147.

Guinote, A. (2008). Power and affordances: When the situation has more power over powerful than powerless individuals. *Journal of Personality and Social Psychology, 95,* 237–252.

Gurr, T. R. (1981). Historical trends in violent crime: A critical review of the evidence. *Crime and Justice, 3,* 295.

Gutman, I. (1995). *Encyclopedia of the Holocaust.* Macmillan.

Guzmán, R. A., Rodríguez-Sickert, C., & Rowthorn, R. (2007). When in Rome, do as the Romans do: The coevolution of altruistic punishment, conformist learning, and cooperation. *Evolution and Human Behavior, 28*(2), 112–117.

Hall, J. H., & Fincham, F. D. (2006). Relationship dissolution following infidelity: The roles of attributions and forgiveness. *Journal of Social and Clinical Psychology, 25,* 508–522.

Hall, J. R. (1987). *Gone from the promised land: Jonestown in American cultural history.* New Brunswick: Transaction Books.

Hamilton, D. L., Dugan, P. M., & Trolier, T. K. (1985). The formation of stereotypic beliefs: Further evidence for distinctiveness-based illusory correlations. *Journal of Personality and Social Psychology, 48,* 5–17.

Hamilton, D. L., & Gifford, R. K. (1976). Illusory correlation in interpersonal perception: A cognitive basis of stereotypic judgments. *Journal of Experimental Social Psychology, 12,* 392–407.

Hamilton, W. D. (1964). The genetical evolution of social behaviour I and II. *Journal of Theoretical Biology, 7,* 1–16, 17–52.

Handley, I. M., Lassiter, G. D., Nickell, E. F., & Herchenroeder, L. M. (2004). Affect and automatic mood maintenance. *Journal of Experimental Social Psychology, 40,* 106–112.

Hang-Pil, S., & Shavitt, S. (1994). Persuasion and culture: Advertising appeals in individualistic and collectivistic societies. *Journal of Experimental Social Psychology, 30,* 326–350.

Hansen, G. L. (1987). Extradyadic relations during courtship. *Journal of Sex Research, 23,* 382–390.

Hardin, G. (1968). The tragedy of the commons. *Science, 162,* 1243–1248.

Hare, R. D. (1998). *Without conscience: The disturbing world of the psychopaths among us.* New York: Guilford Press.

Harrell, W. A. (1978). Physical attractiveness, self-disclosure, and helping behavior. *Journal of Social Psychology, 104,* 15–17.

Harris, C. R. (2000). Psychophysiological responses to imagined infidelity: The specific innate modular view of jealousy reconsidered. *Journal of Personality and Social Psychology, 75,* 1082–1091.

Harris, M. B. (1974). Mediators between frustration and aggression in a field experiment. *Journal of Experimental Social Psychology, 10*(6), 561–571.

Harris, M. B. (1976). Instigators and inhibitors of aggression in a field experiment. *Journal of Social Psychology, 98*(1), 27–38.

Harris, M. B., Benson, S. M., & Hall, C. L. (1975). The effects of confession on altruism. *Journal of Social Psychology, 96,* 187–192.

Harris, M. B., Harris, R. J., & Bochner, S. (1982). Fat, four-eyed, and female: Stereotypes of obesity, glasses, and gender. *Journal of Applied Social Psychology, 12,* 503–516.

Harrison, A. A., & Connors, M. M. (1984). Groups in exotic environments. In L. Berkowitz (Ed.), *Advances in Experimental Social Psychology* (Vol. 18, pp. 49–87). New York: Academic Press.

Harrison, A. A., & Fiscaro, S. A. (1974). Stimulus familiarity and alley illumination as determinants of approach response latencies of house crickets. *Perceptual and Motor Skills, 39,* 147–152.

Harrison, K. (2000). The body electric: Thin-ideal media and eating disorders in adolescents. *Journal of Communication, 50,* 119–143.

Harrison, K. (2001). Ourselves, our bodies: Thin-ideal media, self-discrepancies, and eating disorder symptomatology in adolescents. *Journal of Social and Clinical Psychology, 20,* 289–323.

Harrison, K. (2003). Television viewers' ideal body proportions: The case of the curvaceously thin woman. *Sex Roles, 48,* 255–264.

Harter, S. (1993). Causes and consequences of low self-esteem in children and adolescents. In R. F. Baumeister (Ed.), *Self-esteem: The puzzle of low self-regard* (pp. 87–116). Plenum Press.

Haselton, M. G., & Buss, D. M. (2000). Error management theory: A new perspective on biases in cross-sex mind reading. *Journal of Personality and Social Psychology, 78,* 81–91.

Hassebrauck, M. (1986). Ratings of distress as a function of degree and kind of inequity. *Journal of Social Psychology, 126,* 269–270.

Hatfield, E., & Rapson, R. L. (1987). Passionate love: New directions in research. In W. H. Jones & D. Perlman (Eds.), *Advances in personal relationships* (Vol. 1, pp. 109–139). Greenwich, CT: JAI Press.

Hauck, A., & Finch, A. (1993). The effect of relative age on achievement in middle school. *Psychology in the Schools, 30,* 74–79.

Haugtvedt, C. P., & Petty, R. E. (1992). Personality and persuasion: Need for cognition moderates the persistence and resistance of attitude changes. *Journal of Personality and Social Psychology, 63,* 308–319.

Hawkley, L. C., Burleson, M. H., Berntson, G. G., & Cacioppo, J. T. (2003). Loneliness in everyday life: Cardiovascular activity, psychosocial context, and health behaviors. *Journal of Personality and Social Psychology, 85,* 105–120.

Hazan, C., & Shaver, P. R. (1987). Romantic love conceptualized as an attachment process. *Journal of Personality and Social Psychology, 52,* 511–524.

Hearold, S. (1986). A synthesis of 1043 effects of television on social behavior. In G. Comstock (Ed.), *Public communication and behavior* (pp. 65–133). New York: Academic Press.

Heatherton, T. F., & Nichols, P. A. (1994). Personal accounts of successful versus failed attempts at life change. *Personality and Social Psychology Bulletin, 20,* 664–675.

Heatherton, T. F., Polivy, J., & Herman, C. P. (1989). Restraint and internal responsiveness: Effects of placebo manipulations of hunger state on eating. *Journal of Abnormal Psychology, 98,* 89–92.

Heatherton, T. F., Polivy, J., Herman, C. P., & Baumeister, R. F. (1993). Self-awareness, task failure and disinhibition: How attentional focus affects eating. *Journal of Personality, 61,* 49–61.

Heatherton, T. F., & Vohs, K. D. (2000). Interpersonal evaluations following threats to self: Role of self-esteem. *Journal of Personality and Social Psychology, 78,* 725–736.

Hebl, M. R., & Heatherton, T. F. (1997). The stigma of obesity: The differences are black and white. *Personality and Social Psychology Bulletin, 24,* 417–426.

Hebl, M. R., & Mannix, L. M. (2003). The weight of obesity in evaluating others: A mere proximity effect. *Personality and Social Psychology Bulletin, 29,* 28–38.

Heider, F. (1946) Attitudes and cognitive organizations. *Journal of Psychology, 21,* 107–112.

Heider, F. (1958). *The psychology of interpersonal relations.* New York: Wiley.

Heine, S. J., & Lehmann, D. R. (1997). Culture, dissonance, and self-affirmation. *Personality and Social Psychology Bulletin, 23,* 389–400.

Heine, S. J., Lehman, D. R., Markus, H. R., & Kitayama, S. (1999). Is there a universal need for positive self-regard? *Psychological Review, 106,* 766–794.

Heinz, S., Baron, G., & Frahm, H. (1988). Comparative size of brains and brain components. In H. D. Steklis & J. Erwin (Eds.), *Comparative Primate Biology: Vol. 4. Neurosciences.* New York: Wiley.

Henderson, V., & Dweck, C. S. (1990). Achievement and motivation in adolescence: A new model and data. In S. Feldman & G. Elliott (Eds.), *At the threshold: The developing adolescent* (pp. 308–329). Cambridge, MA: Harvard University Press.

Hendin, H. (1982). *Suicide in America.* New York: Norton.

Hendricks, N. J., Ortiz, C. W., Sugie, N., & Miller, J. (2007). Beyond the numbers: Hate crimes and cultural trauma within Arab American immigrant communities. *International Review of Victimology, 14*(1), 95–113.

Henken, V. J. (1976). Banality reinvestigated: A computer-based content analysis of suicidal and forced-death documents. *Suicide and Life-Threatening Behavior, 6*, 36–43.

Henry, B., Caspi, A., Moffitt, T. E., & Silva, P. A. (1996). Temperamental and familial predictors of violent and nonviolent criminal convictions: Age 3 to age 18. *Developmental Psychology, 32*, 614–623.

Hepworth, J. T., & West, S. G. (1988). Lynchings and the economy: A time-series reanalysis of Hovland and Sears (1940). *Journal of Personality and Social Psychology, 55*, 239–247.

Herdt, G. (1984). Ritualized homosexual behavior in the male cults of Melanesia, 1862–1983: An Introduction. In G. Herdt (Ed.), *Ritualized homosexuality in Melanesia* (pp. 1–82). Berkeley: University of California Press.

Herek, G. M. (2000). The psychology of sexual prejudice. *Current Directions in Psychological Science, 9*, 19–22.

Herek, G. M., & Capitanio, J. P. (1996). "Some of my best friends": Intergroup contact, concealable stigma, and heterosexuals' attitudes toward gay men and lesbians. *Personality and Social Psychology Bulletin, 22*(4), 412–424.

Herek, G. M., & Capitanio, J. P. (1999). AIDS stigma and sexual prejudice. *American Behavioral Scientist, 42*, 1126–1143.

Herlitz, J., Wiklund, I., Caidahl, K., Hartford, M., Haglid, M., Karlsson, B. W., et al. (1998). The feeling of loneliness prior to coronary artery bypass grafting might be a predictor of short- and long-term postoperative mortality. *European Journal of Vascular and Endovascular Surgery, 16*, 120–125.

Herman, C. P., & Mack, D. (1975). Restrained and unrestrained eating. *Journal of Personality, 43*, 647–660.

Herold, E. S., & Mewhinney, D.-M. K. (1993). Gender differences in casual sex and AIDS prevention: A survey of dating bars. *Journal of Sex Research, 30*, 36–42.

Hewstone, M. (1990). The "ultimate attribution error"? A review of the literature on intergroup causal attribution. *European Journal of Social Psychology, 20*, 311–335.

Hicks, E. K. (1996). *Infibulation: Female mutilation in Islamic northeastern Africa.* New Brunswick, NJ: Transaction.

Higgins, E. T., & Bargh, J. A. (1987). Social cognition and social perception. *Annual Review of Psychology, 38*, 369–425.

Higgins, E. T., Rholes, W. S., & Jones, C. R. (1977). Category accessibility and impression formation. *Journal of Experimental Social Psychology, 13*, 141–154.

Hill, C. A., Blakemore, J. E. O., & Drumm, P. (1997). Mutual and unrequited love in adolescence and adulthood. *Personal Relationships, 4*(1), 15–23.

Hill, C. T., Rubin, Z., & Peplau, L. A. (1976). Breakups before marriage: The end of 103 affairs. *Journal of Social Issues, 32*, 147–168.

Hill, G. E. (1934). Cheating among delinquent boys. *Journal of Juvenile Research, 18*, 169–174.

Hilmert, C. J., Kulik, J. A., & Christenfeld, N. J. (2006). Positive and negative opinion modeling: The influence of another's similarity and dissimilarity. *Journal of Personality and Social Psychology, 90*, 440–452.

Hinde, R. A. (1970). *Animal behavior.* New York: McGraw-Hill.

Hirt, E. R., Deppe, R. K., & Gordon, L. J. (1991). Self-reported versus behavioral self-handicapping: Empirical evidence for a theoretical distinction. *Journal of Personality and Social Psychology, 61*, 981–991.

Hirt, E. R., Kardes, F. R., & Markman, K. D. (2004). Activating a mental simulation mind-set through generation of alternatives: Implications for *debiasing* in related and unrelated domains. *Journal of Experimental Social Psychology, 40*, 374–383.

Hirt, E. R., & Markman, K. D. (1995). Multiple explanation: A consider-an-alternative strategy for *debiasing* judgments. *Journal of Personality and Social Psychology, 69*, 1069–1086.

Hirt, E. R., & Sherman, S. J. (1985). The role of prior knowledge in explaining hypothetical events. *Journal of Experimental Social Psychology, 21*, 519–543.

Hitsch, G. J., Hortaçsu, A., & Ariely, D. (2006). What makes you click? Mate preferences and matching outcomes in online dating. MIT Sloan Research Paper No. 4603-06. Available at http://home.uchicago.edu/~hortacsu/onlinedating.pdf

Hoffman, M. L. (1977). Sex differences in empathy and related behaviors. *Psychological Bulletin, 84*, 712–722.

Hoffnung, M. (2006). What's in a name? Marital name choice revisited. *Sex Roles, 55*(11–12), 817–825.

Hofstadter, D. R. (1979), *Gödel, Escher, Bach: An eternal golden braid.* New York: Basic Books.

Hogan, R., Jones, W. H., & Cheek, J. M. (1985). Socioanalytic theory: An alternative to armadillo psychology. In B. R. Schlenker (Ed.), *The self and social life* (pp. 175–198). New York: McGraw-Hill.

Hogan, R., & Kaiser, R. B. (2005). What we know about leadership. *Review of General Psychology, 9*(2), 169–180.

Hogg, M. A. (2005). All animals are equal but some animals are more equal than others: Social identity and marginal membership. In K. D. Williams, J. P. Forgas, & W. von Hippel (Eds.), *The social outcast: Ostracism, social exclusion, rejection, and bullying.* New York: Psychology Press.

Hollingshead, A. B. (1998). Retrieval processes in transactive memory systems. *Journal of Personality and Social Psychology, 74*, 659–671.

Hollingshead, A. B., & Brandon, D. P. (2003). Potential benefits of communication in transactive memory systems. *Human Communication Research, 29*, 607–615.

Holloway, S. D., Kashiwagi, K., Hess, R. D., & Azuuma, H. (1986). Causal attributions by Japanese and American mothers and children about performance in mathematics. *International Journal of Psychology, 21*, 269–286.

Holmes, J. G. (2004, October). The power of positive thinking in close relationships. Paper presented at the Third International Positive Psychology Summit, Washington, DC.

Holtzworth-Munroe, A., & Jacobson, N. S. (1985). Causal attributions of married couples: When do they search for causes? What do they conclude when they do? *Journal of Personality and Social Psychology, 48*, 1398–1412.

Homans, G. C. (1950). *The human group.* New York: Harcourt, Brace, & World.

Homans, G. C. (1961). *Social behavior: Its elementary forms.* New York: Harcourt, Brace, & World.

Honour, J. W. (2004, July 8). The fight for fair play: Can athletes be held responsible for every substance they take? *Nature, 430*, 143–144.

Hooley, J. M., Orley, J., & Teasdale, J. D. (1986). Levels of expressed emotion and relapse in depressed patients. *British Journal of Psychiatry, 148*, 642–647.

Hoorens, V., & Todorova, E. (1988). The name letter effect: Attachment to self or primacy of own name writing? *European Journal of Social Psychology, 18*, 365–368.

Horner, M. (1972). Toward an understanding of achievement related conflicts in women. *Journal of Social Issues, 28*, 157–176.

Hornstein, H. A. (1982). Promotive tension: Theory and research. In V. Derlega & J. Grzelak (Eds.), *Cooperation and helping behavior: Theories and research* (pp. 229–248). New York: Academic Press.

Horowitz, A. V., White, H. R., & Howell-White, S. (1996). Becoming married and mental health: A longitudinal study of a cohort of young adults. *Journal of Marriage and the Family, 58*, 895–907.

Hoshino-Browne, E., Zanna, A. S., Spencer, S. J., Zanna, M. P., Kitayama, S., & Lackenbauer, S. (2005). On the cultural guises of cognitive dissonance: The case of Easterners and Westerners. *Journal of Personality and Social Psychology, 89*, 294–310.

Houston, D. A., Doan, K. A., & Roskos-Ewoldsen, D. (1999). Negative political advertising and choice conflict. *Journal of Experimental Psychology: Applied, 5*, 3–16.

Hovland, C. I., Janis, I. L., & Kelley, H. H. (1953). *Communication and persuasion.* New Haven, CT: Yale University Press.

Hovland, C., Lumsdaine, A., & Sheffield, F. (1949). *Experiments on mass communication: Studies in social psychology in World War II* (Vol. 3). Princeton, NJ: Princeton University Press.

Hovland, C., Lumsdaine, A., & Sheffield, F. (1965). *Experiments on mass communication.* New York: Wiley.

Hovland, C. I., & Sears, R. (1940). Minor studies of aggression: Correlation of lynchings with economic conditions. *Journal of Psychology, 9*, 301–310.

Hovland, C. I., & Weiss, W. (1951). The influence of source credibility on communication effectiveness. *Public Opinion Quarterly, 15*, 635–650.

Howell, S. (1989). "To be angry is not to be human, but to be fearful is": Chewong concepts of human nature. In S. Howell & R. Willis (Eds.), *Societies at peace: Anthropological perspectives* (pp. 45–59). London: Routledge.

Howes, J. J., & Hokanson, J. E. (1979). Conversational and social responses to depressive interpersonal behavior. *Journal of Abnormal Psychology, 88*, 625–634.

Hoyle, R. H., Pinkley, R. L., & Insko, C. A. (1989). Perceptions of social behavior: Evidence of differing expectations for interpersonal and intergroup interaction. *Personality and Social Psychology Bulletin, 15*, 365–376.

Hsee, C. K. (1996). The evaluability hypothesis: An explanation for preference reversals between joint and separate evaluations of alternatives. *Organizational Behavior and Human Decision Processes, 67*(3), 247–257.

Hsee, C. K., & Zhang, J. (2004). Distinction bias: Misprediction and mischoice due to joint evaluation. *Journal of Personality and Social Psychology, 86*(5), 680–695.

Hu, Y., & Goldman, M. (1990). Mortality differentials by marital status: An international comparison. *Demography, 27*, 233–250.

Huesmann, L. R., Moise, J., Podolski, C. P., & Eron, L. D. (2003). Longitudinal relations between childhood exposure to media violence and adult aggression and violence: 1977–1992. *Developmental Psychology, 39*, 201–221.

Hull, J. G. (1981). A self-awareness model of the causes and effects of alcohol consumption. *Journal of Abnormal Psychology, 90*, 586–600.

Hull, J. G., Levenson, R. W., Young, R. D., & Scher, K. J. (1983). Self-awareness-reducing effects of alcohol consumption. *Journal of Personality and Social Personality, 44*, 461–473.

Human security brief 2007. (2008, May 21). Vancouver, BC, Canada: Simon Fraser University, Human Security Report Project. Retrieved May 1, 2009, from http://www.humansecuritybrief.info/

Hupka, R. B. (1981). Cultural determinants of jealousy. *Alternative Lifestyles, 4*, 310–356.

Huston, T. L., Surra, C., Fitzgerald, N. M., & Cate, R. (1981). From courtship to marriage: Mate selection as an interpersonal process. In S. Duck & R. Gilmour (Eds.), *Personal relationships 2: Developing personal relationships.* New York: Academic Press.

Hyde, J. S. (2005). The gender similarities hypothesis. *American Psychologist, 60*, 581–592.

Hyde, J. S., & Kling, K. C. (2001). Women, motivation, and achievement. *Psychology of Women Quarterly, 25*, 264–378.

Hyland, M. E. (1989). There is no motive to avoid success: The compromise explanation for success-avoiding behavior. *Journal of Personality, 57*, 665–693.

Impett, E. A., & Peplau, L. A. (2002). Why some women consent to unwanted sex with a dating partner: Insights from attachment theory. *Psychology of Women Quarterly, 26*, 360–370.

Innes, C. A. (1988). *Drug use and crime.* Washington, DC: U.S. Department of Justice.

Insko, C. A., Schopler, J., Hoyle, R. H., & Dardis, G. J. (1990). Individual–group discontinuity as a function of fear and greed. *Journal of Personality and Social Psychology, 58*, 68–79.

Insko, C. A., Schopler, J., Pemberton, M. B., Wieselquist, J., McIlraith, S. A., Currey, D. P., et al. (1998). Long-term outcome maximization and the reduction of interindividual–intergroup discontinuity. *Journal of Personality and Social Psychology, 75*, 695–711.

Insko, C. A., Smith, R. H., Alicke, M. D., Wade, J., & Taylor, S. (1985). Conformity and group size: The concern with being right and the concern with being liked. *Personality and Social Psychology Bulletin, 11*, 41–50.

Iraq war fuels terror—US report. (2006, September 27). *BBC News*. Retrieved May 1, 2009, from http://news.bbc.co.uk/2/hi/americas/5382762.stm

Isen, A. M. (2000). Positive affect and decision making. In M. Lewis & J. M. Haviland-Jones (Eds.), *Handbook of emotions* (2nd ed., pp. 417–435). New York: Guilford Press.

Isen, A. M., & Levin, P. F. (1972). Effect of feeling good on helping: Cookies and kindness. *Journal of Personality and Social Psychology, 21*, 384–388.

Isen, A. M., & Patrick, R. (1983). The effect of positive feelings and risk taking: When the chips are down. *Organizational Behavior and Human Performance, 31*, 194–202.

"Islamist" held in Van Gogh case. (2004, November 3). *BBC News*. Retrieved January 26, 2005, from http://news.bbc.co.uk/1/hi/world/europe/3978787.stm

Ito, T. A., Miller, N., & Pollock, V. E. (1996). Alcohol and aggression: A meta-analysis on the moderating effects of inhibitory cues, triggering events, and self-focused attention. *Psychological Bulletin, 120*, 60–82.

Iyengar, S. S., & Lepper, M. R. (2000). When choice is demotivating: Can one desire too much of a good thing? *Journal of Personality and Social Psychology, 79*, 995–1006.

Izard, C. E. (1971). *The face of emotion*. New York: Appleton-Century-Crofts.

Izard, C. E. (1990). The substrates and functions of emotion feelings: William James and current emotion theory. *Personality and Social Psychology Bulletin, 16*, 626–635.

Jackson, L. A., Hunter, J. E., & Hodge, C. N. (1995). Physical attractiveness and intellectual competence: A meta-analytic review. *Social Psychology Quarterly, 58*, 108–122.

Jacobs, R. C., & Campbell, D. T. (1961). The perpetuation of an arbitrary tradition through several generations of a laboratory microculture. *Journal of Abnormal and Social Psychology, 62*, 649–658.

James, W. (1884). What is an emotion? *Mind, 9*, 188–205.

James, W. (1890). *Principles of psychology*. New York: Holt.

James, W. (1948). *Psychology*. Cleveland, OH: World Publishing. (Original work published 1892)

James, W. H. (1981). The honeymoon effect on marital coitus. *Journal of Sex Research, 17*, 114–123.

Janis, I. L. (1954). Personality correlates of susceptibility to persuasion. *Journal of Personality, 22*, 504–518.

Janis, I. L. (1967). Effects of fear arousal on attitude change: Recent developments in theory and experimental research. *Advances in Experimental Social Psychology, 4*, 166–224.

Janis, I. L. (1972). *Victims of groupthink*. Boston: Houghton Mifflin.

Janis, I. L. (1982). *Groupthink* (2nd ed.). Boston: Houghton Mifflin.

Janis, I. L., & Feshbach, S. (1953). Effects of fear-arousing communications. *Journal of Abnormal and Social Psychology, 48*, 78–92.

Janis, I. L., & Field, P. (1959) Sex differences and personality factors related to persuasibility. In C. Hovland & I. Janis (Eds.), *Personality and persuasibility* (pp. 55–68, 300–302). New Haven, CT: Yale University Press.

Janis, I. L., Kaye, D., & Kirschner, P. (1965). Facilitating effects of "eating-while-reading" on responsiveness to persuasive communications. *Journal of Personality and Social Psychology, 1*(2), 181–186.

Janiszewski, C., Noel, H., & Sawyer, A. G. (2003). A meta-analysis of the spacing effect in verbal learning: Implications for research on advertising repetition and consumer memory. *Journal of Consumer Research, 30*, 138–149.

Jankowiak, W. (Ed.). (1995). *Romantic passion: A universal experience?* New York: Columbia University Press.

Jankowski, M. S. (1991). *Islands in the street: Gangs and American urban society*. Berkeley: University of California Press.

Janoff-Bulman, R. (1992). *Shattered assumptions: Towards a new psychology of trauma*. New York: Free Press.

Janoff-Bulman, R., & Brickman, P. (1982). Expectations and what people learn from failure. In N. T. Feather (Ed.), *Expectations and actions: Expectancy-value models in psychology* (pp. 207–237). Hillsdale, NJ: Erlbaum.

Janus, S. S., & Janus, C. L. (1993). *The Janus report on sexual behavior*. New York: Wiley.

Jencks, C., & Phillips, M. (Eds.). (1998). *The Black–White test score gap*. Washington, DC: Brookings Institution.

Jensen, A. (1977). Genetic and behavioral effects of nonrandom mating. In C. Noble, R. Osborne, & N. Weyl (Eds.), *Human variation: Biogenetics of age, race, and sex*. New York: Academic Press.

Jensen, L. A., Arnett, J. J., Feldman, S. S., & Cauffman, E. (2002). It's wrong, but everybody does it: Academic dishonesty among high school and college students. *Contemporary Educational Psychology, 27*, 209–228.

Johns, M., Inzlicht, M., & Schmader, T. (2008). Stereotype threat and executive resource depletion: Examining the influence of emotion regulation. *Journal of Experimental Psychology: General, 137*(4), 691–705.

Johnson, D. J., & Rusbult, C. E. (1989). Resisting temptation: Devaluation of alternative partners as a means of maintaining commitment in close relationships. *Journal of Personality and Social Psychology, 57*, 967–980.

Johnson, D. W., & Johnson, R. T. (1983). The socialization and achievement crises: Are cooperative learning experiences the solution? *Applied Social Psychology Annual, 4*, 119–164.

Johnson, W., McGue, M., Krueger, R. F., & Bouchard, T. J. (2004). Marriage and personality: A genetic analysis. *Journal of Personality and Social Psychology, 86*, 285–294.

Johnson, W. G., Schlundt, D. G., Barclay, D. R., Carr-Nangle, R. E., & Engler, L. B. (1995). A naturalistic functional analysis of binge eating. *Behavior Therapy, 26*, 101–118.

Joiner, T. (2005). *Why people die by suicide*. Cambridge, MA: Harvard University Press .

Joiner, T., Pettit, J. W., Walker, R. L., Voelz, Z. R., Cruz, J., Rudd, M. D., & Lester, D. (2002). Perceived burdensomeness and suicidality: Two studies on the suicide notes of those attempting and those completing suicide. *Journal of Social and Clinical Psychology, 21*, 531–545.

Jonas, K., Eagly, A. H., & Stroebe, W. (1995). *Attitudes and persuasion*. In M. Argyle & A. M. Colman (Eds.), *Social psychology*. Harlow, UK: Longman.

Jones, D. (2004, April 9). Obesity can mean less pay. *USA Today*.

Jones, E. E. (1964). *Ingratiation*. New York: Irvington.

Jones, E. E., & Berglas, S. (1978). Control of attributions about the self through self-handicapping strategies: The appeal of alcohol and the role of underachievement. *Personality and Social Psychology Bulletin, 4*, 200–206.

Jones, E. E., & Gerard, H. B. (1967). *Foundations of social psychology*. New York: Wiley.

Jones, E. E., & Harris, V. A. (1967). The attribution of attitudes. *Journal of Experimental Social Psychology, 3*, 1–24.

Jones, E. E., & Nisbett, R. E. (1971). *The actor and the observer: Divergent perceptions of the causes of behavior*. New York: General Learning Press.

Jones, E. E., Rhodewalt, F., Berglas, S., & Skelton, J. A. (1981). Effects of strategic self-presentation on subsequent self-esteem. *Journal of Personality and Social Psychology, 41*, 407–421.

Jones, E. E., & Wortman, E. (1973). *Ingratiation: An attributional approach*. Morristown, NJ: General Learning Press.

Jones, J. T., Pelham, B. W., Mirenberg, M. C., & Hetts, J. J. (2002). Name letter preferences are not merely mere exposure: Implicit egotism as self-regulation. *Journal of Experimental Social Psychology, 38*, 170–177.

Jones, J. W., & Bogat, G. (1978). Air pollution and human aggression. *Psychological Reports, 43*(3, Pt. 1), 721–722.

Jones, W. (1989, August). Address given at the annual convention of the American Psychological Association, New Orleans.

Jost, J. T., & Kay, A. C. (2005). Exposure to benevolent sexism and complementary gender stereotypes: Consequences for specific and diffuse forms of system justification. *Journal of Personality and Social Psychology, 88*, 498–509.

Joyce, W. F., Nohria, N., & Roberson, B. (2003). *What really works: The 4+2 formula for sustained business success*. New York: HarperBusiness.

Judd, C., & Park, B. (1993). The assessment of accuracy of social stereotypes. *Psychological Review, 100*, 109–128.

Jury deliberates in Kevorkian murder trial. (1999, March 25). *CNN*. Retrieved October 27, 2004, from http://www.cnn.com/US/9903/25/kevorkian.06/

Jussim, L., Cain, T. R., Crawford, J. T., Harber, K., & Cohen, F. (in press). The unbearable accuracy of stereotypes. In T. Nelson (Ed.), *Handbook of prejudice, stereotyping, and discrimination*. Mahwah, NJ: Erlbaum.

Jussim, L., & Harber, K. D. Teacher expectations and self-fulfilling prophecies: Knowns and unknowns, resolved and unresolved controversies. *Personality and Social Psychology Review, 9*(2), 131–155.

Jussim, L., HsiuJu, Y., & Aiello, J. R. (1995). Self-consistency, self-enhancement, and accuracy in reactions to feedback. *Journal of Experimental Social Psychology, 31*, 322–356.

Juvonen, J., & Gross, E. F. (2005). The rejected and the bullied: Lessons about social misfits from developmental psychology. In K. D. Williams, J. P. Forgas, & W. von Hippel (Eds.), *The social outcast: Ostracism, social exclusion, rejection, and bullying*. New York: Psychology Press.

Kachadourian, L. K., Fincham, F. D., & Davila, J. (2004). The tendency to forgive in dating and married couples: Association with attachment and relationship satisfaction. *Personal Relationships, 11*, 373–393.

Kachadourian, L. K., Fincham, F. D., & Davila, J. (2005). Attitudinal ambivalence, rumination and forgiveness of partner transgressions in marriage. *Personality and Social Psychology Bulletin, 31*, 334–342.

Kagan, J. (1981). *The second year: The emergence of self-awareness*. Cambridge, MA: Harvard University Press.

Kahn, J., Smith, K., & Roberts, E. (1984). *Familial communication and adolescent sexual behavior* (Final report to the Office of Adolescent Pregnancy Programs). Cambridge, MA: American Institute for Research.

Kahneman, D. (1999). Objective happiness. In D. Kahneman, E. Diener, & N. Schwartz (Eds.), *Well-being: The foundations of hedonic psychology* (pp. 3–25). New York: Russell Sage Foundation.

Kahneman, D., & Frederick, S. (2002). Representativeness revisited: Attribute substitution in intuitive judgment. In T. Gilovich, D. Griffin, & D. Kahneman (Eds.), *Heuristics and biases* (pp. 49–81). New York: Cambridge University Press.

Kahneman, D., Knetsch, J. L., & Thaler, R. H. (1990). Experimental tests of the endowment effect and the Coase theorem. *Journal of Political Economy, 98*(6), 1325–1348.

Kahneman, D., & Miller, D. T. (1986). Norm theory: Comparing reality to its alternatives. *Psychological Review, 80*, 136–153.

Kahneman, D., Slovic, P., & Tversky, A. (Eds.). (1982). *Judgment under uncertainty: Heuristics and biases*. New York: Cambridge University Press.

Kahneman, D., & Tversky, A. (1979). Prospect theory: An analysis of decision under risk. *Econometrica, 47*, 263–291.

Kahneman, D., & Tversky, A. (1982). The psychology of preferences. *Scientific American, 246*, 160–173.

Kahneman, D., & Tversky, A. (1984). Choices, values, and frames. *American Psychologist, 39*, 341–350.

Kahneman, D., Wakker, P. P., & Sarin, R. (1997). Back to Bentham? Explorations of experienced utility. *Quarterly Journal of Economics, 62*, 375–406.

Kallgren, C. A., Reno, R. R., & Cialdini, R, B. (2000). Littering can be reduced by anti-littering norms: A focus theory of normative conduct: When norms do and do not affect behavior. *Personality and Social Psychology Bulletin, 26*, 1002–1012.

Kanazawa, S. (2002). Bowling with our imaginary friends. *Evolution and Human Behavior, 23*, 167–171.

Kanin, E. J., Davidson, K. D., & Scheck, S. R. (1970). A research note on male–female differentials in the experience of heterosexual love. *Journal of Sex Research, 6*, 64–72.

Kant, I. (1924). *Critique of judgment*. Hamburg, Germany: Felix Meiner Verlag. (Original work published 1790)

Kant, I. (1967). *Kritik der praktischen Vernunft* [Critique of practical reason]. Hamburg: Felix Meiner Verlag. (Original work published 1797)

Kantak, K. M., Hegstrand, L. R., & Eichelman, B. (1981). Facilitation of shock-induced fighting following intraventricular 5, 7-dehydroxytryptamine and 6-hydroxydopa. *Psychopharmacology, 74,* 157–160.

Karau, S. J., & Williams, K. D. (1993). Social loafing: A meta-analytic review and theoretical integration. *Journal of Personality and Social Psychology, 65,* 681–706.

Kardes, F. R. (1988). Spontaneous inference processes in advertising: The effects of conclusion omission and involvement on persuasion. *Journal of Consumer Research, 15,* 225–233.

Kasser, T., & Ryan, R. M. (1993). A dark side of the American Dream: Correlates of financial success as a central life aspiration. *Journal of Personality and Social Psychology, 65,* 410–422.

Kasser, T., & Ryan, R. M. (2001). Be careful what you wish for: Optimal functioning and the relative attainment of intrinsic and extrinsic goals. In P. Schmuck & K. Sheldon (Eds.), *Life goals and well-being* (pp. 116–131). Göttingen: Hogrefe.

Katzev, R., Edelsack, L., Reynolds, R., Steinmetz, G., Walker, T., & Wright, R. (1978). The effect of reprimanding transgressions on subsequent helping behavior: Two field experiments. *Personality and Social Psychology Bulletin, 4,* 326–329.

Kearns, J. N., & Fincham, F. D. (2005). Victim and perpetrator accounts of interpersonal transgressions: Self-serving or relationship-serving biases? *Personality and Social Psychology Bulletin, 31,* 321–333.

Keefe, K., & Berndt, T. J. (1996). Relations of friendship quality to self-esteem in early adolescence. *Journal of Early Adolescence, 16,* 110–129.

Keegan, J. (1993). *A history of warfare.* New York: Knopf.

Keillor, G. (1985). *Lake Wobegon days.* New York: Penguin Books.

Keinan, G. (1987). Decision making under stress: Scanning of alternatives under controllable and uncontrollable threats. *Journal of Personality and Social Psychology, 52,* 639–644.

Keinan, G., Friedland, N., & Ben-Porath, Y. (1987). Decision making under stress: Scanning of alternatives under physical threat. *Acta Psychologica, 64,* 219–228.

Keir, G. (1966). The psychological assessment of the children from the island of Tristan da Cunha. In C. Banks & P. L. Broadhurst (Eds.), *Stephanos: Studies in psychology presented to Cyril Burt* (pp. 129–172). New York: Barnes & Noble.

Keizer, K., Lindenberg, S., & Steg, L. (2008, December 12). The spreading of disorder. *Science, 322,* 1681–1685.

Kelley, H. H. (1967). Attribution theory in social psychology. In D. Levine (Ed.), *Nebraska Symposium on Motivation* (Vol. 15, pp. 192–238). Lincoln: University of Nebraska Press.

Kelley, H. H., & Stahelski, A. J. (1970). Social interaction basis of cooperators' and competitors' beliefs about others. *Journal of Personality and Social Psychology, 16,* 66–91.

Kelln, B. R. C., & Ellard, J. H. (1999). An equity theory analysis of the impact of forgiveness and retribution on transgressor compliance. *Personality and Social Psychology Bulletin, 25,* 864–872.

Kelly, M. H. (1999). Regional naming patterns and the culture of honor. *Names, 47,* 3–20.

Keltner, D., Gruenfeld, D. H., & Anderson, C. (2003). Power, approach, and inhibition. *Psychological Review, 110,* 265–284.

Kerr, N. L. (1983). Motivation losses in small groups: A social dilemma analysis. *Journal of Personality and Social Psychology, 45,* 819–828.

Kerr, N. L., & Bruun, S. E. (1983). Dispensability of member effort and group motivation losses: Free-rider effects. *Journal of Personality and Social Psychology, 44,* 78–94.

Kerr, N. L., Rumble, A. C., Park, E. S, Ouwerkerk, J. W., Parks, C. D., Gallucci, M., & Van Lange, P. A. M. (2009). "How many bad apples does it take to spoil the whole barrel?": Social exclusion and toleration for bad apples. *Journal of Experimental Social Psychology, 45,* 603–613.

Kevorkian gets 10 to 25 years in prison. (1999, April 13). *CNN.* Retrieved October 27, 2004, from http://www.cnn.com/US/9904/13/kevorkian.03/

Kiecolt-Glaser, J. K., Fisher, L. D., Ogrocki, P., Stout, J. C., Speicher, C. E., & Glaser, R. (1987). Marital quality, marital disruption, and immune function. *Psychosomatic Medicine, 49,* 13–34.

Kiecolt-Glaser, J. K., Garner, W., Speicher, C., Penn, G. M., Holliday, J., & Glaser, R. (1984). Psychosocial modifiers of immunocompetence in medical students. *Psychosomatic Medicine, 46,* 7–14.

Kiecolt-Glaser, J. K., & Newton, T. L. (2001). Marriage and health: His and hers. *Psychological Bulletin, 127,* 472–503.

Kiesler, S., Sproull, L., & Waters, K. (1996). A prisoner's dilemma experiment on cooperation with people and human-like computers. *Journal of Personality and Social Psychology, 70,* 47–65.

King, K., Balswick, J. O., & Robinson, I. E. (1977). The continuing premarital sexual revolution among college females. *Journal of Marriage and the Family, 39,* 455–459.

Kingston, D. A., Fedoroff, P., Firestone, P., Curry, S., & Bradford, J. M. (2008). Pornography use and sexual aggression: The impact of frequency and type of pornography use on recidivism among sexual offenders. *Aggressive Behavior, 34,* 341–351.

Kinsey, A. C., Pomeroy, W. B., & Martin, C. E., & Gebhard, P. H. (1953). *Sexual behavior in the human female.* Philadelphia: Saunders.

Kipnis, D. (1972). Does power corrupt? *Journal of Personality and Social Psychology, 24,* 33–41.

Kipnis, D. (1976). *The powerholders.* Chicago: University of Chicago Press.

Kirkpatrick, L. A., & Ellis, B. J. (2001). An evolutionary-psychological perspective on self-esteem: Multiple domains and multiple functions. In G. J. O. Fletcher & M. S. Clark (Eds.), *Blackwell handbook of social psychology: Vol. 2. Interpersonal processes* (pp. 411–436). Oxford, UK: Blackwell.

Kirschenbaum, D., Humphrey, L., & Malett, S. (1981). Specificity of planning in adult self-control: An applied investigation. *Journal of Personality and Social Psychology, 40,* 941–950.

Kirschenbaum, D., Malett, S., Humphrey, L., & Tomarken, A. (1982). Specificity of planning and maintenance of self-control: 1 year follow-up of a study improvement program. *Behavior Therapy, 13,* 232–240.

Kitayama, S., & Markus, H. R. (1999) Yin and Yang of the Japanese self: The cultural psychology of personality coherence. In D. Cervone (Ed.), *The coherence of personality: Social-cognitive bases of consistency, variability, and organization* (pp. 242–302). New York: Guilford Press.

Kitayama, S., Snibbe, A. C., Markus, H. R., & Suzuki, T. (2004). Is there any "free" choice? Cognitive dissonance in two cultures. *Psychological Science, 15,* 527–533.

Kitzinger, C. (1987). *The social construction of lesbianism.* London: Sage.

Klein, S. B., & Kihlstrom, J. F. (1986). Elaboration, organization, and the self-reference effect in memory. *Journal of Experimental Psychology: General, 115,* 26–39.

Klinesmith, J., Kasser, T., & McAndrew, F. T. (2006). Guns, testosterone, and aggression: An experimental test of a mediational hypothesis. *Psychological Science, 17,* 568–571.

Kling, K. C., Hyde, J. S., Showers, C. J., & Buswell, B. N. (1999). Gender differences in self-esteem: A meta-analysis. *Psychological Bulletin, 125,* 470–500.

Klinger, M. R., & Greenwald, A. G. (1994). Preferences need no inferences? The cognitive basis for unconscious emotional effects. In P. M. Niedenthal & S. Kitayama (Eds.), *The heart's eye: Emotional influences in perception and attention* (pp. 67–85). Orlando, FL: Academic Press.

Knight, G. R. (1999). *A brief history of Seventh-Day Adventists.* Hagerstown, MD: Review & Herald.

Knight, L. J., & Boland, F. J. (1989). Restrained eating: An experimental disentanglement of disinhibiting variables of perceived calories and food type. *Journal of Abnormal Psychology, 98,* 412–420.

Knoth, R., Boyd, K., & Singer, B. (1988). Empirical tests of sexual selection theory: Predictions of sex differences in onset, intensity, and time course of sexual arousal. *Journal of Sex Research, 24,* 73–89.

Knowles, E. S., & Linn, J. A. (2004). Approach-avoidance model of persuasion: Alpha and omega strategies for change. In E. S. Knowles & J. A. Linn (Eds.), *Resistance and persuasion.* Mahwah, NJ: Erlbaum.

Koch, E. J., & Shepperd, J. A. (2008). Testing competence and acceptance explanations of self-esteem. *Self and Identity, 7,* 54–74.

Kolata, G. (1992, November 22). The burdens of being overweight: Mistreatment and misconceptions. *New York Times,* A1.

Kolditz, T., & Arkin, R. M. (1982). An impression management interpretation of the self-handicapping phenomenon. *Journal of Personality and Social Psychology, 43,* 492–502.

Koss, M. P. (1988). Hidden rape: Sexual aggression and victimization in the national sample of students in higher education. In M. A. Pirog-Good & J. E. Stets (Eds.), *Violence in dating relationships: Emerging social issues* (pp. 145–168). New York: Praeger.

Kouzes, J. M., & Posner, B. Z. (2002). *The leadership challenge* (3rd ed.). San Francisco: Jossey-Bass.

Kraus, S. J. (1995). Attitudes and the prediction of behavior: A meta-analysis of the empirical literature. *Personality and Social Psychology Bulletin, 21,* 58–75.

Krauss, R. M., Freedman, J. L., & Whitcup, M. (1978). Field and laboratory studies of littering. *Journal of Experimental Social Psychology, 14,* 109–122.

Krauthammer, C. (1997, June 29). Apology is not ours to give. *Cleveland Plain Dealer,* p. 2-E.

Kravitz, D. A., & Martin, B. (1986). Ringelmann rediscovered: The original article. *Journal of Personality and Social Psychology, 50,* 936–941.

Kray, L. J., & Galinsky, A. D. (2003). The debiasing effect of counterfactual mind-sets: Increasing the search for disconfirmatory information in group decisions. *Organizational Behavior and Human Decision Processes, 91,* 69–81.

Krendl, A. C., Richeson, J. A., Kelley, W. M., & Heatherton, T. F. (2008). The negative consequences of threat: A functional magnetic resonance imaging investigation of the neural mechanisms underlying women's underperformance in math. *Psychological Science, 19*(2), 168–175.

Krosnick, J. A., & Alwin, D. F. (1989). Aging and susceptibility to attitude change. *Journal of Personality and Social Psychology, 57*(3), 416–425.

Krueger, J., & Clement, R. W. (1994). The truly false consensus effect: An ineradicable and egocentric bias in social perception. *Journal of Personality and Social Psychology, 67,* 596–610.

Krueger, J., Wirtz, D., & Miller, D. T. (2005). Counterfactual thinking and the first instinct fallacy. *Journal of Personality and Social Psychology, 88,* 725–735.

Kruger, J., & Gilovich, T. (2004). Actions, intentions, and self-assessment: The road to self-enhancement is paved with good intentions. *Personality and Social Psychology Bulletin, 30*(3), 328–339.

Krull, D. S., Loy, M. H.-M., & Lin, J. (1999). The fundamental fundamental attribution error: Correspondence bias in individualist and collectivist cultures. *Personality and Social Psychology Bulletin, 25,* 1208–1219.

Kuiper, N. A., & Derry, P. A. (1982). Depressed and nondepressed content self-reference in mild depression. *Journal of Personality, 50,* 67–79.

Kunce, L. J., & Shaver, P. R. (1994). An attachment-theoretical approach to caregiving in romantic relationships. In K. Bartholomew & D. Perlman (Eds.), *Advances in personal relationships* (Vol. 5, pp. 205–237). London: Kingsley.

Kunda, Z. (1990). The case for motivated reasoning. *Psychological Bulletin, 108,* 480–498.

Kunda, Z., Davies, P. G., Adams, B. D., & Spencer, S. J. (2002). The dynamic time course of stereotype activation: Activation, dissipation, and resurrection. *Journal of Personality and Social Psychology, 82,* 283–299.

Kunda, Z., & Thagard, P. (1996). Forming impressions from stereotypes, traits, and behaviors: A parallel-constraint-satisfaction theory. *Psychological Review, 103,* 284–308.

Kunz, P. R., & Woolcott, M. (1976). Season's greetings: From my status to yours. *Social Science Research, 5,* 269–278.

Kuo, Z. Y. (1930). Genesis of the cat's behavior towards the rat. *Journal of Comparative Psychology, 11*, 1–35.

Kurzban, R., & Leary, M. R. (2001). Evolutionary origins of stigmatization: The functions of social exclusion. *Psychological Bulletin, 127*, 187–208.

Lacoursiere, R. B. (1980). *The life cycles of groups: Group developmental stage theory.* New York: Human Sciences Press.

LaFrance, M., & Banaji, M. (1992). Toward a reconsideration of the gender–emotion relationship. In M. S. Clark (Ed.), *Emotion and social behavior: Review of personality and social psychology* (Vol. 14, pp. 178–201). Newbury Park, CA: Sage.

Lagerspetz, K. M., Bjorkqvist, K., & Peltonen, T. (1988). Is indirect aggression typical of females? Gender differences in aggressiveness in 11- to 12-year-old children. *Aggressive Behavior, 14*, 403–414.

Lakin, J. L., & Chartrand, T. L. (2005). Exclusion and nonconscious behavioral mimicry. In K. D. Williams, J. P. Forgas, & W. von Hippel (Eds.), *The social outcast: Ostracism, social exclusion, rejection, and bullying.* New York: Psychology Press.

Landman, J. (1993). *Regret: The persistence of the possible.* New York: Oxford University Press.

Langer, E. J. (1975). The illusion of control. *Journal of Personality and Social Psychology, 32*, 311–328.

Langer, E. J., & Roth, J. (1975). Heads I win, tails it's chance: The illusion of control as a function of the sequence of outcomes in a purely chance task. *Journal of Personality and Social Psychology, 32*, 951–955.

Langer, L. M., & Tubman, J. G. (1997). Risky sexual behavior among substance-abusing adolescents: Psychosocial and contextual factors. *American Journal of Orthopsychiatry, 67*, 315–322.

Langlois, J. H., Roggman, L. A., Casey, R. J., & Ritter, J. M. (1987). Infant preferences for attractive faces: Rudiments of a stereotype? *Developmental Psychology, 23*, 363–369.

LaPiere, R. T. (1934). Attitudes vs. actions. *Social Forces, 13*, 230–237.

Larsen, R. J. (2000). Toward a science of mood regulation. *Psychological Inquiry, 11*(3), 129–141.

Larsen, R. J., & Diener, E. (1987) Affect intensity as an individual difference characteristic: A review. *Journal of Research in Personality, 21*, 1–39.

Larson, R. W., & Pleck, J. (1999) Hidden feelings: Emotionality in boys and men. In D. Bernstein (Ed.), *Nebraska Symposium on Motivation: Vol. 45. Gender and motivation* (pp. 25–74). Lincoln: University of Nebraska Press.

Larson, R. W., Richards, M. H., & Perry-Jenkins, M. (1994). Divergent worlds: The daily emotional experience of mothers and fathers in the domestic and public spheres. *Journal of Personality and Social Psychology, 67*, 1034–1046.

Larwood, L., & Gattiker, U. E. (1995). Rational bias and interorganizational power in the employment of management consultants. *Group and Organization Studies, 10*, 3–17.

Latane, B., & Darley, J. (1968). Group inhibition of bystander intervention in emergencies. *Journal of Personality and Social Psychology, 10*, 215–221.

Latane, B., Eckman, J., & Joy, V. (1966). Shared stress and interpersonal attraction. *Journal of Experimental Social Psychology Supplement, 1*, 80–94.

Latane, B., Williams, K., & Harkins, S. (1979). Many hands make light the work: The causes and consequences of social loafing. *Journal of Personality and Social Psychology, 37*, 822–832.

Lau, R. R. (1989). Individual and contextual influences on group identification. *Social Psychology Quarterly, 4*, 17–52.

Laumann, E. O., Gagnon, J. H., Michael, R. T., & Michaels, S. (1994). *The social organization of sexuality: Sexual practices in the United States.* Chicago: University of Chicago Press.

Lavine, H., Sweeney, D., & Wagner, S. H. (1999). Depicting women as sex objects in television advertising: Effects on body dissatisfaction. *Personality and Social Psychology Bulletin, 25*, 1049–1058.

Lawrence, C., & Andrews, K. (2004). The influence of perceived prison crowding on male inmates' perception of aggressive events. *Aggressive Behavior, 30*(4), 273–283.

Lawson, A. (1988). *Adultery: An analysis of love and betrayal.* New York: Basic Books.

Lea, S. E. G., & Webley, P. (2006). Money as tool, money as drug: The biological psychology of a strong incentive. *Behavioral and Brain Sciences, 29*, 161–209.

Leary, M. R. (2005). Varieties of interpersonal rejection. In K. D. Williams, J. P. Forgas, & W. von Hippel (Eds.), *The social outcast: Ostracism, social exclusion, rejection, and bullying.* New York: Psychology Press.

Leary, M. R., & Baumeister, R. F. (2000). The nature and function of self-esteem: Sociometer theory. In M. Zanna (Ed.), *Advances in experimental social psychology* (Vol. 32, pp. 1–62). San Diego, CA: Academic Press.

Leary, M. R., Kowalski, R. M., Smith, L., & Phillips, S. (2003). Teasing, rejection, and violence: Case studies of the school shootings. *Aggressive Behavior, 29*, 202–214.

Leary, M. R., & Springer, C. A. (2000). Hurt feelings: The neglected emotion. In R. Kowalski (Ed.), *Aversive behaviors and interpersonal transgression.* Washington, DC: American Psychological Association.

Leary, M. R., Springer, C., Negel, L., Ansell, E., & Evans, K. (1998). The causes, phenomenology, and consequences of hurt feelings. *Journal of Personality and Social Psychology, 74*, 1225–1237.

Leary, M. R., Tambor, E. S., Terdal, S. K., & Downs, D. L. (1995). Self-esteem as an interpersonal monitor: The sociometer hypothesis. *Journal of Personality Psychology, 68*, 518–530.

Leary, M. R., Tchividjian, L. R., & Kraxberger, B. E. (1994). Self-presentation can be hazardous to your health: Impression management and health risk. *Health Psychology, 13*, 461–470.

Lebanese food served with a bang. (2008, June 23). *BBC News.* Retrieved May 1, 2009, from http://news.bbc.co.uk/2/hi/middle_east/7468729.stm

Lee, B.-K., & Lee, W.-N. (2004). The effect of information overload on consumer choice quality in an on-line environment. *Psychology and Marketing, 21*, 159–183.

Lee, C. (1995). Prosocial organizational behaviors: The roles of workplace justice, achievement striving, and pay satisfaction. *Journal of Business and Psychology, 10*, 197–206.

Lee, Y., Jussim, L., & McCauley, C. (1995). *Stereotype accuracy.* Washington, DC: American Psychological Association.

Lee-Chai, A. Y., Chen, S., & Chartrand, T. L. (2001). From Moses to Marcos: Individual differences in the use and abuse of power. In A. Y. Lee-Chai & J. A. Bargh (Eds.), *The use and abuse of power: Multiple perspectives on the causes of corruption* (pp. 57–74). New York: Psychology Press.

Leffingwell, A. (1892). *Illegitimacy and the influence of the seasons upon conduct.* New York: Scribner's.

Lehman, D. R., Lempert, R. O., & Nisbett, R. E. (1988). The effects of graduate training on reasoning: Formal discipline and thinking about everyday-life events. *American Psychologist, 43*(6), 431–442.

Leiblum, S. R., & Rosen, R. C. (1988). Changing perspectives on sexual desire. In S. Leiblum & R. Rosen (Eds.), *Sexual desire disorders* (pp. 1–20). New York: Guilford Press.

Leitenberg, H., & Henning, K. (1995). Sexual fantasy. *Psychological Bulletin, 117*, 469–496.

Leitenberg, H., Detzer, M. J., & Srebnik, D. (1993). Gender differences in masturbation and the relation of masturbation experiences in preadolescence and/or early adolescence to sexual behavior and sexual adjustment in young adulthood. *Archives of Sexual Behavior, 22*, 87–98.

Leith, K. P., & Baumeister, R. F. (1996). Why do bad moods increase self-defeating behavior? Emotion, risk tasking, and self-regulation. *Journal of Personality and Social Psychology, 71*, 1250–1267.

Lennox, R. D., & Wolfe, R. N. (1984). Revision of the self-monitoring scale. *Journal of Personality and Social Psychology, 46*, 1349–1364.

Leon, G., & Chamberlain, K. (1973). Emotional arousal, eating patterns, and body image as differential factors associated with varying success in maintaining a weight loss. *Journal of Consulting and Clinical Psychology, 40*, 474.

Leonardelli, G. J., & Brewer, M. B. (2001). Minority and majority discrimination: When and why. *Journal of Experimental Social Psychology, 37*, 468–485.

Lepper, M. P., Greene, D., & Nisbett, R. E. (1973). Undermining children's intrinsic interest with extrinsic reward: A test of the "overjustification" hypothesis. *Journal of Personality and Social Psychology, 28*, 129–137.

Lerner, J. S., Gonzalez, R. M., Small, D. A., & Fischhoff, B. (2003). Effects of fear and anger on perceived risks of terrorism: A national field experiment. *Psychological Science, 14*, 144–150.

Lerner, J. S., & Keltner, D. (2001). Fear, anger, and risk. *Journal of Personality and Social Psychology, 81*, 146–159.

Lerner, J. S., Small, D. A., & Loewenstein, G. (2004). Heart strings and purse strings: Carryover effects of emotions on economic decisions. *Psychological Science, 15*(5), 337–341.

Lerner, J. S., & Tetlock, P. E. (1999). Accounting for the effects of accountability. *Psychological Bulletin, 125*, 255–275.

Lerner, M. J. (1982). The justice motive in human relations and economic model of man: A radical analysis of facts and fictions. In V. Derlega & J. Grzelak (Eds.), *Cooperation and helping behavior: Theories and research* (pp. 249–278). New York: Academic Press.

Lerner, M. J., & Miller, D. T. (1978). Just world research and the attribution process: Looking back and ahead. *Psychological Bulletin, 85*, 1030–1051.

Lerner, M. J., & Simmons, C. H. (1966). Observer's reaction to the "innocent victim": Compassion or rejection? *Journal of Personality and Social Psychology, 4*, 203–210.

Lerner, R. (1969). Some female stereotypes of male body build–behavior relations. *Perceptual and Motor Skills, 28*, 363–366.

Leslie, J. B., & Van Velsor, E. (1996). *A look at derailment today.* Greensboro, NC: Centre for Creative Leadership.

Leung, K., & Bond, M. H. (2004). Social axions: A model for social beliefs in multicultural perspective. In M. Zanna (Ed.), *Advances in experimental social psychology* (Vol. 36, pp. 119–197). New York: Academic Press.

Levenson, R. W., & Gottman, J. M. (1983). Marital interaction: Physiological linkage and affective exchange. *Journal of Personality and Social Psychology, 45*, 587–597.

Levi, K. (1982). *Violence and religious commitment: Implications of Jim Jones's Peoples Temple movement.* University Park: Pennsylvania State University Press.

Levine, J. M., & Moreland, R. L. (1998). Small groups. In D. Gilbert, S. Fiske, & G. Lindzey (Eds.), *Handbook of social psychology* (4th. ed., Vol. 2, pp. 415–469). Boston: McGraw-Hill.

Levine, J. M., & Valle, R. S. (1975). The convert as a credible communicator. *Social Behavior and Personality, 3*, 81–90.

Levitt, S. D., & Dubner, S. J. (2005). *Freakonomics: A rogue economist explores the hidden side of everything.* New York: Morrow.

Lewin, K. (1951). *Field theory in social science: Selected theoretical papers* (D. Cartwright, Ed.). New York: Harper Torchbooks.

Lewinsohn, P. M., Mischel, W., Chaplin, W., & Barton, R. (1980). Social competence and depression: The role of illusory self-perceptions. *Journal of Abnormal Psychology, 89*, 203–212.

Lewis, W. A., & Bucher, A. M. (1992). Anger, catharsis, the reformulated frustration-aggression hypothesis, and health consequences. *Psychotherapy, 29*, 385–392

Liang, D. W., Moreland, R. L., & Argote, L. (1995). Group versus individual training and group performance: The mediating role of transactive memory. *Personality and Social Psychology Bulletin, 21*, 384–393.

Liberman, N., Sagristano, M. C., & Trope, Y. (2002). The effect of temporal perspective on level of construal. *Journal of Experimental Social Psychology, 38*, 524–534.

Liberman, N., & Trope, Y. (1998). The role of feasibility and desirability considerations in near and distant future decisions: A test of temporal construal theory. *Journal of Personality and Social Psychology, 75*, 5–18.

Lickel, B., Hamilton, D. L., Wieczorkowska, G., Lewis, A., Sherman, S. J., & Uhles, A. N. (2000). Varieties of groups and the perception of group entitativity. *Journal of Personality and Social Psychology, 78,* 223–246.

Lieberman, M. A., Yalom, I. D., & Miles, M. B. (1973). *Encounter groups: First facts.* New York: Basic Books.

Lieberman, M. D., Gaunt, R., Gilbert, D. T., & Trope, Y. (2002). Reflection and reflexion: A social cognitive neuroscience approach to attributional inference. *Advances in Experimental Social Psychology, 34,* 199–249.

Liebert, R., & Baron, R. (1972). Some immediate effects of televised violence on children's behavior. *Developmental Psychology, 6,* 469–475.

Liebowitz, M. R. (1983). *The chemistry of love.* Boston: Little & Brown.

Liebrand, W. B. G., Wilke, H. A. M., & Wolters, F. J. M. (1986). Value orientation and conformity: A study using three types of social dilemma games. *Journal of Conflict Resolution, 30,* 77–97.

Lifton, R. J. (1967). *Death in life: Survivors of Hiroshima.* New York: Basic Books.

Lightfoot-Klein, H. (1989). *Prisoners of ritual: An odyssey into female genital circumcision in Africa.* New York: Haworth Press.

Lin, Y.-J., & Wicker, F. W. (2007). A comparison of the effects of thought suppression, distraction and concentration. *Behaviour Research and Therapy, 45*(12), 2924–2937.

Linder, D. E., Cooper, J., & Jones, E. E. (1967). Decision freedom as a determinant of the role of incentive magnitude in attitude change. *Journal of Personality and Social Psychology, 6,* 245–254.

Lindner, E. G. (2002). Healing the cycles of humiliation: How to attend to the emotional aspects of "unsolvable" conflicts and the use of "humiliation entrepreneurship." *Peace and Conflict: Journal of Peace Psychology, 8,* 125–138.

Lindskold, S., & Aronoff, J. R. (1980). Conciliatory strategies and relative power. *Journal of Experimental Social Psychology, 16,* 187–198.

Linnoila, M., Virkkunnen, M., Scheinin, M., Nuttila, A., Rimon, R., & Goodwin, F. K. (1983). Low cerebrospinal fluid 5-hydroxyindoleacetic acid concentration differentiates impulsive from non-impulsive violent behavior. *Life Sciences, 33,* 2609–2614.

Linville , P. W., & Jones, E. E. (1980). Polarized appraisals of outgroup members. *Journal of Personality and Social Psychology, 38,* 689–703.

Lipsey, M. W., Wilson, D. B., Cohen M. A., & Derzon, J. H. (1997). Is there a causal relationship between alcohol use and violence? A synthesis of the evidence. In M. Galanter (Ed.), *Recent developments in alcoholism: Vol. 13. Alcohol and violence: Epidemiology, neurobiology, psychology, and family issues* (pp. 245–282). New York: Plenum Press.

Litt, C. J. (1981). Children's attachment to transitional objects: A study of two pediatric populations. *American Journal of Orthopsychiatry, 51,* 131–139.

Little, B. R. (1989). Personal projects analysis: Trivial pursuits, magnificent obsessions, and the search for coherence. In D. Buss & N. Cantor (Eds.), *Personality psychology: Recent trends and emerging directions* (pp. 15–31). New York: Springer-Verlag.

Locke, E. A., & Kristof, A. L. (1996). Volitional choices in the goal achievement process. In P. M. Gollwitzer & J. A. Bargh (Eds.), *The psychology of action: Linking cognition and motivation to behavior* (pp. 363–384). New York: Guilford Press.

Locke, E. A., & Latham, G. P. (1990). *A theory of goal setting and task performance.* Englewood Cliffs, NJ: Prentice-Hall.

Locksley, A., Ortiz, V., & Hepburn, C. (1980). Social categorization and discriminatory behavior: Extinguishing the minimal intergroup discrimination effect. *Journal of Personality and Social Psychology, 39*(5), 773–783.

Loeber, R., & Hay, D. (1997). Key issues in the development of aggression from childhood to early adulthood. *Annual Review of Psychology, 48,* 371–410.

Loewenstein, G. F., Weber, E. U., Hsee, C. K., & Welch, N. (2001). Risk as feelings. *Psychological Bulletin, 127,* 267–286.

Logue, A. W. (1991). *The psychology of eating and drinking: An introduction* (2nd ed.). New York: W. H. Freeman.

Lopes, L. L. (1987). Procedural debiasing. *Acta Psychologica, 64,* 167–185.

Lopes, P. N., Brackett, M. A., Nezlek, J. B., Schütz, A., Sellin, I., & Salovey, P. (2004). Emotional intelligence and social interaction. *Personality and Social Psychology Bulletin, 30,* 1018–1034.

Lord, C. G., Lepper, M. R., & Preston, E. (1984). Considering the opposite: A corrective strategy for social judgment. *Journal of Personality and Social Psychology, 47,* 1231–1243.

Lord, C. G., Ross, L., & Lepper, M. R. (1979). Biased assimilation and attitude polarization: The effects of prior theories on subsequently considered evidence. *Journal of Personality and Social Psychology, 37,* 2098–2109.

Lord, C. G., & Saenz, D. S. (1985). Memory deficits and memory surfeits: Differential cognitive consequences of tokenism for tokens and observers. *Journal of Personality and Social Psychology, 49,* 918–926.

Lord, R. G., Foti, R. J., & DeVader, C. L. (1984). A test of leadership categorization theory: Internal structure, information processing, and leadership perceptions. *Organizational Behavior and Human Performance, 34,* 343–378.

Lorenz, K. (1966). *On aggression* (M. K. Wilson, Trans.) New York: Harcourt, Brace.

Lucas, R. E. (2007). Long-term disability is associated with lasting changes in subjective well-being: Evidence from two nationally representative longitudinal studies. *Journal of Personality and Social Psychology, 92*(4), 717–730.

Luce, M. F. (1998). Choosing to avoid: Coping with negatively emotion-laden consumer decisions. *Journal of Consumer Research, 24,* 409–433.

Luce, M. F., Bettman, J. R., & Payne, J. W. (1997). Choice processing in emotionally difficult decisions. *Journal of Experimental Psychology: Learning, Memory, and Cognition, 23,* 384–405.

Luce, M. F., Bettman, J. R., & Payne, J. W. (2001). *Emotional decisions: Tradeoff difficulty and coping in consumer choice.* Chicago: University of Chicago Press.

Lydon, J. E., Menzies-Toman, D., Burton, K., & Bell, C. (2008). If-then contingencies and the differential effects of the availability of an attractive alternative on relationship maintenance for men and women. *Journal of Personality and Social Psychology, 95,* 50–65.

Lynch, J. J. (1979). *The broken heart: The medical consequences of loneliness.* New York: Basic Books.

Lyubomirsky, S. (2001). Why are some people happier than others? The role of cognitive and motivational processes in well-being. *American Psychologist, 56,* 239–249.

Maass, A., Cadinu, M., Guarnieri, G., & Grasselli, A. (2003). Sexual harassment under social identity threat: The computer harassment paradigm. *Journal of Personality and Social Psychology, 85,* 853–870.

MacDonald, G., & Leary, M. R. (2005). Why does social exclusion hurt? The relationship between social and physical pain. *Psychological Bulletin, 131,* 202–223.

MacDonald, T. K., & Ross, M. (1999). Assessing the accuracy of predictions about dating relationships: How and why do lovers' predictions differ from those made by observers? *Personality and Social Psychology Bulletin, 25,* 1417–1429.

Macfarlane, A. (1986). *Marriage and love in England: Modes of reproduction, 1300–1840.* New York: Basil Blackwell.

Mack, D., & Rainey, D. (1990). Female applicants' grooming and personnel selection. *Journal of Social Behavior and Personality, 5,* 399–407.

Mackay, C. (1932). *Extraordinary popular delusions and the madness of crowds.* New York: Farrar, Straus and Cudahy. (Original work published 1841)

Mackie, D., & Cooper, J. (1984). Attitude polarization: Effects of group membership. *Journal of Personality and Social Psychology, 46,* 575–585.

Mackie, D. M., Worth L. T., & Asuncion, A. G. (1990). Processing of persuasive in-group messages. *Journal of Personality and Social Psychology, 58,* 812–822.

MacLean, M. J., & Chown, S. M. (1988). Just world beliefs and attitudes toward helping elderly people: A comparison of British and Canadian university students.

International Journal of Aging and Human Development, 26, 249–260.

Macphail, E. (1982). *Brain and intelligence in vertebrates.* Oxford, UK: Clarendon Press.

Macrae, C. N., Milne, A. B., & Bodenhausen, G. V. (1994). Stereotypes as energy-saving devices: A peek inside the cognitive toolbox. *Journal of Personality and Social Psychology, 66,* 37–47.

Maddux, C. D., Stacy, D., & Scott, M. (1981). School entry age in a group of gifted children. *Gifted Child Quarterly, 25,* 180–184.

Major, B., Zubek, J. M., Cooper, M. L., Cozzarelli, C., & Richards, C. (1997). Mixed messages: Implications of social conflict and social support within close relationships for adjustment to a stressful life event. *Journal of Personality and Social Psychology, 72,* 1349–1363.

Malamuth, N. M., & Check, J. V. P. (1981). The effects of mass media exposure on acceptance of violence against women: A field experiment. *Journal of Research in Personality, 15,* 436–446.

Malle, B. F. (2006). The actor-observer asymmetry in causal attribution: A (surprising) meta-analysis. *Psychological Bulletin, 132,* 895–919.

Malle, B. F., Knobe, J. M., & Nelson, S. E. (2007). Actor-observer asymmetries in explanations of behavior: New answers to an old question. *Journal of Personality and Social Psychology, 93,* 491–514.

Maner, J. K., DeWall, C. N., Baumeister, R. F., & Schaller, M. (2007). Does social exclusion motivate interpersonal reconnection? Resolving the "porcupine problem." *Journal of Personality and Social Psychology, 92*(1), 42–55.

Maner, J. K., Gailliot, M. T., & DeWall, C. N. (2007). Adaptive attentional attunement: Evidence for mating-related perceptual bias. *Evolution and Human Behavior, 28*(1), 28–36.

Maner, J. K., Kenrick, D. T., Neuberg, S. L., Becker, D. V., Robertson, T., Hofer, B., et al. (2005). Functional projection: How fundamental social motives can bias interpersonal perception. *Journal of Personality and Social Psychology, 88,* 63–78.

Manning, R., Levine, M., & Collins, A. (2007). The Kitty Genovese murder and the social psychology of helping; The parable of the 38 witnesses. *American Psychologist, 62,* 555–562.

Manucia, G. K., Baumann, D. J., & Cialdini, R. B. (1984). Mood influences on helping: Direct effects or side effects? *Journal of Personality and Social Psychology, 46,* 357–364.

Marcus-Newhall, A., Pedersen, W. C., Carlson, M., & Miller, N. (2000). Displaced aggression is alive and well: A meta-analytic review. *Journal of Personality and Social Psychology, 78,* 670–689.

Maris, R. (1969). *Social forces in urban suicide.* Homewood, IL: Dorsey.

Maris, R. (1981). *Pathways to suicide: A survey of self-destructive behaviors.* Baltimore, MD: Johns Hopkins University Press.

Markman, K., Gavanski, I., Sherman, S., & McMullen, M. (1993). The mental simulation of better and worse possible worlds. *Journal of Experimental Social Psychology, 29,* 87–109.

Marks, G. (1984). Thinking one's abilities are unique and one's opinions are common. *Personality and Social Psychology Bulletin, 10,* 203–208.

Marks, G., & Miller, N. (1987). Ten years of research on the false consensus effect: An empirical and theoretical review. *Psychological Bulletin, 102,* 72–90.

Marks, T., & Hammen, C. L. (1982). Interpersonal mood induction: Situational and individual determinants. *Motivation and Emotion, 6,* 387–399.

Markus, H. R., & Kitayama, S. (1991). Culture and the self: Implications for cognition, emotion, and motivation. *Psychological Review, 98,* 224–253.

Markus, H. R., & Kunda, Z. (1986). Stability and malleability in the self-concept in the perception of others. *Journal of Personality and Social Psychology, 51,* 858–866.

Marques, J. M., Abrams, D., Páez, D., & Hogg, M. A. (2001). Social categorization, social identification, and rejection of deviant group members. In M. A. Hogg & R. S. Tindale (Eds.), *Blackwell handbook of social psychol-*

ogy: Group processes (pp. 400–424). Oxford, UK: Blackwell.

Marques, J. M., & Paez, D. (1994). The "black sheep effect": Social categorization, rejection of ingroup deviates and perception of group variability. European Review of Social Psychology, 5, 37–68.

Marques, J. M., & Yzerbyt, V. Y. (1988). The black sheep effect: Judgmental extremity in inter- and intra-group situations. European Journal of Social Psychology, 18, 287–292.

Marshall, G. D., & Zimbardo, P. G. (1979). Affective consequences of inadequately explained arousal. Journal of Personality and Social Psychology, 37, 970–988.

Maruyama, G., Rubin, R. A., & Kingsbury, G. G. (1981). Self-esteem and educational achievement: Independent constructs with a common cause? Journal of Personality and Social Psychology, 40, 962–975.

Maslach, C. (1979). Negative and emotional biasing of unexplained arousal. Journal of Personality and Social Psychology, 37, 953–969.

Maslow, A. H. (1968). Toward a psychology of being. New York: Van Nostrand.

Mather, B. (2004). Employee theft: How to prevent instead of apprehend. Business Know-How. Retrieved October 18, 2004, from http://www.businessknowhow.com/manage/employeetheft.htm

Maticka-Tyndale, E., Herold, E. S., & Mewhinney, D. (1998). Casual sex on spring break: Intentions and behaviors of Canadian students. Journal of Sex Research, 35, 254–264.

Mayer, J. D. (1993). The emotional madness of the dangerous leader. Journal of Psychohistory, 20, 331–348.

Mayer, J. D., & Salovey, P. (1997). What is emotional intelligence? In P. Salovey & D. Sluyter (Eds.), Emotional development and emotional intelligence: Implications for educators (pp. 3–31). New York: Basic Books.

Mayer, J. D., Salovey, P., & Caruso, D. (2002). Mayer-Salovey-Caruso Emotional Intelligence Test (MSCEIT): User's manual. Toronto: Multi-Health Systems, Inc.

Mayer, J. D., Salovey, P., Caruso D. R., & Sitarenios, G. (2003). Measuring emotional intelligence with the MSCEIT V2. 0. Emotion, 3, 97–105.

McCabe, P. (1987). Desired and experienced levels of premarital affection and sexual intercourse during dating. Journal of Sex Research, 23, 23–33.

McCullough, M. E. (2008). Beyond revenge: The evolution of the forgiveness instinct. San Francisco: Jossey-Bass.

McCullough, M. E., Bono, G., & Root, L. M. (2007). Rumination, emotion, and forgiveness: Three longitudinal studies. Journal of Personality and Social Psychology, 92, 490–505.

McCullough, M. E., Emmons, R. A., & Tsang, J. (2002). The grateful disposition: A conceptual and empirical topography. Journal of Personality and Social Psychology, 82, 112–127.

McCullough, M. E., Pargament, K. I., & Thoresen, C. E. (Eds.). (2000). Forgiveness: Theory, research, and practice. New York: Guilford Press.

McCullough, M. E., Rachal, K. C., Sandage, S. J., Worthington, E. L., Brown, S. W., & Hight, T. L. (1998). Interpersonal forgiving in close relationships: II. Theoretical elaboration and measurement. Journal of Personality and Social Psychology, 75, 1586–1603.

McFarlin, D. B. (1985). Persistence in the face of failure: The impact of self-esteem and contingency information. Personality and Social Psychology Bulletin, 11, 153–163.

McFarlin, D. B., Baumeister, R. F., & Blascovich, J. (1984). On knowing when to quit: Task failure, self-esteem, advice, and nonproductive persistence. Journal of Personality, 52, 138–155.

McFarlin, D. B., & Blascovich, J. (1981). Effects of self-esteem and performance on future affective preferences and cognitive expectations. Journal of Personality and Social Psychology, 40, 521–531.

McGee, R., & Williams, S. (2000). Does low self-esteem predict health compromising behaviours among adolescents? Journal of Adolescence, 23, 569–582.

McGinnis, M. Y., Lumia, A., Breuer, M. E., & Possidente, B. (2002). Physical provocation potentiates aggression in male rats receiving anabolic androgenic steroids. Hormones and Behavior, 41, 101–110.

McGuire, W. J. (1961). The effectiveness of supportive refutational defenses in immunizing and restoring beliefs against persuasion. Sociometry, 24, 184–197.

McGuire, W. J. (1964). Inducing resistance to persuasion: Some contemporary approaches. Advances in Experimental Social Psychology, 1, 191–229.

McGuire, W. J. (1968). Personality and susceptibility to social influence. In E. F. Borgotta & W. W. Lambert (Eds.), Handbook of personality theory and research (pp. 1130–1187). Chicago: Rand McNally.

McGuire, W. J., McGuire, C. V., Child, P., & Fujioka, T. (1978). Salience of ethnicity in the spontaneous self-concept as a function of one's ethnic distinctiveness in the social environment. Journal of Personality and Social Psychology, 36, 511–520.

McGuire, W. J., McGuire, C. V., Child, P., & Winton, W. (1979). Effects of household gender composition on the salience of one's gender in the spontaneous self-concept. Journal of Experimental Social Psychology, 15, 77–90.

McGuire, W. J., & Papageorgis, D. (1961). The relative efficacy of various types of prior belief-defense in producing immunity against persuasion. Journal of Abnormal Social Psychology, 62, 327–337.

McKenna, K. Y. A., & Bargh, J. A. (1998). Coming out in the age of the Internet: Identity "demarginalization" through virtual group participation. Journal of Personality and Social Psychology, 75, 681–694.

McKenna, K. Y. A., & Bargh, J. A. (1999). Causes and consequences of social interaction on the Internet: A conceptual framework. Media Psychology, 1, 249–269.

McKenna, K. Y. A., & Bargh, J. A. (2000). Plan 9 from Cyberspace: The implications of the Internet for personality and social psychology. Personality and Social Psychology Review, 4, 57–75.

McKillip, J., & Reidel, S. L. (1983). External validity of matching on physical attractiveness for same and opposite sex couples. Journal of Applied Social Psychology, 13, 328–337.

McLeod, E. (1982). Women working: Prostitution today. London: Croom Helm.

McMillen, D. L., & Austin, J. B. (1971). Effect of positive feedback on compliance following transgression. Psychonomic Science, 24, 59–61.

McMullen, M. N., Markman, K. D., & Gavanski, I. (1995). Living in neither the best nor the worst of all possible worlds: Antecedents and consequences of upward and downward counterfactual thinking. In N. J. Roese & J. M. Olson (Eds.), What might have been: The social psychology of counterfactual thinking (pp. 133–167). Mahwah, NJ: Erlbaum.

McNeill, W. H. (1982). The pursuit of power: Technology, armed force, and society since A.D. 1000. Chicago: University of Chicago Press.

Mead, G. H. (1934). Mind, self and society. Chicago: University of Chicago Press.

Mead, M. (1928). Coming of age in Samoa: A psychological study of primitive youth for western civilization. New York: Morrow.

Medvec, V. H., Madey, S. F., & Gilovich, T. (1995). When less is more: Counterfactual thinking and satisfaction among Olympic medalists. Journal of Personality and Social Psychology, 69, 603–610.

Meissner, C. A., & Brigham, J. C. (2001). Thirty years of investigating the own-race bias in memory for faces: A meta-analytic review. Psychology, Public Policy, and Law, 7, 3–35.

Mellers, B. A., Schwartz, A., Ho, K., & Ritov, I. (1997). Elation and disappointment: Emotional responses to risky options. Psychological Science, 8, 423–429.

Merton, R. K. (1948). The self-fulfilling prophecy. Antioch Review, pp. 193–210.

Mesquita, B. (2003). Emotions in collectivist and individualist contexts. Journal of Personality and Social Psychology, 80, 68–74.

Mesquita, B., & Frijda, N. (1992). Cultural variations in emotions: A review. Psychological Bulletin, 112, 179–204.

Messick, D. M., Bloom, S., Boldizar, J. P., & Samuelson, C. D. (1985). Why we are fairer than others. Journal of Experimental Social Psychology, 21, 480–500.

Messinger, D., Fogel, A., & Dickson, K. L. (1999). What's in a smile? Developmental Psychology, 35, 701–708.

Messinger, D., Fogel, A., & Dickson, K. L. (2001). All smiles are positive, but some smiles are more positive than others. Developmental Psychology, 37, 642–653.

Meyer, C. B. & Taylor, S. E. (1986). Adjustment to rape. Journal of Personality and Social Psychology, 50, 1226–1234.

Meyer, D. E., & Schvaneveldt, R. W. (1971). Facilitation in recognizing pairs of words: Evidence of a dependence between retrieval operations. Journal of Experimental Psychology, 90, 227–234.

Michaud, S. G., & Aynesworth, H. (2000). Ted Bundy: Conversations with a killer. Irving, TX: Authorlink.

Mick, D. G., & DeMoss, M. (1990). Self-gifts: Phenomenological insights from four contexts. Journal of Consumer Research, 17, 322–332.

Midlarsky, E., Jones, S. F., & Corley, R. P. (2005). Personality correlates of heroic rescue during the holocaust. Journal of Personality, 73, 907–934.

Mikula, G., Petri, B., & Tanzer, N. (1989). What people regard as unjust: Types, structures and everyday experiences of injustice. European Journal of Social Psychology, 20, 133–149.

Milgram, S. (1963). Behavioral study of obedience. Journal of Abnormal and Social Psychology, 67, 371–378.

Milgram, S. (1973, December). The perils of obedience. Harper's, 62–66.

Milgram, S. (1974), Obedience to authority; An experimental view. New York: Harper and Row.

Milgram, S. (1977). The individual in a social world. New York: McGraw-Hill.

Miller, A. G., McHoskey, J. W., Bane, C. M., & Dowd, T. G. (1993). The attitude polarization phenomenon: Role of response measure, attitude extremity, and behavioral consequences of reported attitude change. Journal of Personality and Social Psychology, 64, 561–574.

Miller, C. T., & Downey, K. T. (1999). A meta-analysis of heavyweight and self-esteem. Personality and Social Psychology Review, 3, 68–84.

Miller, D. H., Greene, K., Causby, V., White, B. W., & Lockhart, L. L. (2001). Domestic violence in lesbian relationships. Women and Therapy, 23, 107–127.

Miller, D. T., & Holmes, J. G. (1975). The role of situational restrictiveness on self-fulfilling prophecies: A theoretical and empirical extension of Kelley and Stahelski's triangle hypothesis. Journal of Personality and Social Psychology, 31, 661–673.

Miller, J., Butts, C. T., & Rodes, D. (2002). Communication and cooperation. Journal of Economic Behavior and Organization, 47, 179–195.

Miller, L. C., & Fishkin, S. A. (1997). On the dynamics of human bonding and reproductive success: Seeking windows on the adapted-for human–environmental interface. In J. Simpson & D. Kenrick (Eds.), Evolutionary social psychology (pp. 197–235). Mahwah, NJ: Erlbaum.

Miller, N., Maruyama, G., Beaber, R. J., & Valone, K. (1976). Speed of speech and persuasion. Journal of Personality and Social Psychology, 34, 615–624.

Miller, N. E. (1941). The frustration-aggression hypothesis. Psychological Review, 48, 337–342.

Miller, R. L., Seligman, C., Clark, N. T., & Bush, M. (1976). Perceptual contrast versus reciprocal concession as mediators of induced compliance. Journal of Behavioral Science, 7, 401–409.

Miller, R. S. (1997). Inattentive and contented: Relationship commitment and attention to alternatives. Journal of Personality and Social Psychology, 73, 758–766.

Miller, T. Q., Smith, T. W., Turner, C. W., Guijarro, M. L., & Hallet, A. J. (1996). A meta-analytic review of research on hostility and physical health. Psychological Bulletin, 119, 322–348.

Millhausen, R. R., & Herold, E. S. (1999). Does the sexual double standard still exist? Perceptions of university women. Journal of Sex Research, 36, 361–368.

Mischel, W. (1973). Toward a cognitive social learning reconceptualization of personality. Psychological Review, 80, 252–283.

Mischel, W. (1974). Processes in delay of gratification. In L. Berkowitz (Ed.), Advances in experimental social *psychology* (Vol. 7, pp. 249–292). San Diego, CA: Academic Press.

Mischel, W. (1996). From good intentions to willpower. In P. M. Gollwitzer & J. Bargh (Eds.), *The psychology of action: Linking cognition and motivation to behavior* (pp. 197–218). New York: Guilford Press.

Mischel, W., Ebbesen, E. B., & Zeiss, A. R. (1976). Determinants of selective memory about the self. *Journal of Consulting and Clinical Psychology, 44*, 92–103.

Mischel, W., & Mendoza-Denton, R. (2002). Harnessing willpower and socio-emotional intelligence to enhance human agency and potential. In L. G. Aspinwall & U. M. Staudinger (Eds.), *A psychology of human strengths: Fundamental questions and future directions for a positive psychology* (pp. 245–256). Washington, DC: American Psychological Association.

Mischel, W., & Shoda, Y. (1995). A cognitive-affective system theory of personality: Reconceptualizing situations, dispositions, dynamics, and invariance in personality structure. *Psychological Review, 102*, 246–268.

Mischel, W., Shoda, Y., & Peake, P. K. (1988). The nature of adolescent competencies predicted by preschool delay of gratification. *Journal of Personality and Social Psychology, 54*, 687–696.

Misra, S., & Kalro, A. (1979). Triangle effect and the connotative meaning of trust in Prisoner's Dilemma: A cross cultural study. *International Journal of Psychology, 14*, 255–263.

Mita, T. H., Dermer, M., & Knight, J. (1977). Reversed facial images and the mere-exposure hypothesis. *Journal of Personality and Social Psychology, 35*, 597–60.

Mitchell, N. (1998, April). Testosterone: The many gendered hormone. Radio documentary first broadcast on ABC's *Women Out Loud.*

Mochon, D. (2008, November). *Single option aversion: When the illusion of choices reduces deferral.* Paper presented at the annual meeting of the Society for Judgment and Decision Making, Chicago.

Mokdad, A. H., Marks, J. S., Stroup, D. F., & Gerberding, J. L. (2004). Actual causes of death in the United States, 2000. *Journal of the American Medical Association, 291*(10), 1238–1245.

Moore, B. S., & Underwood, B. (1979). Environmental noise, perceived control, and aggression. *Journal of Social Psychology, 109*, 245–252.

Moore, M. (2003, October 31). Top Israeli officer says tactics are backfiring. *Washington Post,* p. A1.

Moore, R. (1985). *A sympathetic history of Jonestown: The Moore family involvement in People's Temple.* Lewiston, NY: E. Mellen Press.

Moore, R. (1986). *The Jonestown letters: Correspondence of the Moore Family 1970–1985.* Lewiston, NY: E. Mellen Press.

Moreland, R. L., Argote, L., & Krishnan, R. (1996). Socially shared cognition at work: Transactive memory and group performance. In J. Nye & A. Brower (Eds.), *What's social about social cognition? Research on socially shared cognition in small groups* (pp. 57–84). Thousand Oaks, CA: Sage.

Moreland, R. L., Argote, L., & Krishnan, R. (1998). Training people to work in groups. In R. Tindale, L. Heath, J. Edwards, E. Posavac, F. Bryant, Y. Suarez-Balcazar, et al. (Eds.), *Theory and research on small groups* (pp. 37–60). New York: Plenum Press.

Morf, C. C., & Rhodewalt, F. (2001). Unraveling the paradoxes of narcissism: A dynamic self-regulatory processing model. *Psychological Inquiry, 12*, 177–196.

Morgenthau, H. (1962). Love and power. *Commentary, 33*, 247–251.

Mori, D., Chaiken, S., & Pliner, P. (1987). "Eating lightly" and the self-presentation of femininity. *Journal of Personality and Social Psychology, 53*, 693–702.

Morokoff, P. J. (1985). Effects of sex guilt, repression, sexual "arousability," and sexual experience on female sexual arousal during erotica and fantasy. *Journal of Personality and Social Psychology, 49*, 177–187.

Morokoff, P. J. (1986). Volunteer bias in the psychophysiological study of female sexuality. *Journal of Sex Research, 22*, 35–51.

Morris, K. A., & Swann, W. B., Jr. (1996). Denial and the AIDS crisis: Wishing away the threat of aids. In S.

Oskamp & S. Thompson (Eds.), *Safer sex in the '90s* (pp. 57–79). New York: Sage.

Morris, W. N., & Reilly, N. P. (1987). Toward the self-regulation of mood: Theory and research. *Motivation and Emotion, 11*, 215–249.

Moscovici, S., & Zavalloni, M. (1969). The group as a polarizer of attitudes. *Journal of Personality and Social Psychology, 12*, 125–135.

Moya, M., Glick, P., Expósito, F., de Lemus, S., & Hart, J. (2007). It's for your own good: Benevolent sexism and women's reactions to protectively justified restrictions. *Personality and Social Psychology Bulletin, 33*(10), 1421–1434.

Mullen, B., Johnson, C., & Salas, E. (1991). Productivity loss in brainstorming groups: A meta-analysis. *Basic and Applied Social Psychology, 12*, 3–23.

Mullin, C. R., & Linz, D. (1995). Desensitization and resensitization to violence against women: Effects of exposure to sexually violent films on judgments of domestic violence victims. *Journal of Personality and Social Psychology, 69*, 449–459.

Munger, K., & Harris, S. J. (1989). Effects of an observer on handwashing in a public restroom. *Perceptual and Motor Skills, 69*, 733–734.

Murnen, S. K., Perot, A., & Byrne, D. (1989). Coping with unwanted sexual activity: Normative responses, situational determinants, and individual differences. *Journal of Sex Research, 26*, 85–106.

Murphy, S. (1992). *A delicate dance: Sexuality, celibacy, and relationships among Catholic clergy and religious.* New York: Crossroad.

Murray, S., Bellavia, G., Rose, P., & Griffin, D. (2003). Once hurt, twice hurtful: How perceived regard regulates daily marital interactions. *Journal of Personality and Social Psychology, 84*, 126–147.

Murray, S., & Holmes, J. G. (1993). See virtues in faults: Negativity and the transformation of interpersonal narratives in close relationships. *Journal of Personality and Social Psychology, 65*, 707–722.

Murray, S., & Holmes, J. G. (1994). Story-telling in close relationships: The construction of confidence. *Personality and Social Psychology Bulletin, 20*, 663–676.

Murray, S., Holmes, J. G., & Griffin, D. W. (1996). The benefits of positive illusions: Idealization and the construction of satisfaction in close relationships. *Journal of Personality and Social Psychology, 70*, 79–98.

Murray, S., Rose, P., Bellavia, G., Holmes, J., & Kusche, A. (2002). When rejection stings: How self-esteem constrains relationship enhancement processes. *Journal of Personality and Social Psychology, 83*, 556–573.

Murstein, B. I., & Christy, P. (1976). Physical attractiveness and marriage adjustment in middle-aged couples. *Journal of Personality and Social Psychology, 34*, 537–542.

Musch, J., & Grondin, S. (2001). Unequal competition as an impediment to personal development: A review of the relative age effect in sport. *Developmental Review, 21*, 147–167.

Muslim population worldwide. (2009). Retrieved May 22, 2009, from http://www.islamicpopulation.com

Myers, D. G. (1992). The secrets of happiness. *Psychology Today, 25*, 38–46.

Myers, D. G. (2006). *Social psychology* (8th ed.). New York: McGraw Hill.

Najmi, S., & Wegner, D. M. (2008). Thought suppression and psychopathology. In A. J. Elliot (Ed.), *Handbook of approach and avoidance motivation* (pp. 447–459). New York: Psychology Press.

Neely, J. H. (1991). Semantic priming effects in visual word recognition: A selective review of current findings and theories. In D. Besner & G. Humphreys (Eds.), *Basic processes in reading: Visual word recognition* (pp. 264–336). Hillsdale, NJ: Erlbaum.

Nelson, L. D., & Morrison, E. L. (2005). The symptoms of resource scarcity: Judgments of food and finances impact preferences for potential partners. *Psychological Science, 16*(2), 167–173.

Nelson, M. R. (2002). Recall of brand placements in computer/video games. *Journal of Advertising Research, 42*, 80–92.

Nelson, R. J., & Chiavegatto, S. (2001). Molecular basis of aggression. *Trends in Neurosciences, 24*, 713–719.

New studies show strong link between diet and behavior. (2004). Retrieved October 17, 2004, from http://www.kidscanlearn.net/artcri.htm

Newcomb, T. L. (1943). *Personality and social change: Attitude formation in a student community.* New York: Dryden Press.

Newcomb, T. L., Koenig, K. E., Flacks, R., and Warwick, D. P. (1967) *Persistence and change: Bennington College and its students after 25 years.* New York: Wiley.

Newcombe, D., & Arnkoff, D. B. (1979). Effects of speech style and sex of speaker on person perception. *Journal of Personality and Social Psychology, 37*, 1293–1303.

Newman, A. (2001, February 4). Anti-smoking campaign: Rotten teeth and dead babies. *New York Times Magazine,* p. 16. Available at www.nytimes.com/

Newman, M. L., Pennebaker, J. W., Berry, D. S., & Richards, J. M. (2003). Lying words: Predicting deception from linguistic styles. *Personality and Social Psychology Bulletin, 29*(5), 665–675.

Nguyen, H.-H. D., & Ryan, A. M. (2008). Does stereotype threat affect test performance of minorities and women? A meta-analysis of experimental evidence. *Journal of Applied Psychology, 93*(6), 1314–1334.

Nickerson, R. S. (1998). Confirmation bias: A ubiquitous phenomenon in many guises. *Review of General Psychology, 2*, 175–220.

Niedenthal, P. M., Halberstadt, J. B., & Innes-Ker, A. H. (1999). Emotional response categorization. *Psychological Review, 106*, 337–361.

Niederland, W. G. (1961). The problem of the survivor. *Journal of Hillside Hospital, 10*, 233–247.

Nijman, H. L. I., & Rector, G. (1999). Crowding and aggression on inpatient psychiatric wards. *Psychiatric Services, 50*(6), 830–831.

Nisbett, R. E., & Wilson, T. D. (1977). Telling more than we can know: Verbal reports on mental processes. *Psychological Review, 84*, 231–259.

The Nobel Prize Internet Archive. (2008). Retrieved April 20, 2009, from http://nobelprizes.com/nobel/economics/economics.html

Nolen-Hoeksema, S. (1991). Responses to depression and their effects on the duration of depressive episodes. *Journal of Abnormal Psychology, 100*, 569–582.

Noordewier, M. K., van Horen, F., Ruys, K. I., & Stapel, D. A. (2009). What's in a name? 361.708 euros: The effects of marital name change. *Basic and Applied Social Psychology,* in press.

Norton, M. I., Frost, J. H., & Ariely, D. (2007). Less is more: The lure of ambiguity, or why familiarity breeds contempt. *Journal of Personality and Social Psychology, 92*, 97–105.

Nuttin, J. R. (1985). *Future time perspective and motivation: Theory and research method.* Hillsdale, NJ: Erlbaum.

Nuttin, J. R. (1987). The respective roles of cognition and motivation in behavioral dynamics, intention, and volition. In F. Halisch & J. Kuhl (Eds.), *Motivation, intention, and volition.* New York: Springer-Verlag.

Oakes, W. (1972). External validity and the use of real people as subjects. *American Psychologist, 27*, 959–962.

Oaten, M., Stevenson, R. J., & Case, T. I. (2009). Disgust as a disease-avoidance mechanism. *Psychological Bulletin, 135*, 322–338.

Obach, M. S. (2003). A longitudinal-sequential study of perceived academic competence and motivational beliefs for learning among children in middle school. *Educational Psychology, 23*, 323–338.

Oettingen, G., & Gollwitzer, P. M. (2001). Goal setting and goal striving. In A. Tesser & N. Schwarz (Eds.), *Blackwell handbook of social psychology: Intraindividual processes* (pp. 329–348). Oxford, UK: Blackwell.

Ohbuchi, K. I., Kameda, M., & Agarie, N. (1989). Apology as aggression control: Its role in mediating appraisal of and response to harm. *Journal of Personality and Social Psychology, 56*, 219–227.

Okwumabua, J. O., & Duryea, E. J. (2003). Depressive symptoms and decision making among African American youth. *Journal of Adolescent Research, 18*, 436–453.

Olatunji, B. O. (2008). Disgust, scrupulosity and conservative attitudes about sex: Evidence for a mediational model of homophobia. *Journal of Research in Personality, 42*(5), 1364–1369.

Oliner, S. P., & Oliner, P. M. (1988). *The altruistic personality: Rescuers of Jews in Nazi Europe*. New York: Free Press.

Oliver, M. B., & Hyde, J. S. (1993). Gender differences in sexuality: A meta-analysis. *Psychological Bulletin, 114,* 29–51.

Olson, M. A., & Fazio, R. H. (2001). Implicit attitude formation through classical conditioning. *Psychological Science, 12,* 413–417.

Olweus, D. (1994). Bullying at school: Long-term outcomes for the victims and an effective school-based intervention program. In R. Huesmann (Ed.), *Aggressive behavior: Current perspectives* (pp. 97–130). New York: Plenum Press.

Organ, D. W. (1988). Organizational citizenship behavior: The good soldier syndrome. Lexington, MA: Lexington Books.

Ornstein, R. (1991). *The evolution of consciousness: Of Darwin, Freud, and cranial fire: The origins of the way we think.* New York: Prentice-Hall.

Orobio de Castro, B., Veerman, J. W., Koops, W., Bosch, J. D., & Monshouwer, H. J. (2002). Hostile attribution of intent and aggressive behavior: A meta-analysis. *Child Development, 73,* 916–934.

O'Sullivan, L. F., & Allgeier, E. R. (1998). Feigning sexual desire: Consenting to unwanted sexual activity in heterosexual dating relationships. *Journal of Sex Research, 35,* 234–243.

O'Sullivan, L., & Byers, E. S. (1996). Gender differences in response to discrepancies in desired level of sexual intimacy. *Journal of Psychology and Human Sexuality, 8,* 49–67.

O'Sullivan, L. F., Byers, E. S., & Finkelman, L. (1998). A comparison of male and female college students' experiences of sexual coercion. *Psychology of Women Quarterly, 22(2),* 177–195.

Oswald, I., Taylor, A. M., & Treisman, M. (1960). Discriminative responses to stimulation during human sleep. *Brain, 83,* 440–453.

Ottaviani, R., & Beck, A. T. (1987). Cognitive aspects of panic disorders. *Journal of Anxiety Disorders, 1,* 15–28.

Ouwerkerk, J. W., Kerr, N. L., Gallucci, M., & Van Lange, P. A. M. (2005). Avoiding the social death penalty: Ostracism and cooperation in social dilemmas. In K. D. Williams, J. P. Forgas, & W. von Hippel (Eds.), *The social outcast: Ostracism, social exclusion, rejection, and bullying.* New York: Psychology Press.

Ouwerkerk, J. W., Van Lange, P. A., Gallucci, M., & Kerr, N. L. (2005). Avoiding the social death penalty: Ostracism and cooperation in social dilemmas. In K. D. Williams, J. P. Forgas, & W. von Hippel (Eds.), *The social outcast: Ostracism, social exclusion, rejection, and bullying.* New York: Psychology Press.

Overing, J. (1986). Images of cannibalism, death and domination in a "non-violent" society. In D. Riches (Ed.), *The anthropology of violence* (pp. 86–101). Oxford, UK: Blackwell.

Owen, J. (2004, July 23). Homosexual activity among animals stirs debate. *National Geographic.* Retrieved December 18, 2005, from http://news.nationalgeographic.com/news/2004/07/0722_040722_gayanimal.html

Page, S. E. (2008). *The difference: How the power of diversity creates better groups, firms, schools, and societies.* Princeton, NJ: Princeton University Press.

Paik, H., & Comstock, G. (1994). The effects of television violence on antisocial behavior: A meta-analysis. *Communication Research, 21,* 516–546.

Paleari, G., Regalia, C., & Fincham, F. D. (2005). Marital quality, forgiveness, empathy, and rumination: A longitudinal analysis. *Personality and Social Psychology Bulletin, 31,* 368–378.

Palmstierna, T., Huitfeldt, B., & Wistedt, B. (1991). The relationship of crowding and aggressive behavior on a psychiatric intensive care unit. *Hospital and Community Psychiatry, 42(12),* 1237–1240.

Panksepp, J. (1998). *Affective neuroscience: The foundations of human and animal emotions.* London: Oxford University Press.

Panksepp, J., Herman, B. H., Conner, R., Bishop, P., & Scott, J. P. (1978). The biology of social attachments: Opiates alleviate separation distress. *Biological Psychiatry, 13,* 607–618.

Panksepp, J., Najam, N., & Soares, F. (1980). Morphine reduces social cohesion in rats. *Pharmacology, Biochemistry, and Behavior, 11,* 131–134.

Panksepp, J., Vilberg, T., Bean, N. J., Coy, D. H., & Kastin, A. J. (1978). Reduction of distress vocalization in chicks by opiate-like peptides. *Brain Research Bulletin, 3,* 663–667.

Papageorgis, D., & McGuire, W. J. (1961). The generality of immunity to persuasion produced by pre-exposure to weakened counterarguments. *Journal of Abnormal and Social Psychology, 62,* 475–481.

Pargament, K. I. (1997) *The psychology of religion and coping. Theory, research, practice.* New York: Guilford Press.

Park, C. (2003). In other (people's) words: Plagiarism by university students—literature and lessons. *Assessment and Evaluation in Higher Education, 28,* 471–488.

Patterson, F., & Linden, E. *The education of Koko.* New York: Holt, Rinehart, & Winston.

Patterson, O. (1982). *Slavery and social death.* Cambridge, MA: Harvard University Press.

Paul, A. M. (1999, June 28). Promotional intelligence. *Ivory Tower.* Retrieved August 11, 2004, from http://www.salon.com/books/it/1999/06/28/emotional/index1.html

Paul, C., Fitzjohn, J., Herbison, P., & Dickson, N. (2000). The determinants of sexual intercourse before age 16. *Journal of Adolescent Health, 27,* 136–147.

Paulhus, D. L., & Levitt, K. (1987). Desirable responding triggered by affect: Automatic egotism? *Journal of Personality and Social Psychology, 52,* 245–259.

Paulus, P. B., Dzindolet, M. T., Poletes, G., & Camacho, L. M. (1993). Perception of performance in group brainstorming: The illusion of group productivity. *Personality and Social Psychology Bulletin, 19,* 78–89.

Payne, B. K. (2001). Prejudice and perception: The role of automatic and controlled processes in misperceiving a weapon. *Journal of Personality and Social Psychology, 81,* 181–192.

Payne, B. K., Govorun, O., & Arbuckle, N. L. (2008). Automatic attitudes and alcohol: Does implicit liking predict drinking? *Cognition and Emotion, 22(2),* 238–271.

Pedersen, W. C., Miller, L. C., Putcha-Bhagavatula, A. D., & Yang, Y. (2002). Evolved sex differences in the number of partners desired? The long and short of it. *Psychological Science, 13,* 157–161.

Pelham B. W., Carvallo M., DeHart T., & Jones J. T. (2003). Assessing the validity of implicit egotism: A reply to Gallucci (2003). *Journal of Personality and Social Psychology, 85,* 800–807.

Pelham, B. W., Mirenberg, M. C., & Jones, J. T. (2002). Why Susie sells seashells by the seashore: Implicit egotism and major life decisions. *Journal of Personality and Social Psychology, 82,* 469–487.

Penner, L. A. (2002). The causes of sustained volunteerism: An interactionist perspective. *Journal of Social Issues, 58,* 447–467.

Penner, L. A. (2004). Volunteerism and social problems: Making things better or worse? *Journal of Social Issues, 60,* 645–666.

Penner, L. A., Dertke, M. C., & Achenbach, C. J. (1973). The "flash" system: A field study of altruism. *Journal of Applied Social Psychology, 3,* 362–370.

People 'still willing to torture.' (2008, December 19). *BBC News.* Retrieved December 19, 2008, from http://news.bbc.co.uk/2/hi/health/7791278.stm

Peplau, L. A., & Perlman, D. (Eds.). (1982). *Loneliness: A sourcebook of current theory, research, and therapy.* New York: Wiley.

Perez, R. C. (1973). The effect of experimentally induced failure, self-esteem and sex on cognitive differentiation. *Journal of Abnormal Psychology, 81,* 74–79.

Peristiany, J. G. (Ed.). (1965). *Honour and shame: The values of Mediterranean society.* London: Weidenfeld & Nicolson.

Pernanen, K. (1991). *Alcohol in human violence.* New York: Guilford Press.

Perry, C. L., Killen, J., Slinkard, L. A., & McAlister, A. L. (1980). Peer teaching and smoking prevention among junior high students. *Adolescence, 15,* 277–281.

Persons, J. B., & Rao, P. A. (1985). Longitudinal study of cognitions, life events, and depression in psychiatric inpatients. *Journal of Abnormal Psychology, 94,* 51–63.

Persson, A. V., & Musher-Eizenman, D. R. (2005). College students' attitudes toward Blacks and Arabs following a terrorist attack as a function of varying levels of media exposure. *Journal of Applied Social Psychology, 35(9),* 1879–1893.

Peters, K., & Kashima, Y. (2007). From social talk to social action: Shaping the social triad with emotion sharing. *Journal of Personality and Social Psychology, 93,* 780–797.

Peterson, C., & Seligman, M. E. P. (2004). *Character strengths and virtues.* New York: Oxford University Press.

Pettigrew, T. F. (1979). The ultimate attribution error: Extending Allport's cognitive analysis of prejudice. *Personality and Social Psychology Bulletin, 5,* 461–476.

Pettigrew, T. F. (1985) New Black–White patterns: How best to conceptualize them? *Annual Review of Sociology, 11,* 329–346.

Pettigrew, T. F., & Tropp, L. R. (2005). Allport's intergroup contact hypothesis: Its history and influence. In J. F. Dovidio, P. Glick, & L. A. Rudman (Eds.), *On the nature of prejudice: Fifty years after Allport* (pp. 262–277). Malden, MA: Blackwell.

Pettiway, L. E. (1987). Arson for revenge: The role of environmental situation, age, sex, and race. *Journal of Quantitative Criminology, 3(2),* 169–184.

Petty, R. E., & Cacioppo, J. T. (1979). Issue involvement can increase or decrease persuasion by enhancing message-relevant cognitive responses. *Journal of Personality and Social Psychology, 37,* 1915–1926.

Petty, R. E., & Cacioppo, J. T. (1986) *Communication and persuasion: Central and peripheral routes to attitude change.* New York: Springer-Verlag.

Phillis, D. E., & Gromko, M. H. (1985). Sex differences in sexual activity: Reality or illusion? *Journal of Sex Research, 21,* 437–443.

Pickett, C. L., & Gardner, W. L. (2005). The social monitoring system: Enhanced sensitivity to social cues and information as an adaptive response to social exclusion and belonging need. In K. D. Williams, J. P. Forgas, & W. von Hippel (Eds.), *The social outcast: Ostracism, social exclusion, rejection, and bullying.* New York: Psychology Press.

Pickett, C. L., Silver, M. D., & Brewer, M. B. (2002). The impact of assimilation and differentiation needs on perceived group importance and judgments of ingroup size. *Personality and Social Psychology Bulletin, 28,* 546–558.

Piliavin, I. M., Piliavin, J. A., & Rodin, J. (1975). Costs, diffusion, and the stigmatized victim. *Journal of Personality and Social Psychology, 32,* 429–438.

Pilkington, D. (2002). *Rabbit-proof fence.* New York: Miramax. (Original work published 1996)

Pines, A., & Aronson, E. (1983). Antecedents, correlates, and consequences of sexual jealousy. *Journal of Personality, 51,* 108–136.

Pinker, S. (2007, March 19). A history of violence. *New Republic, 236(12),* 18.

Pino, N. W., & Smith, W. L. (2003). College students and academic dishonesty. *College Student Journal, 37,* 490–500.

Pitt, E. L. (2000). Domestic violence in gay and lesbian relationships. *Journal of the Gay and Lesbian Medical Association, 4,* 195–196.

Plant, E. A. (2004). Responses to interracial interactions over time. *Personality and Social Psychology Bulletin, 30,* 1458–1471.

Plant, E. A., & Devine, P. G. (1998). Internal and external motivation to respond without prejudice. *Journal of Personality and Social Psychology, 75,* 811–832.

Plant, E. A., & Devine, P. G. (2001). Responses to other-imposed pro-black pressure: Acceptance or backlash? *Journal of Experimental Social Psychology, 37,* 486–501.

Plant, E. A., & Peruche, B. M. (2005). The consequences of race for police officers' responses to criminal suspects. *Psychological Science, 16,* 180–183.

Platt, C. W. (1988). Effects of causal attributions for success on first-term college performance: A covariance structure model. *Journal of Educational Psychology, 80,* 569–578.

Pliner, P., & Chaiken, S. (1990). Eating, social motives, and self-presentation in women and men. *Journal of Experimental Social Psychology, 26*, 240–254.

Polivy, J. (1976). Perception of calories and regulation of intake in restrained and unrestrained subjects. *Addictive Behaviors, 1*, 237–243.

Polman, J., Orobio de Castro, B., & van Aken, M. (2008). Experimental study of the differential effects of playing versus watching violent video games on children's aggressive behavior. *Aggressive Behavior, 34*(3), 256–264.

Pomazal, R. J., & Clore, G. L. (1973). Helping on the highway: The effects of dependency and sex. *Journal of Applied Social Psychology, 3*, 150–164.

Postmes, T., & Spears, R. (1998). Deindividuation and anti-normative behavior: A meta-analysis. *Psychological Bulletin, 123*, 238–259.

Pottebaum, S. M., Keith, T. Z., & Ehly, S. W. (1986). Is there a causal relation between self-concept and academic achievement? *Journal of Educational Research, 79*, 140–144.

Powers, W. T. (1973). *Behavior: The control of perception.* Chicago: Aldine.

Pratkanis, A. R., & Aronson, E. (1992). *Age of propaganda: The everyday use and abuse of persuasion.* New York: Henry Holt.

Pratkanis, A. R., Greenwald, A. G., Leippe, M. R., & Baumgardner, M. H. (1988). In search of reliable persuasion effects: III. The sleeper effect is dead: Long live the sleeper effect. *Journal of Personality and Social Psychology, 54*, 203–218.

Pratt, T. C., & Cullen, F. T. (2000). The empirical status of Gottfredson and Hirschi's general theory of crime: A meta-analysis. *Criminology, 38*, 931–964.

Prentice, D. A., & Miller, D. T. (1992). When small effects are impressive. *Psychological Bulletin, 112*, 160–164.

Pronin, E., Berger, J., & Molouki, S. (2007). Alone in a crowd of sheep: Asymmetric perceptions of conformity and their roots in an introspection illusion. *Journal of Personality and Social Psychology, 92*, 585–595.

Pryor, J. B., Gibbons, F. X., Wicklund, R. A., Fazio, R. H., & Hood, R. (1977). Self-focused attention and self-report validity. *Journal of Personality, 45*, 513–527.

Pryor, J. B., Reeder, G. D., Yeadon, C., & Hesson-McInnis, M. (2004). A dual-process model of reactions to perceived stigma. *Journal of Personality and Social Psychology, 87*, 436–452.

Pyszczynski, T., Greenberg, J., & Holt, K. (1985). Maintaining consistency between self-serving beliefs and available data: A bias in information processing. *Personality and Social Psychology Bulletin, 11*, 179–190.

Quote without comment. (1975, January). *Consumer Reports*, p. 62.

Raskin, R., & Terry, H. (1988). A principal-components analysis of the Narcissistic Personality Inventory and further evidence of its construct validation. *Journal of Personality and Social Psychology, 54*, 890–902.

Reams, M. A., Geaghan, J. P., & Gendron, R. C. (1996). The link between recycling and litter: A field study. *Environment and Behavior, 28*, 92–110.

Record, J. (2003). *Bounding the global war on terrorism.* Carlisle, PA: U.S. Army War College.

Reich, J. W., & Robertson, J. L. (1979). Reactance and norm appeal in anti-littering messages. *Journal of Applied Social Psychology, 9*, 91–101.

Reifman, A. S., Larrick, R. P., & Fein, S. (1991). Temper and temperature on the diamond: The heat-aggression relationship in major league baseball. *Personality and Social Psychology Bulletin, 17*, 580–585.

Reinholtz, R. K., & Muehlenhard, C. L. (1995). Genital perceptions and sexual activity in a college population. *Journal of Sex Research, 32*, 155–165.

Reinisch, J. (1990). *The Kinsey Institute new report on sex: What you must know to be sexually literate.* Stuttgart: St. Martin's Press

Reis, H. T. (1990). The role of intimacy in interpersonal relations. *Journal of Social and Clinical Psychology, 9*, 15–30.

Reiss, I. L. (1986a). *Journey into sexuality.* New York: Prentice-Hall.

Reiss, I. L. (1986b). A sociological journey into sexuality. *Journal of Marriage and the Family, 48*, 233–242.

Reiss, I. L., Anderson, R. E., & Sponaugle, G. C. (1980). A multivariate model of the determinants of extramarital sexual permissiveness. *Journal of Marriage and the Family, 42*, 395–411.

Reiter, S. M., & Samuel, W. (1980). Littering as a function of prior litter and the presence or absence of prohibitive signs. *Journal of Applied Social Psychology, 10*, 45–55.

Reno, R. R., Cialdini, R. B., & Kallgren, C. A. (1993). The trans-situational influence of social norms. *Journal of Personality and Social Psychology, 64*, 104–112.

Renzetti, C. M. (1992). *Violent betrayal: Partner abuse in lesbian relationships.* Newbury Park, CA: Sage.

Renzi, P. (1990). Effects of acoustic stimulation and pain induced aggression in mice: An experimental model of stress. In P. F. Brain (Ed.), *Fear and defence* (pp. 127–141). Amsterdam: Harwood.

Reston, J., Jr. (1981). *Our father who art in hell.* New York: Times Books.

Reykowski, J. (1982). Motivation and prosocial behavior. In V. Derlega & J. Grzelak (Eds.), *Cooperation and helping behavior: Theories and research* (pp. 352–375). New York: Academic Press.

Rhine, R. J., Hill, S. J., & Wandruff, S. E. (1967). Evaluative responses of preschool children. *Child Development, 38*, 1035–1042.

Rhodes, N., & Wood, W. (1992). Self-esteem and intelligence affect influenceability: The mediating role of message reception. *Psychological Bulletin, 111*, 156–171.

Rhodewalt, F., & Agustdottir, S. (1986). Effects of self-presentation on the phenomenal self. *Journal of Personality and Social Psychology, 50*, 47–55.

Richards, Z., & Hewstone, M. (2001). Subtyping and subgrouping: Processes for the prevention and promotion of stereotype change. *Personality and Social Psychology Review, 5*, 52–73.

Richeson, J. A., & Shelton, J. N. (2003). When prejudice doesn't pay: Effects of interracial contact on executive function. *Psychological Science, 14*, 287–290.

Richeson, J. A., Trawalter, S., & Shelton, J. N. (2005). African Americans' implicit racial attitudes and the depletion of executive function after interracial interactions. *Social Cognition, 23*, 336–352.

Richman, J. A., & Flaherty, J. A. (1986). Sex differences in drinking among medical students: Patterns and psychosocial correlates. *Journal of Studies on Alcohol, 47*, 283–289.

Ridley, M. (1993). *The red queen: Sex and evolution in human nature.* New York: Penguin.

Ridley, M. (2004). *Evolution* (3rd ed.). Oxford, UK: Blackwell Science.

Ringelmann, M. (1913). Recherches sur les moteurs animés: Travail de l'homme. *Annales de l'Institut National Argonomique*, 2e srie, tom 12, 1–40.

Rippere, V. (1977). "What's the thing to do when you're feeling depressed?" A pilot study. *Behaviour Research and Therapy, 15*, 185–191.

Risen, J. L., Gilovich, T., & Dunning, D. (2007). One-shot illusory correlations and stereotype formation. *Personality and Social Psychology Bulletin, 33*(11), 1492–1502.

Ritson, J. (1802). *An essay on abstinence from animal food, as a moral duty.* London: Richard Phillips.

Roberts, W. A. (2002). Are animals stuck in time? *Psychological Bulletin, 128*, 473–489.

Robinson, P. *Schindler's List teaching guide.* (1995). Available at http://www.southerninstitute.info/holocaust_education/schind.html

Roehling, M. V., Roehling, P. V., & Odland, L. M. (2008). Investigating the validity of stereotypes about overweight employees: The relationship between body weight and normal personality traits. *Group and Organization Management, 33*(4), 392–424.

Roese, N. J. (1997). Counterfactual thinking. *Psychological Bulletin, 121*, 133–148.

Roese, N. J., & Olson, J. M. (1997). Counterfactual thinking: The intersection of affect and function. In M. P. Zanna (Ed.), *Advances in experimental social psychology* (Vol. 29, pp. 1–59). New York: Academic Press.

Roese, N. J., & Olson, J. M. (Eds.). (1995). *What might have been: The social psychology of counterfactual thinking.* Mahwah, NJ: Erlbaum.

Rogers, C. R. (1961). *On becoming a person.* Boston: Houghton Mifflin.

Rogers, E. M. (1983). *Diffusion of innovations.* New York: Free Press.

Rogers, T. B., Kuiper, N. A., & Kirker, W. S. (1977). Self-reference and the encoding of personal information. *Journal of Personality and Social Psychology, 35*, 677–688.

Rogow, A. A, Carey, G. L., & Farrell, C. (1957). The significance of aphorisms in American culture. *Sociology and Social Research, 41*, 417–420.

Rohrer, J. H., Baron, S. H., Hoffman, E. L., & Swander, D. V. (1954). The stability of autokinetic judgments. *Journal of Abnormal and Social Psychology, 49*(4, Pt. 1), 595–597.

Roney, J. R. (2003). Effects of visual exposure to the opposite sex: Cognitive aspects of mate attraction in human males. *Personality and Social Psychology Bulletin, 29*(3), 393–404.

Roney, J. R., Mahler, S. V., & Maestripieri, D. (2003). Behavioral and hormonal responses of men to brief interactions with women. *Evolution and Human Behavior, 24*, 365–375.

Rosenbaum, M. E. (1986). The repulsion hypothesis: On the nondevelopment of relationships. *Journal of Personality and Social Psychology, 51*, 1156–1166.

Rosenberg, M. (1979). *Conceiving the self.* New York: Basic Books.

Rosenberg, M., Schooler, C., & Schoenbach, C. (1989). Self-esteem and adolescent problems: Modeling reciprocal effects. *American Sociological Review, 54*, 1004–1018.

Rosenfeld, D. L., Folger, R., & Adelman, H. F. (1980). When rewards reflect competence: A qualification of the overjustification effect. *Journal of Personality and Social Psychology, 39*, 368–376.

Rosenhan, D. L., Salovey, P., & Hargis, K. (1981). The joys of helping: Focus of attention mediates the impact of positive affect on altruism. *Journal of Personality and Social Psychology, 40*, 899–905.

Rosenhan, D. L., & White, G. M. (1967). Observation and rehearsal as determinants of prosocial behavior. *Journal of Personality and Social Psychology, 5*, 424–431.

Rosenman, R. H., & Chesney, M. A. (1982). Stress, Type A behavior and coronary heart disease. In L. Goldberger & S. Breznitz (Eds.), *Handbook of stress: Theoretical and clinical aspects* (pp. 547–565). New York: Free Press.

Rosenthal, R., & Jacobson, L. (1968). *Pygmalion in the classroom: Teacher expectation and pupils' intellectual development.* New York: Rinehart and Winston.

Ross, L., Greene, D. & House, P. (1977). The false consensus effect: An egocentric bias in social perception and attributional processes. *Journal of Experimental Social Psychology, 13*, 279–301.

Ross, L., Lepper, M. R., & Hubbard, M. (1975). Perseverance in self-perception and social perception: Biased attributional processes in the debriefing paradigm. *Journal of Personality and Social Psychology, 32*, 880–892.

Ross, M. (1989). The relation of implicit theories to the construction of personal histories. *Psychological Review, 96*, 341–357.

Ross, M., & Sicoly, F. (1979). Egocentric biases in availability and attribution. *Journal of Personality and Social Psychology, 37*(3), 322–336.

Ross, S. M. (1996). Risk of physical abuse to children of spouse abusing parents. *Child Abuse and Neglect, 20*, 589–598.

Rothbart, M. K. (1989). Temperament and development. In G. A. Kohnstamm, J. A. Bates, & M. K. Rothbart (Eds.), *Temperament in childhood* (pp. 187–247). New York: Wiley.

Rothberg, J. M., & Jones, F. D. (1987). Suicide in the U.S. Army: Epidemiological and periodic aspects. *Suicide and Life-Threatening Behavior, 17*, 119–132.

Rothman, A. J., Bartels, R. D., Wlaschin, J., & Salovey, P. (2006). The strategic use of gain- and loss-framed messages to promote healthy behavior: How theory can inform practice. *Journal of Communication, 56*(Suppl. 1), S202–S220.

Rotton, J. (1979). The air pollution experience and physical aggression. *Journal of Applied Social Psychology, 9,* 397–412.

Rotton, J., & Frey, J. (1985). Air pollution, weather, and violent crimes: Concomitant time-series analysis of archival data. *Journal of Personality and Social Psychology, 49,* 1207–1220.

Rowatt, W. C., Cunningham, M. R., & Druen, P. B. (1999). Lying to get a date: The effect of facial physical attractiveness on the willingness to deceive prospective dating partners. *Journal of Social and Personal Relationships, 16*(2), 209–223.

Rozin, P. (1987). A perspective on disgust. *Psychological Review, 94,* 23–41.

Rozin, P., Haidt, J., & McCauley, C. R. (1993). Disgust. In M. Lewis & J. M. Haviland (Eds.), *Handbook of emotions* (pp. 575–594). New York: Guilford Press.

Rozin, P., Haidt, J., & McCauley, C. R. (2009). Disgust: The body and soul emotion in the 21st century. In B. O. Olatunji & D. McKay (Eds.), *Disgust and its disorders: Theory, assessment, and treatment implications* (pp. 9–29). Washington, DC: American Psychological Association.

Rozin, P., Markwith, M., & McCauley, C. (1994). Sensitivity to indirect contacts with other persons: AIDS aversion as a composite of aversion to strangers, infection, moral taint, and misfortune. *Journal of Abnormal Psychology, 103,* 495–505.

Rozin, P., McCauley, C., & Imada, S. (1997). Body, psyche, and culture: The relationship between disgust and morality. *Psychology and Developing Societies, 9,* 107–131.

Rozin, P., & Nemeroff, C. (1990). The laws of sympathetic magic: A psychological analysis of similarity and contagion. In W. Stigler, R. A. Shweder, & G. Herdt (Eds.), *Cultural psychology: Essays in comparative human development* (pp. 205–232). Cambridge, UK: Cambridge University Press.

Rozin, P., & Royzman, E. B. (2001). Negativity bias, negativity dominance, and contagion. *Personality and Social Psychology Review, 5,* 296–320.

Ruback, R. B., & Juieng, D. (1997). Territorial defense in parking lots: Retaliation against waiting drivers. *Journal of Applied Social Psychology, 27,* 821–834.

Ruble, D. N., Fleming, A. S., Hackel, L. S., & Stangor, C. (1988). Changes in the marital relationship during the transition to first time motherhood: Effects of violated expectations concerning division of household labor. *Journal of Personality and Social Psychology, 55,* 78–87.

Rudski, J. M. (2002). Hindsight and confirmation biases in an exercise in telepathy. *Psychological Reports, 91,* 899–906.

Rusbult, C. E. (1983). A longitudinal test of the investment model: The development (and deterioration) of satisfaction and commitment in heterosexual involvements. *Journal of Personality and Social Psychology, 45,* 101–117.

Rusbult, C. E., & Martz, J. M. (1995). My relationship is better than—and not as bad as—yours is: The perception of superiority in close relationships. *Personality and Social Psychology Bulletin, 21,* 558–571.

Rusbult, C. E., Morrow, G. D., & Johnson, D. J. (1987). Self-esteem and problem solving behavior in close relationships. *British Journal of Social Psychology, 26,* 293–303.

Ruscio, J. (2002). *Clear thinking with psychology: Separating sense from nonsense.* Pacific Grove, CA: Wadsworth.

Rusesabagina, Paul. (2006, September 29). *BBC News.* Retrieved October 22, 2008, from http://news.bbc .co.uk/2/hi/programmes/hardtalk/5393104.stm

Rushton, J. P., Brainerd, C. J., & Pressley, M. (1983). Behavioral development and construct validity: The principle of aggregation. *Psychological Bulletin, 94,* 18–38.

Rushton, J. P., Chrisjohn, R. D., & Fekken, G. C. (1981). The altruistic personality and the Self-Report Altruism Scale. *Personality and Individual Differences, 2,* 293–302.

Rushton, J. P., Fulker, D. W., Neale, M. C., Nias, D. K. B., & Eysenck, H. J. (1986). Altruism and aggression: The heritability of individual differences. *Journal of Personality and Social Psychology, 50,* 1192–1198.

Russell, D., Peplau, L. A., & Cutrona, C. E. (1980). The revised UCLA Loneliness Scale: Concurrent and discriminant validity evidence. *Journal of Personality and Social Psychology, 39,* 472–480.

Russell, J. A. (1980). A circumplex model of affect. *Journal of Personality and Social Psychology, 39,* 1161–1178.

Russell, J. A. (1994). Is there a universal recognition of emotion from facial expressions? A review of the cross-cultural studies. *Psychological Bulletin, 115,* 102–141.

Russell, J. A. (1995). Facial expressions of emotion: What lies beyond minimal universality? *Psychological Bulletin, 118,* 379–391.

Russo J. E., Staelin, R., Nolan, C. A, Russell, G. J., & Metcalf, B. L. (1986) Nutrition information in the supermarket. *Journal of Consumer Research, 13,* 48–70.

Rwanda: How the genocide happened. (2004, December 18). *BBC News.* Retrieved October 22, 2008, from http://news.bbc.co.uk/2/hi/africa/1288230.stm

Ryan, R. M. (1982). Control and information in the intrapersonal sphere: An extension of cognitive evaluation theory. *Journal of Personality and Social Psychology, 43,* 450–461.

Ryan, R. M., & Deci, E. L. (2000). Self-determination theory and the facilitation of intrinsic motivation, social development, and well-being. *American Psychologist, 55,* 68–78.

Ryan, R. M., & Grolnick, W. S. (1986). Origin and pawns in the classroom: Self-report and projective assessments of individual differences in children's perceptions. *Journal of Personality and Social Psychology, 50,* 550–558.

Rydell, R. J., & McConnell, A. R. (2006). Understanding implicit and explicit attitude change: A systems of reasoning analysis. *Journal of Personality and Social Psychology, 91*(6), 995–1008.

Ryff, C. D. (1995). Psychological well-being in adult life. *Current Directions in Psychological Science, 4,* 99–104.

Rynd, N. (1988) Incidence of psychometric symptoms in rape victims. *Journal of Sex Research, 24,* 155–161.

Sackett, P. R., Hardison, C. M., & Cullen, M. J. (2004a). On interpreting stereotype threat as accounting for African American–White differences on cognitive tests. *American Psychologist, 59,* 7–13.

Sackett, P. R., Hardison, C. M., & Cullen, M. J. (2004b). On the value of correcting mischaracterizations of stereotype threat research. *American Psychologist, 59,* 48–49.

Salmivalli, C., Kaukiainen, A., Kaistaniemi, L., & Lagerspetz, K. M. J. (1999). Self-evaluated self-esteem, peer-evaluated self-esteem, and defensive egotism as predictors of adolescents' participation in bullying situations. *Personality and Social Psychology Bulletin, 25,* 1268–1278.

Salovey, P., & Mayer, J. D. (1990). Emotional intelligence. *Imagination, Cognition, and Personality, 9,* 185–211.

Salovey, P., & Rodin, J. (1991). Provoking jealousy and envy: Domain relevance and self-esteem threat. *Journal of Social and Clinical Psychology, 10,* 395–413.

Sandelands, L. E., Brockner, J., & Glynn, M. A. (1988). If at first you don't succeed, try, try again: Effects of persistence-performance contingencies, ego involvement, and self-esteem on task persistence. *Journal of Applied Psychology, 73,* 208–216.

Sanders, S. A., & Reinisch, J. M. (1999). Would you say you "had sex" if . . . ? *Journal of the American Medical Association, 281,* 275–277.

Sanna, L. J., & Schwarz, N. (2003). Using the hindsight bias: The role of accessibility experiences and (mis)attributions. *Journal of Experimental Social Psychology, 39,* 287–295.

Santos, M. D., Leve, C., & Pratkanis, A. R. (1994). Hey buddy, can you spare seventeen cents? Mindful persuasion and the pique technique. *Journal of Applied Social Psychology, 24,* 755–764.

Sapolsky, R. M. (1998). *The trouble with testosterone: And other essays on the biology of the human predicament.* New York: Scribner.

Satow, K. L. (1975). Social approval and helping. *Journal of Experimental Social Psychology, 11,* 501–509.

Savin-Williams, R. C. (1990). *Gay and lesbian youth: Expressions of identity.* New York: Hemisphere.

Savitsky, K., Van Boven, L, Epley, N, & Wight, W. (2005). The unpacking effect in responsibility allocations for group tasks. *Journal of Experimental Social Psychology, 41,* 447–457.

Sawyer, D. (2004, October 21). American sex lives. *Prime-Time Live,* ABC television.

Scarpa, A., & Raine, A. (2000). Violence associated with anger and impulsivity. In J. C. Borod (Ed.), *The neuropsychology of emotion.* New York: Oxford University Press.

Schachter, S. (1951). Deviation, rejection, and communication. *Journal of Abnormal and Social Psychology, 46*(2), 190–207.

Schachter, S. (1964). The interaction of cognitive and physiological determinants of emotional state. In L. Berkowitz (Ed.), *Advances in experimental social psychology* (pp. 49–79). New York: Academic Press.

Schachter, S., & Singer, J. E., (1962). Cognitive, social, and physiological determinants of emotional state. *Psychological Review, 69,* 379–399.

Schaefer, R. T. (2003). *Sociology* (8th ed.). New York: McGraw-Hill.

Schank, R. C., & Abelson, R. P. (1977). *Scripts, plans, goals, and understanding: An inquiry into human knowledge structures.* Hillsdale, NJ: Erlbaum.

Scheibehenne, B., Greifeneder, R., & Todd, P. M. (2008, November). *Can there ever be too many options? Re-assessing the effect of choice overload.* Paper presented at the annual meeting of the Society for Judgment and Decision Making, Chicago.

Scheier, M. F., Fenigstein, A., & Buss, A. H. (1974). Self-awareness and physical aggression. *Journal of Experimental Social Psychology, 10,* 264–273.

Scheirer, M. A., & Kraut, R. E. (1979). Increased educational achievement via self-concept change. *Review of Educational Research, 49,* 131–150.

Scherer, K. R., & Wallbott, H. G. (1994). Evidence for universality and cultural variation of differential emotion response patterning. *Journal of Personality and Social Psychology, 66,* 310–328.

Schlenker, B. R. (1975). Self-presentation: Managing the impression of consistency when reality interferes with self-enhancement. *Journal of Personality and Social Psychology, 32,* 1030–1037.

Schlenker, B. R. (1980). *Impression management: The self-concept, social identity, and interpersonal relations.* Monterey, CA: Brooks/Cole.

Schlenker, B. R., Dlugolecki, D. W., & Doherty, K. J. (1994). The impact of self-presentations on self-appraisals and behaviors: The power of public commitment. *Personality and Social Psychology Bulletin, 20,* 20–33.

Schmidt, R. E., & Gendolla, G. H. E. (2008). Dreaming of white bears: The return of the suppressed at sleep onset. *Consciousness and Cognition, 17*(3), 714–724.

Schmitt, D. P. (2003). Universal sex differences in the desire for sexual variety: Tests from 52 nations, 6 continents, and 13 islands. *Journal of Personality and Social Psychology, 85,* 85–104.

Schopler, J., & Insko, C. A. (1992). The discontinuity effect in interpersonal and intergroup relations: Generality and mediation. *European Review of Social Psychology, 3,* 121–151.

Schopler, J., Insko, C. A., Drigotas, S. M., & Graetz, K. A. (1993). Individual–group discontinuity: Further evidence for mediation by fear and greed. *Personality and Social Psychology Bulletin, 19,* 419–431.

Schopler, J., Insko, C. A., Drigotas, S. M., & Wieselquist, J. (1995). The role of identifiability in the reduction of interindividual–intergroup discontinuity. *Journal of Experimental Social Psychology, 31,* 553–574.

Schopler, J., Insko, C. A., Drigotas, S. M., Wieselquist, J., Pemberton, M. B., & Cox, C. (1995). The role of identifiability in the reduction of interindividual–intergroup discontinuity. *Journal of Experimental Social Psychology, 31,* 553–574.

Schütz, A. (1999). It was your fault! Self-serving biases in autobiographical accounts of esteem threatening conflicts in married couples. *Journal of Social and Personal Relationships, 16,* 193–209.

Schütz, A. (2000). Selbstwertgefühl: Zwischen Selbstakzeptanz und Arroganz. Stuttgart: Kohlhammer.

Schütz, A. (2001). Self-esteem and interpersonal strategies. In J. P. Forgas, K. D. Williams, & L. Wheeler (Eds.), *The social mind: Cognitive and motivational aspects of* interpersonal behavior (pp. 157–176). New York: Cambridge University Press.

Schwartz, B. (2004, April) The tyranny of choice. *Scientific American*, 72–75.

Schwartz, B., Ward, A., Monterosso, J., Lyubomirsky, S., White, K., & Lehman, D. R. (2002). Maximizing versus satisficing: Happiness is a matter of choice. *Journal of Personality and Social Psychology, 83*(5), 1178–1197.

Schwarz, N., & Clore, G. L. (1983). Mood, misattribution, and judgments of well-being: Informative and directive functions of affective states. *Journal of Personality and Social Psychology, 45*, 513–523.

Schwarzwald, J., Raz, M., & Zvibel, M. (1979). The applicability of the door-in-the-face technique when established behavioral customs exist. *Journal of Applied Social Psychology, 9*, 576–586.

Scott, J. P. (1958). *Aggression.* Chicago: University of Chicago Press.

Seabright, P. (2004). *The company of strangers: A natural history of economic life.* Princeton, NJ: Princeton University Press.

Seal, D. W. (1997). Interpartner concordance of self-reported sexual behavior among college dating couples. *Journal of Sex Research, 34*, 39–55.

Sears, D. O. (1986). College sophomores in the laboratory: Influences of a narrow data base on social psychology's view of human nature. *Journal of Personality and Social Psychology, 51*, 515–530.

Sedikides, C. (1993). Assessment, enhancement, and verification determinants of the self-evaluation process. *Journal of Personality and Social Psychology, 65*, 317–338.

Sedikides, C., Gaertner, L., & Toguchi, Y. (2003). Pancultural self-enhancement. *Journal of Personality and Social Psychology, 84*, 60–70.

Segal, N. L. (1984). Cooperation, competition and altruism within twin sets: A reappraisal. *Ethology and Sociobiology, 5*, 163–177.

Sennett, R. (1974). *The fall of public man.* New York: Random House.

Sentyrz, S. M., & Bushman, B. J. (1998). Mirror, mirror on the wall, who's the thinnest one of all? Effects of self-awareness on consumption of fatty, reduced-fat, and fat-free products. *Journal of Applied Psychology, 83*, 944–949.

Sesame Street breaks Iraqi POWs. (2003, May 20). Retrieved June 8, 2004, from http://news.bbc.co.uk/1/hi/world/middle_east/3042907.stm

Seta, C. E., & Seta, J. J. (1995). When audience presence is enjoyable: The influences of audience awareness of prior success on performance and task interest. *Basic and Applied Social Psychology, 16*(1–2), 95–108.

Shackelford, T. K. (2001). Self-esteem in marriage: An evolutionary psychological analysis. *Personality and Individual Differences, 30*, 371–390.

Shah, J. Y. (2003). Automatic for the people: How representations of significant others implicitly affect goal pursuit. *Journal of Personality and Social Psychology, 84*, 661–681.

Shah, J. Y., Friedman, R., & Kruglanski, A. W. (2002). Forgetting all else: On the antecedents and consequences of goal shielding. *Journal of Personality and Social Psychology, 83*, 1261–1280.

Shakur, S. (1993). *Monster: The autobiography of an L.A. gang member.* New York: Atlantic Monthly Press.

Shandall, A. A. (1967). Circumcision and infibulation of females. *Sudan Medical Journal, 5*, 178–212.

Shandall, A. A. (1979). *Circumcision and infibulation of females.* Geneva: Terre des Hommes.

Shaw, B. F., & Beck, A. T. (1977). The treatment of depression with cognitive therapy. In A. Ellis & R. Grieger (Eds.), *Handbook of rational emotive therapy* (pp. 309–326). New York: Springer.

Sheard, M. H., Astrachan, D. I., & Davis, M. (1975, September). Effect of noise on shock-elicited aggression in rats. *Nature, 257*(5521), 43–44.

Sheldon, K. M. (1994). Emotionality differences between artists and scientists. *Journal of Research in Personality, 28*, 481–491.

Sheldon, K. M., & Kasser, T. (1998). Pursuing personal goals: Skills enable progress but not all progress is beneficial. *Personality and Social Psychology Bulletin, 24*, 1319–1331.

Sheldon, K. M., & Lyubomirsky, S. (2004). Achieving sustainable new happiness: Prospects, practices, and prescriptions. In P. A. Linley & S. Joseph (Eds.), *Positive psychology in practice* (pp. 127–145). Hoboken, NJ: Wiley.

Shelton, J. N. (2003). Interpersonal concerns in social encounters between majority and minority group members. *Group Processes and Intergroup Relations, 6*, 171–185.

Sheppard, J. A., & Strathman, A. J. (1989). Attractiveness and height: The role of stature in dating preference, frequency of dating, and perceptions of attractiveness. *Personality and Social Psychology Bulletin, 15*(4), 617–627.

Sherif, M. (1935). A study of some social factors in perception. *Archives of Psychology* (Columbia University), No. 187, 60.

Sherif, M. (1966). *In common predicament: Social psychology of intergroup conflict and cooperation.* Boston: Houghton-Mifflin.

Sherif, M., & Sherif, C. W. (1953). *Groups in harmony and tension: An integration of studies of intergroup relations.* New York: Harper & Brothers.

Sherman, S. T., Zehner, K. S., Johnson, J., & Hirt, E. R. (1983). Social explanation: The role of timing, set, and recall on subjective likelihood estimates. *Journal of Personality and Social Psychology, 44*, 1127–1143.

Shin, J., & Ariely, D. (2004). Keeping doors open: The effect of unavailability on incentives to keep options open. *Management Science, 50*, 575–586.

Shneidman, E. S. (1981). Suicide thoughts and reflections, 1960–1980. *Suicide and Life-Threatening Behavior, 11*, 197–360.

Shoda, Y., Mischel, W., & Peake, P. K. (1990). Predicting adolescent cognitive and self-regulatory competencies from preschool delay of gratification: Identifying diagnostic conditions. *Developmental Psychology, 26*, 978–986.

Shoes thrown at Bush on Iraq trip. (2008, December 15). *BBC News.* Retrieved December 26, 2008, from http://news.bbc.co.uk/2/hi/middle_east/7782422.stm

Shook, N. J., & Fazio, R. H. (2008). Interracial roommate relationships: An experimental field test of the contact hypothesis. *Psychological Science, 19*(7), 717–723.

Shorter, E. (1975). *The making of the modern family.* New York: Basic Books.

Shotland, R. L., & Straw, M. K. (1976). Bystander response to an assault: When a man attacks a woman. *Journal of Personality and Social Psychology, 34*, 990–999.

Shrauger, J. S. (1975). Responses to evaluation as a function of initial self-perceptions. *Psychological Bulletin, 82*, 581–596.

Shrauger, J. S., & Shoeneman, T. J. (1979). Symbolic interactionist view of self-concept: Through the looking glass darkly. *Psychological Bulletin, 86*, 549–573.

Shrauger, J. S., & Sorman, P. B. (1977). Self-evaluations, initial success and failure, and improvement as determinants of persistence. *Journal of Consulting and Clinical Psychology, 45*, 784–795.

Sidanius, J., & Pratto, F. (1999). *Social dominance: An intergroup theory of social hierarchy and oppression.* New York: Cambridge University Press.

Siegman, A. W., & Reynolds, M. A. (1983). Self-monitoring and speech in feigned and unfeigned lying. *Journal of Personality and Social Psychology, 45*(6), 1325–1333.

Silfver, M., Helkama, K., Lönnqvist, J.-E., & Verkasalo, M. (2008). The relation between value priorities and proneness to guilt, shame, and empathy. *Motivation and Emotion, 32*(2), 69–80.

Silk, J. B., Brosnan, S. F., Vonk, J., Henrich, J., Povinelli, D. J., Richardson, A. S., et al. (2005, October 27). Chimpanzees are indifferent to the welfare of unrelated group members. *Nature, 437*, 1357–1359.

Silvia, P. J., & Duval, T. S. (2001). Objective self-awareness theory: Recent progress and enduring problems. *Personality and Social Psychology Review, 5*, 230–241.

Sime, J. D. (1983). Affiliative behavior during escape to building exits. *Journal of Environmental Psychology, 3*, 21–41.

Simpson, J. A. (1990). Influence of attachment styles on romantic relationships. *Journal of Personality and Social Psychology, 59*, 971–980.

Simpson, J. A., Gangestad, S., & Lerma, M. (1990). Perception of physical attractiveness: Mechanisms involved in the maintenance of romantic relationships. *Journal of Personality and Social Psychology, 59*, 1192–1201.

Sinclair, L., & Kunda, Z. (1999). Reactions to a Black professional: Motivated inhibition and activation of conflicting stereotypes. *Journal of Personality and Social Psychology, 77*, 885–904.

Sinclair, L., & Kunda, Z. (2000). Motivated stereotyping of women: She's fine if she praised me but incompetent if she criticized me. *Personality and Social Psychology Bulletin, 26*, 1329–1342.

Sinclair, R. C., & Brown, N. R. (1999, April–May). *Discrepant partner reports: Do women encode sexual experiences more deeply than men do?* Paper presented at the annual convention of the Midwestern Psychological Association, Chicago.

Singer, T., Seymour, B., O'Doherty, J., Kaube, H., Dolan, R. J., & Frith, C. D. (2004). Empathy for pain involves the affective but not sensory components of pain. *Science, 303*, 1157–1162.

Singh, D. (1993). Adaptive significance of female physical attractiveness: Role of waist-to-hip ratio. *Journal of Personality and Social Psychology, 65*(2), 293–307.

Singh, D. (1995). Female judgment of male attractiveness and desirability for relationships: Role of waist-to-hip ratio and financial status. *Journal of Personality and Social Psychology, 69*(6), 1089–1101.

Skaalvik, E. M., & Hagtvet, K. A. (1990). Academic achievement and self-concept: An analysis of causal predominance in a developmental perspective. *Journal of Personality and Social Psychology, 58*, 292–307.

Slovic, P., & Lichtenstein, S. (1971). Comparison of Bayesian and regression approaches to the study of information processing in judgment. *Organizational Behavior and Human Performance, 6*, 649–744.

Sluka, J. (1992). The anthropology of conflict. In C. Nordstrom & J. Martin (Eds.), *The paths to domination, resistance, and terror* (pp. 18–36). Berkeley: University of California Press.

Smith, D. (2004, June 20). Sign writer. *Observer.* Retrieved October 25, 2004, from http://observer.guardian.co.uk/comment/story/0,6903,1243121,00.html

Smith, G. E., Gerrard, M., & Gibbons, F. X. (1997). Self-esteem and the relation between risk behavior and perceptions of vulnerability to unplanned pregnancy in college women. *Health Psychology, 16*, 137–146.

Smith, G. F., & Dorfman, D. D. (1975). The effect of stimulus uncertainty on the relationship between frequency of exposure and liking. *Journal of Personality and Social Psychology, 31*, 150–155.

Smith, G. H., & Engel, R. (1968). Influence of a female model on perceived characteristics of an automobile. *Proceedings of the Annual Convention of the American Psychological Association, 3*, 681–682.

Smith, M. L. (1980). Meta-analysis of research on teacher expectations. *Evaluation in Education, 4*(1), 53–55.

Smith, R. (2003, December 3). The impact of hate media in Rwanda. *BBC News.* Retrieved October 22, 2008, from http://news.bbc.co.uk/2/hi/africa/3257748.stm

Smith, S. M., & Shaffer, D. R. (1991). Celerity and cajolery: Rapid speech may promote or inhibit persuasion through its impact on message elaboration. *Personality and Social Psychology Bulletin, 17*, 663–669.

Smith, T. (1994). Attitudes toward sexual permissiveness: Trends, correlates, and behavioral connections. In A. S. Rossi (Ed.), *Sexuality across the life course* (pp. 63–97). Chicago: University of Chicago Press.

Smith, T. B., McCullough, M. E., & Poll, J. (2003). Religiousness and depression: Evidence for a main effect and the moderating influence of stressful life events. *Psychological Bulletin, 129*, 614–636.

Smith, T. W., Snyder C. R., Perkins S. C. (1983). The self-serving function of hypochondriacal complaints: Physical symptoms as self-handicapping strategies. *Journal of Personality and Social Psychology, 44*, 787–97.

Smuts, B. (1996). Male aggression against women: An evolutionary perspective. In D. Buss & N. Malamuth (Eds.), *Sex, power, conflict* (pp. 231–268). New York: Oxford University Press.

Snyder, C. R., & Higgins, R. L. (1990). *Self-handicapping: The paradox that isn't.* Norwell, MA: Kluwer.

Snyder, C. R., Higgins, R. L., & Stucky, R. J. (1983). *Excuses: Masquerades in search of grace.* Somerset, NJ: Wiley.

Snyder, C. R., & Lopez, S. (Eds.). (2002). *Handbook of positive psychology.* New York: Oxford University Press.

Snyder, M. (1974). Self monitoring of expressive behavior. *Journal of Personality and Social Psychology, 30,* 526–537.

Snyder, M., & DeBono, K. G. (1985). Appeals to image and claims about quality: Understanding the psychology of advertising. *Journal of Personality and Social Psychology, 49,* 586–597.

Snyder, M., & Gangestad, S. (1986). On the nature of self-monitoring: Matters of assessment, matters of validity. *Journal of Personality and Social Psychology, 51,* 125–139.

Soetens, B., Braet, C., Dejonckheere, P., & Roets, A. (2006). When suppression backfires: The ironic effects of suppressing eating-related thoughts. *Journal of Health Psychology, 11*(5), 655–668.

Soetens, B., Braet, C., & Moens, E. (2008). Thought suppression in obese and non-obese restrained eaters: Piece of cake or forbidden fruit? *European Eating Disorders Review, 16*(1), 67–76.

Sommer, K. L., & Rubin, Y. (2005). Maintaining self-esteem in the face of rejection. In K. D. Williams, J. P. Forgas, & W. von Hippel (Eds.), *The social outcast: Ostracism, social exclusion, rejection, and bullying.* New York: Psychology Press.

Sommer, K. L., Williams, K. D., Ciarocco, N. J., & Baumeister, R. F. (2001). When silence speaks louder than words: Explorations into the intrapsychic and interpersonal consequences of social ostracism. *Basic and Applied Social Psychology, 23,* 225–243.

Sommers, C. H. (1994). *Who stole feminism: How women have betrayed women.* New York: Touchstone.

Soubrie, P. (1986). Reconciling the role of central serotonin neurons in humans and animal behavior. *Behavioral and Brain Sciences, 9,* 319–364.

Spangler, G., & Grossman, K. E. (1993). Biobehavioral organization in securely and insecurely attached infants. *Child Development, 64,* 1439–1450.

Spanier, G. B., & Lewis, R. A. (1980). Marital quality: A review of the seventies. *Journal of Marriage and the Family, 42,* 825–839.

Spanier, G. B., & Margolis, R. L. (1983). Marital separation and extramarital sexual behavior. *Journal of Sex Research, 19,* 23–48.

Spencer, S. J., Steele, C. M., & Quinn, D. M. (1999). Stereotype threat and women's math performance. *Journal of Experimental Social Psychology, 35,* 4–28.

Sprecher, S. (1989). Premarital sexual standards for different categories of individuals. *Journal of Sex Research, 19,* 23–48.

Sprecher, S. (1998). Social exchange theories and sexuality. *Journal of Sex Research, 35,* 32–43.

Sprecher, S. (1999). "I love you more today than yesterday": Romantic partners' perceptions of changes in love and related affect over time. *Journal of Personality and Social Psychology, 76,* 46–53.

Sprecher, S., & Regan, P. C. (1996). College virgins: How men and women perceive their sexual status. *Journal of Sex Research, 33,* 3–15.

Sprecher, S., & Regan, P. C. (2002). Liking some things (in some people) more than others: Partner preferences in romantic relationships and friendships. *Journal of Social and Personal Relationships, 19,* 463–481.

Sroufe, L. A., & Waters, E. (1977). Heart rate as a convergent measure in clinical and developmental research. *Merrill-Palmer Quarterly, 23,* 3–27.

Staats, A. W., & Staats, C. K. (1958). Attitudes established by classical conditioning. *Journal of Abnormal and Social Psychology, 57,* 37–40.

Staffieri, J. (1967). A study of social stereotype of body image in children. *Journal of Personality and Social Psychology, 7,* 101–104.

Stanford, W. E. (1999, March–April). Dealing with student credit card debt. *About Campus,* pp. 12–17.

Staples, R. (1973). *Black women in America: Sex, marriage, and family.* Chicago: Nelson-Hall.

Stasser, G., & Titus, W. (1985). Pooling of unshared information in group decision making: Biased information sampling during discussion. *Journal of Personality and Social Psychology, 48,* 1467–1478.

Stasser, G., & Titus, W. (1987). Effects of information load and percentage of shared information on the dissemination of unshared information during group discussion. *Journal of Personality and Social Psychology, 53,* 81–93.

Steele, C. M. (1997). A threat in the air: How stereotypes shape intellectual identity and performance. *American Psychologist, 52,* 613–629.

Steele, C. M. (1999, August). Thin ice: "Stereotype threat" and Black college students. *Atlantic Monthly,* 44–54.

Steele, C. M., & Aronson, J. A. (1995). Stereotype threat and the intellectual test performance of African Americans. *Journal of Personality and Social Psychology, 69,* 797–811.

Steele, C. M., & Aronson, J. A. (2004). Stereotype threat does not live by Steele and Aronson (1995) alone. *American Psychologist, 59,* 47–55.

Steele, C. M., & Josephs, R. A. (1990). Alcohol myopia: Its prized and dangerous effects. *American Psychologist, 45,* 921–933.

Steele, C. M., & Southwick, L. (1985). Alcohol and social behavior: I. The psychology of drunken excess. *Journal of Personality and Social Psychology, 48,* 18–34.

Steffensmeier, D., & Allan, E. (1996). Gender and crime: Toward a gendered theory of female offending. *Annual Review of Sociology, 22,* 459–487.

Steinfatt, T. M. (1973). The Prisoner's Dilemma and a creative alternative game: The effects of communications under conditions of real reward. *Simulation and Games, 4,* 389–409.

Steinfeld, J. (1972). *Statement in hearings before Subcommittee on Communications of Committee on Commerce* (United States Senate, Serial #92-52, pp. 25–27). Washington, DC: U.S. Government Printing Office.

Stern, J. (2004, June 6). Beneath bombast and bombs, a caldron of humiliation: Many seek to restore a dignity damaged by the new world order. *Los Angeles Times.*

Stern, S. E., & Faber, J. E. (1997). The lost e-mail method: Milgram's lost-letter technique in the age of the Internet. *Behavior Research Methods, Instruments, and Computers, 29,* 260–263.

Sternberg, R. J. (1986). A triangular theory of love. *Psychological Review, 93,* 119–135.

Stillman, T. F., Baumeister, R. F., & DeWall, C. N. (2007). What's so funny about not having money? The effects of power on laughter. *Personality and Social Psychology Bulletin, 33,* 1547–1558.

Stone, J., & McWhinnie, C. (2008). Evidence that blatant versus subtle stereotype threat cues impact performance through dual processes. *Journal of Experimental Social Psychology, 44*(2), 445–452.

Stone, L. (1977). *The family, sex and marriage in England: 1500–1800.* London: Perennial.

Stoner, J. A. F. (1961). *A comparison of individual and group decisions involving risk.* Unpublished master's thesis, Massachusetts Institute of Technology.

Storey, A. E., Walsh, C. L., Quinton, R. L., & Wynne-Edward, K. E. (2000). Hormonal correlates of paternal responsiveness in new and expectant fathers. *Evolution and Human Behavior, 21,* 79–95.

Strack, F., & Deutsch, R. (2004). Reflective and impulsive determinants of social behavior. *Personality and Social Psychology Review, 8*(3), 220–247.

Strack, F., Martin, L., & Stepper, S. (1988). Inhibiting and facilitating conditions of the human smile: A nonobtrusive test of the facial feedback hypothesis. *Journal of Personality and Social Psychology, 54,* 768–777.

Straus, M. A. (1997). Physical assaults by women partners: A major social problem. In M. R. Walsh (Ed.), *Women, men and gender: Ongoing debates* (pp. 210–221). New Haven, CT: Yale University Press.

Stripling, J. (2008, January 16). Kevorkian pushes for euthanasia. Retrieved October 1, 2008, from http://www.gainesville.com/article/20080116/NEWS/801160333

Strober, M., & Humphrey, L. L. (1987). Familial contributions to the etiology and course of anorexia nervosa and bulimia. *Journal of Consulting and Clinical Psychology, 55,* 654–659.

Stroebe, W., Diehl, M., & Abakoumkin, G. (1992). The illusion of group effectivity. *Personality and Social Psychology Bulletin, 18,* 643–650.

Stroop, J. R. (1935). Studies of interference in serial verbal reactions. *Journal of Experimental Psychology, 28,* 643–662.

Strube, M. J. (1988). The decision to leave an abusive relationship: Empirical evidence and theoretical issues. *Psychological Bulletin, 104,* 236–250.

Suls, J., & Wan, C. K. (1987). In search of the false uniqueness phenomenon: Fear and estimates of social consensus. *Journal of Personality and Social Psychology, 52,* 211–217.

Suls, J., Wan, C. K., & Sanders, G. S. (1988). False consensus and false uniqueness in estimating the prevalence of health-protective behaviors. *Journal of Applied Social Psychology, 18,* 66–79.

Sundali, J., & Croson, R. (2006). Biases in casino betting: The hot hand and the gambler's fallacy. *Judgment and Decision Making, 1*(1), 1–12.

Surowiecki, J. (2004). The wisdom of crowds: Why the many are smarter than the few and how collective wisdom shapes business, economics, societies, and nations. New York: Doubleday.

Svenson, O. (1981). Are we less risky and more skillful than our fellow drivers? *Acta Psychologica, 47,* 143–151.

Swann, W. B., Jr. (1985). The self as architect of social reality. In B. Schlenker (Ed.), *The self and social life* (pp. 100–125). New York: McGraw-Hill.

Swann, W. B., Jr. (1987). Identity negotiation: Where two roads meet. *Journal of Personality and Social Psychology, 53,* 1038–1051.

Swann, W. B., Jr. (1998). The self and interpersonal relationships. Paper presented at the meeting of the Society of Experimental Social Psychologists, Lexington, KY.

Swann, W. B., Jr., De La Ronde, C., & Hixon, J. G. (1994). Authenticity and positivity strivings in marriage and courtship. *Journal of Personality and Social Psychology, 66,* 857–869.

Swann, W. B., Jr., Griffin, J. J., Predmore, S., & Gaines, B. (1987). The cognitive-affective crossfire: When self-consistency confronts self-enhancement. *Journal of Personality and Social Psychology, 52,* 881–889.

Swann, W. B., Jr., Hixon, J. G., Stein-Seroussi, A., & Gilbert, D. T. (1990). The fleeting gleam of praise: Cognitive processes underlying behavioral reactions to self-relevant feedback. *Journal of Personality and Social Psychology, 59,* 17–26.

Swann, W. B., Jr., & Predmore, S. C. (1985). Intimates as agents of social support: Sources of consolation or despair? *Journal of Personality and Social Psychology, 49,* 1609–1617.

Swann, W. B., Jr., Stein-Seroussi, A., & Giesler, R. B. (1992). Why people self-verify. *Journal of Personality and Social Psychology, 62,* 392–401.

Swann, W. B., Jr., Wenzlaff, R. M., Krull, D. S., & Pelham, B. W. (1992). The allure of negative feedback: Self-verification strivings among depressed persons. *Journal of Abnormal Psychology, 101,* 293–306.

Swim, J. K. (1994). Perceived versus meta-analytic effect sizes: An assessment of the accuracy of gender stereotypes. *Journal of Personality and Social Psychology, 66,* 21–36.

Symanski, R. (1980). Prostitution in Nevada. In E. Muga (Ed.), *Studies in prostitution* (pp. 246–279). Nairobi: Kenya Literature Bureau.

Symons, C. S., & Johnson, B. T. (1997). The self-reference effect in memory: A meta-analysis. *Psychological Bulletin, 121,* 371–394.

Symons, D. (1979). *The evolution of human sexuality.* New York: Oxford University Press.

Symons, D. (1995). Beauty is in the adaptations of the beholder: The evolutionary psychology of human female sexual attractiveness. In P. R. Abramson & S. D. Pinkerton (Eds.), *Sexual nature/sexual culture* (pp. 80–118). Chicago: University of Chicago Press.

Szymanski, S. (2000). A market test for discrimination in the English professional soccer leagues. *Journal of Political Economy, 108*(3), 590–603.

Tajfel, H., & Billig, M. (1974). Familiarity and categorization in intergroup behavior. *Journal of Experimental Social Psychology, 10*(2), 159–170.

Tajfel, H., Billig, M. G., Bundy, R. P., & Flament, C. (1971). Social categorization and intergroup behaviour. *European Journal of Social Psychology, 1*(2), 149–178.

Tamir, M., Mitchell, C., & Gross, J. J. (2008). Hedonic and instrumental motives in anger regulation. *Psychological Science, 19*(4), 324–328.

Tangney, J. P., Baumeister, R. F., & Boone, A. L. (2004). High self-control predicts good adjustment, less pathology, better grades, and interpersonal success. *Journal of Personality, 72*, 271–322.

Tangney, J. P., & Dearing, R. L. (2002). *Shame and guilt.* New York: Guilford Press.

Tangney, J. P., & Fischer, K. W. (1995). *Self-conscious emotions: The psychology of shame, guilt, embarrassment, and pride.* New York: Guilford Press.

Tannahill, R. (1980). *Sex in history.* London: Scarborough House.

Tanner, A. (2003, November 21). Spam rage: Man arrested for threats to company. *Reuters News Service.* Retrieved January 26, 2009, from http://www.globalaffairs.org/forum/archive/index.php/t-17696

Tansey, G., & D'Silva, J. (1999). *The meat business: Devouring a hungry planet.* New York: St. Martin's Press.

Tata, J., Anthony, T., Lin, H., Newman, B., Tang, S., Millson, M., & Suvakumar, K. (1996). Proportionate group size and rejection of the deviate: A meta-analytic integration. *Journal of Social Behavior and Personality, 11*, 739–752.

Taylor, N. (2003). Under-reporting of crime against small businesses: Attitudes toward police and reporting practices. *Policing and Society, 13*, 79–89.

Taylor, S. E. (1983). Adjustment to threatening events: A theory of cognitive adaptation. *American Psychologist, 38*, 1161–1173.

Taylor, S. E., & Brown, J. D. (1988). Illusion and well-being: A social psychological perspective on mental health. *Psychological Bulletin, 103*, 193–210.

Taylor, S. E., & Gollwitzer, P. M. (1995). Effects of mindset on positive illusions. *Journal of Personality and Social Psychology, 69*, 213–226.

Taylor, S. E., Klein, L. C., Lewis, B. P., Gruenewald, T. L., Gurung, R. A. R, & Updegraff, J. A. (2000). Biobehavioral responses to stress in females: Tend-and-befriend, not fight-or-flight. *Psychological Review, 107*, 441–429.

Taylor, S. E., & Pham, L. B. (1996). Mental simulation, motivation, and action. In P. M. Gollwitzer & J. A. Bargh (Eds.), *The psychology of action: Linking cognition and motivation to behavior* (pp. 219–235). New York: Guilford Press.

Tec, N. (1986). *When light pierced the darkness: Christian rescue of Jews in Nazi-occupied Poland.* New York: Oxford University Press.

Tedeschi, J. T., & Felson, R. B. (1994). *Violence, aggression, and coercive actions.* Washington, DC: American Psychological Association.

Tedeschi, J. T., Schlenker, B. R., Bonoma, T. V. (1971). Cognitive dissonance: Private ratiocination or public spectacle? *American Psychologist, 26*, 685–695.

Teigen, H. (1986). Old truths or fresh insights? A study of student's evaluations of proverbs. *British Journal of Social Psychology, 25*, 43–50.

Telch, C. F., & Agras, W. S. (1996). Do emotional states influence binge eating in the obese? *International Journal of Eating Disorders, 20*, 271–279.

Terracciano, A., Abdel-Khalek, A. M., Ádám, N., Adamovová, L., Ahn, C.-K., Ahn, H.-N., et al. (2005). National character does not reflect mean personality trait levels in 49 cultures. *Science, 310*, 96–100.

Tesser, A. (1976). Attitude polarization as a function of thought and reality constraints. *Journal of Research in Personality, 10*, 183–194.

Tesser, A. (1988). Toward a self-evaluation maintenance model of social behavior. In L. Berkowitz (Ed.), *Advances in experimental social psychology* (Vol. 21, pp. 181–227). San Diego, CA: Academic Press.

Tesser, A., & Rosen, S. (1975). The reluctance to transmit bad news. In L. Berkowitz (Ed.), *Advances in experimental social psychology* (Vol. 8, pp. 193–232). New York: Academic Press.

Tetlock, P. E. (1980). Explaining teacher explanations for pupil performance: A test of the self-presentation position. *Social Psychology Quarterly, 43*, 283–290.

Tetlock, P. E. (1981). Pre- to post-election shifts in presidential rhetoric: Impression management or cognitive adjustment? *Journal of Personality and Social Psychology, 41*, 207–212.

Tetlock, P. E. (1992). The impact of accountability on judgment and choice: Toward a social contingency model. In M. P. Zanna (Ed.), *Advances in experimental social psychology* (Vol. 25, pp. 331–376). San Diego, CA: Academic Press.

Tetlock, P. E. (2000). Coping with trade-offs: Psychological constraints and political implications. In S. Lupia, M. McCubbins, & S. Popkin (Eds.), *Political reasoning and choice.* Berkeley: University of California Press.

Thayer, R. E., Newman, R., & McClain, T. M. (1994). Self-regulation of mood: Strategies for changing a bad mood, raising energy, and reducing tension. *Journal of Personality and Social Psychology, 67*, 910–925.

Thompson, A. P. (1983). Extramarital sex: A review of the research literature. *Journal of Sex Research, 19*, 1–22.

Thompson, M. P., Norris, F. H., & Hanacek, B. (1993). Age differences in the psychological consequences of Hurricane Hugo. *Psychology and Aging, 8*, 606–616.

Thornhill, R., & Gangestad, S. W. (1999). The scent of symmetry: A human sex pheromone that signals fitness? *Evolution and Human Behavior, 20*, 175–201.

Thrash, T. M., & Elliot, A. J. (2003). Inspiration as a psychological construct. *Journal of Personality and Social Psychology, 84*, 871–889.

Tice, D. M. (1991). Esteem protection or enhancement? Self-handicapping motives and attributions differ by trait self-esteem. *Journal of Personality and Social Psychology, 60*, 711–725.

Tice, D. M. (1992). Self-presentation and self-concept change: The looking-glass self is also a magnifying glass. *Journal of Personality and Social Psychology, 63*, 435–451.

Tice, D. M., & Baumeister, R. F. (1993). Controlling anger: Self-induced emotion change. In D. M. Wegner & J. W. Pennebaker (Eds.), *Handbook of mental control* (pp. 393–409). Englewood Cliffs, NJ: Prentice-Hall.

Tice, D. M., & Baumeister, R. F. (1997). Longitudinal study of procrastination, performance, stress, and health: The costs and benefits of dawdling. *Psychological Science, 8*, 454–458.

Tice, D. M., & Bratslavsky, E. (2000). Giving in to feel good: The place of emotion regulation in the context of general self-control. *Psychological Science, 11*, 149–159.

Tice, D. M., Bratslavsky, E., & Baumeister, R. F. (2001). Emotional distress regulation takes precedence over impulse control: If you feel bad, do it! *Journal of Personality and Social Psychology, 80*, 53–67.

Tice, D. M., Butler, J. L., Muraven, M. B., & Stillwell, A. M. (1995). When modesty prevails: Differential favorability of self-presentation to friends and strangers. *Journal of Personality and Social Psychology, 69*, 1120–1138.

Tidwell, M., Reis, H. T., & Shaver, P. R. (1996). Attachment styles, attractiveness, and emotions in social interactions: A diary study. *Journal of Personality and Social Psychology, 71*, 729–745.

Tiggemann, M., & Pickering, A. S. (1996). Role of television in adolescent women's body dissatisfaction and drive for thinness. *International Journal of Eating Disorders, 20*, 199–203.

Tiggemann, M., & Rothblum, E. D. (1988). Gender differences in social consequences of perceived overweight in the United States and Australia. *Sex Roles, 18*, 75–86.

Timbergen, N. (1952). The curious behavior of the Stickleback. *Scientific American, 187*, 22–26.

Timeline: Rwanda. (2008, August 8). *BBC News.* Retrieved October 22, 2008, from http://news.bbc.co.uk/2/hi/africa/1070329.stm

Tjaden, P., & Thoennes, N. (1998). *Stalking in America: Findings from the National Violence Against Women Survey* (NCJ Report no. 169592). Washington, DC: National Institute of Justice and Centers for Disease Control and Prevention.

Tobacyk, J. J., & Downs, A. (1986). Personal construct threat and irrational beliefs as cognitive predictors of increases in musical performance anxiety. *Journal of Personality and Social Psychology, 51*(4), 779–782.

Tobacyk, J. J., & Milford, G. (1983). Belief in paranormal phenomena: Assessment instrument development and implications for personality functioning. *Journal of Personality and Social Psychology, 44*, 1029–1037.

Toll, B. A., Sobell, M. B., Wagner, E. F., & Sobell, L. C. (2001). The relationship between thought suppression and smoking cessation. *Addictive Behaviors, 26*, 509–515.

Tomasello, M., & Call, J. (1997). *Primate cognition.* New York: Oxford University Press.

Tomkins, S. S. (1962). *Affect, imagery, consciousness: Vol. 1. The positive affects.* New York: Springer.

Tormala, Z. L., & Petty, R. E. (2002). What doesn't kill me makes me stronger: The effects of resisting persuasion on attitude certainty. *Journal of Personality and Social Psychology, 83*, 1298–1313.

Tremblay, R. E. (2000). The development of aggressive behavior during childhood: What have we learned in the past century? *International Journal of Behavioral Development, 24*(2), 129–141.

Treynor, W. (in press). Are the most mistrustful the least trustworthy? Studies of unethical behavior. *Journal of Ethics and Behavior.*

Triandis, H. C. (1978). Some universals of social behavior. *Personality and Social Psychology Bulletin, 4*, 1–16.

Triandis, H. C. (1989). The self and social behavior in differing cultural contexts. *Psychological Review, 96*, 506–520.

Trinkaus, J. (1984). A bottle law: An informal look. *Perceptual and Motor Skills, 59*, 806.

Triplett, N. (1897). The dynamogenic factors in peacemaking and competition. *American Journal of Psychology, 9*, 507–533.

The triumph of evil. (1995). PBS *Frontline.* Retrieved October 22, 2008, from http://www.pbs.org/wgbh/pages/frontline/shows/evil

Trivers, R. (1972). Parental investment and sexual selection. In B. Campbell (Ed.), *Sexual selection and the descent of man: 1871–1971* (pp. 136–179). Chicago: Aldine.

Trope, Y. (1983). Self-assessment in achievement behavior. In J. Suls & A. Greenwald (Eds.), *Psychological perspectives on the self* (Vol. 2, pp. 93–121). Hillsdale, NJ: Erlbaum.

Trope, Y. (1986). Self-enhancement and self-assessment in achievement behavior. In R. Sorrentino & E. T. Higgins (Eds.), *Handbook of motivation and cognition* (Vol. 2, pp. 350–378). New York: Guilford Press.

Tsai, J. L., Chentsova-Dutton, Y., Freire-Bebeau, L., & Przymus, D. E. (2002). Emotional expression and physiology in European Americans and Hmong Americans. *Emotion, 2*(4), 380–397.

Tsal, Y. (1984). *The role of attention in processing information from advertisements.* Unpublished manuscript, Cornell University, Ithaca, NY.

Tsang, J.-A., McCullough, M. E., & Hoyt, W. T. (2005). Psychometric and rationalization accounts for the religion-forgiveness discrepancy. *Journal of Social Issues, 61*, 785–805.

Turnbull, S. (2003). *The Ottoman Empire 1326–1699.* New York: Routledge.

Turner, C. W., Layton, J. F., & Simons, L. S. (1975). Naturalistic studies of aggressive behavior: Aggressive stimuli, victim visibility, and horn honking. *Journal of Personality and Social Psychology, 31*, 1098–1107.

Turner, R. H. (1976). The real self: From institution to impulse. *American Journal of Sociology, 81*, 989–1016.

Tversky, A., & Kahneman, D. (1974) Judgment under uncertainty: Heuristics and biases. *Science, 185*, 1124–1131.

Tversky, A., & Kahneman, D. (1983). Extensional vs. intuitive reasoning: The conjunction fallacy in probability judgment. *Psychological Review, 91*, 293–315.

Twenge, J. M. (1997). "Mrs. His Name": Women's preferences for married names. *Psychology of Women Quarterly, 21*(3), 417–429.

Twenge, J. M. (2006). *Generation me.* New York: Free Press.

Twenge, J. M., Baumeister, R. F., Tice, D. M., & Stucke, T. S. (2001). If you can't join them, beat them: Effects of social exclusion on aggressive behavior. *Journal of Personality and Social Psychology, 81*, 1058–1069.

Twenge, J. M., & Campbell, W. K. (2001). Age and birth cohort differences in self-esteem: A cross-temporal meta-analysis. *Personality and Social Psychology Review, 5*, 321–344.

Twenge, J. M., & Campbell, W. K. (2003). "Isn't it fun to get the respect that we're going to deserve?" Narcissism, social rejection, and aggression. *Personality and Social Psychology Bulletin, 29*, 261–272.

Twenge, J. M., Campbell, W. K., & Foster, C. A. (2003). Parenthood and marital satisfaction: A meta-analytic review. *Journal of Marriage and Family, 65*, 574–583.

Twenge, J. M., Catanese, K. R., & Baumeister, R. F. (2002). Social exclusion causes self-defeating behavior. *Journal of Personality and Social Psychology, 83*, 606–615.

Twenge, J. M., Catanese, K. R., & Baumeister, R. F. (2003). Social exclusion and the deconstructed state: Time perception, meaninglessness, lethargy, lack of emotion, and self-awareness. *Journal of Personality and Social Psychology, 85*, 409–423.

Twenge, J. M., Ciarocco, N. J., Cuervo, D., Bartels, J. M., & Baumeister, R. F. (2004). Social exclusion reduces prosocial behavior. *Journal of Personality and Social Psychology, 92*, 56–66.

Twenge, J., & Crocker, J. (2002). Race, ethnicity, and self-esteem: Meta-analyses comparing Whites, Blacks, Hispanics, Asians, and Native Americans, including a commentary on Gray-Little and Hafdahl (2000). *Psychological Bulletin, 128*, 371–408.

Twenge, J. M., Konrath, S., Foster, J. D., Campbell, W. K., & Bushman, B. J. (2008). Egos inflating over time: A cross-temporal meta-analysis of the Narcissistic Personality Inventory. *Journal of Personality, 76*, 875–901.

Tybout, A. M., & Yalch, R. F. (1980). The effect of experience: A matter of salience? *Journal of Consumer Research, 6*, 406–413.

Uchino, B. N., Cacioppo, J. T., & Kiecolt-Glaser, J. K. (1996). The relationship between social support and physiological processes: A review with emphasis on underlying mechanisms and implications for health. *Psychological Bulletin, 119*, 488–531.

Udry, J. R. (1980). Changes in the frequency of marital intercourse from panel data. *Archives of Sexual Behavior, 9*, 319–325.

Unger, L. S. (1996). The potential for using humor in global advertising. *Humor, 9*, 143–168.

U.S. Federal Bureau of Investigation. (2008). *Uniform crime reports*. Washington, DC: U.S. Government Printing Office.

United States v. Scheffer. (1998, March 31). Retrieved October 25, 2008, from http://www.law.berkeley.edu/faculty/sklansky/evidence/evidence/cases/Cases%20for%20TOA/Scheffer,%20United%20States%20v.htm

Unkelbach, C., Forgas, J. P., & Denson, T. F. (2008). The turban effect: The influence of Muslim headgear and induced affect on aggressive responses in the shooter bias paradigm. *Journal of Experimental Social Psychology, 44*(5), 1409–1413.

Utman, C. H. (1997). Performance effects of motivational state: A meta-analysis. *Personality and Social Psychology Review, 1*, 170–182.

Vaillancourt, R. (2005). Indirect aggression among humans: Social construct or evolutionary adaption? In R. E. Tremblay, W. W. Hartup, & J. Archer (Eds.), *Developmental origins of aggression* (pp. 158–177). New York: Guilford Press.

Van Beest, I., & Williams, K. D. (2006). When inclusion costs and ostracism pays, ostracism still hurts. *Journal of Personality and Social Psychology, 91*, 918–928.

Van Boven, L., & Epley, N. (2003). The unpacking effect in evaluative judgments: When the whole is less than the sum of its parts. *Journal of Experimental Social Psychology, 39*, 263–269.

Van den Bergh, B., Dewitte, S., & Warlop, L. (2008). Bikinis instigate generalized impatience in intertemporal choice. *Journal of Consumer Research, 35*(1), 85–97.

Van Dijk, E., Van Kleef, G. A., Steinel, W., & Van Beest, I. (2008). A social functional approach to emotions in bargaining: When communicating anger pays and when it backfires. *Journal of Personality and Social Psychology, 94*(4), 600–614.

Van Dijk, W. W., & Zeelenberg, M. (2002). Investigating the appraisal patterns of regret and disappointment. *Motivation and Emotion, 26*, 321–331.

Van Goozen, S. H. M., Cohen-Kettenis, P. T., Gooren, L. J. G. M., Frijda, N. H., & Van de Poll, N. E. (1995). Gender differences in behaviour: Activating effects of cross-sex hormones. *Psychoneuroendocrinology, 20*, 343–363.

Van Kleef, G. A., De Dreu, C. K. W., & Manstead, A. S. R. (2004a). The interpersonal effects of anger and happiness in negotiations. *Journal of Personality and Social Psychology, 86*(1), 57–76.

Van Kleef, G. A., De Dreu, C. K. W., & Manstead, A. S. R. (2004b). The interpersonal effects of emotions in negotiations: A motivated information processing approach. *Journal of Personality and Social Psychology, 87*(4), 510–528.

Van Praag, H. M. (1990). Two-tier diagnosing in psychiatry. *Psychiatry Research, 34*, 1–11.

Vandello, J. A., Bosson, J. K., Cohen, D., Burnaford, R. M., & Weaver, J. R. (2008). Precarious manhood. *Journal of Personality and Social Psychology, 95*, 1325–1339.

Vaughan, D. (1986). *Uncoupling: Turning points in intimate relationships*. New York: Oxford University Press.

Veenhoven, R. (2004). *World database of happiness: Continuous register of scientific research on subjective appreciation of life*. Retrieved September 26, 2004, from http://www.eur.nl/fsw/research/happiness

Vennard, M. (2008, December 26). Iranians join Bush shoe protest. *BBC News*. Retrieved December 26, 2008, from http://news.bbc.co.uk/2/hi/middle_east/7800453.stm

Visser, P. S., & Krosnick, J. A. (1998). Development of attitude strength over the life cycle: Surge and decline. *Journal of Personality and Social Psychology, 75*(6), 1389–1410.

Vohs, K. D., Mead, N. L., & Goode, M. R. (2006, November). The psychological consequences of money. *Science, 314*(5802), 1154–1156.

Vohs, K. D., & Schooler, J. W. (2008). The value of believing in free will: Encouraging a belief in determinism increases cheating. *Psychological Science, 19*(1), 49–54.

Wakslak, C. J., Nussbaum, S., Liberman, N., & Trope, Y. (2008). Representations of the self in the near and distant future. *Journal of Personality and Social Psychology, 95*, 751–773.

Waldman, S. (1992, January 27). The tyranny of choice: Why the consumer revolution is ruining your life. *New Republic*, 22–25.

Walker, I., & Crogan, M. (1998). Academic performance, prejudice, and the jigsaw classroom: New pieces to the puzzle. *Journal of Community and Applied Social Psychology, 8*, 381–393.

Wallace, H. M., & Baumeister, R. F. (2002). The performance of narcissists rises and falls with perceived opportunity for glory. *Journal of Personality and Social Psychology, 82*, 819–834.

Wallace, H. M., Exline, J. J., & Baumeister, R. F. (2008). Interpersonal consequences of forgiveness: Does forgiveness deter or encourage repeat offenses? *Journal of Experimental Social Psychology, 44*, 453–460.

Wallach, M. A., Kogan, N., & Bem, D. J. (1962). Group influence on individual risk-taking. *Journal of Abnormal and Social Psychology, 65*, 75–86.

Walsh, A. (1991a). The biological relationship between sex and love. *Free Inquiry, 11*, 20–24.

Walsh, A. (1991b). Self-esteem and sexual behavior: Exploring gender differences. *Sex Roles, 25*, 441–450.

Walster, E., Aronson, V., Abrahams, D., & Rottmann, L. (1966). Importance of physical attractiveness in dating behavior. *Journal of Personality and Social Psychology, 4*, 508–516.

Walster, E., & Festinger, L. (1962). The effectiveness of "overheard" persuasive communication. *Journal of Abnormal and Social Psychology, 65*, 395–402.

Walters, K. S., & Portmess, L. (Eds.). (1999). *Ethical vegetarianism: From Pythagoras to Peter Singer*. Albany: State University of New York Press.

Wang, C. L., Bristol, T., Mowen J. C., & Chakraborty, G. (2000). Alternative modes of self-construal: Dimensions of connectedness-separateness and advertising appeals to the cultural and gender-specific self. *Journal of Consumer Psychology, 9*, 107–115.

Warneken, F., & Tomasello, M. (2006). Altruistic helping in human infants and young chimpanzees. *Science, 311*, 1301–1303.

Watson, D., & Clark, L. A. (1991). Self- versus peer ratings of specific emotional traits: Evidence of convergent and discriminant validity. *Journal of Personality and Social Psychology, 60*, 927–940.

Watson, D., & Clark, L. A. (1992). Affects separable and inseparable: On the hierarchical arrangement of the negative affects. *Journal of Personality and Social Psychology, 62*, 489–505.

Watson, D., & Clark, L. A. (1997). Extraversion and its positive emotional core. In R. Hogan, J. Johnson, & S. Briggs (Eds.), *Handbook of personality psychology* (pp. 767–793). New York: Academic Press.

Watson, D., & Tellegen, A. (1985). Toward a consensual structure of mood. *Psychological Bulletin, 98*, 219–235.

Wayment, H. A., Silver, R. C., & Kemeny, M. E. (1995). Spared at random: Survivor reactions in the gay community. *Journal of Applied Social Psychology, 25*, 187–209.

Weary, G. (1980). Examination of affect and egotism as mediators of bias in causal attributions. *Journal of Personality and Social Psychology, 38*, 348–357.

Wegner, D. M. (1986). Transactive memory: A contemporary analysis of the group mind. In B. Mullen & G. R. Goethals (Eds.), *Theories of group behavior* (pp. 185–208). New York: Springer-Verlag.

Wegner, D. M. (1989). *White bears and other unwanted thoughts: Suppression, obsession, and the psychology of mental control*. New York: Viking/Penguin.

Wegner, D. M. (1994). Ironic processes of mental control. *Psychological Review, 101*, 34–52.

Wegner, D. M. (2002). *The illusion of conscious will*. Cambridge, MA: MIT Press.

Wegner, D. M., Giuliano, T., & Hertel, P. (1985). Cognitive interdependence in close relationships. In W. Ickes (Ed.), *Compatible and incompatible relationships* (pp. 253–276). New York: Springer-Verlag.

Wegner, D. M., Schneider, D. J., Carter, S. R., & White, T. L. (1987). Paradoxical effects of thought suppression. *Journal of Personality and Social Psychology, 53*(1), 5–13.

Wegner, D. M., Wenzlaff, R. M., & Kozak, M. (2004). Dream rebound: The return of suppressed thoughts in dreams. *Psychological Science, 15*, 232–236.

Weiner, B. (1972). *Theories of motivation: From mechanism to cognition*. Chicago: Rand McNally.

Weintraub, K. J. (1978). *The value of the individual: Self and circumstance in autobiography*. Chicago: University of Chicago Press.

Weiss, B., & Feldman, R. S. (2006). Looking good and lying to do it: Deception as an impression management strategy in job interviews. *Journal of Applied Social Psychology, 36*(4), 1070–1086.

Weissman, M. M., & Paykel, E. S. (1974). *The depressed woman*. Chicago: University of Chicago Press.

Wells, B., & Corts, D. P. (2008). Measuring attitudes towards sorority and fraternity members: Indication of implicit, ingroup favoritism. *College Student Journal, 42*(3), 842–846.

Wenzlaff, R. M., & Wegner D. M. (2000). Thought suppression. *Annual Review of Psychology, 51*, 59–91.

West, S. G., & Brown, T. J. (1975). Physical attractiveness, the severity of the emergency and helping: A field experiment and interpersonal simulation. *Journal of Experimental Social Psychology, 11*, 531–538.

Whatley, M. A., Webster, J. M., Smith, R. H., & Rhodes, A. (1999). The effect of a favor on public and private compliance: How internalized is the norm of reciprocity? *Basic and Applied Social Psychology, 21*, 251–259.

Wheeler, L., & Kim, Y. (1997). What is beautiful is culturally good: The physical attractiveness stereotype has different content in collectivistic cultures. *Personality and Social Psychology Bulletin, 23*, 795–802.

Wheeler, L., & Nezlek, J. (1977). Sex differences in social participation. *Journal of Personality and Social Psychology, 35*, 742–754.

Wheeler, L., Reis, H., & Nezlek, J. B. (1983). Loneliness, social interaction, and sex roles. *Journal of Personality and Social Psychology, 45*(4), 943–953.

Whisman, V. (1996). *Queer by choice*. New York: Routledge.

White, C. M., Reisen, N., & Hoffrage, U. (2008, November). *Choice deferral can arise from absolute evaluation or relative comparison*. Paper presented at the annual meeting of the Society for Judgment and Decision Making, Chicago.

White, G. L. (1980). Physical attractiveness and courtship progress. *Journal of Personality and Social Psychology, 39*, 660–668.

Whitley, B. E. (1988). Sex differences in heterosexuals' attitudes toward homosexuals: It depends upon what you ask. *Journal of Sex Research, 24*, 287–291.

Why We Fight. Retrieved October 15, 2004, from http://history.acusd.edu/gen/filmnotes/whywefight.html

Whyte, M. (2003, November 10). Put your spam to music: Musician culls unwanted e-mail for song titles Compilation CD made, distributed via the Internet. *Toronto Star*. Retrieved August 5, 2004, from http://www.thestar.com/NASApp/cs/ContentServer?pagename=thestar/Layout/Article_Type1&c=Article&cid=1068419407812&call_pageid=991479973472&col=991929131147

Wicker, A. W. (1969). Attitudes versus actions: The relationship of verbal and overt behavioral responses to attitude object. *Journal of Social Issues, 25*, 41–78.

Wicklund, R. A. (1974). *Freedom and reactance*. Potomac, MD: Erlbaum.

Wicklund, R. A., & Gollwitzer, P. M. (1982). *Symbolic self-completion*. Hillsdale, NJ: Erlbaum.

Wiederman, M. W. (1993). Demographic and sexual characteristics of nonresponders to sexual experience items in a national survey. *Journal of Sex Research, 30*, 27–35.

Wiederman, M. W. (1997). The truth must be in here somewhere: Examining the gender discrepancy in self-reported lifetime number of sex partners. *Journal of Sex Research, 34*, 375–386.

Wiederman, M. W. (2004). Self-control and sexual behavior. In R. Baumeister & K. Vohs (Eds.), *Handbook of self-regulation* (pp. 537–552). New York: Guilford Press.

Wiederman, M. W., & LaMar, L. (1998). "Not with him you don't!": Gender and emotional reactions to sexual infidelity during courtship. *Journal of Sex Research, 34*, 375–386.

Wiehe, V. R. (1991). *Perilous rivalry: When siblings become abusive*. Lexington, MA: Heath/Lexington Books.

William, I. M. (1993). *Humiliation: And other essays on honor, social discomfort, and violence*. Ithaca, NY: Cornell University Press.

Williams, A. D. (1992). Bias and debiasing techniques in forensic psychology. *American Journal of Forensic Psychology, 10*, 19–26.

Williams, K. D. (2001). *Ostracism: The power of silence*. New York: Guilford Press.

Williams, K. D., Bourgeois, M. J., & Croyle, R. T. (1993). The effects of stealing thunder in criminal and civil trials. *Law and Human Behavior, 17*, 321–331.

Williams, K. D., & Zadro, L. (2005). Ostracism: The indiscriminate early detection system. In K. D. Williams, J. P. Forgas, & W. von Hippel (Eds.), *The social outcast: Ostracism, social exclusion, rejection, and bullying*. New York: Psychology Press.

Williams, S. S. (2001). Sexual lying among college students in close and casual relationships. *Journal of Applied Social Psychology, 31*(11), 2322–2338.

Williamson, G. M., & Clark, M. S. (1989). Providing help and desired relationship type as determinants of changes in moods and self-evaluations. *Journal of Personality and Social Psychology, 56*(5), 722–734.

Willis, R. (1989). The "peace puzzle" in Ufipa. In S. Howell & R. Willis (Eds.), *Societies at peace: Anthropological perspectives* (pp. 133–145). London: Routledge.

Wills, T.A. (1981). Downward comparison principles in social psychology. *Psychological Bulletin, 90*, 245–271.

Wilson, J., Kuehn, R., & Beach, F. (1963). Modifications in the sexual behavior of male rats produced by changing the stimulus female. *Journal of Comparative and Physiological Psychology, 56*, 636–644.

Wilson, J. Q., & Kelling, G. L. (1982, March). Broken windows. *Atlantic Monthly*, 29–38.

Wilson, M., & Daly, M. (2003). Do pretty women inspire men to discount the future? *The Royal Society Biology Letters, 271*, S177–S179.

Wilson, T. D., Dunn, D. S., Kraft, D., & Lisle, D. J. (1989). Introspection, attitude change, and attitude–behavior consistency: The disruptive effects of explaining why we feel the way we do. In M. P. Zanna (Ed.), *Advances in experimental social psychology* (Vol. 22, pp. 287–343). San Diego, CA: Academic Press.

Wilson, T. D., Hodges, S. D., & LaFleur, S. J. (1995). Effects of introspecting about reasons: Inferring attitudes from accessible thoughts. *Journal of Personality and Social Psychology, 69*, 16–28.

Wilson, T. D., Lindsey, S., & Schooler, T. Y. (2000). A model of dual attitudes. *Psychological Review, 107*, 101–126.

Wilson, T. D., Wheatley, T., Meyers, J. M., Gilbert, D. T., & Axsom, D. (2000). Focalism: A source of durability bias in affective forecasting. *Journal of Personality and Social Psychology, 78*, 821–836.

Winfield, F. E. (1985). *Commuter marriage*. New York: Columbia University Press.

Wing, R. R., Tate, D. F., Gorin, A. A., Raynor, H. A., Fava, J. L., & Machan, J. (2007). "STOP regain": Are there negative effects of daily weighing? *Journal of Consulting and Clinical Psychology, 75*, 652–656.

Witvliet, C. V. O., Ludwig, T. E., & van der Laan, K. L. (2001). Granting forgiveness or harboring grudges: Implications for emotion, physiology, and health. *Psychological Science, 121*, 117–123.

Wood, P. B., & Bartkowski, J. P. (2004). Attribution style and public policy attitudes toward gay rights. *Social Science Quarterly, 85*(1), 58–74.

Worchel, S., Lee, J., & Adewole, A. (1975). Effects of supply and demand on ratings of object value. *Journal of Personality and Social Psychology, 32*, 906–914.

Worldiq.com (2004). Retrieved December 26, 2008, from http://www.wordiq.com/definition/Information_overload

Worthman, C. M. (1999). Faster, farther, higher: Biology and the discourses on human sexuality. In D. Suggs & A. Miracle (Eds.), *Culture, biology, and sexuality* (pp. 64–75). Athens: University of Georgia Press.

Wortman, C. B., & Brehm, J. W. (1975). Responses to uncontrollable outcomes: An integration of reactance theory and the learned helplessness model. In L. Berkowitz (Ed.), *Advances in experimental social psychology* (Vol. 8, pp. 277–336). New York: Academic Press.

Wout, D., Danso, H., Jackson, J., & Spencer, S. (2008). The many faces of stereotype threat: Group- and self-threat. *Journal of Experimental Social Psychology, 44*(3), 792–799.

Wright, E. F., & Jackson, W. (1991). The home-course disadvantage in golf championships: Further evidence for the undermining effect of supportive audiences on performance under pressure. *Journal of Sport Behavior, 14*, 51–60.

Wright, E. F., & Voyer, D. (1995). Supporting audiences and performance under pressure: The home-ice disadvantage in hockey championships. *Journal of Sport Behavior, 18*, 21–28.

Wright, J. C., Giammarino, M., & Parad, H. W. (1986). Social status in small groups: Individual–group similarity and the social "misfit." *Journal of Personality and Social Psychology, 50*, 523–536.

Wright, R. (2000). *Non zero: The logic of human destiny*. New York: Pantheon.

Wright, S. C., Aron, A., McLaughlin-Volpe, T., & Ropp, S. A. (1997). The extended contact effect: Knowledge of cross-group friendships and prejudice. *Journal of Personality and Social Psychology, 73*, 73–90.

Wyer, R. S., & Frey, D. (1983). The effects of feedback about self and others on the cognitive processing of feedback-relevant information. *Journal of Experimental Social Psychology, 19*, 540–559.

Wylie, R. C. (1979). *The self-concept: Vol. 2. Theory and research on selected topics*. Lincoln: University of Nebraska Press.

Wynder, E. L., & Graham, E. A. (1950). Tobacco smoking as a possible etiological factor in bronchiogenic carcinoma. *Journal of the American Medical Association, 143*, 329–336.

Yerkes, R. M., & Dodson, J. D. (1908). The relation of strength of stimulus to rapidity of habit formation. *Journal of Comparative Neurology and Psychology, 18*, 459–482.

Yukl, G. (2006). *Leadership in organizations*. Upper Saddle River, NJ: Prentice-Hall.

Zajonc, R. B. (1965). Social facilitation. *Science, 149*, 269–274.

Zajonc, R. B. (1968). Attitudinal effects of mere exposure. *Journal of Personality and Social Psychology, 9*(2, Pt. 2), 1–27.

Zajonc, R. B., Heingartner, A., & Herman, E. M. (1969). Social enhancement and impairment of performance in the cockroach. *Journal of Personality and Social Psychology, 13*, 83–92.

Zajonc, R. B., Reimer, D. J., & Hausser, D. (1973). Imprinting and the development of object preference in chicks by mere repeated exposure. *Journal of Comparative Physiological Psychology, 83*, 434–440.

Zalar, R. W., Harris, R. B., Kyriacou, D. N., Anglin, D., & Minow, M. (2000). Domestic violence. *New England Journal of Medicine, 342*, 1450–1453.

Zanna, M., & Cooper, J. (1974). Dissonance and the pill: An attribution approach to studying the arousal properties of dissonance. *Journal of Personality and Social Psychology, 29*, 703–709.

Zanna, M., Higgins, E. & Taves, P. (1976). Is dissonance phenomenally aversive? *Journal of Experimental Social Psychology, 12*, 530–538.

Zebrowitz, L. A., Andreoletti, C., Collins, M. A., Lee, S. Y., & Blumenthal, J. (1998). Bright, bad, babyfaced boys: Appearance stereotypes do not always yield self-fulfilling prophecy effects. *Journal of Personality and Social Psychology, 75*, 1300–1320.

Zebrowitz, L. A., & Montepare, J. M. (1992). Impressions of babyfaced individuals across the life span. *Developmental Psychology, 28*, 1143–1152.

Zebrowitz, L. A., Voinescu, L., & Collins, M. A. (1996). "Wide-eyed" and "crooked-faced": Determinants of perceived and real honesty across the life span. *Personality and Social Psychology Bulletin, 22*, 1258–1269.

Zebrowitz-McArthur, L. A., & Montepare, J. M. (1989). Contributions of a babyface and a childlike voice to impressions of moving and talking faces. *Journal of Nonverbal Behavior, 13*, 189–203.

Zhao, W., & Dweck, C. S. (1994). *Implicit theories and vulnerability to depression-like responses*. Unpublished manuscript, Columbia University, New York.

Ziegert, J. C., & Hanges, P. J. (2005). Employment discrimination: The role of implicit attitudes, motivation, and a climate for racial bias. *Journal of Applied Psychology, 90*, 553–562.

Zillmann, D. (1979). *Hostility and aggression*. Hillsdale, NJ: Erlbaum.

Zillmann, D., Katcher, A. H., & Milavsky, B. (1972). Excitation transfer from physical exercise to subsequent aggressive behavior. *Journal of Experimental Social Psychology, 8*, 247–259.

Zimbardo, P. G. (1970). The human choice: Individuation, reason, and order versus deindividuation, impulse, and chaos. In W. J. Arnold & D. Levine (Eds.), *Nebraska Symposium on Motivation* (pp. 237–307). Lincoln: University of Nebraska Press.

Zogby, J., & Zogby, J. J. (2004). *Impressions of America 2004: How Arabs view America; how Arabs learn about America*. Washington, DC: Arab American Institute/Zogby International.

Zuckerman, M. (1975). Belief in a just world and altruistic behavior. *Journal of Personality and Social Psychology, 31*, 972–997.

Zuckerman, M. (1979). Attribution of success and failure revisited, or: The motivational bias is alive and well in attribution theory. *Journal of Personality, 47*, 245–287.

Name Index

A

Abakoumkin, G., 444
Aberly, A.N., 272
Aberson, C.L., 88
Abraham, S.F., 116, 380
Abrams, D., 424
Abramson, L.Y., 82
Achenbach, C.J., 275
Acker, M., 356, 359
Ackerman, J.M., 395
Ackerman, P., 272
Adams, G.R., 85
Adams, H.E., 165, 400
Adewole, A., 233
Adhikary, A.K., 405
Adler, P., 328
Agarie, N., 175
Agras, W.S., 179
Agustdottir, S., 79
Ahlering, R.F., 242
Aiello, J.R., 438
Ailman, W.F., 307
Ainsworth, M.D.S., 327, 362
Ajzen, I., 212
Alebiosu, K.A., 418
Alexander, M.G., 146
Alexander, R.A., 449
Algom, D., 187
Alicke, M.D., 268
Allan, E., 300
Alland, A., Jr., 296
Allen, N.B., 260
Allen, N.J., 445
Allgeier, E.R., 213
Allison, S.T., 149, 263
Alloy, L.B., 82
Allport, Floyd, 4
Allport, G., 406
Allport, Gordon, 4, 200
Altermatt, T.W., 394
Alwin, D.F., 243
Amabile, T.M., 107
Ambady, N., 183
Ames, D.R., 450
Amodio, D.M., 416
Anderson, C., 453
Anderson, C.A., 18, 177, 215, 299, 304, 306
Anderson, Christopher, 103
Anderson, K.B., 299, 306
Anderson, P.B., 302
Anderson, R.E., 380
Andrade, E.B., 189
Andreoletti, C., 420
Andrews, J.D.W., 328
Angleitner, A., 384
Ansell, E., 339
Antonovsky, H.F., 213
Apsler, R., 245
Archer, J., 300, 303
Ard, B.N., 356, 375, 376
Argote, L., 446
Ariely, D., 103, 269, 331
Aries, E.J., 171, 275
Aristotle, 32
Arkes, H.R., 155
Arkin, R.M., 75

Armbrister, R.C., 136
Armkoff, D.B., 236
Aron, A., 454
Aron, A.P., 165, 166
Aronoff, J.R., 453, 456
Aronson, C.A., 17, 73, 241, 330
Aronson, E., 207, 382, 385, 418, 423
Aronson, Elliot, 32
Aronson, J.A., 423
Arvers, P., 308
Asch, Solomon, 52, 226
Ashmore, R.D., 335
Ashton, H., 116
Ashton-James, C., 188
Astrachan, D.I., 306
Asuncion, A.G., 237
Atthowe, J.M., 100
Aunger, R.V., 386
Austin, J.B., 175
Averill, J.R., 172
Aviles, F.E., 308
Axelrod, R., 262, 327
Axsom, D., 180
Aynesworth, H., 174
Azuuma, H., 136

B

Bachman, J.G., 85
Back, K.W., 333
Backteman, G., 79
Bacon, Francis, 147
Badcock, P.B.T., 260
Baggini, J., 147
Bailey, D.S., 16
Bailey, J.M., 379
Bailey, R.C., 386
Baldwin, M.W., 363
Balswick, J.O., 386
Banaji, M.R., 77, 185
Bandura, A., 110, 204, 205, 295
Bane, C.M., 205
Barash, D.P., 327
Barbee, A.P., 334
Barclay, D.R., 179
Bard, P., 163
Bargh, J.A., 6, 42, 77, 111, 132, 162, 202, 327, 332, 455
Barlow, D.H., 181
Barndollar, K., 42
Barnett, P.A., 328
Baron, G., 128
Baron, R., 296
Baron, R.A., 174, 290
Baron, S.H., 227
Barrett, M., 170
Barrick, M.R., 449
Barry, H., III, 39
Bartell, P.A., 281
Bartels, J.M., 341
Bartels, R.D., 133
Bartholomew, K., 361, 362
Bartholow, B.D., 304
Bartkowski, J.P., 401
Bartlett, M.Y., 384
Barton, R., 83
Bassett, R., 229
Bator, R., 230

Batson, C.D., 272, 273
Batson, J.G., 272
Battistich, V., 85
Baumann, D.J., 178
Baumeister, R.F., 37, 47, 48, 60, 65, 66, 76, 81, 84, 85, 86, 87, 89, 90, 104, 106, 114, 116, 117, 119, 146, 168, 172, 173, 175, 176, 177, 179, 186, 202, 213, 264, 274, 276, 289, 298, 302, 308, 311, 325, 326, 327, 328, 333, 337, 339, 341, 346, 359, 364, 375, 387, 433, 437, 439
Bay-Hinitz, A.K., 418
Bazargan, M., 218
Bazargan, S., 218
Bazerman, M.H., 101
Beaber, R.J., 247
Beach, F., 375
Beach, S.R.H., 264
Beaman, A.L., 435
Bean, N.J., 339
Bechara, A., 179
Beck, A.T., 82
Beck, J.G., 213, 375
Becker, A.E., 64–65
Bedford, L., 424
Beggan, J.K., 78, 263
Begue, L., 308
Beilock, S.L., 437
Bejciy-Spring, S.M., 399
Bell, Alexander Graham, 38
Bell, A.P., 377
Bell, C., 366
Bellavia, G., 364
Belsky, J., 177
Bem, Daryl, 71, 377, 378
Bem, D.J., 448
Benbow, C.P., 423
Benjamin, A.J., Jr., 304
Ben-Porath, Y., 187
Benson, P.L., 275
Benson, S.M., 175
Berger, J., 139
Berglas, S., 75, 76, 79, 118
Berkowitz, L., 17, 171, 173, 178, 191, 295, 296, 298, 303, 305, 306
Berman, J., 307
Berman, M., 218
Bernat, J.A., 400
Berndt, T.J., 85
Bernston, G.G., 329
Berscheid, E., 261, 336
Bettencourt, B.A., 300
Bettman, J.R., 49
Beumont, P.J.V., 116
Bezemer, M.D., 398
Bhatti, B., 329
Biddle, B.J., 63
Biel, A., 260
Billig, M., 403
Binder, J., 407, 418
Birch, K., 272
Biryukov, P., 135
Bishop, J.A., 85
Bishop, P., 339
Bjerregaard, B., 346
Bjorkqvist, K., 291

Blackwell, B., 35
Blakemore, J.E.O., 346
Blanchard, F.A., 340
Blaney, N., 418
Blankenship, K.L., 245
Blanton, H., 73, 181
Blascovich, J., 75, 81, 88, 202, 424
Blau, P.N., 374
Blehar, M.C., 362
Block, J., 85
Bloom, S., 301
Blumenthal, J., 420
Blumstein, P., 356, 360, 380, 384
Bochner, S., 399
Boddy, J., 387
Bodenhausen, G.V., 407, 408
Bogaert, A., 364
Bogat, G., 306
Boggiano, A.K., 107
Boland, F.J., 134
Boldizar, J.P., 301
Bollier, T., 410
Bonacci, A.M., 87, 104, 302, 397
Bond, C.F., 437
Bond, M.H., 40
Bond, R.A., 52
Bono, G., 265
Bonoma, T.V., 90
Bonta, B.D., 405
Book, A.S., 306
Boone, A.L., 114
Bornstein, R.F., 203
Bortz, J., 176
Bos, H.M.W., 401
Bosch, J.D., 299
Bosson, J.K., 37
Bostrom, R.N., 204
Bosveld, W., 149, 150
Botta, R.A., 65
Bouchard, T.J., 353
Bourgeois, M.J., 240
Bowdle, B.F., 313
Bowlby, J., 325, 327
Bowles, T., 85
Boyd, K., 375
Boyd, R., 33, 37
Boyle, J., 240
Bozman, A.W., 213, 375
Brackett, M.A., 188
Bradford, J.M., 305
Bradley, G.W., 137
Bradley, S.J., 189
Braet, C., 134
Braginski, B.M., 90
Braginski, D.D., 90
Brainerd, C.J., 212
Branden, N., 82
Brandon, D.P., 446
Bratslavsky, E., 116, 179, 190, 202, 359
Braveman, J., 384
Brechner, K., 442
Brehm, J.W., 17, 104, 331
Brehm, S.S., 104
Brennan, K.A., 362
Breuer, M.E., 306

Brewer, M.B., 403, 435
Brickman, P., 88, 169
Bricout, V., 308
Brigham, J.C., 395
Bristol, T., 243
Brockner, A., 85, 86, 88, 170, 176, 261
Brockner, J., 85, 86, 88, 176
Brody, L.R., 185
Broemer, P., 78
Brooke, J., 400
Brown, G., 82
Brown, Jonathon, 83
Brown, K.W., 170
Brown, N.R., 146
Brownstein, S.C., 152
Brunell, A.B., 450
Bruun, S.E., 440, 441
Bucher, A.M., 173
Buckley, T., 272
Budesheim, T.L., 237, 240
Buehler, R., 112, 180
Buhrmester, D., 85
Bulman, R.J., 216
Bundy, R.P., 403
Bunker, B.B., 328
Burger, Jerry, 266
Burger, J.M., 136
Burleson, M.H., 329
Burnaford, R.M., 37
Burns, D., 82
Burnstein, E., 270
Burris, C.T., 218
Burrows, L., 6, 42, 132
Burton, K., 366
Burton, R.L., 218
Burwell, R.A., 65
Bush, M., 232
Bushman, B.J., 65, 87, 104, 111, 116, 173, 174, 242, 298, 302, 304, 311, 397, 398
Buss, A.H., 185, 291, 373, 375, 380
Buss, D.M., 30, 64, 65, 88, 146, 337, 383
Buswell, B.N., 82
Butler, J.L., 92, 437
Butts, C.T., 263
Butz, D.A., 395
Buunk, B., 383, 384
Buzwell, S., 375
Byers, E.S., 375
Byrne, D., 329

C

Cacioppo, J.T., 161, 203, 229, 241, 242, 244, 246, 329, 342, 343
Cadinu, M., 419
Caesar, P.L., 303
Cairns, K.J., 84, 90
Caldwell, M.A., 328
Calhoun, K.S., 400
Call, J., 108
Call, V., 356
Camacho, L.M., 444
Campbell, A., 168, 177
Campbell, C.A., 364
Campbell, D.T., 14, 15, 17, 227, 433
Campbell, J.D., 81, 84, 85
Campbell, W.K., 82, 85, 87, 88, 137, 168, 364, 365, 450
Cannon, W.B., 163
Cantor, J.R., 238
Capitanio, J.P., 401
Cappell, C., 303
Carey, G.L., 11

Carlsmith, J.M., 17, 180, 208
Carlson, M., 273, 290, 304
Carpenter, G.R., 213
Carr, T.H., 437
Carr, T.S., 307, 309
Carr-Nangle, R.E., 179
Carter, S.R., 135, 176, 261
Caruso, David, 188
Carvallo, M., 78
Carver, C.S., 64, 67, 114
Case, D.A., 155
Case, T.I., 152
Casey, R.J., 336
Cash, T.F., 336
Caspi, A., 79
Catalan, J., 232
Catanese, K.R., 104, 302, 326, 339, 340, 375
Cate, R., 186
Causby, V., 303
Cesario, J., 46
Chaiken, S., 162, 200, 202, 236, 244, 377, 378
Chajut, E., 187
Chakraborty, G., 243
Chamberlain, K., 115
Chaplin, W., 83
Chartrand, T.L., 332, 456
Chassin, L., 248
Check, J.V.P., 305
Cheek, J.M., 327
Chen, E.S., 456
Chen, Keith, 34
Chen, M., 6, 42, 132
Chen, S., 455
Chentsova-Dutton, Y., 183
Cherniss, C., 188
Chesney, M.A., 173
Chew, B., 81
Chiavegatto, S., 307
Child, P., 73
Chiodo, J., 340
Chipman, J., 292
Chivers, M.L., 165
Chown, S.M., 277
Chrisjohn, R.D., 275
Christenfeld, N.J., 52
Christensen, H.T., 213
Christy, P., 330
Cialdini, R.B., 175, 178, 228, 229, 230, 231, 232, 251, 273, 282, 317, 331
Ciarocco, N.J., 341, 364
Clark, C.L., 362
Clark, D., 62
Clark, D.A., 82
Clark, L.A., 161, 453
Clark, M.S., 359, 360, 361
Clark, N.T., 232
Clayson, D.E., 399
Clement, R.W., 149
Clifford, M., 336
Clipp, E.C., 334
Clore, G.L., 179, 275
Coan, J.A., 177
Coccaro, E.F., 307
Cohen, D., 37, 312
Cohen, J., 189
Cohen, M.A., 307
Coie, J.D., 291
Colapinto, John, 26–27
Coleman, J.S., 387
Collins, M.A., 420
Collins, N.L., 361, 362, 363
Collins, R.L., 300

Colman, A.M., 345
Colvin, C.R., 85
Comer, R., 209
Compton, J.A., 249
Comstock, G., 292
Comte, A., 271
Conner, R., 339
Connolly, T., 181
Converse, P.E., 177
Conway, M., 80
Cook, T.D., 14, 15, 17
Cooley, Charles Horton, 68
Cooper, H.M., 116, 136
Cooper, J., 209, 210
Cooper, M.L., 182, 361, 364
Copeland, J.T., 456
Corcoran, D., 361
Corley, R.P., 275
Cornog, M., 375
Correll, J., 395
Cosmides, Leda, 30, 154
Costa, P.T., 170
Cottrell, C.A., 332, 437, 439
Cox, C., 436
Coy, D.H., 339
Coyle, C.T., 264
Coyne, J., 328, 354
Cozzarelli, C., 182
Craig, R., 248
Cramer, P., 399
Cramer, R.E., 281
Crandall, C., 270, 399
Crandall, C.S., 439
Cranston, J.W., 16
Crick, N.R., 300
Crisp, R.J., 424
Critelli, J.W., 85
Croake, J.W., 213
Crocker, J., 82, 84, 88, 89, 421, 422
Crogan, M., 418
Croizet, J.C., 73
Cronin, A.K., 292
Croskerry, P., 155
Croson, R., 149
Crowley, A.E., 275
Croyle, R.T., 240
Cuervo, D., 341
Cullen, F.T., 310
Cullen, M.J., 424
Cunningham, M.R., 277, 314, 334
Cupach, W.R., 346
Curry, S., 305
Cutrona, C.E., 342

D

Dabbs, J.M., Jr., 307, 326
Daby, M., 384
Daly, M.J., 218
Damasio, Antonio, 177, 178, 179
Damasio, H., 179
Danner, D., 170
Danso, H., 423
Darby, B.L., 232, 265, 273
Darby, B.W., 175
Dardenne, B., 410
Dardis, G.J., 406
Darley, J.M., 279, 280, 413
Darwin, Charles, 28, 29, 294
Das, E., 398
David, J.P., 182
Davidson, K.D., 186
Davidson, R.J., 177
Davies, G., 34
Davis, B.P., 234
Davis, J.H., 250

Davis, J.M., 260
Davis, K.E., 346
Davis, M., 306
Davis, M.H., 356, 359
Davis, P.A., 120
Davy, J., 176, 261
Dawkins, R., 301
Dawson, R.E., 243
Day, D., 312, 449
Deacon, T., 128
Dearing, R.L., 48, 175
Deaux, K., 275
DeBono, K.G., 242
de Brouwer, A.-M., 283
deCharms, R., 107
Deci, Ed, 71, 72, 106, 107
De Dreu, C.K.W., 173
DeHart, T., 78
De Hoog, N., 239
Dejonckheere, P., 134
DeJong, W., 399
DeLamater, J., 372
De La Ronde, C., 370
de Lemus, S., 410
Delespaul, P.A.E.G., 48, 176
DeLongis, A., 329, 354
Delucchi, K., 85
DeMarree, K.G., 450
DeMeis, J., 37
DeMoss, M., 189
DeNeve, K.M., 306
Denson, T.F., 308, 398
DePalma, M.T., 277
DePaola, S.J., 237, 240
DePaulo, B.M., 314, 315
Deppe, R.K., 75
Derby, S.L., 142
Derezotes, D., 329
Dermer, M., 203
de Rougemont, D., 355
Derry, P.A., 84
Dertke, M.C., 275
Derzon, J.H., 307
de Saint-Exupery, Antoine, 108
Désert, M., 73
Deshales, P., 35
DeSteno, D.A., 384, 385
Deuser, W.E., 299
Deutsch, M., 225
Deutsch, R., 41, 43
DeVader, C.L., 449
Devine, P.G., 395, 415, 416
DeVries, D., 451
de Waal, Frans, 28, 32, 260
DeWall, C.N., 106, 337, 340, 394
De Wit, J.B.F., 239
Diamond, L.M., 372
Dickenson, D.J., 37
Dickson, K.L., 183
Dickson, N., 86
Diehl, M., 444
Diener, E., 65, 85, 169, 435, 441
Diener, M., 85
Dienstbier, R.A., 316
Dill, K.E., 18, 299
Dilugolecki, D.W., 80
Dion, J., 49, 336
Di Paula, A., 88
Dixon, D.N., 328
Doan, K.A., 240
Dodge, K.A., 291
Dodson, J.D., 187
Doerr, C., 395
Doherty, K.J., 80
Dolan, R.J., 271

Dollard, J., 13, 297
Donnerstein, E., 17, 305
Doob, L., 13, 297
Dorfman, D.D., 241
Dorr, N., 306
Douthait, E.A., 438
Dovidio, J.F., 393
Dowd, T.G., 205, 259
Downey, G., 339
Downey, K.T., 85
Downs, A., 218
Downs, D.L., 86
Doyle, Arthur Conan, 143
Dragna, M., 281
Draper, P., 405
Drigotas, S.M., 406, 436
Driscoll, D.M., 202
Druen, P.B., 314, 334
Drumm, P., 346
D'Silva, J., 35
Dube, K.C., 191
Dubner, S.D., 34
Dubner, S.J., 396
Du Bois-Reymond, M., 387
Dudley, R.T., 149, 150
Dugan, P.M., 411
Dumont, M., 410
Dunbar, Robin, 31, 327
Duncan, B.D., 272
Duncan, C.P., 238
Dunn, D.S., 205
Dunn, E.W., 188
Dunning, D., 84, 146, 148
Dunton, B.C., 200, 415
Duryea, E.J., 181
Dutrévis, M., 73
Dutton, D.G., 165, 166, 416
Duval, Shelley, 64, 65
Dweck, Carol, 105
Dzindolet, M.T., 444

E

Eagly, A.H., 200, 204,
    236, 244, 275, 335
Earleywine, M., 308
Eaterbrook, J.A., 187
Ebbesen, E.G., 84
Eckman, J., 334
Edelsack, L., 175
Edelstein, R.S., 362, 363
Edgerton, R., 313
Edwards, D.J.A., 248
Ee, J.S., 85
Eek, D., 260
Effrein, E.A., 80
Efran, M.G., 237
Eftekhari-Sanjani, H., 423
Egan, G., 327
Ehly, S.W., 85
Eichelman, B., 307
Eichmann, Adolf, 4
Einstein, Albert, 141
Eisenberg, N., 186, 230, 275
Eisner, M., 292
Elder, G.H., 334
Elfenbein, H.A., 183
Ellard, J.H., 264
Elliot, A.J., 170, 182, 364
Ellis, A., 173
Ellis, B.J., 74
Ellsworth, P.C., 182, 183
Emery, G., 82
Emmons, R.A., 108, 170
Emswiller, T., 275
Engel, R., 70

Engler, L.B., 179
Engs, R.C., 191
Enright, R.D., 264
Entman, R.M., 133
Epley, R., 133, 137
Epps, J., 299
Epstein, J.A., 314
Epstein, S., 79
Epstude, K., 152
Erber, M.W., 190
Erber, R., 190, 456
Erez, A., 183
Erickson, B., 236
Eron, L.D., 79, 304
Estrada, C.A., 182
Evans, K., 339
Exline, J.J., 218, 260, 264, 265
Exposito, F., 410
Eysenck, H.J., 275

F

Faber, J.E., 397
Fagg, E., 424
Falck, R., 248
Falender, V.J., 80
Fanning, J.R., 307
Fantino, E., 155
Farberow, N.L., 120
Farrell, C., 11, 108
Farwell, L., 364
Fava, J.L., 116
Fazio, R.H., 65, 80, 200, 202,
    203, 212, 407, 415, 418
Fedoroff, P., 305
Feeney, B.C., 362, 363
Fehr, Beverly, 85, 161, 441
Fein, S., 306, 408
Feingold, A., 330, 335
Fekken, G.C., 275
Felson, R.B., 289, 292, 301
Fenell, D., 264
Fenigstein, A., 64, 65
Fenton-O'Creevy, M., 151
Ferrari, J.R., 119
Ferriere, R., 259
Feshbach, S., 238, 239, 291
Festinger, L., 70, 208, 243,
    244, 333, 441
Fiddick, L., 154
Field, P., 86
Filiberti, A., 260
Finch, A., 37
Fincham, F.D., 264, 265
Fink, B., 336
Finkel, E.J., 88, 264, 265
Finkenauer, C., 202
Finnie, W.C., 317
Firestone, P., 305
Fiscaro, S.A., 203
Fischer, A.H., 172
Fischer, K.W., 175
Fischer, P., 16
Fischhoff, B., 142, 172
Fishbein, M., 212
Fisher, C.D., 107
Fisher, J.D., 259
Fisher, L.D., 329
Fisher, T.D., 146
Fishkin, S.A., 146, 375
Fiske, S.T., 128, 147, 205,
    332, 410, 456
Fiske, Susan, 154
Fitzgerald, N.M., 186
Fitzjohn, J., 86
Fitzsimons, G.M., 111

Flacks, R., 243
Flaherty, J.A., 191
Flament, C., 403
Flanagan, M., 306
Fleming, A.S., 177
Flink, C., 107
Flynn, F.J., 450
Fogel, A., 183
Folkes, V.S., 345
Folkman, S., 329, 354
Forgas, J.P., 398
Forster, J.L., 191
Forsyth, D.R., 85
Foster, C.A., 88, 168, 364, 365
Foster, J.D., 87
Foti, R.J., 449
Frady, R.L., 307
Fraley, B., 454
Francoeur, R.T., 375
Fraser, S.C., 435
Frayser, S.G., 36
Frazier, P., 218
Frederick, S., 43
Freedman, J.L., 264
Freire-Bebeau, L., 183
Freud, Sigmund, 41, 47, 118, 297
Frey, D., 16, 84, 306
Frey, R.G., 35
Friedland, N., 187
Friedman, L.N., 107
Friedman, R., 110
Friesen, W., 170
Frieze, I.H., 346
Frijda, N.H., 178, 182, 183
Frith, C.D., 271
Frost, J.H., 331
Frost, R.O., 340
Fujimoto, Shun, 62
Fujioka, T., 73
Fujita, F., 85
Fukuyama, F., 331
Fulker, D.W., 275
Funder, D.C., 8, 85
Furman, W., 85
Furnham, A., 276

G

Gable, S.L., 177, 182
Gabriel, M.T., 85
Gachter, S., 441
Gaertner, L., 93, 341
Gaertner, S.L., 393
Gagnon, J.H., 146, 302, 356, 401
Gailliot, M.T., 308, 337
Gaines, B., 75
Galinsky, A.D., 155, 454, 455
Gallucci, M., 78, 342, 440
Galton, Francis, 150, 444
Gangestad, S., 330, 337, 369
Gardner, W.L., 161, 329,
    341, 342, 343
Gärling, T., 260
Gartrell, N.K., 401
Garvin, E., 179
Gasper, K., 179
Gattiker, U.E., 399
Gaunt, R., 42
Gaur, S.D., 306
Gavanski, I., 152
Gazaniga, Michael, 42
Gebauer, J.E., 78
Geen, R.G., 173, 295, 306
Gehring, W.J., 201
Gendolla, G.H.E., 135
Gentry, W.A., 450

Gerard, H.B., 71, 225
Gerberding, J.L., 142
Gerrard, M., 65, 181
Gerstel, N., 328
Gesch, B., 309
Giammarino, M., 344
Giancola, P.R., 308
Gibbons, F.X., 65, 181
Giesler, R.B., 76
Gifford, R.K., 148, 411
Gilbert, D.T., 42, 76, 129,
    180, 214, 215, 250
Gilman, S.E., 65
Gilovich, T., 82, 139, 144,
    148, 151, 153, 219
Giuliano, T., 446
Glaser, R., 329, 354
Glass, D.C., 107
Glendenning, A., 85
Glenn, N.D., 177
Gleser, G.C., 121
Glick, P., 410
Glynn, M.A., 88
Gneezy, A., 133
Goethals, G.R., 149
Goffman, Erving, 61, 63, 89, 91
Golding, S.L., 148
Goldman, M., 353
Goleman, Daniel, 188, 202
Gollwitzer, P.M., 42, 83, 92,
    108, 109, 111, 385
Gondolf, E.W., 384
Gonzales, M., 83, 265
Gonzales, P.M., 73
Gonzalez, R.M., 172
Good, T.L., 136
Goode, M.R., 263
Goodie, A.S., 155
Goodwin, F.K., 307
Goodwin, J.S., 329
Gordon, L.J., 75
Gorin, A.A., 116
Gotlib, I.H., 328
Gottfredson, S.D., 310, 423
Gottman, J.M., 185, 186, 366
Gottschalk, L.A., 121
Govaerts, K., 328
Graetz, K.A., 406
Graham, E.A., 18
Grammer, K., 336
Grasmick, H.G., 317
Grasselli, A., 419
Gray-Little, B., 82
Green, B.L., 230
Green, G., 330
Green, S.W., 152, 182
Greenberg, J., 66, 84, 87, 90, 176
Greenblat, C., 356
Greene, D., 149
Greene, K., 303
Greenspan, S.L., 189
Greenwald, A.G., 77, 84,
    200, 203, 236, 395
Greifeneder, R., 103
Gretiemeyer, T., 16
Griffin, D., 112, 370
Griffin, D.W., 364
Griffin, J.J., 75
Griffit, M., 356
Grimbos, T., 165
Grolnick, W.S., 107
Gromko, M.H., 146
Grondin, S., 35, 36, 37
Groom, R.W., 306
Gross, E.F., 341, 344

Gross, H., 328
Gross, J., 340
Gross, J.J., 173
Grossman, D., 307
Grossman, K.E., 363
Grotpeter, J.K., 300
Gruenfeld, D.H., 453, 454, 455
Grunberg, N.E., 191
Gruner, C.R., 238
Guarnieri, G., 419
Guijarro, M.L., 173
Guinote, A., 454
Gupta, S.P., 191
Gurr, T.R., 292
Gutman, I., 256, 257

H
Hackel, L.S., 177
Hafdahl, A.R., 82
Hagtvet, K.A., 85
Haidt, J., 182
Halberstadt, J.B., 180
Hall, J.H., 264, 265
Hall, J.R., 224, 225
Hallet, A.J., 173
Hamburg, P., 65
Hamilton, D.L., 148, 411, 433
Hamilton, W.D., 270, 327
Hammen, C.L., 328
Hanacek, B., 218
Hannon, P., 264
Hansen, G.L., 213
Hanson, D.J., 191
Harber, K.D., 420
Hardin, G., 442
Hardison, C.M., 424
Hare, R.D., 174
Hargis, K., 277
Harkins, S., 440
Harmon-Jones, E., 218, 416
Harrell, K.L., 272
Harris, M.B., 13, 14, 175, 399
Harris, R.J., 399
Harris, S.J., 90, 268
Harris, V.A., 138
Harrison, A.A., 203
Harrison, K., 65
Hart, J., 410
Harter, S., 79
Hauck, A., 37
Haugen, J.A., 265
Haugtvedt, C.P., 242
Hausser, D., 203
Hawkley, L.C., 329, 342, 343
Hay, D., 300
Hazan, C., 361, 362
Headon, C., 48
Healy, M., 88
Hearold, S., 283
Heatherton, T.F., 47, 65, 79, 85,
    90, 114, 175, 399, 424
Hebl, M.R., 399
Hecht, T.D., 445
Hegstrand, L.R., 307
Heider, F., 135, 206
Heine, S.J., 92, 105, 211
Heiner, R.B., 303
Heingartner, A., 437
Heinz, S., 128
Helkama, K., 268
Henderson, V., 105
Hendin, H., 120, 121
Hendricks, N.J., 396
Henken, V.J., 121
Henning, K., 375

Hepworth, J.T., 412
Herbison, P., 86
Herdt, G., 36
Herek, G.M., 400, 401
Herlitz, J., 329
Herman, B.H., 339
Herman, C.P., 65, 134
Herman, E.M., 437
Herold, E.S., 213, 276, 386
Hertel, P., 446
Herzog, D.B., 65
Hess, R.D., 136
Hesson-McInnis, M., 48
Hewstone, M., 276, 394
Hicks, E.K., 387
Higgins, E., 210
Higgins, E.T., 46, 75, 77,
    132, 140, 166
Hight, T.L., 170
Hill, C.A., 346
Hill, C.T., 186
Hill, S.J., 202, 264
Hilmert, C.J., 52
Hilton, J.L., 201
Hinde, R.A., 295
Hirschi, T., 310
Hirt, E.R., 75, 155
Hitler, Adolf, 4
Hixon, J.G., 76, 370
Ho, 449
Ho, K., 181
Hodge, C.N., 335
Hodges, S.D., 205
Hoffman, B.J., 450
Hoffman, E.L., 227, 275
Hoffman, H.G., 395
Hoffrage, U., 104
Hofstadter, Douglas, 152
Hogan, R., 327, 449, 451
Hogg, M.A., 344
Hokanson, J.E., 328
Hollingshead, A.B., 446
Holloway, S.D., 136
Holmes, J., 364
Holmes, J.G., 263, 370
Holt, K., 84
Holtzworth-Munroe, A., 368
Holzberg, A.D., 84
Homans, G.C., 374
Honour, J.W., 315
Hood, R., 65
Hooley, J.M., 328
Hoorens, V., 78
Horner, Matina, 118
Hornstein, H.A., 178
Horowitz, A.V., 353, 362
Hoshino-Browne, E., 211
House, P., 149
Houston, D.A., 240
Hovland, C., 235, 236,
    238, 242, 244, 412
Howell, S., 405
Howell-White, S., 353
Howes, J.J., 328
Hoyle, R.H., 406, 433
Hoyt, W.T., 265
Hsee, C.K., 101, 181
HsiuJu, Y., 75
Hu, Y., 353
Hubbard, M., 215
Huesmann, L.R., 79, 304
Huitfeldt, B., 306
Hull, J.G., 66, 115, 308
Humphrey, L., 111, 340
Hunt, W.C., 329

Hunter, J.E., 335
Hupka, R.B., 382, 383
Huston, T.L., 186
Hutchins, I., 35
Hutton, D.G., 81
Hyde, J.S., 73, 82, 190, 372, 375, 376
Hyland, M.E., 118
Hymes, C., 162, 202

I
Idson, L.C., 133
Imada, S., 152
Inderbitzen, H.M., 85
Inglis, D., 85
Innes, C.A., 307
Innes-Ker, A.H., 180
Insko, C.A., 268, 406, 433, 436
Inzlicht, M., 424
Isen, A.M., 182, 183, 277
Iuzzini, J., 341
Iyengar, S.S., 103
Izard, C.E., 163

J
Jackson, J.R., 200, 423
Jackson, L.A., 335
Jacobs, R.C., 227
Jacobson, L., 420
Jacobson, N.S., 368
James, B., 213
James, W., 60, 162
James, W.H., 356
Janda, L.H., 336
Janis, I.L., 86, 235, 238, 239
Jankowiak, W., 355
Jankowski, M.S., 310
Janoff-Bulman, R., 88, 216
Janus, C.L., 146, 376
Janus, S.S., 146, 376
Jeffery, R.W., 191
Jencks, C., 423
Jensen, A., 330
Johns, M., 424
Johnson, B.C., 236
Johnson, C., 444
Johnson, D.J., 364, 369
Johnson, J.T., 77, 119
Johnson, W., 353, 354
Johnson, W.G., 179
Joiner, T., 27, 119, 121
Jonas, K., 204
Jones, C.R., 132
Jones, Edward E., 9
Jones, E.E., 71, 79, 137,
    138, 209, 329, 331
Jones, F.D., 120
Jones, J.T., 78
Jones, J.W., 75, 90, 118, 306
Jones, S.F., 275
Jones, W.H., 327
Josephs, R.A., 308
Jost, J.T., 407
Joy, V., 334
Judd, C.M., 395, 409, 421
Juieng, D., 17
Jussim, L., 75, 410, 420
Juvonen, J., 341, 344

K
Kagan, J., 64
Kahn, J., 328, 387
Kahneman, Daniel, 43, 77,
    100, 101, 102, 112, 141,
    143, 144, 148, 152, 169
Kaiser, R.B., 449, 451

Kaistanierni, L., 88
Kallgren, C.A., 317
Kalro, A., 263
Kameda, M., 175
Kanazawa, S., 343
Kanin, E.J., 186
Kant, I., 106, 337
Kantak, K.M., 307
Karabenick, S.A., 275
Karau, S.J., 440
Kardes, F.R., 243
Karpinski, A., 201
Kashima, Y., 46
Kashiwagi, K., 136
Kashy, D.A., 314
Kasser, T., 107, 108, 307
Kastin, A.J., 339
Katcher, A.H., 298
Katzev, R., 175
Kaube, H., 271
Kaukiainen, A., 88
Kavenocki, S., 213
Kay, A.C., 407
Kaye, D., 238
Kearns, J.N., 265
Keating, L., 85
Keefe, K., 85
Keeney, R.L., 142
Keinan, G., 187
Keir, G., 405
Keith, T.Z., 85
Keizer, K., 317
Kelem, R.T., 435
Kelley, H.H., 139, 235, 263
Kelley, W.M., 424
Kelling, G.L., 317
Kelln, B.R.C., 264
Kelly, M.H., 312
Keltner, D., 172, 453, 454
Kendall, P.C., 299
Kendrick, D.T., 178
Kerkhof, P., 398
Kerr, N.A., 85, 342, 440
Kerr, N.L., 440, 441
Ketsetzis, M., 85
Key, C.R., 329
Kiecolt-Glaser, J.K., 329, 354
Kiesler, S., 263
Kihlstrom, J.F., 77
Killen, J., 248
Kim, S., 329, 335
King, K., 386
Kingsbury, G.G., 85
Kingston, D.A., 305
Kinney, R.F., 83, 109
Kinsey, A.C., 376
Kipnis, David, 453
Kirk, C.T., 315
Kirkendol, S.E., 314
Kirker, W.A., 77
Kirkpatrick, L.A., 74
Kirschenbaum, D., 111, 112
Kirschner, P., 238
Kitayama, S., 62, 93, 105, 211, 270
Kitzinger, C., 373
Klassen, M.L., 399
Klein, S.B., 77
Klinesmith, J., 307
Kling, K.C., 73, 82
Klinger, M.R., 203
Knetsch, J.L., 77
Knight, G.R., 218
Knight, J., 134, 203
Knobe, J.M., 139
Knoth, R., 375

Knowles, E.S., 234
Koch, E.J., 87
Koenig, K.E., 243
Koestner, R., 72, 107
Kogan, N., 448
Kolata, G., 399
Kolditz, T., 75
Konrath, S., 87
Koomen, W., 149, 150
Koops, W., 299
Kouzes, J.M., 449
Kowalski, R.M., 341
Kozak, M., 135
Krafft, Peter, 58
Kraft, D., 205, 265
Kraus, S.J., 213
Kraut, R.E., 85
Kravitz, D.A., 439
Kraxberger, B.E., 93
Kray, L.J., 155
Krendl, A., 424
Krishnan, R., 446
Kristof, A.L., 108, 109
Krosnick, J.A., 243
Krueger, J., 85, 149, 152
Krueger, R.F., 353
Kruger, J., 139
Kruglanski, A.W., 110
Krull, D.S., 129, 138, 328
Kuehn, R., 375
Kuhnert, K.W., 450
Kuiper, N.A., 77, 84
Kuipers, P., 178
Kulik, J.A., 52
Kumar, A., 191
Kumar, N., 191
Kumashiro, M., 264
Kunce, L.J., 362
Kunda, Z., 71, 84, 410, 412
Kunz, P.R., 259
Kuo, Z.Y., 296
Kusche, A., 364

L
Laan, E., 165
Lackenbauer, S., 211
Lacoursiere, R.B., 327
LaFleur, S.J., 205
LaFrance, M., 185
Lagerspetz, K.M.J., 88, 291, 300
Laird, J.D., 209
Lake, R.A., 416
Lalumiere, M.L., 165
Lancet, M., 213
Landman, J., 153
Lang, M.E., 177
Lange, Carl, 162
Langer, E.J., 78, 86, 151
Langlois, J.H., 336, 337
LaPiere, R.T., 212
Larrick, R.P., 306
Larsen, J.D., 37, 190, 191
Larsen, R.J., 383
Larson, R.W., 185
Larwood, L., 399
Lashley, B.R., 315
Latane, B., 279, 280, 334, 440
Latham, G.P., 108, 109
Lau, R.R., 435
Laumann, E.O., 146, 302, 356, 357, 375, 401
Lavine, H., 65
Lawrence, T., 334
Lawson, A., 381
Layton, J.F., 304

Lazarus, R., 329, 354
Lea, S.E.G., 34
Leary, Mark, 86
Leary, M.R., 93, 177, 325, 339
le Bon, G., 444
Lee, C., 258
Lee, J., 233
Lee, S.Y., 420
Lee-Chai, A., 42, 455
Leffingwell, A., 306
Leggett, E.L., 105
Lehman, D.R., 92, 105, 155, 210, 211
Leiblum, S.R., 375
Leippe, M.R., 236
Leitenberg, H., 375
Leith, K.P., 172
Lema, M., 369
Lempert, R.O., 155
Lennon, R., 186, 275
Lennox, R.D., 330
Leon, G., 115
Leonard, K.E., 16, 300
Leonardelli, G.J., 435
LePage, A., 303
Lepper, M.R., 72, 103, 205, 215, 246
Lerner, J.S., 172, 436, 455
Lerner, M.J., 178, 276
Lerner, R.M., 275
Leung, K., 40
Levav, J., 269
Leve, C., 234
Levenson, R.W., 66, 366
Levine, J.M., 237
Levitt, A.J., 34, 76, 92
Levitt, S.D., 396
Lewin, Kurt, 4, 6, 10
Lewinsohn, P.M., 83
Lewis, A., 433
Lewis, W.A., 173
Leyens, J.P., 73
Li, N.P., 332
Liang, D.W., 446
Liberman, N., 73, 113
Lichtenstein, S., 142, 144
Lickel, B., 433
Lieberman, M.D., 42, 327
Liebert, R., 296
Liebowitz, M.R., 354
Liebrand, W.B.G., 263
Lifton, R.J., 261
Lightfoot-Klein, H., 387
Liljenquist, K.A., 454
Lin, J., 138
Lind, E.A., 236
Linden, E., 314
Lindenberg, S., 317
Linder, D.E., 209
Lindner, E.G., 313
Lindsey, S., 200
Lindskold, S., 453, 456
Linn, J.A., 234
Linnoila, M., 307
Linz, D., 305
Lipsey, M.W., 307
Lisle, D.J., 205
Litt, C.J., 39
Little, B.R., 108
Lloyd, K., 85
Lobel, M., 260
Locke, E.A., 108, 109
Lockhart, L.L., 303
Loeber, R., 300
Loewenstein, G.F., 101
Logue, A.W., 115
Lohr, B.A., 165, 401

Long, J., 218
Longo, L.C., 335
Lonnqvist, J.-E., 268
Lopes, L.L., 155
Lopes, P.N., 188
Lopez, S., 274
Lord, C.G., 73, 205, 215, 246
Lord, R.G., 449
Lorenz, K., 295
Loy, M. H.-M., 138
Lubinski, D., 423
Lucas, R.E., 169
Luce, M.F., 49
Ludwig, T.E., 264
Luhtanen, R.K., 89
Lumia, A., 306
Lumsdaine, A., 235, 238
Lydon, J.E., 366
Lynch, J.J., 329
Lyubomirsky, S., 170, 210

M
Maass, A., 419
Maccoby, N., 244
MacDonald, G., 339
Macfarlane, A., 370
Machan, J., 116
Mack, D., 134
Mackay, C., 444
Mackie, D.M., 237
MacLean, M.J., 277
Macphail, E., 128
Macrae, C.N., 407
Maddux, C.D., 37
Madey, S.F., 144, 277
Maestripieri, D., 326
Magee, J.C., 454, 455
Magnusson, D., 79
Mahler, S.V., 326
Maio, G.R., 78
Major, B., 82, 84, 182, 421, 422
Mak, D., 133
Makhijani, M.G., 335
Malamuth, N.M., 305
Malett, S., 112
Malle, B.F., 139
Malone, P.S., 214
Malpass, R.S., 395
Mandal, E., 334
Maner, J.K., 337, 340, 413
Manning, D., 83, 265
Manstead, A.S.R., 173
Manucia, G.K., 178
Marcus-Newhall, A., 290, 304
Margolis, R.L., 380, 381
Maris, R., 120
Markman, K., 152, 155
Marks, G., 84, 149
Marks, J.S., 142
Marks, T., 328
Markus, H.R., 62, 71, 92, 105, 211
Markwith, M., 48
Marques, J.M., 344
Marques, S., 424
Marshall, G.D., 166
Martin, B., 439
Martin, C.E., 376
Martin, L., 163
Martin, R., 182
Martz, J.M., 367
Maruyama, G., 85, 247
Masicampo, E.J., 106
Maslach, C., 166
Mather, B., 316
Maticka-Tyndale, E., 276

Mayer, Jack, 451
Mayer, John, 188
McAlister, A.L., 248
McAndrew, F.T., 307
McCabe, P., 375, 377
McCain, John, 10
McCauley, C., 48, 152, 182
McClain, T.M., 189
McCloskey, M.S., 307
McConnell, A.R., 415
McCown, W.G., 119, 306
McCoy, S.B., 181
McCrae, R.R., 170
McCullough, M.E., 170, 218, 264, 265
McDougall, William, 4
McElwee, R.O., 84
McFarland, C., 180
McFarlin, D.B., 75, 81, 88
McGee, R., 86
McGhee, D.E., 200, 415
McGinnis, M.Y., 306
McGue, M., 353
McGuire, C.V., 73
McGuire, W.J., 73, 248
McHoskey, J.W., 205
McKenna, K.Y.A., 327
McKillip, J., 330
McLanahan, S., 177
McLeod, E., 328
McMaster, M.R., 281
McMillen, D.L., 175
McMullen, M.N., 152
McNeill, W.H., 405
McWhinnie, C., 423
Mead, George Herbert, 63, 68
Mead, N.L., 263
Medvec, V.H., 144, 153
Meissner, C.A., 395
Mellers, B.A., 181
Mellor, B., 49
Menzies-Toman, D., 366
Mesquita, B., 183
Messick, D.M., 149, 263, 301
Messinger, D., 183
Metcalf, B.L., 155
Mewhinney, D.-M.K., 213, 276
Meyer, D.E., 131, 302
Meyerowitz, J.A., 84
Meyers, J.M., 180
Michael, R.T., 146, 302, 356, 401
Michaels, S., 146, 302, 356, 401
Michaud, S.G., 174
Mick, D.G., 189
Midlarsky, E., 275
Mikula, G., 301
Milavsky, B., 298
Milberg, S., 360
Miles, M.B., 327
Milford, G., 218
Milgram, Stanley, 4–5
Miller, A.G., 205
Miller, C.T., 85
Miller, D., 303
Miller, D.T., 78, 152, 263
Miller, J., 263, 396
Miller, J.A., 229
Miller, L.C., 36, 146
Miller, N., 13, 149, 247, 273, 290, 298, 300, 308
Miller, R.L., 232
Miller, R.S., 366, 369
Miller, T.Q., 173
Millhausen, R.R., 386
Mills, J., 207, 359, 360, 361

Milne, A.B., 407
Mirenberg, M.C., 78
Mischel, W., 49, 83, 84, 114, 295
Misra, S., 263
Mita, T.H., 203
Mitchell, C., 173
Mochon, D., 103
Modan, B., 213
Moise, J., 304
Mokdad, A.H., 142
Moller, A.P., 336
Molouki, S., 139
Monshouwer, H.J., 299
Montepare, J.M., 420
Monterosso, J., 210
Moore, B.S., 306
Moore, M., 292
Moore, R., 224
Moreland, R.L., 446
Morf, C.C., 87, 311, 364
Morgenthau, Hans, 452
Morokoff, P.J., 379
Morris, K.A., 239
Morris, W.N., 298
Morrison, E.L., 336
Morrow, G.D., 364
Mowen, J.C., 243
Mowrer, O., 13, 297
Moya, M., 410
Muehlenhard, C.L., 375
Mullen, B., 444
Muller, D., 308
Mullin, C.R., 305
Munger, K., 90, 268
Munter, P.O., 316
Muraven, M., 92
Muraven, M.B., 116
Murray, S., 364, 370
Murstein, B.I., 330
Musch, J., 36, 37
Musham, C., 66
Musher-Eizenman, D.R., 399
Myers, D.G., 250

N
Nadler, A., 259
Najam, N., 339
Najmi, S., 135
Nault, L.P., 35
Neale, M.C., 275
Neely, J.H., 131
Negel, L., 339
Nelson, J.E., 238
Nelson, L.D., 336
Nelson, M.R., 244
Nelson, R.J., 307
Nelson, S.E., 139
Nemeroff, C., 151
Neuberg, S.L., 332
Newcomb, T., 243, 441
Newcombe, D., 236
Newman, R., 189, 239, 315
Nezlek, J., 107, 188, 328, 329, 342
Nguyen, H.-H.D., 424
Nias, D.K.B., 275
Nichols, P.A., 79
Nicholson, N., 151
Nickerson, R.S., 147
Niedenthal, P.M., 180
Niederland, W.G., 261
Nijman, H.L.I., 306
Nisbett, R.E., 312, 313
Nisbett, Richard, 69, 70, 72, 79, 137, 155

Nolan, C., 155
Nolen-Hoeksema, S., 190
Nooordewler, M.K., 142
Norris, F.H., 218
Norton, M.I., 331
Nussbaum, S., 73
Nuttila, A., 307
Nuttin, J.R., 78

O
Oakes, M.A., 395
Oakes, W., 21
Oaten, M., 152
Obach, M.S., 136
O'Barr, W.M., 236
Odland, L.M., 399
O'Doherty, J., 271
Oettingen, G., 108
Ogrocki, P., 329, 354
Ohbuchi, K.I., 175
Okwumabua, J.O., 181
Olatunji, B.O., 401
Oliner, P.M., 275
Oliner, S.P., 275
Oliver, M.B., 375, 376
Olson, J.M., 152, 153, 179, 415
Olson, M.A., 203
Olweus, D., 88
O'Malley, P.M., 85
Omar, A., 315
Organ, D.W., 258
Orley, J., 328
Orobio de Castro, B., 299, 305
Ortiz, C.W., 396
Osherow, N., 418
O'Sullivan, L.F., 213, 302, 375
Oswald, I., 41
Ottaviani, R., 82
Oubaid, V., 384
Ouellette, R., 360
Ouwerkerk, J.W., 342, 345, 440
Owen, J., 401

P
Paik, H., 292
Palin, Sarah, 10
Palmstierna, T., 306
Pankepp, J., 339
Papageorgis, D., 248
Parad, H.W., 344
Pargament, K.I., 218, 264
Park, B., 395, 409, 421
Park, L.E., 88
Patnoe, S., 418
Patrick, R., 183
Patterson, E.W.J., 237
Patterson, F., 314
Patterson, O., 421
Paul, A.M., 188
Paul, C., 86
Paulhus, D.L., 76, 92
Paulus, P.B., 444
Paxson, L.M., 39
Paykel, E.S., 328
Payne, J.W., 49, 395, 415
Peake, P.K., 114
Pedersen, W.C., 36
Pederson, J., 83
Peekna, H.M., 272
Pelham, B.W., 78, 129, 328
Peltonen, T., 291
Pemberton, M.B., 436
Penner, L.A., 275, 283
Pepitone, A., 441

Peplau, L.A., 186, 328, 342
Peretta, S., 84
Perez, R.C., 88
Perkins, H.W., 191
Perkins, S.C., 75
Perlman, D., 342
Pernanen, K., 307
Perper, T., 375
Perry, C.L., 248
Perry-Jenkins, M., 185
Persons, J.B., 218
Persson, A.V., 399
Peruche, B.M., 395
Peters, K., 46
Peterson, C., 274
Peterson, R.F., 418
Petri, B., 301
Pettigrew, T.F., 138, 393, 407, 418
Pettiway, L.E., 301
Petty, R.E., 203, 241, 242, 244, 246, 249
Peyser, H., 401
Pfau, M., 249
Pham, L.B., 100
Phillips, M., 423
Phillips, T., 298
Phillis, D.E., 146
Pickering, A.S., 65
Pickett, C.L., 342, 435
Piliavin, I.M., 281
Piliavin, J.A., 281
Pillard, R.C., 379
Pinel, E.C., 180
Pines, A., 382, 385
Pinker, S., 292, 293
Pinkley, R.L., 433
Pitre, U., 315
Pitt, E.L., 303
Plaks, J.E., 46
Plant, E.A., 395, 416, 424
Platt, C.W., 136
Pleck, J., 185
Pliner, P., 377, 378
Podolski, C.P., 304
Poletes, G., 444
Polivy, J., 65, 115
Poll, J., 218
Pollock, V.E., 308
Polman, J., 305
Pomazal, R.J., 275
Pomeroy, W.B., 376
Porges, S.W., 189
Portmess, L., 35
Posner, B.Z., 449
Possidente, B., 306
Postmes, T., 442
Pottebaum, S.M., 85
Powell, M., 360
Powell, M.C., 202
Powers, W.T., 115
Pratkanis, A.R., 234, 236, 241
Pratt, T.C., 310
Pratto, F., 407
Predmore, S., 75, 328
Prentice, D.A., 78
Pressley, M., 212
Presson, C.C., 248
Preston, E., 215
Prewitt, K., 243
Pronin, E., 139
Provias, D., 424
Pryor, J.B., 48, 65, 455
Przymus, D.E., 183
Putcha-Bhagavatula, A.D., 36
Pyszczynski, J., 84, 87, 90

Q
Qualtrough, T., 213, 375
Quanty, M.B., 173, 295
Quigley, B., 300
Quilitch, H.R., 418
Quinn, D., 424
Quinn, D.M., 423
Quinton, R.L., 326
Qunisey, V.L., 306

R
Rachal, K.C., 170
Raine, A., 172
Rainey, D., 336
Rao, P., 218
Raskin, R., 311
Ravesloot, J., 387
Raymond, P., 162, 202, 455
Raynor, H.A., 116
Raz, M., 232
Read, S.J., 362
Rector, G., 306
Reeder, G.D., 48, 364
Regan, P.C., 86, 375, 454
Reidel, S.L., 330
Reifman, A., 306
Reilly, N.P., 298
Reimer, D.J., 203
Reinholtz, R.K., 375
Reinisch, J.M., 146, 354
Reis, H.T., 48, 85, 176, 177, 182, 328, 342, 363
Reisen, N., 104
Reiss, I.L., 380, 382
Rennard, Stephen, 12
Reno, R.R., 317
Renzetti, C.M., 384
Renzi, P., 306
Reykowski, J., 178
Reynolds, R., 175
Rhine, R.J., 202
Rhoads, K., 230
Rhodes, A., 259
Rhodes, N., 242
Rhodewalt, F., 79, 87, 311, 364
Rholes, W.S., 132
Riad, J.K., 307
Rice, R.W., 328
Richards, C., 182, 185
Richards, Z., 394
Richardson, D.R., 290, 296
Richerson, P.J., 33, 37
Richeson, J.A., 415, 424
Richman, J.A., 191
Ridley, M., 47
Riketta, M., 78
Rimon, R., 307
Ring, K., 90
Ringelmann, Max, 3–4, 439
Rippere, V., 190
Risen, J.L., 148
Ritov, I., 181
Ritson, J., 35
Ritter, J.M., 336
Rittle, R.H., 437
Roberts, B.W., 79
Roberts, E., 387
Roberts, W.A., 49, 108
Robinson, I.E., 386
Robinson, P., 275
Rodes, D., 263
Rodin, J., 281
Roehling, M.V., 399
Roehling, P.V., 399

Roese, N.J., 152, 153, 179
Roets, A., 134
Rogers, E.M., 238
Rogers, W.L., 77, 177
Roggman, L.A., 336
Rogow, A.A., 11
Rohrer, J.H., 227
Romero, V., 88
Romero-Canyas, R., 339
Roney, J.R., 326, 384
Root, L.M., 265
Rorer, L.G., 148
Rose, E., 218
Rose, P., 364
Roseman, I.J., 172
Rosen, J.C., 340
Rosen, R.C., 375
Rosen, S., 69
Rosenbaum, M.E., 204, 330
Rosenberg, M., 69, 85
Rosenhan, D.L., 277, 282
Rosenman, R.H., 173
Rosenthal, D., 375
Rosenthal, R., 420
Roskos-Ewoldsen, D., 240
Ross, D., 204
Ross, Edward, 4
Ross, L., 149, 205, 215, 246
Ross, M., 80, 112, 137
Ross, S., 204
Roth, J., 151
Rothbart, M.K., 185
Rothberg, J.M., 120
Rothblum, E.D., 399
Rothman, A.J., 133
Rottman, L., 330
Rotton, J., 306
Rovine, M., 177
Rowatt, W.C., 314
Rozin, P., 48, 151, 152, 182
Ruback, R.B., 17
Rubin, R.A., 85, 186
Rubin, Y., 339
Ruble, D.N., 177
Rusbuilt, C.E., 264, 364,
    366, 367, 369
Rush, A.J., 82
Rushton, J.P., 212, 275
Russell, C.S., 177
Russell, James, 155, 161, 184
Russo, J.E., 155
Ryan, A.M., 424
Ryan, Richard, 72, 85, 107, 108
Ryan, R.M., 170
Rydell, R.J., 415
Ryff, C.D., 170
Rynd, N., 302

S
Sackett, P.R., 424
Sadava, S., 364
Sagristano, M.C., 113
Salas, E., 444
Salmivalli, C., 88
Salovey, Peter, 133, 188, 277, 384, 385
Samet, J.M., 329
Samuelson, C., 301
Sandage, S.J., 170
Sandelands, L.E., 88
Sanders, G.S., 150
Sanders, S.A., 146
Sandfort, T.G.M., 401
Sanna, L.J., 155
Santos, M.D., 234

Sapolsky, R., 306
Sarin, R., 169
Satow, K.L., 258
Savitsky, K., 137
Sawyer, D., 146
Schachter, S., 333
Scarpa, A., 172
Schachter, Stanley, 164, 226, 377
Schaefer, H.S., 177
Schaefer, R.T., 442
Schaller, M., 340
Scheck, S.R., 186
Scheibehenne, B., 103
Scheier, M.F., 64, 65, 67, 85, 114
Scheinin, M., 307
Scher, K.J., 66
Scherer, K.R., 183
Scherzer, N.A., 375
Schlenker, B.R., 80, 89, 90, 91, 265
Schlundt, D.G., 179
Schmader, T., 424
Schmidt, R.E., 135
Schmitt, D.P., 30, 373, 375
Schneider, D.J., 135
Schneiderman, E., 188
Schoenbach, C., 85
Schoenthaler, S., 309
Schooler, C., 85
Schooler, J.W., 106
Schooler, T.Y., 200
Schopler, J., 406, 436
Schumacher, J.A., 307
Schumm, W.R., 177
Schunk, D.H., 110
Schure, E., 178
Schutz, A., 188, 365
Schvanveldt, R.W., 131
Schwartz, B., 103, 209
Schwartz, I., 88
Schwartz, J.K.L., 200
Schwartz, N., 181
Schwartz, P., 356, 360
Schwarz, N., 155, 313
Schwarz, P., 179
Schwarzwald, J., 232
Scollon, C.N., 169
Scott, J.P., 339
Scott, M., 37, 295
Scratchley, L.S., 81
Seabright, P., 360
Sears, D.O., 21, 245, 412
Sears, R., 13, 297
Sechler, E.S., 215
Sedikides, C., 75, 93, 137, 364
Segal, N.L., 270
Sekerak, G.J., 437
Seligman, C., 232
Seligman, M.E.P., 274
Sellin, I., 188
Sellmer, G.P., 375
Semmelroth, J., 383
Sennett, 1974, 60
Sentyrz, S.M., 65
Seta, C.E., 437
Seta, J.J., 437
Seto, M.C., 165
Seymour, B., 271
Shackelford, T.K., 88, 382
Shaffer, D.R., 247
Shah, J.Y., 110, 111
Shakur, S., 309
Shandall, A.A., 387
Shaver, P., 361, 363
Shaver, P.R., 361, 362
Shaw, B.F., 82

Shea, D.L., 423
Sheard, M.H., 306
Sheffield, F., 235, 238
Sheldon, K.M., 107, 170, 171
Shelton, J.N., 415, 424
Sheppard, J.A., 335
Shepperd, J.A., 87
Sherif, C.W., 403
Sherif, Muzafer, 227, 403
Sherkat, D.E., 218
Sherman, S., 152, 248, 433
Shin, J., 103
Shneidman, E.S., 121
Shoda, Y., 114, 295
Shoham, I., 213
Shook, N.J., 407, 418
Shorter, E., 370, 381, 382
Shotland, R.L., 279, 375, 377
Showers, C.J., 82
Shrauger, J.S., 68, 75, 88
Sicoly, F., 137
Sidanius, J., 407
Sikes, J., 418
Silfver, M., 268
Silver, M., 403, 435
Silvia, P.J., 65
Sime, J.D., 270
Simmons, C.H., 276
Simons, L.S., 304
Simpson, J.A., 362, 369
Sinclair, L., 146, 412
Singer, B., 375
Singer, Jerome, 107, 164
Singer, T., 271
Singh, D., 335
Sitarenios, G., 188
Skaalvik, E.M., 85
Skaggs, L.M., 315
Skelton, J.A., 79
Slingsby, J.K., 272
Slinkard, L.A., 248
Slovic, P., 142, 144, 148
Sluka, J., 2
Small, D.A., 172
Smart, L., 311
Smith, C.A., 75
Smith, D., 147
Smith, G.E., 65, 86
Smith, G.F., 241
Smith, G.H., 70
Smith, K., 387
Smith, P.B., 52
Smith, R.H., 259, 268
Smith, S.M., 247
Smith, T.B., 218
Smith, T.W., 173
Snapp, M., 418
Snibbe, A.C., 211
Snowdon, D., 170
Snyder, C.R., 75, 140, 274
Snyder, M., 242, 330
Soane, E., 151
Soares, F., 339
Sobell, LC., 135
Sobell, M.B., 135
Soetens, B., 134
Solomon, D., 85
Solomon, S., 87
Solzhenitsym, Alexander, 167
Sommer, K.L., 339, 364
Sommers, Christina Hoff, 10
Sommers, S.R., 89
Sorman, P.B., 88
Southwick, L., 116
Spangler, G., 363

Spanier, G.B., 177, 380
Spears, R., 442
Specht, H., 329
Speicher, C.E., 329
Spencer, Herbert, 29
Spencer, S., 423
Spencer, S.J., 211, 408, 423, 424
Spitzberg, B.H., 346
Sponaugle, G.C., 380
Sprecher, S., 86, 356, 366,
    374, 454
Springer, C.A., 177, 339
Sproull, L., 263
Sroufe, L.A., 363
Staats, A.W., 204
Staats, C.K., 204
Stack, A.D., 173
Stacy, D., 37
Staelin, R., 155
Staffieri, J., 399
Stahelski, A.J., 263
Stanford, W.E., 248
Stangor, C., 177
Staples, S.L., 372
Starzyk, K.B., 306
Stasser, G., 447
Stearns, E., 37
Steele, C., 424
Steele, C.M., 73, 116, 308, 423
Steffensmeier, D., 300
Steg, L., 317
Steger, M., 218
Steinel, W., 173
Steinfatt, T.M., 263
Steinfeld, J., 304
Steinmetz, G., 175
Stein-Seroussi, A., 76
Steinwert, T., 399
Stephin, C., 418
Stepney, R., 116
Stepper, S., 163
Stern, P.C., 292
Stern, S.E., 397
Sternberg, R., 358
Stevenson, R.J., 152
Stillwell, A.M., 92, 114,
    172, 175, 186, 333
Stone, J., 423
Stone, L., 60, 171, 355, 370, 395
Stoner, J.A.F., 448
Storey, A.E., 326
Story, A.L., 84
Stout, J.C., 329, 354
Strack, F., 41, 43, 163, 455
Stratham, A.J., 335
Straub, R.O., 191
Straus, M.A., 300
Straw, M.K., 279
Strober, M., 340
Stroebe, W., 204, 239, 444
Stroop, James, 129
Stroup, D.F., 142
Strube, M.J., 328
Struckman-Johnson, C., 302
Stucke, T.S., 341
Stucky, R.J., 140
Subra, B., 308
Sugie, N., 396
Suls, J., 84, 149, 150, 182
Sundali, J., 149
Surowiecki, J., 444, 445
Surra, C., 186
Suzuki, T., 211
Svenson, O., 82
Swander, D.V., 227

Swann, W.B., Jr., 74, 75, 76, 239, 328, 370
Sweeney, D., 65
Symanski, R., 328
Symons, D., 30, 77, 373, 374

T

Tafarodi, R.W., 214
Tajfel, H., 403
Tambor, E.S., 86
Tamir, M., 173, 190
Tangney, J.P., 48, 114, 175
Tann, E.K., 309
Tannahill, Reay, 36
Tanner, A., 160
Tansey, G., 35
Tanzer, N., 301
Tarpley, W.R., 218
Tashiro, T., 218
Tata, J., 227
Tate, D.F., 116
Taves, P., 166, 210
Taylor, A.M., 41
Taylor, S., 268
Taylor, S.E., 83, 100, 109, 128, 147, 300
Taylor, Shelley, 83, 216
Taylor, S.P., 16, 84, 153
Tchividjilan, L.R., 93
Teasdale, J.D., 328
Tec, N., 272
Tedeschi, J.T., 90, 289, 292, 301
Teigen, H., 11
Telch, C.F., 179
Tellegen, A., 161
Terdal, S.K., 86
Terry, H., 311
Tesser, A., 69, 71, 205
Testa, M., 422
Tetlock, Phillip, 50, 137, 436, 455
Thagard, P., 410
Thaler, R.H., 77
Thayer, R.E., 189, 190, 191
Therriault, N., 190
Thoennes, N., 346
Thomas, E.J., 63
Thompson, A.P., 379
Thompson, M.P., 218
Thoresen, C.E., 264
Thornhill, R., 336, 337
Thrash, T.M., 170
Tice, D.M., 47, 76, 80, 81, 90, 92, 116, 119, 172, 179, 190, 341
Tidwell, M., 363
Tiggemann, M., 65, 399
Tillman, T.C., 277
Timbergen, N., 295
Titus, L.J., 437
Titus, W., 447
Tjaden, P., 346
Tobacyk, J.J., 218
Todd, P.M., 103
Todd, R., 272
Todorva, E., 78
Toguchi, Y., 93
Toll, B.A., 135
Tomarken, A., 112
Tomasello, M., 108, 271
Tomkins, S.S., 163
Tooby, John, 30, 154
Tormala, Z., 249
Towles-Schwen, T., 212
Tracy, J.L., 307
Tranel, D., 179

Treisman, M., 41
Tremblay, R., 300
Triandis, H.C., 61, 259
Trinkaus, J., 317
Triplett, Norman, 3
Trivers, R., 30, 373
Trolier, T.K., 411
Trope, Y., 42, 73, 74, 113, 418
Tropp, L.R., 407
Trötschel, R., 42
Tsai, J.L., 183, 245
Tsang, J., 170, 265
Tubman, J.G., 86
Turner, C.W., 173, 304
Turner, Ralph, 61
Tversky, A., 100, 101, 102, 112, 143, 144, 148, 152
Twenge, J.M., 82, 87, 168, 177, 339, 340, 341, 342, 387
Tybout, A.M., 230
Tyler, T.R., 456

U

Uchino, B.N., 329
Udry, J.R., 356
Uhles, A., 433
Ullom, H.H., 312
Underwood, B., 306
Unger, L.S., 238
Unkelbach, C., 398
Utman, C.H., 107

V

Vaillancourt, R., 300
Valle, R.S., 237
Valone, K., 247
van Aken, M., 305
Van Balen, F., 401
Van Beest, I., 51–52, 173
Van Boven, L., 137
Vance, S.L., 418
Vandello, J.A., 37
Van Den Burg, M.T.C., 384
van der Laan, K.L., 264
Van der Pligt, J., 149, 150
Vanderslice, V.J., 328
Van Dijk, M., 87, 104, 173, 178, 302
Van Kleef, G.A., 173
Van Lange, P.A.M., 342, 440
Van Praag, H.M., 189
Vasquez, E.A., 308
Vaughan, D., 369
Veenhoven, R., 258
Veerman, J.W., 299
Vennard, M., 290
Venus, P., 238
Verkasalo, M., 268
Vermeulen, I.E., 398
Vilberg, T., 339
Vincent, J.E., 175, 232, 273
Virkkunnen, M., 307
Visser, P.S., 243
Vlandis, J.W., 204
Voelki, K., 422
Vohs, K.D., 85, 106, 146, 202, 263, 276, 315, 326, 375
Voinescu, L., 420

W

Wack, D.L., 437
Wade, J., 268
Wagner, E.F., 135
Wagner, S.H., 65
Wakker, P.P., 169

Wakslak, C.J., 73
Waldman, S., 100
Walker, I., 418
Walker, T., 175
Wall, S., 362
Wallace, H.M., 104, 264, 437, 439
Wallach, M.A., 448
Wallbom, M., 65
Wallbott, H.G., 183
Walsh, A., 86, 354
Walsh, C.L., 326
Walster, E., 243, 261, 330, 336
Walters, K.S., 35
Wan, C.K., 84, 149, 150
Wandruff, S.E., 202
Wang, C.L., 243
Ward, A., 210
Warneken, F., 271
Warwick, D.P., 243
Waters, E., 362, 363
Waters, K., 263
Watson, D., 161, 453
Weary, G., 83
Weaver, C.N., 177
Weaver, J.R., 37
Weber, E.U., 181
Webley, P., 34
Webster, J.M., 259
Wegener, D.T., 245
Wegner, D.M., 42, 135, 190, 446
Weinberg, M.S., 377
Weiner, Bernard, 136
Weiss, W., 236, 242, 314
Weissman, M.M., 328
Welch, N., 181
Wenzlaff, R.M., 135, 328
West, S., 275
West, S.G., 412
Westen, D., 383
Wetter, D., 83
Whatley, M.A., 259
Wheatley, T., 180
Wheeler, D., 232, 328, 329, 335, 342
Wheeler, J., 277
White, B.W., 303
White, C.M., 104
White, G., 330
White, H.R., 353
White, K., 210
White, S.B., 101
White, T.L., 135
Whitley, B.E., 401
Whitson, J.A., 454
Whyte, M., 160
Wicker, A.W., 212, 214
Wicklund, Robert, 64, 65, 92, 104, 385
Wieczorkowska, G., 433
Wiederman, M.W., 146, 379
Wiehe, V.R., 301
Wieselquist, J., 406, 436
Wilke, H.A.M., 263
William, I.M., 313
Williams, A.D., 155
Williams, C.J., 200
Williams, K., 440
Williams, K.D., 51–52, 240, 337, 338, 339, 342, 364
Williams, K.J., 73
Williams, S., 86
Willis, R., 405
Willits, J.E., 275

Willman, P., 151
Wills, T.A., 84, 217
Wilson, D.B., 307
Wilson, J., 375
Wilson, J.Q., 317
Wilson, M., 384
Wilson, T.D., 180, 200, 205
Wilson, Timothy, 69, 70
Winfield, F.E., 328
Wing, R.R., 116
Winton, W., 73
Wirtz, D., 152
Wistedt, B., 306
Wittenberg, M.T., 85
Wittenbrink, B., 395
Witvliet, C.V.O., 264
Wlaschin, J., 133
Wohlwend-Lloyd, R., 364
Wolf, I.K., 152
Wolfe, R.N., 330
Wolsic, B., 85
Wolters, F.J.M., 263
Wood, P.B., 401
Wood, W., 242
Woolcott, M., 259
Worchel, S., 233
Worth, L.T., 237
Worthington, E.L., 170, 264
Worthman, C.M., 326
Wortman, C.B., 104, 216
Wortman, E., 331
Wotman, S.R., 186, 328, 333
Wout, D., 423
Wright, L.W., Jr., 165
Wright, R., 175
Wyer, M.M., 314
Wyer, R.S., 84
Wylie, R.C., 85
Wynder, E.L., 18
Wynne-Edward, K.E., 326

Y

Yalch, R.F., 230
Yalom, I.D., 327
Yamamoto, M., 332
Yang, Y., 36
Yerkes, P.M., 187
Young, M.J., 182
Young, R.D., 66
Yukl, G., 449
Yzerbyt, V.Y., 344

Z

Zadro, L., 339, 342
Zajonc, R.B., 203, 437
Zanna, A.S., 211
Zanna, M., 166, 210, 211
Zappa, Frank, 154
Zavalloni, M., 448
Zebrowitz, L., 420, 421, 423
Zebrowitz-MacArthur, L.A., 420
Zeelenberg, M., 178
Zeichner, A., 400
Zeiss, A.R., 84
Zell, A.L., 265
Zhang, J., 101
Zhao, W., 105
Zillmann, D., 164, 174, 298
Zimbardo, P.G., 166, 435, 441
Zonderman, A.B., 170
Zorman, M., 308
Zubek, J.M., 182, 328
Zuckerman, M., 83, 137, 277
Zvibel, M., 232

Subject Index

A

ABCs of intergroup relationships, 393–402
ABC triad, 6
Aborigines, Australian, 392–393
A-B problem, 213
Abstinence and gender, 375
Acceptance. *See also* Rejection; Social acceptance
  private acceptance, 228
  self-acceptance, 365
Accessibility and attitudes, 212–213
Accountability
  aggression and, 442
  in groups, 436
  power and, 455
  social loafing and, 440
Accumulated common wisdom, 11
Accuracy of stereotypes, 409–410
Acquaintance rapes, 302
Action, power and, 455
Actor/observer bias, 137–139
Adaptation
  attitudes and, 202
  power and, 456
Addiction
  to power, 452
  self-regulation and, 114
Adolescence and aggression, 300
The Adventures of Tom Sawyer (Twain), 72
Advertisement wear-out, 241
Advertising. *See also* Persuasion
  classical conditioning and, 204
  introspection and, 70
  negative advertising, 240–241
  wear-out, 241
Affect, 6
  automatic affect, 162
  defined, 161
Affect-as-information hypothesis, 179–180
Affect balance, 167
Affect Intensity Measure (AIM), 171
Affectionate love. *See* Companionate love
Affective forecasting, 180–181
Affect regulation, 189–192
  cheering up and, 189–190
  gender and, 190–191
  goals of, 190
  usefulness of, 191
African Americans
  optimal distinctiveness theory, 436
  self-esteem of, 421–422
  slavery, stereotypes of, 421
Age. *See also* Children
  adolescents and aggression, 300
  and aggression, 299–300

elderly persons and prejudice, 402
  persuasion and age of audience, 243
Agent self, 60
Age of Reason, 292
Aggression. *See also* Antisocial behavior; Crime; Frustration-aggression theory; Violence
  accountability and, 442
  age and, 299–300
  alcohol use and, 307–308
  anger and, 171, 173, 291, 298
  Bobo doll and, 295–296
  chemical influences, 306–308
  conscious overriding and, 44–45
  culture and, 46, 296, 310
  culture of honor and, 312–313
  decrease in, 292–293
  defining, 289–291
  deindividuation and, 441–442
  direct aggression, 290–291
  domestic violence, 301–303
  external causes of, 303–308
  frustration-aggression theory, 13–14, 297–298
  gender and, 300
  hostile cognitive biases and, 299
  hot temperatures and, 306
  humiliation and, 313
  hydraulic model of, 295
  indirect aggression, 290–291
  innate theories of, 294–295
  instinct theories of, 294–295
  internal causes of, 297–301
  interpersonal causes of, 301–303
  learning theories of, 295–296
  mass media and, 304–305
  mood and, 298–299
  narcissism and, 311
  nature *vs.* nurture and, 296–297
  proactive aggression, 291
  reactive aggression, 291
  rejection and, 341–342
  running amok, 309–310
  self-control and, 310–311
  self-esteem and, 311–312
  serotonin and, 307
  sexual media and, 305
  social learning and, 204–205, 295
  testosterone and, 306–307, 326
  theories on, 294–297
  toddler aggression, 300
  video games and, 15
  weapons effect, 303–304
AIDS. *See* HIV/AIDS
Air pollution and aggression, 306
Albania, culture of honor in, 313
Alcohol use
  affect regulation and, 191
  aggression and, 307–308
  monitoring and, 115–116
  self-awareness and, 66
  self-handicapping and, 75–76
  self-regulation and, 114

Alienation, 4
Altruism, 9. *See also* Bystander helping; Helping
  beautiful victims and, 275–276
  educating others about, 282
  emotions and, 277
  gender and, 275
  increasing helping, 282–283
  just world, belief in, 276–277
  models of helping, providing, 282–283
  mood and, 277
  moral inclusion, teaching, 283
  as motive for helping, 271–273
  and personality, 275
  possibility for, 273–274
  similarity and, 275
  volunteering, 283
  willingness to help, 274–277
Altruistic helping, 271–272
Altruistic punishment, 441
Ambiguity
  informational influence and, 228
  and sexual arousal, 165
Amends, making, 175
Amish community, 338
Amok, 309–310
Anchoring and adjustment heuristic, 144–145
Anger, 171–174. *See also* Venting anger
  aggression and, 171, 173, 291, 298
  catharsis theory, 173–174
  causes of, 172–173
  cultivation of, 190
  exercise and, 174
  hiding *vs.* showing, 173–174
  self-destructive aspect of, 172
  self-regulation and, 114
  social benefits of, 173
Animals. *See also* Evolution
  cultural animals, 32
  diversity and, 432
  dogs, hearing of, 50–51
  goals and, 108
  homosexuality in, 401
  loneliness and pets, 343
  social animals, 30–31
  tradeoffs and, 50–51
Anthropology, 7
Anticipated emotions, 180–181
Antisocial behavior. *See also* Aggression
  cheating, 315–316
  defined, 291–292
  deindividuation and, 434–435
  diet and, 309
  littering, 317–318
  lying, 314–315
  prosocial behavior compared, 257
  stealing, 316–317
Anxiety
  decision-making and, 181
  Internet and, 327

irrational beliefs and, 218
  self-regulation and, 114
  stereotype threat and, 424
  suicide and, 121
  suppressed thoughts and, 135
Anxious/ambivalent attachment, 361–362
Apologies and forgiveness, 265
Applied researchers, 10
Appraisal motive, 74–75
Approach/action orientation and power, 455
Arabs. *See also* Islam
  prejudice and, 396–399
Arousal, 186–187. *See also* Sexual arousal
  affect regulation and, 189
  aggression and, 298
  anger and, 171–172
  attention and, 186–187
  cheating and, 316
  dissonance and, 210
  emotional arousal, 162–167
  groups and, 437
  misattribution of, 164–166
  performance and, 186–187
  pleasant arousal, 166
  in Schachter-Singer theory of emotion, 164
  social facilitation and, 438
As Nature Made Him (Colapinto), 26–27
Assembly lines, 431, 433–434
  dominant response and, 438
Assertiveness and leadership, 450
Assisted suicide, 198–199
Assumptive worlds, 216
Athletics. *See* Sports
Attachment, 361–364
  dimensions of, 362–363
  and self-esteem, 364
  and self-love, 364–365
  and sex, 363–364
  and sexuality, 372
  types of, 361–362
Attachment theory, 362–363
Attention
  arousal and, 186–187
  defenses against influence based on, 251
  disrupt-then-reframe technique, 234–235
  pique technique and, 234
  self-deception and, 84
  social influence techniques and, 234–235
Attitudes, 4. *See also* Implicit attitudes
  A-B problem, 213
  accessibility of, 212–213
  aggregation of behavior and, 212
  attack on, 212
  behaviors and, 211–214
  beliefs compared, 200

Attitudes (*continued*)
    classical conditioning
      and, 203–204
    context of behavior and, 212
    defense of, 212–213
    defined, 200
    disgusting foods, eating, 209
    dissonance and, 206–207
    dual attitudes, 200–201
    on extradyadic sex, 380
    formation of, 202–205
    general attitudes and
      behaviors, 212
    inoculation of, 248–249
    mere exposure effect, 203
    money and, 208
    negative attitude change, 249
    operant conditioning and, 204
    persuasion and, 246, 248–249
    polarization and, 205
    predicting behaviors, 211–214
    reasons for, 201–202
    social learning and, 204–205
    stigma and, 201
Attraction, 325, 329–338. *See also* Attractiveness
    complementarity and, 330–331
    mere exposure and, 333–335
    oppositeness and, 330–331
    praise and, 331–332
    reciprocity and, 332–333
    reinforcement theory, 331–332
    shared experiences and, 334
    similarity and, 330–331
    social rewards and, 331–332
    what is beautiful is good
      effect, 335–336
Attractiveness
    altruism and, 275–276
    clothing and, 336
    measurement of, 335
    of source of message, 237
    sources of, 337
    of spouses, 330
    symmetry and, 337
    typicality and, 337
    what is beautiful is good
      effect, 335–336
Attribution cube, 139–141
Attributions, 135–141
    actor/observer bias, 137–139
    criticism and self-esteem, 422
    defined, 135
    excuses and, 139–141
    fundamental attribution
      error, 138–139
    hostile attribution bias, 299
    race and attribution
      theory, 421–422
    in relationships, 368
    self-serving bias and, 137
    success and failure,
      explaining, 136–137
    theory, 5
    ultimate attribution error, 138
Audience, 242–244
    evaluation apprehension
      and, 437
    inhibition, 281
Australian Aborigines, 392–393
Authority and obedience, 266–267
Autokinetic effect, 227–228

Automatic affect, 162
    behavior and, 178
Automatic egotism, 76
Automatic system, 41–45
    goal hierarchies and, 110
    interpersonal functions and, 46
    overriding, 45
    prejudice and, 415
    reasons for, 42
    stigma, dealing with, 48
Automatic thinking, 129–133
    knowledge structures
      and, 130–131
    and power, 455
Automobile industry, 430–431
Availability heuristic, 142–143
Aversive racism, 393
Avoidant attachment, 361–362
    dimensions of, 362–363
    and sex, 364
Awareness. *See also* Self-awareness
    automatic *vs.* controlled
      thinking and, 130
    bystander helping, need for, 279

B

Baby faces and honesty, 420
Bad apple effect, 345
    social loafing and, 440
Bait-and-switch technique, 230
Balance theory, 206
Bankruptcy and self-regulation, 114
Barney, 283
Base rate fallacy, 148–149
Beauty. *See* Attractiveness
Behavior, 4, 6. *See also* Aggression;
    Antisocial behavior; Prosocial
    behavior; Risky behavior
    A-B problem, 213
    aggregation of, 212
    anticipated emotion and, 181
    attitudes and, 211–214
    commons dilemma and, 443
    emotions and, 178
    Freudian psychoanalysis and, 6
    general attitudes and, 212
    guilt and, 175–176
    nature and, 46–47
    rejection and, 341–342, 345
    self-awareness and, 65
    self-defeating behavior, 118–119
    self-presentation and, 90
Behaviorism, 5
Beliefs, 214–219
    altruism and, 276–277
    assumptive worlds and, 216
    attitudes compared, 200
    cognitive coping, 216–217
    coping and, 215–217
    defined, 200
    doubting *vs.,* 214–215
    irrational beliefs, 218–219
    just world, belief in, 276–277
    preservance, 215
    religious belief, 217–218
Belongingness
    emotions and, 177
    failure to achieve, 329
    as need, 325–328
    ongoing relationships
      and, 328–329

options for, 329
regular social contacts
    and, 328–329
Benevolence of life, belief in, 216
Benevolent sexism, 410–411
Better-than-average effect, 150
Between-subjects design, 12
Biases and errors, 145–154. *See also* Prejudice; Self-serving bias; Stereotypes
    actor/observer bias, 137–139
    base rate fallacy, 148–149
    confirmation bias, 147, 413
    conjunction fallacy, 147–148
    correspondence bias, 138
    counterfactual thinking, 152–153
    debiasing people, 155
    false consensus effect, 149–150
    false uniqueness effect, 150
    gambler's fallacy, 149
    hostile cognitive biases and, 299
    illusion of control, 151
    illusory correlation, 148
    magical thinking, 151–152
    omission bias, 103
    optimistic bias, 112–113
    outgroup homogeneity bias, 395
    reducing cognitive
      errors, 154–155
    seriousness of, 154
    statistical regression, 150–151
    status quo bias, 103
Binge eating, 66
    mood and, 179
    self-regulation and, 115
    as socially contagious, 439
Biological psychology, 8
Biology, influence of, 5
Bisexuality, 378
Blame
    aggression and, 301
    coping and, 216
    copying and, 216
    narcissists and, 364
    rape and, 302
    scapegoat theory, 411–412
Bobo doll study, 295–296
Body shape and attractiveness, 336
Boomerang effect, 249
Bosses, bad, 451
Brain. *See also* Emotions
    alcohol use and, 308
    diagram of, 163
    size of, 31
    social brain, 31–32, 45–46
Brainstorming, 443–445
Brainwashing, 79, 215
Broaden-and-build theory of
    emotions, 181–182
Broken Windows Theory, 317–318
Burdensomeness and suicide, 121
Bystander effect, 278
Bystander helping, 278–282
    awareness of need, 279
    busyness and, 281–282
    deciding how to help, 280–281
    educating others about, 282
    five steps to, 278–281
    increasing, 282–283
    indirect help, offering, 281
    interpreting meaning of
      event, 279–280

pluralistic ignorance and, 280
providing help, 281
in public setting, 282
responsibility, taking, 280

C

Cannibalism, 289–291
Cannon-Bard theory of
    emotion, 163–164
Capacity for change and self-
    regulation, 116–117
Casual sex, gender and, 375–376
Categorization process, 394–395
Catharsis theory, 173–174
Central route to persuasion, 245
CEOs (chief executive officers),
    study of, 449
Cerebrum, 163
Certainty effect, 101–102
Change, 29
Charivari, 381–382
Chastity belts, 383
Cheating, 315–316
    free rider problem, 440
    punishing cheaters, 441
    reducing, 315–316
Chemicals and aggression, 306–308
Chewong people, competition
    among, 405
Chicken soup and colds, 12
Child abuse, 303
Childlessness, 168
Children. *See also* Attachment;
    Parenthood
    and aggression, 295–296,
      299–300
    altruism, teaching, 274
    attitudes and, 202
    attractiveness and, 336
    child abuse, 303
    emotions in, 185–186
    gullibility of, 215
    rejection among, 344
    stealing by, 316–317
Choices, 100–103
    attitudes and, 202
    avoidance of, 103
    and change, 104–106
    committees and, 447
    dissonance and, 208–210
    emotions and, 180–181
    entity theorists and, 105
    freedom and, 106–107
    incremental theorists and, 105
    influences on, 100–103
    Maximization Scale, 210
    money and, 101
    omission bias, 103
    postponing choices, 103–104
    power and, 454
    reactance theory and, 104
    status quo bias, 103
    steps in choosing, 100
    tyranny of choice, 209–210
Civil wars, 2
Classical conditioning, 203–204
Climate. *See* Weather
Clinical psychology, 8
Clothing and attractiveness, 336
Cognition, 6
Cognitive coping, 216–217

Cognitive dissonance. *See* Dissonance
Cognitive miser, 128–129
Cognitive processing and
    rejection, 339–340
Cognitive psychology, 8
Cohabitation. *See* Living together
Colds, chicken soup and, 12
Collective wisdom, 432, 443–445
College student samples, 20–21
Colors and Stroop effect, 129–130
Comfort foods, 179
Coming of Age in Samoa (Mead), 382
Commitment
    bait-and-switch technique
        and, 230
    defenses against influence, 250
    foot-in-the-door technique
        and, 229
    labeling technique and, 230
    low-ball technique and, 230
    narcissists and, 365
    social influence and, 228–231
    in Sternberg's triangle of
        love, 358–359
Committees, foolish, 447
Commons dilemma, 442–443
Common sense, 11
Common sense psychology, 135–136
Communal relationships, 359–361
Communication
    and commons dilemma, 443
    convert communicators, 237
    cooperation and, 263
    need for, 325, 327
    overheard communicator
        trick, 243
    social animals and, 38
Communism
    and competition, 406
    private ownership and, 442
Commuter marriages, 328
Companionate love, 354–355
    marriage and, 356
    Sternberg's triangle
        theory and, 359
    transition to, 357
Company citizens, 258
Competition
    cooperation *vs.*, 405
    defined, 404
    discontinuity effect, 406
    instinct for, 436–437
    realistic conflict theory
        and, 404–405
    us *vs.* them and prejudice,
        403–406
Competition machine, 3–4
Competitive instinct, 436–437
Complementarity and
    attraction, 330–331
Compliance
    labeling technique, 230
    public compliance, 228
Conclusions and fundamental
    attribution error, 139
Conditioned response, 203–204
Conditioned stimulus, 203–204
Confederates, 13
Confirmation bias, 147, 413
Conflict
    in commons dilemma, 442–443
    forgiveness and, 264

power and, 456
realistic conflict theory, 404–406
selfishness and self-control, 48
social animals and, 38
stereotypes and, 412–413
Conformity, 267–269
    attributions and, 139
    groupthink and, 446
    normative influence
        and, 226–227
    people first theory and, 52
    restaurants and, 269
Confounded variables, 15
Confounding, 15
Conjunction fallacy, 147–148
Conscience, 258
Conscious emotion, 162
Consciousness, 122
Conscious override of
        prejudice, 414–418
Conscious system, 41–45
    override by, 44–45
    reasons for, 42
Conscious thinking, 129–133
Consensus, 139
Consistency, 206–211. *See
        also* Dissonance
    attributions and, 139
    bait-and-switch technique
        and, 230
    balance theory, 206
    beliefs and, 214
    defenses against influence, 250
    dissonance theory and, 206–207
    drive toward, 211
    in interpersonal sphere, 210–211
    labeling technique and, 230
    low-ball technique and, 230
    P-O-X theory, 206
    religious belief and, 218
    social influence and, 228–231
    trauma, coping with, 217
Consistency motive, 74–75
Construct validity, 14
    of the cause, 14
    of the effect, 14
Contact
    and happiness, 177
    prejudice, contact hypothesis,
        406–407, 418
Contamination concept, 152
Contempt, 172
Conterfactual thinking, 152–153
Contribution, overestimation of, 137
Control. *See also* Self-control
    automatic *vs.* controlled
        thinking and, 130
    illusion of control, 151
    panic button effect and, 107
Controlled thinking, 129–133
    debiasing and, 155
Convert communicators, 237
Coolidge effect, 375–376
Cooperation, 261–263
    communication and, 263
    competition *vs.*, 405
    defined, 404
    money and, 263
    power and, 453
    prisoner's dilemma, 261–263
    realistic conflict theory
        and, 404–405

rejection and, 341
    in Robber's Cave study, 404
Coping
    belief and, 215–217
    cognitive coping, 216–217
    downward comparison, 217
    irrational beliefs and, 218
    religious belief and, 218
Corpus collosum, 163
Correlational approach, 18–19
Correlation coefficients, 18
Correlations, 18
Correspondence bias, 138
Corruption and power, 453
Counterfactual thinking, 179
Counterregulation, 134
Covariation principle, 139
Credibility of source, 236–237
Credit cards, 248–249
    self-regulation and, 114
Crime. *See also* Murder
    alcohol use and, 307
    baby-faced boys and, 420–421
    hate crimes, 414
    in medieval Europe, 381–382
    self-control and, 310–311
    self-regulation and, 114
Crisis, informational influence
        and, 228
Criticism
    self-esteem and, 422
    self-presentation and, 90
    toxic leaders and, 451–452
Crowding and aggression, 306
Cruelty, 293
Cues
    and lying, 315
    and rejection, 340–341
Cults and foot-in-the-door
        technique, 229
Cultural animals, 32
Cultural relativity, 21
Culture, 32. *See also* Social animals
    aggression and, 46, 296, 310
    altruistic punishment and, 441
    body shape and, 336
    common themes of, 53
    competition *vs.* cooperation
        and, 405
    conscious overriding and, 44–45
    defined, 33–35, 99
    differences in people and, 39–40
    domestic violence and, 303
    eating and, 35
    emotions, differences in, 183–184
    groups, cultural, 433
    happiness and, 168
    and homosexuality, 36, 377, 401
    and jealousy, 382–383, 386–387
    love and, 355–356
    money and, 34
    nature and, 28, 35–37
    persuasion and, 243
    as praxis, 34
    reciprocity and, 333
    role differentiation in, 435
    self and, 61–63
    self-regulation standards and, 114
    sex and, 36, 376
    shared ideas, 33
    similarity and, 331
    sleep and, 39

as system, 33–34
    tradeoffs and, 48–50
    and violence, 310
Culture of honor, 312–313
Curiosity, 9
Cynicism and cheating, 315

D

Dating. *See also* Relationships
    eating and, 378
    extradyadic sex and, 381
    race and, 396
Death and dying, 29. *See also* Suicide
    assisted suicide, 198
    self-esteem and, 87
    thanatos, 295
Death drive, 118
Debiasing people, 155
Debt and self-regulation, 114
Decisions. *See* Choices
Defenses against influence
    techniques, 250–251
Deindividuation, 316, 434–435
    and mob violence, 441–442
Delayed gratification, 120
Demeanor and lying, 314
Dependent variables, 13
Depression, 6
    affect regulation and, 190–191
    irrational beliefs and, 218
    power, lack of, 453
    rejection and, 339
    self-esteem and, 82–83
Descriptive norms, 317
Devaluation
    relationships, alternatives in, 369
    and toxic leaders, 451
Developmental psychology, 8
Deviance and rejection, 344–345
Diet and dieting. *See also*
        Eating; Food
    capacity for change and, 116–117
    hunger and, 134
    self-presentation and, 90
    self-regulation and, 115, 116
    vegetarianism, 35
    violence and, 309
Diffusion of responsibility, 280
Direct aggression, 290–291
Disability
    prejudice and, 402
    rejection and, 344
Disbelieving, 214–215
Discontinuity effect, 406
Discrimination
    and Arabs, 397
    as behavioral component of
        intergroup relationships, 394
    defined, 393
    reverse discrimination, 415–416
    sports, racial discrimination
        in, 394
Disgust, 47, 182
    and homosexuality, 401
Dismissing avoidant attachment,
        362–363
Disorder, Broken Windows
        Theory and, 317–318
Disrupt-then-reframe
        technique, 234–235
    defenses against, 251

Dissimilarities and relationships, 331
Dissonance, 206–207
    advances in theory, 210–211
    choice and, 208–210
    effort justification and, 207–208
    low-ball technique and, 230
    post-decision dissonance, 209
    religious belief and, 218
    self-presentation and, 211
Distal goals, 110
Distant future, ideas about, 49
Distinctiveness of information, 139
Distraction
    evaluation apprehension
        and, 438
    and persuasion, 244, 245–246
Distress
    attribution, distress-
        maintaining style of, 368
    empathy and, 272
    negative state relief
        hypothesis, 273
    rejection and, 339
Diversity
    in groups, 432
    movement toward, 331
    and rejection, 432
Divorce and extradyadic sex,
        380–381
DNA testing, 380, 386
Dogs, hearing of, 50–51
Domestic violence, 301–303
    child abuse, 303
    investment theory and, 367
Dominant response theory,
        437–438
    arousal and, 437–438
Donations
    asking for, 231
    prosocial behavior and, 258–259
Door-in-the-face technique, 231–232
Double standard, 386–387
Doubt vs. beliefs, 214–215
Downward comparison, 71, 217
Downward counterfactuals, 152–153
Dreams, suppressed thoughts in, 135
Drilling for oil. See Oil drilling
Drug use
    self-regulation and, 114
    tradeoffs and, 49
Dual attitudes, 200–201
Duchenne smiles, 185
Duplex mind, 41–45
    believing and doubt and,
        214–215
    comparison of systems, 43
    consistency and, 211
    goal hierarchies and, 110
    introspection and, 70
    power and, 454–455
    self-knowledge and, 76
    on thinking, 129
Dyad as group, 432–433

E

Eating
    affect regulation and, 191
    bugs or worms, 209
    dating and, 378
    groups, eating in, 438–439
    nature and, 47
    vegetarianism, 35

Eating disorders, 10. See also
        Binge eating
    rejection and, 339
    self-regulation and, 114
    standards and, 64–65
eBay, 3
EBE (exotic becomes erotic), 377–379
Economics, 7
Education
    jigsaw classroom and
        prejudice, 418
    self-fulfilling prophecies in, 420
    sexuality and, 376
    of spouses, 330
    stereotype threat and, 423
Effects and factorial design, 16
Efficiency and automatic vs.
        controlled thinking, 130
Effort
    automatic vs. controlled
        thinking and, 130
    justification, 207–208
Ego and altruism, 271–273
Egoistic helping, 271–272
Elaboration likelihood model
    (ELM), 244–246
Elderly persons and prejudice, 402
E-mail
    junk e-mail, 160
    lost e-mail technique, 397–398
Emergencies. See also Altruism;
        Bystander helping
    informational influence
        and crisis, 228
Emotional intelligence (EQ),
        188–189, 192
    affect regulation and, 189
Emotions. See also Affect regulation;
        Anger; Arousal; Depression;
        Empathy; Guilt; Happiness;
        Sadness; Shame
    aggression and, 298–299
    altruism and, 277
    anticipated emotions, 180–181
    arousal and, 162–167
    behavior and, 178
    belongingness and, 177
    benefits of positive
        emotions, 182–183
    broaden-and-build theory
        of, 181–182
    Cannon-Bard theory of
        emotion, 163–164
    choices and, 180–181
    conscious emotion, 162
    cultural differences and, 183–184
    decisions and, 180–181
    defined, 161
    emotional intelligence
        (EQ), 188–189, 192
    expression of, 183–184
    financial decisions and, 182
    foods and, 179
    gender and, 185–186
    James-Lange theory of
        emotion, 162–163
    learning and, 178–180
    meaning and, 192
    negative emotions, 181–183
    persuasion and, 238
    positive emotions, 170, 181–183
    power and, 453

reactance, 17
    reasons for, 177–183
    risk-as-feelings hypothesis, 181
    Schachter-Singer theory of
        emotion, 164–166
    simulation heuristic and, 143–144
    social functions of, 46
    thinking and, 178–180
Empathy
    -altruism hypothesis, 272–273
    altruistic helping and, 271–272
    gender and, 275
    prosocial behavior and, 270–271
    sadness and, 178
    -specific punishment
        hypothesis, 273
    -specific reward hypothesis, 273
Empathy-altruism hypothesis,
        272–273
Empathy-specific punishment
    hypothesis, 273
Empathy-specific reward
    hypothesis, 273
Endowment effect, 77–78
Enemies, 177
Energy crisis, 10
Entitlement and toxic leaders, 452
Entity theorists, 105
Environment. See also Nature
    aggression and, 306
    survival and, 29–30
Equality, 260
Equal Opportunity Employment
        Commission, 397
Equity, 260
Eros, 294–295
Erotic plasticity, 376
Error management theory, 102
Errors. See Biases and errors
Ethnic jokes, 414
Evaluation apprehension, 437, 438
Evolution, 28–30
    of brain, 31–32
    gender and, 30
    and groups, 433
    and language, 40
    prejudice and, 406
    prosocial behavior, benefits
        of, 270–271
    survival through, 30
Evolutionary theory
    on extradyadic sex, 380
    on jealousy, 383–384
    of sexuality, 373–374
Exchange relationships, 359–361
Excitation transfer, 164, 174
    and aggression, 298
Executive functions, 60
    alcohol use and, 308
Exercise. See also Sports
    affect regulation and, 189–190
    aggression and, 298
    anger and, 174
Expectancies, violation of, 131
Expectations
    and alcohol use, 308
    hostile expectation bias, 299
    power and, 456
Experiences
    attraction and shared
        experiences, 334
    and homosexuality, 379

Experimental philosophy, 9
Experimental realism, 17
Experimental studies, 3–4, 14–15
    self-correction and, 20
Expertise and persuasion, 236
Explanations and common
        sense psychology, 136
Explicit attitudes, 200
Exploitation, 4
    power and, 453
External Motivation to Respond
        Without Prejudice, 416–418
External validity, 17–18
Extradyadic sex, 379–381
    attitudes about, 380
    and breakup risk, 380–381
    in dating relationships, 381
    evolutionary theory and, 380
    jealousy and, 382
    measurement of, 379–380
Extramarital sex. See Extradyadic sex
Extrinsic motivation, 71–72
Eyewitnesses and racial
        identification, 395–396

F

Facial expression-emotion
        link, 183–184
Facial feedback hypothesis, 163
Factorial designs, 16
Failure, explaining, 136–137
Fairness, 258, 259–261. See also
        Prosocial behavior
    aggression and, 301
    exchange relationships and, 361
    human nature and, 260
    world, belief in fairness of, 216
Fallacies. See Biases and errors
False consensus effect, 149–150
False uniqueness effect, 150
Familiarity and attraction, 333–334
Families. See also Marriage;
        Parenthood
    deviance and rejection, 345
    obedience and, 267
    prosocial behavior and,
        270–271
    violence in, 301–303
Fascism, 435. See also Nazism
Fast-approaching-deadline
        technique, 234
Fast talking and persuasion, 247
Fate, coping and, 216
Favorability vs. plausibility
        tradeoff, 92
Fear
    avoidant attachment and, 363
    behavior and, 178
    decision-making and, 181
    discontinuity effect and, 406
    homophobia and, 401
    misattribution of arousal,
        164–166
    persuasion and, 238–239
    safe sex, persuasion for, 239
Fearful avoidant attachment, 363
Feedback
    belief preservance and, 215
    emotions and, 177
    facial feedback hypothesis, 163
    looking-glass self and, 69
    self-handicapping, 75–76

self-regulation and, 115
skepticism about, 83–84
Female sexuality, 386–387
Field experiments, 17–18
Fight or flight syndrome, 300
Finances. *See* Money
Fipa people, competition among, 405
First instinct fallacy, 152
Flukes, 12
Food. *See also* Eating
　animals and, 51
　mood and, 179
　rejection and, 340
Foolish committees, 447
Foot-in-the-door technique, 229
Ford Motor Company, 430–431
Forewarning about persuasion, 249
Forgiveness, 264–265
　barriers to, 265
　happiness and, 170
Framing, 133. *See also* Reframing
Freedom
　of action, 106–107
　choice and, 105
　panic button effect, 107
　scarcity technique and, 233–234
　self-determination theory
　　and, 106–107
Free rider problem, 440
　punishing free riders, 441
Free will, 106
Frequency
　anchoring and adjustment
　　heuristic, 144–145
　availability heuristic and, 142–143
　representativeness heuristic
　　and, 141–142
　simulation heuristic and, 143–144
Freudian psychoanalysis, 5, 6
Friends. *See also* Relationships
　belongingness and, 328–329
Frustration
　and aggression, 13–14, 297–298
　defined, 297
Frustration-aggression theory,
　　13–14, 297–298
　independent variables in, 16
Frustration and Aggression (Dollard,
　et al.), 297–298
Fundamental attribution
　error, 138–139
　bystander effect and, 278
Future, ideas about, 49

G

Gain-framed appeals, 133
Gambler's fallacy, 149
Gambling
　gambler's fallacy, 149
　irrational beliefs and, 218–219
　as self-defeating behavior, 118
　self-regulation and, 114
Gay gene, 372, 377
Gays. *See* Homosexuality
Gender, 26–27. *See also*
　　Homosexuality; Sexuality
　affect regulation and, 190–191
　aggression and, 300
　altruism and, 275
　choices and, 1021
　domestic violence and, 301–303

emotions and, 185–186
evolution and, 30
jealousy and, 385
littering and, 317
love and, 186
self-esteem and, 82
sex drive and, 375
sexual behavior and, 213
violence and, 297
Generalized other, 68
A General Theory of Crime
　(Gottfredson &
　Hirschi), 310–311
Generation Me, 87
Geneva Convention, 293
Genocide
　humiliation and, 313
　Rwanda genocide, 288–289, 298
Genovese murder, 278
Global warming and violence, 306
Glucose and alcohol use, 308
Goals, 108–111. *See also* Planning;
　　Superordinate goals
　of groups, 433
　happiness and, 169
　hierarchy of, 109–110
　and interrupted activities, 109
　multiple goals, 110–111
　prejudice and achieving, 418
　pursuing, 108–109
　setting, 108–109
　shielding, 110–111
　Zeigarnik effect, 109
Goal shielding, 110–111
Gone With the Wind, 378
Good looks. *See* Attractiveness
Goodness, belief in, 216
Good Samaritan parable, 281–282
Good soldier syndrome, 258
Good to Great study, 449
Graffiti, 317–318
Gratification, delayed, 120
Gratitude and happiness, 170
Great Depression, 4
Great Second Advent Awakening, 218
Greed
　commons dilemma and, 443
　discontinuity effect and, 406
　private ownership and, 442
Group norms
　defined, 227
　normative influence
　　and, 226–227
Group polarization effect, 447–448
Groups. *See also* Belongingness;
　　Ingroups; Outgroups; Race
　accountability in, 436
　action in, 436–443
　arousal and, 437
　attitudes and, 205
　bad apple effect, 345
　benefits of, 433
　binge eating and, 439
　brainstorming, 443–445
　committees, foolish, 447
　commons dilemma, 442–443
　conformity and, 268
　cultural groups, 433
　defined, 432–433
　deindividuation, 434–435
　deviance, rejection for, 344
　discontinuity effect, 406

diversity in, 432
dominant response theory
　and, 437–438
evaluation apprehension, 437
in experimental studies, 15
free rider problem, 440
groupthink, 446–447
individual roles in, 434
intergroup relationships,
　ABCs of, 393–402
leadership of, 449–452
loneliness and, 343
love for teams, 445
moral inclusion, teaching, 283
morality and, 47–48
Nazism and, 435
optimal distinctiveness
　theory, 435–436
polarization of, 447–448
prosocial behavior and, 259
risky shift of, 447–448
shared resources and, 442
social facilitation and, 436–439
social loafing, 439–441
thinking in, 443–447
transactive memory in, 445–446
united identity of, 433
wisdom of, 443–445
Group selection, 47
Groupthink, 446–447
Guilt, 48, 174–176
　effects of, 175–176
　forgiveness and, 264
　littering and, 317
　overbenefit and, 260–261
　power, lack of, 453
　rejection and, 346
　relationships and, 176
　shame compared, 174–175
　suicide and, 121
　survivor guilt, 261
Gullibility, 215
Guns and aggression,
　　303–304

H

Halo effect, 237
Happiness, 167–171
　Affect Intensity Measure
　　(AIM) and, 171
　children and, 168
　defining, 167
　hedonic treadmill, 169
　increasing, 170
　objective roots of, 167–169
　subjective roots of, 169–171
　what is beautiful is good
　　effect, 336
Hate crimes, 414
Health. *See also* Illness
　forgiveness and, 264
　happiness and, 170
　loneliness and, 329, 343
　positive emotions and, 170
　self-esteem and, 89
Hearing of dogs, 50–51
Heart disease and anger, 173
Hedonic treadmill, 169
Height
　and attractiveness, 335
　discrimination and, 393

Helping, 258. *See also* Altruism;
　　Bystander helping;
　　Prosocial behavior
　altruistic helping, 271–272
　egoistic helping, 271–272
　just world, belief in, 276–277
　the world, 10
Herd instinct, 327
Heroic acts, 258
Heuristics, 141–1415
　anchoring and adjustment
　　heuristic, 144–145
　availability heuristic, 142–143
　persuasion, heuristic/systematic
　　model for, 244–246
　representativeness
　　heuristic, 141–142
　scarcity heuristic, 233
　seriousness of errors and, 154
　simulation heuristic, 143–144
　stereotypes as, 407–408
Heuristic/systematic model, 244–246
Hiding anger, 173–174
Hierarchy of goals, 109–110
High-empathy people, 272–273
Higher purpose, belief in, 217
History, 7
　crime in medieval
　　Europe, 381–382
　of social psychology, 3–6
HIV/AIDS
　extradyadic sex and, 379
　safe sex, persuasion for, 239
　survivor guilt and, 261
Holocaust, 4–5, 256–257
　humiliation and, 313
Homicide. *See* Murder
Homophobia, 400–401
Homosexuality, 377–379
　A-B problem and, 213
　culture and, 36, 377, 401
　EBE (exotic becomes
　　erotic), 377–379
　erotic plasticity and, 376
　intimacy and, 372
　prejudice and, 399–402
　roots of prejudice against, 401
　sex partners and, 146
Honesty
　baby faces and, 420
　in relationships, 369–371
Hostile attribution bias, 299
Hostile expectation bias, 299
Hostile perception bias, 299
Hostile sexism, 410–411
Hot hand players, 149
Hot temperatures and violence, 306
Hourglass figure and
　　attractiveness, 336
Human sacrifice, 293
Human Security Brief 2007, 292–293
Humiliation, 313
Humility and self-presentation, 92
Humor
　ethnic jokes, 414
　and persuasion, 238
Hunger, 46
　eating and, 134
Hydraulic model of aggression, 295
Hypocrisy, self-presentation as, 91
Hypothalamus, 163
Hypothesis, defined, 12

I

Idealizing in relationships, 369–371
Ideas. *See also* Shared ideas
    culture and, 46–47
    distant future, ideas about, 49
Identity and self-presentation, 92
Ifaluk people, competition
    among, 405
Ignorance. *See also* Pluralistic
        ignorance
    prejudice and, 406–407
    and social cognition, 154–155
Illness. *See also* Mental illness
    loneliness and, 343
    prejudice and, 402
    rejection and, 339
    sexually transmitted
        diseases (STDs), 114
Illusion of control, 151
Illusions. *See also* Positive illusions
    and self-esteem, 82–83
Illusory correlation, 148
Imitation, 204
Implicit Association Test
    (AIT), 200–201
Implicit attitudes, 200
    measurement of, 200–201
    prejudiced attitudes, 415
Impressionable years hypothesis, 243
Impression-making, 91–92
Improving the world, 10
Impulse, selfish, 47–48
Impulsive system, 41–42
Incremental theorists, 105
Independent self-construal, 62–63
Independent variables, 13
Indirect aggression, 290–291
Individual roles, 434
Infidelity. *See* Extradyadic sex
Influence. *See* Social influence
Information
    conscious system and, 43
    people first theory and, 51–52
Informational influence, 227–228
Information overload, 145–146
    tyranny of choice and, 209–210
Ingratiation, 329
Ingroups
    favoritism and, 403
    members of, 395–396
Inhibitions
    alcohol use and, 307–308
    bystander helping and, 281
    power and, 455–456
Initiative and self-esteem, 85, 88
Injunctive norms, 317
Innate theories of aggression,
    294–295
Inner processes, 411–414
Inoculation of attitudes, 248–249
Insanity. *See* Mental illness
Instinct
    aggression, theories on, 294–295
    competitive instinct, 436–437
    first instinct fallacy, 152
    herd instinct, 327
Instrumental conditioning, 204
Intelligence
    of audience, 242
    credibility and, 237
    emotional intelligence
        (EQ), 188–189

of groups, 444
racial bias in IQ tests, 423–424
and rejection, 344
of spouses, 330
what is beautiful is
    good effect, 336
Intention
    automatic *vs.* controlled
        thinking and, 130
    planning and, 113
Interactions, 16
Interdependence and self, 61–63
Interdependent self-construal, 62–63
Intergroup relationships. *See also*
        Discrimination; Prejudice
    ABCs of, 393–402
Internal-external attributions, 136
Internal Motivation to Respond
        Without Prejudice, 416–418
Internal validity, 15
Internet and belongingness, 327
Interpersonal functions, 32
Interpersonal self, 60
Intimacy
    avoidant attachment and, 363
    homosexuality and, 372
    narcissism and, 88
    in Sternberg's triangle
        of love, 358–359
Intimate-partner violence, 301–303
Intrinsic motivation, 71–72
    freedom of action and, 107
Introspection, 69–70
Intuition, 11, 43
Investment model of
        relationships, 367
Invulnerability, groupthink and, 447
Iraq
    military action in, 292
    shoe throwing in, 290–291
Ironic processes, 134–135
Irrationality, 117–121, 122. *See*
        also Self-destruction
    of beliefs, 218–219
    suicide and, 119
Islam
    prejudice and, 396–399
    Qur'an on punishment, 344

J

Jains, competition among, 405
James-Lange theory of
    emotion, 162–163
Japan, sleeping arrangements
    in, 39–40
Jealousy
    causes of, 384–385
    culture and, 382–383, 386–387
    double standard and, 386–387
    emotional infidelity
        and, 383–384
    evolutionary theory on, 383–384
    gender of interloper and
        jealousy, 385
    sexual infidelity and,
        382, 383–384
    social reality and, 385–386
    suspicions of infidelity, 384–385
    and type of interloper, 385
Jigsaw classroom, 418
Jokes, ethnic, 414
Jonestown suicides, 224–225

*Journal of Personality and
    Social Psychology,* 8
Judaism. *See also* Holocaust
    and prejudice, 402
    scapegoating and, 411–412
    stereotypes of, 410
Judgment and stereotypes, 408
Junk food and violence, 309
Junk mail
    e-mail, 160
    self-deception, theory of, 84
Justice. *See also* Fairness
    and prosocial behavior, 258

K

Kelley's attribution cube, 139–141
*The Kervorkian Suite: A Very Still
    Suite* (Kervorkian), 199
Kin selection, 270
Knowledge, 9. *See also* Self-knowledge
    cultural animals and, 38
    persuasion and, 246
    structures, 130–131
!Kung people, competition
    among, 405

L

Labeling technique, 230
Laboratory experiments, 17–18
Lake Wobegon effect, 150
Language and cultural differences, 40
Lassie, 283
Laughter and power, 454
Law, rule of, 258
Law of least effort, 407
Leadership, 449–452. *See also* Power
    good leaders, traits of, 449
    legitimate leadership, 456
    toxic leaders, 450–452
Learned helplessness, 105
Learned scripts, 131
Learning. *See also* Social learning
    aggression, learniang theory
        and, 295–296
    emotions and, 178–180
    observational learning, 204
Legitimate leadership, 456
Legitimazation-of-paltry-favors
        technique, 230–231
Legitimizing myths, 456
Lesbians. *See* Homosexuality
Lexical decision task, 412–413
Lie to Me, 315
Life, prolonging, 29
Life satisfaction, 167
Likeability of source, 237
Liking. *See also* Attraction
    reciprocity and, 332–333
    rewards and, 331–332
    similarity and, 330
Limited-number technique, 234
Littering, 317–318
    Broken Windows Theory, 317–318
Living together
    jealousy and, 384–385
    sexual activity and, 357
Loafing, social, 439–441
Loneliness. *See also* Belongingness
    health and, 329, 343
    rejection and, 342–343
Loner animals, 31
Long-distance relationships, 328

Looking-glass self, 68–69
    changing, 79
Loss-framed appeals, 133
Lost letter technique, 397–398
Love. *See also* Attachment;
        Companionate love; Passionate
        love; Relationships; Sexuality
    Affect Intensity Measure
        (AIM) and, 171
    attachment drive and, 372
    culture and, 355–356
    defined, 354
    extradyadic sex and, 381
    familiarity and, 334
    fear and, 166
    at first sight, 359
    gender and, 186
    narcissists and, 364–365
    reciprocity and, 332–333
    rejection and, 345–346
    self-love, 364–365
    Sternberg's triangle, 358–359
    for teams, 445
    unrequited love, 345–346
Low-ball technique, 229–230
Low-empathy people, 272–273
Low self-esteem, 81–82
Lying, 314–315
    detecting, 314–315
Lynching, 412

M

Magical thinking, 151–152
Main effects, 16
Manhood
    culture and, 37
    measurement of, 335
Marriage. *See also* Extradyadic sex
    attributions in, 368
    companionate love and, 356
    growth in, 366
    honesty in, 369–371
    idealizing in, 369–371
    investing in, 366–367
    loneliness in, 342
    long-distance relationships, 328
    maintaining, 365–371
    narcissism and, 364–365
    Prince Charles/Princess
        Diana, 352–354
    satisfaction with, 367
    selective confirmation in, 371
    self and, 61
    sexual activity and, 356, 357
    similarity and, 330
    thinking styles in, 367–371
    Victorian practices, 371
    worsening of, 366
Mass media. *See also* Television
    and aggression, 304–305
    rape depiction in, 305
    and Rwanda genocide, 288–289
Masturbation and culture, 36
Matching hypothesis, 330–331
Maximization Scale, 210
Mayer-Salovey-Caruso
        Emotional Intelligence
        Test (MSCEIT), 188
Meaning
    choices and, 106
    defined, 99
    emotions and, 192

Meaningfulness
    children and, 168
    of thought, 122
Media. *See* Mass media
Medulla oblongata, 163
The Memoirs of Sherlock Holmes
        (Doyle), 143
Memory
    knowledge structures and, 131
    priming, 131–133
    self-concept and, 80–81
    self-deception and, 84
    transactive memory in
        groups, 445–446
Mental illness, 6. *See also* Depression
    obsessive-compulsive
        disorder (OCD), 135
    panic disorders, 135
    passionate love and, 355–356
    prejudice and, 402
    self-presentation and, 90–91
    suppressed thoughts and, 135
    toxic leaders and, 451
Mere exposure effect, 203
    and attraction, 333–335
Messages, 237–242
    overheard messages, 243–244
    personal relevance of, 245
    repetition of, 241–242
    stealing thunder technique,
        239–241
    weak arguments in, 245–246
Meta-analysis, 18–19
Meta-cognition, 155
Mexico, sleep patterns in, 39
Midbrain, 163
Milgram experiments, 266–267
Military action and terrorism, 292
Millerite Movement, 218
Mimicry and liking, 332
Minimal group effect, 403
Minority groups. *See* Race
Misattribution of arousal, 164–166
Mob violence, 441–442
Modeling
    aggression, 295
    altruism, 282–283
Modesty
    self-knowledge and, 76
    self-presentation and, 92–93
Money. *See also* Wealth
    attitudes and, 208
    attractiveness and, 335
    choice and, 101
    cooperation and, 263
    culture and, 34
    emotions and financial
        decisions, 182
    power and, 454
    sexual attraction and, 384
Monitoring. *See also* Self-monitoring
    dieting and, 115, 116
    self-regulation and, 114–116
Mood. *See also* Affect regulation
    aggression and, 298–299
    altruism and, 277
    defined, 161
    food and, 179
    good mood, benefits of,
        182–183
    helping and, 273
    weather and, 179–180

Morality
    groups and, 47–48
    groupthink and, 447
    social animals and, 38
    teaching moral inclusion, 283
Motivation
    for aggression, 291
    anger and, 172
    guilt as, 175
    overjustification effect, 71–72
    prejudice, overcoming, 416–418
    self-determination
        theory, 106–107
    sex partners and, 146
Mr. Rogers' Neighborhood, 283
Mundane realism, 17
Murder
    decreasing rates of, 292
    hot temperature and, 306
    in Southern United States, 312
Music and affect regulation, 190
Muslims. *See* Islam
Mutation, 30
Mutuality and communal
        relationships, 361

N
Names, 2
    changing, 142
    and self, 78
Narcissism
    evaluation apprehension and, 439
    forgiveness and, 265
    leadership and, 450
    relationships and, 364–365
    self-esteem and, 87–88
    violence and, 311
Narcissistic Personality Inventory, 311
National Violence Against
        Women (NVAW) Survey
        on stalking, 346
Natural selection, 29
    culture and, 38–39
    emotions and, 178
    suicide and, 119
Nature, 27–28
    aggression and, 296–297
    behavior and, 46–47
    culture and, 28, 35–37
    defined, 28
    eating and, 35
    homosexuality and, 379
    prejudice and, 403
    psyche and, 27–28
    sexuality and, 376
Nazism, 4–5. *See also* Holocaust
    and groups, 435
"Nearer My God to Thee"
        (Kervorkian), 199
Need
    for belongingness, 325–328
    for cognition, 242
Negation and anger, 173
Negative advertising, 240–241
Negative affect, 161
    aggression and, 298
Negative attitude change, 249
Negative state relief hypothesis, 273
Neuroscience, 8
Neurotransmitters
    and aggression, 307
    and love, 354–355

Neutral stimulus, 203–204
Neutrophils, 12
News stories, 2
Night and Fog, 183
1984 (Orwell), 446
Noise
    and aggression, 306
    stress, 107
Nonexperimental studies, 18–19
Nonprejudiced people,
        processes of, 415
Non-zero-sum games, 262
Normative influence, 225–227
Norms
    group norms, 226–227
    littering and, 317
    prosocial behavior and, 259–260
Novum Organum (Bacon), 147
Numbness and rejection, 339

O
Obedience, 265–267
    Milgram experiments, 266–267
Obesity
    prejudice and, 399
    self-regulation and, 114
Objective predictors, 168
Objective roots of happiness, 167–169
Observational learning, 204
Observed scripts, 131
Obsessive-compulsive disorder
        (OCD), 135
Oil drilling, 10
    political tradeoffs, 50
Omission bias, 103
One Day in the Life of Ivan Denisovich
        (Solzhenitzyn), 167
One-shot illusory correlations, 148
One-sided messages, 240
Operant conditioning
    attitudes and, 204
    dissonance and, 207
Operational definitions, 13
Opportunistic flexibility, 454
Oppositeness and attraction,
        330–331
Optimal distinctiveness
        theory, 435–436
Optimism, 83
    happiness and, 170
    and planning, 112–113
    planning fallacy and optimistic
        bias, 112–113
Options and choice, 102–103
Orgasm, 357
Ostracism, 338–339
Outback Steakhouse, 269
Outgroups
    homogeneity bias, 395–396
    identity of groups and, 33
    members, 395–396
Overbenefit, 260–261
Overestimation of contribution, 137
Overheard messages, 243–244
Overjustification effect, 71–72
Overweight. *See* Obesity

P
Pain of rejection, 339
The Painted Bird (Kosinski), 432
Panic button effect, 107
Panic disorders, 135

Parenthood
    Affect Intensity Measure
        (AIM) and, 171
    avoidant attachment and, 362
    child abuse and, 303
    happiness and, 168
    kin selection, 270
Passionate love, 354–355
    companionate love,
        transition to, 357
    idealizing of partner, 370
    and insanity, 355–356
    skepticism about, 356
    Sternberg's triangle
        theory and, 359
Passion in Sternberg's triangle
    of love, 358–359
Paternity testing, 380, 386
Peace Train (Stevens), 396–397
People first theory, 50–52
Perception
    hostile perception bias, 299
    power and, 453
Performance
    arousal and, 186–187
    brainstorming and, 444
    evaluation apprehension and, 437
    rejection and, 344
    social facilitation theory and, 438
    social loafing, 439–441
    transactive memory and, 446
Peripheral route to persuasion, 245
Personality
    and helping, 275
    psychology, 8
*Personality and Social Psychology
        Bulletin,* 8
*Personality and Social
        Psychology Review,* 8
Personal projects, 108
Personal relevance of messages, 245
Person perception, 142
Persuasion, 235–247. *See also*
        Audience; Messages
    age of audience, 243
    attitudes and, 246, 248–249
    central route to, 245
    convert communicators, 237
    credibility of source, 236–237
    culture of audience and, 243
    distraction and, 244, 245–246
    elaboration likelihood model
        (ELM), 244–246
    emotional responses and, 238
    expertise and, 236
    forewarning about, 249
    heuristic/systematic
        model, 244–246
    humor and, 238
    impressionable years
        hypothesis, 243
    inoculation of attitudes, 248–249
    intelligence of audience, 242
    knowledge and, 246
    likeability of source, 237
    need for cognition of
        audience, 242
    negative advertising, 240–241
    overheard messages, 243–244
    peripheral route to, 245
    personal relevance of message, 245
    public image and, 242–243

Persuasion (*continued*)
  repetition of message, 241–242
  resisting, 247–251
  scare tactics and, 238–239
  source of, 235–237
  speed of speech and, 247
  stealing thunder technique,
      239–241
  stockpiling resources to
      resist, 249–250
  trustworthiness and, 236–237
  variation, repetition
      with, 241–242
  weak arguments and, 245–246
Pets. *See* Animals
Phenomenal self, 71, 73
Phenylethylamine (PEA), 354–355
Philosophy, 9
Phobias. *See also* Fear
  suppressed thoughts and, 135
Physical attractiveness. *See*
      Attractiveness
Physiological psychology, 8
Piaroa people, competition
      among, 405
Pique technique, 234
  defenses against, 251
Planning, 111–113
  drawbacks and plans,
      111–112
  mistakes in, 112–113
  optimism and, 112–113
Planning fallacy, 112–113
Plasticity, erotic, 376
Pleasant arousal, 166
Pleasure from helping, 273–274
Pluralistic ignorance, 228
  bystander helping and, 280
Polarization
  and attitudes, 205
  of groups, 447–448
Political science, 7
Politics
  brainwashing and, 215
  oil drilling and, 50
  stereotypes of, 409
Polygraph tests, 315
Pons, 163
Popularity and binge eating, 439
Positive emotions, 181–183
  health and, 170
Positive illusions, 82–83
  and goal-setting, 108–109
Possessiveness. *See* Jealousy
Post-decision dissonance, 209
Poverty and prejudice, 402
Power, 452–456
  action and, 455
  approach/action orientation
      and, 455
  corruption and, 453
  duplex mind and, 454–455
  effects of, 453–456
  emotions and, 453
  followers, effects on, 456
  inhibitions and, 455–456
  laughter and, 454
  money and, 454
  opportunistic flexibility, 454
  outcomes of, 455–456
  punishments and, 453
  rewards and, 453

P-O-X theory, 206
Praise, attraction and, 331–332
Praxis, culture as, 34
Precarious manhood, 37
Pregnancy
  evolutionary theory and, 373–374
  prison inmates and, 50
  self-esteem and risk of, 86
  self-regulation and, 114
Prejudice
  as affective component of
      intergroup relationships, 394
  and Arabs, 396–399
  common targets of, 396–402
  conscious override of, 414–418
  contact and reducing, 418
  contact hypothesis, 406–407
  defined, 393
  discontinuity effect, 406
  evolution and, 406
  goals, common, 418
  and homosexuality, 399–402
  and ignorance, 406–407
  impact of, 418–424
  implicit prejudiced attitudes, 415
  ingroup favoritism and, 403
  inner processes and, 411–414
  and Islam, 396–399
  jigsaw classroom and, 418
  motives for overcoming, 416–418
  nonprejudiced people,
      processes of, 415
  and obese/overweight, 399
  objections to, 394–395
  operation of, 413
  rationalizations for, 407
  realistic conflict theory, 404–406
  reasons for, 402–409
  reducing, 414–417
  Robber's Cave study, 403–406
  and self-defeating
      prophecy, 420–421
  self-esteem and, 88, 408
  and self-fulfilling
      prophecy, 419–421
  self-regulation and, 415
  us *vs.* them and, 403–406
Premarital sex, 387
Preoccupied attachment, 362
Prescription: Medicine
      (Kervorkian), 198
Preservation of beliefs, 215
Priming, 131–133
Prisoners
  communication among, 325, 327
  pregnancy and, 50
Prisoner's Dilemma, 261–263
Private acceptance, 228
Private ownership, 442
Private self-awareness, 64, 94
Proactive aggression, 291
Product placement, 243–244
Prolonging life, 29
Propinquity effect, 333–334
Prosocial behavior. *See also* Altruism
  conformity, 267–269
  cooperation, 261–263
  defined, 257
  empathy and, 270–271
  equality, 260
  equity, 260
  evolutionary benefits of, 270–271

forgiveness, 264–265
  norms and, 259–260
  obedience, 265–267
  reasons for, 269–274
  reciprocity norms and, 259
Prostitutes, 146
Proximal goals, 110
Psyche, 27–28
Psychoanalysis, 5, 6
Psychological disorders. *See*
      Mental illness
Psychology, 8–9
PTSD (posttraumatic stress
      disorder), 135
Public compliance, 228
Public image and persuasion,
      242–243
Public self, 60
Public self-awareness, 64
Public self-consciousness, 66
Punishment
  aggression and, 301
  altruistic punishment, 441
  for cheating, 441
  of children, 303
  for deviance, 344–345
  empathy-specific punishment
      hypothesis, 273
  of free riders, 441
  power and, 453–454
  torture as, 293

Q
Quasi-experiments, 14–15
Qur'an on punishment, 344

R
Race. *See also* Discrimination;
      Prejudice
  dating and, 396
  intelligence testing and, 423–424
  phenomenal self and, 73
  rejection and, 344
  scapegoat theory and, 412
  self-esteem and, 82, 421–422
  slavery, stereotypes of, 421
Racism. *See also* Prejudice
  defined, 393
Random assignment, 14
Rape, 302
  chastity belts and, 383
  mass media and, 305
Reactance theory, 17, 104
Reactive aggression, 291
Realism
  experimental realism, 17
  mundane realism, 17
Realistic conflict theory, 404–406
Reality
  assumptive worlds and, 216
  and self-esteem, 82–83
Reality television shows, 324–325
Real self, 60–61
Reasoning, 43
Receptivity of audience, 242
Reciprocity
  in animals, 260
  cooperation and, 262–263
  defenses against influence
      by, 250–251

door-in-the-face technique,
      231–232
  exchange relationships and, 361
  liking and, 332–333
  as prosocial behavior, 259
  social influence and, 231–233
  suicide and, 260
  that's-not-all technique, 232–233
Recycling and littering, 317
Reflective system, 41–42
Reframing
  affect regulation and, 189–190
  disrupt-then-reframe
      technique, 234–235
Regression to the mean, 150
Regret, 153
  suicide and, 121
Reinforcement theory, 331–332
Rejection, 325, 338–347
  aggression and, 341–342
  bad apple effect, 345
  behavior and, 341–342, 345
  causes of, 343–345
  children and, 344
  deviance and, 344–345
  diversity and, 432
  effects of, 339–341
  loneliness and, 342–343
  ostracism, 338–339
  performance and, 344
  romantic rejection, 345–346
  stalking behaviors, 346
Rejection sensitivity, 339
Relationship-enhancing style
      of attribution, 368
Relationship-oriented
      leaders, 449–450
Relationships. *See also* Attachment;
      Belongingness; Extradyadic
      sex; Marriage
  anticipated emotions and, 181
  attributions in, 368
  avoidant attachment and, 363
  belongingness and, 177
  communal relationships, 359–361
  companionate love and, 356
  devaluing alternatives in, 369
  ending bad relationships, 328
  exchange relationships, 359–361
  forgiveness and, 264–265
  growth in, 366
  guilt and, 176
  helping and, 276
  honesty in, 369–371
  idealizing in, 369–371
  investing in, 366–367
  loneliness and, 343
  long-distance relationships, 328
  maintaining, 365–371
  narcissism and, 88
  prosocial behavior and, 257
  satisfaction with, 367
  selective confirmation in, 371
  self-esteem and, 364
  self-regulation and, 114
  similarity and, 330
  social allergy effect, 334
  temptation and, 366
  thinking styles in, 367–371
  types of, 359–365
  view of partners in, 368–369
  worsening of, 366

Relative age effect, 37
Relevance and persuasion, 245
Religion
    affect regulation and, 190
    belief, religious, 217–218
    brainwashing and, 215
    forgiveness and, 265
    happiness and, 170
    higher purpose, belief in, 217
    modesty and, 92
    self-presentation and, 91–92
    sexuality and, 376
Repetition of message,
        241–242
Replication, 20
Representativeness heuristic,
        141–142
Reproduction, 30
    social animals and, 31
Reputation and helping, 273
Research. *See also* Experimental
        studies; Scientific method
    applied researchers, 10
    between-subjects design, 12
    design, 14–19
    factorial designs, 16
    field experiments, 17–18
    laboratory experiments, 17–18
    within-subjects design, 12
Responsibility
    and bystander helping, 280
    diffusion of, 280
Restaurants and conformity, 269
Reverse discrimination, 415–416
Reverse double standard, 387
Rewards
    aggression and, 301
    attraction and, 331–332
    empathy-specific reward
        hypothesis, 273
    overjustification effect and, 72
    power and, 453–454
    of smoking, 118
Rhetoric (Aristotle), 235, 238
Risk-as-feelings hypothesis, 181
Risky behavior
    choice and, 100
    good mood and, 183
    groups and, 447–448
    risk-as-feelings hypothesis, 181
    as self-defeating behavior, 118
    self-presentation and, 93
    testosterone and, 326
Risky shift of groups, 447–448
Robber's Cave study, 403–406
Roles
    differentiation of, 434–435
    self, social roles and, 63–64
Romantic love. *See* Passionate love
*Romantic Passion: A Universal
        Experience?* (Jankowiak), 355
Romantic Period, 355
Rule of law, 258
Rules
    for communal relationships, 361
    deviance and rejection,
        344–345
    for exchange relationships, 361
    obeying, 258
Running amok, 309–310
Russian roulette, 102–103
Rwanda genocide, 288–289, 298

S
Sadness, 182. *See also* Depression
    empathy and, 178
Sadomasochism, 289–290
Safe sex, persuasion for, 239
Salience, stereotypes and, 411
Samples, student, 20–21
Scapegoat theory, 411–412
Scarcity, 233–234
    defenses against influence by, 251
Scare tactics and persuasion, 238–239
Scent and attractiveness, 337
Schachter-Singer theory of
        emotion, 164–166
Schemas
    self-schemas, 5
    thinking and, 131
Scientific method, 6–7
    overview of, 11–12
Scripts, 131
Secondhand smoke and
        aggression, 306
Secure attachment, 361–362
Selective confirmation in
        relationships, 371
Self
    culture and, 61–63
    defined, 59
    endowment effect, 77–78
    as impulse, 61
    independence *vs.*
        interdependence, 61–63
    information-processing
        and, 77–81
    as institution, 61
    main jobs of, 59–60
    names and, 78
    origins of, 60–64
    philosophy and, 9
    self-reference effect, 77
    social roles and, 63–64
    social world and stability, 79
    study of, 5
Self-acceptance, 365
Self-actualization, 364
Self-awareness, 60, 64–67
    alcohol use and, 308
    behavior and, 65
    binge eating and, 66
    deindividuation, 434–435
    escaping, 65–67
    main effect for, 16–17
    in perspective, 94
    private self-awareness, 64, 94
    standards and, 64–65
    suicide and, 120–121
Self-censorship and
        groupthink, 447
Self-concept, 59
    changing, 78–81
    memory and, 80–81
    in perspective, 94
    promoting change, 79–80
    stories about self, revising, 80
Self-control
    aggression and, 310–311
    alcohol use and, 308
    cheating and, 315
    cultural rules and, 47
    rejection and, 340
    selfishness and, 48
Self-correction, 20

Self-deception
    junk mail theory of, 84
    strategies, 83–84
Self-defeating behavior, 118–119
Self-defeating prophecy
    prejudice and, 420–421
    stereotypes creating, 423
Self-destruction, 117–121
    anger and, 172
    rejection and, 341
    self-defeating behavior, 118–119
    suicide, 119–120
Self-determination theory, 106–107
Self-directed action, 122
Self-enhancement, 74–75
    automatic egotism and, 76
    and modesty, 92–93
Self-esteem, 5, 81–83
    of African Americans, 421–422
    aggression and, 311–312
    benefits of, 84–85
    caring about, 85–87
    criticism and, 422
    illusion and, 82–83
    narcissism and, 87–88
    prejudice and, 408
    pursuing, 88–89
    reality and, 82–83
    rejection and, 339, 346
    self-deception strategies, 83–84
    self-love and, 364
    sexual activity and, 85, 86
    sociometer theory, 86–87
    value of high self-esteem, 87–88
Self-fulfilling prophecy and
        prejudice, 419–421
Self-handicapping, 75–76
    and self-defeating
        behavior, 118–119
Self-image and mere exposure
        effect, 203
The Selfish Gene (Dawkins), 270
Selfishness, 47–48
    aggression and, 301
    altruism and, 273–274
    rejection and, 340
Self-knowledge, 59–60, 67–68
    appraisal motive, 74–75
    automatic egotism, 76
    beginnings of, 74
    changing, 78–79
    conflicts among motives for, 75
    consistency motive, 74–75
    duplex mind and, 76
    introspection and, 69–70
    looking-glass self, 68–69, 79
    in perspective, 94
    phenomenal self, 71, 73
    ranking of motives, 75
    reasons for seeking, 73–77
    self-enhancement motive, 74–75
    self-perception, 71
    social comparison and, 70–71
    working self-concept, 71, 73
Self-love, 364–365
Self-monitoring
    persuasion and public
        image, 242–243
    and social situations, 330
Self-perception theory, 71
    overjustification effect, 71–72
Self-presentation, 5, 89–93

    defined, 90
    dissonance and, 211
    favorability *vs.* plausibility, 92
    identity and, 92
    impression-making, 91–92
    modesty and, 92–93
    risky behavior and, 93
Self-protection, 81
Self-reference effect, 77
Self-regulation, 5, 67, 113–117, 122
    affect regulation, 189–192
    capacity for change and, 116–117
    monitoring and, 114–116
    prejudice and, 415
    rejection and, 340
    standards of, 114
Self-reports on extradyadic sex, 380
Self-schemas, 5
Self-serving bias, 83, 137
    and extradyadic sex, 381–382
    scapegoating and, 411–412
Self-sufficiency and money, 263
Self-worth, 421
Sensitivity
    about being the target of
        a threatening upward
        comparison, 260
    loneliness and, 342
    rejection sensitivity, 339
Serotonin and aggression, 307
Sesame Street, 283
Sexism, hostile *vs.* benevolent,
        410–411
Sex partners, counting, 145–146
Sexual activity. *See also* Sexuality
    A-B problem, 213
    affect regulation and,
        189–190, 191
    aggression and, 302
    attachment and, 363–364
    choices and, 1021
    companionate love and, 356
    counting sex partners, 145–146
    helping and, 276
    marriage and, 356, 357
    phenylethylamine (pea) and, 355
    quality of, 357
    safe sex, persuasion for, 239
    as self-defeating behavior, 118
    self-esteem and, 85, 86
    self-presentation and, 93
    self-regulation and, 114
    testosterone and, 326
Sexual arousal
    ambiguity about, 165
    decision-making and, 181
Sexual coercion, 302
Sexual harassment and
        stereotypes, 419
Sexuality, 372–387. *See also*
        Extradyadic sex;
        Homosexuality; Jealousy;
        Pregnancy; Sexual activity
    attachment and, 372
    casual sex, gender and, 375–376
    culture and, 36, 46, 376
    dating and sex, 377
    desire and gender, 376
    double standard and female
        sexuality, 386–387
    enjoyment and gender, 376
    erotic plasticity, 376

Sexuality (*continued*)
evolutionary theory of, 373–374
female sexuality, 386–387
gatekeepers, women as, 376–377
money and attraction, 384
nature and, 376
social constructionist
theories of, 372–373
social exchange theory
of, 374, 387
stereotypes about gender
and, 374–377
Sexually transmitted diseases
(STDs), 114
Shadow of intelligence, 181
Shame, 174–176
guilt compared, 174–175
Shared experiences, attraction
and, 334
Shared ideas, 33
and praxis, 34
Showing anger, 173–174
Similarity
altruism and, 275
attraction and, 330–331
in groups, 433
optimal distinctiveness
theory, 435–436
prejudice and, 402–403
Simulation heuristic, 143–144
Situational factors, power of, 6
Skinnerian behaviorism, 99
Slavery, 293
stereotypes of, 421
Sleep
automatic system and, 41
culture and, 39
deprivation, 250
loneliness and, 343
Sleeper effect, 236
Slum Dog Millionaire, 444
Smiles, Duchenne, 185
Smoking
aggression and secondhand
smoke, 306
as self-defeating behavior, 118–119
Social acceptance, 45, 325
skills, developing, 45–46
Social allergy effect, 334
Social animals, 30–31, 32
foundations of, 37–38
herd instince of, 327
in perspective, 53
Social brain theory, 31–32, 45–46
Social categorization, 394–395
Social cognition. *See also* Attributions
defined, 127
stupidity of people and, 154–155
Social comparison, 70–71
Social constructionist theories
of sexuality, 372–373
Social exchange, 260
Social exchange theory of
sexuality, 374, 387
Social exclusion. *See* Rejection
Social facilitation, 436–439
social loafing and, 441
Social influence. *See also*
Commitment; Consistency;
Reciprocity; Scarcity
attention, techniques based
on, 234–235, 251
bait-and-switch technique, 230

defenses against techniques,
250–251
disrupt-then-reframe
technique, 234–235
door-in-the-face technique,
231–232
fast-approaching-deadline
technique, 234
foot-in-the-door technique, 229
informational influence, 227–228
labeling technique, 230
legitimazation-of-paltry-favors
technique, 230–231
limited-number technique, 234
low-ball technique, 229–230
normative influence, 225–227
pique technique, 234
techniques of, 228–235
that's-not-all technique, 232–233
Socialism and private ownership, 442
Social learning
of aggression, 204–205, 295
attitudes and, 204–205
Social loafing, 439–441
punishing, 441
social facilitation and, 441
Social networks. *See also* Groups;
Relationships
and happiness, 169
Social psychology
defined, 3
focuses of, 6–7
history of, 3–6
reasons for studying, 9–11
and social sciences, 7–8
Social Psychology (McDougall), 4
Social Psychology (Ross), 4
Social reality and jealousy, 385–386
Social roles. *See* Roles
Social support and affect
regulation, 189
Socioeconomic status (SES)
of spouses, 330
Sociology, 7–8
Sociometer theory, 86–87
Southern United States, culture
of honor in, 312–313
Soviet Union, collapse of, 5
Spam, 160
Spanking, 303
Speaker credibility, 236–237
Speed of speech and persuasion, 247
Spinal cord, 163
Split-brain studies, 42
Sports
culture and, 35–37
drug use tradeoffs, 49
racial discrimination in, 394
relative age effect, 37
Sports Illustrated jinx, 151
Spring break sex, 276
Stable-unstable attributions, 136
Stalking behaviors, 346
Standards
self-awareness and, 64–65
of self-regulation, 114
suicide and, 119
Starbucks, 3
Star Trek, 247–248
Statistical reasoning, 155
Statistical regression, 150–151
Statistics in scientific method, 12
Status quo bias, 103

Stealing, 316–317
Stealing thunder technique, 239–241
Stereotypes
accuracy, element of, 409–410
baby faces and honesty, 420
as cognitive component of
intergroup relationships, 394
confirmation bias, 413
conflict and, 412–413
defined, 394–395
of emotions and gender, 186
as energy-savers, 407–408
of guilt, 176
as heuristics, 407–408
of homosexuality, 399–402
impact of, 418–424
inner processes and, 411–414
as law of least effort, 407
negativity of, 410–411
nonprejudiced people,
processes of, 415
objections to, 394–395
operation of, 413
overcoming, 414–417
rationalizations for, 407
reasons for, 402–409
rejection and eating, 340
salience and, 411
self-fulfilling prophecy and, 420
sexuality and gender, 374–377
slavery and, 421
stigma and, 421–422
stress and, 412–413
threat of, 422–424
Stereotype threat, 422–424
Sternberg's triangle, 358–359
Stigma
attitudes and, 201
homosexuality and, 402
selfish/self-control
conflict and, 48
stereotypes and, 421–422
Stimulants and arousal, 166
Stockpiling resources and
persuasion, 249–250
Stranger rapes, 302
Stress
fight or flight syndrome, 300
religious belief and, 218
stereotypes and, 412–413
tend and befriend syndrome, 300
thinking and, 187
Stroop effect, 129–130
Stroop test, 129
Student samples, 20–21
Stupidity. *See* Ignorance
Subjective roots of happiness, 169–171
Subtypes, 394
Success
emotional intelligence and, 188
explaining, 136–137
salary as index of, 421
what is beautiful is good
effect, 336
Suicide, 119–120
assisted suicide, 198–199
burdensomeness and, 121
credit card debt and, 248–249
fairness and, 260
Jonestown suicides, 224–225
rejection and, 339
self-awareness and, 66, 120–121
Superiority, groupthink and, 447

Superordinate goals, 404
and prejudice, 418
Suppression of thought, 134
Survival, 29–30
Survivor guilt, 176, 261
Symmetry and attractiveness, 337
System, culture as, 33–34

T
Task-oriented leaders, 449–450
Teams, love for, 445
Television
Lie to Me, 315
loneliness and, 343
prosocial programs, 283
reality shows, 324–325
and violence, 304–305
*Who Wants to Be A
Millionaire?*, 444, 445
Temperature. *See* Weather
Temporal discounting and
choice, 100–101, 102
Temptation, 9
extradyadic sex and, 381
Ten Commandments, 46–47, 114
Tend and befriend syndrome, 300
Territoriality, 17
Terrorism
Arabs, discrimination
against, 398–399
humiliation and, 313
military action and, 292
Testosterone
and aggression, 306–307
as mixed blessing, 326
Tests and counterfactual
thinking, 152
Test-score gap, 423–424
Thalamus, 163
Thanatos, 295
That's-not-all technique, 232–233
Theories, 12–14. *See also*
specific theories
Thinking. *See also* Automatic
thinking; Controlled thinking;
Memory; Social cognition
about people, 127–128
conterfactual thinking,
152–153
defined, 99
effort of, 129
emotions and, 178–180
framing, 133
in groups, 443–447
ironic processes, 134–135
marriage, thinking styles
in, 367–371
outside the box, 454
priming, 131–133
reasons for, 128–129
relationships, thinking
styles in, 367–371
schemas and, 131
scripts and, 131
stress and, 187
suppression of thought,
134–135
Thirst, 46
Thought. *See* Thinking
Threat of stereotypes, 422–424
Time and tradeoffs, 48–49
Torture, 293
Toxic leaders, 450–452

Tradeoffs, 48–50
    in perceptual systems, 50–51
    political tradeoffs, 50
    and self-defeating
        behavior, 119
    and suicide, 110
Transactive memory in
    groups, 445–446
Trauma
    coping and, 215–217
    religious belief and, 218
Trespass, 318
Tristan Islanders, competition
    among, 405
The Trouble with Testosterone
    (Sapolsky), 306
True self, 60–61
Trustworthiness
    and liking, 332
    and persuasion, 236–237
Truth and intuition, 11
Two-sided messages, 240
Typicality and attractiveness, 337
Tyranny of choice, 209–210

U

Ultimate attribution error, 138
Unconditioned response, 203–204
Unconditioned stimulus, 203–204
Unconscious, 41
Underachievement and self-
    regulation, 114
Underbenefit, 260–261
United Nations, 293

United States v. Scheffer, 315
Unrequited love, 345–346
Upward counterfactuals, 152–153
Upward social comparisons, 71
U.S. Census Bureau, 49
Us *vs.* them and prejudice,
    403–406

V

Validity
    external validity, 17–18
    internal validity, 15
Variables
    confounded variables, 15
    dependent variables, 13
    independent variables, 13
Variation, repetition with, 241–242
Vegetarianism, 35
Venting anger, 173–174
    affect regulation and, 189–190
    aggression and, 298
Verbal aggression, 291
Vicarious learning, 204
Victorian marriages, 371
Video games and aggression, 15, 305
Violence, 291. *See also* Aggression
    adolescence and, 300
    alcohol use and, 307–308
    culture and, 310
    culture of honor and, 312–313
    deindividuation and, 441–442
    diet and, 309
    domestic violence, 301–303
    gender and, 297

hot temperatures and, 306
humiliation and, 313
jealousy and, 383
mass media and, 304–305
measuring, 292–293
mob violence, 441–442
narcissism and, 311
rejection and, 341
running amok, 309–310
self-esteem and, 311–312
self-regulation and, 114
serotonin and, 307
in sexual media, 305
testosterone and, 306–307, 326
in video games, 15, 305
weapons effect, 303–304
Virginity and culture, 36
Virtue, 9
Vitamins and antisocial behavior, 309
Volunteering, 283

W

Walking and conscious/
    automatic systems, 42
Wants, defined, 329
War, 22
Weak arguments, 245–246
Wealth
    exchange relationships and, 360
    private ownership, 442
Weapons effect, 303–304
Weather
    and aggression, 306
    and mood, 179–180

Weight. *See also* Obesity
    attractiveness and, 336
Western United States, culture
    of honor in, 313
What is beautiful is good
    effect, 335–336
Who Wants to Be A Millionaire?,
    444, 445
Wide-eyed innocence, 420
Willpower, 117
Wisdom
    accumulated common wisdom, 11
    of groups, 443–445
    philosophy and, 9
The Wisdom of Crowds
    (Surowiecki), 444
Within-subjects design, 12
Womanhood, culture and, 37
Words, use of, 6
Working self-concept, 71, 73
World peace, 2
World War II, 2, 4–5. *See also* Nazism
Wounded pride theory, 311–312

Y

Yerkes-Dodson law, 187
Yielding by audience, 242

Z

Zeigarnik effect, 109
Zero-sum games, 262
Zimbabwe, toxic leadership
    in, 450–451
Zrinyi's Sortie (Krafft), 58